The Ypres Times

Ypres Times

The Complete Post-War Journals of the Ypres League
Vol 3. 1933 – 1939

UNIFORM

First published by Uniform
an imprint of the Unicorn Publishing Group LLP, 2021
5 Newburgh Street
London W1F 7RG

www.unicornpublishing.org

All rights reserved. No part of this publication may be reproduced, stored in or introduced into a retrieval system, or transmitted, in any form or by any means (electronic, mechanical, photocopying, recording or otherwise), without the prior written permission of the copyright holder and the above publisher of this book.

Every effort has been made to trace copyright holders and to obtain their permission for the use of copyrighted material. The publisher apologises for any errors or omissions and would be grateful to be notified of any corrections that should be incorporated in future reprints or editions of this book.

© Notes, Mark Connelly 2021
© Unicorn Publishing Group 2021

10 9 8 7 6 5 4 3 2 1

ISBN 978-1-913491-55-0

The publishers are grateful for the support of the In Flanders Fields Museum and City Archives, Ieper, Belgium for their assistance in compiling these volumes.

Design by Unicorn Publishing Group

Printed and bound in the UK

NOTES ON VOLUME THREE

In its last six years the *Ypres Times* maintained many of its core elements. Chief among them was the coverage of pilgrimages. The sheer number of pilgrimages and battlefield tours recorded in its pages reveals that the shadow the Great War did not fade in the thirties. In fact, the opposite could be argued. As tensions rose in Europe and across the globe, the memory of that great conflict became all the sharper. The editions for 1938, the last full year of peace and the one in which the twentieth anniversary of the Armistice was marked, contain a truly remarkable number of accounts. Particularly noticeable about these stories are those produced by old comrades associations. Clearly, even international tension did not dampen the veteran enthusiasm for old stamping grounds. At the other end of the age scale is the increasing number of stories referring to school, cadet and Territorial Army tours (for examples see the editions of July 1934 and July 1936). Youths and young men, and the emphasis was on the male gender, were exposed to the battlefields of the Great War. As the accounts reveal, the objective of the tours combined the intellectual and the deeply emotional. The battlefields were studied as a series of tactical problems and interpreted through the lens of military history. At exactly the same time, those present were exhorted to solemn and respectful remembrance of the myriads who had sacrificed all for God, King, Country and Empire. Deep down in the rhetoric there was an irony: the young were told that the sacrifices were worthy because they had achieved an end to war. At exactly the same time, they were also being told, sometimes explicitly, sometimes implicitly, that it would be their job to emulate that selflessness should it become necessary. Thus, the complexities of remembrance and commemoration in the 1930s find clear expression in the *Ypres Times*.

The waxing of the Eton Memorial School was another strong theme of the period. The League took a deep interest in the foundation it had helped create. The school was staffed by teachers supplied by the London County Council on a secondment basis, and through the pages of the *Ypres Times* the hard work of the heads, their assistants, as well as the enormous input of their wives into the success of the school is made clear. What also becomes apparent is the way the children were perceived. Although many had both a British father and a British mother, large numbers had French or Belgian mothers meaning the children lived a life of dual cultures, and in many cases English was not the primary language of the home. The *Ypres Times* largely avoided this complexity. According to its understanding, these children were solely British, as is shown in the coverage of the school's calendar constructed around the observation

v

of Empire Day, St. George's Day, May Day (complete with maypole dances) and, of course, Armistice Day.

Set against this evidence of vitality, indeed as the thirties progressed almost frenzied activity, the sad signs of decline in the League are palpable. In April 1933 the *Ypres Times* Maintenance Fund was given extensive coverage. Launched in September 1931, the need for additional funds to maintain the journal was urgent by 1933. At the same time the clarion calls for members became shrill with a £5 prize offered to the branch that recruited most new members in a year. As the responses of members reveal, passion for the League remained strong with many volunteering to pay an additional subscription to fund the journal (January, April 1934). In some ways the League was a victim of its early success when it had offered a generous life membership package. Those who had taken advantage by providing a modest lump sum in the early 1920s ensured an immediate boost to funds, but over the longer-term such a model failed to keep the League in financial health. In 1938, the journal was reduced to two editions, and in 1939 it only managed one. The *Ypres Times* never returned, although, somewhat miraculously, the League remained in existence until 1961.

One of the reasons behind the decline may be down to Beckles Willson, who appears to have run out of steam after his continuous exertions. From 1934 much of the editorial writing was undertaken by the League's newest committee member, H.A. Benson, with Beckles Willson contributing the League Secretary's Notes column. Benson's particular speciality was panegyrics to royalty. In April 1934 he led with an extensive obituary of Albert, King of the Belgians. Two years later, he did the same on the death of King George V, which was rapidly followed by a piece welcoming the accession of Edward VIII. A year later it he placed the Princesses Elizabeth and Margaret Rose in the spotlight, and in the following edition turned to Queen Mary. In effect, royal biographies had replaced stories about Ypres as leading articles. Having provided non-stop coverage for so many years, and with the rebuilding of Ypres at such an advanced stage, it was perhaps natural that the supply of compelling stories had dried-up and a new source of inspiration was required. In retrospect, it can be argued that the League's mission was done; it had reached its natural conclusion. And, indeed, the final edition contained the most apt and poignant of codas, as Benson told League members, 'It's "Ieper" Now'. Explaining the desire of Flemings to use their language, he noted that there had been a renaming programme meaning 'on the station platform at Ypres, for example, the familiar "Ypres" has given way to the purely Flemish "Ieper," and the tortuous street "Rue Au Beurre," which winds its way to the Menin Gate, has become "Boterstraat". The world had changed, and was about to change even more cataclysmically than during the last great conflagration.

Ypres may have moved on from 1919, and in far more ways than simply its spelling, but the League played a seminal role in maintaining the memory of the former city, the place of wartime sacrifice and endeavour. And, as any visitor to modern Ieper knows, that memory is still recognised by the city's inhabitants. The pilgrim of today, the inheritor of everything the League worked to inspire, is met with exactly the same friendliness, warmth and understanding as those who made that journey of love and reverence in the 1920s and 1930s. The Ypres League cemented a bond between the Britannic world and a beautiful, historic Flemish market town forced into the inferno of modern war.

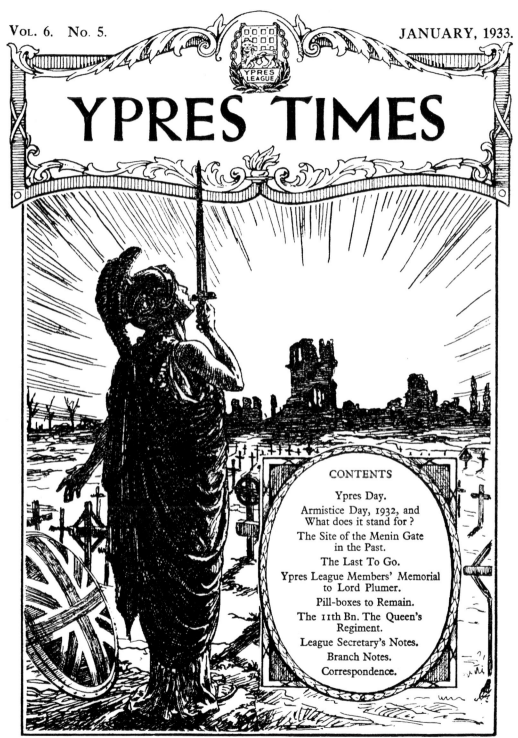

Memory Tablet.

JANUARY — FEBRUARY — MARCH

JANUARY.

Jan. 8th, 1916	Gallipoli evacuation completed.
,, 12th, 1915	The use of poisonous shells by Germans reported.
,, 21st, 1915	Zeebrugge bombarded by British airmen.
,, 24th, 1916	Naval battle off Dogger Bank.

FEBRUARY.

Feb. 3rd, 1917	America broke with Germany.
,, 18th, 1915	U-boat "blockade" of England.
,, 18th, 1918	German invasion of Russia.
,, 21st, 1916	Battle of Verdun begun.
,, 21st, 1918	British capture Jericho.
,, 25th, 1915	Allied Fleet attacked Dardanelles.

MARCH.

Mar. 10th, 1915	British capture of Neuve Chapelle.
,, 11th, 1917	British take Baghdad.
,, 12th, 1917	Revolution in Russia.
,, 15th, 1917	Abdication of the Tsar.
,, 21st, 1917	First British War Cabinet.
,, 21st, 1918	German offensive on the Western Front.

Supplement to YPRES TIMES, *January*, 1933.

GOVERNMENT HOUSE,
FARNBOROUGH,
HANTS.

Message to Members of the Ypres League, 1933.

May I, as the new President of The Ypres League, address a personal message to all members of the League.

Firstly, may I thank you all for your kindness in electing me as your President in the place of our late and beloved Chief—Field-Marshal Lord Plumer—the man who defended Ypres through those long years against tremendous odds.

I can but promise to do my utmost to carry on his great work for The Ypres League as he would wish and expect me to do, but I can naturally only be a shadow of the Chief himself. History will record his great work. History will no doubt tell how he held the Salient by his stout heart, by his thoughtfulness for everyone who served under his command, even the humblest, and by his great courage and sense of justice and honour. He was a great leader, who inspired and won the affection of all those who had the privilege of serving under him.

It is very encouraging to me to know that several hundred new members have joined the League since his death, evidently with the intention of carrying on his great work. To these new members I tender my grateful thanks, and to all members I would say, " Good luck to you all in 1933, and let us make 1933 the year in which we redouble our efforts as a token of respect to our late Chief to whom our Country and Empire owe so much."

C. H. HARINGTON, *General.*
President, The Ypres League.

The Ypres Times

Communications to
The Editor, "Ypres Times,"
9 Baker Street, London, W.1.

PRICE 6d.
POST FREE 7d.

Vol. 6, No. 5   Published Quarterly   January, 1933

[By kind permission of J. Russell & Son.

GENERAL SIR CHARLES H. HARINGTON (NOW G.O.C. OF THE ALDERSHOT COMMAND), WHO HAS SUCCEEDED THE LATE FIELD-MARSHAL VISCOUNT PLUMER AS PRESIDENT OF THE YPRES LEAGUE.

Ypres Day

ON Sunday, October 30th, the twelfth annual commemoration of the Ypres League was held on the Horse Guards' Parade. Among a distinguished company were General Sir Charles H. Harington, President of the League, H.E. The Belgian Ambassador, Colonel H. Nerincx, Military Attaché Belgian Embassy, Field-Marshal Viscount Allenby, and Lieut.-General Sir W. P. Pulteney.

A short but impressive service was commenced by the singing of the hymn "O Valiant Hearts," accompanied by the band of the 1st Surrey Rifles.

The gathering was addressed by the Rev. G. H. Woolley, V.C., M.C., who spoke of the fine sentiment which prompted such a gathering, and paid a glowing tribute to the

Photo] [*By kind permission of The Sport & General Press Agency, Ltd.*

memory of the late Field-Marshal Viscount Plumer, who was with us on the 1931 parade, the last public occasion of his life.

Following the address, the "Lament" was played by the pipers of the 1st Bn. Scots Guards. The last notes of the pipes died away into a dead silence, broken almost immediately by the clear, thrilling notes of the most moving of all bugle calls "The Last Post," while men stood bareheaded and motionless, heedless of wind and rain.

The rain ceased as the whole parade, headed by the band, formed in procession and marched to the Cenotaph, where Field-Marshal Viscount Allenby laid the Ypres League wreath.

The wreath-bearers were Major G. R. P. Roupell, V.C., East Surrey Regiment, and Sergeant O. Brooks, V.C., late Coldstream Guards, while the Ypres League banner and flag were borne by Lieut. W. A. White, V.C., late M.G.C., and Lieut. Michael O'Leary, V.C., late Connaught Rangers. At the conclusion of the parade, a party of members and friends of the League, headed by four of the V.Cs., placed a wreath on the grave of the Unknown Warrior. The service was conducted by Canon C. S. Woodward, M.C., who also paid a tribute to the memory of Lord Plumer.

It has been said that in maintaining these annual parades we are fostering the militarist spirit. Surely, all our members must rise in refutation of such a charge. In keeping alive the memory and spirit of the comradeship learned in the war, we believe we do our part in preparing the only sure road to peace on earth, the growth of goodwill and the spirit of peace in men's hearts. Only so can we really keep faith with those we honour. Otherwise the memory of the horror and sacrifices of Ypres must eventually be blotted out by future tragedies, the magnitude of which may well be beyond our imagination.

Photo] [By kind permission of The Sport & General Press Agency, Ltd.

FIELD-MARSHAL VISCOUNT ALLENBY LAYING THE YPRES LEAGUE WREATH AT THE CENOTAPH.

Yet not all of those in whose honour we keep Ypres Day were the young and keen. On this parade we were reminded only too well of the figure of our late President. When we saw him " out there " he was already the seasoned veteran, with hair and moustache whitened through years of campaigning before some of those he led were born, but now Lord Plumer has passed, as we like to think, to the head of that great army of whom it is no exaggeration to say—they loved him well; and we of the Ypres League, as a personal gesture of tribute to Lord Plumer, are making a great effort to recruit new members to the League's ranks. It is some years now since soldiers were " demobbed " and scattered all over the earth, yet the bond of comradeship, forged in the fires of the Salient, holds them still, and they have " joined up " again—not for war, but for commemoration and mutual service, believing in the value of that comradeship in these difficult and troublous times.

S. H. K. G.

Armistice Day, 1932, and what does it stand for?

ON Armistice Day I paraded at Wellington Barracks at 9.30 a.m. to join the Ypres League Section with the column in its march to the Cenotaph. The parade was in charge of Admiral of the Fleet, Sir Charles Madden. The Guards, with their usual superb efficiency, handled the parade in a fine manner.

During the war I had paraded as a Company Commander at Wellington Barracks, and I recaptured something as I walked on to that Parade Ground. Was there ever such a column as this? I think not. Every station in life was represented, and every man had " taken the knock " in the line. The night before the parade I received from a sergeant of my old Battalion—a man I had not seen or heard from since the March fighting in 1918—a letter that opened as follows:—

" With the near approach of another anniversary of Armistice Day, naturally our minds go back to the days ' out yonder,' and the people with whom we spent our days."

The letter went on to tell me of the deaths of sergeants who had served under me. Now I suppose that letter is typical of thousands received by officers and men all over the country. It speaks of the spirit animating the men on that parade. I noticed one man whose clothing and boots were in a lamentable state but he was bearing himself with a pride that was good to see. Did it not bring back the self-respect of that man to chat with men who had served in the line as he had served in the days when the country was threatened? Of course it did.

One thing was mentioned with a note of bitterness, and that was the fact that the War Office had made no issue of " Battle Clasps." I took the matter up with the Press, and their report to me was to the effect that the War Office received very few letters about the matter from officers and men. Why should officers and men write to the War Office about such a matter? I see a great deal of ex-service men, and I can assure the War Office that it is a very real grievance with them.

The Band of the Coldstream Guards, and Drums and Fifes of the 2nd Battalion of the Scots Guards led the first half of the column; the Band of the Grenadier Guards and Drums of the 2nd Battalion of Grenadier Guards led the second half. The route to the Cenotaph was Birdcage Walk, Horse Guards Arch and Whitehall. His Majesty The King laid a wreath on the Cenotaph, and then the Bishop of London offered a prayer. Leading the March Past at the Cenotaph we returned to Wellington Barracks.

I venture to think that the sentiment regarding Armistice Day is as deep to-day as it was on that November 11th of 1920. It is argued that the actual Two Minutes' Silence throughout the Country cannot be maintained. That may be, but as long as this generation lasts there will always be a group gathered at the Cenotaph on that day.

On Memorial Day in New York, 1931, I was on the Staff of Major-General John F. O'Ryan, who took the salute, and twenty-five veterans of the Civil War marched over the entire route of the parade. The oldest of those veterans was a man of ninety-one years, and as they approached the Reviewing Stand some women began strewing the road with rose leaves. How sentimental and foolish I can hear some of you say. Not at all, gentlemen. It was strangely touching. In an address later the former Assistant Attorney-General of New Jersey said:—

"We are a grateful nation. Because of the sacrifices of the men we gather to honour to-day, we are living in the full security of peace. Let us not forget them."

The burial of The Unknown Warrior at Westminster Abbey on November 11th, 1920, started something that touched the souls of all men, for there were " none so poor to do him reverence."

"THE UNKNOWN WARRIOR"
(In Memoriam)

What Mother's son is this that they bring here
With such high honour, that in all its ways
A nation halts, and dreams of fateful days
The while deep thoughts now beat about the bier?
The son of every Mother, far and near
Who lost a lad in war, and gently prays.
This is the boy brought home, this hour repays!
The Mother comfort finds, though falls the tear.

O, bring him on with music—bring him on,
While we re-capture for a little time
The glory of the hours when first we flung
Our banners high with hope the world upon.
He speaks of bloody sweat in every clime,
And strong love known the fighting men among.
                    R. HENDERSON-BLAND.

Reprinted from " The Graphic," November, 1920.

Set to music by Teresa del Riego, and sung on Armistice Day by Miss Stiles Allen, at the Town Hall, Woolwich.

It is argued that all Military Associations are bad things—keeping alive the spirit of militarism. Now I do not think this is true. Very few men who have been seriously engaged in the line would like to see another war. No, that sort of talk comes from men who have not seen the horrors of war, and have not been called on to possess their souls in the very face of death.

But what does annoy soldiers is the talk of ardent pacifists who never heard a shot fired. A short time ago a very distinguished man, addressing a convention, said of the late war that " it sent to their unmerited death millions of human beings who had not the least notion of what the fighting was all about." That sort of talk is an insult to the men who fought—Germans and Britishers alike. If the gentleman in question had heard the German troops singing their songs of triumph at night in Peronne, during their great drive in March, 1918, he might have been excused for believing, as the British troops waiting to be attacked again in the morning believed, that the Germans knew very well what it was all about.

Let us away with all this false cant. There is no bitterness between soldiers who fought in the Great War, but do not let us, in our eagerness to ensure a world peace hide behind tapestries bitten through with insincerity. I am very much against competitive and armed nationalism, and am all in favour of international co-operation, but why belittle the efforts of the men who laid down their lives in the War?

I have read most of the important war books, and have found many of them most interesting, and some of them have tried my patience. Reading some of them many people might get the idea that war was a bestial and entirely demoralizing experience. To many it may have been so, but I can honestly say that the men I had the privilege to serve with did not find it so, and it was a great test of manhood. The bloody battles of the Somme and Ypres, and the agony of the Fifth Army, tried men as few things could try them.

Let the country choose men who have fought in the Great War as their representatives, and send them abroad, and it will be found that they will prove the best ambassadors of peace the country ever had.

In these days when the voice of poetry is silent, no longer stirring the hearts of men, when no man dares to praise a man set above his fellows because he is so busy observing the feet of clay, the Armistice Day comes as a reminder that we cannot find satisfaction in a life such as led by a squirrel in a cage, and that we must look to the higher reaches of the spirit and dare to believe in immortality. If we do not believe in the immortal spirit of man, then I say that Armistice Day is a joke and a farce, and its celebration should not be tolerated.

I am one who is so foolish as to believe that the Greeks were right in their estimate of men as set forth by the address of Pericles to the Athenians. War is the great sifter of souls, and the men who held the gate in war should be honoured. I would rather trust myself to the company of soldiers than to any other class of men, because they have been tested. Any officer in the line knew how difficult it was to recommend men for "stripes." However excellent a man might be on parade he might prove something very different when he is called upon to act in action. There is a difference in men—make no mistake about that. We are taught to believe that we brought nothing into the world and we take nothing out of it. That I do not believe. I believe that a man when he dies passes with a soul large or mean according to the manner in which he has allowed the forces of life to impinge upon him. In these days of disillusionment men are asking what did the Great War achieve? It achieved more than the wisest of us can ever foresee. Only yesterday you had the Chancellor of the Exchequer pleading in the House of Commons, with a voice shaken with emotion, for the poor of this country. He said:—

"Why should anybody who lives in such conditions vote for me or for my party? If I lived in such conditions I do not think my head would govern my actions. I should feel that the circumstances to which I was condemned were intolerable, that there was something rotten in the State which permitted them to exist so long."

That should have been said years ago by men of his position, and in the same manner. But for the Great War we might have waited for a similar utterance spoken with the same emotion another fifty years.

Armistice Day stands for all such noble utterance.

R. HENDERSON-BLAND.
(*Formerly Gloucestershire Regiment.*)

MESSAGE FROM THE BISHOP OF LONDON.

FULHAM PALACE, S.W.6.
DEAR CAPTAIN BLAND,

I have read your article on Armistice Day with much approval. Often as I take the service and stand by the Cenotaph I never fail to find it deeply moving, and it will be a bad day for the Country when once the sacrifice made by our splendid men is forgotten. Yours sincerely,
A. F. LONDON.

The Site of the Menin Gate in the Past

THE early history of Ypres is wrapped in the darkness of long past ages. Nothing is known for sure about it before A.D. 902, when Baldwin-the-Bald, Count of Flanders, built a castle on a small island on the Yperlee, approximately opposite the site of the Cathedral.

A map, made up from old chronicles, shows the primitive city which, about 930, had gathered under the protection of the castle. The present moat, from the Lille Gate to the Dixmude Gate (" Dead End ") seems to occupy the site of the primitive ditch dug as a defence on the eastern side, the marshy banks of the Yperlee protecting the western part of the city.

At the end of the tenth century the population had already developed at such a rate that they had crossed the western bank of the river and surrounded the chateau. The early moat was crossed by six bridges, one of them approximately on the site of the present Memorial Arch. The defence had also been strengthened with an earthen parapet.

From a document, dated 1269, Ypres was then approximately the same size and shape it is to-day. The defences had been considerably improved and the ditch widened. Ten gates gave passage to many roads, one of them, the " Hengouard Gate," giving entrance to both the Menin and Zonnebeke roads, meeting on the very edge of the moat.

During the next hundred years Ypres largely increased its importance and became one of the leading cities of Western Europe. Its products—mainly cloth—had acquired world-wide fame and were sought for on all markets. During that period of prosperity the wealthy clothmakers built their famous Hall, which survived all events till 1914. The population had increased at such a rate that a second moat and parapet had to be built, the work taking from 1325 to 1328. Between both rings of defences stood hundreds of houses, several churches and monasteries. The Kruisstraat, near the well-known Lunatic Asylum on the Vlamertinghe Road, still reminds one of the Holy Cross Church. At the cross-roads farther west (another favourite target for the Boche gunners) an Augustine monastery gave its name to the road still called Augustine Street. This road was the western boundary of Great Ypres. To the east, the " Ommeloopstraete," or " contour-street," just skirted the western corner of Zillebeke Lake, which was dug in 1295 for the water supply of the town (as was Dickebusch Lake in 1321), and supplied Potijze and Saint Jean. The present existing roads circling round the city seem to be nothing but the covertway of the outer ramparts.

But the disastrous siege of 1383 by the English brought about the downfall of the proud City of the Cloth.

The besieging army, under command of Henry Spencer, Bishop of Norwich, numbered about 75,000 men. In Ypres, including suburbs, were about 80,000 inhabitants, all told, of whom not 20,000 took an active part in the defence. The too extensive first line could not be defended and was given up without resistance, the suburbs were utterly destroyed by the besiegers, whilst the defence was concentrated on the ramparts of the city itself. For the first time Ypres was to be bombarded with artillery ; two guns, of very primitive design, came into action opposite the Messines Gate (now Lille Gate) and fired some 450 stone cannon balls in the course of 45 days, but it is stated they did little actual damage.

The defence was carried out with the utmost energy and gallantry, and on August 8th the siege was given up after 62 days of active operations, during which no less than

23 attacks had been made. The annual "Thuindag" celebrations on the first Sunday of August still commemorates the end of the siege.

Ypres never recuperated from this disaster, the suburbs were not rebuilt. With the stones of the destroyed churches and other buildings the first stone wall was built round the city (from 1388 to 1396).

After this memorable event Ypres enjoyed 180 years of peace, only troubled occasionally by political strife.

On July 20th, 1578, the town was occupied by surprise by the Protestants and retaken by the Spaniards under command of the famous Alexander Farnese, Prince of Parma, five years later, after a seven months' blockade.

The Spanish, in 1640, greatly improved the defence works, reducing the number of gates to six and building in front of the wall and moat a series of demi-lunes, especially on the eastern front, covered by six such works, four of which were south of the old Hengouard Gate then called the Antwerp Gate. The Menin and Zonnebeke road was cut through the second one starting from the north.

To write the military history of Ypres from about this date would mean to copy the history of nearly all the European wars, as since then Belgium deserved the name of Battlefield of Europe.

The King of Spain being then the legitimate ruler of Belgium, this country was involved in the numerous wars fought by the French and the Dutch against Spain. In May, 1648, a French army under Louis de Bourbon, with Marshals de Gramont and Rantzau, arrived in view of the town. The western side of the city was protected by floods. Two saps were dug against the eastern sector, one of them being directed against the Antwerp Gate. In less than a week the French took the demi-lunes south of the gate and the garrison surrendered without defending the walls. The following year the Spanish came back and attacked from the north-west. The French governor surrendered after 26 days' resistance.

Not until 1658 did the French reappear, when on September 11th an army of 30,000 men under Turenne arrived from Dunkirk. After a fierce cannonade the garrison, 4,800 strong, capitulated on the 25th of the same month.

Peace was signed the following year and Ypres returned to the Spanish.

War broke out again in 1665, but Ypres was not attacked during the early period, and this delay was actively used to improve the fortifications. The Antwerp Gate was suppressed, but replaced by an important citadel of pentagonal shape, built just east of the Saint Jacques Church, with two demi-lunes to the north and three to the south. The Menin road was cut right through the citadel itself. (For simplicity's sake I will not mention the works on other sides of the town.)

On March 15th, 1678, Louis XIV, King of France, arrived in sight of Ypres. The small Spanish force, only 3,500 strong, took shelter in the citadel. Though siege operations were at first impeded by rain and mud, the French were able to bring up strong artillery forces and the Governor surrendered on the 25th. The garrison was allowed to leave with military honours and marched past Louis XIV at Wieltje.

Nimeguen Peace Treaty was signed in September, whereby Ypres became French, its position near the border being considered as most important. Modernization of the defence works according to the new bastion-system was entrusted to the famous engineer Vauban. The Spanish citadel disappeared again to be replaced by a strong work called "Corne d'Anvers," linked to other similar works farther north by demi-lunes. One of them, between the "Corne d'Anvers" and the "Corne de Thourout" gave passage to the Menin Road. The old crenulated stone wall was replaced by a stone rampart bastioned except on the southern front This is the rampart you can still see, now battle scarred, but it proves the quality of the work designed by Vauban, as even the heavy German shells failed to pierce it. The casemates in the rampart behind Saint Jacques Church also date from this period (about 1690). The number of

Translation of explanation at the bottom :—
  "The siege of Ypres (1383) by the Bishop of Norwich and the English" (from a 15th Century Manuscript "Chronique de Flandre" in the Library of Angers).

The original writing reads :—
  "Le Xe jour de juing l'an mil iij^{ct} iiij^{xx} et iij assaillirent les engles moult fort la ville dippre."
  (On the 10th day of June, 1383, the English attacked very strongly the town of Ypres.)

gates became reduced to four, three of them being ornated with artistic façades. The Antwerp Gate was the most beautiful of them and bore, facing the city, a long latin inscription to the glory of " Ludovicus-Magnus " with the date 1688.

War broke out again in 1689, illustrated in following years by the victories of Marlborough. Though every Belgian town was taken and retaken several times during these eventful years, Ypres escaped all attacks on account of its strong fortifications. After the Treaty of Utrecht in 1713, Ypres was occupied by a Dutch garrison.

In 1744 the French, under Louis XV, invaded Flanders on June 6th and attacked Ypres, which was only feebly held. The attack took place along both banks of the Yser Canal (dug in 1638) and was so actively pushed that the Governor, Prince William of Hesse-Phillipsthal, surrendered on the 25th. Capitulation was signed at the Royal Headquarters at Vlamertinghe next day.

Belgium, having passed by heritage under the rule of the Emperor Joseph II of Austria, a pacifist, decided to dismantle all the fortresses on Belgian soil. All the works east of the moat were levelled and the ground sold by auction. The Menin and Zonnebeke roads were made to follow the course they have to-day and led through the Antwerp Gate.

In 1792 the successor of Joseph II had to pay for undue pacifism and lack of foresight when the French started war against Austria and had no trouble in occupying Ypres. The Austrians retook it, soon to lose it once more. The French evacuated the town again the following year. Immediately the Austrians decided to rebuild the works outside the moat and on the eastern front alone nine demi-lunes were erected.

The city was attacked on June 1st, 1792, by General Moreau. His army stretched from the Yser Canal to the Vlamertinghe Road. The Austrians, 7,000 strong, surrendered on the 17th, after a very heavy bombardment and weak resistance.

In 1794 the outer works were again levelled.

In 1804 Emperor Napoleon paid a visit to Ypres. The main gate was called after him, and an imperial eagle carved on the stonework. Thus disappeared the old name of Antwerp Gate.

In 1815, during the Hundred Days, all the exterior works were hastily rebuilt under the British R.E. Colonel Carmichael Smyth, and armed with numerous British artillery, landed at Ostend and brought along the Nieuport canal.

After Waterloo, Belgium was united to Holland and during the following years Ypres was strongly fortified against a possible invasion by the French. A large-sized lunette was built in 1821-22 on the site of the old citadel, with three demi-lunes north and as many south of it. Napoleon's Gate, thenceforth called Menin Gate, gave passage to the road after it had passed through the third demi-lune from the north.

In 1852 the Belgian Government decided Ypres should no longer rank amongst the few fortified places of the country. All the outer works were levelled once again, this time even the brick rampart built by Vauban was pulled down on the northern front, and in 1853 also on the western side to make room for the railway works and station. The old gates were pulled down, so as to give wider passage to the roads.

And so it came that, during a dark night early in 1915, when word passed down the single file, " the last man, shut the Menin Gate !" this man, new to the place, swore he could find no gate to shut.

M. DE HASQUE, D.C.M.,
Hon. Lieut., Belgian Army.

* * *

Writer of above avails himself of this opportunity to convey his most respectful greetings and kindest regards to all under whose orders or with whom he served in the Ypres Salient from January, 1915, right up to the great offensive as Belgian Military Interpreter, with the 27th, 6th, 38th, 30th, 56th, 7th, 14th and 29th Divisions, B.E.F., and after the Armistice with 4th Division and XXII Army Corps.

The Last to Go

By Wanderer.

DECEMBER, 1915, found us thoroughly enjoying ourselves on the Island of Mudros, and appreciating to the full, ample leg-room after months in very cramped quarters at Suvla, on the Gallipoli Peninsula, which we had evacuated a short time before.

Had we known that before long we were to return to the Peninsula, we would not have been quite so cheerful possibly, but we did not know, so there was nothing to interfere with our enjoyment.

Mudros was not at all pretty, everything a dull brown, but the climate at that time of year was superb, and as we had got our horses back again, we had a chance to explore the island.

On Christmas Day some of us rode over to the hot springs on the other side of the island from our camp and had a gorgeous hot bath, though in my opinion it was not to be compared to the bath P.N.T.O. gave B. and myself in his private bathroom the morning after the evacuation of Suvla.

Helles had not at that time been evacuated, though it was generally understood that it was only a question of days before it also would be left and the whole of the Gallipoli Peninsula given up to the Turks, so that we were a good deal surprised when orders came for two Brigades of the Division to embark for Helles. We buoyed ourselves up with the thought that we were being sent over to help in the evacuation and not to hang on there, which as it turned out was our mission, though some of us, owing to an accident no foresight could guard against, were very near being left behind.

Our two Brigades held the left of the line, and our Division Headquarters were at Gully Beach, where there was a small jetty.

As soon as we had settled in, we began the preliminary work for evacuation which proved no easy business. Unlike Suvla, where the decision to evacuate had been taken some time before the time to leave, the decision to give up Helles was only made at the last minute, so that everything had to be done in a hurry, and it was not easy to discover dumps of stores which had been "cached" all over the place, and almost forgotten. The Turks having been once bitten were wide awake, and matters were further complicated by the presence of a number of Greek workmen, who were suspected of being in sympathy with the enemy, I think with good reason, so that there was a possibility of the date of the evacuation leaking out.

By giving out the date of the evacuation as one day in advance of the real date it was hoped that the Turks would be deceived, which fortunately they were, as it made all the difference. The evacuation was planned for three successive nights. A very few to go on the first night, the bulk to go on the second night, leaving only the rear-guards, in the case of our Division about 800 men, to go on the last night.

On the morning of the second day of the evacuation the Turks, thinking no doubt that we had very few men left, made an attack on the whole Corps front, a particularly determined one being made on the front of our Division, which got into our front line, and after some pretty stiff fighting was repulsed.

Thereafter the enemy, either because he thought the evacuation business was a hoax, or because he thought he had fired off most of his ammunition, gave us no further trouble, but this behaviour on his part was more than compensated for by that of the sea, which at Suvla had been like a duck pond all through, and so far at Helles had been quite calm.

On the morning of the last day we woke to find a fresh breeze from the south-west which increased as the sun rose, and did not go down at sunset, and by that time there were waves breaking on shore, which was the very last thing we wanted, because we had to embark in K lighters.

These lighters are very much like the ordinary lighter but are completely decked over and have their own motive power. I say are, when perhaps I should have said were, as I very much doubt if they still exist, or ever will exist again.

A vessel of this kind is necessarily very difficult to handle in such a sea as was running that night, and should either of the two lighters detailed to take us off fail to get alongside the jetty, we should be in the deuce of a mess.

The night was very dark. Our rear-guards got away from the front line and down to the beach unknown to the enemy; the first lighter got alongside the jetty all right, when the second lighter, which was following close beind her, suddenly swung off, turned broadside to the shore, and grounded fast.

Our situation was distinctly awkward. We had 800 men to embark in one lighter, the maximum capacity of which was supposed to be 400, and all too little time before dawn, and the Turks probably also, would be on us.

Somehow or other we crammed 650 men into one lighter, who as far as I know were none the worse for being jammed in like herrings in a barrel, though the lighter had all it could do and made no end of fuss in getting away from the jetty on the way to a transport, where she eventually arrived safely.

Orders came from W Beach that we were to send the 150 men remaining down there for embarkation. The General sent me in charge of this party with orders to go by the shore, which between Gully and W Beach was backed by low cliffs, and as we moved off I can still see him in memory moving up the cliff by the land road, carrying his Gladstone bag, which was afterwards the subject of a parody on a well-known song.

We reached W Beach a bit wet as we had to wade through the sea in places, and there found two lighters still alongside the jetty, embarking on the one furthest from the shore.

The jetty, and a considerable distance inland and out to sea was brightly lit by an ammunition dump blazing on the cliff just above us, the S.A.A. crackling like rapid fire, but the gun ammunition was not yet ignited, and I was just going to agree to the Captain's suggestion that we should put off to a transport when W. arrived much perturbed at the General's absence, and demanding that the lighter should remain at the jetty and take him off on arrival.

I could not believe that the General had not already embarked as he had had a much shorter distance to travel than we had, but I agreed to remain, as it seemed impossible that W. could have failed to see him with the jetty lit up as with a dozen arclights.

As a matter of fact the General and the two officers with him were at that moment on the far side of the wire covering W Beach, and had they not providentially met a demolition party coming in, who showed them the gap they could not find, they must have been taken prisoners. They got to the jetty safely, embarking in the inshore lighter. We must have been beside the jetty for some twenty minutes or so after my conversation with W. when there was a terrific explosion in the dump quickly followed by another, flames shooting up to a great height, followed by almost complete darkness.

A number of heavy objects, I do not know what, but they sounded very unpleasant, fell all around us, so that we thought it best to push off without delay, and get ourselves tucked in comfortably in a transport.

But our troubles were not yet over, in fact the worst was yet to come.

We hailed transport after transport, but incredible as it may seem, were told by all, some more rudely than others, but never politely, that they were full up already, and we could go to—Helles.

There was nothing for it, then, but to try to reach Kephalo on the Island of Imbros ourselves, but as the wind was on shore and our lighter was bound to make a lot of leeway, we stood a very good chance of being driven on shore before we could get clear of the Gallipoli Peninsula, and having to say good-morning to the Turks after having, as we hoped, bade them a last farewell.

Photo]   [*Imperial War Museum, Crown Copyright.*

THE ENTRANCE TO GULLY RAVINE, SEPTEMBER, 1915.

The following colloquy which I overheard between our Captain and his First Lieutenant did not increase my hopes of safe passage to Imbros:—

CAPTAIN· "I say, Bill, do you know the Kephalo light?"
BILL: "No, can't say I do, but I daresay we shall pick it up all right."

Off we went hopefully in the direction Imbros was supposed to be. Some ten of us preferred the risk of being washed overboard, a real one as there were no bulwarks and our foreboard was something over 2 feet, to the very thick atmosphere in the hold. As there was not a chink through which fresh air could penetrate to the hold, and most of the passengers there were seasick, the hot air which rushed out when the hatches were opened on arrival at Imbros did not smell like lavender or roses. A hawser was passed round the deck passengers to prevent us falling into the sea. It was a good thing that this was done, as in spite of the cold we all dozed off at times, and but for its restraint should very likely have rolled across the few feet of deck separating us from our ship's side. As a matter of fact I do not think we shipped any sea water at all during our voyage, none certainly came my way, so that luckily we escaped risk and discomfort on that head.

We wallowed on through the night and after what seemed an interminable time, though it could not have been more than two hours, dawn broke, and we found that we were heading straight for Kephalo, which we reached safely in due course.

May I be allowed to say, "Well done, Captain, and well done, Bill," for surely it was no mean thing to bring a lighter from Helles to Imbros in a gale.

Anyway we soldiers, who were your passengers, think so, and will ever be thankful that we had your seamanship to aid us that night.

[*All rights reserved.*]

Ypres Day in Paris

On behalf of the Ypres League, a wreath was placed on the Tomb of the Unknown Warrior, at the Arc de Triomphe, bearing the following inscription :—

TO THE MEMORY OF OUR GALLANT
FRENCH COMRADES WHO DIED IN
THE IMMORTAL DEFENCE OF YPRES
1914–1918

FROM
THE YPRES LEAGUE

The ceremony was performed by Lieut.-Colonel Beckles Willson, accompanied by Brigadier-General Stanley H. Ford, Military Attaché at the American Embassy, Paris.

N.B.—The Chairman and Committee of the Ypres League desire to express their very grateful thanks to Colonel Beckles Willson, and General Stanley Ford for their great kindness in holding this touching ceremony at their personal initiative and expense, to commemorate the twelfth anniversary of the League.

Ypres League Members' Memorial to Lord Plumer

ON November 1st, Lieut.-General Sir W. P. Pulteney, G.C.V.O., K.C.B., etc., Chairman of the Ypres League, addressed a letter to the members of the League asking each to subscribe 2s. towards a worked banner bearing Lord Plumer's arms, the banner to be placed in St. George's Church at Ypres, and any surplus money collected to be placed in trust to form a fund to provide free education to a child at the Ypres British School as a Plumer Scholarship.

So far over a thousand members have generously subscribed and to whom the Chairman expresses his very grateful thanks.

Members will be interested to know that the contract for the banner has been given to the Disabled Soldiers' Embroidery Industry at 40, Ebury Street, London, and the work is being carried out under Lady Plumer's personal supervision.

A special service, conducted by the Bishop of London, will be held at Ypres on June 4th, 1933. The Bishop will dedicate the banner, and on Whit-Monday, June 5th, present the prizes at the Ypres British School.

Particulars of travel and accommodation in connection with above may be obtained from the Secretary, Ypres League, 9, Baker Street, London, W.1.

Ypres " Pill-Boxes " to Remain

IT may interest readers of THE YPRES TIMES to know that arrangements have been concluded with the Belgian Government to preserve some 180 concrete blockhouses, shelters and dug-outs—familiarly termed " pill-boxes " in the neighbourhood of Ypres, as a lasting memorial to the prowess, self-sacrifice, and valour of those of the British infantry who fell in the Immortal Salient.

Up to two years ago several thousands of these " pill-boxes " were standing in the Ypres Salient and on the Messines Ridge, but since then the Belgian Government, at the request of the landowners, has been gradually demolishing them and a number of well-known landmarks have in consequence disappeared, it was felt that slowly but surely the time would arrive when none of these interesting relics would be left, and following a special meeting of representatives of the British Legion, Toc H, and the Ypres League a communication was addressed to the Belgian Government Department concerned with a view to the suspension of the demolitions. This, we are pleased to state, was very courteously received and eventually orders were issued by the Belgian Government for a total suspension of the demolitions and proposals and maps showing the points it was desired to retain were requested to be submitted. The task of preparing the desired information was very kindly undertaken by Colonel E. G. L. Thurlow, D.S.O., of the British Legion, and as a result of his labours it is very satisfactory to learn that the Belgian Government have agreed to the preservation of some 180 of the most interesting concrete shelters, blockhouses and dug-outs.

A brief description of the events connected with each of the "pillboxes" which are to be left is now being prepared by Colonel Thurlow and it is hoped to produce this in handy form sometime in the spring. This interesting guide-book should prove immensely welcome to those fortunate enough to visit the old battle front in the future and who would be pleased to obtain some idea of what actually occurred at these famous landmarks.

Only the tremendous enthusiasm of Colonel Thurlow has enabled him to overcome the difficulties in the preparation of such a unique record, as it will be remembered that following the terrible weather and battles in 1917 the Salient was completely obliterated, landmarks disappeared, streams ceased to exist, woods were effaced and even some of the roads vanished. All that was left were the innumerable pill-boxes, the existence of which were, in hundreds of cases, quite unexpected. Fortunately Divisional and Regimental histories furnish a certain number of clues which together with a close study of trench maps have made it possible in the majority of cases to piece together the story of these pill-boxes.

Colonel Thurlow would nevertheless be extremely grateful to receive anything authentic concerning the large shelter at Essex Farm which was used as a dressing station, the observation post at Hussar Farm, Potijze, Bedford House, Lankhof Chateau and the large concrete German Headquarters on the main road a quarter of a mile east of Gheluvelt.

Any readers of THE YPRES TIMES in possession of information regarding these places are asked to be so good as to communicate with Colonel E. G. L. Thurlow, c/o British Legion, 26, Eccleston Square, London, S.W.1, not later than January 15th, 1933.

"Ypres Times" Maintenance Fund.

Through the columns of the last edition of THE YPRES TIMES, we had pleasure to thank all who have contributed so generously to the above-mentioned fund, and we reported that the total amount subscribed was £400, of which £200 had been placed on deposit and that the balance was being utilized in defraying part cost of the current numbers.

Members will be glad to know that a further sum of £100 has been added to the deposit account, which has only been made possible through the continued generosity of our faithful supporters, to whom we extend our very grateful and hearty thanks, and it is comforting to know that we close the year with promises of donations ahead.

We earnestly hope that each one of our members who have not yet contributed will send some donation, no matter how small, towards the growth of the fund in 1933. However, we know we can look forward to the staunch support from all members who have the continuance of THE YPRES TIMES at heart.

The 11th Bn. The Queen's Royal Regiment : Their Service in the Salient

THIS battalion of the " New Armies " was raised in Lambeth in 1915 by the Mayor, Sir Charles Gibbs, and was commanded by Lieut.-Colonel H. B. Burnaby, D.S.O., from the time of its inception until he was killed at Delville Wood in September, 1916.

After training in Brockwell Park and at Aldershot, the 11th Queen's proceeded overseas with the 41st Division (Major-General Sir Sydney Lawford, K.C.B.,) in May, 1916. For the next two months the unit divided its time between holding the line near Ploegsteert and occupying reserve positions in Le Bizet, on the Franco-Belgian frontier.

For most of September, 1916, and part of October, the battalion was engaged in the long-drawn-out Battle of the Somme. After participating in the capture of Flers, the 11th Queen's, now under command of Lieut.-Colonel R. Otter, M.C., was sent north. During the winter of 1916-17, it held the line in the region of the Bluff, which was taken over from the 52nd Battalion of the Australian Infantry. Battalion Headquarters was at Spoilbank alongside the Ypres-Comines Canal.

When relieved by the 11th Royal West Kents, the 11th Queen's moved back to rest huts in Alberta Camp, near Reninghelst. These inter-battalion changes, which took place usually at five-day intervals, involved a long and tiring march via Ouderdom and Dickebusch. The enemy were not very active during these months, but our men were kept busy improving the system of trenches and repairing damage from shell-fire.

In January, 1917, a very successful raid was made on the trenches opposite our position. Wearing white duck uniforms and white-washed equipment, making them inconspicuous against the snow-covered ground, the raiders, numbering sixty, sprang a surprise on the enemy, inflicted heavy losses on them and brought back two prisoners. Captain E. G. Bowden, who was in command, subsequently received the Military Cross for this night's work.

During the spring of 1917 the battalion was withdrawn from the line to train for the Battle of Messines.

On June 7th, at 3.10 a.m., the 11th Queen's, under command of Major H. Wardell, advanced from the line Mud Patch—Triangular Wood (east of Saint Eloi) to the attack. Both objectives were captured, the second—the Dammstrasse—was consolidated and held, while later in the day another brigade of the division continued the attack through this position. Major Wardell, who was later awarded the D.S.O., was badly wounded in the head during the attack. The battalion continued to occupy the Dammstrasse until June 12th, when it moved back to Voormezeele where it refitted and commenced training for the Third Battle of Ypres.

This protracted engagement opened on July 22nd, 1917, with an eight-day preliminary bombardment. The enemy countered our artillery preparation most vigorously and took a toll of casualties during these days of waiting and preparing. At 3.50 a.m., on July 31st, the 11th Queen's advanced from tapes which had previously been laid out near Battle Wood. In spite of the deep mud, following the creeping barrage, our men captured their first objective with little difficulty. After this the heavy going prevented the troops keeping up with the barrage, and as they drew near to their second and final objective they found themselves held up by German machine guns firing from pill-boxes. In spite of several gallant attempts no further progress could be made and a line was established to secure the ground already won. The well-protected enemy machine guns, firing from the flanks and at short range, resulted in heavy losses to the battalion. Two days later the unit was relieved and moved back for reinforcements and training.

The battalion started marching back to the line on September 15th, reaching Voormezeele after four days on the road. On September 20th, 1917, the 11th Queen's took part in the attack, south of the Menin Road, directed against the Tower Hamlets Ridge. For a week it was busily engaged in this area owing to the enemy's unwillingness to leave the British in possession of their important gains.

The remainder of September and all October, 1917, were spent either on the Belgian Coast defences or in the line near Nieuport. In November, with the rest of the 41st Division, the 11th Queen's were sent to Italy. Returning in March, 1918, the unit was soon engaged in helping to stem the German attack on the Somme. After suffering very heavy casualties in the defence of Bapaume, the battalion was reinforced with drafts from various other units—the Oxfordshire and Buckinghamshire Light Infantry and the King's Own Yorkshire Light Infantry supplying large contingents.

In the middle of April, 1918, we were put into the line in the Salient, after moving north. The retirement from Passchendaele was taking place at this time; when completed we held a position running north from Hell Fire Corner. The trenches were bad, consisting only of breastworks. It was not possible to dig as water was found just a few inches below the surface.

During those days in front of Ypres, the enemy seemed to be closing in around us on all sides. With the capture of Kemmel Hill he was able to overlook practically all our activities in the Salient. Lieut.-Colonel Bowden was in command during this period—the "back to the wall" days—and it was due to his cheerful leadership that there were no signs of discouragement in the battalion. Three months later, at the age of 24 years, he was killed.

Towards the end of April the unit went back through Ypres into reserve, where a few days of comparative comfort were spent among the ruins of Bedford Camp on the Poperinghe Road. While we were in this locality we were joined by Lieut.-Colonel W. L. Owen, M.C., who arrived to take command of the battalion.

May, 1918, provided fine weather which was not without its effect, both physical and moral. Most of the month was spent in the vicinity of what was once Cork Cots Camp, with Battalion Headquarters at Potijze. The rising ground in "No Man's Land" hindered observation between the two front lines, and during the day life was tolerable. But at night both sides were actively patrolling to guard against surprise and secure prisoners.

Early in June, to everybody's gratification, we learned that we were to go back to Saint Omer for a rest. Eventually we were billeted in Tatinghem, a small village a few kilometres out of the town, where we trained hard for a fortnight. At this time we welcomed Brigadier-General M. Kemp Welch, D.S.O., M.C., who came from another battalion of our regiment to take command of the brigade, the 123rd.

We returned to the line from Saint Omer by road, spending several days over the journey. The end of the march found us relieving French troops under the shadow of Kemmel Hill. For some two months we lived under German observation from this prominent height of the Flanders plain. While in the front line we occupied isolated posts in shell-holes, abandoning the old French trenches. This must have saved us many casualties as the enemy could not possibly have known our exact positions. Those were busy nights as the area was in a poor state of defence. The absence of communication trenches was a feature of the place; all reliefs and ration parties had to move above ground.

While in "support" we were near the La Clytte—Westoutre Road. The former village was occupied by one company, but the attention it received from enemy artillery made it a very unhealthy spot. The area we held while "in reserve" included Reninghelst. We found this village in a very dilapidated state when we arrived, but considerably less of it was standing by the time we left. Every few days we moved from one area to the other. During the weeks spent in this district we never saw a civilian, never could we escape the unseen eyes on Kemmel Hill which loomed above us.

July 18th, 1918, was, it had been learned from a captured prisoner, to be the date of a big attack by the enemy with the object of reaching the Coast. It was obvious that he had massed an immense quantity of artillery, and intelligence reports indicated a concentration of troops in front of us. As the day dawned our guns put down heavy barrages. Later we were convinced that there would be no attack that morning.

OFFICERS OF THE 11TH BATTALION THE QUEEN'S, MARCH, 1916.

Subsequently, we learned that the French had advanced farther south a few days previously and that the extra German troops on our front had been hurriedly diverted to deal with the new situation which had arisen.

The same night Captain Furness took up most of his company from Reninghelst and made a very successful raid near Butterfly Farm, obtaining prisoners and valuable information. He and two of his officers, Lieutenants Moon and Trotter, were wounded before they returned to our lines.

It was our privilege to introduce some of the newly arrived American units (100th and 107th Regiments) to the line. This was, perhaps, one of the outstanding events of our tour in this part of the front. Joining forces with one of these New York battalions, we produced two " composite battalions," commanded by our own officers. No better part of the line could have been chosen to give newcomers their initiation, as there was always considerable activity in some form or other.

At the time it was rumoured that our guests would, in the near future, deliver an attack in order to recover Kemmel Hill. If this was the intention of their presence, the enemy frustrated it by abandoning the hill and retiring back to the Wytschaete—Messines line on August 30th, the day following our departure for a much-needed rest at Saint Omer.

After a few days we were suddenly recalled, proceeding to Hazebrouck by train and then continuing the journey to the outskirts of Poperinghe on foot. We understood that the other two brigades of our division were to press back the Germans from the positions to which they had recently retired, while we acted as reserve. In two days' time we relieved the 15th Hampshires, who had suffered badly from an enemy they had failed to surprise, in the vicinity of Vierstraat. This had been the front line previous to the German retirement, but was now occupied by the support battalion of our brigade. A few days later we took our turn in the front line. This consisted of a bank, broken in places, which was under observation from the high ground held by the Germans near Wytschaete. The spell of bad weather which was endured here prevented much activity on either side.

Early in September, 1918, we were relieved by troops of the 34th Division and went into camp near Ouderdom. For three weeks we trained hard for some "show," concerning the nature of which there was much wild speculation. Tactics of quite a new nature were given much time and attention. We were taught to seek the " soft-spots " in the enemy's line, and when they were encountered they were to be exploited by a method of " infiltration," sections in " wormlike " formations pushing on as far as they could. " Waves," "moppers-up," and the like terms, symbolical of trench warfare, were no longer employed.

On September 26th, the plan of campaign of the Second and Belgian Armies was revealed to us. The idea seemed to be beyond the wildest flights of imagination—troops were to advance several miles a day, for days on end !

Before dawn, on September 28th, the battalion set out from Ouderdom. It was the first day of the Great Advance. Although we were in the corps reserve that morning, we spent that night at Verbrandenmolen, and next morning we were in the van of an attack across the Ypres-Comines Canal. By midday we had established ourselves in a position in front of Comines, which we had to hold against a counter-attack in the evening.

After a day's rest we moved, on October 1st, in the direction of Menin. The leading troops were soon brought to a standstill by the enemy, and near Tenbrielen the 11th Queen's received orders to attack at 5.45 p.m. from America cross-roads in the direction of Halluin. While proceeding to America we came under heavy shell-fire, from which we suffered badly. Among the casualties was Major V. Holden, D.S.O., who had commanded the battalion since September 28th. (He died from his wounds, and now lies in Dirty Bucket Cemetery.) Under the command of the Adjutant, Captain T. P. Newman, we advanced until it was dark, when we dug in just short of our objective, south of Gheluwe. That night and during the two succeeding days we lost many of our number while holding a very exposed position. When relieved we went back to Kruiseecke, where we received reinforcements and reorganized.

This, strictly speaking, concludes our activities in the Salient.

On October 14th we helped to take Gheluwe, where a strong resistance against our advance on Menin had been maintained. The next day the British occupied Menin. The 11th Queen's were amongst the first troops to cross the Lys and enter Courtrai. After fighting at Knocke, the battalion was the first over the Scheldt and into Berchem. When it was compelled to halt on November 11th, 1918, it had reached the banks of the Sambre.

After 2½ years of fighting the 11th Queen's had lost 560 officers and men. Their names are preserved in a "Book of Remembrance," which is kept in Lambeth Town Hall.

The battalion was disbanded in Germany early in 1920. It still "goes marching on," however. The O.C.A. holds an Annual Dinner every March, and last Whitsun its members revisited the Salient to pay tribute to their Fallen Comrades.

E. W. J. N.

"A History of the 11th Battalion The Queen's Royal Regiment" has been published. It contains the names of those 560 who were killed, those who served with the Battalion, and those who received decorations or were mentioned in despatches. Any readers of this article who are interested are invited to communicate with the Secretary of the O.C.A., Mr. H. C. Burberry, 5, Troy Road, S.E.19.

Book Review

"BETWEEN THE BIG PARADES." By FRANKLIN WILMER WARD.

The critic of *The Daily Mail*, when reviewing this book, wrote : "This is a book which should be read, because it does present one aspect of the American point of view, and it is important for us to realize the theories on which that point of view is based."

I venture to think that General Franklin W. Ward, the present Adjutant-General for the State of New York, had no thought of theories when writing the book, but I endorse the remark made as to the advisability of reading it.

Perhaps I am not the right person to review it, because I have the privilege of knowing many of the principal figures who appear in the book, and have a genuine admiration for them.

In his foreword to the book the General admits that he was very concerned about whether he should dare to adopt "an apparently light, facetious and careless style." I for one think he has adopted the right method. He writes as a soldier.

The book is packed full of human stories. The one telling of a General taking coffee with two Doughboys without disclosing his rank is a story that could only be told of the Americans Knowing the human side of the General concerned I appreciate it.

The Button Box story is most poignant, and has an authentic note all over it. The chief protagonist in that story was blown to pieces by a shell on the very sector of the line where I had the last glimpse of the enemy at the Battle of Kemmel.

In their attack on the Hindenburg Line the 27th Division (commanded by Major-General John F. O'Ryan), and the 30th Division (commanded by Major-General Lewis), fought with Australian troops under that fine soldier the late Lieut.-General Sir John Monash. The two divisions "captured one hundred and fifty-two enemy officers, and fifty-seven hundred and ninety-four enlisted men, nine heavy guns, seventy-two field pieces, seven hundred and forty machine guns, and forty-seven trench mortars." Not bad going in my opinion.

The French High Command were a little surprised when the American First Division captured Catigny on May 28th, 1918. Anyone who knows that fine soldier Major-General Hanson E. Ely, who had something to do with that show, would not have been surprised. It was largely owing to his personal bravery when things were "hung up" that the attack was a success.

I have been on the field of the Battle of Gettysburg and have had some thoughts there, but I would never have ventured to write this.

"Shades of Gettysburg with its round cannon balls popping from a dozen 'Napoleons,' the grape and canister dropping here and there. The grand old fellows sitting round the village grocery store are going to feel dwarfed to toy proportions when these new veterans get back home, stalk in, and unlimber." Exactly ! And where is Waterloo to-day in comparison with the Third Battle of Ypres—Passchendaele ?

I could write much about this book if space allowed, but I must be content with wishing it success on its way towards helping to make a better understanding between the two countries.

Well written, a great story, a sympathetic and soldierly spirit throughout, it should have many readers.

R. H.-B.

League Secretary's Notes.

LET EACH ONE OF US ENDEAVOUR TO DEFINITELY ESTABLISH FOR OURSELVES IN 1933 A SPECIAL INDIVIDUAL MEMORIAL TO OUR LATE PRESIDENT, FIELD-MARSHAL VISCOUNT PLUMER, BY PUTTING OUR BEST INTO THE WORK OF INCREASING THE MEMBERSHIP OF THE YPRES LEAGUE, AND SO FULFIL ONE OF LORD PLUMER'S EARNEST DESIRES.

Captain G. E. de Trafford wishes to express his very grateful thanks to the Ypres League members who have so generously responded to his personal appeal for new members and offers his sincere good wishes to the remainder, hoping that their noble endeavours to recruit a new member will meet with deserved success early in the New Year.

TO OUR NEW MEMBERS.

The past quarter has been exceedingly happy for the League in that over 300 new members have enrolled, which is more as compared with any other consecutive three months in recent years. It is difficult for us to find an adequate expression of thanks to all who have been instrumental in the recruiting.

Headquarters feel proud to see the League flourishing in times when rapid progress is least expected, so we take this opportunity to welcome most heartily such a splendid muster of new members who have come to strengthen our ranks, and they in their turn are already showing practical interest in joining up quite a number of their friends.

As evidence of this activity we have recently had the pleasure to welcome, as a Life Member, an Indian, in the person of Quartermaster Karam Illahi Havildar of the 13th Mountain Battery at present serving on the North-West Frontier. Quartermaster Havildar served throughout 1915 in the Ypres Salient with the 5th Mountain Battery, and expresses great pleasure to join an Association commemorating the fighting in the Immortal Salient and looks forward to receiving the beautiful scroll certificate. A letter of welcome is being addressed to this new member in Urdu. This recruitment is credited to our enthusiastic Life Member, Captain L. Parrington, of the 5th Mountain Battery, at Waziristan.

The reason why so many ex-warriors are willing to join the Ypres League in distressing times is surely because the highest form of comradeship prevailed during the war, and its memory is a comfort to those who understand, and realize, that the League's motive is to keep that wonderful spirit of fellowship alive and to perpetuate the heroic deeds and sacrifices of their pals.

THE YPRES TIMES helps in great magnitude to keep a constant reunion particularly among our members scattered in distant lands. Indeed, the journal has been described as "the only real link in printed form with the greater past that remains." We, therefore, make a special request to our new members possessing literary ability to help us to fill the pages of future editions. Contributions such as battle articles, personal reminiscences or humorous episodes are exceedingly welcomed by the Editor and received with much gratitude.

We wish our new members a happy New Year and trust that your endeavours for the welfare of the League will be two-fold. Firstly, to do your best to get recruits for which enrolment forms will be gladly sent by your request. Secondly, to submit some article of interest for publication in our popular little journal, THE YPRES TIMES.

We shall look forward to whatever kind support you are able to give.

TO OUR BRANCH SECRETARIES, AND CORRESPONDING MEMBERS.

We have pleasure in sending our best wishes to you all for the New Year, with the hope for better times to come. The past year can be classed as one of the most difficult years on record. Nevertheless, the League, in spite of a long period of depression, continues to display its best fighting qualities, so much so, that we are in the happy position to report that 1932, contrary to expectations, has excelled previous years in the number of new members recruited, and much gratitude is due to those staunch members who have so ably and devotedly helped in this ever-important work.

The Travel Bureau, one of our most progressive activities, has, during the past year, been reduced by 30 per cent., entirely due to the low rate of exchange, and the last moment unavoidable cancellation of the unveiling ceremonies of the Arras and Thiepval Memorials at Whitsuntide naturally proved a considerable financial loss to the League in having to re-organize the same large party of pilgrims for the unveilings in August, for which the services of four conductors were required, namely: Mr. Gordon Steel, Mr. S. H. K. Geller, Captain H. D. Peabody and Mr. O. Mears, to whom grateful thanks are due to the efficient way in which they executed their duties.

The tours of 1932 are tabulated as follows :—

Mar. 25-28	Purley Branch party to Ypres.	
,, 26-29	Easter Pilgrimage to Ypres.	
May 14-17	Whitsuntide Pilgrimage to Ypres.	
,, 14-17	Whitsuntide Pilgrimage to Arras.	

May 20-23   85th Club Tour to Ypres.
June 4-5   Party for special service at St. George's Church at Ypres, combined with a *free pilgrimage* of 23 poor relatives to the war graves.
July 29-Aug. 2   Four parties organized within this period to the unveiling ceremonies of the Arras and Thiepval Memorials.
July 30-Aug. 2   Pilgrimage to Ypres and Thiepval.
Sept. 16-19   Pilgrimage to Arras.

Great assistance had been rendered during the early summer to our independent and party travel as the result of the valuable publicity given in the local Press through the kindness of our Branch Secretaries and Corresponding Members. We thank them sincerely, and hope that we may be favoured with a repetition of their generosity in 1933.

Recruiting Competition.

During the year we have watched with the greatest of interest a higher enthusiasm in competing for the two coveted prizes of £5. Again Purley is top of the Branches with 42 recruits, won by a narrower margin than last year, and we wish to congratulate Bombardier E. A. R. Burden, Major Graham Carr, and Committee on their well-deserved victory, and on the Branch activities throughout the year comprising a reunion dinner, golf competitions, and Armistice Day parade, all of which have been great successes.

The £5 prize to a member or corresponding member has been awarded to Mr. G. Graham S. Grundy, of Headingley, Leeds, who has accounted for 18 recruits. Hearty congratulation to Mr. Grundy for his magnificent individual effort.

Our London County Committee, under the honorary secretaryship of Mr. J. Boughey, are highly commended on their recruiting efforts in 1932, and the work put into the organization of the monthly Informal Gatherings is compensated by the fact that the meetings are so well patronized, and the Committee are to be congratulated on the success of the annual dinner and dance held last April under the chairmanship of General Sir William Heneker, K.C.B., K.C.M.G., D.S.O.

League's Representatives.

The following gentlemen have prominently figured in the year's work:—Messrs. C. J. and W. Parminter, at Ypres; Captain Stuart Oswald, at Amiens; and Mr. P. Vyner, at Arras. They have all done exceptionally valuable services in connection with our tours of the battlefields, and we thank them heartily, and last but not least, our representative in America, Captain R. Henderson-Bland, now on a visit to his home in London, but in spite of his busy life he has found time to write some brilliant articles for the YPRES TIMES, his practical co-operation and forethought for the well-being of the Ypres League is indeed inspiring, and his cheery visits to headquarters are always immensely welcome. We would like to place on record our grateful thanks to Captain Bland for his unfailing interest and support which we are privileged to enjoy.

Space will not permit a longer letter, so we conclude with our renewed good wishes for 1933 and trust that the New Year will bring you much happiness and success in all your interests.

VOTES OF THANKS.

We cannot allow this edition of THE YPRES TIMES to go to press without conveying our sincere thanks to a staunch member, Mr. J. Brunskill, of Monkseaton, Northumberland, for the exceptional kindness he has shown during 1932 in giving such valuable publicity in the "Matters Military" column of the *Newcastle Journal*, in support of the League's membership, travel and other activities. We can assure him that his kindness has proved an immense help.

On November 7th an exceedingly interesting and highly successful lantern lecture on the Ypres Salient, by Captain H. D. Peabody, D.C.M., was held at the St. Andrew's Hall, West Kensington, and organized by the individual effort of Mr. C. J. H. Cope, one of our most loyal London members. At the conclusion of the evening a collection for the Ypres League realized £2 17s. 3d.

Mr. Cope has again proved what individual initiative can accomplish for the good cause of our Association, and we would like to express to him our renewed and sincere gratitude.

BACK NUMBERS OF "THE YPRES TIMES."

If any members can spare the following back numbers of THE YPRES TIMES, the Secretary would be immensely grateful:—January, 1929; April, 1930; October, 1931; April, 1932.

HOTEL
SPLENDID & BRITANNIQUE
YPRES

GRAND' PLACE. Opposite Cloth Hall.

LEADING HOTEL FOR COMFORT AND QUALITY.

COMPLETELY RENOVATED.

RUNNING WATER.   BATHROOMS.

MODERATE TERMS.   GARAGE.

Patronized by The Ypres League.

PRESENTATION SCROLL.

The Chairman and Committee of the Ypres British Settlement have very gratefully accepted from Mrs. R. Henderson-Bland an exceedingly valuable and handsomely framed illuminated copy of the Memoriam Poem written by her husband, Captain R. Henderson-Bland, and which appeared in the supplement of the last (October) edition of THE YPRES TIMES.

The design, 19 inches by 16 inches, has been brilliantly executed by Mr. J. W. Portway, engrosser to the Ypres League, and incorporates the following features :—

An outer border of oak leaves entwined round a gold bar, with an inner border of Flanders Poppies, Cornflowers and Roses. The Flemish Lion is shown in red on gold ground, and the Paschal Lamb on blue, the coat of arms of the late Field-Marshal Viscount Plumer, coat of arms of Ypres, Field-Marshal's baton on cushion, badges of the Second Army, Gloucestershire Regiment, and Ypres League.

Arrangements are being made for the transit of the scroll to Ypres, the placing of which will be left in the hands of the local authority.

YPRES LEAGUE TIE.

At the request of the majority of our members we have been pleased to produce the tie in better quality silk and in a darker shade of cornflower blue relieved by a narrow gold stripe. The price is 3s. 6d. post free.

HOTEL MODERNE

(Place de la Gare) **A R R A S** (Pas de Calais)

F. GRAVIER, Proprietor.

Recommended by the Ypres League.

YPRES

Skindles Hotel

(Opposite the Station)

Proprietor — Life Member, Ypres League

Branch at Poperinghe

(close to Talbot House)

THE BRITISH TOURING SERVICE

Manager—Mr. P. VYNER.

Representative and Life Member, Ypres League.

**10, Station Square
ARRAS
(P.-de-C.) France.**

Cars for Hire, with British Driver Guides.   Tours Arranged.

A Junior Pilgrimage to Ypres.

There has been in Belgium for some time a Voluntary Association called "The Belgian-Luxembourg Students' Travelling Society."

Under the patronage of the Belgian Minister of Science and Arts and the Minister of State of the Grand Duchy of Luxembourg, it is controlled by the Belgian-Luxembourg Touring Office (National official office).

The new Association will arrange and help forward friendly relations between young students of different nationalities with a view of bringing about a better understanding and esteem amongst them.

A start will be made at Easter, 1933, by an Anglo-Belgian Travel Exchange, whereby 750 Belgian and Luxembourg students will visit London, and 750 Britishers will go to Belgium.

Besides visiting Ostend, Bruges, Ghent (where English children will be present at the inauguration of the "Floralies" ceremonies in the presence of the Belgian Royal Family) the programme provides for participation in the Peace Day at Ypres.

The local leaders, namely, the "Last Post" Committee, the schools, and the English Colony at Ypres will arrange the details of this wonderful ceremony which will be staged at the Menin Gate on Friday, April 21st, at 11 a.m. The organizers, by this great show wish to draw the attention of the Youth of Great Britain to the enormous sacrifices made by their parents in the Great War. They want to bring home to them that humanity must be spared a recurrence of such a plague and that every effort must strive for Peace (The Ideal of Peace).

To augment the great significance of the Day of Peace, the organizers would welcome the help and presence of members of the Junior Branch of the Ypres League.

Junior members wishing to join should apply at once to H. W. Barter, Esq., The School Journey Association, 35, Parkview Road, Addiscombe, Croydon, who has all arrangements in hand on the British side.

In conjunction with this visit of the Juniors, adults will be arranged for by "Sobelvoy" Belgian-Luxembourg Travel Society. Those who wish to join the grown-ups are requested to write direct to "Sobelvoy" 48, Place de Brouckere, Brussels.

Branch Notes.

COLCHESTER.

A sound foundation has been laid for an Ypres League, Colchester and District Branch, and Mr. H. Snow's hard spade work and perseverance deserves the greatest praise. We owe him and his faithful supporters a deep debt of gratitude for the valuable time they have so ungrudgingly given to the forming of this Branch to which we offer our earnest support and every good wish.

The following gentlemen have generously accepted office :—Lieut.-Colonel W. H. Herring, M.C. (Chairman), Major G. C. Benham, M.C., Captain A. C. Palmer (Hon. Treasurer), Mr. H. Snow (Hon. Secretary) and Mr. W. H. Taylor (Pilgrimage Hon. Secretary).

MAGOG.

This Branch was originally inaugurated in January, 1929, but the general depression in Canada that followed was responsible for its temporary inactivity. We are, however, exceedingly pleased to announce that this Branch has now been able to re-form, and judging from recent reports we feel confident that it may shortly become one of our most active branches.

Mr. Ed. Kingsland, well known in veteran patriotic work and an old sergeant-major of Sherbrooke's 117th Battalion, to whose fine initiative the re-establishment of the Branch is due, has kindly undertaken the duties of secretary and treasurer, and he is deserving of our grateful thanks and heartiest congratulations.

The Presidency and Vice-Presidency has been accepted by Sergeant W. P. Adams, M.M., and Mr. F. L. Whiting, respectively, and we thank these two gentlemen for their kindness in giving Mr. Kingsland such valued support.

It is really most encouraging to us at Headquarters to know that this loyal interest is being taken to increase the membership of the Ypres League in Canada, and we wish our Magog Branch every success in its great and noble endeavours.

LONDON COUNTY COMMITTEE.

After the vacation, the London County Committee have resumed their monthly meetings which take place on the third Thursday of each month between the hours of 7 and 10 p.m., at the Bedford Head Hotel, Maiden Lane, Strand, W.C.2.

The September programme was kindly given by members and friends and plenty of good talent was immensely enjoyed, and the old war-time choruses again played a great part in fostering the spirit of comradeship.

In October a highly successful evening was due to our friend, Mr. W. B. Steel, in conjunction with his large variety of efficient artists, and we were all sorry when the entertainment came to a close at a late hour.

Our November gathering welcomed Captain H. D. Peabody, D.C.M., who delivered another of his most interesting lantern lectures on the Salient. We are indeed grateful to him and also to Mr. R. S. Beck who kindly operated the lantern. The success of these lectures has prompted members to lend war-time photographs for the preparation of slides which may be useful to Captain Peabody.

Mr. W. G. Foster and his friends gave us a very pleasant evening on December 15th, and he is deserving of our grateful thanks.

We wish to express sincere gratitude to all who have helped us throughout 1932, and the continued popularity of these meetings gives us encouragement, but we must ask our London members to exercise all that is in their power to recruit more new members for the League so that the numbers attending the Gatherings may increase.

The forthcoming fixtures are recorded on page 155, and we hope they will receive the staunch support that has been shown in the past.

We are hopeful of organizing a dance to take place some time in January, and full particulars will be sent out on completion of the arrangements.

THE NINTH ANNUAL
CHILDREN'S CHRISTMAS PARTY

ORGANIZED BY THE

LONDON COUNTY COMMITTEE

WILL TAKE PLACE AT THE

WESTMINSTER CITY SCHOOL

55, PALACE ST., VICTORIA ST., S.W.1

(By permission of the Governors of the School)

On SATURDAY, JANUARY 14TH, 1933,

AT 4 P.M.

Admission :
Junior Division Members, Free. Friends, 6d. each.
Application for tickets should be made to the Hon. Secretary, London County Committee, Ypres League, at 9, Baker Street, W.1., not later than January 12th, 1933.

A Christmas Tree will again be provided. Gifts of Toys or Donations will be very gratefully received, and should be sent to The Hon. Secretary, London County Committee, at 9, Baker Street, London, W.1.

The object of this party is to strengthen the Junior Division. Junior members are admitted to the party free, and a limited number of friends wishing to attend will be charged 6d. each. Last year there was a record attendance, which we hope will be exceeded. Application for tickets should be made not later than January 12th.

Tea commences at 4 p.m., followed by a ventriloquist entertainment.

To some children, this is the only treat enjoyed during the festive season, and it is hoped that members will do all they can to give us their support and make this annual event a great success. There will be a Christmas Tree, and Father Christmas will appear during the evening. Gifts of toys and donations, for which we earnestly appeal, will be received very gratefully by the Hon. Secretary, London County Committee, Ypres League, 9, Baker Street, W.1.

We are very pleased to announce that the Enfield Children's Orchestra under the personal direction of Mrs. Lea Peabody, have kindly promised to come and give selections during the evening.

ANNUAL SMOKING CONCERT.

Pluvius, for some inexplicable reason, seems to cogitate a spirit of antipathy towards the Ypres League's annual reunion of members at the October Smoking Concert. Or is it sympathy—sympathy with the spirit of the occasion ? For was not Ypres, and everything associated with it, synonymous with rain, rain, and yet more rain ? Certainly the gathering on Thursday, October 27th, was no exception to the attention this ethereal person appears to devote to the Caxton Hall of recent years, but if his object was to damp the spirit of conviviality and comradeship within, his efforts were entirely unsuccessful.

This 1932 reunion was especially notable as the tenth occasion of this exceedingly popular annual event, and it was fitting that the League should be honoured with the presence, as chairman, of Field-Marshal The Viscount Allenby, G.C.B., G.C.M.G., LL.D. Lord Allenby has been, for many years, a Vice-President of the Ypres League, but his manifold activities do not often permit of his personal submission to the vociferous welcome accorded him on that night— a greeting which signified unanimously the respect and admiration that is conjured by the name of Allenby of the East. We were glad, indeed, to have him with us.

Of course, Major E. Montague Jones, O.B.E., the ever-genial Chairman of the London County Committee, was there. We dare not imagine a Smoking Concert without him. He spoke of the activities of the League during the past year, and also said how pleased he was to learn from the Secretary that the membership of the League had increased by leaps and bounds during the past few months. We all know to what extent this accomplishment is due to Captain G. E. de Trafford personally. Major Montague Jones also passed an expression of gratitude to that indefatigable worker in the interests of the League, Mr. John Boughey, upon whom, as Hon. Secretary of the London County Committee, falls all the work and worry of organizing the League's social functions in London.

It is said that old soldiers never die and, surely, neither will old war-time choruses. How the rafters rattled ! It has not yet been discovered whether the element of keen business competition now prevailing in all trades and industries was directly responsible for the per-

Please book these dates in your Diary.

THE MONTHLY
Informal Gatherings
FOR JANUARY, FEBRUARY, MARCH AND APRIL,

WILL BE HELD AT

THE BEDFORD HEAD HOTEL, MAIDEN LANE, STRAND, W.C.2

ON

THURSDAY, 19TH JANUARY, 1933.
Illustrated Talk on "With the Grand Fleet in the Great War," by Captain E. L. FREWEN, R.N.

THURSDAY, 16TH FEBRUARY, 1933.
Illustrated Talk on Salonika.

THURSDAY, 16TH MARCH, 1933.
Programme by St. Dunstan's Concert Party.

THURSDAY, 20TH APRIL, 1933.
Programme by "85 Club."

FROM 7 P.M. TO 10 P.M.

Start the year 1933 well by paying us a visit at our Gathering on Thursday, 19th January, 1933. A very hearty welcome awaits you and any ex-Service friend whom you may wish to bring along.

Full particulars of the Gatherings will be sent by the Hon. Secretary, London County Committee, to a friend on receipt of name and address.

Ladies are cordially invited.

---

meation of its influence to a section of the gathering, not entirely unacquainted with field guns and batteries, but the fact remains that it necessitated the best stentorian parade voice of Major Montague Jones to entice a competitive community singing party back to the fold from a position, entrenched but not invulnerable.

The primary object of the Ypres League is commemoration and the fostering of the spirit of comradeship born of the war. These Smoking Concerts surely play their part in this grand purpose. To catch snatches of conversations of old "durationers"; to see that middle-aged man trying his hardest to recognize in another who has just approached him, a comrade of the Menin stunt; to hear those choruses from four hundred throats; indubitably does the heart good. The need of comradeship is as great to-day as it was during those now long-ago days. Many a fellow still finds there's a long, long trail awinding, just as he did along the Pop—Ypres Road on those miserably wet October nights and, not a few find they still have a share of troubles to pack in their old kit bags. But it's hard for some to smile. There is solace, however, in comradeship, and the League offers this.

Eleven o'clock terminated an altogether enjoyable evening. An evening appreciated for its pleasant entertainment, the opportunity afforded of meeting old friends, and its sociable company.

A. R. F.

THE BOMBARDIER'S FOURSOMES.

THIRD, FOURTH AND FIFTH BATTLES.

In the third battle the Bombardier himself and Lindsay were unfortunate enough to be defeated by Kerr and Tissington; this pair played quite blamelessly, and the worst that can be said of them is that it is always very tactless to defeat the C.O., especially on his own course.

Hines and Meredith came through against Adams and Macfarlane at Coulsdon Court, 1 up.

It has already been reported that Rae and Crute beat Mutton and Duncan, 3 and 2.

Featherstone and Carr did well against the pros.—Irens and Ha(g)ine—at Purley Downs in their third battle, and won by the unfriendly margin of 6 and 4.

Up to that point the dates fixed for the various battles had been fairly well kept, but there came delays in the two fourth battles.

In the first of these, Rae and Crute came out to Coulsdon Court to play Feathers and Carr one evening early in September, but Fate and The Staff team were against them, so that they suffered defeat, 6 and 5.

Hines and Meredith would be better named Box and Cox, as when one is not away on holiday the other is, so that a month elapsed before they met Kerr and Tissington one fine afternoon at Coulsdon Court. This was the third occasion that they had had the choice of course and yet had to play on the enemy's home —their own being barred by the rules—a small matter they did not omit to mention in loud protest.

No eye-witness account of the battle is available, but the writer who was engaged some five holes behind, was able to follow progress by the series of loud noises!

Kerr and Tissington were reported the winners, 4 and 2, but Hines says (among other things) that his side won really because he was bluffed out of two tee shots, which cost two holes, added to which there should have been two strokes penalty on Kerr and Tiss. for local knowledge, so that being four holes better off that way, they must have won on the 19th at least!

As it was, the 19th was played in the usual way.

Owing to a multitude of other battle engagements, the fifth (and final) battle could not be staged until November 13th—a fitting conclusion to a summer tournament.

Three of the four being members, and fourth a past member, of Coulsdon Court, it was felt that this course was sufficiently neutral for the purpose.

At zero hour a bleak and Arctic wind was blowing, and it was clear that the fight would be grim, for all four wore the League tie! Feathers led off and Kerr drove against him; Tiss. played a good second, but Carr only bumped it on to the green somehow, and further distinguished himself by failing to negotiate a half-stymie, and knocking the other ball in instead—to lose the hole.

The second was won by The Staff, who got a startling 2 at the third, and won that too.

There followed a half and win for Kerr and Tiss., who enlisted the elements to hole out for them at the 6th, the wind blowing the ball in from the lip of the hole.

A half, a win and another half, left them 2 up at the turn.

Some very undistinguished play followed, resulting in 2 halves, a scrambling win for The Staff, and a complete present by Carr of a half to the enemy at the 13th, their last stroke hole; they immediately showed their appreciation by winning the 14th in a birdie to be 2 up.

Then The Staff did things and got the next two back. All square.

At the 17th, Feathers got a half by a magnificent bunker shot and holing a good putt. Still all square.

Both tee shots went down the middle at the 18th; Kerr was bunkered with his next, just short of the green, Feathers was not. Both on in 3, Kerr putted wide; Feathers just failed to hole the putt—and laid the enemy a blank stymie!

Tiss. could not negotiate it, so The Staff won, 1 up.

The 19th was played in the usual way.

So ended The Bombardier's Foursomes for 1932, after many good and cheery battles.

In the afternoon a party of fifty strong, under command of Bombardier Burden, attended the Armistice Day service.

THE SECRETARY.

KENYA AND MADRID BRANCHES.

Reports have been received, delayed by Christmas post, which will be printed in full in our next issue.

NEW YORK BRANCH.
Obituary.

We regret to record the passing of two very distinguished and well-known personalities of the Great War, especially endeared to the American Expeditionary Force, in the names of Father Francis P. Duffy (Senior Chaplain of the 165th U.S. Infantry, 42nd Division), and Captain Robert W. Hanna (British Liaison Officer to the 27th American Division in France and Flanders).

"**FATHER**" **DUFFY,** as he was affectionately known, had been referred to as "the ideal army chaplain and the ideal parish priest," and in view of his wonderful record this pronouncement is easily understood. Although never a man of robust constitution, he incurred the reputation as an "iron man," and his heroic actions under shell-fire in the Great War were recognized by the United States, France and other governments for which he received the Distinguished Service Cross, the Distinguished Service Medal, the Cross of the Legion of Honour, and the Croix de Guerre with palm. On July 28th, 1918, his regiment crossed the Ourcq and penetrated the German defences to the north, suffering heavy casualties, Father Duffy, spending the whole day on the battlefield, continued to bear wounded men to shelter under heavy machine-gun fire, cheering them by word and example and thrilling them by his total disregard of danger. The incidents of this particular day earned him a citation for the Distinguished Service Cross, but it might have been any day when with his regiment in action. Those fortunate enough to know him in those dark days will for ever remember him for his tenderness and solicitude for the wounded under deadly shell-fire. Apart from military life, which included chaplain in the Spanish-American War, this self-sacrificing officer appears to have been as much beloved by his humble parishioners in New York, where Protestant and Jew and those of no faith at all loved him for his encouragement and advice. He was, indeed, a gift to mankind, and his end was typical of the life he led, a simple unassuming parish priest, clasping the crucifix and rosary beads given him as a lad by his mother and which he treasured above all else.

* * *

CAPTAIN ROBERT W. (MARK) HANNA, the only honorary member of Post 27, Divisional Headquarters, 27th American Division Association of the world war, whose sudden death in London recently came as a shock to his many American friends, was a British officer appointed for his particular abilities as Liaison Officer to the 27th American Division when this division was operating with the British Second and Fourth Armies. This young officer was very highly esteemed by the American High Command, and no more fitting gesture could be shown than by the special cable forwarded to Captain R. Henderson-Bland (Ypres League Representative in America) now on a visit to this country, asking him to represent the 27th Division at the funeral, to which Captain Bland sympathetically complied. Captain Hanna, for his services in the aforementioned post, was awarded the Conspicuous Service Cross of the State of New York, and General J. F. O'Ryan, when recommending him for the honour, referred to his exceptionally meritorious services as Liaison Officer from June 1st to November, 1918. His timely hints and suggestions being of special value during the operations of the division while with the British Second Army in the vicinity of Mt. Kemmel, and with the British Fourth Army at Le Catelet and Le Cateau. An officer possessed of keen perception, energy, tact and great cheerfulness, his loss will be mourned by comrades on both sides of the Atlantic.

Correspondence.

Captain R. Henderson-Bland has very kindly allowed us to reprint the following two personal letters, which we consider of great interest.

October 22nd, 1932

My Dear Bland,

I was particularly interested to hear of your activities in connection with the Ypres League in the United States and to see for the first time THE YPRES TIMES containing your description of the burial of Lord Plumer in Westminster Abbey, and your excellent and dignified sonnet.

As an experienced journalist and editor, I consider THE YPRES TIMES a remarkable journal, well edited and produced, and it is inspiring and touching to find such a vital reminder of the past existing in these days.

Yours sincerely,
A. E. Manning Foster.

* * *

October 30th, 1932

My Dear Mr. Henderson-Bland,

You were most thoughtful and gracious in sending me a copy of your brilliant and moving description of Lord Plumer's funeral. Being in London, and having an engagement in the neighbourhood of the Abbey about the time of that service, I had the privilege of seeing that impressive cortege enter that holy place. After keeping my engagement, again I found myself near the entrance to the nave of the Abbey, just as the service ended. You may be sure I looked with deep interest at those who had taken official part.

I was perhaps more deeply interested because of having been a guest of the General Staff on the British front in September, 1918, stopping at Tramecourt. It was my privilege to see something of the British operations from Bailleul along to a point opposite Cambrai, and I was at Vimy Ridge the day our 27th and 30th Divisions went in against the Hindenburg Line, where in an hour or two we gave the lives of nine of my young parishioners of St. Thomas's Church, New York, who were members of the 107th Regiment of the Old New York Seventh.

All this will simply tell you how sympathetic and how deep is my appreciation of your thoughtfulness. It does not begin to tell you of my admiration for your truly noble picture of Lord Plumer's funeral in the Abbey.

With heartiest good wishes,
I am, ever most faithfully,
Yours,
Ernest Milmore Stires.
Bishop of Long Island.

* * *

Bulawayo.
October 28th, 1932.

Secretary, Ypres League,

Dear Sir,

It will be of considerable interest to you to learn that while the remains of the late Field-Marshal Lord Plumer were being laid to rest, a memorial service was held at the Church of S. John the Baptist, Bulawayo. Seeing that the late Lord Plumer first came into prominence during the Matabele Rebellion in 1896, and there are still a number of Pioneers alive who served under him then and later during the Boer War, it was most fitting that this service should have been held at Bulawayo, the town nearest the scenes of his operations against the Matabele.

The service was conducted by the Ven. Archdeacon A. M. Mylne, Archdeacon of Matabeleland, Rector of Bulawayo, and ex-Chaplain to the Forces. The officers of the British South Africa Police and the officers of the Southern Rhodesia Defence Force attended, while the church was crowded out. Among those who attended were a number of ex-service men, many of whom had served in the Second Army, while among the Pioneers who attended were several who took part in the Matabele Rebellion and Boer War under Plumer. The Pipers of the 2nd Battalion Rhodesia Regiment (Defence Force) played a lament. The Chief Justice, the Hon. Mr. Justice Russell, representing the Government of the Colony, gave the address. The service ended up with the " Last Post " and " Réveillé " sounded by Cadet buglers. The congregation included the Mayor of Bulawayo, in robes of office, and the Town Clerk, while there were special places reserved for the ex-service men who wore medals and decorations.

Yours sincerely,
A. N. Cranswick.

* * *

Brisbane,
October 12th, 1932.

Dear Captain de Trafford,

Both the undersigned are in receipt of your personal letter referring to the unparalleled loss to the Ypres League in the death of our late beloved President, Field-Marshal Viscount Plumer, and urging the members of the Ypres League to strive harder to mantain the maximum membership of our organization. There you can rest assured that we will do our best to comply with your request as we appreciate the splendid work the Ypres League is doing, and furthermore anything associated with Ypres is worthy of the very best that any loyal citizen of the Empire can render.

We should like to take this opportunity of congratulating you personally on your efforts to maintain the League at its very apex, and as far as members in the Dominions are concerned your correspondence helps very much to perpetuate those ties of Empire which are so very necessary to maintain the true spirit of loyalty and co-operation between " His Majesty's Dominions."

Again expressing our appreciation of the splendid service the Ypres League is rendering to the Empire,

Yours sincerely,
(Signed) C. H. Green.
G. Lawson.

"BETWEEN THE BIG PARADES."

By Franklin W. Ward.

A gripping war story of the lives, fortunes and misfortunes of soldiers during the actual hostilities abroad. The characters, from officers of high rank to privates, pulsate with action, sometimes in laugh-evoking comedy and witticism, sometimes in tear-bringing pathos and tragedy.

A war tale built around the New York National Guard (27th American Division), commanded by General J. F. O'Ryan, during the Great War, and which served with distinction with the British Forces under the command of the late Field-Marshal Viscount Plumer in the Immortal Ypres Salient.

CONTENTS.

CHAPTER.
- I. **THE VOYAGERS**—Blasting Submarines.
- II. **FRANCE ON MEMORIAL DAY**—Coloured Soldiers—The Four Horsemen.
- III. **WITH HIS MAJESTY'S ROYAL BRITISH ARMY**—Night Riders à la mode—With a " Furrin" Army, to be sure.
- IV. **THE SANITARY INSPECTOR**—Moving On—The Escarboten Club—Gamblers' Luck.
- V. **PERSHING**—A General Court-Martial—Flanders Fields.
- VI. **THE LINE**—A Slip of the Tongue—The Cup that Cheers—The King Cometh—An "Irish" Promotion—The Inspector Laughs Last—Cassel the Ancient—Pounds, Shillings and Pence.
- VII. **VIA PARIS**—Langres—"Grapevine" Route—The Button Box—Flotsam and Jetsam—A Reunion.
- VIII. **THE HINDENBURG LINE**—The Objective—The Morning of September 27th—The Signal—The Long Day—Night—New Blood—The Shute—The 29th of September—Here Valour Sleeps—" We were in a Crump-hole, 'im and me!"
- IX. **THE COLONEL TAKES ANOTHER TRIP**—Joining Up—The Open Road—Following Heinie—Silk Hats.
- X. **THE TOWN OF ST. SOUPLET**—Mr. Fritz makes a Raid—Digging-in—The Council of War—Under Cover of Darkness—The Rum Ration—The 18th of October—Aerial Combat and Wienerschnitzel.
- XI. **THE LAST DAY**—At the St. Maurice River—The End of the Trail—" Red Cross "—Retrospection.
- XII. **ONE NIGHT STANDS**—A " Rest " Area—Second-story Men—" Quite a' Hoccasion."
- XIII. **A LEAVE OF ABSENCE**—Armistice—Leaving 'is Majesty's Army—Decorations—Horse and Horse—Christmas—Dead-gone—The Come-on—A New Corporal.
- XIV. **HOME**—Loose Leaves—Hail and Farewell.

PRICE $2.50 (postage, 6d. extra).

(or its equivalent outside America and Canada)

Obtainable only in Europe

through

HEADQUARTERS, THE YPRES LEAGUE, 9, BAKER STREET, LONDON, W.1.

N.B.—See review on page 149.

Branches and Corresponding Members.

BRANCHES.

LONDON	Hon. Secretary to the London County Committee: J. Boughey, 9, Baker Street, London, W.1.
	E. LONDON DISTRICT—L. A. Weller, 132, Maxey Road, Dagenham, Essex.
	TOTTENHAM AND EDMONTON DISTRICT—E. Glover, 191, Lansdowne Road, Tottenham, N.17.
	H. Carey, 373, Sydenham Road, S.E.26.
GATESHEAD	Lieut.-Colonel E. G. Crouch, 8, Ashgrove Terrace.
LIVERPOOL	Captain A. M. Webster, Blundellsands.
PURLEY	Major Graham Carr, D.S.O., M.C., 112-114, High Street.
SHEFFIELD	Captain J. Wilkinson, " Holmfield," Bents Drive.
BELGIUM	Colonel L. Aerts, 27, Rue de l'Abbaye, Bruxelles.
CANADA	Ed. Kingsland, P.O. Box 83, Magog, Quebec.
SOUTH AFRICA	L. G. Shuter, Church Street, Pietermaritzburg, Natal.
AMERICA	Representative: Captain R. Henderson-Bland, 110 West 57th Street, New York City.

CORRESPONDING MEMBERS.

GREAT BRITAIN.

ABERYSTWYTH	T. O. Thomas, 5, Smithfield Road.
ASHTON-UNDER-LYNE	G. D. Stuart, Woodlands, Thronfield Grove, Arundel Street.
BANBURY	Captain C. W. Fowke, Yew Tree House, King's Sutton.
BIRMINGHAM	Mrs. Hill, 191, Cattell Road, Small Heath.
	John Burman, " Westbrook," Solihull Road, Shirley.
BOURNEMOUTH	H. L. Pasmore, 40, Morley Road, Boscombe Park.
BRISTOL	W. S. Hook, Stoneleigh, Cotham Park.
BROADSTAIRS	C. E. King, 6, Norman Road, St. Peters, Broadstairs.
	Mrs. Briggs, North Foreland House.
CARLISLE	Lieut.-Colonel G. T. Willan, D.S.O., 3, Goschen Road.
CHATHAM	W. N. Channon, 22, Keyes Avenue.
CHESTERFIELD	Major A. W. Shea, 14, Cross Street.
COLCHESTER	W. H. Taylor, 64, High Street.
CONGLETON	Mr. H. Dart, 61, The Crescent.
DARLINGTON	D. S. Vigo, 125, Dorset Road, Bexhill-on-Sea.
DERBY	T. Jakeman, 10, Graham Street.
DORRINGTON (Salop)	Captain G. D. S. Parker, Frodesley Rectory.
EXETER	Captain E. Jenkin, 25, Queen Street.
GLOUCESTER	H. R. Hunt, " Casita," Parton Lane, Churchdown.
HERNE BAY	Captain E. Clarke Williams, F.S.A.A., " Conway," Station Road.
HOVE	Captain G. W. J. Cole, 2, Westbourne Terrace, Kingsway.
LEEDS	R. G. Rawnsley, The Lilacs, Hawksworth Avenue, Guiseley.
LEICESTER	W. C. Dunford, 343, Aylestone Road.
LINCOLN	E. Swaine, 79, West Parade.
LLANWRST	A. C. Tomlinson, M.A., Bod Estyn.
LOUGHTON	Capt. O. G. Johnson, M.A., Loughton School.
MATLOCK (Derby)	Miss Dickinson, Beechwood.
MELROSE	Mrs. Lindesay Kelsall, Huntlyburn.
NEW BRIGHTON (Cheshire)	E. F. Williams, 5, Waterloo Road.
NEW MILTON	W. H. Lunn, Greycot, Albert Road.

NOTTINGHAM ...	...	E. V. Brown, 3, Eldon Chambers, Wheeler Gate.
ST. HELENS (Lancs.)	...	John Orford, 124, Knowsley Road.
SHREWSBURY ...	...	Major-General Sir John Headlam, Cruck Meole House, Hanwood.
TIVERTON (Devon)	...	Mr. W. H. Duncan Arthur, Surveyor's Office, Town Hall.
WELSHPOOL ...	...	Mr. E. Wilson, Coedway, Ford, Salop.

DOMINIONS AND FOREIGN COUNTRIES.

AUSTRALIA ...	...	Messrs. C. H. Green and George Lawson, Anzac House, Elizabeth Street, Brisbane, Queensland.
		R. A. Baldwin, c/o Government Savings Bank of N.S.W., Martin Place, Sydney.
		Mr. W. Cloves, Box 1296, G.P.O., Adelaide.
BELGIUM	...	Sister Marguerite, Sacré Cœur, Ypres.
		Colonel L. Aerts, 27, Rue de l'Abbaye, Bruxelles.
BUENOS AYRES ...		President, British Ex-Service Club, Calle 25 de Mayo 577.
CANADA	...	Brig.-General V. W. Odlum, C.B., C.M.G., D.S.O., 2530, Point Grey Road, Vancouver.
		V. A. Bowes, 326, 40th Avenue West, Calgary, Alberta.
		W. Constable F. Grece, 4095, Tupper Street, Westmount, Montreal.
CEYLON	...	Captain F. R. G. Webb, M.C., Irrigation Bungalow, Kalmunai, E.P.
EGYPT	...	L. B. S. Larkins, The Residency, Cairo.
INDIA	...	Lieut.-Quartermaster G. Smith, Queen's Bays, Sialkot, India.
		W. J. Cotter, 26, The Crescent, Viceregal, Camp Post Office, New Delhi.
IRELAND		Miss A. K. Jackson, Cloneyhurke House, Portarlington.
KENYA		Harry Shields, Survey Department, Nairobi.
		Corporal C. H. Slater, P.O. Box 403, Nairobi.
NEW ZEALAND ...		Captain W. U. Gibb, Ava Lodge, Puhinui Road, Papatoetoe, Auckland.
		S. E. Beattie, Lowlands, Woodville.
SOUTH AFRICA ...		H. L. Versfeld, c/o Cape Explosives Works, Ltd., 150, St. George's Street, Cape Town.
SPAIN		Captain P. W. Burgess, Calle de Zurbano 29, Madrid.
U.S.A.		Captain Henry Maslin, 942, President Street, Brooklyn, New York.
		L. E. P. Foot, 20, Gillett Street, Hartford, Conn., U.S.A.
		A. P. Forward, 449, East 80th Street, New York.
		J. W. Freebody, 945, McBride Avenue, Los Angeles.
NOVA SCOTIA ...		Will. R. Bird, Amherst.

Membership of the League.

This is open to all who served in the Salient, and to all those whose relatives or friends died there, in order that they may have a record of that service for themselves and their descendants, and belong to the comradeship of men and women who understand and remember all that Ypres meant in suffering and endurance.

Life membership, £2 10s.

Annual members, 5s.

Do not let the fact of your not having served in the Salient deter you from joining the Ypres League. Those who have neither fought in the Salient nor lost relatives there, but who are in sympathy with the objects of the Ypres League, are admitted to its fellowship, but are not given scroll certificates.

There is a Junior Division for children whose relatives served in the Salient. It is open also to others to whom our objects appeal.

Annual subscription 1s. up to the age of 18, after which they can become ordinary members of the League.

The Ypres League (Incorporated).
9 Baker Street, Portman Square, W.1.

Telephone: WELBECK 1446.   *Telegrams:* YPRESLEAG, "WESDO," LONDON.

Patron-in-Chief: H.M. THE KING.

Patrons:

H.R.H. THE PRINCE OF WALES.   H.R.H. PRINCESS BEATRICE.

President: GENERAL SIR CHARLES H. HARINGTON.

Vice-Presidents:

F.-M. VISCOUNT ALLENBY.   GENERAL SIR PHILIP CHETWODE.
F.-M. SIR CLAUD JACOB.   THE LORD WAKEFIELD OF HYTHE.
THE VISCOUNT BURNHAM.   LIEUT.-GENERAL SIR CECIL ROMER.

General Committee:

THE COUNTESS OF ALBEMARLE.
MAJOR J. R. AINSWORTH-DAVIS.
*CAPTAIN C. ALLISTON.
LIEUT.-COLONEL BECKLES WILLSON.
*MR. JOHN BOUGHEY.
*MISS B. BRICE-MILLER.
COLONEL G. T. BRIERLEY.
CAPTAIN P. W. BURGESS.
*MAJOR H. CARDINAL-HARFORD.
REV. P. B. CLAYTON.
*THE EARL OF YPRES.
MRS. CHARLES J. EDWARDS.
MAJOR C. J. EDWARDS.
MR. H. A. T. FAIRBANK.
MR. T. ROSS FURNER.
SIR PHILIP GIBBS.
MR. E. GLOVER.
MAJOR C. E. GODDARD.
MAJOR-GENERAL SIR JOHN HEADLAM.
MR. F. D. BANKS HILL.
MAJOR-GENERAL C. J. B. HAY.

MR. J. HETHERINGTON.
MRS. E. HEAP.
GENERAL SIR W. C. G. HENEKER.
BRIGADIER H. C. JACKSON.
CAPTAIN O. G. JOHNSON.
*MAJOR MONTAGUE JONES.
CAPTAIN H. D. PEABODY.
*THE HON. ALICE DOUGLAS PENNANT.
*LIEUT.-GENERAL SIR W. P. PULTENEY.
LIEUT.-COLONEL SIR J. MURRAY.
LIEUT.-GENERAL SIR CECIL ROMER.
*COLONEL G. E. C. RASCH.
VISCOUNT SANDON.
THE HON. SIR ARTHUR STANLEY.
MR. ERNEST THOMPSON.
CAPTAIN J. LOCKLEY TURNER.
*LIEUT.-GENERAL SIR H. UNIACKE.
*MR. E. B. WAGGETT.
CAPTAIN J. WILKINSON.
CAPT. H. TREVOR WILLIAMS.
     * Executive Committee.

Finance:

LIEUT.-GENERAL SIR W. P. PULTENEY.
LIEUT.-GENERAL SIR HERBERT UNIACKE.
CAPTAIN C. ALLISTON.

Secretary:

CAPTAIN G. E. DE TRAFFORD.

Auditors:

MESSRS. LEPINE & JACKSON,
     6, Bond Court, E.C.4.

Honorary Solicitors:

MESSRS. FLADGATE & CO., 18, Pall Mall, S.W.

Bankers:

BARCLAYS BANK, LTD., Knightsbridge Branch.

Trustees:

LIEUT.-GENERAL SIR W. P. PULTENEY.
MR. E. B. WAGGETT.
MAJOR E. MONTAGUE JONES.

League Representative at Ypres:
CAPTAIN P. D. PARMINTER,
19, Rue Surmont de Volsberghe.

League Representative in America:
CAPTAIN R. HENDERSON-BLAND.
110 West 57th Street, New York.

League Representative at Amiens:
CAPTAIN STUART OSWALD,
7, Rue Porte-Paris.

League Representative at Arras:
MR. P. VYNER,
10, Station Square.

OBJECTS OF THE LEAGUE.

I.—Commemoration and Comradeship.

II.—The arranging of special facilities for travel and transport of members.

III.—The furnishing of information about the Salient ; marking of historic sites and the compilation of charts of the battlefields.

IV.—To secure the erection of a Ypres British Church and School.

V.—The establishment of groups of members throughout the world, through Branch Secretaries and Corresponding Members.

VI.—The maintenance of cordial relations with dwellers on the battlefields of Ypres.

VII.—The formation of a Junior Division.

     All these objects have now been secured, and the upkeep of the Ypres British Settlement (Object IV) is our future policy.

Use the Ypres League Travel Bureau for Ypres and Whole of the Western Front.

FOR THE FOLLOWING PUBLICATIONS, Etc., apply:

Secretary, YPRES LEAGUE, 9, BAKER STREET, LONDON, W.1.

THE BATTLE BOOK OF YPRES. A history of notable deeds contributed by all regiments. 5s.; post free, 5s. 6d. Compiled by Beatrix Brice with the assistance of Lieut.-General Sir William Pulteney, K.C.B., etc.

BOOKS.

YPRES : Outpost of the Channel Ports. By Beatrix Brice. With Foreword by Field-Marshal Lord Plumer, G.C.B. Price 1s. 6d.; post free 1s. 10d.

In the Ypres Salient. By Lt.-Col. Beckles Willson. 1s. net; post free 1s. 2d.

To the Vanguard. By Beatrix Brice. 1s. net; post free 1s. 2d.

The City of Fear and Other Poems. By Gilbert Frankau. 3s. 6d. net; post free 3s. 8d.

With the Cornwall Territorials on the Western Front. By E. C. Matthews. 7s. 6d.; post free 8s.

Story of the 63rd Field Ambulance. By A. W. Westmore, etc. Cloth, 3s. 6d., post free. Paper, 2s. 6d., post free.

War Letters to a Wife. By Colonel Rowland Feilding. Popular Edition. 7s. 6d.; post free 8s.

YPRES LEAGUE TIES. 3s. 6d. each, post free.

YPRES LEAGUE BADGES. 2s. each, 2s. 1½d. post free.

EMBROIDERED BADGES. 4s. each, post free.

Map and List of Cemeteries in the Ypres Salient. Price 9d.; post free 11d.

Map of the Somme. Price 1s. 8d., post free.

PICTURES.

Burning of the Cloth Hall, 1915. A Coloured Print, 14 in. by 12 in. 1s. post free.

The Tomb of the Unknown Warrior. By Bernard Gribble. 10s. 6d., post free.

ENGRAVINGS, 33 in. by 21 in., £1 11s. 6d. each.

Hell Fire Corner.

Heavy Artillery Going into Action before Passchendaele.

" I Won't."

BRITISH WAR CEMETERIES AND MEMORIALS SITUATED IN THE YPRES SALIENT.

Post Cards. Ypres : British Front during the War. Ruins of Ypres. Price 1s. post free.

Photographs in Album Form. 8 in. by 7 in. Price 2s.; post free 2s. 3d.

Photographs of Cemeteries in Booklet Form. Post card size. 4 Series. Price 1s.; post free 1s. 2d.

Photographs of Memorials in Booklet Form. Post card size. 2 Series. Price 1s.; post free 1s. 2d.

Photographs of Menin Gate Unveiling. Size 11 in. by 7 in. 1s. 2d. each, post free.

Hill 60. Complete Panorama Photograph.
12 in. by 3¾ in. Price 3s., post free.
15 in. by 5 in. Price 3s. 6d., post free.

WAR-TIME PHOTOGRAPHS OF THE SALIENT.

6 in. by 8 in. ... 1s. 6d. each.
12 in. by 15 in. ... 4s. each.
List forwarded on application.

YPRES TIMES.

The Journal may be obtained at the League Offices.
BACK NUMBERS 1s.; 1931, 8d.; 1932, 6d.

PHOTOGRAPHS OF WAR-TIME SKETCHES.

Bedford House (Front View), 1916.
Bedford House (Back View), 1916.
Voormezeele Main Street, 1916.
Voormezeele Crucifixion Gate, 1916.
Langhof Chateau, 1916.

Size 8¼ in. by 6¼ in. Price 2s. 6d. each, post free.

ETCHINGS.

Etchings of Menin Gate Memorial. 9 in. by 6 in. Price, 5s. each, post free. Signed proofs, 10s. 6d. each, post free.

Printed in Great Britain for the Publishers by GALE & POLDEN, LTD., 2, Amen Corner, Paternoster Row, London, E.C.4.

Memory Tablet.

APRIL MAY JUNE

APRIL.

April 5th, 1917	...	United States declares war on Germany.
,, 9th, 1917	...	Battle of Vimy Ridge begins.
,, 9th, 1918	...	Battle of the Lys begins.
,, 14th, 1918	...	General Foch appointed Generalissimo of the Allied Armies in France.
,, 22nd, 1915	...	Second Battle of Ypres begins. Germans use asphyxiating gases.
,, 22nd, 1918	...	British Naval attack on Zeebrugge and Ostend.
,, 24th, 1916	...	Rebellion in Ireland.
,, 25th, 1915	...	Allied forces land in Gallipoli.
,, 27th, 1915	...	General Sir Herbert Plumer given command of all troops in the Ypres Salient.
,, 29th, 1916	...	Fall of Kut.

MAY.

May 7th, 1915	...	The *Lusitania* torpedoed and sunk by the Germans.
,, 12th, 1915	...	Windhoek, capital of German South-West Africa, captured by General Botha.
,, 19th, 1918	...	Germans bomb British hospitals at Etaples.
,, 23rd, 1915	...	Italy declares war on Austria.
,, 31st, 1916	...	Sea battle off the coast of Jutland.

JUNE.

June 5th, 1916	...	Loss of Earl Kitchener on H.M.S. *Hampshire*
,, 7th, 1915	...	Flight-Lieut. Warneford attacks and destroys Zeppelin between Ghent and Brussels.
,, 7th, 1917	...	British victory at Messines Ridge.
,, 29th, 1917	...	General Allenby in command in Egypt.

The YPRES TIMES

Communications to
The Editor, "Ypres Times,"
20 Orchard Street, London, W.1.

PRICE 6d.
POST FREE 7d.

Vol. 6, No. 6   Published Quarterly   April, 1933

League Offices: Change of Address

IN consequence of the lease expiring at 9, Baker Street, Portman Square, London, W.1, the premises of which are shortly to be demolished, it became necessary for us to seek suitable quarters for our offices elsewhere, and we are pleased to inform our members that we have been extremely fortunate in securing ideal accommodation on the first floor of

20, ORCHARD STREET, PORTMAN SQUARE, LONDON, W.1.

Our new address is certainly more central and accessible, being only about fifty yards from Oxford Street, and within a few yards of the stopping-place for omnibuses from all parts of London. The exact location is immediately facing Selfridge's Car Park, in Orchard Street. Marble Arch and Bond Street are the nearest tube stations, the latter being no more than eighty yards distant along Oxford Street from Orchard Street.

We trust that the many members and friends we had the privilege and pleasure to receive at our old quarters in Baker Street will honour us with a visit at the new premises and agree that the present headquarters are in every respect worthy of the League.

The Battle of Arras-Vimy Ridge, Easter, 1917

By Lieut. C. J. Hupfield, 2nd Bn. The Suffolk Regt., 3rd Division.

SINCE the finish of the long-drawn-out Somme struggle with the Ancre battle in November, 1916, no major operation had been organized by the British Army until word came round in March, 1917, that things were again on the move.

I may mention that, in all my time in France, I cannot recollect better spirit or morale among the men than just around this period, which culminated in the famous Easter Monday success, east of Arras and Vimy Ridge. The preliminaries to the attack on Easter Monday at dawn were unusual in so far as our particular Division was concerned. On Good Friday, April 6th, two brother officers and myself went round our proposed assembly positions and then reconnoitred the old medieval Spanish caves near Arras station. These had been greatly improved by New Zealand engineers, and were named Auckland, Wellington, Christchurch, etc. Our unit, the 2nd Suffolks and remainder of the 76th Brigade, came in that night, in pouring rain, having marched from Wanquetin, and entered the sewers of Arras in single file and thence into the caves, eighty feet below ground.

Immense preparations had been going on for weeks all around Arras and to the north, all focused on April 9th. On Saturday, the 7th, we had to take our non-commissioned officers round the assembly trenches and issue the usual S.A.A. rations and instructions. It was a glorious day, sunny but very cold. On the Sunday we celebrated Holy Communion underground, and the bulk of the Battalion attended one of the most impressive Easter services on record. The afternoon dragged on, and at night we read out the Divisional "Order of the Day" for the morrow. We were all in fine fettle and anxious to end the suspense of training. There was an eerie silence in these caves after the earsplitting field-guns and howitzers just outside, as about half way down the stairs their explosions became inaudible.

We had a short sleep from about 10 p.m. till midnight, and then put on our battle equipment, loaded revolvers and lined up our men for the long climb up those interminable stairs. About 1 a.m., in inky darkness, we started slowly up and up towards—what ? About half way up our 18-pounder staccato fire became audible outside and grew louder and louder as we reached the top, a little final attention before the gunners shut down for an hour or two to lay in shells in preparation for the barrages. We arrived about 2.30 in our assembly trench, crawling slowly along and keeping very quiet. On this lovely night, with swift-moving clouds overhead, there were scores of thousands of men on a thirty-six-mile front, all doing the same, and it was a mercy there was now not any shelling to speak of. Our artillery had been working very hard since the Wednesday, and we were wondering if the enemy were expecting anything.

I made a final tour of my men and found all correct. Then, at 3.30, the best part of the show came round in the form of dixies of tea and rum rations.

Zero hour was 5.30 a.m., and from 4.30 it became wearisome in the extreme, and colder and colder. We were crouching and sitting in four-foot trenches with our loaded rifles, with bayonets fixed, lying on the parados. Five-fifteen arrived, and with it great clouds blew up from the south, then 5.26, 5.27, and at 5.28 (with apparently two minutes to go) hell broke loose on the Vimy Ridge portion of the front, all guns trained on the Ridge firing their fastest. Simultaneously nearly a dozen large mines, pushed under the Ridge, went up, and the inferno was overpowering by its very suddenness and wonderful timing. Then, on the stroke of 5.30, our own particular few miles of front joined in, and now it was impossible to hear the man next to you, even if he shouted. We couldn't help pitying the Boche—for hadn't we seen the guns of all sizes, wheel to wheel, in and around many parts of Arras? As a final gesture all the machine guns in the upper floors of the houses in the Rue du Temple in our rear loosed off over our heads.

It was dull and misty and the visibility poor, but we had the opportunity to marvel at the enemy's efforts on the Ridge in the S.O.S. direction. Reds, greens and golden rain went up in scores, and were relayed back out of sight to their batteries, for retaliation. Brock's Benefit at the Crystal Palace wasn't in it.

THE ATTACK AT ARRAS.

British infantry, with a tank, going forward. The first line of German trenches had been taken and some of the men and the tank had reached the second line, beyond which was the barrage smashing attempts at sending up German reinforcements. A group of German prisoners can be seen in the left foreground.

The Canadian Corps were digging him out in the teeth of the barrage, and it was obvious they were in a panic.

Suddenly, one of our "sausages" broke loose and drifted away to the north—an extraordinary sight.

Our own job—the taking of the "Harp Redoubt" a particularly tough piece of work—was to start at 7.30, and we had perforce to wait. Meanwhile, the 1st Gordons and other units were clearing our front and attacking Devil's Wood and Tilloy village, where very bloody fighting took place. We were under continuous heavy shell-fire and had some very close shaves. About 6 a.m. it commenced to rain in torrents, and this added to our discomfort, as we were soon soaked through. The enemy were shelling unmercifully now, and in Blangy and St. Sauveur, suburbs on our left, houses were going up about three a minute. About 6.45 it ceased raining and at seven the Royal Welch and others—the second contingent—formed up and, with a cheer from us, set off into the mist, which was still fairly thick.

At 7.25 we climbed out, stretched our legs and formed up on top, moving off at 7.30. We had to go due east over trench after trench for about a mile or more and take the "Harp," a network of defences shaped like an Irish harp. It was most difficult to keep touch, the ground was sodden, and we were laden as usual.

We soon passed the first dead, and many wounded were about. Large batches of prisoners were being propelled towards Arras, and it still further increased our morale. Tanks were waddling about everywhere. Fully twenty were to be seen, and very ludicrous they looked.

We pushed through barrage after barrage and made for the cross-roads near the "Harp," where there was a large shell crater. Much wire had to be negotiated, but we were quite happy as we were moving on a down grade and could take in all that was going on. We duly crossed the front trench of the "Harp," held by the Royal Fusiliers, and with "Go it the Suffolks" in our ears we pushed on to our final objective.

It was now about 8.30, and we were getting very tired, the going and the wire having been shocking. In due course, after many excitements and with great difficulty, a little band of us, including about half my bombing section, my sergeant, servant and myself, were the first in Neuilly Trench, our objective. We had to dislodge some hardy snipers, my sergeant and servant using their rifles and I my revolver, and then bombed all the dugouts, eventually clearing over 200 yards and capturing all their Easter mail in one of the dugouts, before some reinforcements came up to join us.

We had taken about one and a quarter hours to do 2,500 yards, and were more than excited at our success. Later on we were badly sniped from some tall trees east of Tilloy, which was not yet quite clear on our left flank, and we also had quite a bit of shelling still to endure, as, naturally, they had their own trenches well ranged. The company on our right was missing altogether, so we had to extend and take on their section of trench, too. I went round and cut numerous wires running along the trench, to prevent any F.O.O., who might still be about, from signalling.

The morning was beautifully fine, and about noon the 8th Brigade "leap-frogged" us and went on to the "Brown Line" at Feuchy, the enemy's last consecutive line for miles, but Fate was not with us on that venture, and the "Brown Line" held us up for twenty-four valuable hours, during which reinforcements came up from Douai.

Our total gain of territory was about five miles on a large front, with the Canadian success at Vimy as the outstanding event. Our casualties had been comparatively light, and we were very cheery. That night, after relief, a biting snowstorm caught us and, after a day of miserable discomfort on the Tuesday, we had to go forward through ruined Tilloy about 3 a.m., and at 7 a.m. on Wednesday, with absolutely no preparation, and without having slept for three nights, we attacked over open ground in extended order the village of Guemappe, and were mown down by machine guns in enfilade. Just prior to this attack, we had formed up behind hundreds of cavalry horses, tethered in the open in a fold in the ground. I shall never forget that morning breaking, and the enemy, suddenly realizing this target, and dropping 5·9s among all those poor horses and incidentally ourselves. It proved the uselessness of cavalry in modern war, and was the only occasion on which we had experienced their presence.

During the succeeding weeks, further attacks ensued, but things slowly settled down again on the new Scarpe—Monchy front for the summer.

Keeping Faith with the Dead

HOW are we keeping faith with those who gave their lives so simply to protect their homeland from the tyranny of a brutal military dictatorship ? This question ought to be asked, not only on Armistice Day, but day by day.

England has given away much that they fought for. Communism has been allowed to replace Christianity. A Union of the Godless is to be formed in England, and the seed to be sowed in schools, colleges and factories by a certain Bolshevik agent (name in my possession). Moscow has set aside £23,000 a month to subsidize our Press, and to pay their agents from £5 to £10 a week to organize revolution. Moscow has proclaimed that Britain will be converted to atheism in the next five years.

They have caricatured God, derided Christ, and set up Lenin as the god of the godless. They have formed the British Young Communist League to remove from the minds of young English boys and girls all that " Imperial nonsense with which they have been stuffed at school." Their godless agents have been established among the Navy, Army, Air Force, Territorials, Boy Scouts, Girl Guides and Boys' Brigades.

Last Empire Day a Communist school-teacher refused to go to the playground with the children to wave the Union Jack.

The broadcasting centre is being used for Communist propaganda.

All this propaganda has been permitted by our successive Governments. Our laws protect these enemies in our midst, while the law would punish any one of us who might give these agents what they are asking for.

While this subversive warfare is taking place among our people under the guidance of the paid agents from Moscow, the League of Nations, composed of a mixed lot of representatives, including those from Moscow, has succeeded in weakening the Royal Navy to danger point.

In the days of Queen Victoria the Royal Navy was stronger than the navies of the next two most powerful nations at sea, and world peace was maintained. When England scrapped her Fleet, beginning in 1904, the war clouds gathered until, in 1914, when the German Navy had increased to parity with ours, the German war party were encouraged to spur Austria on to acts that made war inevitable.

Our Air Force has been similarly weakened, and the question of air warfare is being seriously considered ; but there can be no question of the need of a super-Navy for England, because, if we cannot guard our sea communications, we should be in the same plight as a man whose arteries are cut—bleeding to death.

In a communication addressed to a very prominent member of the Cabinet on November 24th last, I wrote :—

" I am sure that if those young men who so simply went over the top and gave their lives for England could reappear and be called on to fight again, they would fight for England the same as ever ; but if they were told that a League of Nations composed of a mixed lot of politicians and enemies of England would dominate the world, they would, with one accord, turn their weapons on the politicians who allowed this great betrayal. Therefore, all the sermons and ceremonies on Remembrance Day are turned into mockery of the dead, who look down on the hatless politicians gathered at the Cenotaph with their bowed heads and their calculating minds at work in the two minutes' silence, planning how best to bring to nought the sacrifices they mock at."

We can keep faith with the dead only by being true to ourselves. We must keep our trust in God, and set aside personal advantage when it clashes with duty to our country. Life might be made so lovely and so simple if we would only play the game with one another.

Those boys played the game. They are gone—but they live somewhere. It was not in vain.

We can keep faith with them by upholding England's honour and glory before all nations. If we maintain a strong Navy and make it known that our strength is never to be used for attack, but for protection until the rest of the world settle their differences and learn to live in peace, we shall prevent a great war. We shall also thereby encourage trade and remedy world unemployment. With England on the up-grade other nations will follow ; but, if England is weakened and falls, the world will go down with her.

Let us organize in every village and town to strengthen our Government to rid the country of godless propagandists and revolutionary agents. Let us boycott cinemas that show the least sign of acting as propagandists for subversive and godless influences. Each of us is endowed with talents to be accounted for. We must use them ; expediency is false. We can forgive personal injury ; but we must not turn the other cheek to the enemies of God. If we think these things out and try to act like Christians and like men of British breed, we shall be keeping faith with the dead.

W. E. R. MARTIN,

Paymaster, Rear-Admiral.

What the British Navy Did During The Great War

During the four years of the War, British ships transported no less than *thirteen millions of men overseas*, and only lost 2,700 lives through enemy action! This remarkable achievement was made possible, to a large extent, by British women—*never forget that !*

Speaking about the British Navy, here are a few facts worth remembering :—Five million, five hundred thousand tons of German shipping, and one million tons of Austrian shipping were driven off the seas by Admiral Beatty's squadrons. Oversea trade and oversea colonies of the enemy were cut off, and two million Huns of fighting age were thus prevented from joining the enemy. In 1916, two thousand, one hundred mines were swept up and eighty-nine mine-sweepers were lost. In 1914 there were only twelve mine-sweepers and patrol boats. Four years later these numbered 3,300. In order that British ships patrolled the seas, they had to navigate eight million miles each month. The British Navy transported more than thirteen million men overseas, two million horses and mules, five hundred thousand vehicles, twenty-five million tons of explosives, fifty-one million tons of oil and fuel, one hundred and thirty million tons of food and other war materials for the use of the Allies. In one month, three hundred and fifty thousand men were transported to France from England. Great Britain transported two-thirds of the American Army to France and England, and escorted one-half of their total transports. That, comrades, is only part of what the British Navy accomplished.

Reprinted from " The Listening Post."

An Adventure at Ypres

VERY shortly after joining the Lahore Divisional Artillery, the writer, with his battery, went into action during the latter days of April, 1915, near Ypres. Guns were entirely in the open, and emplacements were built as rapidly as it was possible for the tired men to get them finished.

Meanwhile, rumours were circulating that the Germans were using or were about to use asphyxiating gas, which rumours apparently emanated from the fact that they were already using a certain number of gas-shells.

In this connection, it is interesting to note that the French General Staff, to whom the scribe was attached at one period, had actually received information from a German officer who had been captured some time previously, that the Germans were about to use gas, but owing to this man being so glib with his information, the French Staff refused to believe him, with very nearly irreparably disastrous results to the Allies.

The morning after the battery had got into position, the Major instructed the Senior Lieutenant and the writer to proceed to a farm situated *in between the German and French lines*, and thus observe the enemy for ranging purposes.

At this period the Lahore Divisional Artillery was supporting the junction of the French and Canadian Divisions, holding the line beyond Ypres.

They proceeded with extreme care towards the front lines, owing to the fact that all movements in the Ypres Salient were visible to the enemy, who had command of all the high ground, and found that the French had no trenches worth speaking about, and were lying in little scooped-out places which they had dug for themselves when and where possible in the Flanders mud.

Crossing the Yser Canal and mounting the railway, they passed through groups of French Territorials (elderly men called to the colours) and Senegalese, arriving eventually at French Battalion Headquarters, situated behind the wall of a demolished farmhouse under a corrugated iron shelter.

Here they partook of such hospitality as the headquarters, which consisted of a colonel and four officers, could offer, and then, followed by their signallers, proceeded at a smart trot towards the farm previously mentioned, and more by luck than good judgment arrived unscathed.

The scribe's companion proceeded up the creaking stairs to the first floor, while the writer decided to investigate the contents of the cellar. On his way down, to his amazement—and, be it said, to his dismay—a German non-commissioned officer rushed past him up the stairs, jumped out of the window of the farmhouse, facing the German lines, and, for the first and almost the last time during the war, the writer had the opportunity of using his revolver ; with what effect, however, he cannot say, as the last seen of our friend was his hurried entrance into a German front-line trench.

On examination, it was found that this non-commissioned officer had complete telephone equipment in the cellar, and was evidently reporting on our movements to the German lines. After disabling the telephone apparatus, the scribe picked up several German letters and a notebook that were lying around, also the non-commissioned officer's soft hat and one or two other documents, which he proposed to show to the Staff, and then keep as souvenirs—but more of this anon.

Then, proceeding to the first floor of the house, they brought into action their field-glasses and telephone equipment, and very soon correct ranges were established to the German positions. Shortly after, however, either through the information given by the escaped non-commissioned officer or by messages signalled from our own lines (spies being incredibly numerous in those days, and in that sector in particular), a special bombardment of this farm began to take place, and the writer and his companion were at first driven to the cellar until this became filled with asphyxiating fumes from gas-shells sent over, then, with their two signallers, they were forced to come out and lean with their backs to the best remaining wall.

They were in a highly unpleasant position, owing to the fact that their telephonic communication had been rendered useless through shells breaking the wire in several places, and through the fact that they were completely isolated from their own side of the line.

The shelling then became so severe that it was decided, their job having been done, that, accompanied by the signallers, they should make a desperate effort to regain their front line—or rather, the French front-line trenches—and they had almost started on this project when a shell burst immediately in front of their party, very seriously wounding the writer's companion and shell-shocking one of the signallers.

It now became more vital than ever that the French front-line trenches should be reached, and an attempt was made ; and although subjected to intensive shell and machine-gun fire, all four reached these trenches successfully, without any damage being done, save that the writer's revolver case, which he was wearing at his side, was penetrated by a machine-gun bullet.

Passing down this trench to the French Battalion Headquarters already mentioned, which were in the front line, it was discovered that the entire French staff, with whom they had had lunch, had been wiped out by shell-fire, and a pause was made to give what little medical aid was possible to several officers and men who were lying around wounded and unable to help themselves.

Then, moving a little farther along the line, the party had scarcely regained their breath when one of the signallers remarked that he smelled a peculiar odour and, putting his head slightly above the trench, gave one yell, leapt out and started a rapid retreat down the slopes, across the muddy fields, towards the French rear lines. The second signaller, almost immediately, went through the same procedure, and then the scribe and his companion decided that it was time to see what was happening themselves.

What they saw was a low bank of greenish-yellow fog advancing irresistibly towards them, with an odour which was already becoming nauseating. It did not take long to decide what was to be done. Their job was finished, and it not only was their duty to return as quickly as possible to their battery, but it had become a question of " sauve qui peut."

Therefore, as best they could, they got out of the trench and started off in the general direction of the battery, coughing and choking as they went.

Owing to their heavy equipment and the lack of breath caused by the gas, it was soon found impossible to run, and their retreat, even before they lost track of one another, had degenerated into a stumbling walk.

The writer, having recognized the smell of chlorine, and by great good fortune having his water-bottle with him, soaked his handkerchief with water and placed it in front of his mouth and nose, thereby unquestionably saving his life, as most of the chlorine and phosgene (of which the gas was composed) became dissolved before penetrating to his lungs.

The retreat down the slope was an appalling experience, the whole of the ground being not only continuously swept by German shrapnel, but the Germans, being hidden by their gas throughout the attack, had mounted their machine guns on the parapets of their trenches and swept the retreating forces continuously with intensive machine-gun fire.

In spite of this, however, the scribe arrived at the banks of the Yser Canal, personally unscathed, although one of his shoulder-straps had disappeared, a strap from one of his leggings had been torn off, a bullet had penetrated the heel of one of his boots, and a slight blood-stain above the right eye testified to the fact that a shell had burst within a few feet of him.

At the head of the pontoon bridge, crossing the Canal, stood a French officer with a revolver in each hand, threatening to shoot any man attempting to cross to the rear, but on recognizing that the writer belonged to the Artillery, he inquired the situation, an outline of which he attempted to give him, when a heavy shell struck the bridge, and the next thing that he recalls is his waking up and finding himself immersed up to the neck in the Yser Canal and finding that the pontoon bridge was no longer in existence. Getting out as best he could, he proceeded along the bank of the Canal, picking up such information as he thought would be useful for his battery commander.

A terrible sight was the country-side. When the first gas had appeared, the Senegalese, thinking that it was a devil, had raised shouts of " un diable vert arrive," and in spite of the most heroic efforts on the part of their officers to stay them, they had retreated *en masse*, many being asphyxiated by the wayside, and the majority of the others being mown down by the ruthless shell and machine-gun fire. The same fate had befallen the majority of the French Territorials, while the Canadians to the east, although many had been asphyxiated or killed by shell and machine-gun fire, had, to a large degree, held fast.

It will be recalled that a break of several thousands of yards was left open to the Germans, who, in all probability, at that moment more than any other during the war, had a supreme opportunity of breaking the Allied front, had they but used it.

Down across the fields came a staggering, howling, shrieking, coughing mob of French coloured troops, Territorials and mixed troops of all armies, enveloped in the deadly greenish-yellow mist. Add to this picture the continual bursting of shrapnel shells, the rattle of machine-gun fire and the roar of the battle, and no picture of Dante's " Inferno " can compare, for in the pictures, at least, one is spared one of the worst features of modern warfare—the almost incredible volume of mind-torturing sound.

But to return to the adventure. Separating himself from this mass of struggling humanity, the scribe, in endeavouring to trace his battery, stumbled on two lonely field guns of an isolated Canadian battery. Innocently he asked the way to the Blank Battery of the Lahore Division, and almost immediately the Canadian Sergeant-Major, being quite accountably in a state of nerves, and looking at the writer's dishevelled appearance, and seeing the German hat peeping out of his pocket, placed him under arrest as a spy. To make matters worse, on being asked the name of his battery commander, and to which brigade his battery belonged, the writer was incapable of replying, his memory being temporarily gone, as a result of the experiences he had been through.

A heated debate apparently was then held as to what was to be done, and, being searched, of course, the letters and documents which he had picked up earlier in the day in the cellar were found, and were considered to be damning evidence.

In those days there was short shrift for spies caught in the act, and he would have been shot then and there without mercy, had it not been for the fortunate fact that no officer was available and the Sergeant-Major was loth, under those circumstances, to take the responsibility, after the writer had made what possibly was the best and most impassioned speech he has made or ever will make in his life-time.

And so, stumbling and violently ill, he was marched between a patrol of men, the Sergeant-Major following behind with drawn revolver, some five miles to the nearest General Staff, expecting at any moment that the Sergeant-Major's revolver would " accidentally " go off, to save the trouble of the march. On arrival at General Staff Headquarters, and with great difficulty obtaining an immediate interview with the General, the scribe was quickly able to establish his innocence, and was thunderstruck to hear the General ask him : " Is it really true that they are using gas ?"—a supreme example of the communication difficulties in modern warfare and of its vital importance.

Having obtained permission to rejoin his battery, he was given an escort of an N.C.O. and two men, and plunged across the now dark fields in the general direction of his battery, collecting on the way a number of other lost souls attempting to refind their units.

With the exception of being shot at by friends who thought they were spies, and by spies and snipers in tree-tops who hoped they were the enemy, the little party eventually arrived at battery headquarters at around 11 p.m., where they fell, sick and exhausted, to the ground.

And the Battery Commander, coming up to the writer, gave vent to the following :—
" Why, I have sent a telegram to say you were ' missing, believed killed,' and now, damn it all, I shall have to change it ! "

In such an inglorious manner did the adventure end, and all that remains to be added as an epilogue is that the scribe's companion managed to reach the battery, from which he was evacuated, only to be killed at a later date, while the two signallers, although they escaped unhurt, eventually developed tuberculosis and died from the effects of the gas.

History has told, and will tell for all time, how the gap was filled by officers, servants, cooks, postal orderlies, etc. ; how, with the Canadians holding fast, and fresh French reserves being rushed up the line, the breach was restored ; how the second Battle of Ypres came to an end, finding battered, heroic Ypres still in Allied hands, and how, in later years, a Memorial Gate was erected on the never-to-be-forgotten Menin Road, bearing the superbly simple legend :—

" —To the Officers and Men of the
British Armies Who Stood Here in
1914-1918."

M. P. T.

Ypres, April 22nd-28th, 1915

The surging battle line long since is still,
    And cenotaphs are reared, and flowers are spread
Across the meadow and behind the hill,
    O'er all those hallowed gardens of the dead.

Dead ! Not to us, though all the world forget
    That hideous travail of a nation's birth ;
Your living memory is with us yet
    Despite far scattered mounds of sacred earth.

And those of us—so few—who still remain
    Cherish our scars—sore guerdon of the years—
And, in remembering, almost bless our pain
    That tells of tribute paid in blood and tears.

      *   *   *   *

And so to you we raise this silent glass

      *   *   *   *

And pledge ourselves to keep your memory bright,
And pray we, too, when comes our time to pass,
    May look with fearless eyes into the night.

R. Ross Napier.

Memorials to the late Field-Marshal Lord Plumer

THE following will be unveiled by the Bishop of London at the Ypres British Church on Sunday, June 4th.

(1) Lord Plumer's Banner, subscribed for and presented by members of the Ypres League. It will be hung on the south side opposite the 5th Division Banner.

(2) The beautiful Memorial Brass given by Lady Plumer and the Ypres Settlement Fund, to be placed in the Chancel.

WARRIOR'S CHAPEL.

This Memorial and the furniture thereof will be completed at an early date, and an announcement through the Press made in due course.

ETON MEMORIAL.

The Memorial in the Cloisters at Eton will be unveiled on Messines Day (Wednesday, June 7th) by H.R.H. The Duke of Gloucester, himself an old Etonian.

YPRES BRITISH SCHOOL

MR. and Mrs. Morris complete their four years of office on March 31st, and will be succeeded by Mr. and Mrs. Allen, also kindly lent by the London County Council.

It is not possible to express here all our good wishes for the future of Mr. and Mrs. Morris on their return to England.

Everyone with any knowledge of Ypres will realize the benefits the children in the Ypres Salient have received from them, not only educationally, but in home life and, better still, in preparing them for employment in the Mother Country when their school education has been completed.

It seems scarcely credible that when the Morrises first went to Ypres four years ago, not half a dozen of the children understood English properly; now all do. They started the school with 48 children and they leave it with 112, 90 per cent. of the children attending belonging to the men tending the cemeteries. I understand Mr. Morris is desirous of becoming an Assistant Inspector of Schools, and I sincerely hope he will be successful in his ambition.

The prizes will be given away in the School on Whit-Monday by the Bishop of London.

H.R.H. The Duchess of York has presented a photograph of Princess Elizabeth and Princess Margaret to be hung in the School.

W. P. PULTENEY,
Lieut.-General.

N.B.—We feel sure that many of our members who so generously subscribed towards the Memorial Banner to Lord Plumer will desire to be present at the dedication ceremony and, in connection with this special service, the League's travel facilities are placed at the disposal of all interested.

Applications for prospectuses by the day routes (Ostend or Boulogne) and night route (Dunkerque) should be made as early as possible to the Secretary, Ypres League, 20, Orchard Street, London, W.1.

Prison and Doughnuts

I HAVE been in prison, not once, but many times, always, I must tell you, living up to a profound aversion for variety by going to the same place of incarceration. This jail of mine would have been a place of delight to the hardened criminal, for it was not a lockfast place of detention, such as you may read about, or even hear of secondhand from those who pass the time of day with frequenters of such places. It had no bolts and few bars, and I can say with certainty that there were no walls to speak of, for no man, however given to exaggeration, could fittingly describe the mounds of powdered rubble which surrounded the prison as prison walls. Perhaps the mounds had once dignified the jail as high-class barricades of brick and mortar, but if that be so, some more than ordinary upheaval had visited the place, for it was easy to see that the powdered masonry had not been reduced to that lamentable state directly by the hand of man.

You walked into this prison if not of your own free will at least with something of the gait of a man who is not bound to enter if he wills otherwise. This I do know, you entered without the guidance and restraining arms of gentlemen in blue or other men of the Crown who have to do with prisons. Now this will strike you as being funny; you could walk out again if you willed, and no one would say you nay. Yet you would not roam far—at least, you would not roam far to the north, for men died daily in the low-lying lands thereabouts.

I hated night in my prison cell. Night in prison is a time when the searchings of conscience probe beyond the veil of make-believe, and a man stands pitifully before himself as he really is, a piece of human frailty devoid of all the trimmings of affectation. But I should tell you that it was not the twinges of a guilty conscience that made night hateful to me, for I had little or no conscience, and little or no time to be bothered with such a thing. Nearer and more material things obtruded themselves on me. For one thing, there were many noises which seemed to intensify with the coming of the night, and engendered in you, if you were human at all, that unpleasant mental condition which the facetious describe as " windy." In the stillness of the night when noise carries far, there would be borne to my ears strange rushing, tearing sounds which culminated in explosions that very often would cause the jail to rock. Aeroplanes continually droned overhead, accompanied by much whistle-blowing and shouting in the streets nearby, and to crown all—to give tone to the thing—this untuneful noise was for ever being diligently embellished by the clean-cut, well-articulated oaths of the multitudes of transport drivers who paused, so it seemed to me, beside the prison to give vent to their feelings before passing on.

And all through the night this query drove sleep away—" Do I die to-morrow ?" " Do I die to-morrow ?" and to-morrow always answered as to-morrow ever will.

Ypres prison was a grim place, housing grim men during the years of which I write, for it sheltered for one night only many of those who had to enter the trenches next day. From that charnel house of hope and aspiration there passed on to a muddy tomb thousands of those who had been gathered from the four corners of the earth to defend an ideal which the passing years have caused us to lose sight of. Would that the gods made it possible for us to enrich ourselves with the collated thoughts of those men, garnered from Ypres prison on the night before they crossed the divide. What a touch of human wisdom it would prove to a world which dies slowly by its own hand.

Have you ever looked back from the trenches to where Ypres lay—

" A monument to Man's savagery,
Yet a barrier to his greed."

and wondered if it would ever rise again from its ashes to house those to whom it rightfully belonged ? Have you ever, as you stood knee-deep before the breastworks—wet, cold and perhaps hungry—visualized the future in your mind's eye and asked yourself if the powdered rubble which lay behind you would ever again assume the lines of ordered, well-built streets, wherein the chatter of care-free citizens would once again be heard ?

If you are an ordinary man, you never asked yourself these questions. There were more pressing things to do than merely ruminate over abstract problems. The Sickle, for instance, was for ever being held over your head, and your future—something of real consequence—might end at any moment.

But Ypres has arisen from its ashes, and its citizens do go about their business with the shadow of war relegated to the limbo of almost forgotten things, and you, plain, ordinary you, made the thing possible. You came from Calgary and Melbourne, Dublin and Dundee, London and " Brum," and all the other places which furnished the Salient with its human barriers, possessed of something much more effective and vital than the lethal weapons of war. You had courage, and it was courage alone that barred the door to Ypres. Men may talk of trenches and " strong points," and even lay great stress on the good generalship of our leaders, but none of those things would have prevailed without the high moral and physical courage of the untrained youth of the Empire who stood solid before the ruins, stemming every rush and counteracting every move that was set in motion against them.

Photo] [The Imperial War Museum, Crown Copyright.
THE YPRES PRISON.

The Salient may have had more disadvantages than any other part of the line, but, on the other hand, it had its compensations, even if they were of a minor kind. It will be difficult for you who have trodden its debris-strewn streets, with the smell of death for ever in your nostrils, to associate the place with anything in the nature of worldly compensations. But there were one or two things which made the soldier's life tolerable in his off moments in this rather dreaded part of the line.

I remember our Corps Commander, General Sir Aylmer Hunter Weston, soldier-like and eloquent, with a great flow of well-phrased words, visiting us at " B " Camp near Poperinghe. We were paraded, and the General fired off his customary address :—

" Officers, non-commissioned officers and men," he said, raising himself up in his saddle to give effect to his words, " I bring you good news. You will be pleased to know you are returning to the Somme, where I hope you will get your own back for that cutting up you got on July 1st."

There was a fidget in the ranks behind me, and the voice of McDonald, of Fife, broke a tense silence—" Nae mair hot doughnuts, lads. Albert again, with bully and biscuits." Tough, muscular coal-heaver and full-blooded fighting man that he was, the Somme did not appal him, but the loss of the doughnuts *was* a bitter thought.

McDonald got seven days for talking in the ranks, but he voiced the disappointment of the whole platoon. No more would we sample the piping-hot products of the good wives of Flanders, who traded almost on top of the trenches, carrying round their wares in baskets as they themselves put it " Jus' bake."

And throughout the world, to-day, there will be many of those who helped to add fresh pages to British history by their tenacious defence of a triangle of ground which reeked with the blood of their comrades, who will draw their belts in just another hole and sigh for the doughnuts that were " Jus' bake." And very naturally those men will ask themselves " Did I give my youth for nothing ? Is my sacrifice to be in vain ?"

The ideals that were worth fighting for in 1914 are still the urge of the man who loves his country, and to-morrow, if need be, the youth of the country would fight in defence of those selfsame ideals. Patriotism and love of country are not variable things, and no man who is worth his salt will seek to water down his views just because the wheel of fortune has made a temporary turn against him.

Lack of patriotism *is* rampant to-day. Let us who have fought and who have no use for such a thing draw closer together. By doing that we will be able to help each other and establish once again a comradeship that was bred, fostered and made a real joy of life, when we stood on the very edge of the grave. A friendship that is established when men are faced by the daily hazards which beset the modern soldier is something that will endure for all time and overcome all obstacles. But we must maintain contact with each other. Lack of contact with those who were our comrades during the war years, engenders apathy and indifference. The Ypres League—which has been doing great service in the cause of comradeship for many years—helps those who have lost touch with fighting chums to revive the friendships of days gone by.

There is not so much spring in our step now, and our hair is beginning to grey, and many of us stand quite close to Poverty Corner. "We haven't got much out of life," some of those who have manned the breastworks will say. We haven't got much out of life, because we have forgotten we once worked together on a most important job, and were a very strong trade union. When we get together, and keep there, as we did in the days gone by, those things we fought for may come near to realization.

* * * * *

There will be men in those cells to-night. Different men, housed under different circumstances, and their sleep may be disturbed, although not as mine was. Let them in their quiet moments to-night, take solace from the thought that they will not have to man the breastworks to-morrow.

IAN LOVE.

ETCHINGS OF THE MENIN GATE MEMORIAL.

Major C. J. Hazard, M.C., of Colombo, Guatemala, a life member of the Ypres League, has very generously given Headquarters a number of his fine etchings of the Menin Gate Memorial, stipulating that the proceeds of sales should go towards the financial support of the YPRES TIMES.

Size of etching : 9 inches by 6 inches. Price : 5s. each, post free. Signed proofs : 10s. 6d. each, post free. These etchings are considered wonderful value.

Applications should be addressed to the Secretary, Ypres League, 20, Orchard Street, London, W.1.

"Ypres Times" Maintenance Fund

CONTRIBUTIONS continue to be received under this heading, and we are happy to report that as a result of a recent donation from one of our staunch supporters in India, the grand total generously subscribed by members in response to the appeal of September, 1931, has reached £500. It was reported in the last edition of THE YPRES TIMES that £200 had been already placed on deposit, to which a further sum of £100 had been added.

For an organization of our dimensions, and in view of the depressing conditions through which we have all been passing, the result of the appeal to date is a fine achievement, and only to the sacrifice and loyalty of every one of those members who have so generously responded can we attribute the very life of the popular little Journal in its present standard to-day.

As an adequate testimony to the fact that even time does not efface the memory of those who suffered and endured the agonies of the war years, 1914-1918, we would refer to the many scores of letters that have been received from all parts of the world telling of the eagerness with which THE YPRES TIMES is sought, and hoping for its continuance. Some of these letters have been printed from time to time in the League's Journal, but we should be pleased for any members so interested to view them at the Head Office at any time they are good enough to call.

We look forward to seeing many more kind contributions before it can be safely said that the YPRES TIMES has been placed on a permanent footing, and with this in view we earnestly hope that those members who have not so far felt in a position to contribute will bear us in mind in the near future, when we sincerely trust that conditions both for our members and the League will have materially improved.

Donations should be addressed to the Secretary, Ypres League, 20, Orchard Street, London, W.1., and envelopes should be marked on left-hand corner, "Ypres Times Fund."

1933 Recruiting Competition

IN view of the popularity and immense success of the past two recruiting competitions, and in order to give recently-formed branches an opportunity to compete, we have great pleasure to announce that **A FURTHER PRIZE OF £5** will be awarded this year as follows :—

TO THE BRANCH RECRUITING THE GREATEST NUMBER OF NEW MEMBERS IN 1933.

All membership forms completed must be received at Headquarters bearing on the top left-hand corner the name of the branch responsible for the recruitment.

We shall watch with interest this latest challenge to the proud position now enjoyed by the hitherto all-conquering Purley Branch.

In 1915

Hill 60. Ypres—Comines Railway. Zwarteleen.

TAKEN FROM THE DUMP,

17 Years Later

Hill 60. Ypre—Comines Railway. Zwarteleen. Level Cr

TAKEN FROM THE DUMP,

| Southern End of Armagh Wood. | The Caterpiller. | Battle Wood. |

[*Photo, Imperial War Museum, Crown Copyright*

ANDENMOLEN, 10-4-15.

| The Caterpiller. | Battle Wood. |

ANDENMOLEN, 12-9-32.

THE ABOVE 1915 WAR-TIME PHOTOGRAPH CAN BE PURCHASED
AT 3/- EACH, SIZE 12"× 3¾", AND 3/6 EACH, SIZE 15"× 5"
APPLICATIONS TO SECRETARY, YPRES LEAGUE, 20 ORCHARD STREET, LONDON, W.I.

A Memory of Mesopotamia

"AS things turned out, the Basra—Nasiriya Railway, built as a branch, became the trunk line, and all other lines were dismantled after the Armistice."—*Loyalties, Mesopotamia, 1914-17*, p. 193.

The above extract from Lieut.-Colonel Sir Arnold T. Wilson's finely written book brings vividly to view a picture of one of those now dismantled railways in the early spring of 1918. It was the Basra—Amara line, over 115 miles in length, and only the previous April converted to metre gauge.

We were working under the dignified title of Railway Construction Battalion. Actually, with the exception of a company of Royal Engineers, we were a couple of hundred infantrymen waiting to rejoin our regiments over 300 miles farther up the Tigris, and temporarily borrowed for this work.

Our camp was on the river bank barely thirty miles distant from Amara, but as far as we were concerned it might have been 300 miles away, for in every direction stretched the hard, flat desert, the only signs of life being our railway and the passing vessels on the Tigris. We were engaged in making a double track line of a few hundred yards at places a few miles apart, and digging what we hoped would later be reservoirs filled by the flooded Tigris waters when the snows melted in the mountains away to the north-east.

Cut off entirely from our units, which meant, for some weeks at least, letters and parcels from the outside world, we lived an essay in practical socialism which could never be attained by our Western standards of civilization and theories. In our little world in the desert money was useless, it could buy nothing. Our rations arrived each morning by the night train from our base. Our work was communal, we were working together with one object in view, we had no other life. Each man was judged on his personal merits alone. We lived a life in the open and in ideal climatic conditions, for the much-abused Mesopotamia (why give it the Arabic style—Iraq ?) has a charm quite its own in the early spring when days are sunny and warm, but never too hot for manual work the day through. I often wonder why tourist agencies have not yet exploited these odd months in the heart of the Middle East, for not even Egypt can show such a wealth of historical associations.

To awake to the first streak of dawn on the far-away Persian mountains, and later, at work, to see the sun rise on the peaks, snow-capped at that time of the year ; at midday, when the sun was strong, to look across to our snow mountains, and then, at evening-tide, to turn your backs on them to watch the sun sinking below the desert horizon will always remain in the memory as a wonderful riot of colour and beauty. The spaciousness, the cleanness of your outlook, the last glow of the sun on the distant desert, then the cool evening breezes—the effect can never be captured on canvas and paper.

There was no need for us to bother about half days and holidays and high days ; we had the last two hours of daylight each day to ourselves. We played football—no searching for pitches there, the desert was ours to play on. We dug a small bathing pool by the river bank, and the river itself was never dull, for at that period of the campaign there were over 1,000 vessels in Government commission on the 600-mile stretch of river. Old paddle-boats from Rangoon, stern-wheelers from Calcutta, Thames tugs, local mahaylas, huge sailing-barges, brand new paddle steamers from the Clyde, manned by men from all parts of the Empire—Sierra Leone, Somaliland, Singapore and Sunderland.

With many recollections of other countries and other sights, of exciting times and dull times, I sometimes wonder what particular call that time spent in a desert waste should have that its memory stands out so clear-cut. Was it the magnificent sunrises and equally glorious sunsets, the illimitable space with those snow-capped mountains merging into the horizon ?

Was it our true spirit of comradeship ? Or was it a subconscious knowledge that we were back in the cradle of civilization—following the Assyrian, Babylonian, Persian, Alexandrian, Roman, Arab, Mongol and Turk in their conquests of Mesopotamia ? The majority of us would have flatly denied that ; yet the country held an interest, a hold over one which was indefinable.

W. J. PARRY.

Reverie

MARCH, which is the anniversary month of the culmination of my Army "career," sets me reflecting yet again on certain impressions recollected at random, of my three and a quarter years in the Army, the years when I was 18, 19, 21. I am inclined to smile at the photo of my callow self of that time. I reflect, though, that it might have been the photo of one "killed in France." Of course, if it were, I should not know anything about it ; but even so, I don't like to think of this youth having ended out there. I am glad he came back, even though it was to take part in the universal scramble for hogwash. (I *think* that is how Shaw describes it.)

I am amazed when I reflect that this gap of three and a quarter years should have occurred in my humdrum life—yawning, as it were, between two long periods of un-eventfulness. And although I resent that those precious years should have been wasted in that they were culturally fallow, retrospect, blurring the edges of ugly and unhappy realities, as it always does, has softened the memory of them and (I must admit it) has tinged them lambently with a melancholy romance.

I remember Catterick Camp.—It is a summer evening. In this vast camp of concrete huts are men from every county in the British Isles. Bugles are variously sounding the " Last Post." The first bugle's long sad lingering notes distantly float through the quietness. Before they have expired, the bugle of my own regiment sounds with startling blaringness solemnly. . . . The evening seems to be listening to the last loud note reverentially. . . . All is still. . . . A minute later, from the next camp, sound the same notes less loudly. Before they have all left the bugle the familiar and solemn beginning sounds distantly in three other directions.

The tuneful jangle ceases dancing and wailing discordantly. All is still—the stillness of summer evening peace.

Almost inaudible, ringing out from afar, sound the familiar long solemn tones as from a deserted distant land. The world seems to be listening. . . .

The final inquiring plaintive note wings weakly away as though uncertain of its course in the extensive evening quiet—lost. . . .

* * * * * *

I remember when drafts left the camp for France in dark nights, very late.—We leave our beds or our seats at the stove and rush out. On the pack of each marching man is a little white linen bag containing special rations. These little white bags remain in my mind now as they did then—the sinister brandings of men doomed to take great risks and perhaps to die. The band is playing the draft to the little station. Improvised lamps gleam eerily on the music scores and brasses of the band. In the darkness of the outlandish country road comrades run alongside their departing friends who are branded with the little white bags. They shout their farewells above the noise of the band ; the marching friend takes a hand in both of his, then another, shouting out laughingly his farewell at the face in the dark.

I was A4 then—too young to be sent abroad. But my turn came.—We march away in an autumn evening from the little fishing town of Hornsea on the Yorkshire coast. The band and bugles tactlessly play " Home Sweet Home " and " Swanee River." Now *we* each bear a sinister little white bag, and our friends not on the draft run alongside us and grip our hands. On the platform the band plays while we wait for the train. Despite being burdened with our packs, we dance with each other in bravado, hysteria, desperation. The ranker adjutant, a terror to both officers and men, amazes us by relenting and shaking our hands through the carriage windows and wishing us good luck.

* * * * * *

I remember Corbie, on the Somme.—Our platoon is roused from sleep in an old barn, late at night. Drowsy men stumble about in the straw in the light of a candle like puppets in a shadow-show. Some are surlily silent ; some curse loudly ; some cough and spit ; some joke. A few boys on whose faces their incipient beards are downy, express themselves in strong manly oaths and blasphemies. One lad runs out and along the road pulling his braces over his grey-flannelled shoulders. He has gone to a farmhouse to say farewell to Julie who has loved him since we came here three days ago. Another lad who, the company said, ought to have had the D.C.M., still lies in his blankets in the straw. He swears angrily when attempts are made to rouse him. He is exhausted from his excesses of the earlier evening, when he staggered into the barn, drunk, firing a revolver about us at random.

Later the four platoons of " C " Company assemble in the road to march away. In the dark village we are joined by " A," " B " and " D " Companies. We stand burdened like pack mules. During the calling of the roll some villagers, hastily clad, with dim lights in their rooms, come to doors and windows to watch the battalion's departure. Words of command in various pitches of the voice are shouted. They sound above the noise of soldiers' heavy boots forming fours, and the rattle of their equipment. The big drum, far in front, with solemn grand assurance, booms out quickly—Boom ! boom ! boom ! Boom ! boom ! boom ! and the band blares out into the cold inhospitable night a march tune—defiant, desperate, heartbreaking it seems to me now. Shrill and gruff, there are cries of " *Bon chance ! Au revoir !* " Crash loudly band so that we don't think of home ! *We* don't care ! Over the top and the best of luck ! Play up the band ! We roar out our songs swaggeringly, braggingly, we have forgotten how we scuttled out of the line and along the MULE TRACK last time when coming out on rest. We have forgotten we were asleep an hour ago. We march through the dark . . .

The band ceased playing a long time ago. We trudge along in the late night, sweating, exhausted, silent, along bleak roads unbounded by hedges—dear English hedges—with a dark expanse extending in front and to the right and to the left. The weak hope which had almost left us returns when we see a small shadowy village in the distance, slumbering. Having trudged to the limits of human endurance, we hope to drop there our bodies of pain.

Along, along, along, through the cosy narrow slumbering street we trudge in angry despair. When we do halt we drop down at the side of the road and sleep.

The unpitying words " Fall in ! " drag us up to our painful feet. We continue trudging, dazed. A dark expanse extends in front and to the right and to the left.

Another village appears. And slowly is left behind us, with its Utopian old barns and cowsheds where one might sleep. Young Whitely, a sturdy little lad from a Yorkshire woollen mill, is set up on the captain's horse. The officers relieve staggering men of their rifles.

We have passed through more villages. They were so profoundly asleep that they didn't know we passed through like phantoms.

We have taken off our caps from our wet steaming hair; we have unbuttoned our greatcoats and tunics and cardigans and shirts and vests. Sweat trickles in runlets over our flesh in the keen cold early morning as we trudge along in the silent gloom, along a bleak grey road with an indefinite expanse in front and at the right and at the left. We trudge along in pain.

* * * * * *

I remember the little Somme village of Marcelcave on a peaceful sunny afternoon in March, 1918.—So sunny and warm is the weather that the bareness of the trees seems incongruous. The platoon is in single file in front of a large dixie of good brown tea, dumped in the middle of the narrow street. Some are already served, and are strolling away. Before the others have had theirs an order comes to " Fall in ! " The others are compelled to cease waiting. Thirstily they stick their empty mess-tins in their packs, and very soon we are marching away. We pass through the village square—with its four sides of plane trees—in which, lately, in the evenings our band played happy music while the villagers and Tommies were smoking and sitting and talking and strolling and drinking. We pass the estaminet where, last night, I drank wine with boon companions—bottles of it. Madame is standing at the door sadly, waving her white handkerchief and calling out " *Bon chance! Bon chance!* " despairingly, as though pitting her good wishes against huge inevitable ruthlessness.

* * * * * *

The German offensive is launched against us.—We are straggling wearily in retreat, not having slept for days and nights. We have discarded much of our equipment. Officers and men from various regiments of the Fifth Army, each wearing high upon his sleeves near the shoulders a diamond-shaped piece of cloth of green or blue or red or yellow or of various other shapes and colours, straggle along mixed. A shirt-sleeved gun-crew is seen in a green field where there are cows, loading and firing with feverishly desperate automatism. Later, their last shell expended, they are clinging to their gun which, bumping and jumping behind galloping horses, is being dragged along the road furiously in a cloud of dust. . . .

And young Whitely, who had given me one of his most delicious tinned kippers from home, while we were in deep underground cellars in Ypres, near the Grande Place, last winter—a survivor said of him afterwards, that he had stuck a big Prussian; had jabbed his bayonet up into his ribs; had tugged at it imprisoned in the bones of the supine Prussian; had pressed his small foot on the big body while he tugged; had fired bullets into it to loosen the bayonet, cursing and swearing frenziedly as he tugged—until a German revolver-bullet in his face stilled the curses on his bloody lips. . . . Young Whitely—so gentle, so smilingly round-faced after his tot of rum when he crawled into our "funk-hole" in the front line, singing. . . . Those others . . . the bottles of wine with them under the plane trees. . . .

And " *we that are left grow old.*"

SIDNEY G. KNOTT.

League Secretary's Notes

TO OUR NEW MEMBERS.

It gives us much pleasure to heartily welcome the new members who have enrolled since January, and we thank those who have expressed in writing their gratefulness for the work the League is doing to keep the great memory of Ypres alive.

The following is an interesting record of our four hundred and twenty-four 1932 new members and places from which they were recruited:—

London.
S.W.	33
W.	16
N.	14
N.W.	10
S.E.	9
E.	7
E.C.	4
W.C.	1
	94

Scotland	17
Wales	14

Home Counties.
Surrey	60
Yorks	29
Kent	24
Essex	16
Lancashire	16
Cheshire	9
Oxon	9
Sussex	9
Devon	9
Worcestershire	8
Hampshire	7
Lincolnshire	7
Warwickshire	6
Middlesex	6
Derbyshire	6
Salop	5
Bucks	4
Nottinghamshire	4
Cambs.	3
Staffordshire	3
Suffolk	3
Somersetshire	3
Cornwall	2
Durham	2
Gloucester	2
Berkshire	2
Dorsetshire	1
Norfolk	1
Wiltshire	1

Foreign and Colonial.
U.S.A.	14
Africa	7
Australia	6
Canada	5
India	3
China	2
Newfoundland	1
France	1
Iraq	1
F.M.S.	1
Portugal	1

We hope that the return for 1933 will compare no less favourably, and to this end we earnestly ask the co-operation of all our new members and wish them every success in their good endeavours to swell the membership of the Ypres League. Headquarters will be glad to receive applications for enrolment forms.

TO OUR BRANCH SECRETARIES AND CORRESPONDING MEMBERS.

The first quarter of 1933 has been by no means inactive, and we are delighted to see such excellent progress at Colchester, where the first reunion dinner of the Ypres League, Colchester and District Branch, is being held on March 30th.

Purley are still upholding their wonderful reputation in adding to the membership roll, and their annual reunion dinner was held on March 15th (see Branch Notes). Major Graham Carr has kindly allowed himself to be elected Chairman of the Branch for 1933, and in addition he has very generously taken on the duties of Hon. Secretary and Treasurer. We take this opportunity to thank Major Carr most heartily for his immense enthusiasm, and we wish the Branch every success under his leadership.

Our London County Committee have done good work in holding some very successful Gatherings during the past quarter.

News of Corporal Slater in Kenya and Captain Burgess, of Madrid, will be found in Branch Notes, and we are exceedingly indebted to these gentlemen for their staunch support.

We are now looking forward optimistically to a favourable travel season. A party of members and friends will be spending the Easter week-end at Ypres, and on April 21st we are organizing a party of the 167th Infantry Brigade T.A. on a lecture tour of the Ypres Salient. Whitsuntide will bring us a very busy week-end when a party of the Coldstream Guards journey to Ypres under our auspices, and a special pilgrimage and independent travel will be arranged in connection with the service in St. George's Church, Ypres, to dedicate the banner to Lord Plumer and other memorials (see page 171). Also at Whitsuntide we are organizing a four-day week-end battlefield tour to Arras and a similar tour to Amiens (see pages 188, 189). Both these Battlefield Tours will be repeated at the August Bank Holiday.

On May 26th to 29th the annual trip of the 85th Club will take place, making headquarters at Ypres.

We ask our Branch Secretaries and Corresponding Members to repeat their courtesy of past years by inserting a short notice in their local Press about the League's travel facilities to Ypres and other parts of the Western Front. Such publicity is immensely helpful and exceptionally valuable.

1932 proved a most satisfactory year for the League, particularly in the recruiting department, so we must leave nothing unturned to make the present year's result one of a similar calibre, and, in fact, try to double our efforts with the hope that our more palatial quarters at 20, Orchard Street, W.1, will bring the League the best of luck.

THIRTEENTH ANNUAL REPORT.

We beg to draw attention to the interesting Thirteenth Annual Report of the Imperial War Graves Commission containing photographs of War Cemeteries in France, Italy, Egypt, Syria and South-West Africa, with particularly fine reproductions of the Arras and Thiepval Memorials. Copies of the Report can be obtained on application to the Secretary, Imperial War Graves Commission, 32, Grosvenor Gardens, London, S.W.1, price 1s., post free.

EMBROIDERED BADGES.

These badges can be supplied at 4s. each, post free. A considerable number have already been sold, and we are delighted to hear that the badges have given entire satisfaction to our members who have received them. Applications to the Secretary.

BURNING OF THE CLOTH HALL, 1915.

There are only a few coloured prints, 14 in. by 12 in., now in stock, and, as further supplies are not obtainable, we are selling the remaining prints at 1s. each, post free.

PHOTOGRAPHS OF WAR GRAVES.

The Ypres League has made arrangements whereby it is able to supply photographs (negative, and one print, postcard size, unmounted) of graves situated in the Ypres Salient, and in the Hazebrouck and Armentieres areas, at the price of 10s. each.

WREATHS.

Arrangements are made by the Ypres League to place wreaths for relatives on the graves of British soldiers situated in France and Belgium at the following times of the year :—

EASTER, ARMISTICE DAY, CHRISTMAS.

The wreaths may be composed of natural flowers, laurel, or holly, and can be bought at the following prices—12s. 6d., 15s. 6d., and 20s., according to the size and quality of the wreath.

YPRES LEAGUE TIE.

At the request of the majority of our members we have been pleased to produce the tie in better quality silk and in a darker shade of cornflower blue relieved by a narrow gold stripe. The price is 3s. 6d., post free, and all members of the League should possess one.

Applications to the Secretary, Ypres League, 20, Orchard Street, London, W.1.

YPRES LEAGUE BADGE.

The design of the badge—a lion guarding a portcullis gate—represents the British Army defending the Salient, which was the gate to the Channel Ports.

The badge, herewith reproduced, is brilliantly enamelled with silver finish. Price 2s., post free 2s. 1½d. (pin or stud, whichever is desired). Applications should be addressed to the Secretary, Ypres League, 20, Orchard Street, London, W.1.

HOTEL
SPLENDID & BRITANNIQUE
YPRES

GRAND' PLACE. Opposite Cloth Hall.

LEADING HOTEL FOR COMFORT AND QUALITY.

COMPLETELY RENOVATED.

RUNNING WATER.   BATHROOMS.

MODERATE TERMS.   GARAGE.

Patronized by The Ypres League.

Army Day Parade, U.S.A.

Captain R. Henderson-Bland has received a letter from Colonel Edward Olmsted, D.S.M., inviting him to take his old position on the Staff of the Veterans Division for the Army Day Parade, to be held on April 8th, in New York, U.S.A.

Captain Henderson-Bland has written to Colonel Olmsted regretting that he is unable to be present in New York on that date, and has expressed his deep appreciation of the honour conferred on him. He sends his kind greetings to all members of the Ypres League in America.

Branch Notes

KENYA.

Corporal C. H. Slater very kindly made arrangements last Armistice Day for the placing of a Ypres League wreath on the Cenotaph, Nairobi, and we wish to express our very grateful thanks to him and to the following generous subscribers to the wreath :—Captain D. P. Petrie, Captain C. H. Beer (our latest recruit from Kenya), Rev. J. P. Orr, Major W. N. Mackenzie, Mr. H. R. Petherick, Mr. H. Shields, Brig.-General A. R. Wainwright, Mr. M. C. Wethall, Mr. Angus Macdonald, Colonel G. J. Henderson, M. T. J. Lewis, Mr. S. W. Kemp, Mr. G. J. Robbins, Brig.-General P. Wheatly, Corporal C. H. Slater and Sergeant J. Slater.

COLCHESTER AND DISTRICT.

In the last issue of the YPRES TIMES it was announced that a sound foundation had been laid for a branch, and now the full Committee has been elected as follows :—
Lieut.-Colonel W. H. Herring, M.C. (Chairman)
Major G. C. Benham, M.C. (Vice-Chairman).
Captain A. C. Palmer (Hon. Treasurer).
Mr. H. Snow (Hon. Secretary).
Mr. W. H. Taylor (Pilgrimage Hon. Secretary).
Mr. C. W. Cook.
Mr. G. C. Stanford.
Captain A. E. Leighton.
Mr. J. M. Finn.
Mr. C. E. Rooney, M.C.

We extend our gratitude to these gentlemen for their generous interest and valued support.

The First Reunion Dinner is being held on March 30th, an account of which will appear in the July edition of this Journal.

PURLEY.

Annual Dinner.

The members of the Purley Branch held their Fifth Annual Dinner on Wednesday, March 15th, at the Red Lion, Coulsdon, under the Presidency of Major Graham Carr, who this year combined the office of Chairman with his normal duties as Secretary.

CORPORAL SLATER PLACING THE WREATH.

No more signal honour could be offered him, and none more richly deserved, and this fact was duly appreciated by the large company present.

The presence of General Sir Hubert Gough added lustre to the Chairman's laurels, and the gathering included two distinguished wearers of the V.C., in the persons of Lieut. Boulter and Captain Bill Haine, and our old friend Captain de Trafford.

The C.O. opened the proceedings with "Orderly Room," and in the course of his remarks referred somewhat slightingly to his *alter ego*, the Secretary, much to the amusement of his hearers.

The Bombardier then presented the cups and momentoes appertaining to the Foursome Competition associated with his name. The winners were Captain Featherstone and Major Graham Carr, while the runners-up were Captain Tissington and Gunner Kerr. The final produced a most wonderful battle, and it is worthy of note that the winners never led until the last hole.

The C.O. then called upon the Father of the Branch, Major Harris, to propose the toast of "The Visitors," and the company was treated to a most excellent speech.

The proposer referred to the honour done to the Branch by the presence of General Gough, whose services to the League were gladly and ungrudgingly given. He remarked that the

General would not and must not expect the members of the Purley Branch to be overawed by his presence, as not even a Sergeant-Major could subdue them on that occasion.

The General responded in a speech which charmed and delighted his audience. He spoke of the memories of the Salient which to him, and to most of his hearers, were sacred. In a notable passage, he remarked that, although the English were a non-military race, they turned out the finest soldiers in the world. He informed his audience that he had had to listen to a diatribe from his neighbour on the wickedness and the shortcomings of Generals (this particular neighbour may be identified as the Amphibian), but it was distinctly pleasing to the members of the Branch that the General gave the impression of having enjoyed himself immensely.

The Bombardier, in the last speech of the evening, proposed the health of the C.O. He

Extract from Menu Card.

Oeufs R.F.C.
Whizz-Bangs

Crème DixMud
Consommé Water Tower

Sole Yser (bombé)

Bœuf Route Menin (Rôti Hell Fire)
Yorks. & Lancs. Pudd.
Agneau Passchendæle
Sauce Glycerine
Pommes Mills
Verts Ver(e)y
Petits Shrapnel

Compote PoelcApple
Confiture pavé

Glace du Moat

Fromage Phosgene

Canal Café

said that, while it would be easy to dilate upon the virtues of the C.O. as a Chairman, and as the Secretary of the Branch, he (the speaker) preferred to think of him as a good sportsman, a good fellow and a real friend of the members of the Branch.

This sentiment met with the vociferous approval of the company and, with a brief speech of thanks, the Chairman unloosed the bonds of restraint, and the rest of the evening was spent in enjoying the excellent entertainment provided by Captain Vernon Lee, the Branch's own favourite.

Some excellent stories by Dr. Moon and Lieut. Silvester, and the A. P. Herbert verses recited by the Amphibian, contributed to a most delightful evening, which was enjoyed by no less than 126 members and their friends—the largest number so far gathered together.

THE BOMBARDIER.

LONDON COUNTY COMMITTEE.
Informal Gatherings.

A review of the last three Informal Gatherings, which are held on the third Thursday in each month at the Bedford Head Hotel, Maiden Lane, Strand, W.C.2, from 7 to 10 p.m., recalls the passing of three very interesting and enjoyable evenings.

On January 19th there was a welcome return visit by Captain E. L. Frewen, R.N., who gave a very interesting illustrated talk on " With the Grand Fleet in the Great War." Many present that evening remembered Captain Frewen's previous lecture on " Zeebrugge," and as the unanimous opinion was that the talk on the activities of the Grand Fleet was even more interesting, there remains very little scope for an expression of further appreciation, having in mind the way in which everyone thoroughly enjoyed the thrilling recital of the Navy's exploits at Zeebrugge. These Naval lectures are all the more appreciated by members of the Ypres League, because the average "foot-slogger's" experience of the Navy during the war was strictly limited to visions of ghostly grey forms surrounding his troopship when on the way to Boulogne, Havre, or Etaples, and knowledge of "what the other fellows did" will always be a narrative of great interest. We hope to see more of Captain Frewen.

The following month brought a new experience to the Gatherings in the form of a visit by the "St. Dunstan's Singers" Party on February 16th, an experience which will long be remembered by those present. How those fellows can sing! Individually and collectively they are artistes of the first order. Humour? Yes, more than sufficient to mitigate the feelings of pathos in the members of the audience at the sight of those terribly afflicted heroes. They soon made it clear that they were not there for sympathy but to provide an evening's entertainment for everyone to enjoy, which we most certainly did. The choral singing of the part-songs was perhaps the greatest success, although it is particularly difficult to individualize any one item from the programme. What a splendid chaperon the party has in Miss E. M. McCall, their Music Mistress. The care and attention she bestows upon each member is worthy of the highest commendation.

The March Gathering, which took place on the 16th, was the occasion of another of those most interesting illustrated talks by Captain H. D. Peabody, D.C.M., of which he has already given several. He appears to have an inexhaustible supply of slides at his disposal, and their collation and classification must take hours of his time. This particular evening Captain Peabody's talk was more generalized than usual, and dealt with various sectors of the battle front instead of one particular sphere of activities. The innovation proved most successful, and yet another very interesting talk was thoroughly enjoyed by everyone. Impromptu items provided by staunch supporters of these Informal Gatherings, terminated a very convivial evening. Surely we have the material for a Ypres League

Concert Party in the persons of these particular supporters—our old and extremely versatile friend, Mr. W. B. Steele, of "Immortal Bard" fame; our humorous songster, Mr. C. A. Payne; Mr. W. G. Foster, our inimitable tenor; Mr. A. Hanser, our recently discovered baritone; and Mrs. Furner, our worthy accompanist.

The Committee would like to take this opportunity of thanking all friends for their kind support at these Monthly Gatherings, and trust to see ever increasing numbers during the coming months. Those of you who have been absent of late—please make a special effort to come along next time. Be sure we miss you.

On April 20th next we anticipate the pleasure of a programme by the 85th Club, and arrangements regarding the May and June gatherings are in hand and the programmes will be announced in due course. We earnestly request members to support us not only with their presence, but by encouraging those interested to join the League as full members. A. R. F.

THE CHILDREN'S ANNUAL XMAS PARTY.

The Annual Children's Party, organized by the London County Committee of the Ypres League, was held this year on January 14th last, and as in former years, proved an immense success.

Thanks to the generosity of the Governors of the Westminster City School, their large hall was again placed at our disposal for the occasion which was transformed into a riot of colour by the many willing enthusiasts working a little overtime the night previously. The earlier arrivals among the youngsters lost no time in making full use of the amount of space at their disposal, and very soon were indulging in all manner of games, many of which had certainly not been allowed for in the original programme. It was good to watch these radiantly happy children, and as the hour for tea approached the building could have been easily located at some distance by the hilarious shouting and laughter of some 140 of these youngsters. Tea was launched by the volunteer assistants (now working at top pressure) and was followed by more games and music. The latter was supplied by the Enfield Orchestral Society, kindly provided by Mrs. Peabody, and was thoroughly appreciated by all present. For over an hour the entertainer amused and mystified his young and keenly interested audience with his amazingly clever conjuring, ventriloquism and silhouette throwing, and to end a most happy evening, Father Christmas "parked" his reindeer outfit near Victoria Station and, assisted by Harlequin, who had for the moment forgotten his Columbine, distributed the gifts from a heavily-laden Christmas Tree.

Cordial thanks are extended to Mrs. Peabody, and Mr. Don Craggs for providing the splendid musical and entertainment items, to Captain H. D. Peabody for generous services once again in the arduous role of Father Christmas, and last but not least, to the many willing helpers who so kindly gave their valuable time and services and to whom the great success of the function was largely due.

THE ANNUAL MEETING

of the

LONDON COUNTY COMMITTEE

will take place on

THURSDAY, APRIL 20th, 1933

at the

Bedford Head Hotel, Maiden Lane, Strand, W.C.2,

at 7 p.m.

The business will be to receive the Report of the London County Committee for the past year and to elect the Committee for the ensuing year. Members are earnestly requested to attend, and the Committee will be glad to receive any suggestions to further the interests of the League in the London area. Should any members have proposals to make, will they please forward them to the Hon. Secretary, London County Committee, Ypres League, at 20, Orchard Street, W.1. prior to the date of the above meeting.

LONDON COUNTY COMMITTEE

Informal Gatherings

These will be held at the

BEDFORD HEAD HOTEL,
Maiden Lane, Strand, W.C.2

on

THURSDAY, APRIL 20th, 1933.
(Programme by the 85th Club)
THURSDAY, MAY 18th, 1933.
THURSDAY, JUNE 15th, 1933.

From 7 to 10 p.m.

Members and friends are earnestly requested to support these Monthly Gatherings, not only by their own presence, but by advertising them amongst their friends.

Particulars will be sent to any friend on the name and address being supplied, and members are urged to help all they can in this direction.

Ladies cordially invited.

MADRID.
Armistice Celebration.

There was a large attendance at the service held in the British Embassy Church of St. George, Madrid, on Friday, November 11th, in memory of those who fell in the Great War. H.E. Sir George Grahame, G.C.V.O., K.C.M.G., and members of the British Embassy, and H.E. the Hon. Irwin Laughlin and members of the American Embassy were present.

The Rev. H. B. Firth, Chaplain, conducted the service. Immediately after the two minutes' silence, Mr. E. D. Van Tubergen, representing American ex-servicemen, and Mr. H. M. F. Stow, representing British ex-servicemen, each placed on the altar a wreath bearing the respective national colours, the British wreath also having the Ypres colours and a card with the following inscription:—

TO THE GLORY OF GOD

AND IN MEMORY OF 250,000 BRITISH SOLDIERS WHO LAID DOWN THEIR LIVES IN THE SERVICE OF THEIR COUNTRY IN THE YPRES SALIENT 1914-1918

YPRES LEAGUE

On Saturday, November 12th, a large and brilliant gathering of British and American ex-service men and their families were present at the Dinner held at the Hotel Nacional, Madrid, to celebrate the anniversary of the Armistice. Mr. Baron and Mr. Blanc, President and Secretary respectively of the Cercle Français were guests of the evening.

Colonel J. P. G. Worlledge, O.B.E., presided and proposed the toast to the President of the United States of America and the President of the Spanish Republic. Mr. Van Tubergen replied by toasting " The King."

After dinner, H.E. Sir George Grahame, the British Ambassador, came to the dance, which lasted until the small hours of the morning. Most of the members of the Madrid Branch of the Ypres League were present, and certainly contributed to the success of the evening.

P. W. BURGESS, *Captain*,
Corresponding Member for
Spain Ypres League.

REUNION DINNER AND DANCE.

The London County Committee have pleasure to announce that the Ninth Annual Reunion Dinner will be held on Saturday, May 6th, at the Royal Hotel, Woburn Place, W.C.1. For particulars see page 190. The success of this function depends on individual members and the support they are so kind as to give by advertising the reunion, because a record attendance is desired.

Application for tickets, together with remittance (price 7s. per ticket, double 6s. 6d.) should be sent to the Hon. Secretary, London County Committee, Ypres League, 20, Orchard Street, W.1. Members are asked to apply for tickets not later than May 3rd.

YPRES
Skindles Hotel
(Opposite the Station)

Proprietor — Life Member, Ypres League

Branch at Poperinghe
(close to Talbot House)

HOTEL MODERNE
(Place de la Gare) **A R R A S** (Pas de Calais)

F. GRAVIER, Proprietor.

Recommended by the Ypres League.

THE BRITISH TOURING SERVICE

Manager—Mr. P. VYNER.
Representative and Life Member, Ypres League.

**10, Station Square
ARRAS
(P.-de-C.) France.**

Cars for Hire, with British Driver Guides.   Tours Arranged.

INTRODUCTION TO OUR TRAVEL BUREAU

The Ypres League Travel Facilities are heartily extended to all members or friends desirous of visiting Cemeteries, Memorials and all parts of the old Western Front Battlefields, special care being taken to ensure the complete liberty of action, general comfort and entire satisfaction of the pilgrim, whether travelling with our conducted pilgrimages or independently. Information on all matters connected with Battlefield Tours is gladly given by Headquarters. All tickets issued are accompanied by a detailed Itinerary of Train Services and other helpful information.

The Travel covers the popular Four-Day and Week-End Trips to Ypres, Arras and Amiens by the day and night routes, with inclusive quotations. Special quotations can be given for trips of longer duration to any part of the Western Front, to include board and accommodation in such places as Brussels, Armentières, Albert, Paris, etc. In such cases, circular tickets can be issued so as to avoid the unnecessary trouble of booking tickets on tour and thereby permitting the traveller to break the journey *en route*.

Passports are necessary for trips of longer duration than " week-ends "—*i.e.*, Friday to Monday or Saturday to Tuesday.

The League Representatives at Ypres, Arras and Amiens meet our travellers on arrival, and do everything possible to make their stay of great interest, including the provision of transport (private car or charabanc) at reasonable charges.

In view of the special arrangements concluded by the Ypres League with the Continental Hotel Proprietors, it should be clearly understood that those travelling under our auspices are not expected to give gratuities to hotel staffs.

Do not allow those doubts to postpone that trip you have really always promised yourself.

LET THE YPRES LEAGUE TRAVEL BUREAU HELP YOU !

PILGRIMAGES

TO CEMETERIES, MEMORIALS AND BATTLEFIELDS OF THE YPRES SALIENT.

EASTER (April 15th—18th) ... YPRES.

WHITSUNTIDE (June 3rd—6th) YPRES. ARRAS. AMIENS.
Three Separate Tours

AUGUST 5th—8th (Bank Holiday) YPRES. ARRAS. AMIENS.
Three Separate Tours

JUNE 3rd—6th.
Pilgrimage and independent travel in connection with Special Service at St. George's Church, Ypres, for purpose of dedicating the Memorial Banner to the late F.M. Lord Plumer, and the G.C.B. Banner of the late F.M. The Earl of Ypres. The Bishop of London will officiate.

Prospectuses will be sent on application to The Secretary, Ypres League, 20, Orchard Street, London, W.1.

Cost.—LONDON to YPRES return via Ostend, with full board and best available accommodation, including taxes and service (three nights)—without passports.

	£ s. d.		£ s. d.
2nd Class rail and 1st Class boat ...	4 19 6	3rd Class rail and 1st Class boat ...	4 5 11
2nd Class throughout	4 10 6	3rd Class throughout	3 16 11

INDEPENDENT TRAVEL

WEEK-END FOUR-DAY TRIPS (NO PASSPORTS REQUIRED)
Friday to Monday or Saturday to Tuesday.

THE YPRES BATTLEFIELDS.
LONDON to YPRES return, with full board and accommodation (three nights), including taxes and service.

THE SOMME BATTLEFIELDS.
LONDON to AMIENS return, with full board and accommodation (three nights), including taxes and service.

Via Ostend.	£ s. d.	Via Calais.	£ s. d.	Via Boulogne.	£ s. d.
1st Class ...	5 17 2	1st Class ...	6 8 11	1st Class	7 8 4
2nd Class ...	4 13 0	2nd Class ...	5 4 4	2nd Class	6 3 11
3rd Class ...	3 19 5	3rd Class ...	4 6 9	3rd Class	5 7 3

The above prices do not include meals on the journey or excursions on the Continent

THE ARRAS BATTLEFIELDS.

LONDON to ARRAS return, with full board and accommodation (three nights), including taxes and service.

VIA BOULOGNE.

	£	s.	d.
1st Class rail and boat	7	19	3
2nd Class rail and boat	6	11	9
3rd Class rail and boat	5	12	5

YPRES, ARRAS AND AMIENS (NIGHT ROUTE).

FRIDAY TO MONDAY OR SATURDAY TO TUESDAY, RETURN TICKET FROM LONDON, with two days' full board and one night's accommodation, to include taxes and service.

	Ypres.			Arras.			Amiens.		
	£	s.	d.	£	s.	d.	£	s.	d.
1st Class throughout	5	1	5	5	17	0	6	5	3
3rd Class rail and boat, 2nd Class Continent	3	10	0	4	3	10	4	9	1
3rd Class throughout	3	7	4	3	19	5	4	1	0

The above prices do not include meals on the journey or excursions on the Continent.

Special quotations will be given on application for trips of longer duration to Ypres and to other parts of the Western Front, when Circular Tickets can be issued. Apply Secretary Ypres League, 20, Orchard Street, London, W.1.

SPECIAL FOUR-DAY CONDUCTED TRIPS (SATURDAY TO TUESDAY) AT WHITSUNTIDE (JUNE 3rd to 6th) AND AUGUST BANK HOLIDAY (AUGUST 5th to 8th), WITH HEADQUARTERS AT ARRAS OR AMIENS.

ARRAS
DAY ROUTE.   WITHOUT PASSPORTS.

QUOTATION.—Ticket LONDON to ARRAS return, with full board and accommodation (three nights) at the Hotel Moderne, Arras, to include taxes and gratuities at Hotel.

	£	s.	d.
2nd Class Train and Boat	6	11	9
3rd Class Train and Boat	5	12	5

Transfer from 2nd Class to 1st Class on Boat, 10s. return extra.
Transfer from 3rd Class to 1st Class on Boat, 12s. return extra.

Our Representative at Arras, Mr. P. Vyner, will make necessary provision for such conducted tours of the Battlefields as desired at a very moderate charge, and a popular whole-day tour detailed as under would cost approximately 80 francs per head for party of ten or more persons. Packet lunches would be provided.

Arras Memorial—Roclincourt—Thelus—Vimy—Vimy Ridge—Notre Dame de Lorette—Souchez—La Targette—Ayette—Bncquoy—Serre—Newfoundland Memorial Park—Thiepval Memorial—La Boisselle—Albert—Contalmaison—Delville Wood—Flers—Bapaume—Ervillers—Mercatel—Baurains—Arras.

AMIENS
DAY ROUTE.   WITHOUT PASSPORTS.

Quotation.—Ticket LONDON to AMIENS return, with full board and accommodation (three nights) at Hotel Ecu de France, Amiens, to include taxes and gratuities at hotel.

	£	s.	d.
2nd Class Train and Boat	6	3	11
3rd Class Train and Boat	5	7	3

Transfer from 2nd Class to 1st Class on Boat, 10s. return extra.
Transfer from 3rd Class to 1st Class on Boat, 12s. return extra.

Our Representative at Amiens, Captain Stuart Oswald, will make necessary provision for such conducted tours of the Battlefields as desired at a very moderate charge, and a popular whole-day tour detailed as under would cost approximately 80 francs per head for party of ten or more persons. Packet lunches would be provided.

Amiens—Albert—Delville Wood—High Wood—Thiepval Memorial—Pozières—Newfoundland Memorial Park—Auchonvillers—Mailly-Maillet—Beaussart—Bertrancourt—Acheux—Varennes—Harponville—Vadencourt—Contay—Agincourt—Behencourt—Pont-Noyelles—Querrieu—Amiens.

THE NINTH ANNUAL
REUNION
DINNER AND DANCE

ORGANIZED BY THE

LONDON COUNTY COMMITTEE

OF

THE YPRES LEAGUE

will be held at the

ROYAL HOTEL,
Woburn Place, W.C.1

(nearest Tube Station, Russell Square)

at 7 p.m. for 7.30 p.m.

On SATURDAY, MAY 6th, 1933

Members and their friends are cordially invited by the London County Committee to support the Dinner and Dance, and secure a record Gathering.

EVENING DRESS OPTIONAL   DECORATIONS & MEDALS TO BE WORN

Tickets 7s. 0d. each Single   Ladies Cordially
      6s. 6d. each Double   Invited

Early application for tickets, accompanied by remittance, should be sent to the Hon. Secretary, London County Committee, Ypres League, 20 Orchard Street, Portman Square, London, W.1, not later than May 3rd.

Branches and Corresponding Members

BRANCHES.

LONDON	Hon. Secretary to the London County Committee: J. Boughey, 20, Orchard Street, London, W.1.
	E. LONDON DISTRICT—L. A. Weller, 132, Maxey Road, Dagenham, Essex.
	TOTTENHAM AND EDMONTON DISTRICT—E. Glover, 191, Lansdowne Road, Tottenham, N.17.
	H. Carey, 373, Sydenham Road, S.E.26.
COLCHESTER	H. Snow, 9, Church Street (North) (Hon. Sec.).
	W. H. Taylor, 64, High Street (Pilgrimage Hon. Sec.).
GATESHEAD	Lieut.-Colonel E. G. Crouch, 8, Ashgrove Terrace.
LIVERPOOL	Captain A. M. Webster, Blundellsands.
PURLEY	Major Graham Carr, D.S.O., M.C., 112-114, High Street.
SHEFFIELD	Captain J. Wilkinson, "Holmfield," Bents Drive.
BELGIUM	Colonel L. Aerts, 27, Rue de l'Abbaye, Bruxelles.
CANADA	Ed. Kingsland, P.O. Box 83, Magog, Quebec.
SOUTH AFRICA ...	L. G. Shuter, Church Street, Pietermaritzburg, Natal.
AMERICA	Representative: Captain R. Henderson-Bland, 110 West 57th Street, New York City.

CORRESPONDING MEMBERS.

GREAT BRITAIN.

ABERYSTWYTH	T. O. Thomas, 5, Smithfield Road.
ASHTON-UNDER-LYNE ...	G. D. Stuart, "Woodlands," Thronfield Grove, Arundel Street.
BANBURY	Captain C. W. Fowke, Yew Tree House, King's Sutton.
BIRMINGHAM	Mrs. Hill, 191, Cattell Road, Small Heath.
	John Burman, "Westbrook," Solihull Road, Shirley.
BOURNEMOUTH	H. L. Pasmore, 40, Morley Road, Boscombe Park.
BRISTOL	W. S. Hook, "Stoneleigh," Cotham Park.
BROADSTAIRS	C. E. King, 6, Norman Road, St. Peters, Broadstairs.
	Mrs. Briggs, North Foreland House.
CARLISLE	Lieut.-Colonel G. T. Willan, D.S.O., 3, Goschen Road.
CHATHAM	W. N. Channon, 22, Keyes Avenue.
CHESTERFIELD	Major A. W. Shea, 14, Cross Street.
CONGLETON	Mr. H. Dart, 61, The Crescent.
DARLINGTON	D. S. Vigo, 125, Dorset Road, Bexhill-on-Sea.
DERBY	T. Jakeman, 10, Graham Street.
DORRINGTON (Salop) ...	Captain G. D. S. Parker, Frodesley Rectory.
EXETER	Captain E. Jenkin, 25, Queen Street.
GLOUCESTER	H. R. Hunt, "Casita," Parton Lane, Churchdown.
HERNE BAY	Captain E. Clarke Williams, F.S.A.A., "Conway," Station Road.
HOVE	Captain G. W. J. Cole, 2, Westbourne Terrace, Kingsway.
LEEDS	R. G. Rawnsley, "The Lilacs," Hawksworth Avenue, Guiseley.
LEICESTER	W. C. Dunford, 343, Aylestone Road.
LINCOLN	E. Swaine, 79, West Parade.
LLANWRST	A. C. Tomlinson, M.A., Bod Estyn.
LOUGHTON	Capt. O. G. Johnson, M.A., Loughton School.
MATLOCK (Derby) ...	Miss Dickinson, Beechwood.
MELROSE	Mrs. Lindesay Kelsall, Huntlyburn.
NEW BRIGHTON (Cheshire)	E. F. Williams, 5, Waterloo Road.
NEW MILTON	W. H. Lunn, "Greycot," Albert Road.

NOTTINGHAM ...	...	E. V. Brown, 3, Eldon Chambers, Wheeler Gate.
ST. HELENS (Lancs.)	...	John Orford, 124, Knowsley Road.
SHREWSBURY ...	...	Major-General Sir John Headlam, Cruck Meole House, Hanwood.
TIVERTON (Devon)	...	Mr. W. H. Duncan Arthur, Surveyor's Office, Town Hall.
WELSHPOOL	...	Mr. E. Wilson, Coedway, Ford, Salop.

DOMINIONS AND FOREIGN COUNTRIES.

AUSTRALIA ...	...	Messrs. C. H. Green and George Lawson, Anzac House, Elizabeth Street, Brisbane, Queensland. R. A. Baldwin, c/o Government Savings Bank of N.S.W., Martin Place, Sydney. Mr. W. Cloves, Box 1296, G.P.O., Adelaide.
BELGIUM	...	Sister Marguerite, Sacré Cœur, Ypres. Colonel L. Aerts, 27, Rue de l'Abbaye, Bruxelles.
BUENOS AYRES ...	...	President, British Ex-Service Club, Calle 25 de Mayo 577.
CANADA	...	Brig.-General V. W. Odlum, C.B., C.M.G., D.S.O., 2530, Point Grey Road, Vancouver. V. A. Bowes, 326, 40th Avenue West, Calgary, Alberta. W. Constable F. Grece, 4095, Tupper Street, Westmount, Montreal.
CEYLON	...	Captain F. R. G. Webb, M.C., Irrigation Bungalow, Kalmunai, E.P.
EGYPT	...	L. B. S. Larkins, The Residency, Cairo.
INDIA	...	Lieut.-Quartermaster G. Smith, Queen's Bays, Sialkot, India.
IRELAND	...	Miss A. K. Jackson, Cloneyhurke House, Portarlington.
KENYA	...	Harry Shields, Survey Department, Nairobi. Corporal C. H. Slater, P.O. Box 403, Nairobi.
NEW ZEALAND ...	...	Captain W. U. Gibb, Ava Lodge, Puhinui Road, Papatoetoe, Auckland. S. E. Beattie, Lowlands, Woodville.
SOUTH AFRICA ...	...	H. L. Versfeld, c/o Cape Explosives Works, Ltd., 150, St. George's Street, Cape Town.
SPAIN	...	Captain P. W. Burgess, Calle de Zurbano 29, Madrid.
U.S.A.	...	Captain Henry Maslin, 942, President Street, Brooklyn, New York. L. E. P. Foot, 20, Gillett Street, Hartford, Conn., U.S.A. A. P. Forward, 449, East 80th Street, New York. J. W. Freebody, 945, McBride Avenue, Los Angeles.
NOVA SCOTIA ...	...	Will. R. Bird, Amherst.

Membership of the League.

This is open to all who served in the Salient, and to all those whose relatives or friends died there, in order that they may have a record of that service for themselves and their descendants, and belong to the comradeship of men and women who understand and remember all that Ypres meant in suffering and endurance.

Life membership, £2 10s.

Annual members, 5s.

Do not let the fact of your not having served in the Salient deter you from joining the Ypres League. Those who have neither fought in the Salient nor lost relatives there, but who are in sympathy with the objects of the Ypres League, are admitted to its fellowship, but are not given scroll certificates.

There is a Junior Division for children whose relatives served in the Salient. It is open also to others to whom our objects appeal.

Annual subscription 1s. up to the age of 18, after which they can become ordinary members of the League.

The Ypres League (Incorporated).
20 Orchard Street, Portman Square, W.1.

Telephone: WELBECK 1446.   *Telegrams:* YPRESLEAG, "WESDO," LONDON.

Patron-in-Chief: H.M. THE KING.

Patrons:
H.R.H. THE PRINCE OF WALES.   H.R.H. PRINCESS BEATRICE.

President: GENERAL SIR CHARLES H. HARINGTON.

Vice-Presidents:

F.-M. VISCOUNT ALLENBY.   F.-M. SIR PHILIP CHETWODE.
F.-M. SIR CLAUD JACOB.   THE LORD WAKEFIELD OF HYTHE.
THE VISCOUNT BURNHAM.   LIEUT.-GENERAL SIR CECIL ROMER

General Committee:

THE COUNTESS OF ALBEMARLE.
MAJOR J. R. AINSWORTH-DAVIS.
*CAPTAIN C. ALLISTON.
LIEUT.-COLONEL BECKLES WILLSON.
*MR. JOHN BOUGHEY.
*MISS B. BRICE-MILLER.
COLONEL G. T. BRIERLEY.
CAPTAIN P. W. BURGESS.
*MAJOR H. CARDINAL-HARFORD.
REV. P. B. CLAYTON.
*THE EARL OF YPRES.
MRS. CHARLES J. EDWARDS.
MAJOR C. J. EDWARDS.
MR. H. A. T. FAIRBANK.
MR. T. ROSS FURNER.
SIR PHILIP GIBBS.
MR. E. GLOVER.
MAJOR C. E. GODDARD.
MAJOR-GENERAL SIR JOHN HEADLAM.
MR. F. D. BANKS HILL.
MAJOR-GENERAL C. J. B. HAY.

MR. J. HETHERINGTON.
MRS. E. HEAP.
GENERAL SIR W. C. G. HENEKER.
BRIGADIER H. C. JACKSON.
CAPTAIN O. G. JOHNSON.
*MAJOR MONTAGUE JONES.
CAPTAIN H. D. PEABODY.
*THE HON. ALICE DOUGLAS PENNANT.
*LIEUT.-GENERAL SIR W. P. PULTENEY.
LIEUT.-COLONEL SIR J. MURRAY.
LIEUT.-GENERAL SIR CECIL ROMER.
*COLONEL G. E. C. RASCH.
VISCOUNT SANDON.
THE HON. SIR ARTHUR STANLEY.
MR. ERNEST THOMPSON.
CAPTAIN J. LOCKLEY TURNER.
*LIEUT.-GENERAL SIR H. UNIACKE.
*MR. E. B. WAGGETT.
CAPTAIN J. WILKINSON.
CAPT. H. TREVOR WILLIAMS.
   * Executive Committee.

Finance:
LIEUT.-GENERAL SIR W. P. PULTENEY.
LIEUT.-GENERAL SIR HERBERT UNIACKE.
CAPTAIN C. ALLISTON.

Honorary Solicitors:
MESSRS. FLADGATE & Co., 18, Pall Mall, S.W.

Bankers:
BARCLAYS BANK, LTD., Knightsbridge Branch.

Secretary:
CAPTAIN G. E. DE TRAFFORD.

Trustees:
LIEUT.-GENERAL SIR W. P. PULTENEY.
MR. E. B. WAGGETT.
MAJOR E. MONTAGUE JONES.

Auditors:
MESSRS. LEPINE & JACKSON,
    6, Bond Court, E.C.4.

League Representative at Ypres:
CAPTAIN P. D. PARMINTER,
19, Rue Surmont de Volsberghe.

League Representative at Amiens:
CAPTAIN STUART OSWALD,
7, Rue Porte-Paris.

League Representative in America:
CAPTAIN R. HENDERSON-BLAND.
110 West 57th Street, New York.

League Representative at Arras:
MR. P. VYNER,
10, Station Square.

PRIMARY OBJECTS OF THE LEAGUE.

I.—Commemoration and Comradeship.
II.—To provide special travel facilities for Members and all interested to Ypres and battlefields, and transport of Members.
III.—The furnishing of information about the Salient; marking of historic sites and the compilation of charts of the battlefields.
IV.—The erection of a Ypres British Church and School.
V.—The establishment of groups of members throughout the world, through Branch Secretaries and Corresponding Members.
VI.—The maintenance of cordial relations with dwellers on the battlefields of Ypres.
VII.—The formation of a Junior Division.

Use the Ypres League Travel Bureau for Ypres and Whole of the Western Front.

FOR THE FOLLOWING PUBLICATIONS, Etc., apply:
Secretary, YPRES LEAGUE, 20 ORCHARD STREET, LONDON, W.1.

THE BATTLE BOOK OF YPRES. A history of notable deeds contributed by all regiments. 5s.; post free, 5s. 6d. Compiled by Beatrix Brice with the assistance of Lieut.-General Sir William Pulteney, G.C.V.O., etc.

BOOKS.

YPRES: Outpost of the Channel Ports. By Beatrix Brice. With Foreword by Field-Marshal Lord Plumer, G.C.B. Price 1s. 6d.; post free 1s. 10d.

In the Ypres Salient. By Lt.-Col. Beckles Willson. 1s. net; post free 1s. 2d.

To the Vanguard. By Beatrix Brice. 1s. net; post free 1s. 2d.

The City of Fear and Other Poems. By Gilbert Frankau. 3s. 6d. net; post free 3s. 8d.

With the Cornwall Territorials on the Western Front. By E. C. Matthews. 7s. 6d.; post free 8s.

Story of the 63rd Field Ambulance. By A. W. Westmore, etc. Cloth, 3s. 6d., post free. Paper, 2s. 6d., post free.

War Letters to a Wife. By Colonel Rowland Feilding. Popular Edition. 7s. 6d.; post free 8s.

YPRES LEAGUE TIES. 3s. 6d. each, post free.

YPRES LEAGUE BADGES. 2s. each, 2s. 1½d. post free.

EMBROIDERED BADGES. 4s. each, post free.

Map and List of Cemeteries in the Ypres Salient. Price 9d.; post free 11d.

Map of the Somme. Price 1s. 8d., post free.

PICTURES.

Burning of the Cloth Hall, 1915. A Coloured Print, 14 in. by 12 in. 1s. post free.

The Tomb of the Unknown Warrior. By Bernard Gribble. 10s. 6d., post free.

ENGRAVINGS, 33 in. by 21 in., £1 11s. 6d. each.

Hell Fire Corner.

Heavy Artillery Going into Action before Passchendaele.

"I Won't."

BRITISH WAR CEMETERIES AND MEMORIALS SITUATED IN THE YPRES SALIENT.

Post Cards. Ypres: British Front during the War. Ruins of Ypres. Price 1s. post free.

Photographs in Album Form. 8 in. by 7 in. Price 2s.; post free 2s. 3d.

Photographs of Cemeteries in Booklet Form. Post card size. 4 Series. Price 1s.; post free 1s. 2d.

Photographs of Memorials in Booklet Form. Post card size. 2 Series. Price 1s.; post free 1s. 2d.

Photographs of Menin Gate Unveiling. Size 11 in. by 7 in. 1s. 2d. each, post free.

Hill 60. Complete Panorama Photographs. 12 in. by 3¾ in. Price 3s., post free; 15 in. by 5 in. Price 3s. 6d., post free. See pages 166-167.

WAR-TIME PHOTOGRAPHS OF THE SALIENT.

6 in. by 8 in. ... 1s. 6d. each.
12 in. by 15 in. ... 4s. each.
List forwarded on application.

YPRES TIMES.

The Journal may be obtained at the League Offices.
BACK NUMBERS 1s.; 1931, 8d.; 1932, 6d.

PHOTOGRAPHS OF WAR-TIME SKETCHES.

Bedford House (Front View), 1916.
Bedford House (Back View), 1916.
Voormezeele Main Street, 1916.
Voormezeele Crucifixion Gate, 1916.
Langhof Chateau, 1916.

Size 8½ in. by 6½ in. Price 2s. 6d. each, post free.

ETCHINGS.

Etchings of Menin Gate Memorial. 9 in. by 6 in. Price, 5s. each, post free. Signed proofs, 10s. 6d. each, post free.

Printed in Great Britain for the Publishers by GALE & POLDEN, LTD., 2, Amen Corner, Paternoster Row, London, E.C.4.

Memory Tablet.

JULY — AUGUST — SEPTEMBER

July.

July	1st,	1916	... First Battle of the Somme begins.
,,	2nd,	1918	... 1,000,000 Americans transported to France.
,,	9th,	1915	... Conquest of German South Africa.
,,	18th,	1918	... General Foch's counter-attack.
,,	28th,	1914	... Austria-Hungary declared war on Serbia.
,,	30th,	1915	... First German liquid fire attack.
,,	31st,	1917	... Third Battle of Ypres begins.

August.

Aug.	1st,	1914	... Germany declares war on Russia.
,,	2nd,	1914	... German ultimatum to Belgium.
,,	3rd,	1914	... Germany declared war on France.
,,	4th,	1914	... Great Britain declared war on Germany.
,,	10th,	1914	... France declared war on Austria-Hungary.
,,	12th,	1914	... Great Britain declared war on Austria-Hungary.
,,	16th,	1914	... British Expeditionary Force landed in France.
,,	23rd,	1914	... Japan declared war on Germany.
,,	27th,	1916	... Rumania entered the war.

September.

Sept.	3rd,	1916	... Zeppelin destroyed at Cuffley.
,,	5th,	1914	... End of Retreat from Mons to the Marne.
,,	6th,	1914	... First Battle of the Marne begins.
,,	15th,	1914	... First Battle of the Aisne begins.
,,	23rd,	1914	... First British air raid in Germany.
,,	25th,	1915	... Battle of Loos.
,,	27th,	1917	... Hindenburg Line broken.
,,	29th,	1918	... Bulgaria surrendered.

Communications to
The Editor. "Ypres Times,"
20 Orchard Street, London, W.1.

PRICE 6d.
POST FREE 7d.

Vol. 6, No. 7   Published Quarterly   July, 1933

The Men Who Fought at Ypres

By Robert Blatchford.

IT is well that there should be a Ypres League to keep green our remembrance of the long sustained and victorious defence of the Salient, and to preserve the camaraderie of the trenches.

For four long and awful years that dangerous and difficult position was held, at first by our Expeditionary Force of Regulars, later by Territorials, Kitchener's armies, Canadians, Australians, Indian Divisions, and conscripts. No words can do justice to the epic achievement of those heroic regiments, nor can our deepest gratitude be worthy of their magnificent and ungrudging sacrifice. A quarter of a million of our dead lie on those battlefields—our best men; and what men they were.

Through four tragic years our soldiers held the lines against the stubborn and intrepid attacks of the German armies. Always outnumbered and for the first year outgunned, enfiladed by artillery, raided by aircraft, surprised in the second year by the first attack by poison gas, they stood fast, officers and men, enduring wet and cold, often standing for hours on end knee deep in muddy water. Who that was not in the line can realize the strain and suffering of the terrible winter of 1916? Later, when I saw the shell-holes and the mud, the torn and rusted wire and the unspeakably squalid trenches of the Somme, I was appalled. How could flesh and blood endure such trial? It is something we must try to imagine so that we do not underrate our debt. Tired veterans and green boys of our blood and breed living and sleeping in muddy drains, tried by heat and cold; by rain and snow, plagued by vermin, disgusted by rats and stench and mire; with hidden snipers trying to murder them, with aircraft bombing them; with mortars and howitzers trying to blast them with poison gas and high explosives. This not for days, but for months, for wearing years.

The amazing story of Ypres cannot be told. It was a war, a war of many battles. Desperate feats of arms were recurrent and numerous. The dramas of Thermopylæ and Balaclava were fought again and again in those muddy fields and shattered villages of Flanders. Names like Pilkem, Kruiseeck, Zandvoorde, Wytschaete and Zillebeke have actually no place in the public memory; were never made familiar in the Press; yet the battles fought in those obscure villages were of greater intensity and magnitude than Inkerman or Waterloo, and their names would thrill us if we knew the facts.

I saw the Scots Guards entrain for the front. A splendid regiment they looked, as the Iron Duke said of his men, "Fit to go anywhere and do anything." Four weeks later they were relieved after fighting at Kruiseeck, and numbered only 450 men. That was in September, 1915. In November the German armies, reinforced by the Prussian Guard, attacked along the entire front from Zillebeke to Zonnebeke. In this sanguinary battle the Prussian Guard of fifteen battalions was almost annihilated, and our own losses were alarming. The First Brigade, which met the Guards' attack, went into action 4,500 strong and came out with 5 officers and 468 men. Of the 1st Scots Guards there survived one captain and 69 men; of the Coldstreams there were 150 men and of officers not one. I write here of episodes, incidental battles which established the Salient, battles fought in the first few months of the war. The scale of the fighting loosely spoken of as The Defence of Ypres was too vast for detailed description. It was, as I have said, a war, a war of many battles, and its purpose, successfully accomplished at a tragic cost, was the defence of the Channel ports.

I need not stress the importance of that defence. Had we lost the Channel ports we should have forfeited the security of the Channel crossings. Our reinforcements would have been threatened, our supplies of munitions and stores endangered, and it is not too much to surmise that we might have lost the war. How much then do we owe to the marvellous endurance and self-sacrificing courage of our troops in Flanders. I call their endurance marvellous because I really am amazed when I remember that our men could and did endure such dangers, toils and sufferings and live. There was no lack of courage and devotion amongst enemies and allies in the Great War; but I do not believe that any of the combatants, sorely tried as all were, had to win through such physical hardships as those suffered by the British and Belgian and French soldiers engaged in the long agony of the battles and watches among the oozy fields around the Salient. We must remember these men, and when we remember them we should place above the greatness of their victory the splendour of their sacrifice.

There exists an easy and simple comradeship in the Army which is impossible amid the exigencies of civil life. A regiment is a family; a band of brothers, and those of us who have left the Colours must and do regret the loss of that comradeship so genuine and so intimate. It is good work to re-unite, if only for a brief space, men who stood together in the trenches and moved together on the march.

Of the two hundred and fifty thousand brave and faithful men who died in the great defence we think with a tender reverence and abiding regret, and it is fit we should honour their memory. And no Briton who remembers the war, not as a luminous story, but as a dreadful reality and humiliating human disaster, can think without a thrill of the crowd that once a year stands bare-headed in awed silence round the Cenotaph, that saddest of national monuments; but do not let us neglect the survivors. We have, happily, still amongst us, thousands of the men who fought at Ypres. Let us then say for them as we say for the honoured dead in all sincerity: "At the going down of the sun and in the morning we will remember them."

Memorials to Field Marshal Viscount Plumer

Impressive Whitsun Ceremony at Ypres.

Bishop of London's Glowing Tribute.

WITH simple, yet dignified and impressive ceremonial, the Bishop of London dedicated the memorials to Field Marshal Viscount Plumer, the late President of the Ypres League, in St. George's Church, Ypres, on the morning of Sunday, June 4th.

THE MEMORIAL BANNER.
(Size 3 ft. × 2 ft. 3 in.)

The officiating clergy included the Bishop of Fulham (North and Central Europe) and the Rev. G. R. Milner, British Chaplain at Ypres. The beautiful little church, the foundation stone of which was laid by the late Field Marshal in July, 1927, was filled to overflowing by members of the British community in Ypres and visitors from the British Isles. Amongst those present to honour his memory, were his widow (the Dowager Viscountess Plumer) and his two daughters (the Hon. Eleanor Plumer and the Hon. Mrs. Anthony Orpen), General Sir Charles Harington (General Officer Commanding-in-Chief at Aldershot and President of the Ypres League), Col. F. G. Poole, Major A. S. Orpen, Col. Comte de Maleissye-Melun (Lord Plumer's French Liaison Officer, 1915 to 1917) who came specially from Paris to attend the dedication, Mr. O. L. Gill (representing Major General Sir Fabian Ware and the Imperial War Graves Commission) Mr. and Mrs. Morris (late Master and Mistress of the Ypres British School), Mr. C. J. Parminter, Major Paul Slessor and party of Toc H, Capt. G. E. de Trafford, members of the Ypres League, and a party of widows and mothers of men who fell in the Salient, whom the League had taken over, free of cost, by means of a fund which Lord Plumer had raised during the latter years of his life for the specific purpose of enabling bereaved relatives, who could not personally afford the expense, to visit the graves of their beloved dead.

It is appropriate that permanent tributes to the memory of Viscount Plumer should have been placed in the church at Ypres, for not only will his name for all time be inseparably associated with the Salient, particularly with Messines, but the sacred building itself is due in no small measure to his influence and enthusiasm, to stand as a perpetual memorial to Field Marshal the Earl of Ypres and the 260,000 British soldiers (one-fourth of the Empire's casualties in the Great War) who fell under his command in and around Ypres.

The memorials took the form of a banner (herewith reproduced), bearing the coat of arms of the late Field Marshal and a mural brass, carrying the inscription: "To the Glory of God. In memory of Field Marshal Herbert Charles Onslow Plumer, 1st Viscount, G.C.B., G.C.M.G., G.C.V.O., G.B.E. Born 1857. died July, 1932."

The banner was subscribed for and presented by members of the Ypres League: and the brass, which is placed in the chancel, was the gift of the Dowager Viscountess Plumer, in conjunction with the Ypres British Settlement Fund.

It should be added that the banner—a beautiful example of silk embroidering art—is the work of the Disabled Soldiers' Embroidery Association (Friends of the Poor), 40-42, Ebury-street, S.W.1, and is the handicraft of an ex-soldier of the Suffolk Regiment, namely, Mr. G. Hoy, who lost both his legs at Zonnebeke in the Great War. The Association, which enjoys the patronage of H.M. The Queen, and the services of the Dowager Viscountess Plumer on its committee, gives occupation and interest in life to ninety disabled men who otherwise would have no possibility of employment owing to their cruel disabilities. Many of them have become very skilled embroiderers and have executed orders for Buckingham Palace, the Prince of Wales, the Princess Royal, the Duchess of York and Princess Marie Louise, as well as for Regimental Colours.

The Bishop of London, in the course of an eloquent and inspiring address, paid glowing tribute to the character and life work of the gallant Field Marshal.

No commander, he said, was more trusted and loved by the troops who served under him. Calm in the face of danger, he surrendered his work to God day by day, and he did honour to the Church to which he belonged. Like many other illustrious laymen, he was a saint in the truest sense of the word. " Lord Plumer saved Ypres," concluded the Bishop, " and it was by sacrifice that victory was achieved. It was by Christian sacrifice, and by that alone, that the peace of the world could be assured."

The service terminated with the " Last Post " and " Réveillé," effectively sounded by buglers posted in the school playground which adjoins the church, followed, of course, by the rendering of the National Anthem by the choir and congregation.

H. B.

It should be mentioned that the G.C.B. banner of the late Field Marshal The Earl of Ypres, which during his lifetime hung in Westminster Abbey, has recently been placed in St. George's Church at Ypres. This banner was presented to the Church by the present Earl of Ypres.

In connection with the Special Service we print below a telegram sent to the King from Ypres, and His Majesty's reply:—

HIS MAJESTY THE KING,
BUCKINGHAM PALACE,
LONDON.

June 3rd, 1933.

General Sir Charles Harington, President, members of the Ypres League, of which your Majesty is Patron-in-Chief, and the British community in Ypres, assembled for the Dedication of the Memorials to the late Field Marshal Viscount Plumer, by the Bishop of London in St. George's Church, Ypres, to-morrow, send their loyal and humble greetings on the occasion of your Majesty's birthday.

THE SECRETARY, YPRES BRITISH SETTLEMENT,
THE VICARAGE,
RUE D'ELVERDINGHE,
YPRES.

June 4th, 1933.

Please convey to the members of the Ypres League, assembled to dedicate the memorials to the late Lord Plumer, the King's sincere thanks for their loyal message of birthday greetings.

PRIVATE SECRETARY.

"The Welch"* at Morval
(August 30th to September 1st, 1918.)

BY C. L. BERRY.
(Captain, late 13th Welch Regiment).

THE village of Morval lies mid-way between Le Transloy and Combles, one and a half miles north of the latter and about a mile south-south-east of Lesbœufs, in what was once the starkest wilderness of war's worst devastation —the Somme. On September 26th, 1916, Morval was captured from the Germans by our 5th Division and remained in British occupation until March 24th, 1918 when it was lost, recovered by the enemy in his successful March advance. By that time the village had become, like most Somme towns and villages, unrecognisable except as a collection of scattered ruins. To-day, of course, the wilderness blossoms and the war might be forgotten but for the Morval British Cemetery. This stands like a beautiful garden on the western outskirts of the village on fairly high ground, surrounded by richly fertile and well cultivated fields. The cemetery is only a small one, *but of the 54 graves which it contains, all except one—that of a captured German—are those of soldiers of the Welsh Division killed in or near Morval between August 26th and September 6th, 1918.* Most of them fell during two days only—August 30th and September 1st. There was for a while another cemetery, the Morval New Cemetery, on the north side of the Morval—Sailly Road just before it crosses the side road to Le Transloy and Combles. It contained 39 graves, and these, too, were all of the 38th (Welsh)

---

* " Welch " is the spelling now adopted by what was then known as the Welsh Regiment. This form of the word (which, however, we spell it, is English and not Welsh) is therefore used for that regiment, but not for the Division.

Division—casualties which occurred between August 31st and September 4th inclusive. These graves have now been concentrated into the Sailly-Saillisel British Cemetery, thirty-four being identified burials and five unidentified.

The assaults of the Welch Regiment on Morval on August 30th and September 1st and the eventual capture of the village were but incidents in the Second Battle of Bapaume which had waged since August 21st, but they were marked by unexampled (or, at least, unsurpassed) tenacity, courage and sacrifice. For several days the 38th (Welsh) Division had fought its way eastward until, by the evening of August 29th-30th, the 10th South Wales Borderers (115th Brigade) had taken Lesbœufs. The 113th Brigade on their right were, however, arrested in their advance before Morval by the unexpected strength of the enemy's forces in that village. Although all along the German line the enemy had withdrawn all except essential men and guns, Morval, which occupied a commanding position, was found to be strongly held. Neither of the two divisions on our flanks could move until Morval fell, so that the resistance of that stronghold held up the whole advance. That same evening, therefore, the 113th Brigade (Royal Welch Fusiliers) made another valiant attempt to capture the village, but were again unsuccessful, and during the night were relieved by the 114th Brigade (13th, 14th and 15th Battalions, The Welch Regiment).

The next day, August 30th, was a tragic one for the Welch Regiment. The enemy continued to offer a courageous and effective resistance to our onslaughts. As Morval still held out, the 17th Division was prevented from reaching the clear line in front of us which followed the Peronne—Bapaume Road. The enemy was also still in possession of Beaulencourt, as our patrols found to their cost. All day the reserve troops of the Welsh Division were mercilessly shelled. At 5 a.m. the 13th and 14th Battalions, The Welch Regiment, attacked Morval with disastrous results. Although the position was a commanding one and strongly held, the Welch had to attack in broad daylight and entirely without the usual and necessary artillery support. Naturally, little or no progress was made, while heavy casualties were incurred. After this obvious lesson, a further attack by the same battalions was ordered, preceded this time by a preliminary bombardment and supported by an artillery barrage. Further heavy casualties resulted. The 13th Welch did not receive their orders until it was already too late for them to reach their assembly positions. Thus it happened that the 14th Welch Regiment, already twice depleted by heavy casualties, advanced entirely unsupported and found the enemy in great strength with machine guns and well wired in. Morval still remained uncaptured; and thus the day closed, the 14th Welch Regiment having only four officers left—Lieut.-Col. G. F. Brooke, D.S.O., Capt. R. D. Williams, Lieut. I. Williams and 2/Lieut. L. O. Griffiths.

The whole of the following day, August 31st, was spent in bombarding Morval preparatory to a further assault on that stubborn stronghold on September 1st. Yet even that day brought its casualties, too. Lieut.-Col. T. Parkinson, D.S.O., who had commanded the 15th Welch Regiment since November, 1915, was wounded by shrapnel, and Capt. J. Williams, M.C., took over the command of the Battalion.

The third and last day of the action against Morval—September 1st, 1918—was as successful as the first day was disastrous. According to the plan of campaign, the 114th Brigade (13th, 14th and 15th Battalions, The Welch Regiment) was to capture Morval at all costs; the 115th Brigade (Royal Welch Fusiliers and South Wales Borderers) on their left were to take Sailly-Saillisel, and the 113th Brigade (Royal Welch Fusiliers) to move forward to support them. At 4.45 a.m. the three battalions of the Welch Regiment or what was left of them—attacked under cover of a creeping barrage and, after desperate fighting, finally captured and held their important objective, the village of Morval. It is recorded that " 200 enemy dead could be counted on the ground." The 115th Brigade advanced north of Morval, but was unexpectedly checked by enfilade machine-gun fire from a commanding position on high ground in a gap which had been created between that Brigade and the 17th Division on the left of our own 38th Division. In conseqence of the serious position thus created, the 113th Brigade had to pass through and carry out the attack on Sailly-Saillisel, which eventually fell before their assaults. The 114th Brigade (Welch Regiment)

Photo]   [*Imperial War Museum, Crown Copyright*

THE VILLAGE OF MORVAL, SEPTEMBER, 1916.

was then brought into Divisional Reserve for a brief spell, while the 113th and 115th Brigades followed up the advance.

To-day the graves at Morval remain to remind us of those few days of heroic fighting and tragic loss. The following officers and other ranks of the 14th Welch Regiment were buried in the same grave and beneath one wooden cross (now replaced by separate headstones) in Morval British Cemetery:—

        Capt. T. C. H. Berry, 5th (attached 14th) Welch Regiment ; aged 26.
        Lieut. E. H. Balsom, of Caerphilly ; also aged 26.
        2/Lieut. J. S. Graham, of South Shields ; aged 23.
        2/Lieut. G. Y. P. Jones, of Cardiff ; aged 23.
        Sergt. F. J. H. Hall, also of Cardiff ; aged 26.
        Pte. L. E. M. Matthews, of Hornsey ; aged 19.
        Pte. W. H. Craddock.

All these were killed in the futile attacks on Morval on August 30th. In addition, the same cross marked the graves of:—

>L./Cpl. C. Coleman, of Sutton-in-Ashfield.
>Pte. J. R. Jones, of Pont-y-cymmer.

The former fell earlier in the day at Delville Wood, and Pte. Jones on August 27th. Two of the fallen the writer particularly remembers. Capt. T. C. H. Berry was his own brother and had joined the 14th Welch Regiment only a few days before. He had been severely wounded at Messines in June, 1917, when serving with the 1st/8th City of London Regiment (Post Office Rifles), and had spent most of the year following in hospitals. He fell " whilst gallantly leading his company " against the commanding stronghold of Morval. Lieut. Balsom was another Territorial Officer (4th Welch Regiment), but recently attached to the 14th Welch Regiment. G. Y. P. Jones impressed all who knew him, not less by courage and cheerfulness than by the handsome charm of his youth.

Among others of the Welch Regiment who fell during these actions, and whose graves are in Morval Cemetery, were:—

>Capt. C. J. Boulton, M.C., of Hanley, the brave and deservedly popular Adjutant of the 13th Welch Regiment, killed August 30th.
>2/Lieut. E. Burtonwood, of Maesteg, also of the 13th Welch Regiment ; aged 23.
>2/Lieut. C. H. Hughes, 14th Welch Regiment, killed September 1st ; aged 22.
>2/Lieut. H. J. Bladon, of Cardiff, who, like Graham (above), was attached to the 14th Welch Regiment from the 4th (Territorial) Battalion ; killed September 1st ; aged 28.
>2/Lieut. C. H. Hughes, of Morda, 14th Welch Regiment, killed August 30th ; aged 22.

Two other officers of the Welch Regiment who made the supreme sacrifice at about the same time as those mentioned above were:—

>Lieut. A. D. Morris, 13th Welch Regiment.
>2/Lieut. E. V. Rowe, 13th Welch Regiment.

Their graves have never been identified and so their names are engraved on Panel 7 of the Memorial to the Missing erected by the Imperial War Graves Commission* at Vis-en-Artois. Morris had served continuously with the 13th Welch Regiment since 1915 and, as a result of fearless patrolling work, none knew " No Man's Land " from Weiltje to Boesinghe as he did. His duties as bombing officer earned for him the affectionate name of " Dai Bombs." Six other officers of the Welch Regiment may also be mentioned as their deaths in action belong to this period, though immediately preceding the attack on Morval—2/Lieut. E. G. Jones and 2/Lieut. P. L. Leech, both of the 13th Welch Regiment, whose graves are at Gezaincourt and Longueval (Caterpillar Valley) respectively ; Lieut. C. T. Osmond and 2/Lieut. W. H. Hazard, both of the 14th Welch Regiment, are buried at Gezaincourt Bagneux) and Delville Wood respectively ; 2/Lieuts. R. C. Evans and W. Bowe are buried at Pozières and Fienvillers.

So heavy were the losses among other ranks that it is impossible to refer to them individually, though mention has been made above of those who, in the equality of death, shared a common grave at Morval. During the whole of the Second Battle of Bapaume, which lasted altogether less than a fortnight, *i.e.*, from August 21st to September 3rd, the three Service Battalions of the Welch Regiment lost 15 officers killed and 28 wounded†. Among other ranks the casualties were 208 killed, 900 wounded and 55 missing. The total casualties (killed, wounded and missing) for all ranks were thus 1,206.

---

* The Secretary, Imperial War Graves Commission, has most kindly supplied me with this and other information.

† I am indebted for these figures to the *History of the Welch Regiment*, Part II, by Major General Sir Thomas O. Marden, K.B.E., C.B., C.M.G. This splendid history is a unique source of information for all matters relating to the history of that regiment. Reference may also be made to the brief *History of the 38th (Welsh) Division*, by Lieut.-Colonel Rhys Price, C.M.G., D.S.O., and Lieut.-Colonel J. E. Mumby, C.M.G., D.S.O.

Photo] HILL 60 IN WAR-TIME. [*Antony, Ostend*

Gorse on Hill 60

"Hill 60 in 1914 was merely a low ridge some 150 feet high, and 250 yards from end to end, formed artificially when the railway cutting was dug. . . . Its military importance was due to its being the highest point in this area and consequently commanding views in every direction."
The Battle Book of Ypres.

Several V.Cs. were awarded for valour on this hill.

WRITTEN AFTER A VISIT TO HILL 60, JUNE 4TH, 1933.

So bravely breaks the golden-gorse
    Upon the hill again
That we can see in Nature's mood
    An easement of all pain.

Ah, who could guess when standing here
    That men in fury fought,
And held their wills, and gave their lives,
    To hold a place long sought?

This little hill that any child
    With careless, happy laughter
Could make in one long, gallant run,
    Is left to fame hereafter.

Here late was mud, and long churned earth,
    But also roots that bore
A flaming bush to victory
    From out the insensate maw.

R. HENDERSON-BLAND,
late Gloucestershire Regiment.

Leadership—The British Race

By Lieut.-Col. Graham Seton Hutchison, D.S.O., M.C.
(Author of "Footslogger," "Warrior," "The W Plan," etc.)

The mission of the British Race is not yet ended.

AN AFFIRMATION.

WE, men and women, old and young, who have before our eyes Britain's beauteous landscape—the blue haze of its valleys, the verdant green of its pastures, the spring gold of its moorland gorse, the rolling downs dotted with sheep, the heathered hills, the deep silent woods carpeted with bluebells or tinted with russet of Autumn loveliness—

WE, who scent the first buds of the English rose in June, and gather the perfume of wild flowers from the hedgerow amid deep country lanes—

WE, who hear the magnificent peal of Cathedral chimes; and, echoing across the fields, the bells from some old church tower, which tell of the immortality of England, or sometimes softly intoning of one who has gone back to his rest in her bosom—

WE, who have given our father's blood, our brother's blood, and our children's blood that the great spirit of Britain shall bring knowledge, prosperity and peace among the peoples of the world—

WE, whose word has been our bond, to whom lies do not easily come, and to whom the sanctity of contract means our personal honour—

WE, to whom fair dealing as between man and man implies a moral integrity beyond the Penal Code—

WE, who inspired the freedom of mankind from slavery, and will not endure its imposition on ourselves—

WE, whose spirit responds to the profound and eternal truths traditional in the British character—

WE, whose genius has been inspired by the quiet grandeur, sculptured and painted by the Great Architect of this land—

WE, whose individual souls are cast in the everlasting model of our country—

WE, who are strong as the English oak, and whose endurance has been tested through a thousand years of history—

WE, who, through British fibre, have conquered in every field of manly endeavour, have endured tropical suns and arctic frosts, have held the beleaguered trench, kept the watch before Ypres and have marched to the uttermost ends of the earth—

WE, whose name as Britons, is written fairly upon the great pages of history, and whose great figures occupy the forefront of a World's Pageant—

WE, who have in our bones and blood the matchless tradition of these Islands—

WE, who cherish the ideals for which, in good times and bad Great Britain has stood—

WE, summoning courage from the heart of our land in which it is vested—

WE declare that we stand unmoved for the ideals which have inspired our race, and will go forward renewed, regenerated, united, towards the great destiny which an unerring history contributes as our right.

God Save The King.

Ypres British School
The Bishop of London Distributes the Prizes
PICTURESQUE OPEN-AIR CEREMONIAL.

ON the morning of Monday, June 4th, in brilliant sunshine, the Bishop of London presented the prizes to the successful scholars attending the British School at Ypres.

It was a typical day culled out of "Flaming June," and very wisely the decision was made to hold the picturesque and pleasing little ceremonial out of doors in the school playground. Nevertheless, although a cooling breeze tempered

Photo]   THE CHILDREN OF THE YPRES BRITISH SCHOOL, 1933.   *[Daniel, Ypres*

the extreme heat and fluttered the folds of the Union Jack overhead, the sun's rays beat fiercely on the asphalted pavement. This prompted the Bishop, with characteristic thoughtfulness, to make the request that the youngsters should be brought in the shade under the eastern wall.

There was a goodly company present, which included many proud parents and members of the British community in Ypres. Amongst others I noticed General Sir Charles Harington, the Dowager Viscountess Plumer, who was accompanied by her two daughters, the Bishop of Fulham (North and Central Europe) Col. Higginson (representing the Imperial War Graves Commission), Col. F. G. Poole, Mrs. L. K. Briggs and Miss Briggs, the Rev. G. R. and Mrs. Milner, Mr. and Mrs. Morris (who were visiting the scene of their former labours),

Mr. C. J. Parminter and Mr. and Mrs. W. P. Allen (the new Schoolmaster and Schoolmistress).

General regret was expressed at the enforced absence, through illness, of Sir William Pulteney. Indeed, to the writer, who has been present at previous " Prize Days " at Ypres, the proceedings seemed to bear close resemblance to a performance of " Hamlet " with the character of the Prince of Denmark omitted.

After Mr. Allen had given an interesting and lucid review of the various activities of the school, the Bishop of London presented the prizes, which took the form of instructive and other appropriate books.

They were donated on this occasion by :—

(a) Mrs. L. K. Briggs, of Broadstairs, for ordinary school work.
(b) The Third Army Corps. These were awarded to children on the vote of their fellow scholars, and were won by Muriel Grasham, Priestley Dunn and Irene Fletcher.

There were also five prizes for those pupils who had produced the best plants from bulbs.

In the course of a charming address—now grave, now gay—the Bishop complimented the children upon their bright, happy and healthy appearance. The objects of the school, he said, were to teach them the " Three Rs " and to inculcate in their minds a love for England—the country to which they belonged. Never in history, he declared, had Great Britain stood higher in name and préstige among the nations of the earth than she did to-day. In the colours that comprised the Union Jack, the red stood for Sacrifice, the blue for Honesty in Commerce, and the white for Purity in Life.

Sir Charles Harington, President of the Ypres League, who distributed the prizes in 1932, congratulated the children on the progress that they had made during the past twelve months. He referred to the disappointment that the absence of Sir William Pulteney had caused to all present, but questioned whether the scholars fully realized what a debt they owed Sir William for his tireless energy and enthusiasm. Referring to the fact that, on the previous day he had visited Tyne Cot Cemetery and was paying a second visit that afternoon, he expressed the wish that everyone in the British Isles should see that hallowed God's Acre. In conclusion, he extended a hand of welcome to Mr. and Mrs. Allen and wished them success in the task they had undertaken.

The Bishop of Fulham, in passing a vote of thanks to the Bishop of London, expressed gratitude to Lady Plumer, Sir Charles Harington, Col. Higginson and Col. Poole for gracing the ceremony with their presence. He also paid tribute to Sir Fabian Ware and the Staff of the Imperial War Graves Commission for their loyal and generous support.

Col. Higginson briefly replied, and the proceedings terminated with customary cheering and the National Anthem.

The pupils on the school roll now number 116, the fathers of 98 of these children being employees of the Imperial War Graves Commission. At the opening, four years ago, under the control of Mr. and Mrs. Morris, the attendance totalled only 47. The problem of accommodating this unexpected increase has been overcome by making use of the Pilgrims' Hall and leasing a large room near the building which constituted the original and temporary school. Too much praise cannot be accorded Mr. and Mrs. Morris for the unqualified success they have made of the difficult and uphill pioneer work which faced them during their brief four years' sojourn in Ypres. They have left the school in a state of high efficiency, whilst they have won the affection and regard of all their pupils and the gratitude and respect of their parents. Their successors will find them " good ones to follow, but hard ones to beat."

H. B.

Presentation to Mr. and Mrs. Morris

On the eve of the departure of Mr. and Mrs. Morris to resume duty in England, after a stay of four years as the pioneers of instruction in the British School in Ypres, a social evening was held in the Pilgrims' Room on Thursday, March 30th last, at which a picture in oils of a scene in Bruges—which had been subscribed for by numerous members of the British colony here—was presented to Mr. and Mrs. Morris as a tangible token of the esteem in which they were held.

In making the presentation, the Chaplain, the Rev. G. R. Milner, M.A., expressed the thanks of the members of the community for the unstinted way in which Mr. and Mrs. Morris had entered into the social activities of the colony during their stay, and the regret on every hand at their enforced departure from our midst. He ventured the hope that their future would be a prosperous one and their days no less happy than they had been during their four years in Ypres.

In suitably acknowledging the gift on behalf of Mrs. Morris and himself, Mr. Morris assured all present of the deep regret they felt in leaving Ypres and of the pleasure it had given them to take part in the various activities of the community, and further expressed the hope that Mrs. Morris and he had of visiting Ypres on many occasions in the future.

During an interval, tea, which had been very kindly provided by Mr. and Mrs. Morris, was partaken of by the company and, towards midnight, a most enjoyable evening was brought to a close with the singing of " Auld Lang Syne " and " The King."

A. M.

" Tuindag "

IN 1343 English troops, under the leadership of the then Bishop of Norwich, formed an alliance with the City of Ghent for the purpose of invading France by way of the Flemish marshes. The citizens of Ypres, the intended base of the invaders, however, had other ideas, and proceeded to put their defences in order, and made all preparations for a prolonged siege. The English commander, sure of subduing the city in a short time, was no doubt surprised when, at the end of nine dreary weeks, he was forced to raise the siege and retreat in the face of rapidly advancing French forces. The departure of the invaders coincided with the feast-day of Notre-Dame de Thuyne, to whose good offices the Yprians attributed their successful defence. And from that day began her reign as Patroness of Ypres and of Western Flanders. A popularity that has grown with the years, till to-day the festivities, religious and lay, in connection with " Tuindag," last sixteen days, beginning on the Sunday preceding the 8th of August and closing on the second Sunday following. High Mass is celebrated in the rebuilt Cathedral of Saint Martin by the Dean of Ypres, attended by the Cathedral Chapter and members of the various religious orders in the diocese. The beautifully decorated altars, the brilliant robes of the clergy, the banners of the Guilds and Confraternities, the relics carried on cushions of crimson and gold, all combine to make an unforgettable picture. Later, the Grande Place teems with the thousands who have come from all over Belgium and the Flemish provinces of France to pay tribute to Flanders' Patroness. The centre of the Place is filled with stalls offering sweets and toys, cooked meats and chips, edibles of all kinds suitable for consumption out-of-doors. A travelling theatre boosts its attractions through the medium of a small but very noisy band, which also accompanies and illustrates the antics of Punch and Judy in the stall next door. Liliana—The Fat Lady—one of whose socks, as big as an average bathing suit, is flaunted outside her booth, offers her charms for inspection at the rate of one franc (or 1½d.) per head. A miniature railway running through a circular tunnel, motor-cars on tracks, and weird animals curvetting round on revolving platforms cater for the little ones, while the grandmothers, their daughters and granddaughters, scramble into the swing-boats and aeroplanes, to the huge delight of the perambulating crowds. Various gambling games attract the more sophisticated, and in the shooting gallery is a gaily painted figure of a lady surprised in an advanced state of négligé, and who, on being " potted " in a well marked spot, hastily adjusts her disarray. Here and there among the crowds one meets groups of pilgrims who have come from all over the world to visit the battlefields and cemeteries of the Salient, and who join wholeheartedly in the merriment, forgetting for the moment their travel-weariness. All this and much more under the shadow of the scaffolded walls of the old Cloth Hall. Each day's programme varies.

Religious ceremonies are followed by distributions of prizes to school-children, and gymnastic displays. Guild meetings succeed to classical concerts given in one of the many public squares. Band promenades by the local garrison or by some of the many " club " bands from the provinces, have their crowds of dévotees who sit comfortably on the café terraces and imbibe their bocks while listening with the air of connoisseurs who are not to be too easily pleased. The " Cercle William Tell "—local champions of the bow and arrow, Flanders' favourite sport—hold competitions and reunions for visiting members and teams. And in the rendezvous of the different political organizations there is much talk and disputation, accompanied by the inevitable bock and cigars. Flanders, too, has her Sinn Fein! And all over the city are notices calling on the citizens to re-affirm their loyalty to King and Country, and so signalize their disapproval of those who agitate, and, at times, with force! for " complete independence for West Flanders " and for complete severance of their ties with Belgium and her King. Flanders, the cock-pit of Europe, spoil of any and every adventurer, claims to stand alone. So much for the vaunted lessons of history. In the evening a famous trick-cyclist pays a flying visit to give a short display in the crowded Grande Place and then the crowds begin to thin out. Some drift to the cafés to smoke and gossip till midnight, others to their homes or hotels, and by far the greater number set off on 'buses or bicycles for the neighbouring towns and villages. But, at 9 o'clock, when the festivities are showing signs of quietening down, a crowd of some 200 gathers in and around the immense pile of the Menin Gate. A white-helmeted policemen, at either approach, holds up the road traffic, while four buglers in the red, blue, and gold of the Municipality blow the " Last Post " on silver bugles presented to the city in memory of those who died in her defence. Tired-eyed women stand silent and motionless—tears very near the surface. A crippled ex-officer, stiff as a ramrod on his crutches, chokes convulsively. Black-clad Belgians, who have listened to the Call night after night for years, stare unseeingly —as at some figment of the past recalled by the plaintive notes. A figment of the past—or, mayhap, a haunting fear for the future? A sudden shower of rain fills the cafés to overflowing, and is gone as quickly as it came. A few of the more sturdy, or less tired, of the Pilgrims stroll out past the Gate towards the Menin Road, there to stand and stare across the distances of the night. Tiny lights, almost too distant to be seen, outline roughly the run of the old Salient. St. Jean, Hooge, Zillebeke, and, down south, Wytschaete, with all their wealth of associations, and over all a brooding sense of waiting—for what? A last look round, perhaps a whispered prayer—then back, and so to bed. Tuindag has begun.

JOHN A. SHEAHAN.

A Day on the Somme.

AT the risk of being considered irrelevant, I propose to take my readers away from the Salient with me for a summer day on the Somme. This day is a day in the life of one John Brown, and the date July 20th, 1916. There is, perhaps, little out of the ordinary in the story, but a personal experience has usually some points of interest to those who have had similar adventures.

John Brown was no soldier. At the outbreak of war in 1914 he was a young man of twenty-five, big, strong, and healthy, just an ordinary young Englishman ready to do what he saw as his duty to his country. The war had been in progress a month when he put on his fusilier's uniform, and in 1915 he was in the front line just too late for the Battle of Loos. The Somme was a new experience for him. By this time he was a hardened veteran, but he had, of course, no taste of a real attempt to advance.

When his battalion arrived from the north the battle had been raging for a fortnight, flesh and blood against iron and steel that flew at one red-hot from all directions, tearing and mutilating all the frail human flesh with which it came in contact. How humanity prevailed against it was wonderful; but by sheer weight of numbers, flesh gained against metal, and the British Army was advancing slowly.

On July 20th the brigade of which Brown was a humble member was deputed to capture a wood which could be seen in front of the new lines, a lovely sylvan spot which was to become famous under the name of High Wood. Two battalions were in front, with Brown's in close support, and another in reserve when the attack began at 2 a.m. The men advanced through a wide stretch of " No Man's Land " just as they had done on Salisbury Plain, but there were a good many casualties before they reached the wood, including the gallant Colonel, a Worcestershire man who had won the D.S.O. and a permanent limp with his county regiment in South Africa. Fortunately he was only wounded, and lived on to die a natural death last year. As the men lay on the fringe of the wood, our guns poured into the trees a rain of shells which effectually drove the Germans who survived into a far corner, which they continued to hold throughout the day. The uproar was deafening, and no man could hear the voice of his neighbour. As the barrage lifted the troops raced into the wood with bayonets fixed, Brown and his companions reaching the far side without encountering anything more deadly than various dead Germans, and a few Highlanders who had fallen in a previous attack the week before.

Day was now breaking, the opening of a glorious day of summer, as Brown began, along with some of his own battalion and a party of regular Royal Engineers under a sergeant, to dig a machine-gun emplacement in front of the wood and in full view of the enemy. Work proceeded rapidly, with shrapnel bursting overhead and bullets whistling past. Cover seemed a long time in coming, but all worked with a frenzy natural in men trying to save their lives. By the time the trench was deep enough to afford real protection the party was sadly depleted. Brown had escaped with a bump on the shoulder blade by a piece of spent metal, which was of no account, and a small piece of shrapnel which had hit him in the corner of the mouth, and which caused him annoyance by reason of the attention of a big fly which persisted in sitting on the sore spot; but most of his companions had departed, either killed or gone back wounded. During the morning he had been working beside an R.E., when a shrapnel shell had burst behind them, scorching the back of his neck. He turned to the man beside him, saying: "That was a near one," but the man was dead. What had merely felt hot to Brown had killed the man working shoulder to shoulder with him. Earlier in the day, Brown had been digging next to the R.E. sergeant, when a German sniper crawled out of his trench to a favourably placed shell hole in front of his line. This was too much for the sergeant, who seized his rifle and took careful aim, saying as he did so, "I'll get that blighter," but before he had time to fire the sniper had got him through the forehead. He turned his face to Brown and his lips moved, but a film passed over his eyes, and the words were never uttered. He also had passed on.

The time arrived when Brown found himself alone in front of the wood. The thought that he was entirely alone facing the might of Germany gave him a momentary feeling of panic, though not many yards away were the remains of an

Photo]   [*Imperial War Museum, Crown Copyright*

HIGH WOOD, SEPTEMBER, 1916.

English Brigade. He climbed out of his trench and ran for the wood, with bullets aimed at him cracking in his ears; but he arrived safely, and found shelter in a little trench occupied by two men of another company of his battalion. Here he was on the fringe of the wood, with an uninterrupted view of the enemy lines.

Ere long the German artillery concentrated on the wood, till it seemed that nothing could live in it. The ground rocked, and even the air rocked as the heavy shrapnel burst overhead with loud crashes and great black clouds of fantastic shape. As Brown looked back into the wood he saw a shell burst above a little trench occupied by four men of his own company. Each one of them flung his arms into the air, and fell face downward on the parapet—dead. As the earth rocked and swayed, a giant oak not far distant received a direct hit. Half the tree rose into the air and then came to earth with what must have been a mighty crash, but which was unheard in the dreadful din. Then the Germans got out of their trenches, advancing in short rushes towards the wood. They did not come very far, taking cover in shell holes, and though they came on later in the day Brown was not there to see it.

A Scottish Major now came up with orders to the thinned front line to retire to the middle of the wood. Brown had only gone a few yards before he came upon the Major lying on his face—he must have been killed immediately after he had given the order. As the men ran for their new positions shrapnel burst over, behind, and in front of them, while thousands of machine-gun bullets cracked in the trees like chattering demons.

Brown was destined never to see that line. He had found his way into the main ride through the wood, and had not gone far before he felt something

Photo]   [*Imperial War Museum, Crown Copyright*

AERIAL VIEW OF HIGH WOOD, OCTOBER, 1916.

like a kick at the bottom of the spine, followed by a dull pain somewhere inside. What had happened to him he did not know, but what he did know was that he must get out of that wood while he had strength to do it as he might collapse at any minute. The British had already evacuated part of the wood, and sooner or later the Germans would attack, perhaps retaking what they had lost, together with those wounded who were fortunate enough to escape the shells. So on he went until he was through the wood, and there in front of him he saw the enemy's barrage between our support line and the wood. Though he did not know it, Military Medals were given that day to runners who passed through that barrage. He did not hesitate—anything was better than to lie helpless and unattended in that wood—and through the barrage he went. He was not alone, and one man near him went through at the expense of an arm blown off at the shoulder.

Through the barrage, Brown was soon at the support line, where complete peace reigned. The regimental stretcher-bearers inspected his wound, which they found to be a clean hole with no external bleeding, on which they put a bandage which at once fell off. Every minute it became more evident that he had got a bad internal injury, the pain was steadily growing worse, while his strength was ebbing. He knew where the main dressing station lay, and as he saw no chance of any attention nearer, he began painfully to make for it. It was now that he met a reserve stretcher-bearer of his battalion, a good Samaritan who began to help him on his way, until up came one of those sergeants who never see the line, who proceeded to inform the stretcher-bearer that he had got a better job than that for him. That was a long, long trail, slower and slower every step, with head bent down to his knees, and sweat running from every pore; but he got there.

The doctor at the dressing station was not over worried about a nice little hole which did not bleed, and Brown soon found himself in an ambulance containing four stretcher cases; but he was not one of these, having been termed a sitting case. By this time he could neither sit nor stand, and endured agonies at every jolt of the ambulance. Most of that dismal journey was passed on his hands and knees, with head resting on the arm of a friendly stretcher case.

At the Field Ambulance he met with kindness, and what was more important, intelligence. It was discovered for the first time that things were serious—he was placed on his first stretcher, and labelled for urgent operation. The references of those doctors to the M.O. who had committed him to that agonizing run in the ambulance were far from complimentary.

Without any undue delay Brown found himself at the C.C.S. at Heilly, where he waited on his stretcher behind many others in a similar situation. At last his turn came, the trouble was located, and the friendly chloroform gave him peace after a day of varied emotions. In the night he awoke to find himself in a real bed, but it was not until the next day, when the surgeon paid him a visit, that he discovered that he was wearing a necklace of lint from which hung a pendant in the form of a shrapnel bullet which had been extracted by a skilful hand from one of the vital abdominal organs of his body. Brown still has that bullet.

J. B.

The Ramparts Cemetery (Lille Gate) Ypres at Night

Calm and lovely is the night,
   And the graves are lovely too;
The moon rides high as if it rode
   With deep intent to strew
Its beams upon the water,
   Where peace is born anew.

It is well with you, my brothers, it is well
   Sleeping in the shadows of this immortal place
That saw your comrades pass, and pass again,
   And was the silent witness of their grace,
And all their holy pain.

R. HENDERSON-BLAND,
(Late Gloucestershire Regiment).

The Easter Pilgrimage of 1933

A PARTY of pilgrims, including the "old sweats" and their wives, one of whom was ex-Nursing Sister F. A. Hayden (Mrs. Fry), of the Canadian Army Medical Corps, met at Victoria Station on Saturday, April 14th. We arrived at Ostend just in time to catch the train for the Immortal Salient (Ypres), where we were met by the Ypres League's representative, Mr. C. J. Parminter, and conducted to comfortable accommodation at the Hotel Splendid and Britannique.

CANADIAN MEMORIAL AT ST. JULIEN.

On Sunday morning some of the party visited the British church, while others journeyed to various cemeteries or renewed acquaintance with familiar spots. After lunch we all enjoyed a charabanc tour of the Salient, leaving Ypres by the Rue de Dixmude, and passing White House and Oxford Road Cemeteries, the 50th Northumbria Division Memorial and the magnificent St. Julien Memorial erected in honour of 2,000 Canadians who fell in the first gas attack on April 22nd, 1915. Our next stop was at the Guynemer Memorial to the famous French ace who, after three years of fighting, was killed on September 11th, 1917, at the age of 21 years. Passchendaele Ridge was next on the itinerary where we examined the Canadian Memorial and the Memorial Window to the 66th Lancashire Division, which has been placed in the local church. Tyne Cot Cemetery, with its memorial to the "Missing," was deeply impressive, and the cemetery contains the original Tyne Cot blockhouse captured by the 2nd Australian Division on October 4th, 1917. The tour continued to Polygon Wood, Clapham Junction, Stirling Castle and the Canadian Memorial at Hill 62, consisting of a large tract of land planted with maple trees from Canada, and a large circular stone pavement surrounding a short stone column. Sanctuary Wood still contains some of the old trenches, duck boards, shrapnel scarred tree trunks, old tin hats, rifles rusted with age, and numerous other war materials, all of which reminded us of other days. Hell Fire Corner was passed en route to Hill 60, where we reconnoitred some of the old trenches and tunnels, and saw the memorials to the Queen Victoria Rifles and the 1st Australian Tunnelling Company. This concluded our day's adventure.

The following day was the anniversary of the capture of Vimy Ridge, and I was particularly anxious to visit our old home on the Ridge and to say that sixteen years after I again walked the trenches and tunnels. So bright and early on Easter Monday, a contrast to the dismal rainy days we once knew, we were off down the road past Shrapnel Corner and Dickebusch, passing Mount Kemmel on our right, the London Scottish Memorial, New Zealand Memorial

CHRIST DES TRENCHES AT NEUVE CHAPELLE.

and Hill 63, then on to Ploegsteert Wood and Memorial to the "Missing," Hyde Park Corner, Strand Cemetery, London Rifle Brigade Cemetery and Le Bizet at the French border where the custom officials "do their stuff." We went on through Armentières, La Bassée and Neuve Chapelle. Here we saw the famous "Le Christ des Trenches." It consists of a figure of Christ which was shot to pieces during the war, with exception of the face, which was left untouched, and now rests at the base of a new cross and restored by the Bouquet family in 1929. Further down the road was the beautiful Indian Memorial, after which we passed a Portuguese Cemetery, La Bassée Canal, Hulloch on the left, Höhenzollen Redoubt, Chalk Farm, Hill 70, and entered Lens. A vastly different Lens to the one we knew in the war days; incidentally, the birthplace of Georges Carpentier, the famous French boxer. We eventually arrived at the old Canadian trenches on Vimy Ridge, and descended the Grange Tunnels and examined many names carved in the chalk. At one place there is a nose of a German shell which had just pierced the ceiling after having passed through 13 feet of chalk. Old barbed wire, tin hats, shell craters, etc., are still to be seen in the vicinity. The Canadian Memorial, not yet completed, is a massive structure and will be a magnificent work of art occupying one of the most prominent positions on the Ridge.

We continued our tour past Thelus, Nine Elms Cemetery, St. Catherines, into Arras where we lunched in true French style in a side-walk café. Like Lens, Arras appears to be another thriving city. We now stopped at the old tunnels at La Targette, which are of great interest. On the opposite side of the road is a German cemetery containing 35,000 bodies. Then Notre Dame de Lorette with its similar number of French bodies. Our return journey proceeded via Souchez, rebuilt by the Borough of Kensington, and its Grande Place is named Kensington Square. Then came Aix Noulette, Bully Grenay, Neux-le-Mines, Béthune, Le Touret Cemetery and Memorial to 20,000 "Missing," Estaires and Steenwerck, again reaching the Belgian border at Le Seau. Our route followed through Neuve Eglise, Daylight Corner, Suicide Corner, Sackville Street, Lovers Lane, Kemmel, Irish House Cemetery, La Laiterie Cemetery, also a memorial to the 27th and 30th U.S.A. Divisions, and so on to Ypres.

For the benefit of relatives who have not visited the cemeteries in France and Belgium, I can state without fear of contradiction that there are no better kept cemeteries, and great credit is due to the work of the Imperial War Graves Commission.

I cannot close without a word of appreciation to our genial friend, Capt. de Trafford, the Secretary of the Ypres League, whose untiring efforts made the trip such a huge success.

E. C. F.

1933 Recruiting Competition

IN view of the popularity and immense success of the past two recruiting competitions, and in order to give recently-formed branches an opportunity to compete, we have great pleasure to announce that **A FURTHER PRIZE OF £5** will be awarded this year as follows :—

TO THE BRANCH RECRUITING THE GREATEST NUMBER OF NEW MEMBERS IN 1933.

All membership forms completed must be received at Headquarters bearing on the top left-hand corner the name of the branch responsible for the recruitment.

Our Whitsuntide Arras Pilgrimage.

MEANTIME Capt. de Trafford was assembling the Ypres party of some fifty to sixty pilgrims at Victoria Station, his Chief-of-Staff was piloting a party of twenty-five persons to the coast *en route* to Arras. The programme mapped out for this particular party was very ambitious since the many graves and memorials to be visited were so widely scattered. The tour on the Sunday necessitated a trip of at least 150 miles.

Punctual to the time fixed overnight by the conductor, Mr. Vyner produced a very excellent 22-seater charabanc and also kindly arranged for Mr. "Joe" Harris, one of his henchmen and an extremely popular fellow with all League pilgrims, to accompany the party as a guide. Leaving headquarters at the Hotel Moderne about 8.30 a.m. the party, numbering nineteen, commenced their long trek northwards. Making for the Bethune main road, the first cemetery to be visited was at Anzin St. Aubin where a lady member, recently over from Canada, paid her respects at the grave of one of three brothers apart from her husband who were all killed in the Great War. From Anzin the following three cemeteries were visited, where at least one of the party had a relative buried: Cabaret Rouge Military Cemetery, Souchez, Maroc Military Cemetery at Bully-Grenay and Loos (Dud Corner). The line was then taken to Estaires via Vermelles, La Bassée and Neuve Chapelle, crossing the Belgian frontier at Le Seau and so on to Ypres via Locre and Dickebusch.

The party by this time were quite ready for the splendid lunch awaiting them at the Skindles Hotel, where Mdme. Bentin, who personally supervised the service, must have found the conditions with this influx rather tropical. Quite an hour was spent after lunch visiting the outstanding

SOME OF THE PARTY AT THE AIR FORCE COLUMN—ARRAS MEMORIAL.

places of interest in Ypres, the pilgrims being particularly impressed by the Ypres British Church and, of course, the Menin Gate. The intense heat did not improve matters for the conductor in his efforts to reassemble the party at the Grande Place, but on the eventual report "all present" the charabanc proceeded at a rapid pace to Passchendaele to enable the pilgrims to view the beautiful Tyne Cot British Military Cemetery, and the largest British Line Cemetery. From there the return journey was commenced via Voormezeele, St. Eloi, traversing the Wytschaete and Messines Ridges and on to "Plug Street" Wood where a stop was made to allow a member to visit his son's grave at the Rifle House Cemetery. This obscure but very pretty little cemetery is set deeply in the wood and the many narrow paths makes it difficult to locate. During the long trek through the wood, Joe could be heard estimating the reduction in weight he had been able to effect as a result of the walk, but agreed that the sight of the wonderful colouring of the many flowers now in full bloom in the three cemeteries was worth every inch of the journey.

The next port of call was the notorious Armentières, probably best remembered by the ladies of the party who appeared to be immensely " tickled " by the systematic but general scrutiny of the Douane officials when crossing the frontier again into France. After much effort tea was obtained here for those that way inclined and then, following a raid on a nearby stall for *pommes de terre frites* the route was taken to Lens (mining area) and Vimy Ridge where a stay of some thirty minutes was made to permit the party to inspect the Grange Tunnels and the new Canadian Memorial shortly to be unveiled. When " home " was reached at 10.20 p.m. the waiters at the Moderne appeared more pleased than the pilgrims since dinner had been kept since 7.30 p.m. After such a tiring day not many " see you laters " could be heard following the dinner, but it is believed that a few of the ex-tommy element contrived to spend a convivial hour together at a neighbouring estaminet exchanging reminiscences in connection with the places visited that day.

On Whit Monday the whole party of twenty-five undertook a tour of the Somme battlefields and outstanding memorials covering some ninety odd miles. Primary places of interest included Beaumont Hamel (Newfoundland Park) with its original trenches and war débris, Albert, where a very pleasant hour was spent, La Boisselle, site of the second largest mine crater, Delville Wood (Memorial to the South Africans), Trones Wood, High Wood, Combles, Longueval, Pozières, Martinpuich and Bapaume. None of the party were unduly limited to any special time when visiting either graves, memorials, or noted battlefield spots, and everyone appeared happily indifferent to returning again late for dinner, this time 9.45 p.m. in lieu of the customary set continental hour for this repast of 7.30 p.m., once more to the chagrin of the French waiters.

These two motor tours were conspicuous for the exceptional number of interesting spots visited, together with the buoyant spirit of the party throughout which was due in no small measure to one of our party wits, an old Nottingham ex-service stalwart, namely, Mr. O. H. Weatherall.

Praise was given to the efficient service and general comfort at the Hotel Moderne, and the pilgrims voted the whole trip an immense success.

Many flattering comments on the tour could be heard aboard the boat on the return journey with sincere expression to join further Ypres League pilgrimages in the not distant future.

Book Review

" THE PILL-BOXES OF FLANDERS."

This little book, which is published by Messrs. Ivor Nicholson & Watson, for the British Legion, is now ready and is on sale to the public.

It contains full particulars as to the history and construction of the German pill-box and corroboration of various details was obtained from General Von Salzenberg who, as Commander of the Pioneers of the 15th Corps, was responsible for the building of the earlier examples.

The largest numbers of these pill-boxes are to be found in the vicinity of St. Julien and astride the main road to Bruges, and here it is still possible to get a very complete idea of the skilful way in which the Germans planned their defensive system. There are no less than 112 of these still standing, the majority of which were taken on July 31st, 1917, by the 55th (West Lancashire) and 39th Divisions.

A complete line of 59 of these works—each within a few feet of the next—is particularly interesting, and close by are the two massive blockhouses at Alberta which were captured by men of the Sherwood Foresters.

Other groups are still in existence near Essex Farm, Pilckem, Frezenberg and Sanctuary Wood, whilst at Gheluvelt (a name always associated with the Worcestershire Regiment) there remains an excellent example of a German Headquarter dug-out.

Details are given of the fighting which culminated in the capture of all the above and various incidents connected therewith are related.

On the Messines Ridge the greater number have been demolished, but those few that do remain are directly connected with some of the most heroic episodes which occurred in the course of the Great War, and here also is to be found the sole surviving mine crater of the nineteen which were exploded on June 7th, 1917.

There are references to over fifty British infantry battalions, besides units from the Dominions, all of which were directly concerned in the capture or subsequent defence of these unique strongholds.

Several illustrations are included and the provision of two large-scale plans, together with a chapter on "How to reach the Pill-boxes," should be a means of facilitating access to the different groups. There is in addition an excellent map on a 1/40,000 scale, which indicates clearly not only the exact position of all the pill-boxes, but also shows the whereabouts of all the cemeteries and memorials in the area, so that it serves a triple purpose.

Every pilgrim or visitor to the Ypres neighbourhood and, in fact, everyone who is in any way interested in the "Salient," should be in possession of a copy of this little book.

Copies may be obtained from the Secretary, Ypres League, 20, Orchard Street, London, W.1. Price: 1s. (post free, 1s. 3d.).

A Week End in Ypres

By a Member of the 85th Club.

"VICTORIA—11.0 p.m. Friday." So read the instructions; and a cheery crowd of thirty-five-odd assembles at the appointed time to set out on an annual pilgrimage to Ypres and all the old haunts of the battlefields. What a difference from the journeys we used to make from London to the mud of Flanders.

A few hands of cards and the "last beer before leaving England" and we are soon on the boat and tucked down into our bunks waiting for the early morning arrival in sleepy, dirty Dunkerque, and the hope of coffee and rolls at the station—but, no! only the usual farcical visit to the French Customs, where they try to deprive us of our packs of cards and the only remaining decent "fags" left to us. No bad judges either to take our English cigarettes—for even a French Customs Officer can get tired of the doubtful French variety.

We get through after some argument and set off in the comfort of the Paris express, only to be turned out at Hazebrouck to board the local Belgian "express" with the square wheels.

We start to say "Do you remember . . . ?" almost as soon as we cross the Belgian frontier, and soon reach "Pop." and our beloved Ypres, so new and yet so full of all its old associations.

A hasty wash and brush-up at the hotel and we set off in our cars to visit battlefields, old billets and all the old haunts which can never be wiped from our memories. The day runs away all too quickly and before we know it we are back to the Hotel for dinner followed by our usual visit to the ceremony of the "Last Post" at the Menin Gate, played each year better by the local firemen.

Sunday is "our" day to do as we like and gives a splendid opportunity to consume innumerable foreign drinks of doubtful origin which we even enjoy because it is all such a refreshing change from our usual round.

So much to do and to see that the time is all too short, and much too soon do we have to pack up and return with a friendly call at "Toc H" at "Pop." on our way back.

Thanks to the courtesy and help of the Ypres League we have had a most enjoyable time and look forward already to next year.

Why do we set this time apart each year? No doubt because it lifts us out of our routine life. But surely one of the greatest joys is to feel that once again we have visited the scene of so much that happened in our lives and that once again we have satisfied ourselves that our boys are sleeping in peace round the country-side and are so well cared for.

W. S. B.

League Secretary's Notes

TO OUR NEW MEMBERS.

Each quarter brings its quota of new members, to whom we are always very delighted to extend a most hearty welcome. The recent recruits have come from London, Essex, Kent, Sussex, Bucks, Warwickshire, Wiltshire, and also from Canada, New Zealand and America.

We thank these new members for coming forward to make the League an increasing power for patriotic unity, and we appeal to their loyalty in recommending others to enroll, because personal contact brings the most faithful supporters.

The Ypres League depends entirely on its membership, and it is not easy for a sentimental association to thrive during the present financial difficulties of the world, but nevertheless, past experience has proved that those who are acquainted with the League's aims and objects are willing to pay the 5s. annual subscription to forward the interests of the great cause in which survivors and relatives of the fallen are all united.

Nothing gives headquarters greater pleasure and encouragement than to receive letters from our members requesting application forms with a view to finding prospective recruits, and we have pleasure to publish an extract from a letter received from J. A. (Edinburgh), June 1st :—

"In connection with our worthy League I am very pleased to report to you that I have secured two recruits and very good ones too, but I have only one membership form, so I should thank you much for six more and I will try and enroll more new members."

We earnestly trust that those who have recently joined will follow J. A.'s fine and practical example and so assist so valuably in maintaining the strength of the League.

TO BRANCH SECRETARIES, CORRESPONDING MEMBERS AND REPRESENTATIVES.

April, May and June have been particularly active in the travel department and some 200 persons have visited the cemeteries and battlefields of France and Belgium under the auspices of the League, and what has helped so much to promote our travel facilities is the fact that our Branch Secretaries, Corresponding Members and friends have generously given, at our request, some valuable publicity in their local Press. For this, special thanks are due to Major Graham Carr (Purley), Mr. W. H. Taylor (Colchester), Mr. E. Wilson (Welshpool), Mr. W. N. Channon (Chatham), Major A. W. Shea (Chesterfield), Lieut.-Colonel G. T. Willan (Carlisle), Capt. J. Wilkinson (Sheffield), Mr. J. Burman (Birmingham), Miss J. M. Wilkinson (Matlock), Mr. H. Carey (London), and to our exceedingly staunch friends Mr. H. Benson, Mr. J. Brunskill and Mr. S. H. Geller. Also we are very largely indebted to the Editors of the *News of the World*, *Referee*, and *Empire News* for being so kind as to insert notices of our pilgrimages in the Old Comrades Column of their valuable papers.

Our pilgrimages and tours for the past three months are as follows :—

April 15-18	Easter pilgrimage to Ypres.
April 21-24	167th Infantry Brigade, T.A.: Lecture tour to Ypres.
May 26-29	85th Club tour to Ypres.
June 3-5	Pilgrimage of poor relatives to Ypres at the League's expense.
June 3-6	Whitsuntide pilgrimage to Ypres.
June 3-6	Whitsuntide pilgrimage to Arras and the Somme.

This year, our Sheffield and Colchester Branches were given the privilege of selecting ten poor mothers to accompany the League's pilgrimage to Ypres at Whitsuntide, and an expression of sincere gratitude is due to these two indefatigable workers, namely: Capt. J. Wilkinson and Mr. W. H. Taylor, who went to infinite trouble in choosing most deserving cases, and we congratulate them on having performed this arduous but charitable task so successfully.

The Whitsuntide pilgrimage to Ypres was honoured by the presence of Capt. and Mrs. R. Henderson-Bland. Capt. Bland, as you are all aware, is the Ypres League's representative in America, and we hope that his initial re-visit to the Salient since his fighting days with the Gloucestershire Regiment will convey a deep impression on our members in America and be instrumental in persuading some of them to join our pilgrimages should they find the opportunity during their visits to this country.

A hearty vote of thanks is due to Mr. S. H. Geller, who helped so admirably in capacity of conductor for one of our Whitsuntide parties, and equal gratitude is extended to our representatives at Ypres and Arras, viz. : Mr. C. J. Parminter and Mr. P. Vyner respectively, for the genial and efficient way in which they look after the comfort of each individual member of the party.

We have recently had a very welcome visit to headquarters from Capt. Stuart Oswald, our representative at Amiens, and it would give us great pleasure to avail ourselves of his kind services in conducting a pilgrimage to Amiens, but in spite of liberal advertisement, it is strange to relate that no applications have been received for visits to that centre.

Purley and Colchester are fully alive to the importance of " Recruiting new members," and the first six months of the year result in even marks to these two faithful Branches.

The London County Committee continue their well-organized reunions which have important effect in keeping up the interest among our London members, and we thank Major Montague Jones, Mr. Boughey and the Committee for the sterling service rendered.

The year 1932 was notable for the number of new members recruited and we look optimistically on 1933 not only to swell the membership but to increase the popularity of our pilgrimages to France and Belgium which play such an important part in keeping a reunion of those to whom the Ypres Salient and other parts of the Western Front mean so much.

We conclude by thanking all who have devoted such a big slice of their precious time for the welfare of the League during the past quarter.

EDITOR'S NOTE

Articles appearing in THE YPRES TIMES invariably invoke criticism which is always greatly appreciated and valued, but, for fear of misunderstanding, on the part of our readers, the Editor wishes to point out that extreme personal views that may have been expressed in either articles or letters published in the journal in no way whatever influence the League's original aims and objects.

WREATHS.

Arrangements are made by the Ypres League to place wreaths for relatives on the graves of British soldiers situated in France and Belgium at the following times of the year :—

EASTER, ARMISTICE DAY, CHRISTMAS.

The wreaths may be composed of natural flowers, laurel, or holly, and can be bought at the following prices—12s. 6d., 15s. 6d., and 20s., according to the size and quality of the wreath.

PHOTOGRAPHS OF WAR GRAVES.

The Ypres League has made arrangements whereby it is able to supply photographs (negative, and one print, postcard size, unmounted) of graves situated in the Ypres Salient, and in the Hazebrouck and Armentieres areas, at the price of 10s. each.

BURNING OF THE CLOTH HALL, 1915.

There are only a few coloured prints, 14 in. by 12 in., now in stock, and, as further supplies are not obtainable, we are selling the remaining prints at 1s. each, post free.

HOTEL
SPLENDID & BRITANNIQUE
YPRES

GRAND' PLACE. Opposite Cloth Hall.

LEADING HOTEL FOR COMFORT AND QUALITY.

COMPLETELY RENOVATED.

RUNNING WATER. BATHROOMS.

MODERATE TERMS. GARAGE.

Patronized by The Ypres League.

AUGUST BANK HOLIDAY PILGRIMAGES (CONDUCTED)
(SATURDAY to TUESDAY)
AUGUST 5th to 8th

PILGRIMAGE TO **YPRES**

PILGRIMAGE TO **ARRAS and THE SOMME**

Members and all interested wishing to take part are requested to apply early as possible on account of limited accommodation at the best hotels.

Application for Prospectus should be made to Secretary Ypres League, 20, Orchard Street, London, W.1.

YPRES LEAGUE BADGE.

The design of the badge—a lion guarding a portcullis gate—represents the British Army defending the Salient, which was the gate to the Channel Ports.

The badge, herewith reproduced, is brilliantly enamelled with silver finish. Price 2s., post free 2s. 1½d. (pin or stud, whichever is desired). Applications should be addressed to the Secretary, Ypres League, 20, Orchard Street, London, W.1.

EMBROIDERED BADGES.

These badges can be supplied at 4s. each, post free. A considerable number have already been sold, and we are delighted to hear that the badges have given entire satisfaction to our members who have received them. Applications to the Secretary.

YPRES LEAGUE TIE.

At the request of the majority of our members we have been pleased to produce the tie in better quality silk and in a darker shade of cornflower blue relieved by a narrow gold stripe. The price is 3s. 6d., post free, and all members of the League should possess one.

Applications to the Secretary, Ypres League, 20, Orchard Street, London, W.1.

YPRES

Skindles Hotel

(Opposite the Station)

Proprietor — Life Member, Ypres League

Branch at Poperinghe

(close to Talbot House)

HOTEL MODERNE

(Place de la Gare) **ARRAS** (Pas de Calais)

F. GRAVIER, Proprietor.

Recommended by the Ypres League.

THE BRITISH TOURING SERVICE

Manager—Mr. P. VYNER.
Representative and Life Member, Ypres League.

**10, Station Square
ARRAS
(P.-de-C.) France.**

Cars for Hire, with British Driver Guides.   Tours Arranged.

Branch Notes

Photo] [*J. E. Sutter, Colchester* (*Press Photographer*)

INAUGURATION OF YPRES LEAGUE COLCHESTER AND DISTRICT BRANCH.

Memories of the Ypres Salient—where the flower of the British Army and Overseas Forces fell in an inferno of death and suffering till victory crowned a dauntless courage—were revived on the occasion of the inaugural dinner of the Colchester and District Branch of the Ypres League, held on Thursday, March 30th, at the Red Lion Hotel. The Chairman of the Branch (Colonel H. W. Herring, M.C.) occupied the chair, supported by Brigadier-General F. W. Towsey, C.M.G., D.S.O., Capt. G. E. de Trafford, M.C. (League Secretary), Major G. C. Benham, M.C. (Vice-Chairman), Mr. F. J. Collinge, Mr. Hubert Snow (Branch Hon. Secretary), Capt. A. C. Palmer (Hon. Treasurer), Mr. W. H. Taylor (Hon. Pilgrimage Secretary), Capt. C. Rooney, M.C., Capt. A. E. Leighton, Messrs. G. C. Stanford, J. M. Finn and C.W. Cook (Committee).

Following the loyal toast, Major G. C. Benham proposed " The Ypres League." He recalled exploits in the Salient, and how the 11th Essex Regiment earned the utmost gratitude of the Commander of French troops because of the magnificent work done in a difficult situation. The Salient, he added, outdid all his previously conceived conceptions of hell, and it was in that Salient that a quarter of a million of their comrades fell. The League was founded thirteen years ago, and following the death of Lord Plumer—a magnificent defender of Ypres—that great soldier, Sir Charles Harington, had become President. They sometimes read in the local Press of certain youths and irresponsible people who seemed to think that the term, " King and Country," had no significance. To all those who took any part whatever in the service of their King and Country, and were proud to do so, expressions from such folk had caused more amusement and pity than anything else. They had a good answer, however, to what had been said, and that was that the bulk of people who called themselves British enjoyed meeting together, forming themselves into such a society as this, and doing everything they could to foster and encourage those two great C's—Comradeship and Commemoration. In that spirit he asked them to honour this toast.

Capt. de Trafford, in reply, conveyed to the company a message from Lieut.-General Sir W. P. Pulteney (Chairman of the Ypres League), who commanded the Third Army in the war, and who thanked Colonel Herring, Mr. Snow and the officers of the newly formed Branch for all that had been done and the good progress made. The speaker voiced a tribute to the immense amount of work Mr. Snow had accomplished, and his admiration for the perseverance and enthusiasm which had characterized that labour, and gave a short talk on the League's aims and objects.

Brigadier-General Towsey, who proposed the toast of " The Chairman," said he supposed he was the oldest member of the League present, and he believed it was right to keep alive the memory of the Salient, which was the grave of many reputations and of many illusions.

The Chairman, who was accorded musical honours, briefly responded, and he remarked that he supposed anyone who served even a week in the Salient were now pacifists, but they were not pacifists of the " King and country " type, of whom they had heard ; they belonged to the other type of pacifists, and were determined that if it could be honourably avoided they were not going to let such a thing as the late war occur again.

The artistes for the evening were Messrs. T. A. Doe (comedian), A. J. Durrant (bass singer), and D. J. Durrant (accompanist).

LONDON COUNTY COMMITTEE.

Informal Gatherings and Other Activities.

Gratitude is extended to all who have helped to forward this most important work of reunion.

In April we were honoured by the presence of our friends of the 85th Club, who gave us a truly excellent entertainment. Mr. R. Barnes (Chairman of the Club) kindly presided, and the evening was thoroughly enjoyed—in fact, this concert is regarded by our members as one of the best of the season, and we are deeply grateful to Mr. A. Skinner (Hon. Secretary of the 85th Club) and to Mr. W. F. Taylor who generously undertook the arrangements for the programme.

Two other Gatherings during the past quarter were of an impromptu character, and sincere thanks are due to those members and friends who came forward and helped with some of their excellent talent. These meetings are held to provide the spirit of comradeship and so maintain this important object for which the League stands.

The London County Committee are now busily engaged in preparing next season's programmes and much look forward to renewed support from members and friends. Those wishing to kindly offer their services should send their names to Mr. J. Boughey, who will be glad to send fixture dates for selection. Invitations to the Informal Gatherings will be sent to any friends whose names and addresses are submitted by members.

At the request of members, a Gathering will be held on Thursday, July 20th, at the Bedford Head Hotel, Maiden Lane, Strand, W.C.2, from 7 to 10 p.m. No special programme is being arranged, but it is hoped that many will come and spend an hour or two to chat over old times.

The attendances, during the past few Gatherings, have not been up to the usual high standard so the Committee looks with anticipation to increased support at these meetings.

Several new proposals are being adopted for next year, including a Whist Drive, and any further suggestions will receive the Committee's consideration.

The London County Committee took part in the parade of the League of the Empire Review at St. Paul's Cathedral on Saturday, May 27th, when a small contingent of London members was commanded by Capt. C. Alliston. Larger attendances are called for on future parades so as to keep the League more in the public eye.

The Annual Meeting of the London County Committee was held on Thursday, April 13th, when we were pleased to elect as a member of the Committee, Mr. John W. Franklin, representing the 5th London Field Ambulance. We regret the loss on the Committee of Mr. L. A. Weller, owing to business reasons, but appreciation is recorded of his work done for the London Branch.

The Eleventh Annual Reunion Smoking Concert will take place at the Caxton Hall, Caxton Street, Victoria Street, S.W.1, on Saturday, October 28th, 1933, at 7.30 p.m., and the support of all London members is requested. The preliminary arrangements involve heavy detailed work, so it is earnestly desired that members will do everything in their power to assure a "full house." Particulars will be given in the October edition of the YPRES TIMES, and notices will appear in the Press.

Reunion Dinner and Dance.

This annual reunion was held on Saturday, May 6th, at the Royal Hotel, Woburn Place, W.C.1, and thanks are due to the management for the excellent arrangements. Over ninety members and friends were received by Colonel G. T. Brierley, C.M.G., D.S.O., who presided. Berry's Band was in attendance and gave popular musical numbers during the dinner and played admirably for the dance which followed. Mr. E. C. Stone kindly acted as M.C.

After the toast to His Majesty the King, a one-minute silence was observed in memory of "Absent Friends." The Chairman then rose to propose the toast of "The London County Committee," and recalled the workings of the Branch from the time of its inception when he himself was Secretary of the Ypres League. The names of old friends were mentioned who were connected with the original Committee.

The Colonel congratulated the Committee on their achievements and work they had done for the League and also on the splendid muster present and added what an immense pleasure it was to preside. In mentioning the general work of the League, he expressed his appreciation of the YPRES TIMES, and was sure everybody felt the better for reading it.

Major Montague Jones, Chairman of the London County Committee, thanked Colonel Brierley for his kindness in taking the chair, and said how pleased they all were to see him once more amongst them and also Mrs. Brierley. Major Jones made a very strong appeal to all to do their utmost to increase the membership of the League and proposed the health of Colonel Brierley who replied by expressing his sincere thanks for a very pleasant evening.

At the conclusion of the dinner an adjournment was made to the ballroom, where a happy time was spent, and those who did not brave the floor equally enjoyed themselves exchanging war reminiscences and the friendly atmosphere of an exceedingly successful function. Much thanks are due to all who gave their valued support.

PLEASE RESERVE THIS DATE.

THE
ELEVENTH ANNUAL REUNION
SMOKING CONCERT

(Organized by the London County Committee)

will be held on

Saturday, October 28th, 1933

at 7.30 p.m.

IN

Caxton Hall, Caxton St., Victoria Street, S.W.1

A record attendance is anticipated, and members are requested to give their kind support.

Full particulars will appear in the next (October) edition of THE YPRES TIMES.

PURLEY.

The Spring Golf Meeting of the Purley Branch took place at Coulsdon Court Golf Club on Thursday, May 11th, when 37 members took part in an 18-hole Bogey competition. Early returns gave no indication of what was to come, but gradually improvement took place until the last three matches in produced better scores, and Capt. B. A. Forster (8) last of all, won the Fifth Wipers Cup with a return of one up.

Capt. E. Featherstone (scr.) and Gunner H. M. Brown (18) tied for second prize at one down.

At the supper which followed the first prize was presented to Capt. Forster, who sportingly promised to provide a cup for the Autumn Meeting if this can be arranged. Many members present gave verbal and or other noisy support to the proposal, and the Chairman promised the early reconsideration of the Committee which had proposed to discontinue the Autumn Meetings.

Thanks were expressed to Cmdr. H. D. C. Stanistreet, the Secretary of the C.C.G. Club, and the Chairman, for their part in the proceedings.

The Bombardier's Foursomes, 1933.
FIRST AND SECOND BATTLES.

The day after Operation Orders were issued, some of the troops got to it, Lieuts. Bernard Jones and Brill engaging Commander Monk and Capt. Beatty (sounding supiciously like a strong naval party) at Woodcote Park. After a dog-fight the latter got away with the match on the 18th, more by strategy than golf; the enemy conceding a hole which in fact they had won, to be all square.

Capts. Scott and Green entertained Commander Stanistreet and Capt. McLaurin at Woodcote Park, put up a very good show and won 5—4.

At the same time and on the same course Lieut. Bellingham and Capt. " Bung " Brewer were defeating Major Harris and Capt. Streat 3 and 1; some adventures are reported.

Majors Meakin and Wayte claimed special merit for two reasons : (1) For playing off in very good time ; (2) for defeating Lieut.-Colonel Inglis and Major Alderson, a very hot side, by 3 and 2. They admit, however, laming one of the enemy first ! All done at Croham Hurst.

Capt. Douse and Cpl. Taylor beat Capt. Rae and Sergt. Crute 5 and 3 ; no details.

Cpl. Meredith and Lieut. Hines conceded some strokes to Majors Legg and Forster, and just got away with the match at Woodcote Park at the 20th, after being dormy three down. Some battle.

Capt. Waghorn and Lieut. Hancock met Lieut. Duncan and Capt. George Mutton at Woodcote, and won on the last green one up.

The same evening, on the same course, The Bombardier and Lieut. Jack Lindsay went for Gnr. Kerr and Capt. Tissington, won 3 and 2, and so avenged the previous year's defeat.

It was a wretched wet evening for battle, but turned into quite a wet night after supper, when the Coulsdon Court members are reported to have recovered some of their battle losses at " vingt-y."

Capt. Smither and Major Tomlinson engaged Capt. Lund and Major Russell on their home course, Coulsdon Court, and reported victory at the 20th. Sounds like another dog-fight.

Finally, General Gough and Commander Shelton met Major Leck and Lieut. Wiltshire at Purley Downs, where the latter put up some rough stuff to win 3 and 2, finishing with three " birdies." It is reported that when he made a bad shot, the General swore like the trooper that he is !

So ended the First Battles, all done in time.

The Second Battles started by Lieut. Midgley and Capt. Forster walking over, the enemy capitulating.

Next the Staff team, Capt. Featherstone and Major G. Carr, met the Naval party, Monk and Beatty, at Coulsdon Court ; the latter lost three holes at an unfortunate stage, so that the Staff won 3 and 2. (Naturally the Staff had seen to it that they had choice of course !)

Bellingham and Brewer went over to Croham Hurst and beat Meakin and Wayte 2 and 1. 'Nuff said.

Woodcote Park was the scene of much bloodshed one evening when three matches were played simultaneously. Scott and Green played scratch golf, behaving very rudely and beating Meredith and Hines 7 and 6, and Hines had come up from Sandbanks specially to win this !

Capt. Ray and Pte. Jim Irens had a close match with Leck and Wiltshire, beating them by 2 and 1, after some good golf on both sides.

The Bombardier and Lindsay put up too many 3's to give Waghorn and Hancock a fair chance, finishing the match at the 15th with an "eagle" 3, to win 4 and 3. Waghorn fired off the shot of the evening, in (nearly) holing out for 2 from a bunker.

Pte. Butt and Capt. E. H. Carr met Gnr. McFarlane and Lieut. Adams at Coulsdon Court and won a close battle by 2 and 1.

Douse and Taylor brought the Second Battles to an end in good time, by visiting Chipstead to play Smither and Tomlinson, coming away victors 6 and 4.

The competition this year has proved very popular, 26 pairs having entered and all tell of good battles, well and truly fought. Many remain to be fought yet, and the doings of the eight remaining teams in the Third, Fourth and Fifth Battles will be duly reported later.

THE ADJUTANT.

Correspondence.

THE SECRETARY,
YPRES LEAGUE,

20, SWORDS STREET,
OXMANTOWN ROAD,
DUBLIN.
June 11th, 1933.

DEAR SIR,

Having just returned from holidays we take an early opportunity of sincerely thanking the members of the Ypres League, whom we met on the recent Whitsuntide pilgrimage, for the facilities afforded by them to two ex-service men visiting Ypres.

A friend and myself, revisited Ypres expecting merely to see the Menin Gate Memorial and some of the old landmarks near the town, but hearing that a pilgrimage had been organized for the dedication of the Lord Plumer Memorial on Whit Sunday, we happily decided to approach the principal official at the termination of the service with a view to participating in any tour which might have been arranged on that date, and by his very kind permission we were permitted to join the party which started at 2 p.m. from the Ypres Grande Place. It proved to be a trip which enabled us to see all the important memorials within the Salient which otherwise, as casual visitors, we would not have seen. Besides, we had the services of a thoroughly well-informed guide.

We shall always remember the kindness of our companions on this trip, particularly appreciating the wonderful *esprit de corps* of our fellow ex-service men. A splendid comradeship that has endured among us even despite the passage of many years.

As two "old comrades" unattached to any ex-service organization, we shall always retain pleasant memories of the impromptu gathering at the Café de la Lune that night following the motor trip, when finally we met in joyous reunion. Those who had travelled from London, the Midlands, Brighton, and ourselves from Ireland would certainly like to keep in touch with those friends, through the League, and with a view to doing so, we respectfully ask that you accept our names for enrolment. Kindly notify us regarding the annual subscription and conditions of membership.

Wishing the Ypres League every success.

Yours faithfully,
J. J. ABBOTT.
M. O'HEA.

THE SECRETARY,
YPRES LEAGUE.

June, 1933.

DEAR SIR,

Thoughts, especially the very appreciative ones, are difficult to write down in black and white, but I should like to tell you how great is my appreciation and admiration for the faultless organization of the Whitsun Pilgrimage to Arras.

Everything was perfectly arranged, and only when we realize how extremely easy and comfortable the journey was, the kindness and courtesy extended to us, both here and by our fellow countrymen across the Channel, can we fully appreciate our debt of gratitude to the Ypres League, the silent service whose first consideration is our comfort.

How I wish that everyone could go and see those beautifully kept cemeteries and memorials, even in these days of the world's forgetfulness, maybe they would recapture that wonderful spirit of comradeship and courage that belonged to those happy warriors who walk the Elysian Fields.

I remain,
Yours truly,
MADELEINE RIDDELSDELL.

Branches and Corresponding Members

BRANCHES.

LONDON	Hon. Secretary to the London County Committee: J. Boughey, 20, Orchard Street, London, W.1.
	E. LONDON DISTRICT—L. A. Weller, 132, Maxey Road, Dagenham, Essex.
	TOTTENHAM AND EDMONTON DISTRICT—E. Glover, 191, Lansdowne Road, Tottenham, N.17.
	H. Carey, 373, Sydenham Road, S.E.26.
COLCHESTER	H. Snow, 9, Church Street (North) (Hon. Sec.).
	W. H. Taylor, 64, High Street (Pilgrimage Hon. Sec.).
GATESHEAD	Lieut.-Colonel E. G. Crouch, 8, Ashgrove Terrace.
LIVERPOOL	Captain A. M. Webster, Blundellsands.
PURLEY	Major Graham Carr, D.S.O., M.C., 112-114, High Street.
SHEFFIELD	Captain J. Wilkinson, "Holmfield," Bents Drive.
BELGIUM	Capt. P. D. Parminter, 19 Rue Surmont de Volsberghe, Ypres.
CANADA	Ed. Kingsland, P.O. Box 83, Magog, Quebec.
SOUTH AFRICA ...	L. G. Shuter, Church Street, Pietermaritzburg, Natal.
AMERICA	Representative: Captain R. Henderson-Bland, 110 West 57th Street, New York City.

CORRESPONDING MEMBERS.

GREAT BRITAIN.

ABERYSTWYTH	T. O. Thomas, 5, Smithfield Road.
ASHTON-UNDER-LYNE ...	G. D. Stuart, "Woodlands," Thronfield Grove, Arundel Street.
BANBURY	Captain C. W. Fowke, Yew Tree House, King's Sutton.
BIRMINGHAM	Mrs. Hill, 191, Cattell Road, Small Heath.
	John Burman, "Westbrook," Solihull Road, Shirley.
BOURNEMOUTH	H. L. Pasmore, 40, Morley Road, Boscombe Park.
BRISTOL	W. S. Hook, "Stoneleigh," Cotham Park.
BROADSTAIRS	C. E. King, 6, Norman Road, St. Peters, Broadstairs.
	Mrs. Briggs, North Foreland House.
CARLISLE	Lieut.-Colonel G. T. Willan, D.S.O., 3, Goschen Road.
CHATHAM	W. N. Channon, 22, Keyes Avenue.
CHESTERFIELD	Major A. W. Shea, 14, Cross Street.
CONGLETON	Mr. H. Dart, 61, The Crescent.
DARLINGTON	D. S. Vigo, 125, Dorset Road, Bexhill-on-Sea.
DERBY	T. Jakeman, 10, Graham Street.
DORRINGTON (Salop) ...	Captain G. D. S. Parker, Frodesley Rectory.
EXETER	Captain E. Jenkin, 25, Queen Street.
GLOUCESTER	H. R. Hunt, "Casita," Parton Lane, Churchdown.
HERNE BAY	Captain E. Clarke Williams, F.S.A.A., "Conway," Station Road.
HOVE	Captain G. W. J. Cole, 2, Westbourne Terrace, Kingsway.
LEICESTER	W. C. Dunford, 343, Aylestone Road.
LINCOLN	E. Swaine, 79, West Parade.
LLANWRST	A. C. Tomlinson, M.A., Bod Estyn.
LOUGHTON	Capt. O. G. Johnson, M.A., Loughton School.
MATLOCK (Derby) ...	Miss Dickinson, Beechwood.
MELROSE	Mrs. Lindesay Kelsall, Huntlyburn.
NEW BRIGHTON (Cheshire)	E. F. Williams, 5, Waterloo Road.
NEW MILTON	W. H. Lunn, "Greycot," Albert Road.

NOTTINGHAM	E. V. Brown, 3, Eldon Chambers, Wheeler Gate.
ST. HELENS (Lancs.) ...	John Orford, 124, Knowsley Road.
SHREWSBURY	Major-General Sir John Headlam, Cruck Meole House, Hanwood.
TIVERTON (Devon) ...	Mr. W. H. Duncan Arthur, Surveyor's Office, Town Hall.
WELSHPOOL	Mr. E. Wilson, Coedway, Ford, Salop.

DOMINIONS AND FOREIGN COUNTRIES.

AUSTRALIA	Messrs. C. H. Green and George Lawson, Anzac House, Elizabeth Street, Brisbane, Queensland. R. A. Baldwin, c/o Government Savings Bank of N.S.W., Martin Place, Sydney. Mr. W. Cloves, Box 1296, G.P.O., Adelaide.
BELGIUM	Sister Marguerite, Sacré Cœur, Ypres.
BUENOS AYRES ...	President, British Ex-Service Club, Calle 25 de Mayo 577.
CANADA	Brig.-General V. W. Odlum, C.B., C.M.G., D.S.O., 2530, Point Grey Road, Vancouver. V. A. Bowes, 326, 40th Avenue West, Calgary, Alberta. W. Constable F. Grece, 4095, Tupper Street, Westmount, Montreal.
CEYLON	Captain F. R. G. Webb, M.C., Irrigation Bungalow, Kalmunai, E.P.
EGYPT	L. B. S. Larkins, The Residency, Cairo.
INDIA	Lieut.-Quartermaster G. Smith, Queen's Bays, Sialkot, India.
IRELAND	Miss A. K. Jackson, Cloneyhurke House, Portarlington.
KENYA	Harry Shields, Survey Department, Nairobi. Corporal C. H. Slater, P.O. Box 403, Nairobi.
NEW ZEALAND ...	Captain W. U. Gibb, Ava Lodge, Puhinui Road, Papatoetoe, Auckland. S. E. Beattie, Lowlands, Woodville.
SOUTH AFRICA ...	H. L. Versfeld, c/o Cape Explosives Works, Ltd., 150, St. George's Street, Cape Town.
SPAIN	Captain P. W. Burgess, Calle de Zurbano 29, Madrid.
U.S.A.	Captain Henry Maslin, 942, President Street, Brooklyn, New York. L. E. P. Foot, 20, Gillett Street, Hartford, Conn., U.S.A. A. P. Forward, 449, East 80th Street, New York. J. W. Freebody, 945, McBride Avenue, Los Angeles.
NOVA SCOTIA ...	Will. R. Bird, Amherst.

Membership of the League.

This is open to all who served in the Salient, and to all those whose relatives or friends died there, in order that they may have a record of that service for themselves and their descendants, and belong to the comradeship of men and women who understand and remember all that Ypres meant in suffering and endurance.

Life membership, £2 10s.

Annual members, 5s.

Do not let the fact of your not having served in the Salient deter you from joining the Ypres League. Those who have neither fought in the Salient nor lost relatives there, but who are in sympathy with the objects of the Ypres League, are admitted to its fellowship, but are not given scroll certificates.

There is a Junior Division for children whose relatives served in the Salient. It is open also to others to whom our objects appeal.

Annual subscription 1s. up to the age of 18, after which they can become ordinary members of the League.

The Ypres League (Incorporated).

20 Orchard Street, Portman Square, W.1.

Telephone: WELBECK 1446.   *Telegrams:* YPRESLEAG, "WESDO," LONDON.

Patron-in-Chief: H.M. THE KING.

Patrons:

H.R.H. THE PRINCE OF WALES.   H.R.H. PRINCESS BEATRICE.

President: GENERAL SIR CHARLES H. HARINGTON.

Vice-Presidents:

F.-M. VISCOUNT ALLENBY.   F.-M. SIR PHILIP CHETWODE.
F.-M. SIR CLAUD JACOB.   THE LORD WAKEFIELD OF HYTHE.
THE VISCOUNT BURNHAM.   LIEUT.-GENERAL SIR CECIL ROMER.

General Committee:

THE COUNTESS OF ALBEMARLE.
MAJOR J. R. AINSWORTH-DAVIS.
*CAPTAIN C. ALLISTON.
LIEUT.-COLONEL BECKLES WILLSON.
*MR. JOHN BOUGHEY.
*MISS B. BRICE-MILLER.
COLONEL G. T. BRIERLEY.
CAPTAIN P. W. BURGESS.
*MAJOR H. CARDINAL-HARFORD.
REV. P. B. CLAYTON.
*THE EARL OF YPRES.
MRS. CHARLES J. EDWARDS.
MAJOR C. J. EDWARDS.
MR. H. A. T. FAIRBANK.
MR. T. ROSS FURNER.
SIR PHILIP GIBBS.
MR. E. GLOVER.
MAJOR C. E. GODDARD.
MAJOR-GENERAL SIR JOHN HEADLAM.
MR. F. D. BANKS HILL.
MAJOR-GENERAL C. J. B. HAY.

MR. J. HETHERINGTON.
MRS. E. HEAP.
GENERAL SIR W. C. G. HENEKER.
CAPTAIN O. G. JOHNSON.
*MAJOR MONTAGUE JONES.
CAPTAIN H. D. PEABODY.
*THE HON. ALICE DOUGLAS PENNANT.
*LIEUT.-GENERAL SIR W. P. PULTENEY.
LIEUT.-COLONEL SIR J. MURRAY.
LIEUT.-GENERAL SIR CECIL ROMER.
*COLONEL G. E. C. RASCH.
VISCOUNT SANDON.
THE HON. SIR ARTHUR STANLEY.
MR. ERNEST THOMPSON.
CAPTAIN J. LOCKLEY TURNER.
*LIEUT.-GENERAL SIR H. UNIACKE.
*MR. E. B. WAGGETT.
CAPTAIN J. WILKINSON.
CAPT. H. TREVOR WILLIAMS.

* Executive Committee.

Finance:

LIEUT.-GENERAL SIR W. P. PULTENEY.
LIEUT.-GENERAL SIR HERBERT UNIACKE.
CAPTAIN C. ALLISTON.

Honorary Solicitors:

MESSRS. FLADIATE & Co., 18, Pall Mall, S.W.

Bankers:

BARCLAYS BANK LTD., Knightsbridge Branch.

Secretary:

CAPTAIN G. E. DE TRAFFORD.

Trustees:

LIEUT.-GENERAL SIR W. P. PULTENEY.
MR. E. B. WAGGETT.
MAJOR E. MONTAGUE JONES.

Auditors:

MESSRS. LEPINE & JACKSON,
    6, Bond Court, E.C.4.

League Representative at Ypres:
CAPTAIN P. D. PARMINTER,
19, Rue Surmont de Volsberghe.

League Representative in America:
CAPTAIN R. HENDERSON-BLAND.
110 West 57th Street, New York.

League Representative at Amiens:
CAPTAIN STUART OSWALD,
7, Rue Porte-Paris.

League Representative at Arras:
MR. P. VYNER,
10, Station Square.

PRIMARY OBJECTS OF THE LEAGUE.

I.—Commemoration and Comradeship.
II.—To provide special travel facilities for Members and all interested to Ypres and battlefields, and transport of Members.
III.—The furnishing of information about the Salient; marking of historic sites ond the compilation of charts of the battlefields.
IV.—The erection of a Ypres British Church and School.
V.—The establishment of groups of members throughout the world, through Branch Secretaries and Corresponding Members.
VI.—The maintenance of cordial relations with dwellers on the battlefields of Ypres.
VII.—The formation of a Junior Division.

Use the Ypres League Travel Bureau for Ypres and Whole of the Western Front.

FOR THE FOLLOWING PUBLICATIONS, Etc., apply:
Secretary, YPRES LEAGUE, 20 ORCHARD STREET, LONDON, W.1.

THE BATTLE BOOK OF YPRES. A history of notable deeds contributed by all regiments. 5s.; post free, 5s. 6d. Compiled by Beatrix Brice with the assistance of Lieut.-General Sir William Pulteney, G.C.V.O., etc.

BOOKS.

YPRES: Outpost of the Channel Ports. By Beatrix Brice. With Foreword by Field-Marshal Lord Plumer, G.C.B. Price 1s. 6d.; post free 1s. 10d.

In the Ypres Salient. By Lt.-Col. Beckles Willson. 1s. net; post free 1s. 2d.

To the Vanguard. By Beatrix Brice. 1s. net; post free 1s. 2d.

The City of Fear and Other Poems. By Gilbert Frankau. 3s. 6d. net; post free 3s. 8d.

With the Cornwall Territorials on the Western Front. By E. C. Matthews. 7s. 6d.; post free 8s.

Story of the 63rd Field Ambulance. By A. W. Westmore, etc. Cloth, 3s. 6d., post free. Paper, 2s. 6d., post free.

War Letters to a Wife. By Colonel Rowland Feilding. Popular Edition. 7s. 6d.; post free 8s.

The Pill Boxes of Flanders. 1s.; post free 1s. 3d.

YPRES LEAGUE TIES. 3s. 6d. each, post free.

YPRES LEAGUE BADGES. 2s. each, 2s. 1½d. post free.

EMBROIDERED BADGES. 4s. each, post free.

Map and List of Cemeteries in the Ypres Salient. Price 9d.; post free 11d.

Map of the Somme. Price 1s. 8d., post free.

PICTURES.

Burning of the Cloth Hall, 1915. A Coloured Print, 14 in. by 12 in. 1s. post free.

The Tomb of the Unknown Warrior. By Bernard Gribble. 10s. 6d., post free.

ENGRAVINGS, 33 in. by 21 in., £1 11s. 6d. each.

Hell Fire Corner.

Heavy Artillery Going into Action before Passchendaele.

"I Won't."

POST CARDS, PHOTOGRAPHS AND ETCHINGS.

Post Cards. Ypres: British Front during the War. Ruins of Ypres. Price 1s. post free.

Photographs of Menin Gate Unveiling. Size 11 in. by 7 in. 1s. 2d. each, post free.

Hill 60. Complete Panorama Photographs.
12 in. by 3¾ in. Price 3s., post free; 15 in. by 5 in. Price 3s. 6d., post free. See pages 166-167.

WAR-TIME PHOTOGRAPHS OF THE SALIENT.

6 in. by 8 in. ... 1s. 6d. each.
12 in. by 15 in. ... 4s. each.

List forwarded on application.

PHOTOGRAPHS OF WAR-TIME SKETCHES.

Bedford House (Front View), 1916.
Bedford House (Back View), 1916.
Voormezeele Main Street, 1916.
Voormezeele Crucifixion Gate, 1916.
Langhof Chateau, 1916.

Size 8¼ in. by 6¼ in. Price 2s. 6d. each, post free.

ETCHINGS.

Etchings of Menin Gate Memorial. 9 in. by 6 in. Price, 5s. each, post free. Signed proofs, 10s. 6d. each, post free.

YPRES TIMES.

The Journal may be obtained at the League Offices.
BACK NUMBERS 1s.; 1931, 8d.; 1932, 6d.

Printed in Great Britain for the Publishers by GALE & POLDEN, LTD., 2, Amen Corner, Paternoster Row, London, E.C.4.

Memory Tablet.

OCTOBER - NOVEMBER - DECEMBER

October.

Oct.	4th, 1914	...	Russian ultimatum to Bulgaria.
,,	5th, 1915	...	Allied Forces land at Salonika.
,,	9th, 1914	...	Antwerp occupied by Germans.
,,	10th, 1916	...	Allied ultimatum to Greece.
,,	14th, 1915	...	Bulgaria at war with Serbia
,,	18th, 1918	...	Belgian coast clear.
,,	20th, 1914	...	First Battle of Ypres begun.
,,	25th, 1918	...	Ludendorf resigned.

November.

Nov.	1st, 1918	...	Versailles Conference opened.
,,	3rd, 1918	...	Austrian surrender. Keil Mutiny.
,,	4th, 1917	...	British troops in Italy.
,,	5th, 1914	...	Great Britain declares war on Turkey.
,,	6th, 1917	...	British storm the Passchendaele Ridge.
,,	9th, 1918	...	Marshal Foch receives German Envoys. Abdication of the Kaiser.
,,	10th, 1918	...	Kaiser's flight to Holland.
,,	10th, 1914	...	"Emden" sunk.
,,	11th, 1918	...	Armistice Terms accepted.
,,	18th, 1917	...	General Maude's death in Mesopotamia.

December.

Dec.	8th, 1914	...	Naval Battle off the Falklands.
,,	9th, 1917	...	British capture Jerusalem.
,,	15th, 1915	...	Sir Douglas Haig C.-in-C. in France.
,,	16th, 1914	...	Germans bombarded West Hartlepool.
,,	19th, 1915	...	Withdrawal from Gallipoli.
,,	24th, 1914	...	First air raid on England.

Communications to
The Editor, "Ypres Times,"
20, Orchard Street, London, W.1.

PRICE 6d.
POST FREE 7d.

Vol. 6, No. 8   Published Quarterly   October, 1933

Armistice Day Message to our Members

THIS year sees the 15th anniversary of the signing of the Armistice. Our thoughts naturally go back to the years 1914-18, and especially to that part of the Western Front where so many of us spent the hardest time of our lives—I refer to Ypres.

How can those of us who survived the ordeal at Ypres forget what our gallant soldiers went through? Much has been done in the way of memorials in the Ypres Salient and in Ypres itself, such as the Menin Gate, the Ypres British Church and School and the many beautiful and well-kept cemeteries in that area, but let us not forget another memorial in the Association which was formed soon after the War— The Ypres League.

I would like to take this opportunity to remind the members of the League how much this Association has done and is still doing to retain the splendid friendship and fellowship of the trenches, and to commemorate the immortal deeds and sacrifices of our gallant comrades in the glorious defence of Ypres, which was held firmly by the British Army throughout the whole War.

Let us remember that the peace and quiet which we now enjoy in Britain is due to those who made the great sacrifice, and that we should do all we can to support the Ypres League.

There are still many who served at Ypres who do not belong to the League. It is the duty of every member to do his best to get them to join us.

Every good wish to the Ypres League!

CLAUD W. JACOB,

Field Marshal

Vice-President, Ypres League.

Hand-Made Lace
Increased Activities in Ypres Salient
REVIVAL OF AN OLD-WORLD CRAFT.
(*Specially contributed to the* YPRES TIMES.)
By HENRY BENSON, M.A.

IN the course of the past few weeks I made an extensive tour through Flanders, which included visits to Brussels, Bruges, Thourout, Ypres and Poperinghe. It came as a surprise to me to find what wonderful progress the bobbin-lace industry had made in the last twelve months. In the windows of the principal shops, and even of cafés may be seen the familiar notice of pre-war days—"Dentelles Veritables."

THE CRADLE OF A MEDIÆVAL CRAFT.

The revival of this mediæval industry has been beset by great difficulties for all concerned, and but for the zeal of Queen Elisabeth and that enthusiastic society, "Les Amies de la Dentelle," this occupation, which employs thousands of Belgian women, would probably have perished with the war.

On sentimental grounds alone its death would have been regrettable, for Flanders claims to have founded the art of bobbin-lace making, that claim being based on the existence of the fifteenth-century masterpiece in the Church of St. Gomar (attributed to Quentin Matsys), in which a young girl is represented making lace on a pillow which she holds in her lap. Again, the peasants will tell you a pretty romance of how the art was accidentally discovered by a Flemish fishergirl who, whilst thinking of her absent lover, half unconsciously twisted the weighted strings that fringed her net into a pattern roughly resembling that of a branch of coral which he had given her.

AMERICAN ASSISTANCE DURING THE WAR.

The German invasion of 1914 nearly killed the Belgian lace industry because it became impossible to obtain thread. The blue flax fields of the Lys had been devastated, and instead of the river being filled with boxes floating the finest linen fibre in the world, it was given over to the military requirements of the marauders. Thanks, however, to the kind offices of Mr. Hoover, an international agreement was drawn up in the following year, whereby the United States was permitted to send American thread to Belgium and to take out an equivalent weight in lace, which was sold in the allied countries for the benefit of the Belgian women engaged in the trade. This arrangement afforded each dentellière the opportunity of making three francs worth of lace each week—not a large amount, but sufficient to assure the continuity of the craft. The Committee had 47,000 women on its lists, and I am told that more than 2,000 new patterns were designed between 1914 and 1918.

AN AGED LACE-MAKER SPEAKS HER MIND.

During those terrible years of war many of these women heroically insisted on remaining calmly at their cushions making lace, whilst the shells burst before and behind them. Soldiers in the Ypres Salient will remember the old woman who sat near the station gates and finally had to be forcibly removed by order of the British authorities.

At Thourout, a few weeks ago, I had a long talk with one of these gallant souls, old Madame Souxdorf, a veteran of seventy-eight summers. Daylight was fast melting into a twilight of pink and opaline hues, but there she remained at the door of her little éstaminet before her snow-white cushion and bobbins, twisting and braiding the threads of a mesh of Valenciennes, as she had twisted and braided them for more than six decades. Whether it was due to old age or to the mental and physical sufferings she had endured during the war, I do not know, but she was frankly pessimistic regarding the future of the hand-made lace industry.

"The scale of payment is so low," she told me, "that it can never be more than a side-line, and it is impossible for it to flourish in a modern Belgian town or city. Present conditions are all against it. The attractions of the kinemas and dancing-halls for the younger generation are too great. The age-long patience of the laceworker is the child of monotony and isolation. Before the war, in the long and solitary winter months, when work in the fields was impossible, our peasant women would turn to their lace cushions as much for recreation as for money. Things will never be the same again; the world is travelling too fast." Only once, when she showed me ten treasured Australian sovereigns, to which a real war romance is attached, did the old lady assume a cheerful demeanour.

HER PATIENT TOIL-WORN HANDS
A BRIDAL VEIL CREATE.

A Convent Lace School at Bruges.

From the pessimist let me turn to the optimist! It was my privilege last week to visit one of the largest Convent lace schools in Bruges, and the Mother-Superior very courteously permitted me to watch the children at their various tasks. In the summer, she told me, they commence work at 7.30 a.m., and continue until 8 p.m., with only three half-hour intervals for recreation. The hours, of course, are shorter in the winter, when, in order to obtain the powerful light that is essential for such delicate work, oil lamps are ingeniously placed behind bottles filled with water, so that the magnified rays may pass in spotlights on the cushion. Each girl receives a small remuneration weekly for her toil.

In one class-room I noticed an elder girl, whose cushion supported a mound of bobbins. The Mother-Superior told me that they totalled over one thousand and that the girl was engaged in making a long scarf. "When shall you have finished it?" I asked. "Well, I commenced last March and it should be completed by next April." I must confess that the thought of that fragile maiden of seventeen summers sitting in front of that cushion for thirteen long months has haunted me ever since. I wonder whether the woman who eventually will wear that delicate scarf over her shoulders would care to hear of the dark-eyed dentellière and her thousand bobbins!

"What of the future of the industry?" I asked the Mother-Superior.

"We can find a ready market abroad for all we make," she said, "and the demand for 'Point de Paris' is exceptionally heavy. There is no fine lace that is so much in request, because it combines durability with beauty. Our great enemy is the middleman, for the price we receive for our work compared with that obtained for it in the shops is out of all proportion."

THIRD OF AN INCH—A WEEK'S WORK!

Before I left I was shown a flounce of priceless Valenciennes lace attached to a vestment. This had been made in Ypres. The thread, manufactured from Brabant flax, cost £260 a pound, and it was so fine that it was imperceptible to the naked eye. One third of an inch represented a week's work, and the flounce had taken twelve years to complete.

It is of interest to note that in Turnhout alone 1,800 children are attending the lace schools, whilst there are 500 lace workers in Poperinghe. Most of the latter are engaged in making the world-famed "Point d'Aiguille."

H.B.

Polderhoek Chateau

POLDERHOEK Château, as doubtless many of my readers will remember, was the name given to what was once a château, but which was just a pile of bricks, mortar and mud in the autumn of 1917.

This château was situated approximately one mile north of the Menin Road, above Gheluvelt, and about two and a half miles in front of Stirling Castle.

My brigade (the 13th, 5th Division) had already made several attacks around Tower Hamlets and Inverness Copse in September, 1917. We were at rest, at Dickebusch, when the orders came through to attack Polderhoek Château.

The stunt was to come off on October 4th, and zero hour was fixed for 6 a.m. About 3 a.m. on the fateful day my gun-team (Vickers machine gun) consisting of Lieut. W., my pal Kirk from Newcastle, a young fellow from Manchester, myself, and eight men from the Warwickshire Regiment who were to act as ammunition and water carriers, etc., were assembled in a couple of shell holes some dozen yards or so in front of our first line. On either side of us were other machine-gun teams.

The King's Own Scottish Borderers, Royal Warwickshire Regiment, Royal West Kents, etc., were to advance past us and we were to follow up just behind the first wave, take Polderhoek Château, and hang on.

A steady drizzle of rain was falling and a ground mist added to the general discomfort of our shell hole. Soon we were soaked through, and the equivalent of a thimbleful of rum per man, brought to us by our section officer, was very welcome.

There was the usual rumble of guns, when a shell burst just behind our hole, and in a few seconds we were greeted by the head of some unfortunate comrade, which dropped right among us.

At last, after what seemed an eternity, our barrage opened, and from the British Tommies' point of view it was "some" barrage, but I have no doubt the Germans had a different opinion.

The whole sky for miles around on the British front was lit up with vivid flashes from the massed guns, while a dull red glow hung over the gun-lines behind us. Guns of every calibre added their voices to the inferno, and to make a pal hear one had to shout in his ear.

Machine-gun fire literally poured from the enemy's lines, while shrapnel hurled mud and earth in all directions; even at such a time we pitied the occupants of those trenches, and afterwards marvelled that anyone could come out of such a hell alive.

We were now over the top and could dimly discern the first wave in front, but soon lost sight of them in the increasing smoke which hung everywhere. After advancing some distance up to our knees in mud, we received a temporary check and had to take refuge in a shell hole. Here we found we had already lost five of our ammunition carriers and our water-tin was empty, thanks to a Jerry's bullet. During the wait Lieut. W. handed cigarettes round, and one of the Warwicks, who was evidently superstitious, refused to light third man from the match, whereupon one of his comrades laughingly exclaimed, "I'll light third man." Hardly had he done so when he was shot through the head.

After about ten minutes' delay we advanced again, the rain still coming down in sheets.

Photo　　　　　　POLDERHOEK CHATEAU, 1917.　　[Imperial War Museum, Crown Copyright

Out of our original team of twelve we had already lost six, and were to lose more good men, for we had scarcely covered another hundred yards when the young fellow from Manchester was hit in the stomach; while I was assisting him to the shelter of a "mudbank" there was a rip and crack at my side—a bullet had smashed his elbow. I made the unfortunate man as comfortable as I could, with the pitiless rain beating down on him as he lay in the mud. I promised to send some stretcher-bearers, but I knew his hours were numbered.

By this time I had lost my gun-team, which had advanced some distance farther, and of course it was impossible to locate them in that cloud of smoke and bursting shells, so I had no alternative but to go forward with the second wave and chance stumbling across my comrades later. This I did, and arrived safely within two hundred yards of our objective.

Germans were scampering up the ridge in front with a couple of tanks after them, but tanks were useless in such a sea of mud; they stuck at the foot of the ridge, where ultimately they had to be abandoned.

At that moment I heard a Vickers firing away on my right. Thinking it might be my own team, I made for it with all the speed I could. Some Fritz, who evidently bore me a grudge, sent a hail of bullets about my heels, and, matters becoming decidedly unhealthy, I was forced to jump into a large hole for cover. Here I received a shock, for, standing against the side of the hole, were four Germans complete with rifles and fixed bayonets, and I thought my number was up. But luck was on my side, for they proved to be dead—from concussion, I concluded.

Crawling out of my shell hole, I made my way slowly but surely across to the gun I had heard firing, and found it to be the remainder of my gun-team, viz., Kirk and Lieut. W. These two and myself were the only men left of those who had set out at 6 a.m.

We now carried on and passed Polderhoek Château, where we located quite a decent position, but had to retire to the old emplacement in which I had found the gun.

Here, while the enemy were preparing for a counter-attack, we came to the conclusion that reinforcements were necessary, and it fell to the writer to get through with a message to Headquarters at Stirling Castle. I had not proceeded very far when Jerry dropped his barrage, and I guessed he was counter-attacking from the rattle of rifle and machine-gun fire from the new front line. The front line was really not a trench at all, but just shell holes, many of them half full of stinking water covered with slime and scum, from which here and there an arm or leg protruded.

After what seemed weeks of struggling through that mud bath, but which was actually only an hour or so, I reached Stirling Castle and delivered my message to Lieut. Gibbon, acting Commanding Officer. This gallant officer said he must go to the position himself. So off we started down the duckboards, Lieut. Gibbon leading. But this officer, loved by all his men, and a true gentleman, was picked off by a sniper near Inverness Copse. Almost at the same instant there was a terrific explosion; I was flung off my feet; a shower of mud and filth rained down upon me, and I remembered no more until I regained consciousness some time later. I felt sick and dazed, but luckily had escaped with a few minor scratches only. I can recall wandering around until a driver of one of the big tanks assisted me to Stirling Castle. Here I was given a tot of rum by our Padre and sent into a dug-out to the rear of Headquarters for a sleep—and sleep I did, for nearly twelve hours, with a box for a mattress, a mud-bank for a pillow and my feet in eighteen inches of water; but I did enjoy that sleep, although when I awoke my legs were numbed and dead.

About three days later I returned to the transport lines to find that Kirk and the Lieutenant W., who had given me up for lost, had already arrived back safe and sound. Our brigade had been relieved and several counter-attacks repulsed.

H.W.B.,
(*late 13th M.G. Coy., 5th Infantry Division*).

Greeting

Out of the mist of years to-day,
  Bugles' ringing
Over the far-flung fields of sleep
  Echoes bringing.
Triumphant peals the call on high,
Bearing greeting to you who kept
Unbroken faith before you slept.

You did not stop to count the cost,
  You paid the price:
You broke the bread and drank the wine
  Of sacrifice.
You lived your hour, and went your way;
Be with us now so we too keep
Unbroken faith before we sleep.

AILEEN RADCLIFFE.

Reprinted by the kind permission of
the Editor of the "Sunday Graphic."

St. Andrew's Night in the Salient

By Ian Hay.

MOST of us who served in the Ypres Salient will remember Zillebeke Lake—that big triangular reservoir with its apex pointing to Maple Copse and Sanctuary Wood, and its base confronting the Lille Gate of Ypres, some thousand yards away. I spent nearly three months without a break in the dug-outs in the dam at the foot of the lake, in 1915. We were a Scottish Brigade Headquarters.

Our little Mess—there were only five of us—had decided that if the Boche was on his good behaviour (or as near to good behaviour as a Boche can hope to get) on Saint Andrew's Night, we would have a Saint Andrew's Dinner. So we resolved ourselves into a Dinner Committee of five, with the Brigadier as Honorary Chairman. The Committee commenced its labours by sending home for a haggis. The next item on the *agenda* was the selection of the most suitable solvent for haggis. The light wine of our native land was unobtainable; in fact, our only available beverage was Rum, Service, Diluted. This the Wine Committee (the Staff Captain and the Signal Officer) condemned as too crude an accompaniment to such a delicate dish.

Suddenly the Brigade Machine Gun Officer (myself) remembered that in a former age he had been Secretary to a College Club in Cambridge, which had been accustomed, once a fortnight, to gather round a mahogany table for the purpose of indulging in harmony and drinking some rather innocuous milk punch. I may add that it was part of the Secretary's duty—in fact, all of the Secretary's duty—to make the punch. So I volunteered to brew a bowl for the feast. The offer was accepted —with the stipulation that I drank the first glass.

The difficulty was to obtain all the necessary components—namely, rum, brandy, milk, sugar, lemon-peel, and the yolks of six eggs—rather a large order when you are living within eight hundred yards of the enemy's front line. Our one certainty, thanks to the infallibility of the Army Service Corps, was the rum ration. I commandeered the entire Mess allowance for three days, and then set out to accumulate the remaining ingredients. Sugar was obtained by cajolery from the Quartermaster-Sergeant; milk was provided by that benevolent Swiss neutral, Mr. Nestle. The Brigade Interpreter, the only member of the Mess whose duty permitted him to leave the trenches, set off on a foraging expedition to the farms in rear of us, and returned with five assorted eggs. Lemons were unobtainable, but a spoonful of lime-juice made a fair substitute.

Our most insuperable difficulty was the brandy. Here the silent strong man of the Mess (the Brigade Major) came to our rescue. He seldom spoke, but when he did he was usually worth listening to. On the evening of the twenty-ninth of November, during the final sitting of the Dinner Committee, he spoke for the first time:—

"Divisional Headquarters have plenty. They always have plenty. I will send to them for some."

The following afternoon, during the usual three o'clock bombardment by the enemy of the cross-roads which lay between us and the Lille Gate, a motor-cyclist was observed riding furiously from the direction of Ypres. He dashed across the cross-roads, neatly timing the interval between two German shells, and finally drew up, all standing, at our dug-out entrance and delivered into my hands half a bottle of brandy.

The component parts of our evening's brew being now all present and correct, I set to work and made the punch, in a tin wash-hand basin; the necessary heat was supplied by a bucket of coke. Then, when we had eaten our haggis, we drank the punch. It was much criticised—but finished.

We were rising reluctantly from our seats, and pulling on our equipment in order to set off upon our nightly tasks, when the door opened and a Signal orderly appeared, bearing in his hand a pink telegraphic slip.

"From Divisional Headquarters, sir," he announced to the Brigade Major.

The Brigade Major read the document aloud. It said:—

> "*Divisional General is most anxious to learn nature of casualty for which your Brigade Headquarters required brandy this afternoon.*"

We sat down again and looked at one another. Finally our concentrated gaze was turned upon the Brigade Major. We asked him:—

"What did you say when you telephoned for that brandy?"

The Brigade Major, that monosyllabic man, replied:—

"Don't let your mind dwell on that. The point is that we got it."

Someone—I think it was the Brigadier himself—added:—

"Yes; and what's more, we have had it! They can't take it away from us now!"

Finally we decided to throw ourselves on the mercy of the Court. The following telegram was dispatched to Divisional Headquarters:—

> "*This is Saint Andrew's Night; and we are a Scottish Brigade. We wanted the brandy because the B.M.G.O. had volunteered to brew us a bowl of punch. No casualties, as yet.*"

In the small hours of the morning, as we returned from our nightly round, a reply came through from the Divisional General:—

"*Scotland for ever!*"

The Late Viscount Burnham
Death of One of our Vice-Presidents

An Active and Useful Life.

IT is with deep regret we have to record that, since our last issue, one of our valued Vice-Presidents, Viscount Burnham, has passed away, having died suddenly in his sleep at his London residence on 20th July, in his 71st year.

In the early stages of the formation of the League he rendered assistance of incalculable value; and although of recent years, owing to his multifarious duties, we had not seen quite so much of him, he was always ready to place his unbounded influence freely and unreservedly at our disposal. His death creates a vacancy that it will be difficult to fill.

Open, debonair, restlessly energetic, and large-hearted, the end of the Great War found Lord Burnham occupying a unique status among the public men of his time. Without being in the first flight of politicians, for he never held office, he had achieved, by indefatigable industry, by strict moderation of speech, and by his known willingness to be of service in any good or national cause, the position of being one of those to whom the Government turned almost instinctively when they required a good chairman for a Committee of Inquiry or a painstaking member of a Commission charged with the duty of tackling a difficult problem and presenting a workable report. Again, no one did more to cement more closely a mutual friendship between Great Britain, France and Belgium. Indeed, he was one of those men who helped to make the whole mechanism of the State and of society move smoothly.

For long he was the acknowledged head of the British Press, and even after he relinquished his newspaper, he remained a wise counsellor and friend to all journalists. No good cause went without his support, and the amount of work he did in the last twenty years was colossal. He exhaled wherever he went a warm humanity and a considerate courtesy, before which difficulties melted as snow. Few men can have had more friends.

H.B.

Eton Memorial to Lord Plumer

Photo [Galthorpe & Sons, Ltd.

THIS MEMORIAL, WHICH HAS BEEN PLACED IN THE CLOISTERS AT ETON WAS UNVEILED ON MESSINES DAY (JUNE 7th, 1933) BY H.R.H. THE DUKE OF GLOUCESTER, HIMSELF AN OLD ETONIAN.

Ypres Day

THE Ypres League Annual Commemoration will be held on **Sunday, October 29th,** and the following arrangements have been made :—

2.30 p.m. Assemble on the Horse Guards' Parade.
3.00 p.m. Address by the Rev. P. B. Clayton, C.H., M.C., and Lament by Pipers of the Scots Guards.
3.15 p.m. March to the Cenotaph.
3.30 p.m. Laying of the Ypres League Wreath on the Cenotaph.
3.45 p.m. March back to the Horse Guards' Parade.
4.00 p.m. Dismiss on the Horse Guards' Parade, and at 4.30 p.m. an Ypres League deputation will proceed to the Tomb of the Unknown Warrior in Westminster Abbey and place a wreath.

H.R.H. Princess Beatrice has graciously consented to attend the service and lay the League wreath on the Cenotaph.

Plain clothes and medals to be worn (uniform optional).

We hope that members of the Ypres League will make every effort to attend this Commemoration.

The Ploegsteert Road Barrier

THE owners of Petite Douve Farm had lived in mortal fear when in the early days of the war a troop of Uhlans trotted down the road from the village of Messines but the Germans—beyond giving a passing glance at the farmstead—continued on in the direction of Ploegsteert and the family, who for twenty years had tilled the soil and grown grain and tobacco along the valley of the Douve River, breathed a sigh of relief.

Several weeks later, on being warned by British cavalry of the approach of the enemy and after several shells had fallen in the vicinity of their home, the farmer, with his wife and two daughters went to stay with friends back of Bailleul.

When, in '15, stationary warfare had settled into a routine of interchanging reliefs, madame and her elder daughter took up residence at the Trois Rois, on the Neuve Eglise road on the Franco-Belgian border, and developed a profitable business in catering to the hungry troops in divisional reserve at Aldershot and Bulford camps.

One day, while reaping a share of the soldiers' francs, madame was visited by a British officer accompanied by an interpreter and was asked many questions as to the layout of Petite Douve Farm, their erstwhile home; the construction of the brick walls; the depth and a full description of the cellars under the farmhouse; and details regarding the bridge which crossed the Douve immediately to the south. . . . There had been much talk in the summer of '15 of enemy mining activity in this particular locality.

The troops occupying trenches 132 and 133—known as 63 and 64 prior to July 1st—had frequently reported "evidence" of subterranean workings—certainly, suspiciously concealed trucks had been seen on a trench tramline—nevertheless, our Engineers had been quite emphatic in decrying such operations.

Later, observers reported seeing jets of steam and a large quantity of fresh soil behind the ruins of the farm. From day to day the pile grew and, with no surface work to give reason for same, anxiety increased and the subject of the German underground operations was on everyone's tongue.

Listening posts were strengthened and patrols were sent out and prowled around from dusk till dawn in an endeavour to detect signs of what was going on under cover of darkness. No-man's-land, be it said, had long been in undisputed control of the Canadians. Each hillock and hole and each tree stump were familiar objects to them. The ground, too, had been cleared to a large extent. Various articles of equipment, bombs, and a sack containing holes cut by a sharp instrument—probably a sniper's mask—had been brought in. And a dead cow—believed to have been the notorious carcass commemorated in the lines of the song "My little wet home in the trench"—had been given burial; gas-masks being worn by those who attended the obsequies.

Then came a spell of rest, and the 2nd (Western Canada) Brigade proceeded to Saint-Jans-Cappel, in corps reserve.

During the occupancy of the Douve sector by the relieving troops—also Canadians—the Germans, working from a ruined cottage; east of the Messines road in no-man's-land and, screened by a tree which had been felled conveniently adjacent by our artillery, constructed a barricade across the road. The new work was discovered at noon of 3rd December by the 2nd Canadian Mounted Rifles who, just as soon as it was dusk, sent out a patrol which made a close inspection of the barricade and, after throwing several bombs, returned and made report.

The advanced position was about 110 yards from our front line and about the same distance from the German trenches. It was found to be strongly constructed; being bricked at the base and built up with sandbags:

To permit such boldness with impunity was not to be tolerated and orders were given for its immediate capture. But this was easier said, than done.

Torrential rains had made a quagmire of the trenches; in which the men wallowed around up to their waists. Nepean Avenue—the main communication trench—contained four feet of water and the deepened ditch along the edge of the Messines road was equally impassable. Added to this, the Douve had risen and both flanks of the barricade rested on the flooded river. Such were the conditions under which hasty plans were prepared.

The attack was made in the early morning of December 4th but proved abortive.

General Staffs worked overtime in calling for and digesting reports on the situation. The advanced post, if allowed to remain would have menaced the lives of our listening patrols and wiring parties and generally weakened the defensive system.

Another, unsuccessful, move to drive the enemy out and pull down the barrier was made by Lord Strathcona's Horse on the night of 8th/9th December. On that occasion some twenty Germans swarmed out and showed open fight and a sharp bombing action ensued; resulting in eleven casualties to the attacking party.

CHATEAU DE LA HUTTE.

By this time the news had reached the 2nd Brigade, in corps, reserve, and the 5th Battalion volunteered to return forthwith and make a further determined effort to capture and destroy the stronghold. Accordingly, on 9th December, they moved up to Bulford camp and the following night took over their old position in the line. The scouts went out to make a reconnaissance but their presence was soon made known to the German garrison when they stumbled upon a carefully concealed tripwire which exploded a series of bombs.

For the next few days the situation was the subject of earnest contemplation, and views, as to why the Germans had "met the Canadians half way," were freely aired.

In the early hours of 17th November—sixteen days previous to the erection of the barrier—the 7th Canadian Battalion had raided the German trenches at the junction of Petite Douve Farm and returned with twelve prisoners of the 2nd Battalion, 11th Prussian Regiment. It was, therefore, generally conceded that the new German forward position was to frustrate a repetition of attack by stealth, as, from the flanks of the barrier a wide field of fire was obtained and even though a raiding party might have succeeded in reaching the German line, withdrawal would have been disastrous. There were many, however, who held to the more sinister aspect—that mining activity *may* have been progressing and that the advanced fort was intended to give added protection to the, supposed, gallery entrance shaft.

Finally, a well-conceived plan was devised which was successfully carried out on the morning of 15th December.

A fifteen-minute bombardment was put down in the afternoon and again at night on the 12th, 13th and 14th of December, and for five minutes only, from 4 a.m. of 15th.

An attacking force, consisting of three parties of one officer and fourteen men each, was selected on the 12th and assembled in a hut in Ploegsteert Wood—just west of Hyde Park Corner—where the scheme was gone over in every detail. In fact, leaving nothing to chance, a rehearsal was carried out on the Ash Road barrier on the night of 13th.

During the bombardment on the afternoon of 13th, the defenders once again emerged from the barricade, being driven out by the shell fire. Six were promptly shot—five being accounted for by Sergeant J. S. McGlashan (later, Major, M.C., D.C.M.) of the 5th Battalion—while the remainder scuttled to the cover whence they fled.

On the night of 14th/15th—in preparation for the final phase—the 3rd Battery, C.F.A., placed an 18-pdr. in the front line directly opposite their target. This was a bold piece of work. The gun was towed up the Messines road to the Château de la Hutte by an armoured car of "A" Battery, 1st Cdn. Motor Machine Gun Brigade. From this point it was decided to man-handle the gun the remainder of the way as it was feared the chug of the motor might be heard by the enemy. A pause was made until the 11 p.m. bombardment subsided. But, during the retaliatory fire a tree was felled across the road between the gun and the front line. After the bombardment had ceased, this obstruction was hauled aside; new shell holes were filled in and the gun—whose carriage wheels had been covered with rubber tires—was noiselessly wheeled up to the position that had been cleared for it. An embrasure was made by pulling down the parapet for a width of two and a half feet. The stage was then set.

The attacking parties moved up to the front line to take up their allotted positions. All badges and numerals had been removed from their uniforms, and faces and hands blackened with charcoal. The bayonet-men had affixed small, pocket flashlights to their rifles—being bound on with telephone wire just below the lower band.

The flanking parties crept silently over the parapet and crouched to right and left of the road. These men, in order to deaden the report of the forward gun, had stopped their ears with cotton batten.

Promptly at 4 a.m.—15th December—the artillery opened on the barricade. The forward gun fired three rounds of H.E. followed by twenty-two rounds of shrapnel at point blank range—then something happened to the firing mechanism. . . . Its work, however, had been accomplished.

At 4.05 the attackers rushed the position, this time meeting no opposition. But two occupants remained alive and these were passed back to the trench. Three mangled forms located among the debris bore mute testimony of the effectiveness of the bombardment—a further body was discovered, subsequently.

The raiders, amid the inferno of rifle, machine-gun and shell fire concentrated by the enemy, having satisfied themselves that no other living German remained, mined the position against further occupation, withdrew; bringing with them seven rifles and a bag of bombs.

After a check-up had been made it was found that only two casualties had been sustained by the attacking party and these were but slightly wounded.

Photo] [Canadian Official War Photograph, Crown Copyright

HYDE PARK CORNER (PLOEGSTEERT WOOD)

Following the short but decisive action, it was necessary to withdraw the gun from the front line with the least possible delay, for which purpose it was considered advisable to run the armoured car right up to the gun regardless of risk. However, in following this course unforeseen hindrances arose. Within two hundred yards of the front trench the car ran foul of a cave-in and became ditched. The driver ran down to the gun crew and informed them of his plight. A second car was 'phoned for while the gun crew proceeded to the scene of trouble and commenced to extricate the one that was ditched.

The second car did not get as far as the first. Its wheels sank through a planked bridge that had been thrown across the reserve trench and there it stuck.

In the meantime, number 1 car had been righted; backed to the trench; gun hooked on and was on its way—only to find that the road was blocked by car number 2. Nevertheless, by a precarious manoeuvre a passage was effected. The gun was unhooked and car number 1 hauled car number 2 out on to the road. Then, again acting as limber, with Driver Frank Waghorn (later, Lieut. M.C., D.C.M., M.M.) at the wheel, made Hyde Park Corner at top speed.

The two prisoners, captured that morning, Bernhard Klesse and Paul Rösner, were of the 3rd Battalion, 11th Reserve Infantry Regiment, 117th Division—one a Landwehr and the other an Ersatz Reservist—both had volunteered for duty at the barricade. Although unwounded they had endured a terrible ordeal. Yet, despite their distress, they showed no symptoms of fear. Indeed, they exemplified such fortitude and resoluteness—those soldierly qualities which most of us strived to maintain but, on occasion, gravely feared we would be found wanting when the crucial moment arose—that they commanded the utmost respect of their captors.

The prisoners, on being interrogated, stated that their company—12th—had been sent to replace the 5th Company of the 2nd Battalion; which had been withdrawn in disgrace following the successful raid by the British Columbia Battalion on 17th November.

Both prisoners declared that the light railway was used solely for the purpose of bringing up rations and ammunition, and, that *the Germans were not mining in the Douve Sector*.

Thus ended the episode—and "The Army Commander was pleased——"

EDWIN PYE, 5TH BN., C.E.F.

An Instructional Tour of the Ypres Salient

LAST April, a party of officers of the 1st, 2nd and 3rd City of London Regiments (T.A.) visited the Salient under the guidance of their Brigade Commander with the primary object of studying on the ground certain phases of the first battle of Ypres; in particular the defence and recapture of Gheluvelt on October 31st, 1914.

The travelling arrangements for the tour were made for us by the Ypres League, whose representative came with us, and to whom the warmest thanks of the party are due for all that he did to make the tour a success.

Travelling by the night boat to Dunkerque, we reached Ypres in time for breakfast, and then proceeded by char-a-banc to Kruiseik. There the director recounted the events of the period 19/26th October, 1914; the gradual extension of the Allied line from Vermelles to the Sea; the abortive attempt by the 7th Division to advance to MENIN and the river Lys, and the simultaneous advance of five new German Corps, whose objective was Calais. From this encounter dated the birth of the Salient.

Here, at Kruisecke, by the exercise of a little imagination, it was possible to visualize to some degree the German attack on the 1st Bn. Grenadier Guards on the morning of 29th October, so vividly described in Lord Ernest Hamilton's "The First Seven Divisions."

In a roadside cottage at Kruiseik Cross Roads there is a colour print by a well-known artist, depicting an incident in the fighting at this spot.

Its owner was delighted to show it to us, and it is worth more than a passing glance, for it shows the locality as it then was. It is not easy for anyone visiting the Salient to-day, who was not there in 1914, to realize how remarkably the landscape has altered. It is true that the greater number of the houses, and other buildings have been rebuilt on or near their former foundations, and that most of the old roads have been remade. The writer, who was in the Salient almost continuously from October, 1914, to September, 1917, found little difficulty in identifying localities by the buildings, it was easier in 1933 than in 1917! It was far harder to realize what a great change in visibility has taken place. In October, 1914, trees were tall and still in leaf. Hedges were high and thick, garden and field crops added their screen of foliage. In fact, in 1914, observation in any direction was remarkably limited, whereas to-day the eye travels without hindrance over broad acres of almost treeless cultivation. It requires an effort of the mind to realize how much obstruction to the view there was in 1914, and to understand how it was that the Germans were able to penetrate unseen through gaps in our thin line; and how events in one part of the field could take place unknown to those only a few hundred yards to a flank. In 1914, the field of fire of the rifle was very restricted; now, it is difficult to understand how any troops could advance over such open country in the face of small arm and machine-gun fire, except by night or under the cover of mist or smoke. Then, artillery observers had the greatest difficulty in finding any place from which to direct fire; to-day, any small rise in the ground will provide an excellent observation post.

From Kruiseik we moved to Gheluvelt, and there made a detailed study of the stirring events that took place in and around that village on October 31st. The reader does not need to be reminded that this was the critical day of the battle, perhaps of the whole war. The story of the famous counter-attack of the 2nd Battalion of the Worcesters has been written, and thrills the reader. To stand on the ground itself, to be told the story again by one who was there, is more fascinating than any reading can possibly be.

Eighteen years in a man's life is a long spell, and the memory is apt to become dull, but the writer has recollections of that amazing day which will never fade. He may therefore be pardoned if he recalls only two.

The scene of the first is a battery position not far from the Château which was on that day the Headquarters of the 7th Division, and which was afterwards known as Stirling Castle. It was then a white, square, stone building surrounded by tall trees. Now there is a smaller red-tiled house on the bare side of a low rise.

Some time on the morning of October 31st three figures appeared in the battery position, coming wearily from the direction of Gheluvelt. Two were Guardsmen, a Corporal and another man, the third a private of the Gloucester Regiment. All were incredibly muddy and bloodstained, but not with their own blood. All three had that peculiar stare that a man has who has recently been through heavy fire. The Corporal approached an officer; they had been blown out of their trenches, had lost their way, could we tell them where were Headquarters?

We gave them hot tea and rum, and some food. They sat awhile chatting to the gunners, while we made fruitless inquiries as to the whereabouts of their regiments, or even of their brigade headquarters.

Presently the Corporal stood up, thanked us for the tea, and saluted as though on the barrack square at Chelsea. Then, turning to his companions, he said, "Come, lads, let's get back again." So they went, back to the line, and out of our lives, but not, I am certain, out of the memory of any one of us who saw them go, with heads up.

It is a few hours later. The battery has been ordered out of its position and is standing just off the Menin Road, near Hooge, facing towards Ypres. It is waiting for an opportunity to join the double line of traffic moving slowly eastwards. None of us have any doubts about the seriousness of the situation. The stream of transport coming from the front line, the wounded and stragglers, the set faces of officers, the nearer sound of rifle fire and shelling, all tell the same tale. There is a tenseness in the air that can almost be felt, as before a thunderstorm. Across the road is a group of officers collecting stragglers; when there are about twenty, they are formed up and one of the officers marches them off to fill yet another gap in the line.

Then, with almost dramatic suddenness, the whole atmosphere changes. The tension is over—people are smiling. What has hapened? A Staff Officer walks up, filling a pipe. We ask, "What news?" He lights his pipe, and throws away the match, then, quietly, "The Worcesters have recaptured Gheluvelt, and the London Scottish have taken Messines with the bayonet." It is impossible to put into words the feeling of *security* which that simple statement inspired. The episode is as vivid in the mind to-day as when it occurred.

We visited Nonneboschen Wood, the scene of the failure, on November 11th, 1914, of the attack of the Prussian Guard; Langemarck, where the director told us the story of the attack of the 2nd Bn. Grenadier Guards up to Houthulst Forest on October 9th, 1917; Hill 60, stopping *en route* at Hooge Château to pay our respects to the Baroness, and being shown by her over the grounds of the charming house, built to replace the former mansion, and the "Crater," now transferred into a delightful ornamental water. For the student, each of these places has its lessons; for all who visit them, memories, whether they fought in the salient or not.

Standing later at the Menin Gate at sunset, as the "Last Post" sounded, then walking back in the deepening dusk along the outer margin of the moat to the Station Square, these memories of three years came flooding back. But through this flood one question persisted, and remains unanswered. If it were to happen again, would we still hold the enemy as our incredibly thin line held the Germans in 1914? Pessimists and pacifists may groan and scream as they will, but the writer is convinced that the spirit that inspired the defenders of the Salient is not dead. We pray that it may not again be put to such a test, but if the time should come, it will not fail.

Thousands visit the Salient; some to make a pilgrimage to a certain graveyard; others to see the many memorials, of which few are so beautiful as the lovely Canadian memorial at Sanctuary Wood; many go merely as sight-seers. But for the soldier, a study of a battlefield under the guidance of a capable instructor, who himself took part in the battle, and has since made it his special study, is at once a lesson and an inspiration. Those of us who were privileged to take part in the visit to Ypres here recorded will not soon forget a delightful experience.

One of the Party.

A Transport Incident

AGAIN we were about to move into position. At this date, 13th September, 1918, it was supposed that the battery would take part in a show in support of Belgian troops operating near Ypres. For some days the column (12 S.B.A.C. 70th A.S.C. Brigade) lay parked along the main street of Wormhoudt, whence we had moved from the low hills of Mory and left behind a district of sorry desolation and come to a place where at least there stood houses, populated by civilians who walked in safety in the streets and worked in the fields around. As a matter of fact, before undertaking another bout of hauling gun baulks and "ammo'," some needed repairs would have to be done, and during this temporary respite all hands fell to making a complete overhaul, and with the assistance of M.T. inspectors (Nuts and Bolts) and a whole lot of new spares, "Twelfth Siege" lorries looked equal to any in the Park.

About that time a shortage of petrol occurred and the writer can very well remember the first supply of 600 gallons coming along—the first issue to be drawn for some days.

Various rumours got about but came to nought. Finally orders were received for gun stores to be loaded and for the first two howitzers to be towed to a position approved at Joffe Farm over No. 4 Bridge at Brielen. This bridge was one of several which spanned the Yser Canal.

Tanks were filled and reserves put aboard and two tractors started for their guns. These were picked up at International corner not far from an ammunition dump, nightly the rendezvous of vehicles of all kinds filling up their battery needs. So we clattered away from a green lane overhung with branches to the high road and its iron pave, upon which the track plates beat out a metallic tune.

There are few better guns to draw than 9-2 howitzers dismantled for the road. The weight is well carried by some 12 wheels (sometimes 14), so that it rides well over bad ground, and is not easily ditched. Unlike the Mark 19 gun it can be withdrawn in sections, whereas the latter with its 17 tons supported on two wide wheels had a knack of sinking to its axle in roadside ditches.

For a time we just walk in front and wait till the guns draw up, and step out for another spell. Hereabouts there was little traffic on the road and the dusk was quiet, and later the route turned among the dark shuttered buildings of Poperinghe, more or less deserted at this hour and without lights of any kind.

Here we bear left-handed on to a switch road and halt in order to get spanners busy tightening up loose bolts and to do a minor adjustment to a slipping fan belt. Directly the clutch is let in, the tractor rises a good foot on its tracks, and down comes the front wheel with a violence which brings the water streaming down the radiator and filling the air with steam. Camouflage strung along from tree to tree and black lettered notices to "Drive slowly to avoid dust" indicate that the road into Ypres has been reached. The first gun takes its place in the stream of traffic; the other one is some way behind. Between, before, behind, there is the everlasting stream of horse drawn wagons, M.T. lorries, field guns.

A quivering horizon towards Wytschaete suggests mild summer lightning, but it is flashes from gun pits on both sides to the accompaniment of a low mutter. Then a left-handed turn to a road with little pave but a lot of dust, and here it is quieter running but the valves beat louder. The whine of a spent shell comes over.

A Belgian cart with its wheel broken holds up traffic here as does also a 60-pounder gun with its team waiting for a new shaft pole to be attached.

When we do get on the move the next stop will be to see if the bridge across the canal is intact and to cross it with all speed once it is reached. The timbers creak and groan but hold the load and higher ground is reached. Recently lorry tracks into a steeper runway indicate a likely spot for a gun position and off the road there are figures in the gloom . . . the advance guard were digging out the gun pits, with practised skill. The driver brings his caterpillar in exactly the right angle for the gunners to part first the bed plate, followed by the cradle, into which the piece itself is slung, and we stand by to lend a hand with an obstinate baulk or to strain a hawser. This done we can get clear of the position, and, in growing daylight, take the road back at a steady pace, to where breakfast and a few hours' sleep are welcome.

Subsequently, four other guns were taken up in like manner and load upon load of ammunition. The sequel to be related is that by some means or other the enemy got wind of the impending "push," and a withdrawal had commenced before our heavies had shot off half their shells. Column and battery therefore packed up and commenced another trek, this time via Boeschepe to Berthen where we were employed for a few days hauling stones and conveying roadmenders to Kemmel.

A. H. BOWEN.

The August Pilgrimage, 1933

I HAVE been a member of the Ypres League for a number of years and happy to do all in my power for such a worthy cause. Having been over to Ypres independently on previous occasions, I have found myself at a loss to explain to possible pilgrims the benefit and pleasure derived by travelling under the auspices of the League, so decided to go this year and see for myself. I had doubts about going solo, rather expecting to meet with little parties of friends from various parts of the country who naturally would have their own particular plans, and that I should be somewhat "frozen out"; but let me assure any prospective pilgrim that once you join up with the party you are one of a happy family. It put me in mind of J. B. Priestley's "Good Companions."

Saturday, August 5th, was a glorious morning with a promise of a fine and sunny week-end, when at 7.30 I padded along to Victoria Station wearing the League's cornflower emblem and eager to start on what was one of the happiest week-ends I have ever spent. I found the party about fifty strong being made comfortable in the Dover train by our genial Secretary, Captain de Trafford, and settled down with five other fellows, and there and then ripened a friendship which not only meant such a splendid time during the trip but which we hope to renew on many more occasions. The party consisted of many ladies with an object of spending a few precious hours with their loved ones out there, and how splendid they were. Some getting well into the autumn of their days, but that great fighting spirit of our race keeps them young, and so year after year they go across to be with their men folk who passed on that we might live in peace in this beautiful England of ours.

DECORATIONS IN THE RUE DE LILLE, YPRES.

The conversation en route was not, as one would think, war, quite the contrary, county cricket, latest film shows, etc., although these carriage companions of mine had spent ghastly months in the dirty ditches around Ypres.

After the usual formalities we quickly got aboard the "Princess Marie Jose," and what a glorious crossing with sea like a mill pond. Here we made acquaintance with the rest of the party, taking snaps, light refreshments, and changed our money into Belgian francs. Ostend looked very happy with its wonderful front and old-fashioned bathing machines.

During our run to the tragic City, we spotted a pill box or two, but nothing more to remind us of the past. Brand new buildings and an abundance of growing corn covered the devastation of Armageddon. On arrival at Ypres at 4.40 p.m. we separated to find our respective accommodation, most of which was reserved at the Hotel Splendid and Britannique in the Grande Place, and where we all assembled for meals. An exceedingly comfortable hotel, and I complimented our hostess on the extreme cleanliness of everything; in fact it was impossible to find a complaint about accommodation or service.

We spent the first evening looking around and making our plans for the next two days, getting better acquainted over a friendly glass and attended the "Last Post" at the Menin Gate. At midnight under a full moon de Trafford and I strolled up to the Ramparts for a few moments' quiet with the "boys." It was a wonderful experience and the thought that, could this be the scene of so much slaughter but a few short years before, and now all so quiet and peaceful on this summer night.

On Sunday we made a very interesting battlefield motor tour of the Salient, visiting St. Julien, Passchendaele, Sanctuary Wood and many other famous spots, and everything of interest was explained by our esteemed Mr. Parminter, who so ably represents the League at Ypres. We arrived back in time to witness the great religious Thuindag procession of the various orders, and I must admit I have never seen anything quite like it. For an hour the different bodies threaded their way through the magnificently decorated streets chanting as they went. In the evening the whole town and countryside gave themselves up to the "fun of the fair." I wonder what Tommy would have thought fifteen years ago of roundabouts in the Grande Place!

On Monday an exceedingly interesting whole-day charabanc tour was organised over the battlefields as far as Arras and back, and thoroughly enjoyed by all who took part.

What struck me most forcibly was the extraordinary beauty of the cemeteries we visited. They compare most favourably with any we have in this country, and after a little while when nature exerts itself and the trees and shrubs are grown to maturity, they should be unsurpassed in beauty.

The Belgian populace were most kind and considerate, and in no instance did I see any attempt to profit unduly from the pilgrims' visits to their town. The memorials scattered over the old battlefields are excellent examples of British architecture, from the small regimental column to the immense Menin Gate, which should stand for all time as a tribute to British arms.

THE PARTY STARTING OFF ON TOUR

During our stay several bodies of ex-service men arrived in Ypres and deposited wreaths at the Menin Gate, and I noticed particularly that the Burgomaster was present on each occasion and said a few words. Among the visitors were a party of limbless ex-service men under the auspices of St. Martin Association; 1,300 students from Scottish schools and universities who travelled from Bruges accompanied by the Kilmarnock Cadet Pipers Band; a large party of South-West area British Legion and a contingent of Irish Free State British Legion.

My only regret was that the trip was not longer, because one could spend at least a week exploring and nosing around old haunts. On Tuesday morning we entrained for home and eventually reached Victoria at about 9.30 p.m., full of praise for the efficient arrangements made by the Ypres League. In conclusion I personally thank Captain de Trafford for all he did to make the trip so very enjoyable, and this I am sure is seconded by members of the whole party.

W.S.H., *Corresponding Member, Ypres League, Bristol.*

The Plumer Memorial Fund

ON November 1st, 1932, Lieut. General Sir W. P. Pulteney, G.C.V.O., K.C.B., Etc., Chairman of the Ypres League, addressed a letter to members asking each to subscribe 2s. towards a worked banner bearing Lord Plumer's Coat-of-Arms, and any surplus money over and above the cost of the banner to be placed in trust to form a fund to provide free education to a child at the Ypres British School as a Plumer Scholarship.

For the interest of our members we herewith publish the balance sheet :—

SUBSCRIPTIONS.	£ s. d.	EXPENDITURE.	£ s. d.
Nov. 8th, 1932, to Sept. 30th, 1933	174 10 10	Printing, Stationery, Postages, Cheque Book, Transit of the Banner to Ypres and Custom Duty	17 18 7
		Cost of Banner	27 7 6
		Accountancy Charges	4 4 0
			£49 10 1
		Credit Balance ...	125 0 9
	£174 10 10		£174 10 10

The Banner is placed in the chancel of the Ypres British Church and was dedicated on June 4th, 1933 by His Lordship The Bishop of London.

SCHOLARSHIP FOR THE SCHOOL.

The £125 credit balance will be placed in trust with the Provost of Eton, and the interest on the capital will be devoted to the free education of a boy at the British School at Ypres.

Ypres, 1918-1933

IT was generally surmised at the close of the war that Ypres was so utterly blasted to bits and its environs so irreparably scarred that it was probable that this section of the old battle front would be left as it was as a monument and memorial of the terrific struggle waged there.

Certainly nobody ever anticipated the complete restoration of the town and its surrounding villages and countryside in the comparatively short time that has elapsed since the last "five point nine" soared over the Menin Road, and to anyone who has not watched the annual gradual transition from the wreckage of war to the peaceful pursuits of industry and commerce, with nature adding her quota to the labours of mankind, the revelation now in 1933 must be truly astounding.

Ascend the tower of the Cloth Hall—now once again keeping sentinel over the peaceful Flemish plains, see again the well-wooded nature of the old Salient with its numerous hamlets and churches, look also toward the Yser Canal once blocked with the debris of war but now once more giving Ypres a clear passage to the sea, its miniature dock with wharfside elevator and warehouse all ready for loading and unloading water-borne merchandise from such small craft as can usually be seen on Belgian waterways.

With the rebuilding of the Cloth Hall now in progress the visible links with the war years are now practically effaced and one must search in odd corners for any vestige of war ruin, for this re-born Flemish City is loth to remind one of its wounds.

To walk on and around the ancient ramparts with its surrounding moats and many backwaters the picturesque pre-war appearance of Ypres can now be readily visualised, indeed it seems hard to imagine that the foul breath of war ever blotted out the pretty scenery one finds at the southern edge of the town, the aspect is quite like that of an English park with the summer-clad boating parties wending their way past shady banks and overhanging trees.

The young trees planted along each side of the more important outlying highways to replace those blasted to bits by shellfire are now anything from twenty to thirty feet in height in some places. Nothing gave a more complete battlefield aspect to the Salient than those stunted skeletons of once magnificent trees, and the contrast to-day is most marked to anyone who trod these roads in more stirring times.

Those famous woods east of Ypres whose names will never be forgotten by those condemned to spend deadly hours in and around them are now once again almost impregnable fastnesses, but the kindly hand of nature, not the bloody arms of man, restrains the intruder.

THE YPRES-BOESINGHE ROAD AT ESSEX FARM CORNER.

Tall trees—swiftly growing higher, dense undergrowth, luxuriant shrubs, brambles, wild flowers, all are there in abundance; game, hares and rabbits are again in possession of their rightful domain, blackberries can be picked in galore, the illusion and impression of being somewhere in the English countryside is complete.

Returning to Ypres along the Boesinghe road a relic of a barbaric age gapes in the canal bank near Essex Farm corner, the westering sun glints on the lines of headstones just off the road and on reaching the shadow of the new Cloth Hall tower the strains of the "Last Post" come up from the new Menin Gate.

Present day Ypres resembles its distant past, but to many there is also a past that is ever present.

E.F.W.

League Secretary's Notes

To All Our Members :

Our first duty is to welcome very heartily all those who have enrolled as members of the Ypres League during the past quarter, and we look forward to whatever support they are so kind as to give us, especially in the recruiting of further new members.

We should like to draw the attention of all our members to the revised eight-page explanatory pamphlet of the Ypres League which should prove useful when approaching prospective members. Apart from describing fully the aims and objects, the pamphlet makes most interesting reading, and contains a finely written article on the men who fought at Ypres, by that well-known writer Robert Blatchford, also comments in support of the League by Sir Philip Gibbs and Major General John F. O'Ryan who has given our Association such high prestige in the United States.

In view of the touching Armistice Day Message from our Vice-President, Field Marshal Sir Claud Jacob, which opens this edition of the Ypres Times, we are sure that every member will wish to respond readily to the Field Marshal's call and that, as a result, a goodly influx of new members will be forthcoming, and to this end we earnestly ask our members to apply to us without delay for a supply of the new pamphlet, in order to assist them in their staunch endeavours to swell the League's membership. Last year, between September and December, we welcomed into our ranks 172 new recruits and our ambition is to beat the figure by the end of the present year.

1933 can claim to have been quite a satisfactory year, and we thank our Branch Secretaries, Representatives, Corresponding Members and all who have so generously given their valuable time and devoted services for the welfare of the League.

It is pleasing to record that the Pilgrimages to the Cemeteries and Battlefields of France and Belgium have been more popular than ever this summer despite the disadvantageous rate of exchange, and the fact that we have been favoured with beautiful weather for the trips has added much to their success. We were very pleased to see Mr. W. S. Hook, our enthusiastic Corresponding Member for Bristol, accompanying the August Bank Holiday party to Ypres, and his happy disposition throughout the week-end served in no small way in creating such cheerful atmosphere. A small party was also conducted to Arras during the same week-end.

Grateful thanks are due to the brothers Parminter and to Mr. Vyner at Ypres and Arras respectively for the particular attention they gave to visits to cemeteries and battlefield tours.

The Ypres League Sign Boards marking historic sites in the Salient have all been repaired and repainted, and for this we owe a deep debt of gratitude to Mr. C. J. Parminter for months of strenuous work in accomplishing this heavy task so successfully.

The next edition of the Ypres Times is not due until January 1st, so we take this opportunity to wish you all a very happy Christmas, and to express our renewed thanks to all our faithful supporters.

YPRES LEAGUE TIE.

At the request of the majority of our members we have been pleased to produce the tie in better quality silk and in a darker shade of cornflower blue relieved by a narrow gold stripe. The price is 3s. 6d., post free, and all members of the League should possess one.

Applications to the Secretary, Ypres League, 20, Orchard Street, London, W.1.

OLD WELL-KNOWN SPOTS IN NEW GUISE.

The following prints, size $4\frac{1}{4}$ x $2\frac{1}{2}$, recently taken of famous spots in the Ypres Salient, and which may be of great interest to our readers, are on sale at headquarters, price 4d. each, post free 5d.

Poelcapelle Church.
Ramparts at the Lille Gate.
Hell Fire Corner, Left and Right.
Shrapnel Corner.
Road to Transport Farm.
Zillebeke Lake.
Hill 62, Canadian Memorial.
Hooge from Zouave Wood.
Hooge Crater Cemetery.
Clapham Junction.
Stirling Castle.
Gheluvelt Church.
Cheddar Villa Dressing Station.
Vancouver Cross Roads.
Canadian Memorial : Vancouver Cross Roads.
Hyde Park Corner. (Memorial.)
Wulverghem.
Messines Church.
Potsdam Redoubt at Corner Cott.

Applications should be addressed to Secretary, Ypres League, 20, Orchard Street, London, W.1.

BURNING OF THE CLOTH HALL, 1915.

There are only a few coloured prints, 14in. by 12in., now in stock, and, as further supplies are not obtainable, we are selling the remaining prints at 1s. each, post free.

WREATHS.

Arrangements are made by the Ypres League to place wreaths for relatives on the graves of British soldiers situated in France and Belgium at the following times of the year:—

EASTER, ARMISTICE DAY, CHRISTMAS.

The wreaths may be composed of natural flowers, laurel, or holly, and can be bought at the following prices—12s. 6d., 15s. 6d., and 20s., according to the size and quality of the wreath.

BACK NUMBER OF "THE YPRES TIMES."

If any members can spare copies of the July, 1933, THE YPRES TIMES, the Secretary would be immensely grateful.

YPRES LEAGUE BADGE.

The design of the badge—a lion guarding a portcullis gate—represents the British Army defending the Salient, which was the gate to the Channel Ports.

The badge, herewith reproduced, is brilliantly enamelled with silver finish. Price 2s., post free 2s. 1½d. (pin or stud, whichever is desired). Applications should be addressed to the Secretary, Ypres League, 20, Orchard Street, London, W.1.

EMBROIDERED BADGES.

These badges can be supplied at 4s. each, post free. A considerable number have already been sold, and we are delighted to hear that the badges have given entire satisfaction to our members who have received them. Applications to the Secretary.

PHOTOGRAPHS OF WAR GRAVES.

The Ypres League has made arrangements whereby it is able to supply photographs (negative, and one print, postcard size, unmounted) of graves situated in the Ypres Salient, and in the Hazebrouck and Armentieres areas, at the price of 10s. each.

COLLECTION OF TINFOIL.

A collection of tinfoil has been started by headquarters, eventually to be sold in aid of the funds of the Ypres League, and if members care to co-operate, and post what tinfoil they are kind enough to spare it would be most gratefully accepted by the Secretary.

The tinfoil should be kept flat and free from paper.

GLEANINGS FROM WARWICKSHIRE HISTORY

by JOHN BURMAN, F.R.Hist.S.
Price 3/6 net (by post 3/10).

This book deals with many aspects of the local and family history of Warwickshire from Anglo-Saxon times to the present day, and should be of great interest to natives and residents in the county and to those who have Warwickshire connections.

It contains accounts of such historic Warwickshire families as the Comptons of Compton Wynyates; the Grevilles of Warwick Castle; the Verneys of Compton Verney; the Leighs of Stoneleigh; the Sheldons of Beoley; and many others.

There are chapters devoted to the Warwickshire Subsidy Roll of 1332; the Battle of Birmingham; the Stratford-on-Avon Jubilee of 1769; the Guild of Knowle, Sir Walter Scott's visits to the county; and an account of the North Warwickshire Hunt in the 'sixties.

The book will be appreciated by all who are interested in the history of bygone Warwickshire.

Apply:—
CORNISH BROTHERS, LTD.
39, New Street, Birmingham, 2.

THE BRITISH TOURING SERVICE

Manager—Mr. P. VYNER
Representative and Life Member, Ypres League

**10, Station Square
ARRAS
(P.-de-C.) France**

Cars for Hire, with British Driver Guides   Tours Arranged

FRIENDSHIP.

A company went into action on the Western front. They were badly cut up. When the remnant got back to their trenches one boy discovered that his pal was missing. He asked his officer if he might go out into No-man's-land to look for him.

The officer said: "Yes, you may go, but it isn't worth it."

The boy went, and in a little time returned mortally wounded.

Before he died he said to his officer: "It was worth it, sir, for when I reached him he said: 'I knew you'd come.'"

That is friendship.

BELATED RETURN OF WAR-TIME LETTER.

Mr. A. Brown, of East Street, Leigh, has just received a letter from the War Office which he posted to a Mr. Arnold, who was postmaster at Leigh during the War. Mr. Brown took the letter in the trenches, but was wounded, and he lost his tunic containing it. It has now been returned to him by a Berlin solicitor, who discovered the letter in the tunic, which he found on the Menin-Ypres Road.—*The Times,* July 8th,

Branch Notes

LONDON COUNTY COMMITTEE.

The London County Committee commence a new session of their activities. The chief events are the monthly Informal Gatherings held on the third Thursday of each month from 7.15 p.m. to 10 p.m. at the Bedford Head Hotel, Maiden Lane, Strand, W.C.2.

These meetings are organized with the object of maintaining the spirit of fellowship and good comradeship of the war and to bring the Ypres League's objects before others with a view to increasing its membership. These monthly gatherings involve considerable spade work so we trust that members will do their best to make the functions known in order to provide good attendances. The Hon. Secretary will be glad to forward a notice to anyone interested.

Programmes for the coming season have been arranged and we thank all who have generously offered their support, also those who have assisted us so well in the past.

Two or three dances will be held during the coming season, also several lantern lectures of special interest and we look forward to the success of these popular events.

Eleventh Annual Re-union Smoking Concert.

The London County Committee Smoking Concert will take place on Saturday, October 28th at the Caxton Hall, Caxton Street, Victoria Street, S.W.1.

Major Montague Jones, O.B.E. (Chairman of the London County Committee) will take the Chair, and amongst those who have accepted invitations are the following:—H. E. The Belgian Ambassador; H. E. The French Ambassador; H. E. The American Ambassador; Major A. Nyssens, Military Attaché Belgian Embassy; Colonel R. Voruz, Military Attaché French Embassy; Lieut-Colonel Cortlandt Parker, Military Attaché American Embassy; General Sir Hubert Gough; General Sir W. C. G. Heneker; Lieut-General Sir W. P. Pulteney; Major-General C. P. Deedes; The Rev. G. H. Woolley and Major W. H. Brooke.

Doors will be open at 7 p.m. and the Concert commences at 7.30 p.m. An excellent programme is being arranged under the direction of Mr. A. E. Nickolds, and a very enjoyable evening is anticipated. Community singing of the old war-time choruses will again be a feature of the programme. We want another record gathering and individual help is needed to make this important annual function known amongst those who are not members of the League and who may be pleased to attend. If any members are unable to be present themselves, might we suggest that they be so kind as to purchase a ticket to help the funds of the London County Committee.

Cornflowers will be on sale at the Hall, price 2d. each and we ask everybody to wear this Ypres League emblem.

Application for tickets, prices 1/-, 2/6 and 5/- (including tax) should be made as early as possible to the Hon. Secretary, London County Committee Ypres League, 20, Orchard Street, W.1. Ladies are cordially invited.

A limited number of tables can be reserved for parties of four and upwards on payment of 2/- per table on the 2/6 tickets, and 2/6 per table on the 5/- tickets. Latest date for application is October 21st.

In conclusion, we very much hope that October 28th will see a record attendance and that the function will surpass all previous efforts. See page 254.

Obituary.

Since the last Informal Gathering in July we regret to announce the death of one of our most loyal supporters in London, namely Mr. C. Stocker. Mr. Stocker never failed to attend the League's activities and took a great interest in its work. His help at the Annual Children's Party, despite his eighty years, was greatly appreciated and he has left an example for others to follow in his loyalty to our cause. We extend to his family our deepest sympathy in their sad bereavement.

INFORMAL GATHERINGS

OF THE

LONDON COUNTY COMMITTEE OF THE YPRES LEAGUE

WILL BE HELD AT THE

BEDFORD HEAD HOTEL, MAIDEN LANE, STRAND, W.C.2

From 7 to 10 p.m., on the following dates:

Thursday, October 19th, 1933.

(Lecture by Mr. Dawes on "Comradeship during the War"—France, Salonika and Palestine).

Thursday, November 16th, 1933.

Thursday, December 21st, 1933.

(Programme being arranged by Mr. O. Mears).

We look forward to the best support at these Gatherings, and request members to bring the dates to the notice of their friends in order to ensure another successful season. Invitations will be sent by the Hon. Secretary to any friends on receipt of names and addresses. Ladies are cordially invited.

ETCHINGS OF THE MENIN GATE MEMORIAL.

Major C. J. Hazard, M.C., of Colombo, Guatemala, a life member of the Ypres League, has very generously given Headquarters a number of his fine etchings of the Menin Gate Memorial, stipulating that the proceeds of sales should go towards the financial support of the YPRES TIMES.

Size of etching: 9 inches by 6 inches. Price: 5s. each, post free. Signed proofs: 10s. 6d. each, post free. These etchings are considered wonderful value.

Applications should be addressed to the Secretary, Ypres League, 20, Orchard Street, London, W.1.

PURLEY.

The Bombardier's Foursomes, 1933.

THIRD, FOURTH AND FINAL BATTLES.

Now the competition among the eight teams remaining was very great.

In the first of the Third Battles, The Bombardier and his mate Lindsay met Bellingham and Brewer: and behold, there were many strokes, but the Bombardier's side prevailed 2 and 1, at Woodcote Park.

Then Feathers and G. Carr played Midgley and Forster (strongly tipped by Purley Downs) at Coulsdon Court, and a good battle it was: being 2 down with 5 to go, the Staff finished with 3 birdies and 2 bogies to win 2 up, in a score of 78.

The last two battles were fought at Woodcote Park the same evening: Scott and Green were dormy 2 down to Douse and Taylor, after some good golf, and finally extricated themselves from a desperate situation to win at the 20th.

Butt and E. H. Carr in their match with Ray and Irens started giant killing with a vengeance: there may have been unexpected incidents, but anyway the back markers of the competition, Ray and Irens, were put out 4 and 3.

So to the fourth or semi-final, battles.

Scott and Green invited Feathers and G. Carr to Woodcote Park, but omitted to notice that there were three good reasons why they could not win:—

(1) They were improperly dressed.
(2) Scott had done a practice round of 79 the night before.
(3) It was the 13th of the month.

At any rate, a very close match resulted. Scott and Green won the first, but the Staff got the next 2 and managed to keep just about one nose-length in front to win by 2 and 1, in reasonable figures.

Butt and E. H. Carr went invading to Woodcote Park of their own accord to play the Bombardier and Lindsay, and started taking liberties by winning the first hole with a birdie. Nothing daunted the Bombardier and his mate holed the first 9 in 37, and were exactly one up. (The Chairman arrived while the 10th was in progress, to find the whole army apparently hay-making: but it was only somebody had sliced out of bounds.)

The sides played shot for shot after this: a rainstorm caused a delay: finally they arrived at the 18th and were all square.

It was then that Butt and E. H. Carr took another liberty, playing the 19th in a very good birdie to win the battle, having gone round in many strokes under handicap.

On the Final Battle our Special Correspondent, The Bombardier himself, reports as follows:—

. . . .

The last battle by mutual consent was played at Coulsdon Court, and the Bombardier was invited by the Adjutant to undertake the combined duties of Reporter and Umpire. In the latter capacity he was not required to function: matches between gentlemen rarely require supervision.

The troops were paraded at 6 p.m. on Tuesday, 11th July, and numbered off as follows: Major Graham Carr, Chairman and Secretary of the Branch, and Captain Featherstone on the one side, and Private Butt and Captain Ernest Carr on the other.

The night being wet, the troops were served out with jerkins, mackintosh-capes and gumboots and instructions were given to the canteen to prepare hot rum on return to the bivouac.

The start was somewhat delayed owing to the acquisitiveness of a certain member of the Club (a "Wiper" withal) who purloined Captain Carr's clubs.

The first shot was played by Feathers, who drove a safe but not a very straight ball. Butt pulled his to glory, leaving his 18-handicap partner a difficult shot over the trees, which he accomplished nobly, only to see his partner putt short and lose the hole.

At the second hole, the Adjutant lifted his august head and deposited the ball in a bunker from which he and his partner took four more to get down. All square.

The third gave the Adjutant an opportunity to reinstate himself, and he holed a stout putt of 20 yards for a 2, putting his side one up.

They lost the next hole rather sadly, and also the 5th, where they conceded a stroke.

At the 6th, a magnificent short hole, the Adjutant played a peach, after his brother had made a complete foozle: the 7th was halved in 5, but at the 8th Feathers retrieved a bad second by holing a long putt and his side again took the lead. Bad putting by the challengers, who had a stroke at the 9th, let their opponents off with a half, so at the turn the holders were one up.

They won the 10th and 11th to become 3 up.

At this moment the Bombardier, who was getting wet, almost decided that he could nominate the winners and retire to the Bar, but a change came over the proceedings.

Real bad play by the holders lost them the 12th and 13th.

At the latter hole Butt drove amongst the cars on to a road, from whence his partner played a clever shot back on to the course. It looked, in spite of the stroke they were giving as if the holders would secure at least a half, but a sad tale of bunker shots altered matters and Butt and Ernest Carr won the hole easily.

At the 14th Ernest Carr indulged in the luxury of an air shot, but in spite of that the challengers got a fine half in 5 by laying their opponents a stymie.

The 15th was halved in 4 but the holders won the 16th in 3 to become dormy two.

Even then the challengers were not finished. They won the 17th with a stroke (dormy one) and had a fighting chance of winning the 18th, which they reached in two to three, but whether they thought compassionately of the Bombardier, who was very wet, or whether they were thirsty or merely dam' bad golfers, they took three putts and only got a half, and so lost the match at the 18th.

So ended the second competition of the Bombardiers Foursomes and the winners on the first occasion are still the holders of the Cups.

The Reporter, who with his partner was beaten in the semi-final by Butt and Ernest Carr at the 19th, had a sneaking sympathy for the losers of this great match, and had they putted as well in the final as they did in the semi-final, the Cups would have found new homes.

All credit must be given them for their gallant fight and the Reporter wishes them well in the future.

As regards the winners, they certainly nodded once or twice, but their play all through, especially that of the junior partner, was a model of accuracy and keenness.

It now remains to find a pair to "knock off their blocks."

THE BOMBARDIER.

NEW YORK.

Major General John F. O'Ryan, our esteemed President in the United States, has recently been offered the candidature for the Mayorality of New York.

General O'Ryan, however, has found himself unable to accept, much to the regret of the many good citizens of that City.

OBITUARY.

We regret to record the death of Mr. Robert A. C. Smith, a staunch Life Member of the Ypres League. During a long career he founded the Pilgrims' Association and was associated with at least a hundred Companies. During the Great War he was adviser to the Army and Navy in their use of the port of New York and directed the sailings of transports, and in 1917 gave the use of the city pier to the Red Cross, thus facilitating the task of returning wounded soldiers to American shores.

Captain R. Henderson-Bland, representative of the Ypres League in America, draws attention to a most interesting and impressive article entitled "New Ypres Exalts An Army Of The Dead," by Clair Price, which appeared in the "New York Times Magazine" of August 6th. The article gives worthy mention of the Ypres British Settlement.

CORRESPONDENCE.

191, Lansdowne Road,
Tottenham,
London, N.17.
9.9.1933.
To Secretary, Ypres League.
Dear Sir,

I would like to take this opportunity of stating what I consider to be excellent reasons why so many members of the Ypres League visit the Salient regularly year after year.

I am often asked why I enjoy visiting Ypres so frequently, and my reply is that the place has a peculiar fascination for me, due to the fact that it was there that I shared the hardships of war service with my comrades, many of whom made the supreme sacrifice and others who are now suffering from the after effects of their experiences.

During my visits to Ypres I am very liable to develop sentimental ideas, because various places bring back memories grave and sad of events which are associated with these spots.

The appeal of the war areas must be quite apparent to ex-service men, and like many others I seem to come under the spell of its attraction, so much so that when the time comes to leave, it is with a very deep sense of regret.

Relatives of men who served at Ypres, especially those who have dear ones buried there, are particularly comforted in having the opportunity to visit the cemeteries which are so beautifully kept. It has been a great pleasure to me to have seen several hundreds of parents, widows and other relatives when they have visited the graves, and the happiness which prevails amongst them is due to the fact that they have had the chance to pay their respects to "The Immortal Heroes."

I trust that I may be permitted to contradict the false impression that so many people have, that the parties who visit the battlefields indulge in a disrespectful attitude. I have never yet in any of my frequent trips to Ypres seen a party which did not behave in a respectful way. Although they may be full of the spirit of jollity they always conduct themselves in a proper manner suited to the environment in which they find themselves.

Anyone who is contemplating a visit need not fear that they will have ground for complaint, especially if they avail themselves of the facilities provided by the Ypres League. The League's representatives are always ready to assist and advise pilgrims so as to ensure complete satisfaction.

The Spirit of Comradeship which exists among the members of the League is the finest I have come across since the war.

Wishing the Ypres League every success in arranging pilgrimages to Ypres during the years to come,

I remain,
Yours respectfully,
ERIC GLOVER.

The Ypres League (Incorporated)

Balance Sheet, 31st December, 1932

LIABILITIES AND FUNDS.

	£ s. d.	£ s. d.	£ s. d.
Free Pilgrimage Fund			331 5 11
General Fund—			
Balance at credit, 1st January, 1932	84 17 3		
Add Balance at credit for year to 31st December, 1932	110 18 7		
			195 15 10
Reserve Fund, *re* Life Membership Subscriptions ...			300 0 0
Represented by Investment £300 *as per contra.*			
"Ypres Times" Maintenance Fund			238 2 2
Partly represented by Investment £200 *as per contra.*			
Maintenance Fund—Ypres Salient Notice Boards ...			13 16 5
Sundry Creditors			55 19 3
Note.—No Reserve has been included for possible liability to Income Tax on income other than Interest.			
Hostel Fund—			
Balance at 1st January, 1932 ...	372 8 6		
Add Excess of Income over Expenditure for the year to 31st Dec., 1932	9 10 6		
			381 19 0
			£1,516 18 7

ASSETS.

	£ s. d.	£ s. d.	£ s. d.
Stocks of Publications, etc., on hand ... ... As per Head Office records and Secretary's valuation.			163 13 11
Cash at Bank and in hand—			
Free Pilgrimage Fund	257 13 11		
Head Office Account	202 18 3		
Hostel Fund	66 7 2		
			526 19 4
Reserve Fund Investment			300 0 0
"Ypres Times" Maintenance Fund Investment ...			200 0 0
Cash on Deposit at Barclay's Bank, Ltd.			
War Stock 3½%			
£323 2s. 11d. Stock on Hostel Fund Account.			322 19 10
Sundry Debtors, etc.			3 5 6
			£1,516 18 7

W. P. PULTENEY, *Lieut.-General,*   *Hon Treasurer.*
E. MONTAGUE JONES, *Major* } *Members of the*
O. G. JOHNSON, *Captain* } *General Committee.*

REPORT OF THE AUDITORS TO THE MEMBERS OF THE YPRES LEAGUE, INCORPORATED.

We beg to report that we have examined the above Balance Sheet with the Head Office Books and relative Documents of the Association and have obtained all the information and explanations we have required. In our opinion such Balance Sheet is properly drawn up so as to exhibit a true and correct view of the Association's affairs, according to the best of our information and the explanations given to us and as shown by the Books of the Association.

Dated this 27th day of May, 1933.

LEPINE & JACKSON, Chartered Accountants,
Auditors.

6, BOND COURT, WALBROOK, LONDON, E.C.4.

Head Office

Income and Expenditure Account for the year ended 31st December, 1932

EXPENDITURE.

	£	s.	d.
To Salaries	349	2	6
,, Rent	170	0	1
,, Printing and Stationery	30	2	1
,, Postages and Telegrams	47	10	9
,, Prospectuses, Publicity Leaflets, etc.	39	13	0
,, Telephone and Insurances	16	15	8
,, Gas and Electric Light	13	3	0
,, Accountancy and Audit Charges	15	15	0
,, Office Cleaning	26	0	0
,, General Expenses	78	3	7
,, Income Tax	1	0	0
	787	5	7
,, Balance, Surplus carried to General Fund	207	15	7
	£995	1	2

INCOME.

	£	s.	d.
By Subscriptions	581	0	5
,, Donations	161	1	8
,, Junior Division	4	8	0
,, Travel Bureau	196	18	7
,, Interest on Bank Deposit Account	2	17	4
,, Publications, etc.—Profit on Sales	48	15	2
	£995	1	2

Head Office

General Fund for the year ended 31st December, 1932

EXPENDITURE.

	£	s.	d.	£	s.	d.
To "THE YPRES TIMES"—						
Cost of Printing, etc.	357	10	6			
Less Sales and Advertising Revenue	10	13	6			
				346	17	0
,, BALANCE.—Carried to Balance Sheet				110	18	7
				£457	15	7

INCOME.

	£	s.	d.
By INCOME AND EXPENDITURE ACCOUNT Surplus for the year transferred.	207	15	7
,, "YPRES TIMES" MAINTENANCE FUND Amount allocated towards cost of "The Ypres Times" in 1932.	250	0	0
	£457	15	7

THE ELEVENTH ANNUAL
REUNION OF MEMBERS AND FRIENDS

Organized by the London County Committee of the Ypres League

WILL BE HELD AT THE

CAXTON HALL, CAXTON STREET, VICTORIA STREET, S.W.1

ON

SATURDAY, OCTOBER 28th, 1933

All Members of the Ypres League and their friends are heartily invited by the London County Committee to meet together at the Caxton Hall, on Saturday, October 28th, 1933, when the

GRAND SMOKING CONCERT

will be given. The Chair will be taken by

Major E. MONTAGUE JONES, O.B.E.
(Chairman of the London County Committee).

The following will also be present :

His Excellency The Belgian Ambassador; His Excellency The French Ambassador; His Excellency The American Ambassador; Major A. Nyssens, Military Attache, Belgian Embassy; Colonel R. Voruz, Military Attache, French Embassy; Lieut.-Colonel Cortlandt Parker, Military Attache, American Embassy; General Sir Hubert Gough, G.C.M.G., K.C.B., K.C.V.O.; General Sir W. C. G. Heneker, K.C.B., K.C.M.G., D.S.O.; Lieut.-General Sir. W. P. Pulteney, G.C.V.O., K.C.B., K.C.M.G., D.S.O.; Major General C. P. Deedes, C.B., C.M.G., D.S.O.; Brig.-General A. Burt, C.B., C.M.G., D.S.O.; The Reverend G. H. Woolley, V.C., M.C.; and Major W. H. Brooke, M.C.

The Programme will be under the personal direction of Mr. A. E. Nickolds, and among the Artistes are the following:—

- Miss PEARL JOYCE, Contralto (Queen's Hall, Albert Hall, etc.)
- Miss SUZETTE TARRI, Entertainer (B.B.C., Palladium, etc.)
- Mr. DAVID JENKINS, Bass (Queen's Hall, Coliseum, etc.)
- Mr. A. E. NICKOLDS, Banjoist-Entertainer (B.B.C., Palladium, Plaza, etc.)
- Mr. PAUL FREEMAN, The King of Cards (Maskelyne's).
- Mr. WILFRED LEWE, Humorist (Principal London Halls).
- Miss HELENA MILLAIS, Actress-Entertainer ("Our Lizzie" of the B.B.C.)

Musical Selections by "THE ENFIELD COLLEGE OF MUSIC ORCHESTRA" under the direction of Mrs. Doris Lee Peabody.

Community singing of old war-time choruses will be included in the programme.

Medals and decorations to be worn.   Please wear your League Badge.   Ladies specially invited.

DOORS OPEN AT 7 P.M.   CONCERT COMMENCES AT 7.30 P.M.

Admission - - 1s., 2s. 6d. and 5s. (including tax).

Accommodation at the Hall is limited but tables can be reserved for parties of four and upwards on payment of 2s. per table on the 2s. 6d. tickets, and 2s. 6d. per table on the 5s. tickets. Applications for tables cannot be considered after October 21st.

A large attendance is anticipated, and early application for tickets accompanied by remittance should be addressed to the Hon. Secretary, London County Committee, Ypres League, 20, Orchard Street, London, W.1.

YOUR SUPPORT ON OCTOBER 28TH WILL BE APPRECIATED.

Branches and Corresponding Members

BRANCHES.

LONDON	Hon. Secretary to the London County Committee : J. Boughey 20, Orchard Street, London, W.1.
	E. LONDON DISTRICT—L. A. Weller, 132, Maxey Road, Dagenham, Essex.
	TOTTENHAM AND EDMONTON DISTRICT—E. Glover, 191, Lansdowne Road, Tottenham, N.17.
	H. Carey, 373, Sydenham Road, S.E.26.
COLCHESTER	H. Snow (Hon. Sec.), 9, Church Street (North).
	W. H. Taylor (Pilgrimage Hon. Sec.), 64, High Street.
GATESHEAD	Lieut.-Colonel E. G. Crouch, 8, Ashgrove Terrace.
LIVERPOOL	Captain A. M. Webster, Blundellsands.
PURLEY	Major Graham Carr, D.S.O., M.C., 112-114, High Street.
SHEFFIELD	Captain J. Wilkinson, "Holmfield," Bents Drive.
BELGIUM	Capt. P. D. Parminter, 19, Rue Surmont de Volsberghe, Ypres.
CANADA	Ed. Kingsland, P.O. Box 83, Magog, Quebec.
SOUTH AFRICA	L. G. Shuter, Church Street, Pietermaritzburg.
AMERICA	Representative : Captain R. Henderson-Bland, 110 West 57th Street, New York City.

CORRESPONDING MEMBERS.

GREAT BRITAIN.

ABERYSTWYTH	T. O. Thomas, 5, Smithfield Road.
ASHTON-UNDER-LYNE	G. D. Stuart, "Woodlands,", Thronfield Grove, Arundel Street.
BANBURY	Captain C. W. Fowke, Yew Tree House, King's Sutton.
BIRMINGHAM	Mrs. Hill, 191, Cattell Road, Small Heath.
	John Burman, "Westbrook," Solihull Road, Shirley.
BOURNEMOUTH	H. L. Pasmore, 40, Morley Road, Boscombe Park.
BRISTOL	W. S. Hook, "Stoneleigh," Cotham Park.
BROADSTAIRS	C. E. King, 6, Norman Road, St. Peters, Broadstairs.
	Mrs. Briggs, North Foreland House.
CARLISLE	Lieut.-Colonel G. T. Willan, D.S.O., 3, Goschen Road.
CHATHAM	W. N. Channon, 22, Keyes Avenue.
CHESTERFIELD	Major A. W. Shea, 14, Cross Street.
CONGLETON	Mr. H. Dart, 61, The Crescent.
DARLINGTON	D. S. Vigo, 125, Dorset Road, Bexhill-on-Sea.
DERBY	T. Jakeman, 10, Graham Street.
DORRINGTON (Salop)	Captain G. D. S. Parker, Frodesley Rectory.
EXETER	Captain E. Jenkin, 25, Queen Street.
GLOUCESTER	H. R. Hunt, "Casita," Parton Lane, Churchdown.
HERNE BAY	Captain E. Clarke Williams, F.S.A.A., "Conway," Station Road.
HOVE	Captain G. W. J. Cole, 2, Westbourne Terrace, Kingsway.
LEICESTER	W. C. Dunford, 343, Aylestone Road.
LINCOLN	E. Swaine, 79, West Parade.
LLANWRST	A. C. Tomlinson, M.A., Bod Estyn.
LOUGHTON	Capt. O. G. Johnson, M.A., Loughton School.
MATLOCK (Derby)	Miss Dickinson, Beechwood.
MELROSE	Mrs. Lindesay Kelsall, Huntlyburn.
NEW BRIGHTON (Chesire)	E. F. Williams, 5, Waterloo Road.
NEW MILTON	W. H. Lunn, "Greycot," Albert Road.

NOTTINGHAM ...	... E. V. Brown, 3, Eldon Chambers, Wheeler Gate.
ST. HELENS (Lancs.)	... John Orford, 124, Knowsley Road.
SHREWSBURY ...	... Major-General Sir John Headlam, K.B.E., C.B., D.S.O , Cruck Meole House, Hanwood.
TIVERTON (Devon)	... Mr. W H. Duncan Arthur, Surveyor's Office, Town Hall.
WELSHPOOL ...	... Mr. E. Wilson, Coedway, Ford, Salop.

DOMINIONS AND FOREIGN COUNTRIES.

AUSTRALIA ...	... Messrs. C. H. Green, and George Lawson, Anzac House, Elizabeth Street, Brisbane. Queensland. R. A. Baldwin, c/o Government Savings Bank of N.S.W., Martin Place Sydney. Mr. W. Cloves, Box 1296, G.P.O., Adelaide.
BELGIUM ...	... Sister Marguerite, Sacré Coeur, Ypres.
BUENOS AYRES ...	... President, British Ex-Service Club, Calle 25 de Mayo 577.
CANADA ...	.. Brig.-General V. W. Odlum, C.B., C.M.G., D.S.O., 2530, Point Grey Road, Vancouver. V. A. Bowes, 326, 40th Avenue West. Calgary, Alberta. W. Constable F. Grece, 4095, Tupper Street, Westmount, Montreal.
CEYLON ...	... Captain F. R. G. Webb, M.C., Irrigation Bungalow, Kalmunai, E.P
EGYPT ...	... L. B. S. Larkins, The Residency, Cairo.
INDIA ...	... Lieut.-Quartermaster G. Smith, Queen's Bays. Sialkot, India.
IRELAND ...	... Miss A. K. Jackson. Cloneyhurke House, Portarlington.
KENYA ...	... Harry Sheilds, Survey Department, Nairobi. Corporal C. H. Slater, P.O. Box 403, Nairobi.
NEW ZEALAND ...	... Captain W. U. Gibb, Ava Lodge, Puhinui Road, Papatoetoe, Auckland. S. E. Beattie, Lowlands, Woodville.
SOUTH AFRICA ...	... H. L. Versfield, c/o Cape Explosives Works Ltd., 150, St. Georges Street, Cape Town.
SPAIN ...	... Captain P. W. Burgess, Calle de Zurbano 29, Madrid.
U.S.A. ...	... Captain Henry Maslin. 942, President Street, Brooklyn, New York. L. E. P, Foot. 20, Gillett Street. Hartford, Conn, U.S.A. A. P. Forward. 449, East 80th Street, New York. J. W. Freebody, 945. McBride Avenue, Los Angeles.
NOVA SCOTIA ...	... Will R. Bird, Amherst.

Membership of the League

This is open to all who served in the Salient, and to all those whose relatives or friends died there, in order that they may have a record of that service for themselves and their descendants, and belong to the comradeship of men and women who understand and remember all that Ypres meant in suffering and endurance.

Life membership, £2 10s.

Annual members, 5s.

Do not let the fact of your not having served in the Salient deter you from joining the Ypres League. Those who have neither fought in the Salient nor lost relatives there, but who are in sympathy with the objects of the Ypres League, are admitted to its fellowship, but are not given scroll certificates.

There is a Junior Division for children whose relatives served in the Salient. It is open also to others to whom our objects appeal.

Annual subscription 1s. up to the age of 18, after which they can become ordinary members of the League.

THE YPRES LEAGUE (INCORPORATED)
20, Orchard Street, Portman Square, W.1.

Telephone: WELBECK 1446.   *Telegrams*: YPRESLEAG, "WESDO," LONDON.

Patron-in-Chief: H.M. THE KING.

Patrons:

H.R.H. THE PRINCE OF WALES.   H.R.H. PRINCESS BEATRICE.

President: GENERAL SIR CHARLES H. HARINGTON.

Vice-Presidents:

F.-M. VISCOUNT ALLENBY.
F.-M. SIR CLAUD JACOB.   THE LORD WAKEFIELD OF HYTHE.
F.-M. SIR PHILIP CHETWODE.   LIEUT.-GENERAL SIR CECIL ROMER.

General Committee:

THE COUNTESS OF ALBEMARLE.
MAJOR J. R. AINSWORTH-DAVIS.
*CAPTAIN C. ALLISTON.
LIEUT-COLONEL BECKLES WILLSON.
*MR. J. BOUGHEY.
*MISS B. BRICE-MILLER.
COLONEL G. T. BRIERLEY.
CAPTAIN P. W. BURGESS.
*MAJOR H. CARDINAL-HARFORD.
REV. P. B. CLAYTON.
*THE EARL OF YPRES.
MRS. C. J. EDWARDS.
MAJOR C. J. EDWARDS.
MR. H. A. T. FAIRBANK.
MR. T. ROSS FURNER.
SIR PHILIP GIBBS.
MR. E. GLOVER.
MAJOR C. E. GODDARD.
MAJOR-GENERAL SIR JOHN HEADLAM.
MR. F. D. BANKS HILL.

MAJOR-GENERAL C. J. B. HAY.
MR. J. HETHERINGTON.
MRS. E. HEAP.
GENERAL SIR W. C. G. HENEKER.
CAPTAIN O. G. JOHNSON.
*MAJOR E. MONTAGUE JONES.
CAPTAIN H. D. PEABODY.
*THE HON. ALICE DOUGLAS PENNANT.
*LIEUT.-GENERAL SIR W. P. PULTENEY.
LIEUT.-COLONEL SIR J. MURRAY.
*COLONEL G. E. C. RASCH.
VISCOUNT SANDON.
THE HON. SIR ARTHUR STANLEY.
MR. ERNEST THOMPSON.
CAPTAIN J. LOCKLEY TURNER.
*LIEUT.-GENERAL SIR H. UNIACKE.
*MR. E. B. WAGGETT.
CAPTAIN J. WILKINSON.
CAPTAIN H. TREVOR WILLIAMS.

* Executive Committee.

Bankers: *Honorary Solicitors*:

BARCLAYS BANK LTD., Knightsbridge Branch.   MESSRS. FLADGATE & CO., 18, Pall Mall, S.W.

Secretary: *Auditors*:

CAPTAIN G. E. DE TRAFFORD.   MESSRS. LEPINE & JACKSON, 6, Bond Court, E.C.4.

League Representative at Ypres:
CAPTAIN P. D. PARMINTER.
19, Rue Surmount de Volsberghe.

League Representative in America:
CAPTAIN R. HENDERSON-BLAND.
110 West 57th Street, New York.

League Representative at Amiens:
CAPTAIN STUART OSWALD.
7, Rue Porte-Paris.

League Representative at Arras:
MR. P. VYNER,
10, Station Square.

Hon. Secretary, Ypres British Settlement:
LT. COLONEL F. G. POOLE,

PRIMARY OBJECTS OF THE LEAGUE

I.—Commemoration and Comradeship.
II.—To provide special travel facilities for Members and all interested to Ypres and battlefields, and transport of Members.
III.—The furnishing of information about the Salient; marking of historic sites and the compilation of charts of the battlefields.
IV.—The erection of a Ypres British Church and School which has been completed.
V.—The establishment of groups of members throughout the world, through Branch Secretaries and Corresponding Members.
VI.—The maintenance of cordial relations with dwellers on the battlefields of Ypres.
VII.—The formation of a Junior Division.

Use the Ypres League Travel Bureau for Ypres and Whole of the Western Front.

FOR THE FOLLOWING PUBLICATIONS, Etc., apply:
Secretary, YPRES LEAGUE, 20, ORCHARD STREET, LONDON, W.1.

THE BATTLE BOOK OF YPRES. A history of notable deeds contributed by all regiments. 5s.; post free, 5s. 6d. Compiled by Beatrix Brice with the assistance of Lieut.-General Sir William Pulteney, G.C.V.O., etc.

BOOKS.

YPRES: Outpost of the Channel Ports. By Beatrix Brice. With Foreword by Field-Marshal Lord Plumer, G.C.B. Price 1s. 6d.; post free 1s. 10d.

In the Ypres Salient. By Lt.-Col. Beckles Willson. 1s. net; post free 1s. 2d.

To the Vanguard. By Beatrix Brice. 1s. net; post free 1s. 2d.

The City of Fear and Other Poems. By Gilbert Frankau. 3s. 6d. net; post free 3s. 8d.

With the Cornwall Territorials on the Western Front. By E. C. Matthews. 7s. 6d.; post free 8s.

Story of the 63rd Field Ambulance. By A. W. Westmore, etc. Cloth, 3s. 6d., post free. Paper, 2s. 6d., post free.

War Letters to a Wife. By Colonel Rowland Fielding. Popular Edition. 7s. 6d.; post free 8s.

The Pill Boxes of Flanders. 1s.; post free 1s. 3d.

YPRES LEAGUE TIES. 3s. 6d. each, post free.

YPRES LEAGUE BADGES. 2s. each, 2s. 1½d. post free.

EMBROIDERED BADGES. 4s. each, post free.

Map and List of Cemeteries in the Ypres Salient. Price 9d.; post free 11d.

Map of the Somme. Price 1s. 8d., post free.

PICTURES.

Burning of the Cloth Hall, 1915. A Coloured Print, 14 in. by 12 in. 1s. post free.

ENGRAVINGS, 33 in. by 21 in., £1 11s. 6d. each.

Hell Fire Corner.

Heavy Artillery Going into Action before Passchendaele.

"**I Won't.**"

POST CARDS, PHOTOGRAPHS AND ETCHINGS.

Post Cards. Ypres: British Front during the War. Ruins of Ypres. Price 1s. post free.

Photographs of Menin Gate Unveiling. Size 11 in. by 7 in. 1s. 2d. each, post free.

Hill 60. Complete Panorama Photographs. 12 in. by 3¾ in. Price 3s., post free; 15 in. by 5 in. Price 3s. 6d., post free.

WAR-TIME PHOTOGRAPHS OF THE SALIENT.

6 in. by 8 in. ... 1s. 6d. each.
12 in. by 15 in. ... 4s. each.

List forwarded on application.

PHOTOGRAPHS OF WAR-TIME SKETCHES.

Bedford House (Front View), 1916.
Bedford House (Back View), 1916.
Voormezeele Main Street, 1916.
Voormezeele Crucifixion Gate, 1916.
Langhof Chateau, 1916.

Size 8½ in. by 6½ in. Price 2s. 6d. each, post free.

ETCHINGS.

Etchings of Menin Gate Memorial. 9 in. by 6 in. Price, 5s. each, post free. Signed proofs, 10s. 6d. each, post free.

YPRES TIMES.

The Journal may be obtained at the League Offices. BACK NUMBERS 1s.; 1931, 8d.; 1932, 6d.

Printed in Great Britain for the Publishers by FORD & GILL, 21a/23, Iliffe Yard, Crampton Street, London, S.E.17.

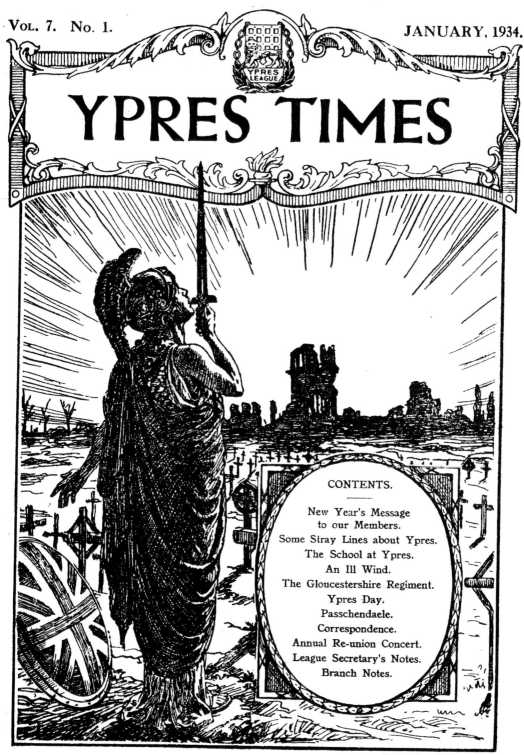

Memory Tablet.

JANUARY - FEBRUARY - MARCH

JANUARY.

Jan. 8th, 1916   Gallipoli evacuation completed.
„ 12th, 1915   The use of poisonous shells by Germans reported.
„ 21st, 1915   Zeebrugge bombarded by British airmen.
„ 24th, 1916   Naval battle off Dogger Bank.

FEBRUARY.

Feb. 3rd, 1917   America broke with Germany.
„ 18th, 1915   U-boat "blockade" of England.
„ 18th, 1918   German invasion of Russia.
„ 21st, 1916   Battle of Verdun begun.
„ 21st, 1918   British capture Jericho.
„ 25th, 1915   Allied Fleet attacked Dardanelles.

MARCH.

Mar. 10th, 1915   British capture of Neuve Chapelle.
„ 11th, 1917   British take Baghdad.
„ 12th, 1917   Revolution in Russia.
„ 15th, 1917   Abdication of the Tsar.
„ 21st, 1917   First British War Cabinet.
„ 21st, 1918   German offensive on the Western Front.

The Ypres Times

Communications to
The Editor, "Ypres Times,"
20, Orchard Street, London, W.1.

PRICE 6d.
POST FREE 7d.

Vol. 7, No. 1   Published Quarterly   January, 1934

New Year's Message to our Members

IN the absence abroad of our President I send all good wishes for the year to all members of the Ypres League.

Last year's work by the League both here and at Ypres were most successful, our thanks are due to our indefatigable Secretary, Captain de Trafford, and Mr. Mears, his Assistant.

No effort should be spared during the present year to interest the growing up generation in the traditions of the Salient.

A special word of congratulation is due to the Purley and Colchester Branches for their splendid enrolment work during last year.

Nothing could give the League more confidence in the future than the remarks sent me by the Dowager Viscountess Plumer, whose message reads as follows:—

"I should like to add my good wishes to those of Sir William Pulteney. When we were at Ypres at Whitsuntide we were all very much impressed with the work that had been achieved. I felt that the aims my husband had in view were being realised and the Settlement was not only a Memorial to the Dead but an incentive to the Living. The School which was especially dear to him seemed in a most flourishing condition: there we hope and believe that the children inspired by the traditions of the Salient will learn the lessons of service and sacrifice which it teaches."

W. P. Pulteney,
Lt. General (Chairman).

Some Stray Lines about Ypres

By Stephen Graham.

Author of "A Private in the Guards"; "Ivan the Terrible"; "Boris Godunof," etc.

ONE always doubted whether the names of Neuve Chapelle, Festubert, Loos would be found in the school history books after the war, whether they would not be dwarfed by much greater battles in later stages of the war. But the name of Ypres we gradually learned must stand. As a nation we were not much concerned with Ypres before 1914, but for ever after we must be associated with it—through the memory of the blood which has been shed and of the dead who have been buried there. What regiment in the British army has not fought or held the line at Ypres? At what expense of lives has it been held? The more ruinous it has become the more sacred it has become, and the more determined we have been to keep it. And not on military so much as on emotional grounds! Some Roman writer describing the ancient Saxons said they fought on the sea with such a spirit that, in course of battle, were there but two planks of a boat left the warriors would somehow be found standing on them and fighting still. So also amidst the ruins of Ypres.

The sentiment about Ypres is not confined to one section of the army, the feeling about it is universal, and almost any soldier, if asked about the town, will give testimony to the one effect. "Oh, I think I'd kill myself if they took Ypres," says a blaspheming old soldier who otherwise would not seem to have an ounce of religion in him. "Ypres was the most beautiful little town you could ever wish to see at the end of a day's march," says another. The most fantastic notions of its beauty have arisen in the mind of the common soldier. Ypres is now part of the substance of a dream. It is legendary already. The havoc wrought there is a sort of picture and symbol of the havoc wrought in our lives by the war, and its ruins have stood for us as a picture in little of the ruins of our civilization as a whole.

On some shattered buildings in France a warning has been set up against making repairs since the Government has the intention of leaving them standing as they are as a witness for all time of what the Germans have done. The same might be put over Ypres, though not because of what the Germans have done but because of what they failed to do.

The battalion of Scots Guards in which at a later date I served, took a vital part in the First Battle of Ypres, for it was there that it received its baptism of fire. It did not take part in what is sometimes called the Second Battle of Ypres, namely, the abortive German attack of May 1915 where they carried the abasement of the profession of arms a stage lower by the introduction of poison gas. But when the battalion came into the town on the 14th March, 1916, it held the salient in company with other regiments throughout the desolating summer of that year, and only left it late in July for the Battle of the Somme.

What a contrast was the Ypres which the battalion left in November 1914 and the one which met its eyes a year and four months later. It had been a flourishing little town, full of eager civilians, with Cathedral and Cloth Tower intact, and many an ancient and old-fashioned building, but when we returned it was a place of the dead, utterly wrecked, with not one whole building left standing, a place where at night the footstep on the cobbled roadway echoed eerily as if one were in a haunted domain. There were no roofs, no upper storeys anywhere, and all was flat except the many jagged pointers of isolated walls and the low stumps of what had been houses and shops.

Ypres was really in the nature of a reserve line for the front which was some 2,000 yards beyond. Instead of being trenches there, as would normally have been the case, the men were in cellars below the ruins. For cellars remained, the worst bombardments cannot destroy them. The open streets were never safe from shell fire and bullets. The men remained in the cellars except when called upon to relieve those in the firing line or to retire to rest billets beyond Poperinghe. There was no coming up to the surface for drill or for "divine service." F. Coy. lived in the old town-prison, fourteen in a cell, deep down below the surface of the street in a silence where no guns were ever heard. It was airless and grey, and murderers had scratched their names on the walls in days gone by, but the soldiers were merry enough and there was even a cinematograph theatre in one of the larger dungeons. There was also a canteen. G. Coy. were in cellars on the Dry Switch; Right Flank Coy. were in Rue Dixmude, opposite the Cathedral; and Left Flank Coy. in Boulevard Malon, near the railway station. The ways to the line were the St. Jean road, the Potijze

YPRES — THE CITY OF MARTYRDOM

and Menin roads; the first started in the Northern part near Dead End, the other two commenced at the Menin Gate which was near the Square and the Cloth Hall and centre of the town. All three roads traversed the trenches and continued beyond the German lines. The Menin Road was that on which the battalion had first come under fire in October 1914.

An officer of the regiment wrote a vivid account of the Ypres to which they returned :—

"It was only by devious passages that you could obtain access to the mysterious internal chambers of the ramparts, centuries old. It was perfectly safe. In all our lines there was not a safe dug-out; this had made it famous. And now it looked curiously seductive and homelike There lay the remains of a late supper; there were two beds and two sets of pyjamas; there was the book left open at the page half-read; and there were the gramophone records lying in an untidy heap beside the gramophone. The atmosphere was pungent with tobacco smoke, but warm and comfortable. . . . Outside the mist crept in, crept out and roundabout. Like a ghost, like a wraith it stole along the dim streets whose secrets were buried beneath tons of bricks and masonry, beneath heaps and heaps of ruins. At first you could see nothing in the filmy darkness after the brilliance of the dug-out; instinct alone guided your footsteps. In the dug-out all sound was deadened; you could hear nothing from without. But now you discovered that the guns were firing in Ypres itself—fitfully yet frequently. Their banging and booming awoke a thousand echoes. Every time a gun fired, the reflection of the flash lit up jagged ruins, a naked wall or the skeletons of houses. . . ."

These words, written by my friend Wilfred Ewart who was afterwards killed when we were out in Mexico together, have the haunting quality of the unforgettable and the unforgotten.

S.G.

The School at Ypres

THE number of children attending the School has now risen to 130. it bears witness to the very successful teaching of Mr. Allen and his assistants.

Lady Plumer has given a cup to be competed for between the two Houses, called Plumer and Pulteney, which have been formed in the School.

An anonymous donor has given an Encyclopædia Britannica for the use of the School and Library.

The parents have given their children at the School, gymnasium tunics, jerseys and caps for the boys, and blue serge tunics and green jerseys with blue berets for the girls. I understand that these outfits are very effective and a tremendous success.

General Sir William Furse has given a Plaque of H.R.H. The Prince of Wales, herewith reproduced, to be hung in the Eton Room at the School.

The Plaque is an excellent impression and should be hung in all schools. It is the work of the badly disabled ex-service men of the Ashtead Potters.

These Plaques can be obtained from the Ashtead Potters Ltd., Ashtead, Epsom, Surrey, price £1 1s. 0d. each with 2/- extra for packing and postage, and every possible encouragement should be given to this fine Institution.

The Trustees of the School have invested the money subscribed by members of the Ypres League to a Memorial to Field Marshal Lord Plumer. This money is allocated at the rate of 10% per annum to start one boy in work in England every year. The Scholarship will last twelve or thirteen years.

W. P. PULTENEY,
Hon. Secretary,
Ypres British School.

An Ill Wind

(Echoes of '15)

AUGUSTE JAEGER, late Private of the 234th Reserve Infantry Regiment (51st Res. Div., 26th Army Res. Corps), is to-day incarcerated, he having been convicted and sentenced at Leipsig, on 17th December, 1932, to ten years in the penitentiary for desertion and betrayal of the German gas attack nineteen years ago. The circumstances surrounding this man's disclosure of the German preparations were made more widely known through an article by General Ferry—ex-Commander of the 11th (French) Division—published in *La Revue des Vivants* of July, 1930, and republished in a book by the same author, entitled, *Des champs de bataille au Désarmement*.

Private Jaeger—23 years of age, automobile driver—deserted to the 4th Battalion Chasseurs at Langemarck on the night of 13th/14th April, 1915, and, to the French interpreter Guth, stated : "An attack against the French trenches is being prepared for the near future. To this end, four batteries of twenty bottles (cylinders) each of asphyxiating gas have been distributed per company in the first line trenches. Each battery is composed of five men. At a given signal—three red rockets set off by the artillery—the bottles will be opened and the gas, escaping, is pushed by a favourable wind towards the French trenches. The said gas will asphyxiate the men occupying these trenches and will enable the Germans to occupy them in turn, without loss of men. In order to avoid being asphyxiated themselves, each man is issued with a pad saturated with oxygen." Jaeger then handed over rudiments of the mask* to the interpreter.

An earlier warning—of equal significance—had come to the French from prisoners captured during the preceding month; a detailed account of which was published in a Bulletin of the VIII (French) Army, dated 30th March; translation of which follows : "According to the prisoners of the XV Corps there exists on the Zillebeke Front a supply of iron bottles of 1.40 m. in length, disposed slightly behind the trench, in camouflaged or even buried shelters. These bottles contain gas intended to put to sleep or to asphyxiate the enemy. It has not yet been put in use, but the pioneers have been instructed in their use; they are laid on the ground, in the direction of the enemy; they are opened by pulling off the cap; the interior pressure releases the gas, which is forced out while remaining near the ground; in order for the operation not to be dangerous to the operator, the wind must be favourable. The pioneer who has charge of opening up the bottles has a special apparatus which he puts over his head. All the men are supplied with an envelope made up of some material and they have orders to place these over their nostrils so as not to inhale the gas." This information was republished in a Bulletin of the X (French) Army, of the same date.

Despite these warnings, further corroborated by the Belgian General Staff—who, on 16th April claimed that the Germans had manufactured in Ghent 20,000 tulle respirators which, soaked in a suitable liquid, were to protect the men against the heavy asphyxiating gases they proposed to discharge—little, if any, credence was placed in the statements.

The French authorities disbelieved the story of Jaeger, partly because they considered he had been primed—as he was so voluble—and mainly because the use of asphyxiating gas was prohibited by the accepted laws of warfare.

---

*The rubber mask subsequently used by the Germans first fell into British hands on November 17th, 1915, when found in possession of prisoners captured by the 7th Canadian Battalion in a trench raid near Ploegsteert.

General Ferry, in his article *Ce qui s'est passé sur l'Yser*, states: "We immediately informed General Aimé, Chief of the 21st Brigade, on duty in the sector, and instructed him:—

1. To reduce, for the time being, the number of troops then accumulated in the front line; to avoid loss of men if the intended attack should take place.

2. To try and locate, and destroy with his artillery, the batteries of said bottles. . . . To despatch an officer to the 28th (British) Division, at Ypres, and the Canadian Brigade at Boesinghe—which was to move up to the sector that night—to be on the greatest alert and to take the necessary measures at hand to prevent the inhaling of gas.

General Ferry's reference to "la brigade Canadienne à Boesinghe" is not clear. The first Canadian brigade to move up to the sector was the 2nd C. I. Bde.—Headquarters of which were at Steenvoorde until the line was occupied, when move was made to Wieltje.

General Putz, in sending the information to Second Army, told the liaison officer that he did not believe it, and considered Jaeger had been sent over with the intention to deceive.

In the V Corps*—immediately to the right of the French—General Plumer passed on the warning to his divisional commanders "for what it is worth."

A staff officer of the 2nd Canadian Infantry Brigade, who had received the warning at 6 p.m. on the evening of the 15th, wrote on 16th April: "Last night we got ready to receive a German attack. Divisional Headquarters notified us that the Germans intended to attack with tubes of poisonous gas; but it didn't materialise."

The reaction seems to have been summed up in the one word DISBELIEF. At any rate, because the attack did not take place almost immediately the subject was all but forgotten.

One factor must, however, be conceded to the High Command, viz., they were greatly handicapped by not knowing the nature of the gas the enemy proposed to employ, and, as a Canadian diarist states: "There was, it is true, knowledge on our part that the enemy was about to use some poisonous gas, but no one knew what would be the effects of that gas, nor how he would follow it up."

About the end of March, the War Office asked Sir William Ramsay's committee to consider what gases might possibly be used, and what would be the best means of protection. But before the committee reported, the cloud attack of April 22nd was made. Sir William Ramsay, on having the circumstances explained to him over the telephone, with the suggestion that the gas was probably chlorine, repaired to the War Office with sample mouth-pads* of flannel soaked in hyposulphite of soda.

On 26th April, Lord Kitchener asked Dr. John Scott Haldane, F.R.S.—brother of Lord Haldane—to proceed to France and investigate the nature of the gas that had been used. Dr. Haldane, thereupon, proceeded to Bailleul and, accompanied by Sir Wilmot Parker Herringham — Consulting Physician to the British forces in France—examined men from the Canadian batallions who were at No. 2 Casualty Clearing Hospital suffering from the effects of gas.

Two days later the War Office issued an appeal through the Press for a half million respirators.

---

* The Official History of the Canadian Forces in the Great War 1914-1919—The Medical Services, p. 299, contains the following: "In the diary of the assistant medical director of the 1st Division, Colonel G. L. Foster, an ominous entry appears under date of April 15: 'Attended consultation of officers of V. Corps, with D.M.S. Second Army presiding. Rumour that this evening the enemy will attack our lines, using an asphyxiating gas to overcome our men in the trenches'."

* J. Grant Ramsay, Principal of the Institute of Hygiene, devised the first effective respirator used by British and Canadian troops.

Lieut.-Col. G. Nasmith, of the Canadian Mobile Laboratory, on 23rd April, 1915, wrote to G.H.Q. direct, to save time, advising that he had diagnosed the gas as chlorine and bromide and suggested the use of a pad soaked in hyposulphite of soda to protect the men.

From 9 a.m. of the morning that the announcement appeared in the English newspapers (28th April), the Chief Ordnance Officer at the Royal Army Clothing Department, Pimlico, was besieged with requests for instructions. A long queue of willing workers—many sitting on the steps—awaited this officer's appearance, and, on receiving the specifications, rushed to the nearest stores to purchase the prescribed material. One lady alone undertook to deliver 5,000 a day. With such alacrity did the public respond that deliveries of the finished article commenced within five hours of receipt of instructions. Some of the stores, including Messrs. Harrods, Ltd., displayed made-up samples in their windows.

Number 1 specification called for bleached cotton gauze and Number 2 specification, stockinette.

Most of the respirators made from No. 1 specification had cheese-cloth (muslin) instead of cotton gauze, this, not being required for surgical purposes, was easier to procure. Many of the stockinette type were made from body-belts—thus serving a more useful purpose.

The size advised was 9in. by 4in., tapering at both ends. Between the folds of the material a small piece of Lancashire-Welsh woollen flannel about 3in. long and ¼in. narrower than the respirator was to be tacked in. About 3in. from both ends a pad of cotton wool was placed to take up as much moisture as possible but not to cover the mouth. This pattern was adjusted by two bands of elastic and tape about ¼in. wide. It was suggested that the respirators be dyed with coffee or Madder or Condy's Fluid.

Such an overwhelming response was made by the women of Britain that on Thursday, 29th April, the War Office made the following announcement: "Thanks to the magnificent response already made to the appeal in the Press for respirators for the troops, the War Office is in a position to announce that no further respirators need be made." Indeed, a superabundance was received which permitted a goodly supply being turned over to the Belgian Army.

The French official despatch of 24th April gives an admirable description of the cloud effect of the gas: "A dense yellow smoke, emanating from the German trenches and blown by a steady wind, produced an effect of complete asphyxiation upon our troops. The appearance and the effect produced are exactly those of feeding a wood fire with sulphur, the yellow vapours of which mingled with the white smoke giving the described appearance."

The effect from the enemy side is given by a German writer as follows: "A heavy yellowish-white, opaque cloud appeared like a wall along the German trenches, on a front of six kilometres. The cloud, at first the height of a man, later increasing in height, travelled with a wind of between two and three metres per second."

Seen laterally, or obliquely, as by most of the Canadians, the cloud appeared unbroken; seen from in front it was in BLOCKS with clear intervals between. An officer of the Canadian Mobile Laboratory reported that the gas cloud took about half an hour to travel an approximate distance of 6,000 yards. And that the cloud looked at least thirty or forty feet high. Another member of the division described the gas as. "a sort of bluish-green mist" and that "it felt cold to breathe, and immediately one felt it in one's lungs and began to cough and gasp for breath."

The troops in the line had not the knowledge of their superiors and were caught at a great disadvantage. The aroma of the gas was at first pleasant to the nostrils —many will recall that it was likened to scented violets—but when the fumes reached the lungs it proved a different story.

During the second discharge of gas on 24th April, the Canadians sought the best means at their disposal for protection from the fumes. Handkerchiefs, towels and cotton ammunition bandoliers were used; being wetted with water or any liquid available, while several members of the 84th (British) Brigade obtained effective relief by using oiled, flannel rifle rags. It was not until May that the official respirators were issued.

By the middle of May the troops were receiving the "Veil" Respirator,* made of black cotton gauze and fitted with a veil of the same material for protection for the eyes.

Later on, owing to the increased use of lachrymal shell† which only affected the eyes, goggles were issued.

The first improvement on the respirator was known as the "Smoke" or Hypo Helmet.‡ This design—a flannel bag, pulled on over the head and the skirt tucked in the collar of the tunic—was fitted with a one-piece mica window. The breath was exhaled into the bag and the window rapidly became "smoked," hence the name. A few of these helmets were being issued by 20th May to machine gunners and other selected personnel—the practice followed with all later patterns. In the gas attack of 24th May, a large number of the mica windows became cracked and broken, rendering the helmets valueless. Further supply was, therefore, suspended till unbreakable cellulose acetate windows could be procured. By 6th July, all British troops in the field had been equipped with this modified pattern—the first to completely cover the head.

In August, the "P" or Tube Helmet was introduced, designed of the same shape as the Smoke Helmet. Two glass eye-pieces replaced the single c.a. window and the helmet was impregnated with phenates to protect against phosgene gas. In January, 1916, by the further addition of hyomine, to ensure protection against prussic acid, it was called the P.H. Helmet. And later, when fitted with metal-rimmed glass goggles—lined inside with a fine rubber sponge which ensured closer fitting and greater comfort—the name was again changed to P.H.G. The P, P.H. and P.H.G. helmets were fitted with an expiratory valve—a metal tube rubber-lined, held in the mouth by the teeth.

Shortly after the Canadian Division had arrived in the Ploegsteert area—on moving north from Givenchy in June, 1915—a new idea as a protective measure against gas was developed. The troops in the trenches were supplied with wooden boxes containing coarse wood shavings and a small glass bottle of gasoline. These boxes were distributed one to each bay and strict instructions were given as to their care and use.

In the event of the enemy releasing gas, the boxes were to be placed on the parapet and the gasoline container—concealed amongst the shavings—smashed with the butt of the rifle, and, after setting fire with a match, the lighted boxes were to be poked over the parapet with the bayonet fixed to the rifle.

---

*These were made by a well-known firm of manufacturing chemists of Bermondsey, London, who for over a year were responsible for the entire output of respirators and anti-gas helmets. May 6th, the first day of manufacture of the veil respirator, 8,000 were produced. By 31st December, 1916, the same firm—employing between four and five thousand hands—had turned out over twenty million of the helmet pattern.

† The Germans experimented with this type of projectile on January 10th, 1915, at Lodz, Poland.

‡ Devised in April by Captain Cluny Macpherson (later Lieut.-Col., M.D., C.M., J.P., C.M.G. —Principal Medical Officer of the Royal Newfoundland Regiment). Captain Macpherson—a native of Terra Nova and a graduate of McGill University, Montreal—arrived in England with the Third Newfoundland Contingent in March, 1915. He was appointed to the Anti-Gas Committee under the Chairmanship of Colonel (later Sir) William H. Horrocks, K.H.S., R.A.M.C. Writing from the War Office—20th June, 1915—to His Excellency the Governor of Newfoundland, he stated in part : "A formal order has now been issued that the helmet of my pattern is to supersede the respirators which were issued. . . . The order is that every man in all ranks is to have two on his person, one at his regimental depôt, and one at the ordnance base. . . . Four for each man."

GAS ATTACK AT YPRES

"The Canadians quickly realised that it was best to face the cloud, and hold on in the hope that the blindness would be temporary, and the cutting pain would pass away."

From "Canada in Flanders," Vol. 1 (Sir Max Aitken, M.P.) The Official Story of the Canadian Expeditionary Force.

By this means it was anticipated the gas would rise clear of the trenches. The fires were estimated to be effective for the space of approximately twenty minutes and the men were, therefore, warned not to light them prematurely.

Gas vacuum bulbs were also distributed at intervals along the forward trenches in order to obtain samples of the cloud gas for analytical purposes.* These were like large electric-light globes, rubber-capped at the neck. The men were instructed to puncture the rubber cap when a gas cloud enveloped the trench and then re-cap with the spare nipple that was attached.

Then followed the Vermorel Sprayer, a manually pumped tank—strapped on the back of the operator — normally employed by horticulturists. This was used to neutralize the gas in trenches and dugouts by spraying them with a solution of hyposoda. The Ayrton Fan*—commonly called the "Flapper" in allusion to the action of this device—was also extensively used for expelling the gas fumes from dugouts.

In the winter of 1915-16, the "Large Box Respirator"† came into use which, like its successor the Small Box Respirator, was worn on the chest, being connected by tube to a facial mask. First issues of the Box Respirator—as it was first called—were made to the Special Brigade R.E. for use during British gas operations.

The dimming of goggles by condensation of moisture still remained a problem but, to a large extent, was overcome by cleaning the eye-pieces with "Glasso"—a white paste—issued in April, 1916.

In June, 1916, the Small Box Respirator was adopted. Issues commenced in August to the Second Army. The First, Third, Fifth and Fourth Armies being completed by the end of January, 1917. All previous patterns were then withdrawn and thenceforth were only used by personnel operating outside of a five-mile limit.

The Small Box Respirator remained the Service pattern to the end of the war. The subsequent minor changes which were effected included an improved container and the adoption of splinterless triplex glass eye-pieces.

Although the Small Box Respirator proved quite adequate for protection against all gases used by the enemy, nevertheless it was not the slightest avail against carbon monoxide. The tunnelling companies who had frequently to face the latter gas were equipped with special oxygen breathing or mine rescue apparatus.

The equine was also provided with a protective mask, the "Tissot" pattern—a French device—being largely used.

AN EYE FOR AN EYE: THE BRITISH RETALIATE.

Within five weeks of the first gas attack the British had fifty gas cylinders in the field, but, as in the case of the Germans—who were fully prepared to project gas in the Zillebeke sector by 10th March — favourable winds and circumstances delayed their use, and it was not until 25th September, at Loos, that the British made their first attack with this new weapon.*

The Germans had made use of gas shell prior to the cloud attack of 22nd April, viz., at Neuve Chapelle on 27th October, 1914; at Bolimow, on the eastern front,

---

*An experimental laboratory had been organized at G.H.Q. on 26th April.

*Invented by Mrs. Hertha Ayrton—the only woman member of the Institute of Electrical Engineers—who, in 1915, presented the device to the War Office for the duration of the war. Over a hundred thousand were used at the front.

†Invented by the late Lieut.-Colonel E. F. Harrison, Controller of Chemical Warfare. Colonel Harrison became a victim of his own discovery; he died on November 4th, 1918, from pneumonia aggravated by exposure to gas during the course of his experiments. He joined the Sportsmen's Battalion at the age of 47—as a private—in 1915, and after the first gas attack was transferred as a corporal to the chemical branch of the Royal Engineers. Shortly before his death he was to have been promoted to the rank of Brigadier-General and awarded the Legion of Honour, but death intervening these honours were not bestowed upon him.

*In the month of October, 1918, the British projected forty-six tons of gas against the Germans.

31st January, 1915; and again on the western front near Nieuport in March and at Hill 60 on 16th April, 1915.

A German official communique, dated 17th April, read: "Yesterday east of Ypres the British employed shells and bombs with asphyxiating gas." Denial and exposure of this was forthcoming in Sir John French's report of April 19th: "The statement in a recent German official communique that we had been using asphyxiating gases in the Ypres district is false, and was doubtless made to justify the use of these gases, which have been freely employed by the enemy in his attacks on Hill 60."

Dr. Rudolph Hanslian, in his treatise, *Der Chemische Kreig*, submits that Germany did not violate the Hague Convention until May, 1916, when the "Green Cross" shell was introduced.* He states: "Her (Germany's) shells and gas mines used previously to May, 1916, contained a high proportion of high explosive and a small charge of purely irritant substances. Neither these nor her gas-cloud attacks —the latter a logical development of the traditional 'smoke-out' operation, and not even mentioned in the Declaration—can be considered as infractions of the agreement."

In further support of his contention, Dr. Hanslian strives to justify German's actions; he states: "Let us consider the provisions of the Hague Convention, 18th October, 1907. Article 23 (a), taken from the Declaration of 28th July, 1899, forbids the use of poison or poisoned weapons. This is intended to prohibit the use of poison in the customary sense, that is to say, the poisoning of wells and food supplies, and of poisoned weapons such as are employed by savage races. Had any intention existed to forbid the use of poison in any other form, such intention would have been clearly expressed.

"Article 23 (e) forbids the use of arms, projectiles, or materials, calculated to cause *unnecessary suffering*. If any of the weapons that first came into use during the war can refute the charge of unnecessary suffering, that weapon is gas. There remains for consideration whether the suffering inflicted by gas goes beyond the intended limits. Statistics on the subject of gas casualties show that such is not the case. German records show that between 1st January, 1918, and 30th September, 1918, for which period exact figures are available, out of about 58,000 cases treated for gas poisoning, only 1,755 died; approximately three per cent. French data (Clemenceau, Secret Session at the end of August, 1918) show us that of 14,578 gas-cases treated in the first ten days of August, 1918, 424 had died; approximately 2.9 per cent. Furthermore, ultimate recovery from gas-poisoning is in most cases complete, and permanent disability rare. The percentage of mortality in cases of gun-shot wounds amounts frequently to as much as twenty-five per cent. Article 23 (e) therefore does not enter into the argument."

The Doctor, however, unwittingly refutes his statement when, later on, he refers to the first gas attack. He continues: "The sector attacked was occupied chiefly by a French colonial division. The gas cloud struck terror and confusion into its ranks, and produced 15,000 casualties, including five thousand dead."

Edwin Pye.
(Ex-5th Bn. C.E.F.)

---

*Later, a more deadly gas was used which, when inhaled in strength, caused the organs of the victim to become blistered throughout his body, and slow and agonising death followed. This was the "Mustard Gas"—also called "Yperite" on account of the Germans' initial use of it in the Ypres Salient—first used on 12th July, 1917.

The Gloucestershire Regiment
(28th and 61st)

Nicknames:
"*The Back Numbers*"—"*The Slashers*"—"*The Old Braggs*"—"*The Fore and Afts.*"

Battle Honours:
Ramillies - Louisburg - Guadaloupe - QUEBEC, 1759 - Martinique - Havannah - St. Lucia - Maida - CORUNNA - Talavera - Busaco - Barrosa - Albuhera - Salamanca - Vittoria - Pyrenees - Nivelle - Nive - Orthes - Toulouse - Peninsula - WATERLOO, 1815 - Chillianwallah - Goojerat - Punjaub - Alma - Sevastopol - Delhi - Defence of Ladysmith - Relief of Kimberley - Paardeberg - South Africa, 1899-1902.

Great War:
MONS - Retreat from Mons - Marne, 1914 - Aisne, 1914 - YPRES, 1914- 1915, 1917 - Langemarck, 1914, 1917 - Gheluvelt - Nonne Bosschen - Givenchy, 1914 - Gravenstafel - St. Julien - Frezenberg - Bellewarde - Aubers - LOOS - SOMME, 1916, 1918 - Albert, 1916, 1918 - Bazentin - Delville Wood - Pozieres - Guillemont - Flers Courcelette - Morval - Ancre Heights - Ancre, 1916 - Arras, 1917, 1918 - Vimy, 1917 - Scarpe, 1917 - Messines, 1917, 1918 - Pilckem - Menin Road - Polygon Wood - Broodseinde - Poelcapelle - Passchendaele - Cambrai, 1917, 1918 - St. Quentin - Bapaume, 1918 - Rosieres - Avre - Estaires - LYS - Hazebrouck - Bailleul - Kemmel - Bethune - Drocourt-Queant - Hindenberg Line - Epéhy - Canal du Nord - St. Quentin Canal - Beaurevoir - SELLE - Valenciennes - Sambre - France and Flanders, 1914-1918 - VITTORIO VENETO - Italy, 1917, 1918 - Struma - DOIRAN, 1917 - Macedonia, 1915, 1918 - Suvla - SARI BAIR - Scimitar Hill - Gallipoli, 1915, 1916 - Egypt, 1916 - Tigris, 1916 - Kutalamara, 1917 - BAGHDAD - Mesopotamia, 1916, 1918 - Persia, 1918.

Uniform: Scarlet, facings white; Head-dress—Helmet, Cap, blue.
Regimental March: "KYNEGAD SLASHERS."
NOTE.—Names in Capitals in great war Battle Honours are borne on the King's Colour.

When Captain de Trafford, the indefatigable Secretary of the Ypres League invited me to write a brief history of the Gloucesters, with whom I had the high honour and privilege to serve during the Great War, I pointed out that there was a danger of exalting one particular regiment unless my article was used with the hope that further contributions setting forth the glorious traditions of other regiments of the British Army followed mine. de Trafford assured me that it was his intention to publish in future editions of THE YPRES TIMES as many articles as he could secure dealing with different regiments.

THE 28th Regiment was raised in 1694 by Sir John Gibson. As usual in those days it was called Gibson's after the Colonel.
In 1705, the Regiment, then De Sal's Regiment, first saw service under Marlborough at Huy, near Liége in Flanders. 1706, it distinguished itself at the Battle of Ramilies. In 1734, Phillip Bragg became Colonel and commanded until 1759. "Old Braggs" is still heard as an honourable nickname of the Regiment. In 1759, as Townsends', it took a glorious part in the capture of Quebec (13th of September). The immortal General Wolfe died at the moment of victory in the arms of Lieut. Brown of the 28th Regiment. In 1773, the Colonel's name to designate regiments fell out of use. In 1775, the Regiment gained the title of "The Slashers" for their gallantry at the Battle of White Plains, and passage of the Bronx River in North America, through the use they made of their sword bayonets when they had run out of ammunition. I have seen the memorial at White Plains and also buttons from Gloucester tunics in a museum dedicated to Washington in New York.

In 1782, the Regiment received the county title of The North Gloucestershire Regiment, but the first Battalion always reverted to the title of 28th when in action. During the Great War, the first Battalion always displayed at Battalion Headquarters a small flag bearing the number 28 surrounded with Battle Honours.

It was in 1801, at the Battle of Alexandria in Egypt that the 28th won its greatest distinction—the right to wear the number at the back as well as in front of the head-dress as the Regiment now wears the Sphinx. The Battle of Alexandria on March 21st decided the fate of Egypt and the morrow saw a change of masters on the banks of the Nile. Another March the 21st, that of 1918, will always be remembered by officers and men of the Gloucestershire Regiment, for on that day started the German Offensive on which hung the fate of the British Empire. One account of the Battle of Alexandria speaks of that splendid soldier Colonel Paget. (The Gloucestershire Regiment have always been fortunate in their Commanding Officers.) "It was completely surrounded by the enemy. It was a crisis of supreme interest. Annihilation seemed to await the 28th Regiment, but the intrepid coolness of their Commanding Officer (Colonel Paget) and the almost unexampled courage of his men saved them. The word of command was given "Rear rank, Right About Face" and obeyed with that calmness and steadiness characteristic of the British soldier in the moment of peril. The French, not meeting, as they had hoped, a feeble and disheartened foe, were received by so vigorous and well directed fire that all their efforts to expel this handful of men from their post were frustrated." These words remind one of something Lord Napier of Magdala once wrote: "With what majesty the British soldier fights."

In Alison's "History of Europe" there is another account of this action which ends in this manner: "The gallant troops without flinching stood back to back and maintained this extraordinary contest for a considerable time. Colonel Paget, who had hitherto directed the proceedings of the Regiment, here fell severely wounded and the next officer in seniority assumed command." Sir Ralph Abercromby was wounded amidst the Gloucesters on that day, and was later taken on board the flagship of the Fleet where he died after the victory had been announced to him. He was buried at Malta, which had been captured by Napoleon in 1798, when he suppressed the Knights of Malta, who were revived in 1834 and are with us to-day under the Order of St. John of Jerusalem.

In 1808, the 28th was with Sir John Moore in the immortal retreat to Corunna. They formed part of the rear guard. Sir John Moore praised their wonderful powers of endurance and fine discipline. The 28th had an important share in the Battle of Corunna. That leader of men, Sir John Moore was killed in this battle. During the battle, he met a Highland Regiment retiring, and asked the reason of the retirement, and was told that the ammunition had given out. He rebuked them by reminding them that they still had their bayonets, and led them into action again. They gave a splendid account of themselves. That was leadership. In my opinion, the British Army owes more to Sir John Moore than to any other soldier. During the remainder of the Peninsular War, the 28th was present in nearly all the important battles. After the Battle of Corunna, the 28th returned to England, when the second Battalion was raised.

In 1811, the 28th absorbed the men of the second Battalion and joined Lord Wellington's Army. The 28th were not in the Battle of St. Sebastian but a Sergeant Ball and six grenadiers were present. They had been sent down to buy supplies and were in charge of 2,000 dollars for that purpose. Hearing that St. Sebastian was to be stormed on the next day, Sergeant Ball reminded his men that the 28th had been engaged in almost every action in the Peninsula, and proposed that, for the credit of the Regiment, they should volunteer for the storming party. His proposition was met with enthusiasm by the six grenadiers. The money was placed in charge of an officer. Sergeant Ball and his men fell in with the 9th Regiment, escaped death and wounds, reclaimed the money and rejoined the 28th with the supplies they had set out to get.

Now we come to the greatest Battle Honour the Regiment possesses—Waterloo. The 28th was at Quatre Bras on the 16th of June, 1815, where they covered themselves with glory, and at Waterloo on the 18th. At Quatre Bras, the Brigadier addressed the square that had stood firm after so many charges of the French Cavalry with these words: "Bravo 28th! The 28th are still the 28th and their conduct this day will never be forgotten." The Duke of Wellington wrote: "They have conducted themselves with the greatest bravery." In 1855, they took part in the Crimean War and fought with honour at Alma, Sebastapool and Inkerman. Fourteen N.C.O.s and men were granted D.C.M.s during that war. In 1858, the 28th went to India, arriving too late to share in the fighting involved by the Indian Mutiny though they were engaged on two occasions. On July the 1st, 1881, the 28th became the 1st Battalion of the Gloucestershire Regiment and the facings were changed from light yellow to white. The 2nd Battalion (61st) was originally a second Battalion of the 3rd Buffs (now East Kent Regiment). It became in 1758, the 61st Regiment and proceeded almost immediately to the West Indies distinguishing itself there. In 1779, the 61st were engaged in Cape Colony, South Africa, in suppressing a rebellion among the Kaffirs. In 1801, the 61st were in Egypt at the same time as the 28th. In 1809, the 61st joined Sir Arthur Wellesley's (later the Duke of Wellington) Army in the Peninsula. The 61st had the misfortune not to be present at the Battle of Waterloo. In 1848, they were again in India and in the Sikh War they were present in many actions, notably Chillianwallah. Of their conduct in that battle the Duke of Wellington said: "The 61st Regiment at the Battle of Chillianwallah decided the action and was greatly instrumental in saving the British Army." During the Indian Mutiny, the 61st were before Delhi and assaulted the Kashmir Gate. In 1881, the 61st became the 2nd Battalion of the Gloucestershire Regiment.

Both Battalions fought in the Boer War, and won four Battle Honours, giving the Regiment at that time the most crowded flag in the British Army. Rifle Regiments do not carry flags. The battle honours borne by a regiment constitute no criterion of the actual number of campaigns or battles in which it has participated. However, it must not be imagined that all the engagements not recorded by honours on its colours were reverses. As a matter of fact many of them were victorious preliminaries to greater battles, such as Quatre Bras, the precursor of Waterloo. Many of our regiments have taken part in battles fought on British soil, such as Sedgemoor, the Boyne and Culloden, but victories like these, won against our own countrymen, are not recorded on the colours of the regiments concerned, for reasons that may be readily understood.

Space will not allow, and it is not my intention to write of the actions in whch the Regiment was engaged in the Great War. Suffice to say that on several occasions they repeated the glorious action that won them the Back Badge in Egypt in 1801. That is they carried on when surrounded by the enemy. General Sir Ian Hamilton, in his despatches from Gallipoli praises at great length the conduct of the 7th Gloucesters for fighting on in an imperturbable manner when all the officers had become casualties. The General need not have been surprised. All men who wear the Back Badge of the Gloucestershire Regiment are so imbued with the traditions of the Regiment that initiative comes naturally to them.

R. HENDERSON-BLAND (CAPT.), *late The Gloucestershire Regiment.*

THE BACK BADGE.

Ypres Day

THE 13th Annual Commemoration of the Ypres League was held on October 29th, the nearest Sunday to the 31st of the month officially known as "Ypres Day." This day marked the crisis of the First Battle of Ypres, 1914, when our line was re-established at Gheluvelt, thus deciding the fate of the Salient.

The Dowager, Viscountess Plumer, very kindly extended us the honour of deputising for Her Royal Highness The Princess Beatrice who, through indisposition, was unable to be present.

Photo] [Sport and General Press Agency Ltd.
THE REV. P. B. CLAYTON, CH., M.C., WITH SERGEANT O. BROOKS, V.C. AND THE YPRES LEAGUE WREATH WHICH WAS PLACED ON THE CENOTAPH.

Amongst the distinguished personages present were: His Excellency The Belgian Ambassador; General A. Nyssens, Military Attaché Belgian Embassy; Commandant Hemeleers-Shenley, Assistant Military Attaché Belgian Embassy; Lieut.-Col. G. P. Vanier, representing the High Commissioner for Canada, and Lieut.-Gen. Sir W. P. Pulteney.

The Commemoration commenced at 3 p.m. with a service on the Horse Guards' Parade conducted by the Rev. "Tubby" Clayton, so well known and respected by the many thousands of men who fought in the Ypres Salient.

THE YPRES TIMES

Photo]

A GENERAL VIEW OF THE YPRES LEAGUE SERVICE HELD ON THE HORSE GUARDS' PARADE

The service opened with the singing of the hymn "O Valiant Hearts" played by the band of the 1st Surrey Rifles after which the Rev. P. B. Clayton addressed the large gathering as follows:—

"Brethren, we are debtors! Here once again, a place of memories where some of us have stood as the years have gone by in their procession since our dear friends departed this life. Here once again are a few survivors, and there stand with them who were spared these things—spared because these same men we commemorate on this day had begun the great procession of huge sacrifice which kept this country free.

"Brethren, we are debtors! As we look back on this Ypres Commemoration we remember that on this particular great day, Lord Plumer, against the doctor's orders came here, and we now stand as we stand each year united by some lovely sacred memory.

"Brethren, we are debtors! Whoever forgets, we will not forget. In actual truth—we know it to be true. There is in one of these great buildings around us, a document which tells us what would have been our fate had these men not done what they did for us. There would

[Planet News Ltd.

...MEMORATION OF "YPRES DAY," DURING THE REV. P. B. CLAYTON'S ADDRESS.

have been upon this country a debt of six thousand millions to be paid; the whole of this country from North to South would have been occupied by the troops of our conquerors until such time as the debt was paid. Every Colony would have been taken away from us; our children would be a helot people. English persons would have to step off the pavement to allow our conquerors to hold it. All these things would have been our fate. Therefore I say in the sight of history we are debtors and more than that within the sight of God these men not only saved us.

"It was not a simple fact this great episode or holding of the immortal line which opened that great chorus of sacrifice which held the salient of Ypres through those years. Not only do we look back on the great leaders who have passed into the 'flame invisible' beyond the sight of man—General Fitzclarence, the 20th Brigade, the second and seventh Divisions, the 3rd Cavalry Corps, and not only these records but the glory of every regiment still fighting on and on. These men, by their lives and character taught us faith, constancy, brotherly love—they taught us unselfishness which leads to sacrifice, and here to-day it is no time for sermons but a time for praise indeed, and to us their sacrifice shall be our example and their inspiration our true legacy.

"Yes, till the boys come home we will keep the old fires burning in us and by them who marched we march in this hour."

The "Lament" was finely played by the Pipers of the Scots Guards, and after a short silence the "Last Post" was sounded followed by the hymn "Oh God our help in ages past," the National Anthem and Réveillé.

The march to the Cenotaph was headed by Major E. Montague Jones, O.B.E., the Commandant of the Parade followed by the band of the 1st Surrey Rifles; O.T.C. and T.A. Units; Old Contemptibles; members of the Ypres League, 85th Club and St. Dunstan's. The wreath bearers were: Lieut. Michael O'Leary, V.C., and Sergeant O. Brooks, V.C.

At the Nation's shrine, the Dowager Viscountess Plumer accepted the wreath from His Excellency The Belgian Ambassador and laid it upon the Memorial. After a few minutes silence the Pipers played the contingents on their return to the Horse Guards' Parade for dismissal.

At 4.30 p.m. a deputation of the Ypres League was received at Westminster Abbey by The Right Rev. W. Foxley-Norris, D.D., and before a good attendance of the general public, Captain R. Henderson-Bland, the League's esteemed representative in America, placed the wreath on the grave of the Unknown Warrior. During a short service of impressive simplicity, the Dean addressed the assembly with the following touching words:—

"Before we stand in silence for a moment's prayer let me remind you—though you need no reminder—what it is we are doing.

"Under this stone there lay the mortal remains of one of our men representatives of the whole British forces. We do not know his name or his achievements. He may himself have been in the Salient through those times we are thinking of to-day—at any rate he represents those who were.

"On this day, a day never-to-be-forgotten in the history of England and more than that in the history of decisive battles of the world. On this day there occurred one of the greatest crises in history when the battle began. On the 31st of October, 1914, as you well know, our line was re-established, but the incredible suffering and sacrifice of the Salient will always be spoken of was not finished then. Before the end of the war 250,000 of our men had given their lives around Ypres; and let us not forget these men. We never will because some of these men went out from our own homes. It is difficult for those who lost their own to speak. They in reverence remember that army called the Old Contemptibles who proved themselves the finest army in the world, and they remember that new army built up around them who won their spurs and reputation; they remember the forces of the Colonial Empire who won their place side by side with them.

"In reverence let us stand a moment in silence remembering all these things as especially those who we ourselves lost."

* * *

Later, the Dean invited the Ypres League deputation to visit the grave of Lord Plumer in the Warrior's Chapel—"A name," he said, "which will always through history be joined to that of Ypres.

Passchendaele

ON the 27th October, 1917, a date which I continue to remember as I do 1066, our draft left Folkestone for Boulogne. I stood on deck gazing at the white cliffs of Albion, thinking that I ought to feel regret proper to the occasion—but I felt seasick instead. So I could have said with any perfervid patriot that I was very eager to get to France.

We were posted to the 8th Battalion, Durham Light Infantry, whose platoons we found in barns scattered about the village of Moulle, near St. Omer. From the distance came the dull boomings of the guns which we heard now for the first time and wondered when we would be among them.

I had read in the newspapers about Passchendaele Ridge and, after a few days at Moulle, that was where we went.

* * *

The "front line" is really an elongated shell-hole. In the enormous darkness of the cold quiet night the noise of a solitary exploded shell echoes like the bang of a door in a baronial giant's deserted gloomy hall. In front, on top, in the distance, the faint "pop" of a Very light sounds from the German lines. This light, attached to a little silken parachute, ascends, irradiating with whiteness an expanding circular space on the ground. In its extending radiance which is creeping and revealing, short tree trunks and branches, bare, black, broken, on what was once a road, are like bony old women's arms stretched out to heaven in silent imprecation. Against the penumbra, is some barbed wire. Hanging on it are effigies, awry and mute, reminding me of the grotesque figures carried round London streets on November the 5th to the shouts from little boys of "Guy! Guy! Guy!" Here and there the ground bulges into a head; booted feet; khaki-covered arms. A man is lying on his back with his knees up and his arms outstretched as though lazily reclining in a field while on leave in the heat of a summer day....

The little silken parachute having come slowly down, the light sputters in a small radius of incandescence on the ground then vanishes. The darkness blacks out the sight of my eyes so that I am blind in the night. Rain commences to patter metallically-sounding on my steel helmet. I am the sentry, and alone. The other fellows are in their holes, one of them muttering uneasily in his cold damp huddled sleep. I wish one of them would wake up and come out. It is about 3 o'clock. I have been here since midnight. The plaintive buzzing "ping" of a bullet sounds overhead. The rain continues to drizzle. The explosion of a distant shell sounds like a gentle tap on a gong ... the thin circles of echo slowly ebb away.

* * *

IT is Chrismas Eve, the last Christmas Eve of the war. The earth is covered with a thick frost. The darkness echoes with the staccato sounds of a distant machine-gun. Through the air the spate of bullets speeds—swish! ping ping ping ping! .... We wait for the East Yorks to relieve us. We wear sheep-skins or leather jerkins over our overcoats. Instead of puttees we have sandbags round our legs untidily. We wait fearfully, "nervily," stamping on the ground and banging together our gloved hands. Our gloves are without fingers, they are of rough white leather and are attached to a long white tape which hangs round our necks and over our shoulders. In the darkness the lighted ends of our cigarettes glow.

"The pass-word is Thistle, pass it on."
"The pass-word is Thistle, pass it on." This sentence is repeated until it fades out of hearing.

"I wouldn't like to be the East Yorks tonight."

"No: yaw right. I wish they'd 'urry up any 'ow."

Hoarsely a young officer says, "Less noise you fellows. Stop shouting and banging about!"

"Windy," murmurs a corporal.

All is still. We are strained with anxiety lest a sudden bombardment should endanger our exit. We wonder fearfully if the silence is evilly ominous. We speak in whispers.

"Halt! Who goes there?" The silence suddenly seems to be, as it were, alert and waiting.

"DETAILS," RETURNED FROM LEAVE, HALTING ON THEIR WAY TO REJOIN THEIR BATTALION IN THE LINE.

"Friends—Thistle."

"Pass friends."

Two short silhouettes whose rifle muzzles stick up from their shoulders jump into our trench, onto the firestep, by the sentry.

"Who are *they*?" whispers a young fellow new to the Company.

"Battalion runners. What cheer, 'Arry."

The runner so addressed, a Durham miner, peers into the face of the man who hails him whisperingly, "We's that? W'y yer beggar o' Hell, it's ard Bwoonie (old Brownie). "War ye gannin on kidder?" (How are you going on? . . .) "As thah jist coom oot agen mun?"

"Yes. Come out with a rush."

"Aye. Thah nahs ard Billy Kelly ye used ter knock aboot wi'? He's jist ketched a nice blighty. 'E went down the dinkie lasst neet."

"'E always *was* jammy."

"Ahl see ye w'en ye cum oot kidder. Ahve got ter find the skipporr."

"Righto 'Arry. 'E's up the end there. I'll see you when we come out."

"W'y aye mun." And he gropes his way along with his companion runner following. . . .

There are muffled sounds of voices in the rear: the relief party has arrived. We stamp on our cigarettes.

We file out, and on top, in the black starless night, pass the sweating reliefs who trudge into the trench with bowed heads, in silence.—What a place on Christmas Eve! Some of our lads looking back call out, "Good luck, Yorks!"

One voice from the doomed-looking reliefs—as though it were the quintessence of the universal human spirit attenuated and dwindled by weariness in the war until it is extant only in one human soul; as though preserving itself from extinction by proclaiming itself into vigorous life—replies into the silent dark vast void, with an only word seeming lone in the universe, "Cheero!"

SIDNEY G. KNOTT.

Correspondence

47, Corona Avenue,
Hollins, Oldham.
17th November, 1933.

To the Secretary, Ypres League.

Dear Sir,

I am interested in the Ypres Salient. I am now sixteen years of age, and was but four months old when my father was killed in that horrible calamity of 1914-18. He was Gunner Charles Goble of the R.G.A. and fell in action at Ypres in 1917.

I shall be glad to receive particulars of the League.

Yours truly,
HARRY G. GOBLE.

7, Waterloo Road,
New Brighton.
4/11/1933.

To the Committee, Ypres League.

Dear Sir,

I am rather concerned about the depleted funds available for the continuance each quarter of our little journal, and should like you to consider my suggestion of making a charge to members of the Ypres League of sixpence per copy for THE YPRES TIMES, but if you think this is asking too much of the members' generosity, I think we might as well say threepence per copy—one shilling per annum which is a fair enough compromise.

I myself am taking the law into my own hands, Committee or no Committee, and shall start sending sixpence per quarter commencing with the next January, 1934, issue, in the meantime I enclose ten shilling which pays for the last five years' editions I have received.

The quarterly YPRES TIMES is the only link we distant and scattered members of the League have, and publication regularly is most essential to all of us. It is worth a penny a month I am sure.

We must get down to business in matters like this, and the journal cannot be published and kept going by the aid of voluntary contributions for long. It is too haphazard and I feel sure that most of our members would prefer to fall in with my suggestion rather than risk losing this link with our memorious past.

Let us all face up to the position and settle the matter in the next issue of THE YPRES TIMES. If difficulties have arisen, we members of the Ypres League would, I am certain, welcome the opportunity of overcoming these obstacles in the only sensible manner possible.

If shot and shell failed to overwhelm us in those distant days surely a few coppers won't do it now.

Let our New Year's resolution therefore be: Threepence per copy in future.

Very best regards,
Yours faithfully,
E. F. WILLIAMS.

The Committee of the Ypres League have written to express their grateful thanks to Mr. E. F. Williams for his keen interest and loyal support of THE YPRES TIMES, and publish the above letter with a view to bringing his proposition before all its members.

The Committee respectfully asks those who desire to conform with Mr. Williams' suggested New Year's resolution, or have any further suggestions, to be so kind as to communicate with the Secretary, Ypres League, 20, Orchard St., London, W.1.

> Modesty almost prevented the following eulogy from inclusion in the columns of this journal, but in view of the contributor's expressed wishes it has been decided to accede to the request.

16th November, 1933.

My dear Secretary,

I recently had great pleasure to make my initial visit to your headquarters since becoming a member of the League some years back, and I am really glad to have done so, and it gave me great pleasure to walk straight into the General Secretary's office without any of the formalities so noticeable with similar organisations which was a very pleasing surprise.

I enjoyed a most interesting hour's chat, and had I known one would be so eagerly and charmingly welcomed I am afraid I should have been guilty, hitherto, of encroaching on many hours of your precious time.

Such circumstances are distinctly encouraging to members, and knowing as I do now, that so fine a fellowship exists at the League's headquarters, I feel honoured to be one of its members and sincerely hope that our Association will be in a position to continue its splendid work for many years.

I am rather ashamed to think that I have done so little to further the good cause, even among my own friends but I assure you this state of things will be speedily rectified.

To a great number of people, one is considered old-fashioned now-a-days to talk of the Great War except on Armistice Day. Why? I can never understand, because those years '14-'18 with all their attendant horrors and sacrifices from which sprang so fine a comradeship among men is to me a very cherished memory. Together with so many more youngsters who withstood mankind's greatest test of courage and endurance at such a tender and certainly very impressionable age, it is not to be wondered that so long as we retain our faculty of mind, war-time reminiscences will always remain a part of conversation when ever our type foregather. I am never happier than when I run across an old ex-Tommy. Would not the world to-day be better off for more of that spirit of comradeship which we once knew and enjoyed, and which now forms so prominent a part in the Ypres League's aims and objects? and to belong to an organisation where this spirit is so splendidly inspired is indeed gratifying and encouraging to its members.

It is most interesting to me to have found out that yourself and your assistant Secretary have, between you, served on five separate battle fronts during the Great War—rather a unique record, and I should imagine that this acquaintance with actual facts does much to instil confidence in the people who visit you from various parts of the world.

I am afraid my little appreciation has become lengthy, but before its closure, may I specially ask that my remarks be brought to the notice of my fellow members, because I feel that others, apart from receiving the regular issue of THE YPRES TIMES may be blissfully ignorant of the wonderful work and spirit behind the League movement. The realisation of such facts will I am sure greatly assist in retaining the complete confidence of members and equally urge them to double their good efforts on the League's behalf.

Thanking you for the courtesy so generously extended to me and assuring you of my loyal support at all time.

Very sincerely yours,
W.P.T. (Mansfield).

Annual Re-union Smoking Concert

THE month of October stands out in the memory of everyone associated with Ypres more than any other month of the year, for was it not really the most momentous month in each of the years of the War? Nineteen years ago, on the 3rd October, 1914, the Germans occupied Ypres. It is true they were not permitted to remain for long, but it was not until October four years later that they were forced from its immediate vicinities. October thus saw the beginning and end of the mighty Teutonic endeavours to force the Salient. What of the intervening years? In October 1917 began both the First and Second Battles of Passchendaele. Three years earlier in October 1914 the battles of Messines, Langemarck, and Gheluvelt began. This historical summary may seem somewhat irrelevant appearing under the heading above, but it is necessary to emphasize the importance the month of October holds for every member of the Ypres League. It is therefore obviously appropriate that the Annual Reunion of Members and their friends should be held in October; in fact, as near as ever possible to the most important day of all—Ypres Day—the 31st October.

Last October was the occasion of the Eleventh Annual Reunion and Smoking Concert which was held on Saturday, the 28th, at the Caxton Hall, Westminster, and a really most enjoyable evening was spent by everyone. The function was an immense success and very well attended, despite the inclemency of the weather. A wet evening is now accepted as a permanent feature of these Reunions, but once inside Caxton Hall, good cheer waits! The Chair was taken by Major E. Montague Jones, O.B.E., the Chairman of the London County Committee, and the following distinguished guests were present:—

His Excellency The Belgian Ambassador; Général-Major A. Nyssens (Military Attaché Belgian Embassy); Général de Brigade R. Voruz (Military Attaché French Embassy); Colonel Cortlandt Parker (Military Attaché American Embassy); Lieut.-Gen. Sir W. P. Pulteney, G.C.V.O., K.C.B., K.C.M.G., D.S.O.; The Rev. G. H. Woolley, V.C., M.C., and Major W. H. Brooke, M.C.

During the evening the following messages were received by the Chairman:—

"The King as Patron-in-Chief of the Ypres League has received with much pleasure the loyal message sent from the Annual Reunion of the London Branch, and will be glad if you will convey to all who are present the expression of His Majesty's sincere thanks."
PRIVATE SECRETARY.

"This is an evening of remembrance and reunion, and since to my regret, I am unable to be with you, will you express to the members of the Ypres League the friendly sentiments of comradeship and admiration that the American people have for the comrades in arms.
ROBERT W. BINGHAM,
American Ambassador."

Major Montague Jones, in a short speech, referred to the activities and progress of the League during the past year, and warmly thanked Captain G. E. de Trafford, M.C., the worthy League Secretary, for all his hard work and continued enthusiasm, and also Mr. John Boughey for his never-ending activities as the Hon. Secretary of the London County Committee. Lieut.-Gen. Sir W. P. Pulteney followed by telling the company about the British School at Ypres, and explaining what a valuable institution it had now become.

A splendid entertainment was provided by a number of well known artistes under the direction of Mr. A. E. Nickolds, who, himself, held the audience under the spell of his banjo. The other artistes were Miss Pearl Joyce, Contralto, Mr. Wilfred Lewe, Humorous, Miss Suzette Tarri in Comedy Impressions, Mr. David Jenkins, Bass, Mr. Paul Freeman, the King of Cards, Miss Helena Millais in "Fragments from Life." Earlier in the evening, and during the Interval, a number of musical selections were rendered by "The Enfield College of Music Orchestra" under the kind and able direction of Mrs. Doris Lee Peabody, and this innovation was much appreciated. The evening closed towards 11 p.m. to the resounding echoes of the inevitable community singing of old war-time choruses, without which these Reunions would not be complete. Altogether, an evening to be remembered, and one upon which to resolve, by all possible means, to attend the next.

The excellent programme was organised by Captain H. D. Peabody, D.C.M., of the London County Committee, who is to be heartily congratulated on mustering such a splendid array of talent.

It is fifteen to nineteen years since the events mentioned at the beginning of this report. Far too long a period in a man's life not to be noticeable, but long enough to thoroughly test that wonderful spirit of Comradeship which is a legacy from those now far off days. For proof that this spirit has most certainly survived the ordeal of years, it is only necessary to attend these Annual Reunions to realize that out of the Comradeship of the War has been born a lasting friendship to help us through the difficult days of Peace.

League Secretary's Notes

IT would greatly facilitate the work at headquarters and at the same time avoid unnecessary trouble and expense, if members changing their addresses would be so good as to notify head office as early as possible of such change, because it is disappointing when copies of THE YPRES TIMES and other correspondence is returned through the post marked "gone away" followed perhaps a year or two later by letters from members revealing their new addresses and enquiring if the YPRES TIMES is still in publication, in which case might they have the back numbers? We regret that it is not always possible to accede to such a request. Firstly, because in the case of annual subscribers, they have unintentionally allowed their subscriptions to lapse, and secondly, when they do eventually renew it is very probable that back editions of the journal, with the exception of an office copy, have become exhausted.

MANY members make it a practice to pay their five shillings subscriptions months, and invariably a year, after they become due.

Certainly better late than never! but it gives us no little anxiety despite the established regulation of allowing members a year and two quarters editions of the YPRES TIMES from the date of last payment due to the fact that annual payments are made in advance. At the end of the two quarter's grace, names are automatically removed from the membership register and the journal curtailed until such time as the dues are received. This unlimited lapsed period causes headquarters a considerable amount of extra clerical work and also additional postage in addressing a second and often a third reminder.

May we therefore respectfully appeal to all our staunch annual subscribers to make every possible endeavour to pay their subscriptions at some convenient time during the month in which the first reminders are received. We feel sure that members will fully appreciate this earnest appeal from a business point of view, and do all they can, from now on, to reduce the already heavy administrative work of the League, accomplished by a minimum headquarter's staff of two persons, namely, the Secretary and his faithful Assistant.

TO ALL OUR MEMBERS.

We wish all members of the Ypres League the best of good wishes for the New Year with the hope that 1934 may bring success to their personal as well as business interests.

The last quarter has been notable for the number of members who have been so kind as to submit to headquarters the names and addresses of relatives and friends possessing treasured associations with Ypres, resulting in many enrolling and whom we are delighted to welcome as members. We thank our staunch members for giving the League such admirable support.

We have no reason to be discontented with the League's work in 1933, in fact the year has proved a successful all-rounder, and special gratitude is due to our Purley, London, Colchester and Sheffield Branches. We congratulate them on their commendable work.

It has been a revelation for us to watch the astonishing progress of our youngest Branch, namely Colchester.

Space does not permit mention of all those Corresponding Members and others who have helped individually, but a word of praise is deserving to Mr. S. C. Allen-Olney, of Hove, who has again come conspicuously to the fore, not only in the promotion of the Junior Branch, but also in his successful efforts to recruit new adult members.

1934 promises to be a year of great activity. A large quantity of the revised Ypres League explanatory pamphlet has been circulated and proving its worth. We would like all members to apply to headquarters for a few of these pamphlets for the purpose of interesting prospective recruits whenever an opportunity arises.

The travel prospects for the coming year are good. We hear from outside sources that the number of persons making pilgrimages to the cemeteries and battlefields is on the decrease, but happily to relate we are unable to corroborate such a rumour in respect of the Ypres League Pilgrimage and Independent Travel, because enquiries to date are already in excess of previous years.

It is especially pleasing to report that many of our 1933 pilgrims have not only joined as members of the League, but signified their intention to travel again this year under our auspices and bring some of their relatives and friends.

May we respectfully ask all our members to add one good resolution to their list for the New Year, and that is:—

To resolve to recruit at least one new member for the Ypres League in 1934.

We earnestly trust that every member will accept our suggested resolution, because no better service can possibly be rendered to the League in its great work of Commemoration. We, at headquarters, are determined to exercise everything in our power to make the Ypres League a stronger force than ever during its fourteenth anniversary year.

We express renewed gratitude and best wishes to all our faithful supporters and look forward to enjoy their same loyal co-operation in 1934.

RECRUITING COMPETITION.

Congratulations to our Purley Branch who have won the £5 prize with a return of 45 new members for 1933, but the race between Purley and Colchester was so close that we have decided to award a very deserving second prize of £2 10s. 0d. to Colchester.

Well done these two Branches

THAT INDIVIDUAL EFFORT.

The Ypres League is fortunate in having such a loyal member in Mr. C. J. H. Cope, who has repeated his kindness of 1932 in organising, so successfully at his own expense, another lantern lecture at St. Andrew's Hall, West Kensington, on November 6th last when a collection was made in aid of the League funds.

The lecturer was Mr. Arthur E. Dawes, D.C.M., formerly of the 20th London Regiment who spoke on Comradeship during the Great War and showed us some exceedingly interesting slides of France, Salonika and Palestine.

Miss E. Booth also deserves an equal share of thanks for her kindness in lecturing at Oxford and for her generosity in organising a collection for the League funds.

Mr. Cope and Miss Booth are to be heartily congratulated on their staunch individual efforts for the welfare of the Ypres League and we owe them both a very deep debt of gratitude.

PILGRIMAGE DEPOSIT ACCOUNT.

In the last October edition of the YPRES TIMES a leaflet was inserted describing the Ypres League's new easy payment scheme for members and friends desirous of visiting cemeteries, memorials and battlefields in France and Belgium under the League's auspices.

There are already favourable signs that this scheme will prove very popular, and all those wishing to avail themselves of the facilities offered are requested to complete the form already in their possession when forwarding the initial deposit.

Headquarters will, of course, be pleased to supply additional forms if at any time required by members and friends.

As we go to Press we hear that Major General John F. O'Ryan, D.S.M., K.C.M.G., C.V.O., President of the Ypres League in the United States, has been appointed Police Commissioner of New York, and we take this opportunity to convey to the General our hearty congratulations.

RE-UNION DINNER.

A re-union dinner of the 128th Field Company Royal Engineers is to take place on April 14th, 1934, at the Leicester Corner House, Leicester Square, London, W.C.2. All members interested are invited to communicate with Mr. A. P. Winsor, 47, Avondale Road, Finchley, London, N.2.

YPRES LEAGUE TIE.

At the request of the majority of our members we have been pleased to produce the tie in better quality silk and in a darker shade of cornflower blue relieved by a narrow gold stripe. The price is 3s. 6d., post free, and all members of the League should possess one.

Applications to the Secretary, Ypres League, 20, Orchard Street, London, W.1.

We have much honour to insert in this current edition of the YPRES TIMES an article entitled "Some Stray Lines About Ypres," from the valuable pen of Mr. Stephen Graham. We would like to add that Mr. Graham wrote a special article on the last Armistice Day Parade for the "Sunday Graphic."

Madam Stiles Allen, the famous dramatic soprano, sang Captain R. Henderson-Bland's poem "Unknown Warrior" (music by Teresa del Reigo) at the Central Hall, Westminster, on Armistice night, and later in the evening at the Town Hall, Woolwich.

This poem, originally printed in "The Graphic" and a few years back sung over the radio on Armistice night by Madam Stiles Allen was reprinted in an article by Captain Bland which was published in the January, 1932 edition of THE YPRES TIMES.

YPRES LEAGUE BADGE.

The design of the badge—a lion guarding a portcullis gate—represents the British Army defending the Salient, which was the gate to the Channel Ports.

The badge, herewith reproduced, is brilliantly enamelled with silver finish. Price 2s., post free 2s. 1½d. (pin or stud, whichever is desired). Applications should be addressed to the Secretary, Ypres League, 20, Orchard Street, London, W.1.

HOTEL
Splendid & Britannique
YPRES

GRAND' PLACE   Opposite Cloth Hall.

LEADING HOTEL FOR COMFORT AND QUALITY.

COMPLETELY RENOVATED.

RUNNING WATER.   BATHROOMS.

MODERATE TERMS.   GARAGE.

Patronized by The Ypres League.

YPRES
Skindles Hotel
(Opposite the Station)

Proprietor—Life Member, Ypres League

Branch at Poperinghe
(close to Talbot House)

Branch Notes

LONDON COUNTY COMMITTEE.

Informal Gatherings.

A new session opened in September last with an impromptu programme given by members. On October 19th, we owed much gratitude to Mr. Dawes who delivered a most interesting lantern lecture on "Comradeship during the Great War," France, Salonika, and Palestine, and we trust that he may favour us with another lecture on some future date. In November our indebtedness went to Captain H. D. Peabody, D.C.M., who generously arranged to show the film "The Battle of the Somme," which was followed keenly by the ex-service members. On December 21st, we mustered a record attendance and thoroughly enjoyed a thrilling programme of splendid variety provided by Mr. Mears of headquarters. All the artistes deserved the highest praise. We extend our grateful thanks to Mr. Mears and hope that he will see his way to arrange another entertainment for us next year. During the evening, a competition resulted in two lucky persons present taking away with them a turkey each which we trust they enjoyed, and another lucky recipient was reminded of his army days by winning a tin of bully beef and two extra thick army biscuits.

We regret the temporary absence from the Informals of our friends, Captain Alliston and Mr. Thrussell who have been in ill health, but we wish them both a speedy recovery.

The forthcoming fixtures will be found on this page, and we look forward to wholehearted support from our members and friends so as to ensure the continuance of these record attendances.

Please book these dates in your Diary.

THE MONTHLY
Informal Gatherings
FOR JANUARY, FEBRUARY, MARCH AND APRIL

WILL BE HELD AT

THE BEDFORD HEAD HOTEL, MAIDEN LANE, STRAND, W.C.2.

ON

THURSDAY, 18TH JANUARY, 1934.
Illustrated Talk on 'The Navy at Gallipoli," by Commander H. M. Denny, D.S.O.

THURSDAY, 15TH FEBRUARY, 1934.
Programme by the St. Dunstan's Concert Party.

THURSDAY, 15TH MARCH, 1934.
Illustrated Talk by Captain H. D. Peabody, D.C.M.

THURSDAY, 19TH APRIL, 1934.
Programme by the "85th Club."

FROM 7.15 P.M. TO 10 P.M.

Start the year 1934 well by paying us a visit at our Gathering on Thursday, 18th January, 1934. A very hearty welcome awaits you and any ex-Service friend whom you may wish to bring along.

Full particulars of the Gatherings will be sent by the Hon. Secretary, London County Committee, to a friend on receipt of name and address.

Ladies are cordially invited.

THE TENTH ANNUAL
Children's Christmas Party
ORGANIZED BY THE
LONDON COUNTY COMMITTEE
WILL TAKE PLACE AT THE
WESTMINSTER CITY SCHOOL
55, PALACE ST., VICTORIA ST., S.W.1
(By permission of the Governors of the School)

On SATURDAY, JANUARY 13TH, 1934,
AT 4 P.M.

Admission:
Junior Division Members, Free. Friends, 6d. each.

Application for tickets should be made to the Hon. Secretary, London County Committee, Ypres League, at 20, Orchard Street, W.1., not later than January 11th, 1934.

A Christmas Tree will again be provided. Gifts of Toys or Donations will be very gratefully received, and should be sent to The Hon. Secretary, London County Committee, at 20, Orchard Street, London, W.1.

Tea commences at 4 p.m., followed by a ventriloquist entertainment.

To some children, this is the only treat enjoyed during the festive season, and it is hoped that members will do all they can to give us their support and make this annual event a great success. There will be a Christmas Tree, and Father Christmas will appear during the evening. Gifts of toys and donations, for which we earnestly appeal, will be received very gratefully by the Hon. Secretary, London County Committee, Ypres League, 20, Orchard Street, W.1. We are very pleased to announce that the Enfield Children's Orchestra under the personal direction of Mrs. Lea Peabody, have kindly promised to come and give selections during the evening.

* * * * *

FIRST ANNUAL BALL OF THE COLCHESTER & DISTRICT BRANCH.

COLCHESTER & DISTRICT BRANCH.

The 1st Annual Ball organised by the Colchester and District Branch was held at the Red Lion Hotel, Colchester, on November 15th. The function was a great success and 150 were present. Among those who brought parties were:— The Chairman, Colonel H. W. Herring, M.C., Major G. C. Benham, M.C., Mr. Gerald Stanford, Captain M. Leach, M.C., and Captain C. P. Thomas.

The dance band of the 4th Queen's Own Hussars provided the music for the dancing, which was kept going until 2 a.m.

Everyone present accorded the Ball as one of the best held in the town recently, so it is hoped that next year even a more successful function will be held.

A special vote of thanks is due to Captain C. P. Thomas, Hon. Secretary of the Ball Committee, and to Mr. M. McKinley for their indefatigable work in making the event such a financial success for the Branch.

Whist Drive.

The Colchester Branch held a very successful whist drive at Jacklin's Café, on November 23rd. There were 88 players at this initial drive in the history of the Branch and the awards were presented to the winners by Mrs. Herring, wife of Colonel Herring, the Chairman of the Branch:— Ladies: 1, Mrs. Howe, 190; 2, Mrs. Lassam, 179; 3, Mrs. Wilkinson, 178; highest half, Mrs. Broom, 98; lowest score, Miss Farrell, 136; lucky competitions, Mrs. T. Richer and Mrs. Bunting. Gentlemen: 1, Mr. F. Wright, 176; 2, Mrs. Snow (playing as a gentleman), 171, after cutting; 3, Mr. Portway, 171; highest half, Mr. Kirkham, 89; lowest score, Mr. Whittaker, 134. There were generous prize-donors. Captain A. C. Palmer was the M.C., and those assisting were Captain C. Rooney, M.C., Captain Leighton and the Branch Hon. Secretary, Mr. Hubert Snow.

PURLEY BRANCH.

The Autumn Golf Meeting took place on Wednesday, October 4th, at Purley Downs Golf Club, when the members competed for the Sixth Wipers Cup, kindly presented by Captain B. A. Forster.

It was a beautiful afternoon when Bombardier E. A. R. Burden and his partner led off at 2 p.m. Fairly rapid fire was kept up from them until 4 p.m., when the 29th and last competitor went off.

The Competition was against Bogey, and Bombdr. Burden (handicap 4) with a return of one-up and a very consistent round won the prize, and a very popular win it was. Pte. E. S. Butt (handicap 2) and Lieut. J. V. Lindsay (handicap 9) with a return of "all square" tied second.

The supper which followed at the Club House was the usual cheery affair and after the presentation of prizes, the winner and the two seconds were called on in turn to explain how it was done. After which the two members who failed to put in their cards were called on for the same thing and satisfied the gathering somehow!

A great many stories were told before the party finally dispersed in high spirits and vowing that there always should be an Autumn Meeting in future.

Memorial Service.

A contingent of 42 members from the Purley Branch attended the Memorial Service held at St. Mark's Church, Purley, on Sunday, November 5th.

The organizers of the service were kind enough to reserve for us accommodation and gave us the privilege of leaving the Church before the general public this year. There was a good congregation and we were treated to a very fine service by the Rev. L. Artingstall.

SHEFFIELD AND DISTRICT BRANCH.

Ten thousand poppy leaves fell from the roof of the Sheffield City Hall on Saturday night, the 11th November, each leaf representing a Sheffield life given in the Great War.

A large Union Jack was hoisted above the platform. A cross, on which hung Flanders poppies, was raised in front, and a white projection light was focussed in front of it. From behind the Union Jack came the solemn tones of the organ playing Mackenzie's "Benedictus."

This was an act of devotion at a Festival of Remembrance, organised by the Sheffield and District Joint Council of Ex-Servicemen's Associations and in which the Sheffield Branch of the Ypres League and Chesterfield Members took part.

The festival began in thought, inspired by one minute's silence. Then, while Regimental marches were played, standard bearers proceeded to the platform followed by representatives of all the Associations concerned.

The Bishop of Sheffield delivered a simple prayer, the Band, each member of which was dressed to represent a different unit, played a Military overture, and Lieut.-General C. P. Deedes (Col. Commandant, King's Own Yorkshire Light Infantry) followed with an address.

After the singing of Ketelby's "Sanctury of the Heart" by Miss Gladys Havenhand, with the band and organ, War-time choruses were taken up with zest by the audience.

The Toc H Lamp of Maintenance was lighted by the Bishop, then a brief silence was shattered by the roll of drums and the "Last Post," the "Reveille" and finally, "Abide with Me."

This was Sheffield's devotion to memory.

In conclusion the writer wishes to thank those of our Members who so kindly supported him on the platform, and trusts that if a similar Festival is arranged next year, that he may rely on their co-operation again.

(P.S.—Someone was terribly "flat" on the writer's left, during the singing of the Choruses, and any efforts taken to rectify this nuisance pending next year's efforts will be greatly appreciated.)

JACK WILKINSON (Capt.).

THE BRITISH TOURING SERVICE

Manager—Mr. P. VYNER

Representative and Life Member, Ypres League

**10, Station Square
ARRAS
(P.-de-C.) France**

Cars for Hire, with British Driver Guides — Tours Arranged

Branches and Corresponding Members

BRANCHES.

LONDON	Hon. Secretary to the London County Committee : J. Boughey 20, Orchard Street, London, W.1.
	E. LONDON DISTRICT—L. A. Weller, 132, Maxey Road, Dagenham, Essex.
	TOTTENHAM AND EDMONTON DISTRICT—E. Glover, 191, Lansdowne Road, Tottenham, N.17.
	H. Carey, 373, Sydenham Road, S.E.26.
COLCHESTER	H. Snow (Hon. Sec.), 9, Church Street (North).
	W. H. Taylor (Pilgrimage Hon. Sec.), 64, High Street.
GATESHEAD	Lieut.-Colonel E. G. Crouch, 8, Ashgrove Terrace.
LIVERPOOL	Captain A. M. Webster, Blundellsands.
PURLEY	Major Graham Carr, D.S.O., M.C., 112-114, High Street.
SHEFFIELD	Captain J. Wilkinson, "Holmfield," Bents Drive.
BELGIUM	Capt. P. D. Parminter, 19, Rue Surmont de Volsberghe, Ypres.
CANADA	Ed. Kingsland, P.O. Box 83, Magog, Quebec.
SOUTH AFRICA	L. G. Shuter, Church Street, Pietermaritzburg.
AMERICA	Representative : Captain R. Henderson-Bland, 110 West 57th Street, New York City.

CORRESPONDING MEMBERS

GREAT BRITAIN.

ABERYSTWYTH	T. O. Thomas, 5, Smithfield Road.
ASHTON-UNDER-LYNE	G. D. Stuart, "Woodlands,", Thronfield Grove, Arundel Street.
BANBURY	Captain C. W. Fowke, Yew Tree House, King's Sutton.
BIRMINGHAM	Mrs. Hill, 191, Cattell Road, Small Heath.
	John Burman, "Westbrook," Solihull Road, Shirley.
BOURNEMOUTH	H. L. Pasmore, 40, Morley Road, Boscombe Park.
BRISTOL	W. S. Hook, "Stoneleigh," Cotham Park.
BROADSTAIRS	C. E. King, 6, Norman Road, St. Peters, Broadstairs.
	Mrs. Briggs, North Foreland House.
CHATHAM	W. N. Channon, 22, Keyes Avenue.
CHESTERFIELD	Major A. W. Shea, 14, Cross Street.
CONGLETON	Mr. H. Dart, 61, The Crescent.
DARLINGTON	D. S. Vigo, 125, Dorset Road, Bexhill-on-Sea.
DERBY	T. Jakeman, 10, Graham Street.
DORRINGTON (Salop)	Captain G. D. S. Parker, Frodesley Rectory.
EXETER	Captain E. Jenkin, 25, Queen Street.
GLOUCESTER	H. R. Hunt, "Casita," Parton Lane, Churchdown.
HERNE BAY	Captain E. Clarke Williams, F.S.A.A., "Conway," Station Road.
HOVE	Captain G. W. J. Cole, 2, Westbourne Terrace, Kingsway.
LEICESTER	W. C. Dunford, 343, Aylestone Road.
LINCOLN	E. Swaine, 79, West Parade.
LLANWRST	A. C. Tomlinson, M.A., Bod Estyn.
LOUGHTON	Capt. O. G. Johnson, M.A., Loughton School.
MATLOCK (Derby)	Miss Dickinson, Beechwood.
MELROSE	Mrs. Lindesay Kelsall, Huntlyburn.
NEW BRIGHTON (Chesire)	E. F. Williams, 5, Waterloo Road.
NEW MILTON	W. H. Lunn, "Greycot," Albert Road.

NOTTINGHAM	... E. V. Brown, 3, Eldon Chambers, Wheeler Gate.
ST. HELENS (Lancs.)	... John Orford, 124, Knowsley Road.
SHREWSBURY ...	... Major-General Sir John Headlam, K.B.E., C.B., D.S.O., Cruck Meole House, Hanwood.
TIVERTON (Devon)	... Mr. W H. Duncan Arthur, Surveyor's Office, Town Hall.
WELSHPOOL ...	... Mr. E. Wilson, Coedway, Ford, Salop.

DOMINIONS AND FOREIGN COUNTRIES.

AUSTRALIA	... Messrs. C. H. Green, and George Lawson, Anzac House, Elizabeth Street, Brisbane, Queensland. R. A. Baldwin, c/o Government Savings Bank of N.S.W., Martin Place Sydney. Mr. W. Cloves, Box 1296, G.P.O., Adelaide.
BELGIUM	... Sister Marguerite, Sacré Coeur, Ypres.
BUENOS AYRES ...	... President, British Ex-Service Club, Calle 25 de Mayo 577.
CANADA	.. Brig.-General V. W. Odlum, C.B., C.M.G., D.S.O., 2530, Point Grey Road, Vancouver. V. A. Bowes, 326, 40th Avenue West. Calgary, Alberta. W. Constable F. Grece, 4095, Tupper Street, Westmount, Montreal
CEYLON	... Captain F. R. G. Webb, M.C., Irrigation Bungalow, Kalmunai, E.P
EGYPT	... L. B. S. Larkins, The Residency, Cairo.
INDIA	... Lieut.-Quartermaster G. Smith, Queen's Bays. Sialkot, India.
IRELAND	... Miss A. K. Jackson, Cloneyhurke House, Portarlington.
KENYA	... Harry Sheilds, Survey Department, Nairobi. Corporal C. H. Slater, P.O. Box 403, Nairobi.
NEW ZEALAND ...	... Captain W. U. Gibb, Ava Lodge, Puhinui Road, Papatoetoe, Auckland. S. E. Beattie, Lowlands, Woodville.
SOUTH AFRICA ...	... H. L. Versfield, c/o Cape Explosives Works Ltd., 150, St. Georges Street, Cape Town.
SPAIN	... Captain P. W. Burgess, Calle de Zurbano 29, Madrid.
U.S.A.	... Captain Henry Maslin, 942, President Street, Brooklyn, New York L. E. P. Foot. 20, Gillett Street, Hartford, Conn, U.S.A. A. P. Forward. 449, East 80th Street, New York. J. W. Freebody. 945, McBride Avenue, Los Angeles.
NOVA SCOTIA ...	... Will R. Bird, Amherst.

Membership of the League

This is open to all who served in the Salient, and to all those whose relatives or friends died there, in order that they may have a record of that service for themselves and their descendants, and belong to the comradeship of men and women who understand and remember all that Ypres meant in suffering and endurance.

Life membership, £2 10s.

Annual members, 5s.

Do not let the fact of your not having served in the Salient deter you from joining the Ypres League. Those who have neither fought in the Salient nor lost relatives there, but who are in sympathy with the objects of the Ypres League, are admitted to its fellowship, but are not given scroll certificates.

There is a Junior Division for children whose relatives served in the Salient. It is open also to others to whom our objects appeal.

Annual subscription 1s. up to the age of 18, after which they can become ordinary members of the League.

THE YPRES LEAGUE (INCORPORATED)
20, Orchard Street, Portman Square, W.1.

Telephone: WELBECK 1446.   *Telegrams*: YPRESLEAG, "WESDO," LONDON.

Patron-in-Chief: H.M. THE KING.

Patrons:
H.R.H. THE PRINCE OF WALES.   H.R.H. PRINCESS BEATRICE.

President: GENERAL SIR CHARLES H. HARINGTON.

Vice-Presidents:
F.-M. VISCOUNT ALLENBY.
F.-M. SIR CLAUD JACOB.   THE LORD WAKEFIELD OF HYTHE.
F.-M. SIR PHILIP CHETWODE.   LIEUT.-GENERAL SIR CECIL ROMER.

General Committee:

THE COUNTESS OF ALBEMARLE.
MAJOR J. R. AINSWORTH-DAVIS.
*CAPTAIN C. ALLISTON.
LIEUT-COLONEL BECKLES WILLSON.
*MR. J. BOUGHEY.
*MISS B. BRICE-MILLER.
COLONEL G. T. BRIERLEY.
CAPTAIN P. W. BURGESS.
*MAJOR H. CARDINAL-HARFORD.
REV. P. B. CLAYTON.
*THE EARL OF YPRES.
MRS. C. J. EDWARDS.
MAJOR C. J. EDWARDS.
MR. H. A. T. FAIRBANK.
MR. T. ROSS FURNER.
SIR PHILIP GIBBS.
MR. E. GLOVER.
MAJOR C. E. GODDARD.
MAJOR-GENERAL SIR JOHN HEADLAM.
MR. F. D. BANKS HILL.

MAJOR-GENERAL C. J. B. HAY.
MR. J. HETHERINGTON.
MRS. E. HEAP.
GENERAL SIR W. C. G. HENEKER.
CAPTAIN O. G. JOHNSON.
*MAJOR E. MONTAGUE JONES.
CAPTAIN H. D. PEABODY.
*THE HON. ALICE DOUGLAS PENNANT.
*LIEUT.-GENERAL SIR W. P. PULTENEY.
LIEUT.-COLONEL SIR J. MURRAY.
*COLONEL G. E. C. RASCH.
VISCOUNT SANDON.
THE HON. SIR ARTHUR STANLEY.
MR. ERNEST THOMPSON.
CAPTAIN J. LOCKLEY TURNER.
*LIEUT.-GENERAL SIR H. UNIACKE.
*MR. E. B. WAGGETT.
CAPTAIN J. WILKINSON.
CAPTAIN H. TREVOR WILLIAMS.

* Executive Committee.

Bankers:
BARCLAYS BANK LTD., Knightsbridge Branch.

Honorary Solicitors:
MESSRS. FLADGATE & CO., 18, Pall Mall, S.W.

Secretary:
CAPTAIN G. E. DE TRAFFORD.

Auditors:
MESSRS. LEPINE & JACKSON,
6, Bond Court, E.C.4.

League Representative at Ypres:
CAPTAIN P. D. PARMINTER.
19, Rue Surmount de Volsberghe.

League Representative in America:
CAPTAIN R. HENDERSON-BLAND.
110 West 57th Street, New York.

League Representative at Amiens:
CAPTAIN STUART OSWALD.
7, Rue Porte-Paris.

League Representative at Arras:
MR. P. VYNER,
10, Station Square.

Hon. Secretary, Ypres British Settlement:
LT. COLONEL F. G. POOLE,

PRIMARY OBJECTS OF THE LEAGUE

I.—Commemoration and Comradeship.
II—.To provide special travel facilities for Members and all interested to Ypres and battlefields, and transport of Members.
III.—The furnishing of information about the Salient; marking of historic sites and the compilation of charts of the battlefields.
IV.—The erection of a Ypres British Church and School which has been completed.
V.—The establishment of groups of members throughout the world, through Branch Secretaries and Corresponding Members.
VI.—The maintenance of cordial relations with dwellers on the battlefields of Ypres
VII.—The formation of a Junior Division.

Use the Ypres League Travel Bureau for Ypres and Whole of the Western Front.

FOR THE FOLLOWING PUBLICATIONS, Etc., apply:

Secretary, YPRES LEAGUE, 20, ORCHARD STREET, LONDON, W.1.

THE BATTLE BOOK OF YPRES. A history of notable deeds contributed by all regiments. 5s.; post free, 5s 6d. Compiled by Beatrix Brice with the assistance of Lieut.-General Sir William Pulteney, G.C.V.O., etc.

BOOKS.

YPRES: Outpost of the Channel Ports. By Beatrix Brice. With Foreword by Field-Marshal Lord Plumer, G.C.B. Price 1s. 6d.; post free 1s. 10d.

In the Ypres Salient. By Lt.-Col. Beckles Willson. 1s. net; post free 1s. 2d.

To the Vanguard. By Beatrix Brice. 1s. net; post free 1s. 2d.

The City of Fear and Other Poems. By Gilbert Frankau. 3s. 6d. net; post free 3s. 8d.

With the Cornwall Territorials on the Western Front. By E. C. Matthews. 7s. 6d.; post free 8s.

Story of the 63rd Field Ambulance. By A. W. Westmore, etc. Cloth, 3s. 6d., post free. Paper, 2s. 6d., post free.

War Letters to a Wife. By Colonel Rowland Fielding. Popular Edition. 7s. 6d.; post free 8s.

The Pill Boxes of Flanders. 1s.; post free 1s. 3d.

YPRES LEAGUE TIES. 3s. 6d. each, post free.

YPRES LEAGUE BADGES. 2s. each, 2s. 1½d. post free.

EMBROIDERED BADGES. 4s. each, post free.

Map and List of Cemeteries in the Ypres Salient. Price 9d.; post free 11d.

Map of the Somme. Price 1s. 8d., post free.

PICTURES.

Burning of the Cloth Hall, 1915. A Coloured Print, 14 in. by 12 in. 1s. post free.

ENGRAVINGS, 33 in. by 21 in., £1 11s. 6d. each.

Hell Fire Corner.

Heavy Artillery Going into Action before Passchendaele.

" I Won't."

POST CARDS, PHOTOGRAPHS AND ETCHINGS.

Post Cards. Ypres: British Front during the War. Ruins of Ypres. Price 1s. post free.

Photographs of Menin Gate Unveiling. Size 11 in. by 7 in. 1s. 2d. each, post free.

Hill 60. Complete Panorama Photographs. 12 in. by 3¾ in. Price 3s., post free; 15 in. by 5 in. Price 3s. 6d., post free.

WAR-TIME PHOTOGRAPHS OF THE SALIENT.

6 in. by 8 in. ... 1s. 6d. each.
12 in. by 15 in. ... 4s. each.

List forwarded on application.

PHOTOGRAPHS OF WAR-TIME SKETCHES.

Bedford House (Front View), 1916.
Bedford House (Back View), 1916.
Voormezeele Main Street, 1916.
Voormezeele Crucifixion Gate, 1916.
Langhof Chateau, 1916.

Size 8¼ in. by 6¼ in. Price 2s. 6d. each, post free.

ETCHINGS.

Etchings of Menin Gate Memorial. 9 in. by 6 in. Price, 5s. each, post free. Signed proofs, 10s. 6d. each, post free.

YPRES TIMES.

The Journal may be obtained at the League Offices.

BACK NUMBERS 1s.; 1932, 8d.; 1933, 6d.

Printed in Great Britain for the Publishers by FORD & GILL, 21a/23, Iliffe Yard, Crampton Street, London, S.E.17.

Memory Tablet.

APRIL - MAY - JUNE

APRIL

April	5th, 1917	United States declares war on Germany.
,,	9th, 1917	Battle of Vimy Ridge begins.
,,	9th, 1918	Battle of the Lys begins.
,,	14th, 1918	General Foch appointed Generalissimo of the Allied Armies in France.
,,	22nd, 1915	Second Battle of Ypres begins. Germans use asphyxiating gases.
,,	22nd, 1918	British Naval attack on Zeebrugge and Ostend.
,,	24th, 1916	Rebellion in Ireland.
,,	25th, 1915	Allied Forces land in Gallipoli.
,,	27th, 1915	General Sir Herbert Plumer given command of all troops in the Ypres Salient.
,,	29th, 1916	Fall of Kut.

MAY

May	7th, 1915	The *Lusitania* torpedoed and sunk by the Germans.
,,	12th, 1915	Windhoek, capital of German South-West Africa captured by General Botha.
,,	19th, 1918	Germans bomb British hospitals at Etaples.
,,	23rd, 1915	Italy declares war on Austria.
,,	31st, 1916	Sea battle off the coast of Jutland.

JUNE

June	5th, 1916	Loss of Earl Kitchener on H.M.S. *Hampshire*.
,,	7th, 1915	Flight-Lieut. Warneford attacks and destroys Zeppelin between Ghent and Brussels.
,,	7th, 1917	British victory at Messines Ridge.
,,	29th, 1917	General Allenby in command in Egypt.

The Ypres Times

Communications to
The Editor, "Ypres Times,"
20, Orchard Street, London, W.1.

PRICE 6d.
POST FREE 7d.

Vol. 7, No. 2   Published Quarterly   April, 1934

Albert The Lion-Hearted
The late King of the Belgians in War and Peace

"A Very Gallant Gentleman."

(Specially contributed to the *Ypres Times*)
By Henry Benson, M.A.

THE first State visit that King Albert made, after his accession in December, 1909, was to Berlin, and few know how great was the pressure which the ex-Kaiser then brought to bear in order to conclude an alliance between Germany and Belgium. Personal friendship, family kinship and the advantages of such a compact to the smaller kingdom were urged in vain.

Then followed the historic interview between the two monarchs in November, 1913, at which General von Moltke, Chief of the German Staff, was a third party. The All-Highest told King Albert that war with France was both necessary and inevitable. Von Moltke supported his Sovereign's opinion, and declared himself certain of success. "Your Majesty must realise the irresistible eagerness with which 'the day' is being awaited by the whole German people." Then in French he added: "Cette fois il faut en finir."

Nevertheless, both the War Lord and his General had failed to form a correct estimate of the lion-hearted man with whom they were dealing. Persuasion followed by covert threats, was as raindrops on the Sphinx, and King Albert's curt reply completely annihilated further argument:—

"The independence of Belgium is guaranteed by the Great Powers, and she will expect both France and Germany to honour their signatures and respect her neutrality."

Faith in His Country's Destiny.

It was my privilege to be present in the Belgian Parliament House in Brussels on 4th of August, 1914, when King Albert, attired in the full dress of a Belgian General, made his memorable speech from the throne. Never in the world's long history has a more dignified defiance been hurled in the face of an arrogant and dastardly foe.

"Not since 1830, has a more grave hour sounded for Belgium," he declared. "Our duty is clear. We must maintain an indomitable resistance, courage and unity. This is the supreme moment for action.

"The stranger who violates our territory will find all the Belgians gathered round their Sovereign, who will never betray his constitutional oath. I have faith in our destiny. A country which takes up arms to defend itself wins the respect of all, and we cannot perish. God be with us!"

Within nineteen hours mobilisation was complete, and King Albert joined his Army, never to leave it until the Armistice in November, 1918.

"Little" Belgium.

I am afraid that people in this country are prone to see both the Sovereign of the Belgians and his nation in a false perspective. The epithet "little" trips off our tongue when we refer to Belgium, and we ignore its politics as if they were those of an English parish. In actual fact, however, it is a country of over 8,000,000 inhabitants—that is, a good deal more than Scotland and the Irish Free State put together—and they are among the most intelligent, industrious and enterprising in Europe. Moreover, in their Congo dependency they govern an empire twice the size of the Union of South Africa, and of a very much higher average fertility.

Again, above all else, Belgium has always been a country of soldiers. From the time of Julius Caesar, who found a tough proposition on "that day he overcame the Nervii" to the era of William of Hohenzollern, the Belgian soldiers have always been men to count with. Belgian neutrality never for a moment meant that her army was like that of Monaco or the Vatican—a mere Sovereign's bodyguard, accoutred and attired for purposes of parade.

The War Cloud Bursts.

The war strength in 1914 was 320,000 men, composed of twelve classes, and King Albert immediately placed himself at the head of that force. Its magnificent defence of Liége and its gallant actions at Namur were blazed throughout the world. But alas! unsupported at the time by his allies, the King was compelled to fall back before superior numbers and withdraw to Antwerp. The Belgians did not retreat easily, and disputed every inch of the way. None the less, the retreat was heart-rendering. They retired on a tranquil and smiling land, rich in the promise of harvest and the products of a long peace. As they went backwards they saw the land behind them made desolate and bare by the ravages of war—the harvest trampled under foot, houses destroyed, spires toppled to the ground, altars overturned.

The last stand before Antwerp was made about Louvain, and on 14th of August a momentary junction was made at Charleroi between the French and Belgian armies; but the French had brought up insufficient men and guns and eventually the Germans broke the connexion. King Albert was obliged to retreat into Louvain during the night of 17th of August; but, in order to avoid drawing the enemy's fire on its ancient churches, its magnificent town hall and its venerated University, he wisely decided forthwith to evacuate the city and permit the Germans to enter without opposition. For a like cause the Belgian Government withdrew from Brussels to Antwerp on the same day.

Antwerp, 1914.

The King, at the head of his Army, retired within the fortifications of Antwerp, where he joined the Queen and their children, who had taken up their residence at the palace in the Place de Meir. I am betraying no secret in stating that at the time he felt his brave soldiers had not been seconded in the manner they should have been. He thought the Allies, who praised the Belgians so much for their stubborn resistance to the Germans, should have come more speedily and in greater numbers to their aid.

The losses of his army had been immense, but once again he sallied forth from Antwerp. The Belgians retook Alost, re-occupied Malines and held strong positions about Cortenberg, between Brusseis and Louvain. For a whole week the cannonading was heard continuously night and day in the capital.

During those momentous seven days King Albert was everywhere in the Belgian lines; now by the roadside consulting with his generals; now in the trenches, with a rifle borrowed from a soldier, firing himself at the foe; and again at the

HIS LATE MAJESTY, ALBERT, KING OF THE BELGIANS

front, encouraging and directing. Still insufficient reinforcements came to him and he was forced to abandon the attack. Once again he withdrew his troops to Antwerp. The sortie, however, had won him more than he lost, for the German casualties were heavy—from between 40,000 to 50,000 killed and wounded.

Queen Elisabeth and her children moved from Antwerp to Ostend, where she busied herself with Red Cross work and attention to the soldiers' needs. She was the last to leave Ostend, and from there she joined King Albert on the Franco-

Belgian frontier, where he had already led his army to carry on the fight, side by side with the French, with the same undaunted bravery as he displayed on the Belgian plains. With him were 120,000 Belgian soldiers. By its gallant defiance and defence the Belgian Army had secured the safety of the Channel ports, had enabled the British Expeditionary Force to land in France and saved civilization.

The March to Victory.

During four weary years King Albert remained on the coastal frontier, with his headquarters on the last few miles of Belgian soil. It was in this area that trench warfare lasted longest; but in September, 1918 he began the recovery of his country with French, British and Belgian soldiers under his command. So rapid was the offensive that by mid-October British troops had entered Armentières, Douai, Lille, Roubaix and Tourcoing; whilst on 11th of November British Divisions were in Grammont, Lessines and Ath—towns that they had never known before— and in Mons!

" Peace Hath its Victories no Less Than Those of War."

It was inevitable, I suppose, that war memories of King Albert should almost monopolise the columns in the British Press of his tragic death; but it was through the wisdom of his leadership in peace no less than by the courage of his leadership in war that he earned the love of his own people and the respect of the whole world.

The Armistice found Belgium ripe for complete social disruption. Its factories had been destroyed by the Germans; its farms denuded of stock and implements; its people, after four years of blind, helpless suffering behind the enemy's lines in an acutely sensitive and psychopathic state. That all these problems and perils were so bravely and quickly surmounted was one of those fine post-war achievements which in our post-1929 pessimism we are apt to forget.

To whom was it due? To many party leaders, no doubt—to Catholics, like M. Jaspar and M. Renkin, to Socialists like M. Vandervelde, to Liberals like M. Hymans, and above all to a fund of sturdy capacity in the Belgian people. But the keystone in the whole arch was the King. Without him it would constantly have fallen to the ground. Time and again, indeed, it almost did so; but always he contrived to save the situation.

Again, his late Majesty's handling of the Flemish question was masterly in its caution. He never forfeited the confidence of either side; and only a short while ago, after everybody else had failed, he was able to bring the parties safely round one of the most dangerous corners.

Yes, King Albert was a greater man than most of us realised during the War— even greater than the measure taken by his eulogists at the time of his death. With the sole possible exception of his own grandfather, Leopold I., he was the best Constitutional Monarch who ever reigned on the Continent of Europe. Soldier and Statesmen, keenly interested in science, engineering, technology and sociology, he was at the same time an intelligent patron of art, literature and music and an enthusiastic devotee of manly sports.

Above all else he set the example of using his talents as a national trust. While he occupied the throne, every Belgian citizen knew that there was one man of extreme ability in public affairs living wholly for the nation's interests. Faction and corruption, lethargy and irresponsibility, shrank ashamed before his noble and unselfish example.

Requiescat in pace!

H. B.

The Scots Guards

By Stephen Graham,
Author of *A Private in the Guards; Ivan the Terrible; Boris Godunof*, etc.

Battle Honours:

The following honorary distinctions are borne upon each of the King's and Regimental Colours:—
"Namur, 1695," "Dettingen," "Lincelles," "Talavera," "Barrosa," "Fuentes d'Onor," "Nive," "Peninsula," "Waterloo," "Alma," "Inkerman," "Sevastopol," "Tel-el-Kebir," "Egypt, 1882," "Suakin, 1885," "Modder River," "South Africa, 1899—1902."

The Great War—3 Battalions.—"Retreat from Mons," "Marne, 1914," "Aisne, 1914," "Ypres, 1914, '17," "Langemarck, 1914," "Gheluvelt," "Nonne Bosschen," "Givenchy, 1914," "Neuve Chapelle," "Aubers," "Festubert, 1915," "Loos," "Somme, 1916, '18," "Flers-Courcelette," "Morval," "Pilckem," "Poelcappelle," "Passchendaele," "Cambrai, 1917, '18," "St. Quentin," "Albert, 1918," "Bapaume, 1918," "Arras, 1918," "Drocourt-Queant," "Hindenburg Line," "Havrincourt," "Canal du Nord," "Selle," "Sambre," "France and Flanders, 1914-18."

Uniform—Scarlet.   *Facings*—Blue.   *Pipers Tartan*—Royal Stuart.

THE redoubted regiment of Scots Guards has been little written about. As I once heard a sergeant explain, "the history of the Scots Guards has never been written, because it cannot be written." This may be partly due to the destruction of the regimental papers by fire in 1841. There the records of its early romantic history were lost, though perhaps not absolutely irretrievably. Research in Scotland and elsewhere would probably be rewarded with some most interesting stories.

Henry VIII at his accession created "The King's Bodyguard of the Honorable Corps of Gentlemen at Arms," the origin of the Guards. Charles II had "His Majesty's Own Troop of Guards," these, of course, were horse. But there were also Foot-Guards. The Scots Guards were raised and maintained in Scotland during the reign of Charles II, according to one writer, but according to another we must put the date back to 1639. Probably it was an irregular force during the Civil War and only received official status at the Restoration, and was placed on the Scottish establishment which at that time was distinct from the English.

It was originally called the Scots Guards, though called upon to change its name at two subsequent points in its history. It was originally a Highland regiment raised by the Earl of Argyle. They seem to have been employed by Charles I against the Irish rebels. Returning to Scotland they remained a royalist force and fought under Leslie at Dunbar. They suffered severe casualties but their numbers were made up and they fought against Cromwell again at the battle of Worcester where they were almost annihilated.

Early in the reign of Charles II they were placed under the command of the Earl of Linlithgow and they fought against the Covenanters at Bothwell Bridge. In 1680 they marched to London where they remained in the English service though they did not come under the English establishment until 1707 the year of the union by Act of Parliament of the two countries, England and Scotland.

In 1689 one battalion embarked for the Netherlands under Marlborough and was engaged in action the same year, and in the next at the battle of Fleurus. In 1691, at the seige of Mons, the rank of lieutenant-colonel was first granted to its captains by William of Orange. In the following years the Scots Guards took part in the battles of Steenkirk and Landen. In 1694 it was quartered at Bruges. In the next year, 1695, it distinguished itself highly at the seige of Namur it advanced without firing a shot exposed to a murderous fire of the enemy behind the town's ramparts. Displaying great steadiness under fire they drew close to the palisades where they poured volley after volley into the ranks of panic-stricken defenders."

There appear to have been two battalions of the Scots Guards from the earliest period of their history. One had been sent to the wars in 1689 and the other followed subsequently. In 1696 one was sent home on the news of a threatened French invasion. But it re-embarked the following year and rejoined the main army in Brabant.

They returned for a while to Scotland during the reign of Queen Anne, but with the failure of the Stuart dynasty they remained in the English service, loyal soldiers of the Hanoverian George I. They took no part in the " Bonny Prince Charlie " movements. On the other hand they distinguished themselves in the foreign wars, especially at the battle of Dettingen, and they took part also in the battle of Fontenoy. They became known as the Third Guards, the territorial designation being perhaps obnoxious to the Georges.

Some detachments of Scots Guards served against the rebellious American colonists, but I have not been able to trace where exactly they were engaged.

The regiment served in France and Spain during the war against Napoleon. It obtained new fame by a very gallant charge at the battle of Lincelles. That was in 1793. In 1799 one battalion was quartered in Holland. In 1800 one battalion was sent to Egypt and took part in the battle of Alexandria. Returning it was sent to Hanover. In 1807 it was sent to Denmark and occupied Copenhagen. The other battalion had been sent to Spain and was soon engaged under Wellington in the Peninsular War. It served in the Peninsular until July 1814 when it had to shift to meet the new menace of Napoleon. It had taken part in the capture of Madrid and of Oporto and fought ruggedly at the passage of the Douro, at Talavera, Barossa, Busaco, Fuentes d'Onor, Salamanca, the seige of Ciudad Rodrigo, the battle of Vittoria, the attack on the heights of St. Jean de Luz, the battle of the Nive, the passage of the Adour and the investment of Bayonne. The other, the 2nd battalion took part in the battle of Barossa.

In 1813 the six companies of the 2nd battalion were sent to the Netherlands, the blockade of Antwerp and the storming of Bergen-op-Zoom. The second battalion also played a distinguished part at Quatre Bras and Waterloo where it was in the second brigade of Guards under Byng. It returned home from Paris in 1816.

King William IV again changed the title of the regiment and it became the Scots Fusilier Guards (1832), and it adopted the bearskin cap. There ensued a quieter period in its history for the Napoleonic struggle had exhausted Europe and it was a generation before the powers could fight again. But when France, England and Italy combined against Russia the Scots Guards were in the army of the invasion of the Crimea and fought gallantly at Inkerman, and took great part in the sustained seige of Sevastopol.

In 1877 Queen Victoria restored to the regiment its original name, The Scots Guards, which it bears until now.

The 1st battalion was brigaded with other battalions of Guards under the command of the Duke of Connaught in the Nile Campaign, 1882-5, fighting in the battles of Hasheen and Tamai and taking part in the expedition to Suakin.

The next active service of the regiment brings us to modern times and the South African War where their chief engagement was at the battle of the Modder River. Their casualties in that battle were thought heavy at the time, something less than a hundred. The war against the Boers seems to shrink in significance when compared with the Great War with the Germans which followed it. But it was a turning point toward " modern war " when soldiers began to wear Khaki instead of the magnificent regimentals of the Crimean War, and men must seek cover and use their wits rather than move forward shoulder to shoulder in an unbroken line.

But it is not within the intended scope of this series to enumerate the exploits of regiments in the recent conflict. It will be enough to say that the Scots Guards were employed continuously throughout and enhanced their established fame, from Mons and the First Battle of Ypres to the occupation of Cologne. At first the two battalions were brigaded in separate divisions. Thus the second went out with " the immortal seventh," but later as is generally known a Guards division was formed, and the two battalions were not separated to the extent that had been witnessed in previous wars.

It will be seen that the Scots Guards have played a glorious part in their country's history and that there has not been much " scrapping " in which they did not take a part. They are popularly known as the " Jocks." They wear a Tartan ribbon. They march past to the strains of Hieland Laddie. Their pipers are among the best in the world.

S. G.

France and Flanders

BY CHARLES DOUIE (Author of *The Weary Road*).

IT was the morning of Palm Sunday, 1929. A little crowd was gathered on the pavement before the Church of St. George at Ypres. A service of dedication was in progress behind the closed doors. A psalm was dimly heard, then the low murmur of prayers. Louder came the most familiar of English hymns. The door of the Church opened, and the buglers of the York and Lancaster Regiment took up their position fronting the Church. There was silence, broken only by the rustle of the crowd baring their heads. The buglers played *The Last Post*. Ypres heard again the call which once echoed daily through the ruins. *Reveillé* followed; then *God Save the King*. The crowd resumed their hats, but two civilians, conspicuous for their old clothes among the neat and orderly Belgian crowd dressed in their Sunday best, bared their heads again and stood to attention, as the Commander of the Second Army, the defender of Ypres, appeared in the porch and answered the salute of the soldiers drawn up in the road.

The night before we had taken the train at St. Pancras for Tilbury with packs on our backs and without any plan other than that of wandering down the Western Front, revisiting villages and battlefields once familiar to us. Arriving at Ypres we had been directed to the Church of St. George. We had arrived too late to take part in the service, and indeed we would not have found room in the little church. We had perforce been content to wander round it, admiring the grace and dignity of its architecture, at once reminiscent of England and yet in harmony with the Flemish streets and houses of rebuilt Ypres. But it was good to hear the English church service in a town, which to our generation at least is for ever England, and to see again in the streets the khaki which once was the only colour.

The crowd surrounding the little church slowly dispersed. We returned to the square, and made our way to the Menin Gate. For a time we sought and found the names there inscribed of many of our friends " to whom the fortune of war denied the known and honoured burial given to their comrades in death." Then we mounted to the ramparts of Ypres and looked out on the grimmest of all battlefields. Ten years before from horizon to horizon there was nothing but desolation, a vast and noisome swamp littered with the wreckage of war, a wilderness peopled only by the unburied dead. Now farms and villages have re-appeared on their old sites, very clean and new, and unremitting toil has levelled the tormented land and re-established cultivation. Over the battlefield the lion which surmounts the arch of this splendid gateway gazes for ever across the Ypres Salient and the graves of the myriad dead. Within the hall of the gateway there is a wonderful sense of power and space and light. The dead are nobly commemorated here for all time.

We continued along the Menin Road to Hooge and Clapham Junction and so to Greenjacket Ride, so full of memories of the far-off days of First Ypres, of the ever-dwindling remnant of the Old Army barring the road to the sea, of the heroic figure of General FitzClarence, " O.C. Menin Road," the inspiration of the defence, dying in the hour of final success.

We found by the Ride the desolate remains of an old German cemetery. No more melancholy scene could be imagined than these rotting wooden crosses overgrown with rank vegetation, against the background of shell-torn woodland, in the oncoming twilight. We hurried on to Zwartelen and to Hill 60, scene of an epic stand by my regiment in the gas attack of Second Ypres. Here my greatest friend, Robin Kestell Cornish, defending the Hill with the four survivors of its garrison, won the first of many honours on the battlefield. Three years later he won the supreme honour, falling on the battlefield of Passchendaele.

Monday found us at the Ypres Railway Station, taking tickets for Moorslede. From there we climbed the hill, if so it can be called, to Passchendaele. How little a hill; how great a cost was paid for it. We passed through the rebuilt Passchendaele and turned south to Tyne Cot and its wilderness of graves, so few with a name, testimony to the conditions under which Third Ypres was fought. We pursued our way along the high ground as far as Broodseinde. On our way home by Zonnebeke and Frezenberg we passed a French cemetery. On one cross there was a crown of thorns, made of barbed wire.

Tuesday found us at Armentières, Wednesday at Loos, Thursday at Arras. Friday brought us to Albert and the battlefield of the Somme, ground very familiar to us both. On the Bapaume Road we met an old soldier. " Were you wounded here? " I asked. " No," he said, " I fell out of a train at Rouen." We continued up the road to La Boisselle and my first front-line trench, still recognisable, for it ran through the old French cemetery on the edge of the mine craters. We looked into the huge crater blown on July 1st, 1916; well I remember the carrying parties to the mines which led at last to that! Then to Ovillers, Crucifix Corner, Aveluy and Bouzincourt, and home to Albert.

Saturday was our longest day. We were in training after a week and we had need to be. How many miles we walked, I do not know, but veterans of the Somme are asked to believe that we touched Aveluy, Authuille Wood, Thiepval, Mouquet Farm, Pozières, Martinpuich, High Wood, Longueval, Delville Wood, Flers, Ginchy and Guillemont. We were prepared to walk home, but we found a railway station at Guillemont, and an evening train to Albert. We were lucky in having filled our pockets with cheese before starting out, as we were unable to get any food in the estaminets and buvettes. Fortunately we found no difficulty in getting enough to drink, especially at Pozières, where we met a party from a Lancashire Territorial Division. I took the opportunity of thanking one of the party for the great courtesy of his division which once relieved us two hours before the appointed time. The memory seemed still to rankle and at his suggestion we left the estaminet in a considerable hurry.

On the morning of Easter Sunday we were up very early, for by a perusal of a French railway guide we had discovered a means of reaching St. Quentin during the day. When in Albert in 1916 I had followed on trench maps the light railway which crossed the Bapaume Road and passed in and out of the German lines in the vicinity of Fricourt, Mametz and Carnoy, and then turned east through Bernafay and Trônes Woods to Guillemont and Peronne. Little did I think then that one day I would proudly buy a ticket from the office of the Chemin de Fer Economique et Agricole in Albert and be transported to Peronne. I have used the word *transport* advisedly, for the movement of the train had a distinct resemblance to that of a G.S. Wagon moving fast on a pavé road. But a bottle of wine from which, and the French guard from whom, we were rarely separated, consoled us. We arrived in good order at Peronne. Here we could get no food at the station, where we had a wait for a bus. But we found a gunsmith's shop in whose window was a stuffed fox encircled by twelve different patterns of shot-guns. Vive le sport.

We were bound for Cepy Farm where my regiment had been heavily engaged when the Germans retreated in March 1917. We never reached it, as at Holnon we met an old friend, the custodian of the War Graves, Corporal Butcher. The re-union lasted some hours and led to the consumption of much Amer Picon. In the afternoon we decided that a long walk would be advantageous and we covered the seven miles to St. Quentin in a straight line and without a halt.

Easter Monday was our last day. We entrained for Lille, with a view to intercepting a fast train to Calais. At Lille Station we purchased a postcard, such as we had not seen for some years. A lady in evening dress, with a tennis racket in the wrong hand, was gazing into the eyes of a French soldier in uniform. The legend ran " Apres le jeu, il faut causer; et ça finit par un baiser." We addressed it to an eminent official in Whitehall. It arrived, very late and embellished with several hundred thumb-marks.

C. O. G. D.

The Slush at Passchendaele

By Charles Smith.

ALTHOUGH I arrived in France in March, 1916, after a short stay in Egypt, I did not see service on the Ypres sector until October, 1917, where I had the most terrible time of all my war experiences.

At that time I was a Bombardier in " B " Battery of the 152nd Brigade, R.F.A. (34th Division).

We had spent the summer in the district of Caulaincourt, a beautiful wooded region where the Germans had not been able to spoil the natural surroundings, although, before his evacuation in the previous spring, the enemy had destroyed every house, bridge, and building. There was a big château in the village, at which it was said the Kaiser had made his headquarters.

Apart from the mosquitos, the district was a pleasant one to soldier in. Our Battery position was in a coppice near Vadencourt. It was a " quiet " front. Here I spent a number of nights at the Observation Post. It was a dull and monotonous job, with hardly a sound of even a rifle shot and Very lights few and far between.

It was the calm before the storm. On the 3rd of October we were relieved by a Battery from the Ypres front, and the gunners told us some lurid stories of their experiences in that sector.

We then had a few days' rest, and entraining at Peronne we arrived at Proven on the 9th of October. Here we were told of the conditions which prevailed at the guns. " They are so bad," so the story ran, " that the gunners have to be relieved every three days."

After four days in Camp at Proven, and nightly air raids, the selected gun teams, of which I was one, journeyed along the boarded tracks over the famous pontoon bridge at Boesinghe, and through the water-logged wilderness of shell-holes to a battery position near the Steenbeek, where we took over the 18-pounders of the battery we were relieving.

The conditions were really terrible, and I do not blame the gunners who were relieved for their haste in getting away from the position. They had suffered some severe losses, and the day before our arrival, had one of their guns blown up, and there it lay, a shattered wreck in a shell-hole nearly as big as a mine crater.

On the right of the position was a concrete " pill-box," in which the officers and men were herded. To get to the guns was to risk drowning in shell-holes, and nearly everywhere one moved was knee-deep in slush.

We had just made an inspection of the guns and taken a record of the registered targets, when the position was heavily shelled, and we had to scramble round the shell-holes to a place of safety, but the shells seemed to follow us. One great burst occurred just behind my sergeant and myself—about ten yards away. It sounded like a 12-inch. We dropped to mother earth, every minute expecting to receive in some part of our anatomy a relic of the German iron foundries, for splinters and mud were dropping round like rain. However, when the firing ceased, it was found that, except for a little damage to clothes and nerves, we had come through the first round with men and guns intact.

This position came in for very heavy shelling during the three days we were in occupation, and our gas drill served us in good stead. Sleep was almost out of the question, and we spent the nights in the pill-box dozing in a sitting position, with frequent gas alarms, which, while they saved many lives, added to the miseries of our existence, for to sit with gas masks on while the enemy pelted the position with gas shells is not exactly a picnic.

After three days of this we handed over the guns to another battery and then went forward with another set of guns. We came into action in some partially-made open positions along the shell-battered valley of the Broombeek. The objective for which the men in front of us were fighting was an advance in the region of Houthulst Forest, but though some progress was made the operations were frustrated by the weather.

Here our Battery did not possess a friendly pill-box or dug-out in which to shelter. During the ten days I spent at this position I was never able to have an hour's sleep or even get my feet and clothing dry. Six of us lived in a shell-hole,

Photo] [Imperial War Museum, Crown Copyright

HAULING A FIELD GUN OUT OF THE MUD ON THE PILCKEM RIDGE

our only cover being a canvas trench shelter which we have carried on the gun through the foresight of the sergeant. As the historian has recorded, " Such fighting was the last word in human misery, for the country was now one irreclaimable bog, and the occasional hours of watery sunshine had no power to dry it."

We were sustained by the thought of our duty to the men in front. I remember on one occasion standing to the guns in readiness for the S.O.S. as the Germans were expected to counter-attack. We got the call to action, and no sooner had we commenced to fire than the enemy guns began to shell our position. Not a man flinched, in fact, we were so eager to serve the guns that we had no time to think of danger. We came through the ordeal with a few minor casualties.

In this position we were firing all hours of the day and night. In between the firing we were unloading the ammunition, which was brought to the guns by pack horses. Many weary hours were spent endeavouring to keep the shells free from mud. The poor little drivers who had struggled through slush and shell-fire to feed the guns can perhaps be forgiven for occasionally unloading the shells and dropping them in the slush near the guns, but this did not lessen our labours.

The plight of the horses was pitiable. They looked at us with their big sad eyes as if to say, " Is this the best that man can do?" If such an existence as I have attempted to describe was the best that man can do it would be a black outlook for the human race.

Few of the gunners escaped without feeling the effects of the gas, and most of us were soon cawing like a flock of crows.

I came away from the guns on the 20th October, and went to the wagon line at Elverdinghe, where I soon recovered from the effects of gas, so far as my voice was concerned, but it left its imprint on my physique, and when we left the district on November 3rd, and I was given a bicycle to ride, I found this was beyond my powers, and so I followed the wagons on foot during a six days' march, in which we took the route of St. Sixte, Godewaersvelde, Calonne, Marles, Mingoval, to Boiry St. Martin, a devastated district about ten miles south of Arras.

On our way there, owing to the casualties among our horses, we could only raise four-horse teams, and all of these were badly in need of rest.

This experience changed my whole philosophy of life. I made up my mind that whatever came I could never go through a worse time and live. It was certainly a cure for " grousing."

C. S.

Albert I
KING OF THE BELGIANS.

In Memoriam

O valorous heart! If the dead acclaim
Great souls, and splendid coming in their ways
Then halls immortal shook with your fair name.
What man of all these days, or other days
Called forth a grief so sudden, and so strong
As you when bidden to the lordly throng
Of those who kept their souls in face of terrible hours?

In days of mockery who mocked this man?
Few kinder ever throned in hearts of men.
Not him to waste his breath while great hours ran—
Not him to loudly boast with voice, or pen
In some proud hour that he had saved the world;
Yet saved it was when he with pride unfurled
The oriflamme of Belgium when the hosts were hurled.

R. HENDERSON-BLAND.

On Feeling Hungry at the Front

A SURE way to enjoy a meal is to make yourself hungry for it. This may seem a trite statement, however little we act upon the advice implied. We are all the creatures of custom—and custom, said the philosopher, does make dotards of us all. Eating, to the majority, is only a habit; and how many of us ever indulge the luxury of hunger? Our meals are prepared for us at set hours, and we eat them, not because we are hungry, but because we did the same thing at the same hours the day before. One of the war's compensations was the state of hunger it conferred upon the soldier; and this condition was created, not only by the absence of sufficient food, but by the strenuous open-air life he was leading. Try to imagine, then, the edge that must have been given to his appetite, and how he must at times have sighed for a slice of the roast beef of old England. Sometimes, when on the march, I would indulge my fancies in the Barmecide manner. I saw myself arriving home on leave just as the household were sitting down to dinner, and in imagination I ate ravenously, never missing a course, and generally making a beast of myself at the table. That some of the others had similar day-dreams was demonstrated on one occasion on the road from Poperinghe to Dickebusche. We were marching at ease at which times the men were usually allowed to smoke and talk. One chap was remarking to his neighbour how easily he could dispose of a pound of steak fried with onions and potatoes. The man addressed at once rejoined that he could quickly put away three or four black puddings and two or three bottles of beer. Those of us who had listened to these savoury speculations smiled sickly; but a corporal, marching near, got so exasperated that he ordered the men to "Stop that dirty talk."

One can only surmise, in the absence of a clue to the mystery, how such an existence was sustained on the scanty fare provided. It may have been that these Spartan days had so drained the entire system of all deleterious and poisonous matter that the body, nurtured mainly on unlimited supplies of air (though not always fresh air) was able to stand up the better in its natural vigour and function healthily on a mere minimum of food.

On the other hand, I have often wondered whether the war would have been won sooner and more thoroughly if the troops could have received their meals direct from Claridge's or the Ritz. Well, I've fed at these places, and I don't think it would. The best compliment I can pay Army feeding is, that the only occasions on which I felt "off colour" were usually after receiving a parcel of food from home. Such food, as a rule did more than appease the appetite—it strangled it, and the sequel was my appearance on the sick parade.

One further remark on pure hunger. As a boy I used often to think, whilst reading of the olden wars, that if I were ever a soldier and at war, I should be too excited to want to eat. I thought of this one morning while we were being shelled out of Zillebeke and I was chewing a crust with the greatest relish.

On the whole we were better fed up the line than at the base, where the rations in quantity were deplorable. Their quality calls for no comment here. I shall mention the breakfast at Le Harve. It consisted of a measure of tea that might or might not have filled an ordinary breakfast cup. With this there was a piece of ham fat with a streak or two of red running through it, and, lastly, a bit of dry bread that weighed perhaps three or four ounces. And on that breakfast we sweated for five hours at the docks before the inner man was renewed. One evening the dinner met with more than the usual disapproval, and a disturbance threatened. One of our captains—a certain Honourable—presently appeared from the seclusion of the officers' quarters, and after making some very tactless remarks had to beat a hasty retreat as the men looked like mobbing him. I may say I have related this event from hearsay, as it did not occur in my platoon. And I am anxious to finish with the base—I hated it. Before leaving for the front a sergeant-major told us we would be better off up the line, and he never said a truer thing, despite the perils that surrounded us. If there were horrors and hardships we felt we were taking a more serious part in the war.

Ex-service men will remember something of the system of feeding and rationing, although it may have varied in different units according to circumstances. Each tent or hut or section of platoon appointed two men as orderlies for the day, these men receiving " warning " of this the previous night from their corporal. In the very early hours—say, at 3.30 a.m.—the camp orderly made his round, rousing the men, not by the blowing of the bagpipes, as at places on the home front, but by quietly projecting his head in at the door and speaking in a loud whisper lest his voice should penetrate to where enemy aircraft may have been hovering—" Corporal," he would say, " half past three—see these men get up." A " Réveillé " given in this way every morning became stereotyped and monotonous. Only, in this instance, it wasn't without a humorous aspect, as the corporal was usually about the last man to get to his feet, which prompted a wag one morning to repeat the corporal's order in the reverse way. " Men," he shouted, " half past three—see that corporal gets up."

Of course, the first to jump to the summons were the orderlies for the day—for time was short. We had to be on parade in half an hour. I am thinking now of the winter of 1917-18 spent at Dickebusch; of those dark hours of the morning groping along towards the cookhouse and stumbling back again carrying in each hand a heavy dixie to the brim with tea. Meanwhile, the other man would be slithering along in the mud, a platter of fried bacon grasped in his arms, the two of us, no doubt, looking as if we were on roller skates. A slip on the part of either would have been serious. It is the case that such a thing did occur to one man, but, by the aid of a lighted match the pieces of bacon were rescued from the soft Flanders soil. On returning to the hut that man's name was, in a very special sense, Mud.

It was then the hut orderly's job to pour the tea into the men's mess-tins ranged ready on the floor, and each man received a piece of bacon to eat with his ration of bread. The consumption of breakfast was often attended with difficulties. In the midst of it a second visit from the camp orderly was no uncommon thing. " Blow out these candles," he would say; " enemy aircraft about." And breakfast, eaten off the floor, was often finished in inky darkness. Thereafter we moved noiselessly into the open where, to more commands eerily whispered, we lined up and tiptoed off to duty like a platoon of ghosts.

In these days we were back again in camp by ten in the morning, and our principal meal was usually ready some time about midday. For this meal all the camp orderlies were paraded before the cookhouse door. " 'Shun," roared the cookhouse sergeant, " Right turn," and we were marched through an atmosphere smelling strongly of stew and out by another door lifting up as we went the appropriate dixies and platters. Despite all this ceremony, however, dinner was always less acceptable than tea. The big meal was invariably stew—and greasy at that. Occasionally it was followed by rice-pudding, with the sugar left out. At times the rice was changed for what looked like or was shaped like a roly-poly. Its main ingredient was meal, with an occasional raisin embedded in it—" Here am I, and where are you? " so to speak. On the whole it made a palatable " sweet." While dinner was being dished, we were usually brought to attention by the camp orderly, who appeared with the orderly officer for the day. Immediately on compliance it was the officer's duty to say " Any complaints? " If the answer was " None, sir," he retreated at once, feeling much relieved, no doubt; but if we had the temerity to plead there wasn't enough of this or that particular item of food, he could always prove to us how completely mistaken we were, and that there was an ample sufficiency for everyone. Then he turned away leaving us looking foolishly at one another. This "Any complaints?" stunt seemed always to be a meaningless gesture.

Later in the day the orderlies paraded for the last time for general rations, which consisted of bread, cheese, jam, and margarine, and occasionally there was an issue of tobacco and cigarettes and green envelopes. It will be remembered that letters for home enclosed in green envelopes were forwarded uncensored. The soldier sealed the envelope, but he had to sign a declaration on the cover to the effect that his letter contained no reference to the war or to his unit's whereabouts. Of course, the military reserved the right to open the envelope if they thought fit, and doubtless not all of these green-shrouded missives were delivered with the seal unbroken.

As to the distribution of the food, each section was given a tin or two of jam and a jar of margarine; and to every man two or three inches of cheese and a quarter of a loaf, or perhaps a third or, at times, even as much as half a loaf. It all depended on circumstances. Note, however, that the loaf wasn't the hefty

Photo! [Imperial War Museum, Crown Copyright
DINNER IN THE TRENCHES

fellow of the baker's window, but often a pale, attenuated lump of dough which only these thin days could provide. The man who fetched these rations sometimes had his theory of the fall in the bread ration when that occurred, say from a half loaf to a quarter. It was the German prisoners who were getting the bread intended for the British Tommy. " Boys," he would announce, as he arrived with the big box of provender on his shoulder, " there's been a huge haul of German prisoners, the bread ration's down to a quarter of a loaf to each man." And whether we believed his story or not we usually took occasion to curse those German prisoners.

As tobacco was only an occasional issue, we couldn't tell whether enemy prisoners were absorbing our supplies or not; and as for the green envelopes, we felt sure they could not be. It was also some satisfaction to know that, while the Quartermaster could say, " One loaf between two men," he couldn't say, " One green envelope between two men." It was said, however, that one envelope did on one accasion do duty for two men. The families of both were known to each other, accordingly the two communications were enclosed, and the Siamese envelope (if the expression may be allowed) was directed to the home of one of them. I cannot vouch for the truth of the story, but of course it was quite a possible arrangement.

Some men there were who never wrote home, either in green or any other colour of envelope, while others couldn't get enough of them. Accordingly a certain amount of trafficking went on in stationery. After a time a man would find himself the possessor of an accumulation of these special covers, and was ready to barter them away for a few cigarettes or perhaps a slice of bread. For the cost of a few smokes I frequently came in for some of these coveted envelopes.

But to return to food. Tea, as I have said, was the meal most enjoyed, with its cheese and Australian jelly. Of course, there was the old joke that the tea at times was so weak it couldn't run out of the dixie. But it was no joke at other times—breakfast for instance—when it tasted strange and heavy, as if it had been infused with oil as well as water; or perhaps the dregs of the previous day's stew were still in the dixie when the tea was made. After tea a long fast ensued—in fact, until next morning's breakfast—intensified by the night ration of rum, for rum, while it warmed the blood, created a great hunger. Notwithstanding, the rum parade was always looked forward to with zest. On cold winter nights it was a real life-renewer, but as I have said, its one unwelcome effect was to make us very hungry. But as we went to bed shortly after swallowing the " tot," sleep mercifully silenced the inner man.

The provisioning of the armies both at home and in the field must have been a huge task, and the story of how it was done would provide a very interesting narrative.

J. M.

"Cheeroh, Comrades!"

By F. H. Snow (Author of *No Names, No Pack-Drill*).

ONE who was not called on to endure the mud, lice and peril of Flanders trenches, begs leave, in his initial contribution to the *Ypres Times*, to speak to those that were. He speaks as an ex-R.A.M.C. corporal—not one whose duties took him even to First-Aid Post or Advanced Dressing Station, but back at Railhead, as sanitary N.C.O., in the unforgettable war years. What, then, his comrades of the Line may ask, has such a one to say to us?—what can he express of value to us whose hardships and dangers far surpassed his?

If passionate zeal to comprehend the life of which he touched the fringe, deep sympathy with those who travailed in it, could bring comprehensive sight, the writer claims that sight was his. Through all the ordeals of the Salient, with its glutinous and barbarous winter conditions, its positional disadvantages, its many crises, the writer strove to visualise and understand what his comrades were experiencing, and not permit the dimming of the picture by his own safe state.

From his comparative luxury he saw ever the tortured Front, the shell-churned, terrible mud or arid, devastated soil, the grim-eyed boys doing the job from which he was exempted.* He never forgot, and to-day, fifteen years after, appreciates still the gulf that lay between their lives and his, honours them, and cordially addresses them.

You who once kept the Line beyond the Cloth Hall, fought in the shallow ruts round Kemmel, moved on your bellies across the pitted slime at Poelcapelle, Messines, Menin—cheeroh! Some of you have done well, many not too well, a lot of you are workless, seemingly prospectless. To you latter the present must often have seemed less palatable than the Past. I have met men who said : " If my choice lay between this and that, I'd have a basin of ' that.' " Poor commendation of the time we live in, but pretty true. I am, however, convinced, despite the pronouncements of axe-grinding politicians, that a better time is near. and my desire is to communicate this optimism to Salient survivors whose faith may have suffered eclipse.

Messages of hope are cheap. Their promiscuous utterance tires those whose lane of difficulty has been long and seems to stretch forth interminably. But is not a beam perceptible in the grey sky—a lessening of the gloom that since the after-war flush has steadily deepened over us? I earnestly think so. The lightening may be slow. The pulse of business is beating stronger, as should be evident to the most prejudiced. The rise of share prices and tendency to loose money-bags in industrial and commercial enterprise, the factory-building fillip, must show that blood is pumping at the heart of things. In due course it will reach the veins and capillaries and animate local industry. It *must* come. It is on the way.

Lest it be thought the writer speaks from a comfortable height above the mud-flats of adversity, he hastens to say that his feet are hardly dry, and have been sometimes embedded since his farewell to the war and the Salient. He therefore feels qualified to counsel those who have found the mire of Peace as sticky as that round Ypres. If he did not mount the fire-step or crawl from one foul shell-hole to the next across No Man's Land, he has missed the duckboards since. But he sees dry weather ahead, a firmer footing in prospect, and ventures to express his faith.

In the rugged days out there you " stuck it " when the very bottom seemed to have fallen out of things, and life at Home, in any conditions, appeared Heaven. The soberest minds hardly foresaw the length of the inevitable slump. The Peace has tried the nation almost as severely as the War, and many of those who carried Britain on their khaki backs have been embittered by the long depression and the dark aspect of the future. Their brighter day, I believe, is soon coming.

Spring is here again. 1914—1934!

Twenty Springs ago Ypres was meaningless to us—Kemmel, St. Eloi, Poperinghe, Messines, Menin, undreamt of in our philosophy. Twenty Springs since, they are significant to us—to *you*, perhaps, I should have said—though the New has grown up over the Old, and time has somewhat dimmed their images. Our aspirations will not expunge them.

The sap is moving where wire and trench held sway—buds thrusting forth in the Salient. There and here Nature is rejuvenating. Let us also rejuvenate. Let us renew our hopes of substantial betterment for Britain and ourselves, believing our Spring at hand.

Comrades of the Line, cheeroh!

F. H. S.

* Not as an objector, but by his duties, being Pre-War enlisted,

Don't Forget the Four-Foots

By Peter Shaw Baker (Author of *Animal War Heroes*).

IT has been estimated that altogether some sixteen million animals took part in the War—a figure that will surprise many, even those who saw for themselves the endless stream of remounts plodding, day and night, up to the advance area. Official statistics reveal that over 500,000 horses and mules paid the supreme sacrifice with the British Forces alone. It is no exaggeration to say that the part played by the animals was an important factor in the ultimate vicitory of the Allied Forces. " The power of an army as a striking weapon " said the late Earl Haig in one of his final despatches, " depends on its mobility. Mobility depends largely upon the fitness and adaptability of animals for army work."

Those who bore the brunt and burden of the day will readily call to mind the way in which the dumb creatures responded to the call in the hour of need. Who is there that cannot recall a picture of a pair of those grossly libelled creatures, the mules, plodding on and on in front of a swaying general service wagon, doing work that no man-made machine could ever accomplish? It was their very stubbornness, for which they are so often maligned, that kept them going till they dropped from exhaustion, or were felled by enemy fire. And was there a single gunner in the whole British Force who did not come to love his horses, and grieve as for a comrade when they were parted from him? There were many other dumb creatures too, who did their bit uncomplainingly—dogs, pigeons, oxen, camels, elephants, mice, canaries, even reindeer. Many a man will remember pausing for a moment in the grim business of war, to glance in wonder at the lithe form of a messenger dog as it bounded along, heedless of all the chaos and confusion, intent only on its mission. And then, of course, there were the mascots; if the truth were but known, there is probably more than one man in England to-day who owes his sanity to those animal pals, whose cheerfulness no adversity or discomfort could damp.

It is one of the primary objects of the Ypres League to keep alive the wonderful spirit of comradeship that was born on the battlefields of Flanders. It will, therefore, perhaps interest members of the League to know what has become of some of those other " old comrades," members of the " silent force," whose companionship and loyalty in the time of stress, although inarticulate was none the less manifest.

Many who took part in the First Battle of Ypres will recollect how, during that critical period, Sir John French rode amongst the troops, making impromptu little speeches of encouragement, and there is no doubt the words he spoke went a long way to put new hope into many a despairing heart. It may be remembered by those to whom the words were addressed that Sir John was mounted on a handsome bay thoroughbred. This horse, Warrior by name, is now living a life of ease and contentment in the Isle of Wight. Warrior was not Sir John's own charger, but was loaned to him by Major-General Seely (now Lord Mottistone). The horse is twenty-three years old now, but is still so vigorous that Lord Mottistone is able to ride him to hounds occasionally. Quite recently Lord Mottistone wrote of him, " . . . this very morning I rode him over Mottistone Downs. The gay old horse was quite fit and well, and it took me all my time to hold him. But before we started to ride down the hill back to his stable, I jumped off, threw the reins over his head, and lit a cigarette while I looked over the sea. Warrior bent his head down and rubbed it against my cheek. I patted his neck and he gave a whinny of pleasure. Such can friendship be between man and horse." Warrior was in France throughout the War; he had an adventurous career, spending much of his time under fire. Space will not permit a full account of his escapades, so suffice to say that he has been described as " 'the luckiest horse on the Western Front."

Survivors of the defence of the Salient may also remember a team of the R.H.A. which played a prominent part in the great struggle. They belonged to the Eagle Troop, and were popularly known as the " Old Blacks." They are reputed to be the only team that went out in 1914 and returned complete at the end of the War. Partly for this reason, and partly on account of their distinguished record, they were chosen to draw the cortege of the Unknown Warrior to Westminster in 1920. Only one of the six remains alive to-day. He is a pensioner on

Photo] [Imperial War Museum, Crown Copyright

THAT NOBLE FOUR-FOOT, "THE HORSE," UNDER ADVERSE CONDITIONS

a farm at Bexley, Kent, and passes his days browsing in an orchard, perhaps—who knows?—thinking of those dark days of long ago, when he floundered about knee deep in mud. He carries on his belly a large scar, caused by a shell that exploded almost between his legs.

Another war veteran still alive is " Jimmy " a donkey, who was mascot of the 1st Battalion the Cameronians. Jimmy was born in the trenches, his mother being a captured German transport animal, and he now lives at Peterborough as mascot of the local branch of the Royal Society for the Prevention of Cruelty to Animals. Frances, Countess of Warwick has three war veterans—Nobby, Dobby, and Bobby—on her estate at Dunmow, Essex. All three horses served throughout the War.

Of the other notable War animal survivors, mention must be made of Ragtime, Lord Middleton's handsome grey Arab, who saw fierce fighting in the desert during the Mesopotamia Campaign, and is now, at the age of twenty-four, living with his master at Malton, Yorks. Rocky, a dog who was born in the front line near Roclincourt in 1918, and is now living in Dundee; and Dickybush, a wire-haired terrier who was born within a few miles of the Salient — his mother being one of the numerous strays rendered homeless by the invading hordes—and who is now living at Toulon, South of France, having attained the ripe age of eighteen years. Dickybush (he takes his name from the village, Dickebusch) experienced a most remarkable escape from death when only a few weeks old. A bomb fell on the house he was in, and, exploding in the room, killed his mother and four brothers and sisters. Dickybush escaped unharmed and was nursed through puppyhood by Major Hall of the Intelligence Service who had previous to the arrival of the litter found the mother-dog wandering vainly amid the ruins in search of a haven of rest.

Photo] [Imperial War Museum, Crown Copyright
SUBMARINE OFFICER ATTACHING MESSAGE TO LEG OF CARRIER PIGEON

It is now nearly twenty years since the drums of war first echoed across the fair plains of Flanders, and the ranks of our four-footed comrades of the battle-fields are becoming sadly thinned. True, there are still quite a few left with us, some in private ownership, others continuing to ply the daily round and common task of useful employment. But their number is dwindling day by day, and, by the natural order of things, the time is rapidly approaching when they all will have passed from us. Even so, their memory will remain ever green in the minds of those who enjoyed their companionship during the long drawn-out struggle.

There is no national memorial to the War Animals in this country, but several practical schemes have been inaugurated to commemorate the great sacrifices they made. The Governors of the Royal Veterinary College have opened a special " Lest We Forget " Fund with the object of

Photo] [Imperial War Museum, Crown Copyright
GERMAN DOG CARRYING APPARATUS FOR LAYING TELEPHONE WIRES

rebuilding the College and equipping it with modern appliances. The R.S.P.C.A. too, have opened an Animals' War Memorial Dispensary in Cambridge Avenue, Kilburn, and over 6,000 animals were treated there during 1932. The Dispensary is designed and equipped on modern lines to provide every facility for the efficient treatment of the sick animals, and the secretary is always pleased to show visitors around. On the outside of the building there is a tablet inscribed :—

> "This building is dedicated as a Memorial to the countless thousands of God's humble creatures who suffered and perished in the Great War 1914—1918. Knowing nothing of the cause, looking forward to no final victory, filled only with Love, Faith and Loyalty, they endured much and died for us. May we all remember them with gratitude, and in the future commemorate their suffering and death by showing kindness to living animals."

In this age of mechanisation the rising generation are apt to overlook the sacrifice made on our behalf by the War Animals. We should, therefore, make it our duty to tell our sons and daughters about these silent battlefield comrades of ours. By so doing we shall inculcate a greater love and understanding in the human heart for all dumb creatures; thus, even as we now enjoy the peace and quiet of England given us by our fallen comrades, so will the animals of to-day and to-morrow reap the benefit of their fellow-creatures' sacrifices.

P. S. B.

Ypres Times Maintenance Fund

OUR January edition of the *Ypres Times* contained a copy of a letter that had been received at Headquarters from one of our most loyal members, namely Mr. E. F. Williams of New Brighton, offering a suggestion backed by his own initial contribution for raising funds for the maintenance of the popular League journal. Since Mr. Williams' letter was published we have been touched by the ready response by many other members supporting his proposition and we wish to record here how immensely grateful we are to those who have so generously extended us such encouraging support. We have pleasure to reproduce below a few of the many letters received.

Several members have urged us to establish a fixed charge per quarter for the journal but while appreciating very much indeed their kind sentiment, the Committee wish to point out quite clearly that there is no intention whatever of considering any official charge over and above the annual membership subscription of 5/- and that any support generously extended to us under this heading must be entirely voluntary and such amounts received to be added to the sum already on deposit at the bank for this specific purpose.

25/2/34.

I, as a Life Member, wish to be associated with the excellent suggestion put forward by Mr. E. F. Williams in your current issue, and enclose a postal order for 12/- representing 10/- to cover the past five years, and 2/- in advance for the next four editions.

E. A. M. (Gravesend).

25/1/34.

Mr. E. F. Williams' example in paying 6d. a copy for the *Ypres Times* seems a sound one to follow under the circumstances. I therefore enclose a P.O. for 2/- advance payment for my copies for the current year of which I already possess the January number. Trusting other members of the League will follow suit.

Mrs. E. S. (Belmont).

15/1/34.

Having read Mr. E. F. Williams' letter in the January *Ypres Times*, I should like to say that I am entirely in accord with his suggestion that a charge of 3d. or 6d. per copy should be made in future. Since the death of my son, 2nd Lieut. D. G. W. Hewitt, V.C., Hampshire Regt., at St. Julien in 1917, I have visited Ypres several times and will always take a special interest in the town and its surroundings. The *Ypres Times* is practically the only means of information to many, who, like myself are no longer able to go there often, but who will always be keenly interested in the place and its future welfare. It would indeed be a matter of regret were one deprived of the various items of news which the excellent little quarterly contains. I enclose 2/- to pay for my own copy for 1934.

Mrs. E. M. H. (Winchester).

22/1/34.

I think that the suggestion of Mr. E. F. Williams of New Brighton is an excellent idea and I have therefore very much pleasure in enclosing a postal order for 2/6 for my four *Times* of the current year. I trust that many members will fall into line in a similar way and thus help to make our financial world a little more stable than it has been in the past. I shall hope to send you a P.O. for this amount each succeeding year and wishing the League all prosperity in this New Year.

Capt. L. B. (Penrhos Bay).

20/1/34.

I think 3d. per copy in future is a good suggestion on the part of one of your correspondents, so in future when I send my yearly subscription I will try and bear that in mind.

G. A. B. (Bp. Auckland).

27/1/34.

I should like to inform you of the great pleasure I derived from this quarter's *Ypres Times*, I am sure that the letter of Mr. Williams will not go unheeded—a splendid suggestion and I enclose a small donation, wishing I could make it more, but I have been saving up to join your trip to Ypres at Easter, and being a "son of the soil" it has been hard work. Wishing you all success.

H. W. D. (Reading).

16/1/34.

Many thanks for my copy of the *Ypres Times*. May I congratulate you on another very interesting issue this quarter. I have read with much interest the letter from Mr. Williams and his suggestion which I think splendid. I beg to hand you the sum of 2/6 as my contribution for 1934 and hope that many members will fall in with the suggestion. I only wish that the journal was a monthly one instead of quarterly.

F. W. S. (London, N.19).

On February 16th last we were reminded again of the loyalty and strength of our Purley Branch in the form of a cheque for £5 from the Branch Funds contributed as a mark of appreciation of the *Ypres Times*, and almost before we had time to adequately convey our sincere appreciation of this noble gesture we have been brought nearer still to the gold standard by a further gift of £20 to the *Ypres Times* Maintenance Fund handsomely subscribed among those faithful Purley stalwarts at their Annual Re-Union Dinner on March 2nd.

We would like also to record our grateful thanks to Mrs. L. K. Briggs, our Corresponding Member for Broadstairs, for so kindly coming again to the rescue with a most generous donation of £5.

N.B.—It is a very great encouragement to Headquarters to feel that the *Ypres Times* is worthy of such staunch support. Adequate gratitude cannot be measured in terms, but expressing our most sincere thanks to all our faithful donors we can assure them that their encouragement has thrown a welcome ray of light on the efforts which we are making for the continuity of the *Ypres Times*.

Thursday, June 7th

A Reunion will be held on Messines Day on the Horse Guards' Parade at 5 p.m. Plain clothes will be worn.

Units that took part in the Battle of Messines will be formed up on the South side of the Parade.

Those who served in the Ypres Salient but did not take part in the actual Battle of Messines will be formed up on the North side of the Parade.

It will be of great assistance to those responsible for the arrangements that day if those people desirous of attending the Reunion would notify the fact by postcard before the 1st of June to:—

>The Secretary,
>Ypres League,
>20, Orchard Street,
>Portman Square,
>London, W.1.

The Divisions which took part in the Battle of Messines were:—11th, 16th, 19th, 23rd, 24th, 25th, 36th, 41st, 47th, 3rd Australian, 4th Australian, New Zealand.

In addition to above there were the Army and Corps Troops:—

34 Army Brigades, R.F.A., 47 Heavy or Siege Batteries, R.G.A., 10 Tunnelling Companies, R.E., 8 Companies Special Brigade, R.E., 17 Army Troop Companies, R.E., 1 Field Company Survey, R.E., 4 Signal Companies, 48 Tanks.

7th—14th of June, 1917.

Cobbles

When Yper town was built anew
Upon its ancient site,
When hotels grew like mushrooms
Upon a summer night,
When shops appeared like magic,
When churches grew apace,
When fields were dug and planted
And the landscape changed its face;—
I wonder why the streets were left
As knobbly as of yore,
Why cobbles were not changed for roads
That make the feet less sore.
Perhaps 'tis done that pilgrims
May not have an easy shoe
But should hobble on the cobbles
As good pilgrims ought to do.

L. K. BRIGGS.

GRANDE PLACE, YPRES

League Secretary's Notes

The first quarter of the New Year has been one of increased activity both in membership and travel.

On March 16th to 19th, the League had privilege to organise a battlefield lecture tour for a sydnicate party of the Honourable Artillery Company and resulted in a most interesting week-end at Cambrai with two days char-a-banc itineraries to the Etreux, Elouges and Mons areas. Seventy-two officers took part and Major General W. J. Dugan, C.B., C.M.G., D.S.O., Commander of the 56th (1st London) Division accompanied the tour throughout.

A fortnight following our Easter Pilgrimage to Ypres, a four day Public Schools' tour to Ypres and battlefields as far as Vimy Ridge and Arras is being organised under the auspices of the Ypres League and O.T.C. Club, April 14th—17th. The War Office have kindly given permission to Colonel C. T. Tomes, D.S.O, M.C., Major F. L. McNaughton, D.S.O., and Captain H. Redman to accompany the tour for purpose of lecturing the boys whose ages will rank between 15 to 19 years. During the same week-end, April 13th to 16th, the League is having the honour to again organise a battlefield tour for Officers of the 167th Infantry Brigade T.A. Headquarters will be made at Cambrai. Apart from the usual Whitsuntide and August Bank Holiday mixed Pilgrimages we are arranging trips for at least two other Regimental Associations to Ypres, namely our old friends of the 85th Club on May 25th to 28th and the 2nd North Midland Brigade 46th Divison during the August Bank Holiday.

Two most successful reunion dinners were held by our Colchester and Purley branches on February 1st and March 2nd respectively. The London County Committee Informal Gathering have been retaining their popularity and the Committee is looking forward to a large gathering of members and friends at the reunion dinner to be held in London on April 21st at which General Sir Hubert Gough will preside. Captain J. Wilkinson, Hon. Secretary of our Sheffield Branch is making a splendid effort to recapture the old interest in the League in his district which has been badly hit by the trade depression resulting in many staunch members having to relinquish their annual subscriptions *pro tem*. We wish Captain Wilkinson every success in his fine endeavours in bringing our old supporters back to the active membership list.

It is most pleasing for us to record the interest shown in the Ypres League by the 13th Belgian Field Artillery at Liege, and we have heartily welcomed, through the good services of Commandant R. Castadot, quite a number of Life and Subscribing Members together with excellent prospects of further enrolments. The 13th Belgian Battery participated in the Defence of the Ypres Salient during two years under the command of the British Army, and to record that fact, the Belgian Artillery Regiment has been authorised to place a memorial in the town of Ypres.

1934 has started well and we convey our sincere thanks to our Branches, Corresponding Members and faithful individual supporters.

HOTEL
Splendid & Britannique
YPRES

GRAND' PLACE. Opposite Cloth Hall.

Leading Hotel for Comfort and Quality.

Completely Renovated.

Running Water. Bathrooms.

Moderate Terms. Garage.

Patronized by The Ypres League.

WAR BOOK.

We recommend to our readers "*The Cambridgeshires*" by Brig. General E. Riddell and Colonel M. C. Clayton, published by Bowes & Bowes, price 10/6. A most excellent account of a regiment during the Great War, and those interested in Ypres should read chapters 4 and 15 to 20, but it is all good reading.

COLLECTION OF TINFOIL.

We announced in the last October edition of the "Ypres Times" that a collection of tinfoil had been started by headquarters eventually to be sold in aid of the funds of this League. We are indeed most greatful for the kind co-operation of many members who have so generously responded and we shall be pleased to receive, at 20, Orchard Street, whatever further supplies can be spared.

OLD WELL-KNOWN SPOTS IN NEW GUISE.

The following prints, size 4¼ x 2½, recently taken of famous spots in the Ypres Salient, and which may be of great interest to our readers, are on sale at headquarters, price 4d. each, post free 5d.

- Poelcapelle Church.
- Ramparts at the Lille Gate.
- Hell Fire Corner, Left and Right. (2 photos).
- Shrapnel Corner.
- Transport Farm Cemetery.
- Transport Farm Corner.
- Zillebeke Lake.
- Hill 62, Canadian Memorial.
- Hooge from Zouave Wood.
- Hooge Crater Cemetery.
- Clapham Junction.
- Stirling Castle.
- Gheluvelt Church.
- Cheddar Villa Dressing Station.
- Vancouver Cross Roads.
- Canadian Memorial: Vancouver Cross Roads.
- Hyde Park Corner. (Memorial.)
- Wulverghem.
- Messines Church.
- Potsdam Redoubt at Corner Cott.

Applications should be addressed to Secretary, Ypres League, 20, Orchard Street, London, W.1.

BACK NUMBER OF "THE YPRES TIMES."

If any members can kindly spare their copies of the January, 1934, edition of the *Ypres Times*, the Secretary would receive them most gratefully.

YPRES LEAGUE PILGRIMAGES FOR 1934
(CONDUCTED)

For Prospectuses apply to the Secretary.

Two Separate Tours Whitsuntide (May 19th-22nd) { Ypres, Arras and the Somme

August 4th-7th (Bank Holiday) Two Separate Tours { Ypres, Arras and the Somme

YPRES

Skindles Hotel

(Opposite the Station)

Proprietor—Life Member, Ypres League

Branch at Poperinghe

(close to Talbot House)

THE BRITISH TOURING SERVICE

Manager—Mr. P. VYNER
Representative and Life Member, Ypres League

**10, Station Square
ARRAS
(P.-de-C.) France**

Cars for Hire, with British Driver Guides   **Tours Arranged**

1934 Recruiting Competition

IN view of the popularity and immense success of the past three recruiting competitions, we have great pleasure to announce that **A FURTHER PRIZE OF £5** will be awarded this year as follows :—

TO THE BRANCH RECRUITING THE GREATEST NUMBER OF NEW MEMBERS IN 1934.

All membership forms completed must be received at Headquarters bearing on the top left-hand corner the name of the branch responsible for the recruitment.

Branch Notes

LONDON COUNTY COMMITTEE.

Informal Gatherings.

The London County Committee have pleasure to report continued good attendances at the monthly informals, organised to promote the spirit of fellowship and re-union of all who have the welfare of the Ypres League at heart.

We feel immensely grateful to the staunch supporters who have done so much to make the Gatherings so regularly successful during the first quarter of the New Year.

At the January meeting we had pleasure to welcome Commander H. M. Denny, who gave an exceedingly interesting talk in the Navy in Gallipoli. Our grateful thanks are expressed to Commander Denny and also to the Navy League for so kindly arranging the lecture.

On Thursday, February 15th, we enjoyed an admirable entertainment by the St. Dunstan's Singers under the personal direction of Miss E. McCall. Every item on the programme was excellently rendered and the party is deserving of our warmest thanks.

In March we were indebted to Captain H. D. Peabody, D.C.M., who was so kind as to deliver a lecture and showed us some of his wonderful collection of slides in which all who served in the Ypres Salient were deeply interested.

We beg to remind our members and friends that the Informal Gatherings are being held on the third Thursday in April, May and June at the Bedford Head Hotel, Maiden Lane, Strand, W.C., from 7.15 p.m. to 10 p.m.

Our old and esteemed friends of the 85th Club come to us on April 19th and hope we may welcome them with a " full house " when Mr. F. Underhill, Chairman of the Club, will preside.

London members will be pleased to know that Captain C. Alliston and Mr. Thrussell, who have been on the sick list for a considerable period, are progressing favourably. We wish them both speedy recovery and hope they will be able to join with us in our re-unions in the near future.

ANNUAL RE-UNION DINNER AND DANCE.

The London County Committee have pleasure in announcing that the tenth Annual Dinner and Dance will take place on Saturday, April 21st at the Royal Hotel, Woburn Place, W.C.1., when the Chair will be taken by General Sir Hubert Gough, G.C.M.G., K.C.B., K.C.V.O. (see page 62). The Committee look forward to the co-operation of all London members to ensure the success of the function. Application for tickets, together with remittance (price 7s. per ticket, double 6s. 6d.), should be sent to the Hon. Secretary, London County Committee, Ypres League, 20, Orchard Street, W.1. Members are asked to apply for tickets not later than Apr1 18th.

CHILDREN'S ANNUAL CHRISTMAS PARTY.

Anyone passing the Westminster City School on Saturday, January 13th would have paused to listen to the unaccustomed sounds of revelry issuing from that classic building.

The occasion was the Annual Christmas Party arranged by the London County Committee of the Ypres League, and once again the large hall of the School had been made available by the kindness of the Governors and lavishly decorated with bunting by several energetic and agile members of the Committee. An extra large Christmas Tree shared the platform with the music stands of the Enfield Orchestral Society, whose members gave a splendid selection of lively and appropriate airs under the skilled direction of Mrs. Peabody.

The 146 children present proved to be "good mixers" and by the time tea was served the ice had been broken and a real Christmas spirit of goodwill and comradeship prevailed. After tea came the excitement of "Musical Chairs," "Musical Bumps" and other games dear to the juvenile heart, and shall it be whispered that not a few grown-ups also took part with evident enjoyment! Then came an hour or more of the most thrilling conjuring tricks and the youngsters were held spellbound as endless yards of ribbon were produced from a borrowed hat, coins and eggs were extracted from the most unlikely places and a bottle of milk was found to be in two places at once! This was followed by more games, after which there was a distribution of Xmas Crackers and numbered tickets which entitled each child to a present from the Christmas Tree. Father Christmas himself then appeared and carried on the good work of presenting the gifts and addressed a few homely and kindly words to the kiddies. On leaving, every child received a further gift of fruit and sweets and as one watched the tired but happy crowd filing past, the words of Tiny Tim in the immortal "Christmas Carol" came distinctly to my mind—"God bless us, every one."

During the evening we had the pleasure of a visit from Captain and Mrs. R. Henderson-Bland, whose work for the Ypres League in America is so much appreciated.

To all who in any way contributed to the success of the party, we tender our grateful thanks. Especially are we indebted to Mrs. Peabody and her Orchestra, to Mr. Elsee for the conjuring entertainment, to Mrs. Glover, Miss Greaves and Miss Riddelsdell for their efforts on "cook-house fatigue" and to Captain H. D. Peabody for again impersonating Father Christmas in his own inimitable way.

J.W.F.

THE ANNUAL MEETING

of the

LONDON COUNTY COMMITTEE

will take place on

THURSDAY, APRIL 26th, 1934

at the

YPRES LEAGUE OFFICES

20, Orchard Street,

Portman Square, W.1.

at 7.30 p.m.

The business will be to receive the Report of the London County Committee for the past year and to elect the Committee for the ensuing year. Members are earnestly requested to attend, and the Committee will be glad to receive any suggestions to further the interests of the League in the London area. Should any members have proposals to make, will they please forward them to the Hon. Secretary, London County Committee, Ypres League, at 20, Orchard Street, W.1., by April 19th.

LONDON COUNTY COMMITTEE

Informal Gatherings

These will be held at the

BEDFORD HEAD HOTEL,

Maiden Lane, Strand, W.C.2

on

THURSDAY, APRIL 19th 1934.

(Programme by the 85th Club)

THURSDAY, MAY 17th 1934.

THURSDAY, JUNE 21st 1934.

From 7.15 to 10 p.m.

Will you kindly make these gatherings known amongst your own circle and interest some ex-Service man in the Ypres League in order to increase our membership?

Particulars will be sent to any friend on the name and address being supplied, and members are urged to help all they can in this direction.

Ladies cordially invited.

COLCHESTER BRANCH.

The second annual re-union of the Colchester and District Branch of the Ypres League, held at the Red Lion Hotel on February 1st, was a remarkable gathering of some of "The Old Brigade" who, assisted in keeping the Channel ports free of a foreign foe, and in the final destruction of military might which sought the conquest of our island. The silent toast in memory of the fallen—a quarter of a million of the flower of the Empire—was honoured at the call of the Chairman (Lieut.-Colonel H. W. Herring, M.C.), and there were interesting speeches, and, above all, a fine comradeship, which country and Empire held out because of the defence of the Salient and those of us who served there must take some pride in being members of the League and commemorating the service which those who still lay in the Salient rendered, and which should never be underrated."

Captain G. E. de Trafford, M.C., the secretary of the League, ably replied, and brought from Lieut.-General Sir W. P. Pulteney, the League chairman, a message of congratulation upon the astonishing advance of the Colchester Branch and the fine work of its officials, including Mr. W. H. Taylor, pilgrimage hon. secretary, and Mr. Hubert Snow, the branch hon. secretary, whose perseverance, enthusi-

2nd ANNUAL REUNION DINNER OF THE COLCHESTER AND DISTRICT BRANCH.

found vent in community singing, during which the Rector of Lexden (Rev. S. L. Dolph) delighted a large company with parodies on a famous song. Among those at the head table was the Colonel of the Essex Regiment (Major-General J. C. Harding-Newman, C.B., C.M.G., D.L.). After the repast, Major G. C. Benham, M.C., in proposing the toast of "The Ypres League," spoke of the considerable growth of the Colchester infant of the League, and stressed the desirability of keeping in remembrance the long and marvellous and well-sustained defence put up in the Salient, which, he claimed, was a war in itself, and one which had a tremendous bearing on the conclusion of hostilities. "Out-gunned in the Ypres Salient in the early stages, as we were, yet the Salient still held out; and I don't think it is putting it too strongly to say that this asm and co-operation with headquarters had contributed largely to the big increase in membership.

Mr. G. J. Collings proposed "The Visitors" and in response Rev. S. L. Dolph recounted the story in brief of the three main battles of the Salient, and, as an ex-Australian soldier, gave, amid laughter, reminiscences of his career as an unpaid infantry lance-corporal who "fell foul" of the sergeant-major, lost his stripe, and transferred to the artillery..

Rev. F. R. P. Carrick, an ex-padre, proposed the toast of "The Colchester Branch," remarking that it was an interesting fact that the oldest town in our realm should be in the forefront of the League's branches in regard to increase of membership.

The Chairman, in response, described the Colchester Branch as one of the bright spots in the League's organisation. At the last dinner their membership was 48, and to-day it had increased by 75 per cent. to 84, and they had a bank balance of £20. Colonel Herring added that it was proposed to hold a Branch pilgrimage to Ypres in July.

Mr. M. McKinley thanked the artists of the evening, who were Miss Jenny Bradley, Mr. Granville Offord, Sergt.-Major J. Bird, and also the quintette of the band of the 4th Q.O. Hussars, who played during the repast by permission of the Colonel and officers.

PURLEY BRANCH.

The Sixth Annual Re-union Dinner of the Purley Branch took place on Friday, March 2nd at the Red Lion Hotel, Coulsdon.

Every year this popular function sees a large number present, so that it was natural to find a record attendance (132) this year, with Captain R. L. Haine, V.C., M.C., in the Chair.

As an entirely ex-Service dinner this is an occasion of great good comradeship, all Arms, all Services and all ranks joining in an evening entirely given up to the lighter side of war; the guests of honour, General Sir Hubert Gough, G.C.M.G., K.C.B., K.C.V.O., etc, and Lieut. General Sir William P. Pulteney, G.C.V.O., K.C.B., etc., being among those who enjoyed the whole programme as much as anyone.

According to Operation orders, troops began to assemble at 7 p.m. ready for zero hour and rations at 7.30 p.m. Rations were expressed on the menu in code—a copy of this, the Super B.A.B. Code, being attached for exercise; but all members and guests got very well fed, whether they solved the thing or not.

After "The King" and The Silent Toast had been properly honoured, the C.O. held a pow-wow, opening the proceedings with a very witty speech, in the course of which he welcomed the two distinguished guests, recited a list of units and fronts represented, announced a dance to be held in October, eulogised the Adjutant and presented the prizes won in the 1933 Bombardier's Foursomes.

Capt. Vernon Lee, M.C., next entertained the company and continued in his usual wonderful form when called on for duty throughout the evening.

Then the Adjutant reported, sometimes seriously and sometimes extremely flippantly; the membership of the Branch stood at 200 before the Dinner; for the third consecutive year the recruiting prize was won. G.H.Q. might frown if we won it again! all the 1933 golf and other news; plans for bigger entries; and how remarkably members responded to his notices, or otherwise. At this point all the guests were enrolled as members without resistance.

"Our Gallant Allies" were proposed by Father Major H. G. Harris, who cordially greeted all guests, especially General Gough who enjoyed the previous dinner sufficiently to come again, who had played golf with us too and was still a friend; there was also a great welcome for the Chairman of the Ypres League.

The Army Commander and the Corps Commander replied. They enjoyed this meeting with those who had served in the war; those who went through those different forms of hell had something in common, something which others had not; this comradeship was a fine thing.

The troops were much cheered to think they really had enjoyed it.

General Pulteney expressed his very grateful thanks to the Branch and complimented the Committee on the efficient organisation of the re-union.

Capt. Ray next read a paper concerning one Queen, Sheba. It was a clever work (and too clever for some); well rendered.

The toast of the evening, "The C.O." was proposed by Bombardier Burden (there are others, but he is *The* Bombardier).

Here was our Bill in command; we liked and honoured him for himself, apart from his V.C.; he had always met the enemy unafraid; when adversity came later, he still met it smiling; a very modest and withal a very weighty C.O.

And when the troops sang that he was a jolly good fellow, they meant it.

Capt. Haine acknowledged briefly, and turned on the entertainment again.

The songs that won the war were, as usual, a feature of the evening, rendered by the full company.

Stretcher bearers were scheduled for 11 p.m. but were not required.

On the way home, however, one field officer was heard insistently explaining that if ever there were another war, here was the "nuclus" of at least an Army ready made!

KENYA BRANCH.

Since the publication of the January "Ypres Times," we have received very welcome news from Corporal C. H. Slater informing us, that on Armistice Day he arranged for the placing of a Ypres League wreath on the Cenotaph at Nairobi. We desire to express our very grateful thanks to Corporal Slater, and to the following gentlemen who so generously subscribed towards the wreath:—Brig. General A. R. Wainwright, D.S.O., M.C.; Captain D. P. Petrie; Cpl. S. W. Kemp; Major W. N. Mackenzie, Colonel G. J. Henderson, Cpl. C. H. Slater, Cpl. C. H. Beer. The fact that this commemoration is carried out each year by our staunch Kenya Branch is most gratifying to us at headquarters.

THE TENTH ANNUAL
RE-UNION
DINNER AND DANCE

ORGANIZED BY THE

LONDON COUNTY COMMITTEE

OF

THE YPRES LEAGUE

will be held at the

ROYAL HOTEL
Woburn Place, W.C.1

(nearest Tube Station, Russell Square)

at 6.30 p.m. for 7 p.m.

On SATURDAY, APRIL 21st, 1934

The Chair will be taken by
GENERAL SIR HUBERT GOUGH, G.C.M.G., K.C.B., K.C.V.O.

Members and their friends are very earnestly requested by the London County Committee to support the Dinner and Dance, in order to secure a record Gathering.

Evening Dress Optional.   *Decorations and Medals to be Worn.*

Tickets 7s. 0d. each Single   **Ladies Cordially**
6s. 6s. each Double   **Invited**

Early application for tickets, accompanied by remittance, should be sent to the Hon. Secretary, London County Committee, Ypres League, 20, Orchard Street, Portman Square, London, W.1, not later than April 18th.

Branches and Corresponding Members

BRANCHES.

LONDON	Hon. Secretary to the London County Committee : J. Boughey, 20, Orchard Street, London, W.1.
	E. LONDON DISTRICT—L. A. Weller, 132, Maxey Road, Dagenham, Essex.
	TOTTENHAM AND EDMONTON DISTRICT—E, Glover, 191, Lansdowne Road, Tottenham, N.17.
	H. Carey, 373, Sydenham Road, S.E.26.
COLCHESTER	H. Snow (Hon. Sec.), 9, Church Street (North).
	W. H. Taylor (Pilgrimage Hon. Sec.), 64, High Street.
GATESHEAD	Lieut.-Colonel E. G. Crouch, 8, Ashgrove Terrace.
LIVERPOOL	Captain A. M. Webster, Blundellsands.
PURLEY	Major Graham Carr, D.S.O., M.C., 112-114, High Street.
SHEFFIELD	Captain J. Wilkinson, "Holmfield," Bents Drive.
BELGIUM	Capt. P. D. Parminter, 19, Rue Surmont de Volsberghe, Ypres.
CANADA	Ed. Kingsland, P.O. Box 83, Magog, Quebec.
SOUTH AFRICA	L. G. Shuter, Church Street, Pietermaritzburg,
AMERICA	Representative : Captain R. Henderson-Bland, 110 West 57th Street, New York City.

CORRESPONDING MEMBERS

GREAT BRITAIN.

ABERYSTWYTH	T. O. Thomas, 5, Smithfield Road.
ASHTON-UNDER-LYNE	G. D. Stuart, "Woodlands,", Thronfield Grove, Arundel Street.
BANBURY	Captain C. W. Fowke, Yew Tree House, King's Sutton.
BIRMINGHAM	Mrs. Hill, 191, Cattell Road, Small Heath.
	John Burman, "Westbrook," Solihull Road, Shirley.
BOURNEMOUTH	H. L. Pasmore, 40, Morley Road, Boscombe Park.
BRISTOL	W. S. Hook, "Stoneleigh," Cotham Park.
BROADSTAIRS	C. E. King, 6, Norman Road, St. Peters, Broadstairs.
	Mrs. Briggs, North Foreland House.
CHATHAM	W. N. Channon, 22, Keyes Avenue.
CHESTERFIELD	Major A. W. Shea, 14, Cross Street.
CONGLETON	Mr. H. Dart, 61, The Crescent.
DARLINGTON	D. S. Vigo, 125, Dorset Road, Bexhill-on-Sea.
DERBY	T. Jakeman, 10, Graham Street.
DORRINGTON (Salop)	Captain G. D. S. Parker, Frodesley Rectory.
EXETER	Captain E. Jenkin, 25, Queen Street'
GLOUCESTER	H. R. Hunt, "Casita," Parton Lane, Churchdown.
HERNE BAY	Captain E. Clarke Williams, F.S.A.A., "Conway," Station Road.
HOVE	Captain G. W. J. Cole, 2, Westbourne Terrace, Kingsway.
LEICESTER	W. C. Dunford, 343, Aylestone Road.
LINCOLN	E. Swaine, 79, West Parade.
LLANWRST	A. C. Tomlinson, M.A., Bod Estyn.
LOUGHTON	Capt. O. G. Johnson, M.A., Loughton School.
MATLOCK (Derby)	Miss Dickinson, Beechwood.
MELROSE	Mrs. Lindesay Kelsall, Huntlyburn.
NEW BRIGHTON (Chesire)	E. F. Williams, 5, Waterloo Road.
NEW MILTON	W. H. Lunn, "Greycot," Albert Road.

NOTTINGHAM	E. V. Brown, 3, Eldon Chambers, Wheeler Gate.
ST. HELENS (Lancs.)	John Orford, 124, Knowsley Road.
SHREWSBURY	Major-General Sir John Headlam, K.B.E., C.B., D.S.O., Cruck Meole House, Hanwood.
TIVERTON (Devon)	Mr. W. H. Duncan Arthur, Surveyor's Office, Town Hall.
WELSHPOOL	Mr. E. Wilson, Coedway, Ford, Salop.

DOMINIONS AND FOREIGN COUNTRIES.

AUSTRALIA	Messrs. C. H. Green, and George Lawson, Anzac House, Elizabeth Street, Brisbane, Queensland.
	R. A. Baldwin, c/o Government Savings Bank of N.S.W., Martin Place, Sydney.
	Mr. W. Cloves, Box 1296, G.P.O., Adelaide.
BELGIUM	Sister Marguerite, Sacré Coeur, Ypres.
BUENOS AYRES	President, British Ex-Service Club, Calle 25 de Mayo 577.
CANADA	Brig.-General V. W. Odlum, C.B., C.M.G., D.S.O., 2530, Point Grey Road, Vancouver.
	V. A. Bowes, 326, 40th Avenue West, Calgary, Alberta.
	W. Constable F. Grece, 4095, Tupper Street, Westmount, Montreal.
CEYLON	Captain F. R. G. Webb, M.C., Irrigation Bungalow, Kalmunai, E.P.
EGYPT	L. B. S. Larkins, The Residency, Cairo.
INDIA	Lieut.-Quartermaster G. Smith, Queen's Bays, Sialkot, India.
IRELAND	Miss A. K. Jackson, Cloneyhurke House, Portarlington.
KENYA	Harry Sheilds, Survey Department, Nairobi.
	Corporal C. H. Slater, P.O. Box 403, Nairobi.
NEW ZEALAND	Captain W. U. Gibb, Ava Lodge, Puhinui Road, Papatoetoe, Auckland.
	S. E. Beattie, Lowlands, Woodville.
SOUTH AFRICA	H. L. Versfield, c/o Cape Explosives Works Ltd., 150, St. Georges Street, Cape Town.
SPAIN	Captain P. W. Burgess, Calle de Zurbano 29, Madrid.
U.S.A.	Captain Henry Maslin, 942, President Street, Brooklyn, New York.
	L. E. P. Foot, 20, Gillett Street, Hartford, Conn, U.S.A.
	A. P. Forward, 449, East 80th Street, New York.
	J. W. Freebody, 945, McBride Avenue, Los Angeles.
NOVA SCOTIA	Will R. Bird, Amherst.

Membership of the League

This is open to all who served in the Salient, and to all those whose relatives or friends died there, in order that they may have a record of that service for themselves and their descendants, and belong to the comradeship of men and women who understand and remember all that Ypres meant in suffering and endurance.

Life membership, £2 10s.

Annual members, 5s.

Do not let the fact of your not having served in the Salient deter you from joining the Ypres League. Those who have neither fought in the Salient nor lost relatives there, but who are in sympathy with the objects of the Ypres League, are admitted to its fellowship, but are not given scroll certificates.

There is a Junior Division for children whose relatives served in the Salient. It is open also to others to whom our objects appeal.

Annual subscription 1s. up to the age of 18, after which they can become ordinary members of the League.

THE YPRES LEAGUE (INCORPORATED)
20, Orchard Street, Portman Square, W.1.

Telephone: WELBECK 1446.　　　　　　　　　*Telegrams*: YPRESLEAG, " WESDO," LONDON.

Patron-in-Chief: H.M. THE KING.

Patrons:
H.R.H. THE PRINCE OF WALES.　　　H.R.H. PRINCESS BEATRICE.

President: GENERAL SIR CHARLES H. HARINGTON.

Vice-Presidents:
F.-M. VISCOUNT ALLENBY.　　　　　F.-M. SIR CLAUD W. JACOB.
THE LORD WAKEFIELD OF HYTHE.　　F.-M. SIR PHILIP CHETWODE.
GENERAL SIR CECIL ROMER.　　　　F.-M. LORD MILNE.

General Committee:
THE COUNTESS OF ALBEMARLE.　　　MAJOR-GENERAL C. J. B. HAY.
MAJOR J. R. AINSWORTH-DAVIS.　　 MR. J. HETHERINGTON.
*CAPTAIN C. ALLISTON.　　　　　　　MRS. E. HEAP.
LIEUT-COLONEL BECKLES WILLSON.　 GENERAL SIR W. C. G. HENEKER.
*MR. J. BOUGHEY.　　　　　　　　　CAPTAIN O. G. JOHNSON.
*MISS B. BRICE-MILLER.　　　　　　 *MAJOR E. MONTAGUE JONES.
COLONEL G. T. BRIERLEY.　　　　　 CAPTAIN H. D. PEABODY.
CAPTAIN P. W. BURGESS.　　　　　　*THE HON. ALICE DOUGLAS PENNANT.
*MAJOR H. CARDINAL-HARFORD.　　　*LIEUT.-GENERAL SIR W. P. PULTENEY.
REV. P. B. CLAYTON.　　　　　　　 LIEUT.-COLONEL SIR J. MURRAY.
*THE EARL OF YPRES.　　　　　　　 *COLONEL G. E. C. RASCH.
MRS. C. J. EDWARDS.　　　　　　　 VISCOUNT SANDON.
MAJOR C. J. EDWARDS.　　　　　　　THE HON. SIR ARTHUR STANLEY.
MR. H. A. T. FAIRBANK.　　　　　　MR. ERNEST THOMPSON.
MR. T. ROSS FURNER.　　　　　　　 CAPTAIN J. LOCKLEY TURNER.
SIR PHILIP GIBBS.　　　　　　　　 *LIEUT.-GENERAL SIR H. UNIACKE.
MR. E. GLOVER.　　　　　　　　　　*MR. E. B. WAGGETT.
MAJOR C. E. GODDARD.　　　　　　　CAPTAIN J. WILKINSON.
MAJOR-GENERAL SIR JOHN HEADLAM.　CAPTAIN H. TREVOR WILLIAMS.
MR. F. D. BANKS HILL.

* Executive Committee.

Bankers:　　　　　　　　　　　　　　*Honorary Solicitors*:
BARCLAYS BANK LTD., Knightsbridge Branch.　MESSRS. FLADGATE & CO., 18, Pall Mall, S.W.

Secretary:　　　　　　　　　　　　*Auditors*:
CAPTAIN G. E. DE TRAFFORD.　　　　MESSRS. LEPINE & JACKSON,
　　　　　　　　　　　　　　　　　　6, Bond Court, E.C.4.

League Representative at Ypres:　　**League Representative in America:**
CAPTAIN P. D. PARMINTER.　　　　　CAPTAIN R. HENDERSON-BLAND.
19, Rue Surmont de Volsberghe　　　110 West 57th Street, New York.

League Representative at Amiens:　**League Representative at Arras:**
CAPTAIN STUART OSWALD.　　　　　　MR. P. VYNER,
7, Rue Porte-Paris.　　　　　　　　10, Station Square.

Hon. Secretary, Ypres British Settlement:
LT. COLONEL F. G. POOLE,

PRIMARY OBJECTS OF THE LEAGUE

I.—Commemoration and Comradeship.
II.—To provide special travel facilities for Members and all interested to Ypres and battlefields, and transport of Members.
III.—The furnishing of information about the Salient ; marking of historic sites and the compilation of charts of the battlefields.
IV.—The erection of a Ypres British Church and School which has been completed.
V.—The establishment of groups of members throughout the world, through Branch Secretaries and Corresponding Members.
VI.—The maintenance of cordial relations with dwellers on the battlefields of Ypres
VII.—The formation of a Junior Division.

Use the Ypres League Travel Bureau for Ypres and Whole of the Western Front.

FOR THE FOLLOWING PUBLICATIONS, Etc., apply:

Secretary, YPRES LEAGUE, 20, ORCHARD STREET, LONDON, W.1.

THE BATTLE BOOK OF YPRES. A history of notable deeds contributed by all regiments. 5s.; post free, 5s. 6d. Compiled by Beatrix Brice with the assistance of Lieut.-General Sir William Pulteney, G.C.V.O., etc.

BOOKS.

YPRES: Outpost of the Channel Ports. By Beatrix Brice. With Foreword by Field-Marshal Lord Plumer, G.C.B. Price 1s. 6d.; post free 1s. 10d.

In the Ypres Salient. By Lt.-Col. Beckles Willson. 1s. net; post free 1s. 2d.

To the Vanguard. By Beatrix Brice. 1s. net; post free 1s. 2d.

The City of Fear and Other Poems. By Gilbert Frankau. 3s. 6d. net; post free 3s. 8d.

With the Cornwall Territorials on the Western Front. By E. C. Matthews. 7s. 6d.; post free 8s.

Story of the 63rd Field Ambulance. By A. W. Westmore, etc. Cloth, 3s. 6d., post free. Paper, 2s. 6d., post free.

War Letters to a Wife. By Colonel Rowland Fielding. Popular Edition. 7s. 6d.; post free 8s.

The Pill Boxes of Flanders. 1s.; post free 1s. 3d.

From Mons to the First Battle of Ypres. By J. G. W. Hyndson, M.C. Price 5s., post free 5s. 2d.

YPRES LEAGUE TIES. 3s. 6d. each, post free.

YPRES LEAGUE BADGES. 2s. each, 2s. 1½d. post free.

EMBROIDERED BADGES. 4s. each, post free.

Map and List of Cemeteries in the Ypres Salient. Price 9d.; post free 11d.

Map of the Somme. Price 1s. 8d., post free.

PICTURES.

Burning of the Cloth Hall, 1915. A Coloured Print, 14 in. by 12 in. 1s. post free.

ENGRAVINGS, 33 in. by 21 in., £1 11s. 6d. each.

Hell Fire Corner.

Heavy Artillery Going into Action before Passchendaele.

" I Won't."

POST CARDS, PHOTOGRAPHS AND ETCHINGS.

Post Cards. Ypres: British Front during the War. Ruins of Ypres. Price 1s. post free.

Photographs of Menin Gate Unveiling. Size 11 in. by 7 in. 1s. 2d. each, post free.

Hill 60. Complete Panorama Photographs. 12 in. by 3¾ in. Price 3s., post free; 15 in. by 5 in. Price 3s. 6d., post free.

WAR-TIME PHOTOGRAPHS OF THE SALIENT.

6 in. by 8 in. ... 1s. 6d. each.
12 in. by 15 in. ... 4s. each.

List forwarded on application.

PHOTOGRAPHS OF WAR-TIME SKETCHES.

Bedford House (Front View), 1916.

Bedford House (Back View), 1916.

Voormezeele Main Street, 1916.

Voormezeele Crucifixion Gate, 1916.

Langhof Chateau, 1916.

Size 8¼ in. by 6¼ in. Price 2s. 6d. each, post free.

ETCHINGS.

Etchings of Menin Gate Memorial. 9 in. by 6 in. Price, 5s. each, post free. Signed proofs, 10s. 6d. each, post free.

YPRES TIMES.

The Journal may be obtained at the League Offices.

BACK NUMBERS 1s.; 1932, 8d.; 1933, 6d.

Printed in Great Britain for the Publishers by FORD & GILL, 21a/23, Iliffe Yard, Crampton Street, London, S.E.17.

Memory Tablet.

JULY — AUGUST — SEPTEMBER

JULY.

July 1st, 1916	...	First Battle of the Somme begins.
,, 2nd, 1918	...	1,000,000 Americans transported to France.
,, 9th, 1915	...	Conquest of German South Africa.
,, 18th, 1918	...	General Foch's counter-attack.
,, 28th, 1914	...	Austria-Hungary declared war on Serbia.
,, 30th, 1915	...	First German liquid fire attack.
,, 31st, 1917	...	Third Battle of Ypres begins.

AUGUST.

Aug. 1st, 1914	...	Germany declares war on Russia.
,, 2nd, 1914	...	German ultimatum to Belgium.
,, 3rd, 1914	...	Germany declared war on France.
,, 4th, 1914	...	Great Britain declared war on Germany.
,, 10th, 1914	...	France declared war on Austria-Hungary.
,, 12th, 1914	...	Great Britain declared war on Austria-Hungary.
,, 16th, 1914	...	British Expeditionary Force landed in France.
,, 23rd, 1914	...	Japan declared war on Germany.
,, 27th, 1916	...	Rumania entered the war.

SEPTEMBER.

Sept. 3rd, 1916	...	Zeppelin destroyed at Cuffley.
,, 5th, 1914	...	End of retreat from Mons to Marne.
,, 6th, 1914	...	First Battle of Marne begins.
,, 15th, 1914	...	First Battle of Aisne begins.
,, 23rd, 1914	...	First British air raid in Germany.
,, 25th, 1915	...	Battle of Loos.
,, 27th, 1917	...	Hindenburg Line broken.
,, 29th, 1918	...	Bulgaria surrendered.

The Ypres Times

Communications to
The Editor, "Ypres Times,"
20, Orchard Street, London, W.1.

PRICE 6d.
POST FREE 7d.

VOL. 7, No. 3. PUBLISHED QUARTERLY JULY, 1934

Leopold III, King of the Belgians
NEW REIGN OPENS AUSPICIOUSLY AMID MANIFESTATIONS OF LOYALTY.
"BELGIUM INDIVISIBLE AND INDEPENDENT."

Specially contributed to the *Ypres Times*.
By HENRY BENSON, M.A.

IT will be generally conceded that King Leopold III. has ascended the throne of Belgium in the face of exceptional difficulties, both at home and abroad, and that, in succeeding a father whose name must always rank high on the roll of constitutional monarchs, although he has a fine heritage to start from, he has a lofty standard to maintain.

KING ALBERT'S NOBLE EXAMPLE.

In a very literal sense the late King Albert incarnated the unity and permanent life of his country; he was the rallying-point for all good citizens; he bridged the gulf between classes and peaceably adjusted the conflict between parties. Ministries came and went in almost bewildering succession, but he remained continuously hiving a store of disinterested experience, which came to exceed that of any politician. Moreover, outside Parliamentary and Ministerial affairs, he fostered sympathetically all the main developments of Belgium's national life—its industry and trade, its local government and philanthropy, its science and technology, its art and literature, its festivities and sport, its culture and education; whilst in all these important activities he had the supreme good fortune to receive the wholehearted co-operation and support of his gracious Consort, Queen Elisabeth.

KING LEOPOLD'S PERSONAL CHARACTERISTICS.

Although King Albert's death was both premature and tragic, Belgium has not been called upon to suffer the misfortune of a minority succession. King Leopold is thirty-two years of age, he has been carefully trained, he worked hard at his apprenticeship, and has already shown that he has inherited character and capacity.

His " accession " speech justifies the fairest hopes. " Belgium indivisible and independent " was its keynote; whilst admirable and courageous were the words in which he affirmed his faith, that social peace and justice could be achieved " in orderly and legal fashion " within the constitution of the country. In these days of dictatorships one warms to the spectacle of a people and King who have not yet despaired of combining liberty with progress.

I recall that on one occasion the late King Albert passed the remark, " I want both my sons to be workers, and for that reason the principal condition I insist upon being observed in the selection of their companions is that they shall be children of honest men and workers—not children of idlers." King Leopold was sent for a time to Eton and afterwards served as a young soldier in Belgium during the latter part of the war. " Duty First " is his adopted motto, and each morning sees him at his study in Brussels at nine o'clock sharp, going through a mass of correspondence and State documents with his staff. Then he is ready to receive ambassadors, ministers and other visitors. It is usually late when his business day is done, but he makes a practice of taking a short walk before dinner.

That his sympathies are with his people in an hour of national sorrow is demonstrated by the fact that, as soon as he heard of the mine disaster at Paturges, near Mons, last May, in which forty-three lives were lost, he hastened to the pithead and on the following day inaugurated a relief fund with a handsome donation.

In Belgium there is no crown, no regalia, and consequently no coronation ceremony, but last month a special mission was sent from Brussels to London for the purpose of announcing officially to the Court of St. James's the new King's accession to the throne.

The dedication of the carillon of the Ypres Belfry—part of the reconstruction scheme of the immortal Cloth Hall—will take place on Sunday, 29th of the present month, when King Leopold and Queen Astrid are to make a State entry into the resurrected city. The rejoicings are to extend over several days, and the British colony is making arrangements for a personal participation.

It is interesting to recall that three years ago his Majesty, then Duke of Brabant, unveiled at Ploegsteert the memorial erected there to the 11,447 " missing " British soldiers who fell in that area ; whilst in the speech he delivered before the African Society in London, last year, he gave strong evidence of his affection and regard for the British Empire.

Queen Astrid.

It was said of the late King Albert in 1909 that " he did not mount the throne alone —his family mounted it with him." So, likewise, it may be claimed on behalf of his son, for the popularity of Queen Astrid and her children is manifest in all parts of Belgium.

The Queen has a special interest for the British people, on account of her relationship to their own Royal family, and the fact that she was brought up with the Duke of Connaught's only grand-daughter, Princess Ingrid. At Fridhem, the family seat in the heart of Sweden, the children grew up in the happy atmosphere of freedom and unpretentiousness. When in Stockholm they attended a public cookery school together, and went through all branches of the work, from vegetable cleaning to cake making. The cakes were allowed to be taken home. It was Princess Astrid's special delight to take her turn marketing. Carrying a capacious basket, she would descend upon the barrows in the Östermalm Square and spend a happy time arguing with the peasant women over the price and quality of their wares. It was also a special privilege, on her way home from school, to walk arm-in-arm with a girl friend, stopping now and then to admire the pretty shops along Strandvagen or the Hamngatan. It may be mentioned that needlework is not her strong point. She prefers the more active, even menial, tasks of housewifery to patient hours spent in fine sewing. In this respect she resembles her great-aunt, the late Queen Alexandra, who was seldom, if ever, known to take up the needle.

The Royal Children.

In Belgian Court circles, where etiquette is very strictly observed, Princess Astrid's informality at first caused a little stir of surprise. On the other hand, the great mass of the people loved her for it.

Nothing could have been better calculated to win their hearts than to see her sitting, like any humble house-mother, on the sands at Ostend, building castles with her little girl, Josephine Charlotte. The absolutely natural behaviour of this small princess and her baby brother, Prince Baudouin, is the outcome of the young Queen's belief in freedom from restraint. Their brightness, rosy health and obvious happiness are the finest tributes to the wisdom of her theories of upbringing, which offset the brain-tax that is bound to attach to children of royal birth in a bi-lingual country. From babyhood these children have been taught to lisp French and Flemish with equal facility, and naturally they have picked up their mother's Swedish as well. The birth of a second son, Prince Albert (named after his late grandfather) last month, was hailed with acclamation throughout the length and breadth of Belgium.

Three Far-seeing Monarchs.

The reign of King Leopold III. has opened auspiciously amid remarkable manifestations of loyalty and goodwill on the part of all sections of the community. Belgians recall with pride that throughout the past hundred years each of their three Sovereigns

THEIR MAJESTIES THE KING AND QUEEN OF THE BELGIANS.

served the nation well. Leopold I. strove hard to consolidate his little kingdom; Leopold II. transformed the little kingdom to which he succeeded into a wide empire; Albert I. prepared his country for peace as well as for war. He girt his sword about him fearlessly, but he also opened books and taught the Belgian world to admire the works of the Belgian poets and novelists in the same way that they had long admired those of Belgian scientists and historians. It is for Leopold III. to aim at embodying in himself the virtues of his three illustrious predecessors, and the whole world will applaud his efforts. At present, of course, he cannot be expected always to exhibit that sure touch which only follows in the wake of long experience. On the other hand, nothing else seems lacking to his equipment as a powerful factor in international affairs. That his reign may be happy, peaceful and prosperous is the wish of all men of goodwill. H.B.

Lieut.-General
Sir Herbert Crofton Campbell Uniacke
K.C.B., K.C.M.G.

APPRECIATIONS.

THE death of General Sir Herbert Uniacke is a very sad loss to all who knew him, and indeed to England, for he was one of her great sons.

Brought up in the Artillery, there was no one who understood how to handle that great arm better than he did, even when its power and magnitude during the course of the late war had increased beyond anything that any of us could have foreseen.

But it was not his professional knowledge alone that entitled him to the admiration, the respect, and the affection of those who served with him; it was his great character, one that was typical of the race.

I saw him in many moments of intense storm and stress, when a lesser soul would have collapsed under the strain, but he never faltered, his great spirit never quailed, nor did he ever fear responsibility nor shirk a great decision.

Moreover, he had other splendid human qualities which endeared him to his fellows, for he possessed a sense of humour and a merry wit, he never deserted a friend, he was the soul of loyalty. His loss is a very heavy one for us all.

HUBERT GOUGH,
General.

On May 17th, Herbert Uniacke was laid to rest by the River, in the Parish Churchyard at Marlow.

It would be safe to say that no reader of this journal, no gunner and few members of the B.E.F., can have seen the notice of his death, without feeling keen regret that a great figure of the 1914-1918 war has passed on at the comparatively early age of 67; but, mingled with that regret, his friends must feel glad that the suffering and pain which he has patiently endured for the last three years has been ended, and that a good and faithful servant has gone to his last home.

Before the war Uniacke had been for some years a member of the R.A. Committee, and was therefore largely responsible for the equipment of the Artillery of the B.E.F.

He went to France in command of a Brigade of Horse Artillery, but early 1915 he was selected to the Command of one of the two Heavy Artillery Groups which were then being formed and held this command in the Ypres Salient until November, 1915, when he went to the Somme as G.O.C., R.A. of the 3rd Corps. When the 5th Army was formed in 1916, General Uniacke was selected for its Major-General, R.A., and it was in this rôle that he was best known.

A cheery optimist in fair weather and foul, no one went to his office or was visited by him, who did not feel the better for it. He brought a great mind to bear on the problems of war and instilled confidence and affection in those of all ranks who served under him.

With a real knowledge of the possibilities and the limitations of artillery fire, he was always ready to try out any improvement which was suggested to him and with a versatility, which was not too common, he was continually thinking out new methods of bombardment and new ways of surprising the enemy. There was nothing small about Uniacke, he never belittled the work of others, and all who served under him were certain of his advice and support in any difficulties.

When the 5th Army disappeared after its fine retreat in March, 1918, Uniacke was employed on the lines of communication until the end of the war.

After the war he commanded the Rawalpindi Division and for some months the Northern Army in India. He was made Colonel Commandant of the Regiment in 1927 and Lieutenant of the Tower of London the same year. To the end of his life and during his long illness he took the keenest interest in the Regiment and in old soldiers generally. He was Chairman of the Executive Committee Artillery House and Vice-President of the Old Contemptibles' Association.

Requiescat in pace!

R. P. BENSON,
Brig.-General.

Photo] [Vandyk, London
THE LATE SIR HERBERT UNIACKE

The Ypres League has sustained a great loss in the death of Sir Herbert Uniacke, who has been for many years a most staunch and highly esteemed supporter of our cause. Sir Herbert was a familiar figure at our "Ypres Day" Commemoration Parades in London, and frequently presided at the League's Annual Reunion Dinners and Smoking Concerts. The practical help he so generously extended can never be measured in words and his wise counsel as a member of the Executive Committee will be sadly missed.

We express our deepest sympathy to Lady Uniacke and family in their great bereavement.

Public Schools Battlefield Tour

BETWEEN the hours of nine and ten on Saturday morning, April 14th last, the environment of Victoria Station was considerably enlivened by the arrival of some 150 boys of our Public Schools who were bound for Dover, *en route* for their initial tour of the battlefields of France and Flanders, all wearing the Ypres League cornflower emblem.

These exuberant spirits of expectancy most certainly did their best to make their presence felt when three cheers were called for His Excellency The Belgian Ambassador, his Military Attaché, Lieut.-General Sir W. P. Pulteney and the Dowager Viscountess Plumer who all so generously spared the time in order to bid the party *bon voyage*.

The occasion was a somewhat unique one, in that it was the first officially organised Public Schools Battlefield Tour, and moreover, fulfilling the desire expressed by the late Lord Plumer, that the younger generation should visit the scenes where their fathers and near relatives had fought.

The tour which these lads were to make had been organised by the Ypres League and the Officers Training Corps Club, and a most interesting and extensive itinerary was prepared. Every boy taking part belonged to the Junior Division of the Officers Training Corps and accompanying the party were several officers of the O.T.C. headed by Major E. Montague Jones, O.B.E., M.A.

The Schools represented were as follows :—City of London, Cheltenham, Clifton, Eton, Glasgow, King Edward's (Bury St. Edmunds), King's (Worcester), Lancing, Malvern, Marlborough, Oundel, Repton, Rossall, Rugby, St. Albans, Shrewsbury, Stowe, Wellington and Winchester.

The official duties of conductor throughout the tour were admirably carried out by Mr. O. Mears, the Assistant Secretary of the Ypres League. The journey to Ypres, our headquarters, was accomplished without a single hitch, and on our arrival it seemed only a matter of minutes before everyone was safely deposited in their allotted rooms equally divided between the two leading hotels, namely the Splendid & Britannique and Skindles.

During dinner on the first night we were honoured by the presence of the Ypres League's Chairman, Sir William Pulteney, who had shown his practical interest and support in the tour by making a special mid-day journey to Ypres—a gesture which received the unanimous appreciation it deserved. At 8.30 p.m. the whole party congregated at Skindles Hotel for a lantern lecture delivered jointly by three regular officers, namely, Colonel C. P. Tomes, D.S.O., M.C., late Warwickshire Regt., Major F. L. McNaughton, D.S.O., Royal Artillery, and Captain H. Redman, K.O.Y.L.I. They described how the British Army came to find itself at Ypres and how the Salient was formed and defended. In view of the Salient tour on the following day this lecture proved most helpful and instructive.

Sunday dawned sunny and warm and after breakfast a visit was made to Talbot House at Poperinghe, where Padre Pat Leonard, who had travelled to Ypres with the party, related with great vividness and feeling, the uses and life of the "Old House" during the war. We returned to Ypres in time for the 11 o'clock service at St. George's Church, after which a wreath was laid at the Ypres Town War Memorial by Major E. Montague Jones. The remaining period before lunch was spent in exploring the town, viewing the Menin Gate, ramparts, Cathedral and the war museum.

Punctually at 2.30 p.m. a convoy of char-a-bancs conveyed the party on a tour of the Salient and between Wieltje and St. Julien, Colonel Tomes claimed the attention of all with his animated account of an attack made by his company in their first contact with the Germans in 1914. The tour continued broken now and again with brief halts

REPRESENTATIVE PARTY OF THE PUBLIC SCHOOLS TOUR ASSEMBLED IN THE YPRES BRITISH SCHOOL PLAYGROUND.
[Daniel, Ypres

for explanations via St. Julien, Gravenstafel, Tyne Cot, Broodseinde, Becelaere, Gheluvelt, Hooge and thence to Sanctuary Wood and Hill 60 where we examined with interest the reconstructed trenches and tunnels. The barrage of questions put by the cadets at these particular spots were as much as the officers could be expected to cope with in the limited time available!

Ypres was reached at 7 p.m. and after a welcome repast, the whole party assembled at the Menin Gate Memorial where the resident Padre, the Rev. G. R. Milner, M.A., ushered a few prayers prior to the sounding of the "Last Post." The senior officer present then placed a wreath as an act of homage to the 55,000 British soldiers who fell in the immortal defence of Ypres and whose graves have never been located. At 9 p.m., Hotel Skindles was the concentration centre for a further lantern lecture on the battles of Neuve Chapelle, Loos, and the Vimy Ridge, which places were to be visited on the next day. On Monday we were again favoured with summer-like conditions and with haversack rations our compass was set for "La Belle France," via Wytschaete. Talks were given on the Messines Ridge, "Plugstreet" Château, Neuve Chapelle and Loos. Passing through rebuilt Lens our itinerary was continued to the Canadian trenches on Vimy Ridge. Here we relished our packet lunches and explored the formidable tunnels, mine shafts and dug-outs which are to-day lighted by electricity and have a more wholesome smell than when they were in original use! It was amusing to observe how the whole party seemed to suddenly disappear beneath the earth's surface and it was only with much persuasion and blowing of whistles that everybody was finally recovered.

An interval of half-an-hour in Arras enabled us to visit the Cathedral which is shortly to be dedicated and the two "Places" with their wonderfully restored Spanish type buildings were worthy of note.

On the return to Ypres intermediate points of interest were Souchez, Bethune, Neuve Eglise and Kemmel and we entered the town by the Lille Gate at about 7.30 p.m. After dinner, the evening was spent very pleasantly in an atmosphere singularly reminiscent of the old comradeship of the war, and time was found for the selection and purchase of little souvenirs of this memorable trip.

Our reserved train steamed out from Ypres at 9 o'clock on Tuesday morning to the accompaniment of a goodly send off by the Yprians with whom we had become quite friendly in the course of our brief visit. After another smooth passage across the Channel and through the customs we finally reached Victoria at 4.42 p.m. thoroughly satisfied and pleased with our experience.

Naturally, those of us who had known France and Belgium in war-time often found it extremely difficult to recognise the various reconstructed areas, but there still remains, here and there, a few scattered concrete pill-boxes, a heap of rusty barb wire, a crater, an occasional collection of "duds" and Mills bombs as a reminder of sixteen years ago, but there is now so little evidence of the squalor, misery, destruction and awfulness of modern war and we ask ourselves: What were the younger generation making of it? This, perhaps was in their minds—" Here we are on the spot where our elders fought, struggled, and died during four long weary years and what is the result of it all? At home, money troubles and unemployment. Out here, painfully new villages, cemetery after cemetery, endless memorials with their vast lists of 'Missing' such as the Menin Gate, Tyne Cot and Thiepval—the tragedy, stupidity, and futility of it all."

If, as well, we made these young men even dimly realise the mental torture, the heroism, the despair, and courage of those who had fought and died for them, the tour was indeed not made in vain, and further, if our efforts have enabled them to understand that they must work for an honourable peace so that such a catastrophe can never be repeated, we may have added another stone to the Peace Structure which this country is striving so earnestly to build.

J. M. WEST (*Major*).

N.B.—As a result of this tour, Cheltenham College have kindly promised to present a book prize each year to the Ypres British School.

The Gordon Highlanders

By JOHN MALCOLM BULLOCH.

Battle Honours :

"MYSORE," "SERINGAPATAM," "EGMONT-OP-ZEE," "MANDORA," "CORUNNA," "FUENTES D'ONOR," "ALMARAZ," "VITTORIA," "PYRENEES," "NIVE," "ORTHOS," "PENINSULA," "WATERLOO," "SOUTH AFRICA, 1835," "DELHI, 1857," "LUCKNOW," "CHARASIAH," "KABUL, 1879," "KANDAHAR, 1880," "AFGHANISTAN, 1878–80," "TEL-EL-KEBIR," "EGYPT, 1882, 1884," "NILE, 1884–85," "CHITRAL," "TIRAH," "DEFENCE OF LADYSMITH," "PAARDEBERG," "SOUTH AFRICA, 1899–1902."

The Great War—21 *Battalions.*—"MONS," "LE CATEAU," "Retreat from Mons," "MARNE, 1914, '18," "Aisne, 1914," "La Bassée, 1914," "Messines, 1914," "Armentières, 1914," "YPRES, 1914, '15, '17," "Langemarck, 1914," "Gheluvelt," "Nonne Bosschen," "Neuve Chapelle," "Frezenberg," "Bellewaarde," "Aubers," "Festubert, 1915," "Hooge, 1915," "Loos," "SOMME, 1916, '18," "Albert, 1916, '18," "Bazentin," "Delville Wood," "Pozières," "Guillemont," "Flers-Courcelette," "Le Transloy," "ANCRE, 1916," "ARRAS, 1917, '18," "Vimy, 1917," "Scarpe, 1917, '18," "Arleux," "Bullecourt," "Pilckem," "Menin Road," "Polygon Wood," "Broodseinde," "Poelcappelle," "Passchendaele," "CAMBRAI, 1917, '18," "St. Quentin," "Bapaume, 1918," "Rosières," "Lys," "Estaires," "Hazebrouck," "Béthune," "Soissonnais-Ourcq," "Tardenios," "Hindenburg Line," "Canal du Nord," "Selle," "Sambre," "France and Flanders, 1914–18," "Piave," "VITTORIO VENETO," "Italy, 1917–18."

Uniform—Scarlet.   *Facings*—Yellow.   *Tartan*—Gordon.

TO my mind one of the chief distinguishing features of the British Army is its recognition of the personal equation which is, indeed, inherent in the individualism of our race. Under it, soldiers are not regarded merely as "troops" to be moved about like pawns on a chessboard, and then forgotten on the cease fire. They are human beings with rights as citizens and a fine set of intensely personal military traditions.

This personal equation aspect of our army is seen at its best in the case of Infantry, divided as it is into regiments representing different districts, especially when those districts are the areas in which the units were originally raised. The method is to be found in a very marked degree in the Scots regiments, and especially the kilted ones, which were raised in the eighteenth century by Highland lairds to meet the national emergency caused by the long war with France, and which retain, in spite of the tendencies to standardise uniforms, the picturesque tartans of their corps as originally raised.

The Gordon Highlanders form a striking example of such a corps. They were raised in 1794 by the 4th Duke of Gordon, assisted by his very unconventional consort, Jane Maxwell. In his time his Grace raised four different corps, and supplied a company each to two others, the Fraser Highlanders and the Black Watch. His own regiments were the 89th Foot (1759–65) which fought in India under Sir Hector Munro; the Northern Fencibles (1778–83); a second corps of Northern Fencibles (1793–99); and the Gordon Highlanders, raised in 1794, as the 100th, and then in 1798 renumbered as the 92nd, by which they were known for nearly a century.

Legend says that the men were recruited by the Duchess with a guinea and a kiss. Her Grace, a very capable woman, who managed to annex three dukes and a marquis for her daughters, for one of whom she even tried to get Napoleon's stepson, Eugene

Beauharnais, was quite capable of such a dramatic gesture. But when the regiment was raised, the countryside had been squeezed so dry, and the competition of rival recruiters was so intense, that with all her blandishments she could not have got even a drummer boy for so small a bounty as a guinea. Furthermore, one doubts the story from the fact that it was told of her eldest daughter, Lady Madelina Sinclair, in the matter of the Caithness Fencibles, and was laughingly dismissed by the girl's husband as a canard started by jealous recruiting rivals to discredit her.

The family feeling in the Gordons is shown by the fact that Inverness-shire and Aberdeenshire, where the Duke had huge estates, supplied respectively 240 and 124 men out of 894. Only nine came from England, 51 from Ireland, and two from Wales; while 361 were Macs of one kind or another. It may surprise some people to know that the original recruits were not the giants usually supposed. Being essentially Highland, they averaged only 5 ft. 5½ in., and only six men were 6 ft. or over.

The family feeling was further emphasised by the command of the regiment being given to the Duke's heir, the dashing Marquis of Huntly, for whom his father raised a company on his joining the Black Watch in 1790. It was the Black Watch, indeed, which suggested Gordon tartan, for that sett was designed by William Forsyth, a manufacturer at Huntly, Aberdeenshire, for the Northern Fencibles in 1793. What Forsyth did was simply to run a yellow strip through Black Watch tartan.

The tartan and badge of the Highland regiments illustrate the personal equation element in the Army, because it must be remembered that they were really the monopoly of private families just like the uniform of the old feudal levy. But what is far more remarkable is the fact that the piper of each company carries on his pipe banner the arms of the captain of that company for the time being. The city of Aberdeen was the first rendezvous of the new regiment, and though other regiments were subsequently quartered there, it remains the depot of the Gordons to this day.

The regiment received its baptism of fire in the mismanaged Walcheren expedition of 1799, on setting out for which the Marquis of Huntly, who was wounded at Egmont-on-Zee, was greeted with Mrs. Grant of Laggan's song, "Highland Laddie." Sir John Moore, who was also wounded, was carried off the field by the Gordons, and always kept in touch with them. That is why the officers wear a thread of black in their gold braid to remember his death at Corunna, while it is said the black buttons on the men's gaiters are for the same purpose.

The achievement of the Gordons in the field, including Egypt, the Peninsula, Waterloo, Afghanistan, Transvaal, Tirah, South African and the Great War, are part and parcel of our military history and need not be detailed.

In 1881 the 92nd was linked with the 75th and became the 2nd battalion of the Gordon Highlanders. The 75th was raised in 1787 by General Sir Ralph Abercromby (1734–1801) of the Tullibody family, and became known as the Stirlingshire Regiment. But in 1809 its Highland dress was abandoned, and to all intents and purposes the 75th became an English regiment, being ultimately, under the "linked" system, semi-attached to the Dorsetshire Regiment (the 39th). In 1881, under the territorial system, it was amalgamated with the Gordons, and as if in verification of the old alliterative rhyme about the family, "the Gordons hae the guidin' o't," the 75th took the tartan and the kilt—not without a humorous protest. But as Col. Greenhill Gardyne, the admirable historian of the Gordon Highlanders, says in "The Life of a Regiment," the union has been "a happy one."

During the Great War, the Gordons had eleven battalions in the field, including seven battalions of Territorials. One of these battalions, the 4th, had an (Aberdeen) University Company, which was the only distinctly university battalion in the war. Its history will shortly be published.

The Gordons, who will be installed this year in their barracks in Aberdeen, have a first rate magazine, "The Tiger and Sphinx," which deals with all the battalions. Sir Ian Hamilton, who is a child of the regiment, is colonel, and the Gordons have allied regiments in Toronto, Melbourne and Capetown. In fact, the Gordon Highlanders—a vast family—grow stronger the older they become. But then that only is living up to its motto, " Bydand," which means steadfast.

July 27th, 1917

By A. H. ASHCROFT, D.S.O., M.A.

RICH as the Ypres Salient is in thrilling stories, there is something particularly dramatic, and possibly unique, in the tale of what happened on July 27th, 1917.

How many battalions shared the experience of my own, I do not know to this day ; in the line one rarely had the opportunity of learning what was happening on any but one's own immediate front. I can thus only write of a small Brigade sub-sector, which included amongst other familiar landmarks, Lancashire, Fusilier, and Turco Farms. We were holding and improving the line in preparation for the 51st Division, who were to take part in a large scale attack on the 29th.

For the Salient, the gun-fire was astonishingly subdued, but, as often happened in the War, we were congratulating ourselves in utter ignorance of what was in store. Early in the afternoon we received a message to the effect that air observation suggested that the Germans were evacuating their front system, declining, that is to say, the battle which they knew to be imminent. We were therefore to be in readiness to push out fighting patrols and maintain contact. An hour later more detailed instructions were received, and the three company commanders holding the front line were summoned to receive their orders.

Not until after four in the afternoon did we get the word " go," and—a common experience—the telegram gave little time for further preparation, zero hour having been put at five o'clock. This was not so serious, as somewhat ominously the telegram stated that there would be no artillery barrage for this advance. What was serious was the sentence " If patrols are heavily fired on they will not persevere, but will return to our lines." The event proved that the units on our flanks read this to mean that a number of casualties from snipers was not justified, and they quickly returned to their own trenches. My own C.O. assumed that snipers and machine guns were bound to be left behind as a screen for the enemy, and ordered a withdrawal only in face of greatly superior numbers and a stable defence.

But to come to the narrative of the action. Five patrols, each of an officer and twenty-five other ranks, left our lines shortly after five, and all except one, which was held up by machine gun fire from Canadian Farm, worked their way into the enemy front line—a distance in this sector of about two hundred yards. The first patrol to cover this unsupported journey in broad daylight had hardly got into Calendar Trench, when a body of fifty Germans was seen moving forward in an endeavour to get in on its right flank. These were dispersed by controlled fire, but having thus obtained sufficient proof that the enemy was present in force, the officer in charge decided not to attempt a deeper thrust, but to work his way back and report. Meanwhile No. 2 Patrol under 2nd Lieut. R., had managed to get into Calendar Support, when he found himself threatened by the same enveloping tactics. At the same time he received No. 1's message that he was about to withdraw. Lieut. R. therefore decided to conform, but not before he had captured a prisoner who confirmed the impression, which the events had forced upon the patrols, that the enemy had hoped to entice us forward by lying low, and to obtain from prisoners the exact hour of the forthcoming attack. That the ruse did not altogether succeed was only due to the fighting qualities of our patrols, and the excellent leadership of their subalterns.

Meanwhile, No. 3 Patrol on our left-centre had much the same experience, but unfortunately the officer in charge was badly wounded in the enemy front line. The patrol, however, pushed on under its sergeant to the second line. Here the fire was very hot and our Lewis gun was simply riddled by bullets. Under the pressure it was impossible to locate the fallen officer, and later on we learnt that he had died in enemy hands.

The most difficult task of all fell to our left flank platoon. They could find no support on their left, and though they dealt faithfully with many snipers, they came up against a nest of concrete defences between Cake Lane and Cake Walk. In trying to work round the first of these the whole of the Lewis gun team became casualties, and the withdrawal had to be carried out with rifle-covering-fire only.

Slowly but steadily the little body of men extricated itself out of a menacing position, mainly due to the superb marksmanship and coolness of a boy not yet out of his teens —17114 Private T. Barratt. In each successive rush he was the last to go back, and he set an example to his fellows beyond all praise. With her strange fickleness Fortune deserted him just as he got back—the last of his patrol—to our line. He was killed instantaneously during the very heavy shell-fire which the Germans had maintained on our front line from the moment the patrols had left it. He was posthumously awarded the Victoria Cross, and we felt the Divisional Commander did not put it too highly when he said " I know of no award of the V.C. more richly merited, amongst the records of stirring deeds ; this stands out as second to none."

This is a bald and simple narrative, but it requires no colouring for readers who have knowledge of the Salient, and any spark of imagination. One hundred and thirty men had left our trenches in the clear light of a summer day in the hottest sector on the whole of the Western Front without the support of a single gun or maxim, or tank. Casualties were indeed heavy, but a far greater number had been inflicted on the enemy. If one may compare a Battalion's achievement with a great historical event, it had succeeded in tweaking the Kaiser's moustache at Ypres as effectively as Drake singed the King of Spain's beard at Cadiz.

A. H. A.

Gift to the Ypres British Church

AN interesting and very beautiful gift has come into the possession of St. George's Church, Ypres, by the recent death of the Rev. C. W. Prangley, of Downham Market, Norfolk.

His son, 2nd Lieutenant C. D. Prangley, 1st Lincolnshire Regiment, fell in the advance on Gueudecourt on 25th September, 1916, and in his memory, Mr. George Smith, of Downham Market, designed for the family an illustrated Holy Communion Service Book. This was bequeathed to St. George's Church on the death of Mr. Prangley, the father, and has now been received from the Archdeacon of Wisbech, Norfolk, his great friend.

The book is of unique design, and unusual skill and care must have been exercised in its execution.

Battle of the Aisne

SEPTEMBER, 1914.

By CAPTAIN J. G. W. HYNDSON, M.C.
(*Late*) The Loyal Regiment.
(Author of *From Mons to the First Battle of Ypres*).

AT nightfall on September 13th, my battalion, the 1st Loyal North Lancashire Regiment, together with the units of the 2nd Brigade, were billeted in the village of Moulin. The day had been spent in close contact with the enemy who, after severe fighting, had been driven back from the River Aisne and were known to have established themselves on the Chemin Des Dames ridge overlooking the Aisne Valley.

To protect the advance of the 1st Division next day, the 2nd Brigade was ordered to seize before daybreak the top of the Chemin Des Dames in the neighbourhood of Cerny-En-Laonnois.

At 2 a.m. we were roused in the grey dawn. A thick mist blotted out the whole country-side and the rain was coming down in a steady drizzle, making everything round us look drab and dismal.

After a hasty breakfast of rashers of very salty bacon, bread and jam, with mugs of tea to wash it down, we hurriedly fell in and marched off in the wake of the leading units of the 2nd Brigade who had already preceded us.

We had no sooner got clear of the village when rifle and machine-gun fire broke out some distance in front of us and we knew that the leading units of the Brigade were already in action. We hurried on under a barrage of stray bullets which sounded most unpleasant as they zipped over our heads, cutting down small branches of trees from time to time in their passage. The road twisted for about a mile down to the village of Vendresse, where we halted to seek cover under a very over-grown hedge and to await orders. Meanwhile the volume of fire had increased to an intensity we had not yet experienced and we realised that we were about to plunge into a pretty big battle. The ground in front of us sloped up in a steep ridge along the top of which ran the Chemin Des Dames. There was a big sugar factory on the highest point of the ridge, and the ground was undulating and broken with innumerable small woods and clumps of trees scattered here and there. Nestling in the valley on the British side and sheltered by the ridge, were the villages of Vendresse and Troyon.

From Vendresse the road wound steeply for about a mile until it dipped down into the village of Cerny-En-Laonnois. The Germans, it was discovered, had found time to dig themselves in and were well entrenched on the ridge. They had chosen an excellent position from which they could overlook all our movements and they obviously meant to try and stop any further advance on our part.

We remained in the shelter of the hedge, such as it was, for some time, and several men were wounded in the arms or legs. While we waited, the 1st Guards Brigade swung past and disappeared up the road. From the direction of the firing a batch of some 500 prisoners appeared, escorted to the rear by a few soldiers. Everything was apparently going in our favour. At 9 o'clock orders arrived for us to move up the road and we accordingly moved off in fours. As we toiled up the hill we saw many signs of the struggle. In one place a gun had been knocked into the road, dead men and horses were lying about and a stream of slightly wounded men kept passing us on their way to the First Aid post in Troyon.

We soon reached the top of the hill and halted just short of a point where the road turned left-handed over the ridge. Here the Brigadier met us and issued his orders which were to the effect that we must advance, capture the factory and assist the 1st Guards Brigade, 2nd K.R.R.C., and the Royal Sussex Regiment, who were held up.

In the position where we had halted, we were in comparative shelter beneath a bank bordering the road, but a terrific fire of all kinds swept over our heads and we realised we should be exposed to it in a very few moments. The signal to advance was soon given, and I watched the leading platoon jump over the bank and move forward into the inferno.

A minute or two passed before it was my turn, and then I gave the signal to advance. We leaped on to the bank and rushed forward widely extended. As soon as we topped the bank we were exposed to a devastating fire. Many of the men were struck down at once, but nevertheless we went on by rushes of from sixty to eighty yards. Almost at once two 8 in. shells pitched into the left half of my platoon and seven or eight men disappeared entirely. We were bewildered by the noise of battle and as yet could see nothing of the enemy, but continued to dribble forward, passing through scores of our own dead and wounded. Many of the latter were calling for water and stretcher bearers, but it was not possible to help them as we had to go on. Suffering severe losses, we at last reached the firing line and mixed up with the regiments in the Guard's and our own brigades. Here the casualties were appalling, our men were lying on the ground in heaps. It was impossible to get on any further, so heavy had been the losses during the advance, and, as we were entirely in the open without a vestige of cover, I ordered the men to dig themselves in with their entrenching tools.

The noise of battle was so great that I had to crawl up and down the line to issue instructions. By this time the rain had ceased altogether and visibility was good, so I was able to look round to see if I could take in the situation, and almost at once I spotted the movements of several groups of Huns doubling forward towards us, and also saw others trying to work round our right, near the sugar factory.

I ordered the men to fire at the different targets and had the satisfaction of seeing many of the enemy fall, whilst the remainder stopped and lay down to engage us with rifle fire.

By this time I had only some thirty men left out of the original fifty-six with whom I started the advance, but several men from the units of the Guards' brigade had attached themselves to me. After about an hour, during which time many more men were hit, the Germans brought some fresh batteries of machine guns into action and so accurate was the shooting that we dared not show a head. It was nerve-racking to hear the machine gun bullets traversing up and down the line, especially during the few seconds when they passed directly over us. Meanwhile, under cover of these machine guns and also of several fresh batteries of artillery which had got our exact range, the Germans launched a strong counter attack, and it took us all our time to bring them to a standstill. They came on bravely, surging forward in mass formation, although scores of them were shot down. It was a target of a life-time!

They managed to get to within two hundred yards of our firing line, but the reception they got was too much for them, and the survivors fell back rapidly to their original starting point. Once again the Germans poured a terrific fire of all arms into us. Our numbers diminished, but we hung on grimly, digging ourselves farther and farther into the ground, until the whole of our bodies were under cover of mother earth.

By this time my platoon was reduced to about twenty men unwounded and ammunition was beginning to run short. In anticipation of a fresh effort on the part of the Germans I ordered the men to husband their ammunition and to collect what they could from the dead and wounded as there was no other method of obtaining fresh supplies. The duel continued until about 2.30 p.m., when the expected attack developed. It met with the same fate as the previous one on my particular section of the battlefield, but succeeded in forcing back the troops on the right, thus enabling the Germans to break through, and I watched them sweep on in dense masses far to the rear. It was an awful moment. I thought nothing could prevent us being captured if we were fortunate enough to escape being killed. However, fresh troops from the reserves were available to counter-attack and the German advance was brought to a standstill before they could penetrate too deeply into our position. The danger of being surrounded was for the moment averted, but the fact remained that we were now too far forward and must go back.

I received orders from my Company Commander to withdraw, and, waiting for a lull in the firing, dashed back to a new alignment. Our move was the signal for a fresh outbreak of firing on the part of the Germans, and we doubled back under a perfect tornado of shell and bullets. By a miracle I was not hit, but only ten men in the platoon survived to find shelter in a nullah which we fortunately happened to stumble into. As it appeared impossible to move either backwards or forwards under the hail of bullets, I decided to remain where I was for the present, and did my best to assist in the retirement of the other troops who were all coming back.

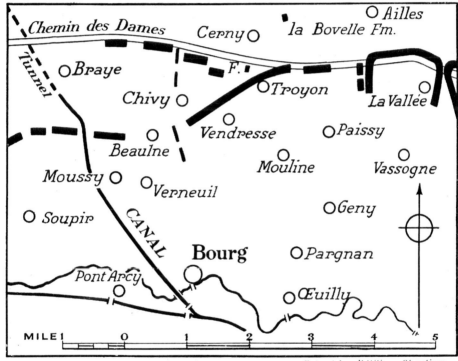

Extract from " Military Operations, France and Belgium, 1914." Volume 1.

The Germans made no attempt to follow the retiring troops and were quite content with their gains. After a time a further withdrawal was carried out to a sunken track just in front of the main Vendresse-Cerny road and here we dug ourselves into the bank and prepared to hold on to the last man.

However, the Huns had suffered untold losses and were far too exhausted to make any further efforts except artillery fire, and this became gradually more spasmodic until the rapidly approaching darkness put an end to the struggle.

It had been a nightmare of a day, and our losses had been awful. In my platoon six men answered the roll call out of a fifty-six who had started the day. The other units in the 1st and 2nd Brigades had suffered equally heavily, but the 3rd Brigade, who were in reserve most of the day, had come off comparatively lightly.

On the other hand, the Germans had sustained appalling losses. Their attacks were generally made in close order and several times we saw whole companies practically annihilated by our accurate marksmanship.

If only our artillery, sadly hampered by the mist, had been able to obtain better observation in the early part of the morning, and been able to find more advantageous positions than the configuration of the ground on our side allowed, the result of the battle would have been very different, and it is conceivable that we might even have gained possession of the Chemin Des Dames, which was the key to the whole position, and given the Germans no option but to continue their rearward movement.

The German artillery on the other hand were not handicapped by the mist to any great extent, more especially as they unhesitatingly fired on both combatants when any doubt existed as to the exact position of their own troops.

J. G. W. H.

85th Club Tour

THE 85th Club has just paid its fifth annual visit to Ypres, but pressure of business prevented a number of keen members from taking part, so on May 25th, nineteen of us started our journey from Victoria by the 11 p.m. service (night route) accompanied by the League's Secretary, Captain de Trafford.

We were blessed with a calm crossing between Folkestone and Dunkerque, and at Hazebrouck we refreshed ourselves with coffee and rolls before boarding the slow Belgian train for Ypres. Just before we reached Poperinghe we passed the Old Military Cemetery by the railway line where one of our comrades lies buried—then the Sacré Cœur Asylum, our billet in 1915, is on our right as we approach Ypres.

On arrival at Skindles Hotel we were accorded the usual hearty welcome by Madame and her efficient staff, and after a good English breakfast we boarded Captain Parminter's cars for a battlefield tour.

An interesting trip was in store for us this year, for we had with us Captain J. G. W. Hyndson, M.C., late of the Loyal North Lancs, who served through the Aisne, the Marne, the Retreat from Mons and the first Battle of Ypres. We passed through Potijze, Zonnebeke and Gheluvelt where Captain Hyndson showed us the very fields on which his battalion fought, and described the German break-through, our rally before Hooge, the historic charge of the Worcesters, the retaking of Gheluvelt and the desperate fighting in the château grounds where gallant General Fitzclarence, V.C., fell leading his Brigade towards Polygon Wood. We continued our journey to Westoutre to visit the grave of a comrade. Passing Hooggraaf, a place of our encampment during the first gas attack, and eventually reached Cassel for an excellent meal provided by the Hotel Sauvage. After lunch we climbed up to the Château grounds, now a public park, from where the clear visibility afforded us a magnificent panoramic view of the Ypres Salient and we were even able to locate the Vimy Ridge, a distance of approximately thirty-five miles. Here, on the summit of Cassel, stands the fine equestrian statue of Marshal Foch gazing out towards the battle area, a replica of this memorial has been erected in Grosvenor Gardens, London.

Our next halt was Talbot House, Poperinghe of sacred memory, a haven of rest to many, both during and since the war. A beautiful garden lies at the back of the Old House, just now, full of many flowering shrubs and all kept trim and neat. Following tea at Skindles we proceed via Elverdinghe to Boesinghe and the Pilckem Ridge from where Captain Hyndson gave us a vivid account of the 1914 Bixchoote scrap, and after a stop at Essex Farm we reached Ypres in time for dinner at which we welcomed the Rev. G. R. Milner and Mr. W. Parminter as guests. At 9 o'clock we all lined up at the Menin Gate for the "Last Post" perfectly rendered by two buglers of the Ypres Fire

Brigade. A most impressive little ceremony and one which is greatly respected by the town's folk.

Late evening a sing-song was enjoyed of the old choruses so familiar in our camping days, on the march and in our own unit's pantomimes.

Sunday morning we visited friends and places of interest, not forgetting the British Church and School. At noon we assembled on the Ramparts by the "Gate" to hold our annual service of remembrance, conducted by the Rev. G. R. Milner, and to place a wreath before the names of the R.A.M.C. fallen. In the afternoon Captain Hyndson took some of us to Tyne Cot and Polygon Wood. Many of the local inhabitants with their

Photo] [Daniel, Ypres
85th CLUB PARTY AT THE MENIN GATE.

children visit these cemeteries of ours' on Sunday afternoon, parking their bicycles outside. These are the only places where they can tread upon real English green sward which the children seem to enjoy, but we were glad to notice that due reverence is observed.

At 5 p.m. we entrained for Dunkerque, where we were once more the guests of the Seamen's Memorial Institute. Here the Chaplain showed us the historic Consul's room in which Lord Kitchener promised Joffre the full support of the whole British Empire.

A calm crossing to Folkestone enabled us to get several hours wanted sleep, and we arrived at Victoria at 7.40 Monday morning, in time to turn into our offices, tired, but full of such happy memories and already looking forward to an equally pleasant trip a year hence. Many thanks to all responsible for our comfort and safe journey.

First Shots

IN March, 1914, the White Nile was lower than it had been for many years. All steamers running northwards were consequently late, and a subaltern, who had been spending his leave big game shooting, was constrained to cable from Khartoum to the Commandant of the Cavalry School, that an " act of God " prevented him from reaching Netheravon by the 1st April.

There was little thought in his head that the King's Enemies would send him on his travels again within six months.

Hectic days at the Cavalry School—three or four horses to ride a day, either to school or be schooled on—occasional dashes to catch the 1.40 at Salisbury to play polo in London and back again for 6 a.m. parade the following day.

Then rumours of war, impatience with the Government and bets on the chances and orders to mobilise. Would anyone there kill a German with his own hand?

One Instructor was prepared to bet even money with every student there against it, perhaps to encourage the cavalry spirit!

Mobilisation was simple but strenuous. It took every hour of daylight and every hour was a full one.

Horses arrived to make the Regiment up to war strength often ill shod and coats of hair of at least two inches thick.

All draught horses had to be fitted into new harness from mobilisation store and tried out in teams to see if they would go kindly together. Reservists had to be clothed and equipped and got fit.

Yet they disembarked at Havre on the 17th August, and only one horse in the Brigade fell out of its slings into the sea and that was fished out again.

Rest Camp at Havre meant a few hours before the train was ready, and time for a bathe in the sea.

A dozen French interpreters joined up in the quaintest variety of uniform including one volunteer without any uniform at all.

Inhabitants were enthusiastic with gifts of flowers and fruits and the Dragoons were " en fete " and happy.

No time for more than a glad eye *en passant* or a kiss blown from the saddle. That they could not talk French worried them not at all.

A great joke was the dyeing of all the grey horses with permanganate of potash; in a night all became liver chestnuts—and the next day? Entrainment always to the unknown destination which proved to be Aulnoye, near Beaufort—a first experience of billets.

Addresses of welcome from the Mayor and more flowers.

On this day the first instance on record of the mechanisation of cavalry occurred in the form of a motor cycle smuggled out with the motor transport and delivered at Beaufort. The owner whose first servant rode it throughout the retreat, saw little of either, but his Commanding Officer had many reasons to bless the irregularity that brought him so swift a despatch rider. (The cycle was blown up by a shell at Braisne on the Aisne and the D.R. killed in 1917 at Monchy, near Arras.)

On 21st August they advanced South of Maubeuge, crossed the Belgian frontier at Erquelinnes to take up an outpost line at Binche, the Brigade covering about ten kilometres of front. For miles to the north every building seemed to be on fire.

At about 10 a.m. of the 22nd, the first real live enemy were seen. An officer's patrol towards Nivelles saw large numbers of cavalry on that road, another to Haine St. Paul, near La Louviere, had a scrap, and then two mounted men rode down to the crossing of the river Senne into the small village of Peronnes.

A wire obstacle had been constructed here and sentries posted. The troop, under cover, were playing " House."

One learns many things big game shooting. A moving target is not easy to hit, and many hits may not " stop " or kill. The excitement by the thrill of firing at a living target is not conducive to a steady hand.

The men of this troop learn something of these lessons now.

Their positions are swiftly and silently manned. Some hundreds of their comrades lie and watch the arena from the hill behind.

No one breathes. The two Germans ride on down half-a-mile of straight pavé.

They come right up to the wire obstacle within a few yards of the ambushed troop. Then half-a-dozen men fire. One German falls dead, the other disappears in a clatter up the road hanging round his horse's neck.

Both horses seem to escape ; but who can say ?

An enterprising man goes out to take the shoulder tab of the fallen warrior, for identification is all important. There is a crack and a ricochet passes unpleasantly close. In his dive back to cover his glasses get caught up in the wire and he struggles ludicrously like a rabbit in a snare. For a minute or two there is quiet. Then for all the world like peace manœuvres, a party of German Staff Officers ride up on to the sky line. Laboriously they dismount, hand over their horses, and start to take out maps and glasses.

Still no sound from the watchers. As they group themselves conveniently against their led horses, one machine gun opens fire.

Too far to hear their oaths, but men on the ground and horses loose, men running, and a scene of chaos, are plainly visible through glasses.

Again an interval of quiet and no sound. One battery comes into action and a few shells burst high in air and harmlessly.

Lines of skirmishers appear on the far hillside, and move slowly down the slope at over two thousand yards range. They bunch in the gaps of the wire fences, and more machine guns start to take toll.

Meanwhile, two miles away to the left front and not far from the machine gunners first target, a detached post of a troop are lying up in the village of Manage.

They are watching the battle and the villagers are cooking them a stew, for it is now 1 p.m.

A strong company of German infantry march up to the edge of Manage, pile arms and prepare their dinners.

The Troop Leader's plan is to crawl up to a garden wall, fire fifteen rounds rapid, and then beat a hasty retreat.

The Regimental Sergeant Major arrives with a message—" You are to retire at once." The Regiment is already on the move. The Brigade has to move to the west and replace another Brigade of the Division.

So the action is broken off. The players in the first act of the drama, hardly yet realising that they are not on manœuvres, get back to their horses and trek.

One officer had his thigh broken, his ammunition was removed and he was placed in an ambulance cab to be taken prisoner the following day.

When his leg was healed he escaped and returned to England.

A man was wounded in the hand and made nothing of his wound which afterwards proved serious.

There was a gap of nine miles between the British right and the French on this day. The incident occurred in covering this gap.

In history a little more than a Squadron had bumped against the advanced guard of the 7th German Army Corps, and caused the 13th Division to deploy, thereby delaying it by four hours.

TWENTY YEARS AGO.

A Farewell to Ypres

IN the July, 1933, edition of the *Ypres Times*, I described John Brown's last day on the Somme in 1916, and here I propose to give a short account of his last day in the Salient.

Having made a good recovery from his wounds, he returned to the front as an officer in a north-country regiment during the first week of June, 1917. After a few days of discomfort in the hot sandy desert of Etaples, where time was divided between the Bull Ring and a very indifferent Mess, varied by the thrill of two violent thunderstorms and news of the Battle of Messines, he received orders to join his battalion. He found them enjoying a rest in a French village after having had a rough time at Arras. This was a pleasant change after the trials of Etaples, and although it did not last long, he enjoyed every minute of it. The hot weather continued, and the march up towards Ypres was carried out during the small hours of the morning, spread over three or four days; but even so it tried many of the men, and Brown often carried three or four rifles slung over his shoulder. After nearly a year away from the line he found a great difference in the physique and stamina of the men, and when at the end of the march he was ordered to take the crocks to the Divisional General for inspection, under the eyes of the Flemish peasants, he did not appreciate his task.

That summer was spent on the new front at Wytschaete. The battalion was in the attack of July 31st, the first day of the third Battle of Ypres, and otherwise was in and out of the line in the usual monotonous fashion. A pleasant feature of the summer was a rest in the woods of Kemmel Hill, with a wonderful view of the German lines and the country beyond. Towards the end of September the Division took over another sector to the north, and Brown's battalion found itself in tunnels near Hill 60. These were most depressing places, with the pumps continually at work clearing the water, but they could not clear the atmosphere, which was certainly not conducive to good health. The shells regularly thudded on the earthen roof, and in one portion had penetrated it, but on the whole it was a safe spot, which, however, was not to afford shelter to Brown for very long. During the evening of the 24th September, he received instructions from his C.O. to proceed at 2 o'clock the following morning with a Sergeant and twenty men, led by a guide, to the front line with trench mortar ammunition, which must be delivered without fail.

Punctually at 2 a.m. on the 25th, the little party crawled through the entrance to the tunnel on their way to the dump. It was very dark, and this probably caused their troubles to begin early, as the guide soon announced that he had lost his way. After considerable time had been wasted in groping about, a duck-board track was struck, and the guide reported that he was now on the right road for the dump, although Brown did not feel too confident. However, right or wrong, they were destined never to see that dump. Before long shells began to burst around them and officer and sergeant were kept busy in preventing the men from scattering. Orders were orders, and it was imperative that the ammunition must be got to the front line, so Brown had no thought of retreat. In any event, there was no cover, and it seemed as dangerous to go back as to go forward.

The shells fell faster and faster, and soon—a blinding flash, and Brown found himself lifted off his feet and deposited on his back on a disordered heap of duck-boards. The sergeant was wounded, but on his feet, while others lay dead and wounded around. The completion of his task was now impossible, Brown ordered the unwounded to return to headquarters, and to come back with stretchers, by which time the shelling would probably have ceased. On either side of the wounded officer lay a man groaning, and he now turned his attention to them. The one on his right told him that his leg was blown off, and the poor fellow was right. Before long he became delirious, begging Brown not to go without him, adding: "You have always been a good friend to me, Mr. Brown, and so has Mr. ——." He died the following night in the C.C.S. On the left lay groaning a mere boy, who told his officer that he was dying. In this case what appeared to be a tragedy turned to comedy, for the dying boy suddenly rose to his feet and ran for his life towards safety. Brown's right leg was badly mangled, and splinters had hit him in the chest, the hand and the throat. His pipe was blown to atoms in his pocket, and may easily have saved him from a further wound. The shells continued to burst on all sides, and his worst wound was yet to come. As each shell came near he bent his head in the direction of the burst in the hope that his tin hat would afford some protection, but at last came one that burst through that frail defence. It took his unwounded leg, fracturing the femur, with a distinctly heard crack, sending a shudder through his body from head to foot, but for the time there was no pain. That came later! Providentially he did not lose consciousness, and with

Photo] [Imperial War Museum, Crown Copyright
CARRYING THE WOUNDED BACK THROUGH THE MUD—YPRES, 1917.

a constant appeal of " Don't leave me, sir," always in his ears, called for help as his strength allowed him. Day was now breaking, and two artillerymen located them in the dim light. They had heard Brown's calls, and had only been waiting for the shelling to abate a little before coming to the rescue. Away they went again, soon returning with reinforcements and stretchers. As those good fellows gently lifted his mangled thirteen-stone body on to the stretcher, and carried him over shell-holes, the considerable distance to the dressing station, real hard labour willingly given for a complete stranger, Brown realised more than he had ever done before, the self-sacrificing comradeship of the Great War.

After attention at the dressing station, the ambulance carried him away past Hell-Fire Corner, the Menin Gate, and through the immortal ruins of Ypres, on to the 3rd Canadian C.C.S., the exact location of which he did not discover. What took place here was afterwards wrapped in mist. He remembered passing his companion in distress lying in bed, and wishing him good luck, to which he received a cheery but weak reply from a man who had only a few hours to live. He remembered the Sister putting hot water bottles in bed with him, and he remembered asking her if she was an American, and being told that she was a Canadian. He afterwards learned from his "case-sheet" that he had undergone an operation here. but he knew nothing of it.

In a few days he left for Rouen, and said "good-bye" to the Salient in war-time, and farewell to the war as a fighting soldier. He arrived at Rouen in the middle of the night, and did not forget the painful journey from the station to the hospital, or the smell of petrol fumes which pervaded the ambulance. Dreary weeks followed, with both legs suspended on splints at an angle of about forty-five degrees to the roof of what was known as a Sinclair bed, a wooden framework fitted with pulleys which raised and lowered him as required. The brightest spot in his stay at Rouen was a visit from H.R.H. The Duke of Connaught, with whom he had a pleasant chat which left behind a permanent feeling of admiration for that fine old soldier.

On the last day of November he set sail for England, but his troubles were far from over. More than once he was to lie at the point of death, but he refused to die, and a fine constitution eventually pulled him through. After many operations, his left leg was amputated on Armistice Day, and he was one of the few who did not celebrate that memorable day in some way or other. In fact he knew nothing of the Armistice until the following day.

This was his final operation, and it doubtless saved his life; which may be said to have been a happy ending to the war so far as John Brown was concerned.

J. B.

The Smell of "Wipers"

By ARTHUR LAMBERT (Author of *Over the Top*).

SURVIVORS of the long years in the Salient are now approaching the sere and yellow. Bones are aching, teeth are beginning to decay, hair is beginning to go grey, and all the senses commencing to lose their youthful vigour. Even the unforgettable memories of those battles in which we all wallowed in indescribable filth and misery are becoming dim, as each year places them another step away.

Our work and our homes are filling our minds just a modicum more, as each month flits quickly by. The babies of twenty years ago have reached maturity and are now supplying the daily details of the present to the exclusion of the past. The back-fire of a motor engine in the High Street is replacing the memory of the 5·9 shells that kept trying to bury us in Jolting House Trench, and the fragrance of our gardens, and the fresh green English fields are replacing the odours of Ypres, the charnel house of Europe.

Did the smell of the Salient permeate your being during your martyrdom? Was that sickly aroma always in your nostrils, affecting your breathing, and your eating and smoking, and sleeping if you ever did any?

There was never anything quite like it, and many ruminations as to its source, during those interminable hours in the dug-out or trench failed to produce a reasonable theory as to its origin. Probably a combination of swampy earth, rotting wood, dead animals, stagnant water, poison gas, high explosives, phosphorus, and the dozens of natural gases rising from the shattered earth, combine to produce a pungent, slightly aromatic odour that was unique and omnipresent. A trifling discomfort to one sense in a life of agony that outraged all the senses and one that was forgotten when there was a sea between us and that patch of tortured earth.

How strange to experience it again after fifteen years!

Time had taken its toll of me, and memories of the Salient were very deep down, only coming to the surface, when sudden, unexpected meetings with old comrades brought a gleam to the eye, and a flood of reminiscence to the tongue.

I was wandering round Poole Harbour, that lovely stretch of water comparable to Naples Bay, and so far away was the Army that no thought of a Sergeant Major's comments on my dress ever came to mind. Khaki tunic, ammunition belt, water bottle and bayonet had been replaced by tennis shirt (outrageously open at the neck) loose and comfortable flannel bags, and "blazer." There was no peaked cap, and indeed no cap at all, and the light south-westerly wind ruffled my greying hair, as it ruffled the thousand pennants of the yachts rocking gently on the green waters.

It was a clean and refreshing breeze, with a tang of the salt that it had borrowed from the English Channel, and it combined with the blue sky, and the bright sun to produce a feeling of peace and contentment as I crossed the swing bridge leading to Hamworthy Island.

There was no thought of the stagnant mud of Hooge or Gheluvelt, as I watched the swift waters running along the quay sides, or of poisoned air, as I sniffed the breeze into my lungs.

Suddenly my nostrils distended and a look of disgust must have crossed my tanned face. Borne on the back of the invisible wind had come, an odour, langorous and sickly, that stirred up some memory that had been buried for many a year, and which was difficult of identification.

A heavier puff of wind brought a stronger reminder, and then conviction, that from the direction of jolly Sandbanks, and pretty Swanage, and those lovely Purbeck Hills was coming the smell of Ypres!

For a few seconds Poole with its ancient houses, and its harbour alive with shipping faded away, and in its place was a pock-marked swamp, with a few tree-trunks, lolling drunkenly at various angles, and a confused clutter of rusty wire, squat concrete buildings and a number of silent and mournful tanks, deep in clinging mud. There was a main road running out of a ruined town, with tracks of heavy timber radiating from it in all directions, and over the whole district a pall of smoke and rising from it an odour precisely similar to that now sweeping along from the noble, peaceful Dorset coast.

A nausea overcame me and a desire to retreat followed by a determination to discover the cause of this evil imposition of a forgotten horror on a pleasant holiday. A smart walk for a quarter-mile revealed that the sense of smell had not been in error.

On the pleasant banks of the harbour, facing the pine covered cliffs of Bournemouth was a graveyard of War. Masses of torn and shattered guns, rolls of rusty wire and shell cases, tin-hats, old Lewis guns and rifles, portions of submarines encrusted with barnacles and weeds from ocean beds, limbers with shattered wheels, wrecked lorries, and the thousand and one battered remnants left on a battlefield after the battle has died away.

From the heap of filthy junk came the unmistakeable smell of Ypres, and for a few seconds I surveyed the scene with twitching nostrils and a mind full of memories of those long-dead months. Then lugging a pipe out of a hip pocket, and filling and lighting it, I turned tail and hurried back to the town, puffing furiously, and determining to have a long swim in clean, cold English sea-water at the earliest possible moment.

A. L.

Sporting Days in the Salient and Elsewhere

By Lieut.-Col. G. J. Henderson.

THE day before the battle of Neuve Chapelle, in March, 1915, I was posted to command a battery in the 6th Division at Armentieres. Straight in front of Armentieres, and in the German lines, was the village of Wesmacar which contained a church with a fairly high tower, still standing, and fairly complete except for a few shell holes through its sides. I had observed flashes of light at one of these shell holes in the tower, which I took to be field glasses of a German observing officer. I therefore reported the fact, and the 60-pounder guns were turned on to knock the tower down. I witnessed the shoot from my O.P. It was one of the prettiest pieces of pin-point shooting I have ever seen done. Sixteen rounds were fired, and never one far off a direct hit. Six or seven shots actually hit the tower, and the sixteenth brought it down with a crash. So we were rid of that very annoying fellow with the field-glasses.

The whole performance seemed to annoy the enemy, for he retaliated by violently shelling Chapelle d'Armentieres, one of our observing stations. He fired 60 or 70 rounds but failed to bring it down, which, I think, was one up to us.

Shortly after this the Second Battle of Ypres took place, and we at Armentieres could see the bursting shells and hear the guns quite plainly. When it finished the 6th Division was sent up to Ypres to relieve one of the British Divisions that had fought in that infernal gas battle.

A friend of mine, who commanded another battery in the same brigade, was very keen on attacking the enemy's guns with his 18-pounders. I caught the infection, and we used to sort of hunt in couples for the hostile guns; and with fairly good effect, as was proved by the fact that we saw the German gunners running away from their guns in a certain battery of which we could see the position—a shocking sight which I have seen more than once in the German Artillery, but never once in our own. Later on, when I commanded a brigade, I had to order the men away from the guns of one of my batteries, whose guns were being steadily blown up by a German 8-inch battery with aeroplane observation. It made me think that we had established a superiority over the German artillery in morale, if not in weight and numbers.

To return to our muttons. We got comfortably settled down in the Salient, and a month or two later I put one gun of my battery right forward about 800 yards behind the front line. This I called the subalterns' gun, as it was very useful for training young subalterns who were a little shy of bringing the battery into action to shoot at things they fancied. They did not have any shyness about bringing the single gun into action.

I used to use it for attacking hostile anti-aircraft batteries. One could spot these batteries fairly easily as they shot up into the air, and their slight puffs of smoke were generally visible.

One of these batteries took up a position near the Frezenberg Road and we called him the Frezenberg Battery. He had four guns. I located his position on the map by a compass-bearing from my O.P. and by taking the time by stop-watch between his flash and report. That I got him fairly accurately was proved by the fact that whenever I saw one of our aeroplanes going out I turned my single gun on to the Frezenberg Battery. The moment he opened fire I used to give him three rounds gun-fire repeated several times. He never fired more than three or four shots at the aeroplane, and then stopped firing.

He found his position unhealthy and left it, but we traced him again and repeated the treatment with similar effect. I went home on five days' leave about this time, and my captain continued the chase. He told me when I returned that he had hunted this battery out of six different positions. Eventually it disappeared altogether, and our sport in that direction ceased.

The enemy took a great dislike to my single forward gun, and used to keep an aeroplane cruising up and down behind the lines. The moment my subalterns' gun opened fire the aeroplane used to make a bee line for it. Eventually they thought they had found its position, and they nearly had—but not quite.

They opened fire on it one day from almost directly to our right and slightly to the rear with a 5.9 and 4.2 battery. They searched up and down 200 or 300 yards for several hours. Their longest shots were range exactly, but about 20 yards off the line. One 4.2 shell took a different line from the rest and just hit the corner of the gun emplacement, but did not damage the gun, although it satisfied the Germans who left it severely alone in the future.

The detachment sat by all this time in a cellar of a ruined house watching the "strafe," and, I have no doubt, praying that no shell would hit the gun.

Shortly after this I left the battery to do a job at Corps Headquarters in connection with locating the enemy's batteries with a view to counter-battery work.

Just before I left the battery one of my subalterns came tearing down from the O.P. in a great state of excitement and announced that he had shot a railway engine in Zonnebeke station. I laughed and said, "Good man, how did you do it?" He said that he had seen a train come into Zonnebeke, cocked up the single gun to its extreme range, about 10,000 yard, and let fly a high explosive shell. He said the engine went up in a cloud of steam and puffed slowly out of the station. No doubt what had happened was that the shell had burst near the engine and a splinter had gone through the boiler.

I developed quite an affection for this single gun. We used to change the detachments weekly, and I think the men enjoyed their tours of duty with this forward gun. Anyway it produced a sense of rivalry between the different detachments as to who should do the most good work with it.

G.H.J.

War Book Review

"From Mons to the First Battle of Ypres."—By J. G. W. HYNDSON, M.C.

This straightforward account of the personal experience of a regimental officer during the opening stages of the Great War is well worth reading. Captain Hyndson has made good use of the original British Expeditionary Force. He went out in August, 1914, as a platoon commander of the 1st Loyal North Lancashire Regiment (2nd Brigade, 1st Division) and served through the retreat from Mons, the battles of the Marne and the Aisne, and the terrific struggle before Ypres during October and November. He describes faithfully the reaction of the professional soldier to the first sights and sounds of modern war, but the best portion of the narrative is his simple, vivid account of "First Ypres." Here the Loyals were part of the great sacrifice made by the Regular Army. Captain Hyndson, who soon found himself commanding a company, and for a short space the remnants of his battalion, tells us that it lost in all 30 officers and 1,000 men. The attack near Bixchoote, the 23rd of October, and the struggle near Gheluvelt on the last day of the month, are remembered by the Regiment with particular pride. General Sir Edward Bulfin, who commanded the 2nd Brigade at the time, contributes an appreciative introduction.

"THE ARMY QUARTERLY."

The above-mentioned war book can be obtained from the Secretary, Ypres League, 20, Orchard Street, London, W.1. Price 5s., post free 5s. 3d.

League Secretary's Notes

There are persons who actually survived the Great War period generously extending their imaginative discouragement by asserting that memories of war are merely matter for the historian, but it is obvious that such persons, however good their intentions, are completely devoid of practical knowledge of the fighting man and the wonderful comradeship of the trenches.

Why, then, has every belligerent nation of the world war set up their respective ex-service associations, thereby dispelling any doubt whatever that the great comradeship of the war is something unmeasured in the lives of those who served and suffered Happily, because there are the many thousands who "understand" and are comforted to know that there exists, after all this lapse of time, associations not only to maintain the good fellowship, but to keep the heroic deeds and sacrifices before those who were too young to participate in the 1914-18 grim encounter, as a preventative of a further catastrophe.

The younger generation's desire to grasp such education was proved as a result of our recent Public Schools O.T.C. battlefield tour to Ypres, when the keenest interest was expressed by the cadets in the League's aims and objects, and a letter which we have pleasure to publish in the correspondence column contains similar appreciation. Further, many young Territorial Officers of the H.A.C., and 167th Infantry Brigade, who travelled to the battlefields last spring under our auspices, have also shown their admiration of the Ypres League and its work.

It is our pleasant duty to welcome very heartily all who have enrolled as members of the League since the publication of our April *Ypres Times* and to thank our staunch Branch Committees and individual supporters who have been instrumental in the recruitments.

Our annual Easter and Whitsuntide pilgrimages to Ypres were again a great success and patronised by goodly musters of members and friends, many of whom were enjoying their first visits to the old battle haunts since the war. At Whitsuntide, the League defrayed expenses of a number of specially selected poor mothers and widows from Gateshead, Colchester, Canterbury and London for their initial visits to the graves of their sons and husbands situated in the Salient, and for the recommendations we are greatly indebted for the kind co-operation of Colonel E. C. Crouch, Mr. W. H. Taylor, "The Kentish Gazette," and to our London County Committee respectively.

On Sunday, July 29th, H.M. the King of the Belgians has graciously consented to visit the Yrpes British School. Members of the Ypres British Settlement Committee will be present.

The last April edition gave considerable space to the subject of the "*Ypres Times*, Maintenance Fund," and we cannot allow this letter to close without conveying our sincere thanks to many members who continue to signify their willingness to contribute donations towards the heavy expense of the journal when remitting their annual subscriptions. Letters of appreciation of our little "quarterly" seem to increase, and, needless to say, it is a great encouragement to headquarters to know that the *Ypres Times* is so well received and enjoyed.

OBITUARY.
Major J. R. Ainsworth-Davis, M.A.

We regret to announce the death of Major Ainsworth-Davis, a valued member of our General Committee. Major Davis always showed a very keen interest in the League's activities, and he rendered splendid service during the time he was Chairman of our London Branch.

Our deepest sympathy is extended to Mrs. Ainsworth-Davis and family.

MR. HENRY BENSON, M.A.

It is with extreme pleasure that we are able to announce the acceptance by Mr. Benson of the Ypres League's invitation to become a member of the General Committee.

Mr. Benson's high prestige in the literary world is well known, and the fine articles that he has from time to time contributed gratis to the columns of the YPRES TIMES have been greatly valued by the Committee and much enjoyed by our readers. The impressive narrative from his pen on the late King Albert, which we had privilege to publish in the last April edition, elicited many letters of praise, including one from His Excellency, The Belgian Ambassador, requesting six additional copies to send to friends in Belgium, and another from the 13th Belgian Field Artillery Association at Liège asking for five extra copies.

Mr. Benson has always had the cause of the Ypres League at heart, and he has continually expressed his admiration of our movement, particularly in regard to the League's charitable work in defraying expenses of specially selected poor mothers and widows to Ypres to see the last resting places of their sons and husbands for the first time.

We consider it an honour to welcome Mr. Benson as a member of our General Committee, and we have pleasure to record our gratitude for all he has so willingly done for us in the past and for the kind way in which he has now closely associated himself with the Ypres League.

YPRES LEAGUE BADGE.

The design of the badge—a lion guarding a portcullis gate—represents the British Army defending the Salient, which was the gate to the Channel Ports.

The badge, herewith reproduced, is brilliantly enamelled with silver finish. Price 2s., post free 2s. 1½d. (pin or stud, whichever is desired).

AUGUST BANK HOLIDAY PILGRIMAGES (CONDUCTED)

(SATURDAY to TUESDAY)

AUGUST 4th to 7th

PILGRIMAGE TO **YPRES**

PILGRIMAGE TO **ARRAS and THE SOMME**

Application for Prospectus should be made to Secretary, Ypres League, 20, Orchard Street, London, W.1.

YPRES
Skindles Hotel
(Opposite the Station)

Proprietor—Life Member, Ypres League

Branch at Poperinghe
(close to Talbot House)

HOTEL
Splendid & Britannique
YPRES
GRAND' PLACE. Opposite Cloth Hall.

LEADING HOTEL FOR COMFORT AND QUALITY.

COMPLETELY RENOVATED

RUNNING WATER. BATHROOMS.

MODERATE TERMS. GARAGE.

Patronized by The Ypres League.

THE BRITISH TOURING SERVICE

Manager—Mr. P. VYNER
Representative and Life Member, Ypres League

**10, Station Square
ARRAS
(P.-de-C.) France**

Cars for Hire, with British Driver Guides   Tours Arranged

Branch Notes

LONDON COUNTY COMMITTEE.

Re-union Dinner and Dance

"St. George for England" is the motto we generally connect with our Patron Saint—a day which will always be held in memory by Englishmen throughout the world, for was it not on this day that the bold and glorious raid on Zeebrugge took place

It was therefore particularly appropriate that the Saturday preceding St. George's Day should have been chosen for the occasion of our tenth Re-union Dinner and Dance, meanwhile our comrades in arms were celebrating the Zeebrugge

how Ypres stood out so eminently during the dark days of the war as an example of the indomitable courage and endurance of our soldiers and why a little of this spirit was so necessary now in the trying days of peace.

Major E. Montague Jones, Chairman of the London County Committee, then gave a resumé of the work of the Committee and thanked each member for their admirable support, mentioning in particular the good work of the Hon. Secretary, Mr. J. Boughey, and concluded a brief but spirited speech with an earnest appeal to all with regard to the necessity of enrolling new members. A call was made for all present to rise and drink

Photo]   YPRES LEAGUE RE-UNION DINNER, 1934   [Ed Sharp, London.

anniversary at an adjacent hotel. In the spacious dining-hall of the Royal Hotel, Woburn Place, W.C.1, some eighty members and friends gathered under the Chairmanship of that distinguished soldier, General Sir Hubert Gough, and sat down to enjoy the splendid meal that was provided.

During the dinner a message conveying the heartiest greetings from the Zeebrugge Association was received from their Chairman, Admiral of the Fleet, Sir Roger Keyes to which our own assembly suitably reciprocated.

Following the loyal toast to His Majesty, our Chairman, in his frank and soldierly manner, spoke of the reasons for this Re-union, and added

the health of our distinguished Chairman for the evening, whom we were greatly honoured in having to preside, and one who will be remembered for his gallant services to the Empire during the Great War. Sir Hubert, on rising to reply amid cheers, thanked the assembly for giving him so enthusiastic a welcome.

At the conclusion of the dinner the room was cleared to enable the dance to proceed, and after a most enjoyable evening another successful function was brought to a close with the singing of the National Anthem. The absence of many of our friends who are regular attendants at the Informal Gatherings was regretted, but we hope they may join us on the next occasion so that instead of 80 we may have 180 present.

Informal Gatherings.

Another successful season is drawing to a close, and our gratitude is extended to the many staunch helpers who have come forward to give us such enjoyable evenings.

These Gatherings, held for members and friends at the "Bedford Head Hotel," Maiden Lane, Strand, on the third Thursday of each month, continue to be well attended and revive in no small way the good fellowship of the war.

On Thursday, April 19th, an excellent entertainment was provided by our good friends of the 85th Club, over which their able Chairman, Mr. F. Underhill, presided. The two following monthly Informals in May and June were of an impromptu character and we were agreeably surprised to discover such marked talent available. We thank all who gave their valued services, and look forward to hearing them again in the future and also others who may be kind enough to add similar support. The organizing of a fresh series of Informal Gatherings involve considerable work on the Committee, and any kind offers from members and friends expressing their willingness to arrange an evening's programme would indeed be very greatly appreciated.

On behalf of the Committee and all its London members we extend heartiest congratulations to our esteemed Patron, Viscount Wakefield of Hythe, on the honour recently bestowed upon him by His Majesty the King.

The London County Committee record with deep regret the loss of two great friends, namely, Major J. R. Ainsworth-Davis, former Chairman of the Committee, and Lieut.-General Sir Herbert Uniacke, both of whom displayed very keen and valued interest in the London functions, which have profited greatly by their help and presence.

The London County Committee express their grateful thanks to Mr. W. C. Parker for the admirable way in which he carried out the duties of M.C. for the Dance that followed the Re-union Dinner.

Dances.

Arrangements have been made for dances to take place at the Veterans' Club, Hand Court, Holborn, W.C.1, on Friday, November 23rd, 1934; Wednesday, January 23rd; and Friday, March 8th, 1935. Full particulars will be announced later.

PLEASE RESERVE THIS DATE.

THE
TWELFTH ANNUAL REUNION

SMOKING CONCERT

(Organised by the London County Committee)

will be held on

Saturday, October 27th, 1934
at 7.30 p.m.
IN
Caxton Hall, Caxton St., Victoria Street, S.W.1

Tickets 1/-, 2/6d., 5/- (Including Tax)
Now available

The support of all members is earnestly solicited as we hope very much to record a bumper attendance this year.

Full particulars will appear in the next October edition of the "Ypres Times."

COLCHESTER.

Obituary.

We deeply regret to record the sudden death of Captain C. P. Thomas, a very active member of our Colchester Branch Committee. It will be remembered that the success of the first Annual Ball held by the Branch last year was very largely due to his fine organising ability, and by his death we have lost one of the keenest supporters. The funeral was attended by the following members of the Branch, who took a wreath composed of irises and cornflowers:—Capt. A. S. Palmer, Mr. M. McKinley, Mr. A. Wooton, Mr. D. Shadrach, Mr. S. C. Nixon and Mr. H. Snow.

1934 Recruiting Competition

IN view of the popularity and immense success of the past three recruiting competitions, we have great pleasure to insert a reminder that **A FURTHER PRIZE OF £5** will be awarded this year as follows :—

TO THE BRANCH RECRUITING THE GREATEST NUMBER OF NEW MEMBERS IN 1934.

All membership forms completed must be received at headquarters bearing on the top left-hand corner the name of the branch responsible for the recruitment.

PURLEY BRANCH.

The Spring Golf Meeting of the Purley Branch took place on Thursday, the 10th May, at Woocote Park Golf Club, in the afternoon, and 43 Members played for the Seventh Wipers Cup.

It was a beautifully fine afternoon throughout, and members began to fire off soon after 2 p.m.; the greater number came down to play after tea, when the first tee was quite gay with the League ties.

The early starters provided only two good returns: Pte. H. Boon and Capt. L. R. Ray, a previous winner, two down to bogey; this was equalled later by Capt. E. C. Ashby, but all three were beaten by Capt. M. K. Scott, who played a very good round to be all square.

Thirty-seven sat down to the supper which followed in the Club House, when the Chairman of the Branch, Capt. R. L. Haine, V.C., M.C., presided. He made a remarkably good opening by telling a story, then presenting the Seventh Wipers Cup to Capt. M. K. Scott, calling upon the Adjutant, Major Graham Carr, D.S.O., M.C., to explain how the Committee solved the problem of which of the three next best, with two down, should receive the prize. This turned out to be fairly simple, as Pte. H. Boon won by having the better return of the last nine holes.

The Adjutant commented on the many fine scores that had been made, and drew the Chairman's attention to the fact that a nil-return stood to the discredit of several members who would, of course, be invited to stand up later and explain why.

Capt. Scott and Pte. Boon responded very happily, and later many members contributed to the amusing evening by some vivid stories.

The proceedings could not terminate without the Chairman thanking the host Club, in the person of the reigning captain, J. Kingsley-Jones, who was present in the Vice-Chair, for the courtesy and kindness extended to our members, then we all went home.

Correspondence

53, St. Barnabas Road,
Essex.

To Secretary, Ypres League   10.5.34.

Dear Sir,

By mere chance a copy of the YPRES TIMES has come into my possession, and after reading its pages I am truly amazed that a spirit of fellowship born almost twenty years ago should be so much alive to-day as to be able to produce such material evidence of its existence.

I am one of the new generation, being only a schoolboy when the war ended, and I have heard and read much of the comradeship of the trenches, but with the passing of years I had thought that comradeship had passed. I must even confess that I was unaware of the existence of the Ypres League, as no doubt are many of my age. Alas! how ignorant we are. Nevertheless, I have always been keenly interested in anything having connection with those four years which remain so vividly impressive in my childhood memories.

May I, therefore, take this opportunity of wishing the Ypres League and "Times" a long, long, life, and at the same time I would mention that I should regard it as an honour to join the ranks of the League. Will you kindly let me have full particulars with a view to my joining? My age is 25.

Yours very sincerely,

GEORGE A. WILSON.

7, Waterloo Road,
New Brighton,
Wallasey.

The Secretary,   18.6.34.
Ypres League,
20, Orchard St., W.1.

Dear Sir,

May I once again intrude in the columns of the *Ypres Times* to express my sincere thanks to all those members of the Ypres League who have responded—or intend to respond—to my call for financial aid in order that the continued and regular publication of the *Ypres Times* may be assured.

I hope that by this time you will have received many more letters written in the same fine spirit as those which graced the correspondence columns in the last issue, and to these pioneers (not forgetting those whose early communications were "crowded out") I desire to show my keen appreciation of their loyalty and sustained interest.

To most of us members living away from London, and necessarily out of touch with all meetings and events in connection with the "League," it can be definitely stated that the *Ypres Times* IS the Ypres League.

So do not forget that little "extra" all you good scouts, we all want our journal to be as firmly founded as the Menin Gate itself—and to mean as much.

Very best regards,

Yours sincerely,

E. F. WILLIAMS.

Branches and Corresponding Members

BRANCHES.

LONDON	Hon. Secretary to the London County Committee : J. Boughey, 20, Orchard Street, London, W.1.
	E. LONDON DISTRICT—L. A. Weller, 132, Maxey Road, Dagenham, Essex.
	TOTTENHAM AND EDMONTON DISTRICT—E. Glover, 191, Lansdowne Road, Tottenham, N.17.
	H. Carey, 373, Sydenham Road, S.E.26.
COLCHESTER	H. Snow (Hon. Sec.), 9, Church Street (North).
	W. H. Taylor (Pilgrimage Hon. Sec.), 64, High Street.
GATESHEAD	Lieut.-Colonel E. G. Crouch, 8, Ashgrove Terrace.
LIVERPOOL	Captain A. M. Webster, Blundellsands.
PURLEY	Major Graham Carr, D.S.O., M.C., 112-114, High Street.
SHEFFIELD	Captain J. Wilkinson, "Holmfield," Bents Drive.
BELGIUM	Capt. P. D. Parminter, 19, Rue Surmont de Volsberghe, Ypres.
CANADA	Ed. Kingsland, P.O. Box 83, Magog, Quebec.
SOUTH AFRICA	L. G. Shuter, Church Street, Pietermaritzburg.
AMERICA	Representative : Captain R. Henderson-Bland, 110 West 57th Street, New York City.

CORRESPONDING MEMBERS

GREAT BRITAIN.

ABERYSTWYTH	T. O. Thomas, 5, Smithfield Road.
ASHTON-UNDER-LYNE	G. D. Stuart, "Woodlands,", Thronfield Grove, Arundel Street.
BANBURY	Captain C. W. Fowke, Yew Tree House, King's Sutton.
BIRMINGHAM	Mrs. Hill, 191, Cattell Road, Small Heath.
	John Burman, "Westbrook," Solihull Road, Shirley.
BOURNEMOUTH	H. L. Pasmore, 40, Morley Road, Boscombe Park.
BRISTOL	W. S. Hook, "Stoneleigh," Cotham Park.
BROADSTAIRS	C. E. King, 6, Norman Road, St. Peters, Broadstairs.
	Mrs. Briggs, North Foreland House.
CHATHAM	W. N. Channon, 22, Keyes Avenue.
CHESTERFIELD	Major A. W. Shea, 14, Cross Street.
CONGLETON	Mr. H. Dart, 61, The Crescent.
DARLINGTON	D. S. Vigo, 125, Dorset Road, Bexhill-on-Sea.
DERBY	T. Jakeman, 10, Graham Street.
DORRINGTON (Salop)	Captain G. D. S. Parker, Frodesley Rectory.
EXETER	Captain E. Jenkin, 25, Queen Street.
GLOUCESTER	H. R. Hunt, "Casita," Parton Lane, Churchdown.
HERNE BAY	Captain E. Clarke Williams, F.S.A.A., "Conway," Station Road.
HOVE	Captain G. W. J. Cole, 2, Westbourne Terrace, Kingsway.
LEICESTER	W. C. Dunford, 343, Aylestone Road.
LINCOLN	E. Swaine, 79, West Parade.
LLANWRST	A. C. Tomlinson, M.A., Bod Estyn.
LOUGHTON	Capt. O. G. Johnson, M.A., Loughton School.
MATLOCK (Derby)	Miss Dickinson, Beechwood.
MELROSE	Mrs. Lindesay Kelsall, Darnlea.
NEW BRIGHTON (Cheshire)	E. F. Williams, 5, Waterloo Road.
NEW MILTON	W. H. Lunn, "Greycot," Albert Road.

NOTTINGHAM	... E. V. Brown, 3, Eldon Chambers, Wheeler Gate.
ST. HELENS (Lancs.)	... John Orford, 124, Knowsley Road.
SHREWSBURY ...	... Major-General Sir John Headlam, K.B.E., C.B., D.S.O., Cruck Meole House, Hanwood.
TIVERTON (Devon)	... Mr. W H. Duncan Arthur, Surveyor's Office, Town Hall.
WELSHPOOL ...	... Mr. E. Wilson, Coedway, Ford, Salop.

DOMINIONS AND FOREIGN COUNTRIES.

AUSTRALIA	... Messrs. C. H. Green, and George Lawson, Anzac House, Elizabeth Street, Brisbane, Queensland. R. A. Baldwin, c/o Government Savings Bank of N.S.W., Martin Place Sydney. Mr. W. Cloves, Box 1296, G.P.O., Adelaide.
BELGIUM	... Sister Marguerite, Sacré Coeur, Ypres.
BUENOS AYRES ...	... President, British Ex-Service Club, Calle 25 de Mayo 577.
CANADA	.. Brig.-General V. W. Odlum, C.B., C.M.G., D.S.O., 2530, Point Grey Road, Vancouver. V. A. Bowes, 326, 40th Avenue West, Calgary, Alberta. W. Constable F. Grece, St. Hilaire Station, Ronville County, Quebec.
CEYLON	... Captain F. R. G. Webb, M.C., Irrigation Bungalow, Kalmunai, E.P.
EGYPT	... L. B. S. Larkins, The Residency, Cairo.
INDIA	... Lieut.-Quartermaster G. Smith, Queen's Bays, Sialkot, India.
IRELAND	... Miss A. K. Jackson, Cloneyhurke House, Portarlington.
KENYA	... Harry Sheilds, Survey Department, Nairobi. Corporal C. H. Slater, P.O. Box 403, Nairobi.
NEW ZEALAND ...	... Captain W. U. Gibb, Ava Lodge, Puhinui Road, Papatoetoe, Auckland. S. E. Beattie, Lowlands, Woodville.
SOUTH AFRICA ...	... H. L. Versfield, c/o Cape Explosives Works Ltd., 150, St. Georges Street, Cape Town.
SPAIN	... Captain P. W. Burgess, Calle de Zurbano 29, Madrid.
U.S.A.	... Captain Henry Maslin, 942, President Street, Brooklyn, New York. L. E. P, Foot. 20, Gillett Street, Hartford, Conn, U.S.A. A. P. Forward, 449, East 80th Street, New York. J. W. Freebody, 945, McBride Avenue, Los Angeles.
NOVA SCOTIA ...	... Will R. Bird, Amherst.

Membership of the League

This is open to all who served in the Salient, and to all those whose relatives or friends died there, in order that they may have a record of that service for themselves and their descendants, and belong to the comradeship of men and women who understand and remember all that Ypres meant in suffering and endurance.

Life membership, £2 10s.

Annual members, 5s.

Do not let the fact of your not having served in the Salient deter you from joining the Ypres League. Those who have neither fought in the Salient nor lost relatives there, but who are in sympathy with the objects of the Ypres League, are admitted to its fellowship, but are not given scroll certificates.

There is a Junior Division for children whose relatives served in the Salient. It is open also to others to whom our objects appeal.

Annual subscription 1s. up to the age of 18, after which they can become ordinary members of the League.

THE YPRES LEAGUE (INCORPORATED)
20, Orchard Street, Portman Square, W.1.

Telephone: WELBECK 1446.   *Telegrams*: YPRESLEAG, " WESDO," LONDON.

Patron-in-Chief: H.M. THE KING.

Patrons:
H.R.H. THE PRINCE OF WALES.   H.R.H. PRINCESS BEATRICE.

President: GENERAL SIR CHARLES H. HARINGTON.

Vice-Presidents:

F.-M. VISCOUNT ALLENBY.   F.-M. SIR CLAUD W. JACOB.
THE VISCOUNT WAKEFIELD OF HYTHE.   F.-M. SIR PHILIP CHETWODE.
GENERAL SIR CECIL ROMER.   F.-M. LORD MILNE.

General Committee:

THE COUNTESS OF ALBEMARLE.
*CAPTAIN C. ALLISTON.
LIEUT-COLONEL BECKLES WILLSON.
MR. HENRY BENSON.
*MR. J. BOUGHEY.
*MISS B. BRICE-MILLER.
COLONEL G. T. BRIERLEY.
CAPTAIN P. W. BURGESS.
*MAJOR H. CARDINAL-HARFORD.
REV. P. B. CLAYTON.
*THE EARL OF YPRES.
MRS. C. J. EDWARDS.
MAJOR C. J. EDWARDS.
MR. H. A. T. FAIRBANK.
MR. T. ROSS FURNER.
SIR PHILIP GIBBS.
MR. E. GLOVER.
MAJOR C. E. GODDARD.
MAJOR-GENERAL SIR JOHN HEADLAM.

MR. F. D. BANKS HILL.
MAJOR-GENERAL C. J. B. HAY.
MR. J. HETHERINGTON.
MRS. E. HEAP.
GENERAL SIR W. C. G. HENEKER.
CAPTAIN O. G. JOHNSON.
*MAJOR E. MONTAGUE JONES.
CAPTAIN H. D. PEABODY.
*THE HON. ALICE DOUGLAS PENNANT.
*LIEUT.-GENERAL SIR W. P. PULTENEY.
LIEUT.-COLONEL SIR J. MURRAY.
*COLONEL G. E. C. RASCH.
VISCOUNT SANDON.
THE HON. SIR ARTHUR STANLEY.
MR. ERNEST THOMPSON.
CAPTAIN J. LOCKLEY TURNER.
*MR. E. B. WAGGETT.
CAPTAIN J. WILKINSON.
CAPTAIN H. TREVOR WILLIAMS.

* Executive Committee.

Bankers:
BARCLAYS BANK LTD., Knightsbridge Branch.

Honorary Solicitors:
MESSRS. FLADGATE & CO., 18, Pall Mall, S.W.

Secretary:
CAPTAIN G. E. DE TRAFFORD.

Auditors:
MESSRS. LEPINE & JACKSON,
6, Bond Court, E.C.4.

League Representative at Ypres:
CAPTAIN P. D. PARMINTER.
19, Rue Surmont de Volsberghe

League Representative at Cambrai:
MR. A. WILDE,
9, Rue des Anglaises.

League Representative at Amiens:
CAPTAIN STUART OSWALD.
7, Rue Porte-Paris.

League Representative at Arras:
MR. P. VYNER,
10, Station Square.

Hon. Secretary, Ypres British Settlement:
LT. COLONEL F. G. POOLE,

PRIMARY OBJECTS OF THE LEAGUE

I.—Commemoration and Comradeship.
II.—To provide special travel facilities for Members and all interested to Ypres and battlefields, and transport of Members.
III.—The furnishing of information about the Salient ; marking of historic sites and the compilation of charts of the battlefields.
IV.—The erection of a Ypres British Church and School which has been completed.
V.—The establishment of groups of members throughout the world, through Branch Secretaries and Corresponding Members.
VI.—The maintenance of cordial relations with dwellers on the battlefields of Ypres
VII.—The formation of a Junior Division.

Use the Ypres League Travel Bureau for Ypres and Whole of the Western Front.

FOR THE FOLLOWING PUBLICATIONS, Etc., apply:

Secretary, YPRES LEAGUE, 20, ORCHARD STREET, LONDON, W.1.

THE BATTLE BOOK OF YPRES. A history of notable deeds contributed by all regiments. 5s.; post free, 5s. 6d. Compiled by Beatrix Brice with the assistance of Lieut.-General Sir William Pulteney, G.C.V.O., etc.

BOOKS.

YPRES: Outpost of the Channel Ports. By Beatrix Brice. With Foreword by Field-Marshal Lord Plumer, G.C.B. Price 1s. 6d.; post free 1s. 10d.

The City of Fear and Other Poems. By Gilbert Frankau. 3s. 6d. net; post free 3s. 8d.

With the Cornwall Territorials on the Western Front. By E. C. Matthews. 7s. 6d.; post free 8s.

Story of the 63rd Field Ambulance. By A. W. Westmore, etc. Cloth, 3s. 6d., post free. Paper, 2s. 6d., post free.

War Letters to a Wife. By Colonel Rowland Fielding. Popular Edition. 7s. 6d.; post free 8s.

The Pill Boxes of Flanders. 1s.; post free 1s. 3d.

From Mons to the First Battle of Ypres. By J. G. W. Hyndson, M.C. Price 5s., post free 5s. 3d.

YPRES LEAGUE TIES. 3s. 6d. each, post free.

YPRES LEAGUE BADGES. 2s. each, 2s. 1¼d. post free.

EMBROIDERED BADGES. 4s. each, post free.

Map and List of Cemeteries in the Ypres Salient. Price 9d.; post free 11d.

Map of the Somme. Price 1s. 8d., post free.

PICTURES.

Burning of the Cloth Hall, 1915. A Coloured Print, 14 in. by 12 in. 1s. post free.

Old Well-known Spots in New Guise. Prints, size 4¼ x 2½, recently taken of famous spots in the Ypres Salient, and which may be of great interest to our readers, are on sale at headquarters, price 4d. each, post free 5d. For particulars apply Secretary.

POST CARDS, PHOTOGRAPHS AND ETCHINGS.

Post Cards. Ypres: British Front during the War. Ruins of Ypres. Price 1s. post free.

Photographs of Menin Gate Unveiling. Size 11 in. by 7 in. 1s. 2d. each, post free.

Hill 60. Complete Panorama Photographs. 12 in. by 3½ in. Price 3s., post free; 15 in. by 5 in. Price 3s. 6d., post free.

WAR-TIME PHOTOGRAPHS OF THE SALIENT.

6 in. by 8 in. ... 1s. 6d. each.
12 in. by 15 in. ... 4s. each.

List forwarded on application.

PHOTOGRAPHS OF WAR-TIME SKETCHES.

Bedford House (Front View), 1916.

Bedford House (Back View), 1916.

Voormezeele Main Street, 1916.

Voormezeele Crucifixion Gate, 1916.

Langhof Chateau, 1916.

Size 8½ in. by 6½ in. Price 2s. 6d. each, post free.

Photographs of the Thiepval and Arras Memorials. Post card size, price 1s. each, post free.

YPRES TIMES.

The Journal may be obtained at the League Offices. BACK NUMBERS 1s.; 1932, 8d.; 1933, 6d.

Printed in Great Britain for the Publishers by FORD & GILL, 21a/23, Iliffe Yard, Crampton Street, London, S.E.17.

Memory Tablet.

OCTOBER — NOVEMBER — DECEMBER

October.

Oct. 4th, 1914	...	Russian ultimatum to Bulgaria.
„ 5th, 1915	...	Allied Forces land at Salonika.
„ 9th, 1914	...	Antwerp occupied by Germans.
„ 10th, 1916	...	Allied ultimatum to Greece.
„ 14th, 1915	...	Bulgaria at war with Serbia.
„ 18th, 1918	...	Belgian coast clear.
„ 20th, 1914	...	First Battle of Ypres begun.
„ 25th, 1918	...	Ludendorf resigned.

November.

Nov. 1st, 1918	...	Versailles Conference opened.
„ 3rd, 1918	...	Austrian surrender. Keil mutiny.
„ 4th, 1917	...	British troops in Italy.
„ 5th, 1914	...	Great Britain declares war on Turkey.
„ 6th, 1917	...	British storm the Passchendaele Ridge.
„ 9th, 1918	...	Marshal Foch receives German envoys. Abdication of the Kaiser.
„ 10th, 1918	...	Kaiser's flight to Holland.
„ 10th, 1914	...	"Emden" sunk.
„ 11th, 1918	...	Armistice Terms accepted.
„ 18th, 1917	...	General Maude's death in Mesopotamia.

December.

Dec. 8th, 1914	...	Naval Battle off the Falklands.
„ 9th, 1917	...	British capture Jerusalem.
„ 15th, 1915	...	Sir Douglas Haig C.–in–C. in France.
„ 16th, 1914	...	Germans bombarded West Hartlepool.
„ 19th, 1915	...	Withdrawal from Gallipoli.
„ 24th, 1914	...	First air raid on England.

The Ypres Times

Communications to
The Editor, "Ypres Times,"
20, Orchard Street, London, W.1.

PRICE 6d.
POST FREE 7d.

VOL. 7, No. 4.   PUBLISHED QUARTERLY   OCTOBER, 1934

The Battle of Bixchoote
(First Battle of Ypres)
By CAPTAIN J. G. W. HYNDSON, M.C.
Late Loyal Regiment.
Author of "*From Mons to the 1st Battle of Ypres.*"

LATE in the afternoon of October 22nd, 1914, the 1st battalion Loyal North Lancashire Regiment marched into the village of Boesinghe on the Yser Canal and were allotted billets.

As the evening drew in, the sky was lit up by a distant glare of the burning houses, which had been set on fire by the German artillery; and the small arms fire became more distinct in the calm night air.

Before we were able to settle down, fresh orders arrived and we were hurriedly called out, and marched off without the slightest idea where we were going. After trudging along a twisting road for a few miles we landed up at St. Jean, here we slept (in the houses) for a few hours. Called out at midnight we marched off again, eventually arriving at Pilckem, the railway crossing, where we turned off into a turnip field and lay down to await daylight but not to sleep as the rest of the night was interrupted by rifle firing which went on continuously, and the Germans sent up a constant stream of different coloured Very Lights, which light up a limited area as brightly as sunlight.

At daybreak the firing increased in volume directly to our front, and a good many stray bullets fell amongst us, but although there was an unpleasant "Zip" about them as they struck the turnip leaves, surprisingly little damage was done and casualties were negligible.

Soon after nine o'clock, all officers were sent for by the Colonel and he addressed us as follows :—

"Gentlemen, yesterday the Germans attacked and penetrated into the position held by the 1st Guards' Brigade in Bixchoote, which you will see by your maps is about two miles in front of us. The Guards' Brigade and particularly the Cameron Highlanders, have been severely handled but are hanging on to the ends of the break. The reserve company of the Camerons has been sent up to fill in the gap, and has managed to prevent the Germans from exploiting their success.

We are to attack and re-establish the original line, and we will be supported by the 2nd South Staffordshire Regiment from the 6th Infantry Brigade. "A," "B" and "C" Companies are to lead and "D" Company is to remain in reserve under my direct orders. The machine-guns will support the attack from the best possible position. Any questions? No? Then off you go; the attack will begin in half an hour from now."

Since the ground over which this attack was to be made was completely open, as far as the slightly rising ground on which Bixchoote was perched, we realized that the task we were about to undertake would be both difficult and costly.

At 10.45 having explained details of the plan to the men, the attack began.

The Company I belonged to was on the extreme right and we at once came under long-distance rifle fire. Consequently I ordered the men to extend to four paces interval and on we went without returning fire.

Supported by a field brigade of artillery, the advance went on steadily until the German shooting became more accurate and several casualties occurred. I therefore called a halt and looking through my field glasses was able to see the German trenches in front of Bixchoote, although the occupants were invisible. To get closer and deal with the garrison in the trenches I ordered the advance to continue but now only by sections, widely extended, and covered by those awaiting their turn, whom I ordered to fire at the German trenches and also at the houses, which were obviously occupied by the enemy. On we went, gradually working forward by rushes, which decreased in length as we got nearer and nearer. At every rush men fell and had to be left to their fate until the fighting was over.

Disdaining the bullets which hurtled past us—" tack, run, swish, tschin, tschin, tack, tack, tack, tschin " on we went to gain our objective, which was to close with the enemy. Soon we had worked up to within two hundred and fifty yards of the German position, where we joined the survivors of the Cameron Highlanders. Full of fight and much cheered up by our arrival they had been supporting our advance manfully. They were sheltered by some partly dug trenches which they had been able to construct during the night and we thankfully dumped ourselves down amongst them, glad to gain a temporary respite from the enemy bullets. From this position we could now occasionally catch sight of the Germans whose firing had become less accurate, owing, I presumed, to their terror at seeing us approach nearer and nearer, in spite of their efforts to stop us, and also to some of their bravest men being killed by our deadly markmanship.

We were now so close to the German trenches that we paused to concentrate all our energies on wearing down his nerves until he dared not show a hair.

Therefore we began to fire for all we were worth at selected portions of their position. Little by little we got the upper hand, but the slightest attempt on our part to advance was met by angry bursts of fire and several officers and men who bravely tried to gain a little ground were shot down.

During this time I noticed the Germans dodging past a gap in the hedge, about 250 yards directly to our front. I ordered the men nearest to me to fire at them as they attempted to slip past the gap. Remembering their snap shooting practice in peace time on the range, the men entered into this task with zest, and many of the flitting figures were seen to fall. We afterwards found twenty or thirty dead Germans lying there. A red house in front also gave us a lot of trouble, as it contained several rifle men who bravely continued to shoot at us, but eventually the garrison ceased fire, and were afterwards found inside, dead or wounded to a man.

On looking to our rear I saw the Regimental stretcher bearers, under the Sergeant-Drummer much in evidence, removing the wounded to the first-aid post, although they were forced to carry out their task under a gruelling fire. As the Germans were no respectors of the Red Cross, they were repeatedly fired at, but casualties did not deter them in the least from carrying many wounded from the stricken field.

And so the fight went on until about one o'clock, when the firing from the enemy trenches almost died down. The time had now come to put the finishing touch to the engagement and we began to work forward in small groups until only some two hundred yards separated us from the enemy. From this point of vantage the whole regiment rose up, and with rousing cheers, which must have put fear into the hearts of the Germans, we surged forward with fixed bayonets and charged. The next few minutes were brim-full of thrills and incidents. Some of the bravest Germans continued to fire at us as we crossed the intervening ground, and I expected to be struck down at any moment, but although the men on my immediate right and left were hit, I escaped unscathed. On we dashed, yelling with all our might, and, storming the front German trench, we bayonetted the surviving defenders, and passed on to the reserve trenches. Here we expected

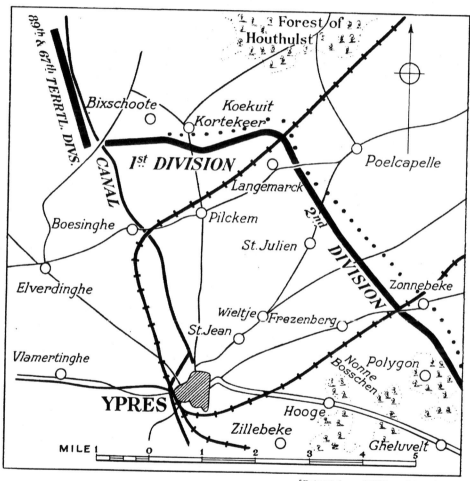

[Extract from "Military Operations, France and Belgium, 1914." Volume 2.

to meet with a stout resistance, but the Germans had enough and suddenly to our amazement we saw the glorious sight of masses of grey-coated men standing up to surrender. The main battle was over, and the only thing left for us to do was to gather in the prisoners, numbering some 400 all told, send them under escort to the rear, and round up isolated bodies of Germans who still continued to resist. One particularly brave man had established himself on the top of the village windmill and continued to fire at us in spite of being repeatedly called upon to surrender. We set fire to the windmill but in spite of this he went on firing until the building collapsed and its brave defender perished in the flames.

I took some men and went on past a house flying the Red Cross flag, when suddenly an awful thing happened. From the rear a screaming noise, followed in rapid succession by others with resounding crashes, as one after another shells landed amongst us. What had happened? In a second it was only too clear. Our guns had mistaken us for retreating Germans as we were now well ahead of the remainder of the battalion. For a moment we paused, and then I shouted to the men to get back to the house flying the Red Cross flag. Back we sprinted, with the exception of a few unfortunate men who were knocked out, and we got out of the danger zone. On reaching the house a ghastly sight met my gaze. The entire outer yard and interior of the place was crammed with German dead, dying and wounded, all lying together on the ground, packed as tightly as sardines. I also found one or two unwounded Germans hiding amongst the others so stationing a guard at the exits I proceeded to make a very thorough search. The result was a bag of twenty men, and as the shelling had now died down I proceeded to report to headquarters.

Everything was now peaceful on the battlefield and in its neighbourhood. We had inflicted a crushing defeat on the enemy, and evidently they had not got fresh troops at hand to counter-attack.

We set to work to consolidate our position and to collect the wounded. Besides the four hundred odd unwounded prisoners captured, the Germans killed numbered tour hundred and fifty, and the wounded approximately twelve hundred. This victory had been dearly bought and cost the battalion six officers (four killed) and one hundred and seventy five other ranks killed and wounded.

We remained undisturbed in the position we had captured until relieved by the French on the night of October 24th when we marched to Ypres for a well earned twenty-four hours' rest.

While we were resting there we were all delighted to receive a " Special Order of the Day " from the Brigadier, which read as follows :—

> " In spite of the stubborn resistance offered by the German troops, the object of the engagement was accomplished, but not without many casualties in the Brigade. By nightfall, the trenches captured by the Germans had been reoccupied, about six hundred prisoners captured, and fully 1,500 German dead were lying out in front of our trenches. The Brigadier-General congratulates the 1st Loyal North Lancashire Regiment, the 1st Northamptonshire Regiment and the 2nd King's Royal Rifle Corps, but desires especially to commend the fine soldier-like spirit of the 1st Loyal North Lancashire Regiment, which, advancing steadily under heavy shell and rifle fire, and aided by the machine-guns, was enabled to form up within a comparatively short distance of the enemy trenches. Fixing bayonets, the Battalion then charged, carried the trenches, and then occupied them, and to them must be allotted the majority of the prisoners captured.
>
> The Brigadier-General congratulates himself on having in his Brigade a Battalion which, after marching the whole of the previous night without food or rest, was able to maintain its splendid record in the past by the determination and self-sacrifice displayed in the action.

(Signed) E. S. BULFIN, *Brigadier-General.*

Ypres British School

King Leopold's Memorable Visit
Viscountess Plumer Distributes the Prizes

By Henry Benson, M.A.

WHEN King Leopold of Belgium went to Ypres on Sunday, 29th July, for the purpose of inaugurating the restored belfry tower of the Cloth Hall and the carillon which has been installed therein, he took advantage of the occasion to

Photo]   [Daniel, Ypres
LITTLE MISS BARBARA ALLEN PRESENTING BOUQUET TO KING LEOPOLD

pay a brief visit to the British School, where 120 British children are being educated, With few exceptions, the pupils are sons and daughters of employees of the Imperial War Graves Commission, who tend the British cemeteries and memorials in the Salient. and they are receiving a first-rate general education, on parallel lines with that which obtains in our elementary schools at home.

Readers of the "*Ypres Times*" will recollect that the school was built and equipped five years ago by Etonians as a memorial to those 342 Etonians who made the supreme sacrifice in and around Ypres during the tragic years, 1914-18.

King Leopold was at school at Eton during the early period of the War, and it was in the rôle of an Etonian that he paid his much-appreciated visit. His Majesty, who displayed a lively interest in all he saw, was received by Countess Haig, Viscountess Plumer, Lieut.-General Sir William and Lady Pulteney, the Rev. E. H. Thorold (Chaplain-General to the Army), the Hon. Mrs. Adeane, the Rev. Archibald Fleming,

Mr. and Mrs. E. L. Vaughan of Eton College, Colonel and Mrs. F. G. Poole and the Rev. G. R. and Mrs. Milner. The little daughter of Mr. and Mrs. W. P. Allen, the headmaster and headmistress, presented King Leopold with a bouquet, which had been prepared for Queen Astrid, whose unexpected absence was universally regretted.

The annual prize-giving took place on the following morning, and it was a happy inspiration that the Dowager Viscountess Plumer was present to distribute the awards. The spirit of the gallant old Field Marshal seemed to hover in benediction over the proceedings. In imagination one could almost hear him whispering, " Adsum ! " or recalling his own words, " I am not missing ; I am here."

It has been my privilege to attend these annual prize-days since their institution, and it is gratifying to notice, year by year, the improvement in the appearance of the children. Mentally alert and physically healthy, they reflect the greatest credit upon both the curriculum and tuition. This feature is the more remarkable when one remembers the difficulties that beset their teachers at the onset. For example, when the school opened its doors, many of the youngsters were unable to speak a word of English ; others spoke it with a pronounced foreign accent ; whilst, practically without exception, all were woefully backward in general education. Books, however simple in character, were useless ; because the pupils could not understand the meaning of any sentence they contained. Were ever teachers more heavily handicapped? Mr. Morris, the first headmaster, came to the conclusion that the only solution to the problem lay in concentrating almost exclusively on the teaching of English ; and that for a time, at any rate, other subjects would have to be entirely subsidiary. Consequently, English became " the headstone of the corner," the sequel to that wise decision being the pleasing spectacle of well-educated and well-mannered boys and girls which was presented to us on 30th July, 1934.

The day being brilliantly fine, the proceedings, as in 1933, took place in the open-air, the school play-ground being thronged with visitors and proud mothers.

After a really excellent rendition of Elgar's "*Land of Hope and Glory*" by the whole school, General Sir William Pulteney delivered a brief but impressive address. After calling attention to the signal honour that had been accorded the school on the previous afternoon by the visit of King Leopold, he thanked the prize-givers and congratulated Mr. and Mrs. Allen on the wonderful progress that had been made during the past twelve months. He added that the essays, which it had been his good fortune to read, reflected great credit on the youthful writers.

Mr. Allen prefaced his annual report by stating that the school was most fortunate in the powerful driving force behind it. The past year, he said, had been in many respects memorable. The health of the children had been good, despite the prevalence of local epidemics, and the attendances had never fallen below 85 per cent. Elementary book-keeping and shorthand had been added to the subjects taken by the top class ; and science and chemistry were new features which were immensely appreciated by the pupils. The swimming contests, which took place in the public baths, evoked keen competition.

Lady Haig addressed the children and their mothers in a charming little speech, and after distributing the awards, Lady Plumer referred to the deep affection in which her husband had always held both church and school. " Nothing would have delighted him more," she added, " than to have seen the wonderful improvement in the children."

Mr. Vaughan congratulated the teachers and pupils on the excellence of the drilling displays, the singing, and the dancing which had just been given, and remarked that real progress had been made in all directions.

The generous donors of prizes, which were numerous this year, were :—

The Third Army Corps.
Mrs. L. K. Briggs.
Hon. Alice Douglas Pennant.
Lady Pulteney.
Sir Charles Harington.
Waterman's Ideal Pen Company.
Cheltenham College.

In conclusion, I would mention how greatly parents, children and teachers appreciate the presence of so many distinguished visitors on Prize-day, which they regard as the red-letter day of the year. It is not only that they see them intimately; but the fact that they have crossed the Channel for the specific purpose of attending the function proves that they take an active interest in the welfare of the school and all that pertains to it.

H.B.

Instructional Tours of the Battlefields of France

Readers of this magazine will, I feel sure, be interested to read of further accounts of Battlefield Tours carried out by certain units of the 56th (1st London) Division, T.A. during the training year,

Incidently we are again much indebted to the good offices of the Ypres League for their ready assistance in making all the necessary travelling arrangements, accommodation and transport over the battlefields.

Tours of this kind are becoming more and more popular as time passes on—some may ask themselves—why are they called "Instructional"? Are they not more in the nature of "JOY RIDES"?
Well, perhaps, an explanation and a brief account of what is actually done may not be out of place.

Firstly, the object of these tours :—

It is now twenty years ago since our grand little army first embarked on the soil of France, and in consequence every opportunity should be taken to pass on some of the lessons to the new generation of officers—some of whom were only just born when the mighty struggle began. New weapons of war have since appeared, modern armaments have changed many of our ideas of warfare of the future, still the fact remains—The principles of war stand unaltered; hence the value of study.

A battlefield tour entails a mass of work in preparation, both for the directors and to those who partake in it. Tours are initiated in this way :—

Particular battles or incidents are chosen for study; the next step is to scrutinise all the relevant and Official History connected with the event, combined when possible, with personal experiences of officers who were present, to supplement the detail and to add the touch of local colour.

When the Directing Staff is satisfied that every point of detail is known and thrashed out, the next step is to pass the complete story to those partaking in the tour.

This is done either in the form of lectures, or exercises, or both.

With all this preliminary work completed, the tour begins, all fully conversant with what they are about to see.

ITINERARY. WEEK-END TOUR.

Leave London 11 p.m. Friday.
Arrive Cambrai 9 a.m. Saturday.
Embus on Tour 10.30 a.m.
Return Hotel 6.30 p.m.
Embus on Tour 8.30 a.m. Sunday.
Return Hotel 6.p.m. Sunday.
Entrain for London 10 p.m. Sunday.
Arrive London 7 a.m. Monday.
To work in the City as usual 9.10. a.m.

The Tour may be an excellent change of air—a sea voyage and a trip across France thrown in—but a "JOY RIDE", NO !

To continue :—

This year, our studies have been varied and all extremely interesting and instructive. Here they are :—

"A." Action of the Cheshires and Norfolks at ELOUGES, 23rd August, 1914.
"B." Rearguard action of the Royal Munster Fusiliers at ETREUX, 27th August,1914.
"C." Battle of CAMBRAI 1917.
    (I) The attack on the village of Fontaine Notre Dame and Bourlon Wood by the 2nd Guards Brigade Nov. 27th.
    (II) Counter-attack by the 1st Guards Brigade on Gouzeaucourt Nov. 30th.
    (III) Attack by the Guards Division (1st and 3rd Guards Brigades) on the St. Quentin Ridge Gonnelieu Dec. 1st.
"D". Battle of the SELLE, and the crossing of the Oise Canal, 1918.
    (I) The attack of the SOUTH AFRICAN BRIGADE, 66th Division north of LE CATEAU October 16th 1918.
    (II) The crossing of the SAMBRE and OISE CANAL at Lock No. 1 by the 2nd Bn. Royal Sussex Regiment (2nd Brigade 1st Division.)

A few words on some of these actions may be of interest. The Official History deals with all at length, but few of us have either the time or the inclination to delve into history. "Sufficient unto the day", is a motto common to many.

In most of these actions, we were fortunate enough to have one or more officers who had actually been present during the fighting, it was possible, therefore, to trace almost every footstep taken.

ELOUGES.

Little did we realise, in these early days of 1914, what a deluge of strength the Germans were about to let loose.

Elouges was one of the early experiences—two days after Mons. The tidal wave was sweeping upon us—difficult enough to stop in ordinary circumstances, but this was was a case of the 5th British Division being over-lapped by two German divisions on the left flank.

The 1st Cheshires, 1st Norfolks and the 119th Bty. R.F.A. were in reserve, and at 11 a.m. were ordered to stem the tide.

An excellent fire position had been taken up, normally strong enough to hold up three times their strength, but alas not strong enough to hold the world.

The Germans came on regardless of casualties—came on again and again, but not until late in the day did they succeed in winning the position.

The Norfolks, less exposed and having a better line of retreat managed to extricate themselves, but the Cheshires were decimated and the remnants taken prisoners.

The following are extracts from an account of the battle by the O.C. Norfolks :—

"Just as I was dictating a message for our Brigadier that we were in a strong position and everything seemed quiet on this flank, suddenly an officer shouted,—'Great Heavens, Colonel, look over there' ! Through glasses we could see a mass of Germans moving in dense columns over open ground just North of QUIEVRAN. We could see at least four or five thousand and knew that there must be many others out of sight."

"And what targets our men had seen ! The worst shot in the Regiment, who never hit a bulls-eye in his life, believed he had killed a thousand Huns."

ETREUX. 27th, August, 1914.

The retreat from Mons was in progress and those who were in it know all they want to know.

On this fateful day, the Royal Munster Fusiliers with the 118 Bty. R.F.A. attached had been given the task of rearguard duties. The odds were somewhat similar to those at Elouges already described.

It is now known that opposed to them were :—
- 1 Sqn. Cavalry.
- 4 Btys. Field Artillery.
- 9 Bns. Infantry.

from 8 a.m. till 9-30 p.m. the Royal Munster Fusiliers fought for their lives, and only when completely surrounded, with but one unwounded officer remaining and a handful of men left, were they forced to surrender.

No finer display of gallantry or devotion to duty was seen during the whole war.

CAMBRAI AND THE ATTACK ON FONTAINE NOTRE DAME.

Here we come to a different period of the War.

Long years had been spent in a stalemate position, but now we come to the era of the tank and the means of overcoming the German barbed wire.

The British attack in Nov., 1917 was planned to take place in the Cambrai area, because the ground there was favourable for the employment of tanks which were to play an important part in the enterprise, and facilities existed for the concealment of the necessary preparations for the attack.

It had been planned months beforehand, but the decision to put the plan into execution at this particular date was influenced by the necessity of helping Italy after her Caporetto disaster.

It was continued for the same cause after the initial success had ended.

The attack on the village of Fontaine Notre Dame and Bourlon Wood formed an isolated action in the battle as a whole and the main object in studying the action was to impress on the young officer, some of the many difficulties entailed in wood and village fighting.

Against a determined enemy there is no harder task to perform; it demands the greatest courage and determination from all ranks, and above all, leadership of the highest order. None of these qualities were lacking in this instance, success was complete but temporary.

Casualties were very severe and as fortune would have it, the Germans had already planned to carry out an attack at the same place but we had forestalled him, his attacking troops were therefore available for an immediate counter-attack.

GOUZEAUCOURT. Nov. 30th.

Our initial success at Cambrai and later the German counter-offensive on the salient thus made is too well known to repeat the story.

So swift and complete indeed was the German advance that at one stage the position of the Third Army was seriously endangered.

No military record of the battle would be complete, however, without a mention of the magnificent resistance of the 47th, 2nd, and 56th Divisions on the northern flank of the salient. They held their ground against the repeated attacks of seven German divisions. On the southern side certain British divisions were holding dangerously extended lines and here it was that the German thrust became the serious danger, having broken through to a considerable depth.

Again we wish to take this opportunity of thanking Captain de Trafford and the staff of the Ypres League for their courtesy and much appreciated assistance in making our tours as comfortable as continental travel knows how.

ONE OF THE PARTY.

Liège—Twenty Years After

AT 10 p.m. on Friday, July 31st, 1914, the churches all over Belgium suddenly started ringing alarm through the stillness of the dark night. The population already under the influence of disquieting news of the past few days immediately understood that something of importance was happening. Neighbours gathered on the door-steps. Soon, bugle calls were sounded, inviting people (according to a very old custom) to listen to an official proclamation—in this case, the general mobilisation order, whilst the gendarmes started knocking at the doors to hand written orders to the reservists. But we still believed ourselves safe behind what we thought the surest protection of all—the signature of the Great Powers.

On Sunday, August 2nd at 7 p.m., the German Minister at Brussels handed over the ultimatum to the Belgian Minister for Foreign Affairs. This document had been prepared on July 26th by the German G.H.Q., and the answer was requested within twelve hours. What happened that night at the Crown Council held by King Albert has been described often enough and so needs no repetition here.

On Monday, August 3rd at 7 a.m. the ultimatum expired and the Belgian refusal to give passage to the German Army was delivered at the Legation. The wording of this proud answer was immediately wired to Berlin, and the original document was conveyed to Aix-la-Chapelle by the German Military Attaché in a very powerful car which had been kept in readiness.

At 4.15 a.m. on Tuesday, August 4th, the first of the millions of Germans to invade Belgium crossed the border at Henri-Chapelle, and at 10.15 a.m., the first Belgian soldier Lancer Fonck, was killed at Thimister—he had attacked single handed, a mounted German patrol.

The Germans now began their atrocities against harmless civilians. At 1 p.m., Madame Xhignensse who stood at the road-side was killed by a soldier at Petit-Rechain near Verviers, and at about the same hour, at Herve, German officers in a motor car shot Dieudonné Duchene, aged sixteen years, who did not understand their questions. From now, and for the next four years, floods of innocent Belgian blood and tears were shed as a result of this inexcusable and savage invasion.

Liége, situated on the river Meuse, is the junction of the roads following the valley of the Meuse (North-South) and the international highroads and railways from the countries East of the Rhine. The twelve forts, divided into two sectors by the river

DISPOSITION OF THE LIEGE FORTS—1914

were keeping these roads and rails under cover of their guns, but only a single Division under Lieut.-General Leman was holding this all important position of defending the areas between the forts.

The first shots were exchanged between the Liége outposts and the invaders on the afternoon of August 4th, and later in the evening strong German forces crossed the Meuse at Visé, close to the Dutch frontier. The enemy had only to resist a reduced battalion of the 12th Belgian Infantry Regiment—very gallant troops, but totally inadequate to defend a 4 kilometre front (approximately 5,000 yards) with 450 men and without any machine guns or Artillery support. Thus, the German cavalry was able

FORT FLERON **FORT PONTISSE**

Nothing remained of the Liége Forts after the German bombardment except an indistinguishable mass of shattered steel and concrete

from the very first day to raid all round Liége but their success proved very weak compared with what they might and should have achieved.

At 10 a.m. on August 5th, the enemy, after a short Artillery bombardment, suddenly attacked Fort Barchon on the Eastern sector and surrounded it for nearly four hours when Belgian reinforcements arrived and threw the enemy back with heavy losses. All day, the Germans massed troops in the dead ground behind the slopes of the hills and out of sight of the forts in readiness for a night attack which proved of a very desperate character, but the onslaught of the invaders was met with most stubborn resistance and again some of the forts were surrounded but later relieved by Belgian counter attacks. Desperate bayonet fighting took place throughout the night along the whole line. On the five of the six attacked fronts the Germans were repelled with appalling losses : at Herstal, hundreds of field-grey bodies littered the battlefield and amongst whom were the Colonel of the 89th Mechlemburg Grenadiers, the flag-carrier and three officers with drawn swords, all killed together. At Rhees, 239 prisoners were captured including five officers. At Liéry, General von Wussow and regimental Colonel Kruger lost their lives. At Beyne-Heusay, Colonel Schultze of the 20th Infantry Regiment was shot. At Ougrée, 150 prisoners were captured from the 38th Brigade and amongst those killed in action was Prince Friedrich Wilhelm von Lippe, Colonel of the 74th I.R.

In one area between the forts of Evegnée and Fléron, the 14th Brigade, after having lost in quick succession, two commanding officers, was firmly taken in hand by Major of the General Staff von Ludendorff who happened to arrive on the spot. He managed to pierce the opposing line by a powerful attack on a weakened Belgian Infantry position and pushed right towards the city of Liége. At dawn, a detachment of the 7th Battalion German Jaegar Regiment reached the outskirts of the town. Some of the inhabitants of the suburbs, seeing these unknown uniforms believed them to be the vanguard of the British reinforcements shouted " Vivent les Anglais ! " The Germans, through sheer luck, reached the Rue de Sainte Foi where General Leman's headquarters were situated. After a fight with the Staff Officers, clerks, orderlies and gendarmes, the enemy were either killed or put to flight, after which the headquarters were removed to the fort of Loncine on the Western side of the Meuse. This measure, taken at such a critical time when nobody knew what was happening in adjacent areas completely disorganised the defence. Without higher leadership and devoid of reinforcements where help was most urgently needed, the Infantry gradually vacated their improvised trenches after expending all their ammunition. Repeated counter attacks held the enemy *pro tem.*, but one area after another was eventually lost and the forts left to defend themselves.

The emplacements of the forts were perfectly known to the German General Staff who for more than twenty five years were aware that they would have to be attacked. In peace time, German officers were sent to spend their holidays in the neighbourhood of Liége so as to become familiar with the ground, and the Belgian Government having no reason to expect a breach of the neutrality treaty never passed a law against spying.

The large area occupied by the forts made them huge targets and they were built at a time when no guns exceeding a calibre of 8 inches were conceived. Their walls and vaults had been made to withstand nothing heavier than 21 centimeter shells. They were unable to survive the terrific detonations of the Krupp 12 inch howitzers or the Skoda 17 inch mortars.

The garrisons left to themselves without any hope of relief, resisted to the extreme limit of human endurance. One by one, the forts were shelled to pieces, their gunners suffocated by the fumes in the underground cellars or in the turrets, the magazines were blown up. Few men escaped a horrible but heroic death. The last fort to be destroyed was Fort Loncine where General Leman had established his headquarters and from where he had done his best to keep in touch with the other forts through the precarious means of despatch runners. On August 16th, Loncine's powder magazine exploded and General Leman was picked up unconscious from amongst the ruins of his last fort.

The guns of Liége had thus been silenced and the flood of the German invasion started rolling through central Belgium towards Paris.

M. DE HASQUE,
Honorary Lieutenant, Belgian Army, Late Belgian Interpreter and Liaison Officer with B.E.F. Ypres Area from January, 1915 *to the end of the War.*

Civilians on the Canal

By SIDNEY ROGERSON,

Author of "*Twelve Days.*"

ON November 1917, the Dead End of the Canal was a more salubrious locality than it had been at any time since the war began. Not for nothing had the great Ypres offensive been fought. It had at least pushed the invader away from the immediate outskirts of the city, until by November the outposts of both armies faced each other across the sea of mud at Passchendaele. For three years the Canal had been almost a part of the front line system. Now it was the seat of a double Divisional H. Qrs., safe therefore from any attentions of the enemy except an occasional long range shell fired as much with the idea of agitating the "officials of the rearward services" as of hurting anyone.

On the top of the forward bank the terrain was almost uncomfortably congested with the huts and elephant shelters which housed the personnel of infantry Divisional H.Qrs., the rear H.Qrs. of batteries, medium and heavy, the balloon sections, the sappers of all varieties, and the other odd specialists who clung round the outskirts of the battle line. For them, the comparative unprotectedness of the upper ground. The staffs of the two divisions, better advised if less venturesome, adhered to custom and had their abode in the ancient dug-outs driven into the forward bank itself and reached by a duckboard track built on piles just above the turbid water. Once these had been funk-holes for weary infantry, with all the dirt and discomfort their use implied. Now they were very commodious residences, some of them boasting brick fire-places, eloquent reminders of Canadian occupation. (Surely the Canadians were the war's greatest fire and grate builders!) Of course they had their minor disadvantages. They were damp. Moreover their chimney pots protruding through the earth were indistinguishable to the casual soldier from the latest pattern urinal tin. Was there not an occasion when a gallant Major-General entertaining his staff after dinner nearly had his fire put out by a careless bombardier on the floor above? Taking it all in all they were comfortable quarters. They were safe from all ordinary risks from artillery. The enemy was separated from them by five impassable miles of mud, while above them rode in daylight a line of balloons, swaying pig-like at their mooring ropes.

It was this aerial display which provided our only source of amusement. The Boche could never resist the temptation of having a go at the balloons. On fine days his "frightfulness" would take the form of air-burst H.E. There would be a scream and a crash and a ball of yellowish-green smoke would appear near a balloon, expanding slowly before it evaporated, while the sharp, armour-piercing head would hurtle down into the rubble heaps behind the canal where the transport lines stood. Down the offended balloonist would be hauled, only to ascend again after a spell, and the whole performance would be re-enacted. On days when the clouds hung low there would be a buzz and drone, a flurry of machine guns, and German triplanes, spitting fire from their spandaus, would hurtle down on the balloon line. In a trice the sky would resemble some umbrella-maker's advertisement on a grand scale as the observers jumped out with their parachutes. Seldom were there any casualties to the crews, whatever might happen to the balloons, though there was one memorable day when two observers made an amusing if watery landing in the canal itself.

There were in short many worse places for a divisional H.Qrs., as we were destined to learn a few months later when the offensive rôles were reversed. For the moment we were reasonably comfortable even by the civilian standards of those days. It is doubtful how many of us realised how lucky we were. Certainly there were a handful who did, but these were the "temporary" staff officers, the "creepers," "gate-crashers" into the red-tabbed hierarchy, whose experience of war was confined to the front line, from which they had most of them not long been absent. They had not had time to become blasé and still uttered a silent prayer of thanks each night they undressed and got into their pyjamas instead of lying down fully clad on a muddy firestep, or crawling into some rat-ridden dug-out. They realised in short that this sort of life was a privilege. They did not enjoy it by right, and in all probability it would only be a respite, a short peep into civilisation before a return to the trenches.

It was all so new to us that we took every opportunity of visiting friends in other units. I was particularly lucky in that I found that the rear H.Qrs. of my brother's battery were at Kruisstraat, about a mile away, and we had some cheery re-unions. But that's another story, as Kipling would say.

One bright morning I was wending my way across to have a word with the R.E. doctor, when someone drew my attention to a little group of men in mufti, moving with bowed heads and hurried gait towards Divisional H.Qrs. They looked like a party of official visitors come to see how the gallant defenders of democracy lived in the battle zone. Curious as always, I hastened back to see what was afoot, to find that the party were indeed English north-country town councillors on a tour of inspection. I was spotted by someone and told to stand by in case I might be wanted to take the visitors further up the line. Meanwhile the Divisional Commander would entertain them to lunch in "A" mess.

I should rather have liked the job of taking them into the forward area and of showing them what the ground looked like around Gravenstafel, but all chances of my doing so were destroyed by the wretched Hun, who had to start his trick of firing at the balloons during the time the delegates were enjoying a very excellent meal in what they probably imagined was a typical dug-out. With a resounding crash, two heavy shells burst near the balloon line. I do not say that those shells definitely influenced the visitors, but it is a fact that they came out from lunch determined to get back as quickly as possible to the safety of G.H.Q. or wherever they were being billeted for the night.

As they went they turned to pour out their thanks to their host, not only for the refreshment he had provided, but as a representative of the men who were fighting their country's battle. Their protestations of admiration for Mr. Atkins were most effusive. They praised the divisional commander to his face, and told him what a wonderful fellow he was; and one of them finished up by declaring, " If you ever come to Bootle " —I think it was Bootle—" we will be ready to black your boots for you." With which offer they departed.

In the years since, I often wondered about those words. What would be the feelings of the parties concerned now ? What are they all doing ? The divisional commander, after a distinguished career, is probably now retired, having to stint himself no doubt in order to keep his sons in the army. And what of the town councillors ? One of them may probably be a leading Labour M.P., another a profiteer who did well out of the war and is now sitting back to enjoy the luxuries that his money can buy. Does one of them remember the sentiments uttered in 1917, or were they to meet again, would there be the same sense of gratitude and fellowship ?

S.R.

Impressions of Passchendaele

By W. R. Bird.

GRAF HOUSE is a splendid farm in the low ground below Passchendaele. I went eagerly in '32 to see what manner of place it might be in civilized years, and spent the day in wonderment. There was scarcely a feature to be recognized. The pillboxes were gone, vanished, with no trace of their site, or of the machine gun emplacements near them, or the gouged trenches leading up the ridge. There is nothing left at Passchendaele but graves of the men who died there.

Photo] [Imperial War Museum Crown Copyright.
VIEW OF PASSCHENDAELE BATTLEFIELD, 1917, SHOWING DERELICT TANK

Passchendaele means, to the soldier who fought there, more tragic memories than any other part of the line, pictures burned in his brain, never to be erased. Men who cannot recall the name of the village at which they spent weeks of rest can tell you how many burned lorries they saw on the old plank road that dreadful night they " went in," and the exact markings on the pillbox opposite the shell hole they occupied. There was a frightfulness in those late autumn days more livid than any words can express, a horror as heavy and almost as visible as the blanketing, clammy, soul-searching mists that clung to every shell-tortured acre.

Memories. . . . I can see now as plainly as then the dripping ruins of Ypres as we huddled there that late October afternoon, listening to the big ones as they "crumped" back of the Prison. The little lane among piled wreckage where we sat and shivered until waiting became intolerable and we scrambled over debris into a dank, shadowy passage with a film of moisture on its walls, ending at a door as cold and rigid as anything in death. . . . I can see again, in its dreadful scum and desolation, the part of California Trench we occupied on a night of incessant rain, with a foot of water in its depths and no place where any man could lie. We sprawled against the slimy, sloping banks of the trench, which was only a huge ditch, our heads and shoulders covered with ground sheets, our feet ankle deep in the mire, trying to hold ourselves there while we dozed. Every now and then some poor chap, worn beyond resistance, would slide down into the muck. His comrades would pull him, whimpering, back to his place and try to hold him there. It was a night of incredible weariness and the drizzle in the ghoulish dawn chilled us to the bone. Plastered with mud, red-eyed from lack of rest, irritable beyond measure, we stood about like cattle huddled in a storm, and watched an officer slide into the trench actually to see if it were *clean*, that we had not left a cigarette butt visible. And the shell came, one of those heart-stopping, high velocity brutes, as if sent to complete the gruesome picture. I can see again the men standing there, scarcely looking a second time at the mangled remains.

And the tents at St. Jean, leaking, rain-soaked, filthy, with wooden flooring covered with mud and water, where we placed our steel helmets and packs on the floor and sat on them, back to back, cramped and doubled, trying not to topple over when we reached a comatose state that answered for sleep, sitting there in the dark, unmoving, without speaking, numbed by the awfulness of everything while icy water pooled inches deep wherever the floor might sag.

Then rain and rain, and more rain, and we, in kilts, so soaked and bedraggled that rain had ceased to mean more misery, in assisting gunners to drag their guns through quagmires in which mules bogged and drowned, toppling the guns over and over in the soupy morass, twenty or thirty pulling on the ropes.

Memories. . . . I see now, as then, those big, black-winged Gothas overhead, dropping bombs on the shell-laden mules and long files of working parties.

The plunging, wading, labouring move we made from Abraham Heights to the front line stands out among all the frightfulness of that first tour as the one that tested every ounce of our endurance. We had had nothing warm in our stomachs for two days and we had spent hours in craters unfit to shelter any living thing. The night was pitch-black, and drenching, the mud more than knee-deep in many places. Somehow, we reached our line—to relieve a remnant of a company who had simply squatted in the swamp and made no attempt at trenching. They were exhausted beyond word or gesture. We slumped down where they had been, then, lashed by our wills, sluggish muscles responded. A sort of line was dug, and one hole in which our platoon had placed its machine gun was deepened enough to permit a cavity in its side over which we hung a groundsheet, and in which we placed a mess tin and tommy cookers. We made tea, boiling, strength-giving tea, getting the water from a shell-hole in front of the post I had made. As one mess tin was being emptied another was being heated, and so it went until morning.

From out in front, where shattered stubs protruded like fingers of a dead hand reaching to high heaven in protest, there came a constant groaning, long shuddering moans, and at last two sergeants clambered from our ditch and went exploring. They came back, labouring and gasping, carrying a German soldier. He had been terribly wounded and gangrene had already set in. In lucid minutes before daylight he gritted his teeth and snarled at us like a cornered animal. But in the first light he was carried back, an hour of frightful labour, to the pillbox that was being used as a first aid post and there, before he could be taken inside, a shell killed him and one of the lads who helped the stretcher-bearers.

Memories. . . . That long day, crouching in our ditch in helpless, freezing, unnerving waiting while shells burst behind, in front, overhead, all around us, but never quite reaching our refuge. Then, at night, a patrol that rivalled the imagination, a crawling for hours, in kilts, through what had been a farmyard. I see again, as then, the outline of pot helmets a shell flash revealed, the German heads, so close together. We crawled on, because they never moved, and grouped about them. They were wedged there, close-packed, long dead. Then the dreadful six hours' crawl back again.

And, that next night . . . the attack on Graf House. It was of better weather and not so dark, but confusion reigned. . . . There was the long waiting, spread-eagled in no man's land, until 2 a.m., and another frightful crawl. Then—chaos . . . too little knowledge, but that was Passchendaele to every unit. Cries, shoutings in the dark, machine guns, shells, wild orders . . . Germans scant yards from us, shooting point-blank from cover of a road embankment. One of the shells had dropped almost beside me.

It seemed an eternity after when I roused. The fight had gone on . . . I had lost sense of direction . . . there was frantic shooting everywhere. Two German gunners, huge men, passing within feet of me, placing their tripod and gun there, beginning to shoot . . . the slow realization that I had a Mills bomb in my pocket . . . the waiting before my brain cleared enough to comprehend its worth . . . drawing the pin . . . the throw . . . the red explosion . . . the overturned tripod . . . the hunched figures in the mud. . . .

Daylight. . . . More shell fire. Wonderment as to where I was, stiffened in a cavity, caked with mud, wretched beyond words. Comrades with hot tea . . . no orders . . . no other men . . . no officers . . . nothing. . . . Just wait and wait, until reckoning is lost, and shell fire is a drumming on your brain, and nothing is quite clear, a condition of merciful coma. Then night once more. Years ago you came to the Salient. Years ago you were at California Trench. . . . Years ago at Abraham Heights. There was a night attack, years, long years ago. But now . . . At Graf Farm a few youths worked among the cabbages and turnips and dogs barked savagely from the yard. It seemed incredible, standing there, that such things had really happened, that the Salient was no more.

That was not Passchendaele, those acres of grass and roots and grain, those farms and hedges, and cobbled roads. It is not the Passchendaele the veteran knows. His Passchendaele is carried forever with him—in his memory.

W.R.B.

Ypres Day

THE Ypres League Annual Commemoration will be held on **Sunday, October 28th,** and the following arrangements have been made.—

2.30 p.m. Assemble on the Horse Guards' Parade.
3.00 p.m. Address, followed by the "Lament" by Pipers of the 2nd Btn. Scots Guards.
3.15 p.m. March to the Cenotaph.
3.30 p.m. Laying of Ypres League Wreath on the Cenotaph.
3.45 p.m. March back to the Horse Guards' Parade.
4.00 p.m. Dismiss on the Horse Guards' Parade, and at 4.30 p.m. an Ypres League deputation will proceed to the Tomb of the Unknown Warrior in Westminster Abbey and place a wreath.

H.R.H. Princess Beatrice has graciously consented to attend the service and lay the League wreath on the Cenotaph.

Plain clothes and medals to be worn (uniform optional).

We hope that members of the Ypres League will make every effort to attend this Commemoration.

2nd North Midland Brigade R.F.A. Old Brigade's Association

IMAGINE long months ago a few war-time pals of the Association sitting in a member's best room, awaiting the arrival of the rest of the party who were to discuss the event of the Annual Dinner. Conversation drifts from one topic to another, and one remark arouses extreme interest—" I'd like to see again some of the places we knew during the War "; " So would I "; Me, too "; " Why not all go? " were the rejoinders.

There came to life the germ of an idea to take a trip. The later arrivals were acquainted with the subject, and so the plan gathered adherents.

This being a new line of activity for the Association, we were somewhat at a loss as to the best way to proceed, but fortunately we had one member who had heard of the services rendered by the Ypres League in this direction, and he was commissioned to " find out things " and report at our next gathering. He faithfully carried out his task and presented schemes for our choice along with approximate costs and periods, so that when our Annual Dinner took place early in March we were able to present a concrete proposal which was favourably received by the company.

From now on enthusiam got warmer and memories were searched for incidents that had occurred during the Brigade's four years' service on the Western Front.

Intending participants in the tour wondered if a particular place of interest could still be recognised, what had happened to the shattered villages and hamlets? Are the roads improved? Should we see any graves of comrades who had gone " West "? How many will the contingent eventually number?

Progress was made and Saturday, August the 4th, 1934 (a significant date) saw 14 of us greeting our conductor, Capt. G. E. de Trafford, M.C., at Victoria Station. We were an assorted crowd of civilians ranging in age from 29 to 54, some of whom had carried through their bat with the 2nd N.M. R.F.A. from February, 1915, until the conclusion of hostilities, some had suffered the pain of wounds and been dismissed from the activities at various stages of the game, but all were now imbued with the same idea—to make the most of the opportunity, and satisfy the mind on points that had been recurring since the germ had taken root.

A pleasant rail and boat journey found us at Ostend on Sunday morning with a couple of hours to spare. After a light repast at the Buffet and a ramble round the unawakened town, we entrained for Ypres, arriving in good time for breakfast at the Hotel de la Gare.

Then commenced in real earnest our quest for enlightenment. The morning was spent according to the desire of the individual, exploring Ypres and environs on foot, and in security hitherto not experienced.

In Ypres itself one marvelled at the enormity of the work entailed in rebuilding, from the vast scrap heap we had formerly known, the Cathedral, Cloth Hall, business places and habitations. We saw the Menin Gate Memorial and the vast proportions of the edifice were in keeping with all that it symbolised.

Following lunch a 'bus tour of the Salient was the programme, and halts were made at points of special interest for members, who recalled their experiences of more hectic times and saw spots of tragic or humorous moment. " This is where we had an O.P."; " Somewhere about here we had a forward gun "; " That's the blinking village Jerry used to shell us from with his 6-inch; " Here's the very cellar I kipped in "; " This is the road where we had six horses wounded in one afternoon "; were the remarks heard in turn.

Everywhere we were amazed at the prolific crops of corn, vegetables, tobacco and hops, where at one time we saw only mud and the havoc of war. The site of Tyne Cot was significant of all that our operations in the Salient involved.

Dinner in the evening was the time for the summing up of our day's activities, and at 9 p.m. all members of the party attended the sounding of the "Last Post" at Menin Gate which was in accord with all that had previously impressed us.

Monday comprised a whole day tour of the country further South, including Armentieres, Fleurbaix, Neuve Chapelle, La Bassee, Hohenzollern Redoubt, Vimy Ridge, Bethune, Bailleul, and Meteren, and again at the various halts events of long years ago were recounted—" This is where we had our Officer's Mess " ; " Our first Officer casualty occurred here."

Some time was spent at Hohenzollern Redoubt, as although our Brigade was not in action there, a number of gunners and drivers were employed on carrying parties to the Infantry Brigade, who were relatives or neighbours at home and whose exploits were closely followed by our mob, and who gave a good account of themselves there on October the 13th, 1915.

Bethune also held considerable interest, for had we not entrained there for leave to England, and well did we remember the concert party's efforts in the glass-domed theatre in " cushy " times ?

A note of a different tone was struck when we found ourselves at a Cemetery behind the old line where a scrutiny of the register divulged the names of 28 of our former comrades who rest beneath the soil of a foreign land. We were reminded of a fateful day when 14 of them were killed together.

Tuesday morning entailed a short run round Ypres district, including a call at the renowned Talbot House, Poperinghe. At Kemmel we located our first bit of Front and recollected the days when ammunition was strictly limited and where spare time was devoted by the gunners to cultivating bits of garden : a feature which was out of the question when matters subsequently livened up.

The time after lunch on Tuesday was originally intended to be spent at Ypres, but the general desire was to have a look at Zeebrugge, so an earlier train was taken to Ostend from whence the electric tram was used to have an enjoyable run along the Belgian Coast to the Mole, where an interesting time was spent on the scene of the Navy's exploits on April 23rd, 1918.

Dinner at the Avenue Hotel, Ostend on Tuesday night was the final item on the itinerary, and 15 tired pilgrims journeyed to Victoria, there to disperse after a three days' tour crowded with interest and good fellowship.

It is of interest to mention that in addition to the small snapshot cameras carried by members of the party, one enthusiast took along his cinema camera and exposed a number of reels on the places visited and the activities of his pals, and if results are successful, our next Annual Dinner will see the innovation of a news reel, which if not up-to-date on current events, will be of outstanding interest to the members of the Association and no doubt whet the appetite of those who were unable to be numbered among this year's party.

Warmest thanks are due to the Ypres League for the great care and consideration extended on this, our first, collective tour, every minute of which was smooth running. One point which added to our pleasure was the provision of a British Ex-Service driver who knew every inch of the ground covered. His answers to our many queries helped us considerably to locate objects of the landscape, and link up our memories with events of almost a score years ago.

Our talks with the natives and grave attèndants also gave us some impression of the procedure of re-establishing the devastated areas, and in one meandering we were pleased to assure a troubled mind that we were not reconnoitering for another war, but that our visit was of a purely peaceable nature.

Maybe some of the party will carry out their promises to keep in touch by correspondence with people they met, for this trip has made us realise that the objects of the Ypres League are very worthy ones, and that each individual can add his weight towards their achievement.

The one regret is that we allowed so many years to elapse between visits.

H. B. S.

August Bank Holiday Pilgrimages

The Ypres League pilgrimages and tours of the Battlefields of France and Flanders are in no way receding with the passing of years, in fact 1934 has found larger musters of members and friends participating.

At August Bank Holiday, despite the disadvantageous rate of the £ sterling abroad we were successful in being able to organise and conduct two parties to Ypres by the day and night route respectively and a third party to Arras. In each case the battlefield motor tours were organised in accordance with the combined wishes of each member of the party, and those who had cemeteries to visit en route were afforded ample time in which to fulfil their sacred duties. It was touching to watch the personal interest shown by the other pilgrims of the party and their anxiety to share in some small way the sorrow endured by the bereaved relatives whenever a particular grave was visited. The cemeteries were all very beautiful notwithstanding the long period of drought, and great credit is due to our ex-service gardeners of the Imperial War Graves Commission who take such devoted interest and pride in their arduous and lonely tasks.

The Ypres "day route" party was sixty four strong under the faithful and friendly guidance of Mr. S. H. K. Geller. Quite a number of this party who had re-visited Ypres periodically since the war found a further advancement in the reconstruction of the famous City's Cloth Hall Tower. After attending the sounding of the "Last Post" each night at the Menin Gate, some of the pilgrims walked out to their various old battle haunts while others found amusement in the Thuindag Fair which was in full swing in the Grande Place. Sunday afternoon was spent on a tour of Ypres Salient passing such places as St. Jean, Wieltje, St. Julien, Gravenstafel, Tyne Cot (Passchendaele), Broodseinde, Becelaere, Clapham Junction, Observatory Ridge, Hill 60 etc., and on the Monday a whole day charabanc expedition was made over the battlefields from Ypres to Vimy Ridge via Wytschaete Ridge, Messines, Ploegsteert, Armentieres, Neuve Chapelle, La Bassee and Lens, and the return journey via Arras, Faubourg d'Amiens Memorial to the "Missing" and on through Bethune, Estaires, Bailleul, Dranoutre and Kemmel reaching Ypres again about 7 p.m.

The Ypres night route party of members of the 2nd North Midland Old Boys (46th Division) from Stoke-on-Trent was conducted by Captain de Trafford, an account of which appears on page 114.

The Arras party was ably shepherded by Mr. O. Mears, and a full programme with even more extended motor itineraries because the cemeteries are very scattered in the Arras and Somme districts. The following places were visited:— Ayette, Bucquoy, Beaumont Hamel (Newfoundland Park), Thiepval, Ovillers, La Boiselle, Aveluy Wood, Albert, Pozieres, Longueval, Combles, Ginchy, Les Boeufs, Le Transloy, Bapaume, Louveral, Boursies, Cambrai, Marquion, Vis-en-Artois, Monchy, Neuville St Vaast, Arras Memorial, Vimy Ridge (Grange Tunnels and Canadian Memorial) Givenchy, Souchez, Notre Dame de Lorette (French Memorial) and Mont St. Eloy.

Many kind letters of appreciation have been received at headquarters from those who took part in the above mentioned tours, and it is pleasing to hear that no small number have already expressed the hope of being able to embark on another trip next year and also to persuade their friends to join them.

The Secretary.

New Novel Competition

OPEN TO MEMBERS ONLY

"YPISODES"

With a view to still further increasing the popularity of our little quarterly, the "Ypres Times" it has been decided to introduce a competition for the best Great War episode or to which we intend to refer as "Ypisode" submitted by any Life Member or Annual Subscriber during the year, 1935.

Each quarter's edition will contain a selection from those received and we feel that they will provide excellent reading and create great interest amongst our members.

Ypisodes may be written on any incident at home or abroad which occurred during the Great War period and may be submitted, not necessarily by members of the fighting services because the competition is open to both sexes. Most of us can recall some particular incident, humorous or otherwise, which if broadcast would provide much interest and amusement to others.

We publish herewith two examples for guidance :—

1. Scene: back of Lancashire Farm on a pitch black December night, 1916.
"C" Coy filing out through long wet grass and self (after first spell in line) bringing up the rear with Sergt X.
Silence only broken by continuous strange whistling noises at our feet and in long grass.
Puzzled at this, I ask: "Are those rats squeaking Sergeant"
Rats, Sir, laughs the Sergeant—them's bullets and there's too many of'em for *my* liking.

2. Scene: Ypres Infantry Barracks, 1917: programme of work-parties by night and stay-at-home by day.
To make a diversion I had made a fine set of "shadowgraphs" of "C" Coy officers and placed the life-sized heads in a row high up on the wall of our mess before we cleared out for a spell in the line.
Heard later that the incoming unit was was not greatly impressed by this martial array, one officer remarking that there was plenty of "frightfulness" outside.
"*Forester.*"

Ypisodes will be judged by their merit and briefness will be strictly taken into account.

From what in the opinion of the Judges are considered the six best Ypisodes submitted throughout the year, the Editor will be asked to nominate the winner, and the result will be published together with the winning Ypisode in the January, 1936 edition of the "Ypres Times".

The successful competitor will be awarded the following prize :—

A WEEK-END TRIP TO YPRES (SATURDAY TO TUESDAY) WITH AN YPRES LEAGUE PILGRIMAGE AT EASTER, WHITSUNTIDE, OR AUGUST BANK HOLIDAY, 3RD CLASS RAIL 2ND CLASS BOAT WITH FULL BOARD AND 3 NIGHTS ACCOMMODATION TO INCLUDE TAXES AND GRATUITIES AT THE HOTEL, AND A HALF-DAY MOTOR TOUR OF THE YPRES SALIENT.

Members may submit any number of entries and the Secretary will be prepared to receive them from the receipt of this October issue until December 15th, 1935 which will definitely be regarded as the closing date.

All entries bearing member's full name and address should be directed as follows :-

"Ypisodes"
Ypres League,
20, Orchard Street,
LONDON W.I.

Coincidence

I FIRST met him at Kut-el-Amara when he was a prisoner under escort. He was a cheerful, happy, individual, very willing, and always crooning his native songs while he was at work; he never bothered to learn the British Tommies' songs of that day, for which we were thankful. Somehow they always seemed a little shallow when sung by a man of another colour and race. The only name we knew him by was 'Pea Soup,' and he was one of the blackest, shiniest, natives that ever came out of Central Africa. At that time he was learning from the Army Authorities what discipline means, for he had wilfully disobeyed an order, and was now a prisoner awaiting trial.

He had signed on for duty as a fireman on one of the Tigris river boats under the control of the Inland Water Transport, and while his vessel was awaiting orders at Kut, he had been ordered ashore to assist in some work going on at the quayside. He had the temerity to point out that he was a ship's fireman, and had only signed for that work. It was fatal of course; he was under escort now waiting to be sent down river to Basrah for a court martial and disgrace. A few days later I went up to the line, and Pea Soup and his court martial went out of my memory.

* * *

Two years later, when I was idling on the deck of a West African liner at Freetown, Sierra Leone, I was hailed with a shout of delight from a Kroo Boy who was working one of the winches at a forward hatch. A sling of palm kernels was dumped hurriedly down the hold, the winchman left his work, and came rushing up a gangway to greet me as an old friend. " I savvy you for Mesopotamia, massa ; you savvy me, Pea Soup?" He hurried on to remind me of all the details of our last meeting in far away Kut, and, like the majority of men of his race, he had a vivid, retentive memory, calling completely to mind all those little details of the past which in the whirl of life is apt in an European to become slurred and misty. The last I saw of him he was going ashore in a lighter, a wave of his hand, the same cheerful grin on his face.

* * *

A year before I first ran into Pea Soup I spent many a long hour of the night listening to exciting yarns and experiences of pre-war days on the veldt from a South African, a hardened old campaigner if ever there was one. At that time we were sharing sentry duty in the front line on the Somme, waiting for the fatal First of July, 1916.—Those escapades of his in the earlier years of this century were shared with a bosom friend, one Scholey by name, but during one of their affairs in 1913 Scholey had been left behind in a hospital in Windhoek; (they were " working " German territory at the time) and all efforts my friend had made to trace him when he returned later had failed; Scholey had disappeared. Three years later here was Scholey's friend a British Infantryman in France with,—as he used to say,—" no hopes of ever seeing Africa and my pal again."

* * *

A few weeks later I was in a London Hospital, and in the next cot was a man from one of the South African Regiments. While we were exchanging news and reminiscences during those long days of idleness I found myself listening to exactly the same story I had heard a few weeks previously. You will have guessed of course who it was. Actually the name over his cot was not Scholey, but that was a small matter of his own. How delighted he was to learn that I could put him in touch with his old partner again. There was no doubt about it. He struggled through a letter, got it away that evening for France, and during the next few days joyfully awaited a reply. He got one about a week later, but it was from a kindly R.A.M.C. orderly to say that his friend had been killed in action that week.

You, too, probably have your own vivid recollections of strange coincidences, and, viewed from the level of everyday life, how unusual and fantastic they appear.

If this page sets memories stirring then I aver that coincidences such as these will be legion. And yet no novelist or playwright of standing introduces them to the world of fictional realism; they only allow for their existence in the unrealistic world of farce and impossibility, while in everyday life we accept these coincidences without demur.

The writers, of course, discovered long ago the fundamental truth that strange coincidences, such as we have in mind, have usually not the slightest effect on our lives; they pass by and we neither gain nor lose by them.

I make this plea for coincidence; are we not, in this transitory age of disbelief, (when "debunking" is such a popular pastime) in danger of going to the other extreme and denying even the possibilities of coincidence as apart from chance?

W. J. PARRY.

The 13th Belgian Field Artillery Memorial Unveiling

ON Sunday, September 9th, the bronze plaque to the memory of the 13th Belgian Artillery was unveiled at Ypres. This plaque is let into the wall at the side of the Ypres Town Memorial and inscribed in Flemish, French and English.

The unveiling took place in the presence of a very large assembly. The pavements from the station to the Grande Place were thronged with interested spectators and Belgian and British flags were flying from every window. A special train brought the members of the 13th Belgian Field Artillery Old Comrades Association with its President, Baron de Rosée, and after a reception at Hotel Skindles, the cortege, headed by the Ypres Town Band playing the old British march tunes, proceeded to the Town Memorial, where the Burgomaster, Monsieur Vanderghote was awaiting to receive the members, a number of whom are also members of the Ypres League and take particular interest in our Association owing to the fact that the 13th Belgian Field Artillery Regiment was the only Belgian Artillery unit which served for two years of the Great War under British Command at Ypres.

The Ypres League was officially represented by Brig.-General Stephen Lushington, C.B., C.M.G., and Captain P. D. Parminter, the League's Ypres representative, and on behalf of all our members, General Lushington placed a beautiful wreath at the Memorial composed of Flanders Poppies tied with the League's colours and inscribed as follows:—

<blockquote>
FROM THE YPRES LEAGUE
In memory of its fallen comrades of the
13th Belgian Artillery Regiment who gave
their lives in the immortal defence of Ypres.
</blockquote>

Wreaths were placed at the Menin Gate and on the Munsters' Memorial. Amongst those present at the ceremony were:—Lieut. General Gillieaux, representing King Leopold, Colonel L. Aerts, Colonel Ashwanden, the National Vice-Chairman of the British Legion, who delivered a most impressive speech at the unveiling, Major P. Slessor, of Toc H., Mr. H. Reeder, of Haig House and members of the Brussels, Antwerp, Ostend, and Ypres Branches of the British Legion.

A special service was held in the Cathedral in which the band of the "Guides" from Brussels took part. After the ceremony the official lunch was held in the Salle Lapierre at which nearly four hundred persons attended under the Presidentship of General Lushington, who proposed the health of the King and Queen of the Belgians. During the lunch the gathering lustily joined in the musical items, comprising many of the old British war-time songs and it certainly appeared that the members of the 13th B.F.A. knew the words of the songs as well if not better than the rest of the community.

The organising of the whole ceremony was of the highest efficiency intermixed with an atmosphere of real good comradeship.

League Secretary's Notes

A hearty welcome is extended to all those who have enrolled as members of the Ypres League since the publication of our last quarterly edition of the "Ypres Times". The summer is not usually regarded as a successful recruiting season, because people are rightly saving up in contemplation of their deserved holidays, but despite this we are encouraged to have enrolled quite a number of new members, many of whom have joined as a result of accompanying our pilgrimages to the battlefields.

In August we had the honour to record the collective Life Membership of the 9th (Scottish) Divisional Association, and the Ypres League scroll certificate, suitably inscribed, has been gratefully acknowledged by the Hon. Secretary, Major A.A. Tyer, M.V.O., T.D.

During 1934 our pilgrimages have been exceedingly well represented and it may be of interest to insert the following summary :—

March 16th—18th	Honourable Artillery Company. Battlefield lecture tour with headquarters at Cambrai.
March 31st—Apl. 3rd	Easter Pilgrimage to Ypres
Apri 13th—16th	167th Infantry Brigade T.A. Battlefield lecture tour with headquarters at Cambrai.
April 14th—17th	Public Schools O.T.C. Battlefield lecture tour with headquarters at Ypres
May 19th—22nd	Whitsuntide Pilgrimage to Ypres.
May 19th—21st	Free Pilgrimage of poor mothers and widows to Ypres.
May 25th—28th	85th Club tour with headquarters at Ypres.
July 14th—17th	Ypres League Colchester and District Branch tour to Ypres.
July 28th—30th	Ypres British Settlement Committee party to Ypres for dedication of the Cloth Hall Belfry and Ypres Britsh School prize-giving.
August 4th—7th	August Bank Holiday Pilgrimages to Ypres and Arras respectively.
August 4th—8th	2nd North Midland Brigade (46th Division) tour to Ypres.
September 15th-18th	Pilgrimage to Ypres.

In addition we have had pleasure to make travel arrangements for our members and friends who preferred to proceed independently to the cemeteries and battlefields. As last year, the pilgrimages and tours have been carried out in most favourable weather which added considerably to their success, and our sincere thanks are due to the Ypres League representatives at the battlefield centres for their efficient transport arrangements.

We would like to draw attention to the Ypres League Deposit Scheme for those desirous of visiting France and Flanders under the League's auspices and for which forms will be sent on application to the Secretary.

With regard to our Branches, Purley have set the pace in recruiting and their popular golf competitions during the summer months have created great interest and pleasure. We are pleased to hear that December 6th next has been earmarked for the first Branch Dance and we extend our hearty good wishes for its success.

Our Colchester Branch have also embarked on summer activity by making a pilgrimage to Ypres under the auspices of the League. The party was accompanied by the Branch Chairman Lieut. Colonel H.W. Herring, M.C.

The London County Committee are busily preparing their winter programmes for monthly Informal Gatherings and Annual Smoking Concert to be held in October, and at the same time they are secretly hoping to land at last that elusive recruiting prize.

We earnestly appeal to all our staunch supporters to continue to bear in mind the importance of recruiting a new member whenever an opportunity occurs. The League has, so far, successfully extricated itself out of the prolonged depressing period of the past few years and now we want each member to make a further special effort to recruit one relative or friend during the forthcoming winter months, because the united endeavour of doing just "this little bit" will cement the position of the League for years to come.

In view of the fact that this is the last quarterly edition of 1934, we would like to wish our faithful members a very happy Christmas, and at the same time ask them to accept our grateful thanks for their generous co-operation which we have so much enjoyed and valued in the old year.

COLLECTION OF TINFOIL

We have announced in previous editions of the "Ypres Times" that a collection of tinfoil is being made by headquarters eventually to be sold in aid of the League's funds. We are immensely indebted to those who have given their valuable time to the collection of this silver paper and hope that we may look forward to receiving further supplies during the winter months.

A DIFFERENT HISTORY.

It is refreshing to pick up a history through which one does not "wade", but by which one is carried interestedly through to the end; a book in which the author has blended historical accuracy with intimate anecdote and has made the story of his Battalion a splendid record of his comrades' deeds (and misdeeds), whilst he has, in addition, given the public a thoroughly interesting book.

One feels, by the time that one reaches the final page, that one knows the chief characters in this "Big Family" almost as well as did the author, who, indeed, had plenty of opportunity of knowing them, having served with them practically throughout the existence of the unit.

Such is the History of the 11th (Lewisham) Battalion of The Queens's Own, Royal-West Kent Regiment, (41st. Division) by Captain R.O. Russell, M.C., and published by the Lewisham Newspaper Co., Ltd., Loampit-vale, S.E.13, at 5s. 9d. post free, with a de luxe edition at a guinea.

The History has several unique features apart from the unconventional manner in which it is written. There are messages from its Colonel, its Brigade Commander and its Divisional Commander. It is copiously illustrated, and the maps and aerial photographs are splendid: a number of them being now published for the first time. Delightful thumb-nail sketches, too, add a further charm.

As for the fighting history of this Battalion we read that its Colonel won the D.S.O. three times in seven months. We need add nothing further.

The Battalion served continuously in the Salient for over twelve months in 1916-17 and this alone should make the book particularly interesting to members of the Ypres League.

The publishers are to be congratulated on producing one of the best battalion histories we have yet come across.

Branch Notes

PURLEY BRANCH.
THE BOMBARDIER'S FOURSOMES, 1934.
4th, 5th and 6th Battles.

Just when the Fourth Battles were in progress, a shadow fell on the competition : Capt. E. H. Carr, one of last year's finalists and again fighting strongly, passed away suddenly, after an illness which he appeared to be overcoming.

The Chairman and a contingent of Members attended the funeral to accord him the last honours.

The Fourth Battles were the Quarter-finals and at the top Alderson and Meredith, who played Mutton and Duncan at Coulsdon Court, got beaten by them on the last green, 2 up.

The next two matches were all Woodcote Park parties : Fitton and Zinn played Frost and Green and lost to them, 4 up and 3 ; Green and Scott played Taylor and Wiltshire, and won 2 up.

In the last match Harris and Streat played Featherstone and G. Carr at Coulsdon Court, and the holders did their stuff quite well and won, 3 and 1.

The Semi-finals or Fifth Battles were exciing affairs : Frost and Green went invading to Coulsdon Court, established an early lead on Mutton and Duncan and beat them handsomely by 5 and 3. Green's already high reputation has gone higher after every match : clearly his partner Frost always does his share too.

The other battle developed into a desperate show : having survived for some years there was just a possibility that the holders, Featherstone and Carr might win one more battle, but this time they were unable to take the one chance of winning at the 18th (Carr looked up !) and Scott and Green won at the 20th. The latter played very fine golf and each made a match-winning shot at the right moment, and so won a great game. The losers were round in 78, Featherstone playing like a hero.

The Sixth and Final Battle was an all-Woodcote-Park affair : Capt. R. L. Haine, V.C., M.C., the Chairman, reports as follows :—

Final of the Bombardier's Foursomes played at Woodcote Park on Sunday 29th July. S. Green (12) and Scott (9) gave five strokes to Frost (17) and G. Green (18).

The final this year was a ding-dong battle from start to finish, and it was not until they reached the 18th green that Scott and Green (S) succeeded in finishing off their opponents by winning 2 up.

Scott and Green took the lead at the first hole but Frost and Green won the second which was a stroke hole. The third was halved in four, and Scott and Green again took the lead at the fourth. The fifth was halved and the sixth won by Green and Frost, to make the match all square once again.

By this stage of the game all the players had settled down and we enjoyed some really fine golf. Frost in particular was playing magnificently, and his driving was worthy of a scratch player.

At the seventh Frost hit a real peach which finished within a few yards of the green and he and his partner got their par 4 to win the hole and become one up. The short eighth saw the match all square once again, for Scott was nicely on whilst his opponent was not so fortunate. The ninth, a stroke hole, was halved, and the game was all-square at the turn.

At the 10th, Green (S) sank a 5 yard putt for a birdie, for Scott and Green to become one up. The eleventh was halved in 4, and the twelfth won by Scott and Green in a par 4. The thirteenth saw Green (S) sink a putt of about 6 yards to save the hole, but the fourteenth was won by Frost and Green in a par 4.

Frost and Green got into trouble at the next hole, Frost driving out of bounds and Green also fluffing his tee shot. They eventually gave up this hole, to make Scott and Green 2 up once again.

At the sixteenth both pairs took 6 to get down, but this was a stroke hole, and a win for Frost and Green.

The seventeenth was halved in 5, leaving Scott and Green dormy 1.

The eighteenth was a very exciting hole with everybody showing signs of nerves. Green (G) drove a nice shot down the fairway but Scott hooked his drive into the rough. Green (S) failed to get out and Scott wisely played up the first fairway on the left of the green. In the meantime Frost had trundled his shot along the fairway (head up) and Green (G) had sliced their third shot to the right of the green. Both were on in four, and Scott clinched matters by sinking a ten-yard putt and winning the hole and the match by 2 up.

The players and their friends adjourned to the Club House to celebrate with the victors and condole with the vanquished. When the party finally broke up it was decided that Scott and Green (S) had also won the 19th.

THE ADJUTANT.

LONDON COUNTY COMMITTEE.
Twelfth Annual Re-union Smoking Concert.

The Smoking Concert will take place at the Caxton Hall, Caxton Street, Victoria Street, S.W.1, on Saturday, October 27th, 1934, when Major E. Montague Jones, O.B.E. (Chairman of the London County Committee) will preside, and amongst the guests who have already accepted invitations to be present are :—
H. E. The Belgian Ambassador; H. E. The French Ambassador; Major A. Nyssens, Military Attaché, Belgian Embassy; Colonel R. Voruz, Military Attaché, French Embassy; Representative of the American Embassy; General Sir W. C. G. Heneker, K.C.B., K.C.M.G., D.S.O., Lieut.-General Sir W. P. Pulteney. G.C.V.O., K.C.B., K.C.M.G., D.S.O., Colonel G. E. C. Rasch, D.S.O., Colonel G. Brierley, C.M.G., D.S.O., The Rev. G. H. Woolley, V.C., M.C., and Major W. H. Brooke, M.C.

Doors will be open at 7 p.m., and the Concert commences at 7.30 p.m. The programme will be given by the "Bubbles" Concert Party under personal direction of Mr. Will Seymour and in addition, Mr. A. E. Nickolds entertains with Songs at the Piano. Musical selections will be played by "The Enfield College of Music Orchestra," under the direction of Mrs. Doris Lee Peabody. Buglers from the 12th London Regiment (The Rangers) have been engaged, through the kind permission of the Officer Commanding, Lieut.-Colonel G. M. B. Portman. A feature of the programme will again be the singing of the old war-time choruses. We want another record gathering, and we depend on individual help to make this important annual function known to those who are not members of the Ypres League, and who may be glad to attend. If any members of the London area are unable to be present themselves, might we take the liberty to suggest that they be so kind as to purchase a ticket in order to assist the funds of the London County Committee.

Cornflowers will be on sale at the Hall, price 2d. each, and we respectfully request everybody to wear this League emblem.

Application for tickets, prices 1/-, 2/6d. and 5/- (including tax), should be made as early as possible, to the Hon. Secretary, London County Committee Ypres League, 20, Orchard Street, W.1. Ladies are cordially invited.

A limited number of tables can be reserved for parties of four and upwards, on payment of 2/- per table on the 2/6d. tickets, and 2/6d. per table on the 5/- tickets. Latest date for application is October 20th.

We look forward to a record gathering on October 27th. *See* page 126.

Informal Gatherings.

From now until July, the Informals are held on the third Thursday in each month, and take place at the Bedford Head Hotel, Maiden Lane, Strand, W.C.2, from 7.15 a.m. to 10 p.m.

These gatherings which have afforded so much pleasure in the past to the many members and friends attending them, are promoted to enable ex-service men to meet together in a convivial atmosphere, to renew old acquaintances and to further that wonderful spirit of the Great War. Admission is free to all members and friends who are cordially invited. Ladies are also exceedingly welcome at these gatherings.

Programmes for the coming season are being arranged, and we thank those who have already offered support and also our staunch members and friends who have helped so generously in the past. *See* page 123.

In conclusion, we appeal to every London member to introduce at least one friend to the membership of the Ypres League during the forthcoming season, and we earnestly hope that serious consideration will be given to this important matter of recruiting. A substantial response to this appeal will be very greatly appreciated by the London County Committee.

INFORMAL GATHERINGS

OF THE

LONDON COUNTY COMMITTEE, YPRES LEAGUE

WILL BE HELD AT

The Bedford Head Hotel, Maiden Lane, Strand, W.C.2.
7.15 p.m. to 10 p.m. on following dates :—

Thursday, October 18th, 1934.
   (Lantern talk on "Sea Power"
         by Lieut.-Commander D. S. E. Thompson, R.N.)
Thursday, November 15th, 1934.
Thursday, December 20th, 1934.
Thursday, January 17th, 1935.

We request members to bring these fixtures to the notice of their friends in order to ensure another successful season, and invitations will be gladly sent by the Hon. Secretary to any friends on receipt of names and addresses. Ladies are cordially invited.

DANCES

Three dances will be held during the coming season as follows:—

Friday, November 23rd, 1934.
Wednesday, January 23rd, 1935.
Friday, March 8th, 1935.

AT THE

VETERAN'S CLUB, HAND COURT, HOLBORN, W.C.1.
(Entrance at 47, Bedford Row)
7.30 p.m.

Tickets 1/6d. each, and it is hoped that these dances may be well supported.

THE BRITISH TOURING SERVICE

Manager—Mr. P. VYNER
Representative and Life Member, Ypres League

10, Station Square
ARRAS
(P.-de-C.) France

Cars for Hire, with British Driver Guides   Tours Arranged

The Ypres League (Incorporated)

Balance Sheet, 31st December, 1933.

LIABILITIES AND FUNDS.

	£ s. d.	£ s. d.
Free Pilgrimage Fund		131 19 6
General Fund—		
Balance at credit, 1st January, 1933	195 15 10	
Less Balance at debit for year to 31st December, 1933	135 2 7	60 13 3
Reserve Fund—		
In respect of Life Membership Subscriptions	300 0 0	
"Ypres Times" Maintenance Fund ...	208 18 10	
Maintenance Fund—		
Ypres Salient Notice Boards		6 16 9
Sundry Creditors, etc.		69 19 10
Hostel Fund—		
Balance, 1st January, 1933	381 19 0	
Less Amount transferred to General Fund	70 8 5	
	311 10 7	
Add Net Income for the year to 31st December 1933	8 13 5	320 4 0
		£1,098 12 2

ASSETS.

	£ s. d.	£ s. d.	£ s. d.
Stocks of Publications, etc., on hand ... As per Head Office records and Secretary's valuation.			94 4 6
Cash at Bank and in hand—			
Free Pilgrimage Fund	135 2 6		
Head Office Account	25 5 11		160 8 5
Halifax Building Society—			
Deposit Account "A"	300 0 0		
Deposit Account "B"	200 0 0		
		500 0 0	
Add Interest accrued		8 15 0	508 15 0
Sundry Pre-payments, etc.			12 4 5
War Stock 3½%			322 19 10
£323 2s. 11d. Stock on Hostel Fund Account.			
W. P. PULTENEY, *Lieut.-General.*			
Hon. *Treasurer.*			
E. B. WAGGETT, *Major* } *Members of the*			
E. MONTAGUE JONES, *Major* } *General Committee.*			
			£1,098 12 2

REPORT OF THE AUDITORS TO THE MEMBERS OF THE YPRES LEAGUE, INCORPORATED.

We beg to report that we have examined the above Balance Sheet with the Head Office Books and relative Documents of the Association and have obtained all the information and explanations we have required. In our opinion such Balance Sheet is properly drawn up so as to exhibit a true and correct view of the Association's affairs, according to the best of our information and the explanations given to us and as shown by the Book of the Association.

Dated this 29th day of June, 1934.

6, BOND COURT, WALBROOK, LONDON, E.C.4.

LEPINE & JACKSON, Chartered Accountants,
Auditors.

Head Office

Income and Expenditure Account for the year ended 31st December, 1933.

EXPENDITURE.

	£	s.	d.
To Salaries	281	15	0
,, Rent and Rates	211	4	9
,, Printing & Stationery	31	6	3
,, Postages & Telegrams	38	11	5
,, Prospectuses, Publicity Leaflets, etc.	26	10	9
,, Telephone & Insurances	16	8	6
,, Lighting & Heating	11	12	8
,, Accountancy & Audit Charges	12	12	0
,, Office Cleaning	7	10	0
,, General Expenses	67	10	1
,, Income Tax		15	0
	738	19	8
,, Balance, Surplus carried to General Fund	17	18	1
	£756	**17**	**9**

INCOME.

	£	s.	d.
By Subscriptions	518	3	6
,, Donations	91	13	4
,, Junior Division	4	14	0
,, Travel Bureau	111	2	3
,, Publications, etc.—Profit on Sales	25	10	2
,, Interest	5	14	6
	£756	**17**	**9**

Head Office

General Fund for the year ended 31st December, 1933.

EXPENDITURE.

	£	s.	d.	£	s.	d.
To "The Ypres Times":—						
Cost of Printing, etc.	326	2	5			
Less Sales and Advertising Revenue	14	15	4			
				311	7	1
,, Expenses in connection with removal to new Offices				20	2	0
				£331	**9**	**1**

INCOME.

	£	s.	d.
By Income and Expenditure Account Surplus for the year transferred.	17	18	1
,, Trustees of Hostel Fund—Special Donation	70	8	5
,, Free Pilgrimage Fund	50	0	0
In respect of Administration Charges, 1927 to 1933 Pilgrimages.			
,, "Ypres Times" Maintenance Fund	58	0	0
Amount allocated towards cost of "The Ypres Times" in 1933.			
,, Balance—Carried to Balance Sheet	135	2	7
	£331	**9**	**1**

THE TWELFTH ANNUAL
REUNION OF MEMBERS AND FRIENDS
Organised by the London County Committee of the Ypres League

WILL BE HELD AT THE

CAXTON HALL, CAXTON STREET, VICTORIA STREET, S.W.1.

ON

SATURDAY, OCTOBER 27th, 1934

All Members of the Ypres League and their friends are heartily invited by the London County Committee to meet together at the Caxton Hall, on Saturday, October 27th, 1934, when the

GRAND SMOKING CONCERT

will be given. The Chair will be taken by

MAJOR E. MONTAGUE JONES, O.B.E.
(Chairman of the London County Committee).

The following will also be present

H. E. The Belgian Ambassador; H. E. The French Ambassador; Major A. Nyssens, Military Attaché, Belgian Embassy; Colonel R. Voruz, Military Attaché, French Embassy; Representative of the American Embassy; General Sir W. C. G. Heneker, K.C.B., K.C.M.G., D.S.O., Lieut.-General Sir W. P. Pulteney, G.C.V.O., K.C.B., K.C.M.G., D.S.O., Colonel G. E. C. Rasch, D.S.O., Colonel G. Brierley, C.M.G., D.S.O., The Rev. G. H. Woolley, V.C., M.C., and Major W. H. Brooke, M.C.

An excellent programme has been arranged by **"The Bubbles"**
Concert Party under the personal direction of Mr. Will Seymour.

Musical Selections by "THE ENFIELD COLLEGE OF MUSIC ORCHESTRA" under the direction of Mrs. Doris Lee Peabody.

Buglers from the 12th London Regiment (The Rangers) will be present through the kind permission of the Officer Commanding, Lieut.-Colonel G. M. B. Portman.

Community singing of old war-time choruses will be included in the programme.
Medals and decorations to be worn.   Please wear your League Badge.   Ladies specially invited.

DOORS OPEN AT 7 P.M.   CONCERT COMMENCES AT 7.30 P.M.
Admission - - 1s., 2s. 6d. and 5s. (including Tax).

Accommodation at the Hall is limited but tables can be reserved for parties of four and upwards on payment of 2s. per table on the 2s. 6d. tickets, and 2s. 6d. per table on the 5s. tickets. Applicants for tables cannot be considered after October 21st.

A large attendance is anticipated, and early application for tickets accompanied by remittance should be addressed to the Hon. Secretary, London County Committee, Ypres League, 20, Orchard Street, London, W.1.

YOUR SUPPORT ON OCTOBER 27TH WILL BE APPRECIATED.

Branches and Corresponding Members

BRANCHES.

LONDON	Hon. Secretary to the London County Committee: J. Boughey, 20, Orchard Street, London, W.1. E. LONDON DISTRICT—L. A. Weller, 132, Maxey Road, Dagenham, Essex. TOTTENHAM AND EDMONTON DISTRICT—E. Glover, 191, Lansdowne Road, Tottenham, N.17. H. Carey, 373, Sydenham Road, S.E.26.
COLCHESTER	H. Snow (Hon. Sec.), 9, Church Street (North). W. H. Taylor (Pilgrimage Hon. Sec.), 64, High Street.
GATESHEAD	Lieut.-Colonel E. G. Crouch, 8, Ashgrove Terrace.
LIVERPOOL	Captain A. M. Webster, Blundellsands.
PURLEY	Major Graham Carr, D.S.O., M.C., 112-114, High Street.
SHEFFIELD	Captain J. Wilkinson, "Holmfield," Bents Drive.
BELGIUM	Capt. P. D. Parminter, 19, Rue Surmont de Volsberghe, Ypres.
CANADA	Ed. Kingsland, P.O. Box 83, Magog, Quebec.
SOUTH AFRICA	L. G. Shuter, Church Street, Pietermaritzburg.
AMERICA	Representative: Captain R. Henderson-Bland, 110 West 57th Street, New York City.

CORRESPONDING MEMBERS

GREAT BRITAIN.

ABERYSTWYTH	T. O. Thomas, 5, Smithfield Road.
ASHTON-UNDER-LYNE	G. D. Stuart, "Woodlands," Thronfield Grove, Arundel Street.
BANBURY	Captain C. W. Fowke, Yew Tree House, King's Sutton.
BIRMINGHAM	Mrs. Hill, 191, Cattell Road, Small Heath. John Burman, "Westbrook," Solihull Road, Shirley.
BOURNEMOUTH	H. L. Pasmore, 40, Morley Road, Boscombe Park.
BRISTOL	W. S. Hook, "Wytschaete" Redland Court Road.
BROADSTAIRS	C. E. King, 6, Norman Road, St. Peters, Broadstairs. Mrs. Briggs, North Foreland House.
CHATHAM	W. N. Channon, 22, Keyes Avenue.
CHESTERFIELD	Major A. W. Shea, 14, Cross Street.
CONGLETON	Mr. H. Dart, 61, The Crescent.
DARLINGTON	D. S. Vigo, 125, Dorset Road, Bexhill-on-Sea.
DERBY	T. Jakeman, 10, Graham Street.
DORRINGTON (Salop)	Captain G. D. S. Parker, Frodesley Rectory.
EXETER	Captain E. Jenkin, 25, Queen Street.
GLOUCESTER	H. R. Hunt, "Casita," Parton Lane, Churchdown.
HERNE BAY	Captain E. Clarke Williams, F.S.A.A., "Conway," Station Road.
HOVE	Captain G. W. J. Cole, 2, Westbourne Terrace, Kingsway.
LEICESTER	W. C. Dunford, 343, Aylestone Road.
LINCOLN	E. Swaine, 79, West Parade.
LLANRWST	A. C. Tomlinson, M.A., Bod Estyn.
LOUGHTON	Capt. O. G. Johnson, M.A., Loughton School.
MATLOCK (Derby)	Miss Dickinson, Beechwood.
MELROSE	Mrs. Lindesay Kelsall, Darnlea.
NEW BRIGHTON (Cheshire)	E. F. Williams, 5, Waterloo Road.
NEW MILTON	W. H. Lunn, "Greycot," Albert Road.

NOTTINGHAM ...	... E. V. Brown, 3, Eldon Chambers, Wheeler Gate.
ST. HELENS (Lancs.)	... John Orford, 124, Knowsley Road.
SHREWSBURY ...	... Major-General Sir John Headlam, K.B.E., C.B., D.S.O., Cruck Meole House, Hanwood.
TIVERTON (Devon)	... Mr. W H. Duncan Arthur, Surveyor's Office, Town Hall.
WELSHPOOL ...	... Mr. E. Wilson, Coedway, Ford, Salop.

DOMINIONS AND FOREIGN COUNTRIES.

AUSTRALIA	... Messrs. C. H. Green, and George Lawson, Anzac House, Elizabeth Street, Brisbane, Queensland. R. A. Baldwin, c/o Government Savings Bank of N.S.W., Martin Place Sydney. Mr. W. Cloves, Box 1296, G.P.O., Adelaide.
BELGIUM	... Sister Marguerite, Sacré Coeur, Ypres.
BUENOS AYRES ...	... President, British Ex-Service Club, Calle 25 de Mayo 577.
CANADA	.. Brig.-General V. W. Odlum, C.B., C.M.G., D.S.O., 2530, Point Grey Road, Vancouver. V. A. Bowes, 326, 40th Avenue West, Calgary, Alberta. W. Constable F. Grece, St. Hilaire Station, Ronville County, Quebec.
CEYLON	... Captain F. R. G. Webb, M.C., Irrigation Bungalow, Kalmunai, E.P.
EGYPT	... L. B. S. Larkins, The Residency, Cairo.
INDIA	... Lieut.-Quartermaster G. Smith, Queen's Bays. Sialkot, India.
IRELAND	... Miss A. K. Jackson, Cloneyhurke House, Portarlington.
KENYA	... Harry Sheilds, Survey Department, Nairobi. Corporal C. H. Slater, P.O. Box 403, Nairobi.
NEW ZEALAND ...	... Captain W. U. Gibb, Ava Lodge, Puhinui Road, Papatoetoe, Auckland. S. E. Beattie, Lowlands, Woodville.
SOUTH AFRICA ...	... H. L. Versfield, c/o Cape Explosives Works Ltd., 150, St. Georges Street, Cape Town.
SPAIN	... Captain P. W. Burgess, Calle de Zurbano 29, Madrid.
U.S.A.	... Captain Henry Maslin, 942, President Street, Brooklyn, New York. L. E. P. Foot. 20, Gillett Street, Hartford, Conn, U.S.A. A. P. Forward. 449, East 80th Street, New York. J. W. Freebody, 945, McBride Avenue, Los Angeles.
NOVA SCOTIA ...	... Will R. Bird, Amherst.

Membership of the League

This is open to all who served in the Salient, and to all those whose relatives or friends died there, in order that they may have a record of that service for themselves and their descendants, and belong to the comradeship of men and women who understand and remember all that Ypres meant in suffering and endurance.

Life membership, £2 10s.

Annual members, 5s.

Do not let the fact of your not having served in the Salient deter you from joining the Ypres League. Those who have neither fought in the Salient nor lost relatives there, but who are in sympathy with the objects of the Ypres League, are admitted to its fellowship, but are not given scroll certificates.

There is a Junior Division for children whose relatives served in the Salient. It is open also to others to whom our objects appeal.

Annual subscription 1s. up to the age of 18, after which they can become ordinary members of the League.

THE YPRES LEAGUE (INCORPORATED)
20, Orchard Street, Portman Square, W.1.

Telephone: WELBECK 1446.   *Telegrams*: YPRESLEAG, " WESDO," LONDON.

Patron-in-Chief: H.M. THE KING.

Patrons:
H.R.H. THE PRINCE OF WALES.   H.R.H. PRINCESS BEATRICE.

President: GENERAL SIR CHARLES H. HARINGTON.

Vice-Presidents:

F.-M. VISCOUNT ALLENBY.   F.-M. SIR CLAUD W. JACOB.
THE VISCOUNT WAKEFIELD OF HYTHE.   F.-M. SIR PHILIP CHETWODE.
GENERAL SIR CECIL ROMER.   F.-M. LORD MILNE.

General Committee:

THE COUNTESS OF ALBEMARLE.   MAJOR-GENERAL C. J. B. HAY.
*CAPTAIN C. ALLISTON.   MR. J. HETHERINGTON.
LIEUT-COLONEL BECKLES WILLSON.   MRS. E. HEAP.
MR. HENRY BENSON.   GENERAL SIR W. C. G. HENEKER.
*MR. J. BOUGHEY.   *CAPTAIN O. G. JOHNSON.
*MISS B. BRICE-MILLER.   *MAJOR E. MONTAGUE JONES.
COLONEL G. T. BRIERLEY.   CAPTAIN H. D. PEABODY.
CAPTAIN P. W. BURGESS.   *THE HON. ALICE DOUGLAS PENNANT.
*MAJOR H. CARDINAL-HARFORD.   *LIEUT.-GENERAL SIR W. P. PULTENEY.
REV. P. B. CLAYTON.   LIEUT.-COLONEL SIR J. MURRAY.
*THE EARL OF YPRES.   *COLONEL G. E. C. RASCH.
MRS. C. J. EDWARDS.   VISCOUNT SANDON.
MAJOR C. J. EDWARDS.   THE HON. SIR ARTHUR STANLEY.
MR. H. A. T. FAIRBANK.   MR. ERNEST THOMPSON.
MR. T. ROSS FURNER.   CAPTAIN J. LOCKLEY TURNER.
SIR PHILIP GIBBS.   *MR. E. B. WAGGETT.
MR. E. GLOVER.   CAPTAIN J. WILKINSON.
MAJOR-GENERAL SIR JOHN HEADLAM.   CAPTAIN H. TREVOR WILLIAMS.
MR. F. D. BANKS HILL.

* Executive Committee.

Bankers: *Honorary Solicitors*:
BARCLAYS BANK LTD., Knightsbridge Branch.   MESSRS. FLADGATE & CO., 18, Pall Mall, S.W.

Secretary: *Auditors*:
CAPTAIN G. E. DE TRAFFORD.   MESSRS. LEPINE & JACKSON, 6, Bond Court, E.C.4.

League Representative at Ypres: **League Representative at Cambrai:**
CAPTAIN P. D. PARMINTER.   MR. A. WILDE,
19, Rue Surmont de Volsberghe   9, Rue des Anglaises.

League Representative at Amiens: **League Representative at Arras:**
CAPTAIN STUART OSWALD.   MR. P. VYNER,
7, Rue Porte-Paris.   10, Station Square.

Hon. Secretary, Ypres British Settlement:
LT. COLONEL F. G. POOLE.

PRIMARY OBJECTS OF THE LEAGUE

I.—Commemoration and Comradeship.
II.—To provide special travel facilities for Members and all interested to Ypres and battlefields, and transport of Members.
III.—The furnishing of information about the Salient; marking of historic sites and the compilation of charts of the battlefields.
IV.—The erection of a Ypres British Church and School which has been completed.
V.—The establishment of groups of members throughout the world, through Branch Secretaries and Corresponding Members.
VI.—The maintenance of cordial relations with dwellers on the battlefields of Ypres
VII.—The formation of a Junior Division.

Use the Ypres League Travel Bureau for Ypres and Whole of the Western Front.

FOR THE FOLLOWING PUBLICATIONS, Etc., apply:

Secretary, YPRES LEAGUE, 20, ORCHARD STREET, LONDON, W.1.

THE BATTLE BOOK OF YPRES. A history of notable deeds contributed by all regiments. 5s.; post free, 5s. 6d. Compiled by Beatrix Brice with the assistance of Lieut.-General Sir William Pulteney, G.C.V.O., etc.

BOOKS.

YPRES: Outpost of the Channel Ports. By Beatrix Brice. With Foreword by Field-Marshal Lord Plumer, G.C.B. Price 1s. 6d.; post free 1s. 10d.

In the Ypres Salient. By Lt.-Col. Beckles Willson. 1s. net; post free 1s. 2d.

With the Cornwall Territorials on the Western Front. By E. C. Matthews. 7s. 6d.; post free 8s.

Story of the 63rd Field Ambulance. By A. W. Westmore, etc. Cloth, 3s. 6d., post free. Paper, 2s. 6d., post free.

War Letters to a Wife. By Colonel Rowland Feilding. Popular Edition, 3s. 6d.; post free 4s.

The Pill Boxes of Flanders. 1s.; post free 1s. 3d.

From Mons to the First Battle of Ypres. By J. G. W. Hyndson, M.C. Price 5s., post free 5s. 3d.

YPRES LEAGUE TIES. 3s. 6d. each, post free.
YPRES LEAGUE BADGES. 2s. each, 2s. 1½d. post free.
EMBROIDERED BADGES. 4s. each, post free.
Map and List of Cemeteries in the Ypres Salient. Price 9d.; post free 11d.
Map of the Somme. Price 1s. 8d., post free.

PICTURES.

Burning of the Cloth Hall, 1915. A Coloured Print, 14 in. by 12 in. 1s. post free.

Old Well-known Spots in New Guise. Prints, size 4¼ x 2½, recently taken of famous spots in the Ypres Salient, and which may be of great interest to our readers, are on sale at headquarters, price 4d. each, post free 5d. For particulars apply Secretary.

POST CARDS, PHOTOGRAPHS AND ETCHINGS.

Post Cards. Ypres: British Front during the War. Ruins of Ypres. Price 1s. post free.

Photographs of Menin Gate Unveiling. Size 11 in. by 7 in. 1s. 2d. each, post free.

Hill 60. Complete Panorama Photographs. 12 in. by 3¾ in. Price 3s., post free; 15 in. by 5 in. Price 3s. 6d., post free.

WAR-TIME PHOTOGRAPHS OF THE SALIENT.

6 in. by 8 in. ... 1s. 6d. each.
12 in. by 15 in. ... 4s. each.

List forwarded on application.

PHOTOGRAPHS OF WAR-TIME SKETCHES.

Bedford House (Front View), 1916.
Bedford House (Back View), 1916.
Voormezeele Main Street, 1916.
Voormezeele Crucifixion Gate, 1916.
Langhof Chateau, 1916.

Size 8½ in. by 6¼ in. Price 2s. 6d. each, post free.

Photographs of the Thiepval and Arras Memorials. Post card size, price 1s. each, post free.

YPRES TIMES.

The Journal may be obtained at the League Offices.

BACK NUMBERS 1s.; 1932, 8d.; 1933, 6d.

Printed in Great Britain for the Publishers by FORD & GILL, 21a/23, Iliffe Yard, Crampton Street, London, S.E.17.

Memory Tablet.

JANUARY - FEBRUARY - MARCH

JANUARY.

Jan. 8th, 1916 ... Gallipoli evacuation completed.
„ 12th, 1915 ... The use of poisonous shells by Germans reported.
„ 21st, 1915 ... Zeebrugge bombarded by British airmen.
„ 24th, 1916 ... Naval battle off Dogger Bank.

FEBRUARY.

Feb. 3rd, 1917 ... America broke with Germany.
„ 18th, 1915 ... U-boat "blockade" of England.
„ 18th, 1918 ... German invasion of Russia.
„ 21st, 1916 ... Battle of Verdun begun.
„ 21st, 1918 ... British capture Jericho.
„ 25th, 1915 ... Allied Fleet attacked Dardanelles.

MARCH.

Mar. 10th, 1915 ... British capture of Neuve Chapelle.
„ 11th, 1917 ... British take Baghdad.
„ 12th, 1917 ... Revolution in Russia.
„ 15th, 1917 ... Abdication of the Tsar.
„ 21st, 1917 ... First British War Cabinet.
„ 21st, 1918 ... German offensive on the Western Front.

The Ypres Times

Communications to
The Editor, "Ypres Times,"
20, Orchard Street, London, W.1.

PRICE 6d.
POST FREE 7d.

VOL. 7, No. 5.   PUBLISHED QUARTERLY   JANUARY, 1935

Ypres Day, 1934

Photo]   ["Reproduced by courtesy of The Associated Press of Great Britain."

H.R.H. THE PRINCESS BEATRICE AT THE CENOTAPH

A MOST impressive and dignified commemoration on Sunday, October 28th, marked the 14th anniversary of the Ypres League.

The large assembly was honoured by the presence of Her Royal Highness The Princess Beatrice who was received on the Horse Guards' Parade by His Excellency The Belgian Ambassador, and amongst those present included Lieut. General Sir. W. P. Pulteney, Chairman of the Ypres League, The Military Attaché Belgian Embassy, Lieut. Colonel G. P. Vanier, representing the High Commissioner for Canada, and the Dowager Viscountess Plumer. The parade comprised contingents of Officers Training Corps cadets, 5th Army, O.C.A., 85th Club, Old Contemptibles, St. Dunstans and the Ypres League.

The service commenced at 3 p.m. with the singing of the Hymn, "O Valiant Hearts," played by the band of the 1st Surrey Rifles, after which the Rev. M. P. G. Leonard, D.S.O. gave the following touching address:—

"We are here this afternoon, whether we be young or old, as legates; that is, we have entered into possession of something which belonged originally to those who are now dead, something which the dead created and which, though dying, they bequeathed to us. It is something so precious that not on grounds of sentiment alone are we bound to treasure and to preserve it. For we are trustees of a spirit and of an example shiningly displayed and associated for all time with the heroic defence of Ypres.

"The men who held the Salient exhibited in their living no less than in their dying, a spirit of cheerful endurance, of indomitable courage, of dogged devotion and of ungrudged self sacrifice. They gave their friendship to each other as gaily and as recklessly as they gave their lives for others. It is of that spirit that we are trustees.

"We mourn the passing during the last twelve months of two of our fellow trustees of that spirit, namely, that very gallant kingly lover and leader of his people, Albert, King of the Belgians and General Sir Herbert Uniacke, that prince of gunners. We know that their passing leaves the Ypres League immeasurably impoverished. We will remember them.

"One example of that spirit of which I speak must suffice this afternoon. During the Passchendaele offensive there was found a scrap of blood-stained paper in a smashed pill-box. On that scrap of paper were the orders signed by the N.C.O. in charge of the Machine Gun section.

"These were the orders:—

(1) This position will be held and the section will remain here until relieved.
(2) If the section cannot remain here alive it will remain here dead; but, in any case, it will remain here.
(3) Should any man through shell-shock or other cause attempt to surrender he will remain here dead.
(4) Should all guns be blown up, the section will use mills bombs, grenades and other novelties.
(5) The position will be held as stated.

"Nor was that an idle boast, for when the relief arrived, the position was held by dead men—every single member of that Machine Gun section lying dead across their broken guns. That is the glorious spirit which to-day we commemorate, and any commemoration worthy of that spirit and of our inheritance of that spirit must be more than just one yearly act of remembrance, and the laying of a wreath on the Cenotaph for all remembrance of the past is sterile, unless it be a spring of courage in the present and a dynamic for the future.

"Our task as trustees of that spirit is to embody it to give it a body—so that it may be used in a creative service of the world of men to-day. Those of you who lived sixteen years ago will remember how the very soul of Belgium was broken, battered, martyred. The Ypres Salient was the abomination of desolation spoken of by the Prophet. One may say that the body of the salient was killed just as truly as the bodies of its quarter of a million defenders died. But its spirit lived on! The spirit of the Salient lived on and has been embodied in a new Ypres and in a new and smilingly fruitful countryside. With the re-building of the Cloth Hall, the last scar of the war will disappear. So, the spirit of Ypres and its defenders must live on. That spirit must be re-embodied and we, its trustees, must see that the spirit of our dead is reclothed, is re-enthroned, in living men and women, so that dreams of a new world for which our dead were quite content to die, shall not miscarry, and since they died before their task was finished we must realise the dreams of the new world undiminished by one

[Photo   [Reproduced by kind permission
                                           of Planet News Ltd.
GENERAL VIEW OF THE COMMEMORATION IN PRESENCE OF H.R.H. PRINCESS BEATRICE SEATED IN THE ROYAL CAR.

particular of the splendour which they planned on earth. And that is not done by sword, tongue or pen.

The service continued with " The Lament " played by the Pipers of the 2nd Battalion Scots Guards, followed by the " Last Post," then the Hymn, " O God, our help in ages past," the National Anthem and Reveille.

The whole parade now formed up for the march to the Cenotaph, headed by the band, and Princess Beatrice, after taking the salute at the Horse Guards' Arch, layed the beautiful Ypres League wreath composed of lilies, chrysanthemums and cornflowers on the National Shrine. The bearers of the wreath were Captain W. A. White, V.C., late Machine Gun Corps, and Sergeant O. Brooks, V.C., late Coldstream Guards.

A few moments silence at the Cenotaph terminated the official ceremony, and at 4.30 p.m. we followed the custom of past years in placing a similar, but smaller, wreath upon the grave of the Unknown Warrior. This unofficial deputation of the Ypres League Committee and members was headed by Major E. Montague Jones, O.B.E., and received at the Abbey by the Venerable Archdeacon Storr, M.A., who conducted a short service and addressed a few appropriate words.

Ypres Day in Paris

In Paris, on October 31st, the twentieth anniversary of the First Battle of Ypres, a wreath was placed by Colonel Beckles Willson on behalf of the Ypres League, on the Tomb of the Unknown Soldier at the Arc de Triomphe bearing the following inscription:—
"In Memory of our Gallant French Comrades who sacrificed their Lives in the Immortal Defence of Ypres (1914-1918) The Ypres League."

Do You Remember?

By IAN HAY.

I WRITE this on Armistice Day 1934—the twentieth anniversary of the outbreak of the Great War. Memories will be busy: they will not all be unhappy memories, by any means.

Those four long years, although they were grim and sometimes horrible, were profoundly interesting—if only because they plucked millions of men and women out of a groove of monotonous routine and gave them a chance to show the stuff they were made of.

Ability came to its own with a bound. Anybody with a capacity for organisation or leadership went right up to the top; a railway manager became First Lord of the Admiralty, and a London taxi-driver finished up the war as a Brigadier-General.

Those years brought recognition to scores of unknown scientists and inventors; and they did more to emancipate women than half a century of ladylike agitation.

They were coarse, barbaric years, but they were dominated by an inspiring atmosphere of courage and fellowship. The men in the trenches had all things in common, while women of all walks of life worked devotedly side by side in factory and canteen.

Charity, public and private, abounded. More than five million pounds were raised for the Prince of Wales's Fund, and nearly every great house in England was a hospital or convalescent home.

And they were days of astonishing material prosperity. There was employment for all, and at fancy wages. There was very little to buy, especially towards the end. and at least everybody had money.

I hope no one will imagine that in recalling some of the alleviating circumstances of those days I am arguing in favour of war or suggesting that we should start another. There are a million sufficient and permanent reasons against that kind of madness lying in British Military Cemeteries over three continents to-day. I am merely setting down in haphazard fashion a few odd memories which may be of interest to the generation which has grown up since then—there is not a British boy or girl at school to-day who was an inhabitant of this globe when the Great War broke out—and perhaps, too, to my own contemporaries.

It is always interesting to look back; and the odd part of it is that the experiences which we often recall with most satisfaction are the unpleasant ones—perhaps because we like to realise that they are safely over.

Do you remember London during the war—say in 1917? Silent, ghostly streets, except in the amusement quarters—dilapidated houses—unpainted shopfronts—no fountains in Trafalgar Square—never a window-box anywhere.

The petrol shortage? 'Buses were scarce and packed to suffocation; taxicabs were pearls of price, and their drivers were gentlemen who took full advantage of the possibilities of the economic situation. (Thirty shillings it cost to hire him for dinner and theatre in the evening, as many a subaltern home on leave discovered.)

Do you remember, too, the private limousines, with great flopping balloon-like gasbags on top, which fed coal-gas direct into the engine in place of petrol? (You could often purchase a lift on one of these if the chauffeur was by himself.)

Do you remember the food shortage? In normal times 50,000 tons of food from abroad are landed in this country every day. How impossible it seemed at that time that we could escape national starvation; yet somehow the Navy—and Lord Rhondda's ration-cards—pulled us through.

Restaurants and eating-houses did a roaring trade, for it was easier to expend a coupon on a plate of beef than queue up at a butcher's shop.

"Have a nice sole, sir; fish is only half a coupon." "Try a slice of ham, sir; that's not rationed at all just now."

And we finished every scrap of food on our plates! We had healthy appetites in those days, chiefly because we all had something to do. Doctors will tell you that fashionable ailments—the ailments of self-indulgence—died out almost entirely during the war.

Do you remember the night life? Every theatre crammed with a roaring audience in khaki. Violet Loraine? George Robey? The streets outside dimmed down almost to invisibility, and an air-raid during the performance a perfectly usual occurrence.

On these occasions it was a point of honour, with the anti-aircraft guns barking all round London, that the audience should keep their seats and the actors carry on. Or perhaps one should say actresses, for in most of the shows there was a plethora of girls and an almost entire absence of men of military age. It was a great time for the fifty-year-old chorus man.

Do you remember our women in the war? The curiously-named Waacs and Wrens and Wrafs? The munition-workers, with their faces stained bright orange colour by picric acid? Honourable scars indeed. Do you remember "Winnie the Window-cleaner," and others of her race—the women 'bus-conductors and railway workers? I recall in a tiny Scottish town which I used to frequent, when on leave, a lusty lass, in a railway porter's cap, who ran an entire station—collected tickets, worked the signals, and carried an incredible quantity of suitcases at a time.

"I'm daen' it for ma man," she explained. "He's oot in yon Gally Polly with the Royal Scots."

Those years were testing years and tragic years, but they gave people an opportunity to bring out what was best in themselves and rise superior to almost incredible difficulties. To-day we are passing through a period quite as testing and infinitely more depressing, because it offers no hope of a speedy or spectacular victory. The pendulum, too, has swung over to a dangerous extreme: for the moment we seem to have lost faith and confidence in ourselves, and—strangest of all—our love of country and pride of race.

But these things will pass, and the pendulum in due course will swing back to normal. Meanwhile, it may hearten us to remind ourselves, especially on days like this, of something which we are in danger of forgetting—namely, how gallantly we bore the burden during those four terrible, splendid years.

Battle of Gheluvelt
(1st Battle of Ypres)

By Captain J. G. W. Hyndson, M.C.
(Author of *From Mons to the First Battle of Ypres*).

SATURDAY, the 31st October, 1914, was to prove the most critical day in the struggle for Ypres and the day upon which the British Expeditionary Force suffered the heaviest casualties since the commencement of the war. The fight for Gheluvelt, which turned out to be the key to the position on this day, was of a particularly desperate nature.

As a result of the fighting on the 30th, our troops were driven back and had taken up a new line East of the village. This position was on the forward slope and very exposed, the enemy having an uninterrupted view of the entire line.*

During the night frantic efforts were made by the weary troops to dig fresh trenches, with their hand shovels, but it was impossible to complete them in time, and, when daylight came, most units had only half finished trenches in which to shelter from the inevitable bombardment.

At the first signs of daybreak the Germans commenced to shell our positions and concentrated an overwhelming fire on the front line and support positions. Special attention was paid to Gheluvelt which was almost obliterated by smoke and very soon burning furiously. After two hours of intensive bombardment the German infantry attacked, carried the front line and killed or captured the defenders to a man.

After a slight pause they swarmed on the masses, offering a splendid target to our rifleman, but despite heavy losses they were able to reach the outskirts of Gheluvelt.

From our two companies in the front line we could get no news and feared that they must have been captured with the others. At about eleven o'clock we were called upon, together with the two companies of the 2nd K.R.R.C. to counter attack and drive the Germans away from the outskirts of the village.

We left our trenches and moved forward to try and carry out our task. The ground all round was literally alive with bursting shells, and about a score of men were struck down as they emerged from the trenches. However, on we went, in extended order, and pushed on into the village which was by this time well alight. German shells were bursting against the houses, throwing bricks and dust in all directions and there was the added danger of being killed by flying masonry.

My Company Commander was unfortunately soon killed and I found myself in command. Shortly afterwards I had a narrow escape from a bullet which knocked me down, and thinking I had been hit I glanced down and found that the bullet had entered my compass case, cleaned it out and passed on without doing me any harm. We progressed into the centre of the village only to find it was impossible to move forward any further. The Germans had established themselves in the houses in front of us and in spite of all our efforts we were unable to make any ground. We took cover as best we could, and engaged the enemy in a rifle duel. This proved too one-sided and costly to last for long and we received orders to withdraw from the village and re-occupy our former trenches. Back we ran. More khaki figures were left on the ground dead and dying but the survivors managed to get back to the trenches in a very exhausted condition.

Here we remained for about an hour, then orders arrived to withdraw to Hooge as we were told the Germans had broken our front line beyond repair. The 2nd K.R.R.C. on our left were to conform to our movement. Seizing a favourable moment

* For detail distribution of troops see sketch.

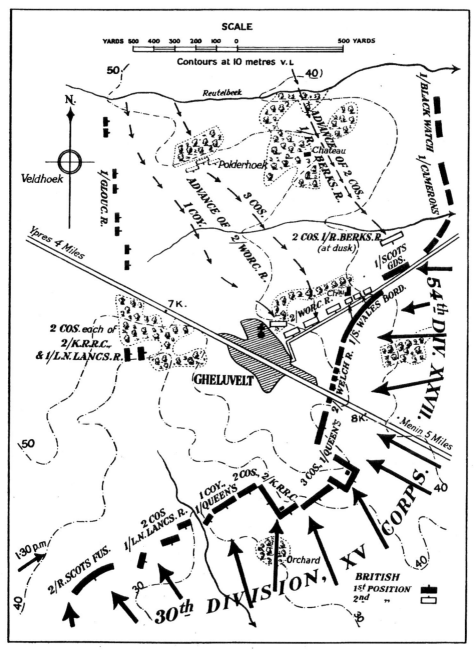

[Extract from "Military Operations, France and Belgium, 1914," Volume 2

we began to retire and moved back widely extended, pursued by the German shells, to which were now added the nerve-racking machine gun and rifle fire.

Crossing the Menin road we made a detour through the thickly wooded country and proceeded in the direction of Hooge. On the way we passed one of our batteries limbering up preparatory to moving back. As soon as they got on the move the German gunners spotted them and judging the range nicely smothered the guns and teams in bursting shrapnel. We were struck dumb with horror and expected to see nothing but their mangled remains, but much to our joy, when the smoke from the shells cleared away, not a man or horse was seen to be hurt, and they galloped off back to take up a new position. We were all filled with admiration at the cool manner in which they handled the situation. Soon afterwards we passed some of the Gordons and Royal Scots Fusiliers of the 7th Division, who were also retiring to conform to the general backward movement.

We reached Hooge to find staff officers busy halting all troops and fresh orders were issued to turn round and in conjunction with other units to advance and counter-attack. "At all costs," the order read, "the Germans must be stopped from advancing any nearer to Ypres."

By this time we were sadly reduced in numbers and only five officers (the commanding officer, Adjutant and three others), and about 125 other ranks were left. Just as we began to move forward, our quartermaster and the transport arrived, so roping in some twenty-five transport drivers, we moved forward with our left on the Menin Road. After going about 400 yards we struck the advancing German infantry and a real soldiers' battle began. So confident were the enemy that they had swept aside all opposition that they came on in massed formation without taking any protective precautions, and we very soon made holes in their ranks. In one instance I noticed German mounted officers leading troops forward in formation of fours and calling on the men nearest to me to open fire at this splendid target, we very soon shot down the officers, horses and a great number of men.

As each body of Germans was destroyed we surged forward and took on the next; shooting and charging alternately and bayoneting the survivors until by sheer exhaustion and losses we came to a standstill. The 2nd Worcester Regiment and the troops on our left recaptured Gheluvelt in a glorious charge which swept all before them and most of the ground lost during the day was regained, though unfortunately at an awful price.

Our Quartermaster, Wilkinson, was killed in a most gallant manner, serving an abandoned machine gun which he had acquired and he must have accounted for scores of Germans before he was killed. Undoubtedly he denied the use of the road to the Germans who were trying to debauch from Gheluvelt and so materially aided the counter attack preparations. Our own losses were appalling and only ninety were present to answer the roll call that evening.

The shades of night were now closing in, and we set to work to dig in and consolidate the ground we stood on, but owing to our extremely exhausted condition could make very little progress. The units of the 1st and 7th Divisions were inconceivably intermixed and a good deal of time was spent in sorting out the men and reorganizing in preparation for the next day. All available men, including non-fighting troops, such as spare transport drivers and Royal Engineers, were placed in the firing line, and we had literally no reserves should the Germans attempt another break through next day. As many of the wounded as possible, both friend and foe, were collected and sent back to the field hospitals, but, alas, hundreds of our own men had to be left to the tender mercy of the Germans, whom we knew were not usually inclined to treat these unfortunate men with any degree of kindness.

During the night several attempts on the part of the Germans to penetrate our line at a number of points were easily repulsed without loss to ourselves, and although we did not realize it at the time, the German effort to break through was definitely frustrated on the 31st of October, 1914, a day which will be ever remembered by those who fought at Ypres on this day and will go down in history as one of the most glorious achievements of the British Army.

N.B.—It is of interest to note that October 31st is known as "Ypres Day," chosen by the Ypres League for the date of its annual commemoration which is held on the nearest Sunday to the famous date and in its actual memory.   J. G. W.

Review of "Days on the Wing"

By Major the Chevalier Willy Coppens de Houlthulst, D.S.O., M.C.

WE must all feel grateful to Willy Coppens for producing an autobiography which, though written in a style somewhat bombastic to the English taste, is of interest to all and a valuable contribution to the inner history of the war.

The author established a great reputation for his attacks on German kite-balloons. To those who were not on the Western Front, a kite balloon may seem rather a tame quarry. We in the R.F.C. thought so at the Battle of Aisne in 1914. On the 22nd September a German kite-balloon was sighted and there was considerable competition amongst the pilots who saw it as to who should be allowed to carry out the apparently easy task of bringing this monstrosity down. Lt. Mapplebeck was allowed to try; about an hour later he came back seriously wounded and the balloon was still there. Kite-balloons were of greater value to the Germans than to us because aeroplane observation for artillery fire by the Germans was a long way below our standard. They made, therefore, every effort to protect them and their attack required not only a high degree of bravery but forethought and ingenuity. New methods were sometimes very successful, but successful on one occasion only and the mere list of Coppens' numerous victims is a sufficient tribute to his efficiency as a war pilot.

Many points are constantly recurring throughout his book which should be read, marked, learnt and inwardly digested by all who now hold responsible positions in the air or aspire to do so in peace or in war. First and foremost is the value of skill in handling the aeroplane; this with discipline forms the foundation on which the whole efficiency of an Air Force must be built. Next comes the importance of good maintenance; time and again throughout the book one reads of attacks being broken off or aeroplanes returning because their guns jammed. Whilst this must reflect principally on the armament staff, one remembers how some of our best pilots, such as McCudden, devoted unceasing care and attention to their own guns, made themselves thorough masters of its mechanism and saw personally to every detail of its maintenance.

The book brings out very clearly the adverse effect on morale of wasted energy, of pilots being kept idle for lack of equipment or lack of organisation. Although Coppens was sent to Calais to start his training in the Flying Corps on the 6th September, 1915, it was not until the winter of 1916 that he joined a squadron and during those 15 months he only put in some 75 hours' flying.

There are many complimentary references to the British Flying Services in the latter half of the book.

The author also discloses the interesting fact that he kept up a regular correspondence with his parents in Brussels.

R. B. P.

The Regret of Scotty Smith

A True Story of the German South West Campaign.

By A. Cecil Alport, M.D. (Major, R.A.M.C., T.F.)

(*Late*) Captain, South African Medical Corps.

ON the 11th February, 1915, a force of 200 men with Major Carrol, of the 18th Mounted Rifles, in command and myself as Medical Officer, occupied Zwart Modder near the German South West border. We were the advance guard of the troops which were assembling at Upington preparatory to the march on Keetmanshoop and the conquest of the Southern portion of German South West Africa.

On the trek to Zwart Modder I noticed that one of our scouts was a very old man and that he always had a small coffee grinder fastened on to the front of his saddle. On enquiry I found that he was the famous Scotty Smith. He was 69 years of age, as hard as nails, could ride all day without feeling fatigued, and having no teeth, carried the coffee-mill in order to grind up the hard army biscuits before endeavouring to masticate them with his toothless gums.

Old Scotty had a South African reputation as a horse and cattle lifter but was never known to rob a poor man. He was, in fact, the Robin Hood of the Veld and, moreover, had taken part in every war in South Africa during the previous forty years. His real name was George St. Ledger Lennox and he was said to come from a good Scottish family. He is mentioned in many South African stories. Probably his most noteworthy exploit was lifting cattle from the German farmers, altering the brand and selling them to the German Government at exorbitant prices, during the Hereros rebellion in German South West Africa in 1904. For this act the Germans put a price of 5,000 marks (£250) on his head, dead or alive. It says much for his pluck that he went on active service at his age seeing that, had he been captured, the Boche would have shot him out of hand.

I took a good deal of interest in the old man and tried to draw him out about some of his experiences but with no great success, until the night we retreated on Cynidas.

Zwart Modder (Black-mud) is situated in a river bed surrounded by enormous red sand dunes which had to be picketed every night in case of a surprise attack. The defence of the place was nearly impossible with the number of troops at our disposal. Apart from this we were comfortable enough. We had our headquarters in the house of a Jewish trader whose store had been looted by the Germans. The house boasted a piano which three of us undertook to tune, with disastrous results, and we made the day and part of the night hideous with our musical endeavours. We slept in our boots and the fear of being cut off and captured was always hanging over us. It was no joke being made a capture of by the Germans as they were short of food and clothing. One of the first things they always did was to exchange a prisoner's clothing for a grain sack with three holes cut in it for the head and arms. A man's appearance in this get-up was most undignified. The treatment meted out by the rebels was just as bad. A local rebel commando captured two loyal scouts who came from a village on the Orange River, and were engaged to girls in that village. Taking the captives to the top of the main street, they stripped them, dressed them in a " stuck-up " collar and tie each, made them wear their spurs upside down on their bare feet and marched them through the place. They then released them, but the girls broke off the engagements.

Our men did not like the situation at Zwart Modder, even though the tints on the dunes in the early morning, varying from red to many shades of brown, and the splashes of colour due to an interspersion with small yellow wild-flowers, made it a lovely spot to live in. The result was that my sick parades were extremely popular.

One youth who appeared regularly was half-witted. He had the sleep-walking habit and one night was nearly shot by a sentry. On another occasion coming back from one of his peregrinations he turned into bed, by mistake, with the sergeant-major. Anyone who has got into bed, my mistake, with a sergeant-major will readily appreciate what happened. The whole camp stood to arms under the impression that we were being attacked by an army corps of Germans.

On the 13th February our sentries fired on an advance patrol of the enemy. The next evening Scotty Smith reported that a body of Germans about two thousand strong with artillery were within ten miles of our outposts and were trying to cut our communications. We immediately wirelessed down to Cynidas for reinforcements, but the commanding officer of the commandos stationed there answered that their scouts reported their own position to be a precarious one, and advised us to fall back on them. This we proceeded to do.

It was a beautiful moonlight night and I sat on the stoop in front of our headquarters listening to the sound of preparations being made for a speedy departure. Out of the shadows the figure of a man appeared and silently seated himself near me.

" Hullo Scotty ! " I said, " We are going to get out of this death-trap at last, it seems."

He appeared to be rather depressed, and in an unwonted burst of confidence told me that he reckoned this would be his last campaign and that he would not get through it.

" As you know," he observed, " I have a price on my head and if I am captured to-night, my time will have come."

I felt very sorry for the old man.

" I quite see that you will be in an awkward position, should we fall into the hands of the Germans," I replied, " still let us hope for all our sakes that this will not happen."

For a long time he remained silent, then he got up and prepared to depart.

" Sit down again, Scotty," I said, " You have something on your mind. Sit down and tell me about it. Perhaps it will relieve you to do so."

After a moment's hesitation he resumed his seat. " Yes," he muttered, " perhaps you are right."

I sat quite quiet afraid to speak lest he should change his mind.

" I am getting an old man now," he began, " and I feel to-night that I am standing very close to death. A man's life is what he makes of it and when it comes to the last, few of us are troubled with regrets; yet when I cast my eyes back upon the long vista of the past there is one act, and, strange as it may seem, one only that I regret."

For nearly a minute he sat gazing into space, then he proceeded: " In 1876, when I was a young man, I took an active part in the Carlist rebellion, in Spain. This was my first campaign. It is not necessary for me to enter into the question of my social position or rank at the time, let it suffice that in those days I was not as near the bottom rung of the ladder as I am now. One night, I remember it was a beautiful moonlight night such as this, I attended a Ball in, let us say, Madrid. After supper while I was dancing with a Spanish Senorita of great beauty, a certain officer inadvertently or through carelessness, stepped upon the train of my partner's dress, and tore a huge hole in it.

Being young and hot-tempered I turned on the fellow and, before realising what I was doing, struck him a blow in the face. Now you know what that meant in Spain in those days."

As a matter of fact I did not, but I made no comment so he continued: "The seconds of the Spaniard called upon me and on behalf of their principal challenged me to a duel."

"Great Scott!" I exclaimed, "What did you do, kick them out?"

"No, I accepted—I was forced to, but I stipulated that the weapons should be pistols, and to this they agreed. On arriving at the field at daybreak next morning with my seconds, I found my opponent waiting eagerly to wipe out the insult he considered he had sustained at my hands. The arrangements for the duel were quite simple. We were instructed to stand back to back, take five paces forward, and at the command one—two—three, turn round and fire."

"Well," I said, "what happened, did you kill your man?"

"Yes," he replied—and he hesitated—"but I forgot to wait for the 'three!' That has been my one regret and the skeleton in my cupboard for forty long years."

"Good Lord!" I murmured.

Perhaps nothing, except my meeting with one of the assassins of the Archduke Francis Ferdinand, the deed that precipitated the war, impressed me so much as the story told me by Scotty Smith that night on the stoop at Zwart Modder.

The twinkling of the fires, the shadowy forms flitting about—some saddling their mounts, other packing their equipment. The cries of the native drivers as they hastened to inspan the transport wagons, the occasional neigh of a horse eager to be off and lastly the soft voice of old Scotty, telling me how in a moment of panic, some forty years earlier, he had saved his life at the expense of his honour. I have often thought that when he is called upon to meet his Maker and account for his many misdemeanours the real regret expressed that night will count heavily in his favour and perhaps earn for the old man some remission of his sins.

It is a great tribute to the sense of proportion of our race that the actions we regret most in our lives are nearly always those in which we have failed to "play the game." So it was with old Scotty the Scout—an adventurer, a fighter, an outcast from his class, a man with a price in his head, but to the end, always—A MAN.

Before I could enquire how he got away after the incident narrated, the order came to march, and I was never able to get the old man to discuss the matter again.

Our scouts who had been in touch with the enemy had come in post haste to report that the Germans were only five miles away moving South towards our line of retreat. It is needless to say that we did not delay, but treked with the greatest expedition.

Boer War veterans and those who have been fortunate enough to take part in night marches with mounted troops know that it has a charm of its own—a wonderful charm. For myself I enjoyed every moment of that retreat. The rhythmic beat of the horses' feet upon the road, the champing of the bits, the rattle of the wagons, the subdued murmur of the men's voices, are as music to the ears of those who have experienced them.

I remember thinking how lucky we were to be there rather than in the water and blood drenched trenches of Flanders. By forced marching we arrived safely at Cynidas at daybreak the following morning. The mobility of the Germans was hampered by having to drag their guns along roads, with sand three or four inches deep. On finding we had escaped, they turned back across the border without attacking our position, which at Cynidas was a very strong one.

I have since heard that my old friend Scotty died some years ago. May his soul rest in peace.

Published by the kind permission of Dr. A. Cecil Alport, M.D., Author of *The Lighter Side of the War* (published by Messrs. Hutchinson & Co.).

We reproduce the first of a series of sketches on the humorous side of the German South West African Campaign, 1914/15, and other sketches will appear in future editions of the "Ypres Times."

These pictures explain why the authorities were so particular about the teeth of intending volunteers. Another excellent way of softening these biscuits is to use dynamite.

[Reprinted by the courtesy of the Argus Printing and Publishing Company, and with the compliments to the author, Mr. W. H. Kirby.

Memories

By H. GREGORY, M.M.,

Author of *Never Again* (Stockwell), 3/6 Nett., and
Prisoners of War, a Play in 4 Acts (Stockwell) 2/- Nett.

ANOTHER year. Each succeeding year brings back memories. To realise that it is now sixteen years since the last shots were fired across " No Man's Land." As each anniversary comes round we pay homage to our Glorious dead, around the Cenotaphs throughout the Empire.

Everything stilled. Not a sound to be heard. Then as the pent up feelings of the relatives of the Glorious departed, the ones who failed to return, sobs are heard to break the silence.

A poor mother shedding tears for her departed son. A wife for a loved and devoted husband. A sweetheart for her lover. Poor little orphans weep for their father. All in sympathy and accord with the fallen in the Great War.

What the glorious dead lived through, we the living survivors of the Great War know, and this is the symbol of what Armistice Day should stand for. To the memory of the fallen. The Glorious dead. What hardships and sufferings they endured in the name of freedom so that the rising generation might live.

Armistice Day is their day. A reminder of the years 1914-18 in solemn remembrance

Every respect is due to their memory. Great and noble deeds were done. The greatest sacrifices endured, and the ex-serviceman as he stands at the Cenotaphs to celebrate another anniversary to his fallen comrades, his mind will run back through the years and in a few fleeting moments he will visualise the battle front again.

He will smell the mud. The stench of the powder will again be in his nostrils. The strain of the waiting, as they linger for the signal to go over the top, will again come back to him.

The nerve racking bombardment will again flit across his mind. Again he will be reminded of wading in the trenches up to the thighs in mud and water, slithering and sliding as they tried to get a grip on the duckboards underneath.

With a cold chill running down his back he will remember the terrible winter when he was practically frozen to death, and of the thaw that followed leaving him to wallow about in a sea of mud and water, always facing obstacles, but never beat. Super men every man of them that nothing could daunt.

As I throw my mind back on this one day of the year I cannot forget my first glimpse of war. Marching in a storm. Laying down in the side of the road to rest, with the water rushing past, sleep overtaking us. A little later as we approached where the Somme offensive commenced we saw, as each Veery light went up, the trees standing out stripped of every branch and cut down by shells, standing there in all their stark reality. Shell holes everywhere, and a sea of mud and water Barbed wire twisting this way and that. Desolation and destruction all around, giving a weird and uncanny appearance as each Veery light ascended, lit this scene dimly for a few seconds, and then inky blackness once again. Later the front line where men had to endure ten thousand Hell's. Day after day. Week after week. Year after year. The years rolled on and there seemed no end. Endurance and sacrifice being patiently borne every minute of the day in the glorious name of freedom.

The Glorious dead have built a noble monument which should be respected by all, and as the adolescent grow up to years of intelligence and understanding they will realise to the full the true meaning of Armistice Day, when all noises are hushed, and we stand bareheaded at 11 a.m. on each anniversary of this one day of the year, to the memory of the fallen in the Great War.

Each succeeding year sees the annual parade of ex-servicemen grow less and less. Their step slower, and more feeble. Their bearing not as erect as of yore. Hair greying. Father Time overtaking many of them, leaving the survivors to carry on the tradition of upholding the memory of their fallen comrades.

As I look back to Armistice Day, 1918, my mind goes back to a Salt Mine in Germany, held as a Prisoner of War. Underfed and overworked.

Photo] [Imperial War Museum, Crown Copyright

FILE OF MEN PICKING THEIR WAY AROUND SHELL-CRATERS IN NEWLY-WON GROUND ON THEIR WAY TO THE FRONT LINE

Black despair our portion. The weary days, weeks, months crept on, each succeeding day bringing another day like the one before it. Our homes, our loved ones ever before our mind's eye, praying for the day when we should be liberated, and able to see them once again.

And then Peace. The glorious Peace the whole world had been waiting for arrived at last. We stood bereft of speech. Could it be true. A new world was opening up before us. Home. Loved ones. Work. Friends. We should return to them once again and take up our accustomed place. Our joy unbounded. Release from captivity. No one can ever understand our feelings as Prisoners in a Foreign land, and to regain our freedom, to breathe the pure air, to stretch out our arms, and exclaim free, free, free, thank God I am a free man.

In conclusion I will quote a leaflet that we were given before leaving Germany, and which at the present time will be appropriate. This leaflet is quoted in full in my book *Never Again*, and is as follows:—

A parting word, Gentlemen, the war is over. A little while, and you will see your native land again, your homes, your loved ones, your friends, you will once more take up your accustomed work. The fortunes of war brought you into our hands as prisoners, you were freed even against your will from the fighting, from danger, from death. But the joys of peace could not be yours, for there was no peace. Now peace is coming, and peace means liberty. When you are already united to your families, thousands of our countrymen will still be pining in far off prison camps with hearts as hungry for home as yours. You have suffered in confinement, as who could not, it was the fate of every prisoner in every prison camp in the world to eat his heart out with longing, to chafe against loss of liberty, to suffer from home sickness, brooding, discouragement, black despair. The days, the weeks, the weary years crept by, and there was no end in sight. There were many discomforts, irritations, misunderstandings.

Your situation has been a difficult one, our own has been desperate. Our country blockaded, our civil population and Army suffering from want of proper and sufficient food and materials, the enormous demands made on our harassed land from every side these and many other afflictions made it impossible to do all that we should have liked to do. Under the circumstances we did our best to lessen the hardships of your lot, to ensure your comfort, to provide you with pastime, employment, mental and bodily recreation. It is not likely that you will ever know how difficult our circumstances have been.

We know that errors have been committed and that there have been hardships for which the former system was to blame. There have been wrongs and evils on both sides. We hope that you will always think of that, and be just.

You entered the old Empire of Germany, you leave the new Republic, the newest and, as we hope to make it, the freest land in the world. We are sorry that you saw so little of what we are proud of in the former Germany, our Arts, our Sciences, our Model Cities, our Theatres, Schools, Industries, our Social Institutions, as well as the beauties of our scenery, and the real soul of our people, akin in so many things to your own.

But these things will remain part of the new Germany. Once the barriers of artificial hatred and misunderstandings have fallen, we hope that you will learn to know, in happier times, these grander features of the land whose unwilling guests you have been. A barbed wire enclosure is not the proper point of view from which to survey or judge a great nation.

The war has blinded all nations. But if a true and just peace will result in opening the eyes of the peoples to the fact, that their interests are common, that no difference in flags, governments, speech or nationality, can alter the great truth of the fraternity of all men, this war will not have been fought in vain.

We hope that every one of you will go home carrying a message of goodwill, of conciliation, of enlightenment. Let all men in our new epoch go forth as missionaries of the new evangel, as interpreters between nation and nation.

The valiant dead who once fought against each other have long been sleeping as comrades side by side in the same earth. May the living who once fought against each other labour as comrades side by side upon this self same earth.

That is the message with which we bid you farewell.

Let us all work in the spirit of the above message, and carry the message of peace far and wide. Let us by all means give full respect to the fallen in the Great War, but let us see to it that it is " NEVER AGAIN." H. G.

(*Copyright, All Rights Reserved*).

The South Staffordshire Regiment

(38th Foot AND 80th Foot).
THE SPHINX SUPERSCRIBED "EGYPT."

Battle Honours :

"GUADALOUPE, 1759," "MARTINIQUE, 1762," "MONTE VIDEO," "ROLICA," "VIMIERA," "CORUNNA," "BUSACO," "BADAJOZ," "SALAMANCA," "VITTORIA," "ST. SEBASTIAN," "NIVE," "PENINSULA," "AVA," "MOODKEE," "FEROZESHAH," "SOBRAON," "PEGU," "ALMA," "INKERMAN," "SEBASTOPOL," "LUCKNOW," "CENTRAL INDIA," "SOUTH AFRICA, 1878-79," "EGYPT, 1882," "KIRBEKAN," "NILE, 1884-85," "SOUTH AFRICA, 1900-02."
The Great War—18 *Battalions*.—"MONS," "Retreat from Mons," "MARNE, 1914," "AISNE, 1914, '18," "YPRES, 1914, '17," "Langemarck, 1914, '17," "Gheluvelt," "Nonne Bosschen," "Neuve Chapelle," "Aubers," "Festubert, 1915," "Loos," "SOMME, 1916, '18," "Albert, 1916, '18," "Bazentin," "Delville Wood," "Pozieres," "Flers-Courcelette," "Morval," "Thiepval," "Ancre, 1916," "Bapaume, 1917, '18," "Arras, 1917, '18," "Scarpe, 1917, '18," "Arleux," "Bullecourt," "Hill 70," "Messines, 1917, '18," "Menin Road," "Polygon Wood," "Broodseinde," "Poelcappelle," "Passchendaele," "CAMBRAI, 1917, '18," "St. Quentin," "Lys," "Bailleul," "Kemmel," "Scherpenberg," "Drocourt-Queant," "Hindenburg Line," "Havrincourt," "Canal du Nord," "ST. QUENTIN CANAL," "Beaurevoir," "Selle," "Sambre," "France and Flanders, 1914-18," "Piave," "VITTORIO VENETO," "Italy, 1917-18," "SUVLA," "Landing at Suvla," "Scimitar Hill," "Gallipoli, 1915," "Egypt, 1916."
REGULAR AND MILITIA BATALIONS.   *Uniforms*—Scarlet.   *Facings*—White.

OVER a century ago William Corbett, famous for his sound sense wrote in glowing terms of Staffordshire men.
He said:—
" Of all the bull-baiting in England, one half is carried on in Staffordshire and Lancashire. The best soldiers in the Kingdom, the most brave and the most faithful to their colours come out of those counties, particularly Staffordshire. The bravery and fidelity of Staffordshire men are proverbial through the army and have been so for two hundred years past. The Staffordshire Regiment of Militia is not only the finest but the best behaved regiment of Militia in the Kingdom. Wherever this regiment goes, it is followed by a score or two of bull-dogs, no bad emblem of the character of the soldiers themselves. The King has had this regiment about his person for several years past, and prefers it to any other. If the manners and morals of the people were injured by bull-baiting, the injury would certainly be rendered manifest in a regiment of Militia, which is composed of young men from every part of the county, from that class of the people who follow such : ports."

After such a tribute, and from such a man, we are not surprised to find that the South Staffordshire Regiment has one of the finest records in the Army, and one of the longest lists of battle honours, not only holding its own on many a famous field, but serving equally well in campaigns, on four of the five Continents, some of them now almost forgotten, but each contributing in some degree to the expansion of our Empire.

The regiment has been connected with Staffordshire from its earliest days, the 1st Battalion having been formed as the 38th Foot at Lichfield in 1702, its headquarters are still in that city and its colours rest in the Cathedral. In 1706 it embarked for the West Indies and remained there nearly sixty years, winning its first battle honours in attacks on the French at Guadaloupe 1759 and Martinique 1762. In 1775 it was in North America for the War of Independence taking part in the battles of Bunker's Hill and Lexington.

Meanwhile the second battalion had been raised as the 80th Foot (Staffordshire Volunteers) and proceeded to India. It was shipwrecked on its voyage from India to Egypt, to take part in Abercrombie's campaign against the French in 1801, and again on its return voyage. Incidentally it was shipwrecked a third time in 1844 on a voyage from Australia to India.

The first battalion having returned from America took part in the expedition of 1805 to recapture the Cape of Good Hope from the Dutch. This successfully accomplished we find them two years later in South America, where a little expedition attempted to annex the southern part of that Continent. The South Staffords covered themselves with glory at the capture of Monte Video not only by their gallantry in attack, but by their perfect discipline when the town had been captured, complete order being restored within a few hours of the engagement. This expedition failed ultimately, but in 1809 the regiment took part in the ill-fated Walcheren expedition, when nearly half the men fell victims to Flanders fever. The Peninsular War they saw through from the early battles of Rolica and Vimiera, and the retreat of Sir John Moore, to the storming of San Sebastian and the entry into France. Then followed garrison duty in France and in Cape Colony just afterwards, with minor operatons for the protection of the colonists against the Kaffirs.

The second battalion now come into action in the Burmese Wars 1824 and 1852, and the Sikh Wars. And so the records go on though the Crimean War, Indian Mutiny and Zulu War, where a sergeant was awarded the V.C., Egypt 1882, where the Staffords were the first to land after the bombardment of Alexandria, and on to the South African War, where we find them on the " Starving " 8th Division under General Rundle. Incidentally in the South African War, besides a line battalion, two militia regiments of South Stafford men served at the front, while companies from the volunteer battalion also went out.

Coming now to the Great War, it will suffice to mention that one line battalion was present at Mons, and both took part in the First Battle of Ypres, where the 2nd battalion held the very apex of the Salient for nineteen days without relief, and were called by their Brigadier " The Unbreakable Coil "—an apt reference to their badge, the Staffordshire Knot. The Territorial Battalions were among the first of these units to land in France, and from their action at the taking of the Hohenzollern Redoubt in 1915, to the swimming of the Canal du Nord at St. Quentin in 1918, they gallantly upheld the county traditions. One service battalion worthily represented the county at the Suvla landing, and the others in France, Flanders and Italy.

The South Staffords are typical of many English County Regiments—unostentatiously serving their country, wherever duty calls. William Corbett recognised their sterling qualities. This brief history has been written to justify his opinion.

A. E. S.

Annual Re-union Smoking Concert

When you were up to your neck in mud in the Salient sixteen to twenty years ago, perhaps sitting disconsolately on an upturned ammunition box, chewing the end of a saturated woodbine, feeling the incessant rain trickling down the back of your neck and perhaps, for the want of a better occupation at the moment counting the drops of rain as they fell into the neck of an uncorked empty rum jar and wondering how long it would take to fill, would you have been in any mood to have discussed with your comrades the possibility of meeting them again at a re-union twenty years hence?

What an interminable step into the future such a suggestion would have sounded then. At that time we could visualise certainly no farther than " when we got our civvy clothes on, oh! how happy we should be."

What a splendid tribute, therefore, to that wonderful spirit of comradeship which still survives the test of the passing years and to the organisation which holds the members together that close on 500 old comrades and their friends met together at Caxton Hall, Westminster, on Saturday, 27th October last. The occasion was the Twelth Annual Re-union Smoking Concert organised by the London County Committee of the League, conducted under the chairmanship of the Committee's indefatigable Chairman, Major E. Montague Jones, O.B.E.

These annual concerts have proved extremely popular functions of the League's activities in London and certainly this occasion was no exception, the usual excellent attendance being recorded, and amongst those present were:—His Excellency The Belgian Ambassador; General-Major A. Nyssens (Military Attaché Belgian Embassy); General de Brigade R. Voruz (Military Attaché French Embassy); Lieut.-General Sir W. P. Pulteney, G.C.V.O., K.C.B., K.C.M.G., D.S.O.; Colonel G. T. Brierley, C.M.G., D.S.O., and Major W. H. Brooke, M.C.

His Excellency who, although so obviously indisposed, paid the following remarkable tribute to the memory of his late King, Albert of the Belgians:—

" I should like to take this opportunity of prefacing my remarks to-night with a few words of thanks, spoken from my heart, for the very real sympathy extended to the Belgian people by the whole world, but by Great Britain in particular, at a time of deep and heartfelt mourning on the occasion of the tragic death of Albert, King of the Belgians, last February. This was an irreparable loss for my country, but it served to prove to us, yet once more, that our English allies are indeed our very good friends, and that our loss was their loss too. We were specially touched by the messages of condolence from the Ypres League, for we felt that, more than any other body, perhaps, it could understand and take part in our national mourning.

" Yet every sorrow, however black, is relieved by some ray of hope, and the ray of hope that is now lighting our future is the knowledge that our King Leopold III is admirably qualified to follow in his father's footsteps. He has already proved, on many occasions, that our high expectations will be fully justified. With such a Sovereign at the helm, Belgium can look forward with confidence to the unknown future."

All those present were impressed by the eloquence of the Ambassador's speech which we report verbatim:—

" There is no deeper bond, between individuals as between nations, than the memory of sacrifice shared, in the same cause. Quite rightly, that picturesque little town of Ypres, which was rased to the ground during the War and was so miraculously restored to life in recent years, remains for you an emblem of British effort. It represents for Great Britain what Verdun may represent for France and the Yser Front for Belgium.

" It is useful to remind ourselves sometimes of these early events. We were so much taken by surprise in 1914 that we were unable to judge them in their true perspective. The fall of Liège, that of Namur, and later that of Antwerp, appeared to meet the Belgians as so many unexpected catastrophes. But if we study detailed accounts of the events, as recorded for instance in the book of Lieut. General Galet, who was, at the time, King Albert's military adviser, the retreat of the Belgian Army from Antwerp, and its stubborn resistance on the Yser, appear nothing short of miraculous. This book, " Albert, King of the Belgians in the Great War " has been admirably translated by Major General Ernest Swinton.

"' The Battle lasted from the 16th to the 31st of October, 1914, and was the fierce prelude to the first Battle of Ypres, which was prolonged until November 17th. From that moment, the two armies were in co-operation.

" You have chosen as your " Ypres Day " the nearest Sunday to the 31st October. That is to-morrow. May I remind you that, on the same date, the battle of the Yser came to a successful end, and the Belgian troops, which had fought valiantly and almost alone for three months, under most difficult conditions, were at last allowed some respite to reorganise and recuperate.

" While glancing the other day through the excellent review published by your League, the " Ypres Times," I found several articles referring to my country. One on " Liège Twenty Years After," recalling the staunch resistance of the forts in the very first days of the struggle, another on a visit paid by His Majesty King Leopold III to the Ypres British School. His Majesty enjoyed his visit, and you all know that King Leopold spent several years at Eton, going to our trenches in Flanders for His holidays.

" I was particularly pleased to hear that Countess Haig, Viscountess Plumer, Lieut.-General Sir William and Lady Pulteney were among those who received the King on this occasion. A third article refers to the unveiling of the 13th Belgian Field Artillery Memorial at Ypres. I should like to be allowed to add a few details to the information given by the " Ypres Times " on this occasion, because we were rather proud of this Regiment, and because many people in this country are still unaware of the origin and activities of the 13th Belgian Artillery. After the Battle of the Yser, the Belgian Artillery was sorely depleted and the very first work undertaken by King Albert and His Minister of War was its complete re-organisation and re-equipment. Guns were purchased from France, horses from Great Britain, and the number of batteries soon became more than adequate for Belgian requirements. It was thus possible to lend a Belgian unit to the British forces in the Ypres Salient, and the 13th Belgian Artillery thus remained attached to the British Army and took part in all their operations. By the way, you will be interested to know that one of the Belgian Officers attached to the 13th Belgian Artillery was yesterday appointed Chief of the General Staff of the Belgian Army, —General Cumont.

"Before concluding, I want most heartily to congratulate the Ypres League on its many achievements. It seems at first a most easy undertaking to keep the Lamp of Memory burning when a whole nation and a great Empire have been stirred to the depth of their souls by great sacrifice made in a noble cause, but life, we know, is very relentless, generation succeeds generation and the future seems always more attractive than the past ....

"With the lapse of time it becomes more and more difficult to maintain numbers and to find financial means to carry on one's work. Individual energy has to come to the rescue, and the wonder is that such individual energy is never lacking. I do not pretend to explain this wonder, though I may perhaps suggest that part of that heroic strength which spent itself so generously on Flanders Fields remains with you still, and prompts you to fresh action."

Sir William Pulteney, then expressed a cordial vote of thanks to His Excellency, The Belgian Ambassador and other distinguished guests for the honour they had given us by their presence.

The Chairman, Major Montague Jones, also spoke and recounted the League's activities throughout the past year, again stressing the urgent need of enrolling new members. He paid tribute to the untiring work and energy of the League's worthy Secretary, Captain G. E. de Trafford, M.C., who conducted affairs so ably from headquarters, and also to Mr. John Boughey who continues to perform innumerable tasks connected with the London County Committee.

An exceptionally fine concert was given by the "Bubbles" Concert Party under the personal direction of Mr. Will Seymour and the individual performance of the artistes were warmly appreciated, as were those of the Enfield College of Music, whose members, under the able direction of Mrs. Doris Lee Peabody, provided musical items throughout the evening.

In keeping with the occasion, the memory of those destined to pay the full sacrifice was hallowed by everyone standing in silent reverence whilst the immortal words of Laurence Binyon's *To the Fallen* were recited by Captain H. D. Peabody, D.C.M. This was preceded and followed by the strains of *The Last Post* and *Reveille* respectively.

The inevitable conclusion to these affairs is the community singing of old war-time choruses and Mr. A. E. Nickolds conducted the gathering in vociferous efforts of their vocal talents.

During the evening a message of loyalty was sent to His Majesty the King from whom a telegram was received in reply, reading :—

"The King has received with much pleasure the message you have sent on behalf of the Members of the Ypres League asembled at their annual reunion. In thanking them, His Majesty wishes all present a very enjoyable evening."

A further message was received as follows :—

"Thank you for giving me an opportunity of conveying to the members of the Ypres League on this occasion of their Annual Re-union an expression of friendship and admiration from comrades in arms across the sea. I regret that I am unable to be with you."

ROBERT W. BINGHAM.
American Ambassador.

A. R. F.

A Hard Case

Having dissipated our remaining few piastres on such army pastimes as Crown and Anchor and Housey ! Housey ! aboard the transport from the Near Eastern battlefields, we arrived at Marseilles in January, 1919, thoroughly broke and with rather mixed feelings.

The thought of being back again to civilisation, particularly in so colourful an atmosphere as Marseilles with its inviting gay cafes, shops and general night life without a bean, was a little too much for one of the party, so a regular debate followed on just how we might raise the wind. An examination of personal effects brought us to the conclusion that nothing we possessed amongst us was of any marketable value and the prospect of a very early night in our temporary camp more evitable than a trip into town.

Quietly observing one of the lads fingering an old and battered metalic watch, Dusty, our wit, suddenly brought us to life with a wild snatch at the watch and an enthusiastic request to follow him. Faithful to our army training, we obeyed the command and eventually found ourselves seated outside a cafe at which some Senegalese soldiers (French Colonial troops) were enjoying a hectic round of bieres. Dusty, still eyed by us in amazement, straightaway proceeded to get on friendly terms with these Senegalese and after many " bon comrade," one of them, a little under the weather, called for drinks for the soldats Anglais which according to our leader's ejaculation was just what the doctor ordered ! Noticing Dusty looking intently at the aforementioned watch, a Senegalese also became interested, and suppressing our mirth, we instinctively felt that this miserable trinket might yet prove our salvation. After a most wonderful tale as to its real worth, and how it came into Dusty's possession via a Turkish General a sale at fifteen francs seemed imminent. On hearing a member of our party jocularly mention that the —— thing wouldn't go, the Sengalese immediately turned and exclaimed " No go, eh ! " Dusty, however, having got so far, did not intend this faux-pas to spoil the transaction, so he replied that his friend meant, no sell ! sell only for twenty francs ! Viewing our party a little suspiciously he eventually said, " Yez ! Comrade, den I give twenty francs ! Following the handing over of the necessary, we suddenly realised we were due back in camp, which of course was not the case, and hastily bid them our very warm adieus, which were heartily reciprocated. Knowing full well it would only be a short time ere they discovered they had been rather badly fooled, we hiked it to the furthermost part of the town and continued to drink their health until only a franc or two remained.

Bearing in mind the fervour of their friendship at our initial meeting, we did not intend to disturb the peace, but dodging shells and bullets appeared easy as compared with playing hide and seek with these Senegalese for the remaining few days that we were at Marseilles, because sure enough if one of us dared stray into a back area café he would be immediately confronted with the cry " You sella de watch," followed by the demand for the return of the twenty francs.

We were certain that the joke would be ultimately appreciated by these good fellows, but our trek across France en route to dear old Blighty gave us an opportunity to tell Dusty a few home truths.

SURVIVOR.

A Dream in Ypres

By A. DOUGLAS THORBURN, M.A. (CAPT. R.F.A., S.R. retd.)
(Author of " *Amateur Gunners.*")

THE Fortunes of War did not bring me to The Salient during the period of hostilities. The battery with which I served for over three years, holding various ranks from 2nd Lieut. to Captain did yeoman service in France, Salonica, Palestine and again in France without being employed farther North than La Bassée.

My visit to Ypres in the summer of 1920 was therefore my first to the area since the outbreak of war. The occasion was a motor tour of the battle areas of Belgium and Northern France in which I had for companion an ex-officer of the Cheshire Regiment who had stopped a bullet in one of the Gallipoli assaults and been permanently lamed thereby.

Our tour included the town of Ypres which in 1920 was still in a state of almost total ruin. By then little had been done in the way of restoration, the Cloth Hall still reared its jagged and gaunt towers to the sky in a sort of protest to the heavens against the destructive powers of man, the Menin Road had been rebuilt but the town and its surroundings still presented a picture of desolation and ruin as dismal and depressing as possible.

My companion's War experiences had not included fighting on the Western front, so that it was interesting to watch his reaction to our surroundings. We spent our day in Ypres visiting cemeteries, Tank cemetery and others in the neighbourhood, memorials to various regiments that had won fame in the countless local battles against picked Divisions of the " finest army that ever went to war " (Marshal Foch's own description of the German Army).

Finally we put up for the night in the only accommodation that then existed, a varnished wooden structure that formed a comfortable hotel in the centre of the town.

And then happened the remarkable experience which is the subject of my story: it is entirely a true story in every particular.

The following personal details are essential if what I am about to tell is to be fully appreciated. The writer is not an imaginative individual. He does not readily believe in the mystical and declines to give any serious credit to such matters as are investigated by Societies for Psychical Research. Such phenomena as Ghosts and their manifestations, communications from the departed and such things have no part in his mental make-up. He regards those who give serious consideration to all such things (whether they be distinguished men of science, eminent writers of fiction, or uninstructed persons with little knowledge of the rules of evidence or of the demands of commonsense) as deluded and possibly unbalanced people who allow their credulity to mislead them.

With this personal explanation let me relate in simple language what happened to me on that summer night in Ypres in 1920.

After a good if simple dinner my friend and I retired to bed, our minds undoubtedly attuned to thoughts of many astonishing memories of the war; to use the jargon of psychology our minds were likely to be extremely receptive of external influences.

I should think, without knowing positively, that my friend is more imaginative, or, if you will, more inclined to be receptive than I, and yet nothing came to him. Neither of us suffer from impaired digestions.

So rarely does the writer, the soundest of sleepers, dream that every dream which comes to him is vivid and pictorial in the extreme and remains permanently embedded in his memory. On this summer night a dream came, vivid and unmistakable in detail, picturing a War incident which I certainly never saw with my eyes. A line of kite-balloons was to be seen against the sky, an enemy aeroplane attacked them, firing incendiary bullets, one of the balloons caught fire and sank down blazing, the observer left the basket in the regulation manner by parachute, *the parachute caught fire and the observer crashed to the ground and was killed.*

All of this scene was presented to me in my dream as vividly as if it had been displayed on the screen of a cinema. It did not awaken me.

To appreciate the singularity of this incident it is necessary to realize that the average number of my dreams is certainly less than one a year. It is also a fact that I must have watched more than a score of kite-balloons attacked by enemy aeroplanes and set on fire by incendiary bullets. I saw the kite-balloon near Gugunci in Macedonia attacked over and over again by enemy airmen and shelled repeatedly, and the balloon behind Bethel (Beitin) in Palestine set upon by Turkish airmen. I saw very many British kite-balloons and German " Sausages " set on fire by aeroplane attack. In every single case flames darted upwards from the top of the balloon and the parachute decended safely long before any fire could endanger the flimsy white " umbrella."

Why then did this vivid dream come to me? Why did I on the one night that I slept in Ypres see in a dream a vivid picture of an incident that I had never seen with my eyes or in a picture?

If any reader of this true story knows of any such incident among the observers who, high in the air, kept their lonely watch on the movements of the attackers who lay in wait around this vital bastion of the Allied armies, I should be most grateful to hear if this curious dream reproduced an actual happening. There seems no other probable explanation of it.

As I have written of an incident which may or may not have happened to an observer of a Kite-Balloon section of the R.A.F. or R.F.C. I should like to record here my complete admiration of the spirit of this very gallant section of the armies of the Great War.

It must be want of imagination that has allowed the services of these devoted men to pass almost unnoticed.

As a gunner I know how much of the information that came to hand from our Intelligence departments was due to their untiring services. It needed a very special kind of courage to hang suspended high in the air at the end of a cable fastened to a lorry, an easy mark for every prowling enemy airman, with a huge bag of inflammable gas overhead, and a flimsy-looking cable and a telephone wire as the sole connection with the ground. In high wind the gyrations of the balloon caused dreadful seasickness and both hands were needed for safety. In spite of these things they managed by determination and doggedness to register our guns on essential targets and enabled us to keep down machine gun fire from pill-boxes sited so as to enfilade the attacking waves of infantry.

They presented an eternal target to long-range guns that fired H.E. airbursts at them. No trench or dugout was there for them to dive into when the crash of an airburst shook the air beside them or when the whine of machine-gun bullets was heard. Should the cable part in a high Westerley wind an immediate parachute descent was the only way to avoid a trip to a German prison camp, and in one case at least this fate was only avoided by so rapid a drop as to involve a pair of broken legs.

Photo] [Imperial War Museum, Crown Copyright.
PARACHUTE COMING DOWN FROM A BLAZING KITE-BALLOON

All of this cold courage had to be produced without the encouragement of the presence of any fellow-soldier, the hardest test of all.

So let every fighting soldier join with me in saying " HATS OFF TO THE BALLOONATICS " as we used to call them. A. D. T.

Mist at Vierstraat

By Donald Boyd.

THE mist which occupied Vierstraat cross-roads, when I woke in the O.P., had changed the whole place. In the December of 1915 we had come to know the village as a broken row of houses parallel with the front line, and standing nearly upon the same level. It looked upon the slope which was crowned by Wytschaete; that was its value to us; and the roof-line of Vierstraat's houses was high enough to conceal the path which led to the street. We spent most of the daylight hours on the first floor of the forge, looking through a window shaped like a segment of orange, but when the day was quiet we sometimes came down, leaving the slit in the occupation of a telephonist, and then took the liberty of sitting on the window-sill upon the street, or walked fifty yards in either direction in the cover of the houses, on the one hand to the crown of the hill where it dipped towards Ypres, or on the left to the actual cross-roads. Further we could not go because the crossing was under German observation.

But now, in the thick mist, the appearance of the place was changed. The short view along the street was closed and the neighbouring houses acquired an enlarged importance, with such alleys and fractures as lay between their walls. Their height and solidity appeared to be greater at this short range. From the broken roofs the condensing mist dropped loudly. The obscurity had stopped the war for the time being. There was no shooting on the front, and the distant traffic of the army, rolling along the cobble stones by Locre and La Clytte could be heard plainly. I was joined on the road by the garrison gunner who occupied the next house. We exchanged some comment upon the kindness of the weather. It had lately snowed and the snow had been persistent enough to drive through the holes in our houses and cover our blankets, so that we woke up rather wetter then we had been when we went to bed. Now it had changed to this mist, which we agreed was a pleasant deviation; a holiday in fact. We both had a complaint to make—that there was an uncomfortable draught through the slits which our predecessors had made behind the window openings. For in each O.P. a separate structure stood just behind the windows, for protection, and also so that the effective opening should be as small as possible. This prevented enemy observers from seeing movements in the window openings. We also talked about the "strafe," or bombardment, which Vierstraat had suffered the day before.

This decided us to go round to the front of the houses to see how much they had been damaged on that side. We went to the cross-roads and turned left towards the front line, which was about three hundred yards ahead. We could see the road only for a few yards, perhaps twenty or thirty, but it had all the marks of desertion. A forlorn look; the grass had sprouted between the setts, and crept forward on the unpaved margins. The trees were all down and here and there the craters had torn up the paving and left the stone blocks lying about in disorder. We explored for a short distance and then turned back for an examination of the gardens of Vierstraat. The grass was long and hung in plumes upon the earth, beaded with mist. Our foot-steps left a black trail behind us. The house fronts reared themselves up suddenly, crowned with a triangular lattice-work of broken rafters. We stopped by a broken fruit-tree to study their appearance. It was with some difficulty that we could identify the ones we used. Indeed we only made sure by going close up to the wall and spying into the peep-holes in the upper windows. We then found the wound that a 5.9 had made in the front wall of the Garrison gunner's house. It had struck exactly at the base of the house and had even blown the wall through to the flooring, whose broken tiles showed a little in the gap. A smaller shell had hit the top of my wall under the roof, and had blown half the slates away. There were also a number of fresh shell-holes in the gardens. We looked at them curiously and poked about among the ravaged plantings. Close at hand the stump of the mill chimney rose through the mist. The German artillery used it as a zero point, a fixed mark upon which they could register their guns, and though it was so often their target there was a substantial amount left. The shell-fire had fetched the bricks tumbling about the base, which was now twice or three times the size of the original chimney. We were just about to enter the old building when we stopped.. Someone was calling. We moved on irresolutely a step and then stopped again. There was another hail. We moved back towards the houses and stared at them. Then I recogized the voice of the major calling me. I could not see him, but assumed he must be looking out of the slit. " Hurry ! " he shouted.

We both ran back to the road and into Vierstraat. I climbed the ladder to the O.P. and found the major squatting there, and then I saw that the mist was rapidly clearing. Already the top of the little fruit-tree was sticking out of the swathe, and I saw that we should have been plainly visible if we had stopped a minute longer. As I listened meekly to Byron's admonition a German shell came over and burst in a pink cloud at the base of the chimney. " Good shooting," the major said. The war had started again.

D. B.

League Secretary's Notes

We now enter the 15th Anniversary year of the life of the Ypres League with the optimism that our Association, with the staunch support of is faithful members, will continue to cement the valuable ground recovered in 1934, which year introduced a distinct note of welcome confidence after a period of many difficulties brought about as a result of the world's trade depression. Members can be assured that headquarters are determined to strive even harder than ever to establish the good position that has momentarily been created, and this can be achieved by inviting the united co-operation in " recruiting," because the sole source of the League's revenue is the annual membership subscription on which the life of the League depends. Before attempting to increase the membership we must first of all focuss our attention on filling up the gaps made by the regrettable number of our supporters who pass away each year, and 1934 has proved all too prominent in this respect. It is most touching to report that quite a number of our ex-service members, though being out of employment, are keeping themselves on the " live register " by paying their five shillings for the year in instalments, and we are indeed very grateful to their stout hearts and fine example.

Much gratitude is extended to a great number of our annual subscribers who have contributed donations over and above their annual subscriptions with the wish that the balance should go towards the " Ypres Times Maintenance Fund," and in many cases to " The Poor Pilgrims' Fund," established for the purpose of assisting financially, specially selected poor mothers to visit, for the first time, the graves of their sons at Ypres, and it is our earnest hope that adequate funds will enable us to reduce our waiting list during 1935. We are greatly encouraged to feel that the League's charitable work is so well approved.

In the January, 1934 edition of this journal, we appealed to all members to notify headquarters in the event of changing their addresses, and we are pleased to say that the response has enabled us to keep our records up-to-date and we hope that members will continue to advise us similarly in the future.

A very hearty expression of thanks goes to our Branches, Corresponding Members and individual supporters who have worked so hard for us in the old year, and Mr. S. C. Allen-Olney is to be specially complimented for his valuable work in respect of the Junior Branch.

The prospects for 1935 are decidedly promising in all departments, and there could not be a more fitting gesture than for our united efforts to record an even more successful year in loyal and respectful acknowledgement of the Jubilee of our Patron-in-Chief, His Majesty the King.

In conclusion we ask all our members to kindly accept our very best wishes for good health and happiness in the New Year.

Attention is again drawn to the League's **easy payment scheme** for those desirous of visiting cemetries, memorials and battlefields in France and Belgium.

Our Saturday to Tuesday 4 day trips at EASTER, April 20th to 23rd, WHITSUNTIDE, June 8th to 11th, and AUGUST BANK HOLIDAY, August 3rd to 6th will be organised as in past years and forms with particulars will be gladly forwarded on application to those wishing to avail themselves of these easy payment facilities.

For the fourth successive year, our Purley Branch have kept abreast of other Branches in the matter of recruiting, and although very closely pursued by both the London and Colchester Branches in 1934, they retain the honour of enrolling the greatest number of new members for the year and thereby win the £5 prize.

Purley members themselves must indeed feel proud of their Branch's recruiting achievements, and we are sure that by extending headquarter's heartiest congratulations and gratitude to their Committee we are also voicing the sentiments of all our members.

The London and Colchester Branch Committees are to be highly commended for their respective efforts and strong challenge they have given to the successful branch, and it gives us great pleasure to announce that a similar prize will be offered for 1935. We shall watch with interest to see whether Purley can complete a nap hand.

Copies of the October, 1933 edition would be very welcomely received by headquarters from members who can reasonably spare them.

We are exceedingly disappointed to announce that our Ypisode Competition, full details of which appeared in the last October edition of the "Ypres Times," has met with such a poor response that we have very reluctantly decided to cancel the competition.

We have had an exceedingly welcome visit to headquarters from Mr. James Armstrong of Edinburgh, one of our most ardent of supporters. During his visit he generously presented to the League, a specimen of the veritable seal of Robert Burns, Scotland's National Bard. The design was executed by the bard himself and bears the following inscription:

WOOD NOTES WILD
BETTER A WEE BUSH THAN NAE BIELD

The original seal was gifted by the ladies and gentlemen of Edinburgh to Robert Burns in the year 1786-87.

We express our sincere thanks to Mr. Armstrong for his very generous gift which we are having framed for the headquarter office.

HOTEL
Splendid & Britannique
YPRES

GRANDE PLACE. Opposite Cloth Hall.

Leading Hotel for Comfort and Quality, and Patronized by The Ypres League.

Completely Renovated.

Running Water. Bathrooms

Moderate Terms. Garage.

Proprietor—Life Member, Ypres League.

YPRES
Skindles Hotel

(Opposite the Station)

Proprietor—Life Member, Ypres League

Branch at Poperinghe

(close to Talbot House)

Branch Notes

5th Army Re-union.

On Saturday evening, November 24th, a representative party of some twenty to thirty members of our London Branch attended he first Trench Supper organised by the Fifth Army, 1916-18, O.C.A.

The Bedford Head Hotel, Maiden Lane, Strand, W.C.2 was made headquarters for this auspicious occasion and the whole function was a marked success. The Ypres League contingent, headed by Captain C. Alliston, was accorded an extremely warm reception and emphasised another instance of the keenness of our members in supporting their old comrades in the activities of kindred Associations.

The surroundings were typical of trench life as only the tommy knew it: bare tables, copies on the wall of La Vie Parisienne, humerous remarks pencilled or chalked here and there, sand-bags, tin hats, etc., in fact most things that one found or did not find in dug-outs of years back. The atmosphere of trench life was re-captured again at the sight of orderlies bringing the rations along in sand-bags following the sounding by the bugler of the familiar "cook-house."

Our *now* rather delicate digestions were sorely taxed with a combination of machonachies, bully-beef, ration biscuits very hard, rice and raisins, margarine, plum and apple jam, pickles, marmalade, cheese, etc., with ten sharing in one loaf. Following the sampling of the above varied ingredients, there were only a few very weak replies to the Orderly Officer's question of " any complaints " and most interest at this period was centred on the Quarter-bloke's parade with the familiar rum-jar. It did not escape notice, however, that the evening's Orderly Sergeant felt compelled to taste two or three times before reporting the contents suitable for issue. This of course started the gathering singing that immortal army ballad " If the Sergeant drinks your rum never mind," although the words applied did not seem to appear on the song-sheet.

After the feed, the company settled down to enjoy an impromptu concert interspersed with full-blown rendering of favourite war-time choruses. Altogether the evening was voted an exceptionally pleasant one and then came the call for " stretcher-bearers." Many of the old swets could be heard asking whether there would be another held next year.

N.B.—The Hon. Secretary, London Branch, desires to express his grateful thanks to the 5th Army O.C.A. for its kind invitation and warm welcome extended to the members of the Ypres League at the above function; and also thanks the many members of the London Branch of the League who supported him so admirably.

THE ELEVENTH ANNUAL
Children's Christmas Party
organised by the
LONDON COUNTY COMMITTEE
will take place at the
**WESTMINSTER CITY SCHOOL,
55, PALACE ST., VICTORIA ST., S.W.1.**
(By permission of the Governors of the School)
On SATURDAY, JANUARY 12th, 1935,
at 4 p.m.

Admission:
Junior Division Members, Free. Friends 6d. each.

Application for tickets should be made to the Hon. Secretary, London County Committee, Ypres League, at 20, Orchard Street, W.1., not later than January 10th, 1935.

Tea commences at 4 p.m., followed by a ventriloquist entertainment.

To many children who attend, this is perhaps the only treat enjoyed by them during the Christmas season, so we earnestly request our members' generous support to enable us to give them a real good time. Father Christmas will again be there in state, and with your kind co-operation we are looking forward to seeing him supplied with a sufficient number of toys to ensure each child receiving at least one present from his bag.

Gifts of toys or donations will be very gratefully received and welcomed by the Hon. Secretary, London County Committee, Ypres League, 20, Orchard Street, London, W.1.

If members are in the vicinity of Palace Street, Westminster on the evening of January 12th, they are cordially invited to pay us a visit and join in the fun with the kiddies.

Informal Gatherings.

At the Bedford Hotel on October 18th last, an exceedingly instructive lantern lecture on " Sea Power " was delivered through the kindness of the Navy League, by Lieut.-Commander D. S. E. Thompson, R.N., and which was followed with keen interest.

Our November gathering welcomed Mr. Walter J. Morrison who gave us a talk on " Five Years with the Y.M.C.A. in France " and his numerous slides enabled us to realise the great work accomplished by that organisation during the Great War. We are glad to say that Mr. Morrison has promised to favour us with a further talk on some future occasion.

The December Informal was very kindly arranged by Mr. O. Mears of headquarters and to whom we express our grateful thanks and congratulate him on mustering such a party of accomplished artistes. The whole programme was excellent throughout in its appropriateness of the festive season, and presented a fitting climax to another successful year. During the evening's entertainment, a draw was held which resulted in two persons, namely Miss E. Dunn and Regan (artiste) receiving a turkey each, generously presented by an anonymous donor.

Notice of forthcoming gatherings appears on this page.

It is a great pleasure for us to report that Captain Alliston and Mr. Thrussell after their illnesses, are able to join us again in our London activities.

Two dances will be held at the Veteran's Club, Hand Court, Holborn, W.C.1., on January 23rd and March 8th respectively at 7.30 p.m. It is earnestly hoped that many members and friends will join us on these two occasions when they are assured of a hearty welcome. See page 156. The London County Committee wishes all its members a very happy 1935, and look forward to the fullest support from everybody during the present year.

Please book these dates in your Diary.

THE MONTHLY
Informal Gatherings
FOR JANUARY, FEBRUARY, MARCH AND APRIL
will be held at
THE BEDFORD HEAD HOTEL, MAIDEN LANE, STRAND, W.C.2
on
THURSDAY, 17th JANUARY, 1935.
THURSDAY, 21st FEBRUARY, 1935.
   Programme by the St. Dunstan's Concert Party.
THURSDAY, 21st MARCH, 1935.
   Illustrated Talk by Captain H. D. Peabody, D.C.M.
THURSDAY, 18th APRIL, 1935.
   Programme by " Anon."
      From 7.15 p.m. to 10 p.m.

Start the year by paying us a visit at our Gathering on Thursday, 17th January, 1935. A very hearty welcome awaits you and any ex-service friend whom you may wish to bring along.

Full particulars of the Gatherings will be sent by the Hon. Secretary, London County Committee, to a friend on receipt of name and address. Ladies are cordially invited.

DANCES.
Dances will be held as follows :—
WEDNESDAY, January 23rd.
FRIDAY, March 8th.
   at the
VETERAN'S CLUB, Hand Court, Holborn, W.C.1.   Tickets 1/6

KENYA BRANCH.

Corporal C. H. Slater, our indefatigable representative in Kenya has repeated his past kindness in placing a wreath, on behalf of the Ypres League, on the Nairobi Cenotaph on Armistice Day.

NAIROBI CENOTAPH SHOWING THE LARGE YPRES LEAGUE WREATH OF HAIG POPPIES

We take this opportunity to convey our very grateful thanks to the following gentlemen who very generously subscribed towards the wreath, namely, Mr. S. W. Kemp, Colonel G. J. Henderson, Major W. N. Mackenzie, Captain D. P. Petrie, D.S.O., Mr. G. J. Robbins, Brig. General H. K. Jackson, C.B., D.S.O., Corporal C. H. Slater, Brig. General P. Wheatley, C.B., C.M.G., D.S.O., and Brig. General A. R. Wainwright, C.M.G., D.S.O.

COLCHESTER BRANCH.

Second Annual Ball.

Much interest was evinced in the second annual ball of the Colchester and District Branch of the Ypres League which took place at the Red Lion Hotel on Wednesday, November 21st, when a company of 100 spent a very enjoyable evening. Old and modern dances were intermingled in the programme. The band of the 1st Lancashire Fusiliers (by permission of Lieut. Colonel L. H. K. Finch, D.S.O., O.B.E.) was in attendance and dancing continued from 8 p.m. until the early hours of the morning.

The M.C.'s were Major G. C. Benham, M.C., Captain A. C. Palmer and Mr. A. McKinley.

Competitions were won by Mrs. Gerald Stanford and Mrs. E. Eyres, and among those present, most of whom brought parties were: Colonel H. W. Herring (President), Major General Harding-Newman, Colonel E. H. Clarke (President Royal Engineers Old Comrades' Association), Mr. Ralph Wright, Mr. Gerald Stanford, Mr. F. J. Collinge, Mr. D. Shadrach and Dr. Fripp.

The arrangements were carried out by a special committee, of which Major G. C. Benham was chairman and Mr. H. Snow, Secretary.

Armistice Day Service.

Lieut. Colonel W. H. Herring and a representative gathering of members of the Colchester Branch attended the Service of Remembrance at Colchester on November 11th and placed a wreath on the Monument. The address was given by the Right Worshipful the Mayor (Councillor A. H. Cross) and the " Last Post " and Reveillé were sounded by buglers of the 2nd Bn. the King's Shropshire Light Infantry.

PURLEY BRANCH.

Autumn Golf Meeting.

The autumn Golf Meeting of this Branch was held at the Purley Downs Golf Club on the 2nd October in a steady drizzle.

Notwithstanding the poor conditions 35 of the 41 who had entered went out and completed 18 holes.

The number constitutes a record for any Autumn Meeting so far held by the Branch and enabled the provision of 2nd prize in addition to the 8th Wipers Cup.

The late starters provided all the excitement, as improving scores were received almost up to the last couple and Commander R. H. Shelton, D.S O., a native of Purley Downs, was the winner with the return of one up.

Captain A. S. Green, one of the successful pair in the Bombadier's Foursomes this year, was second with a return of all square: his partner in the Foursomes, Captain W. K. Scott, won the Spring Meeting, so they may be considered to have had a very successful season. Other good returns were one down by T. G. Crump and C. N. Bellingham.

At the supper in the evening, the Chairman of the Branch, Captain R. L. Haine, V.C., M.C., presented the prizes expressing unbounded surprise that " Sockety Bob " had won a prize at last: with Green it was different, as he was a coming player. The Commander suitably replied.

During the course of liquid refreshment that followed, the Secretary reported other returns, notably the Chairman's own effort which brought up the rear going strong at 14 down! Two members who failed to return their cards were reported and called upon for an explanation in the usual way. After certain stories had been circulated, the Chairman concluded the evening by thanking the Host Club for giving us the privilege of playing there, not forgetting the attention of Howes, the Steward, an ex-service man himself.

Armistice Day Parade.

A very successful Armistice Day Parade was held on November 11th, when the Purley branch mustered a party of 46 to attend the United Memorial Service at the Purley Congregational Church in the afternoon. As usual the parade was under the command of the Chairman, and it is satisfactory to note that Captain R. L. Haine, was so well supported.

Dance.

The Ypres League Dance arranged by this Branch took place on Thursday, December 6th at the Greyhound Hotel, Croydon, and was attended by a company of 314.

There was all-round regret that General Sir Hubert Gough and Lieut. General Sir William Pulteney were unable to be with us on that night, but some recompense was forthcoming in the presence of the League's Secretary, Captain G. E. de Trafford who is always welcome at Branch functions.

The Chairman of the Branch, Captain R. L. Haine, was in command of the Committee which had made all arrangements. Marius B. Winter and his Band provided the music: the Western Brothers provided half an hour's considerable laughter and the Committee provided further diversion in the way of " funny hats," hand grenades and balloons.

The revelry went with a swing and all reports indicated an entirely successful evening which is very likely to become an annual fixture in the future.

Thanks of the Branch are due to the Dance Committee composed of the Chairman already mentioned, N. A. Zinn the M.C., Captain G. B. Mutton (Dance Hon. Secretary), Captain A. S. Green, J. R. Garbutt, M.C., and Major Graham Carr (General Hon. Secretary).

Military Memorial to the Late King Albert of Belgium

Sir,

The recent tragic death of King Albert has revived many memories of one of the truly heroic figures of the Great War. Surely there could be no more fitting tribute to his work for the allied cause than a memorial in the historic town of Ypres erected by those who served with the British Army in Flanders.

With this object in view, a small Committee has been formed, of which I am Chairman.

Fortunately a very fitting opportunity has presented itself to us, namely, that of filling the great Rose Window at the Main South entrance of the restored Cathedral of Ypres with stained glass of British design and make.

The artist selected by the Committee is Miss Geddes, whose work in Canada and Ireland is well known.

His Majesty The King has approved of the scheme, and I am glad to say that His Majesty King Leopold has also expressed his approval of our proposal and considers that it would form a most acceptable memorial to his illustrious father.

The sum required is two thousand pounds (£2,000), and I make this appeal to all ranks 'of those who served in the Great War, and to the Regular and Territorial Armies of to-day to assist me in raising this comparatively modest sum.

The work will be put in hand immediately the Committee feel justified in doing so, and should be finished during next year. The window will be shown to the public in this country before being handed over as a gift from British soldiers to Belgium.

Any surplus funds will be handed over to the Anglo-Belgian Union to be used for providing beds for ex-soldiers in St. Andrew's Hospital, Dollis Hill: if feasible to build a "King Albert Ward."

All cheques should be made payable to "The King Albert Army Memorial" and addressed :

To the Organising Secretary,
King Albert Memorial Fund,
c/o Ypres League Headquarters,
20 Orchard Street,
London, W.1.

Or to :—
Lloyds Bank, Ltd. (City Office),
72 Lombard Street,
London, E.C.

Postal orders or stamps will be gladly received at either of these addresses.

Acknowledgements and records of donations will in all cases be sent by Captain Guy Cassie, c/o Ypres League Headquarters, 20, Orchard Street, London, W.1.

(Signed) ATHLONE,
Chairman.

Committee.

MAJOR-GENERAL THE EARL OF ATHLONE, K.C. (*Chairman*).

HIS EXCELLENCY THE BELGIAN AMBASSADOR.

LIEUT.-GENERAL SIR W. P. PULTENEY (*Chairman Ypres League*).

L'ABBE VERMAUT, THE DOYEN OF YPRES.

MAJOR-GENERAL SIR NEILL MALCOLM.

Organising Secretary :—
CAPTAIN GUY CASSIE
(Late Argyll and Sutherland Highlanders),
c/o Ypres League Headquarters,
20 Orchard Street,
London, W.1.

It is hoped that all members of the Ypres League will support Lord Athlone's appeal and encourage others to do likewise.

There can be no more fitting Memorial to the late King Albert than to restore the famous Rose Window in the Ypres Cathedral with stained glass of British design.

W. P. PULTENEY,
Chairman.
(Ypres League)

THE BRITISH TOURING SERVICE

Manager—Mr. P. VYNER
Representative and Life Member, Ypres League

**10, Station Square
ARRAS
(P.-de-C.) France**

Cars for Hire, with British Driver Guides   Tours Arranged

Branches and Corresponding Members

BRANCHES.

LONDON ... ... Hon. Secretary to the London County Committee : J. Boughey, 20, Orchard Street, London, W.1.
E. LONDON DISTRICT—L. A. Weller, 132, Maxey Road, Dagenham, Essex.
TOTTENHAM AND EDMONTON DISTRICT—E, Glover, 191, Lansdowne Road, Tottenham, N.17.
H. Carey, 373, Sydenham Road, S.E.26.
COLCHESTER ... ... H. Snow (Hon. Sec.), 9, Church Street (North).
W. H. Taylor (Pilgrimage Hon. Sec.), 64, High Street.
GATESHEAD ... ... Lieut.-Colonel E. G. Crouch, 8, Ashgrove Terrace.
LIVERPOOL ... ... Captain A. M. Webster, Blundellsands.
PURLEY ... ... Major Graham Carr, D.S.O., M.C., 112-114, High Street.
SHEFFIELD ... ... Captain J. Wilkinson, "Holmfield," Bents Drive.
BELGIUM ... ... Capt. P. D. Parminter, 19, Rue Surmont de Volsberghe, Ypres.
CANADA ... ... Ed. Kingsland, P.O. Box 83, Magog, Quebec.
SOUTH AFRICA ... L. G. Shuter, Church Street, Pietermaritzburg,
KENYA ... ... C. H. Slater, P.O. Box 403, Nairobi.
AMERICA ... ... Representative : Captain R. Henderson-Bland, 110 West 57th Street, New York City.

CORRESPONDING MEMBERS

GREAT BRITAIN.

ABERYSTWYTH ... ... T. O. Thomas, 5, Smithfield Road.
ASHTON-UNDER-LYNE ... G. D. Stuart, "Woodlands,", Thronfield Grove, Arundel Street.
BANBURY ... ... Captain C. W. Fowke, Yew Tree House, King's Sutton.
BIRMINGHAM ... ... Mrs. Hill, 191, Cattell Road, Small Heath.
John Burman, "Westbrook," Solihull Road, Shirley.
BOURNEMOUTH ... ... H. L. Pasmore, 40, Morley Road, Boscombe Park.
BRISTOL ... ... W. S. Hook, "Wytschaete" Redland Court Road.
BROADSTAIRS ... ... C. E. King, 6, Norman Road, St. Peters, Broadstairs.
Mrs. Briggs, North Foreland House.
CHATHAM ... ... W. N. Channon, 22, Keyes Avenue.
CHESTERFIELD ... ... Major A. W. Shea, 14, Cross Street.
CONGLETON ... ... Mr. H. Dart, 61, The Crescent.
DARLINGTON ... ... D. S. Vigo, 125, Dorset Road, Bexhill-on-Sea.
DERBY ... ... T. Jakeman, 10, Graham Street.
DORRINGTON (Salop) ... Captain G. D. S. Parker, Frodesley Rectory.
EXETER ... ... Captain E. Jenkin, 25, Queen Street.
GLOUCESTER ... ... H. R. Hunt, "Casita," Parton Lane, Churchdown.
HERNE BAY ... ... Captain E. Clarke Williams, F.S.A.A., "Conway," Station Road.
HOVE ... ... Captain G. W. J. Cole, 2, Westbourne Terrace, Kingsway.
LEICESTER ... ... W. C. Dunford, 343, Aylestone Road.
LINCOLN ... ... E. Swaine, 79, West Parade.
LLANWRST ... ... A. C. Tomlinson, M.A., Bod Estyn.
LOUGHTON ... ... Capt. O. G. Johnson, M.A., Loughton School.
MATLOCK (Derby) ... Miss Dickinson, Beechwood.
MELROSE ... ... Mrs. Lindesay Kelsall, Darnlee.
NEW BRIGHTON (Cheshire) E. F. Williams, 5, Waterloo Road.
NEW MILTON ... ... W. H. Lunn, "Greycot," Albert Road.

NOTTINGHAM	... E. V. Brown, 3, Eldon Chambers, Wheeler Gate.
ST. HELENS (Lancs.)	... John Orford, 124, Knowsley Road.
SHREWSBURY ...	... Major-General Sir John Headlam, K.B.E., C.B., D.S.O., Cruck Meole House, Hanwood.
TIVERTON (Devon)	... Mr. W H. Duncan Arthur, Surveyor's Office, Town Hall.
WELSHPOOL ...	... Mr. E. Wilson, Coedway, Ford, Salop.

DOMINIONS AND FOREIGN COUNTRIES.

AUSTRALIA	... Messrs. C. H. Green, and George Lawson, Anzac House, Elizabeth Street, Brisbane, Queensland. R. A. Baldwin, c/o Government Savings Bank of N.S.W., Martin Place, Sydney. Mr. W. Cloves, Box 1296, G.P.O., Adelaide.
BELGIUM	... Sister Marguerite, Sacré Coeur, Ypres.
CANADA	... Brig.-General V. W. Odlum, C.B., C.M.G., D.S.O., 2530, Point Grey Road, Vancouver. V. A. Bowes, 326, 40th Avenue West, Calgary, Alberta. W. Constable F. Grece, St. Hilaire Station, Ronville County, Quebec.
CEYLON	... Captain F. R. G. Webb, M.C., Irrigation Bungalow, Kalmunai, E.P.
EGYPT	... L. B. S. Larkins, The Residency, Cairo.
INDIA	... Lieut.-Quartermaster G. Smith, Queen's Bays, Sialkot, India.
IRELAND	... Miss A. K. Jackson, Cloneyhurke House, Portarlington.
NEW ZEALAND ...	... Captain W. U. Gibb, Ava Lodge, Puhinui Road, Papatoetoe, Auckland. S. E. Beattie, Lowlands, Woodville.
SOUTH AFRICA ...	... H. L. Versfield, c/o Cape Explosives Works Ltd., 150, St. Georges Street, Cape Town.
SPAIN	... Captain P. W. Burgess, Calle de Zurbano 29, Madrid.
U.S.A.	... Captain Henry Maslin, 942, President Street, Brooklyn, New York. L. E. P, Foot. 20, Gillett Street, Hartford, Conn, U.S.A. A. P. Forward. 449, East 80th Street, New York. J. W. Freebody. 945, McBride Avenue, Los Angeles.
NOVA SCOTIA ...	... Will R. Bird, 35, Clarence Street, Amherst.

Membership of the League

This is open to all who served in the Salient, and to all those whose relatives or friends died there, in order that they may have a record of that service for themselves and their descendants, and belong to the comradeship of men and women who understand and remember all that Ypres meant in suffering and endurance.

Life membership, £2 10s.

Annual members, 5s.

Do not let the fact of your not having served in the Salient deter you from joining the Ypres League. Those who have neither fought in the Salient nor lost relatives there, but who are in sympathy with the objects of the Ypres League, are admitted to its fellowship, but are not given scroll certificates.

There is a Junior Division for children whose relatives served in the Salient. It is open also to others to whom our objects appeal.

Annual subscription 1s. up to the age of 18, after which they can become ordinary members of the League.

THE YPRES LEAGUE (INCORPORATED)
20, Orchard Street, Portman Square, W.1.

Telephone: WELBECK 1446. *Telegrams*: YPRESLEAG, " WESDO," LONDON.

Patron-in-Chief: H.M. THE KING.

Patrons:
H.R.H. THE PRINCE OF WALES.   H.R.H. PRINCESS BEATRICE.

President: GENERAL SIR CHARLES H. HARINGTON.

Vice-Presidents:

F.-M. VISCOUNT ALLENBY.   F.-M. SIR CLAUD W. JACOB.
THE VISCOUNT WAKEFIELD OF HYTHE.   F.-M. SIR PHILIP CHETWODE.
GENERAL SIR CECIL ROMER.   F.-M. LORD MILNE.

General Committee:

THE COUNTESS OF ALBEMARLE.   MAJOR-GENERAL C. J. B. HAY.
*CAPTAIN C. ALLISTON.   MR. J. HETHERINGTON.
LIEUT-COLONEL BECKLES WILLSON.   MRS. E. HEAP.
MR. HENRY BENSON.   GENERAL SIR W. C. G. HENEKER.
*MR. J. BOUGHEY.   *CAPTAIN O. G. JOHNSON.
*MISS B. BRICE-MILLER.   *MAJOR E. MONTAGUE JONES.
COLONEL G. T. BRIERLEY.   CAPTAIN H. D. PEABODY.
CAPTAIN P. W. BURGESS.   *THE HON. ALICE DOUGLAS PENNANT.
*MAJOR H. CARDINAL-HARFORD.   *LIEUT.-GENERAL SIR W. P. PULTENEY.
REV. P. B. CLAYTON.   LIEUT.-COLONEL SIR J. MURRAY.
*THE EARL OF YPRES.   *COLONEL G. E. C. RASCH.
MRS. C. J. EDWARDS.   VISCOUNT SANDON.
MAJOR C. J. EDWARDS.   THE HON. SIR ARTHUR STANLEY.
MR. H. A. T. FAIRBANK.   MR. ERNEST THOMPSON.
MR. T. ROSS FURNER.   CAPTAIN J. LOCKLEY TURNER.
SIR PHILIP GIBBS.   *MR. E. B. WAGGETT.
MR. E. GLOVER.   CAPTAIN J. WILKINSON.
MAJOR-GENERAL SIR JOHN HEADLAM.   CAPTAIN H. TREVOR WILLIAMS.
MR. F. D. BANKS HILL.

* Executive Committee.

Bankers: *Honorary Solicitors*:
BARCLAYS BANK LTD., Knightsbridge Branch.   MESSRS. FLADGATE & CO., 18, Pall Mall, S.W.

Secretary: *Auditors*:
CAPTAIN G. E. DE TRAFFORD.   MESSRS. LEPINE & JACKSON, 6, Bond Court, E.C.4.

League Representative at Ypres: **League Representative at Cambrai:**
CAPTAIN P. D. PARMINTER.   MR. A. WILDE,
19, Rue Surmont de Volsberghe   9, Rue des Anglaises.

League Representative at Amiens: **League Representative at Arras:**
CAPTAIN STUART OSWALD.   MR. P. VYNER,
7, Rue Porte-Paris.   10, Station Square.

Hon. Secretary, Ypres British Settlement:
LT. COLONEL F. G. POOLE,

PRIMARY OBJECTS OF THE LEAGUE

I.—Commemoration and Comradeship.
II.—To provide special travel facilities for Members and all interested to Ypres and battlefields, and transport of Members.
III.—The furnishing of information about the Salient ; marking of historic sites and the compilation of charts of the battlefields.
IV.—The erection of a Ypres British Church and School which has been completed.
V.—The establishment of groups of members throughout the world, through Branch Secretaries and Corresponding Members.
VI.—The maintenance of cordial relations with dwellers on the battlefields of Ypres
VII.—The formation of a Junior Division.

Use the Ypres League Travel Bureau for Ypres and Whole of the Western Front.

FOR THE FOLLOWING PUBLICATIONS, Etc., apply:
Secretary, YPRES LEAGUE, 20, ORCHARD STREET, LONDON, W.1.

THE BATTLE BOOK OF YPRES. A history of notable deeds contributed by all regiments. 5s.; post free, 5s. 6d. Compiled by Beatrix Brice with the assistance of Lieut.-General Sir William Pulteney, G.C.V.O., etc.

BOOKS.

YPRES: Outpost of the Channel Ports. By Beatrix Brice. With Foreword by Field-Marshal Lord Plumer, G.C.B. Price 1s. 6d.; post free 1s. 10d.

In the Ypres Salient. By Lt.-Col. Beckles Willson. 1s. net; post free 1s. 2d.

With the Cornwall Territorials on the Western Front. By E. C. Matthews. 7s. 6d.; post free 8s.

Story of the 63rd Field Ambulance. By A. W. Westmore, etc. Cloth, 3s. 6d., post free. Paper, 2s. 6d., post free.

War Letters to a Wife. By Colonel Rowland Feilding. Popular Edition, 3s. 6d.; post free 4s.

The Pill Boxes of Flanders. 1s.; post free 1s. 3d.

From Mons to the First Battle of Ypres. By J. G. W. Hyndson, M.C. Price 5s., post free 5s. 3d.

YPRES LEAGUE TIES. 3s. 6d. each, post free.
YPRES LEAGUE BADGES. 2s. each, 2s. 1½d. post free.
EMBROIDERED BADGES. 4s. each, post free.
Map and List of Cemeteries in the Ypres Salient. Price 9d.; post free 11d.
Map of the Somme. Price 1s. 8d., post free.

PICTURES.

Burning of the Cloth Hall, 1915. A Coloured Print, 14 in. by 12 in. 1s. post free.

Old Well-known Spots in New Guise. Prints, size 4¼ x 2¼, recently taken of famous spots in the Ypres Salient, and which may be of great interest to our readers, are on sale at headquarters, price 4d. each, post free 5d. For particulars apply Secretary.

POST CARDS, PHOTOGRAPHS AND ETCHINGS.

Post Cards. Ypres: British Front during the War. Ruins of Ypres. Price 1s. post free.

Photographs of Menin Gate Unveiling. Size 11 in. by 7 in. 1s. 2d. each, post free.

Hill 60. Complete Panorama Photographs.
12 in. by 3¼ in. Price 3s., post free; 15 in. by 5 in. Price 3s. 6d., post free.

WAR-TIME PHOTOGRAPHS OF THE SALIENT.

6 in. by 8 in. ... 1s. 6d. each.
12 in. by 15 in. ... 4s. each.

List forwarded on application.

PHOTOGRAPHS OF WAR-TIME SKETCHES.

Bedford House (Front View), 1916.
Bedford House (Back View), 1916.
Voormezeele Main Street, 1916.
Voormezeele Crucifixion Gate, 1916.
Langhof Chateau, 1916.

Size 8½ in. by 6½ in. Price 2s. 6d. each, post free.

Photographs of the Thiepval and Arras Memorials. Post card size, price 1s. each, post free.

YPRES TIMES.

The Journal may be obtained at the League Offices. BACK NUMBERS 1s.; 1933, 8d.; 1934 6d.

Printed in Great Britain for the Publishers by FORD & GILL, 21a/23, Iliffe Yard, Crampton Street, London, S.E.17.

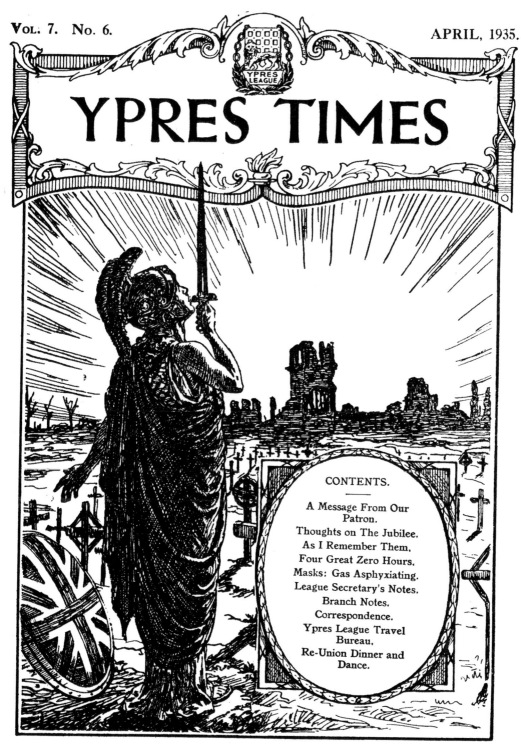

Memory Tablet.

APRIL - MAY - JUNE

APRIL

April	5th, 1917	United States declares war on Germany
,,	9th, 1917	Battle of Vimy Ridge begins.
,,	9th, 1918	Battle of the Lys begins.
,,	14th, 1918	General Foch appointed Generalissimo of the Allied Armies in France.
,,	22nd, 1915	Second Battle of Ypres begins. Germans use asphyxiating gases.
,,	22nd, 1918	British Naval attack on Zeebruge and Ostend.
,,	24th, 1916	Rebellion in Ireland.
,,	25th, 1915	Allied Forces land in Gallipoli.
,,	27th, 1915	General Sir Herbert Plumer given command of all troops in the Ypres Salient.
,,	29th, 1916	Fall of Kut.

MAY

May	7th, 1915	The *Lusitania* torpedoed and sunk by the Germans.
,,	12th, 1915	Windhoek, capital of German South-West Africa captured by General Botha.
,,	19th, 1918	Germans bomb British hospitals at Etaples.
,,	23rd, 1915	Italy declares war on Austria.
,,	31st, 1916	Sea battle off the coast of Jutland.

JUNE

June	5th, 1916	Loss of Earl Kitchener on H.M.S. *Hampshire*.
,,	7th, 1915	Flight-Lieut. Warneford attacks and destroys Zeppelin between Ghent and Brussels.
,,	7th, 1917	British victory at Messines Ridge.
,,	29th, 1917	General Allenby in command in Egypt.

The Ypres League
[INCORPORATED]

SPECIAL JUBILEE MEMBERSHIP APPEAL

(Actual size, 11 in. x 9¼ in.)
Specimen of Scroll Certificate issued to Members who have served in the Salient.

(Actual size, 11 in. x 9¼ in.)
Specimen of Certificate issued to Members who are relatives of the Killed.

Membership in the League is open to all who served in the Salient and to all whose relatives or friends died there, in order that they may have a record of that service for themselves and their descendants, and belong to the comradeship of men who understand and remember all that Ypres meant in suffering and endurance.

We also welcome to our fellowship those who sympathise with our objects, even if they neither served nor lost relatives at Ypres.

To the Secretary, Ypres League,
    20, Orchard Street, London, W.1.

I HEREBY REQUEST *that I may be enrolled as a Member of the Ypres League.*

(a) * I having served in the Ypres sector in the ....
    in the year ....   (Name of Unit)

                                    ....(rank and name)
(b) * My father ⎫
      husband   ⎬ or other   ⎰ *relative or ....
      son   ⎪   ⎱ comrade   (name and rank)
      brother   ⎭

having died on the............(date) *in the defence of Ypres while serving in the*...............................
                                                                              (name of unit)
(c) Being in sympathy with the objects of the League,
    I enclose £   :   s.   d., being ⎰ *5/- Annual Subscription
                                         ⎱ £2 10s. Life Subscription
        and balance donation for furtherance of the objects of the League

Name and Address ....
    (In Block Letters)

    ....

Date........................   ....

* Please cross out wording not applicable.   P.T.O.

Vol. 7, No. 6.   Published Quarterly   April, 1935

A Message from our Patron

IT gives me great pleasure as Patron of the Ypres League, to send greetings to every member of that body which so admirably and successfully keeps alive the memory of the heroic defence of the Salient and of the sacrifice of those who gave their lives for their Country.

I trust I may yet be spared to perform the Annual Ceremony of the laying of the wreath which, year by year, symbolizes our commemorative work.

We are celebrating this year the twenty-fifth anniversary of His Majesty The King's accession; his reign will always be memorable as that in which the greatest war in history took place, and also for the wonderful display of loyalty and devotion from every corner of his Empire. During such a year the League should make a special effort, and I should like to see each member try to swell our numbers by enlisting at the very least one from among his comrades of the Salient. Success in such a combined effort will ensure both the expansion and the continuance of our special aim, which is to keep green the memory of heroic devotion and noble self-sacrifice.

Beatrice.

(Copyright reserved).

Thoughts on the Jubilee

Twenty-Five Years of Trial and Triumph.

Retrospect and Appreciation.

(Specially Contributed to the "*Ypres Times*" by Henry Benson, M.A.)

THIS summer the British Empire will be all "for George and Merrie England!" When Queen Victoria, crowned with the glory of her Diamond Jubilee, drove through the streets of her great London in June, 1897, it was "roses, roses all the way." Now, thirty-eight years later, her grandson, King George, is to set forth from Buckingham Palace amidst the plaudits of his loyal subjects to give thanks in St. Paul's Cathedral for his Silver Jubilee—a quarter of a century, which spans the most difficult and anxious, if in some respects the most glorious, period of our Empire's history.

To old and young, to great and small, to rich and poor, the Jubilee is of personal significance. Each unit in the land feels an individual sense of proprietorship in the preparations for this festival of a nation, and Nature herself will hang out her banners of green leaves and lovely blossoms to wave, we hope, in the glittering light of a glorious May day.

Three Great Monarchs.

Victoria's task as a Sovereign was comparatively easy. She came to the throne at a time when the political clouds left by the wars with Napoleon were beginning to clear, and her reign coincided with a growth of national prosperity for which there have been few parallels in the world's history. Moreover, the young Queen had the advantage of engaging sentiment, whilst her virtues were enhanced by the unpopularity of her predecessors. At the end of her reign the British Crown had gathered an Elizabethan nimbus, partly from her outstanding political wisdom, partly from her length of years, and partly from the prosperous times, which had extended more than six decades.

Her son, Edward VII., possessed the happy gift of appealing to crowds and traits of character which commanded attention everywhere. He maintained the Crown in the prestige which he had inherited; but his reign—an epilogue to one epoch and a prologue to another—was far too short to test the quality of his political abilities as a Sovereign, remarkable as they doubtless were.

The testing time came under George. He became King in the middle of the greatest constitutional crisis since 1688, and from that day onwards he has been under a constant strain, more severe, perhaps, than any British King has been called upon to endure. One slip, a single failure of judgment or temper, and the accumulated popularity of the Crown might have crumbled.

Crisis Succeeds Crisis.

Let us look back!

When the King came to the throne in 1910 he was, as far as the general public was concerned, what the Germans call "ein unbeschriebenes Blatt"—an unwritten page. In the broad sense he was virtually unknown, save that, as the result of his Empire tours, he had shown himself ahead of many of our statemen in grasping the true greatness of the Empire idea. For the rest, his early youth and manhood had been overshadowed by a great Queen and her brilliant and tremendously popular successor. History, however, was to show, when in the fulness of time G.R. replaced E.R. as the Royal monogram, that, although the ship of State had changed its owner, the ballast was the same.

Queen Victoria, nominally a constitutional monarch, was in truth the last of our autocrats; Edward VII, represented the transitional stage, forced by the rising tide of democracy to relinquish some of the prerogatives which his predecessor had battled desperately to maintain; King George was monarch of the new order. He succeeded, as I have pointed out, in the midst of a political crisis which was none of his own making —one which all King Edward's tact and experience had been unable to avert.

His Majesty faced it, as he faced others that were to follow, with an entire absence of panic. The warring parties found themselves in the presence of an umpire above them all, whose good sense and impartiality of judgment was clearly manifest. In

Photo] [Imperial War Museum, Crown Copyright

HIS MAJESTY THE KING, H.R.H. THE PRINCE OF WALES, AND F.M. SIR DOUGLAS HAIG AT BEAUQUESNE ON AUGUST 8th, 1916.

the first year of his reign King George, single-handed, established that respect for the Crown which, based upon his rigid interpretation of his duties as a constitutional monarch, was later to be loyally maintained in the Irish crisis of 1914.

Who can forget that fateful crisis? Was ever a ruler of this country called upon to employ such momentous words as those in which His Majesty summoned the Home Rule conference at Buckingham Palace in the July of that year? "The cry of Civil War," he declared, "is on the lips of the most responsible and sober-minded of my people." In those dark days, when argument had completely been exhausted and it seemed that internecine strife was imminent, the King stepped into the breach and in very truth became the "Adviser of his Advisers." It is idle to speculate what would have happened but for the European outbreak a fortnight later; but it is quite possible that dissolution from within would have destroyed the British Empire.

Ordeal of War.

When war broke out the King was not unduly depressed, but went about his weighty daily tasks composedly. In the blackest hours of our ordeal, though his advisers were sometimes dismayed, he never swerved from his profound belief in the ultimate triumph of the right. He set a personal example of austerity and self-discipline which contributed immensely to the maintenance of the united front the Empire presented during those long and agonising years. Indeed, his attitude throughout personified the lines of Kipling :

> ." No easy hope or lies
> Shall bring us to our goal,
> But iron sacrifice
> Of body, will and soul."

He paid many quiet, unheralded visits to the front, which greatly cheered the troops, and there were almost daily inspections of soldiers and sailors at home. Moreover, during the four war years he conferred over 15,000 decorations. In each case he had made himself acquainted beforehand with the individual services of the recipients.

The truth is, of course, that, before anything else, King George is just an Englishman. He has shown himself imbued with the Englishman's sense of justice, the Englishman's pluck, the Englishman's old habit of doing his job. To no King of England has duty ever spoken with a harsher tone ; no King of England has ever obeyed her voice more submissively and courageously.

"Our Beloved Sovereign"

Facile phrases lie ready made to the hand of him who would write of Kings. But King George's record of sterling service, unassumingly and uncomplainingly rendered, is there before the whole world to take any Byzantine ring out of the phrase which usage has applied to rulers good and bad alike, the phrase, "Our Beloved Sovereign." If it is hard to be a King at all, as many monarchs have lamented, it is harder still to be a good king, especially in the circumstances of George the Fifth's accession and during the epoch-making twenty-five years he has reigned over us.

The King's is not a masterful personality. His distinguishing traits—probably inherited from his mother, Queen Alexandra—are rather kindliness, humanity and balance, and it may be that these qualities have helped him in trials where the more flamboyant attributes of kingship would have been a danger. But mere amiability would not have achieved what he has done. The late Lord Oxford is credited with the saying that if King George had been born in a private station, his political abilities would have made him Prime Minister. The two were close friends, as we well know, but Asquith was never the man to pay idle compliments, even to the best of friends. He recognised behind the King's sauvity and moderation political gifts of an exceptionally high order. Indeed, nothing else will account for the success with which he has helped the country through the many crises of his reign.

The Jubilee's Solemn Significance.

May I offer just one word of warning ? These Jubilee celebrations, culminating as they do in a Thanksgiving Service in St. Paul's Cathedral and in other services of a similar character throughout the whole Empire, should not be regarded as mere pageantry. No doubt, in a sense they are that, and as pageantry should be made as splendid as possible. But the Jubilee is much more. It links the present with the past. It seems to visualise what the monarchy has done for the Empire, and to show, as in a glass, not altogether darkly, what the monarchy may do for it in the future.

It is a call to loyalty—loyalty to the King as the Empire's head, and loyalty towards the Empire's highest and honest ideals of beneficent justice. And in its religious character—never surely to be overlooked after the trials and triumphs of the past twenty-five years—it is a re-dedication and a re-consecration, an almost visible placing of the King and his people into the very hands of Almighty God.

HOMAGE TO OUR PATRON-IN-CHIEF.

In conclusion, as a member of the Ypres League, may I offer on behalf of all its members, as well as those of the British Colony in Ypres itself, our homage and tribute to King George, our gracious Patron-in-Chief, assuring him, as in the past, of our continued and unwavering loyalty throughout the years that lie ahead? Long may he reign!

His "kingly crown" has been beset with many a thorn, and his regal path has bristled with many an obstacle; but assuredly the thorns have been rendered less acute and the path has been smoothed by the love and devotion his subjects in every part of the Empire have at all times offered to him as their Sovereign and Protector.

H.B.

As I Remember Them

By A. Douglas Thorburn, M.A. (Capt. R.F.A., S.R., retd.)
Author of "Amateur Gunners."

"*The Memory of the past will stay
and half our joys renew.*"
Thomas Moore.

EVERY man who served his country in the firing-line during the Great War has a possession of his own which can never be taken from him. No other men have it ; it is the soldier's most treasured piece of property—his memories.

We are **not** " The Lost Generation " but the generation that lived for years on clear and cloudless heights of endeavour of which ordinarily only the poets catch even a fleeting glimpse.

Some people retain in their minds a sharper picture than others of the things that happened to them. Good memories are not conferred upon favoured individuals at birth by fairy godmothers or bad memories by evilly-disposed wizards. A good memory, for incidents at any rate, is merely the result of an active and observant mind and the things in which we have taken the deepest interest leave the deepest impressions on our memories.

If the above be true, and I am sure that it is, it is quite evident that the memories of the " front-line " soldier will be clear-cut and lasting. In the firing-line a man had to use his wits and keep his eyes wide open and his brain active or lose the number of his mess.

London streets were not the only localities in those memorable days which were inhabited by two sorts of people—" the quick and the dead."

All real ex-soldiers of the Great War have a way of setting about recalling memories of the old days ; most of their sentences begin with the words " Do you remember how —?" This is all the more pleasant an exercise because, as a modern French writer has observed, the Memory serves the mind much as the liver serves the body, acting as a kind of filter, which eliminates what is offensive and poisonous and allows to pass only that which is wholesome and pleasant.

As the fortunate survivors of 20th Century War run over their recollections of the years 1914/1919 it will usually be found that memories of the fine things come up the most sharply defined and that, except in the minds of the neurotic and prurient, the hateful experiences are only dimly pictured and time fades the image.

We all know that among the millions who fought in the war there were some who were shirkers, some who had piggish habits and instincts, and some who should never have been there. The thoughts of the right sort of man turn instinctively away from recollections of what was hateful, to memories of what was fine and admirable.

It is quite an untrue picture which paints all the scenes in sombre or lurid colours. There is not one decent man who wore the King's uniform in those memorable years who cannot find tucked away in his mind memories of unselfishness, comradeship, kindness, courage, determination and gallantry, displayed by someone or other of the "greathearted gentlemen" who served with him, in the same rank, or as a subordinate or a superior.

When an ex-soldier tells me that he finds such a book as "All Quiet" true to his own experiences he was, so I think, certainly one of a rotten bad unit or probably deserved to be. To the kind of ex-soldier to whom I am writing, these lurid books do not ring true.

* * * *

I want to tell of several instances of splendid unselfishness that came my way when I was an amateur Gunner.

I will begin with a simple example of absolute unselfishness which I met with one night when, as Forward Observation Officer (F. O. O.) of my battery, I was lodging at Company H. Q. of a London Scottish battalion. The usual Company H. Q. dugout had been blown in during the morning that I arrived and a hurried move had had to be made to another and smaller dugout where the accomodation was so far below requirements that the few wire-netting bunks had to be used in rotation by three sleepers.

I came in shortly after midnight, my share of the bed being from twelve midnight (0001 hours) to 5.30 a.m. (0530 hours) "stand to." As I climbed down the forty foot deep staircase slippery with lumps of mud I trod upon a man sleeping across the stairway. He rose without a word, took me by the hand, and turning on an electric torch led me down to the dugout and carefully steered me between and over the weary men asleep all over the floor. As I was a newcomer to this Company and, of course, to this dugout, it would have been impossible for me to have reached my bed in the dark unaided without disturbing some of the sleepers.

As careful hands tucked the muddy blankets round me the kilted soldier's shirt gaped open and I saw in the dim candle-light that he was wearing a large ebony crucifix hung from his neck on a slender silver chain.

Next morning in reply to my enquiries the Company Commander, whose batman the man turned out to be, told me how this private had asked him for duties which would not involve taking lives as he was a monk in civil life. Finding that the job of officer's batman in France was entailing less hardships than fell to the lot of other privates he had tried to level things up by sleeping on the stairs so that each latecomer to the dugout would awaken him to act as guide to prevent disturbance of any of those sleeping on the floor.

* * * *

Next I will tell of an episode which illustrates excellently the spirit of comradeship displayed in the Army. Just as we were preparing to embark at Marseilles for Salonica there joined our battery a Maltese cart with mule and driver attached from the Army Service Corps.

The driver, who is the subject of this story, was middle-aged, sturdy of build, and of the toughest possible appearance. It was not long after we had landed at Salonica that it became obvious to all of us that this driver was no novice serving "for the duration" but an extremely capable and efficient soldier. He was a "lone wolf" who kept apart, ate his meals and slept by himself under his little cart. His sense of discipline was remarkable, he was as reliable as a ship's chronometer, he was neat, punctual, conscientious, an admirable horseman and horsemaster, the finest long rein driver that I ever saw. He was as tough as the sole of a boot and in spite of his age won two important lightweight boxing contests open to the whole Division. He kept Mary, the fine roan mare he soon got hold of, in show condition and his harness was always a picture.

Our Battery Sergeant Major was a superb specimen of the efficient professional senior N. C. O. After 22 years service there was literally no department of military proficiency that he had not got at his finger-tips. He was a very kindly human character, "a holy terror to the weak-kneed crocks" who was nevertheless ready to help lame dogs over stiles too high for them, and he was respected and admired by all hands.

But the B.S.M. had a weakness. Never when the battery was in action did he let it get the upper hand but on most of the rare occasions when we were out of the line he would make one night at least hideous, shouting, bawling at the top of his voice about how much he loved the Major and the horses and nonsense of that kind.

Time after time this weakness of his was reproved and forgiven, steps were taken to cover things up as far as possible, the C.O. even went so far as to take him out for a ride one morning to keep him out of sight of the General who was due for a visit of inspection.

After this the Major, a very considerate Regular officer, decided to have no more of these scenes and warned the B.S.M. that his patience was at an end and that he would take the necessary steps to have him reduced in rank and transferred to another brigade. All of us begged and implored the Major not to do this, and pointed out that the battery might not find his equal in a thousand years, but to no purpose. The C.O. was adamant.

That night when the officers of the battery were having dinner in the bell tent which served as a mess, one of the batmen said that Driver Welsh wanted to speak to the Major.

The Major, somewhat annoyed that an A.S.C. Driver should demand such a thing during dinner, sent out a message that he would see him at "office" next morning ("Office is the Artillery equivalent of Infantry "Orderly Room") but the batman returned with a reply that Driver Welsh insisted on seeing the Major at once.

"Very well" said the C.O. "Show him in."

Then there appeared in the tent doorway a little humble figure twiddling his cap in his hands and displaying every sign of agitation.

He said "I hear you're going to break the Sergeant Major. That's what I was once. Please don't."

Having disclosed this tragedy of his past, which until then had been a secret unknown to anyone, our little A.S.C. driver left the tent without another word.

His action saved the Sergeant Major.

* * * *

Pictorially stated it is correct to say that the Great War presented itself to the mind of all of us as a huge weight which had to be lifted and could only be moved out of the way by the co-operative efforts of millions of hands belonging to little figures heaving at the immense obstacle. One of these little figures was Driver Brown.

This gallant little man contrived to do his bit to help his country in spite of natural handicaps. In private life a house-painter, he was conspicuous among the drivers—mostly very small men—for his lack of inches, he was no more than 5 feet 2, and in addition he was of poor physique. As a driver his abilities were not even equal to steering satisfactorily the depressing pair of spare horses which helped in the lead of the G.S. Waggon when the battery was on the march. He was, however, a lovable little duffer and everyone overlooked his many failures, recognizing that if the flesh was weak the spirit was very willing.

One day this little fellow asked me—as his Section Commander—if he might be allowed to give up his horses and take on cutting the hay with the chaffcutter in the forage-barn. He said he hated being so useless as a driver and wanted to show us what he was worth. This was the spirit that we all tried to foster in the battery, so I at once conferred on Driver Brown the rank of O.C. chaffcutter.

In the days of horse draught in the Field Artillery the effectiveness of a battery was limited by the ability of the teams to haul guns and ammunition to where they were needed. In Macedonia and Palestine such transport included the crossing of rivers by fords, scaling of considerable mountains in roadless country, and the crossing of bogs and swamps and other obstacles. The horses had to be kept, often in spite of totally inadequate forage, in the pink of condition to be able to do their work and to make the scanty supply of hay go as far as possible, every bit was chaffed and fed in the nosebags. This meant that the chaffcutter must be kept turning round and round almost continuously. It is truly "hard labour" turning the wheel of that machine, but little Driver Brown never faltered either in the bitter cold of a Macedonian Winter or in the tropical heat of the desert. What this meant to so small a man as him may be imagined when I say that in the days when the long "field service" boots were issued in 1916 to soldiers whose duties took them into the deep mud at the horselines, no pair could be found short enough in the leg to allow this tiny driver's knees to bend, and so he had to walk about without bending them until the saddler could find time to cut the legs of his long boots down to allow him to walk properly.

Much of the splendid services of the horses was only made possible by the unceasing toil of this stout-hearted little incompetent driver at the chaffcutter. He was very proud of his office and well deserved to be.

* * * *

The reinforcements which reached us in the big Somme battle in the summer of 1918 were totally untrained. One of them was a middle-aged German Jew, Gunner Rosenberg, who was so unlikely a recruit that I made him extra-assistant-cook and part-time boot-repairer, as in civil life he had been a cobbler in the East End.

In the course of a severe German gas bombardment many of our best gunners were seriously gassed and had to be forthwith evacuated to hospital. I sorted out the less seriously disabled as they arrived at the waggon-lines riding on the ammunition waggons, and ordered them, if they were able, to sit by the fire in the cookhouse until morning. They choked if they attempted to lie down.

When daylight came a pitiable group of men, hoarse and with streaming eyes, coughing and spluttering, were still sitting round the cookhouse fire; with the exception of the Jew cobbler they were our most valuable men, layers and limber-gunners, and these I begged to try and stick it out, and they all agreed like the willing sportsmen that they were.

Gunner Rosenberg was different. He was a newcomer, an untrained foreign Jew, by birth presumably not interested in a British victory. I thought it unnecessary even to ask him to stay with us (one does not order men in the plight of these poor fellows to go or stay) and told him he'd better get off to hospital.

But this grey-haired German Jew stranger would not hear of it. He staggered to his feet and whispered hoarsely "No, Zir, I don't vant to go. I could still go on helping mit der cooking."

I shook his hand for I had no words to express my appreciation of gallantry such as his.

* * * *

To conclude these anecdotes illustrative of the unselfish spirit of the Firing Line, I want to set down an instance of self-sacrifice which reaches the summit of its splendour. All of us have read with admiration the famous story of how the dying Sir Philip Sidney at Zutphen gave the cup of water to a wounded soldier with the classic words "Thy need is greater than mine."

My own War Memories include a parallel incident which took place on the Somme Sector about September, 1918. In the 44th Brigade R.F.A. our Battery, "D" Battery, was invariably associated with "A" Battery in all operations. Our Colonel knew that the two units combined well and were united by ties of friendship in all ranks and consequently he always detailed "A" and "D" Batteries to work together.

One bright autumn morning the two Majors went forward together and selected their O.P.s not far from Epéhy and began the day's shooting. The C.O. of "A" Battery, a young Regular Captain, R.H.A., was accompanied by a telephonist and his Sergeant Major. He had not been ranging for many minutes before a 5.9 landed right on top of the little party, killed the signaller and severely wounded both the Sergeant Major and his Battery Commander. An Infantry company nearby sent a stretcher-party to the scene of the little catastrophe. There was only one stretcher. The Sergeant Major was unconscious. The Major, whose name was Miles Stavely, though very severely wounded was still in possession of all his faculties and ordered the stretcher-bearers to leave him and take the Sergeant Major to the First Aid Post.

When the stretcher-bearers returned Major Stavely was dead.

We were all proud to think that we had been his friends. His last act was of a piece with everything we knew of him, and I dare to say that this bit of utter unselfishness will shine brightly in the memories of all the men of the 44th Brigade for the rest of their lives.

Such splendid acts were not rare in those days. I am delighted to have the opportunity of setting on record the story of one of them in the " Ypres Times."

A.D.T.

The Song of Picardy (1918)

By PATRICK MACGILL.

Author of: "The Red Horizon"; "The Great Push"; "The Brown Bretheren"; Etc.

Oh! barren hearth of Picardy
    And trampled harvest field,
Say, who will light your fire at night
    Or mill your autumn yield?
No more the reaper plies his trade,
    The hours of peace are o'er,
And gone the matron and the maid,
    And they return no more.

The poppies blow in Picardy,
    The skylark sings o'erhead,
And flower and bird their vigil keep
    Above the nameless dead;
But though above the dark sky lowers,
    Beneath its gloom is set
The little seeds of Freedom's flowers,
    To rim the parapet.

And hearts are strong in Picardy,
    Where Hope is still aflame,
Where Freedom's heroes see ahead
    The goal at which they aim;
Though drear and cold the ruined hearth
    And barren fields are dumb,
A voice breathes soft across the earth
    Of peace that is to come.

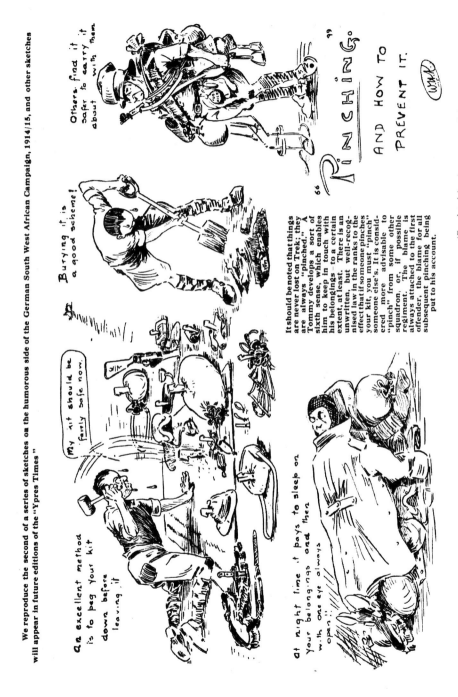

[Reprinted by the courtesy of the Argus Printing and Publishing Company and with the compliments to the author, Mr. W. H. Kirby.

Four Great Zero Hours

By Colonel Neil Fraser-Tytler, D.S.O., T.D.

Extracted from " Field Guns in France " price 3s. 6d. and obtainable from Messrs. Hutchinson, Paternoster Row, London, E.C.4.

3.10 a.m., 7th June, 1917—Battle of Messines Ridge.

PONGO, the Brigade H.Q. dog, turned up at 1 a.m. with an orderly bringing the synchronised watch and the news that Zero was at 3.10 a.m. I remember noting down that 3.10 a.m., plus 13 seconds, by our battery watch was the moment the flag should fall. After that I slept till the guard woke me at 2.30 a.m. Having made final corrections from the thermometer for the range, which was somewhat anxious work, as we were one of the creeping batteries, and had to shoot just over our infantry's heads the whole time, I got my army dressed in their gas masks at the " alert," though once they saw the enemy's number was up, they rapidly reverted to their usual state of undress while working.

It was difficult not to get the fidgets during the last ten minutes. There was gas-shelling a little on our right, and one knew if by some miracle of spy work had made known the Zero hour, a barrage might have opened on our packed assembly trenches. It was a reeking night, hot, damp, and dark, with a clouded moon. Mist rose from the marsh, and a poisonous smell of gas permeated everything.

At 30 seconds before Zero the whole earth shook with a sideways vibration, as the whole line of mines went off together. The sappers had been working at them for nearly a year, and even longer in some places, and they extended for a great distance under the German lines. I forget how many hundred tons of explosives were in each. The stupendous roar as they went up was followed 15 seconds afterwards with one rippling crash as the whole world broke into gun flashes. What an intoxicating and exhilarating noise is a " full steam " barrage. It reminds one somehow of the glorious thunder of hoofs down a hard polo ground. Once it had started all cares and troubles vanished, and beyond strolling round to visit each gun there was nothing to do. But the concussion of the myriad guns stirred up all the latent gas lying in the shell holes, and that, mixed with the N.C.T. and cordite fumes and the dense clouds of dust, made the atmosphere like nothing on earth.

The pace of our fire varied according to what was going on, e.g., during the periods of consolidation of each captured line, it would drop to a round per gun per minute, which gave us the chance of resting the guns and doing small repairs. Then as soon as the infantry were ready to move on the barrage re-formed in front of them, and having gradually worked up to " intense," crept forward once more. Very soon it grew light, but the mist persisted as usual before a hot day till late in the morning. Clarke, our F.O.O., who went over with the third wave, saw a tank trying to squash a small M.G. fort by sitting on the roof and rocking to and fro, but the reinforced cement was too strong, so it waddled back a few yards and spat its 6-pounder H.E. shells through the slits for the necessary few minutes.

To return to the guns. They stood the strain pretty well on the whole, but by 5 a.m. they were almost red hot. The scenes in the gun-pits were rather like the battle pictures of Nelson's day, a bunch of gunners stripped to the waist, covered with oil, a mount of empty shell cases, clouds of steam rising from pools of water raised to boiling point even though poured only once through the bore ; mops, rammers, more oil, dust, and debris of sand-bags made up the picture, the whole being veiled by the green mist made by the bower of verdant spotted netting which encircles the gun-pit—netting which never loses an opportunity of catching fire.

7.30 a.m., 1st July—Battle of the Somme, 1916.

The 1st of July opened with a glorious though very misty morning. Dense belts of fog were hanging in the valleys, and only the tops of the hills were to be seen. After an early breakfast at 4.30 a.m. and a final inspection of the guns, I went up to the O.P., and by six o'clock the other three battery commanders and their F.O.O.'s had also turned up, and the party for the great spectacle was complete.

All night long the bombardment had continued, but at 6.25 a.m. the final intense bombardment started. Until 7.15 a.m. observation was practically impossible owing to the eddies of mist, rising smoke, flashes of bursting shells, and all one could see was the blurred outline of some miles of what appeared to be volcanoes in eruption. At 7.20 a.m. rows of steel helmets and the glitter of bayonets were to be seen all along

AN INFANTRY ATTACK ON THE SOMME, 1916.

the front line. At 7.25 a.m., the scaling ladders having been placed in position, a steady stream of men flowed over the parapet, and waited in the tall grass till all were there, and then formed up; at 7.30 a.m. the flag fell and they were off, the mist lifting just enough to show the long line of divisions attacking—on our right the 39th French Division; in front of us our 30th Division; on our left the 18th.

The line advanced steadily, scarcely meeting any opposition in the first three lines of trenches. Every point was reached at scheduled time, so the automatic artillery barrage was always just in front of the infantry. At 9 o'clock we could see our flags waving in the trench behind German's Wood, and by 8.20 the formidable Glatz Redoubt was captured, an advance of 700 yards with very little loss. This redoubt had been submitted to a terrific bombardment, and the infantry reported that the maze of strong points, machine-gun emplacements, etc., had all been swept away, and that the trenches were crammed with dead. By 8.40 a.m. we had captured Casement Trench, and from there a dense smoke barrage was created with a view to hiding the advance of the second wave (90th Brigade), their objective being Montauban village. They went across in perfect formation up to Glatz Redoubt; there they made a short pause, and then continued the attack and captured the whole village of Montauban by 10 a.m., establishing our line on the north side of the village, overlooking Caterpillar Valley.

Between 10 and 12 noon there was a lull in the operations, and then came the capture of the Briquetterie, preceded by half-an-hour's intense bombardment. During all this time the country was dotted with little parties of prisoners, each with an escort of two men—one Tommy behind to whip up the laggards, while the one in front was usually surrounded by a crowd of prisoners, all eager to show him the quickest way back to safety and food in our lines!

After the mist lifted, the light for observing was perfect. I had of course my own glass, and also a 7-foot monster recently arrived from the Lady Roberts' Telescope Fund, and every detail showed up with the utmost accuracy. There was no enemy shelling, and gradually people emerged from their tunnels and sat on the top of the shafts till it felt quite like a "Point to Point" crowd. On the whole we had a very delightful day, with nothing to do except send numerous reports through to Headquarters and observe the stupendous spectacle before us. There was nothing to do as regards controlling my battery's fire, as the barrage orders had all been prepared beforehand and any fresh targets were dealt with by one officer, who sat all day in a dug-out by himself, with map board and battery watch before him. All orders were written on slips and sent by runners to each gun. Another officer was with the guns, while the third remained with me ready to go forward if necessary, and also to supervise the visual signalling arrangements in case our cable was broken.

5.30 a.m., 9th April, 1917—Battle of Arras.

I had a front seat in the stalls; in fact was nearly on the stage itself for this show, as my O.P., having been blown in on the previous night, I decided to see it out from a 6-ft. slit dug at night in No Man's Land, with a treble laddered 'phone line running back from it. The prospects did not look too healthy, but it was preferable to being crowded in among the observers of fifty other batteries on the popular railway embankment, ever so far back too. I intended to occupy my hole at noon, in full view of the Fritz, trusting to him being too fussed to worry about me, and so he was.

Z day, which was the 9th, began with heavy rain and hail. For the Northern Division zero hour was 5.30 a.m. Our own band, however, did not start playing till after 11 a.m. There was Hell let loose all the morning up North; by 10 a.m. we heard that Telegraph Hill was captured, and that our Tanks were careering onwards like rabbits. Just before eleven I went forward with my telephonist, and advancing across the open in full view of the enemy dropped quickly into our slit, and we awaited the first act of the drama.

About noon the 56th Division streamed across the ridge on our left, the left half of the attack getting through the wire, but the right eventually had to come back and line a sunken road some four hundred yards from the Hindenburg wire. Our counter-battery work was most vigorous, and the enemy only put up a very slight barrage, although our infantry must have presented a perfect target during their long advance across the open. About 2 p.m. the Brigades of the 30th Division commenced their attack, advancing down the slope and passing right over the holes in which we were standing. They were naturally surprised to see us there, and much chaff was in the air about our having secured front seats for the show. They had a long advance in full view the whole time, and did not launch the actual attack on the Hindenburg Line till 3.30 p.m. Previous to their final attack they had had very few casualties, which shows how nonplussed the enemy was for the moment.

While the 30th Division were advancing along the bottom of the valley, the 21st Division attacked all along the high ridge of Henin Hill on our right flank. During the last few days we had all reported time after time that the wire across the bottom of the valley was quite untouched, and sure enough the infantry found this was the case, and had to dig themselves in along a stretch of dead ground about 400 yards from the wire. However, in spite of this attack failing, our losses were not heavy, and I really think that the wire was so dense and strong that the Germans could neither see nor shoot through it from their front line.

The 21st Division did better and got through by two gaps on the extreme summit of the hill, and disappeared from view. But while we, the right-hand pivot of the attack, were being held up to some extent the divisons which had attacked earlier in the morning to the north of us began to press down almost in the rear of the enemy on our immediate front; from our perfect O.P. we could see great confusion on the roads behind Heninel, and our set programme being over at 5 p.m. we were able to engage some glorious targets—roads congested with gun limbers, retreating enemy

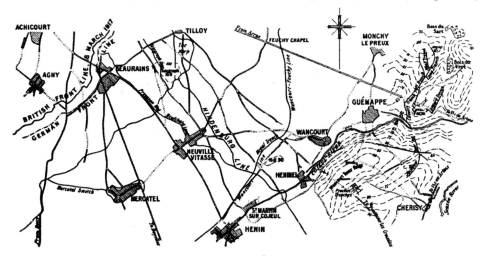

Reprinted from the history of the 2nd City of London Regiment (Royal Fusiliers) in The Great War.

and vehicles of every sort, all went into the hash together. The Germans asked for war, and now at last they were getting it in good measure, heaped up and overflowing.

3.50 a.m., 31st JULY, 1917—THIRD BATTLE OF WYPERS.

The curtain rose at 3.50 a.m., accompanied by the usual racket, reek of H.E., and rocket display by the Germans. On the whole our area was fairly peaceful, and Wilshin arrived with gun limbers at 5.45, having made an easy advance. We were due to cease firing and advance at 6.10 a.m., so at that hour the backs of the gunpits having been previously pulled down, we started the heavy labour of manhandling the guns out of their sunk pits. Luckily at that very moment a Highlander came down the track escorting 25 prisoners. I called to him to go into the cook-house and have some tea and to hand over his rifle and the prisoners to my tender mercies. The enemy was sending over some 8-inch shells, and when I ordered the prisoners to man the drag ropes they started to argue that they ought not to be made to do it, but the argument only lasted 30 seconds; the well-known sound (almost " Esperanto ") of a rifle bolt going to full cock and a few well-chosen words of abuse learnt on a Pomeranian barrack square, quickly got them to work and meanwhile our gunners were safely under cover and able to have breakfast.

We then limbered up to make our next jump of about 2,000 yards forward, moving chiefly along tracks deep in mud, and covered with new craters. A trestle bridge on our route gave way at one side, letting the leading gun fall half into the stream, which caused delay and much " heaving ". We were the last battery to advance, and all the previous batteries had to pass over our future position to reach theirs, so when we reached Potijze Chateau we found the narrow strip of ground (our position) a solid block of vehicles, with horses down everywhere, and a good deal of hostile shelling all around. It was useless waiting until they cleared off our position, so we managed to get the guns up one by one across the shell holes.

Masks: Gas Asphyxiating

By JOHN STAFFORD GOWLAND.
Author of " War is like that."

THE thunder of guns had continued steadily for forty-eight hours, and at night we could see the lurid flashes away to the North. "Ell of a do" on, up at that there perishin' " Wipers " agen," quoth Johnnie, our uncrushable cockney.

It was April, 1915 and we were blissfully ignorant of the fact that the Canadians had for the first time been faced with that new and terrible weapon, gas. How splendidly they stood their ground, totally unprepared for that horrible ordeal we all know. In an extraordinarily short time after that dreadful affair, the first gas masks made their appearance; and the subsequent evolution of that vital piece of equipment caused a number of humorous incidents. It is with this lighter side of a very unpleasant business that I partly propose to deal.

There are, alas, comparatively few of us left who remember the first gas masks. They arrived one day with the rations; little rubberized pouches resembling an ordinary tobacco pouch, but rather larger. These contained a pad of absorbent stuff sewn into a long strip of muslin which was doubled. In fact these 'gags' were suspiciously like an ordinary field dressing steeped in the vilest tasting concoction imaginable. In the event of a gas attack, this contraption was to be tied tightly over the nose and mouth, as our friend, Johnnie, expressed it after trying one on:—" If this 'ere h'asphixiation gas tystes worse'n this 'ere, it aint 'uman." But had Jerry decided to give us a taste of his gas, I have no doubt this first crude contrivance would have been a thousand times better than nothing at all: anyway they gave us a certain amount of confidence for which we were sincerely grateful to those who organized the manufacture and distribution of the gags with such amazing rapidity.

Gas mask No. 2 soon arrived. This was contained in a larger pouch with a strap for carrying across the shoulders and was known as ' gas bag '—for a bag it was; made of flannel, having two mica eye-pieces sewn in, and about where the eyes *should* come when the bag was pulled over the head providing of course that one did not place it back to front. These gas bags were saturated with the same poignantly flavoured chemical, and the open end was to be tucked in the collar of our tunics which were then buttoned and our caps perched on top of the ensemble. It was possible to breathe with difficulty, but the eye-holes became misty immediately and seeing was quite out of the question. But with all its faults, the gas bag greatly minimised our fear of gas and the morale of the troops rose accordingly.

No. 3 was a great improvement if treated with respect, but should one become too familiar and start breathing ' out of turn ' the result was somewhat embarrasing. Gas bag No. 3 still took the form of a flannel bag, but the eye-pieces were much superior and then there was the valve. This was a tin tube some six inches long, two inches of which was inside the bag and a rubber mouth piece, the remaining three or four inches protruded outside and its end was adorned by a rubber valve which must be described in detail. This valve was composed of two triangular pieces of rubber stuck together around the edges, the apex of the triangle being left open, so that the tin tube could be inserted and firmly fastened with cement. Then the two corners at the base of our triangle were cut off leaving two slits. It will now be seen that the tube could be blown through from the inner end, but to inhale was impossible, the two slits closing immediately one tried to do so. Having donned the gas bag, the procedure was to inhale through the nose and then blow through the tube which was kept tightly clenched in the teeth. This kept the eye-pieces from becoming misted to a certain extent except when one perspired, which was almost inevitable. The whole thing seemed very simple but it was amazing how easy it was to get ' out of step.'

We were on one of those alleged rests when gas bag No 3 was used, and of course in the interests of military discipline, gas mask drill by numbers was the order of the day. Our Sergeant, whom we will call Rawlings, was one of those gentlemen with a very red face, a large moustache, a pronounced chest hung rather low and always seemed rather short of breath, but Sergeant Rawlings liked things done right, and having been initiated into the mysteries of the new gas drill, he was determined that we should go through the movement with a click, in fact several clicks, and having delivered himself of a lengthy harangue, proceeded to give us a demonstration going through the motions in excellent style, unfortunately, however, he managed to end up with the wretched thing on backwards. A humorous retort from the irrepressible Johnnie produced an immediate epidemic of mirth. The Sergeant snatched off his mask, roared silence and growled something about insubordination and Cheshire cats, but as the Company C.O. was approaching the scene of operations, the Sergeant commenced again. This time he got it right and breathed as he had carefully instructed us. His first inhalation produced a deep growl ur-r-rgh to be followed as he exhaled through the tube by an extremely high and wavering ' peep ' finally terminating into a barrage of ' urghs ' and ' peeps '. The Officer looked startled, and beat a hasty retreat in direction of the Mess. Sergeant Rawlings, seeing that his demonstration was not being taken in quite the right spirit, got out of tune and lost his grip on the mouth-piece, the whole bag then began to inflate and deflate violently. The demoralization of the troops was now complete, and the Sergeant unmasked hurriedly ; the following ten minutes or so was taken up with profuse and rather impolite verbiage. Order being restored, the whole company donned their masks and the resulting musical effect was beyond description, each valve seemed to have some peculiar characteristic. Some made a deep gurgle others a shrill scream, a number waggled and a few curled up as though in disdain. The parade was doomed to failure, as far as Sergeant Rawlings was concerned, his sense of humour being considerably below par.

A few days later we went back into the line without a further exhibition of the musical qualities of gas mask No 3. The rumours that filtered through concerning the gas attack at Ypres were anything but encouraging and the decision of the wind was noted twenty times a day by everyone from the cook to the Colonel. Nothing transpired until we had been in the line for a few days, then one morning just before dawn, an overstrained sentry gazed horror-stricken over the parapet at a slowly approaching mass of vapour. For a moment or two he watched the swirling eddying menace, then grabbing an entrenching tool handle, he lustily pounded the shell-case hung on the side of the trench. In a few seconds, gas gongs were going all along the line and within a couple of minutes everyone was ' standing to .' The gas cloud was some distance away and although every man had his mask ready, none had yet put them on. The clang of the gongs faded into silence and for a short interval there was a weird and unnatural stillness. All were wondering just how efficient the masks would prove to be. Officers were giving instructions, and endeavouring to appear nonchalant, suddenly the silence was broken; from the direction of the Sergeant's dug-out came a long drawn out wail, a blubbering sound and another wail and for a moment as the sounds rapidly approached the situation was tense. Then Sergeant Rawlings appeared round a traverse wearing his mask, it appeared that in the scramble of the alarm, Rawlings could not find his own mask, someone having knocked it into the floor of the dug-out together with the only candle. All this happened in in a very short time, and our Artillery suddenly going into action, having received word of the expected attack, rather spoilt the effect. Subsequently a patrol reported that the 'gas' was merely a very heavy mist being stirred by the slight morning breeze, but its formation and the fact that numerous 'Very' lights gave it an ominous colour, we, who had not experienced the real thing can be excused for our alarm. Of course the Germans did not know what it was all about, and no doubt thinking the Artillery fire presaged an attack from our side, they retaliated with everything they had, thereby making the ensuing few hours very unpleasant.

The 4th edition of the gas mask was practically the same as its predecessor, except that the eye-pieces were made of glass and had metal frames, also tubes of paste for use in preventing misting of the glass were issued, and as Johnnie remarked, "They tystes a 'ell of a lot better". In due course the respirator with which all are familiar arrived, and a very efficient appliance it proved during our first experience with that very hideous weapon, poison gas. It was rumoured that Sergt. Rawlings, after his second experience with mask No 3, proceeded at the first opportunity to the Quartermaster's store and tried on every mask until he found one that was reasonably silent and had a well behaved valve.

A word to the younger generation who may read this narrative :—Although war undoubtedly had its lighter moments, they were but moments in those months, years, of courage, filth, suffering and utter discomfort. As an example of the horrors of that inhuman weapon, gas :—Living in Western Canada, I come in almost daily contact with some of the survivors of that debacle at Ypres twenty years ago. Every year a few of them pass on to join their comrades whose bodies lie in the cemeteries around Ypres.

Those who still linger on, constantly suffer in one way or another, and their injured lungs are and ideal breeding ground for tuberculosis, a disease that has already carried off many and gained a foothold in others. There are men who are tortured periodically with horrible gas boils, or suffer from dreadful coughs, dizzyness or fainting spells. In short, all these men gave their lives in April, 1915, for they have certainly not *lived* since.

So much for gas. If space permitted, I would like to tell of the hundreds of thousands of other sufferers who receive no pensions and were not even seriously wounded, and yet their spirit, the joy of life, was literally burned out of them. If the Ypres League impresses upon only a few of the new generation, the debt they owe to their fathers, uncles, aye and mothers who spent dreadful years of anxiety waiting for an almost daily expected telegram bearing the tidings that another loved one was gone, and further, if the League passes on the spirit of remembrance to the youngsters, then God bless it. There will come a time when a practical remembrance will be sorely needed : ceremonies held on anniversaries of an almost forgotten Great War will become rites with but little significance. It is then the remaining survivors of the war will have to look for help, (and many will need it) to the few upon whom the Ypres League and hindred organizations have passed on a spirit of genuine and grateful remembrance.

J.S.G.

Ypres Cathedral

LORD ATHLONE'S appeal for funds for an Army and Air Force Memorial to the late King Albert has brought to light some interesting relics saved from the ruins of the old Cathedral.

One parcel contained a piece of stained glass with the lead partly melted, portions of wood carving and a French rifle cartridge; they were packed in old newspapers of the "Daily Mail" and the "Reading Standard."

The "Daily Mail" was dated Wednesday, 27th January, 1915, which was the Kaiser's war birthday, and contains:

1. Picture of the Kaiser at the age of five years sitting on Queen Victoria's knee.
2. "What the Kaiser has said."
   Birthday war memories.
   To his Western Army:— "It is my Royal and Imperial Command that you concentrate your energies for the immediate present upon one single purpose, that is, that you address all your skill and all the valour of our soldiers to exterminate first the treacherous English and to walk over French's contemptible little army."
3. Among an Estate Agent's advertisement :
   "Come inland for safety."
   Houses to let or for sale.

Another packet contained a beautiful piece of stained glass from the Cathedral.

These souvenirs will be returned to the authorities at Ypres in due course.

We trust that anyone who has souvenirs of a similiar description which come from the Cathedral at Ypres will return them to the Headquarters of the Ypres League, 20, Orchard Street, Portman Square, London, W.1.

W. P. PULTENEY,
Lieut-General.

British Legion Reunion

A large reunion of the Surrey British Legion visit Ypres at Easter, when they will hand over to the authorities at Ypres, the sum of £400 to perpetuate the sounding of the "Last Post" at the Menin Gate, and the ceremony on Easter Sunday will be followed with great interest by all members of the Ypres League.

Our most hearty congratulations to the Surrey British Legion on having raised such a magnificent sum.

True Story from Ypres

By A Machine Gun Officer

Mules.

THE trouble all began with a mule, or rather two mules.

Now our Transport Officer had gone on leave and it fell to me to take his place; presumably because I knew a lot about machinery and motors but nothing whatever about mules and horses.

All our mules were carefully paired, and were the pride and joy of our Transport with the exception of one white mule.

A neighbouring battalion also had one white mule, and naturally both wanted to make a pair, so the result had been trouble for some time past and a matter of serious consequence, as I was well aware.

You can imagine my dismay when one morning along came a deputation from this battalion stating that I was to hand over our mule, as our Commanding Officer had told their people, up the line, that it would be alright ; so they had brought along another one for exchange.

Obviously they had heard that J— was on leave and dark deeds were afoot.

Indignantly I faced them " What ! hand over our precious white mule, certainly not, any way, where is your authority to make the exchange ? "

This bothered them considerably and they departed, muttering darkly, " That I should hear more of the matter."

Now something was undoubtedly at the back of it all and I was uneasy ; what would J— say on his return, if I lost the battle and failed in my charge ?

I had a decidedly bad night's sleep with dismal forebodings, and next day, sure enough, the blow fell—a message from Headquarters—I was to hand over our white mule to the battalion.

Desperately I sent a note back saying " There was surely some mistake, as J— had told me not to let them have it at any price "

I was bitterly determined to fight—if only I could hold out until J— came back.

One more day of peace, then came the worst blow of all; this time from the C. O. himself, from the line.

Dear S. " Have lost white mule at cards to C. O. Nth. Battalion, very sorry, cannot get out of it, hand it over to their T. O. at once, and get a good one in exchange."

This was awful—what was I to do ? Desperately I consulted the Transport Sergeant— no help there—we were lost.

Ideas come even to the oppressed and feeble in moments of great crisis, and I got one then.

The scheme was carefully explained to the Sergeant as we went along leading the white mule, which was evidently feeling the crisis acutely, as it was looking very depressed.

Our arrival was greeted with triumphant grins " Well so you've got to hand him over at last " said the T. O. " Won't J— be sick when he gets back."

" I'll bet he will " I replied, keeping one eye on the Sergeant, who was by now patting a very fine brown mule further down their lines.

" Of course, I must have an equally good one in exchange."

" Oh yes—of course " he replied, " Here are one or two "—"No thanks " I interrupted " They are obviously not a patch on our's—now that one over there—that brown one, is the one we must have."

I pointed to where the Sergeant was standing and the triumphant grin faded ; this was turning the tables with a vengeance ; as, according to plan, the Sergeant had spotted one of their most precious pair, which he knew quite well.

In vain their T. O. pointed out the virtues of the others ; I declined with firm dignity and the procession returned victoriously.

That night I sent the following note up to our C.O.

Sir.— I beg to report that the white mule was duly handed over to the Transport Officer Nth. Battalion ; asking for an equally good one in exchange.

For some reason, he now states that he no longer wants our mule.

The battle was over, our honour was saved. S. L. S.

"Patriotism"

OVER the ridge in Picardy the sun was setting. Its dying rays lighted up the crosses on the hillside, yet gleamed faintly through the gloom in the valley as though afraid to reveal its story.

A valley once smiling and peaceful, where men worked and little children played, where the clear stream rippled through the orchards and fields near their homes and by the church where they worshipped.

Gone now are the men and the children, their homes a heap of stones, their church a ruin, the stream, murky and foul, oozes inconsequently into the thousand holes rent in the fields and between the blackened and twisted trees of the orchards. Rude crosses mark the spot where the men died defending their homes and little ones.

Near the ruin of their church the figure of a Saint untouched still stands, stretching out its arms over the ruin and desolation as if in supplication. We read on the crosses the word " Patria." " Patriotism " to the French people has a great meaning, a word to be used not lightly, but rather with reverence. Do we ever think of it in this way ?

The present-day misuse of words and the use of exaggerated expressions by all classes of English-speaking peoples is regrettable, regrettable because the true meaning of words and phrases are lost.

Trivial things and occurrences in life are spoken of as being wonderful, awful, marvellous, fearful and terrible until their use, or rather, misuse, has long since ceased to convey to the mind any conception of their true meaning.

The word " Patriotism " is no exception. In our school days we were taught that " Patriot " meant a lover of his Country. This, too, we think has a deeper meaning —a man must prove his love by sacrifice.

It is not necessary to die like those who lie beneath the rough crosses to prove a love of your Country, but you must sacrifice something willingly for its betterment in peace or its relief in time of danger.

We say willingly sacrifice because a man out here may grumble at the hardships, render his service unwillingly, and seek only his own comfort on every occasion. His sacrifice, like the one in the early Bible story, will not be accepted as it is made grudingly. Likewise, in giving something to the betterment or relief of one's country we must give, by self-denial, of that we are in need of ourselves. The widow's mite was accepted in heaven before the rich man's gift, for, whereas he gave of his riches without denying himself, the widow sacrificed her all.

If we could therefore dissociate patriotism from services grudingly rendered, from displays, concerts, demonstrations, the singing of songs and making of speeches in which it is so freely used, and often wrongly, as these things do not prove love — and use it with reverence, a man in life or death could wish for no finer tribute to his memory than that written on the crosses in Picardy. In Picardy, where the sun sets on ruin and strife and where lie men at peace who sacrificed their all.

Pro Patria.
—*Reprinted from " The 6th K.S.L.I. News."*

League Secretary's Notes

The gracious act of Her Royal Highness Princess Beatrice in contributing an introductory message to this edition of the "Ypres Times" will be received with unanimous appreciation by every member of the Ypres League, and our Patron's solicitation to us all in this Jubilee Year will surely result in wholehearted response, and with this in view, we are enclosing a membership form with each copy of this journal headed "Jubilee Membership Appeal" and we trust that every form will play a practical part in helping to swell the League's membership before the end of 1935 when we shall look forward to the pleasure of conveying to Her Royal Highness, a good report of our loyal endeavours.

We struck an optimistic note in the last January edition of the "Ypres Times" and the first quarter of our 15th anniversary year has shown that, so far, our forecast was justified. February is usually regarded as the month in which time can be given more leisurely to office records and to the preparation for the summer pilgrimages and independent travel to the cemeteries and battlefields, but this year, the month proved a happy exception and even busier than any period during the height of a summer season for no less than four regimental lecture battlefield tours were organized to take place this March, namely :—March 1st to 4th thirty three Officers of the 168th Infantry Brigade to Amiens., March 15th to 18th thirty one Officers of the 167th Infantry Brigade to Ypres., March 18th to 22nd, 33 Officers of the 4th Guards Brigade on a circular tour Paris—Compiégne—Cambrai—Ypres—Boulogne., March 22nd to 24th a syndicate party of 90 Officers and other ranks of the Honourable Artillery Company with headquarters at Arras. We consider it a privilege and a great honour to be entrusted to carry out the arrangements for these official Regimental Tours.

Membership, so important an item in our sphere of activities, is also very satisfactory, and for an exceptionally good start to the year in the matter of new members recruited, we are indebted very much to our three principal Branches, namely :—Purley, Colchester and London, all of whom have already shown extremely creditable returns. There certainly appears every prospect of a highly interesting competition between these Branches for the honour of winning the fifth annual recruiting prize in this 1935 Jubilee year.

The outstanding effort of the Purley Branch in recruiting 31 new members at their last Re-union Dinner deserves special praise.

The London County Committee have continued to hold their popular monthly gatherings and an account of the Childrens Christmas Party will be found in Branch Notes. Successful annual re-union dinners have proved the strength of our Purley and Colchester Branches and the Purley Branch again deserves special thanks for their extremely generous gesture in contributing ten guineas towards the League's charitable work. Also during the past quarter our Brisbane representatives, Mr. C. H. Green and Mr. G. Lawson have been prominent in their recruiting of new members and we owe them gratitude for the way in which they have retained the interest among our existing Brisbane members.

It is pleasing to note that the January, 1935 edition of the "Ypres Times" was so well received by our members. Many letters have been received emphasising the interesting reading of this particular number—a great encouragement, because as the years roll on it is becoming increasingly difficult to procure suitable articles of the standard required, and we appeal to all our ex-service members possessing literary ability, who have not already contributed to the columns of the journal to help in this direction either by writing their own reminiscences or forwarding to headquarters the name and address of any of their friends whom we might approach. Such valuable assistance would be immensely appreciated.

Financial aid for the maintenance of our journal is still very gratefully being received from both Subscribing and Life Members and we would like to place on record, a recent and most generous cheque for £5 to the fund from our true and faithful friend, Mrs. L. K. Briggs of Broadstairs who has also conformed with many other members and paid in advance for the next four quarterly editions.

As Secretary of the Ypres League I would like to add a personal word to conclude this note, and that is my desire for all members to strive their hardest in loyal support of our distinguished Patron's message. Let us all make a firm resolution to recruit one new member for the Ypres League before Christmas and double our membership in this Silver Jubilee Year of our Patron-in-chief, His Majesty The King.

BURNING OF THE CLOTH HALL, 1915.

A few remaining coloured prints now in stock are being offered to our members at the reduced rate of 1s. each, post free.

Since further copies are unobtainable we would advise those interested to make their purchase without delay.

EMBROIDERED BADGES.

These badges can be supplied at 4s. each, post free. A considerable number have already been sold, and we are delighted to hear that the badges have given entire satisfaction to our members who have received them. Applications to the Secretary.

YPRES LEAGUE BADGE.

The design of the badge—a lion guarding a portcullis gate—represents the British Army defending the Salient, which was the gate to the Channel Ports.

The badge, herewith reproduced, is brilliantly enamelled with silver finish. Price 2s., post free 2s. 1½d. (pin or stud, whichever is desired).

Obtainable from Secretary, Ypres League, 20, Orchard Street, London, W.1.

YPRES LEAGUE TIE.

Dark shade of cornflower blue relieved by a narrow gold stripe. In good quality silk.

Price 3/6d., post free.

Obtainable from Secretary, Ypres League, 20, Orchard Street, London, W.1.

OLD WELL-KNOWN SPOTS IN NEW GUISE.

The following prints, size 4¼ x 2½, recently taken of famous spots in the Ypres Salient, and which may be of great interest to our readers, are on sale at headquarters, price 4d. each, post free 5d.

Poelcapelle Church.
Ramparts at the Lille Gate.
Hell Fire Corner, Left.
Hell Fire Corner, Right.
Shrapnel Corner.
Transport Farm Cemetery.
Transport Farm Corner.
Zillebeke Lake.
Hill 62, Canadian Memorial.
Hooge from Zouave Wood.
Hooge Crater Cemetery.
Clapham Junction.
Stirling Castle.
Gheluvelt Church.
Cheddar Villa Dressing Station.
Vancouver Cross Roads.
Canadian Memorial: Vancouver Cross Roads.
Hyde Park Corner. (Memorial.)
Wulverghem.
Messines Church.
Potsdam Redoubt at Corner Cott.

Obtainable from Secretary, Ypres League, 20, Orchard Street, London, W.1.

WREATHS.

Arrangements are made by the Ypres League to place wreaths for relatives on the graves of British soldiers situated in France and Belgium at the following times of the year:—

EASTER, ARMISTICE DAY, CHRISTMAS.

The wreaths may be composed of natural flowers, laurel, or holly, and can be bought at the following prices—12s. 6d., 15s. 6d., and 20s., according to the size and quality of the wreath.

THE BRITISH TOURING SERVICE

Manager—Mr. P. VYNER
Representative and Life Member, Ypres League

**10, Station Square
ARRAS
(P.-de-C.) France**

Cars for Hire, with British Driver Guides — Tours Arranged

Branch Notes

PURLEY BRANCH.

The Seventh Annual Dinner of the Purley Branch was held on Thursday, March 7th, at the Red Lion Hotel, Coulsdon, when a still larger company was present than on any previous occasion, and the evening was unanimously voted a great success. In spite of a few unavoidable absences, 136 members and their guests attended and enjoyed an excellent dinner — or, as the menu termed it, " Engagement."

The Chairman of the evening was once again Major H. G. Harris, who was the first Chairman of the Branch, and his harangue of the troops was quite properly labelled, the C.O.'s Gas Attack! Major Harris drew attention to the fact that we were in danger of losing some members owing to their allowing membership annual subscriptions to lapse which was surely not the wish or the spirit of the Purley Branch, and he also spoke very kindly and sympathetically of the members who had passed over during the previous year. The C.O. continued by saying that it was five years since any reference had been made to the control and constitution of the Branch, and he felt he should ask the members if they were satisfied as things were, or whether any changes were desired, such as Committee personnel: the response left no room for doubt that nobody thought they could run it and better. In conclusion, the Cups were presented to last year's winners of the Bombardier's Foursomes, namely: Captain A. S. Green and Captain W. K. Scott, and the Runners-up Prizes to Lieut. C. J. Frost and Rfm. G. D. Green.

An entertainment by Fred Gwyn and Sam Mann was then turned on and continued throughout the evening and during the intervals between the speeches: the artists were in very good form and contributed largely to the success of the evening.

The Adjutant called on for his report attributed the success of the previous year to Bill Haine, the Chairman, who was such a forceful and successful leader, and to the troops who followed him so well wherever he led. News of the annual receipt of the Ypres League Branch Recruiting Prize was received with acclamation. All the events of the year were then reported, including the golf competitions, Armistice Sunday Parade, and the Branch Dance last December, which was so successful that the Committee found it possible to send Ten Guineas to the Ypres League for ex-service purposes, and Ten Guineas to Earl Haig's Fund for Officers. After referring to the part played by the Committee in the year's work, as well as the Orderly Room, the Adjutant then suggested that all the guests(who had already been provided with the necessary forms) should forthwith be enrolled as members of the Branch, in order that Bombardier O. Mears, who was deputising for Captain de Trafford, should see how it was done This immediately led to the surrender of 31 guests present.

Major S. F. Wood proposed the Toast of our Gallant Allies, and welcomed amongst many others, Lieut.-General Sir W. P. Pulteney, Major-General P. R. C. Commings, Lieut.-Colonel F. G. Poole, and Bombardier O. Mears, from Headquarters.

After the toast had been honoured, Sir William Pulteney and General Commings, each made a most delightful speech, and we were happy to think that our Corps Commander of the past had enjoyed last year's function sufficiently to come again.

The final Toast of the C.O. was proposed very appropriately by Captain " Plug " Street, who gave us what he termed the public and private life of the Chairman to the great edification and no small amusement to new and old members alike. The C.O. responded in his usual modest way, and then we found that one more of these delightful functions had concluded — perhaps a little later, but certainly better than ever.

LONDON COUNTY COMMITTEE.

The London Informal Gatherings continue to maintain their popularity at the Bedford Head Hotel, Maiden Lane, Strand, W.C.1, and good attendances are mustered on the third Thursday in each month. These Gatherings which have afforded so much pleasure to the many members and friends attending them in the past, are promoted with the double object of enabling ex-service men to meet together in convivial atmosphere, to renew old acquaintances, and to further the wonderful spirit of comradeship of the Great War which is so prominent a feature in the League's great work of Commemoration.

It has been a great pleasure for us to observe the presence of so many members of the 5th Army O.C.A. at recent Gatherings and we are most grateful to them for extending us such valuable support. We sincerely hope that they may continue to patronise our functions at which they may always be assured of a hearty welcome.

The February meeting was honoured by the " St. Dunstan's Singers Party " under the personal direction of Miss E. McCall and the truly excellent programme will be long remembered by all who were fortunate enough to be present.

At our March Informal, we enjoyed an illustrated talk on Ypres and other places by Captain H. D. Peabody, D.C.M.

The April Gathering will be held at the Bedford Hotel at 7.30 p.m. on the fourth Thursday in that month, instead of the third.

Annual Reunion Dinner and Dance.

The London County Committee announce that the Eleventh Annual Dinner and Dance will be held on Saturday, May 4th, at the Royal Hotel, Woburn Place, W.C.1, at 7 p.m. The Committee hope for a record attendance to mark this Jubilee Year. Application for tickets, together with remittance (Tickets, 6s. 6d. each), should be sent, not later than May 4th, to the Hon. Secretary, London County Committee, Ypres League, 20, Orchard Street, London, W.1.

We regret to report the severe illness of Mr A. R. Ford, one of our most esteemed members of the London Branch Committee. We wish Mr. Ford a speedy and complete recovery.

Children's Christmas Party.

Saturday, January 12th, marked the annual fixture of the Children's Christmas Party organised by the London County Committee. The large hall at the Westminster City School was placed at our disposal by the kind permission of the Governors of the School. The hall had been tastefully decorated over-night by several energetic members, and in thanking them for their labours we do not forget the valuable help given by other staunch members who worked such long hours in preparing the Christmas tea feast.

The music was again supplied most admirably by the Enfield College of Music, under the able direction of Mrs. Peabody.

At 4 p.m. some 160 children sat down to enjoy a thoroughly good tea after which the room was cleared and all present assembled for a conjuring entertainment by Mr. Winchcombe, who delighted both children and adults alike with his amazingly clever tricks which provided an hour's continual laughter. The children then indulged in various games of musical chairs, bumps, etc.

Father Christmas made his expected appearance to the greeting of cheers loud and long, and taking charge of the party, expressed his pleasure at being able to attend and addressed a few appropriate words on the aims and objects of the Ypres League. A present was then distributed to each child from the well decorated and heavily-laden tree, and an exceedingly happy and successful evening terminated with the singing of "Auld Lang Syne" followed by The National Anthem. A further gift of fruit and sweets was presented to each youngster on leaving the hall.

The London County Committee would like to tender very grateful thanks to all who so generously contributed to the great success of the function giving special mention to Mrs. Peabody and her Orchestra, to Mr. Winchcombe, the conjurer, to Mrs. Glover, Miss M. Riddelsdell, Miss N. Greaves and last, but not least, to Captain H. D. Peabody, D.C.M., for his excellent impersonation of Father Christmas.

LONDON COUNTY COMMITTEE

Informal Gatherings

These will be held at the

BEDFORD HEAD HOTEL,

Maiden Lane, Strand, W.C.2

on

THURSDAY, APRIL 25th, 1935.

THURSDAY, MAY 16th, 1935.

THURSDAY, JUNE 20th, 1935.

From 7.15 to 10 p.m.

Will you kindly make these gatherings known amongst your own circle and interest some ex-Service man in the Ypres League in order to increase our membership?

Particulars will be sent to any friend on the name and address being supplied, and members are urged to help all they can in this direction.

Ladies cordially invited.

THE
ANNUAL MEETING
of the
LONDON COUNTY COMMITTEE

will take place on

FRIDAY, MAY 17th, 1935

at the

YPRES LEAGUE OFFICES

20, Orchard Street,

Portman Square, W.1.

at 7.30 p.m.

The business will be to receive the Report of the London County Committee for the past year and to elect the Committee for the ensuing year. Members are earnestly requested to attend, and the Committee will be glad to receive any suggestions to further the interests of the League in the London area. Should any members have proposals to make, will they please forward them to the Hon. Secretary, London County Committee, Ypres League, at 20, Orchard Street, W.1., by May 12th.

COLCHESTER BRANCH

Thursday, February 7th marked the occasion of the Third Annual re-union dinner of the Colchester & District Branch of the Ypres League held at the Red Lion Hotel.

The date unfortunately co-incided with another important local celebration, nevertheless a very representative gathering of some 70 Great War veterans assembled under the presidency of Lieut-Colonel H. W. Herring, M.C. (Chairman of the Branch) and enjoyed an extremely pleasant evening.

The chief guest of honour was the Chairman of the Ypres League, Lieut.-General Sir W.P. Pulteney, G.C.V.O., K.C.B., K.C.M.G., D.S.O., and amongst those present were :—Brigadier H.N.A. Hunter, D.S.O., (Commanding the 11th Infantry Brigade at Colchester), Brig. General qualification because those who served overseas were equally welcomed as members.

A rousing reception was accorded to Lieut.-General Sir William Pulteney when he rose to reply. The General heartily congratulated the Branch on its growth, remarking that to have started so many years after the war and to achieve such success was a wonderful performance and showed that those who have joined the Branch had the real spirit of comradeship. The speaker said that the Ypres League had assisted that comradeship, not only among its members, but also among all who served in the war including the ex-service men who were employed in the Ypres Salient at the present time, and the organisation of pilgrimages to the Salient for poor relatives to see the graves of those they loved had done a great deal of good

3rd Annual Re-union Dinner of the Colchester Branch.

F.W. Towsey, C.M.G., C.B.E., D.S.O. (wartime Commander of the Colchester Garrison) Major G. C. Benham, M.C., Captain C. J. Round, D L., Dr T.M. Fripp., Mr. Alec E. Blaxhill., Revd. S. L. Dolph and Revd. F.R.P. Carrick.

Through the kind permission of the Officer Commanding, the band of the 5th Inniskilling Dragoon Guards was present and rendered selections during the dinner.

After honouring the loyal toast, the esteemed Chairman proposed the " Ypres League " and in course of his remarks, Colonel Herring stated that the League stood for three things, namely :—comradeship, faith, and love of our country, for he did not think anyone in the front line of the Ypres Salient ever thought that we were going to lose the war. It was their faith, probably more than anything else which pulled them through and he considered that faith was based on love of their country. In conclusion, the Chairman informed the gathering that the strength of the Branch was 43 country members and a similar number of town members. All present were urged to assist in recruiting further members for the Branch, adding that service at Ypres was not an essential and brought extraordinary expressions of gratitude. Sir William Pulteney then spoke briefly on the British School at Ypres which had been built for the children of the employees of the Imperial War Graves Commission and that there were now 120 children in attendance. All these children had previously been receiving their education in Belgian schools. They could hardly speak a word of English and in consequence were rapidly becoming lost to their own country. The appreciation of the parents well recompensed the promotors in the work they had accomplished in respect of the school.

" The Visitors " was proposed by Major Benham who observed that the presence of so distinguished a soldier as Lieut.-General Sir William Pulteney was the greatest honour and reward that could be extended to the Branch for the effort made to establish the Ypres League in Colchester. The Branch was fortunate in possessing a very keen Chairman in Colonel Herring and a splendid Secretary in Mr. Snow. After referring to the great deeds and sacrifices of the Salient, Major Benham emphasised very strongly that the Ypres League did not, as some people seemed to imagine, glorify in war, but was doing everything possible to advance the cause of peace which we all held so dear.

The Revd. S. L. Dolph responded humorously and touched a happy note, after which the company settled down to enjoy a programme of mirth and melody by the Regina Concert Party from Ipswich. A special word of praise and thanks was due to these very capable and clever artistes who maintained the close attention of the whole gathering throughout their delightful entertainment.

In the arrangements of this particularly successful function, Mr. H. Snow was ably assisted by Captain A. C. Palmer, Mr. Nixon, (Toast-master) and members of the Branch Committee.

Correspondence

CHIPPENHAM.
January 18th, 1935.

To The Editor, " Ypres Times"
Dear Sir,

Captain Thorburn's account of his dream in Ypres in 1920 and appeal to any reader of his story to enlighten him as to whether any such incident ever occurred, prompts me to write you of another incident, although I am afraid it has no connection with Captain Thorburn's dream, but it does, however, help to show how well merited is the praise he utters in regard to work done and risks run by members of the Kite-Balloon Section, which as he says was passed almost unnoticed amidst the possibly more strenuous but not less heroic events of the war.

May I therefore add my humble but intense admiration of the quiet gallantry of the "Balloonatics" as Captain Thorburn calls them. Did I not see twelve of them in the air at the same time with parachutes open early in June 1917 when just before the Battle of Messines, Fritz came over single-handed and set alight six balloons in a row, situated between Wulverghem and Armentieres, and all within less than six minutes ! Such was the hardness of war that far from any anxiety as to the safety of the parachutists or regret at the loss of the balloons, I can remember nothing but laughter from all spectators. But the incident which I intended to relate happened shortly after and though more tragic, I regret to say, also ended with a laugh.

On the early morning of July 31st 1917, I was riding down the almost deserted main road from Vlamertinghe and arrived at the outskirts of Ypres and noticed Gold Fish Chateau immediately on my left front. It was just previous to Zero hour for the commencement of the lamentable Passchendaele affair. Everything seemed deathly still, the barrage not having started, there was a thick mist and one of our planes appeared from nowhere and roared over my head from right to left, flying so low that it seemed to barely clear the tree stems lining the pave causing my hardened old horse to halt abruptly. I looked up and gave a wave of my hand and the pilot, to my surprise, waved back. I still focussed my eyes on him and was wondering what his job was when, to my dismay, saw him suddenly nosedive and crash. I galloped across to discover that both pilot and observer had been killed. The position of the disaster, if my memory serves me, was approximately 300 yards North of the Ypres-Poperinghe road, the immediate locality, which a minute before, had appeared destitute of all humanity was at once crawling with various details emerging like rabbits from their burrows.

I had no idea at first what had caused the sudden calamity to my, even now, unknown friend who had waved his hand to me one moment and whom I helped to lift out of his cockpit a minute later with his brains dashed out.

I heard a group near-by, laughing, and though accustomed to the priceless and invaluable callousness of Tommy at war, which was I think assumed to some extent by us all, partly to cloak our real feelings and partly an innate consciousness that if every casualty was taken too seriously, it would be impossible to get through the war at all, but on this occasion I looked up with some indignation, soon to find myself also smiling, for we discovered that owing to the mist, the unfortunate pilot had flown into the wire rope holding a Kite-Balloon which had caused the crash and furthermore severed the hawser. In consequence the balloon was freed, and the wind being from the West set it careering gallantly towards the enemy's lines. The two occupants of the Basket were making a very hurried escape per parachute. However, I heard later that day, they had both just succeeded in reaching terra firma on our side of the front line and were unhurt despite the barrage of German rifle fire.

I never even knew the names of the two poor fellows of the aeroplane and I can only end my account of one of the small and unrealised incidents of war with the hope that if either of the two parachutists are alive to-day and should happen to read this letter, they will forgive my admitted smiles at the time of their unfortunate predicament and let us know if their descent really did end as happily as was reported that evening and I have always most sincerely hoped it did.

Yours truly,
H.R. Yorke (*Major*),
War-Yeo Attached No. 2.
Traffic Control Squadron.

Episode

IN May, 1915 — after the first gas attack — some of the exhausted troops were billeted in farms adjacent to the village of Outtersteene, south-west of Bailleul. Here a large number of the men having recovered from the long and tiring march from the Salient, which all but proved the last straw, congregated in an estaminet and, having pooled their finances, ordered champagne to the limit of their funds.

The quaffing of the contents of the five-franc bottles served by " madame " and her daughter greatly accelerated the reaction from the tremendous strain of the past two weeks. In a very short time the hilarious crowd burst forth into song.

One fellow endeavoured to teach madame a step-dance to the tempo of a mechanical contraption which emitted weird noises — acclaimed by mademoiselle as " MUZEEK." Several men danced on the rickety tables, causing glassware to crash to the floor. While onlookers fed five-sou pieces into the slot of the barrel organ and shuffled and stamped their feet. This rumpus, accompanied by the vocal efforts and the intermittent popping of corks, created an uproarious din ; which drifted down the street to where the commanding officer was billeted. The C.O., an austere disciplinarian, forthwith despatched an officer to investigate the cause of the disturbance, and put an end to the racket.

The officer needed no directing. He straightway made for the estaminet, arriving just as madame had mastered the double-shuffle and the terpsichorean tutor was turning his attention to mademoiselle.

Exercising diplomacy the officer persuaded the men to desist, and to ensure against a repetition of the orgy, urged the men to quit the premises.

With the " MUZEEK " belching forth at full blast, the men — whose francs had rapidly diminished — ceased from their revelry and dejectedly sauntered out to the road. Here they gathered in a group and debated the prospects of raising further funds with a view to visiting another estaminet.

At this juncture a horseman, at walking pace, passed the group of men, wheeled about, and rode up to the disorderly crowd.

" Men," said he, " I was never more proud of this (as he tapped the red band on his arm, inscribed with the word ' CANADA ') than I am to-day." — It was General Alderson, apparently still absorbed with the words of the Commander-in-Chief : *" The Canadians saved the situation."*

EDWIN PYE.

HOTEL
Splendid & Britannique
YPRES

GRANDE PLACE. Opposite Cloth Hall.

LEADING HOTEL FOR COMFORT AND QUALITY, AND PATRONIZED BY THE YPRES LEAGUE.

COMPLETELY RENOVATED.

RUNNING WATER.   BATHROOMS

MODERATE TERMS.   GARAGE.

Proprietor—Life Member, Ypres League.

YPRES
Skindles Hotel

(Opposite the Station)

Proprietor—Life Member, Ypres League

Branch at Poperinghe

(close to Talbot House)

Ypres League Travel Bureau

CONDUCTED PILGRIMAGES FOR 1935

EASTER (APRIL 20th—23rd, Saturday to Tuesday) YPRES (Day route via Ostend).

WHITSUNTIDE (JUNE 8th—11th, Saturday to Tuesday) (Two separate pilgrimages):
    YPRES (Day route via Ostend).
    ARRAS (Day route via Boulogne).

AUGUST BANK HOLIDAY (AUGUST 3rd—6th, Saturday to Tuesday) (Two separate pilgrimages):
    YPRES (Day route via Ostend).
    ARRAS (Day route via Boulogne).

SEPTEMBER (SEPTEMBER 21st—24th, Saturday to Tuesday) YPRES (Day route via Ostend).

YPRES. *Cost.* LONDON to YPRES return via OSTEND, with full board and best available accommodation (three nights) including taxes and gratuities at hotel.

Second Class Train (1st Class Boat)	£5 5 0
Second Class Train and Boat	£4 16 6
Third Class Train (1st Class Boat)	£4 10 0
Third Class Train and Boat	£4 1 6

ARRAS. *Cost.* LONDON to ARRAS return via BOULOGNE, with full board and best available accommodation (three nights) including taxes and gratuities at hotel.

Second Class Train (1st Class Boat)	£6 18 10
Second Class Train and Boat	£6 8 10
Third Class Train (1st Class Boat)	£6 0 11
Third Class Train and Boat	£5 8 11

The above quotations do not include meals on the journey or excursions on the continent.

(Battlefield tours arranged by the Conductor at Ypres or Arras to suit the requirements of the party at moderate charges).

Prospectuses will be gladly forwarded on application to The Secretary, Ypres League, 20, Orchard Street, London, W.1.

INDEPENDENT TRAVEL.

To those contemplating individual travel, our Travel Department would be pleased to furnish information on all matters connected with trips to any part of the Old Western Front Battlefields.

Apply to Secretary, Ypres League, 20, Orchard Street, London, W.1., for the Ypres League Travel Guide for 1935.

THE ELEVENTH ANNUAL

RE-UNION
DINNER AND DANCE

ORGANIZED BY THE

LONDON COUNTY COMMITTEE

OF

THE YPRES LEAGUE

will be held at the

ROYAL HOTEL

Woburn Place, W.C.1

(*nearest Tube Station, Russell Square*)

at 6.30 p.m. for 7 p.m.

On SATURDAY, MAY 4th, 1935

Members and their friends are very earnestly requested by the London County Committee to support the Dinner and Dance, in order to secure a record Gathering.

Evening Dress Optional.   *Decorations and Medals to be Worn.*

Tickets 6s. 6d. each   **Ladies Cordially Invited**

Early application for tickets, accompanied by remittance, should be sent to the Hon. Secretary, London County Committee, Ypres League, 20, Orchard Street, Portman Square, London, W.1., not later than May 2nd.

Branches and Corresponding Members

BRANCHES.

LONDON	Hon. Secretary to the London County Committee : J. Boughey, 20, Orchard Street, London, W.1.
	E. LONDON DISTRICT—L. A. Weller, 40, Lambourne Gardens, Hornchurch, Essex.
	TOTTENHAM AND EDMONTON DISTRICT—E. Glover, 191, Landowne Road, Tottenham, N.17.
	H. Carey, 373, Sydenham Road, S.E.26.
COLCHESTER	H. Snow (Hon. Sec.), 9, Church Street.
	W. H. Taylor (Pilgrimage Hon. Sec.), 64, High Street.
GATESHEAD	Lieut.-Colonel E. G. Crouch, 8, Ashgrove Terrace.
LIVERPOOL	Captain A. M. Webster, Blundellsands.
PURLEY	Major Graham Carr, D.S.O., M.C., 112-114, High Street.
SHEFFIELD	Captain J. Wilkinson, "Holmfield," Bents Drive.
BELGIUM	Capt. P. D. Parminter, 19, Rue Surmont de Volsberghe, Ypres.
CANADA	Ed. Kingsland, P.O. Box 83, Magog, Quebec.
SOUTH AFRICA	L. G. Shuter, Church Street, Pietermaritzburg.
KENYA	C. H. Slater, P.O. Box 403, Nairobi.
AMERICA	Representative : Captain R. Henderson-Bland, 110 Wet 57th Street, New York City.

CORRESPONDING MEMBERS

GREAT BRITAIN.

ABERYSTWYTH	T. O. Thomas, 5, Smithfield Road.
ASHTON-UNDER-LYNE	G. D. Stuart, "Woodlands,", Thronfield Grove, Arundel Street.
BANBURY	Captain C. W. Fowke, Yew Tree House, King's Sutton.
BIRMINGHAM	Mrs. Hill, 191, Cattell Road, Small Heath.
	John Burman, "Westbrook," Solihull Road, Shirley.
BOURNEMOUTH	H. L. Pasmore, 40, Morley Road, Boscombe Park.
BRISTOL	W. S. Hook, "Wytschaete" Redland Court Road.
BROADSTAIRS	C. E. King, 6, Norman Road, St. Peters, Broadstair.
	Mrs. Briggs, North Foreland House.
CHATHAM	W. N. Channon, 22, Keyes Avenue.
CHESTERFIELD	Major A. W. Shea, 14, Cross Street.
CONGLETON	Mr. H. Dart, 61, The Crescent.
DARLINGTON	D. S. Vigo, 125, Dorset Road, Bexhill-on-Sea.
DERBY	T. Jakeman, 10, Graham Street.
DORRINGTON (Salop)	Captain G. D. S. Parker, Frodesley Rectory.
EXETER	Captain E. Jenkin, 25, Queen Street.
GLOUCESTER	H. R. Hunt, "Casita," Parton Lane, Churchdown.
HERNE BAY	Captain E. Clarke Williams, F.S.A.A., "Conway," Station Road.
HOVE	Captain G. W. J. Cole, 2, Westbourne Terrace, Kingsway.
LEICESTER	W. C. Dunford, 343, Aylestone Road.
LINCOLN	E. Swaine, 79, West Parade.
LLANWRST	A. C. Tomlinson, M.A., Bod Estyn.
LOUGHTON	Capt. O. G. Johnson, M.A., Loughton School.
MATLOCK (Derby)	Miss Dickinson, Beechwood.
MELROSE	Mrs. Lindesay Kelsall, Darnlee.
NEW BRIGHTON (Cheshire)	E. F. Williams, 5, Waterloo Road.
NEW MILTON	W. H. Lunn, "Greycot," Albert Road.

NOTTINGHAM ...	E. V. Brown, 3, Eldon Chambers, Wheeler Gate.
ST. HELENS (Lancs.)	John Orford, 124, Knowsley Road.
SHREWSBURY ...	Major-General Sir John Headlam, K.B.E., C.B., D.S.O., Cruck Meole House, Hanwood.
TIVERTON (Devon)	Mr. W H. Duncan Arthur, Surveyor's Office, Town Hall.
WELSHPOOL ...	Mr. E. Wilson, Coedway, Ford, Salop.

DOMINIONS AND FOREIGN COUNTRIES.

AUSTRALIA ...	Messrs. C. H. Green, and George Lawson, Anzac House, Elizabeth Street, Brisbane, Queensland.
	R. A. Baldwin, c/o Government Savings Bank of N.S.W., Martin Place, Sydney.
	Mr. W. Cloves, Box 1296, G.P.O., Adelaide.
BELGIUM ...	Sister Marguerite, Sacré Coeur, Ypres.
CANADA ...	Brig.-General V. W. Odlum, C.B., C.M.G., D.S.O., 2530, Point Grey Road, Vancouver.
	V. A. Bowes, 326, 40th Avenue West, Calgary, Alberta.
	W. Constable F. Grece, St. Hilaire Station, Ronville County, Quebec
CEYLON ...	Captain F. R. G. Webb, M.C., Irrigation Bungalow, Kalmunai, E.P.
EGYPT ...	L. B. S. Larkins, The Residency, Cairo.
INDIA ...	Lieut.-Quartermaster G. Smith, Queen's Bays, Sialkot, India.
IRELAND ...	Miss A. K. Jackson, Cloneyhurke House, Portarlington.
NEW ZEALAND ...	Captain W. U. Gibb, Ava Lodge, Puhinui Road, Papatoetoe, Auckland
	S. E. Beattie, Lowlands, Woodville.
SOUTH AFRICA ...	H. L. Versfield, c/o Cape Explosives Works Ltd., 150, St. Georges Street, Cape Town.
SPAIN ...	Captain P. W. Burgess, Calle de Zurbano 29, Madrid.
N.S.A. ...	Captain Henry Maslin, 942, President Street, Brooklyn, New York.
	L. E. P, Foot. 20, Gillett Street, Hartford, Conn, U.S.A.
	A. P. Forward, 449, East 80th Street, New York.
	J. W. Freebody, 945, McBride Avenue, Los Angele.
NOVA SCOTIA ...	Will R. Bird, 35, Clarence Street, Amhert.

Membership of the League

This is open to all who served in the Salient, and to all those whose relatives or friends died there, in order that they may have a record of that service for themselves and their descendants, and belong to the comradeship of men and women who understand and remember all that Ypres meant in suffering and endurance.

Life membership, £2 10s.

Annual members, 5s.

Do not let the fact of your not having served in the Salient deter you from joining the Ypres League. Those who have neither fought in the Salient nor lost relatives there, but who are in sympathy with the objects of the Ypres League, are admitted to its fellowship, but are not given scroll certificates.

There is a Junior Division for children whose relatives served in the Salient. It is open also to others to whom our objects appeal.

Annual subscription 1s. up to the age of 18, after which they can become ordinary members of the League.

THE YPRES LEAGUE (INCORPORATED)
20, Orchard Street, Portman Square, W.1.

Telephone: WELBECK 1446.   *Telegrams*: YPRESLEAG, " WESDO," LONDON.

Patron-in-Chief: H.M. THE KING.

Patrons:
H.R.H. THE PRINCE OF WALES.   H.R.H. PRINCESS BEATRICE.

President: GENERAL SIR CHARLES H. HARINGTON.

Vice-Presidents:
F.-M. VISCOUNT ALLENBY.   F.-M. SIR CLAUD W. JACOB.
THE VISCOUNT WAKEFIELD OF HYTHE.   F.-M. SIR PHILIP CHETWODE.
GENERAL SIR CECIL ROMER.   F.-M. LORD MILNE.

General Committee:

THE COUNTESS OF ALBEMARLE.
*CAPTAIN C. ALLISTON.
LIEUT-COLONEL BECKLES WILLSON.
MR. HENRY BENSON.
*MR. J. BOUGHEY.
*MISS B. BRICE-MILLER.
COLONEL G. T. BRIERLEY.
CAPTAIN P. W. BURGESS.
*MAJOR H. CARDINAL-HARFORD.
REV. P. B. CLAYTON.
*THE EARL OF YPRES.
MRS. C. J. EDWARDS.
MAJOR C. J. EDWARDS.
MR. H. A. T. FAIRBANK.
MR. T. ROSS FURNER.
SIR PHILIP GIBBS.
MR. E. GLOVER.
MAJOR-GENERAL SIR JOHN HEADLAM.
MR. F. D. BANKS HILL.

MAJOR-GENERAL C. J. B. HAY.
MR. J. HETHERINGTON.
MRS. E. HEAP.
GENERAL SIR W. C. G. HENEKER.
*CAPTAIN O. G. JOHNSON.
*MAJOR E. MONTAGUE JONES.
CAPTAIN H. D. PEABODY.
*THE HON. ALICE DOUGLAS PENNANT.
*LIEUT.-GENERAL SIR W. P. PULTENEY.
LIEUT.-COLONEL SIR J. MURRAY.
*COLONEL G. E. C. RASCH.
VISCOUNT SANDON.
THE HON. SIR ARTHUR STANLEY.
MR. ERNEST THOMPSON.
CAPTAIN J. LOCKLEY TURNER.
*MR. E. B. WAGGETT.
CAPTAIN J. WILKINSON.
CAPTAIN H. TREVOR WILLIAMS.

* Executive Committee.

Bankers:
BARCLAYS BANK LTD., Knightsbridge Branch.

Honorary Solicitors:
MESSRS. FLADGATE & CO., 18, Pall Mall, S.W.

Secretary:
CAPTAIN G. E. DE TRAFFORD.

Auditors:
MESSRS. LEPINE & JACKSON,
6, Bond Court, E.C.4.

League Representative at Ypres:
CAPTAIN P. D. PARMINTER.
19, Rue Surmont de Volsberghe

League Representative at Cambrai:
MR. A. WILDE,
9, Rue des Anglaises.

League Representative at Amiens:
CAPTAIN STUART OSWALD.
7, Rue Porte-Paris.

League Representative at Arras:
MR. P. VYNER,
10, Station Square.

Hon. Secretary, Ypres British Settlement:
LT. COLONEL F. G. POOLE,

PRIMARY OBJECTS OF THE LEAGUE

I.—Commemoration and Comradeship.
II.—To provide special travel facilities for Members and all interested to Ypres and battlefields, and transport of Members.
III.—The furnishing of information about the Salient; marking of historic sites and the compilation of charts of the battlefields.
IV.—The erection of a Ypres British Church and School which has been completed.
V.—The establishment of groups of members throughout the world, through Branch Secretaries and Corresponding Members.
VI.—The maintenance of cordial relations with dwellers on the battlefields of Ypres
VII.—The formation of a Junior Division.

Use the Ypres League Travel Bureau for Ypres and Whole of the Western Front.

FOR THE FOLLOWING PUBLICATIONS, Etc., apply:

Secretary, YPRES LEAGUE, 20, ORCHARD STREET, LONDON, W.1.

THE BATTLE BOOK OF YPRES. A history of notable deeds contributed by all regiments. 5s.; post free, 5s. 6d. Compiled by Beatrix Brice with the assistance of Lieut.-General Sir William Pulteney, G.C.V.O., etc.

BOOKS.

YPRES: Outpost of the Channel Ports. By Beatrix Brice. With Foreword by Field-Marshal Lord Plumer, G.C.B. Price 1s. 0d.; post free 1s. 3d.

In the Ypres Salient. By Lt.-Col. Beckles Willson. 1s. net; post free 1s. 2d.

With the Cornwall Territorials on the Western Front. By E. C. Matthews. 7s. 6d.; post free 8s.

Story of the 63rd Field Ambulance. By A. W. Westmore, etc. Cloth, 3s. 6d., post free. Paper, 2s. 6d., post free.

War Letters to a Wife. By Colonel Rowland Feilding. Popular Edition, 3s. 6d.; post free 4s.

The Pill Boxes of Flanders. 1s.; post free 1s. 3d.

From Mons to the First Battle of Ypres. By J. G. W. Hyndson, M.C. Price 5s., post free 5s. 3d.

YPRES LEAGUE TIES. 3s. 6d. each, post free.
YPRES LEAGUE BADGES. 2s. each, 2s. 1¼d. post free.
EMBROIDERED BADGES. 4s. each, post free.
Map and List of Cemeteries in the Ypres Salient. Price 9d.; post free 11d.
Map of the Somme. Price 1s. 8d., post free.

PICTURES.

Burning of the Cloth Hall, 1915. A Coloured Print, 14 in. by 12 in. 1s. post free.

Old Well-known Spots in New Guise. Prints, size 4¼ x 2½, recently taken of famous spots in the Ypres Salient, and which may be of great interest to our readers, are on sale at headquarters, price 4d. each, post free 5d. For particulars apply Secretary.

POST CARDS, PHOTOGRAPHS AND ETCHINGS.

Post Cards. Ypres: British Front during the War. Ruins of Ypres. Price 1s. post free.

Photographs of Menin Gate Unveiling. Size 11 in. by 7 in. 1s. 2d. each, post free.

Hill 60. Complete Panorama Photographs. 12 in. by 3¼ in. Price 3s., post free; 15 in. by 5 in. Price 3s. 6d., post free.

WAR-TIME PHOTOGRAPHS OF THE SALIENT.

6 in. by 8 in. ... 1s. 6d. each.
12 in. by 15 in. ... 4s. each.

List forwarded on application.

PHOTOGRAPHS OF WAR-TIME SKETCHES.

Bedford House (Front View), 1916.
Bedford House (Back View), 1916.
Voormezeele Main Street, 1916.
Voormezeele Crucifixion Gate, 1916.
Langhof Chateau, 1916.

Size 8½ in. by 6½ in. Price 2s. 6d. each, post free.

Photographs of the Thiepval and Arras Memorials. Post card size, price 1s. each, post free.

YPRES TIMES.

The Journal may be obtained at the League Offices. BACK NUMBERS 1s.; 1934, 8d.; 1935, 6d.

Printed in Great Britain for the Publishers by FORD & GILL, 21a/23, Iliffe Yard, Crampton Street, London, S.E.17.

Memory Tablet.

JULY — AUGUST — SEPTEMBER

JULY.

July	1st, 1916	...	First Battle of the Somme begins.
,,	2nd, 1918	...	1,000,000 Americans transported to France.
,,	9th, 1915	...	Conquest of German South Africa.
,,	18th, 1918	...	General Foch's counter-attack.
,,	28th, 1914	...	Austria-Hungary declared war on Serbia.
,,	30th, 1915	...	First German liquid fire attack.
,,	31st, 1917	...	Third Battle of Ypres begins.

AUGUST.

Aug.	1st, 1914	...	Germany declares war on Russia.
,,	2nd, 1914	...	German ultimatum to Belgium.
,,	3rd, 1914	...	Germany declared war on France.
,,	4th, 1914	...	Great Britain declared war on Germany.
,,	8th, 1918	...	Great British Offensive launched in front of Amiens.
,,	10th, 1914	...	France declared war on Austria-Hungary.
,,	12th, 1914	...	Great Britain declared war on Austria-Hungary.
,,	16th, 1914	...	British Expeditionary Force landed in France.
,,	23rd, 1914	...	Japan declared war on Germany.
,,	27th, 1916	...	Rumania entered the war.

SEPTEMBER.

Sept.	3rd, 1916	...	Zepplin destroyed at Cuffley.
,,	5th, 1914	...	End of retreat from Mons to Marne.
,,	6th, 1914	...	First Battle of Marne begins.
,,	15th, 1914	...	First Battle of Aisne begins.
,,	23rd, 1914	...	First British air raid in Germany.
,,	25th, 1915	...	Battle of Loos.
,,	27th, 1917	...	Hindenburg Line broken.
,,	29th, 1918	...	Bulgaria surrendered.

Communications to
The Editor, "Ypres Times,"
20, Orchard Street, London, W.1.

PRICE 6d.
POST FREE 7d.

VOL. 7, No. 7.   PUBLISHED QUARTERLY   JULY, 1935

By kind permission of] [Central Press Photos Ltd.
JUBILEE DAY PROCESSION PASSING THROUGH LUDGATE CIRCUS.

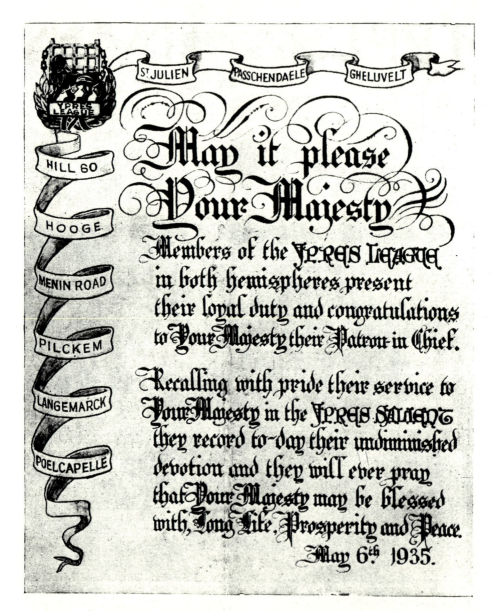

The above Loyal Address (*Actual Size 13½ ins. × 12 ins.*) was forwarded to His Majesty The King through the Home Office and the Royal reply is printed on the opposite page.

HOME OFFICE,
WHITEHALL.
8th May, 1935.

SIR,

I am directed by the Secretary of State to say that he has been commanded by The King to convey to you His Majesty's thanks for the loyal and dutiful Address from

THE YPRES LEAGUE

on completion of the Twenty-fifth Year of His Majesty's Reign and to assure you that His Majesty deeply appreciates the sentiments of loyalty and affection to which it gives expression.

I am,
Sir,
Your obedient Servant,
H. A. STRUTT.

The Chairman,
Ypres League.

[By kind permission of the Central Press Photos Ltd.

JUBILEE DAY SERVICE OF THANKSGIVING IN ST. PAULS CATHEDRAL.

"Trooping the Colour"

ORIGIN OF THE ROYAL BIRTHDAY CEREMONY.

(*Specially contributed to the* YPRES TIMES *by* HENRY BENSON, M.A.)

I WONDER how many of the thousands who witnessed the "Trooping the Colour" — the most picturesque ceremony in the drill book of the British Army — on the Horse Guards' Parade on the occasion of the King's Birthday, last month, were aware of the fact that originally it was nothing further than a guard-mounting formality?

The King's Colour, of course, is the symbol of the Sovereign, and therefore it is very appropriate that honour should be paid to it upon successive anniversaries of the Royal birthday. Ordinarily it is neither touched nor borne except by an officer, but the "Trooping the Colour" opens with the emblem in charge of a sergeant, with two sentries; whilst similarly each guard is formed into line without officers. Afterwards the sergeants in command of the guards join with the officers at the saluting base — a survival of the old custom when they so assembled for the joint purpose of drawing lots for their guard and learning the pass-word.

THE DUKE OF CUMBERLAND'S RUSE.

As the drums beat the "Assembly," the officers and N.C.O.'s proceed to their posts, moving by the slow march to take over their command. Tradition has it that the Duke of Cumberland ("The Butcher") introduced the slow march as a means of testing whether they were sober enough to perform the duty! Slow and quick marches, played by the bands and drums, constitute the first honour paid to the Colour, followed by its reception into the ranks of the battalion. The "Drummers' Call" is the signal for the captain of the escort — in olden days the Grenadiers always formed the escort — to leave his command and to hand it over to the lieutenant. The band and drums play the "British Grenadiers," and the escort moves across the front of the parade to where the Colour is posted.

THE SERGEANT MAJOR.

The sergeant-major, representing the rank and file, takes it from the sergeant in charge, and hands it to the officer who is to bear it. The Colour is received by the escort with full honours. Arms are presented, and in the case of the King's Colour, the band plays the National Anthem in salute.

When the Regimental Colour is being trooped the regimental slow march is played. It may be mentioned that the sergeant-major salutes with the sword, this being the only occasion on which he does so.

Subsequently, the escort with the Colour moves back in slow time, to the music of "Scipio," which is the Grenadiers' slow march. They file through the ranks, arms are presented, and each man is afforded the opportunity of seeing the Colour carried past and of rendering it honour. The impressive ceremony concludes, with a march past in slow and quick time.

THE SIGNIFICANCE OF THE COLOURS.

From time immemorial bodies of people have always had their sign — something symbolic of the spirit of the whole. The Prairie Braves had their totems, the children of Israel, the Egyptians, Assyrians, Greeks and Romans, their ensigns and standards. To the Roman soldiery their standard was definitely their God of War in a mobile or portable form. As soon as a Roman army halted an altar of turf was constructed, upon which were placed the Eagles of the Legions. To this attitude may be traced the origin of the Consecration of the Colours in Christian countries, one of the earliest instances being that of the Pope consecrating the standard carried by William the Conqueror at the Battle of Hastings.

In bygone days the Colours were the rallying point in battle of each British regiment, and round them the last stand was always made. Indeed, a regiment's colours are very largely that regiment's history; and further, when one considers the countries and the causes in which these colours have been unfurled, they become nothing less than an epitome of the history of the British Empire during the last three centuries.

The Suffolks, Cheshires and Marines.

In some fashion the Sovereign's birthday has always been observed for many centuries wherever a British regiment is to be found, and it has usually been associated with the Colour. Some variations there are, according to the regiment's own customs.

Among the most interesting of these exceptional celebrations is that of the 1st Battalion, the Suffolk Regiment, the old 12th of the Line. On the King's Birthday red and yellow roses are worn on the headgear of all ranks, and the drums and colours are decorated in the same way. By a train of reasoning which strikes one as somewhat Irish for so essentially an English regiment, the roses are not worn in honour of the King, but in commemoration of Dettingen Day. The Suffolks do not celebrate the actual date of the battle by any ceremonial, but at Dettington in 1743, King George II, the last King of England who personally led his troops into battle, placed himself at the head of the 12th Foot. Hence the time-honoured birthday roses.

The oak sprigs, which the Cheshire Regiment wear in their headgear on the King's Birthday, together with an oak wreath on their colours, are also in memory of Dettingen, where the 22nd Foot saved the King's life under an oak tree in the thick of the battle. In many places, both at home and abroad, infantry regiments " Troop the Colour " on the King's Birthday, and a distinctive ceremony is that of the Royal Marines, who troop one of their divisional Regimental Colours.

The Navy's " Parade."

At the principal naval commands also the Royal Navy " parade " their King's Colour with ceremonial which is in all essentials the same as that of the Foot Guards on the Horse Guards' Parade. It was only in 1923 that the King approved the use of the White Ensign with the Royal cipher as the King's Colour for the Navy; but, new as the actual colours may be, they seem already to embody all the ancient traditions of the sea service.

George IV. took part in no parade. In 1822, although his birthday fell on 12th August, he kept it more or less appropriately on St. George's Day, when " the morning was ushered in with the customary demonstrations of rejoicing." It was a general holiday, and the King himself, in field marshal's uniform, held a Drawing Room from twelve to five, " when a most splendid and costly gathering assembled, headed by an extraordinary large number of bishops, with the Archbishop of Canterbury, who delivered a lengthy address."

King George's Addition.

In the early years of Queen Victoria's reign there was a special Birthday Drawing Room, and the Guards and the Postmen received new uniforms. There were also illuminations at night, the last being a great feature, since the clubs, public buildings and West-End shops vied with each other in splendour and brilliance, especially when " the new inflammatory agent, gas, was available."

In the " forties " there were military inspections on the Horse Guards' Parade by the Prince Consort on " the birthday," though there is no mention of the Queen's Colour being trooped. After the Crimean War the ceremony seems to have begun to take the present form, although the Queen herself was rarely, if ever, present. The Duke of Cambridge, or one of the Princes, usually took the salute on her behalf.

King George, in 1914, initiated a very popular addition to the ceremony. For the first time he rode off the parade at the head of his own guard, attended only by those of his escort who were themselves Guards officers. It has now become a marked and appropriate feature of the fine ceremony, and one which acquires added beauty and grandeur with the passing of years.

H. B.

Salient Patrols

By WILL R. BIRD.

Ex-Corporal of the 42nd Canadians.

THE SALIENT was a drastic school for every new battalion. Men and officer learned there the importance of initiative, the value of their own resourcefulness. Every unit learned its lesson of watchfulness; there was no other part of the western front where so much depended on your knowing what was doing over the way.

The 42nd Canadian Black Watch, a splendid battalion, was thorough in all its duties; they learned early the value of patrols and listening posts, and throughout the war maintained a fine record. In February, '16, while they were in the Kemmel area, a German bombing party, twenty strong, attempted a surprise attack. Listening posts gave warning, and the raiders were met with such quick resistance that two of them were killed and one captured before the rest could take to flight. Not one of the 42nd were wounded.

But one of the enemy had hidden in a shell hole during the action and he remained there for more than an hour, waiting till everything had quieted. He then spotted our listening post, and threw a bomb right into it, killing the man on duty there; he made his escape immediately after.

It was a lesson for the " Forty-twos ". Had they patrolled the vicinity after the brief scrap they would have discovered the skulker in the shell hole.

Lieut. O. B. Jones came to the 42nd as a private in March, 1916. From that time until he was seriously wounded on the Somme the story of his adventures would make an epic of the Great War. He joined the scouts, won the Distinguished Conduct Medal, and Bar, rose to the rank of sergeant, then won his commission, and the Military Cross. His name was constantly in the Intelligence Summary of the Brigade.

While the battalion was at Hooge he began his work. With two officers and a sergeant, he walked over in the darkness, crossing ground absolutely without cover, and reached the parapet of a trench in which the Germans were working. After watching and listening for a time, Jones left the others and entered the trench within yards of the workers. He explored some distance along it, then returned to a point near where he had entered and removed the steel loophole plate from a sniper's post. He did this while faithful soldiers of the Fatherland were placing sandbags within fifteen feet from him, and succeeded in getting his trophy back to his own trench.

The 42nd was in Brigade Support when the famous attack of June 2nd began. After a hurricane of shell fire that blasted the Canadian trenches from existence, the Germans simply walked over and took possession of their objectives. A fortnight later the diary of one of the German officers was captured. He had entered, on that date of June 2nd, the following : " The attack was completely successful. We are in possession of the important double hill. Our enemies after their continual failures must soon recognise their helplessness and make an end of it."

Under date of June 13th, he wrote : " The catastrophe happened today. The double hill was lost back. The English fired like mad. The trenches were quite destroyed and besides this fearful devastation is the dreadful spectacle of the many dead. Now that the English have enfeebled us with artillery fire and re-occupy their trenches and can sweep us with machine gun fire from the hill, they are content." He made no mention of what their artillery fire did to our trenches, nor did he state that during the *second* action they still had more batteries and guns and men than the Canadians. However, that is by the way.

The 42nd had been called into the line as soon as possible, and helped hold the new line. They fought magnificently and had severe losses. On June 4th the Higher Command was satisfied that the enemy offensive had been checked effectively, and counter measures were decided on, but these had to be postponed until the exact situation could be clearly defined. The 42nd sent out a patrol of six, and these explored the vicinity of the Gourock Road and brought back much useful information. It was then decided to send out Sergeant Jones and a corporal on a daring daylight reconnaissance.

Photo] [Imperial War Museum. Crown Copyright
AN OFFICER LEADING THE WAY OUT OF A SAP FOLLOWED BY THE REST OF THE RAIDING PARTY—SHELLS BURSTING

They wormed from their trench under cover of a heap of debris and worked forward slowly, crawling, taking advantage of all available cover. They reached an old communication trench, battered and useless, and proceeded along it. A German block faced them, but after half an hour's watching they resolved that it was not occupied, and chanced a bold advance. Reaching it, they found the post deserted, and saw a second block beyond. Jones knew every foot of ground. He knew they could not expect to use the second block as an observation post, yet learned, by close scrutiny that the Germans had grown careless, and that no sentries were keeping watch in his immediate vicinity. He crawled down what had been Warrington Avenue trench until he reached a spot dangerously near the enemy block, where there had been a sort of shallow dugout, but which faced into another trench. They had secured a shovel during their crawl. One man kept watch and the other worked swiftly, cutting through the soil, driving a small tunnel. Jones' guess had been accurate. After two hours' hard work they entered the dugout. Its entrance had been blocked and buried, and faced the wrong way, but they proceeded to carry on their tunnelling. They burrowed a hole through the back of the old shelter, carefully removing the last few inches with their hands—and looked through directly into the new German trench.

Old roots and tangled grass were matted with the sod and screened Jones quite effectively, and no one came to that part. He estimated that there were at least 250 men in view all working strenuously to dig a very deep and strong trench. A strong machine gun post was under construction just north of his peeping place. He watched until he detected the posts of three enemy snipers, all the sentries on duty, and after an hour and three-quarters of close observation realized that the Germans did not know the position of the Canadian lines and thought them much nearer than they actually were. He saw that Warrington Avenue in their territory was being improved for use as a C. T. and that wire was being freely used. In places a double barrier was being erected, concertina barbed wire staked down with iron corkscrew standards.

The results of this daylight patrol were that the artillery were provided with accurate targets. They were given the exact range of the German strong points and machine gun posts, knew every contour of the enemy front line, and where the wire was thickest. When the attack took place these strong points were blasted out of existence, and the wire was shredded.

The 42nd, exploring, found an N.C.O. of the Princess Pats in a wrecked shelter where he had lain, alone, two days and nights, blind, his thigh fractured, wounded in a dozen places. He had been hastily placed there during the battle, and forgotten. He was carried half a mile on a bath mat to a point on the Menin Road where a wheeled stretcher was provided.

Jones continued his patrolling, and did grand work in July while the battalion was in the Steenvoorde area. He and four men went out from St. Peter's Street into No Man's land one dark night and crawled to an enemy sap. They found it dry and in good shape, with much evidence of very recent shovelling. Jones went along the sap to the entrance into the main trench. A sentry there shot up two flares directly over him, but he was not detected. The flare man moved along a distance and Jones went into the trench. He was astounded to see another man not more than ten feet from him but the German was peering over the top and did not glance toward him. Crouched, Jones peered in the other direction and saw a third man about twenty feet away. A faint drizzle of rain was falling and it was cloudy. He stayed half an hour, hidden at the sap entrance, remained there while five flares were shot over the sap, and was not seen.

Another night Jones and three men crawled out to the German entanglements, and remained hidden there, for twenty hours. One of the scouts spoke German, and he overheard all that was said in the trench. The party had thirty hand grenades with them, and when a working party congested the trench in the early evening Jones signalled for action. They threw the thirty grenades among the crowded men and escaped safely to their own lines.

The 42nd, when at Crab Crawl, wanted to establish an advanced post. Thirty-five men went out at dark and built a barricade thirty yards long and two feet high, behind which they dug a shallow trench. Jones and an officer crawled to the German wire while the work was in progress. They examined it thoroughly and cut it at several points. They then dislodged a number of iron standards to which the wire was anchored and attached a rope to a long section of the wire. This rope, which had been paid out from a point in the 42nd line, was then passed over the parados to a large party of men lined up as for a tug-of-war. At a given signal they began to pull and drew over a large section of the German wire to their own barricade. Lively minutes followed. Flares went up by the dozen, all colours, bombs were thrown wholesale and machine guns raved, but not a casualty was suffered by the 42nd.

The next night another patrol went out on the left flank and, in the murky darkness, discovered many German outposts placed to prevent a second wire-stealing incident. The patrol selected one post that could be reached easily, and returned with a load of grenades. They hurled their missles and their aim was splendid, while the surprise was so complete that they were back in their own trench before the German machine guns got into action.

During July '16, the Canadians continually harassed the enemy by raiding and patrolling. On the 1st a 26th Battalion party crossed over to the German line. They found three posts, and the sentries opened fire on them, staying right there. The officer in charge, however, rushed in with his revolver and shot the defenders of one post, whereupon the others ran. They explored forty yards of the German trench, gathered the equipment that lay around, and got back to their own lines with slight casualties.

On the night of the 4th a patrol of the 22nd Battalion saw a German patrol coming toward them, and the fact that they were of equal numbers did not scare them. They promptly attacked, killed two of the enemy and captured two; the prisoners yielded very valuable information.

A little later a patrol of the 25th met an enemy patrol, and they, too, attacked. The enemy fled leaving several dead and one wounded, who was taken prisoner. Three nights later a patrol from this same battalion were entering a German trench after disposing of the sentry when they were attacked from the rear by a party of eight. As they only totalled five in strength it seemed a desperate situation, but the Canadians disposed of the eight, having three men wounded in the doing. Five of the Germans were killed outright. Sentries along the trench had been aroused and these opened fire, killing a sergeant with the 25th party. It was not discovered that he was missing until the others had returned to the trench, but the officer at once returned to the German sap to find him.

The 19th Battalion made a daylight raid on the St Eloi front, entered the German trench, bombing and shooting all its length. They captured four machine gun emplacements, killing a large number of the enemy who were Royal Wurttembergers. Then the 27th made a raid. They captured three Germans in the enemy line but these put up such desperate resistance that they had to be killed. A week later another party from the same battalion went over to the German trench, entered it, seized a prisoner and returned, having but one man slightly wounded.

After these enterprises the Germans were very nervous, so a dummy raid was planned. Scouts crawled over and attached wires to the German barriers. In the middle of the night white flares were sent up in threes as if for a signal, and the wires were pulled so that the German barriers rocked and made alarm. A perfect deluge of bombs descended all along the German wire, and continued. Rifle fire was opened, and machine gun fire, then the artillery barraged No Man's land. When the excitement was at its height our artillery opened on the German trenches and added to the din. A German five-point-nine battery dropped thirty-five shells in their own lines.

It is small wonder that in a captured diary taken on the Somme this entry was translated: "It is a relief to get from the trenches opposing those verdammte " Canadian redskins." They are terrible, and fight without any rules whatsoever. One never knows what they may do."

W.R.B.

The Kings' Shropshire Light Infantry

(53RD AND 85TH FOOT.)

BATTLE HONOURS :

"Nieuport," "Tournay," "St. Lucia, 1796," "Talavera," "Fueutes d'Ouor," "Salamanca," "Vittoria," "Pyrenees," "Nivelle," "Nive," "Toulouse," "Peninsula," "Bladensburg," "Aliwal," "Sobraon," "Goojerat," "Punjaub," "Lucknow," "Afghanistan, 1879-80," "Egypt, 1882," "Suakin, 1885," "Paardeberg," "South Africa, 1899-1902." *The Great War*—13 Battalions.—"Aisne, 1914, '18," "ARMENTIERES, 1914," "YPRES, 1915, '17," "Gravenstafel," "St. Julien," "FREZENBERG," "Bellewaarde," "Hooge, 1915," "Mount Sorrel," "SOMME, 1916, '18," "Albert, 1916,'18," "Bazentin," "Delville Wood," "Guillemont," "Flers Courcelette," "Morval," "Le Transloy," "Ancre, 1916," "ARRAS, 1917, '18," "Scarpe, 1917," "Arleux," "Hill 70," "Langemarck, 1917," "Menin Road," "Polygon Wood," "Passchendaele," "CAMBRAI, 1917, '18," "St. Quentin," "Bapaume, 1918," "Rosieres," "Lys," "Estaires," "Messines, 1918," "Hazebrouck," "Bailleul," "Kemmel," "Bethune," "BLIGNY," "Hindenburg Line," "EPEHY," "Canal du Nord," "Selle," "Valenciennes," "Sambre," "Francez Flanders, 1914, '18," "DOIRAN, 1917, '18," "Macedonia, 1915, '18," "Gaza," "JERUSALEM," "Jericho," "Tell Azur," "Palestine,1917, '18."

Note.—Names in small capitals in Great War Honours are borne on the King's Colour.

Uniform—Scarlet.   Facings—Blue.

FEW regiments in the British Army have had a more chequered career than the 85th Foot — the 2nd Battalion, The King's Shropshire Light Infantry.

There have been three regiments that have been numbered as the 85th, and although it is the intention here to narrate a brief history of the survivor, it is of interest to refer to the two previous regiments now long ago disbanded.

The first 85th was raised in 1759 and disbanded in 1763. The official designation was "the 85th Light Infantry Regt." — or "Royal Volontiers" and it was without doubt the first Light Infantry regiment in the British Army. The first Colonel Commandant was Colonel Craufurd, with William Lord Viscount Pulteney as Lieut.-Colonel. The regiment seems to have been very fully officered, having a total of 67, or a greater number than in any of the 124 Regiments of Foot, except the 42nd and 60th Regiments and the 1st or Royal Regiment of Guards of Foot, which regiment had two battalions. The rendezvous of the regiment was Shrewsbury, and here, on January 2nd, 1760, Colours were presented and consecrated. This ceremony, which appears to have been the earliest one of a regular consecration in the British Army, was carried out with unusual éclat. During the prayers and sermon in the old Church of St. Chad the colours were held over the heads of the Lieut.-Colonel Commandant and the Lieut.-Colonel. The regiment then marched to the Quarry, where the Colours, held by these two officers were saluted and kissed. In 1761 the 85th took part in the seige of Belle Isle (off the coast of Brittany), which memory still survives in the Common North Shropshire saying : "We'll give 'em Belle Isle," and in 1762 was sent to Portugal where it fought at Valencia d'Alcantara and Villa Villia against the Spanish. Returning to England in 1763, the Regiment was disbanded.

In the summer of 1779 when England was again involved in war with France and Spain, another 85th Regiment of Foot was formed, popularly known as the "Westminster Volunteers," and commanded by Colonel the Earl of Harrington. This Regiment had a brief and very unfortunate existence. After 18 months' service in the West Indies it embarked in 1782 for home in the fleet of Admiral Graves, and thus came to participate in one of the most terrible disasters which have ever befallen the British Navy ; many of the ships being sunk in a terrible gale in the Atlantic. The remnants of the Regiment were disbanded in 1783.

In 1793 the existing 85th was formed under the auspices of the first Marquis of Buckingham, and commanded by his cousin Lieut.-Colonel (afterwards Field Marshal) Sir George Nugent. It was known as the 85th (Bucks. Volunteers) Regiment of Foot, and was destined early in its career to become associated with Shropshire, being quartered in this County in 1794, and again in 1798, after its return from the Netherlands (where it received the particular thanks of the Commander in Chief for its gallant services during the actions near Bergen). 1801 saw the 85th taking part in the occupation of the island of Madeira and after six year's service in the West Indies it was transformed in 1808 into a Light Infantry Regiment again, thus becoming with the 68th Regiment, fourth in the order of seniority of the Light Corps. In 1809 it took part in the Walcheron expedition and the capture of Flushing, and in 1811 proceeded to the Peninsula where it was in action at Fuentes d'Onor. Having been very much reduced in strength during this campaign, it was ordered home to recruit, and in 1813 again embarked for the Peninsula and served there till the war ended in 1814, distinguishing itself at the battles of Neville and the passage of the Nive. Trouble in America in 1814 found the 85th with other units being hurried to that continent where it took a particularly active part in the successful actions at Bladensburg and Baltimore (a diary kept by Lieut.-Gleig of the 85th is in existence, and gives detailed and personal accounts of all the numerous incidents during this campaign). Arriving back home in 1815 it was given by Royal Command the title of 85th (or Duke of York's Own) Regiment of Light Infantry, and the appropriate motto — " Aucto Splendore Resurgo " — " I rise again with augmented splendour."

In 1820, when stationed at Brighton and providing guards over the Royal Pavilion, the story goes, that a hostile demonstration was made against His Majesty, King George IV. by some of the audience at the theatre. Officers of the 85th were present, and turned the rioters out, at which His Majesty expressed his approbation and was afterwards pleased to command that the Regiment should in future bear the title of the 85th or "King's Light Infantry Regiment," and that the uniform should be faced with Blue and laced with Silver.

For some sixty years the Regiment saw no active service, being on garrison duty in many parts of the Empire, but in 1879, it formed part of the field force under Sir Frederic Roberts, V.C., in Afghanistan, where it served till hostilities ceased. On the reorganization of the Army in 1881, it was linked with the 53rd Regiment, and in the following year received the official title of 2nd Battalion " The King's " (Shropshire Light Infantry).

On the outbreak of the South African War, in 1899, it immediately proceeded to the Cape, and served till the end, taking an active part in the capture of General Cronje and his large force at Paardeberg. It also provided a mounted Infantry Company which operated from 1900 throughout the war.

At the commencement of the Great War, the Regiment was brought to France from India, and formed part of the 80th Brigade, which earned for itself the title of " The Stonewall Brigade." St. Julien, Frezenburg and Bellewaarde in the 2nd Battle of Ypres, brought honours to the Regiment, and in October, 1915, the 80th Brigade were transported to Salonica, and in the final offensive against the Bulgarians the Battalion was amongst the first troops to enter the enemy country. Thence it proceeded to Bartoum on the Black Sea, where it did garrison duty until its return to

England. Serving in Ireland in 1922, it was the last regular Battalion to provide a guard for Dublin Castle, while in 1926 it was the last to evacuate Cologne — this involving the hauling down of the Union Jack from the G. H. Q. building, and handing over the keys of barracks. This flag is now in the possession of the Officers' Mess.

On April 16th last — 117 years since it last entered the county — the Regiment started from Lichfield, where it is now stationed, on an historic march through Shropshire and Herefordshire, and on April 25th, in the presence of an immense gathering, H.R.H. The Duke of York presented new colours in the Quarry, Shrewsbury, where, in the same grounds, the first 85th Light Infantry Regiment had received its first colours in January, 1760.

In connection with this latter ceremony, it is interesting to relate that after the trooping of the old colours, they were received on behalf of the Old Comrades (numbering over 2,000) for escort to the Regimental Depot, by three Ex-Warrant Officers, all of whom were on parade at Lucknow in January, 1877, when they were presented by the Duke of Buckingham and Chandos, whose ancestor helped to form the existing Regiment.

E. W.

Public Schools Battlefield Tour

THE second official Public Schools O.T.C., Battlefield Tour, took place from April 27th to 30th last, and the arrangements were again entrusted to the capable hands of the Ypres League in co-operation with the Officers Training Corps Club.

This Tour was another great success and all who had pleasure to take part were much indebted to the organisers for the care taken to ensure our comfort and interest throughout. In consequence of activities at many of the schools in preparation for Jubilee Celebrations, our numbers were smaller than last year, nevertheless, some seventy officers and cadets assembled at Victoria Station on Saturday morning, April 27th, all in buoyant mood and greatly looking forward to their forthcoming adventure. The party, as a whole, were in the charge of Major E. Montague Jones, O.B.E., T.D., M.A., Hon. Secretary and Treasurer, O.T.C., Club and a member of the Ypres League Committee, with Mr. O. Mears from the League Headquarters as business manager for the Tour.

Alighting from our reserved compartments at Dover, we proceeded to board the Belgian s.s. *Prince Leopold* with slightly mixed feelings as to the nature of the trip ahead for in the distance we could observe a somewhat turbulent sea. Any doubts on this point were quickly dispelled, for we were soon tested by a strong north-easter and rough passage, but the Captain apparently considered our comfort by hugging the coast from Calais to Ostend, incidentally affording us an excellent view of Dunkerque and the battlefield of Nieuport. I am afraid the motion of the boat had proved a little too much for quite a number of the party, but once on terra firma, it was amazing how quickly spirits revived.

On reaching Ypres, again our headquarters, the party was equally divided between the Hotel Skindles, Station Place, and the Hotel Splendid and Britannique, Grand Place. The writer can vouch for the excellence of Skindles Hotel, and he has no reason whatever to believe the other hotel was not as good. Following a refresher in the way of a wash and brush-up all appeared ready and eager for the inviting dinner prepared, after which a quiet saunter was made round the famous old city prior to congregating at " Skindles " for an illustrated talk by the official lecturers to the Tour. The War Office extended us a great favour by so kindly granting special permission to Lt.-Colonel Sir Colin Jardine, Bart., D.S.O., M.C., and Major H. Redman, to accompany the Tour and our sincere thanks are due to these two officers for the efficient and highly interesting manner in

Photo] [Daniel, Ypres
REPRESENTATIVE PARTY OF THE SECOND ANNUAL PUBLIC SCHOOLS TOUR ASSEMBLED IN THE YPRES BRITISH SCHOOL PLAYGROUND

which, both the two evening lantern lectures and their talks when traversing the battlefields by day, were conducted.

It was regretted that Lieut.-General Sir William Pulteney, G.C.V.O., K.C.B., K.C.M.G., etc. (Chairman of the Ypres League), who has evinced such interest in these particular Schoolboy Battlefield Tours, was unavoidably prevented from being with us on this occasion.

On Sunday morning, many of us availed ourselves of the opportunity to pay a visit to "Talbot House," Poperinghe, and I should say that none of those who made the trip will ever forget this wonderful place. We were sorry that neither " Tubby " Clayton nor " Pat " Leonard, were available to receive us, but the caretaker deputised very ably in their absence, and showed us as much as possible in our limited time. The Chapel itself is certainly something to remember, and the " Old House " is most reverently kept in memory of those elder brethren of ours who partook of its hospitality during the trying years of the Great War.

On the return from " Pop," the party rejoined for the 11 a.m. service in the Ypres British Church, where I am sure no more whole-hearted singing of the hymns has been heard in that noble building for some time. Following the service admirably conducted by the resident padre, the Rev. G. R. Milner, M.A., a photograph, herewith reproduced, was taken in the adjacent school play-ground, and our last good deed that morning was to place a wreath on the Town Memorial in honour of those whom it commemorates. The wreath was laid by Major Montague Jones, and the inscription on the card attached was as follows :—

> " In respectful memory of the fallen soldiers of our gallant Belgian Ally who fought side by side with our British Armies in the Immortal Defence of Ypres, 1914 - 1918."
>
> *From the Officers and Cadets of the English Public Schools, O.T.C.*

A char-a-banc tour of the Ypres Salient Battlefields was arranged on Sunday afternoon and the previous night's lecture considerably helped the party to comprehend the strategy that governed the battles of Ypres. The visibility was good, and the lecturers at each outstanding place of interest, explained to us the reason for their significance. A personal impression I gained during this particular tour was that the Canadian Front line at Hill 62 is now rather too much of a museum, although it appeared instructive to the boys. Colonel Jardine's old battery position was a most interesting personal touch, and the Canadian and Australian Memorials are magnificently worthy of the gallantry they commemorate. Actually, the most impressive sight was Tyne Cot Cemetery and Memorial to the " Missing " at Passchendaele : no person could view this huge concentration of known and unknown war dead without being deeply moved and firmly resolved in the longing for a real and lasting peace among nations of the Earth. " A Soldier of the British Army," " A soldier of the ——shire Regiment " was seen inscribed on the headstones north, south, east and west in this cemetery whose walls bear the inscription " Their names live for evermore."

At 9 p.m. on this evening, the whole party assembled at the Menin Gate to hear that impressive rendering of " The Last Post," when a wreath was placed by Major J. M. West of the Shrewsbury School, O.T.C., the card attached bearing the following inscription :—

> " In proud memory of our glorious British Dead who fell in the Immortal Defence of the Ypres Salient, 1914 - 1918, and who have no known graves but whose names are inscribed on this Memorial."
>
> *From the Officers and Cadets of the English Public Schools, O.T.C.*

Monday was the occasion for a whole-day char-a-banc tour into France as far as Arras, and whereas the previous days had been cold, this particular day was more or less ideal, which added materially to our comfort. The route followed *via* the Wytschaete-Messines Ridge where a halt was made to observe the huge mine craters, then on past the London Scottish Memorial, recalling a day of tragic heroism, and thence to Le Bizet where prior to crossing the border we were subjected to a rather amusing but very thorough Customs examination. Leaving Armentieres we soon found ourselves close to the chimney at Aubers Ridge which some of the more elderly among us had observed so often from the British positions in the Fauquissart sector. Our course was then directed to the Loos battlefield where Colonel Jardine gave us an extremely interesting talk on the battle of September, 1915, in which he himself took a very active part. In explanation of the action it was necessary to indulge in a miniature route march over fields, ploughed and otherwise, for some distance, but which nevertheless, came as a welcome relief after the lengthy period in the char-a-banc. Vimy Ridge with its miles of subteranean tunnels was our next objective, and proved as interesting to the boys as anything we had so far seen, and after viewing the unfinished Canadian War Memorial on the Ridge, the party re-assembled for the final phase of our journey to Arras. The short stay in Arras permitted us to see a little of this ancient French city, notorious for its underground tunnels and shelters. The restoration of the cathedral is not yet completed, but we were struck by its apparent beauty. The Grande and Petite Places were other objects of special interest. The return itinerary northward was slightly to the rear of the old British front line, the outward journey having been made behind the old German front line. A halt was made at Bethune in order to permit one of our boys to visit the grave of his father who lay buried in a British Military Cemetery near-by. Our tour continued subsequently *via* Estaires, crossing the frontier at Le Seau and so on past the foot of Kemmel Hill, that dominant feature overlooking the Salient which figured so prominently in the critical 1918 German offensive, eventually reaching Ypres in time for the excellent hot meal already prepared for us. Our last evening in Ypres was spent at leisure, visiting the war museum, exploring the ramparts, and purchasing souvenirs. The facility with which the return journey to London on the Tuesday was accomplished bore further tribute to the organisers, and we were favoured this time by a splendid sea crossing in glorious sunshine. It was certainly a very happy band of pilgrims that detrained from the 4.27 p.m. at Victoria.

To an old soldier — a memorable week-end, but what did it mean to the boys? It told them of the many deeds of heroic devotion and self-sacrifice, it enabled them to comprehend a little of the magnitude of modern warfare with the hundred and one intricate problems of battles and last, but by no means least, the terrific and useless slaughter of young lives. That these youngsters will carry back with them to their homes indelible impressions of this pilgrimage admits of no doubt, but if, in the course of their maturity the full significance of it all is fully appreciated then I am sure such Tours will in every respect be justified.

To the organisers of this English Public Schools O.T.C., Battlefield Tour, — we thank you!

G.C.

Four-Footed Friends

By A. Douglas Thorburn, M.A. (Capt. R.F.A., S.R., Retd.)

(Author of *Amateur Gunners.*)

No. I.—Gunteam after the Armistice in Belgium.

THE three Drivers in the picture drove the original No. 1 Gun out from England and the final one back to Calais. No other drivers ever had charge of "A" Sub-section Gunteam. They were the leading team of the battery from first to last.

Any horseman will appreciate the keen bold stamp of the leaders in this splendid team of Australian horses. The six horses were bright bays perfectly matched in colour. The centre pair were as active as cats, the wheelers were gluttons for work, indomitable and great-hearted.

Both the horses and drivers of this team were, in my experience, incomparable, " that most lordly spectacle on earth " a team that knew its job supremely well and did its work faultlessly on every occasion.

No apology is due for including the animals among my memories of those who gave our country devoted service in the War years. The services of our four-footed friends were as distinguished as their sufferings, I have never seen any figures of the casualties among the horses, mules, camels, and donkeys in the Great War ; they must have been colossal.

Some men are lovers of horses ; to others these creatures are merely useful slaves. To the horseman they are much more, friends as well as servants. Their war-life was a lesson to all of us in endurance, fearless determination in the face of unutterable fatigue, physical misery, and, at times, semi-starvation.

SIDNEY.

Just as we were on the point of embarking on the s.s. *Manitou* for Salonica there was attached to us an A.S.C. driver with a Maltese cart (a sort of box on wheels with neither seat nor springs) and a black mule in the shafts. The mule was in so dilapidated a condition that it was barely able to draw the empty Maltese cart. To ensure the safe arrival of this apparently useless equipage at the dockside we found it necessary to harness a spare horse with " marker's traces " in front of the black mule, which was so weak that it fairly reeled with the effort required to pull the empty cart.

In spite of the tropical heat and the scandalous lack of ventilation in the lower hold of our transport, our solitary mule improved out of all recognition, and a little while after we had landed, ridden by the A.S.C. driver, won the Brigade mule race in a common canter.

As this was the first mule that we had "owned" he naturally became the battery mascot, and for some unknown reason, got the pet name of Sidney.

I think that, although he was only a mule, he was the handsomest quadruped that I ever saw. He was fully sixteen hands, coal black with a coat like satin, and a natural carriage of the head which always reminded me of the chariot horses in the Assyrian sculptures. He was young, intelligent, gentle and obedient. Excepting trained pacers and Bishareen camels, nothing on four legs ever trotted at such a speed as Sidney.

One sunny frosty morning I set off to Salonica town in the Maltese cart with the A.S.C. driver seated beside me on an empty biscuit-box. The branch of the Topsin-Monastir road on which we travelled was about as smooth as a frozen ploughed field. To make a pair we had harnessed Sidney and an even bigger black mule called Johnny to the little cart, and we were literally bouncing up and down on the biscuit-box as our speed reached about fifteen miles an hour.

As we approached the town we saw on the left a small camp of very clean bell-tents. Leaning over the fence by the roadside was our C.R.A. with another General.

The C.R.A. signalled halt ! Driver Welsh and I hauled on the long reins with all strength (no light hand is needed to stop a pair of 16-hand mules trotting at full speed). I expected a severe reprimand for furious driving, but that was not it at all. The C.R.A. bade me a smiling " Good morning," and said he had stopped me because the other General wanted to look at my mules, and fairly beamed with good nature and amusement at my regimentally correct salute with the long whip.

The other General looked the mules over (they were glittering in the sun as brightly as the burnished steel of the harness), and said to our C.R.A., " I congratulate your subaltern on his turnout. It's the smartest team I have ever seen in the whole of my life."

Two Generals, an A.S.C. driver, and a 2nd Lieutenant became just four men who knew and cared enough about mules and horses to appreciate and admire a magnificent pair.

I look back upon this little incident as the pleasantest of all my memories of war service. Differences in rank and status were forgotten and all four of us felt that, war or no war, the world was a fine place on that sunny morning.

Archie and Arthur.

Archie and Arthur were a pair of entire Egyptian donkeys. We acquired them unofficially one very dark night. These pure white donkeys, popularly called "Allenby's white mice," were used for transport after the rains in the Judæan mountains.

There never were such useful animals as Archie and Arthur. They pulled the little cart which carried our portable forge and the coal for it, so we were never reduced to the abomination of cold shoeing. The cart was a capture from the Turks; the harness was made by our wonderful saddler out of bits of broken reins.

Almost every sick and wounded man who had to go to hospital rode there on one or other of these little donkeys. On slippery mountain tracks a camel is a terrifying carriage for the seriously sick or badly wounded; camels fall down quite frequently on slippery going, but donkeys never do.

The illustration shows well what a charming pair they were. The late Brig.-General Hext, our C.R.A., never failed to ask how our donkeys were every time we saw him.

Water Camel.

This is one of the 30,000 camels which carried water both for men and horses for the Beersheba-Sheria operations. The labour was terrific; camels and their drivers —

who have to drag them along in pairs — marched daily twenty hours out of every twenty-four for a fortnight on end; the endurance of both was almost incredible in the scorching sun.

Camels, sour-tempered vicious beasts, never give it up on the march until they are actually dying. Their drivers were equally plucky; they were willing and cheery rascals who took a beating from their Reis (foreman) without a whimper when found in some small dereliction of duty.

The camel is a strange survival from prehistoric times. They have been bred in domestication for centuries. There are no wild camels in existence.

It is not wise to stand chatting with your back to a camel : his neck is extremely elastic, and his bite is often poisonous. No other animal can work without drinking for a week because no other animal can hold thirty gallons inside him.

THE ROANS.

When I joined the Battery with which I was to serve so long, the left section team-horses were a wretched lot with the exception of the leaders of "C" sub Gun-team, and the wheelers of the Gun-team of "D" sub-section (high class enough to win later first prize for the best pair of wheelers in the 268th Brigade in Palestine).

The latter were the only well-known horses in the Battery which had no pet names ; they were simply called The Roans.

The mare was considerably older than the gelding, and I believe, was his mother. They were like two peas in a pod. In spite of the fact that the mare was noticeably chicken-hocked, they were, probably, the most powerful pair of wheelers that ever pulled a gun.

This is no exaggeration as the following incident will demonstrate.

On our march up the line in Salonica we went across country in pitch darkness from Karasouli to Gugunci. The Battery in column-of-route was being led by a sub-altern so lacking in column-of-route intelligence that, after fording a stream which crossed the dirt-track we were following, he marched on quite unaware that only the two leading teams were following him, and that the rest of the column was halted on the other side of the river.

I trotted up from the tail of the column to find out why the Battery had halted, and discovered that the third vehicle was stuck in a hole in the river bottom, and that the two vehicles that had crossed over had disappeared in the dark.

Wading into the ice-cold river up to the waist, I found that a ten-horse team had been unable to move the waggon and so, after half-an-hour of frantic man-handling, I passed the word back for the roans from "D" sub.

By that time all hands engaged were soaked to the bone and half frozen.

In less than a minute up came the roans trotting through the scrub beside the track ; the ten-horse team was unhitched and the two gun-wheelers were hooked in in place of them. One colossal heave and out the waggon came like a cork out of a champagne bottle. Oh, those Roans ! I could have hugged them both.

About thirteen years later (!) I saw the mare standing in her old age in the shafts of a coal cart in Oldhall Street in Liverpool. The carter, like most Liverpool carters, a splendid horsemaster, had the old mare in wonderful condition and told me how, for all her shaky old legs, she still brought the courage of a lion to her comparatively easy work. It was fine to see how well this ex-service veteran was being cared for.

DAISY.
By Major C. F. MILES, M.C.

In 1915 I was appointed to the battery with which I was to serve the whole of my commissioned active service. Having reported for duty I was invited to walk round the horse lines and choose a charger, but there was nothing that suggested itself to me as a " charger " and the fact became apparent that the best I could do was to select one of what in my innocence I had regarded as the light-draught horses. Thus I encountered "Daisy," black and ugly when one looked at her head, but with beautiful legs, a choice I never regretted. She was compact and possessed wonderful powers of endurance, and a fair turn of speed, but perhaps the characteristic that most endeared her to me was her air of nonchalance and imperturbability. No matter what excitement or clamour was going on, Daisy still preserved the expression of the wise old owl and " carried on." One amusing experience will illustrate this characteristic. It was at Marseilles in December, 1916, en route to Salonica, when a yapping little terrier rushde along snapping at the horses' heels, until he chose Daisy for his victim. Some of the other horses not unnaturally had been disturbed by these attentions, but Daisy, without appearing to look at the dog or changing her stride, neatly and cleanly kicked him under the chin and continued on the even tenor of her way. When the dog had recovered from his back-somersault he wisely decided that the game was not worth playing.

The campaign in Palestine was very arduous and strenuous for the horses, but Daisy was always fit and did all that was asked of her, and was the real friend that only such a horse can be.

My last ride on her was from half-way between Jerusalem and the Jordan to Jaffa returning home to England, and as I said good-bye to her I wondered if I should ever see her again. During my absence, the battery was transferred to France, leaving the horses behind. I hope she went to someone who appreciated her qualities — not showy, but very sound.

C. F. M.

JERRY.

As the War struggled on to its last stage our teams declined to a level so low that it became an almost insoluble problem to keep the whole Battery mobile. Teams consisting of four animals were all that could be provided and, except in the case of the gun-teams, these were composed of anything at all that could be called horses or mules.

One of the animals provided by Remounts out of the dregs of their stock was Jerry.

Originally he had probably been a pony in a country butcher's cart. He was a nondescript bay of about 14 hands without weight or substance, poorly muscled and altogether rather a vulgar little " galloway."

One of the six sergeants had a mount with pretensions to value as a team-horse, and he unwillingly took Jerry in exchange for it, surprisingly reporting that he couldn't want a handier saddle-horse. Later, as various horses and mules on the march showed signs of imminent collapse from exhaustion, Jerry often took the place of the weakest team-horse in the column and proved himself a useful worker in an emergency. Eleven a.m. on November 11th, found us in a village called Ostiches in Belgium. We halted outside a brewery and billeted horses and men in a farm belonging to M. Dubrule, the brewer's brother.

After a few days the kind and hospitable brewer came to ask if I could lend him a horse to pull his two-wheeled trap in search of yeast for the brewery.

I inspected the trap and the harness. The collar was a narrow wooden affair with a long pointed top, the kind commonly used by country people in the North of France.

None of our animals, so far as I knew, had ever worn any kind of collar except a breast-collar. I told M. Dubrule that I doubted if any of our horses could be induced to put his head through a contraption of that kind, although we were perfectly willing to try. I went myself for Jerry, the most likely animal I could think of.

I led him up to the strange vehicle, took up the fantastic collar, and showed it him, expecting a decided and possibly violent protest.

But Jerry's versatility was equal to the occasion. He greeted his new job by holding out his head sideways so that I could slip the collar over it more easily, and then trotted off through the village as though he had never done anything else in all his life.

It was just a delightful instance of the willingness of every member of a fine Battery to do anything whatever that was needed of him, a willing spirit that ran through the whole unit like a glowing stripe in a piece of cloth.

That stripe was of pure gold.

A. D. T.

N.B.—The illustrations of this Article have been reproduced by the kindness of William Potter, Publisher, of " Amateur Gunners."

The Late
Field-Marshal Viscount Byng

APPRECIATIONS.

All members of the League will regret the death of that great leader of men, Lord Byng.

As an old school fellow at Eton I had known him well and like everyone else, followed and admired his military career.

No one who ever served with him, no matter of what rank, will forget his friendly grip, his cheery smile and confidence that he inspired. A splendid soldier with a charming personality.

Let us hope that the youth of the present day will follow his life as an example of what that of a great soldier should be—always straightforward in peace and war.

W. P. PULTENEY, Lieut.-General.

One by one the principal figures of the British fighting forces of the Great War are taken from us, each leaving a poignant grief in the hearts of the thousands who served under them, learnt their sterling qualities and honoured them accordingly.

On 6th June, 1935, Field-Marshal Viscount Byng of Vimy passed away. No one who came into close contact with Julian Byng could ever escape the charm of that kindly, simple, generous nature. A man of extreme modesty and strong religious feeling, he had an intense dislike of ostentation and of self-advertisement. Chicanery and subterfuge were anathema to him. His very great sense of duty was never tempered by personal inclination. Loyalty was the keynote of his conduct, perhaps above all, loyalty to his subordinates. No word of criticism would he ever utter, or permit to be uttered, of anyone who had genuinely tried to serve him. Recrimination and controversy after the event he always discouraged.

A deep and discerning student of human nature, endowed with a great sympathy for any kind of suffering, he strove quietly but unceasingly to ameliorate the conditions obtaining for the rank and file of the army.

By nature humble-minded, he usually referred to himself in terms of disparagement. Actually he possessed mental attainments of a very high order. He had an unusually quick brain, logical, analytical and far-seeing ; stored, in addition, with knowledge, often of an unusual and unexpected nature. His sense of humour was proverbial. He possessed great determination and the power of quick decision. Yet there was nothing hard about him. His iron will was sweetened by the artistic understanding and sympathy given to the lover and connoisseur of music. He possessed, in particular, two especial attributes of the great leader. His quiet but magnetic influence quickly welded any group of individuals into a harmonious team, and he had the rare ability to state clearly what he wanted done and then to leave it to those concerned to do it.

A great leader, a most lovable personality, a loyal and true friend, he was a shining example of what the army understands by the phrase " an officer and a gentleman." He will always remain an inspiration to those who served him, and not least to

" ONE OF THEM."

T. E. Lawrence

By Captain Raymond Savage.

THERE is no need for me to write of Colonel Lawrence's war-time exploits. They have been told often and again by various people and posterity will judge of their value and greatness.

It is of Lawrence, the man, that I would write for old comrades of the Great War. I was attached to Lord Allenby's staff in Palestine and, meeting Lawrence many times, was always duly impressed by the modesty and humanity of this great little man. There may have been, and indeed it would seem impossible that it should not be so, an element of vanity about him, but it was a vanity not of self but of achievement.

He welded the Arab tribes together in such a magical manner that in some ways it may be claimed that his success was the breaking point as far as the Central Powers were concerned. He told me that upon the occasion when he was actually captured, but mercifully unrecognised, he had only one fear as he was lashed with a hide whip by the Turks, and that was that he might in his anguish cry out in English. Then his death would have been a slow matter of weeks or months and not of a moment. His detachment and personal bravery were quite amazing, and yet there was a softness in his character which made him seem at times almost ethereal. Those who really knew him loved him in the very best sense of the word, and yet curiously enough, and in some unexplainable way, he does not seem to have left us entirely.

His attitude in refusing all honours and decorations after the War was an attitude of rectitude. It was no grandiloquent gesture, but a deep conviction that as his beloved Arabs had been let down by the Allies, he could in no way accept any honours from those whom he considered had basely broken their word. It cannot be often enough repeated, and I can personally vouch for the fact as I have been his personal agent ever since he began writing, that he refused to accept for himself one penny out of the huge sums that were received from the sales of his book *Revolt in the Desert.* Every penny went to the Royal Air Force Memorial Fund. He steadfastly refused to profit by one farthing from his Arab campaign, and told me that he never intended doing so. There are many living to-day who have benefited by his extraordinary kindness, and it is a shocking thing that many so-called friends tried immediately after his death to profit in mean and petty ways.

There are those who think that he posed, that he was vain and that he sought publicity. This is utterly untrue, and again, only those who knew him intimately realised that he genuinely wished to hide his identity, and that he thought in all innocence that by changing his name he could vanish into oblivion. He just could not realise that any attempt to suppress his identity would lead to greater mystery, and that he would be all the more sought after.

He is gone. His personal friends have lost a trusty loyal friend, and the Nation a great and honoured figure. At his funeral there was only one floral tribute — a little posy of violets and lilies of the valley from a young girl who wrote on a card : " To T. E. L., who should sleep among the Kings." Little did she realise the significance of her simple devoted action.

T. E. sleeps, as he would have wished, in the little Dorset Churchyard, but his memory is enshrined in the hearts of his grateful fellow men throughout the four quarters of the world.

R. S.

Easter Pilgrimage to Ypres, 1935

A PARTY of twenty-one assembled at Victoria Station at 10 a.m. on Saturday, April 20th, and were greeted by our conductor, Captain G. E. de Trafford, M.C., who by his kindly attention made us all feel at home. At Dover we boarded the new mail boat " Prince Baudouin " for Ostend, and enjoyed an excellent crossing. Some of the party were making their first visit since the war, others had never been and were full of expectations while those who had re-visited many times were just as keen and felt drawn to this place, Ypres, by some invisible power which the writer can fully appreciate.

We reached our destination at 6.45 p.m. and walked to the Grande Place in a thunderstorm. The terrific crashes above reminded some of us of a similar welcome by high explosive shells in days gone by. We were heartily welcomed at the Splendid Hotel and made most comfortable. Dinner at 7.30 was much enjoyed after our long journey. Our first duty was to attend the sounding of the " Last Post " at the Menin Gate at 9 p.m. in memory of our fallen comrades. Members of the 61st Division were also there holding a short service of remembrance in which we joined and seeing the 55,000 names inscribed on the panels made us feel and realise the remarks of the late Field-Marshal Lord Plumer that "They are not gone from us, They are here." Some of us walked up the Menin Road and tried to imagine the scene as we used to know it and then to bed, tired, but satisfied with our first day.

Easter Day saw many of us about early, some attending one of the early services in the English Church, the rest of the morning

SOME OF THE PARTY

being spent by members of the party going and doing just what they liked. The writer was much struck with the beauty of the Cathedral, the fine organ, full orchestra and the singing of the choir during High Mass was very beautiful. Mid-day saw the visit of 300 members of the Surrey Branch of the British Legion who officially presented the Burgomaster with a cheque for £400 to complete the endowment fund to ensure the ceremony of the " Last Post." After lunch, we embarked on a battlefield tour of the Salient and the following places were visited : St. Jean, Wieltje, the Canadian Memorial which marks the battlefield where the Canadians withstood the first German gas attack early 'fifteen. We then turned right towards the Passchendaele Ridge stopping for a time at the beautiful Tyne Cot Cemetery and viewed the fine Memorial bearing the names of another 35,000 who have no known graves. Let me add here, that the terrible nature of the battles in the Salient needs no further comment than to say that there are nearly 100,000 who gave their lives for their country and have no known graves, these together with the known total some 250,000 officers and men. One has only to stand in this cemetery to appreciate the dominating position held by the German Army for three years. Our tour continued *via* Zonnebeke, Gheluvelt, Polygon Wood, Glencorse Wood, Hooge, Maple Avenue, Hill 62, and preserved trenches in Sanctuary Wood, then to Hill 60, returning to Ypres through Zillebeke, Hell Fire Corner,

White Chateau and Menin Gate. Our thanks are due to Mr. C. J. Parminter for pointing out all the places of interest which made the tour most enjoyable.

On Monday some of the party were off early for a visit to the Somme battlefields, including the Vimy Ridge, Arras, Serre, Bapaume, Beaucourt, Albert and the Memorial to the 73,000 Missing at Thiepval. Others visited Poperinghe where we were fortunate in finding Major Slessor who showed us over Talbot House and its historical chapel.

The writer has been asked to describe his visit to a certain Pill-Box at St. Julien which he used in September, 1917, when serving with the 58th Division in the attack on the Ridge on September 20th, of that year. The actual Pill-Box was found in nearly perfect condition. This large concrete shelter on the bank of the Steenbeek now known as A.II.62, a former German H.Q., and used as a Battalion H.Q. in September, 1917, consists of semi-circular compartments, 6-ft. to 7-ft. in height. Each compartment was entered from a covered way running the full length at the back and this is the only part damaged to-day as it faced the enemy. When occupied by us and subjected to heavy shell fire it provided safe shelter for 200 to 300 men at a pinch, and was occupied by a company as well as a Battalion H.Q. just prior to the attack. The writer had been in the Somme attack of July 1st, 1916, that was bad enough, but the conditions here were infinitely worse with no cover, what with rain, incessant shell fire pounding the ground, wiping out water courses and in consequence the earth became one large swamp of slimy slush with deep shell-holes full of water into which men fell wounded, and many were drowned. Such were the conditions on September 19th at 11 p.m., when we took up our positions for the attack, lying in the mire awaiting Zero hour soon after 5 a.m.

A. II. 62.

A miserable night indeed, in which I lost quite a number of my men, and was blown up myself by a shell, but strange to relate, unharmed. The attack was directed with the St. Julien-Poelcapelle Road at our rear, Springfield on the left, and Winnipeg to the right. Zero hour arrived and down came the barrage from over 2,000 guns, a wall of bursting shells fell in front of us and crept forward almost as fast as one could walk through the slush — an awe-inspiring sight which will never be forgotten. Machine guns raked us and we lost very heavily. I was shot through the jaw and left shoulder, consequently knocked out, and lost touch with the attack. After a two hours struggle I managed to get back to the first-aid post in St. Julien, and so ended my share in the battle for the ridge.

It is good to hear that the Belgian Government have agreed to the preservation of some 180 of the most interesting concrete shelters, block-houses and dugouts. There were several thousand of them in the Salient — a wonderful system with one batch covering another batch to a great depth, and one wonders at the super-human bravery shown by the Allied Forces in being able to capture them. In a large number of cases they stand unharmed to-day despite their subjection to bombardments such as the world has never seen before.

To those who have not been able to visit the war cemeteries, I say that no greater care could be taken of the graves for they are beautiful gardens, not a weed, not a blade of grass out of place, flowering shrubs abound, spring bulbs and in the rose season a magnificent sight. Your dear ones are in the care of a grateful country, and tended by those who love their work.

Should everyone make a pilgrimage to Ypres? Of course you should go, and pay tribute to our brave comrades who lie out there, they saved England, they were a wall unto us both by day and night. Go for a trip with one of the Ypres League parties! You will have the time of your life, English is spoken everywhere, the Belgian people will give you a hearty welcome and it will be an education.

Tuesday morning we left Ypres soon after 9 a.m. boarding the boat "Princess Astrid" and after another good crossing reached London at about 5 p.m. Incidentally, we had a most interesting conversation with a German officer en route from Dover who had served on both the Somme and Ypres fronts. May this be one of many trips that the "Guard" will make to Ypres and on behalf of the party I convey to Captain de Trafford our best thanks for all his kindness to us which will be long remembered.

A. C. K.

A Week-end in Ypres with the 85th Club

By a Visitor with the 85th Club.

FOR the sixth consecutive year, a pilgrimage to Ypres, under the auspices of the Ypres League, was made by members and friends of the 85th Field Ambulance O.C.A., and despite the passing of time, this annual trip is still looked upon as one of the outstanding events in their social calendar.

The enthusiasm of those assembled at Victoria Station on the night of May 17th was good to witness. Their prospect of once again re-visiting the old battlefield haunts was indeed infectious and the journey to Folkestone appeared particularly short amongst this happy band. The inevitable pack of cards was produced and unfinished games continued on the boat, meanwhile others proceeded to their allotted bunks to snatch a little sleep. Our arrival at grimy old Dunkerque was the signal for the Douane officials to prepare to relieve "Les Anglais" of their good English fags, a procedure, which the party are by now quite accustomed! To rather tired limbs, the comfortable train journey from Dunkerque was welcomed and crossing the frontier Ypres was soon reached looking so new in the early morning sunshine, but so full of old memories and associations. A hasty wash, brush-up and good breakfast at Hotel Skindles, the party were again on the move, this time for a motor tour of the battlefields accompanied by the League's representative, Mr. C. J. Parminter. Many old billets and haunts were visited en route to Cassel where an excellent lunch was eagerly enjoyed at the Hotel Sauvage. Then on the return journey a call was made at Talbot House, Poperinghe and Skindles where tea was taken eventually arriving back in Ypres at about 6.30 p.m.

After dinner the party assembled at the Menin Gate for the ceremony of the "Last Post." Then followed an enjoyable whist drive and dance at the Pilgrims Rest Room adjacent the English Church where the British community congregated in aid of the British Settlement Benevolent Fund.

Sunday was a day of leisure, apart from a short service at the Menin Gate at 12 noon, very kindly conducted by the Resident Chaplain, the Rev. G. R. Milner, M.A., when a wreath of Haig Poppies was placed by the Chairman, Mr. W. F. Taylor.

All too soon, the time arrived to pack up, but what an enjoyable experience made possible by the courtesy and helpful assistance of the Ypres League. It is indeed very inspiring to visit the Immortal Salient to-day and to observe the beautiful manner in which the graves of our fallen comrades are tended and cared for, also to note the marvellous strides made by the Belgians in the re-building of their sorely striken towns and villages and the cultivation of their lands.

C. H. M. R.

League Secretary's Notes

We welcome very heartily all who have enrolled as members during the past quarter, and we desire to convey to them our grateful thanks for their valued support. Thanks are also due to our Branches, Corresponding Members and individual help that we have received in the recruitments. Members are working hard in response to the message of our distinguished Patron, H.R.H. Princess Beatrice, which appeared in the last April edition of the YPRES TIMES, expressing the hope that all members will endeavour to swell our membership by enlisting at the very least one from among their comrades of the Salient. As a result we expect to have the honour to record a goodly influx of new members before the end of the present year.

Welcome tidings have been received from a faithful supporter in Mr. Edward Thomas, of Auckland, New Zealand, signifying his good intention to form a Branch of the Ypres League in Auckland. We wish Mr. Thomas every success in his staunch endeavours, and look forward to report favourably in a future issue of the journal. It is also possible that we may be able to inaugurate a new Branch in Co. Tipperary, where ex-service men are showing their interest in the League through the kindness of Mr. J. Kennedy, ex-Sergeant, R.A.S.C.

The Ypres League travel bureau is happily out to break all previous records in this Jubilee Year, and since March 1st, parties have been conducted to the battlefields of France and Belgium as follows :— 168th Infantry Brigade, 167th Infantry Brigade, 4th Guards' Brigade, Honourable Artillery Company, Easter Mixed Pilgrimage, 85th Club, Whitsuntide Mixed Pilgrimage, Public Schools, and 236th Siege Battery, R.G.A. In prospect, we have the August Bank Holiday Mixed Pilgrimage to Ypres and over the same week-end a party of 60 or more members of the Old Coldstreamers' Association. In addition, the 128th Infantry Brigade are negotiating with us for a battlefield tour in the Autumn, and our last Mixed Pilgrimage to Ypres in 1935 will take place from September 21st to 24th.

Space does not allow us to dwell too much on the travel activity, but it has all-important bearing on the League's work. Firstly, because headquarters staff is brought in personal contact with Army units, ex-service men, and relatives of the fallen and the rapid growth of our travel organization is the outcome of their recommendations. Secondly, this activity is a substantial aid to the recruiting of new members who join the League at their own free will in appreciation, not only of our facilities, but in entire approval of the aims and objects of our Association. Indeed, practical interest does not cease here — After the 85th Club had concluded their sixth consecutive annual tour last May under our auspices, their Committee, as a token of appreciation and regard, most generously contributed a cheque for five guineas to the Ypres League Poor Pilgrim's Fund, and we may add that in connection with this charitable work, a further donation of five pounds has recently been subscribed by the South Kensington Branch of the British Legion. We cannot emphasise our thanks too deeply, and only trust that the respective Committees realise our debt of gratitude for their extremely thoughtful gestures and benevolent support, and they may rest assured that these generous donations will give immense consolation to the poor mothers and widows who are specially selected to see, for the first time, the graves of their sons and husbands at Ypres. Since 1927 the Ypres League has expended over a thousand pounds on this charity and we expect to reduce our anxious " Waiting List " still further during the summer of 1935.

In order to increase the popular appeal of the " YPRES TIMES," we are hoping, provided the kindly co-operation of our friends and readers is forthcoming, to publish in the near future a series of short articles on " The Regimental Customs of the British Army."

We are asking all who are in a position to do so to send us brief details of any traditional customs that may be associated either with their own or any other individual unit.

Contributions, under this heading, will be gratefully received and acknowledged by the Editor.

We cannot conclude these notes without a feeling of deep regret in the sudden death of Captain J. G. W. Hyndson, M.C., one of our best all-round supporters, not only active in recruiting new members, but he contributed three fine battle articles for the YPRES TIMES, which were published in the April, July and October, 1934, editions, respectively, and which must have been read with great interest. In addition, he allowed us to sell his book *From Mons to the First Battle of Ypres* with a commission to the League funds on each copy sold, and once he accompanied one of our parties to Ypres in order to give some lecturettes on his 1914 experiences. Such an active member as Captain Hyndson cannot easily be replaced, and we shall always miss his welcome and encouraging visits to headquarters. Our deepest sympathy is extended to his father, the Rev. Jas. Hyndson, in his great bereavement.

During the last year or two, our ranks have been sadly depleted in the death of some valuable workers, but the League is particularly fortunate, in that it possesses an exceptionally loyal membership and, as in war-time, when so often the best are taken, others are ready to come forward and exercise even greater efforts in their memory.

BURNING OF THE CLOTH HALL, 1915.

A few remaining coloured prints now in stock are being offered to our members at the reduced rate of 1s. each, post free.

Since further copies are unobtainable we would advise those interested to make their purchase without delay.

WREATHS.

Arrangements are made by the Ypres League to place wreaths for relatives on the graves of British soldiers situated in France and Belgium at the following times of the year:—

EASTER, ARMISTICE DAY, CHRISTMAS.

The wreaths may be composed of natural flowers, laurel, or holly, and can be bought at the following prices—12s. 6d., 15s. 6d., and 20s., according to the size and quality of the wreath.

YPRES LEAGUE TIE.

Dark shade of cornflower blue relieved by a narrow gold stripe. In good quality silk.

Price 3/6d., post free.

Obtainable from Secretary, Ypres League, 20, Orchard Street, London, W.1.

BAR-LOCK (1925) CO.
NOTTINGHAM, ENGLAND

TYPEWRITER MANUFACTURERS

by Appointment to His Majesty the King

Makers of

BAR-LOCK   **BAR-LET**
STANDARD   PORTABLE

TYPEWRITERS
MADE IN ENGLAND
AND IN USE ALL OVER THE WORLD

Branch Notes

PURLEY.

The Spring Golf Meeting of the Branch was held on May 21st, at Woodcote Park, Coulsdon, and thirty-three members played for the Ninth Wipers Cup.

The Meeting was distinguished by one of the members, namely, Lieut. B. R. Brill, producing an exceptionally brill-iant round and making a return of four up on Bogey having holed the course in 78 strokes. This naturally left the rest of the troops gasping for breath, and the two nearest for second place at one down: they were Lieut. J. D. Mill and the Adjutant, who was awarded second prize on account of a better last nine holes.

A supper followed the Meeting, and a very enjoyable function it was, with Major H. G. Harris in the Chair. As usual, the prize-winners and delinquents who made no return were called upon for an explanation. The Bombardier and the Amphibian also joined in with a speech and entertainment, and after a hearty vote of thanks to the Host Club, the Meeting terminated.

MILITARY WHIST DRIVE AT COLCHESTER.

The Colchester and district branch of the Ypres League held a military whist drive at Kacklin's Cafe, High Street, Colchester, on Monday evening.

The object was to raise funds to assist poor people to visit the graves of relatives who fell in the war.

There were 92 players, and the winning table was Ireland (Mr. and Mrs. Cook, Mrs. Bunting and Mrs. Millbourn); 2, Denmark (Mrs. Sargeant, Mrs. Finch, Mrs. Langley and Mrs. Borer). The lowest was Egypt (Mrs. Imms, Mrs. Snow, Mrs. Powell and Mrs. Barford). The M.C. was Mr. Eves. During the evening other prizes were won by Mr. Firmin and Mr. Scott.

Mr. H. Snow, the branch's hon. secretary was responsible for the general arrangements, assisted by Capt. C. Rooney, Capt. A. C. Palmer and Mr. W. H. Taylor.

ELEVENTH ANNUAL REUNION DINNER AND DANCE.

On Saturday, the 4th May, the Annual Reunion Dinner and Dance of the London County Committee was held at the Royal Hotel, Woburn Place, W.C.1, members and friends to the number of 134 being present.

This attendance was a great improvement on last year, and the whole of the proceedings were marked by a spirit of sociability and enthusiasm which augurs well for future occasions.

The Dinner was presided over by Brig. General A. Burt, C.B., C.M.G., D.S.O., and supported by the Hon. Alice Douglas Pennant and Major E. Montague Jones. The Chairman, by his geniality and businesslike handling of his duties, did much to make the reunion a great success. In proposing the Loyal Toast he spoke at some length, in view of the near approach of the Silver Jubilee celebrations, and emphasized the fact that their Majesties The King and Queen, and the other Members of their Family, exercise an enormous influence for good throughout the length and breadth of our Empire. The Toast was received by tremendous enthusiasm by all present.

Later, the Toasts of " Absent Friends " and the London County Committee, were submitted, the latter being replied to in his own inimitable way by Major Montague Jones, our hard working and ever genial Committee Chairman. Major Jones thanked all present for their support, gave a resume of the years work, and completely " brought down the house " by a recital of one or two anecdotes in connection with a recent Battlefields Tour, of which he was in charge.

The Chairman of the London County Committee then proposed the toast of " The Chairman " which was received with musical honours, to which General Burt suitably replied.

The following telegrams were received during the evening :—

" *The King sincerely thanks the members of the London Branch of the Ypres League for their kind and loyal message which His Majesty, as Patron-in-Chief, much appreciates.*"—*Private Secretary.*

" *The Fifth Army Old Comrades send greetings and hope you will have a pleasant re-union.*"

At the conclusion of the Dinner the Company adjourned to the Ball Room for the second part of the evening's Programme and the Dance which followed can only be described as the best we have ever held. The duties of M.C. were carried out by Mr. W. C. Parker in his cheery and efficient manner and the Music was provided by the " AL BERRY'S BAND." The Programme of Dances was well assorted, both the modern and older schools being well represented, and this, together with a perfect floor, made the function a great success. The whole of the arrangements for this most enjoyable evening were carried out by Mr. John Boughey, the Secretary of the London County Committee. Mr. Boughey is no lover of limelight, but some of us know and appreciate how much hard work, thought, and energy, he puts into the various activities of the Ypres League in London, and it is earnestly desired that members will back up his efforts by their presence at as many of the Leagues fixtures as possible.

J. W. F.

LONDON COUNTY COMMITTEE.

Informal Gatherings.

The season's Informal Gatherings are now drawing to a close, and we are grateful for the interest that has been shown in these reunions during the past twelve months. The attendances have been satisfactory, although we should like to welcome larger musters. Our indebtedness is due to those who have voluntarily come forward to arrange evening's programmes, and we hope that others will follow the good example during the next series which commence in September. Fixture dates will be gladly sent on application to the Hon. Secretary, Mr. J. Boughey.

The London County Committee are already at work planning the forthcoming Gatherings, when it is expected to introduce into the programmes some new items of interest which we trust will meet the approval of the audiences.

Annual Reunion Smoking Concert.

The Thirteenth Annual Smoking Concert will be held at the Caxton Hall, Victoria Street, S.W.1, on Saturday, October 26th, 1935, at 7.30 p.m., and we shall look forward to the full support of the London members. Full details will be announced in the next quarterly journal and notices will appear in the Press.

PLEASE RESERVE THIS DATE.

THE
THIRTEENTH ANNUAL REUNION

SMOKING CONCERT

(Organised by the London County Committee)

will be held on

Saturday, October 26th, 1935

at 7.30 p.m.

IN

Caxton Hall, Caxton St., Victoria Street, S.W.1

The support of all members is earnestly solicited as we hope very much to record a bumper attendance this year.

Full particulars will appear in the next October edition of the " Ypres Times."

Ypres League Travel Bureau

CONDUCTED PILGRIMAGES

The undermentioned are the last of our Conducted Mixed Pilgrimages for 1935 and open to all interested.

In view of the heavy bookings expected, particularly for the August Bank Holiday Pilgrimage, early application is advised in order to secure the best available accommodation.

AUGUST BANK HOLIDAY (August 3rd—6th, Saturday to Tuesday):

    YPRES (Day route *via* Ostend).

SEPTEMBER (September 21st—24th, Saturday to Tuesday) YPRES (Day route *via* Ostend).

    YPRES. *Cost.* London to Ypres return *via* Ostend, with full board and best available accommodation (three nights) including taxes and gratuities at hotel.

Second Class Train (1st Class Boat)	£4 18 11
Second Class Train and Boat	£4 10 5
Third Class Train (1st Class Boat)	£4 5 0
Third Class Train and Boat	£3 16 6

The above quotations do not include meals on the journey or excursions on the continent.

(Battlefield tours arranged by the conductor at Ypres to suit the requirements of the party at moderate charges.)

Prospectuses will be gladly forwarded on application to The Secretary, Ypres League, 20, Orchard Street, London, W.1.

INDEPENDENT TRAVEL.

To those contemplating individual travel, our Travel Department would be pleased to furnish information on all matters connected with trips to any part of the Old Western Front Battlefields.

Apply to Secretary, Ypres League, 20, Orchard Street, London, W.1, for the Ypres League Travel Guide for 1935.

HOTEL
Splendid & Britannique
YPRES

GRANDE PLACE. Opposite Cloth Hall.

Leading Hotel for Comfort and Quality, and Patronized by The Ypres League.

Completely Renovated.

Running Water. Bathrooms

Moderate Terms.   Garage.

Proprietor—Life Member, Ypres League.

YPRES
Skindles Hotel

(Opposite the Station)

Proprietor—Life Member, Ypres League

Branch at Poperinghe

(close to Talbot House)

THE BRITISH TOURING SERVICE

Manager—Mr. P. VYNER

Representative and Life Member, Ypres League

**10, Station Square
ARRAS
(P.-de-C.) France**

Cars for Hire, with British Driver Guides   Tours Arranged

Branches and Corresponding Members

BRANCHES.

LONDON	Hon. Secretary to the London County Committee : J. Boughey, 20, Orchard Street, London, W.1.
	E. LONDON DISTRICT—L. A. Weller, 40, Lambourne Gardens, Hornchurch, Essex.
	TOTTENHAM AND EDMONTON DISTRICT—E, Glover, 191, Landowne Road, Tottenham, N.17.
	H. Carey, 373, Sydenham Road, S.E.26.
COLCHESTER	H. Snow (Hon. Sec.), 9, Church Street.
	W. H. Taylor (Pilgrimage Hon. Sec,), 64, High Street.
GATESHEAD	Lieut.-Colonel E. G. Crouch, 8, Ashgrove Terrace.
LIVERPOOL	Captain A. M. Webster, Blundellsands.
PURLEY	Major Graham Carr, D.S.O., M.C., 112-114, High Street.
SHEFFIELD	Captain J. Wilkinson, "Holmfield," Bents Drive.
BELGIUM	Capt. P. D. Parminter, 19, Rue Surmont de Volsberghe, Ypres.
CANADA	Ed. Kingsland, P.O. Box 83, Magog, Quebec.
SOUTH AFRICA	L. G. Shuter, Church Street, Pietermaritzburg,
KENYA	C. H. Slater, P.O. Box 403, Nairobi.
AMERICA	Representative : Captain R. Henderson-Bland, 110 West 57th Street, New York City.

CORRESPONDING MEMBERS

GREAT BRITAIN.

ABERYSTWYTH	T. O. Thomas, 5, Smithfield Road.
ASHTON-UNDER-LYNE	G. D. Stuart, "Woodlands,", Thronfield Grove, Arundel Street.
BANBURY	Captain C. W. Fowke, Yew Tree House, King's Sutton.
BIRMINGHAM	Mrs. Hill, 191, Cattell Road, Small Heath.
	John Burman, "Westbrook," Solihull Road, Shirley.
BOURNEMOUTH	H. L. Pasmore, 40, Morley Road, Boscombe Park.
BRISTOL	W. S. Hook, "Wytschaete" Redland Court Road.
BROADSTAIRS	C. E. King, 6, Norman Road, St. Peters, Broadstairs,
	Mrs. Briggs, North Foreland House.
CHATHAM	W. N. Channon, 22, Keyes Avenue.
CHESTERFIELD	Major A. W. Shea, 14, Cross Street.
CONGLETON	Mr. H. Dart, 61, The Crescent.
DARLINGTON	D. S. Vigo, 125, Dorset Road, Bexhill-on-Sea.
DERBY	T. Jakeman, 10, Graham Street.
DORRINGTON (Salop)	Captain G. D. S. Parker, Frodesley Rectory.
EXETER	Captain E. Jenkin, 25, Queen Street.
GLOUCESTER	H. R. Hunt, "Casita," Parton Lane, Churchdown.
HERNE BAY	Captain E. Clarke Williams, F.S.A.A., "Conway," Station Road.
HOVE	Captain G. W. J. Cole, 2, Westbourne Terrace, Kingsway.
LEICESTER	W. C. Dunford, 343, Aylestone Road.
LINCOLN	E. Swaine, 79, West Parade.
LLANWRST	A. C. Tomlinson, M.A., Bod Estyn.
LOUGHTON	Capt. O. G. Johnson, M.A., Loughton School.
MATLOCK (Derby)	Miss Dickinson, Beechwood.
MELROSE	Mrs. Lindesay Kelsall, Darnlee.
NEW BRIGHTON (Cheshire)	E. F. Williams, 5, Waterloo Road.
NEW MILTON	W. H. Lunn, "Greycot," Albert Road.

NOTTINGHAM ...	... E. V. Brown, 3, Eldon Chambers, Wheeler Gate.
ST. HELENS (Lancs.)	... John Orford, 124, Knowsley Road.
SHREWSBURY ...	... Major-General Sir John Headlam, K.B.E., C.B., D.S.O., Cruck Meole House, Hanwood.
TIVERTON (Devon)	... Mr. W H. Duncan Arthur, Surveyor's Office, Town Hall.
WELSHPOOL ...	... Mr. E. Wilson, Coedway, Ford, Salop.

DOMINIONS AND FOREIGN COUNTRIES.

AUSTRALIA ...	... Messrs. C. H. Green, and George Lawson, Anzac House, Elizabeth Street, Brisbane, Queensland. R. A. Baldwin, c/o Government Savings Bank of N.S.W., Martin Place, Sydney. Mr. W. Cloves, Box 1296, G.P.O., Adelaide.
BELGIUM ...	... Sister Marguerite, Sacré Coeur, Ypres.
CANADA ...	.. Brig.-General V. W. Odlum, C.B., C.M.G., D.S.O., 2530, Point Grey Road, Vancouver. V. A. Bowes, 326, 40th Avenue West, Calgary, Alberta. W. Constable F. Grece, St. Hilaire Station, Ronville County, Quebec.
CEYLON ...	... Captain F. R. G. Webb, M.C., Irrigation Bungalow, Kalmunai, E.P.
EGYPT ...	... L. B. S. Larkins, The Residency, Cairo.
INDIA ...	... Lieut.-Quartermaster G. Smith, Queen's Bays, Sialkot, India.
IRELAND ...	... Miss A. K. Jackson, Cloneyhurke House, Portarlington.
NEW ZEALAND ...	... Captain W. U. Gibb, Ava Lodge, Puhinui Road, Papatoetoe, Auckland S. E. Beattie, Lowlands, Woodville.
SOUTH AFRICA ...	... H. L. Versfield, c/o Cape Explosives Works Ltd., 150, St. Georges Street, Cape Town.
SPAIN ...	... Captain P. W. Burgess, Calle de Zurbano 29, Madrid.
U.S.A. ...	... Captain Henry Maslin, 942, President Street, Brooklyn, New York. L. E. P, Foot. 20, Gillett Street, Hartford, Conn, U.S.A. A. P. Forward, 449, East 80th Street, New York. J. W. Freebody, 945, McBride Avenue, Los Angeles.
NOVA SCOTIA ...	... Will R. Bird, 35, Clarence Street, Amherst.

Membership of the League

This is open to all who served in the Salient, and to all those whose relatives or friends died there, in order that they may have a record of that service for themselves and their descendants, and belong to the comradeship of men and women who understand and remember all that Ypres meant in suffering and endurance.

Life membership, £2 10s.

Annual members, 5s.

Do not let the fact of your not having served in the Salient deter you from joining the Ypres League. Those who have neither fought in the Salient nor lost relatives there, but who are in sympathy with the objects of the Ypres League, are admitted to its fellowship, but are not given scroll certificates.

There is a Junior Division for children whose relatives served in the Salient. It is open also to others to whom our objects appeal.

Annual subscription 1s. up to the age of 18, after which they can become ordinary members of the League.

THE YPRES LEAGUE (INCORPORATED)
20, Orchard Street, Portman Square, W.1.

Telephone: WELBECK 1446. *Telegrams*: YPRESLEAG, " WESDO," LONDON.

Patron-in-Chief: H.M. THE KING.

Patrons:
H.R.H. THE PRINCE OF WALES.   H.R.H. PRINCESS BEATRICE.

President: GENERAL SIR CHARLES H. HARINGTON.

Vice-Presidents:

F.-M. VISCOUNT ALLENBY.	F.-M. SIR CLAUD W. JACOB.
THE VISCOUNT WAKEFIELD OF HYTHE.	F.-M. SIR PHILIP CHETWODE.
GENERAL SIR CECIL ROMER.	F.-M. LORD MILNE.

General Committee:

THE COUNTESS OF ALBEMARLE.	MAJOR-GENERAL C. J. B. HAY.
*CAPTAIN C. ALLISTON.	MR. J. HETHERINGTON.
LIEUT-COLONEL BECKLES WILLSON.	MRS. E. HEAP.
MR. HENRY BENSON.	GENERAL SIR W. C. G. HENEKER.
*MR. J. BOUGHEY.	*CAPTAIN O. G. JOHNSON.
*MISS B. BRICE-MILLER.	*MAJOR E. MONTAGUE JONES.
COLONEL G. T. BRIERLEY.	CAPTAIN H. D. PEABODY.
CAPTAIN P. W. BURGESS.	*THE HON. ALICE DOUGLAS PENNANT.
*MAJOR H. CARDINAL-HARFORD.	*LIEUT.-GENERAL SIR W. P. PULTENEY.
REV. P. B. CLAYTON.	LIEUT.-COLONEL SIR J. MURRAY.
*THE EARL OF YPRES.	*COLONEL G. E. C. RASCH.
MRS. C. J. EDWARDS.	VISCOUNT SANDON.
MAJOR C. J. EDWARDS.	THE HON. SIR ARTHUR STANLEY.
MR. H. A. T. FAIRBANK.	MR. ERNEST THOMPSON.
MR. T. ROSS FURNER.	CAPTAIN J. LOCKLEY TURNER.
SIR PHILIP GIBBS.	*MR. E. B. WAGGETT.
MR. E. GLOVER.	CAPTAIN J. WILKINSON.
MAJOR-GENERAL SIR JOHN HEADLAM.	CAPTAIN H. TREVOR WILLIAMS.
MR. F. D. BANKS HILL.	

* Executive Committee.

Bankers:
BARCLAYS BANK LTD., Knightsbridge Branch.

Honorary Solicitors:
MESSRS. FLADGATE & CO., 70, Pall Mall, S.W.

Secretary:
CAPTAIN G. E. DE TRAFFORD.

Auditors:
MESSRS. LEPINE & JACKSON, 6, Bond Court, E.C.4.

League Representative at Ypres:
CAPTAIN P. D. PARMINTER.
19, Rue Surmont de Volsberghe

League Representative at Cambrai:
MR. A. WILDE,
9, Rue des Anglaises.

League Representative at Amiens:
CAPTAIN STUART OSWALD.
7, Rue Porte-Paris.

League Representative at Arras:
MR. P. VYNER,
10, Station Square.

Hon. Secretary, Ypres British Settlement:
LT. COLONEL F. G. POOLE,

PRIMARY OBJECTS OF THE LEAGUE

I.—Commemoration and Comradeship.
II.—To provide special travel facilities for Members and all interested to Ypres and battlefields, and transport of Members.
III.—The furnishing of information about the Salient; marking of historic sites and the compilation of charts of the battlefields.
IV.—The erection of a Ypres British Church and School which has been completed.
V.—The establishment of groups of members throughout the world, through Branch Secretaries and Corresponding Members.
VI.—The maintenance of cordial relations with dwellers on the battlefields of Ypres.
VII.—The formation of a Junior Division.

Use the Ypres League Travel Bureau for Ypres and Whole of the Western Front.

FOR THE FOLLOWING PUBLICATIONS, Etc., apply:
Secretary, YPRES LEAGUE, 20, ORCHARD STREET, LONDON, W.1.

THE BATTLE BOOK OF YPRES. A history of notable deeds contributed by all regiments. 5s.; post free, 5s. 6d. Compiled by Beatrix Brice with the assistance of Lieut.-General Sir William Pulteney, G.C.V.O., etc.

BOOKS.

YPRES: Outpost of the Channel Ports. By Beatrix Brice. With Foreword by Field-Marshal Lord Plumer, G.C.B. Price 1s. 0d.; post free 1s. 3d.

In the Ypres Salient. By Lt.-Col. Beckles Willson. 1s. net; post free 1s. 2d.

With the Cornwall Territorials on the Western Front. By E. C. Matthews. 7s. 6d.; post free 8s.

Story of the 63rd Field Ambulance. By A. W. Westmore, etc. Cloth, 3s. 6d., post free. Paper, 2s. 6d., post free.

War Letters to a Wife. By Colonel Rowland Feilding. Popular Edition, 3s. 6d.; post free 4s.

The Pill Boxes of Flanders. 1s.; post free 1s. 3d.

From Mons to the First Battle of Ypres. By J. G. W. Hyndson, M.C. Price 5s., post free 5s. 3d.

YPRES LEAGUE TIES. 3s. 6d. each, post free.
YPRES LEAGUE BADGES. 2s. each, 2s. 1¼d. post free.
EMBROIDERED BADGES. 4s. each, post free.
Map and List of Cemeteries in the Ypres Salient. Price 9d.; post free 11d.
Map of the Somme. Price 1s. 8d., post free.

PICTURES.

Burning of the Cloth Hall, 1915. A Coloured Print, 14 in. by 12 in. 1s. post free.

Old Well-known Spots in New Guise. Prints, size 4¼ x 2½, recently taken of famous spots in the Ypres Salient, and which may be of great interest to our readers, are on sale at headquarters, price 4d. each, post free 5d. For particulars apply Secretary.

POST CARDS, PHOTOGRAPHS AND ETCHINGS.

Post Cards. Ypres: British Front during the War. Ruins of Ypres. Price 1s. post free.

Photographs of Menin Gate Unveiling. Size 11 in. by 7 in. 1s. 2d. each, post free.

Hill 60. Complete Panorama Photographs. 12 in. by 3¼ in. Price 3s., post free; 15 in. by 5 in. Price 3s. 6d., post free.

WAR-TIME PHOTOGRAPHS OF THE SALIENT.

6 in. by 8 in. ... 1s. 6d. each.
12 in. by 15 in. ... 4s. each.

List forwarded on application.

PHOTOGRAPHS OF WAR-TIME SKETCHES.

Bedford House (Front View), 1916.
Bedford House (Back View), 1916.
Voormezeele Main Street, 1916.
Voormezeele Crucifixion Gate, 1916.
Langhof Chateau, 1916.

Size 8½ in. by 6½ in. Price 2s. 6d. each, post free.

Photographs of the Thiepval and Arras Memorials. Post card size, price 1s. each, post free.

YPRES TIMES.

The Journal may be obtained at the League Offices.
BACK NUMBERS 1s.; 1934, 8d.; 1935, 6d.

Printed in Great Britain for the Publishers by FORD & GILL, 21a/23, Iliffe Yard, Crampton Street, London, S.E.17.

Memory Tablet.

OCTOBER - NOVEMBER - DECEMBER

OCTOBER.

Oct.	4th, 1914	...	Russian ultimatum to Bulgaria.
,,	5th, 1915	...	Allied Forces land at Salonika.
,,	9th, 1914	...	Antwerp occupied by Germans.
,,	10th, 1916	...	Allied ultimatum to Greece.
,,	14th, 1915	...	Bulgaria at war with Serbia.
,,	18th, 1918	...	Belgian coast clear.
,,	20th, 1914	...	First Battle of Ypres begun.
,,	25th, 1918	...	Ludendorf resigned.

NOVEMBER.

Nov.	1st, 1918	...	Versailles Conference opened.
,,	3rd, 1918	...	Austrian surrender. Keil Mutiny.
,,	4th, 1917	...	British troops in Italy.
,,	5th, 1914	...	Great Britain declares war on Turkey.
,,	6th, 1917	...	British storm the Passchendaele Ridge.
,,	9th, 1918	...	Marshal Foch receives German Envoys. Abdication of the Kaiser.
,,	10th, 1918	...	Kaiser's flight to Holland.
,,	10th, 1914	...	"Emden" sunk.
,,	11th, 1918	...	Armistice Terms accepted.
,,	18th, 1917	...	General Maud's death in Mesopotamia.

DECEMBER.

Dec.	8th, 1914	...	Naval Battle off the Falklands.
,,	9th, 1917	...	British capture Jerusalem.
,,	15th, 1915	...	Sir Douglas Haig C.-in-C. in France.
,,	16th, 1914	...	Germans bombarded West Hartlepool.
,,	19th, 1915	...	Withdrawal from Gallipoli.
,,	24th, 1914	...	First air raid on England.

The Ypres Times

Communications to
The Editor, "Ypres Times,"
20, Orchard Street, London, W.1.

PRICE 6d.
POST FREE 7d.

Vol. 7, No. 8.   Published Quarterly   October, 1935

Queen Astrid

A Message of Sympathy to the Belgian People.

SINCE our last issue a terrible tragedy, sudden and relentless, has fallen upon the Belgian Royal Family and the Belgian people, and our members, particularly those resident in and around Ypres, will desire to offer, in conjunction with the whole world, their sympathy and condolence to our neighbours across the Channel in the hour of their national grief.

Ties of mutual sacrifice and suffering, woven in a past still recent, have united our two countries in warm kinship and have made the welfare of the Belgians one of our close interests, to foster which it has been the constant endeavour of the Ypres League. The bereavement—coming so soon after the tragedy which deprived them of their late heroic and beloved King—calls forth from our members the sincerest and most profound sorrow.

Queen Astrid, who came from the North, from the Royal Family of Sweden, had won widespread admiration and affection by her simplicity and whole-hearted loyalty to the Belgian people. She was a devoted mother, a loving wife and companion, a woman who looked and acted as a Queen. Her marriage had been one of real affection, and in both the discharge of their public duties and in their personal relationship the King and Queen proved themselves an ideal pair.

For King Leopold's preservation his own people and Belgium's friends will thank Providence, and to him, above all, and his three children, bereaved of a mother who, amid the obligations of State, set an example to all mothers, our hearts go out in their own personal and most bitter sorrow.

His Majesty now faces the future with a heavy handicap, for the love that crowned his youth has been taken from his side. Still, his courageous and gallant bearing ever since the hour of the tragedy is an earnest to his people that he will not fail under the blow that has made desolate his heart and his home.

Members of the Ypres League share in a very real sense the bereavement which has fallen upon the Belgian nation.

H.B.

An Almost Forgotten Phase

By Captain G. Spencer Pryse, M.C., Author of "Four Days."

ON arrival at Ostend during the first week of September, 1914, I went straight to the Commandant to ask for a car for conveyance into Antwerp. It transpired that a small cortège would be leaving early next morning, and discretion prompted me to join them ; for in the event of an encounter with the enemy, in civilian dress and in such company, there would be every chance to pass unnoticed as a member of a little party of citizens occupied with their own affairs.

The roads were crowded and spectators lined the streets as though it were a gala day. It had even been found necessary to post handbills advising the population to refrain from following the Uhlan cavalry as their curiosity might be misunderstood. Nevertheless, every cross road had its barricade of felled trees and overturned carts held by the Garde Civique in quaint top hats and long ulsters, carrying weapons that may have done good service in the Napoleonic campaigns. They stood in sombre groups in the market squares ; hesitating, knowing that the invader had announced his intention to treat them as civilians and to shoot at sight any taken with arms in their hands.

Patriots leaned over the parapets of church towers and clung to the roofs of windmills, scanning the country. Once or twice excited éclaireurs warned us of the presence of Uhlans ahead and we turned into tortuous narrow lanes with volunteer guides clinging to our mudguards and an escort of enthusiastic children. There was occasional firing very close by, though no uniformed troops were to be seen. Certainly at that stage some ground existed for the policy of reprisals. After an entire day spent in this manner, night found us feeling our way through Moerbeke.

Further progress being out of the question, good luck provided the perfect host in the person of M. Maurice Lippens, since Governor of the Belgian Congo, whose property lay alongside the road. The servant who conducted me to my bedroom spoke proudly of the Brunswickers his friends had already killed. The night was hot and the distant heavy thud of gunfire came through open windows, while nearer to hand the occasional sharp report of a rifle rang out. After breakfast, M. Lippens showed me over his house. Very tall, and imperturbable he awaited alone and unarmed the arrival of the enemy, anxious only for the safety of his people. It was noon when we crossed the bridge of boats that spanned the Scheldt and constituted the solitary means of entry into the beleaguered city.

A few moments afterwards I found myself deposited at the St. Antoine, where accommodation had been provided for various members of the court exiled from Brussels, together with the entire corps diplomatique. The hotel resembled nothing so much as the Tower of Babel. In the crowded lounge, Spaniards, Roumanians, Dutch, Portuguese, Scandinaveans, Serbians, Greeks and Japanese chatted together in little groups over the aperative. Functionaries and staff officers hurried in with the latest news from the outer ring of forts. After lunch, an old General assured me over his cognac that Antwerp being the thrid strongest place in the world, might be considered impregnable. But others fresh from the fighting a few miles away, seemed less confident. Later, M. Davignon, Minister for Foreign Affairs, a rotund personage with a patriarchal beard and charming manners, made his appearance in the lounge, bringing copious despatches from the ends of the earth, which he proceeded to read aloud to a rather flippant audience. Meanwhile, in a secluded corner, Webber, of the British Legation, drank tea with the Countess Ghislaine, Lady-in-Waiting to the Queen, as though there had been no war at all.

I recollect my first dinner at the Antoine. Each nationality had its own table but the British alone was still graced by feminine society, Lady Villiers having elected to remain notwithstanding the Zeppelin raids which had driven away the rest of her sex; and with her Miss Marjorie Villiers, a handsome girl of 17. There was also the Russian Minister, Prince Koudashef, whose own entourage had deserted him, full of information about the progress of the " Russian steam-roller " progress so irresistible that one felt the war might fizzle out at any moment. " A charming fellow, Koudashef," I remember Sir Francis remarking, " It's a pity one can't believe a word of it."

[By kind permission of Captain G. Spencer Pryse and courtesy of the Leicester Galleries

From a lithograph made by Captain G. Spencer Pryse at a cross-road near Soissons on August 30th, 1914. Captain Spencer Pryse was in France before the Belgium period dealt with in this article. Only six proofs are in existence of the original lithograph from which our reproduction is taken. One is in the possession of H.M. The Queen Dowager of Belgium and another in the Metropolitan Museum in New York.

In addition to officials and diplomats, a few others were to be found at the Antoine, the oddest assemblage when one thinks of it. A retired major, incapable of putting together two words in any language except English, who had arrived with a string of much-needed ambulance cars and remained to pick up a collection of Prussian spiked helmets from the battlefields. And Mr. Walter Savage Landor preparing to write a history of the European War and determined to see something of the fighting before it ended, and along with him his cousin the Duc de Morny, whose presence did not appear to serve any purpose whatever. Then there was Gibson, First Secretary to the American Legation, an occasional visitor whose comings and goings invariably caused a stir;

for his presence was also necessary in Brussels in charge of American relief work, and he dashed to and fro through the lines in his car, petted by both sides, full of human sympathy and understanding for either, yet preserving a correct detachment and incidentally bringing together a collection of spiked helmets that promised to rival the Major's own. Finally, to round off the party, a couple of newspaper men from New York, indebted for their presence to the good offices of their Minister and kept well pruned with atrocities. " I guess we can turn every one of those yarns into dollars before we're through," being the slightly unfeeling if munificent comment that reached my ears.

At this stage events crowded one on the heels of the other. Atrocities were in the air. Spectacular trips were arranged, the entire corps diplomatique, not to speak of the two newspaper men, enjoyed a personally conducted excursion to Malines and Termonde where, at the sight of so much wanton damage, resentment became general. Private houses had been knocked about in a perfectly inexcusable way. A shell had even fallen on the Archiepiscopal Palace, and all were shocked by the state of the apartment in which it had exploded. Happily, as the Cardinal explained, " nobody was in the room at the time." Meanwhile things went from bad to worse around the forts. The eventual debacle must have come sooner had not somebody had the happy thought of cutting the dykes and inundating the country with the result that enemy troops were everywhere marooned and drowned, and entire batteries of siege howitzers put out of action. Upon which fresh excursions were organised to view the floods. With Belgian friends I spent a day charging about in an auto blindeè through mud and water for mere curiosity's sake, in the effort to obtain a close up view of the great guns lying half submerged. These reconnaissance officers in their auto blindeès, carried on a game of chance with death between petit déjeuner and diner that could hadly have been more sporting, and on one occasion at least a dinner for three had been ordered that was never eaten, all three being casualties. Baron de Braqueville dropped in occasionally, I suspect he early realised the forlorn nature of the position. What use was it for Lord Kitchener in London to talk about three years of war and men in millions with the enemy siege guns battering in the forts one after another. One day a newcomer appeared in the lounge. He asked for Sir Francis Villiers and was told by the Suisse that he would find him in the chancery, " it will be all right now," he called out, and dashed up the staircase like an enthusiastic schoolboy. It was Winston Churchill. That evening he dined with the Legation and it had to be hinted to the American newspaper men that their presence was undesirable. They refused to budge however. " What was Mister Winston Churchill doing in South Africa 15 years ago " being their somewhat irrevelant retort.

Notwithstanding the arrival of the Naval Division the bombardment steadily increased. Then one morning I left Antwerp for Bordeaux by car in company with Phillippe de Caramen Chimay. We two had become the solitary link uniting the Government of King Albert with the French Cabinet in hiding by the sea, every railway being cut and the Allied airmen not yet commanding confidence as postmen. Along with the bag of despatches we carried a bottle of petrol and a revolver to make sure that no papers should find their way into enemy hands. The sun had just risen as our hundred horse power Mercedes rattled over the rickety bridge of barges that swung with the tide. On the far side lay an armoured car and in its wake we made for St. Nicholas by pavé roads encumbered with sentry posts and barricades and droves of cattle and sheep crowding in for the revictualing of the garrison. Hours must have been wasted while rustic soldiers inspected our numerous permis de circuler. I remember my travelling companion evolved a simple formula more effective than any paper, " Cochon ! Je suis le Prince de Chimay," although its application in face of a rifle pointed unsteadily over the windscreen called for a considerable degree of nerve.

From the first detours had been necessary to avoid falling into enemy hands. We arrived eventually in Ostend by way of Ghent, Ecloo and Bruges, clinging to the sea.

At Furnes our escort left us and in a flick of the eye we passed from the seething life of Belgium into a deserted land. The road stretched wide and empty through villages silent and shuttered without any sign of life. A fortnight earlier I had passed through such country but this time the feeling was intensified. There were no barricades, no sentries.

As the armies fell back, the order had gone out that all obstacles must be removed and defences razed. Northern France lay open to the enemy. We rattled through Dunkerque, Calais and Boulogne that had so recently seen the debarkation of the British Expeditionary Army. We made no stop, knocked at no door. Harvests stood perishing in the fields. Beyond Montreuil we were fired on, a bullet penetrating the hood and making a clean hole in the cap that Phillippe was wearing. But our assailants remained invisible and the journey carried on full tilt.

We had gone through Abbeville and were running between fields of dry corn when a car sprang into view ahead, drawn in alongside the white dusty Route Nationale with what looked terribly like a machine-gun projected over its rear and several persons standing about. An attempt to turn would have been suicidal. Speed and surprise seemed our only friends. The dark grey car stood axle deep in grass to the left of the road. Though only a few seconds can have passed, her crew were already extending with trained precision in the grass on either hand, rifles to shoulder. On the back seat another had swung the gun into action. We were actually on top of them when I recognised a British Naval officer and stood up in my place gesticulating wildly. We had run into one of our own patrols. They gave us the cheeriest of welcomes along with chicken sandwiches and whiskey to fortify the champagne which my travelling companion considered essential on a journey. In reply to enquiries as to the whereabouts of the enemy the Lieutenant in charge explained that the enemy happened to be precisely the fellow he himself was looking for. "Point of fact, the beggar blew up the Dieppe-Paris railway track at two points last night and he's probably lurking close by. As likely as not you'll see something of him yet." As it turned out, however, we crossed the damaged railway without incident and before sundown were negotiating the advanced picquet posts of the fortified place of Rouen. Night had fallen by the time the last hair-pin obstacle had been left behind and we eventually entered the town.

What remained of the journey proved to be merely a matter of speed and patience. On the road again at dawn we passed through Alencon into Le Mans, there to burst upon a refilling point in the British Supply Column, with G.S. wagons and lorries, motor 'buses from Clapham, the Elephant and Castle and West Hampstead packed together in the Place de la Cathedrale and A.S.C. stores piled mountain high. There an ordnance officer told us about the new base at St. Nazaire and we realised that the war would continue.

Through Tours and Poietiers and Angouleine, with barriers steadily growing in frequency and complexity as the danger diminished. The possibility of entering Bordeaux after dark had become a burning question when an encounter with a French Staff car settled it. "Suicide to try. Monsieur le President knows how to protect himself."

So there we were in open country in the evening sunshine. At this point my friend very happily recollected a house he knew of not far away and we thereupon coasted through Libourne and down lanes to pull up eventually in front of a chateau set in woods and overhanging a river. In the salon the Duchesse Decazes and her sister-in-law, Daisy de Broglie, were sewing bandages for the Croix Rouge. There we spent the night, to reach Bordeaux next morning in time for breakfast.

G.S.P.

Ypres British School

Sir William Pulteney presents the Prizes.
Pupils acclaim their Benefactor.

FRIDAY, 26th July, was Prize-day at the Ypres British School, when the awards were presented to the successful scholars by Lieut.-General Sir William Pulteney. There were fewer visitors from England than in past years, but compensation was made by the large attendance, not only from the British colony in Ypres itself, but from all parts of our war graves area in Belgium and Northern France.

The morning being delightfully fine, the picturesque little function took place, as has been customary since 1932, in the school playground. It has been my privilege to be present on each anniversary, and on no previous occasion have I seen the children who now total 109, looking so bright, healthy and happy. Completely free from the slightest suspicion of self-consciousness, they were well mannered and in every respect a credit to their parents and their school. Moreover, what is so very unusual at a school prize-day, when parents and strangers put in an appearance, probably in critical mood, the youngsters obviously enjoyed themselves and revelled in their exhibitions of dancing and calisthenics.

It was somewhat disappointing, however, that the programme contained only one song, "In Loyal Bonds." A little more singing, intermingled with the dancing, would have given a better balance. Perhaps this will be remembered in 1936.

With regard to the prizes, I know of no other school which, in proportion to its size, presents so many awards for merit,—all of them well worth winning, and some of intrinsic value. There is a story that the late Lord Balfour once met in Paris a Frenchman, who proudly informed him that he was the most distinguished of all Parisians. "Why?" queried the British Foreign Minister. "Because I am the only Frenchman in Paris who has not been accorded the Legion of Honour," came the unexpected reply. Well, I am almost tempted to suggest that, if there be any youngster at Ypres School who did not receive a prize from Sir William Pulteney on 26th July, he, or she, can claim to be its most distinguished pupil. In any case, I venture a hazard that, if a show of hands had been demanded at the conclusion of the proceedings, the "haves" would have outnumbered the "have-nots."

Much progress has been made during the past twelve months and the curriculum has been considerably extended. A cookery class was inaugurated during the winter months, which has proved an unqualified success, the attendance being thirty-five. The Dickens Fellowship Association, of London, recently offered prizes to school-children for the best essays on the "Life of Charles Dickens," and its bearing upon incidents in his novel, "David Copperfield." Thirty-seven awards were made and of these four fell to Ypres British School, including a "first" to Irene Gallagher, a lassie of fair promise. Social functions included Jubilee celebrations, a day at the seaside, swimming contests and tennis tournaments.

Sir William Pulteney, who was evidently pleased with the ovation he received, which was as whole-hearted and spontaneous as it was well-merited, told the children that their improvement was more pronounced during the past twelve months than in any other corresponding period. This reflected great credit on the care their mothers bestowed upon them, as well as showing that they themselves were taking an interest in their young lives and the future that lay before them. He made reference to the scheme of the committee for finding employment for them upon leaving school, and emphasised the difficulty of obtaining posts in the British Isles. "I wish you all the very best of health, the very best of luck and God bless you," said Sir William. This homely conclusion stirred both children and parents to rounds of applause.

Colonel Higginson, in moving a vote of thanks to Sir William, said that he was "the rock upon which the school was founded and the sheet-anchor on which it relied for protection and help in times of difficulty." The gratitude of the Imperial War Graves Commission to the school's committee of management, he continued, was very deep and real; and he reminded those present that the Commission also was contributing its share by a financial grant, as well as by the provision of free medical attendance and periodical examination of the scholars.

The Rev. G. R. Milner seconded the vote of thanks.

Letters of regret for enforced absence were read from the Provost of Eton, the Chaplain-General to the Forces and the Bishop of Fulham (Anglican Bishop for North and Central Europe).

H. B.

The Australians at Ypres

By C. E. W. BEAN.

THE Australian Infantry Divisions were twice in the Ypres Salient—first in September and October of 1916, after the fighting at Pozières in the First Battle of the Somme, when the 1st Anzac Corps changed places with the Canadian Corps. The Salient was then unnaturally quiet, the troops on both sides having been withdrawn thither after taking part in the great struggle farther south; there was consequently an opportunity, seldom offered at Ypres, for fortification, and two months were spent in hastily improving the front defences and in establishing new lines farther back so as to increase the security. Then came the order for the return of the 1st Anzac Corps to the Somme in order to take part in a new development of that battle.

Just a year later the Australians returned to the Salient for the Third Battle of Ypres. Only the artillery of their divisions took part in its first stage, which began on July 1st, and gradually came to an end in the morass caused by the rains of that month. It was not until the 20th of September, 1917, after three weeks of dry weather, that the infantry of the 1st Anzac Corps (then comprising the 1st, 2nd, 4th and 5th Australian Divisions) took part in the launching of the second phase of the great battle. Only part of the ridge overlooking the Salient had by then been wrenched from the Germans. If that ridge is likened to a sickle, with its handle at Messines and its blade curving from the Menin Road heights through Broodseinde to Passchendaele, the British had then seized the handle and the junction of handle and blade, but the Germans still held the blade. The phase which now commenced saw the launching, during a fortnight's fine weather, of a series of tremendous hammer-strokes by which the Germans were thrust back about a mile at a time, precisely as planned, until they held only the northern part of the ridge, from Passchendaele onwards. The 1st Anzac Corps, later with the 2nd Anzac Corps (New Zealand, 3rd Australian, and two British divisions) on its left, occupied a more or less central position in each of these strokes, which they delivered in conjunction with a larger number of British divisions. There was no especial secrecy about the operations; the Germans knew well that they were to be attacked, and that the operation would take place at dawn. They were uncertain only of the precise British plans as to date and front. The retaliatory fire was consequently heavy; the roads back to the city were perpetually barraged—Birr Cross-Road and "Hellfire Corner" are names which, in Australia as elsewhere, bring a shudder even to this day; the nearer bivouacs were drenched with "mustard" gas. But so overwhelming was the power at that time of the British artillery that no counter-measures which the enemy could take availed him in the least. On the day appointed for each attack the British advance rolled on exactly as intended. The Germans counter-attacked, as they had been wont to do successfully in the earlier stages of the battle ; but, so long as the fine weather lasted, these attempts were easily detected either by the front-line infantry or by aeroplanes, and the tremendous barrage, descending like a dense curtain, engulfed them. In several cases counter-attacks were thus utterly crushed without the front-line infantry ever knowing that it had even been threatened.

Only once within Australian experience in this phase of the battle was a German counter-attack even partly successful. This was immediately before the second attack of the series. In the first—that of September 20th (usually known as the " Battle of the Menin Road ")—the Germans had been pushed back from Nonne Bosschen and " Glencorse Wood " into Polygon Wood, across which their line now lay. The Butte was still in German possession, and in the next operation, planned for September 26th, it was intended to thrust the Germans back from this position, and, farther north, to reach the neighbourhood of Zonnebeke. The 1st and 2nd Australian Divisions, which had played a central part in the battle of the 20th, had been relieved, and the troops of the 4th and 5th Australian Divisions, which were to deliver the next attack in this sector, were partly in position and partly on the way thither, when, after an unusually severe concentration of artillery fire, the Germans counter-attacked immediately south of the 5th Division's flank. Only the southern edge of that division was involved, but the Germans forced their way into the line farther south by the Reutelbeek. A handful of Scottish troops held out magnificently, although entirely surrounded, but their survival was at the time unknown to anyone on the British side. The 5th Australian Division by heavy fighting made good its own flank and part of the ground adjoining ; but the plans for the next day had been seriously upset, and the authorities were forced to consider whether the intended operation could be carried out. It was, however, decided to " carry on," and the third brigade of the 5th Australian Division was accordingly hurried forward at the last moment to assist its southernmost brigade in the task. On September 26th, at the appointed hour, the great attack moved forward, the southernmost Australian brigade making special arrangements to protect its flank, since the intended advance of the line south of that point could not be fully carried out. This advance went like a whirlwind to its objective. Though fired into from its right rear, the 5th Division seized The Butte ; and, when the Germans presently debouched to counter-attack, an Australian machine-gun from the mound assisted in sweeping away their attempt. Farther south the gap in the line about the Reutelbeek was presently filled, the brave Scots being found still holding their own against a surrounding enemy.

The next operation of the series resulted in the heaviest blow sustained by the Germans during the Third Battle of Ypres. Although the British line now ran over the heights at Polygon Wood, farther north it lay in the lowlands of Zonnebeke facing the Germans whose front line still lay near the foot of the ridge. This was to be assaulted on October 4th, the Australians having shifted slightly northwards so that the 1st Anzac Corps (1st and 2nd Australian Divisions) was opposite Broodseinde, with the 2nd Anzac Corps (New Zealand and 3rd Australian Divisions) on its left. Both Australian and New Zealand troops were especially elated, since this was the first time that four Australasian divisions had fought together in line. Moreover, on their southern flank was the 7th British Division, which had fought beside Australians some months before at Bullecourt and for which they had an especial affection and regard.

The battalions allotted for this attack had marched up during the night along the tracks taped out for them, and were lying down in the dark along other tapes marking the " jumping-off line," with the graceful white flares of the Germans rising and falling from the opposing line 300 yards in front, when there shot up another sort of flare, bursting into hundreds of golden spangles. This was followed by others of the same sort, until these were rising thickly along the enemy's front. It appeared almost certain that the Germans had seen the waiting troops, and that this was his call to his artillery for barrage. Within a few minutes the German artillery opened, its shells falling fairly across the waiting lines of the 1st and 2nd Australian Divisions, and for half-an-hour the officers and men lying out in shell-holes had to endure this tempest. Losses were heavy, and officers were wondering whether their units could possibly carry out the assault, when, at 6 a.m. (the hour for the attack), the German fire suddenly ceased and simultaneously the British barrage, enormously greater in volume, descended. The troops rose to their feet and began to advance. In the dim light a man would be visible about 40 yards away, and they had gone 100 yards when they saw before them another

Photo]   [Imperial War Museum, Crown Copyright.

VIEW OF THE YPRES SALIENT BATTLEFIELD AT GARTER POINT ON OCTOBER 22nd, 1917

line of men, also rising to its feet, its members looking round them as if puzzled, waiting for an order.

It was a line of Germans. The German command had planned an assault at exactly the same hour as the British, but on a smaller scale. The attacking troops of each side had been lying out in No-Man's Land at 5.30 a.m. without the other's knowledge. The yellow flares probably meant the detection of some part of the Australian force, but the German bombardment was part of the normal preparation for their own attack. At 6 a.m. the two lines met, and the Australian rolled over that of the Germans and continued on up the Broodseinde heights to where some of the German staffs and the artillery observers were awaiting news of their own operation. The officers and men at these headquarters, beside the road along the ridge-top fought sternly, but the heights were captured : from its muddy trenches the new front line looked out, at last, into the comparatively green country beyond the ridge, and the Germans were thrust form the observation posts from which they had so long directed the fire of their batteries upon the Salient.

The weather then broke, but so striking had been this last success that it was decided to accept the risk of failure, and make, at last a definite attempt to break through the German front by attacking Passchendaele. To bring forward infantry, guns, and stores over the morass of mud-pools, miles of plank-road and " duckboard " track were laid by the pioneers. Two battles were fought on October 9th and 12th. In these operations the New Zealand, 2nd, 3rd, and 4th Australian, and a number of British divisions took part ; but the mud of that dreadful battlefield clogged the effort both of infantry and artillery, and, in spite of their most gallant efforts, the final advance broke down in the wire of " Bellevue Spur " and the mud of the Ravebeek.

The conditions of the battlefield had now changed, and so did the policy of the high command. The main task of attacking Passchendaele—no longer in an attempt to break through—was transferred to the Canadian Corps, which, despite the mud, tackled the operation in three stages and carried it to success. In this phase—the third (and last) of that battle—several Australian divisions played only subsidiary parts on the flank of the main attack, though all the Australian divisions suffered in the mud and in the bombardments of the back area. In November they were withdrawn to spend the winter at Messines, leaving the New Zealanders at Polderhoek. In the spring the Somme again took them, and they never again returned to the Salient.

List of Members of the A.I.F. who won the Victoria Cross near Ypres

Capt. Robert Cuthbert Grieve, 37th Batt.

Pte. John Carroll, 33rd Batt.

2nd-Lieut. Frederick Birks, Late 6th Batt.

Pte. Reginald Roy Inwood, 10th Batt.

Lce.-Cpl. Walter Peeler, 3rd P. Batt.

Sgt. John James Dwyer, Aust. M.G. Corps.

Pte. Patrick Bugden, Late 31st Batt.

Sgt. Lewis McGee, Late 40th Batt.

Capt. Clarence Smith Jeffries, Late 34th Batt.

THE YPRES TIMES

HOOGE CHATEAU, 1914

IDENTICAL SITE IN 1919 SHOWING TEMPORARY CHURCH AND THE HUT WHICH WAS OCCUPIED BY BARON DE VINCK

Visit of 236th Siege Battery, R.G.A. to Ypres

Whitsun, 1935.

WHEN the Battery left the Salient in May, 1918, after seventeen months unrelieved strenuous fighting, it heaved a great sigh of relief. Not one member wanted to see the " blasted " place again.

Yet, in 1935, when the project was mooted for a visit to our old positions—and, alas, the graves of our dead—the response was instant and eager. Finally 31 pilgrims —for such we were—assembled at Victoria Station on the evening of 8th June. The party included representatives of all ranks from Major to Gunner with some wives, sons and friends.

Under the very able supervision of the League Secretary, who honoured us by personally conducting the tour, assisted by our old Mess Secretary, we were safely shepherded on to the train. The crossing from Folkestone to Dunkerque was uneventful and the subsequent train journey was comfortable, enlivened for many of us by a stand-up snack in the kitchen-car—the first opportunity for many to discover how "rusty" was their French. Those who had expected to travel by cattle truck were agreeably disappointed, and the train proceeded without the bumpety-clank refrain of " Hommes et chevaux, hommes et chevaux," although the old marking, " hommes 40, chevaux 8," was still visible on many cattle trucks in the sidings. An hour's break at Hazebrouck enabled us to stretch our legs. Even at the early hour of 7 a.m. the estaminets were open, and ready for a good trade, while to judge by the noise and speed of the motorists, there is room for a " Hore-Belisha " in the French Government. Soon after leaving Hazebrouck : " Look there's Mont de Cats ! They've never rebuilt the Scherpenberge Mill ! Good old Kemmel ! Do you remember when———? " and the floodgates were opened.

An excellent breakfast at Skindles was followed by a charabanc and motor car tour, our numbers having meanwhile been swelled by the addition of four who had journeyed direct to Ypres, three from Paris and one from Le Touquet. Out from Ypres, through the Lille Gate, past Shrapnel Corner to Lock 8 on the Ypres-Comines Canal— our first stop. Everyone piled out in great excitement. Along the derelict Canal the banks were still pitted with the Battery's old dugouts. A position had been occupied here in 1917. Cameras clicked, tongues wagged, and off we set to St. Eloi and thence to the Brasserie Cross Roads on the York Road. A cemetery occupies the place where the guns had been during the 1918 retreat, but the beer in the Estaminet was just the same. At this position the Battery, after pulling out from its position near Lock 7 under machine-gun fire, had received a target at 11° First charge. (Look up your range tables you old 6 in. How. Gunners !)

On and away to Wytschaete, to the old crater position of 1917, and an inspection of the one remaining crater. Our energetic photographer finished the war here on the third day of the retreat in April, 1918, on the spot where the new church now stands ; he was then occupying, as an O.P., a Pillbox which was blown in by a shell ; of its other occupants two were killed and the other two wounded.

From there to Kemmel Village (we had no time to visit the old O.P. on top) and Kleine Vierstraat cemetery where a number of the Battery's personnel lie at rest. Each headstone was photographed while a solemn hush fell over the party. Away by Swan and Edgar Corner, leaving Dickebusch Lake—a sparkling jewel—on the right. " Do you remember when we had to switch 94° right the day Bailleul fell ? " " Do I not ! That was the day the guns were red-hot and———" That happened behind the Lake.

Past Hellblast Corner—where the big shell dump went up—through La Clytte and Locre—on to Bailleul, leaving behind us several positions which could not be visited because of the state of the roads. It would have been exciting to have seem Busseboom again where the Battery, in spite of very heavy gas shelling mixed with 11 inch armour-piercing, finished with a glorious burst of firing, completing 28,000 rounds in the consecutive 30 days during which the final German attack on the Salient was stemmed. " Do you remember the twenty mules that were buried in one shell-hole ? " " And the Major called them pip-squeaks ! "

At Bailleul we were astonished to find that the Mayor desired to accord us a civic reception, but somewhat to our relief, owing to electioneering activities, this did not take place. Lunch was followed, however, by a visit to the new Town Hall under the personal guidance of the Secretary-General to the Town ; he encouraged most of the party to

Photo] [G. C. Crispin (Press Photo Co.)

GROUP OF THE PARTY TAKEN OUTSIDE SKINDLES HOTEL, YPRES

climb to the top of the splendid belfry—200 ft. above the Square—and while there, spurred on one member to play an obligato on the carillon, much to the astonishment of the local inhabitants. A visit was also paid to the War Memorial, a really magnificent monument to the destruction and resurrection of the town.

Armentières was the next place of call, and the ladies simply had to be shown where Mademoiselle used to live. Unfortunately, as every one asked separately, naturally the famous maiden was given several domiciles. However, that did not spoil the party.

On the way back to Ypres we journeyed through Ploegstreet, past Hill 63, to Lock 7, where the world's biggest shell hole is now a duck pond. There we de-bussed and tried to get to the old position behind Ridgewood, but found the going too rough at the end of a long day, but a walk up the Canal to Spoil-Bank was well rewarded when an entrance to Canada tunnel was discovered beside Lock 6. That tunnel had indeed been a " cushy billet." And so back to Ypres and to dinner, dropping some of the party at Lock 8, where they wanted to explore a little further.

At 8.45 p.m. we assembled at the Menin Gate where a short service was held, the "Last Post" was sounded, and two wreaths were laid on behalf of all ranks of the Battery and their friends. The grandeur of the Memorial and the 55,000 names around us - including some well known and loved — has created a memory which none of the party will ever forget. It was strange to wander back to the hotel through the peaceful streets where once all was desolation and death.

Monday morning we each did our own exploring, the local War Museum being well worth a visit—and after an early lunch we set off for Sanctuary Wood.

Photo] [G. C. Crispin (Press Photo Co.)
AT TYNE COT MEMORIAL

There we inspected the trenches that still remain on the slope of Mount Sorrel. The view from the Canadian Memorial on the top was beautiful, and not a single shell-burst to be seen. Marvellous !

From there we made our final pilgrimage to Tyne Cot cemetery, which is situated close to the village of Passchendaele, and where the names of the two Corporals who were killed in the O.P. at Wytschaete, already referred to, were found amongst the 38,000 names of the missing commemorated in this beautiful tribute to the fallen. The two undemolished pill-boxes afford a striking contrast to the well kept graves grouped around them which are a constant reminder of the sacrifice necessary to capture them.

Photo] [G. C. Crispin (Press Photo Co.)
AT HILL 63 (CANADIAN MEMORIAL)

From here we raced back to Ypres as a storm was obviously approaching from the west ; barely had we reached Skindles when a terrific hail-storm swept the town, the like of which had rarely, if ever, been experienced by any of the party. Windows were smashed, water poured through the hotel roof, and pandemonium reigned. Severe as it was, it was soon over—in time for us to catch our train—and its passing left the party in really fine spirits, and, of course, someone simply had to pull the communication cord after the train had started. Oh, La—La ! !

At Dunkerque a huge supper was followed by toasts and some good speeches, and the opportunity was taken to pay tribute to those principally responsible for the trip. First of all our old Mess Secretary, who in addition to organising this tour, has kept all members of the Battery in touch with each other since demobilisation, received a tremendous ovation. Then Capt. de Trafford was thanked for his most helpful and successful organisation through the whole tour, which had primarily contributed to the happiness of all concerned while demonstrating so clearly the efficiency of the Ypres League service, including, as it did, the personal and most capable supervision of our charabanc tours by Mr. C. J. Parminter. Finally an entertainment by the Battery humorist made everyone laugh till they cried. " Star of the Evening " was sung reverently, solemnly, gladly, and, finally, hilariously, with accent on the " *Cook*-house door ! "

Then we embarked and enjoyed another "mill-pond" crossing, reaching Victoria in the early hours of Tuesday morning.

A fitting finish to the party was the question loudly asked by our humorist at breakfast in an A.B.C. shop near Victoria, " Does anybody here speak English ? "

The trip was a complete success, and can be recommended to all Units who fought in the Salient, who should go and see for themselves what God, Nature and Man can do. Verily, " I shall restore unto you the years that the locusts have eaten."

CHAS. E. SALVESEN,
Major, R.G.A. (T).

"Sunshine and Shadow"

By W. J. PARRY.

NEARLY seventeen years later the most vivid impression of those war years, an impression which remains scarified in my memory, is the sight of starvation. We seldom hear anything of that aspect of war. When it is referred to at all it is generally in a glib sort of way, as though it denoted nothing more than discomfort of hardship. That, of course, is because in our country few have met it, and by starvation I do not mean hunger.

We have all experienced hunger in those years gone by, many, unfortunately, have known it since. And in mid-winter, in those memorable years, when "jocund day stood tip-toe " above the mists of Messines Ridge, and in the front line your daily ration of bread, mysteriously arriving during the night, proved to be one-third of a half-pound loaf. And someone had placed his army boot on your third. Even then, there was often a " dog " biscuit to be found to keep you going during the next twenty-four hours and during those nights, when the official communique assured us that " the night was quiet on the Western Front," there was always the consolation that in a few days time you would be back at rest behind Neuve Eglise, — if your luck held.

No ; I mean starvation. A frightful thing ; the most pitiable, cruel, helpless form of suffering ; just the sight of it remains with me now as surely as a terrifying, recurrent nightmare. Impressions which have seared most deeply into one's very soul are just those which the average Englishman keeps most silent about, but recently I came across the following statement by a financial expert.

"Wheat and coffee," he said, "was burnt because, — well, because there was too much of it."

We have travelled far since 1918, you see, but if you will travel a few minutes with me I will try and show you a sight which even the aforementioned financier might have been hard pressed to explain away.

* * * * *

In the summer of 1918, the 39th Infantry Brigade, operating N.E. of Baqubah on the Diala river, and on the extreme right flank of our army in Mesopotamia was ordered to follow Major General Dunsterville's famous "Hush-Hush Brigade" right across Persia in the new dash to Baku on the Caspian Sea and operating, roughly, seven hundred miles from our railhead in Mesopotamia.

Gifted authors, the late Major M. H. Donohoe, Lt.-Col. Sir Arnold J. Wilson, Mr. Ernest Raymond, General Dunsterville himself, and others, have written in varied ways of the enthralling drama in this, a side-show of the Great War, and I need only state here how on the fourth day after we had passed the frontier town of Khaniquin and had crossed into Persia, our detachment came to a halt in Bisitum, some twenty miles north east of Kermanshah.

Here, carved out of the rocks, on the wall of a perpendicular cliff, and some three hundred feet above the ground is the famous Darius inscription : "The King of Kings," chiselled there by Persian workmen five-hundred years before the dawn of the Christian era, and still in a marvellous state of preservation. And three-hundred feet below it we met starvation.

They were remnants of the Nestorians, Christians who inhabited Kurdistan and North West Persia, followers of the Patriarch of Constantinople, who was condemned for heresy in the year A.D. 431. We know them to-day as Assyrians and, to every right thinking Englishman, their troubles are still with us, or should be.

From 1915, following the Russian retreat from the Assyrian countryside, to the summer of 1918, they had suffered all the most indescribable horrors that war could bring and now the survivors, about 40,000 of them, were marching hundreds of miles down country in the hope of obtaining sanctuary behind the British lines in Mesopotamia. The story of those who survived and reached British protection is magnificently told in Lt.-Col. Sir Arnold T. Wilson's book, *Mesopotamia 1917-1920 : A Clash of Loyalties."*

I would tell you here of those who failed to arrive. The Persia they had to traverse was in the grip of a famine ; in part owing to the fact that the Persians had never grown more wheat than was absolutely necessary for local requirements, but chiefly owing to the method of successive Turk and Russian invaders who had commandeered, often without payment, and had left the mark of destruction wherever they had gone, while yet another unpleasant cause was the cupidity and selfishness of local officials.

We would round a bend and come across several families "resting" by the road-side. Their clothes were mostly in rags. Clothes ! Beside their elders, some toddlers had nothing but a piece of rag to cover them, and nights, even in summer, can be chilly in those Persian uplands, some thousands of feet above sea level. Their poor bodies were emaciated and shrunken, their bones stood out as a frame with nothing to cover it. Many were obviously in the last stage of exhaustion. Unsatisfied hunger, slow starvation, and physical suffering showed in their wild, burning eyes. Some would obviously go no further, they laid waiting for merciful death to put an end to their sufferings.

We were to meet hundreds of these starving people in the days that followed. Death, met along the road-sides of those quiet Persian uplands, appeared to me more horrific, more pitiable ; there was no background such as one knew on the Western Front, no familiar crashes of 5.9's, no whining of bullets, no distant rattle of a machine gun. That was it ; no background. Possibly even Darius, the "King of Kings," looking down on that road for the last two thousand odd years had not seen such sights as our vaunted civilisation could show him in A.D. 1918.

In an endeavour to satisfy the pangs of starvation some of these unhappy exiles would gnaw at roots growing by the wayside. Some became herbivorous and clutched at, and ate, the grass like animals, the result often being an agonizing death. Later we were to hear of poor Persians driven to such like extremities and even to eating human flesh.

Our soldiers did what they could to help these poor, ravenous people. They would share their chipattees, their black bread, or biscuits, with them, but this kindness must in many cases have had the reverse effect than intended, for many of the refugees and local Persians were below the state of health when they could take such food with safety, and, in many cases, after prolonged starvation, the consequences must have been disastrous.

I should like to pay tribute here to what must have been magnificent staff organization and heroic endeavour which, in addition to arranging the supplies and rations of a force working with lines of communications about seven hundred miles long, could also establish soup kitchens in a starving town like Hamasan, feeding as many as two thousand of the poor inhabitants each day. And those, I think, are the stories which should be told, and handed down to future generations. Yet this was only an incident in as exciting a war drama as has ever been enacted, — the British dash from Baghdad to Baku — Khaniquin, Kasr-i-Shirin, Kirind, Kermanshah, Kangavar, Kasvin, Resht, and the Caspian Sea ! Many will know them, and of what incidents could each place tell ! But I do not believe that anyone, once they have seen it, can forget starvation.

Often, in these prosiac years, its sights come back to me in the form of a nightmare. Strangely enough, not in its proper background of immense plains, locked in the summer heat of mid-day by the blue tinted Persian mountains and under the loviliest blue of those Persian skies, but always under grey skies, and as background, — there is Ypres. And the road, — the Menin Road.

W. J. PARRY.

Why I wanted "Hello My Dearie!"

A Story of a Song.
By Temp. 2nd Lieut. F. C. MORGAN, M.C.,
Bowdre Apartments, Augusta, Georgia.

I WISH I had a copy of ' Hello, My Dearie ! ' " — The words were spoken somewhat wistfully. In a moment weighted with tender memories I had spoken, I think to my sister, in Philadelphia, in December, 1932. I had done so in the hearing of my mother — Years had fallen away and I was back in an old Y.M.C.A. hut at Boisleaux, France. It was October, 1927 ; I had crossed the Channel and spent the inevitable days in Etaples. At last orders had come through and I found myself on the train bound for Boisleaux, the railhead ; from thence with two or three others (Bruce and Smith, I recall, for we had been together in the 10th Officer Cadet Battalion at Gailes, Ayrshire). I was to report at the Battalion Headquarters of the First Lancashire Fusiliers, situated somewhere near Blaireville. I had just passed my 19th birthday, and was a terribly green subaltern, so green that when I had been asked as a cadet whether I desired a permanent commission in the Regular Army, a temporary commission in the Regular Army, or a commission in the Territorials, I had replied, " A temporary commission in the Regular Army," just because " it sounded better " ! (Like many others, I had no thought of remaining in the army once " the job was done.") Now I discovered I had been commissioned to the most illustrious unit (six V.C.'s in half-an-hour before breakfast at Gallipoli) in the fighting Twenty-Ninth Division, commanded by that prince among soldiers, Lieutenant-General Beauvois-De Lise. At Etaples I had heard thrilling and blood-curdling accounts of their exploits, it was " a stunting division."

"it was never used for mere holding of the line," "always fattened-up like turkeys for some show," "just been in a bloody battle up at Ypres" . . . !

We arrived at Boisleaux, as near as I can recall, late in the afternoon. It was getting dark ; we discovered it was some little distance to Blaireville, so we decided to spend the night in the Y.M.C.A. hut at Boisleaux. I thought then that it was a bleak sort of place (I was to discover in subsequent months, it was almost as " cushy " a billet as there was to be found in France !), but we were glad of any place with a bed after the tiresome journey from Etaples. The hut was lighted with candles and the Y.M.C.A. man in charge allotted each of us a rude kind of cot in a long row down the side of the building. Tables occupied the centre, and at one of these we sat down together to eat our simple and meagre supper. After supper it was still comparatively early and we had nothing much better to do than think sentimentally and sadly of the loved ones at home, or contemplate with forebodings that which awaited us on the morrow and in the days to come with the " stunting " division . . . Such reflections we knew were unhealthy and sometimes disastrous, so we proceeded to explore the hut. On a shallow sort of platform at one end of it we found a table on which was an old, time-worn, often-used (and sometimes abused) gramophone. It was of the ancient type, having a trumpet to increase the volume of sound, but the trumpet was missing ! Such is the vividness of the memory that I recollect the table and the gramophone were to the left of the platform as we faced it. As far as I can recall, there was only one record, there may have been others, but at any rate only one made a sufficient impression upon my mind to have remained through the years, it was " Hello, My Dearie ! " I shall never hear that song to my dying day without thinking of that old gramophone in that bleak, candle-lit hut ! We played that record not merely once or twice, but over and over again. During its oft-repeated performance I stepped out of the hut into the blackness of the night to get a breath of air and gaze heavenwards at the same bright-shining stars as were shedding their light on the old folks at home.

The flash and boom of the guns were not the only things that made an indelible impression upon my mind. Ever and anon there ascended the streak of a verey light which burst in a white, shimmering glow seeming for a moment to illumine the distant scene and enable me to envisage the line of men who occupied the front line trenches and was the only barrier between me and the enemy. Once there sped heavenwards a red light, followed by a green and then by another green ; it was the S.O.S. sent up by men who must have imagined the enemy to be coming over the top in force, it was only a matter of seconds before the occasional flash and boom became a quick-flashing roar of a barrage, so heavy that my friends (they had not yet become " pals ") joined me in the darkness and all of us stood awe-inspired; we had visions of that line of men being driven back and of ourselves coming face to face with the grey-clad figures of the foe !

However, it proved to be a false alarm, a common occurrence among men whose nerves were at breaking-point and who supposed they had seen ominous movements in no-man's-land and wanted the immediate comfort of a wall of fire between them and those supposed movements. How familiar I became with it all in subsequent days ! At the moment, however, it was a moving experience. Soon the quick-flashing roar slackened to the occasional flash and boom interspersed by the rattle of a machine-gun. . . . We returned to the companion-like warmth of the candle-lit hut and the more cheerful and more familiar strains of " Hello, My Dearie ! " Is it any wonder that I wished I had a copy of the old song ? * *

The conclusion of my story is a large envelope addressed to me in Augusta, Georgia, in my mother's bold handwriting, bearing a London post-mark in December, 1934. It contained a folded copy of " Hello, My Dearie ! " for which she had persistently ransacked the music shops of the Metropolis of the Empire. . . .

P.S. If either Smith, who afterwards became attached to the " Toc-Emmas," or Bruce, who remained with me in the battalion until he was wounded, should still be alive and happen to read these words ; I wish he would communicate with an old pal in a foreign land.

The Sausage Balloon

By Captain W. J. Voss, M.C., Author of "The Light of the Mind."

THE farm lay at the end of a secluded lane, far from the main road. Away to the East was the British front line, whence came the rumble of a heavy bombardment. It was the opening bar of the first battle of the Somme. From the drowsy, peaceful aspect of that Picardy farm, bathed in the hot, dog-day sun, you would not have thought that only a few miles away the great nations of Europe were wallowing in a ghastly blood-bath. Low buildings looked down on the farm-yard from three sides. In the middle some hens were scrabbling and pecking in a heap of manure. A sow, with swollen teats, lay among some straw. An Australian soldier, hands in pockets, lounged against a wall.

Outside the farm ran a line of trenches and several rows of rusty barbed wire. They had never been used, and now nature was reclaiming them with weeds and thistles. A goat was standing on its hind-legs nibbling off the lower leaves of an apple tree. A mangy dog scratched for fleas, another lay asleep in its kennel. Some hens sat on the shafts of a cart, waiting to lay.

In a low wooden building near-by was the officers' mess. Pictures of nude ladies, taken from the pages of "La Vie Parisienne" were pasted on the walls. A telephone stood on an upturned case in the corner, and down the centre of the room was a trestled table. There was a bottle of whisky and soda-water syphon on a shelf which was strewn with magazines, books and trench-maps. Through a tiny window at the side one looked across a field of waving corn. The reflector of the lamp which hung from the ceiling was dotted with flies—like us, they were waiting for death. It was war.

There were three long blasts on a whistle. The captive balloon was about to go up. Men wearing clean, double-breasted uniforms, unlike the mud-stained soldiers of the front line, began to emerge from all sorts of habitations, even from boxes covered with tarpaulins, or holes in the ground, and to walk slowly across the field. The war would be a long one. There was plenty of time. Some had forgotten their gas-masks and turned back to fetch them. They fell in, numbered off (there were about 60 of them), formed fours and marched away across a flat field. I followed them.

One was carrying something which resembled a Russian icon. This was the map-rest. Presently we came to the balloon, screened from the enemy by a line of tall poplar trees. Like a long naked caterpillar, it squatted over its little bags of ballast as if hatching its eggs. The men formed a line on both sides of the huge beast, and each one took hold of the ropes which hung from its belly. The fat worm staggered like a drunken elephant, whilst some khaki-clad figures pushed a basket under it—perhaps the jovial monster was going to lay!

The two principal actors, the observers, now came strolling over from the officers' mess. One of them, Basil Hallam, had made a hit just before the war with his song, "Gilbert the Filbert." The motor on the winding-lorry began to splutter and bark, and orders, unintelligible to my gunner mind, were shouted by the sergeant-major. With the aid of orderlies the two observers laced themselves into complicated corsets, which they connected later to their parachutes by means of a cord. One of them put on a helmet with earphones and mouthpiece attached. Attired in this strange garb, and resembling revived mummies from the British Museum, they climbed into the "nacelle."

The order, "Let go," rang out. The balloon took the air. She rose slowly, gracefully, the rumble of the windlass bidding her farewell. She was at home now, immobile at the end of her wire. Suspended high up in the blue sky, she looked like a sleeping salmon in a pool of still water. You expected her to wake suddenly out of her reverie, give a flick of her fins and shoot away into space. There were many other balloons in the heavens. They stretched in an irregular line from North to South, becoming smaller and smaller near the horizon, and finally disappearing in a haze. Some were high up, some were low down.

Presently, just as we were beginning to bring our eyes back to earth, something happened. The wire rope broke and the balloon, freed from its ground-anchor, pointed its nose upward and rose rapidly. A westerly wind was blowing and the great gas-bag drifted over towards the German lines. Silence fell on the little group round the lorry and every eye was strained upwards. A few seconds passed, then a little white mushroom opened out under the salmon, which had now shrunk to the size of a mackerel—one of the observers was safely launched in his parachute. Breathlessly we waited for the other mushroom to grow, but it never came. The balloon was only a tiny minnow now. Soon it had disappeared in the distant haze. The soldiers standing round the winding-lorry began to set about their duties in silence. In all our minds was the question, " Why had the other mushroom not appeared ? "

I strolled back across the field to the officers' mess. The telephone on the box in the corner of the wooden building buzzed, and I took up the receiver. The officer commanding an adjacent captive-balloon section was speaking. " I have just had a message from the infantry in the line," he said, " saying that Basil Hallam's body has been picked up, attached to an unopen parachute. His companion landed safely just behind our support trenches." So London music-hall audiences could never again applaud " The Colonel of the Knuts " !

W. J. V.

Ypres League Battlefields Pilgrimage

ON Saturday, August 3rd, a party of some 50 pilgrims assembled at Victoria Station at 7.30 a.m., and were greeted by Captain de Trafford, M.C., who conducted the pilgrimage. Those unknown to each other very soon made acquaintance of their fellow passengers and it was not long before one heard the well-known phrase, " Do you remember . . . etc."

At Dover we embarked on the steamer, " Princess Josephine Charlotte," in which a comfortable crossing was made in glorious weather, and after the usual Customs procedure at Ostend, we walked the short distance to the Town Station to entrain for Ypres. At each station *en route*, heads craned forward to see if any old landmarks still remained, especially in the vicinity of Poelcapelle, Langemarck and Boesinghe. The whole countryside is changed, and only two or three pill-boxes could be observed. At 4.30 p.m. we arrived at the tragic city where the party split up to go to their respective hotels. After an excellent dinner, we attended the sounding of the " Last Post " at the Menin Gate, where we found a party of Old Contemptibles lined up beneath the Arch on both sides of the roadway. On the stroke of 9 o'clock all traffic stopped and the silvery notes from the bugles sounded and re-echoed from the lofty roof of the wonderful Hall of Memory. The ceremony concluded, the crowd gradually melted away and all was silent again. Some returned to the Grande Place to watch the erection of stalls, etc., for the " Tuindag " Fair which was to open on the Sunday morning, others proceeded to the old Ramparts to look across the country in safety, whilst others sat at the tables outside numberous estaminets for a smoke and chat over a friendly glass.

Sunday morning was free to enable those who desired to attend Divine Service in the English Church, others could be seen around the Fair, now in full swing with roundabouts, organs playing, showmen shouting, etc. Later in the morning the religious procession wended its way through the streets with nuns carrying the various decorated altars, firemen, bands and banners and lastly the Clergy in their brilliant robes—a most impressive and unforgettable sight.

In the afternoon, coaches conveyed us for a tour of the Salient, and the route taken was *via* St. Jean, St. Julien with its Canadian Memorial, Tyne Cot Cemetery, Zonnebeke, Gheluvelt, Clapham Junction, Hooge, Maple Avenue, Hill 62, Sanctuary Wood—where the preserved trenches with their duckboards and water made a realistic picture. At Hill 60, the trenches and tunnels were entered and the tower with a telescope at the top drew some of the more energetic for a fine panoramic view of the Ypres Salient. We

PHOTOGRAPH OF THE PARTY PRIOR TO DEPARTURE FROM YPRES

returned *via* Hell Fire Corner—now a very peaceful one—and so back to our starting point.

Monday morning at 9 a.m. we set off again, this time for a whole-day tour as far as Arras, passing through St. Eloi, Messines, Ploegsteert, crossing the frontier at Le Bizet. On the Belgian side, a merry-faced Customs officer appeared at the coach window and enquired if there were any on board fro' Yorkshire, as he had spent some time in that county during the war. On the French side, things wery different and enumerable formalities delayed us for a long time. A pompous officer made enquiries if we possessed tobacco, cigarettes, chocolates, etc., but received negative replies. Our coach, in column of route with other transport was unfortunately positioned half-way over a bridge under which was stagnant water and the odour that emanated did not exactly remind one of " ottar of roses ! " At length we reached Armentieres from which the notorious madamoiselle originated, and near the outskirts, high across the road were two stuffed figures, one of which was a female. This led to questions if that might be the lady, but no reply could be given. We now passed the La Bassee Canal, the Indian Memorial and Portuguese Cemetery at the Neuve Chapelle Cross Roads, then La Targette *en route* to Arras where a halt was made for a couple of hours, during which time some of the party were able to visit a cemetery near Bapaume.

Our homeward journey commenced with a visit to the Vimy Ridge, where we explored the Grange Tunnels and the 5.9 shell which had pierced the roof of a dug-out and failed to explode interested many who saw it, also the Canadian and German trenches and various machine guns, trench mortars, etc., were closely examined. Our journey continued through Lens, Hulloch and back to Armentieres, crossing the frontier, this time, without delay. The Belgian officer was still on duty and greeted us as follows : " Of course you have nothing to declare ; Oh no ! and lifted the barrier. Just on 8 p.m. the Lille Gate loomed into sight, and not long after we were seated to a thoroughly enjoyable meal.

Great tribute is due to the British gardeners and officials of the cemeteries for the splendid manner in which the hallowed spots, which are forever England, are kept.

Tuesday morning found us assembled at Ypres Station bound for Ostend, where the party split into two, one portion embarking on the 11 a.m. boat for Dover, and the rest remaining until the afternoon service. The writer, who has made a number of battlefield tours with other organisations, would like to pay the highest possible praise to Captain de Trafford for the manner in which he conducted the party. He was untiring in his efforts to be of service to everyone and his constant care and attention for the comfort of all and sundry was wonderful.

F.W.S.

Ypres Day, 1935

THIS year, the Ypres League Annual Commemoration will be held on **Sunday Morning, October 27th**, and the following programme has been arranged:—

- 11.00 a.m.   Assemble on the Horse Guards' Parade.
- 11.30 a.m.   Address by the Revd. A. T. A. Naylor, O.B.E., M.A., (Guards' Chaplain) who will conduct a short service, followed by the " Lament " by Pipers of the 2nd Battalion, Scots Guards.
- 11.45 a.m.   March to the Cenotaph.
- 12.00 noon   Laying of the Ypres League wreath on the Cenotaph.
- 12.15 p.m.   March back to the Horse Guards' Parade.
- 12.30 p.m.   Dismiss on the Horse Guards' Parade, and at 1.0 p.m. a deputation of the Ypres League will proceed to the Tomb of the Unknown Warrior in Westminster Abbey and place a wreath.

H.R.H. Princess Beatrice has graciously consented to attend the service and lay the League wreath on the Cenotaph.

Plain clothes and medals to be worn (uniform optional).

We hope that members of the Ypres League will make every effort to attend this Commemoration.

League Secretary's Notes

We have great pleasure to welcome all our new members who have been enrolled since the publication of the last edition of the *Ypres Times*, and we are fully expectant that the New Year will witness an appreciable increase of membership in the inauguration of a Branch at Auckland, New Zealand, where very considerable enthusiasm is being shown in the Ypres League through our faithful promoter, Mr. Edward Thomas, who has been working very hard to spread the interest of the League in his country, and in extending to Mr. Thomas our sincere thanks we trust that his devoted efforts will shortly be crowned with deserved success.

We feel that our readers will be interested in the year's travel activities, so following the procedure in past October editions, we give a summary of Pilgrimages and Battlefield Tours which the League has arranged and conducted during 1935:—

March 1st—4th:	35 Officers of the 168th Infantry Brigade to La Fère area with H.Q. at Amiens.
March 15th—18th:	31 Officers of the 167th Infantry Brigade to Ypres and Hazebrouck areas. H.Q. Ypres.
March 18th—22nd:	33 Officers of the 4th Guards Brigade on circular tour from Paris to Compeigne-Cambrai-Ypres-Boulogne.
March 22nd—24th:	Syndicate party of 90 Officers and O.R.'s to Le Cateau and Aisne areas. H.Q. Arras.
April 20th—23rd:	Easter mixed Pilgrimage to Ypres.
April 27th—30th:	Public School Tour of 70 boys to Ypres.
May 17th—20th:	85th Club Tour to Ypres.
June 8th—11th:	Whitsuntide mixed Pilgrimage to Ypres.
June 8th—11th:	236th Siege Battery, R.G.A. Tour to Ypres.
August 3rd—5th:	62 members of the Old Coldstreamers' Association to the Somme. H.Q. Arras.
August 3rd—6th:	Mixed Pilgrimage to Ypres.
August 3rd—6th:	Mixed Pilgrimage to Arras.
Sept. 21st—24th:	Mixed Pilgrimage to Ypres which included a Free Pilgrimage of poor mothers and widows.
Sept. 27th—30th:	30 Officers of the 128th Infantry Brigade to the Elouges and Aisne areas. H.Q. Cambrai.

This sphere of activity has now become one of extreme importance and seldom a day passes without headquarters being approached for information on many questions affecting battlefield travel. Whether it be the organisation of comprehensive tours for small and large parties or giving advice to independent pilgrims wishing to visit graves or memorials, we are, in the course of our duty, only too glad to offer the benefit of our experience in this particular work.

Conforming with the League's charitable work, we had the privilege to defray inclusive expenses of eight poor mothers and widows to Ypres on September 21st. These poor relatives were selected from London, Colchester and Sheffield, and in this connection we would like to place on record our unanimous thanks for the valuable financial assistance rendered by the South Kensington Branch of the British Legion, and by the 85th Club, whose benevolence has been a source of great consolation to three of the most deserving cases on our "waiting list."

Space, unfortunately, does not permit a longer letter, but we cannot conclude without conveying a most sincere expression of gratitude to our Branches, Corresponding Members, Representatives and all individual supporters, for their extremely valued co-operation with headquarters in the various departments of the League's work, and it is our wish that all our members may enjoy a very happy Christmas, and a peaceful and prosperous 1936.

BAR-LOCK (1925) CO.
NOTTINGHAM, ENGLAND
MADE IN ENGLAND
AND IN USE ALL OVER THE WORLD

FOR SERVICES RENDERED.

The General Committee of the Ypres League have been pleased to confer Honorary Life Membership on the following gentleman :—

Mr. Henry Benson, M.A.

In grateful recognition of his valuable services to the League for so many years in contributing many fine articles to the columns of the "Ypres Times" which have greatly enhanced the prestige of the journal, also of the assistance of Mr. Benson in giving frequent publicity to the League's activities through the medium of the Press and the keen interest in which he has always taken in the Leagues' charitable work of defraying the expenses of specially selected poor relatives to Ypres.

YPRES LEAGUE TIE.

Dark shade of cornflower blue relieved by a narrow gold stripe. In good quality silk.

Price 3/6d., post free.

Obtainable from Secretary, Ypres League, 20, Orchard Street, London, W.1.

WREATHS.

Arrangements are made by the Ypres League to place wreaths for relatives on the graves of British soldiers situated in France and Belgium at the following times of the year:—

EASTER, ARMISTICE DAY, CHRISTMAS.

The wreaths may be composed of natural flowers, laurel, or holly, and can be bought at the following prices—12s. 6d., 15s. 6d., and 20s., according to the size and quality of the wreath.

In connection with the Battlefield Tour of the Old Coldstreamers' Association we, herewith, reproduce the above photograph of the Guards' Memorial at Les Boeufs showing the wreath which was placed on, behalf of the party by Major W. A. C Wilkinson, M.C. accompanied by the officers and guardsmen who actually participated in the 1916 "Somme" fighting in the area mentioned.

BURNING OF THE CLOTH HALL, 1915.

A few remaining coloured prints now in stock are being offered to our members at the reduced rate of 1s. each, post free.

Since further copies are unobtainable we would advise those interested to make their purchase without delay.

THE BRITISH TOURING SERVICE

Manager—Mr. P. VYNER

Representative and Life Member, Ypres League

**10, Station Square
ARRAS
(P.-de-C.) France**

Cars for Hire, with British Driver Guides   Tours Arranged

Branch Notes

THIRTEENTH ANNUAL RE-UNION SMOKING CONCERT.

The London County Committee have much pleasure in drawing attention to the arrangements for this year's Annual Smoking Concert. Particular care has been taken to ensure a very convivial evening, and the Committee are hopeful that the attendance will exceed that of previous functions which have always been popular. The success, however, is dependent on individual support, and a cordial invitation is extended to all our London members and their friends to the Caxton Hall on October 26th.

The Smoking Concert will take place at the Caxton Hall, Caxton Street, Victoria Street, S.W.1, on Saturday, October 26th, 1935, when Major E. Montague Jones, O.B.E. (Chairman of the London County Committee) will preside, and amongst the guests who have already accepted invitations to be present are :—H.E. The French Ambassador ; General R. Voruz, Military Attache, French Embassy ; Lieut.-Colonel Raymond E. Lee, Military Attache, American Embassy ; General Sir W. C. G. Heneker, K.C.B., K.C.M.G., D.S.O. ; Lieut.-General Sir W. P. Pulteney, G.C.V.O., K.C.B., Etc. ; Colonel G. T. Brierley, C.M.G., D.S.O. ; The Rev. G. H. Woolley, V.C., M.C. ; and Major W. H. Brooke, M.C. Doors will be open at 7 p.m. and the Concert commences at 7.30 p.m.

The programme is being provided by "The Rogues" Concert Party, under the personal direction of Mr. Bart Brady, and musical selections will be played by "The Enfield College of Music Orchestra," directed by Mrs. Doris Lee Peabody. Community singing of popular war-time choruses will again be a feature of the programme.

Apart from the actual entertainment provided, this annual re-union affords unique opportunity to renew war-time acquaintances and exchange of reminiscences of those never-to-be-forgotten days. If any members of the London area are unable to attend the Concert, might we take the liberty to suggest that they purchase tickets to help the funds of the Branch Committee. Cornflowers will be on sale at the Hall, price 2d.

INFORMAL GATHERINGS

OF THE

LONDON COUNTY COMMITTEE, YPRES LEAGUE

WILL BE HELD AT

The Bedford Head Hotel, Maiden Lane, Strand, W.C.2. 7.15 p.m. to 10 p.m. on following dates:—

Thursday, October 17th, 1935.
 (Lantern talk on "Destroyers in The Great War"
  by Commander H. M. DENNY, D.S.O., R.N.)

Thursday, November 21st, 1935, Steak Supper.

Thursday, December 19th, 1935, programme to be arranged.

Thursday, January 16th, 1936, talk
  by BRIG. GENERAL A. BURT, C.M.G., D.S.O.

We request members to bring these fixtures to the notice of their friends in order to ensure another successful season, and invitations will be gladly sent by the Hon. Secretary to any friends on receipt of names and addresses. Ladies are cordially invited.

each, and we respectfully ask everybody to wear this League emblem.

Application for tickets, prices 1s., 2s. 6d. and 5s. (including tax), should be made as early as possible to the Hon. Secretary, London County Committee, Ypres League, 20, Orchard Street, W.1. Ladies are cordially invited. A limited number of tables can be reserved for parties of four and upwards, on payment of 2s. per table on the 2s. 6d. tickets, and 2s. 6d. per table on the 5s. tickets. Latest date for application is October 21st.

We look forward to a record gathering on October 26th. (*See* page 254).

INFORMAL GATHERINGS.

The Gatherings commenced again on September 19th and will continue to be held on the third Thursday in each month at the Bedford Head Hotel, Maiden Lane, Strand, W.C.2, from 7.15 p.m. to 10 p.m. These re-unions are organised to enable ex-Service men and their friends to meet and renew old acquaintances and to further that wonderful spirit of comradeship.

We hope that the list of fixtures announced on page 249 will be duly noted and the Gatherings well patronised. The Hon. Secretary of the London County Committee will be pleased to send invitations to any friends interested on receipt of names and addresses. Ladies are cordially invited.

PURLEY BRANCH.
The Bombardier's Foursomes.

A larger number than ever entered for this knock-out competition this year—the total being 38 pairs including all previous winners and finalists: the draw was made and posted to each competitor at the commencement of summer time and the first battle was played on April 24th. In view of the number of matches on which to report only brief results can be given:

First Battle.

Corp. A. A. Meredith (10) and Lieut. J. H. Hines (13) bt. Pte. A. K. Irens (4) and Capt. L. R. Ray (6), 3/2 ; Capt. C. F. Tissington (11) and Gnr. W. Kerr (9) bt. Lieut. S. Vaughan (17) and R. M. Simpson (13), 5/4 ; Lieut. C. J. Frost (14) and Rfm. G. Green (15) bt. Lieut. F. St. John North (17) and Lieut. K. May (14), 4/3 ; Pte. H. Boon (20) and Lieut. A. C. Stewart (17) bt. Major L. Meakin (14) and Major J. Wayte (18), 6/5 ; Capt. B. Smither (12) and Capt. C. D. Lovering (10) bt. Major J. L. Menzies (18) and Lieut. J. D. Mills (16), 2/1 ; Capt. W. K. Scott (7) and Capt. A. S. Green (11) bt. Lieut. A. D. Duncan (11) and Capt. G. B. Mutton (18), 2/1.

Second Battle.

Capt. Tissington and Gnr. Kerr bt. Corpl. Meredith and Lieut. Hines 4/3 ; Lieut. Frost and Rfm. Green bt. Lieut. R. W. Pullen (22) and Corpl. H. R. Turnock (24), 7/5 ; Lieut. J. K. Jones (14) and Lieut. H. S. Panchaud (12) bt. Capt. D. H. Morgan (24) and Capt. R. L. Haine (20) Capt. E. Featherstone (1) and Major Graham Carr (7) bt. Q.M.S. S. J. Brown (6) and Lieut. S. G. White (9), 1 up ; Major S. F. Wood (7) and Capt. E. A. S. Lund (18) bt. Capt. E. C. Ashby (8) and Lieut. B. R. Brill (10), 5/4 ; Pte. E. S. Butt (2) and Major L. W. Alderson (7) bt. Major J. S. Hall (18) and Capt. G. E. E. B. Nicholls (24), 2 up ; Gnr. J. K. Macfarlane (13) and 2nd-Lieut. C. E. Reeves (18) bt. Lieut. N. A. Zinn (24) and Lieut. H. J. Fitton (22), 1 up ; Major H. G. Harris (16) and Capt. N. W. Streat (14) bt. Gnr. H. M. Brown (18) and Lieut. E. A. Adams (18), 3/2 ; Lieut. R. R. Birrell (17) and Capt. J. G. Rae (8) bt. Lieut. C. E. Terrell (15) and Lieut. H. L. W. Hancock (12) ; Capt. S. T. Grant (15) and Lieut. T. G. Crump (10) bt. Capt. D. L. Waghorn (14) and Lieut. F. H. Hayns (24) 8/7 ; Bmdr. E. A. R. Burden (3) and Lieut. J. V. Lindsay (7) bt. Capt. F. W. Douse (9) and Corpl. C. T. Taylor (9), 1 up ; Pay-lieut. N. Bell (20) and Pay-Cmdr. F. Monk (16) bt. Lieut. J. J. Mellon (14) and Corpl. E. A. Satchell (15), 3/2 ; Lieut. E. W. Bennett (16) and Capt. H. St. G. Ralling (10) bt. Major D. H. Scott (18) and Major J. F. Legg (22) at 21st ; Major A. Grutchfield (18) and Corpl. C. Stroud (16) bt. Lieut. S. Murray (16) and Driver C. C. Wood (15), 2 up ; Pte. H. Boon and Lieut. A. C. Stewart bt. Capt. B. A. Forster (8) and Lieut. C. G. H. Midgley (8), 1 up ; Capt. W. K. Scott and Capt. A. S. Green bt. Capt. Smither and Capt. Lovering, 2 up.

Third Battle.

Lieut. Frost and Rfm. Green bt. Capt. Tissington and Gnr. Kerr, 3/2 ; Lieut. Jones and Lieut. Panchaud bt. Capt. Featherstone and Major Graham Carr, 2/1 ; Pte. Butt and Major Alderson, w/o ; Major Wood and Capt. Lund, scratched ; Major Harris and Capt. Streat bt. Gnr. Macfarlane and 2nd-Lieut. Reeves at 19th; Lieut. Birrell and Capt. Rae, w/o ; Capt. Grant and Lieut. Crump, scratched ; Bmdr. Burden and Lieut. Lindsay bt. Pay-Lieut. Bell and Pay-Cmdr. Monk, 6/5 ; Lieut. Bennett and Capt. Ralling bt. Major Grutchfield and Corpl. Stroud, 2/1 ; Pte. Boon and Lieut. Stewart, w/o ; Capt. Scott and Capt. Green, scratched.

Fourth Battle.

Lieut. Frost and Rfm. Green bt. Lieut. Jones and Lieut. Panchaud at Woodcote, 2/1 ; Pte. Butt and Major Alderson bt. Major Harris and Capt. Streat at Purley Downs by 6/4 ; Lieut. Birrell and Capt. Rae bt. Bmdr. Burden ann Lieut. Lindsay at Woodcote by 2/1 ; Pte. Bood and Lieut. Stewart bt. Lieut. Bennett and Capt. Ralling at Woodcote by 4/2.

Fifth Battle.

Lieut. Frost and Rfm. Green met Pte. Butt and Major Alderson at Woodcote and receiving 6 shots won 4/3. Alderson made a famous remark on the 10th tee, but—no, we won't give him away. Pte. Boon and Lieut. Stewart played Lieut. Birrell and Capt. Rae on Purley Downs : the Scots meant to put up a dour fight but Boon and Stewart had other views and won 5/4. Up to this point every match had been played well up to programme time—a matter of congratulation on the part of the Adjutant who recognises that either the members have a greater consideration for him or wind up !

Sixth and Final Battle.

Both sides spent a little time sharpening their niblicks before the Adjutant could get them to fix a date for the final which was played on Wednesday, 24th July. By this date the Chairman of the Branch had gone abroad (on leave of course) so the Captain of Woodcote Park, himself a Wipers Member, took the match and reported as follows : —" We are rather proud that this Club has provided all the finalists for the second year in succession : our men are very keen so we hope they may keep on doing it. The entry of 76 players was very encouraging, and the Bombardier may well feel that it was more than usually worth while inaugurating such a competition." Unfortunately for everybody else, the four finalists have been winning all round and all had reductions in handicap since the start. Having seen the play I am sure the strongest pairs reached the last stage and the stronger pair won. Frost and Green beating Boon and Stewart—a thoroughly deserved success particularly after running-up last year. Boon and Stewart will be heard of again for they are very keen and great triers.

Autumn Golf Meeting.

The weather excelled itself on September 24th when we held our Autumn Golf Meeting and played for the Tenth Wipers Cup. It was not merely bad or only rough : a driving rain and gale from the very start reduced an already small entry of 26 down to 18, but the eighteen braved the elements although only 10 actually finished. Under these very difficult conditions the back marker, Bombardier E. A. R. Burden playing from scratch, won the Cup with the score of 5 down which was an extremely good performance on such a day.

The Purley Downs Club extended the usual hospitality and the dripping players were reinforced for the supper by several other members who were unable to get down to play so that a very cheery evening was spent.

Five players qualified as runners-up with the return of 7 down and Captain B. A. Forster secured the second sweep by the best return on the last nine holes.

THE ADJUTANT.

CORRESPONDENCE.

Peterborough,
Ontario.
June 13th, 1935.

The Secretary,
Ypres League.
Dear Sir,

My annual subscription being due this month, I have pleasure to enclose the usual remittance. I have also had in mind your membership campaign in celebration of the King's Jubilee and although it is rather difficult to interest eligible candidates at this distance, it is a great pleasure to add at least one member whose application form and subscription I enclose. It is my hope that in the course of time others may be encouraged to join.

The " Ypres Times " of which I treasure every copy since the first issue, is practically our only link, out here, with old times and comradeships and I would not miss it for anything.

Have you ever considered issuing binders in which to file them ?

Long life to the League !

Yours very truly,
B.O.

Highgate, N.6.
August 13th, 1935.

The Secretary,
Ypres League,
Dear Sir,

I should be glad if you would forward me some membership forms of the League and any literature you may have describing the aims and objects. I think I can obtain at least one new member, and if I had some forms I might hear of some other people who would like to join. You will see from your records that I myself am a Life Member of long standing. I think it is an excellent thing to keep the spirit of the Salient and to join the League is certainly the best way to do it.

Yours faithfully,
C. E. P.

Hartford,
Conn., U.S.A.
August 14th, 1935.

Dear Sir,

I am very much pleased to send you the enclosed application for membership together with a money order for five shillings.

It has been a little difficult in finding recruits in these parts, but you can rest assured that I am always on the alert for new members. I was in casual conversation with Doctor———when he was treating me for a badly sprained back and the subject of the war and Ypres arose and (without any loss of time) the Ypres League. This application and cash is the result.

What pleases me most is that the new member is being enrolled during the Jubilee year, and indeed I should have been much disappointed had I failed to respond to our esteemed Patron's appeal. With kindest regards and all good wishes for the League.

Yours faithfully,
L. E. P. F.

The Ypres League (Incorporated)
Balance Sheet, 31st December, 1934

FUNDS AND LIABILITIES.		£ s. d.	£ s. d.	£ s. d.
Free Pilgrimage Fund	...			91 1 10
General Fund—				
Balance at credit, 1st January, 1934	...	60 13 3		
Add Balance at credit for year to 31st December, 1934	...	15 3 2		
				75 16 5
Reserve Fund—In respect of Life Membership Subscriptions				300 0 0
"Ypres Times" Maintenance Fund	...			223 0 0
Hostel Fund	...	...		322 19 10
Maintenance Fund—Ypres Salient Notice Boards	...			6 16 9
Sundry Creditors, &c.	...	...		114 12 2
				£1,134 7 0

ASSETS.		£ s. d.	£ s. d.	£ s. d.
Stocks of Publications, &c., on hand As per Head Office records and Secretary's valuation.	...			74 3 5
Cash at Bank and in hand—				
Free Pilgrimage Fund	...		93 8 4	
Head Office Account	...		42 17 11	
				136 6 3
Halifax Building Society—				
Deposit Account "A"	...		306 0 0	
Deposit Account "B"	...		204 0 0	
			510 0 0	
Add Interest accrued	...		14 0 5	
				524 0 5
Hostel Fund Investment—				
£323 2s. 11d. War Stock, 3½%				322 19 10
Sundry Pre-payments, &c.	...			76 17 1
				£1,134 7 0

W. P. PULTENEY, *Lieut.-General,*
                                Hon. Treasurer.
MONTAGUE JONES, *Major* ⎱ *Members of the*
E. B. WAGGETT, *Major* ⎰ *General Committee.*

REPORT OF THE AUDITORS TO THE MEMBERS OF THE YPRES LEAGUE, INCORPORATED.

We beg to report that we have examined the above Balance Sheet with the Head Office Books and relative documents of the Association and have obtained all the information and explanations we have required. In our opinion such Balance Sheet is properly drawn up so as to exhibit a true and correct view of the Association's affairs, according to the best of our information and the explanations given to us and as shown by the Books of the Association.

Dated this 21st day of May, 1935.
    6, BOND COURT, WALBROOK, LONDON, E.C.4

LEPINE & JACKSON, Chartered Accountants,
Auditors.

Head Office

Income and Expenditure Account for the year ended 31st December, 1934

EXPENDITURE.	£	s.	d.	INCOME.	£	s.	d.
To Salaries ...	293	10	0	By Subscriptions ...	489	14	9
,, Rent and Rates ...	242	13	2	,, Donations ...	187	9	10
,, Printing and Stationery ...	31	10	10	,, Travel Bureau ...	309	16	6
,, Postages and Telegrams ...	45	19	1	,, Publications, &c. ...	7	18	2
,, Prospectuses, Publicity Leaflets, &c. ...	20	12	4	,, Interest ...	20	12	4
,, Telephone and Insurances ...	26	9	0				
,, Lighting and Heating ...	8	16	10				
,, Accountancy and Audit Charges ...	15	15	0				
,, General Expenses ...	94	10	3				
,, Income Tax ...	5	12	9				
	785	9	3				
,, Balance, Surplus carried to General Fund	230	2	4				
	£1,015	11	7		£1,015	11	7

Head Office

General Fund for the year ended 31st December, 1934

EXPENDITURE.	£	s.	d.	£	s.	d.	INCOME.	£	s.	d.
To "THE YPRES TIMES,"—							By INCOME AND EXPENDITURE ACCOUNT Surplus for the year transferred.	230	2	4
Cost of Printing, &c ...	278	0	6				,, "YPRES TIMES" MAINTENANCE FUND Amount allocated towards cost of "The Ypres Times" in 1934.	44	7	0
Less Sales and Advertising Revenue ...	18	14	4	259	6	2				
,, BALANCE.—Carried to Balance Sheet ...				15	3	2				
				£274	9	4		£274	9	4

THE THIRTEENTH ANNUAL
REUNION OF MEMBERS AND FRIENDS

Organised by the London County Committee of the Ypres League

WILL BE HELD AT THE

CAXTON HALL, CAXTON STREET, VICTORIA STREET S.W.1

ON

SATURDAY, OCTOBER 26th, 1935

All Members of the Ypres League and their friends are heartily invited by the London County Committee to meet together at the Caxton Hall, on Saturday, October 26th, 1935, when the

GRAND SMOKING CONCERT

will be given. The Chair will be taken by

Major E. MONTAGUE JONES, O.B.E.
(Chairman of the London County Committee).

The following will also be present

His Excellency The French Ambassador; Général de Brigade R. Voruz (Military Attaché French Embassy); Lieut.-Colonel Raymond E. Lee (Military Attaché American Embassy); General Sir Wm. C. G. Heneker, K.C.B., K.C.M.G., D.S.O.; Lieut.-Gen. Sir W. P. Pulteney G.C.V.O., K.C.B., K.C.M.G., D.S.O.; Colonel G. T. Brierley, C.M.G., D.S.O.; The Rev. G. H. Woolley, V.C., M.C., and Major W. H. Brooke, M.C.

An excellent Programme has been arranged by "THE ROGUES" CONCERT PARTY *under the personal direction of Mr. Bart Brady.*

Musical Selections by "THE ENFIELD COLLEGE OF MUSIC ORCHESTRA" under the direction of Mrs. Doris Lee Peabody.

Community singing of old war-time choruses will be included in the programme.

Medals and decorations to be worn. Please wear your League Badge. Ladies cordially invited.

DOORS OPEN AT 7 P.M.   CONCERT COMMENCES AT 7.30 P.M.

Admission - - - - 1s., 2s 6d. and 5s. (including Tax).

Accommodation at the Hall is limited, but tables can be reserved for parties of four and upwards on payment of 2s. per table on the 2s. 6d. tickets, and 2s. 6d. per table on the 5s. tickets. Applicants for tables cannot be considered after October 21st.

A large attendance is anticipated, and early application for tickets accompanied by remittance should be addressed to the Hon. Secretary, London County Committee, Ypres League, 20, Orchard Street, London, W.1.

YOUR SUPPORT ON OCTOBER 26th WILL BE APPRECIATED.

Branches and Corresponding Members

BRANCHES.

LONDON	Hon. Secretary to the London County Committee: J. Boughey, 20, Orchard Street, London, W.1.
	E. LONDON DISTRICT—L. A Weller, 40, Lambourne Gardens, Hornchurch, Essex.
	TOTTENHAM AND EDMONTON DISTRICT—E, Glover, 191, Landowne Road, Tottenham, N.17.
	H. Carey, 373, Sydenham Road, S.E.26.
COLCHESTER	H. Snow (Hon. Sec.), 9, Church Street.
	W. H. Taylor (Pilgrimage Hon. Sec.), 64, High Street.
LIVERPOOL	Captain A. M. Webster, Blundellsands.
PURLEY	Major Graham Carr, D.S.O., M.C., 112-114, High Street.
SHEFFIELD	Captain J. Wilkinson, "Holmfield," Bents Drive.
BELGIUM	Capt. P. D. Parminter, 19, Rue Surmont de Volsberghe, Ypres.
CANADA	Ed. Kingsland, P.O. Box 83, Magog, Quebec.
SOUTH AFRICA	L. G. Shuter, Church Street, Pietermaritzburg,
KENYA	C. H. Slater, P.O. Box 403, Nairobi.
AMERICA	Representative: Captain R. Henderson-Bland, 110 West 57th Street, New York City.

CORRESPONDING MEMBERS

GREAT BRITAIN.

ABERYSTWYTH	T. O. Thomas, 5, Smithfield Road.
ASHTON-UNDER-LYNE	G. D. Stuart, "Woodlands,", Thronfield Grove, Arundel Street.
BANBURY	Captain C. W. Fowke, Yew Tree House, King's Sutton.
BIRMINGHAM	Mrs. Hill, 191, Cattell Road, Small Heath.
	John Burman, "Westbrook," Solihull Road, Shirley.
BOURNEMOUTH	H. L. Pasmore, 40, Morley Road, Boscombe Park.
BRISTOL	W. S. Hook, "Wytschaete" Redland Court Road.
BROADSTAIRS	C. E. King, 6, Norman Road, St. Peters, Broadstairs.
	Mrs. Briggs, North Foreland House.
CHATHAM	W. N. Channon, 22, Keyes Avenue.
CHESTERFIELD	Major A. W. Shea, 14, Cross Street.
CONGLETON	Mr. H. Dart, 61, The Crescent.
DARLINGTON	D. S. Vigo, 125, Dorset Road, Bexhill-on-Sea.
DERBY	T. Jakeman, 10, Graham Street.
DORRINGTON (Salop)	Captain G. D. S. Parker, Frodesley Rectory.
EXETER	Captain E. Jenkin, 25, Queen Street.
GLOUCESTER	H. R. Hunt, "Casita," Parton Lane, Churchdown.
HERNE BAY	Captain E. Clarke Williams, F.S.A.A., "Conway," Station Road
HOVE	Captain G. W. J. Cole, 2, Westbourne Terrace, Kingsway.
LEICESTER	W. C. Dunford, 343, Aylestone Road.
LINCOLN	E. Swaine, 79, West Parade.
LLANWRST	A. C. Tomlinson, M.A., Bod Estyn.
LOUGHTON	Capt. O. G. Johnson, M.A., Loughton School.
MATLOCK (Derby)	Miss Dickinson, Beechwood.
MELROSE	Mrs. Lindesay Kelsall, Darnlee.
NEW BRIGHTON (Cheshire)	E. F. Williams, 5, Waterloo Road.
NEW MILTON	W. H. Lunn, "Greycot," Albert Road.

NOTTINGHAM	E. V. Brown, 3, Eldon Chambers, Wheeler Gate.
ST. HELENS (Lancs.)	John Orford, 124, Knowsley Road.
SHREWSBURY	Major-General Sir John Headlam, K.B.E., C.B., D.S.O., Cruck Meole House, Hanwood.
TIVERTON (Devon)	Mr. W H. Duncan Arthur, Surveyor's Office, Town Hall.
WELSHPOOL	Mr. E. Wilson, Coedway, Ford, Salop.

DOMINIONS AND FOREIGN COUNTRIES.

AUSTRALIA	Messrs. C. H. Green, and George Lawson, Box 1153 P., 2nd Floor, Griffiths House, Queen Street, Brisbane, Queensland. R. A. Baldwin, c/o Government Savings Bank of N.S.W., Martin Place, Sydney. Mr. W. Cloves, Box 1296, G.P.O., Adelaide.
BELGIUM	Sister Marguerite, Sacré Coeur, Ypres.
CANADA	Brig.-General V. W. Odlum, C.B., C.M.G., D.S.O., 2530, Point Grey Road, Vancouver. V. A. Bowes, 326, 40th Avenue West, Calgary, Alberta. W. Constable F. Grece, St. Hilaire Station, Ronville County, Quebec.
CEYLON	Captain F. R. G. Webb, M.C., Irrigation Bungalow, Kalmunai, E.P.
EGYPT	L. B. S. Larkins, The Residency, Cairo.
INDIA	Lieut.-Quartermaster G. Smith, Queen's Bays, Sialkot, India.
IRELAND	Miss A. K. Jackson, Cloneyhurke House, Portarlington.
NEW ZEALAND	Captain W. U. Gibb, Ava Lodge, Puhinui Road, Papatoetoe, Auckland S. E. Beattie, Lowlands, Woodville.
SOUTH AFRICA	H. L. Versfield, c/o Cape Explosives Works Ltd., 150, St. Georges Street, Cape Town.
SPAIN	Captain P. W. Burgess, Calle de Zurbano 29, Madrid.
U.S.A.	Captain Henry Maslin, 942, President Street, Brooklyn, New York. L. E. P, Foot, 20, Gillett Street, Hartford, Conn, U.S.A. A. P. Forward, 449, East 80th Street, New York. J. W. Freebody, 945, McBride Avenue, Los Angeles.
NOVA SCOTIA	Will R. Bird, 35, Clarence Street, Amherst.

Membership of the League

This is open to all who served in the Salient, and to all those whose relatives or friends died there, in order that they may have a record of that service for themselves and their descendants, and belong to the comradeship of men and women who understand and remember all that Ypres meant in suffering and endurance.

Life membership, £2 10s.

Annual members, 5s.

Do not let the fact of your not having served in the Salient deter you from joining the Ypres League. Those who have neither fought in the Salient nor lost relatives there, but who are in sympathy with the objects of the Ypres League, are admitted to its fellowship, but are not given scroll certificates.

There is a Junior Division for children whose relatives served in the Salient. It is open also to others to whom our objects appeal.

Annual subscription 1s. up to the age of 18, after which they can become ordinary members of the League.

THE YPRES LEAGUE (INCORPORATED)
20, Orchard Street, Portman Square, W.1.

Telephone: WELBECK 1446. *Telegrams*: YPRESLEAG, "WESDO," LONDON.

Patron-in-Chief: H.M. THE KING.

Patrons:
H.R.H. THE PRINCE OF WALES.   H.R.H. PRINCESS BEATRICE.

President: GENERAL SIR CHARLES H. HARINGTON.

Vice-Presidents:

F.-M. VISCOUNT ALLENBY.   F.-M. SIR CLAUD W. JACOB.
THE VISCOUNT WAKEFIELD OF HYTHE. F.-M. SIR PHILIP CHETWODE.
GENERAL SIR CECIL ROMER.   F.-M. LORD MILNE.

General Committee:

THE COUNTESS OF ALBEMARLE.   MR. F. D. BANKS HILL.
*CAPTAIN C. ALLISTON.   MAJOR-GENERAL C. J. B. HAY.
LIEUT-COLONEL BECKLES WILLSON.   MR. J. HETHERINGTON.
MR. HENRY BENSON.   GENERAL SIR W. C. G. HENEKER.
MR. J. BOUGHEY.   *CAPTAIN O. G. JOHNSON.
MISS B. BRICE-MILLER.   *MAJOR E. MONTAGUE JONES.
COLONEL G. T. BRIERLEY.   MAJOR GENL. C. G. LIDDELL.
CAPTAIN P. W. BURGESS.   CAPTAIN H. D. PEABODY.
BRIG.-GENL. A. BURT.   *THE HON. ALICE DOUGLAS PENNANT.
MAJOR H. CARDINAL-HARFORD.   *LIEUT.-GENERAL SIR W. P. PULTENEY.
REV. P. B. CLAYTON.   LIEUT.-COLONEL SIR J. MURRAY.
THE EARL OF YPRES.   *COLONEL G. E. C. RASCH.
MRS. C. J. EDWARDS.   THE HON. SIR ARTHUR STANLEY.
MAJOR C. J. EDWARDS.   MR. ERNEST THOMPSON.
MR. H. A. T. FAIRBANK.   CAPTAIN J. LOCKLEY TURNER.
MR. T. ROSS FURNER.   *MR. E. B. WAGGETT.
SIR PHILIP GIBBS.   CAPTAIN J. WILKINSON.
MR. E. GLOVER.   CAPTAIN H. TREVOR WILLIAMS.

* Executive Committee.

Bankers: *Honorary Solicitors*:
BARCLAYS BANK LTD., Knightsbridge Branch.   MESSRS. FLADGATE & Co., 70, Pall Mall, S.W.

Secretary: *Auditors*:
CAPTAIN G. E. DE TRAFFORD.   MESSRS. LEPINE & JACKSON, 6, Bond Court, E.C.4.

League Representative at Ypres: **League Representative at Cambrai:**
CAPTAIN P. D. PARMINTER.   MR. A. WILDE,
19, Rue Surmont de Volsberghe   9, Rue des Anglaises.

League Representative at Amiens: **League Representative at Arras:**
CAPTAIN STUART OSWALD.   MR. P. VYNER,
7, Rue Porte-Paris.   10, Station Square.

Hon. Secretary, Ypres British Settlement:
LT. COLONEL F. G. POOLE,

PRIMARY OBJECTS OF THE LEAGUE

I.—Commemoration and Comradeship.
II.—To provide special travel facilities for Members and all interested to Ypres and battlefields, and transport of Members.
III.—The furnishing of information about the Salient; marking of historic sites and the compilation of charts of the battlefields.
IV.—The erection of a Ypres British Church and School which has been completed.
V.—The establishment of groups of members throughout the world, through Branch Secretaries and Corresponding Members.
VI.—The maintenance of cordial relations with dwellers on the battlefields of Ypres.
VII.—The formation of a Junior Division.

Use the Ypres League Travel Bureau for Ypres and Whole of the Western Front

FOR THE FOLLOWING PUBLICATIONS, Etc., apply:

Secretary, YPRES LEAGUE, 20, ORCHARD STREET, LONDON, W.1.

THE BATTLE BOOK OF YPRES. A history of notable deeds contributed by all regiments. 5s.; post free, 5s 6d. Compiled by Beatrix Brice with the assistance of Lieut.-General Sir William Pulteney, G.C.V.O., etc.

BOOKS.

YPRES: Outpost of the Channel Ports. By Beatrix Brice. With Foreword by Field-Marshal Lord Plumer, G.C.B. Price 1s. 0d.; post free 1s. 3d.

In the Ypres Salient. By Lt.-Col. Beckles Willson. 1s. net; post free 1s. 2d.

Story of the 63rd Field Ambulance. By A. W. Westmore, etc. Cloth, 3s. 6d., post free. Paper, 2s. 6d., post free.

War Letters to a Wife. By Colonel Rowland Feilding. Popular Edition, 3s. 6d.; post free 4s.

The Pill Boxes of Flanders. 1s.; post free 1s. 3d.

From Mons to the First Battle of Ypres. By J. G. W. Hyndson, M.C. Price 3/6, post free

YPRES LEAGUE TIES. 3s. 6d. each, post free.

YPRES LEAGUE BADGES. 2s. each, 2s. 1½d. post free.

EMBROIDERED BADGES. 4s. each, post free.

Map and List of Cemeteries in the Ypres Salient. Price 9d.; post free 11d.

Map of the Somme. Price 1s. 8d., post free.

PICTURES.

Burning of the Cloth Hall, 1915. A Coloured Print, 14 in. by 12 in. 1s. post free.

Old Well-known Spots in New Guise.
Prints, size 4¼ x 2½, recently taken of famous spots in the Ypres Salient, and which may be of great interest to our readers, are on sale at headquarters, price 4d. each, post free 5d. For particulars apply Secretary.

POST CARDS, PHOTOGRAPHS AND ETCHINGS.

Post Cards. Ypres: British Front during the War. Ruins of Ypres. Price 1s. post free.

Photographs of Menin Gate Unveiling. Size 11 in. by 7 in. 1s. 2d. each, post free.

Hill 60. Complete Panorama Photographs. 12 in. by 3¾ in. Price 3s., post free; 15 in. by 5 in. Price 3s. 6d., post free.

WAR-TIME PHOTOGRAPHS OF THE SALIENT.

6 in. by 8 in. ... 1s. 6d. each.
12 in. by 15 in. ... 4s. each.

List forwarded on application.

PHOTOGRAPHS OF WAR-TIME SKETCHES.

Bedford House (Front View), 1916.
Bedford House (Back View), 1916.
Voormezeele Main Street, 1916.
Voormezeele Crucifixion Gate, 1916.
Langhof Chateau, 1916.

Size 8½ in. by 6½ in. Price 2s. 6d. each, post free.

Photographs of the Thiepval and Arras Memorials. Post card size, price 1s. each, post free.

YPRES TIMES.

The Journal may be obtained at the League Offices. BACK NUMBERS 1s.; 1934, 8d.; 1935, 6d.

Printed in Great Britain for the Publishers by FORD & GILL 21a/23, Iliffe Yard, Crampton Street, London, S E.17.

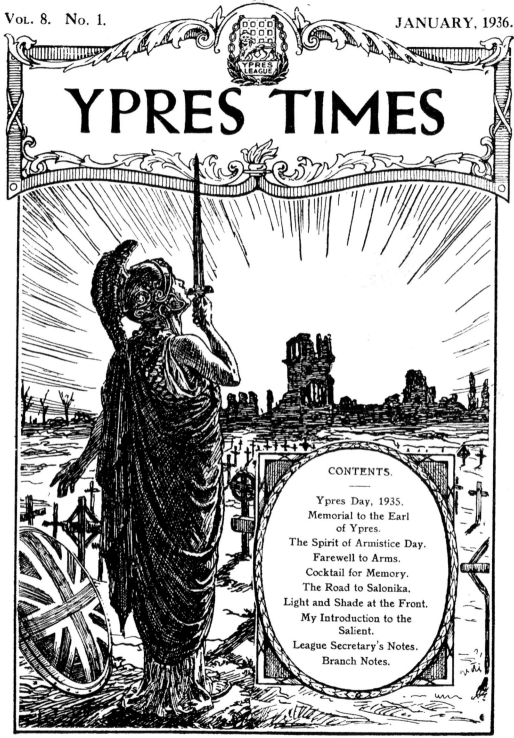

Memory Tablet.

JANUARY - FEBRUARY - MARCH

January.

Jan. 8th, 1916	...	Gallipoli evacuation completed.
„ 12th, 1915	...	The use of poisonous shells by Germans reported.
„ 21st, 1915	...	Zeebrugge bombarded by British airmen.
„ 24th, 1916	...	Naval battle off Dogger Bank.

February.

Feb. 3rd, 1917	...	America broke with Germany.
„ 18th, 1915	...	U-boat "blockade" of England.
„ 18th, 1918	...	German invasion of Russia.
„ 21st, 1916	...	Battle of Verdun begun.
„ 21st, 1918	...	British capture Jericho.
„ 25th, 1915	...	Allied Fleet attacked Dardanelles.

March.

Mar. 10th, 1915	...	British capture of Neuve Chapelle.
„ 11th, 1917	...	British take Baghdad.
„ 12th, 1917	...	Revolution in Russia.
„ 15th, 1917	...	Abdication of the Tsar.
„ 21st, 1917	...	First British War Cabinet.
„ 21st, 1918	...	German offensive on the Western Front.

The Ypres Times

Communications to
The Editor, "Ypres Times,"
20, Orchard Street, London, W.1.

PRICE 6d.
POST FREE 7d.

VOL. 8, No. 1.   PUBLISHED QUARTERLY   JANUARY, 1936

Ypres Day, 1935

[Photo]   [Reproduced with kind permission of Planet News Ltd.

H.R.H. PRINCESS BEATRICE AFTER LAYING THE YPRES LEAGUE WREATH UPON THE CENOTAPH

WITH customary solemnity and dignity, the Ypres League commemorated its fifteenth anniversary on Sunday, October 27th, when a record gathering assembled on the Horse Guards' Parade which was particularly appropriate in the Jubilee Year of our Sovereign.

At 11.20 a.m., the officiating Padre, the Rev. A. T. A. Naylor, O.B.E., M.A., senior Chaplain of the 1st Cavalry Brigade arrived on the parade ground preceded by the Choristers in red cassocks and a standard bearer with a famous war-time Union Jack which is described in the Address.

Punctually at 11.30 a.m. Her Royal Highness Princess Beatrice was received by the Chairman of the Ypres League, Lieut.-General Sir W. P. Pulteney, G.C.V.O., K.C.B., K.C.M.G., D.S.O., accompanied by His Excellency The Belgian Ambassador, and amongst those present included: The Military Attachés of the Belgian, French and American Embassies, Lieut.-Colonel G. P. Vanier, representing the High Commissioner for Canada, The Dowager Viscountess Plumer, also contingents of the O.T.C. Cadets, Old Contemptibles, 5th Army O.C.A., St. Dunstan's, 85th Field Ambulance O.C.A., and Ypres League. The service opened with the singing of the hymn " O Valiant Hearts " accompanied by the Band of the 1st Surrey Rifles. Then followed the Address by the Rev. A. T. A. Naylor, from which we quote :—

" A deep sense of reverence and humility fills our hearts as we meet here to-day. Memories of Ypres are among the most sacred we possess for Ypres was the furnace which proved the temper of our armies, old and new. There they made themselves worthy of the highest traditions of the British Army, and our presence here is to express our gratitude to those who, knowing what laid before them, made the supreme sacrifice in stemming the mass attacks of a determined foe.

" This Union Jack we have here on the Parade is a well-worn flag which was used in the Salient at Ypres to cover bodies of those who upheld these high traditions. It was also used at the funeral of Lord Roberts when the sorrowing army fired the last three volleys that are fired in the name of the Father, the Son and the Holy Ghost. This same flag has covered men of every rank and every walk in life, who fought to prevent the complete possession of the country of our Ally, our brave Ally to whom we now tender our affection and sympathy in her recent grief. Nothing that touches Belgium fails to touch the deep places in our hearts, and thank God for the understanding between our nations, understandings which are based on sentiment created by mutual appreciation of courage and loyalty such as shown in the individual cases of heroism at Ypres, the sum total of which was founded upon the righteousness of the cause.

" Much has been written about the thoughts and feelings of those who were engaged in the Great War. The last thoughts of men were for their friends at home, loving thoughts, and in solemn letters that had to be written to those who were left there was always the feeling " No greater love hath any man than this, that a man lay down his life for his friends.'

" Let nations and individuals realise their need for and how God longs for and yearns for their feelings to express ' Our Father which art in Heaven,' and there will come Peace to the world. There is one virtue in the Lord's Prayer to-day in the fact that it unites us to those who are already in His Presence, beyond earthly limitations."

At the conclusion of the Address, seven Pipers of the 2nd Btn. Scots Guards played the " Lament," and after a short silence the " Last Post " was sounded by the Buglers of the 1st Surrey Rifles — then all joined in the singing of " O God our help in ages past," and the National Anthem which was followed by the " Reveille."

The whole parade now formed up for the march to the Cenotaph headed by the Band, and Princess Beatrice, after taking the salute at the Horse Guards' Arch, layed the beautiful Ypres League wreath composed of its cornflower emblems, lilies and

[Photo] [By kind permission of Planet News Ltd.

A GENERAL VIEW OF THE HORSE GUARDS PARADE DURING THE ANNUAL "YPRES DAY" MEMORIAL SERVICE, WHICH WAS ATTENDED BY H.R.H. PRINCESS BEATRICE.

chrysanthemums on the National Shrine. The wreath bearers were Sergeant O. Brooks, V.C., late Coldstream Guards, and Ex Sgt. A. Marhoff, 4th Dragoon Guards, Chairman of the Old Contemptibles' Association, Finchley Branch.

Despite the passing of years since the Armistice it was amazing to observe the fine bearing on parade of the 120 Old Contemptibles under the command of Brig.-General E. Segrave, C.B., C.M.G., D.S.O., and the smartness in which these old warriors of the Salient responded to the stentorian commands of one of their number, an ex-sergeant major. They moved with the precision of young serving soldiers and elicited the admiration of all present, and it was a very fitting conclusion when Lieut.-General Sir W. P. Pulteney took the salute for their march past prior to dismissal on the return to the Horse Guards' Parade.

At 1 p.m. a deputation of the Ypres League headed by Major E. Montague Jones, O.B.E., T.D., was received at Westminster Abbey by the Ven. Archdeacon Storr, M.A., and a wreath was placed on the grave of the Unknown Warrior. During a short service of touching simplicity the Archdeacon addressed the assembly as follows :—

"Let me begin by saying on behalf of the Dean and Chapter how very glad we are to welcome representatives of the Ypres League year by year. I suppose we all know something of the admirable work the League has done. We receive the wreath which is being placed on the Unknown Warrior's grave, and it will be duly noted in the records of the Abbey.

"It is inevitable on these annual celebrations that their character should tend to sameness, but we shall never forget the heroism and self-sacrifice of those men who gave their all for God and liberty and justice and to their country. As the years go by, that immemorial association unplants more and more upon us the idea of Peace which we want and for which 'they' fought. Though even now the clouds hang very low in this respect, we must work for the cause of fellowship, brotherhood, peace and justice.

"Standing here by this hallowed grave in close proximity of the grave of one of the greatest commanders in the war, Lord Plumer, I would ask you to be silent in prayer for a moment."

After observing a two minutes' silence, prayers followed, and then a visit to the private chapel wherein lies Lord Plumer's remains.

Memorial to the Earl of Ypres

Tablet in Canterbury Cathedral.
Tribute from Personal Friends.

A MOVEMENT started by Sir Charles Warde, Bart., nearly two years ago, for the provision of some permanent memorial in a suitable place to Field-Marshal the Earl of Ypres has come to fruition. Last Armistice Day, a mural tablet in marble, adjoining the Warriors' Chapel of Canterbury Cathedral, was dedicated with simple, yet solemn, ceremony. This, appropriately enough, followed the annual Armistice Day service in the Cathedral.

This little country churchyard in which Lord Ypres is buried is that of the parish in which he was born, Ripple, near Dover. It was here — at Ripple Vale —that his father lived till the future Field-Marshal was four years old. In a simple little grave his bones rest with those of other members of his family.

The execution of the memorial was entrusted to the late Sir Walter Tapper, R.A., F.S.A. whose design, as will be judged from the accompanying photographic reproduction, shows both dignity and refinement. Surmounted by Lord Ypres' coat of arms, bearing the motto "Malo mori quam foedari," the tablet bears the folllowing inscription : " This memorial was erected by his friends in memory of Field-Marshal the Right Honble. Sir John Denton Pinkstan French, Earl of Ypres, P.C., K.P., C.B., O.M., G.C.V.O., K.C.M.G., born 1852, died 1925. He commanded the British Army in France from the outbreak of the Great War to December, 1915. His courageous leadership in front of Ypres helped to save the Allied Forces in the great crisis of the War."

DEDICATION CEREMONY.

The dedication ceremony was performed by the Dean (Dr. Hewlett Johnson), who was asked by Sir Charles Warde to accept the tablet on behalf of the Cathedral body, in the presence of the vast congregation which had assembled for the Armistice service, and the present Earl of Ypres then placed a wreath of Flanders poppies beneath the tablet.

The 15th/19th King's Royal Hussars sent a Trumpet-Major and four trumpeters to sound the Last Post and Reveille after the dedication ceremony. Thus the ceremony was concluded with the most poignant of all forms of military ritual in honour of the dead.

Amongst those present in addition to the Earl of Ypres and Sir Charles Warde were Major the Hon. Gerald French, Lady Patricia French, Lieut.-General Sir William Pulteney, Maj.-General Geoffrey White, Col. Stanley Barry (representing the King's Royal Hussars), Col. H. M. Hayward, Lieut.-Col. Moloney, Sir Hugh Weston, Lady Brougham and Vaux, Lady Violet Beaumont, Capt. Ralph Carr-Greig, the Rev. and the Hon. Mrs. Ivo Carr-Greig, and Mrs. Vyvyan Drury.

The above photograph is copyright and reproduced by kind permission of Mr. A. F. Kersting, 37, Frewin Road, Wandsworth Common, S.W.18, and courtesy of "The Times."

The Spirit of Armistice Day

By Philip Gibbs.

BEFORE and after each anniversary of Armistice Day one hears the plea here and there that it is time this commemoration should be abandoned. Some of those who served during the war prefer that its memory should be forgotten, and there is the younger generation, many of whom are already grown up, who do not realise, it is said, the full meaning of Armistice Day and the spiritual significance of the Two Minutes' Silence. Certainly one young man I know frankly confessed that all this meant absolutely nothing to him. He could not remember the war, he disliked what he had read about it, he regarded it as a great crime and a great folly, and he failed to understand why its memory should be perpetuated. Then there are the young children. They are mystified by this annual silence when their elders stand bareheaded before some cross where there are many wreaths and red poppies. "What does it mean?" I was asked by one of them. "What are all those poppies for? Why does everybody stand so quiet?" I confess I find it difficult to answer such questions by child minds. I hate to tell them of all the slaughter, and to let them know so soon the ugliness of war, and all the death and agony it caused to the young manhood of the world. Yet one day they must know . . . and will want to know, and have a right to know.

There is no glorification of war in this annual remembrance of that day in 1918 when the bugles blew the Cease Fire, and the guns were silent after four years, and death no longer demanded the enormous sacrifice of young life. On the contrary it seems to me — I am certain — that the Two Minutes' Silence each year is the time when vast multitudes of men and women realise most deeply and poignantly the blessing of peace and make a vow in their hearts, consciously or unconsciously, that they will dedicate themselves anew to the spirit of peace and goodwill among nations so that never again, if they can make this spirit prevail, shall there be a war among civilised nations. In this country, anyhow, where Armistice Day is most solemnly celebrated, that is the deeply abiding resolve of the silent crowds, if I have any glimpse into the soul of our people; and I believe that the abandonment of this memorial would not mean that we had put war out of our minds, but had put peace out of our minds, in despair, or in cynical forgetfulness of past emotion.

But there is another reason for Armistice Day. Shall we forget, shall we allow the forgetfulness of, those millions of young men of ours who went into the trenches and endured everything that modern warfare demanded of them year after year? Shall we forget their valour? Shall we forget the sacrifice of a million dead? Shall we forget the heroic humour with which they marched along the roads of war knowing what was ahead of them at journey's end, or that comradeship of the trenches which had in it all the best quality of youth, or that laughter which rang out behind the lines in all their billets and camps and sometimes even — as I heard it, between bursts of high-explosive fire searching for their bodies? We should be untrue to our own heritage and spirit, we should be unfaithful to all those boys, if we allowed remembrance of them to fade out of our minds even because of hatred of war itself.

As a looker on of that war — a chronicler of its daily history — I am obsessed still by its tragedy and by its abomination. Year after year I walked amidst all this death of youth — our most splendid youth — and saw the price that was paid in the blinding and gassing and maiming of manhood. I have written about all that side of war with bitterness, and sometimes with rage. I have pledged myself to use any power of words I may have to prevent any repetition of such history, if it is possible in this age and world of passion and fear. I am I confess deeply apprehensive of the future — even of the near future, because the human tribes are arming again and the drums are beating in the jungles. But none of that will ever blot out of my mind the spirit of those battalions of youth who fought in the last war, nor the courage and cheerfulness and patience with which they faced every hardship. I remember the Cockney humourists who made jokes even in No Man's Land, the Scottish battalions whose valour was beyond all words, the Canadians, as hard as steel, the Australians, very wild and free in their ways, and the divisions recruited from the English counties who were the back-bone of our armies from first to last. I remember the thousands of young officers of the New Army, as we called it. They had been brought up in good homes. They had been taught to wash behind the ears. They had gone to good schools where they had been taught the code of good manners and the tradition of young gentlemen. Now they had to sit in verminous dug-outs, and to crawl into the mud of No Man's Land, and to lead their men across shell holes and mine craters through infernal barrage fire. But they always said "Good morning" very brightly when I met them in sinister places and they tried to see the bright side of things even in an O.P. overlooking the enemy's sandbags. Between battles when they were out of the line for a spell in the ancient city of Amiens, or in Cassel on the hill behind the Salient they were wonderfully successful in forgetting the horrors of war which lay three days behind them and a week or two ahead. Is it possible or right to draw a veil of forgetfulness over all that splendid courage, that heroic quality of youth, under the plea that the war should now be forgotten? Should we not rather cherish every record which brings back to us the memory of those boys — our noblest and best — with their songs, their laughter, their sacrifice, and their idealism? Shakespeare has immortalised the men who fought at Agincourt. We do not forget or wish to forget, the soldiers of the Peninsular war as Thomas Hardy has brought back their ghosts in his "Dynasts." There is still to be written the Saga of the men of Ypres and the Somme — though so many war books have been published. The Ypres League, for which I write this article, stands for the immortal memory of the men who served from 1914 to 1918, and to keep their valour, suffering and sacrifice, undimmed in the mind of the nation, as a great heritage of heroic tradition. That surges up again in our hearts and souls each year on November 11th during the Two Minutes' Silence. It will be a betrayal of our dead if ever we give up that reminder; and those who love peace best should be the strongest advocates of the annual remembrance because in that silence when life stands still — so still that the very birds are astonished — there is a spiritual emotion which is deeper and higher than any hatreds or hostilities. In these moments we remember also the dead who were our enemies, and who now perhaps in another No Man's Land are the comrades of our own dead youth.

Armistice Day, 1935
"Lest We Forget"

You, falling nobly for the righteous nations
Reveal the unknown, the unhoped for face of God.
After long toil, your labours shall not perish.

Through grateful generations yet to come,
Your ardent gesture, dying, love shall cherish,
And like a beacon, you shall guide us home.

CAMPBELL OF SADDELL, F.S.A. (Scot.), J.P.,
The Captain of Saddell Castle.

"Farewell to Arms"

"K.1" PACKS ITS LAST KIT-BAG.

By R. J. T. HILLS.

TWENTY-ONE years ago Kitchener's First Hundred Thousand stood mustered. You remember how we sat back amazed at the great War Minister's demand— merely a preliminary. Such a reinforcement the Army had never known. Kitchener's Army the new force became by its own and popular acclaim. Officialdom insisted on 'New Armies'— a name without a soul.

There were placards to urge us — strikingly different from those old types that used to hang outside the local post office, with their gentlemen in elegant red and blue. A tattered man in khaki cried " Will they never come ? " A cheery soul cupped a match to a gasper and muttered "Half a mo' Kaiser." Lord Kitchener himself pointed grimly out from the hoardings and said " Your Country needs YOU."

Photo]   [Imperial War Museum, Crown Copyright

Never a thought had we given to soldiering — the most of us. Even when it came we imagined it was to be — for the country at large — an affair of coloured flags to be stuck into a map.

Not an ornamental force — K.1. So unwarlike was Britain that it could not produce khaki cloth fast enough for its new soldiers. The blue serge issued in lieu was ugly in cut and blue only to the colour-blind. You remember ? actually it ranged from heliotrope to purple. Still, it served. Occasionally one might see old red militia jackets. Squads of men drilled plain clothes to rags in Hyde Park.

Light-hearted we were. We cared little for war ; less for the foe ; less, of all for the future. There was much painful learning in store. As far as we calculated at all we should be lucky, save the word, if hostilities lasted long enough for us to get out there. That we should win none doubted.

Remember the early days of our soldiering ? Rather remarkable the way we shook ourselves into the harness. The sharper tongued the sergeant major the more we revelled in it. And they were the real stuff, some of those sergeant-majors. Tough old dogs of war, many of them, that had stormed their way in through the barrack gates from retirement as soon as the 'balloon went up,' and led orderly room a dog's life because they wouldn't draft 'em abroad.

* * * *

Now it's all twenty-one years ago — the span of a full army life time. Old ? We shall never admit that. Once a year we say again ' as we that are left grow old,' — the only part of a marvellous creed we don't believe whole-heartedly. In our comradeship with the good fellows that were, we retain the spirit of their youth. But the survivors of the First Hundred Thousand are packing civilian suit-cases and walking out past a new generation of sentries.

Comparatively few soldiered on at all, of course. The great majority enlisted for the famous 'duration.' Most of the battalions, even, to which we belonged were for the 'duration' too. They proved, those temporary formations, the value of the regimental system which the Army is based on. Nothing else could have served us so well. New regiments might have been raised, indeed. But they would have had no tradition on which to base a new reputation. Instead, we were able to put on those precious stamped bits of white metal or brass which made us 'Die Hards,' 'Green Jackets' or 'Notts and Jocks' like the rest.

It was over. Some had originally joined for the regular army. More found prospects of civilian life dull and volunteered to stay on. So the peace-time army was formed and 'K.1' passed on like the others. At least one man signed peace-time papers without knowing it.

"Geordie" was always inconsequential. He drifted into a Glasgow Recruiting Office to enlist.

"Time serving or duration," inquired the colour-sergeant.

"Aye, that'll do me fine," said Geordie.

Not until 1919, when his comrades were being demobilized, did he realize that he had still some years to do. Not that it mattered much — to Geordie.

We've been pretty snug, after all. We fall easily into two rough groups. One consists of fairly senior N.C.O.'s The other inhabits the inconspicuous, more remote corners of barracks. For them the trumpet rarely brays. The effective parts of their uniforms are a pair of slacks and a be-ribboned jacket.

They may be storemen, or cooks. Possibly they attend upon nervous young officers, or keep a friendly eye upon the regimental library. Plump men on the whole, owning allegiance somewhere along the married landing.

* * * *

"K.1" forms the real link between the old and the new. The men we served with were the old type. The King's Scarlet was their true wear. South African medals were not uncommon among them. Moustached and stalwart, up to all the tricks of a close guarded trade — they were our idols They would have been horrified had they guessed it. Our one hope was that we might eventually be nearly as good.

Those men, never let it be forgot, were the creators of the Salient. Before we joined, many of us, they were scrabbling their pitiful holes in the ground, working desperately at clogged rifle bolts, forming a thin but unpassable barrier athwart the path to the Channel Ports and maybe England itself. Many others won the war. They made sure that there was a war left to win.

They never spelt it with a capital letter — never designated it 'Great.' To them it was a job of work, one of a series merely. Perhaps they of all people had the true focus. They answered no conscious call, refused to see beyond the working motto which had carried the army successfully through so many wars. "It's all in the day's work."

To accompany an old-timer into the Salient was to get the impression of accompanying a rather proud owner round his estate. They remembered a previous incarnation of the wretched City. They had actually strolled about the streets and squares, even sat down in its cafés.

* * * *

Our horizons were narrow, in K.1, — limited by France and Flanders. Even while the war lasted more fronts were found than our simple philosophy had ever dreamed of. There are names on the colours that are almost mysteries, put there by battalions the youngsters have never heard of.

The Army has not stood still since. Among us are those who could make Marco Polo hide a modest head, and Munchausen believe his own tales. And how we love to talk.

What matter though the tales be old? We all know word for word what 'Dusty' — not to be confused with 'Dapper' Smith said to the Brigadier on the road to Renescure. Nothing delights us more than to hear it all again from Dusty's own lips. We've never yet got to the bottom of the great Arras Rum Scandal. But we recall as we look at him the exact expression on Lackery Wood's face when he drew the cork and sipped the creosote. And he had no right to the jar at all, anyway.

* * * *

It's all over. Every day one or the other of us sees his name in orders — 'Discharged to Pension.' We're going to miss a lot — find a lot changed. Even our time has been Army time. " Just sounded the ' Quarter ' " — " nearly dismiss." We'll even regret the Reveille sounded by a pestiferous boy Trumpeter.

There have been joys the civilian never knows : joys we never admitted were such. There is comfort in the pawing of horses in the stables below the barrack-rooms : philosophic joy in hanging over the verandah watching new recruits at drill : ecstasy in the smell of wood fires at the end of a long day's manoeuvres.

The future? A bit of a snag perhaps. We've had ample warning, and most of us have managed to find a hole, which, if not a 'better 'Ole' will serve the purpose. Not so easy to start a new life at forty. The Pension consoles us vastly. It won't be large, but it's 'buckshee' — the Army's most delicious word. We feel we've 'won' something in the true soldier sense — and off the Government at that.

The end comes in a final whirl of documents. Each of us has a red-covered official discharge. Kew has sent buff unemployment cards : Chelsea a blue pension paper. Very inquisitive, is Chelsea. It refuses to pay a halfpenny unless we supply the Christian names of father and mother, wife and children.

There have been 'sales of kit,' 'final settlements' new quarters to seek — a long farewell to arms. Henceforth we shall be of those who emerge on Armistice Parade Old Comrades' Sundays and the like, something for the young 'uns to wonder a little at. A pension, a row of medals — and our memories. These things make it worth while — especially the last.

A young corporal has said to me, wistfully, I thought " We can never be quite like you others — we shall never have such memories to share."

Kitchener's First Hundred Thousand is disbanded at last. The War is really over.

"Cocktail for Memory, 1914-1918"

(September Pilgrimage to Ypres).

By Rex Sargeant.

LAST September I paid a visit to the battlefields of the Western Front to see some of the old haunts, and to look on the graves of the 'men who stayed behind.'

There are many ex-service men who long to go, but are afraid of the difficulties. These are purely imaginary if the pilgrim travels under the auspices of the Ypres League whose genial representatives on both sides of the Channel have every detail worked out to three decimal places. They are old soldiers to the last man, and it was sheer delight to talk to them of the days of the 'war to end war.'

I had to travel from the north, and, being alone, and somewhat shy with strangers, I wondered what manner of people would make up the party. There was no need for worry, however. I was met by Captain de Trafford, the Secretary of the Ypres League in London, who soon made me feel as though I had known him for years, a true type of British Army officer, with shrewd eyes ; born to wear a ' Sam Browne ' belt.

Having regard to the ground covered and first-class hotel accommodation provided, the pilgrimage is very cheap, and there were no worries about passports ; indeed, under the guidance of the League, it is almost as easy to get to the Salient now as it was in **1914-1918** !

The Pilgrimage really begins at Victoria Station, London, that place of hateful memory ; for many thousands the gateway to death, and the Road to Golgotha. In those tragic days when troubles came to all of us tied up in bunches — and not in pink ribbon either ! — the station presented a busy scene as we watched the hands of the big clock move towards the time of departure of the ' Trench-train.'

After twenty years there still remain memories that are veritable nightmares for some of us, and other memories we would not part with for any consideration. Strangely enough, the killing part of the business is fading away, but there were certain periods of time during those four years that stand out in bold relief against the background of drama by virtue of some trivial event closely preceding, or following, the period in question — like the pattern of the wall-paper in a dentist's waiting-room !

What a strange emotion all objects stir when we look upon them wondering if we do so for the last time. Going back from a ' little drop o' leaf ' there was our own railway station crowded with khaki figures thinly interspersed with civilians, mostly women dressed in black, who had come to watch their menfolk off back to the Line ; the men in khaki loaded up until they looked like a cross between an ironmonger's shop and a travelling ' Scotchman ' ; waiting as though, for some ghost-train, sticking fast to the soldier's ' Best Friend,' and wondering who among one's acquaintances would soon be wearing wings instead of waders. We were all afraid, for in spite of mass-production death in its 57 varieties every man had to die ' all by himself.'

Came the inevitable moment of parting. The air was electrical, charged with repressed emotion. The main topic of conversation was : How long will it last ? We searched the latest editions of the newspapers for some crumb of comfort.

Standing there, one was conscious of a desire to fix impressions, even of common-place things, like the curve of the shining rails when they enter the tunnel, with the lighted signal-box at its entrance, the silhouette of a factory chimney against a wintry sky, and the picture of the ' Pompey ' sailor on the next platform, he with the cast-iron face and a ' Mona Lisa ' smile, advertising cigarettes that suit old and young.

Came the last fierce moment of parting and a clatter of gear drowned by the noise of the approaching train as it glides round the bend. We move off at length and a girlish figure with her heart in her eyes walks along the platform still waving. Then we settle down with heavy brooding looks like Town Councillors frowning at the naughtiness of a modern world.

But we are keeping that Continental train waiting at No. 1 Platform, Victoria — !

The party reaches Skindles Hotel at length, and we hear again that familiar accent which somehow reminds us of the accent of a Tyneside ' Geordie ' with its rising inflexion. This is my first visit since the war, and, of course, tremendous changes have taken place. It is a brand-new country from the sub-soil up : roads, houses, shops, churches, public buildings, estaminets, all are new, and every tree from ' Pop ' to Passchendaele is a sapling.

Yet in spite of the change in the countryside, it is still possible to find many landmarks. We rode up that main artery, the famous Poperinghe Road, where first impressions broke on our minds and we began to feel the tragic event laying hold of our lives ; when fear came as a deep depression, a wet misery. Then the Salient was a wilderness of mud, an abomination and desolation of mud ; beastly, sticky stuff that seeped into one's very soul, mucking up one's rifle and clothes, making the fingers rough when they dried. The world must have been something like the Salient before the coming of the Piltdown sub-man and the ground-ape. Even now, when riding down the ' Pop ' road, one can easily visualise the rhythmic swing of entrenching-tool handles and ' boots, boots, boots, boots, moving up and down agen — ! '

There is the estaminet where we first met the girl with the ravishing eyes and deliciously tilted nose. She was a cross between Anna Neagle and Helen Twelvetrees, but Anno Domini has ' fortified her breastworks.' Several new editions of her helped to serve us with Bock. These lovely girls were the result of an international agreement between England and Belgium. Their father, an ' old sweat,' was delighted to ' let the peg fly ' in the accent of the north of England, and everybody was ' matey.'

Travelling round the Salient on the Sunday afternoon we passed the studs that carried the chain that held the Channel Ports : St. Jean, St. Julien, Zonnebeke, Gheluvelt, Clapham Junction, Hooge, Maple Avenue, Hill 62, Sanctuary Wood, Hill 60 and Hell Fire Corner ; quiet enough now with the damper shut off ! Up on Passchendaele there were fields of waving poppies and huge tomatoes growing out in the open. We thought of the men who went through Ypres along the Menin Road, seeking cover in the slimy ditches of Hooge, whose bodies enriched this soil.

TYNE COT CEMETERY

In Sanctuary Wood, left untouched since the war, one can imagine hostilities to be still in progress. There is the spot where Sandy Logan instinctively turned up the collar of his coat when there came crescendo scream and a ringing crash. Sandy was a complete variety show and cabaret on two legs. He had a deep and husky voice — a whisky voice ! In civil life he was a rag and bone dealer, and his loaded cart had the sound of a tin chariot going into action over a corrugated-iron bridge, while his familiar call seemed to get chewed up by the only couple of teeth in his head. It was here where Sandy was killed in 1917. He died bloodily, and his end was terrible. Sanctuary Wood is still a gruesome place. Memory plays strange tricks while one is standing in these trenches. We remember the old haunting fear of being buried alive and the Wrath to Come — from Jerry ! the parcel from home, and of how the familiar handwriting of wife or mother seemed to carry one nearer that desirable spot.

The most impressive sight was Tyne Cot Cemetery and Memorial to the ' Missing ' at Passchendaele. Nobody could look on this vast cemetery with ' Lines Properly Dressed Everywhere ' without being deeply moved. " A soldier of the British Army," " A soldier of the —— Regiment " with cap badge chiselled in the headstone were to be seen on all sides, while on the impressive walls was the inscription : " Their names live for evermore." With the help of the Ypres League I easily found the panel on which was the name of a younger brother missing at Passchendaele.

Turning to lighter things : the League places no restrictions on the movements of individual members of the party. On the contrary, it enables groups to cross the frontier into France without fuss. Some of the Bright Lads decided on a trip to Lille on the Sunday night. We had some fun ! The female of the species in this French town is a fast worker and seems to know *all* the answers. Verb. Sap !

Every night at 9 o'clock down at the Menin Gate all traffic stops, and every man bares his head while the "Last Post" is sounded. As the clear, piercing notes ring out one is conscious of searching emotions and a swelling heart that seems to get too big for one's chest, bringing contact across a gap of twenty years. Was it a great week-end? I'll say ——— !

Ypres Memorials

LORD HAIG'S BANNER

FIRST ARMY FLAG

(Campbell's Press Studio
57, St. Paul's Churchyard, E.C.

The Banner of Sir Douglas Haig and the Flag of the First Army, herewith reproduced, are to be hung in the British Church at Ypres.

The work has been beautifully executed by the "Friends of the Poor," 42, Ebury Street, London, S.W. The embroidery of the Banner is the work of Mr. E. Roy, of the Suffolk Regiment, and that of the Flag by Mr. A. Mapletoft, of the London Regiment, who were both seriously wounded in the Great War.

The Banner and Flag will be on view at Headquarters of the Ypres League, 20, Orchard Street, Portman Square, London, W.1, from Monday, January 13th to Saturday, January 25th, 1936. Hours: 11 a.m. to 4 p.m. Saturday, 11 to 1 p.m,. Sunday excepted.

A Dedication Service will be held at Ypres on Thursday, July 16th, 1936.

The Road to Salonika

By B. GRANVILLE BAKER.

WONDERFUL and mysterious are the ways of the War Office, of any other body of Olympians for that matter. Therefore he who would be accounted wise should never be surprised at anything the War Office may be pleased to contribute towards the general Gaiety of Nations. This result is easily attained by uprooting one or other faithful servant from a familiar sphere of activity into surroundings concerning which he is entirely unbiassed by any knowledge whatever. It must have been this consideration that set me in motion towards Salonika from rest on the peaceful Italian front, after years of front line in France. War time travel had this advantage over the deadly precision to which international communications have now been reduced, that you started feeling that anything might happen, firmly convinced with R. L. Stevenson, that it is better to travel hopefully than to arrive. Hope required strong support at times, so for instance when Taranto settled down to complete inertia, and refused to provide transport across the Adriatic merely because German U.-boats had been reported. However, there is generally a way out, and on this occasion the Italian Admiral in Command found it. He was sending a destroyer across, and I should sail in her. A pretty little ship who lived up to her name "Animoso." She danced over the heaving track made by the moonlight and crept into Valona harbour as a pale golden dawn brought into high relief the mountains of Albania.

That feeling of "anything might happen" was almost painfully strong as the Admiral's two-seater, another "Animoso," with an Italian Petty Officer R.N., at the wheel, plunged into Valona where early rising seems to be the rule. Everybody was out in the street, men with all the day before them, women collecting small children from under the hoofs of ponies that wandered about in strings led by absent-minded Kutzo-Vlachs, and Italian carabinieri trying to look as if they did not mind the disorder. But it must have been painful to those picturesque and useful officials. You met them everywhere along the splendid high road constructed by those who claim direct descent from Imperial Rome. Up in the hills overlooking the blue Sea of Adria were the Headquarters of the Italian Army that was steadily transforming Albania, a villa built not only in the style, but in the spirit of Imperial Rome. Here in this country of great and varied natural beauty, Italy was overcoming those difficulties that confronted Rome, and with success except perhaps, in its campaign against the lesser fauna, against which even Keatings may struggle in vain. This particular difficulty reacts on the traveller's attitude towards places that should inspire him with reverence, places with a picturesque and historic past, such as Agyrocastron.

As night falls on Koritza the mountains seem to close in until a sense of oppression comes over you. This may possibly account for a certain touchiness among the inhabitants; they are divided in allegiance between Greeks and Albanians, and this difference became so marked in course of the war than an Inter-allied Commission proceeded to examine the question on the spot. This visit was considered a first-class historic event by the townsfolk, so said the deputation that called upon me on my arrival. Courteous gentlemen, they offered to show me the sights. There was only one sight really, it was just across the market place, but as sightseeing should be conducted decently and in order, the deputation formed up and escorted me until we stood below a small balcony. The only one in the town, I gathered, but it had taken part in the making of history, quite recently too, was you might say, still warm, for here the Inter-allied Commission had gathered and looked down over the market place. A stirring sight it must have been. All the school-children in white with blue ribbon colours of Greece, waving

Greek flags, singing Greek hymns until one of the Inter-allied tossed a handful of coppers among the crowd. At once the Greek hymns ceased, the Greek flags were dropped, and angry little voices were heard uttering remarks such as " drop that coin, you thief, its mine," in Albanian.

Many of those whom the War moved about from one front to another, from the Triangle perchance, to Salonika, may remember that curious and interesting country. The stark outlines of the mountains, the gentle, wooded foothills with little white huts looking so comfortable, yet many of them but empty shells as different armies had

Photo]   [Imperial War Museum, Crown Copyright

This photograph is reproduced to convey an idea of the difficult Balkan Country the British Troops had to negotiate during the fighting on the Salonika Front.

passed by. The blue lakes, and the willows, fringing the banks of streams, hurrying away to the Vardar Valley. And there is the broad plain, the railway junction from which a line runs North to Lake Doiran and towards Beles Planitza. As the rays of the setting sun fade from the heights of Chalcidice, lights begin to call for reflections from the Gulf. Many British soldiers have watched the sight of Salonika lighting up for the night. Some may even have declared that the place looked its best under illumination, especially on the occasion when it was almost burnt out. It may have occurred to these that the Thessalonians of their day were not strictly observing St. Paul's injunction : " that ye may walk honestly toward them that are without."

Whatever opinion the British soldier held and maybe, expressed in his best descriptive vein, of the modern Thessalonian, he was as ever, ready to help in the time of trouble. In Salonika as in every other part of the world, where the British soldier has gone about his lawful occasions, he has been the best propagandist for his country. Be it remembered that the truth is always the best propaganda, and the British soldier always shows himself without guile or self-consciousness, as the world's champion peacemaker. When he marched up the Vardar Valley and helped the Serbs to regain their country, he left innumerable friends behind and made new ones wherever he rested for a while. After Old Serbia had been successfully cleared of people who did not belong there, you would find a little settlement of British soldiers chiefly Motor Transport, tucked away in quaint little Serbian towns, some almost hidden from view, but for the indispensible white-washed stones that marked the roadway to it. Here British soldiers had settled as if for life. All the dogs of the town were " on the strength " for rations, all the children were known by their Christian names, and every notable had been fitted with a suitable nickname. No wonder then that legend has already grown up round those places where British soldiers did bide a while. One such legend, surely based on elemental truth as legend generally is, tells of a British and a Serbian soldier meeting at a wayside wine-shop. Both being single-hearted men, purposeful and direct, they foregathered and understood each other perfectly, though they both talked at the same time each in his own language. Came the hour of parting and exchange of souvenirs to find the British soldier without anything suitable to the occasion ; he had been visiting friends, collectors all, that afternoon. Then in a flash came the brilliant thought. Outside, hitched to a post was the commissariate mule, a suitable present for a Serb. The happiest of Serbs then vanished into the night precariously balanced on a mule.

At dawn next day the Serbs' return to mental alertness was hastened by the sight of a fiddleheaded mule flopping its ears at him. There is only one course open to the good soldier of any army, when in doubt report to the Captain. The report went up and up in the Serbian Army till it reached the Voivod, the Field-Marshal, when it was switched over to the corresponding Emminence in the British Army of Occupation. From that serene height came the answer straight and direct : " What the British soldier gives he never takes back."

Christmas Day

" Peace on earth "—the drums of war
Roll their defiance o'er the bells ;
" Goodwill towards men "—the murderous roar
    Up from the trenches swells.

Is this the offering, this the day,
The triumph of the dripping sword ?
In lowliness the nations pray
    Thy pitying mercy, Lord.

Thou knowest all ; Thou readest deep ;
The heart of man is in Thine eyes ;
It is a vigil grim we keep
    Only that Peace arise.

Peace is not dead ! she waits rebirth
Stirring within the womb of War ;
And from its death shall tread the earth
    More queenly than before.

Reprinted from " Days of Destiny," by kind permission of R. Gorell Barnes.

We reproduce the third of a series of sketches on the humourous side of the German South West African Campaign, 1914/15, and other sketches will appear in future editions of the "Ypres Times."

[Reprinted by the courtesy of the Argus Printing and Publishing Company and with the compliments to the author, Mr. W. H. Kirby.

Light and Shade at the Front
A Few Impressions.
By an Ex. R.B.

IT occurred to the writer a few days ago, after seeing one of Meissonier's pictures in a shop just off Great Portland Street, "A halt by the wayside," that pictorial records of the Great War are still incomplete. No doubt a difficulty lay in the many incidents that would need to be depicted, in the manner of "The Advance of the 3rd Worcesters"; "The Guards at Landrécies"; "The Canadians meeting the first gas attack," differing therein from campaigns which were decided mainly by a single battle ("Meeting of Wellington and Blucher," by Maclise; "Waterloo by Night," by J. M. W. Turner), and inspiration must be sought also in the lulls of battle as in Meissonier's "1814" and Lady Butler's "The Roll Call." Another point; As readers know only too well, much of the duty in the line was done by night, and being mostly shades and little or no lights attempts at illustration would fail through lack of outline. And last but not least, a faithful artist must round off the major scenes with those of minor incidents both in and out of the line.

Pictures visualise actions but not always conditions. For example: Only ex-service men, seeing a picture of troops in action, would discern that the equipment may at times be a handicap, and this although it becomes a second habit when men work, fight, sleep, eat, wash and shave in it. But its weight tells on a man over soft ground, especially if he be loaded up like a walking ironmonger's shop, and also when jumping a trench or other obstacle. Apropos of this: Added to the normal joys of a soldier's life was that, in the Passchendaele Sector, of getting drowned if he slipped off a duckboard. Just as two or three chums were trying to rescue a friend who slipped in this way and was sinking deeper the Colonel came up. Said he : "I'll have this man out even if it costs every man in the Battalion," and a determined effort then met with success.

A quality one noticed about one Section (the S.B.'s) was the efficient, matter-of-fact way they did their job. One night in the Salient when the Company was on its way up, but still some distance from its objective, the enemy put over a heavy shelling and the troops took meagre cover in a trench which was much battered about. The firing was prolonged, and at a moment when a shell bursting on the slope killed a chum who was crouching next the writer a stretcher party led up from the left and lay low for a brief interval, the casualty being covered with a great coat. The "going" was very difficult as the party presently went forward, and it is certain many a casualty owes his life to the S.B.'s dogged and unfaltering sense of duty.

Readers may have observed how custom holds good even when at variance with the work in hand, and so it was on a Christmas night in the Arras Sector. As the writer stood on the fire step looking through the wire and across the snow at the enemy line, and listening to the Germans lustily singing carols, it did strike one as being funny. Like the Angels of Comfort and Joy masquerading in the armour of Mars. But the singers soon fell back into their bad old ways. On Boxing Night the troops "stood to" ready for a German gas attack, and here Luck took a hand; the wind dropped. The Luck still held at noon next day; the wind blew towards the enemy and a two hour's shelling broke up his cylinders, as well as other things, and dosed him with his own medicine. He vacated his front line and the skeleton force in ours had an undisturbed view.

It is highly probable that War makes a soldier a fatalist. How can it be otherwise when, for example, the Company gets an order to be ready to move at a minute's notice (Ypres) and unexpectedly this order is cancelled and the movement delayed until next day. Or, the Company is under cover and listens to the din of attack (Tour de Wancourt) waiting for the order to "go," but presently is ordered back to shell-holes for the time being and the enemy vacates the contested position overnight. And again (to be prosaic on an occasion when the writer side-stepped a plank in the dark (Australian Huts) and "sloshed" full length into a ditch. (" Wet, J——?" Oh-h-h! N-n-n-o-t at all! Only a bit damp. Where can I get a change?") At St. Quentin a small party was about to look round when a distant machine gun bullet, fired at random, cut through the leading man's collar and shirt just missing the nape of his neck. In the same Sector a party was called from cover on a short fatigue and returned to find the place upside down and its four erst-while companions all casualties. And so on *ad. infinitum.*

A feature one noticed about our French allies was a knack they had of making themselves comfortable under adverse conditions. Not only in the line (wooden bunks, light tables and wine-racks in dug-outs), but also of course elsewhere. The writer recalls being on a baggage party from the line which, after two days, found itself late at night on the outskirts of St. Omer. Rations were low and a forage in the town drew blank and he was standing in a Square, black as pitch, thinking "It doesn't look like corn in Egypt here," when a door opened in the far corner disclosing a bright interior. He was admitted and put five francs down on the table as a start-off, (Best not to risk going back empty-handed, thought he!) at the same time reflecting what a change was there from the wind-swept exterior. Lights all on, a mixed company of French soldiers on leave and villagers, refreshments on the table, the stove blazing hot, and everybody happy and cheerful. Later on some provisions, payment declined, were taken away; also this picture of a pleasant little episode. A trait that impressed one in certain parts of the battle zone was the fortitude shown by the weaker sex under fire. The writer was being served at a little shop in Riviera (the last shop on the left leading from the monastry of St. Sepulcre to the open fields) when a shell burst just to the rear, but except for turning a little pale the young woman carried on without a pause. At pleasant little Sombrin gunfire was heard day and night, and at night the flashes lit up the skyline. And when aged people and children straggled out of Bailleul, then being shelled, and rested with their few belongings on the country road they were quite composed. And as to moral : There were two old ladies who sold milk at a farmhouse in Riviera and their parlour was a masterpiece of cleanliness. Old oak furniture, stone mosaics, settles, brackets, pewter-ware, the French windows opening on the fields ; everything was cleaned and polished in keeping with the spotless white caps worn by these old dames.

1. On the firestep.   2. Two in a shellhole.
3. Wet and warm.
4. Dugout.   5. Estaminet.

Each scene recalls many, and the total effect is like parading a number of units into a Company. The burial of the Major within the shadow of the Old Cloth Hall.

A distant view of Lille pointed out by a friend in the trenches. A night of alarms at Polygon Wood. Here, as one moved towards this small area of stumps the Germans seemed to display their whole armoury; continuous bursts of " rapid " at seemingly no object in particular, shell fire, Véry lights, the rise and fall of sprays of liquid fire, and general uneasiness. The archway at Poperinghe brings to mind more than one supper of eggs and chips ; the ruins of Neuve-Eglise are associated with raw potatoes dug up near by, also for supper. The little town of Meteren, whence one looked out at the Véries going up in the line, suggests of all things — Chess. Chess problems were the hobby of a friend (an S.B.) later wounded at Passchendaele. And Meteren was the only place where the writer heard a striking clock from billets, this being built in a little square turret situate the other side of the street. The nearest " close-up " to enemy aircraft was an occasion when the platoon was out in shell holes in the Salient, and two German planes scouted low spitting machine gun bullets at likely objects. But a pleasant set-off to this was a little confectioner's shop near Mont Noir where, foraging round, the writer saw a real Madeira cake for sale and bought it. (" Est ce pour vendre ce gâteau, m'm'selle ? " " Oui, m'sieur ; certainment."). Firewood usually was plentiful. A ruined farm shed, resting on one support, lost this one very cold night, and the whole box of tricks fell down with a terrible clatter. Still, it was only a minor detail, and there was certainly no need for the old farmer to verge almost on the border of apoplexy. And so we go on and all the strings lead to one place, and that's Victoria Station. And how lacking now is Victoria compared with those times when it throbbed with the life and movement of the troops *en route*, and the busy scenes at the leave trains.

As one looks about it is clear science is still making big strides, and it is probable that future efforts to spread culture among unwilling peoples may be attended not only by abundant supplies of sausage and smash, but also with other inventions. However, readers may have noticed scientists are always up against a " quid pro quo." High explosive is countered by " tin-hats," tanks and trenches, and soon our enlightened civilisation may drag from oblivion the hidden shelters of the cave-men. The latest thing in aerial attack closely resembles a little masterpiece in the National Gallery ; this depicts in a graphic manner the destruction of two ancient cities by fire from above. And even the synthetic niceties of the bun-shop are only a short cut to the multi-coloured nastities at the chemist's shop in the next street, not to mention the undertaker's at the corner.

If one may venture an opinion it is to say that an immutable law of Nature's is that of Contrast, and this leads to the statement that after a storm there comes a calm, and this in turn brings to mind an episode in the Salient when the troops were marking time on the relief. Things had been very active, including an attack in which some ground was gained and held, and it was only a matter of routine to expect a counter-attack. The evening was very quiet until, just before dusk, a single enemy shell whined over and burst. Another shell followed and then the sentries sighted the leading wave coming on to the attack. Up went the S.O.S.'s the while the Germans opened up with a heavy supporting fire. All ranks leapt out of the shallow trench on to the front of the parapet and directed their rifle fire towards the flanks, to avoid the men in shell holes in front. The Divisional and Anzac artillery, quick to respond to the enemy's attack, put up an intense fire at the same time dropping a barrage a little in front of the defenders, and as these shells burst in a line the smoke rose from them like a long curtain. Machine guns, posted at the rear, enfiladed the enemy's approaches with an incessant stream of bullets and added to the general pandemonium. Meanwhile rain fell heavily, dripping off the helmets and making the mud still more liquid. Mud, like oil, gets everywhere without let or hindrance, and it mucked up the hands and even worked into the rifle bolts. A few Germans broke through on the left flank, but were quickly bombed back ; the attack was met and the struggle subsided into the quietude that preceded it, save for the rain which pelted down harder than ever.

On a Christmas Day the Company was in the line on Passchendaele Ridge. The writer was in the outpost where the ground fell backwards to the front line on a slight gradient, and it sloped in a like manner to the enemy line, held by Saxons, thus affording a clear view all round. The parapet of the post was at ground level and was carefully camouflaged with cross pieces, petrol tins, old sacking, a waterproof sheet and some snow, the squad's time being taken up between keeping a close watch and making hot " char " with some melted snow and candles. (" Phew ! This char tastes funny." " And no wonder. Look, there's a candle in it." " Candle ? Why, that's the bit we couldn't find.")

PHEW ! THIS CHAR TASTES FUNNY.

Snow lay about thickly and covered with its soft mantle the scenes of carnage. There was a desultory shelling during the day but it broke off towards the evening and as night closed in the moon came out slowly to a full brilliance and illumined with its clear, compassionate beams the tranquil sleep of these fallen legions. It also rounded off the snowy wastes and here and there, with a touch of crystal, gave unreal beauty to a gruesome shape. Indeed, but little was needed in the way of detail to impart to this shambles, as by enchantment, the attractive charm of a Christmas Card.

J. EDWARDS.

(To be continued.)

My Introduction to the Salient

I WAS one of a numerous party of Scottish Rifle Officers who, destined to reinforce various battalions of the Rifle Brigade and King's Royal Rifle Corps, crossed the Channel in January, 1917. The weather in the early part of 1917, as all who were in France at that time will remember, was bitterly cold, hard frost succeeding a heavy fall of snow. Etaples, our base, with its ill-famed " Bull Ring," was far from being a pleasure resort, even under good weather conditions, and it was with a sigh of relief that we heard, after a week's stay there, that instructions had been received for us to proceed to the line the following morning.

The two trains conveying the various drafts were timed to leave at 7.30 a.m., one train going south with the contingents for Arras and the Somme, and the other north to the Salient. No sooner were we seated in our compartments than the rumour went round that neither train would start for at least an hour and, in consequence, most of us took the opportunity of a last chat with the friends who were leaving us, in many cases, alas, for ever. Suddenly, right on time, the south bound train commenced to draw out of the station, and there was a wild rush on the part of its passengers, many of whom just managed to scramble on board before the train cleared the platform. The gallant " Ypres Express " was in no such hasty mood, and it was 2.30 p.m. before it condescended to start. By that time its occupants had become thoroughly tired of reading the warning notice about " The wise old owl that sat in an oak," and, in addition, they were almost chilled to the bone, despite the relief afforded by numerous braziers that had been unearthed from apparently nowhere at all.

In my compartment were B., H. and A., all of whom had served in France before. When we reached Hazebrouck H. was most anxious to impress on me the fact that the Bosche had got as far as that point in 1914. This, at the time, conveyed nothing to me, but I was to realize, in 1918, what it meant. At Abeele H. and A. left us to join their unit, the 21st King's Royal Rifle Corps, and there, for the first time, I heard the sound of the guns. It is interesting to recall my first impressions of gun-fire. Probably owing to the still, frosty air, the noise was greater than I had expected, and when one particularly loud report was heard I felt sure that it must be a mine going up. B., however, soon convinced me that it was only one of the heavy batteries firing.

At length, about 10.30 p.m., we arrived at Poperinghe where I was to spend so many happy off-duty hours in the days to come. While we were collecting our kit, a runner came up to B. and myself and asked if we were the officers for the 17th Battalion King's Royal Rifle Corps. On our replying that we were, he informed us that the Adjutant had instructed him to say that it was too late to join the Battalion that night, and we had, therefore, to put up at the Officers' Club. Accompanied by four other fellows whose Adjutants had not been so considerate as to send them directions, we followed him to the Club. When we arrived there we found that there were only three beds left, and though our four friends very decently urged that B. and I had a prior claim, we, of course, insisted on all tossing for them. Needless to say, I was not one of the lucky ones. After supper we who had drawn blanks lay round the fire, keeping all our clothes on, including our British warm. I soon found that I could keep my feet warmer by taking off my boots, but it *was* a cold night, especially when the fire died out, and we *did* envy the other fellows in their warm, comfortable beds.

Next morning we had a jolly good wash and an excellent breakfast, and then B. and I spent the forenoon looking round " Pop." Immediately after lunch our runner appeared to show us the way to the Battalion, which lay at " A " camp, I think it was, near Brandhoek. For the first time, I tramped up the famous Poperinghe — Ypres road. It was, I remember, a fine, bright winter day, with a light wind raising the dust slightly. As I have already mentioned, B. had been out before, but everything was entirely new to me, and I gazed with great interest on our surroundings. Along the straight tree-lined road passed a continual stream of traffic — transport wagons, limbers, motor lorries, horsemen, and a few humble foot sloggers like ourselves, while on either side of the road were the camouflaged camps composed mostly of wooden or Nissen huts. Occasionally a gun would fire, from a position well back from the road, and, to complete the picture, overhead hovered one or two planes, obviously British. They were not to have the air entirely to themselves, however, for suddenly, far ahead in the direction of Ypres, there appeared a couple of silver specks which soon proclaimed themselves Germans, from the way in which they drew immediately the fire of our "Archies." The sight of the white shell-bursts in the sunny sky made a pretty picture and did not appear to trouble the enemy 'planes much.

At length we reached our camp and were received by the Adjutant, and by him posted to our respective companies. In the battalion mess, at tea that afternoon, we were introduced to our brother officers, and I was told, rather to my dismay, by one of them, whom I had known in England, that the Commanding Officer was not keen on Territorials. That battalion mess never attracted me. To begin with, one unfortunate batman was expected to do the waiting for the whole party, and a dreadful time the poor fellow had. I am inclined to be rather diffident amongst strangers, and I think I should almost have starved had not Denny, a kind-hearted and sympathetic young officer from the London Regiment, looked after me for the first meal or two. One thing in the mess interested me — the table covers. They were composed of sheets of " The Christian Science Monitor," and provided one with excellent reading at meals without the trouble of balancing a paper.

The 17th King's Royal Rifle Corps had suffered very badly in the Somme battles of the previous autumn, and practically none of the original officers were left ; in fact, I soon discovered that quite half the company officers had only been with the battalion a week or so longer than I had myself. Next day I met the men for the first time. While our officers came from all parts of the world, the rank and file were Londoners to a man and an excellent lot of fellows they were, not big and many not young, but all cheery, even-tempered and not afraid of hard work. It would be too much to claim that we were amongst the outstanding battalions in France, but the 17th/60th, like the 39th Division of which it was a part, could be relied on to do its bit. Very few troops had such a long gruelling experience of the Salient. The 39th Division arrived in the St. Omer area in November, 1916, and did not leave the Ypres neighbourhood till the beginning of February, 1918. Nor was that the end of our connection with Flanders, for in April, 1918, we spent another month in the Salient assisting in repelling the German offensive round Wytschaete and Dickebusch. On the day after I joined the battalion we moved up to Ypres and were billeted in the Prison. The weather still being bitterly cold, each man had provided himself with a piece of firewood, and that, and the fact that my company commander, Haynes, a tall, handsome youngster of twenty-one, carried a great staff like a shepherd's crook, interested me more than anything else. It is strange what trifling incidents imprint themselves on one's memory. We waited till dusk before moving off, in case the German observers in 'plane or balloon would spot us, and it was quiet dark when we reached our destination. The prison may have proved a comfortable home to ordinary peace-time prisoners, but then it would have glass in the window frames, no doubt, and the walls would be intact ! The extreme cold drove us to attempt lighting a fire in our cell, which, however, owing to the lack of a chimney, soon filled with smoke, and we gave up the effort in despair and resigned ourselves to the lesser evil.

The following day, Haynes received instructions to go up the line to arrange for our taking over from the 16th Rifle Brigade, which battalion we were to relieve in a few days' time, and he asked me to go with him. Never shall I forget our walk that morning through the deserted streets of Ypres, the ruined buildings standing stark and white in the brilliant sunshine, accentuated by the glare of the snow which lay all around.

As we skirted the Grande Place a shell whizzed through the air. I had not the least idea whence it had come or where it was going, but within the next few days I soon acquired the " shell sense," a most valuable attainment for anyone in the forward area. The 16th Rifle Brigade lay in the Potijze sector, and the company we were to relieve was in reserve. When we arrived at company headquarters we found their officers, a cheerful lot and all youthful, discussing the short tour they were to commence in the front line the following day. One fellow had been detailed to take over Mill Cott., and the others were telling him he had " clicked," because on no account was anyone occupying that spot to show himself in the daytime. I imagined that Mill Cottage must be a rather terrible place, so exposed to the enemy that to be seen was to fall a certain victim to a sniper, but it soon appeared that the reason of the prohibition was not quite so exciting. The ruins of the cottage constituted a strong point, about 400 yards behing the front line, and our Higher Command did not wish the Bosche to know that it was occupied.

As we had been ordered to do some wiring behind the front line that evening, Haynes and I went up the communication trench to have a look at the ground. Had I known that the Commanding Officer was going to select me to take the company up to do the job, I should have studied the lie of the land a great deal more carefully. After the wiring expedition I had the experience of one or two other working parties, and then our company did its spell in the Potijze sector, where I was introduced to trench life and intitiated into the mysteries of " stand-to," the issuing of the rum ration, the examination of rifles, the care of the men's feet, and all the other details that went a long way towards preventing trench warfare becoming monotonous.

J.D.

HOTEL

Splendid & Britannique

YPRES

GRANDE PLACE. Opposite Cloth Hall.

LEADING HOTEL FOR COMFORT AND QUALITY, AND PATRONIZED BY THE YPRES LEAGUE.

COMPLETELY RENOVATED.

RUNNING WATER. BATHROOMS.

MODERATE TERMS. GARAGE.

Proprietor—Life Member, Ypres League.

YPRES

Skindles Hotel

(Opposite the Station)

Proprietor—Life Member, Ypres League

Branch at Poperinghe

(close to Talbot House)

League Secretary's Notes

At the commencement of 1935 we signalled a note of welcome confidence after a most trying and prolonged period due to the general depression, but united efforts, especially during the past year, have brought about a still more happy situation. We are looking forward to further good tidings in 1936 and to welcome many more new members with the additional co-operation of our good comrades of New Zealand. The last mail has brought favourable news from Auckland and we shall soon have the pleasure to announce the official inauguration of a new Branch, but the present is to report that a temporary Committee has now been formed under the Presidency of Mr. M. A. Ferguson, the Belgian Consul, and the Right Hon. J. C. Coates has generously accepted to be Patron of the Branch. The loyal support of the ex-Ypres warriors of New Zealand is not only greatly appreciated and valued, but we are sure that, as a result, the interest in the Ypres League will spread more widely in other Dominions.

Our Purley Branch takes the recruiting honours in winning the £5 prize for the fifth consecutive year—a most praiseworthy achievement in which we all extend to the Branch Committee our thanks and hearty congratulations, and it is the intention of headquarters to acknowledge, in some concrete form, the unique record of this wonderfully progressive Branch, but while placing mention of our Purley Branch first and foremost, we do not under-estimate the successful work of other Branches in their recruiting during the year and we convey to the respective Committees our gratitude.

The 1935 battlefield tours and pilgrimages surpassed all previous records, and according to recent enquiries it is not premature to judge that 1936 will present an equally full programme. These tours to the battlefields serve as a valuable medium in keeping personal touch with representatives of the Regular and Territorial Army Units, Ex-Service Officers and men, relatives of the fallen, and the Public Schools O.T.C. who have shown marked enthusiasm in their trips to France and Flanders: these members of the young generation display sympathetic interest in all that is related to them and value the education that such visits offer.

In the January, 1935 "YPRES TIMES" we made an urgent appeal to all members to notify us of any changes of address, and in consequence, we were able to amend the membership register to date, but we are now beginning to observe that a few copies of the "YPRES TIMES" are filtering their way back to headquarters bearing the postmark "gone away," so we respectfully emphasise how anxious we are to be informed of change of addresses and we trust that members will very kindly remember to advise us from time to time.

We are optimistic in this 16th anniversary year of the Ypres League, backed up by complete confidence in the continued support of our Branches, Corresponding Members, Individual Members and friends. The headquarter keyword for 1936 is "*Membership*"—not only to be content to fill the gaps caused by many deaths during the past year, but to substantially increase our forces at home and overseas. We would like more members to apply to H.Q. for a small stock of explanatory pamphlets and enrolment forms, and if desired, a few back numbers of the YPRES TIMES will be gladly sent for propaganda purposes.

In conclusion, we repeat our October message in wishing all members a very happy and prosperous 1936, and we thank in advance those who are intending to devote some of their precious time for the future welfare of our League.

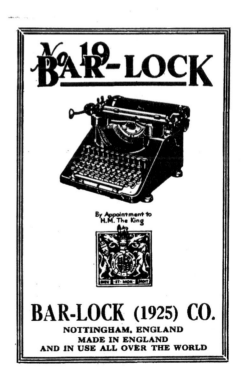

BAR-LOCK (1925) CO.
NOTTINGHAM, ENGLAND
MADE IN ENGLAND
AND IN USE ALL OVER THE WORLD

EMBROIDERED BADGES.

These badges can be supplied at 4s. each, post free. A considerable number have already been sold, and we are delighted to hear that the badges have given entire satisfaction to our members who have received them. Applications to the Secretary.

YPRES LEAGUE BADGE

The design of the badge—a lion guarding a portcullis gate—represents the British Army defending the Salient, which was the gate to the Channel Ports.

The badge, herewith reproduced, is brilliantly enamelled with silver finish. Price 2s., post free 2s. 1¼d. (pin or stud, whichever is desired).

Obtainable from Secretary, Ypres League, 20, Orchard Street, London, W.1.

WREATHS.

Arrangements are made by the Ypres League to place wreaths for relatives on the graves of British soldiers situated in France and Belgium at the following times of the year:—

EASTER, ARMISTICE DAY, CHRISTMAS.

The wreaths may be composed of natural flowers, laurel, or holly, and can be bought at the following prices—12s. 6d., 15s. 6d., and 20s., according to the size and quality of the wreath.

YPRES LEAGUE TIE.

Dark shade of cornflower blue relieved by a narrow gold stripe. In good quality silk.

Price 3/6d., post free.

Obtainable from Secretary, Ypres League, 20, Orchard Street, London, W.1.

BURNING OF THE CLOTH HALL 1915.

A few remaining coloured prints now in stock are being offered to our members at the reduced rate of 1s. each, post free.

Since further copies are unobtainable we would advise those interested to make their purchase without delay.

Branch Notes

LONDON COUNTY COMMITTEE.

Informal Gatherings.

At the season's first meeting at the Bedford Head Hotel on October 17th, we enjoyed a very interesting and instructive lecture on "The Navy of To-day and its Historical Background," delivered by Commander The Hon. S. M. A. J. Hay, O.B.E., R.N., through the kindness of the Navy League.

A "full house" attended the first Steak Supper on November 21st, over which the London County Committee Chairman, Major E. Montague Jones, O.B.E., M.A., presided. It was a very happy band that filled the four long tables and full justice was done to the excellent meal supplied by mine host of the Bedford Head Hotel. After supper, a musical programme was provided by members present, Messrs. Evenden, Hanser, Payne, John Boughey and Captain Peabody led the Community singing. Mr. Thompson gave us some recitations, including an amusing burlesque on how our Hon. Secretary went home after the 5th Army O.C.A. Barrack Supper. As one of the rank and file of the Ypres League, Mr. Schlienger paid tribute to the hard work put in by our Chairman, Major Montague Jones, and said how pleased we were to have his company. The happy evening closed with "Auld Lang Syne" and the National Anthem.

The December gathering took the form of a variety entertainment, very kindly organised by Mr. O. Mears of Headquarters, and we congratulate him on having procured artistes of such high standard : comedians, vocalists, jugglers and dancers were all deserving of the enthusiastic reception accorded them by the large assembly, and the whole show was readily in keeping with the close approach of the festive season. We cannot conclude our reference to this particular re-union without expressing our most grateful thanks to Mr. Mears who, it will be remembered, has generously provided the

London members with a first-rate December entertainment during the past four consecutive years.

Notice of forthcoming gatherings appears on page 28.

We are glad to hear that Mr. A. R. Ford has recovered from his serious illness, but we much regret his resignation from the Committee, necessitated through his decision to live away from London, and in recognition of his faithful services to the Ypres League for the past six years, the Committee have unanimously awarded him a certificate of merit.

We also regret to announce the illness of Mr. L. H. Tunbridge, one of our very staunch London members, and we trust that he will soon be restored to good health.

The London County Committee extends the compliments of the season to all its members whom, it is hoped, will continue to favour them with their loyal support during the year 1936.

CHILDREN'S CHRISTMAS PARTY.

The Twelfth Annual Christmas Children's Party organised by the London County Committee, takes place at the Westminster City School, 55, Palace Street, London, S.W., by kind permission of the Governors of the School, on Saturday, January 4th. A full report will appear in the April edition of the YPRES TIMES. The Committee convey their very sincere thanks to all who have so generously subscribed, and the Hon. Secretary would be most grateful for any further donations towards the cost of this function.

ANNUAL SMOKING CONCERT.

Minus the wonderful comradie that existed among the legions who withstood the German onslaught for four years in the dreaded Ypres Salient and the complete confidence in one to another as comrades, perhaps the successful defence of Ypres against such odds might very well have been an unwritten page in our history. Crouched in a front line trench, chilled to the bone, wet by incessant rain, water knee-deep, nerves jarred almost beyond endurance by concussion of high explosives and " minnies " to the staccato music of those hateful machine guns, a mud-covered rifle that might fail to work in the expected enemy attack, how possibly could one carry on ? Well, one just did !—the knowledge that there was a khaki-clad chum somewhere near-by, often in a worse plight than your own and yet ever ready to help was a wonderful source of comfort and inspiration. A picture of the good times ahead in old Blighty as depicted by doleful " Bert." with his imaginary sumptuous banquets, the cheerful cockney wit of " Slinger Jones " interspersed with droll and exceptional humorous wisecracks of " Scotty " all helped to maintain one's spirit during those testing periods. No wonder that these old comrades of the line, mostly amateur soldiers, of the greatest war in history, who shared so cheerfully such ordeals over so long a period for the love of their King and Country, look forward so much to a re-union of their erstwhile brothers-in-arms.

Many find it possible to give expression to these feelings through the medium of the Ypres League whose London Branch, as a result of its annual re-union Smoking Concert, enables old pals to foregather in convivial atmosphere with the additional attraction of an entertainment of melody and mirth. For this privilege we owe much to that splendid organisation, the Ypres League, who have worked to commemorate the valorous deeds of our departed brothers apart from fostering that fine spirit of fellowship of the trenches which we old Tommies still treasure.

Under the Presidency of the popular London County Committee Chairman, Major E. Montague Jones, O.B.E., M.A., some five hundred members and friends gathered at the Caxton Hall, Westminster, on Saturday, October 26th, for the Thirteenth Annual Re-union Smoking Concert. A number of distinguished guests were present, including : General de Brigade R. Voruz, Military Attaché, American Embassy ; Lieut.-Colonel Raymond E. Lee, Military Attaché American Embassy ; Lieut.-General Sir W. P. Pulteney, G.C.V.O., K.C.B., K.C.M.G., D.S.O., and Major W. H. Brooke, M.C. H.E. The Belgian Ambassador, was unavoidably absent owing to the mourning for the late Queen Astrid ; this being the first occasion since the inauguration of the Smoking Concerts that His Excellency has not been present, and a message of regret was read by the Chairman to a silent and sympathetic audience. The American Ambassador also kindly sent a message regretting his absence and conveying personal greetings together with warm-hearted remembrance of the people of his country for their comrades of the Ypres League. After the sounding of the " General Salute " by trumpeters of the Legion of Frontiersmen, the gathering settled down to a most entertaining programme provided by THE ROGUES CONCERT PARTY, under the direction of Mr. Bart Brady. A feature of the programme was an impression of an old time music hall, Mr. A. E. Nickolds being in his happiest vein as the " old time " music hall chairman. His dry humour and many asides to the waitresses for just one more drink, evoked roars of laughter from the audience.

During the evening a message of loyalty was sent to His Majesty The King and the Royal reply was read by the Chairman.

Major Montague Jones then spoke briefly on the London Branch activities during the past year and paid tribute to its Honorary Secretary, Mr. J. Boughey, and the Committee who have worked so indefatigably in arranging the annual functions and monthly Informal Gatherings which have proved so helpful in maintaining the strength of the London Branch. Reference was also made to the sterling work performed at the League headquarters.

Lieut.-General Sir William Pulteney, after welcoming the Military Attachés, expressed his personal regret that the Belgian Ambassador was unable to attend and concluded his address with some interesting remarks on the Memorial Rose Window which is to be erected in St. Martin's Cathedral at Ypres in memory of the late King Albert of the Belgians.

During the short interval, opportunity was afforded many to renew old acquaintance and relate reminiscences of the stirring time spent together in those far-off days. Continuing the programme, various turns were alternated with musical selections ably rendered by the "Stewart-Carter Octet," under direction of Mr. J. A. Shepherd. These musicians offered their services again when it became known that the Enfield College of Music Orchestra was prevented for the first time from performing at this particular function owing to the illness of their Conductor, Mrs. Doris Lee Peabody. After the sounding of the "Last Post," Captain H. D. Peabody, D.C.M., recited Laurence Binyon's "To The Fallen," which was followed by the "Reveille."

An extremely pleasant evening closed about 11 p.m. with the assembly joining lustily in Community Singing of well-known war-time choruses, an item that is always most popular in these programmes.

Hearty congratulations are extended to those responsible for the arrangements of such an excellent entertainment, and most of those present must have felt that it is a jolly good thing for us, the almost forgotten old warriors, that there still exists a link with those epic times of 1914 to 1918 in the form of the Ypres League.

SHEFFIELD BRANCH.

The Fourth Festival of Remembrance was held at the City Hall, Sheffield, on Armistice Day, and arranged by the Sheffield and District Joint Council of Ex-Servicemen's Associations.

A large audience included the Master and Mistress Cutler (Sir Samuel and Lady Roberts), Captain Matt Sheppard presided and was supported by Lieut.-Colonel A. N. Lee and Canon W. A. Baker (Rector of Handsworth). On the terraced platform seats were representatives of serving units : The Navy, Territorials, Ex-Servicemen's Associations, which included members of the Ypres League, Sheffield Branch, headed by Captain Jack Wilkinson, who were joined by the Chesterfield Sub-Branch, Ambulance workers and others.

The second part of the programme was given over to a delightful entertainment by the Roosters Concert Party, who have acquired national fame from small beginning in the Balkans in 1917. Their show comprised some humorous sketches of life in the Army.

Please book these dates in your Diary.

THE MONTHLY
Informal Gatherings
will be held at

THE BEDFORD HEAD HOTEL, MAIDEN LANE, STRAND, W.C.2

on

THURSDAY, 16th JANUARY, 1936.
Talk by Brig.-General A. Burt, C.M.G., D.S.O.

THURSDAY, 20th FEBRUARY, 1936.
Programme by the St. Dunstan's Concert Party.

THURSDAY, 19th MARCH, 1936.
Programme to be arranged.

THURSDAY, 16th APRIL, 1936.
Illustrated Talk by Captain H. D. Peabody, D.C.M.

From 7.30 p.m. to 10 p.m.

Members are earnestly requested to advertise these Informal Gatherings as much as possible. Give the year a good send-off by attending our next Gathering on Thursday, January 16th, when you and your friends may be sure of a hearty welcome and a pleasant evening.

COLCHESTER & DISTRICT BRANCH.

Armistice Day Memorial Service.

The Service was held at the Cenotaph, Colchester, on November 11th, and the Chairman, Lieut-Colonel H. W. Herring, M.C., in company with a representative party of the Branch, placed a wreath on the Memorial bearing the following inscription : "In proud memory. From the Colchester and District Branch of the Ypres League." Prayer was said by The Right Rev. The Lord Bishop of Colchester, M.A., D.D. ; an address by The Right Worshipful The Mayor, Councillor The Rev. F. E. Macdonald Docker, M.A., B.D. (Hon. Chaplain to the Forces) ; The "Last Post" and Reveille sounded by the Buglers of the 2nd Battn. The Somerset Light Infantry ; the Band of the 2nd Battn. The Bedfordshire and Hertfordshire Regiment accompanied the hymns ; and the Benediction was given by the Rev. L. J. Tizard, B.A., B.D., B.Litt.

Third Annual Ball.

The Third Annual Ball of the Colchester and District Branch of the Ypres League was held on Thursday, December 12th last, at the Red Lion Hotel, Colchester, and a very successful evening was enjoyed by all present, numbering 130, which exceeded the previous year's gathering. The music was provided by the Dance Band of the 5th Inniskilling Dragoon Guards (by kind permission of Lieut-Colonel H. O. Wiley, M.C., and Officers) and the duties of M.C. were ably carried out by Major G. C. Benham, M.C.

During the evening Admiral Sir Roger Keyes honoured the dancers by his presence and made a short speech following the musical honours that were accorded him. Among those who brought parties were:—Lieut.-Colonel H. W. Herring, M.C. (Branch Chairman), Major G. C. Benham, M C. (Vice Chairman), Captain A. C. Palmer, Mr. McKinley, Mr. D. E. Shadrach and Mr. G. Stanford. The arrangements werde in the hands of a capable Ball Committee consisting of Major G. C. Benham, Captain A. C. Palmer, Mr. M. McKinley, Mr. D. E. Shadrach and Mr. W H. Taylor.

PURLEY BRANCH.
Annual Dance.

On Friday, November 8th, the Second Annual Dance of the Branch was held at the Greyhound Hotel, Croydon. The function, brimful of good comradeship, was a huge success and greatly enjoyed by the company of 313. Tom Newman and his band ably provided the dance music, and during the evening Giovanni and Leonard Henry were both in excellent form in their individual entertainments. The Committee filled in any small gaps by supplying the usual splendid hats, balloons, spot dance prizes, etc.

Lieut. N. A. Zinn again kindly undertook the duties of M.C., and his graceful figure stamps him as particularly suitable for the job, which he admirably carried out as expected.

Grateful thanks are due to the Committee, especially to the Chairman, Captain R. L. Haine, V.C., M.C.; Captain A. S. Green, the Dance Secretary; also to Mrs. Zinn and Mrs. Mutton, who co-operated most successfully.

Armistice Day Parade.

On Sunday, November 10th, the Annual Armistice Day Parade was held when a party of 41 members of the Purley Branch attended a united Memorial Service at St. Mark's Church, Peaks Hill, Purley.

KENYA BRANCH.

Through the staunch work of Colonel G. J. Henderson, the Kenya Branch of the Ypres League found it possible to repeat the ceremony of past years in placing a wreath, herewith reproduced, on the Nairobi Cenotaph on Armistice Day, and we would like to express our gratitude to Colonel Henderson and other generous subscribers whose names are not yet to hand but will be mentioned in the next edition of the YPRES TIMES.

The wreath was a very beautiful one and composed chiefly of cornflowers, groups of lilies with a few red carnations and attached was a card inscribed as follows:—

" In Memory of the Noble Dead, 1914-1918.
From the Ypres League,
Kenya Branch."

THE BRITISH TOURING SERVICE

Manager—Mr. P. VYNER

10, Station Square

Representative and Life Member,
Ypres League

ARRAS

(P.-de-C.) France

Cars for Hire, with British Driver Guides

Tours Arranged

Ypres League Travel Bureau

CONDUCTED PILGRIMAGES FOR 1936

EASTER (APRIL 11th—14th, Saturday to Tuesday) YPRES (Day route via Ostend).

WHITSUNTIDE (MAY 30th—JUNE 2nd, Saturday to Tuesday) (Day route via Ostend).

AUGUST BANK HOLIDAY (AUGUST 1st—4th, Saturday to Tuesday) (Two separate pilgrimages) :
        YPRES (Day route via Ostend).
        ARRAS (Day route via Boulogne).

SEPTEMBER (SEPTEMBER 19th—22nd, Saturday to Tuesday) YPRES (Day route via Ostend).

    YPRES. *Cost.* LONDON to YPRES return via OSTEND, with full board and best available accommodation (three nights) including taxes and gratuities at hotel.
        Second Class Train (1st Class Boat) ... £4 18 11
        Second Class Train and Boat £4 10 5
        Third Class Train (1st Class Boat) £4 5 0
        Third Class Train and Boat £3 16 6

    ARRAS. *Cost.* LONDON to ARRAS return via BOULOGNE, with full board and best available accommodation (three nights) including taxes and gratuities at hotel.
        Second Class Train (1st Class Boat) ... £6 18 10
        Second Class Train and Boat £6 8 10
        Third Class Train (1st Class Boat) £6 0 11
        Third Class Train and Boat £5 8 11

The above quotations do not include meals on the journey or excursions on the continent.

(Battlefield tours arranged by the Conductor at Ypres or Arras to suit the requirements of the party at moderate charges).

Prospectuses will be gladly forwarded on application to The Secretary, Ypres League, 20, Orchard Street, London, W.1.

INDEPENDENT TRAVEL.

To those contemplating individual travel, our Travel Department would be pleased to furnish information on all matters connected with trips to any part of the Old Western Front Battlefields.

Apply to Secretary, Ypres League, 20, Orchard Street, London, W.1, for the Ypres League Travel Guide for 1936.

Branches and Corresponding Members

BRANCHES.

LONDON	Hon. Secretary to the London County Committee: J. Boughey, 20, Orchard Street, London, W.1.
	E. LONDON DISTRICT—L. A. Weller, 26, Lambourne Gardens, Hornchurch, Essex.
	TOTTENHAM AND EDMONTON DISTRICT—E. Glover, 191, Landowne Road, Tottenham, N.17.
	H. Carey, 373, Sydenham Road, S.E.26.
COLCHESTER	H. Snow (Hon. Sec.), 9, Church Street.
	W. H. Taylor (Pilgrimage Hon. Sec.), 64, High Street.
LIVERPOOL	Captain A. M. Webster, Blundellsands.
PURLEY	Major Graham Carr, D.S.O., M.C., 112-114, High Street.
SHEFFIELD	Captain J. Wilkinson, "Holmfield," Bents Drive.
BELGIUM	Capt. P. D. Parminter, 19, Rue Surmont de Volsberghe, Ypres.
CANADA	Ed. Kingsland, P.O. Box 83, Magog, Quebec.
SOUTH AFRICA	L. G. Shuter, Church Street, Pietermaritzburg.
KENYA	C. H. Slater, P.O. Box 403, Nairobi.
AMERICA	Representative: Captain R. Henderson-Bland, 110 West 57th Street, New York City.

CORRESPONDING MEMBERS

GREAT BRITAIN.

ABERYSTWYTH	T. O. Thomas, 5, Smithfield Road.
ASHTON-UNDER-LYNE	G. D. Stuart, "Woodlands,", Thronfield Grove, Arundel Street.
BANBURY	Captain C. W. Fowke, Yew Tree House, King's Sutton.
BIRMINGHAM	Mrs. Hill, 191, Cattell Road, Small Heath.
	John Burman, "Westbrook," Solihull Road, Shirley.
BOURNEMOUTH	H. L. Pasmore, 40, Morley Road, Boscombe Park.
BRISTOL	W. S. Hook, "Wytschaete" Redland Court Road.
BROADSTAIRS	C. E. King, 6, Norman Road, St. Peters, Broadstairs.
	Mrs. Briggs, North Foreland House.
CHATHAM	W. N. Channon, 22, Keyes Avenue.
CHESTERFIELD	Major A. W. Shea, 14, Cross Street.
CONGLETON	Mr. H. Dart, 61, The Crescent.
DARLINGTON	D. S. Vigo, 125, Dorset Road, Bexhill-on-Sea.
DERBY	T. Jakeman, 10, Graham Street.
DORRINGTON (Salop)	Captain G. D. S. Parker, Frodesley Rectory.
EXETER	Captain E. Jenkin, 25, Queen Street.
GLOUCESTER	H. R. Hunt, "Casita," Parton Lane, Churchdown.
HERNE BAY	Captain E. Clarke Williams, F.S.A.A., "Conway," Station Road.
HOVE	Captain G. W. J. Cole, 2, Westbourne Terrace, Kingsway.
LEICESTER	W. C. Dunford, 343, Aylestone Road.
LINCOLN	E. Swaine, 79, West Parade.
LLANWRST	A. C. Tomlinson, M.A., Bod Estyn.
LOUGHTON	Capt. O. G. Johnson, M.A., Loughton School.
MATLOCK (Derby)	Miss Dickinson, Beechwood.
MELROSE	Mrs. Lindesay Kelsall, Darnlee.
NEW BRIGHTON (Cheshire)	E. F. Williams, 5, Waterloo Road.
NEW MILTON	W. H. Lunn, "Greycot," Albert Road.

NOTTINGHAM	E. V. Brown, 3, Eldon Chambers, Wheeler Gate.
ST. HELENS (Lancs.)	John Orford, 124, Knowsley Road.
SHREWSBURY ...	Major-General Sir John Headlam, K.B.E., C.B., D.S.O., Cruck Meole House, Hanwood.
TIVERTON (Devon)	Mr. W. H. Duncan Arthur, Surveyor's Office, Town Hall.
WELSHPOOL ...	Mr. E. Wilson, Coedway, Ford, Salop.

DOMINIONS AND FOREIGN COUNTRIES.

AUSTRALIA	Messrs. C. H. Green, and George Lawson, Box 1153 P., 2nd Floor, Griffiths House, Queen Street, Brisbane, Queensland. R. A. Baldwin, c/o Government Savings Bank of N.S.W., Martin Place, Sydney. Mr. W. Cloves, Box 1296, G.P.O., Adelaide.
BELGIUM	Sister Marguerite, Sacré Coeur, Ypres.
CANADA	Brig.-General V. W. Odlum, C.B., C.M.G., D.S.O., 2530, Point Grey Road, Vancouver. V. A. Bowes, 326, 40th Avenue West, Calgary, Alberta. W. Constable F. Grece, St. Hilaire Station, Ronville County, Quebec.
CEYLON	Captain F. R. G. Webb, M.C., Irrigation Bungalow, Kalmunai, E.P.
EGYPT	L. B. S. Larkins, The Residency, Cairo.
INDIA	Lieut.-Quartermaster G. Smith, Queen's Bays, Sialkot, India.
IRELAND	Miss A. K. Jackson, Cloneyhurke House, Portarlington.
NEW ZEALAND ...	Captain W. U. Gibb, Ava Lodge, Puhinui Road, Papatoetoe, Auckland S. E. Beattie, Lowlands, Woodville.
SOUTH AFRICA ...	H. L. Versfield, c/o Cape Explosives Works Ltd., 150, St. Georges Street, Cape Town.
SPAIN	Captain P. W. Burgess, Calle de Zurbano 29, Madrid.
U.S.A.	Captain Henry Maslin, 942, President Street, Brooklyn, New York. L. E. P. Foot, 20, Gillett Street, Hartford, Conn, U.S.A. A. P. Forward, 449, East 80th Street, New York. J. W. Freebody, 945, McBride Avenue, Los Angeles.
NOVA SCOTIA ...	Will R. Bird, 35, Clarence Street, Amherst.

Membership of the League

This is open to all who served in the Salient, and to all those whose relatives or friends died there, in order that they may have a record of that service for themselves, and their descendants, and belong to the comradeship of men and women who understand and remember all that Ypres meant in suffering and endurance.

Life membership, £2 10s.

Annual members, 5s.

Do not let the fact of your not having served in the Salient deter you from joining the Ypres League. Those who have neither fought in the Salient nor lost relatives there, but who are in sympathy with the objects of the Ypres League, are admitted to its fellowship, but are not given scroll certificates.

There is a Junior Division for children whose relatives served in the Salient. It is open also to others to whom our objects appeal.

Annual subscription 1s. up to the age of 18, after which they can become ordinary members of the League.

THE YPRES LEAGUE (INCORPORATED)
20, Orchard Street, Portman Square, W.1.

Telephone: WELBECK 1446.   *Telegrams*: YPRESLEAG, " WESDO," LONDON.

Patron-in-Chief: H.M. THE KING.

Patrons:
H.R.H. THE PRINCE OF WALES.   H.R.H. PRINCESS BEATRICE.

President: GENERAL SIR CHARLES H. HARINGTON.

Vice-Presidents:

F.-M. VISCOUNT ALLENBY.   F.-M. SIR CLAUD W. JACOB.
THE VISCOUNT WAKEFIELD OF HYTHE.   F.-M. SIR PHILIP CHETWODE.
GENERAL SIR CECIL ROMER.   F.-M. LORD MILNE.

General Committee:

THE COUNTESS OF ALBEMARLE.
*CAPTAIN C. ALLISTON.
LIEUT-COLONEL BECKLES WILLSON.
MR. HENRY BENSON.
*MR. J. BOUGHEY.
*MISS B. BRICE-MILLER.
COLONEL G. T. BRIERLEY.
CAPTAIN P. W. BURGESS.
BRIG.-GENL. A. BURT.
*MAJOR H. CARDINAL-HARFORD.
REV. P. B. CLAYTON.
*THE EARL OF YPRES.
MRS. C. J. EDWARDS.
MAJOR C. J. EDWARDS.
MR. H. A. T. FAIRBANK.
MR. T. ROSS FURNER.
SIR PHILIP GIBBS.
MR. E. GLOVER.

MR. F. D. BANKES-HILL.
MAJOR-GENERAL C. J. B. HAY.
MR. J. HETHERINGTON.
GENERAL SIR W. C. G. HENEKER.
*CAPTAIN O. G. JOHNSON.
*MAJOR E. MONTAGUE JONES.
MAJOR GENL. C. G. LIDDELL.
CAPTAIN H. D. PEABODY.
*THE HON. ALICE DOUGLAS PENNANT.
*LIEUT.-GENERAL SIR W. P. PULTENEY.
LIEUT.-COLONEL SIR J. MURRAY.
*COLONEL G. E. C. RASCH.
THE HON. SIR ARTHUR STANLEY.
MR. ERNEST THOMPSON.
CAPTAIN J. LOCKLEY TURNER.
*MR. E. B. WAGGETT.
CAPTAIN J. WILKINSON.
CAPTAIN H. TREVOR WILLIAMS.

* Executive Committee.

Bankers:
BARCLAYS BANK LTD., Knightsbridge Branch.

Honorary Solicitors:
MESSRS. FLADGATE & CO., 70, Pall Mall, S.W.

Secretary:
CAPTAIN G. E. DE TRAFFORD.

Auditors:
MESSRS. LEPINE & JACKSON,
6, Bond Court, E.C.4.

League Representative at Ypres:
CAPTAIN P. D. PARMINTER.
19, Rue Surmont de Volsberghe

League Representative at Cambrai:
MR. A. WILDE,
9, Rue des Anglaises.

League Representative at Amiens:
CAPTAIN STUART OSWALD.
7, Rue Porte-Paris.

League Representative at Arras:
MR. P. VYNER,
10, Station Square.

Hon. Secretary, Ypres British Settlement:
LT. COLONEL F. G. POOLE,

PRIMARY OBJECTS OF THE LEAGUE

I.—Commemoration and Comradeship.
II.—To provide special travel facilities for Members and all interested to Ypres and battlefields, and transport of Members.
III.—The furnishing of information about the Salient; marking of historic sites and the compilation of charts of the battlefields.
IV.—The erection of a Ypres British Church and School which has been completed.
V.—The establishment of groups of members throughout the world, through Branch Secretaries and Corresponding Members.
VI.—The maintenance of cordial relations with dwellers on the battlefields of Ypres.
VII.—The formation of a Junior Division.

Use the Ypres League Travel Bureau for Ypres and Whole of the Western Front.

FOR THE FOLLOWING PUBLICATIONS, Etc., apply:

Secretary, YPRES LEAGUE, 20, ORCHARD STREET, LONDON, W.1.

THE BATTLE BOOK OF YPRES. A history of notable deeds contributed by all regiments. 5s.; post free, 5s. 6d. Compiled by Beatrix Brice with the assistance of Lieut.-General Sir William Pulteney, G.C.V.O., etc.

BOOKS.

YPRES: Outpost of the Channel Ports. By Beatrix Brice. With Foreword by Field-Marshal Lord Plumer, G.C.B. Price 1s. 0d; post free 1s. 3d.

In the Ypres Salient. By Lt.-Col. Beckles Willson. 1s. net; post free 1s. 2d.

Story of the 63rd Field Ambulance. By A. W. Westmore, etc. Cloth, 3s. 6d., post free. Paper, 2s. 6d., post free.

War Letters to a Wife. By Colonel Rowland Feilding. Popular Edition, 3s. 6d.; post free 4s.

The Pill Boxes of Flanders. 1s.; post free 1s. 3d.

From Mons to the First Battle of Ypres. By J. G. W. Hyndson, M.C. Price 3/6, post free.

YPRES LEAGUE TIES. 3s. 6d. each, post free.

YPRES LEAGUE BADGES. 2s. each, 2s. 1½d. post free.

EMBROIDERED BADGES. 4s. each, post free.

Map and List of Cemeteries in the Ypres Salient. Price 9d.; post free 11d.

Map of the Somme. Price 1s. 8d., post free.

PICTURES.

Burning of the Cloth Hall, 1915. A Coloured Print, 14 in. by 12 in. 1s. post free.

Old Well-known Spots in New Guise.
Prints, size 4¼ x 2¼, recently taken of famous spots in the Ypres Salient, and which may be of great interest to our readers, are on sale at headquarters, price 4d. each, post free 5d. For particulars apply Secretary.

POST CARDS, PHOTOGRAPHS AND ETCHINGS.

Post Cards. Ypres: British Front during the War. Ruins of Ypres. Price 1s. post free.

Photographs of Menin Gate Unveiling. Size 11 in. by 7 in. 1s. 2d. each, post free.

Hill 60. Complete Panorama Photographs. 12 in. by 3¼ in. Price 3s., post free; 15 in. by 5 in. Price 3s. 6d., post free.

WAR-TIME PHOTOGRAPHS OF THE SALIENT.

6 in. by 8 in. ... 1s. 6d. each.
12 in. by 15 in. ... 4s. each.

List forwarded on application.

PHOTOGRAPHS OF WAR-TIME SKETCHES.

Bedford House (Front View), 1916.
Bedford House (Back View), 1916.
Voormezeele Main Street, 1916.
Voormezeele Crucifixion Gate, 1916.
Langhof Chateau, 1916.

Size 8½ in. by 6½ in. Price 2s. 6d. each, post free.

Photographs of the Thiepval and Arras Memorials. Post card size, price 1s. each, post free.

YPRES TIMES.

The Journal may be obtained at the League Offices.
BACK NUMBERS 1s.; 1934, 8d.; 1935, 6d.

Printed in Great Britain for the Publishers by FORD & GILL, 21a/23, Iliffe Yard, Crampton Street, London, S.E.17.

Memory Tablet.

APRIL - MAY - JUNE

APRIL

April 5th, 1917	United States declares war on Germany.
,, 9th, 1917	Battle of Vimy Ridge begins.
,, 9th, 1918	Battle of Lys begins.
,, 14th, 1918	General Foch appointed Generalissimo of the Allied Armies in France.
,, 22nd, 1915	Second Battle of Ypres begins. Germans use asphyxiating gases.
,, 22nd, 1918	British Naval attack on Zeebruge and Ostend.
,, 24th, 1916	Rebellion in Ireland.
,, 25th, 1915	Allied forces land in Gallipoli.
,, 27th, 1915	General Sir Herbert Plumer given command of all troops in the Ypres Salient.
,, 29th, 1916	Fall of Kut.

MAY

May 7th, 1915	The *Lusitania* torpedoed and sunk by the Germans.
,, 12th, 1915	Windhoek, capital of German South-West Africa captured by General Botha.
,, 19th, 1918	Germans bomb British hospitals at Etaples.
,, 23rd, 1915	Italy declares war on Austria.
,, 31st, 1916	Sea battle off the coast of Jutland.

JUNE

June 5th, 1916	Loss of Earl Kitchener on H.M.S. *Hampshire*.
,, 7th, 1915	Flight-Lieut. Warneford attacks and destroys Zeppelin between Ghent and Brussels.
,, 7th, 1917	British victory at Messines Ridge.
,, 29th, 1917	General Allenby in command in Egypt.

The Ypres Times

Communications to
The Editor, "Ypres Times,"
20, Orchard Street, London, W.1.

PRICE 6d.
POST FREE 7d.

VOL. 8, No. 2.   PUBLISHED QUARTERLY   APRIL, 1936

His Late Majesty King George V.

PASSING OF A GOOD AND WELL-BELOVED MONARCH.
THE SERVANT OF HIS PEOPLE.
(SPECIALLY CONTRIBUTED TO THE " YPRES TIMES ")
By
HENRY BENSON, M.A.

JANUARY'S issue of this journal was hardly in the hands of our readers before the Empire was called upon to mourn the loss of its revered Sovereign, King George, who had been the gracious Patron-in-Chief of the Ypres League since its inauguration in September, 1920.

The King thus passed away within a few months of the Silver Jubilee of his reign.

It is precisely a year ago that I was privileged to pay a humble tribute in the columns of the YPRES TIMES to the priceless services which his late Majesty had rendered to the realm during that momentous quarter of a century and to give a brief sketch of outstanding incidents in his long and useful career.

There is a note of tragedy in this close conjunction of triumph and death, and the sudden change from thanksgiving to mourning ; but I doubt whether we are right to dwell on the tragedy. Perhaps, rather, we should feel that George V was happy in the ending of his reign. The memory of that Silver Jubilee is still with us. The echoes of his voice as he addressed his widespread family last Christmas Day—less than a month before his death—are still fresh in our ears. But the King has gone from us. After a few short days of illness, as simply and unostentatiously as he had lived, he passed away from our midst. Truly, his life had been beautifully and nobly spent, and as time rolls on this will be more and more fully realised. The symmetry, the balance, the proportion of King George's three score years and ten, all sprang from the simplicity and native goodness of his character. He served both his God and his people with just the same direct sense of duty and of unquestioning obligation. He was destined to pass through a fiery ordeal such as none of his predecessors had ever endured, and he has now gone to join that long line of ancestry which comprises so much of the Empire's history. He will probably go down to posterity as the greatest of our constitutional monarchs, and he was King over his people because in whatever he did he was King over himself. He died with the love of his many subjects lapping him round, and with the respect and homage that the world always renders to worth and goodness.

" NUNC DIMITTIS."

I think that the most memorable moment in my life took place on the night of January 20th, when at 9.30 I turned on my " wireless " and found that no news was coming through. Instinctively I knew that something momentous was happening. There was a stilled silence which, like the Egyptian darkness of old, could almost be felt. It was a silence which cannot possibly be explained ; and it prepared me for the message at 9.38, which must have touched every soul who heard it : " *The King's life is moving peacefully towards its close."*

We had been familiar with the strictly medical terms of previous announcements ; and when at last the end was apparent we awaited something poignant — but in similar strain. Instead, we were given a line of inspired figurative language, a simile of such transcendent beauty that it gave healing as it wounded. Whoever wrote that line must have had supreme inspiration, for the mournful news could not have been announced in tenderer words. It was such a line as only comes from a great poet ; to which in our moments of strong emotion, the poet in each one of us intuitively responds :—" The King's life is moving peacefully towards its close."

Then there followed the great appeal to all the Empire to offer up silent prayer for the King, as he passed to the nearer presence of his God. I know not how that appeal and the beautiful rendering of the 23rd Psalm, " The Lord is my Shepherd," reacted on others. To me, however, it seemed as though all men and women of the realm — snow-bound trappers in Canada, sheep-ranchers in Australia, tea-planters in Malay, prospectors in Africa, negroes in Jamaica, and all the tribes that fill India up to the Himalayan frontier, together with millions of many colours in between the fringes of the Empire — had suddenly assembled in some vast cathedral kneeling and praying for their Sovereign. Never before has the Empire been so welded together on its knees in prayer to Almighty God, never before has the " wireless " been used for such a tremendous declaration or appeal.

It was then announced that the British Broadcasting Stations would close down. Talk ceased, music ceased and the world held its breath. The citizens of the Empire kept vigil, as vigil had never been kept in the long history of mankind, whilst they waited for those bulletins, each quarter of an hour apart, which, like the tolling of the passing bell, brought us to the end a few minutes before midnight. Truly may it be said that the sunset of our King's death tinged the whole world's sky.

The War Years.

I suppose that the Great War, which put so many persons and institutions to the test, brought home the real character of their King to the consciousness of the British peoples. From the very beginning of the conflict he took his place as the visible embodiment of the national spirit and feeling. He was head of his Army, but he did not glory in war. He was a naval man by choice and by position, and he loved the sea and the men who serve on it, but he took no delight in destruction. Fragments of his war messages and speeches linger unforgettably in the memory, such as his assurance to Jellicoe in the early days of national confidence that, " under your direction, the officers and men of the fleets will revive and renew the old glories of the Royal Navy, and prove again the sure shield of Britain and of her Empire in the hour of trial," and his promise to the troops going overseas, which was kept to the letter : " I shall follow your every movement with deepest interest and mark with eager satisfaction your daily progress. Indeed, you will never be absent from my thoughts."

King George paid frequent visits to the munition factories, the hospitals and the training camps, and everywhere helped to stimulate the national effort by unaffected kindly words to wounded soldiers, to hard-driven workers in the factories and to poor parents in country villages who had given their sons to the service of the Empire. His first journey to the Front took place in the grim autumn of 1914 when the Allied troops were still being forced back by the invaders. He was in France again in October, 1915, and on this occasion he met with a bad accident. His horse slipped while he was inspecting some troops, and his Majesty was thrown and badly bruised and strained. The injuries were more serious than the public at the time knew, and it was not until

the end of the following month that he was allowed to leave his bed. When he was being conveyed to the hospital train from the scene of the accident he insisted on investing Lance-Sergeant Oliver Brooks, of the Coldstream Guards, with the Victoria Cross. Characteristic, too, was the King's command that the two Canadian nurses, who attended him when he was taken after his accident to a Canadian field hospital and accompanied him back to London as a " casualty " should stay with him until he was convalescent.

Among repeated visits to the troops in Belgium and France none was more memorable, if more painful, than when in March, 1918, he hurried across the Channel to carry words of confidence, sympathy, and congratulation to the soldiers who had so bravely — and barely — stemmed the fierce German onrush.

The King's Supreme War Service.

" Foremost of the Allied Chiefs to realise the value of the unity of Command, and the one to bring it into being, was the King of England, George the Fifth." This is a passage, which now appears in print for the first time, from the unpublished diaries of the late Marshal Foch, and it is confirmed by a note found among the papers of the war-time French Premier, Georges Clemenceau. In amplifying notes Foch reveals that the King had first of all expressed in strong terms his conviction that the weakness of the Allies lay in the lack of cohesion between the different armies, and that the only remedy was in some form of unity of command.

The political, as well as the army chiefs of the Allied Powers in the West, with the exception of Belgium, would not hear of unity that did not mean handing the command over to themselves. King George made many helpful suggestions for overcoming the difficulties, but nothing came of them until the fateful spring and summer of 1918, when his Majesty had won over the more important of the British political chiefs to the view that for the Allies the choice was between unity of command or defeat. The King then made known to Sir Douglas Haig and his other generals his firm conviction that the cause of the Allies could best be served by accepting the lead of Foch and Sir Douglas's famous letter, placing himself and his troops under the orders of the Generalissimo, followed.

" It was the King of England who saved the unity of command when it was menaced, and, in saving it, he saved the Allies from defeat," declared Clemenceau. Foch's comment is : " I say nothing of what I am told was the intervention of the King when I personally was involved, but I do say without fear of contradiction that his foresight and firmness on the question of unity of command brought to the Allies victory instead of the defeat that threatened them."

The Hour of Victory.

Victory, overwhelming and complete, swiftly followed. For those who lived in London through that unforgettable Armistice Day, November 11th, 1918, one of its abiding memories will always be that of the scene outside Buckingham Palace, when, as if by magic, the broad causeway was alive with an immense and thronging multitude. The mighty concourse poured round the Palace railings and surged about the base of Queen Victoria's statue, raising urgent loyal voices for the King. He, the Queen and others of their family, came out upon a balcony and stood there long, showing themselves to that vast crowd, which seemed as if it would never tire of cheering, shouting and singing patriotic airs. The popular instinct was right. That quiet gentleman — I use the word advisedly — in service uniform, with his grave face and kindly smile, seemed to personify the Britain of the war years, its courage, its tenacity, its placid strength, its invincible good temper. Mighty thrones had fallen and ancient dynasties had been extinguished before the World War ended, but the British Monarchy still stood " four-square to all the winds that blow," erect and solid. That this was largely due to the conduct and character of King George is beyond question. During the whole of his reign, he must have been subjected to all the demoralising obsequiousness, sycophancy, and flattery which monarchs must endure, yet after twenty-five years of it, he could still say to the

Archbishop of Canterbury: "I am only a very ordinary sort of fellow." When we remember that so many commoners cannot even be promoted to be acting-lance-corporal without thinking themselves very superior people, then we get some measure of King George's really royal character. Any homage paid to that kind of royalty is not amazing — it is merely a right and proper tribute.

BURDEN WHICH IS NEVER LIFTED.

One who was constantly with King George during the past ten years recently told me that if he could have stopped work and wintered abroad his life might have been considerably prolonged. But he was of duty compact, and allowed nothing to come before the calls of State. There is no respite for the King. One of the most moving and impressive passages in Mr. Baldwin's broadcast address on the evening following the King's death, was that in which he contrasted his Majesty's lot with that of the politicians : " We can and do have our old age, if we live, to ourselves, but a King's burden is never lifted . . . the only release from it is death."

The Empire mourns the man and the King. He faced throughout his reign great moments of politics and statesmanship, times when the realm itself steered near the edge of disaster, if not defeat. He spoke much of the family, and that is a word the British understand. He gave it a fuller meaning, and besides being a British King, he was also a British father.

The Mighty Monarch, the centre of an Empire's homage, was none the less, in the hour of death, only a man who must yield, as all men must, when the great call comes. He was one of us in the face of eternity. Still, if heredity, rank and place had not made him an Emperor, he would have raised himself to Imperial stature when in the last weakness and frailty of his death-bed he asked the question, " How is the Empire ? "

With the lapse of time the first sense of loss is bound to pass. Not so the memory of a great King who would ask, I believe, from his people no prouder epitaph than this : *" Like his Unknown Soldier, he did his duty."*   H.B.

The Address of the Archbishop of Canterbury
On January 23rd, at the House of Lords, following the Lying-in-State in the Westminster Hall.

I doubt very much whether anyone in our long history has ever enjoyed an affection so intimate and personal. It was the knowledge of this, as I well know, that inspired and cheered King George during all these anxieties. Your lordships may remember the words which he used on the Christmas Day before his Silver Jubilee year. They are worth reminding your lordships of. He said : " If I may be regarded as in some true sense the head of this great and widespread family, sharing its life and sustained by its affection, this will be a full reward for the long and sometimes anxious labours of my reign."

Let me in a closing moment lay some emphasis upon his steadfast devotion to duty.

I do so because it was revealed in a most moving manner in the very last day of his life. At noon on that day, propped up in his chair, looking so frail and weak, he received his last Privy Council. To the Order constituting a Council of State he gave in his own clear tone the familiar " Approved." Then he made deliberate and repeated efforts, most gallant but most pathetic, to sign his last State paper with his own hand.

Then, when the effort was too great for him, he turned to his Council with a last kindly and kingly smile. My lords, it was a scene which those of us who beheld it will never forget. I hope I have been guilty of no impropriety in describing it. I think it is worthy of record, because it showed that what rallied him in his last conscious hours was his old and undeviating response to the claim of duty.

May I say one word about her Majesty Queen Mary ? I should like to give my personal testimony to the truly wonderful fortitude and courage which her Majesty has shown, as I have seen during these last most anxious days. The one who might have been expected to be most overwhelmed was the one from whom to all others surrounding her there radiated calmness and strength. Truly admiration must blend with the sympathy with which she is this day surrounded. We pray with all our hearts that she may be spared to live many years of beneficent activity, to be in ever fuller measure as these years pass the true Queen Mother of her people, and to enjoy her secure possession of their hearts.

I think that the death of King George was singularly fortunate in its time and in its manner — to be spared any lingering weakness, the memory so fresh in his heart of that overflowing gift of the love of his people which he had received. As I looked on his face for the last time on Tuesday morning I saw that there lay upon it a most beautiful tranquility and peace.

—*Reprinted by kind permission of " The Times."*

On behalf of the members of the Ypres League, a wreath composed of white chrysanthemums and cornflowers was despatched to Windsor Castle, and bore the following inscription :—

In Humble Sympathy and Imperishable Memory
of our
Most Gracious and Beloved Patron-in-Chief
His Majesty King George the Fifth
from the
Ypres League.

To the
KING'S MOST EXCELLENT MAJESTY
*The Dutiful Address of the Chairman
and Members of the Ypres League*

May it please Your Majesty

We Your Majesty's Dutiful and Loyal Subjects who served His Late Majesty King George of blessed memory in the Defence of the Ypres Salient beg leave to express our respectful and heartfelt sorrow at the heavy affliction that has fallen upon Your Majesty by the death of our Beloved Sovereign our Patron-in-Chief, and we earnestly pray that your Majesty's Reign may be long, illustrious and blessed with peace.

W. P. Pulteney,
Lieut.-General,
Chairman.

To the
QUEEN'S MOST EXCELLENT MAJESTY
*The Dutiful Address of the Chairman
and Members of the Ypres League*

May it please Your Majesty

We the Members of the Ypres League who were privileged to serve our late beloved Sovereign His Majesty King George of blessed memory in the Defence of the Ypres Salient beg leave to express to Your Majesty our respectful and heartfelt sorrow at the heavy and irreparable affliction which has befallen upon Your Majesty by the death of our Most Beloved Sovereign, Patron-in-Chief of the Ypres League.

W. P. Pulteney,
Lieut.-General,
Chairman.

The following replies were received from the Home Office :—

Sir,
    I have had the honour to lay before The King the Loyal and Dutiful Address of the Members of the Ypres League on the occasion of the lamented death of His late Majesty King George the Fifth, and have received The King's Commands to convey to you His Majesty's grateful Thanks for the assurances of sympathy and devotion to which it gives expression.

I am,
Sir,
Your obedient Servant,
John Simon.

The Chairman,
  Ypres League.

Sir,
    I am directed by the Secretary of State to inform you that the Address of Condolence of the Members of the Ypres League on the death of His late Majesty King George the Fifth has been laid before Queen Mary, whose grateful Thanks I am to convey to you.

I am,
Sir,
Your obedient Servant,
R. R. Stott.

The Chairman,
  Ypres League.

Special Service at St. George's Church and Menin Gate

A special service in memory of His late Majesty King George V. was held in St. George's Church, Ypres, on Tuesday, January, 28th at 10.30 a.m., conducted by the Chaplain, the Rev. G. R. Milner, M.A., Hon. C.F., at which a very large congregation attended consisting of the British Colony of Ypres and surrounding neighbourhood, also the Burgomaster and the Secretary of the town in addition to a number of distinguished local residents.

The Chaplain in his address made a fitting reference to the sterling qualities of King George and to the manner in which he endeared himself to the people of his vast Empire.

A number of our local friends expressed a wish to associate themselves in the loss which our country had sustained, and a Memorial Service was also held at the Menin Gate at 7.45 p.m. on the same day, when a large number of local residents as well as many of the British Colony were present. The service was conducted by the Chaplain, the Rev. G. R. Milner, and the Dean of St. Martin's Cathedral, assisted by other members of the local clergy. The Dean addressed the assembly in English, and made sympathetic reference to the loss which the British people had suffered in the death of their King, a grief which was keenly felt by the Belgian people to whom his late Majesty had always proved himself a very loyal friend.

The service was deeply moving and at its conclusion, the "Last Post" was sounded by the buglers who perform that ceremony every night throughout the year.

The Last Bulletin

Midnight at Buckingham Palace,
January, 20-21, 1936.

"For God's sake, let us sit upon the ground
And tell sad stories of the death of Kings."
—Shakespeare.

We knew his life was passing peacefully —
   The message on the little board told that :
We waited still, with never hearts less free,
   For they were with the dreams our minds begat.
Across the courtyard with slow steps there came
   A man who in his hand a paper limply held.
His gloved hands fumbled the string, and frame,
   And we looked on, and all impatience quelled.
The fumbling hands spoke like a tolling bell —
   Yes, told in silence all there was to tell
And then a policeman read the message hanging there.

Now crownless, sceptreless, alone he lies,
   And yet he reigns as no king ever reigned.
The grief I note about me is a sign
   That he has empery yet, and dies
To live once more in hearts he haply gained
With kind sincerity, and with Love's wine.

The Lying-in-State — Westminster Hall

Here things majestical jostle eye, and mind —
   Lift the heart singing to another sphere :
For History like flames about the bier
   Now breathes, and lives, and forges ties that bind.
   Now England speaks ! This is her hour !
      She has in keeping
        A Monarch sleeping,
      And symbols of power.
   O England ! Patient, noble England !
      What of the dead ?
   He was the very front of her,
      And her inmost soul.
   Wherever Englishmen confer
There is he set in the whole
   Grand scheme of things
That beats with imponderous wings
   On the shores of the world.

R. HENDERSON-BLAND, *Capt.*,
(late Gloucestershire Regiment).

A Short History of the First Guards

The King's Colours :—
 1st Battalion.—Gules (crimson) : In the centre the Imperial Crown ; in base a Grenade fired proper.
 2nd Battalion.—Gules (crimson) : In the centre the Royal Cypher reversed and interlaced or, ensigned with the Imperial Crown ; in base a Grenade fired proper ; in the dexter canton the Union.
 3rd Battalion.—As for 2nd Battalion, and for distinction, issuing from the Union in bend dexter a pile wavy or.
The Regimental Colours :—
 The Union : In the centre a Company Badge ensigned with the Imperial Crown ; in base a Grenade fired proper. The 30 Company Badges are borne in rotation, 3 at a time, one on the Regimental Colour of each of the Battalions.
 The following honorary distinctions are borne upon each of the King's and Regimental Colours :—
  "Tangier, 1680," "Namur, 1695," "Gibraltar, 1704-5," "Blenheim," "Ramillies," "Oudenarde," "Malplaquet," "Dettingen," "Lincelles," "Egmont-op-Zee," "Corunna," "Barrosa," "Nive," "Peninsula," "Waterloo," "Alma," "Inkerman," "Sevastopol," "Tel-el-Kebir," "Egypt, 1882," "Suakin, 1885," "Khartoum," "Modder River," "South Africa, 1899-1902."
The Great War—5 *Battalions*.—" Mons," " Retreat from Mons," " Marne, 1914," " Aisne, 1914," " Ypres, 1914, '17," " Langemarck, 1914," " Gheluvelt," " Nonne Bosschen," " Neuve Chapelle," " Aubers," " Festubert, 1915," " Loos," " Somme, 1916, '18," " Ginchy," " Flers-Courcelette," " Morval," " Pilckem," " Menin Road," " Poelcappelle," " Passchendaele," " Cambrai, 1917, '18," " St. Quentin," " Bapaume, 1918," " Arras, 1918," " Lys," " Hazebrouck," " Albert, 1918," " Scarpe, 1918," " Hindenburg Line," " Havrincourt," " Canal du Nord," " Selle," " Sambre," " France and Flanders, 1914-18."
 Uniform—Scarlet.   *Facings*—Blue.

DURING his exile in France, Charles II, in 1656, formed the nucleus of an army with which to recover his throne. Five regiments were formed, of which one consisted of 400 loyal Englishmen, mostly of gentle birth, who had followed him to exile. To this body Charles gave the name " The Royal Regiment of Guards," and with slight changes of title it has survived to this day as Senior Regiment of Foot in the British Army.

The regiment's first engagement was at the Battle of the Dunes in 1658, when Charles, in alliance with Spain, attempted to relieve Dunkirk, which was being besieged by Cromwell's English Army and the French. Charles' allies fled from the field, but the Royal Regiment stood firm and only laid down its arms when surrounded by the whole French and English army.

After his restoration in 1660, Charles left his loyal regiment in Flanders and formed another of the same name in England, but in 1665 the former were brought home and the two regiments amalgamated. During the next few years the Royal Regiment was engaged in many minor actions, some of them at sea, but it was not until 1680 that the first " battle honour " was won. This was " Tangier," where the Moors vigorously attacked the English garrison, but were twice defeated. The unhappy period of James' II reign and overthrow did not seriously shake the " moral " of the Royal Regiment, and under William they had their first taste of the prolonged continental warfare that lay before them. Louis XIV of France was the great menace to the peace of Europe at that time, and against him William led an army of allies too heterogeneous to be easily handled. His first serious engagement was at Steenkirk (1692), where, in an attempt to relieve Namur, he was at first successful in a surprise attack, but finally had to retire owing to the slowness or jealousy of the Dutch general, Count Solmes. The First Guards (as they were by this time called, to distinguish them from the Coldstream and the Scottish Regiment of Guards) were brilliantly successful in their initial attack, capturing a battery and turning it upon the enemy ; it was only when overwhelmed by the full force of the French counter-attack that, unsupported, they fell back in good order, leaving half their number on the field.

In the following year, 1693, William was again defeated by the French Marshal Luxembourg, this time in a defensive battle at Landen. Two battalions of the First Guards, with their comrades of the Scottish Guards and the Coldstream, defended the key-point, Neerwinden, throughout the day until the line was broken further east by the French cavalry. These two battles rank as British defeats and do not appear as "battle honours," but they hold an honourable place in the records of the Regiment.

Then came the great period of Marlborough's campaigns. Battalions of the First Guards took a prominent part in each one of his famous victories. At Schellenberg (1704), they formed part of the advanced attack delivered by Marlborough before his ally, Louis of Baden, could come up with the main body. Grenadiers of the First Guards led the "forlorn hope" and suffered terrible loss, but held on to their footing in the French lines until the main body came up and broke the line where it had been weakened to resist the advance attack. This grenadier company lost three quarters of its strength and in the battalion as a whole only 5 out of the 17 officers were untouched. In the more famous action at Blenheim in 1704, the 1st Battalion formed part of Rowe's Brigade which led Cutts' assault upon Blenheim itself. The attack, though repeated, failed, but pinned the flower of the French infantry to that spot, leaving the centre to be weakly held and broken by Marlborough's celebrated cavalry attack. At Ramillies (1706), the First Guards were again employed in the holding attack on the village of that name while the cavalry broke the French right. At Oudenarde (1708) they played their part in the "encounter battle" which shattered the reviving "moral" of the French army. Finally, at Malplaquet (1709) they took part in the final and decisive attack of the allied centre which turned impending disaster into overwhelming victory. Among these great campaigns it should not be forgotten that British troops were fighting at the same time in Spain and particularly at Gibraltar, which Admiral Rooke captured in 1704. A composite battalion of Guards took part in all these engagements and particularly in two bloody actions at Barcelona, which was won in 1705 and held against a fierce attack in 1706. The picture is clouded by the disaster at Almanza in 1707, where, thanks to the cowardice of their Portuguese allies, the British force was isolated and forced to surrender.

In the war of the Austrian Succession, the 1st Battalion, part of a Guards Brigade, fought under the command of King George II himself at Dettingen (1743) and later at Fontenoy (1745), under Cumberland, took part in one of the most glorious battles of the British army. It ended in defeat, but never have British soldiers, or the Guards themselves, fought more magnificently. Once again it was a case of an allied army against the French. The British on the right attacked across open ground swept by artillery fire from both flanks ; decimated by this fire they held on and topping the crest came face to face with the French infantry. Here occurred the celebrated incident in which the Captain of the King's Company of the First Guards called upon the French Guards to fire first. Whatever may be the truth of the story the fact remains that the French Guards *did* fire first, at rather too great a range, and while they were reloading the British advanced to within point blank range and fired a volley which mowed the gallant Frenchmen to the ground like grass before the sickle. Every French counter-attack withered away before the British fire, but alas ! the Dutch and Austrian allies on the left had failed to play their part, and the British had to retire, their rear-guard of Guards and Hanoverians halting again and again to pour their deadly volleys into the enemy, who abandoned the pursuit. Each battalion of Foot Guards lost over 250 officers and men, more than half their strength, but the glory of the British infantry reached a height that day which was acclaimed by friend and foe alike.

After a hurried recall to England to protect London against the threat of the Young Pretender, the First Guards returned to the Continent and took part in the battle of Lanffeldt (1746), another allied defeat in which, however, the British contingent upheld its growing reputation.

After a short period of peace inaugurated by the Treaty of Aix-la-Chapelle, Europe was soon involved in the Seven Years' War. The First Guards, together with other British troops, took part in the battles of Vellinghausen (1761), Amöneberg and Wilhelmsthal (1762). There followed the treaty of Utrecht, and then England found herself for once engaged in a struggle of her own making — the tragic War of the American Secession. In July 1776, a combined Battalion of Guards was sent out as part of a reinforcement to Lord Howe, and was at once engaged at Brooklyn, Fort Washington, and the operations on the Hudson. In 1777, there were sharp engagements at Brandywine and Germantown, but it was at Guildford Court House, in 1781, that the Guards now expanded to two battalions, gave the most emphatic evidence of their discipline and courage, losing half their numbers before finally breaking the resistance of the stubborn American rebels. At Cornwallis' capitulation at Yorktown, over 500 Guardsmen became prisoners, a greater number than have ever suffered that fate in one engagement, before or since.

In 1789 began the long series of campaigns caused by the French Revolution, but it was not until 1793 that a British force became actively involved. Then a Guards Brigade, including one battalion of each regiment and a composite battalion of grenadier companies, was sent to Holland, and soon was engaged at Vicoigne, Famars, and the siege of Valenciennes. At Linselles and Dunkirk, in 1793, at Tourcoing in 1794, the Guards gave brilliant proof of their dash in attack, their steadiness in defence, but the feeble policy and generalship of the allies ended in the gloomy retreat into Holland, and inglorious return home.

Then came the rise of the brilliant star, Napoleon Bonaparte, and in 1799, two Guards Brigades were back in Holland, landing in the face of opposition at Helder, and fighting sharp engagements at the Zype, Bergen, Egmont-ann-Zee, and Bakkum, before the expedition was withdrawn. In 1801 came the brilliant little campaign in Egypt, the historic landing at Aboukir and the defeat of the French attack at Roman Camp, Alexandria.

In 1808 began the long and bitter struggle of the Peninsular War. Battalions of the Foot Guards took part in practically every engagement, but it was not until nearly the end that Wellington realised the true worth of the stolid and unbreakable Guards, his earlier trust being placed principally upon the more volatile and dashing Light Infantry. The First Guards, as it happened, were absent from some of the campaigns, though they played a prominent part both at the beginning and the end. Two battalions of the Regiment were included in Sir John Moore's force which, thrusting towards the capital and distracting Napoleon from his settled plan of campaign, was forced into a retreat which has become an epic. The First Guards formed part of Moore's rear-guard throughout and undoubtedly their steadiness played a major part in saving his army from disaster. In the culminating battle of Corunna they took part in a fierce counter-attack which checked Soult's onslaught and might have led to a decisive victory had not Moore himself been mortally wounded at the critical moment.

There followed the disastrous expedition to Walcheren (1809) where 230 men of the First Guards died of fever, but not one in battle. In 1810 a British force, including a Guard Brigade of which the 3rd Battalion First Guards formed a part, was sent to Cadiz and remained there for many weary months, besieged but never attacked. In February, 1811, a large part of this force left the town by sea and, landing at Tarifa, set out to attack the French besieging army from the rear. There followed the singularly bloody battle of Barrosa, where, after being abandoned by their Spanish allies, 4,000

British attacked and defeated 7,000 veteran French soldiers. In 1812 the French siege of Cadiz was finally raised and the British force, including the 3rd Battalion First Guards joined Wellington during his retreat from Burgos, while the 1st Battalion First Guards came up almost at the same time from Corunna. Owing to sickness these battalions were unable to take part in the advance which culminated at Vittoria in 1813, but they were present at the assault on San Sebastian, at the crossing of the Bidassoa, at the engagements on the Nivelle, the Nive, and Adour, also at the final futile sortie from the Bayonne. Before Napoleon was safely in Elba, however, a detachment of the Regiment took part in the calamitous failure to capture Bergen-op-Zoom (1814).

The tale of the Hundred Days is full of glory for the First Guards. At Quatre Bras (1815) the 2nd and 3rd battalions with their comrades of the Third and Coldstream Guards carried out the counter-attack through the Bois de Bossu which turned imminent defeat into victory. At Waterloo the light companies of the three Guards Regiments, later re-enforced by nearly the whole of the 2nd Guards Brigade, held the farm of Hougoumont throughout the day against repeated assaults, while on the main ridge Maitland's Brigade of the First Guards, after enduring heavy bombardment throughout the day, in partnership with Adam's Brigade crushed the final assault of the Old Guard and led the great counter-advance which swept Napoleon's army for ever from the field. For this achievement the Regiment was awarded the title of Grenadiers.

In 1854 the Crimean War broke out, and a Guards Brigade, including the 3rd Battalion First Guards sailed for Scutari. After some preliminary skirmishing the first pitched battle was fought on the Alma, where the Guards Brigade captured the Great Redoubt. There followed the long siege of Sevastopol, interrupted by the Russian sortie at Inkerman, the bloody "Soldiers' Battle" during which Grenadiers and Russians fought all day for possession of the Sandbag Battery, the Regiment losing 233 out of the 430 men engaged. The wounds of battle were, however, nothing to the rigours of the siege, probably the most severe in which troops have ever been engaged.

From 1882-1885, detachments of the Regiment were engaged in Egypt, taking part in the engagements of Tel-el-Keber and Abu-Klea, while in 1897, the 1st Battalion was present at Omdurman, where Kitchener finally subdued the Dervishes.

Two battalions of the Regiment were engaged throughout almost the whole of the South African War (1899-1902), one or other being present at the battles of Belmont, Graspan, Modder River, Magersfontein, Diamond Hill and Biddulphsberg, besides being employed in the system of block-houses and drives which marked the closing stages of the campaign.

The huge scale of the Great War (1914-1918) makes it impossible to record the doings of the Regiment in any detail, but there was hardly a battle of any note in which Grenadiers were not engaged. The 2nd Battalion went out with the Expeditionary Force, and was present at Mons, through the Retreat, at the Aisne and at Ypres. The 1st Battalion went out with the 7th Division in October, 1914, and, after attempting to relieve Antwerp in October, 1914, retired to Ypres and actually began the battle that never really ceased for four years. In 1915, after Neuve Chapelle and Aubers had been fought and lost, two further battalions of Grenadiers were sent to France, all four being together in the newly formed Guards Division which fought its first action at Loos. Two major attacks on the Somme (September 15th and 25th) were the principal feature of 1916; three similar attacks at the Third Battle of Ypres in 1917 were followed by the surprise attack at Cambrai and the great counter-attack by the Germans, which was stopped in the nick of time by the Guards Division. In the German offensive in 1918, the Guards did not yield one yard of ground, and, when the time came to advance, they were almost continuously engaged until the recovery of Mauberge and the Armistice crowned their great effort.

H. L. AUBREY-FLETCHER.

The Capture of Vimy Ridge

PERSONAL EXPERIENCES ON APRIL 9th - 10th, 1917.

Prefatory Note.

With the completion of the great Canadian Memorial on Vimy Ridge in July, 1936, the last link with the famous battle of April 9th, 1917, will have been forged. It is not generally realized that English and Scottish troops also took part in the assault and capture of the Ridge. On my last visit to it in 1922, I found a Memorial to them in the shape of a wooden Cross, surrounded by a small garden, close to that part of the Lens-Arras road where the 1st Battalion Royal West Kent Regiment formed up to continue the attack after passing through the Canadians.

It is to be hoped that this has been re-made in some more permanent material. The following article is based largely on one that appeared in the *Marlburian* for February, 1918.

By Captain H. U. S. NISBET,
late 3rd attached 1st Royal West Kent Regiment.

BEFORE recounting my experiences on Vimy Ridge, it may not be out of place to touch upon happenings prior to the launching of the attack. The 13th Brigade, consisting of my own battalion, 2nd King's Own Scottish Borderers, and 14th and 15th Royal Warwicks, together with our (5th) Divisional Artillery had been attached for the operation to the 2nd Canadian Division, and for a week or two we had been practising daily over specially marked out country behind the line. Although this bore little, if any, resemblance to the ground we were to fight over, the tapes and flags with which it was accurately bedecked not only familiarized us with the names and relative positions of trenches and woods on the Ridge, but also inculcated in all ranks an instinctive sense of direction that no amount of map reading would have done. In fact, there is no doubt that these elaborate preparations, coupled with the perfecting of the creeping barrage time-table, were responsible for our immense confidence and contributed significantly to the overwhelming success of the whole attack. This, we had been given to understand, was to commence on Easter Sunday, but was postponed until the following day.

On Sunday, April 8th, we marched to within four or five miles of the line and spent the afternoon resting under cover of a small wood. The weather, which for a long time had been vile, was mild and sunny. It seemed, indeed, like the beginning of summer.

I had been allotted the job of liaison officer with the 27th Canadians, who were to advance on our right. That evening I set out with Flynn, my batman, to join them. Owing to the darkness, the slippery state of the ground, and the weight of our rifles, ammunition, packs, and two days' rations, the journey took nearly two hours. Eventually after several sousings in liquid mud, we reached their camp dead beat at the moment they were about to move off.

A short respite, while their C.O. completed his preparations, and we were away again. He had allowed his battalion a quarter of an hour's start and now expressed his intention of getting ahead of it. As he carried nothing but a couple of gas helmets he succeeded without much difficulty in accomplishing this feat. To me it was a nightmare. Somewhere on the route I passed Flynn my sack of rations and told him to follow on later!

After a while, we left the road and struck across fields near Neuville St. Vaast, guided by a line of tape. Parallel to it the tracks of tanks could be dimly seen. We passed some batteries that were being gas shelled. In consequence box respirators were adjusted, and we crept along at a snail's pace until the air cleared again.

At last the trench system began, and, after losing our way once or twice, we reached the dug-out that was to house us 'till dawn. As the official despatch stated later, there had been twenty days' intense bombardment of the enemy's front and rear positions. This had quietened down on the night of the 8th-9th to allow the troops to get into position with as few casualties as possible from retaliatory fire. So far as the battalion I was with was concerned, there were only two or three wounded. In spite of the hard going everyone was in high spirits, and although the French were commonly reported to have lost 60,000 killed in their assaults on the Ridge, failure was unthought of.

We slept for a few hours as best we could. In these more comfortable days it is extraordinary to recall how luxurious a table used to be for this purpose, even when one's legs were too long to be supported by it!

At 5.25 a.m. I was awakened to witness the start. It was scarcely light outside — very cold and drizzling. We mounted the fire-step and waited for zero-hour, watching the strangely quiet seconds tick by. Suddenly a gun fired, and immediately the whole sky from Arras to Lens seemed to explode into flame. From our position we could

Photo]   [Imperial War Museum, Crown Copyright

VIMY RIDGE — BOMBARDING THE GERMAN LINES PREVIOUS TO THE ATTACK IN APRIL, 1917

see lines of dark figures and tanks advancing behind the barrage, and, beyond them, the coloured rockets of the enemy, calling for help.

The din was so continuous that one soon forgot it.

After a scratch breakfast of sardines and tinned ham, we set off up the trench to the front line. The first prisoners now appeared with some of our own wounded, whom they were helping along. One of them was wearing the ribbon of the Iron Cross. They were obviously very thankful to have got through alive.

As we neared the front line we came under the German shell fire, which was being concentrated on our advanced trenches. An officer a few yards ahead of me was killed, but I and my batman, who had reappeared during the night, safely reached our reserve line, from which a deep tunnel had been dug up to the front. This was crowded with troops moving up, also with R.A.M.C. men, wounded, and stretcher-bearers. When at last we emerged at the far end the trench had suffered such damage from the heavy rains and shelling, that for a moment we could neither haul ourselves out of it, nor tell which way to proceed. However, we got through a gap and more by chance than skill found ourselves in No Man's Land.

From here onwards the ground was a boggy wilderness of shell craters. The early morning drizzle had turned to snow. It needed all one's strength to drag one leg after the other.

About half-way across this first stretch I just had time to hear that terrible sound of a "dead-on" shell when its wind bowled me over like a ninepin. This, and the violence of its explosion, convinced me that I was finished. It was therefore curious and somewhat disheartening to come back to the realization that I was still alive without even a " blighty." There was nothing for it but to go on.

During the next hour we covered a thousand yards, passing two derelict tanks which had been defeated by the mud, and reached our first (official) halting place — the Lens-Arras Road, where the troops detailed to attack the second and later objectives were forming up. The road, which was quite unrecognizable as such, was being heavily shelled, but both the West Kents and the Canadians were exceedingly fortunate, casualties being few.

Great work was done here by the former's C.O. in getting companies sorted out, and all ranks behaved as though on parade. The result was that the leading waves were ready to advance precisely according to schedule.

At the pre-arranged moment our great barrage lifted and moved forward at the rate of 100 yards every three minutes. During practice we had thought that this might necessitate our waiting, very much exposed, in front of the objectives, but on the actual day the pace was quite fast enough for anyone. The accuracy of the barrage called forth loud praise from the Canadians. Co-operating with it were two hundred machine guns, firing over us at long range targets. Their combined effect was devasting. No sooner had the curtain of shells cleared an enemy trench than the leading wave dashed in, and the succeeding one passed through to continue the attack. Meanwhile, the weather remained atrocious ; occasionally the snow became so thick that the Ridge was entirely hidden. At other times the sun shone brilliantly for a few minutes, but it was mainly dull and bitterly cold. Through all this our aeroplanes carried out their observation work, flying low over objectives. There were very few enemy 'planes about.

By 10 a.m. the Canadian were in possession of the village of Thelus. Nearby we descended a deep shaft and to our surprise found that it led to a vast underground system of dug-outs and tunnels. So unexpected and rapid had been the advance that the inhabitants were blissfully cooking or awaiting their breakfasts. They offered no resistance. Among them was an artillery colonel, who owned a nicely papered bedroom and a feather bed with sheets. In addition to quantities of maps, documents, and souvenirs of all kinds, there were crates of Vichy water, German sausages, excellent cigars, cigarettes, potatoes, coal, rice and other luxuries, which were by no means wasted. Above ground in the village itself, the troops captured several guns and then continued the attack towards the crest of the Ridge — a distance of about 4,000 yards.

The enemy were now thoroughly demoralized, and by early afternoon we had gained the final objectives. For the first time since the early days of the War, our infantry looked down across the wide panorama of the Douai Plain. It was a sight for the gods ! We could see the German gunners working their guns, then limbering up and moving back. Transport waggons were in full retreat with hundreds of fugitives from the Ridge. There appeared to be nothing at all to prevent our breaking through — nothing, that is, except the weather. So appalling was the state of the battlefield that neither tanks nor cavalry could cross it.

My own battalion, the 1st Royal West Kents, captured nine guns and a most realiste dummy, made up of two old wheels and a log of wood. That night we consolidated our position along the crest and threw out strong posts in front. The cold was intense, and there was no cover of any kind. Rations, which had to be brought up on pack animals and officers' chargers, took nine hours to reach battalion headquarters. The Germans made no attempt to counter-attack ; it was not until the next day that we saw lines of men advancing in extended order across the snow covered Plain. They were dealt with fairly effectively by our artillery, and gave us no trouble. During that day there was a good deal of sniping on our sector, but little else, what shell-fire there was being spasmodic and directed for the most part on fixed spots which we left severely alone.

On the night of the 10th-11th, the 13th Brigade was relieved and rejoined the rest of the Vth Division in reserve. Elation at the victory no doubt helped the exhausted and mud-plastered troops over the half-dozen miles back to Villers-au-Bois. My job having terminated, I avoided this anti-climax by wangling a lift on an ammunition limber returning for fresh supplies.

The Fifth Division in the Great War gives the total captures for the Battle of Arras on April 9th as 15,000 prisoners and 200 guns, and the total losses of the 13th Brigade as 7 officers and 280 other ranks. Of these, 2 officers and 136 other ranks belonged to the 1st Royal West Kents.

So ended the first of many trudges over Vimy Ridge. In the following month the Division was engaged in heavy local fighting in the Douai Plain, its terrible casualties being out of all proportion to the results obtained. The vital necessity of careful preparations before attacks were launched did not seem to be appreciated by those who controlled our destinies. After the lesson of April 9th one may well demand why? For " Vimy " was from first to last an outstanding example of the way to win a battle. As such it should have been regarded. As such it cannot fail to interest future students on the Art of War.

H. U. S. N.

The Late Baroness de Cartier de Marchienne
The Passing of a Very Gracious Lady.

IT is with deep regret that we have to record the death of the Baroness de Cartier de Marchienne, wife of the Belgian Ambassador in London, who passed away at the Embassy on February 18th. She was taken ill during the private visit of King Leopold last December, and never made any marked recovery. Consequently, the end was not unexpected.

The Baroness had many friends and admirers in Brussels, Paris and the United States, and to these, since 1929, she had added a large circle in London, by whom she will be sadly missed. She married Baron de Cartier de Marchienne in 1919, when he was Belgian Ambassador in New York.

An American by birth, but of Scottish ancestry, she had all the best qualities of the cultured American woman — charm, taste and distinction. She was an admirable hostess — a hostess, moreover, who did not confuse entertainment with ostentation. Mr. Kellogg once described her as the most remarkable American woman of her generation. To her guests she was a superb hostess ; to her intimates she was more than that — a lady of high ideals, warm-hearted and generous.

Her duties as the wife of the Belgian Ambassador to the Court of St. James's were regarded by her as of the first importance, and, as a result, the influence of the Embassy in London has considerably strengthened the ties between the two countries. Her interest in the welfare of Belgium was very real, and to a marked extent she identified herself with many activities which were beneficial to the Belgian people.

Baron de Cartier de Marchienne has always been a staunch supporter and friend of the Ypres League, and the sympathy of its members are extended to him in his irreparable loss.

H. B.

Light and Shade at the Front

War's Little Uncertainties.

By an Ex. "R.B."

"THIS isn't the route we took to the line." "No, we've come further; but there's no other track leading from that Anzac battery." "Hullo! There's Corporal P——. Any shacks about here, corporal?" "You don't half look a proper couple o' wonks! Bear left when you come to the petrol tins. Where are the others?" "Coming out in two's and three's " . ...

Sometimes a chance word or incident will switch one's thoughts back vividly to the past, and the writer had proof of this the other evening when, jumping on to a passing omnibus, his eyes lighted on a sign : " Departures every half-hour." A simple announcement, but acting like a spark which fires the train and explodes the charge it blew away in a flash all the dimness which obscured the past and revealed, as if it were yesterday, a whole sequence of incidents and scenes which were familiar in the purposeful times of the War. "Departures every half-hour." ...

THEY CAME IN SIGHT OF ZILLEBEKE

"This is our shack. What about a wash?" "Where, in that shell-crater?" "Yes, it's fresh rain water" ..... The troops were back from the line in the late afternoon, and waited for dinner. " How long are we out for? " " Oh! the usual, I expect ; three or four days." " Well, there's nothing doing before dinner ; after that " — " Stop! Listen! " " Listen what? " " Thought I heard the corporal shouting." " For Orderly Men, I suppose, and " — (the corporal looked in) — " Be ready to move off in half-an-hour!"

The wise old philosophers who composed certain sayings designed to act as a sort of salve did something which often has just the opposite effect. Apply it to the line. " There's nothing so bad but it might be worse " to a man who had just flopped on his back into a puddle? Or, " Swearing won't make things better," to somebody else when, leaving the dug-out without his steel helmet, he struck his napper a tidy crack against the lintel at the top? And, " It's no use grousing," when three days out were cut down to half-an-hour? Very well, but " Orders being orders," the only question was : " Which will come first, bully-stew, or moving-off ? " The corporal again looked in : " Fall in everybody, battle order! " and the troops quickly paraded in the darkness. Some trays of steamed bacon were drawn from the cooker — a dark blotch in the gloom, just a chink of light glowing from its fire — but as it was being eaten : " Get ready! " (into pockets goes the uneaten bacon). " Move to the left in fours ; form fours! " " Left! " " By your right! Quick March! " " Left wheel! "— tramp, tramp, tramp, tramp—" March at ease! " — tramp, tramp, tramp, tramp — " March easy! " and so away back towards the line . . . . . . A short distance only was covered and then : " HALT ! " (" Why are we 'alting ? " " We're staying here ") An order was given and a move was made for the night to the lee of an embankment.

Next day: "Just got it from the cooker; we're moving off after tea." "They moving back?" "Suppose so, to where they were last night," and this proving to be correct . . " In single file ; March easy ! " and the route led off parallel to a light field railway. Flat trucks rattled by bringing wounded from the line with a sprinkling of prisoners in field grey, and then direction turned off across open country. The boom and crash of heavy gunfire was heard a little way off (" Somebody's gettin' the dirt ! " " They are an' all ") and on cresting a slope the leading sections came in sight of Zillebeke, centred in a desolate waste of broken ground and hidden under dense clouds of smoke. By way of contrast, further ahead and clear of the shelling was Zillebeke Lake, its calm waters reflecting as in a mirror the silvery sheen of the afternoon sky. As the smoke clouds rolled slowly along little bright points of light broke through where shrapnel came over and burst, and the lads were weighing up their chances when, quite unexpectedly, the route turned sharp left up a steep incline (" Ere, keep y'r blinking rifle out of a feller's eye ! ") and on to a raised road. This road led away to the south on a curve, but northerly it turned in roughly parallel to Zillebeke, and all the debris had been heaped into a big dump at the side.

Some time ago, at a shop near the site of John Broughton's Academy (of the Noble Art ; colour schemes in black and claret) the writer saw an excellent picture entitled " A Roman Chariot Race." But he must confess that the one place in this best of all worlds where he did not expect to see a close-up of that ancient scene was on a shell-swept road near Zillebeke. Yet so it was. As the troops began to cross at about the centre an empty limber, drawn by two mules, cantered into sight round the southern bend. The driver, who was standing feet well apart and was bending slightly forward, gave one glance around ; then : Crack ! went his whip ; crack ! " Gallop y' blighters ! " Crack ! and on they came at breakneck speed, galloping past and rattling out of sight almost, as it seemed, in the twinkling of an eye. One is apt to regard mules as stolid, slow moving animals, but these moved all right ; were quite frisky, in fact. The sections nipped across the road and down the other side, and keeping Ypres on their left they cut in on to the Menin Road.

Anyone who was not at the Front, but who has seen a rough sea beaten about by contrary winds, may with a little care readily visualise the Ypres Sector of the War. To begin with, keeping to the outline, let one suppose that the motion of the waves has given place to the immovable solidity of mother earth. Then, taking a map, annotate the many places that came into prominence. As a general idea, and to give our enquirer a start, let him mark down the grey tumbled ruins of Ypres itself, and the Menin Road leading E.S.E. to Menin. Set out the approximate extent of line involved in the battles. Attend to that section of line where the allied forces faced a new weapon — poison gas — used on that occasion for the first time in military history. Mark off places like Meteren, Dickebusch, Zillebeke, Wytschaete, Kemmel, Messines and Neuve Église, to name only a few. There is also the tangled trench of Ploeg Straat ; the blackened tree stumps which stood for Sanctuary and Polygon Woods. And he must not overlook Hazebrouck whence the rail carried the troops north to Poperinghe, Vlamertinghe and the like, all close to Ypres.

Having set out the ground one must now conjure up the men that held it ; the divisions that ceaselessly made their way by muddy roads and greasy winding paths to their allotted tasks in the struggle, and later on wended their way back behind the line to rest, and to make good their losses ready for another turn in ; being careful not to omit such branches of the service as the A.S.C., the Engineers and the R.A.M.C. Further, keeping to our simile of a broken sea and as evidence of the fighting, let him call to mind the abundant flotsam and jetsam that lay about drifting or cast up on the ebbs and flows of furious attack, from wrecked batteries down to old barbed wire, rotting equipment and — mortal remains. Just one thing more is needed to round off our enquirer's rough and ready impression of the Salient ; the weather. Mostly cloudy, with persistent rains (which gave rise to copious mud) bleak winds and some ground mist. Destruction held sway there, and the Sergeant Grim, enwrapped in his black shroud, reaped day and night to his full content.

"Now then, you blokes ; what about it ! Let's hear from yer !" . . . (Chorus). "There's a sil-ver lin-ing thro' the dark clouds shin-ing" . . . Readers of these lines who enlivened the march with song and shouted forth the bright refrain ("the silver lining") must feel glad to have been spared to see the sequel to that chapter of world history. Rebuilt cities and villages replace former scenes of carnage. The echoes relay, not the fierce tumult of battle, but waft along the everyday sounds of normal industry. In truth, the worst incidents of the War are becoming softened by the mellowing influence of Time.

LIKE OUTPOSTS OF HOPE

On the Menin Road the sections met a stretcher party turning in for the First Aid Post from the line. Just a ramshackle hut set back a little to the left (leading from Ypres), but as readers may have reflected it stood, as did others in all parts of the line, like an outpost of Hope throwing her bright light shimmering across the dark wastes of the battlefields . . . . "Well, what d'ye think of his hand, Bobby ? " " It's pretty bad, but if it's kept clean and dressed regularly it will get all right," and so it proved. Bobby B—— (an expert at making incubators) was in the R.A.M.C., and he effected a goodly number of excellent cures with quite simple materials.

The route now turned off into an area which was being "searched" by enemy fire, and shells falling near the track ("Look like brinkin' coal-boxes to me") caused a momentary halt. Promptly and boldly the platoon officer gave an order . "Cross over in one's and two's as you can to where you see me standing ! " and away he doubled with two men to a point about twenty-five yards away. Whizzz-zzz-zz Crash ! (just to the right) Whizzz-zzz-zz Crash ! (just to the left) and right on its heels came number three, quite close : WHIZZZZ-ZZZ-ZZZ CRASH ! but before the scattered earth ceased to fall (" Now ! ") a man rose and dashed over pell-mell through the smoke to where the small party stood. Other shells fell wider of the track, and soon the whole platoon was over and leading on in single file not far from its objective. Dusk and the troops arrived at the same time . . . "Paper ! Paper ! Close of play, Paper ! " " Paper, Sir ? " Only memories, after all.   J. EDWARDS.

(*To be continued*).

The German East African Campaign

By F. E. Baily *(late Lieut., R.A.S.C.)*

I HAVE never been able to understand why the German East African Campaign was continued after Dar-es-Salaam, the railway and the remaining ports such as Lindi and Kilwa had been captured. From that point onwards there is nothing the Germans could have done except wander about in the hinterland, or possibly occupy Portuguese East Africa, which after all was the affair of the Portuguese, locally known as " our gallant allies."

I don't think the Germans would have got much change out of Rhodesia, as one of the toughest outfits with the B.E.A.E.F. were what was left of the Rhodesian Mounted Rifles.

I was only a subaltern, and what does a subaltern know about anything? But as there were said to be a hundred and fifteen generals mixed up in our side of the affair, and in East Africa one drew an extra allowance called colonial allowance, that may have had something to do with it. Alternatively, seeing that a number of South African troops were engaged, and in my time the G.O.C., General van de Venter, was a South African, there may have been some political motive.

My first-hand knowledge dates from June, 1917, previous to which there had been an incredible amount of bungling, for example the disastrous attack on Tanga and the heavy loss over the capture of Dar-es-Salaam. The Navy could have shelled the place flat, but all they did was take the roof off the Governor's palace and drop a shell into the railway station as a kind of awful warning. Thereafter troops were sent off in boats to take the place, and suffered severely from machine gun fire from the very excellent series of trenches which the Germans had dug along the coast.

It is one of the major bits of bad luck which were encountered during the war that a few days before it broke out Colonel von Lettow Vorbeck landed at Dar-es-Salaam. He was a most experienced African soldier, and one of the most successful commanders in the war. The Governor of German East Africa, von Schnee, was all for surrendering to what he considered the overwhelming British naval forces, but von Lettow insisted on taking over the defence, and for about four years kept a large British army playing a game of tag in which he was always the winner.

I think von Lettow would still be carrying on operations if the war had not been decided on the Western Front. He surrendered on the Rhodesian border after having been chased all through what was then German East Africa and is now Tanganyika Territory to the Portuguese border, which he crossed only to begin the same game all over again in Portuguese East Africa.

The Portuguese kindly placed Port Amelia, which is one of the most magnificent harbours in the world, at our disposal, and we started once more in Portuguese East Africa, finally chasing the Germans up to the Rhodesian border where they surrendered in November, 1918.

I was engaged in the operations which took place on our advance from Kilwa to the river Rovuma, which marks the boundary between Tanganyika Territory and Portuguese East Africa. These operations began in the autumn of 1917 and continued till the following rainy season, though I was knocked out of them at Christmas by a bad attack of malaria, and the general hardships of the campaign.

At that time the only white troops in the country were the R.A., R.E., R.E. Signals (now the Royal Corps of Signals), my own corps, the A.S.C. (now the R.A.S.C.), and the R.A.M.C. except the remains of the 25th Fusiliers (Legion of Frontiersmen) under their famous C.O., Colonel Driscoll. It had been found impossible to keep white infantry in the field owing to the climate, and transport difficulties which prevented the necessary comforts for white infantry to be taken up to the front line. Thus apart from these specialist troops the war was being carried on by the King's African Rifles, greatly expanded on a war footing, the Nigerian Brigade from West Africa, and a large contingent of Indian troops.

I will take it upon myself to say quite frankly that the Indian troops were no good. They may function very well in their own country, but in a strange country and strange surroundings they become homesick and miserable. Possibly the Indian troops I knew were war-time levies, but they belonged to various famous Indian regiments. No names, no pack drill. The only unit which impressed me was the 29th Baluchis, a very military-looking regiment.

I can only speak of the advance to the Portuguese border from my own point of view — that of a convoy officer running mechanical transport, but this may be mildly interesting from the light that it throws on the Italian Campaign in Abyssinia, where the country and the climate are similar, and the transport difficulties similar also.

A convoy consisted of about thirty Model T Ford lorries, and the Italians in Abyssinia are very unlucky in that this inestimable vehicle is no longer produced. It was of 24 h.p. rating, and very light, so that it had a high power-to-weight ratio. Owing to the peculiar transmission system almost any fool could be taught to drive it in a quarter of an hour.

It had no orthodox gear box, and the only wear and tear was on the transmission bands, which could be re-lined quite simply, and there were only two forward speeds first and top, first being very low. Thus, in the hands of an experienced driver, a Model T Ford could be made almost to climb trees.

Except battalion transport in the form of native carriers, there was no other transport but the M.T., for animal transport such as the Italians are employing could not be kept in the field on account of the tsetse fly. This insect is harmless to human beings (except when it is infected with sleeping sickness, which only occurs in certain districts near the Great Lakes), but deadly to animals, so that even donkey transport could not survive. The veterinary officers used to estimate the life of a horse on active service in Tanganyika Territory at three weeks.

The only railway consisted of a few miles of tramway line built from Lindi by a Sapper Colonel, so that transport from the Base to the front line consisted entirely of M.T. vehicles. These when I took over my convoy resembled scrap-iron, owing to having been a long time on active service.

The daily trip for a convoy was supposed to be fifty miles out and back, but as lorries were not fitted with speedometers, I cannot verify this, and as there were no maps of the country one could not measure the distance on a map. Convoys were supposed to pull out at 5 a.m., which meant waking up the personnel at 4 a.m., so that they could get some breakfast, start their engines, and pull out to the supply dump in order to load up.

Nobody who did not experience it can imagine the wear and tear of that campaign on convoy officers, and drivers, because they were running all day, seven days a week, until they went into hospital, and there was never a day off. Consequently, one seldom took out the same lot of drivers two days running, as several had invariably gone sick with malaria or dysentery overnight.

Officially, there was supposed to be a driver and his mate on a lorry, but the shortage of personnel prohibited this, and we only had one driver per lorry. Thus there often occurred the interesting problem of what to do when Driver Smith in the heat of the day suddenly developed a temperature of anything up to 104 deg., and a pulse that rattled like a machine gun, while he shivered from head to foot at the same time. One cannot tow a lorry with no one to steer it, and a man in the throes of a sudden acute attack of malaria is in no condition to drive.

The health of the men was greatly affected by the fact that they had no comforts whatever at any time, except when they went into hospital. It was a war of continual movement, they slept on their lorries, and there were no cooks or cook-houses, or camps within the meaning of the act. They drew their rations from a supply dump, and did any cooking there was to be done themselves, as best they could, but a man who has been driving a lorry in an equatorial climate from 5 a.m. till 11 or 12 p.m., with no interval for rest except when his lorry is being off-loaded, is far too exhausted to bother about cooking. Thus they fed very badly, became covered with veldt sores, and deteriorated very rapidly.

It was a little easier for a convoy officer to keep fit because he was allowed a native servant, but the ideas on cookery and cleanliness of a fifteen or sixteen year old African boy are rudimentary, and as officers drew exactly the same rations as their men, there

INDIAN ARMY TRANSPORT IN G.E.A.

being nothing else obtainable, the boy did not have much scope for his cooking operations.

At remote intervals when one got far enough down the line one could buy supplies from a Field Force Canteen run by the Y.M.C.A., but these didn't last long enough to make much difference.

The convoy officer aroused his exhausted men at 4 a.m., and they scratched up what breakfast they could, and started the engines of the Ford lorries. This usually meant a heart-breaking struggle, and we considered ourselves lucky if we could get one engine started and start the other twenty-nine by towing them.

The convoy then lined up at the supply dump, engaging in a vicious dog-fight with every other convoy to get there first and be loaded up first. Loading was done by the supply dump native boys, who moved with incredible slowness while a *nyempara* (headman), chanted a running count of the packages put on each lorry, thus: *moja, mbili, tatu,* etc., which is Swahili for one, two, three. This was done in a sing-song rather resembling a sea-shanty.

The convoy was finally loaded up, after a bitter controversy between the convoy officer and the supply officer. All the supply officer wanted to do was to shove the supplies indented for on the convoy and get them out of his sight. The convoy officer had very strong views as to how much should be put on each lorry, partly because he had to get it over the ground, and partly because the lorry bodies were in such a ram-shackle state that if they were over-loaded everything fell off. Finally, the convoy officer was requested to sign for the lift of the convoy.

I don't know whether this word " lift " was used in any other theatre of war, and I have never heard it anywhere except in Tanganyika. With us the lift of a convoy was the total amount it could carry. A Ford lorry was supposed to carry five hundred pounds in weight, so that the lift of a convoy of thirty Ford lorries would be 15,000 pounds.

As everyone knows, one of the great arts of war as far as an officer is concerned, is a capacity to sign for anything in the world without a second thought, for obviously a convoy officer could not possibly check what was put on his convoy, since to do so would have taken him all day.

The convoy then moved off. The lucky convoy officer had received some vague instructions that he was to rendezvous with Number 2 Column at say Nidisi Chini. He never had the faintest idea of the situation of this place, and there were no maps to help him, so he could only take the track leading from the supply dump in the direction indicated, and follow his nose, hoping for the best. Nidisi Chini might be a native village of some sort, or merely a temporary camp of grass huts, and as likely as not when he reached it he would find the whole place deserted, and possibly a bit of paper tied to a tree with the legend " Number 2 Column has gone this way." If the luck was against him, the bit of paper would have come adrift from the tree, and then supposing the track forked he did a little boy-scout stuff, trying to gather from the surface of the track which way Number 2 Column had gone.

He had also to decide whether to follow it or not, because his orders were to rendezvous at Nidisi Chini, and orders are supposed to be orders. If he went on he must take various factors into consideration: (*a*) whether he had enough petrol to make the additional journey and return to re-filling point ; (*b*) whether he would find any water for his radiators ; (*c*) as the further distance covered by the Column was incalculable, whether he would be able to reach it and return in time to pull out next morning because if not, some column would go on half rations ; and (*d*) whether the track was more or less safe or whether there was a chance of an enemy patrol cutting back and lying up for the convoy.

M.T. personnel and vehicles were so scarce that no unjustifiable risks of having a convoy cut up could be undertaken. Moreover, if attacked, a convoy was perfectly defenceless, because although every man had some sort of rifle lying about somewhere in his lorry, it was practically unusable from dust, he might or might not have any cartridges, and in any case probably he had never fired a rifle in his life.

Officially, the convoy officer was supposed to lead the convoy in case it fell into an ambush, when he was supposed to do goodness knows what, but unless I had definite warning of enemy patrols being about I always went at the tail of the convoy in order to pick up the breakdowns. Few if any of the men had any mechanical knowledge, or tools, and so it meant my tackling all the breakdowns myself.

The number of breakdowns one might have in a day was only limited by the number of vehicles in a convoy. The so-called roads were merely the soil of Africa exposed when the Road Corps had cut down sufficient trees to make a path through the bush. Consequently after a couple of days running of convoys over them they became a mass of enormous pot-holes. As the Road Corps made a bee-line from X to Y without troubling about the topography one might find two or three dry river beds with banks of varying steepness to be tackled on a day's run, and one in three gradients up which it would be necessary to man-handle every lorry, because they could not climb under their own power.

There were also dizzy hairpin bends on young mountains with precipices yawning for the unlucky driver who lost his nerve, and it invariably happened that on one of the hairpin turns on one of these mountain tracks, with a sheer wall on one side and a precipice on the other, one met a returning convoy head-on. The two convoy officers would then argue the point as to which should reverse, until the tracks became wide enough to let the other pass by.

It was the incredible labour of doing long distances every day of the week under these appalling conditions that laid out M.T. personnel and filled the hospitals with them. By the time the convoy had struggled with the difficulties of the road from 5.30 a.m. till mid-day, practically carrying its vehicles over the bad spots, with an equatorial sun beating down on the convoy officer and his men, everyone's temper was in shreds, and any of my troops could have murdered me with pleasure, and I could have murdered them with equal pleasure.

MOTOR TRANSPORT IN G.E.A. The vehicle on left is an Autocar with engine under the driver's feet and he sat on the ignition It had a quadrant gear change which no one could ever work silently.

It was the most odd kind of war in which one could possibly have been engaged. A convoy officer was a kind of bandit chief who never saw any of his superiors, for they remained at re-filling point and he was out on the road all day and by the time he returned they were fast asleep in bed, except the S.M.T.O.'s sergeant-major who came round at midnight to give the weary convoy officer his instructions for the morrow.

There was no question of criming a man in order to preserve discipline, because no punishment available was half so bad as his daily job of driving a lorry in a convoy. Thus one maintained discipline by tackling rather more work than anybody else on the convoy, shoving with the men when any lorry needed shoving up a hill, and a flow of language. They saw that the officer was no better off than they were, made the best of a bad job, and got on with it, except a minority of lead-swingers who fortunately managed to get themselves into hospital after a couple of days on convoy running. We were well rid of them, as they were no use on the road.

I managed to stick six months of this, but it was a pretty long life for a convoy officer, and many people cracked up sooner.

The lot of the M.T. in Tanganyika was additionally hard since the R.A.M.C. were forbidden to invalid them to South Africa unless it was a matter of life or death. Once he had escaped from the Tanganyika show any officer or man would move heaven and earth not to be sent back there.

However, after being invalided initially to Nairobi, one of the most charming places in the world, I was eventually invalided to South Africa, where a medical board took a gloomy view of me and invalided me home.

My return coincided more or less with the end of the war, and that is the end of the story.

Up Ypres Way!

The Newfoundlanders' Impressions of the Salient.

By Captain L. C. Murphy, *Royal Newfoundland Regiment.*

IT was after that tragic attack at Beaumont Hamel on the Somme — with its terrible toll — that the First Newfoundland Regiment, moved, with the 29th Division, to the Salient ; the remnants of a fine, sturdy Colonial Battalion which had already made good its name in the Gallipoli Adventure.

To us, " Ypres " was already an historic name. It conjured up pictures of popular lined roads, of little red roofed cottages nestling in picturesque settings ; of magnificent buildings, steeped in romance. Stories had reached us of the excellent work of our Canadian Cousins ; of a ghastly gas attack, and of the stern fighting of our British troops and our gallant Belgian allies.

We seemed to move in an atmosphere where voices whispered demands for reverance, and the whole sector breathed of a place —
" . . . . where the Poppies lighted,
The fragrant fields with gleams of flaming red."

* * * * * *

Our Battalion Headquarters were located in a cellar opposite the Barracks ; "A" Company was at the Ramparts, and nearby we saw the Moat where once the graceful swans disported themselves. " D " Company was at the Horn-works, a place honey-combed with innumerable subterranean passages, where the platoons slept on wire-covered beds. "C" Company was in the ruins of the Old School — a picturesque memorial to the German shelling.

Our " H.Q." was like a scene from Bairnsfather. The front wall of the brick building had been ripped away, and the rooms and contents exposed to view. Twisted beds, a large bath-tub, the remains of a stove — all told their story. Our cooker took up its place under a camouflage screen left behind by a thoughtful Artillery Officer, and empty sand-bags, sewn together, made temporary partitions.

A little winding path, along which hung signalling wires, led you through the grounds of the " White Chateau," where you passed three wooden crosses. In a quiet corner was the private Oratory, the windows were shattered and the roof gone, but the altar was intact, and a large statue of the crucified Saviour lay on the grass. Here, one day, the air was filled with joyous melody, as a lark sang, and the slow-drifting clouds moved on, for this was in September, 1916, and the sector was quiet.

* * * * * *

The road from Ypres had its memories, too, as had the adjoining country. We were once quartered at Elverdinghe and Vlamertinghe, while " L4 " and " L8 " bore the handiwork of the Newfoundlanders, who had constructed new trenches there, and re-modelled and improved " strong-points." The latter was accomplished without the supervision of the Engineers, and was not done without danger, as a German observation balloon once spotted us, and brought down a hail of shrapnel on the fillers of sand-bags and drainage experts.

* * * * * *

Our short stay at Poperinghe, however, fully compensated us for any of the more hazardous experiences near the Menin Gate, Hell Fire Corner or Railway Wood.

Our Billets at " Pop " were fairly comfortable, and some of us found refuge in the home of a Curé, who was serving with the Belgian Force. One room was particularly interesting, for behind the pictures on the plaster walls, we found sketches and cartoons, which were pleasant reminders of the Artists' Rifles, and of other units which had spent a brief period of rest before going into the line and into action, from which very few returned.

Across the Square was " La Poupée," where Marie Louise and her little Sister, " Ginger," were pleasant hostesses. Few officers passed the Grand Place without dining there, to enjoy the quaint repartee of these Belgian lasses, and tap out some of the revue songs on the little piano.

* * * * * *

These are only a few impressions of some of our memories of the Ypres we used to know ; but these are of 1916. It was nearly two years later that the flood of battle swept us across the Salient again, and the heavy fighting took us once more to Flanders.

Out of all the wrack of war, however, through the poignancy and sad thoughts, of the terrible conflict — there are a few places which stand out clearly limned through our vista of these years.

Included in the sectors over which we have followed the trail of the Caribou, we linger, thoughtfully and reverently, at one spot — YPRES.

There — in some well-ordered rows the crosses stand embowered in dainty blooms ; there, in tiny plots of hallowed earth, once showered with blood and tears, now sleep soundly the dead of many of our Newfoundland, Imperial and Overseas Colonial Forces.

HOTEL
Splendid & Britannique
YPRES

GRANDE PLACE. Opposite Cloth Hall.

LEADING HOTEL FOR COMFORT AND QUALITY, AND PATRONIZED BY THE YPRES LEAGUE.

COMPLETELY RENOVATED.

RUNNING WATER. BATHROOMS.

MODERATE TERMS.   GARAGE.

Proprietor—Life Member, Ypres League.

YPRES
Skindles Hotel

(Opposite the Station)

Proprietor—Life Member, Ypres League

Branch at Poperinghe

(close to Talbot House)

League Secretary's Notes

DEAR READERS,

Each year is memorable to all of us in some form or another, either individaully or collectively, but 1936 will be particularly remembered for the sadness with which the year commenced by the death of our graciously beloved head of the British Empire, King George V, whose passing is something more than a collective sorrow to the Great War generation. Thousands of ex-service men and women were privileged during those fateful years 1914-1918 to come in direct contact with the late King, many indeed being accorded the honour of speaking personally with him either in training camps at home, on service at the Front, in hospitals, or at investitures, and we shall always treasure his courteous regard and the kindly and homely atmosphere of encouragement His Majesty conveyed irrespective of rank or position we may have held as members of his services. Many of us, therefore, can claim his loss as a personal as well as a collective bereavement, and we of the Ypres League deeply lament the death of our gracious Patron-in-Chief. In respectful condolence and in humble sympathy with His Majesty, Queen Mary, and members of the Royal family, we issued instructions to our Branches requesting them to postpone all official social functions until after the period of Court Mourning.

Our thanks are extended to the respective Committees for their sympathetic response and loyal compliance in effecting the cancellation of arrangements already made for their Annual Re-union Dinners.

First of the many messages of sympathy received at headquarters were those from the 13th Belgian Field Artillery at Liége, and the Military Corps of Interpreters, Antwerp, both units of which served under the command of the British Army in Belgium, many of their old comrades having enrolled as members of the Ypres League. We desire, through these columns, to repeat our expression of gratitude to the two mentioned Associations, and to all others who have similarly shown their sentiments in such true form.

COLLECTION OF TIN-FOIL.

We wish to notify our members that no further collections are now required, and we would like to express our very sincere thanks to those who so kindly contributed.

The municipality of Ypres, at a ceremony on February 17th last which was attended by Belgian, British, and French ex-Service men, changed the name of the Grand Place, which will henceforth be known as the Place Roi Albert.

MODELS OF DEMARCATION STONE.

Plaster models of the Demarcation Stone can be supplied from Head Office.

All members are aware that 240 granite demarcation stones stretch from the Swiss border to the sea, marking the extreme line of advance of the German invasion.

The model, which is 6 inches in height, may be used for a paperweight or as an ornament. Price 5s., post free in United Kingdom. Applications to the Secretary, Ypres League.

YPRES LEAGUE TIE.

Dark shade of cornflower blue relieved by a narrow gold stripe. In good quality silk.

Price 3/6d., post free.

Obtainable from Secretary, Ypres League, 20, Orchard Street, London, W.1.

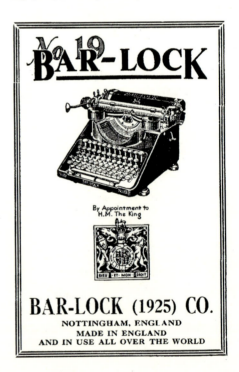

BAR-LOCK (1925) CO.
NOTTINGHAM, ENGLAND
MADE IN ENGLAND
AND IN USE ALL OVER THE WORLD

EMBROIDERED BADGES.

These badges which can be suitably worn on pockets of sports jackets may be supplied on application to the Secretary, Ypres League, 20, Orchard Street, London, W.1. Price 4/- post free.

YPRES LEAGUE BADGE.

The design of the badge—a lion guarding a portcullis gate—represents the British Army defending the Salient, which was the gate to the Channel Ports.

The badge, herewith reproduced, is brilliantly enamelled with silver finish. Price 2s., post free 2s. 1½d. (pin or stud, whichever is desired).

Obtainable from Secretary, Ypres League, 20, Orchard Street, London, W.1.

PHOTOGRAPHS OF WAR GRAVES.

The Ypres League has made arrangements whereby it is able to supply photographs (negative, and one print, postcard size, unmounted) of graves situated in the Ypres Salient, and in the Hazebrouck and Armentieres areas, at the price of 10s. each.

All applications for photographs should be sent to the Secretary, together with remittance, giving the regimental particulars of the soldier, name of cemetery, and number of plot, row and grave.

OLD WELL-KNOWN SPOTS IN NEW GUISE.

The following prints, size 4¼ x 2¼, recently taken of famous spots in the Ypres Salient, and which may be of great interest to our readers, are on sale at headquarters, price 4d. each, post free 5d.

- Poelcapelle Church.
- Ramparts at the Lille Gate.
- Hell Fire Corner, Left.
- Hell Fire Corner, Right.
- Shrapnel Corner.
- Transport Farm Cemetery.
- Transport Farm Corner.
- Zillebeke Lake.
- Hill 62, Canadian Memorial.
- Hooge from Zouave Wood.
- Hooge Crater Cemetery.
- Clapham Junction.
- Stirling Castle.
- Gheluvelt Church.
- Cheddar Villa Dressing Station.
- Vancouver Cross Roads.
- Canadian Memorial: Vancouver Cross Roads.
- Hyde Park Corner. (Memorial.)
- Wulverghem.
- Messines Church.
- Potsdam Redoubt at Corner Cott.

Obtainable from Secretary, Ypres League, 20, Orchard Street, London, W.1.

WREATHS.

Arrangements are made by the Ypres League to place wreaths for relatives on the graves of British soldiers situated in France and Belgium at the following times of the year:—

EASTER, ARMISTICE DAY, CHRISTMAS

The wreaths may be composed of natural flowers, laurel, or holly, and can be bought at the following prices—12s. 6d., 15s. 6d., and 20s., according to the size and quality of the wreath.

THE BRITISH TOURING SERVICE

Manager—Mr. P. VYNER

Representative and Life Member, Ypres League

**10, Station Square
ARRAS
(P.-de-C.) France**

Cars for Hire, with British Driver Guides   Tours Arranged

Mr. Will R. Bird, of 36, Clarence Street, Amherst, Nova Scotia, is making a collection of Canadian Expeditionary Force cap badges and willing to purchase, or exchange C.E.F. for Imperial or other cap badges. Further, Mr. Bird would be agreeable to exchange one copy of the last hundred copies of his book "The Communication Trench," for any four C.E.F., or any six Imperial cap badges.

If any of our readers are interested will they very kindly communicate direct with Mr. Bird.

1936 Recruiting Competition

IN view of the continued popularity of the recruiting competition we have great pleasure to announce that **A FURTHER PRIZE OF £5** will be awarded this year as follows :—

TO THE BRANCH RECRUITING THE GREATEST NUMBER OF NEW MEMBERS IN 1936.

All membership forms completed must be received at headquarters bearing on the top left-hand corner the name of the branch responsible for the recruitment.

Branch Notes.

LONDON COUNTY COMMITTEE.

Children's Christmas Party.

How time rolls on ! Once again the London County Committee has pleasure to report that a very successful Children's Christmas Party was held on Saturday, January 4th, when approximately 150 children and a number of adult friends were present.

The large Hall of the Westminster City School was kindly placed at our disposal and gaily decorated with flags in honour of the occasion : this involved some gymnastic feats on the part of several members of the Committee, but there were no casualties !

At 4 p.m. the children sat down to enjoy a substantial tea and they were well looked after by the adults who turned themselves into most efficient "mess orderlies," after which the young guests joined heartily in a number of popular songs and choruses conducted by Captain H. D. Peabody, D.C.M. This served a double purpose of aiding digestion and giving time for Mr. Mander, the conjurer, to prepare his gadgets. The conjuring tricks held the youngsters spell-bound for an hour, and the fact that some of the latter were invited to the platform to assist in the proceedings, added greatly to the interest and amusement of the entertainment. A ventriloquist then took charge with a clever and witty back-chat between the " doll " and his master, and caused roars of merriment, the climax being reached when the " doll " led the company in a good old children's song, " Quack, quack, quack." The Hall was then turned into a playground, and the children were able to let themselves go in such old favourites as " Musical Chairs," " Musical Bumps," and other games dear to the hearts of youth, the necessary music being skilfully provided at the piano by Mrs. Furner. Bonbons were then distributed, also the numbered tickets entitling each child to a gift from the beautifully illuminated Christmas Tree.

We were glad to welcome the esteemed Chairman of the London County Committee, Major E. Montague Jones, O.B.E., T.D., who, after speaking a few kindly words to the children, called upon our old friend, Father Christmas, to come forward and distribute the gifts. Captain Christmas — as you were ! Father Peabody appeared in appropriate costume, and following a few words to the children on the Junior Branch of the League. proceeded with the work in hand until each child had received either a toy or some useful article. The whole company now gathered for " Auld Lang Syne " followed by the National Anthem which terminated another exceedingly happy Children's Party.

It is a great privilege to take part in this annual function, and to all those who helped in any way to make the event such a success, the London County Committee tenders its most hearty and grateful thanks. To those who lent the Hall, to those who decorated it, to those who directed the games and especially to that devoted band of ladies who " kept the home fires burning " in the kitchen below stairs in order to provide the feast, we say again, thank you !

J. W. F.

INFORMAL GATHERINGS.

Informal Gatherings.

At the 16th of January meeting we were honoured by a visit from Brig.-General A. Burt, C.M.G., D.S.O., who gave a thrilling discourse on the Riff Spanish War, which was followed keenly by the goodly muster present. Also that evening we had pleasure to welcome Mrs. Horsburgh and Colonel Cranston of the Officers' Association who both gave short interesting talks.

Our gratitude is extended to "The St. Dunstan's Singers" who generously provided an excellent entertainment under the personal direction of Miss E. McCall on the occasion of our February Informal.

It is our pleasure to announce that Mr. F. W. Stevenson has been co-opted to fill the vacancy on the Branch Committee caused by the unavoidable resignation of Mr. A. R. Ford.

We greatly regret to announce the death of Mr. L. H. Tunbridge who was one of our keenest workers. The funeral was attended by members of the London Committee and a wreath was composed of white chrysanthemums and cornflowers.

LONDON COUNTY COMMITTEE

Informal Gatherings

These will be held at the

BEDFORD HEAD HOTEL,
Maiden Lane, Strand, W.C.2

on

THURSDAY, APRIL 16th, 1936.
Lantern Talk by :
Captain H. D. PEABODY, D.C.M.

THURSDAY, MAY 21st, 1936.
Talk by Mr. W. J. MORRISON.

THURSDAY, JUNE 18th, 1936.
Programme to be arranged.

From 7.30 to 10 p.m.

Your support is solicited in order to make these Gatherings a success. Will you come along and bring a friend with you?

Particulars will be sent to any friend on the name and address being supplied, and members are urged to help all they can in this direction.

Ladies cordially invited.

THE ANNUAL MEETING

of the

LONDON COUNTY COMMITTEE

will take place on

MAY 22nd, 1936

at the

YPRES LEAGUE OFFICES
20, Orchard Street,
Portman Square, W.1.

at 7.30 p.m.

The business will be to receive the Report of the London County Committee for the past year and to elect the Committee for the ensuing year. Members are earnestly requested to attend, and the Committee will be glad to receive any suggestions to further the interests of the League in the London area. Should any members have proposals to make, will they please forward them to the Hon. Secretary, London County Committee, Ypres League, at 20, Orchard Street, W.1., by May 15th.

KENYA BRANCH.

The last edition of the "Ypres Times" gave particulars and reproduction of a wreath placed on the Nairobi Cenotaph on Armistice Day, 1935, and we are now able to record the names of those generous subscribers to whom we desire to express our renewed thanks : Brig.-General A. R. Wainwright, D.S.O., M.C., Major W. N. Mackenzie ; Lieut.-Colonel G. J. Henderson ; Major G. Clauder, D.S.O., M.C. ; Mr. Sydney Carlier, Mrs. Clause, Miss Heather Henderson, Miss Josephine Henderson, and Mr. B. O. Lea.

COLCHESTER BRANCH.

The Colchester Branch Committee were represented at a special service at St. Peter's Church, Colchester, on Tuesday, January 28th, 1936, held in commemoration of His late Majesty King George, and among the large representative assembly were : The Right Worshipful The Mayor, The Aldermen, Councillors and Corporate Officers of the Borough of Colchester.

Ypres League Travel Bureau

CONDUCTED PILGRIMAGES FOR 1936

EASTER (April 11th—14th, Saturday to Tuesday) YPRES (Day route via Ostend).

WHITSUNTIDE (May 30th—June 2nd, Saturday to Tuesday) (Day route via Ostend).

AUGUST BANK HOLIDAY (August 1st—4th, Saturday to Tuesday) (Two separate pilgrimages):

    YPRES (Day route via Ostend).

    ARRAS (Day route via Boulogne).

SEPTEMBER (September 19th—22nd, Saturday to Tuesday) YPRES (Day route via Ostend).

    YPRES. *Cost.* London to Ypres return via Ostend, with full board and best available accommodation (three nights) including taxes and gratuities at hotel.

        Second Class Train (1st Class Boat) ... £4 18 11
        Second Class Train and Boat £4 10 5
        Third Class Train (1st Class Boat) £4 5 0
        Third Class Train and Boat £3 16 6

    ARRAS. *Cost.* London to Arras return via Boulogne, with full board and best available accommodation (three nights) including taxes and gratuities at hotel.

        Second Class Train (1st Class Boat) ... £6 18 10
        Second Class Train and Boat £6 8 10
        Third Class Train (1st Class Boat) £6 0 11
        Third Class Train and Boat £5 8 11

The above quotations do not include meals on the journey or excursions on the continent.

(Battlefield tours arranged by the Conductor at Ypres or Arras to suit the requirements of the party at moderate charges).

Prospectuses will be gladly forwarded on application to The Secretary, Ypres League, 20, Orchard Street, London, W.1.

INDEPENDENT TRAVEL.

To those contemplating individual travel, our Travel Department would be pleased to furnish information on all matters connected with trips to any part of the Old Western Front Battlefields.

Apply to Secretary, Ypres League, 20, Orchard Street, London, W.1, for the Ypres League Travel Guide for 1936.

Branches and Corresponding Members

BRANCHES.

LONDON	Hon. Secretary to the London County Committee : J. Boughey, 20, Orchard Street, London, W.1.
	E. LONDON DISTRICT—L. A. Weller, 26, Lambourne Gardens, Hornchurch, Essex.
	TOTTENHAM AND EDMONTON DISTRICT—E, Glover, 191, Landowne Road, Tottenham, N.17.
	H. Carey, 373, Sydenham Road, S.E.26.
COLCHESTER	H. Snow (Hon. Sec.), 9, Church Street.
	W. H. Taylor (Pilgrimage Hon. Sec,), 64, High Street.
LIVERPOOL	Captain A. M. Webster, Blundellsands.
PURLEY	Major Graham Carr, D.S.O., M.C., 112-114, High Street.
SHEFFIELD	Captain J Wilkinson, "Holmfield," Bents Drive.
BELGIUM	Capt. P. D. Parminter, 19, Rue Surmont de Volsberghe, Ypres.
CANADA	Ed. Kingsland, P.O. Box 83, Magog, Quebec.
SOUTH AFRICA	L. G. Shuter, Church Street, Pietermaritzburg,
KENYA	C. H. Slater, P.O. Box 403, Nairobi.
AMERICA	Representative : Captain R. Henderson-Bland, 110 West 57th Street, New York City.

CORRESPONDING MEMBERS.

GREAT BRITAIN.

ABERYSTWYTH	T. O. Thomas, 5, Smithfield Road.
ASHTON-UNDER-LYNE	G. D. Stuart, "Woodlands,", Thronfield Grove, Arundel Street.
BANBURY	Captain C. W. Fowke, Yew Tree House, King's Sutton.
BIRMINGHAM	Mrs. Hill, 191, Cattell Road, Small Heath.
	John Burman, "Westbrook," Solihull Road, Shirley.
BOURNEMOUTH	H. L. Pasmore, 40, Morley Road, Boscombe Park.
BRISTOL	W. S. Hook, "Wytschaete" Redland Court Road.
BROADSTAIRS	C. E. King, 6, Norman Road, St. Peters, Broadstairs.
	Mrs. Briggs, North Foreland House.
CHATHAM	W. N. Channon, 22, Keyes Avenue.
CHESTERFIELD	Major A. W. Shea, 14, Cross Street.
CONGLETON	Mr. H. Dart, 61, The Crescent.
DARLINGTON	D. S. Vigo, 125, Dorset Road, Bexhill-on-Sea.
DERBY	T. Jakeman, 10, Graham Street.
DORRINGTON (Salop)	Captain G. D. S. Parker, Frodesley Rectory.
EXETER	Captain E. Jenkin, 25, Queen Street.
HERNE BAY	Captain E. Clarke Williams, F.S.A.A., "Conway," Station Road.
HOVE	Captain G. W. J. Cole, 2, Westbourne Terrace, Kingsway.
LEICESTER	W. C. Dunford, 343, Aylestone Road.
LINCOLN	E. Swaine, 79, West Parade.
LLANWRST	A. C. Tomlinson, M.A., Bod Estyn.
LOUGHTON	Capt. O. G. Johnson, M.A., Loughton School.
MATLOCK (Derby)	Miss Dickinson, Beechwood.
MELROSE	Mrs. Lindesay Kelsall, Darnlee.
NEW BRIGHTON (Cheshire)	E. F. Williams, 5, Waterloo Road.
NEW MILTON	W. H. Lunn, "Greycot," Albert Road.

NOTTINGHAM ...	E. V. Brown, 3, Eldon Chambers, Wheeler Gate.
ST. HELENS (Lancs.)	John Orford, 124, Knowsley Road.
SHREWSBURY ...	Major-General Sir John Headlam, K.B.E., C.B., D.S.O., Cruck Meole House, Hanwood.
TIVERTON (Devon)	Mr. W. H. Duncan Arthur, Surveyor's Office, Town Hall.
WELSHPOOL ...	Mr. E. Wilson, Coedway, Ford, Salop.

DOMINIONS AND FOREIGN COUNTRIES.

AUSTRALIA ...	Messrs. C. H. Green, and George Lawson, Essex House, (Opposite Anzac Square) Brisbane, Queensland.
	R. A. Baldwin, c/o Government Savings Bank of N.S.W., Martin Place, Sydney.
	Mr. W. Cloves, Box 1296, G.P.O., Adelaide.
BELGIUM ...	Sister Marguerite, Sacré Coeur, Ypres.
CANADA ...	Brig.-General V. W. Odlum, C.B., C.M.G., D.S.O., 2530, Point Grey Road, Vancouver.
	V. A. Bowes, 326, 40th Avenue West, Calgary, Alberta.
	W. Constable F. Grece, St. Hilaire Station, Ronville County, Quebec.
CEYLON ...	Captain F. R. G. Webb, M.C., Irrigation Bungalow, Kalmunai, E.P.
EGYPT ...	L. B. S. Larkins, The Residency, Cairo.
INDIA ...	Lieut.-Quartermaster G. Smith, Queen's Bays, Sialkot, India.
IRELAND ...	Miss A. K. Jackson, Cloneyhurke House, Portarlington.
NEW ZEALAND ...	Captain W. U. Gibb, Ava Lodge, Puhinui Road, Papatoetoe, Auckland
	S. E. Beattie, P.O. Box 11, Otaki Railway, Wellington.
SOUTH AFRICA ...	H. L. Versfield, c/o Cape Explosives Works Ltd., 150, St. Georges Street, Cape Town.
SPAIN ...	Captain P. W. Burgess, Calle de Zurbano 29, Madrid.
U.S.A. ...	Captain Henry Maslin, 942, President Street, Brooklyn, New York.
	L. E. P. Foot, 20, Gillett Street, Hartford, Conn, U.S.A.
	A. P. Forward, 449, East 80th Street, New York.
	J. W. Freebody, 945, McBride Avenue, Los Angeles.
NOVA SCOTIA ...	Will R. Bird, 35, Clarence Street, Amherst.

Membership of the League

This is open to all who served in the Salient, and to all those whose relatives or friends died there, in order that they may have a record of that service for themselves and their descendants, and belong to the comradeship of men and women who understand and remember all that Ypres meant in suffering and endurance.

Life membership, £2 10s.

Annual members, 5s.

Do not let the fact of your not having served in the Salient deter you from joining the Ypres League. Those who have neither fought in the Salient nor lost relatives there, but who are in sympathy with the objects of the Ypres League, are admitted to its fellowship, but are not given scroll certificates.

There is a Junior Division for children whose relatives served in the Salient. It is open also to others to whom our objects appeal.

Annual subscription 1s. up to the age of 18, after which they can become ordinary members of the League.

THE YPRES LEAGUE (INCORPORATED)
20, Orchard Street, Portman Square, W.1.

Telephone: WELBECK 1446. *Telegrams*: YPRESLEAG, " WESDO," LONDON.

Patron-in-Chief: H.M. THE KING.

Patron:
H.R.H. PRINCESS BEATRICE.

President: GENERAL SIR CHARLES H. HARINGTON.

Vice-Presidents:

F.-M. VISCOUNT ALLENBY. F.-M. SIR CLAUD W. JACOB.
THE VISCOUNT WAKEFIELD OF HYTHE. F.-M. SIR PHILIP CHETWODE.
GENERAL SIR CECIL ROMER. F.-M. LORD MILNE.

General Committee:

THE COUNTESS OF ALBEMARLE. MR. F. D. BANKES-HILL.
*CAPTAIN C. ALLISTON. MAJOR-GENERAL C. J. B. HAY.
LIEUT-COLONEL BECKLES WILLSON. MR. J. HETHERINGTON.
MR. HENRY BENSON. GENERAL SIR W. C. G. HENEKER.
*MR. J. BOUGHEY. *CAPTAIN O. G. JOHNSON.
*MISS B. BRICE-MILLER. *MAJOR E. MONTAGUE JONES.
COLONEL G. T. BRIERLEY. MAJOR GENL. C. G. LIDDELL.
CAPTAIN P. W. BURGESS. CAPTAIN H. D. PEABODY.
BRIG.-GENL. A. BURT. *THE HON. ALICE DOUGLAS PENNANT.
*MAJOR H. CARDINAL-HARFORD. *LIEUT.-GENERAL SIR W. P. PULTENEY.
REV. P. B. CLAYTON. LIEUT.-COLONEL SIR J. MURRAY.
*THE EARL OF YPRES. *COLONEL G. E. C. RASCH.
MRS. C. J. EDWARDS. THE HON. SIR ARTHUR STANLEY.
MAJOR C. J. EDWARDS. MR. ERNEST THOMPSON.
MR. H. A. T. FAIRBANK. CAPTAIN J. LOCKLEY TURNER.
MR. T. ROSS FURNER. *MR. E. B. WAGGETT.
SIR PHILIP GIBBS. CAPTAIN J. WILKINSON.
MR. E. GLOVER. CAPTAIN H. TREVOR WILLIAMS.

* Executive Committee.

Bankers: *Honorary Solicitors*:
BARCLAYS BANK LTD., Knightsbridge Branch. MESSRS. FLADGATE & CO., 70, Pall Mall, S.W.

Secretary: *Auditors*:
CAPTAIN G. E. DE TRAFFORD. MESSRS. LEPINE & JACKSON, 6, Bond Court, E.C.4.

League Representative at Ypres: **League Representative at Cambrai:**
CAPTAIN P. D. PARMINTER. MR. A. WILDE,
19, Rue Surmont de Volsberghe 9, Rue des Anglaises.

League Representative at Amiens: **League Representative at Arras:**
CAPTAIN STUART OSWALD. MR. P. VYNER,
7, Rue Porte-Paris. 10, Station Square.

Hon. Secretary, Ypres British Settlement:
LT. COLONEL F. G. POOLE.

PRIMARY OBJECTS OF THE LEAGUE

I.—Commemoration and Comradeship.
II.—To provide special travel facilities for Members and all interested to Ypres and battlefields, and transport of Members.
III.—The furnishing of information about the Salient; marking of historic sites and the compilation of charts of the battlefields.
IV.—The erection of a Ypres British Church and School which has been completed.
V.—The establishment of groups of members throughout the world, through Branch Secretaries and Corresponding Members.
VI.—The maintenance of cordial relations with dwellers on the battlefields of Ypres
VII.—The formation of a Junior Division.

Use the Ypres League Travel Bureau for Ypres and Whole of the Western Front.

FOR THE FOLLOWING PUBLICATIONS, Etc., apply:

Secretary, YPRES LEAGUE, 20, ORCHARD STREET, LONDON, W.1.

THE BATTLE BOOK OF YPRES. A history of notable deeds contributed by all regiments. 5s. ; post free, 5s. 6d. Compiled by Beatrix Brice with the assistance of Lieut.-General Sir William Pulteney, G.C.V.O., etc.

BOOKS.

YPRES: Outpost of the Channel Ports. By Beatrix Brice. With Foreword by Field-Marshal Lord Plumer, G.C.B. Price 1s. 0d.; post free 1s. 3d.

In the Ypres Salient. By Lt.-Col. Beckles Willson. 1s. net; post free 1s. 2d.

Story of the 63rd Field Ambulance. By A. W. Westmore, etc. Cloth, 3s. 6d., post free. Paper, 2s. 6d., post free.

War Letters to a Wife. By Colonel Rowland Feilding. Popular Edition, 3s. 6d.; post free 4s.

The Pill Boxes of Flanders. 1s.; post free 1s. 3d.

From Mons to the First Battle of Ypres. By J. G. W. Hyndson, M.C. Price 3/6, post free

YPRES LEAGUE TIES. 3s. 6d. each, post free.

YPRES LEAGUE BADGES. 2s. each, 2s. 1½d. post free.

EMBROIDERED BADGES. 4s. each, post free.

Map and List of Cemeteries in the Ypres Salient. Price 9d.; post free 11d.

Map of the Somme. Price 1s. 8d., post free.

PICTURES.

Burning of the Cloth Hall, 1915. A Coloured Print, 14 in. by 12 in. 1s. post free.

Old Well-known Spots in New Guise.
Prints, size 4¼ x 2½, recently taken of famous spots in the Ypres Salient, and which may be of great interest to our readers, are on sale at headquarters, price 4d. each, post free 5d. For particulars apply Secretary.

POST CARDS, PHOTOGRAPHS AND ETCHINGS.

Post Cards. Ypres: British Front during the War. Ruins of Ypres. Price 1s. post free.

Hill 60. Complete Panorama Photographs.
12 in. by 3¾ in. Price 3s., post free; 15 in. by 5 in. Price 3s. 6d., post free.

MODELS OF DEMARCATION STONE.

The model, which is 6 inches in height, may be used for a paperweight or as an ornament. Price 5/-, post free.
Applications to the Secretary, Ypres League.

PHOTOGRAPHS OF WAR-TIME SKETCHES.

Bedford House (Front View), 1916.
Bedford House (Back View), 1916.
Voormezeele Main Street, 1916.
Voormezeele Crucifixion Gate, 1916.
Langhof Chateau, 1916.
Size 8¼ in. by 6½ in. Price 2s. 6d. each, post free.

Photographs of the Thiepval and Arras Memorials.
Post card size, price 1s. each, post free.

YPRES TIMES.

The Journal may be obtained at the League Offices.

BACK NUMBERS 1s.; 1934, 8d.; 1935, 6d.

Printed in Great Britain for the Publishers by FORD & GILL, 21a/23, Iliffe Yard, Crampton Street, London, S.E.17.

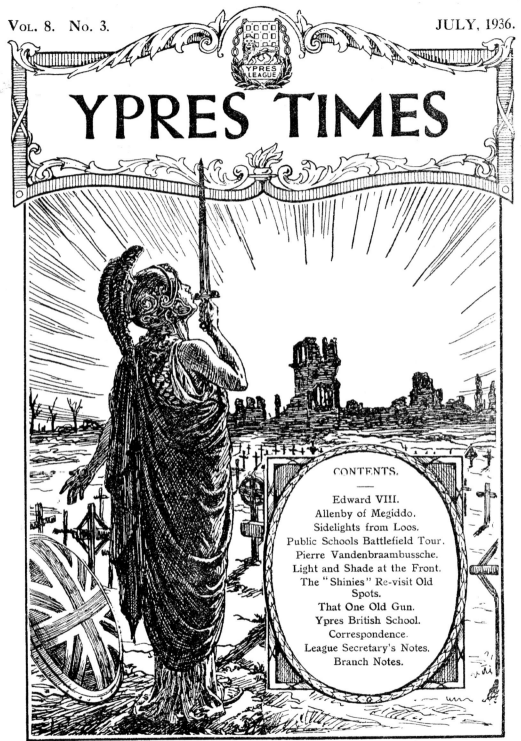

Memory Tablet.

JULY — AUGUST — SEPTEMBER

July.

July	1st, 1916	...	First Battle of the Somme begins.
,,	2nd, 1918	...	1,000,000 Americans transported to France.
,,	9th, 1915	...	Conquest of German South Africa.
,,	18th, 1918	...	General Foch's counter-attack.
,,	28th, 1914	...	Austria-Hungary declared war on Serbia.
,,	30th, 1915	...	First German liquid fire attack.
,,	31st, 1917	...	Third Battle of Ypres.

August.

Aug.	1st, 1914	...	Germany declares war on Russia.
,,	2nd, 1914	...	German ultimatum to Belgium.
,,	3rd, 1914	...	Germany declared war on France.
,,	4th, 1914	...	Great Britain declared war on Germany.
,,	8th, 1918	...	Great British Offensive launched in front of Amiens.
,,	10th, 1914	...	France declared war on Austria-Hungary.
,,	12th, 1914	...	Great Britain declared war on Austria-Hungary.
,,	16th, 1914	...	British Expeditionary Force landed in France.
,,	23rd, 1914	...	Japan declared war on Germany.
,,	27th, 1916	...	Rumania entered the war.

September.

Sept.	3rd, 1916	...	Zeppelin destroyed at Cuffly.
,,	5th, 1914	...	End of retreat from Mons to Marne.
,,	6th, 1914	...	First Battle of Marne begins.
,,	15th, 1914	...	First Battle of Aisne begins.
,,	23rd, 1914	...	First British air raid in Germany.
,,	25th, 1915	...	Battle of Loos.
,,	27th, 1917	...	Hindenburg Line broken.
,,	29th, 1918	...	Bulgaria surrendered.

The Ypres Times

Communications to
The Editor, "Ypres Times,"
20, Orchard Street, London, W.1.

PRICE 6d.
POST FREE 7d.

VOL. 8, No. 3.   PUBLISHED QUARTERLY   JULY, 1936

"Thy choicest gifts in store, on him be pleased to pour"

Edward VIII.
Our Royal Patron-in-Chief.

EX-SERVICE MEN'S STAUNCHEST FRIEND.
BONDS OF LOVE BETWEEN KING AND PEOPLE.

(Specially contributed to the "YPRES TIMES" by HENRY BENSON, M.A.)

IT was with pride and gratitude that the President of the Ypres League, General Sir Charles Harington, received the notification that King Edward VIII had consented to succeed his father, the late King George, as Patron-in-Chief of the Ypres League—a sentiment which will be shared by every member.

* * *

The letter containing the official intimation was couched in the following terms :—

PRIVY PURSE OFFICE,
BUCKINGHAM PALACE, S.W.
MARCH 24TH, 1936.

DEAR SIR,
I AM COMMANDED BY THE KING TO INFORM YOU THAT HIS MAJESTY HAS BEEN GRACIOUSLY PLEASED TO GRANT HIS PATRONAGE TO THE YPRES LEAGUE.

YOURS TRULY,
WIGRAM,
KEEPER OF THE PRIVY PURSE.

THE PRESIDENT,
20, ORCHARD STREET,
PORTMAN SQUARE, W.1.

* * *

ENCOURAGEMENT FOR LEAGUE'S MEMBERS.

This gracious act on the part of the King will have the effect of stimulating the members of the Ypres League to renewed effort on behalf of its prosperity and to insure that its activities are forthwith strengthened and extended.

Everything that tended to the welfare of ex-service men and their kith and kin always found a warm and responsive place in the heart of Edward, Prince of Wales. To-day, he is King-Emperor, but as yet we have not quite adjusted ourselves to that view of him. " Yesterday," he was " The Prince "—youthful and impulsive, standing for all that was fresh and gallant, and as such we shall think of him for a long time to come. Indeed, he himself recognises this fact, for in his soul-awakening broadcast message to the Empire last March, he said : " I am better known to most of you as Prince of Wales—as a man who during the War and since, has had the opportunity of getting to know the people of every country of the world, under all conditions and circumstances. And though I now speak to you as King, I am still that same man who has had that experience and whose constant effort it will be to continue to promote the well-being of his fellow-men."

What a youth our Sovereign has had ! No Monarch in all history has ever received such an education, or seen so much of men and affairs. Moreover, he has come into his inheritance at a time when the nation mourned the passing of one whose life of devoted service and self-sacrifice had made the Crown and the people as one.

War Service on the Western Front.

It is said that a man changes every seven years. In other words, the development of personality and character goes forward in seven-year periods.

By this reckoning His Majesty, who was 42 a few days ago, has just completed the sixth of the determining periods of his life, and he has ascended the throne before middle age has claimed him. To date, however, the period from 1915 to 1922, was probably the most important, because it embraced the war years and the first of those great Empire journeys in which, to quote his own words, " he found his manhood."

When war broke out he was not yet twenty-one, and at that young for his age. Still like thousands of his fellow-Britons, he was quick to realise that his place was with the Regular Army at the front. Whether or not he then foresaw that no man would be able to understand the British Empire of to-morrow who had not tasted the high comradeship of the firing line, his instinct then, as so often since, was right. Single-handed he undertook to overcome the opposition both official and private to his heart's desire, and, in finally achieving it, suggested that the great Victoria had handed down with her crown something of her own extreme pertinacity to her descendants.

Nor was he content, having reached General Headquarters in France, to remain indefinitely attached to the Commander-in-Chief's Staff as extra A.D.C. His one ambition was to get to the front. But here he had to contend with Lord Kitchener who, probably with parental authority behind him, was adamant. The young subaltern urged his claims hard, pointing out, according to a famous story, that a Prince with four brothers is perfectly entitled to get killed if he likes. " But not taken prisoner, sir ! " was the equally famous reply.

The late Earl of Ypres (then Sir John French), who had no fear in him, probably turned a blind eye to the unofficial excursions into the danger zone with which his young A.D.C. diversified the strictly humdrum duties allotted to him behind the line. But the members of the Prince's entourage lived in a nightmare of fear. There was, for example, the occasion on which the Prince insisted on going to call upon the 2nd Battalion of the Rifle Brigade at Laventie, that " shell-trap " of sinister memory. The ruins had been shelled all the morning and would certainly be shelled all the afternoon. But the Prince and his companion got in during a lull and, having reached one of the company's messes, the Royal visitor proclaimed his intention of remaining to luncheon. His companion, at least, never forgot that meal. With every mouthful he expected to hear the whining of an approaching shell, which might spell the irrevocable ; the historic calamity.

But the young ensign of Grenadiers, as King Edward then was, wanted to live up to the time-honoured device of his escutcheon, " Ich Dien." He wanted *to serve*. The

thought of being the only junior officer of his famous fighting regiment to be deprived of the honour of going into action with his platoon perpetually galled him.

Since service with his battalion had to be denied him, the Prince was ultimately suffered to take up an appointment on the staff of the newly-formed Guards Division under the command of Lord Cavan. Here, at least, Lieutenant the Prince of Wales, K.G., was a Guardsman amongst Guardsmen. As was only to be expected, he played his part in the best of spirits with that famous corps.

He did his full share of duty; he was often under fire—on one occasion his car, which he had left outside Vermelles, in the ill-omened Loos sector, was hit by a shell and the chauffeur, I think, killed. More than this, he took the most practical means of making up for his disability to share the life of the trenches by constituting himself the advocate of all manner of petitions, not only from the men in the front line but from their folk at home. If " a spot of leave " had to be urgently " wangled " or a missing man traced, even if it were only a fugitive husband, in the last resort the help of the Prince was solicited and never without avail.

A Very Gallant Gentleman.

Like all the young men, King Edward left part of his youth, and, no doubt, part of the illusions of youth, upon the battlefields of Flanders and Italy; but he brought back in their place a sense of human values that has served his country well. The lesson was there to be learnt and he learned it. After the war, although heir to the most wonderful throne in the history of the world, he could visit a cottage in the country, a poor room in the East End, talk to out-of-work miners, entertain neighbours on his Western ranch, get up early on purpose to wave from a train to some lonely settler at an Australian station, accept a bunch of wild flowers with a smile from a terrified small child, or assist at a Toc H. ceremony, and be equally at home everywhere. Like his grandfather, King Edward VII, he possesses that invaluable gift called tact, which is really the sympathy that enables him to put himself in the place of another, and teaches him to say and do the right thing.

Possibly his greatest asset is a particularly timely and winning sense of humour. Once he was purchasing some small article from a disabled ex-service man and he gave the man a pound note. " I'll have this framed," said the latter. " In that case," replied the Prince, " you can hand it back to me and I'll send you a cheque."

Again, whilst journeying to a function in the country, his car broke down. A small crowd gathered round, ignorant, however, of the identity of the occupant. " One of the idle rich," remarked an elderly man. The Prince overheard it, and immediately took up the challenge. " Rich, if you like, old chap," he said, " but no, not idle."

His Majesty and the Dying Soldier.

From end to end of the British Empire there are men and women who tell little stories of the actions and words which have made them loyal to King Edward till death. Here is one of the most moving of them all, which, so far as I am aware, has not appeared in print. It is true in every detail. To this at least two members of the General Committee of the Ypres League can testify.

Some years after the conclusion of the war, an ex-soldier lay dying in one of the London hospitals. He had no friends in the Metropolis, his only visitor being a well-known padre, who came to the hospital almost daily. Their conversation frequently turned to the war, the days at Toc H at Poperinghe, and the man's close association with the Prince in the Ypres Salient, of which naturally he was very proud. One evening it was obvious that not only were the man's days, but also his hours, numbered. The Padre asked him if he had any special wish. " Yes, sir," he replied, " but it cannot be fulfilled. If only it were possible for me to see the Prince once again, then I would die happy."

Pitying the poor fellow's loneliness and knowing that the Prince would remember him, the Padre decided to seek an interview with his Royal Highness, and to ask whether his engagements would permit of a visit to the hospital on the morrow. It was then 11 p.m., and he knew that H.R.H. was attending a certain evening function. Thither he proceeded, reaching his destination shortly before midnight, only to find that the Prince had already gone home. Nothing daunted, he went on to York House, where he was informed that His Royal Highness was in bed.

"Then I'll leave a message for him," he said. But the Prince must have heard and recognised his voice; for a few minutes later, clad in his pyjamas and dressing-gown, he came down the stairs. "Well, Padre," he exclaimed. "What are you doing here at this hour of the night?" The latter explained. "I remember the man," replied the Prince, "and I must see him. I'm jolly tired; but as he is so ill, we'd better go at once. To-morrow may be too late. Wait a moment whilst I slip on my clothes."

A quarter of an hour later, in the still hours of the morning, they were on their way to the hospital.

Tip-toeing along the ward, so as not to disturb the sleeping patients, the Prince went straight to the man's bedside. He took the poor fellow's hand in his own, and remained with him for some time. He was too far gone to speak, but he opened his eyes and gave a smile of recognition and gratitude. Then he lapsed into a state of coma. A few hours later he beckoned to the sister and whispered, "Was it a dream?" "No," she answered, "it was true." The same afternoon he passed away, happy in the knowledge that the Prince had been to visit him on his lonely death-bed.

Strong Views on Social Problems.

King Edward VIII has personal qualities that are his own. If he has seen no more of the world than did his ever-lamented father, he is perhaps in more intimate touch temperamentally with the sentiment of the great Dominions; his orientation of Royalty is away from the Courts and closer to the common people. Ex-service men think of him as "one of us," and the unemployed know who, of his own initiative, remembered them in their dire distress. He does not think of "classes," but only of human beings, with the same emotions, the same sorrows, the same temptations.

"Who are the unemployed?" he asked in a broadcast speech last year. And at once he proceeded to answer his own question. "Just our fellow country-men and women, the same as ourselves, only far less fortunate. Any of us might find ourselves having to face the same weeks, months, and very often years, of enforced idleness."

Few people realise that, when he sold his hunters in the winter of 1928, the fact was not unconnected with his visit to the workless miners, which made a deep impression on him. "The unemployed are dead sick of these days," he said at Newcastle, "and there is a growing feeling that a special effort should be made to bring this protracted misery to an end." His democratic qualities, his determination to see for himself, his human approach, his interest in the welfare of the unfortunate, his love of daring and his tireless energy have endeared him to his subjects throughout the Empire. The King has always made a point of keeping himself physically fit, and insists upon having the plainest of food served at his table, luncheon often comprising only two pieces of thinly sliced cold beef, two vegetables and a sweet. Dinner is an equally unpretentious meal.

"The Happiness of My Subjects."

Four years younger than his father at the time of his accession, he has ascended the Throne at a period which gives some sinister promise of resemblance to events in the early years of the late reign, and much happy certainty of divergence from them. Then, as now, there is lacking, perhaps even more ominously, a settled prospect of stability in international relations; but at home it is otherwise. Never has our policy been more united, fundamentally, in its conception and pursuit of national needs both at home and abroad. It would, of course, be presumptuous to attempt a forecast of the contribution which King Edward may feel specially qualified to make towards those needs, but his words to the Privy Council on the day of his accession supply a sure index to his general policy :—

"When my father stood here twenty-six years ago he declared that one of the objects of his life would be to uphold constitutional government. In this I am determined to follow in his footsteps and to work, as he did throughout his life, for the happiness and welfare of all classes of my subjects."

A noble,—kingly vow ! May God bless His Majesty with health and length of days for its complete and happy fulfilment !

H.B.

Allenby of Megiddo

ALLENBY has passed over, and the world is poorer for a great heart, a great commander, and a great gentleman.

No man sought the limelight less than he did and few were forced into it more. Few men were less understood than he was, only those who knew him well, grasped his real character ; few people were more abused than he was, even by his own arm of the Service, and few received more praise or honours.

Perhaps that was because, even to those who knew him best, he was to some extent a paradox.

By no means forthcoming on first acquaintance, gruff, direct and forcible to the point of rudeness in his dealings with his officers and men, one came to realise that this was due partly to a curious shyness, partly to his passion for straightness, and partly to a great softness of heart at the back of it all, which he was at pains to conceal.

No one could say he was popular before the Great War when he was a Brigadier and Inspector of Cavalry. He was more feared than loved.

When one knew him, as I was privileged to do, it came as a surprise to find how different his real character was to the popular conception of it.

Ask a man who did not know Allenby well before the war to summarise his character and I think most would have said : " most able and efficient, stern, hard, even ruthless, aloof, forceful, pretty certain to get on if he gets the chance."

When you came to know him well, some of those characteristics remained, in what one might call his public " make up," but behind them you found the real Allenby, almost an entire contradiction. Straight as a ram-rod, strong and supple as the steel it is made of, and behind it all, a great soft heart for women, children and animals, and though he did not wear it on his sleeve, for those men who were fortunate enough to gain his confidence ; and with tastes and hobbies which few would have given him credit for.

I think the most outstanding thing about him was his " straightness." If one can say so about such a thing — it was almost quixotic. He simply did not understand a man who could not say straight out exactly what he thought or meant, without any sort of prevarication or reservation, " even tho' it were to his own hindrance " — let alone an untruth. Next to that I think came his inability to understand the man who was not doing his best, all out, at his job. I think he must have thought that laziness or shirking was some sort of disease he did not understand.

Next, undoubtedly, came the softness of his great heart for children and animals, especially birds and nature.

He knew all the children anywhere near his different headquarters in France, and always had small presents ready for them and plans for entertaining them. They knew and were not frightened of a man whose name and reputation caused alarm among soldiers of many years' service and experience.

His love of nature and birds was well known and to the day of his death he always had a large aviary of birds about which his knowledge was profound. As also about flowers, especially the wonderful ones which have such a brief but lovely existence after the rains in Palestine.

He was a profound student of the Bible, and was wont to declare that his knowledge of it was of the greatest use to him in the Palestine campaign.

He was a brilliant conversationalist and could " hold a table " on one of his own subjects as few men could. His military triumphs have been fully recorded. He wrested the Holy places from the Crescent and restored them to the Cross at a moment when the morale of the allied Powers was at its lowest, and though the final decision must always have come in Europe, his victory, coming when it did, was worth far more than the actual gain of territory ; it gave confidence to one side, and it depressed the other.

Allenby—with the help of English, Scottish, Irish, Australian, New Zealand, Indian and West Indian troops —did what had been the ambition of generations of Crusaders, and I venture to think that no one of them would have behaved so modestly as Allenby in the moment of his triumph.

To serve under him as one of his commanders was an education. There was never the slightest doubt in your mind when he gave you your tasks, as to what his exact intentions were. He always left you to plan your part of it in your own way, and when you explained it to him, and he approved of it, he always said, " a good plan, now remember it is mine, and I take full responsibility." And that was no empty phrase. When he said that, if the operation was successful—you got the praise, if it was not, he took the blame. I wonder how many great commanders in war have always done that—not many I think.

Allenby laughed at the "smallness" and self-seeking of some of the politicians he had to deal with, but he was always very insistent on the terrible responsibility which rests on ministers in war and how it is the soldiers business to help them all they can, and theirs to direct and the soldiers to implement.

Photo] [J. Russell & Sons
LORD ALLENBY

After the war, he showed much skill and more patience in the difficult civil appointments he held. He has had more blame than praise for his work in Egypt, but as usual he did what he thought right, and supported his political chiefs without the least thought of whether it would benefit him personally or not.

Lastly, with reverence, I touch on his most happy married life, and on the tragic loss of his only son — killed in action.

He has gone, and the Empire has lost a great son.

PHILIP W. CHETWODE, F.M.

Sidelights from Loos

By Captain G. A. Brett, D.S.O., M.C.
(Late 23rd London Regiment.)

ONLY a small portion of the 23rd Londons went " over the top " twenty years ago during the battle of Loos, but the whole battalion was in the forward zone from shortly after the commencement of the fighting until the captured ground was handed over to the French a fortnight later. As privileged onlookers, therefore, we saw a great deal, perhaps more than those closely engaged could do, for our attention was not distracted by proximity to the enemy.

* * * * *

Early morning of the 25th September, 1915—very early morning, bleak and damp—darkness intensified by enormous black slag-heaps, the tops of which were but vaguely visible in the first cold, grey light of dawn.

Gradually the shafts of light broadened, showing up the irregular shapes of the heaps, and slowly strengthening until greyish lumps could be discerned at the bases of the mounds. Then, quite suddenly, silence was shattered by the crash of many guns, the greyish lumps stirred, shook themselves, and the 23rd Londons awoke to the Battle of Loos.

* * * * *

The battalion was in reserve, but by 10 o'clock it had been ordered forward to Maroc, and into the old British front trenches, still reeking with the first gas discharged by our army in the war. Next day it was further forward on the outskirts of Loos village, bolstering up where things had not gone so well as expected with the neighbouring division on the left, and here with some minor moves it remained throughout the battle.

Headquarters were established first in Loos Chateau, and we found there a delightfully filled hamper of provisions left behind by a Brigade Staff of the neighbouring Division. The Chateau unfortunately proved a magnet for German shells and, after some nasty jars, we evacuated it at night and re-opened under a tool-cart which had also been abandoned by our neighbours. A wall sheltered us on one side, we let down the wagon tarpaulin to windward, and there the C.O. and I slept two nights. We rather unwisely made use of some blankets found in the cart—the fact that they were damp did not affect us, but they had earlier inhabitants and these did. Owing to the inadvisability of using lights, we did not discover until daylight that we had shared our shelter the first night with a German corpse.

* * * * *

Our wagon stood on the road leading into Loos from the main highway between Bethune and Lens. The late German second line trench now occupied by our men skirted the road, traversing for a short distance the edge of the village cemetery. Whether the enemy need have disturbed the harmless dead is a question for them to answer, but Londoners finding bones all ready for use were not to be disturbed by fanciful fears of desecration, with the result that a C.Q.M.S. arriving at night with the rations was not a little startled when, on rounding a traverse, he found himself confronted in the pale moonlight by a complete skeleton standing menacingly erect.

* * * * *

This road into Loos was a source of considerable interest. Trees in the cemetery covered it from German eyes for the first hundred yards, and the walls of the Chateau hid the last hundred yards into Loos, but between lay a stretch of some three hundred yards with no kindly veil. Traffic of all kinds proceeded unimpeded for a few hours, but eventually a hostile machine gun commenced to make the crossing of the open stretch precarious. Sentries were posted at each end to give warning, and dismounted parties were told to make use of the trench. Mounted people had to take their chance, and bets were freely offered and taken at Battalion Headquarters whenever such a party appeared.

The first race was provided by the Headquarters Staff of a Cavalry Brigade. The Staff Captain won by two lengths, a short head separating second and third, a groom and the Brigadier in that order. A second groom came in fourth, and the Brigade Major also ran, he having dismounted at the starting gate to pick up the Brigadier's cap, which came off when his horse plunged at the first burst of fire.

Another good race was given by a cyclist party, which from a slow start was travelling really fast long before the finish. The real thrill in this race lay in that one of their number had been dropped, the only casualty of the day, and the moment the road was clear the Battalion Signal Officer sprinted from my side down the road, picked

Photo] [Imperial War Museum, Crown Copyright
A STREET IN LOOS; 30th SEPTEMBER, 1915.

up the wounded man, and carried him into the cover of the trench alongside, an act which well merited the M.C. with which he was subsequently decorated.

* * * * *

Three or four days after the first attack, Germans were still being found in cellar and dug-outs, the waves of British having passed unseeing over them, for in those days "mopping-up parties," which became a feature of all attacks later in the war, had not been devised. So when one day mysterious signalling was reported to be going on from a cottage in Loos, elaborate precautions were taken to surprise the party at work. The building was carefully surrounded, and a noiseless entrance made. The first floors yielded no secrets, but a ladder was found leading up to an attic. An officer went quietly up this, revolver in hand, and surprised two men, one asleep and the other operating a signal lamp. They were signallers of the neighbouring Brigade, and the expedition faded quietly away.

Panic ! Came a flying figure from the forward zone, unarmed, capless and without equipment, leaping over obstacles, gasping for breath. He plunged into our trench and tried to clamber out on the rearward side, but was seized by an officer. He struggled wildly, articulating hoarsely : " Let me go ! Germans coming in thousands ! Let me go ! " But a couple of men came to the officer's aid and held him fast.

The company stood to, but could see nothing for alarm. Ordered by the officer to mount the fire-step and point out the enemy, the captive at first refused, but when the officer drew his revolver, he decided that the more distant devil was better than the one standing before him, and reluctantly climbed up. He was very obviously amazed at seeing nothing whatsoever, and burst into tears with mortification. A young soldier of a unit being tried in the flame for the first time, his leaders killed, wounded or at least bewildered by their fearful environment, it is not a matter for surprise that his nerve snapped. Yet an hour later, after a meal of sorts and kindly treatment, the lad completely recovered and voluntarily went forward to rejoin his comrades.

* * * * *

After the storm of an indecisive battle comes a lull, in which both sides pause for breath. Such a day dawned, a day of the sunshine and warmth which sometimes comes before autumn surrenders to winter. Only the occasional rattle of a distant machine gun or the boom of a shell revealed that this was war and not peacetime training. Looking backward from the village into Loos Valley, the late " No Man's Land," across which two armies had gazed at each other with malevolent eyes from their parallel trenches for nearly a year, was plainly visible, while beyond it the ground, straw-coloured, rose gently up to form the ridge on which Philosophe, that quaintly named mining hamlet, and Maroc stood in bold outline against the sky some 1,500 yards away.

But change came with the afternoon. A platoon of troops appeared over the sky line near Maroc marching in fours towards us. Another showed to their right, then another and another, until the crest of the ridge was dotted with moving black squares. More and more followed, echeloned in rear, and the whole straw-coloured slope took on the appearance of a gigantic moving chess-board.

Soon after the leading platoons came over the crest, German batteries opened fire upon them, and quickly every possible enemy gun was concentrating on the chess-board. The platoons never hesitated, but came steadily on, more and more of them, through a veritable hell of explosion, flame, death and agony—no halting, every gap filled immediately it was made. " It's the Guards," said someone, " the Guards Division coming into action for the first time."

Under the influence of this mighty scene, played by men only seen previously by the Battalion in their glitter and splendour outside the Royal palaces in London, our men leapt spontaneously from their cover into machine gun fire to pull aside barbed wire and throw plank bridges across the trenches, anything to help these magnificent soldiers through. They reached and passed through us, every man in step, ranks closed up, heads erect, probably the finest men the world has ever seen. The platoon to pass nearest to me was led by an officer with an empty sleeve thrust through his belt. Those who saw the Guards entering into the maelstrom of Loos will never think again of them as ornamental but not useful soldiers.

* * * * *

A cavalry brigade, dismounted, came through Loos, and we received orders that if and when they attacked Hill 70 we were to follow in close support. We got into touch with their headquarters, gave orders to the companies to be ready to move at fifteen minutes' notice and stood by on tenter-hooks, for Hill 70 was no joke,—even the Guards had failed to take it.

When a motor-cyclist dashed up, his speed as usual accelerated by machine gun fire as he crossed the uncovered stretch of road, the whole battalion saw him ; packs were adjusted, belts tightened up, rifle magazines inspected—in fact there was nowhere the slightest doubt regarding the purport of the message in his haversack.

With nervous fingers I ripped open the envelope and tore out the letter. Twice I read it, not understanding. The C.O. snatched it from me, with a remark concerning "blithering idiots." His face was a study as he read the message, which was as follows : "In future, lasts, shoemakers' will be indented for by battalions direct, and not through brigades as heretofore."

* * * * *

G.A.B.

Public Schools Battlefield Tour

THE third official Public Schools O.T.C. Battlefield Tour left London on Saturday April 18th. Major E. Montague Jones, O.B.E., T.D., was in charge of the party, which numbered 64 officers and cadets ; the business arrangements were again in the hands of Mr. O. Mears of the Ypres League Headquarters.

It was a cheerful party that were greeted at Victoria by Lieut.-General Sir William Pulteney, G.C.V.O., K.C.B., K.C.M.G., whose interest in the Public Schools O.T.C. tours is always so active, and General Nyssens, the Belgian Military Attaché. Not even predictions of rough seas damped our spirits, although later some of us were not particularly glad to see these predictions come true. Fortunately the Captain of the s.s. *Josephine Charlotte* considered the feelings of his passengers and hugged the Belgian coast for the last part of the crossing. In consequence, no one arrived much the worse for wear, and the "laissez passer" so courteously granted by His Excellency, the Belgian Ambassador, made our passage through the Customs a mere formality. Indeed, throughout the tour the kindliness and courtesy of the Belgian officials and people made things easy for us.

After a rather slow journey in an "omnibus" train, we came at last to Ypres. The city welcomed us with sunshine, and we were able to appreciate the beauties of the Cloth Hall and Cathedral. It was difficult to realise that the city had been so completely devastated and rebuilt, and, as we came into the Grande Place, the only reminders of war were the still ruined north end of the Cloth Hall and the imposing mass of the Menin Gate in the evening sunshine. Accommodation had again been reserved for the party at the Hotel Skindles and the Hotel Splendid Britannique. Dinner was very welcome that night, and refreshed by this, we all assembled at the latter hotel for an excellent illustrated lecture by Lieut.-Colonel Viscount Bridgeman, M.C. and Lieut.-Colonel Sir Colin Jardine, Bt., D.S.O., M.C. Our thanks are due to the War Office for supplying us with two such capable and interesting lecturers. They guided us infallibly through the entanglements of the battles of the Ypres Salient, and in the two following days their further explanations and personal reminiscences on the ground made the picture they painted alive and real.

That night we fell asleep to the chimes of the newly restored Cloth Hall clock, and were up betimes to visit Talbot House at Poperinghe. This visit was an unforgettable experience, and here we had the privilege of listening to Major P. Slessor. He first talked to us of the past and present work of "Toc H," and, as we listened to him in that quiet garden, we seemed to see it again thronged with weary but cheerful men of all ranks and units. He then led us through the house itself pointing out the old notices, signed by "Tubby" Clayton, until at last we climbed the stairs to the Chapel, which has been preserved almost exactly in its original state — a more striking memorial to the men who fought in the Ypres Salient than any pile of stone, however impressive.

We returned to Ypres in time to attend a service in the British Church. After this we met in the playground of the British School for the customary ordeal of a photograph and had a short time to inspect its admirably equipped classrooms with a professional eye before our last duty of the morning, to gather at the Ypres Town War Memorial, where on our behalf Major E. Montague Jones placed a wreath of red poppies.

In the afternoon we started our sightseeing in earnest with a tour in char-a-bancs round the Salient. Driving out to the end of the Yser Canal, from which we could see Boesinghe Church, the left extremity of the Salient, we passed on through St. Julien to a point near Hannebeke. This first stopping place was admirably chosen; from it we were able to see the whole Salient, and could realise how much depended on the command of the hills, or rather of the high ground; for even Hills 62 and 60 are but hillocks and the only hill in the neighbourhood is dignified with the name of mountain. Here Lord Bridgeman pointed out the landmarks and gave us a vivid account of the experiences of a company of the Rifle Brigade in the 2nd Battle of Ypres.

Our next halt was at the Tyne Cot Cemetery, where lie 11,512 British soldiers, many of whose names are only "known to God." On paper the huge lists of casualties in the Great War defy the imagination; but here among these ranks of white stones we could realise, many of us for the first time, the terrible waste of war. This cemetery, like all the others we saw, was beautifully kept by its six gardeners. Then on to a point near Polygon Wood, where Sir Colin Jardine carried on the story. He had occupied a battery position here during the 3rd Battle of Ypres, and his own experiences gave a special interest to his talk and helped us to imagine the mud and desolation to which the whole district had been by this time reduced; for apart from the memorials of the fallen and the absence of aged or even middle-aged trees there is little trace left of war. An amusing entr'acte was provided by Major Montague Jones' encounter with a friendly but frisky young horse. We finished our tour of the Salient with a visit to Hills 62 and 60. The Canadian trenches " uniques sur tous les fronts " were disappointing, a self-conscious rubbish heap of old iron, but the tunnels were interesting.

Before bed that night we met at the Menin Gate to pay our tribute to the fallen and to stand in silence while the Belgian buglers sounded the British " Last Post " and while Major C. E. Esnouf of the Rossall School O.T.C. placed our wreath in honour of those whose graves are unknown.

Monday's programme was a whole day tour into France as far as Arras. We halted first to hear the story of the battle of Messines from Lord Bridgeman. He told us how he had himself watched the great explosions of the mines from the point at which we stood, and how later in the day he had advanced with C. Coy. 3rd Battn. Rifle Brigade to the top of the coveted ridge. Extracts from his own diary illuminated the picture, and, when we moved on to the top of the ridge, we could recapture with him the feelings of the troops as they looked out over country which the Allied forces had not seen since 1914.

There followed a long 'bus journey across the French frontier. Here again the kindness of the Belgian and French Embassies had provided us with a laissez passer, which exempted us from any personal scrutiny at the Customs. Unfortunately, the petrol tanks of our buses did not receive immunity from a searching investigation; that, and the shortage of tax stamps caused a long wait. At last we drove on through Armentières to the battlefield of Loos. The sunshine of the previous day had deserted us; but the cold wind did not lessen our appreciation of Sir Colin Jardine's masterly description of the battle. Here again we had the advantage of personal reminiscences and he described to us how "T" Battery R.H.A. galloped into action under rifle fire along the Vermelles-Hulluch road " in the approved style of the illustrations of the Sphere."

After passing through the industrial centre of Lens, we came at last to a real hill, Vimy Ridge. The tunnels here are a most striking relic of the war, and we could see enough of the unfinished Canadian Memorial to realise that it will be a more dignified memorial in its prominent position even than the beautiful memorial at St. Julien. The weather was now steadily deteriorating, and we regretted that in consequence, our lecture here had to be curtailed, and that those who wished to visit Mt. Kemmel had to be disappointed . We did, however, find time to visit the interesting city of Arras, and

REPRESENTATIVE PARTY OF THE THIRD ANNUAL PUBLIC SCHOOLS TOUR ASSEMBLED IN THE YPRES BRITISH SCHOOL PLAYGROUND
[Daniel, Ypres

stopped for a moment at the German Cemetery of La Maison Blanche. It is neatly and reverently kept, but some of us regretted the absence of grass plots, and of stone memorials to those with whom all differences are at an end. From accounts we received on our return to Ypres we learnt that we had really been lucky in our weather; the rain there would have made sight-seeing almost impossible.

The journey back to London was uneventful, and the sea was calm; our comfort was all the greater because we found ourselves on board the new s.s. *Prince Baudouin*, which is equipped more like a luxury liner than the usual Channel steamer.

What we had learnt from the tour no doubt differed in each case, but we were all unanimous in agreeing that we had thoroughly enjoyed ourselves. We felt too that the Great War was less remote than before, and all could realise what folly it would be if Europe allowed it to be repeated. We have so many to thank for the striking success of the tour that it is difficult not to leave some out, but we owe a special debt of gratitude to Major E. Montague Jones and the O.T.C. Club, to all the organisers of the Ypres League, to our lecturers, and to the War Office which provided them, to Major P. Slessor and, above all, to our Belgian hosts.

R.R.T.

In Piam Memoriam
Pierre Vandenbraambussche, O.B.E.

Death of Police Commissaire who Founded "Last Post" Ceremony.

Ypres Mourns a Trusted Servant.

(A Tribute by an English Friend.)

MANY of my readers will learn with a sense of personal sorrow of the death of M. Pierre Vandenbraambussche, O.B.E., Commissaire of Police at Ypres, which took place on April 6th, in his sixty-first year. His passing will be mourned, not only by the Yprois, the members of the British community in the Salient and his fellow-countrymen throughout Western Flanders, but also by thousands of British pilgrims and tourists, to whom he was ever a courteous and willing mentor in any of those little dilemnas which so frequently beset travellers in a foreign land. Those of us, whom duty compels to make frequent visits to Ypres, deplore the loss of a genial, staunch and never-failing friend.

Born at Brussels on November 6th, 1875, where he received his education, the late Commissaire, whilst still in his early 'teens, joined the Belgian Infantry as a volunteer. Leaving the 6th Regiment of the Line as a corporal, he transferred to the Grenadiers, eventually rising to the rank of sergeant-major. It may be mentioned that the late King Albert, then heir to the Throne, held a commission in that famous regiment at the same time.

On his discharge from the Army, M. Vandenbraambussche entered the service of the Grands Magasins de la Bourse, followed by a position as usher in the Chamber of Representatives. Here it was that he met M. Colaert, then Burgomaster of Ypres and representative of that area in the Chamber. This chance acquaintance altered the whole trend of his life and led to his nomination and appointment in 1902 as Commissaire of Police at Ypres, when in his twenty-eighth year—a post which he continued to hold until his recent death. Comparatively young for such a responsible office, as well as being a stranger to the city, it was some little time before he gained the complete confidence of the Yprois in the execution of his difficult and exacting task, but gradually his sterling worth and fearless devotion to duty won the full recognition and appreciation it deserved. It is no exaggeration to state that in post-war years he was the most popular and trusted figure in Ypres.

M. Vandenbraambussche's strongest claim to perpetual remembrance and gratitude on the part of peoples of the British Empire rests on the fact that he was co-founder of the beautiful ceremony of sounding the "Last Post" each evening under the central arch of the Menin Gate Memorial.

It so chanced that I was staying at Ypres when it originated, and the first intimation the English public had of the proposed ceremonial was embodied in an article I wrote at the time. It is now, perhaps, permissible to tell the full story.

The idea was the joint conception of the late Commissaire and M. Koch, proprietor of the Hotel Splendide and Britannique. As many of my readers know, M. Koch's delightful hostelry, nestling unpretentiously in the Place Roi Albert, is the hub of the British colony in Ypres, and in the summer months its genial host is frequently called upon to cater for parties of 200 to 500 British tourists daily. M. Koch, who for many years has enjoyed the patronage of the Ypres League, is known to and respected by almost every visitor to the Salient from King Edward downwards. This country has had no stauncher friends in the whole of Belgium than the late Commissaire and M. Koch.

I was present at the inaugural night of the Menin Gate ceremony, when "La Retraite," which is the Belgian equivalent to the "Last Post," was sounded on four clarions by members of the local Fire Brigade. This was obligatory, and was perforce continued for some little time afterwards, because the Belgian buglers did not know the notes of the "Last Post." Later, the Ypres League prepared the score and the British Legion presented four silver bugles.

It was the original intention of the two founders that the ceremony to have been a "summer-time" function only, but to meet the earnest desire of bereaved relatives it is now continued throughout the year. For a long period the funds to pay the buglers and certain other incidental expenses were subscribed by the hotel proprietors and the trades folk of Ypres, this being in the nature of a personal tribute to our gallant dead. Two years ago, however, the Surrey Branch of the British Legion raised a capital sum, now invested in Belgian securities and in the hands of local trustees, the annual interest from which will assure the continuity of the ceremony for all time.

Pierre Vandenbraambussche

I know of no more touching moments than those spent in watching, as twilight fades and darkness falls, the local employees of the Imperial War Graves Commission, soldierly as ever, standing stiffly to attention in the Hall of Memory at the Menin Gate, in company with ex-service men visitors, some of whom proudly display medals on their breasts, and their women-folk, united, as the first mournful notes of the "Last Post" burst forth, in paying their homage to those 54,896 unknown warriors of all ranks who fought and died for the allied cause in the Salient of Ypres.

May I suggest that the Imperial War Graves Commission place a bronze tablet in a prominent position at Menin Gate recording the fact that M. Vandenbraambussche, upon whom King George bestowed the Order of the British Empire, was co-founder of the ceremony of the "Last Post," so that the origin of this beautiful little function may not pass into oblivion?

M. Vandenbraambussche was laid to rest, with the full rites of the Catholic Church and amid general manifestations of grief, in the Communal Cemetery of Ypres. The Benediction was pronounced by the Dean of St. Martin's, and funeral orations were delivered at the graveside by M. Vanderghote, Burgomaster of Ypres, and M. Deltoier, of Courtrai, on behalf of the Federation of Commissaires of Police. As a mark of respect, the British School was closed during the hour of the funeral.

Ypres mourns the passing of a faithful and trusted servant.

Requiescat in Pace.

H.B.

Light and Shade at the Front

"Get In There."

By An Ex-"R.B."

IT is reasonable to assume that the wide improvements and changes that have been made in armaments since the Great War have brought with them new words of command. It is also tolerably certain that some of the routine commands which were familiar to readers in those distant days will remain, for a while at least, the basic formulae for infantry movements both individual and collective. "On parade!" for instance. Or, "To the right, three paces, ex-ten-n-nd!" Also, "Platoon, dou-b-l-l-e march!" And, "Head turning quickly, to the right (wait for it!) Turn!" As well as, "Backward swing, thr-o-w!" Not to mention, "At the throat-and-stom-m-m-ach—make a good point—Point!" And in all sorts of cadences, starting from the sergeant-major's forcible tones and so along the scale diminuendo.

Or when, after a rest, the Division received marching orders for the Salient and bade farewell to the sweet scented rural scenes of its brief sojourn (Bertrancourt). And to tins of salmon, chunks of canteen cake, buckshee tea and mess-tins of new milk, the latter from a farmhouse set in idyllic surroundings and served by a tall stately young lady of gravely courteous mien. Farewell all. Packing up was done over-night ; an extra necessary or so for some, and for one or two who intended to do the march " de luxe," a bottle of grenadine in the water bottle.

The battalion paraded on the country road after early breakfast and when all was ready the Colonel, mounted at its head, gave the order in full, rolling tones : " The Battalion will move off by order of companies ! " (A pause.) " By your right ! Quick march ! " and scarcely had he spoken the word when the drums beat and the companies moved off briskly in step to the lively bugle notes of " Over the hills and far away ! " The route to the siding, about an hour or two's march away, led through Doullens, and as the troops, marching at scheduled intervals, wound through its old fashioned main street to the strain of the bands, tramp, tramp, tramp, tramp, battalion by battalion of hard knit, active warriors, with the cookers belching smoke along the column and the infantry alternating with the slower movements of the artillery train, there was seen the fine sight (witnessed but seldom) of a division on the move. Alas ! How many soon to be laid low.

A retrospect. Readers will agree that music is at its best when each sort is played in its own proper environment. The jaunty rhythm of a "Hansel and Gretel" polka, for example, is enlivening when heard among the swings and roundabouts of a country fair, or in the dining hall of a major hotel, but it would be wholly distasteful if played, let us say, within the sacred precincts of Winchester Cathedral. Late one night when the company was billeted on the outskirts of Arras, shortly before the offensive, some Jocks passed along a road in the near distance and were being played up to billets by their pipers. These pipes, heard in the midnight watches on the eve of a general engagement, strident, forceful and clear, seemed to presage the very clash of the onset. It is common knowledge that the artillery on the Arras front steadily shelled the German lines for several months before the Easter Monday, allowing for a brief space when it became known that the enemy had secretly fallen back along certain parts of his line. The shelling increased by degrees till it rose to a great volume in the last forty-eight hours, and it reached its peak in the final twelve hours when every available gun on that front was firing. On top the noise was impressive. The air seemed to vibrate and the ground to shake. Down in the caves where the troops were billeted, perhaps some twenty feet or more below ground level, muffled reports of the guns were clearly audible. These caves were said to have been made by Spanish prisoners many years back, but probably this meant they were of natural origin and labour was brought in to fashion them. They were reached by a steep series of steps and were of virgin chalk, lofty, spacious, well ventilated, dry, and were lit by electric light bulbs strung along the sides. A few tons of chalk fell on the Easter Sunday, but most of the troops were out working and casualties were nil.

Rouse at 3 a.m. on the Monday and the company was soon in the open where batteries of 18-pounders, more or less in alignment as the ground permitted, were firing away like little pop-guns. Wounded led back from the ridge, also long lines of German prisoners, the latter helping with the walking cases and giving a hand with the stretchers. The morning opened bright, but it rapidly changed to cold and a dry powdery snow started to fall. While Brigadier S—— was up with the advance looking over the ground in person, and stopped to talk with the O.C., a brief halt was called. A few of the lads scrounged a German mess-tin, "mucked in" with their tea and water rations, and started to boil the water over a tiny fire. Steam was just showing when an order was given : " Lead on ! " The mess-tin was hastily snatched up as the sections moved forward, the tea was thrown in and each of the " co-ops " drank of the mixture as the mess-tin passed from hand to hand. When the Company, in support, reached the left front of its final objective, Wancourt, in the afternoon, that village was being heavily shelled. Objects on the plain were quickly spotted, and as the lads strung out to deepen a German firing trench, enemy shells began to come over whizzing and bursting " thick and heavy." Said a comrade-in-arms to the writer (the former was a Regular, a slim, quiet, young fellow who had volunteered to carry the platoon number board nailed to a long stick), " Dig, J——, as you've never dug before ; it's life or death now ! " At this moment, the sergeant, who having to nip about hadn't brought a shovel, asked the writer to lend him his ; however, the captain, seeing things were warming up, ordered a prompt move into shell holes and then trenching tools did the work. There was another empty German trench about fifteen yards in front of the shell holes, and a little later on a section of it blew sky high with a roar ; the enemy had mined it.

During the night shells splashed the darkness with their vivid light. " Any of you chaps about ? " asked a familiar voice out of the pitchy black. " Yes, two of us over here," and the first speaker nipped in with a Lewis gun. On Tuesday morning the attack on Wancourt was still going on, and some 18-pounders were brought up in the afternoon just to the rear of the troops to press it. These guns were withdrawn about dusk. So as not to draw a barrage one gun was left firing while the others withdrew, and then that gun was harnessed up and it doubled out. That morning some cavalry led on to the plain (4th Dragoons, if the writer's memory is correct on the point) and formed up some distance back to the left rear. Horses—noble companions of man— reared and plunged as enemy shells screamed over and struck, but the rest of the formations were steady as on a barrack square. They were withdrawn out of sight after about twenty minutes and fallen horses and riders strewed the plain. It was said these cavalry were waiting to break through, but as they offered such an easy mark and, moreover, the enemy could rake the plain from his positions beyond Wancourt, it seems more likely, on reflection, they were there to deter the enemy from trying a rush over with superior numbers. Wancourt was entered on Tuesday night (supports in Tilloy) and the Germans were shelling it on Wednesday.

The day after the Company came out the captain made an informal inspection of billets, and he suggested to the writer a visit to the M.O.'s for a slight biff from a bit of earth sustained near the ivy bower. The M.O. : " I've put you down for a day or two at the F.A.", so a quick packing up, a cup of black coffee and away in the car. A few days later again *en route*, this time for the railhead and the R.T.O. This R.T.O. had a fine soldierly bearing. Florid complexion and an alert look, he was about 5 ft. 10 in., shoulders well back, arms a little akimbo, legs a bit astride, and a way of balancing himself slightly on the soles of his feet which seemed to suggest he was a cavalryman. He turned to the new comer. " Yes ! " " Division ? " " Battalion ? " and then pointing to a train by the siding he said, in even tones, " Get in there." The writer found two other spare files in the carriage, and the Battalion being, as they thought, only a short distance away, they didn't trouble to open rations.

The train jogged away, halting now and again by the countryside (restful old trains these). It took a few civilians aboard at Hazebrouck (Hazebrouck gave colour to a rumour then current that the Division was destined for Dunkirk), and in the afternoon

Front parlour. Romville, Arras.   A garden Beaucreampre.

it halted at a stores dump where the spare files jumped out into a bright sunshine, reported to the R.T.O., and helped on a fatigue. Early rouse next day and a ration issue and back into the same friendly old train. Away through Hazebrouck and on by the country. There seemed to be a complete absence of man power, but a few elderly rustics were sighted. It was a sign of their industrious habits that these old folk seemed always to holding something ; a pail, a pitchfork or a few faggots of wood. The engine crew packed up about noon and on looking out the three passengers saw—shades of London town ! — a Vanguard omnibus. The driver : " Where'ye from ? " " All right ! GET IN THERE," and when this 'bus stopped and its cargo alighted : " Was this real ? " (Beaucreampre, to be exact.)

Readers may have noticed that sharp contrasts heighten effects. When the meat in the " gippo " had, well, simmered into thin soup one's attention then was focussed on to the bones. Likewise a little picture of rural charm which in normal times might have passed unobserved, now fixed itself indelibly on one's notice. A fine sunshine, the road white with dust, hedges trimmed, a neat little courtyard, trees in foliage and, exceptionally, the bright twittering of birds. A few wild flowers, fragrant reliquiae of ruined gardens, were sprinkled here and there. Next day some more details arrived, and early the day after that : " On parade ! " . . . " In fours, by the right ! Quick march!" and away went the little party *en route* to the line. Up to the neck in dust and into Arras, then a hub of activity with troops on the move and all the impedimenta of war, while little groups of men off duty stood in the sun outside their billets. How different this from such wintry scenes as little Simoncourt, standing in wide fields and covered with snow. Here long strings of horses and mules used to pass incessantly day and night, and always in the same direction ; towards the line.

"Are those Red-tabs?" "March to attention!" (A grouse: "Marchin' to attention 'ere!'") "a'Heyes left!" "a'Heyes fr'nt!" "March at ease!" "March easy!"... "Left wheel!" (round the corner) "Right turn!" (into a side street of tall, narrow old houses) "Form two deep!" (along a circuitous route by heaps of broken timber, bricks and rubble)..."'Alt!" and into billets on the ground floor where two casualties were already installed. One of these, an upright piano, was injured internally, and the other was a cracked little picture on the wall. As to the former an examination revealed that, failing a new set of "innards," the patient's chances of recovery were at a low ebb. A shell lobbed over into the top floor about midnight and cascaded it with a crash and a rumble into the road. At this a belated party on the first floor tumbled down the stairs and urgently inquired for the cellars. ("There are two beautiful rooms on the first floor which the Agents highly recommend." "Thank you! What about the cellars!")

A fateful coincidence.

"On parade!" with the lark; details were split up and the writer reached the Battalion about mid-day, finding it in reserve at the right rear of some batteries but on slightly higher ground. A kite balloon swung to the left rear of the guns and an enemy plane was showing up from Monchy. About a fortnight before, when the Arras offensive was at its height, the enemy counter attacked along this stretch in strong force (so said a gunner) and looked like reaching the batteries, which were emplaced in the form of a right angle behind a small slope. On this the gunners put their guns out of gear and drew their revolvers.

The writer in the company of a friend (a sturdy lad from St. Albans, in the Yeomanry before it dismounted) witnessed a remarkable coincidence just before the Division left the Arras sector for good. A corporal was taking over for some new troops and stopped to look at a tiny cemetery, which had been dug recently and stood out in sharp relief on a wide expanse of ground. Suddenly he saw on one of the crosses—his brother's name and number. A colonel also was buried here ; his steel helmet in its khaki cover was left on the grave, and a jagged hole in it showed plainly how he was killed.

All things have a beginning, to quote a platitude, and all things must come to an end, and so the pleasant command "Get in there," open sesame to scenes anew, was now in the limbo of the past.

J. EDWARDS.

(*To be continued*)

The "Shinies" Re-visit Old Spots

By C. D. PLANCK.

ON Easter Sunday a representative body of the 7th (City of London) Battalion Old Comrades Association left Victoria for a Battlefield Tour, travelling under the auspices of the Ypres League. A very comfortable journey was made to Dover, yarns were spun *en route*, and very quickly the old Army spirit of comradeship prevailed.

The sea proved a " choppy " one, but our team survived without any casualties ! Ostend was reached according to schedule, and we entrained for Ypres, eventually obtaining a view of the famous Flemish city which has arisen from the ashes. A description of the wonderful change in Ypres has been given many times, so I will carry on to the Hotel Splendid where we all enjoyed an excellent dinner, afterwards inspecting the Menin Gate and attending the Ceremony of the " Last Post." On behalf of the O.C.A. a wreath was laid by Mr. Geo. Hill, in memory of our departed comrades.

Upon returning to the Hotel, a thoroughly good hour of both sad and mirthful reminiscences were related to us by Holmes (late of the Drums) in the true Holmes manner.

The " Cyclist " member of the party requested all to be " on parade " for breakfast at 8.30 a.m. sharp, as we were due to move off at 9 a.m. The Carillion tunes of the Cloth Hall made a good substitute for reveille and all were seated for breakfast in time, except the prime mover of this night light savings bill, who sat down twenty minutes late amid a " barrage " of stinging comments. We boarded our specially chartered char-a-banc like a party of Staff Officers, bearing in mind that to get up the line from Ypres in War days, one had to " foot slog," The sun was shining on the " Shinies " and the hood was pushed back. Reader, please remember it was snowing in Blighty over Easter !

The " troops " were delighted to have with them Capt. de Trafford, he " saved our lives " several times during the day. Travelling *via* Messines, past the London Scottish memorial, we quickly reached the frontier where Custom Officials got busy with the dip stick in the petrol tank. This formality was soon over, and we travelled on through Armentiéres and made our first stop to inspect the Memorial to the Indians at Neuve Chapelle with 4,847 names inscribed. Le Touret Cemetery close by was visited, and here, among the names of over 13,000 missing, we found a long list of " Shinies."

En route to Neuve Chapelle we passed the " Christ of the Trenches," this crucifix stood intact the whole period of the War, practically in the front line.

We were now reaching a part of the country very familiar to some of the party. Our next stop permitted us to stand and survey the site of the Loos battle, which took place on 25th September, 1915, and in those days had such a sinister expression of death. The Double Crassier, Loos village and other landmarks, were clearly distinguishable.

We entered Dud Corner Cemetery and found several graves of 7th men, including the late S. M. Howes, C. L. Crossingham and Drummer B. B. Boast. Around the walls of this beautifully kept cemetery are the names of the missing, about ninety names appear on the panel allotted to the 7th, among which is the name of Adair (Tich) of whom an appreciation was written by a " Shiny " comrade.

Two other cemeteries close to Loos Village were visited, St. Patricks and Loos British Cemetery. In the former we found seven more graves and in the latter are buried Lieutenants Smith, Donaldson, Major W. Casson, and H. V. Moss. Here also is a whole row of headstones (about forty all told), with the 7th badge and underneath the inscription " Known unto God."

Our journey continued through Lens to Vimy, and as we climbed the hill we had a view of the gigantic memorial erected in memory of the Canadians. Vimy stands 475 feet above sea-level, the scene of much mining, and many tunnels were constructed; several of these have been strengthened with concrete and may now be explored. Trenches have concrete sandbags and duckboards.

The " Shinies " were in this area from February to July, 1916, here on May 21st, the Germans made the largest artillery demonstration of the War up to then. This was the first " box barrage " and was followed by a mass attack, resulting in the capture of many 7th men, including Capt. Davies and Lieut. Brooks. The 47th Division suffered 63 Officers and 2,044 other ranks, killed, wounded and missing.

We went into the tunnels which were constructed during the War by British engineers. The average length of these is half a mile; they are 6 ft. 6 ins. high and 3 ft. wide, and there are about twenty-two miles of these all told, complete with mine shafts

THE PARTY AT WARLENCOURT BRITISH CEMETERY

nearly 100 ft. deep. Crests and names carved by the troops while resting can be seen. These tunnels are extremely interesting and well worth visiting.

We were running late according to our schedule, but Capt. de Trafford filled the breach and 'phoned the Hotel at Arras to say we were on our way, so that when we pulled up at the Hotel Moderne everything was ready for us, and no time was wasted in getting down to a good hot lunch.

One of the party, who shall be nameless, scored a point over his thirsty comrades in the following manner: Entering the Hotel he told a waiter to " hurry up with a drink." The garcon, taking him for an individual customer, brought him a drink immediately, whilst we had to sit for some minutes and watch him lower it before we were served.

Our fortune at Arras was to witness the passing of the great road cycle race from Paris to Lille, about one hundred competitors were still going strong at this stage of the contest; each one appeared to have a following of cars and the pavements were lined on both sides by the inhabitants to see these many coloured, begrimed and goggled cyclists on their way.

Off we went again, fortified by good fare, then slowly we drove around the Grand Place and the Petit Place, taking the road to Bapaume. Our driver was exceedingly careful, frequently sounding his loud klaxon horn at a cyclist half a mile before he reached him, much to our amusement and at times the horn went continually for three or four minutes.

From Bapaume we took the road to Albert, and shortly reached the Warlencourt Cemetery where we found more than two dozen graves of "7th" men including Capt. Flower, Sgt. Lovelock, Eagles and Sec. Lt. Coles, M.M. Further along the road we had a view of the Butte de Warlencourt which, although it was attacked by three other Divisions after the efforts of the 47th Division, was never captured until the general retirement of the Germans in 1917.

Our next stop was at the London Cemetery High Wood. Strange to say, we failed to find any 7th graves, but in the extension under construction at the rear, we found the grave of Williams.

Just south of the Cemetery on the edge of High Wood, stands the 47th Divisional Memorial and here a wreath was placed in memory of those gone but not forgotten, after which cameras were out and snaps taken. High Wood will long be remembered, as it was here that Tanks were first used.

We carried on to Guillemont, passing on the way the New Zealand and South African Memorials, then Delville Wood and on past Trones Wood, through Montauban and Mametz to Fricourt. Here we turned north to La Boïsselle *via* Contalmaison.

At La Boïsselle, a walk of about one hundred yards, past several chalk heaps with barbed wire projecting, we found a dump of old rusty Mills bombs, stick grenades, water-bottles, etc., and then we came to the Crater which is gigantic. I should like to give you the dimensions, but I am no good at guessing. I moved back from the edge for it made me feel giddy to look at the bottom.

One famous "Eye-witness" in the War, wrote of this Crater, that it was large enough to hold a battalion of men complete with horses and waggons, and he was not exaggerating. One of our number remarked that he thought "he knew what a Crater was," until he saw this one.

47th DIVISIONAL MEMORIAL
Showing the poppy wreath placed by the party.

Off we went again through Pozieres, and up to see the enormous and cleverly planned Thiepval memorial to the missing of the Somme. This memorial has a perfect setting and is exceedingly well laid out, the names of over 73,000 appear on the panels and, unfortunately, the "7th" are too well represented here.

Back to the Albert - Bapaume road, straight through to Arras where we made a stop at an Estaminet for some liquid refreshment. Here we examined the holes made by bullets in the mirror fixed to the wall, and still in the same position as throughout the War. On the way out of Arras we held a jolly fine "Roosters" concert party in the char-a-banc. Tommy Atkins was choirmaster, ably assisted by our Chelsea comrade, and well supported by the remainder of the company.

We had the pleasure of returning *via* Lille, which permitted a little additional sight-seeing. The 47th Division entered Lille on 28th October, 1918, and received a tremendous reception from the inhabitants who had been under German rule for four years, red, white and blue posters had been printed with the inscription, " Honour and Glory for 47th Division our Deliverers."

On reaching our Hotel at 10.45 p.m. after having accomplished a wonderful circular tour of over 145 miles, a jolly fine dinner prepared by the Splendid's famous chef was enjoyed by all and so to bed.

Monday morning came with more brilliant sunshine, and some of us were out early inspecting the town. After breakfast, one party travelled by 'bus to Zonnebeke to visit Tyne Cot Cemetery and on to Passchendaele whilst we took a 'bus past Shrapnel Corner as far as the Canal Bank, I can recollect that when we went up the line — always by night — we followed the duck board track which hugged the Canal Bank, but now we were walking along the top of the Bank. We continued past the lock ruins up to Spoilbank and Chester Farm Cemeteries. In the latter are several "7th" men, here lies one who won the M.M. in 1917 for killing two unwanted visitors and capturing another, only to meet his fate on the 7th June, here an old pal was accidentally shot by one of our own men, and another killed by a sniper's bullet at " stand to " one morning. What a tale the dates on the stones tell ! Here three artillerymen were all killed on the same date, and one imagines a direct hit on a gun team, then the grave of a German killed during a raid on Hedge Row front.

It seems strange to see an Estaminet at the foot of the Bluff, but it is a fact, how welcome something of this nature would have been during the time when the "7th" spent eleven months in this area.

Some of the party climbed up on top of the Bluff and looked down to where the old Wynde trench (the drain of the front line) used to be, and walked along to the Crater later joining the others at a spot, which to readers familiar with the lay of the land, was known as the Mudpatch. It was here that one of our Sergeants and another man (who had just been reduced in rank), went out on patrol one night and finding it too light to return had to stay close to the German lines in a shell-hole all day. They came in the following night and, if I remember rightly, one got the D.C.M. and the other got his three stripes back.

Then on to the remnants of the White Chateau where Lieut. J. Preston won his M.C. when the "7th" captured the stronghold in 1917. It was in front of this place, just after its capture, on 7th June, that the writer was wounded. The White Chateau is now a grass covered mound surrounded with a grass track.

We returned to the road and carried on to St. Eloi, joining the main road at The Chateau de la Mine, the old Crater appears to have been converted into a duck-pond.

Our next visit was to Bus House Cemetery where Drummers Barnes and Jiggings lay buried. It was nice to see in the visitors book that the parents of both these Drummers had visited these graves recently. We also came across the writer's signature dated 1930.

On down the road to the Canal Bank and Bedford House Cemetery, where we took our 'bus to Ypres. Before leaving a visit was paid to the Cathedral and the British Church, the remainder of our time being spent shop-gazing and making small purchases for those at home.

Ypres on this Easter Monday presented a rare sight to us, the Grande Place was filled with cars and the pavements full of people, a music festival was in progress, about eight bands from surrounding parts were in competition.

Taking our reserved seats in the train this Band of Pilgrims took a farewell glance at hospitable Ypres and settled down to the journey to Ostend where we embarked for home. A lovely smooth crossing being enjoyed, Victoria was reached at 7.40 a.m., and so ended what was voted by all a most memorable and enjoyable week-end.

Before closing I should like to pay two compliments. Firstly, to one of our members, who lost a leg towards the end of the War, and is now fitted up with an artificial one, he accompanied us everywhere and thoroughly enjoyed every minute from start to finish ; the other is to Capt. de Trafford, and to thank him on behalf of all who took part in the Tour. We award him full marks for the attention he gave to our requirements and for all the arrangements made to ensure our tour being a success. We hope he will give his valuable help again next year.

Finally, what a surprise when we opened the morning paper and read, " the coldest Easter for a century " ; we could not believe it, for once in a way the " Shinies " had been lucky with sunny weather.

That One Old Gun

By " Pop " Wright (" Daily Express ").

THE scene, a wood in the Somme country, France. The date, June 30th, 1916. For two days and nights unceasingly British shells have blasted the German line. Miles of guns, big, medium and small have stood shoulder to shoulder on our front pouring shrapnel over. A fly on the other side, it seems to us, would be lucky to escape with its life.

Each night for a week, infantry bombing parties have carried out their smash and grab operations on the enemy trenches. A few Germans have been kidnapped alive. Many British bombers, the flower of their battalions, have never returned. That is why we called them the " Suicide Club."

Parties of us have been marched out into the open bare fields to be taught how to take part in a " great push." The coming battle on July 1st will be the first real test of Kitchener's army as storm troops.

We sit in the fields in circles. Our instructions explain how the " waves " will go over. We shall wear ribbons of different colours on our shoulders to indicate the " wave " we are in.

Dull faced civilians, apparently French peasants, hang around . . . listening. Hovering over the horizon are German " sausage " balloons . . . their occupants watching.

The evening of June 30th has arrived. We have handed to the Quartermaster's staff our valises and personal belongings. The haversack with emergency rations is strapped on our backs. Our equipment is reduced to battle order.

The bellow of our guns across yonder becomes more intense.

Letters have been written to mothers, sisters and wives in England. They are just the same ordinary letters we have been writing to them for nearly two years. The same old white lie . . . " Don't worry. I am in a safe job behind the line. Hope to get leave soon."

The June sun has sunk to the tops of the poplar trees. Some of us, indulging in a few human thoughts, give him a long look.

Our band in a glade near is playing. It sounds plaintive. The air we hear is " The End of a Perfect Day."

Men who have been strapped to trees " doing first field " are released to join their comrades.

Then there is a sudden movement in the woods all around. Words of command reach us. We fall in . . . for the first day of the Battle of the Somme.

Our pouches are bulging with ammunition. We carry spades, bombs, rifles and gas masks. It is a peaceful summer dusk. But a few miles in front of us the horizon growls and thunders. The sky as far as the eye can reach reflects from below a furness of bursting shells, artillery flashes and Verey lights.

A rest on the roadside. A general and his staff appear before us from the shadows. He halts and addresses us. " Good luck, men," he says, " To-morrow afternoon you will be in Serre orchard. Our bombardment has prevented the enemy from bringing up supplies for three days. They have only one old gun in front of you."

My battalion, the 12th York and Lancasters (Sheffield) again falls in. We reach the rear trenches. Any talk is now impossible. We grope our way through the narrow burrows sweating beneath our burdens of metal, and gasping for air. Avenues of field guns above us crash and roar unceasingly and from our rear we hear the diabolical bass of heavy artillery.

Throughout the night we continue our slow struggle through the trenches. Trench boards floating in slime sink feet down as we step on them. Here and there we meet a party of R.A.M.C. men carrying a silent, blanket-wrapped form on a stretcher. How we manage to pass them in that narrow space is a mystery. These little processions increase as the dawn begins to show in the strip of sky visible to us.

And I hear through the inferno a voice in front of me, " One old gun ! "

We reach our posts. The sun is now up. It is about half-past six, and " zero " is not until 7.30 . . . an uncanny hour and a quarter, and a haunting memory.

Added to the shell fire we now hear the busy chatter of machine guns a few yards away. One of our men comes staggering along the trench, his mouth torn almost from ear to ear. For great shells are now screaming over our trench. Company officers are engrossed in their watches. Sergeants are eyeing the faces of the men of their platoons. Here and there faintly I hear a joke—perhaps grim, but effective.

Zero comes.

Arms of officers are raised towards the sandbags. The first wave of men, the ribbons on their shoulders flashing in the sun, scramble over the top.

A sudden hurricane of machine gun fire from the German trenches . . . a mine explodes near us. The sky seems to rock, but in reality it is the country around us. Masses of " No Man's Land " rise to the heavens under the shell fire. Men who are not wiped out by shrapnel are swept down by a hail of machine gun bullets. A quarter of an hour . . . and it is all over on this sector.

Then I find myself seated in the unwrecked part of a trench. I have been bomb carrying. The canvas bucket strapped over my shoulder is still full. No one is left to use them.

I seem to be the only person surviving in the world. Then a figure, his face a mere mask of blood, gropes his way towards me. He addresses me by name. He falls . . . and is still. One of my platoon mates.

Night descends over a growling front. Still dragging my bombs I find myself more by chance than by sense of direction in a trench with a mixed company of survivors of different regiments. Our units have melted away. My own battalion has been reduced to about 25 men.

Our R.S.M. appears later from somewhere among the wreckage. He is an iron old soldier of the regulars. He orders the shattered group to " stand to " for the second sleepless night. We are, he grunts, to go over the top again . . . over the top into that eerie region our battalion had entered that morning never to return.

We wait for death. But the sentence does not come.

And at daybreak as I am falling asleep on a mattress of mud in a sap, I hear a weary Yorkshire voice :

' That one owd gun," it says, " must have had pups in t'neet."

Ypres British School

The Prize-giving at the School will take place at 9.45 a.m. on July 13th, 1936.

T. Blake, who was educated at the British School at Ypres has obtained a First Class Certificate of Education at the Technical School at Chepstow.

* * * *

The Committee of the British School desire to acknowledge with grateful thanks the donation of Twenty Pounds from the Earl Haig and First Army Corps Fund. The money to be devoted to helping in the expenses of children coming over to England for employment.

The unveiling of the Haig and First Corps Memorial has been posponed until October next.

Correspondence

The Editor,   West Worthing.
   YPRES TIMES.   May 3rd, 1936.

SIR,

The Cloth Hall in Ypres was one of the most celebrated medieval buildings in Europe. As all the world knows, it was destroyed in the late war. One of its most striking features was the Great Hall or Salle Pauwels, measuring some 190 feet long by 39 feet wide. The walls of this noble place of assembly were covered by paintings depicting great events in the history of Ypres, one of the best known being the Defence of Ypres against the English in 1383.

For some time past the rebuilding of the Cloth Hall has been in progress, and it is proposed ultimately to restore the whole, including the paintings in the Salle Pauwels, to its ancient grandeur. The authorities of Ypres, however, consider that some outstanding event of the Defence of Ypres by the British during the War of 1914-18 should be depicted and with this object are prepared to put the East wall of the great Hall, measuring some 39 feet by 16 feet, at the disposal of the British people in the hope that something worthy of the Hall and of the Defence may be shown thereon. Doubtless opinions will vary greatly as to the subject to be selected, especially in view of the lack of spectacular effect in modern warfare, but the proposal is well worthy of attention and support.

                                     Your obedient Servant,
                                                               W.G.P.

N.B.—The Ypres League Headquarters support the above scheme, and the Editor, "YPRES TIMES" would welcome any suggestions from members.

* * *

                            THE END HOUSE,
                                  MALCOLM ROAD,
                                          S.W. 19.
The Secretary,   27th May, 1936.
   Ypres League.

DEAR SIR,

If it is permissible I should like to become a subscriber to the Ypres League.

My reasons being :—
    (1) In memory of my brother, S. Milsom, of the Rifle Brigade, killed at Hooge on 30th July, 1915.
    (2) In acknowledgment of the courtesy and kind hospitality shewn to the Officers of the 129th Brigade who visited the Salient, 22nd to 25th of May.

                                           Yours very truly,
                                                  H. L. MILSOM.

League Secretary's Notes

In the last edition of the YPRES TIMES we were lamenting the death of our beloved King George and Patron-in-Chief, but we have received no small measure of consolation by the gracious act of His Majesty King Edward in granting his Patronage to the Ypres League, so in loyal respect to our Royal Patron we must continue our endeavours to strengthen the membership of our Association and leave nothing unturned to uphold the good name and prestige of the Ypres League for many years to come.

Despite the lapse of time since the Great War, sacrifice and good fellowship still remains a vivid picture to members of the League and to those of kindred Ex-service Associations who are working to keep that precious memory alive, not only amongst the ex-service men themselves, but to educate the younger generation in all that the Great War commemorates : our annual Public School O.T.C. Battlefield Tour is an excellent example of how the realistic view can be interestedly conveyed and remembered by the cadets of our leading Public Schools. Further, the League has had privilege to organise a number of Battlefield Tours each year for young officers of Territorial Brigades, and these tours are now recognised as an official part of their Divisional Training. The first regimental tour of 1936 was for that of the 2nd London Infantry Brigade ; then came the 1st London Infantry Brigade party accompanied by such distinguished soldiers as Major-General P. R. C. Commings, Commanding The London Division and Major-General Sir Cecil Pereira ; after which, took place the tours of the 56th Divisional Engineers ; the Public Schools O.T.C., and the 129th Infantry Brigade. In addition to serving units, a party of members of the 7th London O.C.A. embarked on a visit to Ypres and the Somme at Easter, and at next August Bank Holiday we are arranging a circular tour for members of the Old Coldstreamers' Association to Mons and Arras. No less important are the mixed pilgrimages which continue to be well represented and greatly enjoyed by all who take part, and such reunions at Ypres do much to promote our main objects of commemoration and comradeship. The progress of our travel bureau during the past few years has been outstanding, and it now appears that this branch of activity has become a thoroughly established force in the League's work.

From now on, our attention should be focussed more widely on the important sphere of recruiting new members, because the life of the Ypres League solely depends on its membership. We trust that each one of us will make a very special effort between now and the end of 1936 to do our little bit by enroling some relative or friend and thus make the first year of our work under King Edward's Patronage something of which we shall have reason to feel proud.

OBITUARY.

In the death of Viscount Allenby, the Ypres League suffers the loss of one of its distinguished Vice-Presidents and an Appreciation by Field-Marshal Sir Philip Chetwode is published in this edition of the "YPRES TIMES."

It will be remembered that in 1932, the late Field-Marshal showed his practical support of our cause in laying the wreath on the Cenotaph on the "Ypres Day" Commemoration Parade, and in the same year granted us the distinctive honour of presiding at the London Branch Re-union Smoking Concert.

We wish to extend our respectful and heartfelt sympathy to Lady Allenby and family in their great bereavement.

We have pleasure to record that Captain L. Murphy has most generously offered the Ypres League his services as Corresponding Member for St. John's, Newfoundland.

In accepting Captain Murphy's kind offer, we extend to him our sincere thanks and good wishes in his noble endeavours for the welfare of our cause.

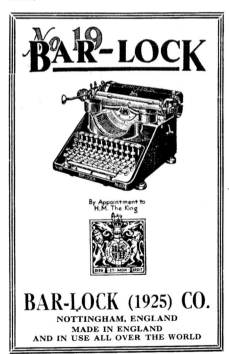

BAR-LOCK (1925) CO.
NOTTINGHAM, ENGLAND
MADE IN ENGLAND
AND IN USE ALL OVER THE WORLD

YPRES LEAGUE POOR PILGRIMS FUND.

We desire to acknowledge with very grateful thanks the following two donations recently received in support of our charitable work:—
1. £20 from The Earl Haig and First Army Corps Fund.
2. £10 from the South Kensington Branch of the British Legion.

We cannot emphasise how greatly we value such benevolence and the kind donors may rest assured that their generous contributions will be deservingly expended this year on poor mothers to enable them to visit, for the first time, the graves of their sons situated in the Ypres Salient.

BACK NUMBERS OF THE "YPRES TIMES."

If any members can kindly spare their copies of the following editions of the "Ypres Times," the Secretary would be most grateful:—
January, April, July and October, 1933 also January, 1934.

EMBROIDERED BADGES.

These badges which can be suitably worn on pockets of sports jackets may be supplied on application to the Secretary, Ypres League, 20, Orchard Street, London, W.1. Price 4/- post free.

MODELS OF DEMARCATION STONE.

Plaster models of the Demarcation Stone can be supplied from Head Office.

All members are aware that 240 granite demarcation stones stretch from the Swiss border to the sea, marking the extreme line of advance of the German invasion.

The model, which is 6 inches in height, may be used for a paperweight or as an ornament. Price 5s., post free in United Kingdom. Applications to the Secretary, Ypres League.

YPRES LEAGUE TIE.

Dark shade of cornflower blue relieved by a narrow gold stripe. In good quality silk.

Price 3/6d., post free.

Obtainable from Secretary, Ypres League, 20, Orchard Street, London, W.1.

YPRES LEAGUE BADGE

The badge is brilliantly enamelled with silver finish. Price 2s., post free 2s. 1½d. (pin or stud, whichever is desired).

HOTEL
Splendid & Britannique
YPRES

GRANDE PLACE. Opposite Cloth Hall.

Leading Hotel for Comfort and Quality, and Patronized by The Ypres League.

Completely Renovated.

Running Water. Bathrooms.

Moderate Terms. Garage.

Proprietor—Life Member, Ypres League.

YPRES
Skindles Hotel

(Opposite the Station)

Proprietor—Life Member, Ypres League

Branch at Poperinghe

(close to Talbot House)

1936 Recruiting Competition

IN view of the continued popularity of the recruiting competition we have great pleasure to announce that **A FURTHER PRIZE OF £5** will be awarded this year as follows :—

TO THE BRANCH RECRUITING THE GREATEST NUMBER OF NEW MEMBERS IN 1936.

All membership forms completed must be received at headquarters bearing on the top left-hand corner the name of the branch responsible for the recruitment.

Branch Notes

PURLEY.

On Thursday, May 21st, the Purley Branch held the Spring Golf Meeting and 36 members competed for the Eleventh Wipers Cup. The competition was 18 holes Bogey, under the Stapleford system, which proved a great success and every competitor enjoyed the round.

The winner was Lieut. S. Newman with $36\frac{1}{4}$ and the second our eminent Chairman, Private A. K. Irens, playing from a handicap of four, returned 36.

At the supper which followed, the prizes were presented, and in addition the Chairman awarded the Cups and replicas to the 1935 winners of the Bombardier's Foursomes which would normally have been given at the Annual Reunion Dinner last March, postponed until the expiry of Court Mourning.

LONDON COUNTY COMMITTEE.
Informal Gatherings.

At the May informal, Mr. W. J. Morrison very kindly gave us an extremely interesting illustrated talk on Y.M.C.A. work with the British Forces in the Field, and in June, an excellent programme was organised under the direction of Mrs. Stratton and Mrs. Heap to whom we offer our grateful thanks.

We have now completed the season's monthly meetings and desire to express our gratitude for the generous assistance that has been extended to these Gatherings during the past twelve months. Further, we shall look forward to seeing even more representative attendances during the next series which will be announced in due course in the columns of the "Ypres Times," and we trust that members and friends will see their way to repeat the voluntary help in connection with these evening entertainments.

We greatly regret to announce that, since the last edition of the "Ypres Times," the London Branch has suffered the loss of a most valuable supporter in the death of Mr. C. Schleinger, one of our original members and whose work for the Ypres League will remain an example of successful individual effort.

PLEASE RESERVE THIS DATE.

◆ ········ ◆

The

FOURTEENTH ANNUAL REUNION

SMOKING CONCERT

(Organised by the London County Committee)

will be held on

Saturday, October 31st, 1936

at 7.30 p.m.

in

Caxton Hall, Caxton St., Victoria Street, S.W.1.

◆ ········ ◆

The Programme will be given by

THE ROOSTER'S CONCERT PARTY.

◆ ········ ◆

The support of all members is earnestly solicited as we hope very much to record a bumper attendance this year. Tickets will shortly be on sale, and full particulars will appear in the next October edition of the "Ypres Times."

Ypres League Travel Bureau

CONDUCTED PILGRIMAGES FOR 1936

AUGUST BANK HOLIDAY (August 1st—4th, Saturday to Tuesday) (Two separate pilgrimages) :

    YPRES (Day route *via* Ostend).

    ARRAS (Day route *via* Boulogne).

SEPTEMBER (September 19th—22nd, Saturday to Tuesday) YPRES (Day route *via* Ostend).

(Battlefield tours arranged by the conductor at Ypres to suit the requirements of the party at moderate charges).

Prospectuses will be gladly forwarded on application to The Secretary, Ypres League, 20, Orchard Street, London, W.1.

INDEPENDENT TRAVEL.

To those contemplating individual travel, our Travel Department would be pleased to furnish information on all matters connected with trips to any part of the Old Western Front Battlefields.

Apply to Secretary, Ypres League, 20, Orchard Street, London, W.1, for the Ypres League Travel Guide for 1936.

THE BRITISH TOURING SERVICE

Manager—Mr. P. VYNER

10, Station Square

Representative and Life Member, Ypres League

ARRAS

(P.-de-C.) France

Cars for Hire, with British Driver Guides   Tours Arranged

Branches and Corresponding Members

BRANCHES.

LONDON	Hon. Secretary to the London County Committee : J. Boughey 20, Orchard Street, London, W.1.
	E. LONDON DISTRICT—L. A. Weller, 26, Lambourne Gardens, Hornchurch, Essex.
	TOTTENHAM AND EDMONTON DISTRICT—E, Glover, 191, Landowne Road, Tottenham, N.17.
	H. Carey, 373, Sydenham Road, S.E.26.
COLCHESTER	H. Snow (Hon. Sec.), 9, Church Street.
	W. H. Taylor (Pilgrimage Hon. Sec.), 64, High Street.
LIVERPOOL	Captain A. M. Webster, Blundellsands.
PURLEY	Major Graham Carr, D.S.O., M.C., 112-114, High Street.
SHEFFIELD	Captain J. Wilkinson, "Holmfield," Bents Drive.
BELGIUM	Capt. P. D. Parminter, 19, Rue Surmont de Volsberghe, Ypres.
CANADA	Ed. Kingsland, P.O. Box 83, Magog, Quebec.
SOUTH AFRICA	L. G. Shuter, Church Street, Pietermaritzburg,
KENYA	C. H. Slater, P.O. Box 403, Nairobi.
AMERICA	Representative : Captain R. Henderson-Bland, 110 West 57th Street, New York City.

CORSPONDING MEMBERS

GREAT BRITAIN.

ABERYSTWYTH	T. O. Thomas, 5, Smithfield Road.
ASHTON-UNDER-LYNE	G. D. Stuart, "Woodlands,", Thronfield Grove, Arundel Street.
BANBURY	Captain C. W. Fowke, Yew Tree House, King's Sutton.
BIRMINGHAM	Mrs. Hill, 191, Cattell Road, Small Heath.
	John Burman, "Westbrook," Solihull Road, Shirley.
BOURNEMOUTH	H. L. Pasmore, 40, Morley Road, Boscombe Park.
BRISTOL	W. S. Hook, "Wytschaete" Redland Court Road.
BROADSTAIRS	C. E. King, 6, Norman Road, St. Peters, Broadstairs.
	Mrs. Briggs, North Foreland House.
CHATHAM	W. N. Channon, 22, Keyes Avenue.
CHESTERFIELD	Major A. W. Shea, 14, Cross Street.
CONGLETON	Mr. H. Dart, 61, The Crescent.
DARLINGTON	D. S. Vigo, 125, Dorset Road, Bexhill-on-Sea.
DERBY	T. Jakeman, 10, Graham Street.
DORRINGTON (Salop)	Captain G. D. S. Parker, Frodesley Rectory.
EXETER	Captain E. Jenkin, 25, Queen Street.
HERNE BAY	Captain E. Clarke Williams, F.S.A.A., "Conway," Station Road
HOVE	Captain G. W. J. Cole, 2, Westbourne Terrace, Kingsway.
LEICESTER	W. C. Dunford, 343, Aylestone Road.
LINCOLN	E. Swaine, 79, West Parade.
LLANWRST	A. C. Tomlinson, M.A., Bod Estyn.
LOUGHTON	Capt. O. G. Johnson, M.A., Loughton School.
MATLOCK (Derby)	Miss Dickinson, Beechwood.
MELROSE	Mrs. Lindesay Kelsall, Darnlee.
NEW BRIGHTON (Cheshire)	E. F. Williams, 5, Waterloo Road.
NEW MILTON	W. H. Lunn, "Greycot," Albert Road.

NOTTINGHAM	E. V. Brown, 3, Eldon Chambers, Wheeler Gate.
ST. HELENS (Lancs.) ...	John Orford, 124, Knowsley Road.
ST. JOHN'S (Newfoundland)	Captain L. Murphy, G.W.V.A. Office.
SHREWSBURY	Major-General Sir John Headlam, K.B.E., C.B., D.S.O., Cruck Meole House, Hanwood.
TIVERTON (Devon) ...	Mr. W H. Duncan Arthur, Surveyor's Office, Town Hall.
WELSHPOOL	Mr. E. Wilson, Coedway, Ford, Salop.

DOMINIONS AND FOREIGN COUNTRIES.

AUSTRALIA	Messrs. C. H. Green, and George Lawson, Essex House, (Opposite Anzac Square) Brisbane, Queensland.
	R. A. Baldwin, c/o Government Savings Bank of N.S.W., Martin Place, Sydney.
	Mr. W. Cloves, Box 1296, G.P.O., Adelaide.
BELGIUM	Sister Marguerite, Sacré Coeur, Ypres.
CANADA	Brig.-General V. W. Odlum, C.B., C.M.G., D.S.O., 2530, Point Grey Road, Vancouver.
	V. A. Bowes, 326, 40th Avenue West. Calgary, Alberta.
	W. Constable F. Grece, St. Hilaire Station, Ronville County, Quebec.
CEYLON	Captain F. R. G. Webb, M.C., Irrigation Bungalow, Kalmunai, E.P.
EGYPT	L. B. S. Larkins, The Residency, Cairo.
INDIA	Lieut.-Quartermaster G. Smith, Queen's Bays. Sialkot, India.
IRELAND	Miss A. K. Jackson, Cloneyhurke House, Portarlington.
NEW ZEALAND	Captain W. U. Gibb, Ava Lodge, Puhinui Road, Papatoetoe, Auckland
	S. E. Beattie, P.O. Box 11, Otaki Railway, Wellington.
SOUTH AFRICA	H. L. Versfield, c/o Cape Explosives Works Ltd., 150, St. Georges Street, Cape Town.
SPAIN	Captain P. W. Burgess, Calle de Zurbano 29, Madrid.
U.S.A.	Captain Henry Maslin, 942, President Street, Brooklyn, New York.
	L. E. P, Foot. 20, Gillett Street, Hartford, Conn, U.S.A.
	A. P. Forward, 449, East 80th Street, New York.
	J. W. Freebody, 945, McBride Avenue, Los Angeles.
NOVA SCOTIA	Will R. Bird, 35, Clarence Street, Amherst.

Membership of the League

This is open to all who served in the Salient, and to all those whose relatives or friends died there, in order that they may have a record of that service for themselves and their descendants, and belong to the comradeship of men and women who understand and remember all that Ypres meant in suffering and endurance.

Life membership, £2 10s.

Annual members, 5s.

Do not let the fact of your not having served in the Salient deter you from joining the Ypres League. Those who have neither fought in the Salient nor lost relatives there, but who are in sympathy with the objects of the Ypres League, are admitted to its fellowship, but are not given scroll certificates.

There is a Junior Division for children whose relatives served in the Salient. It is open also to others to whom our objects appeal.

Annual subscription 1s. up to the age of 18, after which they can become ordinary members of the League.

THE YPRES LEAGUE (INCORPORATED)
20, Orchard Street, Portman Square, W.1.

Telephone: WELBECK 1446.   *Telegrams*: YPRESLEAG, " WESDO," LONDON.

Patron-in-Chief: H.M. THE KING.

Patron:
H.R.H. PRINCESS BEATRICE.

President: GENERAL SIR CHARLES H. HARINGTON.

Vice-Presidents:
THE VISCOUNT WAKEFIELD OF HYTHE.   F.-M. SIR CLAUD W. JACOB.
F.-M. LORD MILNE.   F.-M. SIR PHILIP CHETWODE.
GENERAL SIR CECIL ROMER.

General Committee:

THE COUNTESS OF ALBEMARLE.
*CAPTAIN C. ALLISTON.
LIEUT-COLONEL BECKLES WILLSON.
MR. HENRY BENSON.
*MR. J. BOUGHEY.
*MISS B. BRICE-MILLER.
COLONEL G. T. BRIERLEY.
CAPTAIN P. W. BURGESS.
BRIG.-GENL. A. BURT.
*MAJOR H. CARDINAL-HARFORD.
REV. P. B. CLAYTON.
*THE EARL OF YPRES.
MRS. C. J. EDWARDS.
MAJOR C. J. EDWARDS.
MR. H. A. T. FAIRBANK.
MR. T. ROSS FURNER.
SIR PHILIP GIBBS.
MR. E. GLOVER.

MR. F. D. BANKES-HILL.
MAJOR-GENERAL C. J. B. HAY.
MR. J. HETHERINGTON.
GENERAL SIR W. C. G. HENEKER.
*CAPTAIN O. G. JOHNSON.
*MAJOR E. MONTAGUE JONES.
MAJOR GENL. C. G. LIDDELL.
CAPTAIN H. D. PEABODY.
*THE HON. ALICE DOUGLAS PENNANT.
*LIEUT.-GENERAL SIR W. P. PULTENEY.
LIEUT.-COLONEL SIR J. MURRAY.
*COLONEL G. E. C. RASCH.
THE HON. SIR ARTHUR STANLEY.
MR. ERNEST THOMPSON.
CAPTAIN J. LOCKLEY TURNER.
*MR. E. B. WAGGETT.
CAPTAIN J. WILKINSON.
CAPTAIN H. TREVOR WILLIAMS.

* Executive Committee.

Bankers:
BARCLAYS BANK LTD., Knightsbridge Branch.

Honorary Solicitors:
MESSRS. FLADGATE & CO., 70, Pall Mall, S.W.

Secretary:
CAPTAIN G. E. DE TRAFFORD.

Auditors:
MESSRS. LEPINE & JACKSON,
6, Bond Court, E.C.4.

League Representative at Ypres:
CAPTAIN P. D. PARMINTER.
19, Rue Surmont de Volsberghe

League Representative at Cambrai:
MR. A. WILDE,
9, Rue des Anglaises.

League Representative at Amiens:
CAPTAIN STUART OSWALD.
7, Rue Porte-Paris.

League Representative at Arras:
MR. P. VYNER,
10, Station Square.

Hon. Secretary, Ypres British Settlement:
LT. COLONEL F. G. POOLE.

PRIMARY OBJECTS OF THE LEAGUE

I.—Commemoration and Comradeship.

II.—To provide special travel facilities for Members and all interested to Ypres and battlefields, and transport of Members.

III.—The furnishing of information about the Salient; marking of historic sites and the compilation of charts of the battlefields.

IV.—The erection of a Ypres British Church and School which has been completed.

V.—The establishment of groups of members throughout the world, through Branch Secretaries and Corresponding Members.

VI.—The maintenance of cordial relations with dwellers on the battlefields of Ypres.

VII.—The formation of a Junior Division.

Use the Ypres League Travel Bureau for Ypres and Whole of the Western Front.

FOR THE FOLLOWING PUBLICATIONS, Etc., apply:

Secretary, **YPRES LEAGUE, 20, ORCHARD STREET, LONDON, W.1.**

THE BATTLE BOOK OF YPRES. A history of notable deeds contributed by all regiments. 5s.; post free, 5s. 6d. Compiled by Beatrix Brice with the assistance of Lieut.-General Sir William Pulteney, G.C.V.O., etc.

BOOKS.

YPRES: Outpost of the Channel Ports. By Beatrix Brice. With Foreword by Field-Marshal Lord Plumer, G.C.B. Price 1s. 0d.; post free 1s. 3d.

In the Ypres Salient. By Lt.-Col. Beckles Willson. 1s. net; post free 1s. 2d.

Story of the 63rd Field Ambulance. By A. W. Westmore, etc. Cloth, 3s. 6d., post free. Paper, 2s. 6d., post free.

War Letters to a Wife. By Colonel Rowland Feilding. Popular Edition, 3s. 6d.; post free 4s.

The Pill Boxes of Flanders. 1s.; post free 1s. 3d.

From Mons to the First Battle of Ypres. By J. G. W. Hyndson, M.C. Price 3/6, post free

---

YPRES LEAGUE TIES. 3s. 6d. each, post free.

YPRES LEAGUE BADGES. 2s. each, 2s. 1½d. post free.

EMBROIDERED BADGES. 4s. each, post free.

Map and List of Cemeteries in the Ypres Salient. Price 9d.; post free 11d.

Map of the Somme. Price 1s. 8d., post free.

PICTURES.

Burning of the Cloth Hall, 1915. A Coloured Print, 14 in. by 12 in. 1s. post free.

Old Well-known Spots in New Guise.
Prints, size 4¼ x 2½, recently taken of famous spots in the Ypres Salient, and which may be of great interest to our readers, are on sale at headquarters, price 4d. each, post free 5d. For particulars apply Secretary.

POST CARDS, PHOTOGRAPHS AND ETCHINGS.

Post Cards. Ypres: British Front during the War. Ruins of Ypres. Price 1s. post free.

Hill 60. Complete Panorama Photographs.
12 in. by 3¾ in. Price 3s., post free; 15 in. by 5 in. Price 3s. 6d., post free.

MODELS OF DEMARCATION STONE.

The model, which is 6 inches in height, may be used for a paperweight or as an ornament. Price 5/-, post free.
Applications to the Secretary, Ypres League.

PHOTOGRAPHS OF WAR-TIME SKETCHES.

Bedford House (Front View), 1916.
Bedford House (Back View), 1916.
Voormezeele Main Street, 1916.
Voormezeele Crucifixion Gate, 1916.
Langhof Chateau, 1916.

Size 8½ in. by 6½ in. Price 2s. 6d. each, post free.

Photographs of the Thiepval and Arras Memorials.
Post card size, price 1s. each, post free.

YPRES TIMES.

The Journal may be obtained at the League Offices.

Back Numbers 1s.; 1934, 8d. 1935, 6d.

Printed in Great Britain for the Publishers by FORD & GILL, 21a/23, Iliffe Yard, Crampton Street, London, S.E.17.

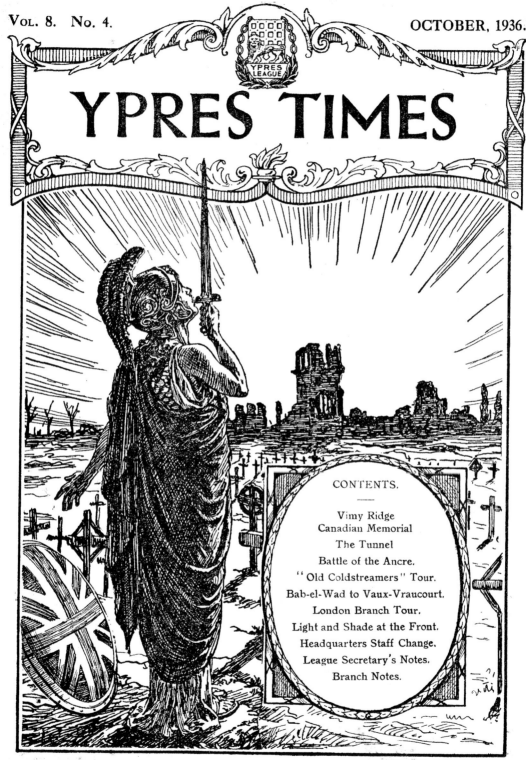

Memory Tablet.

OCTOBER — NOVEMBER — DECEMBER

October.

Oct.	4th, 1914	...	Russian ultimatum to Bulgaria.
,,	5th, 1915	...	Allied Forces land at Salonika.
,,	9th, 1914	...	Antwerp occupied by Germans.
,,	10th, 1916	...	Allied ultimatum to Greece.
,,	14th, 1915	...	Bulgaria at war with Serbia.
,,	18th, 1918	...	Belgian coast clear.
,,	20th, 1914	...	First Battle of Ypres begun.
,,	25th, 1918	...	Ludendorf resigned.

November.

Nov.	1st, 1918	...	Versailles Conference opened.
,,	3rd, 1918	...	Austrian surrender. Kiel mutiny.
,,	4th, 1917	...	British troops in Italy.
,,	5th, 1914	...	Great Britain declares war on Turkey.
,,	6th, 1917	...	British storm the Passchendaele Ridge.
,,	9th, 1918	...	Marshal Foch receives German envoys. Abdication of the Kaiser.
,,	10th, 1918	...	Kaiser's flight to Holland.
,,	10th, 1914	...	"Emden" sunk.
,,	11th, 1918	...	Armistice Terms accepted.
,,	18th, 1917	...	General Maude's death in Mesopotamia.

December.

Dec.	8th, 1914	...	Naval Battle off the Falklands.
,,	9th, 1917	...	British capture Jerusalem.
,,	15th, 1915	...	Sir Douglas Haig C.-in-C. in France.
,,	16th, 1914	...	Germans bombarded West Hartlepool.
,,	19th, 1915	...	Withdrawal from Gallipoli.
,,	24th, 1914	...	First air raid on England.

Vol. 8, No. 4.   Published Quarterly   October, 1936.

H.M. THE KING

Making his speech before unveiling the Canadian Memorial at Vimy Ridge, July 26th, 1936.

Photo]   [Topical Press

Unveiling of the Canadian National War Memorial on Vimy Ridge

THE YPRES LEAGUE were very kindly invited to nominate a Representative as the Guest of the Canadian Government on the occasion of the Unveiling Ceremony at Vimy Ridge which took place there on July 26th last. I had the privilege of being that nominee and formed one of the 60 guests from the United Kingdom.

The great kindness and courtesy of the Canadian Government's High Officials, together with the arrangements made for the comfort of the guests was the ideal of hospitality. A warm welcome from the French Government added to an experience not easily forgotten.

Leaving Victoria Station at 11 a.m. on the 25th by the "Golden Arrow," we reached Paris at about 6 p.m. The Gare du Nord was draped with flags in honour of the occasion, and we were taken by car to the Hotel George V near the Champs Elysses.

In addition to the Under Secretary of State for War and of the Dominions, the Chief of the General Staff, the High Commissioners of Canada, India, and Southern Rhodesia, our party consisted of the widows of famous leaders, Lady Byng, Lady Currie, Lady Jellicoe, representatives of the British Legion, of Toc H, and officers who had served with the Canadian Forces.

At 8 p.m. we attended a banquet given at the Cercle Interallié by Mr. Philippe Roy, Canadian Minister to France, in honour of the Canadian Cabinet Ministers.

The Canadian Minister of Justice, Mr. Lapointe, a French Canadian, spoke of the connection between France and Canada and of the honoured place occupied by Vimy in Canadian history. That distinguished statesman, M. Herriot, now President of the Chamber of Deputies, then paid generous tribute to the Canadian efforts in France in the Great War. My place at table was between the British Consul-General and a former Staff Officer of Marshal Foch, and a most interesting and entertaining evening was enjoyed. Both being in full uniform, there was no difficulty in recognising that famous soldier, the one-armed General Gouraud, "Lion of the Argonne," now Military Governor of Paris, and the sturdy figure of the gallant Marshal Franchôt D'Asperey of Macedonian fame, sometimes known as "Frankly Desperate" to his British comrades.

At 11 a.m. on Sunday, the 26th, our party, together with many French notables, left Paris by special train and at 1.15 p.m. reached Vimy Station, which was be-flagged and where French infantry were beginning to line the roads toward the Ridge. On our way to the Memorial we passed notice boards marked "Canadians de-bus here, Canadian Assembly Post," and already the 8,000 pilgrims were moving to their stations, grizzled, hard-bitten war veterans, women and children. Those who had served wore khaki berets and their medals, while widows of the fallen wore the same berets with the medals of their husbands. Relatives of those who served wore blue berets, while all pilgrims had the maple leaf badge in their caps, and many men and women wore a special pilgrimage medal on the right breast. French war veterans were also assembling with their banners to take part in the ceremony.

Approaching the central avenue leading to the South-western face of the Memorial, which looks towards the original Canadian lines, we passed on the right of the road Guards of Honour furnished by the Canadian Legion, a splendid body of veterans, and "blue jackets" from H.M.S. Saguenay, smart, well trained specimens of young Canada. Behind them were the Canadian Scottish pipers and the band of the Royal Canadian Horse Artillery. On the left was a squadron of Spahis in their picturesque flowing cloaks, two troops mounted on grey barbs, and two on brown, while the outer cordon round the

Memorial was kept by French Infantry in khaki with great-coats and steel helmets. Canadian Mounted Police in red tunics were on duty at the enclosure to the Memorial.

This Memorial to Canada's 60,000 fallen in the Great War, of whom 11,000 have no known grave, but whose names are inscribed on the base, is familiar to many by photograph and is surely one of the most impressive in position and design.

It is situated on the Ridge itself, which gives direct observation for miles around of both the agricultural and industrial areas, the green Plain of Douai and the grimy slag heaps of Lens.

The two pylons of the Memorial, representing France and Canada, are 138 feet high, and the figure of mourning Canada to the right of the pylons was then veiled with Union Jacks.

At 2.15 p.m. His Majesty the King arrived, accompanied by Prince Arthur of Connaught, the Canadian Minister of Justice and the Canadian Minister to France. As the site of the Memorial and the Ridge round about, a total of 240 acres, has now become Canadian soil, by the gift of the French Government, the King had a Canadian Minister in attendance. He was now received by the Canadian Minister of National Defence and of Pensions and National Health, and inspected the Guards of Honour. Descending into the arena on the opposite side of the Memorial, the King moved bareheaded slowly among the pilgrims, paying special attention to a small group of blind men and widows and mothers of the fallen. Loud cheers and great enthusiasm attended his progress and a large number of French Ex-Service men kept shouting " Vive le Roi." and following him.

At 2.50 p.m. the President of the French Republic, M. Lebrun, was received at the Memorial enclosure by H.M. The King, who walked together to the platform overlooking the veiled figure of Canada. Two squadrons of the Royal Air Force now flew overhead and dipped in salute, followed by two squadrons of the French Air Force. A short religious service conducted by Canadian chaplains followed, and on the dais was observed a Commissioner of the Salvation Army with his staff.

The pipers now played " The Flowers of the Forest," and a message from the Prime Minister of Canada, Mr. Mackenzie King, was broadcast from Ottawa. After speeches from Mr. Lapointe and Mr. Mackenzie, both Canadian Ministers, the King was invited to unveil the memorial.

Speaking slowly and clearly, the King commenced by expressing his thanks in French to the President on his own behalf and that of the Canadian people for joining their ceremony. Continuing an impressive speech in English he came to the words " I unveil this Memorial to Canada's Dead." and pulled the cord on the dais. As the flags dropped from the figure of Canada, the 'Last Post' was sounded, followed by two minutes' silence and then the Reveillé.

President Lebrun now delivered his address, after which the band played " Land of Hope and Glory."

The King then presented the Canadian Ministers and others to M. Lebrun, after which the band played the National Anthems. During the playing of " God Save the King " thousands of pilgrims and spectators joined in the words and the King waved his hand in acknowledgment to the crowds below.

Then the King and the President laid wreaths on the Memorial, and left the Ridge amid loud cheers from every side. Lesser folk could now stand where King and President had stood and see the plain and arena below filled with thousands of khaki-capped pilgrims now eagerly waiting to ascend the Ridge from where the enemy had attacked and from which he had been driven. Many were bearing wreaths brought from 3,000 miles distance to lay on their national Memorial, a most moving sight, and as I unwillingly left, they were swarming up the steps with the glow of achievement in their hearts.

As we moved slowly, on account of crowds, towards the station, we saw the base of the Memorial being covered by thousands of contented pilgrims.

The King in his speech had reminded the listening thousands of the inscription over the door of the Memorial Chamber at Ottawa. " All's well, for over there among his peers a happy warrior sleeps." But what of the happy warrior who survives after 20 years absence from the Ridge ? We saw him laying a wreath on the Memorial, or with stained war map in hand seeking old unsavoury haunts, or refreshing himself on the grass where time has healed the war-scarred ground, or with wife and lusty children in blue berets hanging on his arm. Can anything lessen the glory of his achievement ?

F. G. POOLE, Lieut.-Colonel.
(*Hon. Secretary, Ypres British Settlement.*)

The Tunnel

By MARK SEVERN.

THE village of Bellenglise, a strong point in the Hindenburg Line, had been fortified by the Germans according to the latest and most modern ideas and contained, amongst other features, a tunnel, dug under the village some thirty feet below ground level, about a quarter of a mile long, with side galleries and numerous exits, capable of sheltering a thousand men. In front of the village lay the St. Quentin Canal and, in front of the canal, a trench defensive system. Along the whole length of the canal concrete machine gun emplacements had been built which enfiladed the thick belts of wire on the opposite bank. This was the obstacle my brigade was detailed to attack in September of the last year of the war.

The preliminary artillery bombardment lasted three days and was heavy even for those times. I believe over sixteen hundred guns took part on a front of twelve miles and I have been told that they fired something like a million rounds. But mere figures can convey nothing of the magnitude and terror of that storm of fire nor is it any use my attempting to describe it. It began by being stupendous, awe-inspiring, terrible. It ended by shattering all power of thought and feeling.

Zero hour was fixed for 6 o'clock on the morning of the 29th. Under cover of the barrage and a dense mist the leading troops stormed the trenches west of the canal, killed most of the garrison and proceeded to plunge into the canal itself. One battalion, crossing north-west of the village, found very little water and were able to wade across. Having overcome all resistance they advanced into the village, secured the tunnel entrances and captured some hundreds of prisoners. The other two battalions in the centre and on the left were forced to swim for it. The officers went first with ropes, their men followed using life belts, rafts, portable boats and in some places the bridges which had been only partially destroyed. Making short work of the Germans on the other side the whole brigade then moved forward and, within three hours from zero, had captured all their objectives.

My own remembrance of those hours is vague and disconnected. A few incidents stand out bright and sharp on a black background of horror, but they are mostly meaningless, without sequence or shape or the bones of right reason to hold them together, a vague general impression of thunder and chaos in which individual pictures flash and flicker like lightning on a darkened sky. The roar of the bombardment, the senseless chatter of the machine guns, the yells of the attackers, the shrieks of the wounded and the groans of the dying are all blurred, and, clear and distinct above the tumult, I hear the cry of a boy who has been all but disembowelled by a bursting shell. The long lines of advancing men, the groups of Germans with their hands up, the blood red waters of the canal, the carnage, the smoke and the nightmare desolation are hazy and confused, and I see two men carrying a stretcher across a crazy bridge. Over the side of the stretcher a hand trails, but the body to which it is attached has no longer the semblance of a man. I stop to ask a question. The stretcher-bearers, too dazed with all they have been through to answer me, gibber like creatures bereft of mind and stagger blindly on.

About noon I went down into the tunnel which was by then filled with our own men resting after the fight. It was a marvellous place, more like an underground barracks than anything else, with officers' quarters and men's quarters, stores, dormitories, cookhouses, offices, messes and lavatories all complete. I explored it pretty thoroughly and the more I saw the more impressed I became. The various rooms were lined with wood ; walls, ceiling, floor were all wood. There were elaborate arrangements for heating, lighting and ventilation. Nothing had been forgotten. And all to no purpose. That was the point. If the enemy had not taken shelter in it from our bombardment many more would probably have been killed, but enough might have been left alive to bear off our attack. As it was they were caught like rats in a trap.

There was something almost uncanny in wandering round a place so lately occupied by the enemy. At least that is how it struck me. The half-eaten breakfast lying on the table, the untouched cup of substitute coffee, the disordered bunk whence some German had flung himself a few short hours before, these things were silent witnesses of a life in which I had no part. It was like examining the room of a stranger who has just been arrested for murder. The tables, chairs, carpets, mirrors and pictures, the books, photographs and clothes, these things gained an additional, almost fearful interest, from the fact that they belonged to the murderer. Then again, it was all so still and quiet. I found it hard to believe that the faint rumbling overhead was the roar of the battle I had just left.

Except for a few candles the tunnel was in darkness. Stumbling over the prostrate bodies of tired men, I eventually found my way to the engine room where the huge flywheel of an electric light plant loomed still and ghost-like in the gloom. There I found the Colonel. We were examining it and wondering if we could make it work, when an Australian Major, a sapper, burst in on us shouting that the tunnel was mined and that we had better clear our men out quick if we did'nt want to be all blown sky-high. He had found a panelled chamber by the main entrance packed with ammonal with wires leading direct from it to the power plant. He had cut the wires, but felt certain there were other similar explosion chambers and that the moment we started the engine and switched the lights on we should blow ourselves up.

There were two battalions in the tunnel—what was left of them that is—and the Brigade Headquarters. Everyone cleared out in quick time as you may imagine. The shelling was still very heavy up above and the Brigadier gave orders that, as soon as all the mines had been located and the electric light engine had been put in working order, the tunnel was to be re-occupied.

Soon afterwards a German electrician was sent up from the Prisoners of War Cage. He was a little white-faced person with mild eyes and an apologetic manner. I pictured him in a neat black suit carrying the bag round in church at home and somehow I couldn't help feeling sorry for him. He looked so out of place on a battlefield, especially beside the Australian Major, who was a great, big bull of a man.

The Colonel, who knew a little German, soon discovered that the electrician knew about the plan to blow up the tunnel. *What he didn't know was how many mines there were.*

I have never seen anyone so easily excited as that Australian. He flourished his revolver in the poor little man's face. He shouted and swore and waved his arms. One didn't need to know English to understand what he meant. That engine had got to be started even if it blew up the whole of the Western Front. The Boche went a delicate pea-green and looked imploringly at me. I looked at the Colonel. There was no means of knowing if we *had* found *all* the mines, yet it seemed to me that the only way to make sure was to go down again and start the engine. For the life of me I couldn't think of any other method. On the other hand, I didn't like the idea of the " Aussy " being down there alone with the little Boche. Nor did the Colonel. Of course it was not his duty, any more than it was mine, to get blown up if we could avoid it, but we neither of us thought of that at the time.

We must have made a queer quartette as we walked in single file through the now empty tunnel. First the Colonel, very grim and serious with a torch, then the little Boche, trembling but silent, the big Australian close behind, his revolver closer still, and finally myself, fingering a few candle ends that I had had the forethought to put in my pocket. We reached the central chamber, a wooden cube about twelve feet square by eight feet high where, silent and inert, lay the engine. While the mechanic fiddled with the controls the rest of us set to work cleaning plugs and connections. In half-an-hour all was ready. The Colonel and I sat down. The Austalian moved towards the Boche who was panting in short gasps like an animal that is being hunted to death.

Watching them I had a queer feeling that we were already in our graves buried but alive. The room was deathly silent. The only sounds were the scraping of the nails of the Australian's boots on the wood floor and the gasps of the little Boche.

The engine started. The big fly-wheel began to spin. All was well so far. Then suddenly the Boche made a last despairing gesture.

If I live to be a hundred I shall never forget that moment ; the little Bosche half-fainting with terror ; the inexorable Australian driving him on with fists and boots and revolver ; the big fly-wheel slowly spinning ; the Colonel and I, cleaning rags in our hands, sitting on upturned boxes, waiting.

It is customary, I believe, in moments of extreme danger, to review one's whole life in a flash. Those who have been nearly drowned and brought to life again always seem to do this. At the exact moment of extinction they remember everything that has ever happened to them. Others recall some well-known place so vividly that they believe they are really there. Nothing of this sort happened to me. My mind was a blank. I might have been already dead for all that I could see and hear and feel. Only one pin-point of consciousness remained and that was fixed with agonising intensity on the switch-board.

Slowly, with shaking hands, the little Boche pulled the lever across the row of studs . . . The light of the candles gradually paled as the electric bulbs began to glow. The lights went on, the room became clear, the machinery had a uniform note. But none of us moved. For seconds, for hours, for eternity, there was no change in sight or sound or anything palpable to the senses. My impression was that the explosion had come. I was dead. We were all dead. But my mind had survived and dominant in it, perhaps fixed for ever like a photograph, was the impression of a last moment on earth.

Gradually it faded. Our very breathing had stopped and the lungs demanded air. Someone moved. The tension slackened and broke. The lttle Boche, who had collapsed into a corner, began to sob, great hacking sobs which tore his whole body. The Australian, fired his revolver into the air. But I and the Colonel, the grim and solemn Colonel looked at each other and laughed and laughed and laughed.

To the Summer of 1936

Time was when Phoebus, in no miser mood
   Flung all abroad his warm health giving beams,
Then glorious sunshine gilded fields and wood
   And flashed like jewels in the sparkling streams.
But now, alas our Sun God hides his face
   Behind a very continent of cloud,
In vain his ruddy disc we strive to trace
   No welcome ray can pierce that inky shroud.
We call it " Summer Time " — an hour we gain
   From night, by nice adjustment of the clock
But still we suffer everlasting rain
   And at our hopes and prayers high Jove doth mock.—(F.N.L.)

The End of the Somme Phase

BATTLE OF THE ANCRE, NOVEMBER 13th, 1916.

By LIEUT. C. J. HUPFIELD,
2nd Battalion, The Suffolk Regiment, 3rd Division.

THIS battle was distinguished by several unusual features. It was a wonderful success in the centre, but not so fortunate on the wing facing Serre village. The 37th Division and our 3rd Division had to act as pivot to the assault on Beaumont Hamel and Beaucourt in the centre. I wonder, too, how many of the dozen or so Suffolks, who had entered " No Man's " land with me from the bowels of the earth, at the height of the barrage, are still alive to-day. Certainly a most unique way to join in the "fun," and in my case, it was my first big " show."

Photo]   [Imperial War Museum, Crown Copyright

RUINS OF THE SUGAR REFINERY NEAR SERRE, MARCH, 1917

Acting as Lewis Gun Officer to the Battalion, it had been arranged during weeks and weeks of preparation in conjunction with Brigade, to form forward dumps of Lewis drums in the captured objectives (four deep lines of trenches fronting Serre, heavily wired). Many will recollect the nervous strain occasioned by the fact that this battle was announced and postponed four times in all, once within twelve hours of zero hour. The weather was the cause and incessant rain made such a morass of " No Man's " land that we had many men actually drowned in the course of the attack.

At last, on the afternoon and night of Sunday, November 12th the troops commenced to pour into the line in front of Courcelles and Hebuterne and the trenches to the South. The Brigade had decided to open two tunnels (Mark and John) which were a survival of July 1st. These two tunnels led from our front line posts direct to the enemy, terminating near their wire. I was to take a Lewis Gun team and some bombers through " John " and emerge in sufficient time to keep the enemy engaged pending the arrival of our infantry. All excellent in theory.

I will not dwell on the many exciting incidents of the night, which was terribly damp and cold; the accidental shooting from our reserve line by machine guns on to some of our outposts; the rum issue and the last farewells. At 5.30 a.m. I entered the tunnel with my splendid " Mons " orderly and soon after 5.45 a.m. when we were crouching in dead silence, lest the enemy should be listening in *their* tunnels, a terrific rumble as of thousands of drums beating in unison, commenced overhead. The barrage had begun, and after five minutes of this, the awful weeks of suspense and work were at an end. The enemy were supposed to be about 220 yards away and we would emerge 70 to 100 yards from them after pulling down about ten feet of soil at the end of the sloping tunnel. A short ladder was soon put up and out we clambered. For a minute or two, we sat on the lip, completely stupified by the din ; the flashes in the heavy fog prevailing ; the hoarse cries and the shadowy shapes of men in the gloom. An awe-inspiring sight.

Soon we went forward until near the wire, which proved to be of immense depth and hardly cut. There we took stock of the position. It grew lighter and then began a terrible hour, during which we few helpless onlookers (our infantry wave having gone on ahead) saw the attack broken up before our eyes, caused by (*a*) machine gun fire, (*b*) the appalling nature of the ground which had to be crossed. Men were shot down all around us, while we took advantage of what cover there was to be had in a large shell-hole half filled with water. We lay around the lip of this shell-hole trying to piece together such news as we could gather, as I had been ordered by the C.O. to obtain all information of value and transmit to him. This duty had to be abandoned as we were being continually sniped by rifle and machine gun fire.

It resulted in our being pinned down to that spot for the day, one of the most awful I am ever likely to spend. At 6.30 a.m. our part of the attack had been completely shattered and the wounded were lying and crawling around in the mud and filth.

I witnessed some amazing bravery by one of our stretcher bearers who, most of the morning, crawled around on his stomach ; tending the wounded ; collecting pay-books, etc. We survived until " lunch time " when a few mess sandwiches, wrapped in the *Continental Daily Mail* and a small flask of whiskey sufficed for eight men, whom I had collected and who were all sound. I concluded that our bombs and my revolver would come in useful in the event of a further attack being launched in the afternoon. From our knees downwards our legs were in water all day, and this was a *good* shell hole. Many were quite full of water and a 5.9 makes a good hole in the ground. By " lunch time " we were so cold that our teeth were chattering quite audibly and we kept pummelling one another for warmth. The hours dragged on and I decided that at 4.30 p.m. it would be dark enough for us to attempt to regain our lines. All the time whistling, screeching and wobbling shells were flying overhead, but we were, except for the machine guns mentioned above, comparatively immune, until about 2 p.m. when the " fun " started. The enemy had undoubtedly spotted all the crawling humanity in front of them and commenced systematically " searching " with 5.9 shells and trench mortars.

We went through two hours of " hell," great chunks of clay and debris descending on us and shells dropping as close as five yards away. Shrapnel whistled all around us and we were all " strung up." I counted seven hits alone, the last, a small piece of shell penetrating my neck. Only a miracle saved us. We then arranged the order of our return, in pairs, and in different directions. How we ever traversed the 150 yards or so ; through water, falling over wire and with bullets whistling over us, I can hardly remember, but certainly it was not dignified.

Eventually I reached our front trench and found it practically empty, dead lying everywhere, and I had to negotiate a heavy barrage of H.E. before regaining the " close support line " where I found the Battalion Headquarters. There I heard the sorry story of the casualties we had sustained. I was one of three Officers left out of 14 who had been in the attack who were either dead, prisoners or badly wounded.

That night, fortunately, the news filtered through of the success of the Highlanders and the Naval Division in the centre, and this helped to re-establish our morale. Many poor fellows must have died of exposure in " No Man's " land that night, since it was impossible to attend to them all.

Photo]   [Imperial War Museum, Crown Copyright
IRON GIRDERS ON THE ROADSIDE USED BY THE ENEMY AS A BARRICADE AT SERRE VILLAGE

Our M.O. and his orderlies performed wonderful work, and a day later we heard the report of some " Gordons " of our Brigade, lying near the enemy wire, wounded, whom a German doctor had bandaged. We subsequently recovered them.

Months later, when the enemy evacuated this front one night, silently, a few of us went over the ground and for the first time we were able to realise the impregnability of the village of Serre, and we saw many an unburied Suffolk soldier in his position.

Ypres Day

THIS year, the Ypres League Annual Commemoration will be held on **Sunday Morning, November 1st,** and the following programme has been arranged :—

11.00 a.m.   Assemble on the Horse Guards' Parade.
11.30 a.m.   Address by the Rev. J. Lynn, D.D., B.A., Deputy Chaplain General to the Forces, Hon. Chaplain to H.M. The King, who will conduct a short service, followed by the " Lament " by Pipers of the London Scottish.
11.45 a.m.   March to the Cenotaph.
12.00 noon   Laying of the Ypres League wreath on the Cenotaph.
12.15 a.m.   March back to the Horse Guards' Parade.
12.30 p.m.   Dismiss on the Horse Guards' Parade, and at 1.0 p.m. a deputation of the Ypres League will proceed to the Tomb of the Unknown Warrior in Westminster Abbey and place a wreath.

H.R.H. Princess Beatrice has graciously consented to attend the Ceremony.

"Old Coldstreamers" Battlefield Tour

August Bank Holiday 1936.

ZERO hour for parading the party of members taking part in the annual battlefields tour of the London Branch of the Old Coldstreamers Association was timed this year for 7.30 a.m. August 1st, Victoria Station, and when the roll was called at 7.45 a.m. only one absentee from a party of fifty-five was reported, and this was duly notified as a case of last moment urgent business. Of the fifty-four present thirty eight were serving soldiers from the three Coldstream Battalions and the Depot Companies. But for the strenuous summer season and the exceptionally large number of Public Parades, many more would undoubtedly have been included in the tour.

With six Officers and at least a dozen Other Ranks, all with varied war experience, included in the party, it was felt that this particular tour could be no other than one of outstanding interest, especially so when once the battlefields were reached.

The necessary travel arrangements were again in the hands of the Ypres League and Major L. J. L. Pullar, M.C., assisted by Mr. S. H. K. Geller, accompanied the party as their representatives to look after its interests in the matter of transport and accommodation.

Following a pleasant Channel crossing the party arrived at Ostend entirely self-contained. Two large char-a-bancs were in readiness at the Maritime Station as conveyance to Tournai *via* Roulers, where the late tea provided was eagerly welcomed. Headquarters for the night had been arranged for the party at Mons, and it was to this town that the journey continued. Every member appeared interested to see Mons, although no Coldstream Battalion had actually been there during the Great War.

In view of the fact that no hotel large enough to accommodate everyone was available, billeting required the services of half-a-dozen small hotel proprietors, although the rendezvous was the Hotel Dupuis where all met to dine together and enjoy the very excellent dinner prepared.

The next morning, after an English breakfast, char-a-bancs were boarded and the route followed was along the line of the Retreat to Landrecies, where the 3rd Battalion Coldstream Guards fought it's first important engagement. Mr. Adams who had been the C.O.'s orderly on that occasion, gave a graphic account of the engagement on the site of the outpost station, and close to where Corporal Wyatt

The Party at Mons.

won the Victoria Cross for extinguishing two burning haystacks under point-blank fire. It transpired that there were more Old Coldstreamers who had been present at the engagement, and Messrs. Marks, Drury and Leist all contributed to the story. Then followed some friendly debate regarding the actual position of the haystacks, and also whether the fields were planted with beet or stubble. It was while the foregoing reminiscences were being related that a hefty Frenchman appeared on the scene and making himself quite at home, joined in the conversations in French, which was interpreted by the Officers. It subsequently transpired that this particular individual happened to be in the vicinity of a building close to where, and at the very time, Inspector Leist, then a Non-Commissioned Officer, was posting his picquet to stop the advancing Uhlan patrol.

M. Monier, to give this person his name, confirmed in detail what had been related and amused everyone by naively adding that when the first clash came he was compelled to hide himself in the building as he was being shot at by both sides.

At Le Cateau an early lunch was provided and afterwards the battlefields tour continued to Gouzeaucourt, where from two vantage points Major W. A. C. Wilkinson, M.C., gave a vivid narrative of the advance of the 2nd Battalion in the famous counter-attack on the village and the Quentin Ridge beyond.

From Gouzeaucourt to Fontaine, where Major A. G. Salisbury-Jones, M.C., who had a panoramic view of the battle as a Machine-Gun Officer described the action of the 1st Battalion on the 27th November, 1917.

At the Canal du Nord, Dr. C. P. Blacker, M.C., who had commanded No. 1 Company, 2nd Battalion, on the 27th September, 1918, gave his personal impressions of the battle. Finally, at Bourlon Wood, Major Wilkinson found those very trenches which his Company had occupied behind an embankment after the battle of Fontaine. His vivid description of the conditions then prevailing undoutedly impressed the young soldiers of the party with the grim realities of war. At the same time it was difficult to visualise the reeking battlefields of 1917 and 1918, with the smiling fields and ordered villages of 1936. Only the beautifully tended graveyards remain as evidence, too eloquent of the losses.

M. Monier, photographed outside his Estimanet, Landrecies.

The tour continued to Arras, now rebuilt, and at the Hotel Moderne, opposite the station, the party was accommodated for the night. Monday morning was spent visiting the recently unveiled Canadian Memorial at Vimy Ridge and afterwards the Memorial to the missing at Loos. From the " Dud Corner " Memorial, Loos, a magnificent view of the Old Loose battlefield could be seen, and from this viewpoint, Major A. de L. Cazenove, M.V.O., greatly interested the party with a description of the battle, outlining the salient features. Puits 14 bis, and the chalk pits, where the 1st Battalion had suffered so heavily, were then visited and Mr. Hermes, who had been Company Sergeant Major to No. 3 Company on that occasion, was supported in his reminiscences by Mr. Drury. Both of these Old Coldstreamers were able to give an eye-witness account of Sergeant O. Brooks' gallant performance at the Hohenzollern Redoubt which earned him the coveted Victoria Cross.

At this stage it was observed that time was beating the schedule, so the char-a-bancs were rapidly boarded and the route continued to Ypres *via* Laventie (the Guards Division spent a fairly quiet winter here in 1915). A little delay at the frontier necessitated a rather hasty lunch at Skindles Hotel, Ypres. Immediately following this repast the party assembled at the Menin Gate Memorial where a sheaf of red roses was placed by Major Wilkinson on behalf of the London Branch, Old Coldstreamers Association.

Punctually at 2.15 the party left Ypres *en route* to Ostend fro the return journey to London, and if a little tired, it was indeed a happy and contented contingent of Old Coldstreamers who arrived at Victoria Station on the boat train from Dover on August 1st last.

For so pleasant and interesting a trip the sincere thanks of all who took part are heartily extended to the Ypres League, but for whose organisation and kindness the tour could hardly have been brought within the means of serving soldiers.—L. B. W.

From Bab-el-Wad to Vaux-Vraucourt

By CAPTAIN A. F. L. BACON,
(Author of *The Wanderings of a Temporary Warrior*.)

AS the war years recede ever more into the dim distance, two experiences remain as vividly in my mind as any, on different fronts, but both at much the same time of day, that eerie time between nightfall and dawn.

The first in Palestine on the way to Jerusalem in November, 1917 :—On the previous night that portion of the Divisional Staff to which I was then attached were lying on the floor of a deserted monastery when orders came to go at once to Bab-el-Wad. This proved impossible of attainment that night and long hours had to be spent in this narrow pass on the morrow, while shells fell on the road above, rendering repairs necessary before the advance could continue. Bab-el-Wad is said to mean " the Key of the Pass," and it consisted of a rude tenement at a most precipitous turn of the road, with rugged rocks running up to a great height on either side. We were a mixed Division of British and Indian troops, and it was a wise choice which sent us for the duty of clearing the Turks from this road and the surrounding hills, the Indian troops being well versed in hill fighting and picketing, and some of the British troops also who had, like ourselves, come from India.

At last after nightfall I pushed ahead, sometimes on foot, sometimes on horseback, with the rain pelting down and making the all pervading blackness the more distressing. The pass to Jerusalem ran through most precipitous rocks, like a defile in the Highlands, weird and winding. In one cavern, where I tried to shelter for a time from the rain, all the room was wanted for casualties, and an opposite enclosure was tenanted by a dead man. Dark oppressive mist and rain was the chief accompaniment, as the road went ever upward, until the mixed welter of guns, horses and details of transport of all sorts issued at length on to the rocky sides of a valley, where morning light subsequently revealed the village of Enab, seven miles from Jerusalem. It also revealed the Turks still holding the heights commanding the valley, and their presence was soon felt when shells began to plump among the crowded troops, who had bivouacked anywhere in the darkness of the night, on a most restricted space. For a few hours Battalions, Brigades and, Divisional H.Q. all shared this somewhat unpleasant terrain, while the road behind us through the pass was seemingly choked with transport. The rapid pursuit of the Turks had prevented them from standing in the pass however, and the most important Key to Jerusalem was in our hands.

Memory retains various impressions of that morning. A General running for shelter, from bursting shells ; helping a wounded man under cover till he could be evacuated ; the poor stiff bodies of Gurkhas lying unheeded ; the formation of a column to advance into the hills ; hasty improvisations and activities after such an advance ; but the shrouded mystery of the passage up the pass in the mud and rain of the previous nght is still more vivid than the rest.

The second in France at Vaux-Vraucourt in early September, 1918 :—For six days or so the battalion had been holding a hard won advance from Achiet, after successful attack, and the night for relief had come. Three companies had reported at Battalion H.Q. on relief by the incoming battalion. The fourth had failed to do so, and it was 1 a.m. In three-quarters of an hour the new attack was timed to begin. I was sent up therefore with two orderlies to make sure that relief had come. Speed was necessary, as any failure to be back before the attack, meant catching the enemy's barrage which would fall behind the attacking troops. Through the darkness came the rush of shells now this side, now the other, for the Germans had scented danger and were already making a desultory bombardment. At last we safely "made" the Company H.Q. only to find the new men ensconced and ready for their forward spring. The Company Commander was not so engrossed in his own affairs as to be unable to spare a thought for us, and counselled our waiting till the German " strafe " had died down before we tried our luck in the dash back. However, anxious lest worse befall, I decided to go, while the going was moderately good, and off we started back again to the accompaniment of more projectiles. Safely back at Battalion H.Q. I reported all well to my waiting C.O., and we pushed off towards quieter areas, and soon afterwards, as dawn broke, heard the thunderous roar from our own guns which ushered in the dawn, and the successful launching of one more push at the tottering power of Germany.

The darkest hour is before the dawn, and these two experiences taking place during the dark hours led in each case to a successful dawn. Taking a wider view the same applies. In Palestine there had been two unsuccessful battles at Gaza with heavy casualties, till at last the third attack swept all before it, flowed over the plains of Philistia, and before the Turks could reform, pushed them up through the pass in the Judean mountains and came within hail of Jerusalem. There may be two views of the value of the whole Palestine campaign ; but this was the first step towards the subsequent rounding up of the Turkish armies which put them out of the fight.

In France the fearful years which included the fighting at Mons, the heroic defence of the Salient, the Somme battle, Passchendaele and other fateful struggles, had worn down the vigour and manhood of the German nation, and opened the way to that gradual rolling back of the enemy at the Second Marne, and now further North at Vaux-Vraucourt and elsewhere. Not many months remained before the final collapse and the joyful news of Armistice and surrender.

London Branch Tour

A MOST interesting and enjoyable eight-day tour was undertaken by 21 members of the London Branch of the Ypres League, commencing Saturday, August 12th. A reserved carriage had been arranged for us by Headquarters on the 9.35 a.m. train from Victoria, and after a very comfortable rail and boat journey, our arrival at Ostend was greeted with brilliant sunshine, where a luxurious coach was waiting in readiness to convey our party to the first day's destination—Ypres. Well-known places passed *en route* included Nieuport, Dixmude, Houthulst Forest, Poelcappelle, Langemarck, Boesinghe and Salvation Corner. A hearty welcome was accorded the party at Ypres by our friend " Madame " at Skindles Hotel, and very shortly afterwards we were all seated and ready for the dinner arranged for us and which was unanimously voted as excellent. At 9.00 p.m. we assembled at the Menin Gate Memorial for the sounding of the " Last Post " and the remainder of the evening was spent at leisure.

The following morning we boarded our coach and departed Ypres at 8.30 a.m. for Cambrai. A circuitous route was chosen and we proceeded by way of Brielen, Elverdinghe, Vlamertinghe, Poperinghe (a special visit was made here to the Lijssenthoek Cemetery situated just outside the town), Bailleul and Estaires. A visit was made to the Indian Memorial and the Portuguese Cemetery at Neuve Chapelle before passing on to the Le Touret Cemetery and Memorial near La Bassee. This latter Memorial commemorates the names of 13,000 Missing who took part in the battles of La Bassee, Neuve Chapelle, Aubers Ridge and Festubert, 1914-1915. It was while visiting this Memorial that we had the pleasure of meeting another lady member of our Branch over on a visit to friends at Bethune, and who had hoped that by making for this place she would meet our party. The half-way stage of this day's tour was reached at Lens and lunch was taken at the Hotel de Flandre. Continuing our journey after lunch we eventually reached Cambrai *via* Bapaume, and headquarters for the night was made at the Continental Hotel in the Station Place. After dinner many of us paid a visit to the fair which was in full swing in the Grande Place, and many francs found their way into the pockets of the various showmen.

Monday morning punctual to schedule we set out, this time for Albert. Proceeding in the direction of Solesmes, a pilgrimage was made to Romeries Cemetery to visit a certain grave, and then to the Military Cemetery at Le Cateau. Passing Reumont, Honnechy, Busigny and Bohain, we reached Peronne to partake of lunch at the Hotel St. Claude, and due justice was given to the fare provided. One member, a little overcome with the pungent odour of the cheese, caused much amusement among the waitresses by placing his portion on the window-sill. However, he was compensated a little later, when they made him a present of a parcel of very excellent fruit tart for which he had previously expressed a weakness. Continuing our tour after lunch, visits were made to

THE PARTY AT HOTEL DES LONDRES, OSTENDE.

Longueval Cemetery, Delville Wood and Caterpillar Valley Cemetery, thence to Méaulte, and so on to Albert, where we encountered a terrific storm which rather prevented our exploring those old haunts in the town that we remembered from the war years. Accommodation for this night had been arranged for us at the Hotel le Grand.

At 8.30 a.m. the next morning we left Albert and headed for Lille, visiting on the way Dernancourt Cemetery, Varennes, La Boisselle Crater, Thiepval Memorial and Newfoundland Park. Stops were also made at Bucquoy to visit Queen's Cemetery and Pommier Communal Cemetery near Bienvillers, the latter reached only after a walk of a quarter of a mile along a narrow lane. On the road into Arras we stopped to visit the Arras Memorial, and several photographs were taken of the panels of this beautiful Memorial. Following lunch at the Hotel Moderne (well known to Ypres League Pilgrims) our itinerary included a visit to the Canadian Memorial at Vimy Ridge, the Grange Tunnels and trenches, passing *en route* the large French and German Cemeteries at La Targette. Lille was reached in good time for dinner, and those not too fatigued spent a pleasant hour afterwards in the town.

Wednesday morning, August 12th, our party left Lille and proceeded on the return journey to Ostend. This was to be accomplished in easy stages, the route selected being *via* Roubaix, Tourcoing, Menin, Courtrai and Ghent. Lunch had been arranged for us at Ghent, and it was here that we were welcomed to the oldest hotel in the world, the Cour St. George. After doing justice to their excellent menu we were conducted by one of the hotel guides over the castle, visiting torture chambers, chapels, banquetting hall, etc. One of our members, very anxious to feel what it was like to be placed on the guillotine, was duly lifted on the structure and placed in position, but not wishing to leave an old comrade behind, the knife was not released. In the vaults we were shown bones of females that had been found during digging operations. A visit was made to the Cathedral where our guide explained everything of interest. Time did not permit a longer stay at Ghent unfortunately, and very soon we were again on the road, this time to Bruges. A most interesting time was spent in this old-world city prior to the drive to Ostend. This sea-port town was to be our headquarters for the next three days and the morning after our arrival a tour to Holland was arranged. Taking the coach as far as Brisken, we boarded the ferry to Flushing and from there by tram to Middelburg for the market and butter-market. Here a few of the male members of the party were observed to be missing but were seen later fraternising with the gretchens who had come to Middelburg for the market. Altogether a most happy day was spent and rather regretfully we boarded the tram for return to Flushing. On our return journey to Ostend a visit was made to the Mole at Zeebrugge.

Our remaining two days were mostly spent in sight-seeing and leisurely shopping in Ostend prior to catching the Saturday afternoon boat to Dover. Nearly 550 miles were covered during this tour and before concluding this brief account of our wanderings, we should like to extend our thanks to the coach driver appointed to our party from the Wipers Auto Service, Ostend, for the very courteous and efficient manner in which he carried out his duties.

F. W. S.

(Our sincere thanks are extended to Mr. F. W. Stevenson for his kind co-operation and guidance in the organisation of this tour and to Mr. E. G. Holmes, the " Knocker-up.")

J. B.

Ypres British School

Monday, July 13th, this year, was Prize-day at the Ypres British School, and 107 bright, healthy and happy children were assembled in the school playground in eager anticipation of welcoming their benefactor, Lieut.-General Sir William Pulteney who had crossed from England accompanied by the Chaplain-General to the Forces and R. J. N. Parr, Esq , Master at Eton and Hon. Treasurer of the School.

A number of the prizes were again kindly provided for the children by Mrs. L. K. Briggs. The awards were presented to the successful scholars by the Chaplain-General, The Rev. E. H. Thorold, C.B.E., O.B.E., M.A., and present at the distribution were: Lieut.-General Sir W. P. Pulteney, G.C.V.O., K.C.B., K.C.M.G., D.S.O., R. J. N. Parr, Esq., Hon. Treasurer, Ypres British School, Lieut.-Colonel F. G. Poole, D.S.O., O.B.E., Hon. Secretary, Ypres British Settlement, The Rev. G. R. Milner, and Mrs. Milner, Major A. Macfarlane and Mr. Gill, Representatives of Imperial War Graves Commission, and Mrs. L. K. Briggs and Miss Briggs.

Following the prize distribution the children entertained their elders with a splendid programme of song and dance, a physical training display by both boys and girls and in conclusion, a play and more dancing by the smaller children. To those responsible for the organisation, efficiency and general deportment of the children, the visitors spoke in glowing terms. A very happy day indeed, many hand-shakes with the parents and finally a resounding cheer for the General.

Light and Shade at the Front

"Outpost Duty."

(*By an ex-R.B.*)

Scene: A Toy Shop.
SHOPMAN : " Yes, Madam ? "
CUSTOMER : " A small box of lead soldiers, if you please, for my little boy."
YOUNG HOPEFUL (*in a loud voice*) : " Soldiers with guns ! "

What was it that gave one his first impression of soldiering ? Probably the little cardboard boxes of lead men and toy cannon which were common to early childhood days ; each little soldier as stiff as a ramrod ; uniforms buttoned and belted just so ; rifles held immovably at the shoulder or else at the six o'clock aim. This view was encouraged when the erstwhile little boy, now a civilian grown to man's estate, saw the bugler at Wellington Barracks stepping forward to sound a call, and paused to watch the drill. Or perhaps he was strolling through the Mall and saw an N.C.O. and " relief " march by the wall which skirts St. James's Palace, and so to the sentry's post opposite the plane trees.

In fact, the more he saw of " soldiering " the more his early impressions were strengthened. Sentry-go at Kensington Gardens ! Left, left, left-right, left ! The sentry smartly " turned out " in trousers, dark cloth with thin red stripe, boots, ammunition ; great coat, grey ; bearskin ; greatcoat girt about with equipment pipe-clayed, and rifle and bayonet like new. Business taking our civilian to a Thames wharf he passes the tower, and sees a squad in white drill jackets, drilling. Later on, on his way back by the embankment he hears a steady tramp, tramp, tramp, and looking up sees — the Bank Guard marching citywards with fixed bayonets. Why, it's the very thing !

The excellence of this training as a means of handling men is of course exemplified in the classic example of Fuentes de Oñoro (5, May, 1811), where Wellington moved his right wing backwards (Light Division, R. Craufurd ; Cavalry, Cotton), in the full heat of action — Fortescue, L. of W., 1925. But when our civilian found himself in the line he became aware of new formations and new words of command. His early ideas about taking a squad into an outpost, for example, underwent a certain change.

" Squad ! " " In fours, by the right ! QUI-I-CK MARCH ! " " Hold y'r 'ead up, that man ! Keep out of the wire ! " " Number two in the front rank, dress by your right ! . . . . . ALT ! Left turn ! INTO YOUR POST, DOUB-L-L-E MARCH ! "

" Didn't the N.C.O. say that ? " " He did not." " And why not ? " " Well, there is a reason." But stay ; let us " Fall in ! " once more, and try to re-awaken some half-forgotten echoes of the line . . . . .

Some new line was taken over in the sector St. Quentin. It was late at night, weather drizzly and a ground mist, and the Company moved along the trenches in single file by sections, each platoon following a guide. Everything was done silently ; the fire-step was occupied and the troops " relieved " filed out. The men detailed for outpost duty reached these along a sap, if there was a sap, and in each case the squad relieved moved back and tailed on to its comrades who were filing out.

In the outpost : Five tree-stumps to the right, some wiring stakes just in front, a small shelf hollowed out for bombs, sentries placed and timed front and rear with an eye to the flanks ; total strength of post, six men and an N.C.O. About two o'clock in the morning it was noticed that the five tree-stumps had increased to six. Inference that somebody was there. " Eyes down ! " and a quiet challenge : " Who are you ? " Promptly stump No. 6 detached itself : " Willoughby " (the password), and it was seen to be a platoon officer. Risky ? Well, just a little.

This St. Quentin sector was thinly held and the distance from post to post was considerable. At night one could walk seemingly endless distances without meeting a soul; in fact at times one might almost have been excused for thinking that all the soldiers had gone home. The enemy machine guns sounded — a long way off; as to the outposts of the "Flying-foxes"; these were like little oases set in a silent desert of space, and " no man's land " was an ideal area for raiding parties and scouting.

There was an outpost (St. Quentin) which, in common with others, was occupied over the top each night and the squad withdrawn before dawn. A few coils of barbed wire on frames and some wiring stakes were dumped in front. Raiding parties were active and in the small hours it was noticed that the darkness thickened at one point into vague shadows. No patrols out : " Enemy in front ; Open fire ! " and as the rifles opened out the N.C.O. (in the person of the writer) lobbed over a couple of bombs. Presently : " Cease fire ! " and the shadows were gone. This brought the platoon officer and sergeant over. About fifteen minutes later bombing and rifle fire broke out from a post to the left, held by another Company, and in the morning two casualties were discovered. An enemy party had blundered from one post to the other.

It burst like a beautiful Star.

It is fairly correct to say that the men present at an action see least of its general incident. For one thing, each man's attention is limited to his immediate front. And at times visibility may be bad, as was the case in the early hours of Ludendorf's offensive on 21st March (St. Quentin) when a thick white fog prevailed. A lot of gas was mixed up with the high explosive and gas masks had to be worn. A platoon officer accompanied the writer to his post about one o'clock in the morning, groping along by a low shelving bank, and then branched off to glean some news from the batteries, both sides pounding away " hell for leather." Visibility was nil ; the irreducible minimum.

" . . . . . Now, how did the soldiers manage for meals ? "

" Oh, we managed all right ; mustard wasn't an issue, but we had mustard gas. Besides, there were periods of slackening off."

" Slackening off ? "

" Well, you see, Mr. Perky, it was like this . . . . "

The squad were looking out into a drizzle one night (St. Quentin), when the sentry challenged and an officer and three men appeared leading from the front line. Said the Officer to the writer : " I want you on this scouting party." The " going " was a rifle and two bombs and the little party waited while the writer took his straps to pieces and put them under some sacking. Then the scouts went out. The night was dark; no moon or stars. And quiet. Save for an occasional " crack " far away on the flanks there was not a sign of life. The scouts roamed over " no man's land " for hours, looking here, poking there, crawling somewhere else, and at times lying " doggo." The obstacles were varied ; old bits of trench, shell holes, discarded dumps, level stretches and obscure paths. One of the obstacles was a short sunken road heavily flanked with thick wire and filled several feet deep with close concertina wire. The task was to work through this and see what lay at the further end. The party dropped the writer at his post on its way back and he set to work with his straps in the dark (no light job) only pausing as the officer said, tailing into the drizzle : " . . . . and on my way back I'll bring a rum ration."

So far as one can see proverbs seem to be based on truth. Take this one : " Next to being late is the fault of being too early." There was proof of this one night (St. Quentin) when the writer was on a fighting patrol thirty strong. It was cold but fairly clear. After moving round a good while the patrol sighted a large enemy party in the distance, all strung out, and it extended in the prone position so as to intercept the enemy's line of approach, and waited. One man seized old Time by the forelock ; he took the pin out of his bomb ready. But the Fates were at work that night. When still some way off the enemy suddenly went " backwards " instead of " towards " ; their movements seemed uncertain. The patrol's tactics on this night were to surprise the enemy and the pinless bomb had to be held at all costs. For one thing the man couldn't put it back in his pocket. The patrol returned after a while to its starting point, and then the luckless wight hurled his bomb into the night — CRASH !

" *Rat-tat-tat-tat-tat-tat-tat-tat-tat* ! " This at another post (St. Quentin) opposite which an enemy-machine gunner kept the night awake by persistently putting over bursts. " What's that blankety blank firing at ? " " Can't see anything about ; perhaps it's spoof." " *Rat-tat-tat-tat-tat-tat-tat-tat* ! " " There he goes again ; fire back at him ; not the whole drum." " What if he doesn't know we're 'ere ? " " Not half he doesn't ! Now ! " and the flashes pierced the darkness and the rival teams pegged away merrily.

This watery summer, Anno Domini, 1936, reminds one of a battle holiday spent at Boulogne ; the first day or so were all right ; the rest were stormy. A strong Channel gale blew, the seas dashed over the shingle and the wind drove the rain hard. Late at night a furious gust caught the tent flap, away went the pegs, down went the pole, and the six sleepers (not seven), were mixed up in a whirl of flying canvas. This was the close to an episode the opening of which was quite commonplace . . . .

" What's it like, Yorky ? "

" Money for jam, an' all," said a bomber of the Yorks and Lancs. as he picked up a small bag of bombs on his way out.

This outpost was round and about the Messines sector. To reach it the squad climbed out of the trench at a lone tree, moved outwards and slant-wise over the top for about twenty-five yards, then crawled left along an upward gradient between shell-holes. To the left of the post a shallow trench stretched away a good distance to a Lewis gun post. Below the bombing post a sunken road trended slightly right to the enemy line ; the foremost point of the enemy line to the left front of the Lewis gun post was marked by an old windmill.

The second night in there was a stir on the further side of the windmill, and the artillery to our right rear fired diagonally over our heads. Next night the sentry challenged and Sergeant H—— came up. Said he : " Captain S—— wants a second man to go out scouting and report on the state of the German wire," and it fell to the writer. The instructions were : " Go out from the bombing post as soon as a Véry light is sent up " (the night was dark and no Véries were showing). " A second Véry light will be fired twenty minutes later to help the scouts to see the wire.

The two scouts went out at the first Véry and took direction by the sunken road on the right. This sub-divided and they took the left branch till the enemy wire was

sighted, the first thing being the stakes. The scouts turned left, keeping the wire on their right, and after a while flattened out and waited. SzzzzzzzzSzzzzzzzSzzzzzz .....
Up went Véry No. 2. It described a wide curve and burst overhead like a beautiful star ; then fell slowly and burnt out to their right rear. In the brilliant glare a fair view was taken of the wire, and the scouts pushed on. A point was reached where an enemy party was working on the other side of the wire, and the scouts listened to the " chug, chug, chug," of the shovels. Something one of the party said in gutteral German made the others laugh. Perhaps it had reference to soup ; the consistency of the ground would suggest soup, and judging by the size of their mess-tins soup was a staple ration. The scouts finished the tour and turned for home. In taking direction care was needed ; the ground was much cut up and neither side was sending up Véries. After a while, peeping round a shell hole, they saw two shadowy heads in front a little above ground

Go on! Go on!

level. The helmets were not clear so the scouts waited awhile. A movement by one of the watchers decided that point, and the scouts crawled nearer. Presently : Thud ! Over came a lump of earth, followed by a quiet voice : " Come in, you blokes." " What about the swords ? " " Oh ! Move those swords back and let these two blokes get in." This was the Lewis gun post. The report ran : " . . . . and the wire is damaged a good bit. Wiring stakes are beaten down, but a fair number are still more or less upright."
Next night the sentry challenged and Brigadier S—— in person came stumbling up to the post over the broken ground, followed by Major M. Said the Brigadier :
" What are you men doing here ? What ! What ! "
" Sir, a sharp look-out is being kept on front, rear and both flanks of post. So far there is no movement to report."
The Brigadier : " I want the enemy to know you are awake ! Keep putting over bursts of ' rapid ! ' Let them know you are here ! Keep firing at them ! " And he moved

off with Major M. towards the Lewis gun post. There was an excellent reason for that order, as the sequel proved.

The squad levelled their rifles, aimed low and fired five rapid into the night. Presently another five ; and another five after that. And yet another. They thought : The ammo. won't last long at this rate. Then came the familiar whine of an enemy shell — Crash ! Still another five rapid — and another shell — Crash ! This began a strafe. It was now not a question how long the ammo. would last, but how long the squad would last to fire it. The post began to go to pieces, and a runner doubled up breathlessly : " Captain's orders : Get back to the trench ! " and away he went. Quite ! The squad filed out, crouching low. The shelling was formidable. Further along, as the leading man reached the corner of a traverse, a shell screamed over almost " dead on " and burst in the traverse with stunning force. Showers of earth fell, the nose caps of the two leading rifles were blown off, and the squad were befogged and half-choked by thick clouds of acrid smoke. This was " Colonel Bogey " with a vengeance. A pause and then forward again. Shouted a voice : " Make for the lone tree ! " and away they went, helter-skelter, skirting a communication trench full of "A" Company's men waiting on events.

One of the killed in this shelling was Corporal Perkins, packed up for home leave. The night opening quiet, he came up from the Transport Lines to take a message or two back to England. Memory is one of Nature's marvels. The mention of a name and instantly one visualises a sequence of scenes. His appearance : Thick set, about 5-ft. 7-ins., eyes light grey, hair close cut and slightly auburn, nose slightly concave, features square, manner unemotional, voice quiet and a midland or north country burr. A quick backward look of enquiry as a shell burst to his left rear ; the first evening's halt on the Division's way out, a clean tent, candles alight, rations dished out, and letters being read ; or again, when out at rest — tea-time — someone made a remark and he looked across and laughed ; and again, on a ration party, pitch dark, and the route to shell holes indicated by the men (yellow shoulder tabs) who had fallen in that morning's attack. And now — the end.

At the first streak of dawn : " Move up again ! " followed by " Alt in front ! " a few yards short of the post. An "A" Company officer viewed the ground the day before, passing through the post. He was of medium height, Georgian features and build, clean shaven and of fresh complexion. Ladders were fixed left of the post during the night, the men of "A" Company filed in and soon after dawn, at a given signal, they scaled the ladders and rushed over on a silent raid. Some shots were fired, there was a quick scuffle in the enemy trenches, some prisoners were seized, and the men doubled back. Then both sides opened out with shells of all calibre, and the air was laced with streams of machine guns bullet whistling and hissing from all points of the compass. A rum issue was dished out to the raiders when they got back, and to expedite its issue the jar was emptied into a tin. Never did trench reek with a more glorious odour. A call for " S.B." and Taffy worked his way to the casualty by his knees and elbows against the sides of the trench over the heads of crouching men. Then another order came : " Move up to the post." !

Bullets crackled against the post like hail stones on a tin roof. Just at this moment, when it seemed that one had only to poke his head above the parapet to get it shot off, a small party appeared leading from the right of the enemy line to our trench. There were two tall prisoners, helmets askew and jackets unbuttoned, a tall strenuous officer of Dutch descent (from South Africa ; later wounded at Polygon Wood) and an escort of two small riflemen. Opposite the post the prisoners faltered. The tumult was deafening. The officer moved up from the left rear, pointed towards our line with left arm outstretched, and shouted in a tremendous voice : " Go on ! Go on ! " The escort closed in and the little party moved out of sight towards the trench.

The raid was a success and casualties were few, but the officer who viewed the ground was killed.

The firing slackened off and at about eleven o'clock rations arrived. These were a bit the worse for wear, but the squad soon apportioned them and " polished them off." The Frey Bentos being in tins made it easier. The expected counter-attack in the evening did not occur, and the " relief " filed in about midnight. Away back from the line the platoon halted for a guide to billets and at this point the platoon officer (Lieut. S.) produced a small box of Abdullah's, which he passed round, and the fragrant odour of Turkish leaf beguiled the time of waiting.

J. EDWARDS.

(*To be continued.*)

Our First Legacy

ONE of our oldest and most generous members, Miss Eveline Greene, who suffered bereavement in the War, has passed away, and her family has the sincere sympathy of the League. Through her kind thought the League receives a legacy of fifty pounds. This is our first legacy, and Miss Greene has started a precedent which if followed by others will secure our finances on a permanent basis ; for it is the case of all institutions of long standing that their Capital assets consist very largely of legacies.

We greatly appreciate the example that Miss Greene has set us.

* * * * *

Retirement of Captain G. E. de Trafford

NOTHING but the most urgent family call would have induced Captain de Trafford to retire from the Secretaryship of the Ypres League, to which he has given his whole soul for the past eleven years. All who have been in personal touch with him, either at the office, on visits to Ypres, or at our social gatherings, cannot have failed to observe how entirely devoted he was both to the purpose of the League and to its individual members.

Eloquent testimony of his loyal devotion, of his tact, and of his generous lovable nature, may be gathered from the pile of appreciative letters which have poured into our headquarters office during the past few weeks.

The success of the League under his ægis has been a source of great pleasure to him and, as he used to say, this more than fully rewarded him for the time and labour he gave ; often working till near midnight. But he has a reward, the most precious that any man can gain, the sincere and lasting affection of a host of friends.

We all wish him long life and every possible happiness, and we can say with real sincerity, that we shall keep his devotion to our Cause and his lovable personality always in our memory ; de Trafford has left a mark upon the League which will permanently enrich it.

* * * * *

Testimonial Fund

The Committee desire to thank through these columns all those who have so kindly and generously contributed to the " de Trafford Testimonial Fund." The response undoubtedly justifies the opinion unanimously expressed at the last General Committee Meeting that members of the Ypres League, at home and abroad, would wish to be given the opportunity of associating themselves with some form of mememto to mark their appreciation of his eleven years devoted services as Secretary and their affection for him as a comrade. Contributions continue to be received at the time of going to Press, and to give those loyal members resident in far-off places an opportunity of being included in this Testimonial, as well as those who may have been on holiday and away from their permanent address for some time, it is proposed to keep the Fund open for a further few weeks.

For the information of those who may not, for some reason or other, have received the special notice in the form of an addenda sheet with their July copy of the *Ypres Times*, we repeat here that donations not exceeding the sum of 2s. 6d. should be addressed to Barclays Bank, Ltd., Knightsbridge Branch, London, S.W.3, and not forwarded to the League offices. Cheques and Postal Orders should be made payable to the " de Trafford Testimonial Account."

The January, 1937, edition of the *Ypres Times* will contain a complete list of all subscribers to this Fund, and it is intended to present in suitable form a similar list to Captain de Trafford as a permanent souvenir.

* * * * *

Our New Secretary

Major L. J. L. Pullar, M.C., of the Seaforth Highlanders has been working with Captain de Trafford for some weeks, and as he has earned the praise of that " whale for work." we may take it that the League is fortunate in it's new Secretary, and all those who have been in touch with him feel very happy and confident about the future.

A side-light which the writer has culled from a certain letter will commend itself to many of us : " This officer performed very distinguished conduct in the recent operations N.E. of Ypres and would have been recommended for a decoration had he not expressed a wish to be recommended for promotion in the Regular Army in lieu."

The Captain, however, failed to avoid decoration for he was awarded the Military Cross for gallantry at St. Julien in September, 1917, and a bar to his Military Cross for conspicuous gallantry and devotion to duty in the Machine-gun defence of the battle-zone during the retreat in March, 1918.

It is certain that Major Pullar will find many old comrades within the League, for he was Brigade Machine-gun Officer to the 162nd Infantry Brigade at the Suvla Bay landing in August, 1915 ; Company Commander in the Machine-gun Corps ; Commander of Armoured Cars in Mesopotamia, 1921-22 ; with the Seaforth Highlanders on the North West Frontier, 1923-25 ; and in the Royal West African Frontier Force in 1925-29, where he attained the rank of Battalion Commander.

Add to his service record the fact that he is a noted revolver shot, was Captain of Athletics at New College, Oxford University, and it becomes evident that the Major is an Officer of outstanding initiative, accuracy and energy, and we welcome him confidently and very cordially as our Secretary.

E. B. WAGGETT (*Vice-Chairman, Executive Committee*).

The Plumer Memorial Scholarship

Congratulations to Arthur Batchelor, student of the Ypres British School, on being awarded the "Plumer Memorial Scholarship" of £10 for the year 1936.

It may be remembered that this Scholarship is in connection with the Memorial raised in 1933 to the memory of our late beloved President Field-Marshal The Viscount Plumer of Messines.

Funds were raised by members and friends for the purpose of a Worked Banner bearing Lord Plumer's Arms, to be placed in St. George's Church at Ypres, and any surplus money collected to be placed in trust to provide free education to a child at the Ypres British School as a "Plumer Scholarship."

EMBROIDERED BADGES.

These badges which can be suitably worn on pockets of sports jackets may be supplied on application to the Secretary, Ypres League, 20, Orchard Street, London, W.1. Price 4/- post free.

YPRES LEAGUE BADGE.

The design of the badge—a lion guarding a portcullis gate—represents the British Army defending the Salient, which was the gate to the Channel Ports.

The badge is brilliantly enamelled with silver finish. Price 2s., post free 2s. 1½d. (pin or stud, whichever is desired).

Obtainable from Secretary, Ypres League, 20, Orchard Street, London, W.1.

PHOTOGRAPHS OF WAR GRAVES.

The Ypres League has made arrangements whereby it is able to supply photographs (negative, and one print, postcard size, unmounted) of graves situated in the Ypres Salient, and in the Hazebrouck and Armentieres areas, at the price of 10s. each.

All applications for photographs should be sent to the Secretary, together with remittance, giving the regimental particulars of the soldier, name of cemetery, and number of plot, row and grave.

WREATHS.

Arrangements are made by the Ypres League to place wreaths for relatives on the graves of British soldiers situated in France and Belgium at the following times of the year:—

EASTER, ARMISTICE DAY, CHRISTMAS

The wreaths may be composed of natural flowers, laurel, or holly, and can be bought at the following prices—12s. 6d., 15s. 6d., and 20s., according to the size and quality of the wreath.

OLD WELL-KNOWN SPOTS IN NEW GUISE.

The following prints, size 4¼ x 2½, recently taken of famous spots in the Ypres Salient, and which may be of great interest to our readers, are on sale at headquarters, price 4d. each, post free 5d.

Poelcappelle Church.
Ramparts at the Lille Gate.
Hell Fire Corner, Left.
Hell Fire Corner, Right.
Shrapnel Corner.
Transport Farm Cemetery.
Transport Farm Corner.
Zillebeke Lake.
Hill 62, Canadian Memorial.
Hooge from Zouave Wood.
Hooge Crater Cemetery.
Clapham Junction.
Stirling Castle.
Gheluvelt Church.
Cheddar Villa Dressing Station.
Vancouver Cross Roads.
Canadian Memorial: Vancouver Cross Roads.
Hyde Park Corner. (Memorial.)
Wulverghem.
Messines Church.
Potsdam Redoubt at Corner Cott.

Obtainable from Secretary, Ypres League, 20, Orchard Street, London, W.1.

YPRES LEAGUE TIE.

Dark shade of cornflower blue relieved by a narrow gold stripe. In good quality silk.

Price 3/6d., post free.

Obtainable from Secretary, Ypres League, 20, Orchard Street, London, W.1.

MODELS OF DEMARCATION STONE.

Plaster models of the Demarcation Stone can be supplied from Head Office.

All members are aware that 240 granite demarcation stones stretch from the Swiss border to the sea, marking the extreme line of advance of the German invasion.

The model, which is 6 inches in height, may be used for a paperweight or as an ornament. Price 5s., post free in United Kingdom. Applications to the Secretary, Ypres League.

7th (City of London) Battalion, The London Regiment Old Comrades' Association

24, Sun Street,
Finsbury Square, E.C.2.

Arising from the visit of the Old Comrades' Association to Ypres last Easter, it has been suggested that past and present members of the Regiment should hang a Banner in memory of fallen comrades, in the English Church at Ypres. This proposal has been received with enthusiasm, and the Banner is already designed.

The Whitsun Tour of the Battlefields in 1937 will be made the occasion of the dedication and handing over of the Banner. It is hoped that all ranks will be represented on this Tour.

Subscriptions will be taken at the Annual Dinner on December 5th. After providing for the cost of the Banner, etc. it is proposed that the surplus shall form a Benevolent Fund of the Regimental O.C.A. This Fund will be devoted to the relief of distressed ex-Seventh Men who are not members of the O.C.A. and under the Rules are unable to receive assistance from existing funds.

The Committee hope to arrange for the Banner to be viewed by subscribers who may be unable to make the journey to Ypres for the Dedication Ceremony.

On behalf of the Committee,

G. HILL, *Chairman.*

PROPOSED WHITSUN TOUR
(Under the auspices of the Ypres League)

Including ticket—London to Ypres, return via Ostend.

3rd class on train, 2nd class on steamer, char-a-banc from Ostend to Ypres via Langemarck, Tyne-Cot, Passchendaele, Zonnebeke, Clapham Junction, Hooge and Menin Road.

Full Board, commencing with evening dinner at Ypres on Whit-Saturday, and ending with lunch at Ypres on Whit-Monday, arriving Victoria 9 p.m. To include two nights' accommodation with all taxes and gratuities at Hotel. Also whole day char-a-banc tour of the Somme.

Dedication Service of 7th London Banner at St. George's Church, Ypres. Return to Ostend by char-a-banc after visiting St. Eloi, site of White Chateau and the Bluff.

LADIES INVITED

NO PASSPORTS REQUIRED £4 5s. 0d.

Early application for tickets should be made to the Hon. Secretary, **G. Percy Rossiter**, at Headquarters, 24, Sun Street, Finsbury, E.C.2.

MONTHLY INFORMAL GATHERINGS
WILL BE HELD AT
THE BEDFORD HEAD HOTEL,
Maiden Lane, Strand, W.C.2

On THURSDAY, 15th OCTOBER, 1936
THURSDAY, 19th NOVEMBER, 1936
THURSDAY, 17th DECEMBER, 1936
From 7.30 p.m. to 10 o'clock p.m.

Particulars of programmes arranged for these evenings will be forwarded on application being made to the Hon. Secretary, London Branch Committee.

OBITUARY.

From Madrid we have received the sad news from Captain P. W. Burgess, our Corresponding Member, of the death of Captain Logan N. Rock, a Life Member of the League and a very enthusiastic supporter of the Madrid Branch. Captain Rock was American born and came to Europe during the Great War with the 38th Division, American Expeditionary Force. At one period he was attached to Princess Patricia's Canadian Light Infantry and saw service in the Ypres Salient with the British Forces. After the War he studied and qualified in Spanish law, eventually being given charge of the legal part of the transaction between the Spanish Government and the International Telephone and Telegraph Corporation, New York, for the automatic telephone installation in Spain which is considered to-day among the best organised telephone systems in Europe. In 1925 Captain Rock expressed a desire to become associated with the aims and objects of the Ypres League, forwarding as a contribution a draft for £5, half of which was to be in respect of a Life Membership and the balance for the funds of the League whose objects he wrote at the time claimed his complete sympathy. The funeral took place at the British Embassy Church of St. George, Madrid, on June 22nd last, and among the seven to eight hundred mourners present were several members of the Ypres League resident in Madrid with Captain P. W. Burgess as official Representative. A Cross of Sacrifice in cornflowers from the Madrid Branch of the Ypres League was placed at the foot of the coffin.

UNE BELLE PENSÉE.

It is thought that members would like to learn of the following touching incident in connection with a gracious donation made by one of our members to a Canadian Pilgrim. The money was sent to us for forwarding to the proper authority for distribution to a deserving member of the Canadian Pilgrimage attending the Unveiling Ceremony at Vimy Ridge.

The gift was presented to a poor widow, who had eleven sons in the war, six of them were killed. The recipient's means were very slender and the windfall was of great assistance to her. On our informing the donor as to how the money has been used we received a reply of which the following is an extract.

" I feel that I must tell you with all modesty that it is really a strange coincidence that . . . should have been the recipient, as at the Vimy Ridge Unveiling Ceremony a wreath was put on the Memorial for me, and since then I have heard that she happened to notice it, and told a friend of mine (who placed it) that the words I had written on the card had helped to make her brave. How little I thought I should be helping her in that way, and now again through you acting so promptly, I have been able to do so a second time, and I feel very happy to think it should be so."

Branch Notes

THE PURLEY BRANCH,
The Bombardier's Foursomes, 1936.

There was again a large entry for this competition, 35 pairs being engaged. The draw was made and posted to each competitor at the commencement of summer time, and the First Battle then immediately began.

Only brief results can be given owing to the large number of matches.

First Battle.
Pay-Lieut. N. Bell (20) and Pte. H. Boon (14) bt. Corpl. A. A. Meredith (10) and Lieut. J. H. Hines (13), 3/2 ; Lieut. E. W. Bennett (14) and Driver C. C. Wood (15) bt. Lieut. F. B. Jones (10) and Major D. H. Lock (6), 2/1 ; Capt. G. G. Boston (13) and Lieut. C. E. Terrell (14) bt. Capt. E. Featherstone (1) and Major G. Carr (7), 5/3.

Second Battle.
Bennett and Wood bt. Bell and Boon, 4/2 ; C.S.M. N. L. Way (12) and Corp. E. A. Satchell (16) bt. Major L. Meakin (14) and Major J. Wayte (18), 5/3 ; Major F. Roberts (13) and Pte. E. S. Butt (2) bt. Lieut.-Col. A. Wilkinson (20) and Lieut. W. R. Pullen (22), 7/5 ; Lieut. R. R. Birrell (17) and Capt. J. G. Rae (8) bt. Major J. F. Legg (22) and Major D. H. Scott (18), 1 up ; Major A. G. Grutchfield (18) and Corp. C. Stroud (16) bt. Lieut. C. J. Frost (10) and Rfm. G. D. Green (10), 3/1 ; Gnr. J. K. Macfarlane (13) and Gnr. W. Kerr (10) bt. Pte. A. Milne (18) and Trooper F. Skade (24), 6/4 ; Capt. G. B. Mutton (18) and Lieut. A. D. Duncan (11), walk-over ; Bmdr. E. A. R. Burden (2) and Lieut. H. L. W. Hancock (10), scratched ; Major J. S. Hall (18) and Capt. G. E. E. B. Nicholls (24) bt. Lieut. S. V. Smith (11) and Capt. D. Morgan (24), 2/1 ; Lieut. H. F. Smith (9) and Lieut. S. B. Silvester (5) bt. Lieut. S. J. O. Panchaud (12) and Lieut. J. K. Jones (14), 3/2 ; Pte. A. K. Irens (4) and Major L. W. Allerson (6), walk-over ; Capt. E. A. S. Lund (18) and Major S. F. Wood (8), scratched ; Capt. E. C. Ashby (7) and Lieut. J. V. Lindsay (7) bt. Lieut. F. St. John North (16) and Commdr. H. D. C. Stanistreet (7), 2/1 ; Capt. B. A. Forster (8) and Commdr. R. H. Shelton (11) bt. Major H. G. Harris (16) and Capt. N. W. Streat (12), 6/5 ; Lieut. N. A. Zinn (20) and

Lieut. A. J. Fitton (18) bt. Lieut. S. Vaughan (17) and Major R. H. Forster (20), 2/1 ; Pay-Commdr. F. L. Monk (16) and Lieut. S. Murray (14) bt. 2nd Lieut. H. G. Smith (5) and Capt. A. S. Green (11), 2 up ; Lieut. C. H. S. Cox (18) and Lieut. B. R. Brill (8) bt. Corp. C. T. Taylor (9) and Capt. F. W. Douse (8), 2 up ; Bmdr. H. J. Knight (8) and Lieut. J. J. Mellon (15) bt. Boston and Terrell, 7/6.

Third Battle.
Bennett and Wood bt. Way and Satchell, 1 up ; Birrell and Rae bt. Roberts and Butt, 2 up ; Macfarlane and Kerr bt. Grutchfield and Stroud, 4/3 ; Mutton and Duncan bt. Hall and Nicholls, 4/3 ; Irens and Alderson bt. Smith and Silvester, 2/1 ; Forster and Shelton bt. Ashby and Lindsay, 1 up ; Monk and Murray bt. Zinn and Fitton, 5/3 ; Knight and Mellon bt. Cox and Brill, 5/4.

Autumn Golf Meeting.
Two new members joined the League immediately before going out to compete with twenty-one others for the 12th " Wipers Cup " on the afternoon of the 22nd September, 1936, and signalised their joining by returning the 1st and 2nd scores. These were Major C. W. Pulford and Mr. W. W. D. Redwood, both members of the Purley Downs Club, where the competition took place.

As a welcome change from the previous year, the weather was beautifully fine and still, and the course was in grand order as usual ; the general standard of play was really excellent and at least the first six players beat their handicap comfortably, one outstanding return being Major L. W. Alderson, who went round in the bogey score of 76, playing from a six handicap.

A supper in the Club House followed, when the Chairman, Pte. A. K. Irens, presented the prize to the fortunate winner. A number of members afterwards told anecdotes, which were very well received, and after congratulating the Committee of Purley Downs and thanking them for their hospitality, the members dispersed in good time.

THE ADJUTANT.

LONDON BRANCH COMMITTEE.
Fourteenth Annual Re-union Smoking Concert.

The London Branch Committee have arranged to hold the Fourteenth Annual Re-union Smoking Concert on Saturday, October 31st (Ypres Day), 1936, at 7.30 p.m., at the Caxton Hall, Caxton Street, Victoria, S.W.1, when Major E. Montague Jones, O.B.E., (Chairman of the London Branch Committee), will preside. The following distinguished guests have kindly accepted invitations to be present :—

H.E. The Belgian Ambassador, H.E. The French Ambassador, Lieut.-General Baron Vincotte (Military Attaché, Belgian Embassy), General A. Lelong (Military Attaché, French Embassy), Lieut.-Colonel Raymond E. Long, General Sir Hubert Gough, G.C.M.G., K.C.B., K.C.V.O., Lieut.-General Sir W. P. Pulteney, G.C.V.O., K.C.B., K.C.M.G., D.S.O., Brig.-General A. Burt, C.B., C.M.G., D.S.O., and Colonel G. T. Brierley, C.M.G., D.S.F.

The programme of entertainment is being arranged by the " Roosters " the famous Wireless Entertainers and late of the 60th Divisional Concert Party.

(1) In view of the fact that this Re-union is being held on Ypres Day, a strong appeal is made to members to do their best to be present, and so help to make this year a record for this particular function. If each member attending can manage to bring along at least one friend then such record can be easily achieved.

(2) Cornflowers will be on sale at the Hall, price 2d. each, and all present are kindly asked to wear one.

(3) Applications for tickets, price 5/-, 2/6d., and 1/-, should be made as early as possible to the Hon. Secretary, London Branch Committee, Ypres League, 20, Orchard Street, London, W.1. Ladies are cordially invited.

(4) A limited number of tables can be reserved for parties of four and upwards on payment of 6d. per ticket extra on 2/6d. tickets, and 2/6d. per table on the 5/- tickets. Closing date for applications, October 26th.

It is hoped that as many members as possible will apply for tickets for sale among friends, and in the case of those prevented from being present, the Committee respectfully appeal to them to purchase a ticket on behalf of some ex-service man who would otherwise not be able to attend, or to assist their funds.

Informal Gatherings.

The London Branch Committee desire to draw the attention of members to the season's Informal Gatherings, just commenced, and sincerely hope that greater efforts will be made to make these Gatherings more widely known. The Informal Gatherings are promoted with the Ypres League's principal objects in view, Commemoration and Comradeship. Members and friends are cordially welcomed, and opportunity is afforded ex-service men of meeting together in convivial atmosphere, renewing old acquaintances, and thereby strengthening that wonderful spirit of comradeship and good fellowship fostered in the Great War.

Notice of these Gatherings will be gladly sent to any of your friends upon name and address being supplied to the Hon. Secretary.

Monthly Informal Gatherings

will be held at The Bedford Head Hotel, Maiden Lane, Strand, W.C.2, on
Thursday, 15th October, 1936
Thursday, 19th November, 1936
Thursday, 17th December, 1936
from 7.30 p.m. to 10 p.m.

Particulars of programmes arranged for these evenings will be forwarded on application being made to the Hon. Secretary, London Branch Committee.

League Secretary's Notes

Since notes were penned under this heading for our last edition the Ypres League has sustained a great loss as a result of the resignation of Captain G. E. de Trafford, M.C., it's indefatigable Secretary for so many years. Never sparing himself where the league's welfare was concerned, his administrative qualities, wide experience in battlefields travel organisation, and his charming personality will be sadly missed.

Following an urgent family recall in June last, circumstances compelled him to reluctantly vacate the Secretaryship of the Ypres League a position he had so honourably held for over eleven years, and a last moment circular was inserted in the July number notifying members to this effect.

It was indeed with deep sorrow that we were to subsequently learn of the death of his aged father and every member, at home and abroad, will join with us in extending to Captain de Trafford and his family, our deepest sympathy in their great bereavement and irreparable loss. Every good wish goes with this message for our late Secretary's future prosperity and happiness, with added prestige in the new position he now finds himself called upon to fill.

During the short period under his instruction I was particularly impressed by the wonderful *camaraderie* between headquarters and it's members and the various Branches; a good sign and also essential for the successful continuance of an organisation such as ours.

In introducing myself as the successor to Captain de Trafford, I hope that this happy state of affairs will continue during my tenure of office, and that members will extend to me that same loyal support accorded my predecessor.

Our frontispiece portrays our beloved Patron-in-Chief, H.M. The King, at the Unveiling Ceremony of the Canadian War Memorial, Vimy Ridge, on July 26th. On this occasion the Ypres League were invited, through our Chairman, Lieut.-General Sir William Pulteney, to nominate a Representative to be present at this historic Ceremony. Lieut.-Colonel F. G. Poole, D.S.O., O.B.E., Hon-Secretary of the Ypres British Settlement, was eventually nominated, and this distinguished officer duly crossed to France in company with other guests invited and on his return kindly wrote an account of the Ceremony for the interest of our members (*vide* pages 98, 99, 100).

This past quarter our Travel Bureau has been actively engaged with the organisation of several party battlefield tours. Successful Tours having been arranged for the "Old Coldstreamers" London Branch, O.C.A., August Bank Holiday mixed Pilgrimage; an Ypres League "London Branch" Party, a mixed Pilgrimage, September 19th-22nd, which included our annual Free Pilgrimage and September 25th-29th, a contingent from the Leominster Branch of the British Legion. The Free Pilgrimage consisted of poor mothers and widows specially selected from London, Essex, Middlesex, Bristol, Lancashire and Durham.

We extend a hearty welcome to all new members who have enrolled since the publication of our last edition of the YPRES TIMES, the total of which has been most gratifying. With regard to Branch recruitment of new members the Purley Branch appear to be slightly ahead in the competition for the prize of £5 awarded annually for the highest number recruited during the year.

The London Branch Committee are busily engaged in preparing their autumn and winter programmes for the Informal Gatherings and the Annual Smoking Concert at which a number of distinguished guests have accepted invitations.

A number of journals continue to be returned to us through the "dead letter office" as a result of members changing their address without advising headquarters. We are anxious to ensure that members receive their copy regularly and it would, therefore, be greatly appreciated if we could be so notified.

This being the last quarterly edition of 1936 we are desirous of wishing all members a very happy Christmas.

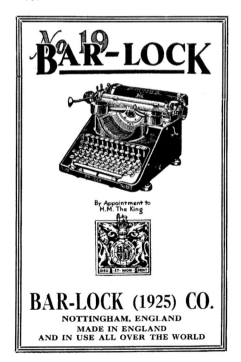

BAR-LOCK No. 19

By Appointment to H.M. The King

BAR-LOCK (1925) CO.
NOTTINGHAM, ENGLAND
MADE IN ENGLAND
AND IN USE ALL OVER THE WORLD

The Ypres League (Incorporated)

Balance Sheet, 31st December, 1935

FUNDS AND LIABILITIES.

	£ s. d.	£ s. d.
Free Pilgrimage Fund		63 11 9
General Fund—		
Balance at credit, 1st January, 1935	75 16 5	
Add Balance at credit for year to 31st December, 1935	137 10 5	
	213 6 10	
Less YPRES TIMES Maintenance Fund— Restoration of amount appropriated at 31st December, 1934	44 7 0	168 19 10
Reserve Fund—In respect of Life Membership Subscriptions		300 0 0
YPRES TIMES Maintenance Fund		275 18 5
Hostel Fund		322 19 10
Maintenance Fund—Ypres Salient Notice Boards		6 16 9
Sundry Creditors, etc.		89 8 8
		£1,227 15 3

ASSETS.

	£ s. d.	£ s. d.
Stocks of Publications, etc., on hand As per Head Office records.		50 13 8
Cash at Bank and in hand—		
Free Pilgrimage Fund	65 18 3	
Head Office Account	213 13 2	279 11 5
Halifax Building Society—		
Deposit Account "A"	315 3 7	
Deposit Account "B"	210 2 4	
	525 5 11	
Add Interest accrued	13 16 9	539 2 8
Hostel Fund Investment—		
£323 2s. 11d. War Stock 3½%		322 19 10
Sundry Debtors and Pre-payments, etc.		35 7 8
		£1,227 15 3

E. B. WAGGETT } *Members of the*
JOHN BOUCHEY } *General Committee.*

W. P. PULTENEY, *Lieut.-General,*
Hon. Treasurer.

REPORT OF THE AUDITORS TO THE MEMBERS OF THE YPRES LEAGUE, INCORPORATED.

We beg to report that we have examined the above Balance Sheet with the Head Office Books and relative Documents of the Association and have obtained all the information and explanations we have required. In our opinion such Balance Sheet is properly drawn up so as to exhibit a true and correct view of the state of the Association's affairs, according to the best of our information and the explanations given to us and as shown by the Books of the Association.

Dated this 26th day of June, 1936.

LEPINE & JACKSON, Chartered Accountants,
Auditors.

6, BOND COURT, WALBROOK, LONDON, E.C.4.

Head Office

Income and Expenditure Account for the year ended 31st December, 1935

EXPENDITURE.

	£	s.	d.
To Salaries	303	10	0
,, Rent and Rates	247	5	2
,, Printing and Stationery	35	7	5
,, Postages and Telegrams	45	0	11
,, Prospectuses, Publicity Leaflets, etc.	16	7	1
,, Telephone and Insurances	25	15	11
,, Lighting and Heating	8	7	7
,, Accountancy Charges	18	18	0
,, General Expenses	94	1	3
,, Income Tax	2	9	6
	797	2	10
,, Balance—Surplus carried to General Fund	410	4	3
	£1,207	7	1

INCOME.

		£	s.	d.	£	s.	d.
By Subscriptions					442	17	1
,, Donations					144	9	9
,, Travel Bureau					599	12	9
,, Sales of Publications, etc.—							
Publications		3	8	0			
Badges, Ties, Photographs and Heraldry		8	19	8			
		12	7	8			
Less Applied to reduce Publications Stock Value							
		12	7	8			
,, Interest					20	7	6
					£1,207	7	1

Head Office

General Fund for the year ended 31st December, 1935

EXPENDITURE.

	£	s.	d.	£	s.	d.
To The Ypres Times—						
Cost of Printing, etc.	291	11	1			
Less Sales and Advertising Revenue	18	17	3			
				272	13	10
,, Balance—Carried to Balance Sheet				137	10	5
				£410	4	3

INCOME.

	£	s.	d.
By Income and Expenditure Account Surplus for the year transferred.	410	4	3
	£410	4	3

THE FOURTEENTH
RE-UNION OF MEMBERS AND FRIENDS

Organized by the London Branch Committee of the Ypres League,

WILL BE HELD AT THE

CAXTON HALL, CAXTON STREET, VICTORIA STREET, S.W.1.

ON

SATURDAY, OCTOBER 31st, 1936

All Members of the Ypres League and their friends are cordially invited by the London Branch Committee to meet together at the Caxton Hall, when a

GRAND SMOKING CONCERT

will be given. The Chair will be taken by

Major E. MONTAGUE JONES, O.B.E., M.A.

(Chairman of the London Branch Committee)

The following will also be present:

H.E. The BELGIAN AMBASSADOR; H.E. The FRENCH AMBASSADOR; LIEUT.-GENERAL BARON VINCOTTE, Military Attaché, Belgian Embassy; GENERAL A. LELONG, Military Attaché, French Embassy; LIEUT-COLONEL RAYMOND E. LEE; GENERAL SIR HUBERT GOUGH, G.C.M.G., K.C.B., K.C.V.O.; LIEUT.-GENERAL SIR W. P. PULTENEY, G.C.V.O., K.C.B., K.C.M.G., D.S.O.; BRIG.-GENERAL A. BURT, C.B., C.M.G., D.S.O., and COLONEL G. T. BRIERLEY, C.M.G., D.S.O.

An excellent programme has been arranged by

"THE ROOSTERS"

(The Famous Wireless Entertainers)—and late of the 60th Divisional Concert Party.

DOORS OPEN AT 7 P.M.   CONCERT COMMENCES AT 7.30 P.M.

ADMISSION ... 5/-, 2/6, and 1/-.

Owing to limited accommodation at the Hall, tables will be very restricted and can only be reserved for parties of four and upwards on payment of 6d. extra per ticket on the 2/6 tickets, and 2/6 per table on the 5/- tickets. Applications for tables cannot be considered after October 26th.

A record attendance is anticipated, therefore early application, accompanied by remittance, should be sent to the Hon. Secretary, London Branch Committee, Ypres League, 20, Orchard Street, Portman Square, London, W.1.

MAY WE HAVE YOUR SUPPORT FOR OCTOBER 31st?

Branches and Corresponding Members

BRANCHES.

LONDON	Hon. Secretary to the London County Committee: J. Boughey 20, Orchard Street, London, W.1.
	E. LONDON DISTRICT—L. A. Weller, 26, Lambourne Gardens, Hornchurch, Essex.
	TOTTENHAM AND EDMONTON DISTRICT—E. Glover, 191, Landowne Road, Tottenham, N.17.
	H. Carey, 373, Sydenham Road, S.E.26.
COLCHESTER	H. Snow (Hon. Sec.), 9, Church Street.
	W. H. Taylor (Pilgrimage Hon. Sec.), 64, High Street.
LIVERPOOL	Captain A. M. Webster, Blundellsands.
PURLEY	Major Graham Carr, D.S.O., M.C., 112-114, High Street.
SHEFFIELD	Captain J Wilkinson, "Holmfield," Bents Drive.
BELGIUM	Capt. P. D. Parminter, 19, Rue Surmont de Volsberghe, Ypres.
CANADA	Ed. Kingsland, P.O. Box 83, Magog, Quebec.
SOUTH AFRICA	L. G. Shuter, 381, Longmarket Street, Pietermaritzburg.
KENYA	C. H. Slater, P.O. Box 403, Nairobi.
AMERICA	Representative: Captain R. Henderson-Bland, 110 West 57th Street, New York City.

CORRESPONDING MEMBERS

GREAT BRITAIN.

ABERYSTWYTH	T. O. Thomas, 5, Smithfield Road.
ASHTON-UNDER LYNE	G. D. Stuart, "Woodlands,", Thronfield Grove, Arundel Street.
BANBURY	Captain C. W. Fowke, Yew Tree House, King's Sutton.
BIRMINGHAM	Mrs. Hill, 191, Cattell Road, Small Heath.
	John Burman, "Westbrook," Solihull Road, Shirley.
BOURNEMOUTH	H. L. Pasmore, 40, Morley Road, Boscombe Park.
BRISTOL	W. S. Hook, "Wytschaete" Redland Court Road.
BROADSTAIRS	C. E. King, 6, Norman Road, St. Peters, Broadstairs.
	Mrs. Briggs, North Foreland House.
CHATHAM	W. N. Channon, 22, Keyes Avenue.
CHESTERFIELD	Major A. W. Shea, 14, Cross Street.
CONGLETON	Mr. H. Dart, 61, The Crescent.
DARLINGTON	D. S. Vigo, 125, Dorset Road, Bexhill-on-Sea.
DERBY	T. Jakeman, 10, Graham Street.
DORRINGTON (Salop)	Captain G. D. S. Parker, Frodesley Rectory.
EXETER	Captain E. Jenkin, 25, Queen Street.
HERNE BAY	Captain E. Clarke Williams, F.S.A.A., "Conway," Station Road.
HOVE	Captain G. W. J. Cole, 2, Westbourne Terrace, Kingsway.
LEICESTER	W. C. Dunford, 343, Aylestone Road.
LINCOLN	E. Swaine, 79, West Parade.
LLANWRST	A. C. Tomlinson, M.A., Bod Estyn.
LOUGHTON	Capt. O. G. Johnson, M.A., Loughton School.
MATLOCK (Derby)	Miss Dickinson, Beechwood.
MELROSE	Mrs. Lindesay Kelsall, Darnlee.
NEW BRIGHTON (Cheshire)	E. F. Williams, 5, Waterloo Road.
NEW MILTON	W. H. Lunn, "Greycot," Albert Road.

NOTTINGHAM	E. V. Brown, 3, Eldon Chambers, Wheeler Gate.
ST. HELENS (Lancs.) ...	John Orford, 124, Knowsley Road.
ST. JOHN'S (Newfoundland)	Captain L. Murphy, G.W.V.A. Office.
SHREWSBURY	Major-General Sir John Headlam, K.B.E., C.B., D.S.O., Cruck Meole House, Hanwood.
TIVERTON (Devon) ...	Mr. W. H. Duncan Arthur, Surveyor's Office, Town Hall.
WELSHPOOL ...	Mr. E. Wilson, Coedway, Ford, Salop.

DOMINIONS AND FOREIGN COUNTRIES.

AUSTRALIA	Messrs. C. H. Green, and George Lawson, Essex House, (Opposite Anzac Square) Brisbane, Queensland. R. A. Baldwin, c/o Government Savings Bank of N.S.W., Martin Place, Sydney. Mr. W. Cloves, Box 1296, G.P.O., Adelaide.
BELGIUM	Sister Marguerite, Sacré Coeur, Ypres.
CANADA	Brig.-General V. W. Odlum, C.B., C.M.G., D.S.O., 2530, Point Grey Road, Vancouver. V. A. Bowes, 326, 40th Avenue West, Calgary, Alberta. W. Constable F. Grece, St. Hilaire Station, Ronville County, Quebec.
CEYLON	Captain F. R. G. Webb, M.C., Irrigation Bungalow, Kalmunai, E.P.
EGYPT	L. B. S. Larkins, The Residency, Cairo.
INDIA	Lieut.-Quartermaster G. Smith, Queen's Bays, Sialkot, India.
IRELAND	Miss A. K. Jackson, Cloneyhurke House, Portarlington.
NEW ZEALAND ...	Captain W. U. Gibb, Ava Lodge, Puhinui Road, Papatoetoe, Auckland S. E. Beattie, P.O. Box 11, Otaki Railway, Wellington.
NEWFOUNDLAND ...	Captain Leo. Murphy, G.W.V.A. Office, St. John's.
NOVA SCOTIA ...	Will R. Bird, 35, Clarence Street, Amherst.
SOUTH AFRICA ...	H. L. Versfield, c/o Cape Explosives Works Ltd., 150, St. Georges Street, Cape Town.
SPAIN	Captain P. W. Burgess, Calle de Zurbano 29, Madrid.
U.S.A.	Captain Henry Maslin, 942, President Street, Brooklyn, New York. L. E. P. Foot, 20, Gillett Street, Hartford, Conn., U.S.A. A. P. Forward, 449, East 80th Street, New York. J. W. Freebody, 945, McBride Avenue, Los Angeles.

Membership of the League

This is open to all who served in the Salient, and to all those whose relatives or friends died there, in order that they may have a record of that service for themselves and their descendants, and belong to the comradeship of men and women who understand and remember all that Ypres meant in suffering and endurance.

Life membership, £2 10s.

Annual members, 5s.

Do not let the fact of your not having served in the Salient deter you from joining the Ypres League. Those who have neither fought in the Salient nor lost relatives there, but who are in sympathy with the objects of the Ypres League, are admitted to its fellowship, but are not given scroll certificates.

There is a Junior Division for children whose relatives served in the Salient. It is open also to others to whom our objects appeal.

Annual subscription 1s. up to the age of 18, after which they can become ordinary members of the League.

THE YPRES LEAGUE (INCORPORATED)
20, Orchard Street, Portman Square, W.1.

Telephone: WELBECK 1446.   *Telegrams*: YPRESLEAG, "WESDO," LONDON.

Patron-in-Chief: H.M. THE KING.

Patron:
H.R.H. PRINCESS BEATRICE.

President: GENERAL SIR CHARLES H. HARINGTON.

Vice-Presidents:

THE VISCOUNT WAKEFIELD OF HYTHE.   F.-M. SIR CLAUD W. JACOB.
F.-M. LORD MILNE.   F.-M. SIR PHILIP CHETWODE.
GENERAL SIR CECIL ROMER.   GENERAL SIR HUBERT GOUGH.

General Committee:

THE COUNTESS OF ALBEMARLE.
*CAPTAIN C. ALLISTON.
LIEUT-COLONEL BECKLES WILLSON.
MR. HENRY BENSON.
*MR. J. BOUGHEY.
*MISS B. BRICE-MILLER.
COLONEL G. T. BRIERLEY.
CAPTAIN P. W. BURGESS.
BRIG.-GENL. A. BURT.
*MAJOR H. CARDINAL-HARFORD.
REV. P. B. CLAYTON.
*CAPTAIN G. E. DE TRAFFORD.
*THE EARL OF YPRES.
MRS. C. J. EDWARDS.
MAJOR C. J. EDWARDS.
MR. H. A. T. FAIRBANK.
MR. T. ROSS FURNER.
SIR PHILIP GIBBS.
MR. E. GLOVER.

MR. F. D. BANKES-HILL.
MAJOR-GENERAL C. J. B. HAY.
MR. J. HETHERINGTON.
GENERAL SIR W. C. G. HENEKER.
*CAPTAIN O. G. JOHNSON.
*MAJOR E. MONTAGUE JONES.
MAJOR GENL. C. G. LIDDELL.
CAPTAIN H. D. PEABODY.
*THE HON. ALICE DOUGLAS PENNANT.
*LIEUT.-GENERAL SIR W. P. PULTENEY.
LIEUT.-COLONEL SIR J. MURRAY.
*COLONEL G. E. C. RASCH.
THE HON. SIR ARTHUR STANLEY.
MR. ERNEST THOMPSON.
CAPTAIN J. LOCKLEY TURNER.
*MR. E. B. WAGGETT.
CAPTAIN J. WILKINSON.
CAPTAIN H. TREVOR WILLIAMS.

* Executive Committee.

Bankers: *Honorary Solicitors*:
BARCLAYS BANK LTD., Knightsbridge Branch.   MESSRS. FLADGATE & CO., 70, Pall Mall, S.W.

Secretary: *Auditors*:
MAJOR L. J. L. PULLAR.   MESSRS. LEPINE & JACKSON, 6, Bond Court, E.C.4.

League Representative at Ypres:
CAPTAIN P. D. PARMINTER.
19, Rue Surmont de Volsberghe.

League Representative at Cambrai:
MR. A. WILDE,
9, Rue des Anglaises.

League Representative at Amiens:
CAPTAIN STUART OSWALD.
7, Rue Porte-Paris.

League Representative at Arras:
MR. P. VYNER,
10, Place de la Gare.

Hon. Secretary, Ypres British Settlement:
LT. COLONEL F. G. POOLE.

PRIMARY OBJECTS OF THE LEAGUE

I.—Commemoration and Comradeship.
II.—To provide special travel facilities for Members and all interested to Ypres and battlefields, and transport of Members.
III.—The furnishing of information about the Salient; marking of historic sites and the compilation of charts of the battlefields.
IV.—The erection of a Ypres British Church and School which has been completed.
V.—The establishment of groups of members throughout the world, through Branch Secretaries and Corresponding Members.
VI.—The maintenance of cordial relations with dwellers on the battlefields of Ypres.
VII.—The formation of a Junior Division.

Use the Ypres League Travel Bureau for Ypres and Whole of the Western Front.

FOR THE FOLLOWING PUBLICATIONS, Etc., apply:

Secretary, YPRES LEAGUE, 20, ORCHARD STREET, LONDON, W.1.

THE BATTLE BOOK OF YPRES. A history of notable deeds contributed by all regiments. 5s.; post free, 5s. 6d. Compiled by Beatrix Brice with the assistance of Lieut.-General Sir William Pulteney, G.C.V.O., etc.

BOOKS.

YPRES: Outpost of the Channel Ports. By Beatrix Brice. With Foreword by Field-Marshal Lord Plumer, G.C.B. Price 1s. 0d.: post free 1s. 3d.

In the Ypres Salient. By Lt.-Col. Beckles Willson. 1s. net; post free 1s. 2d.

Story of the 63rd Field Ambulance. By A. W. Westmore, etc. Cloth, 3s. 6d., post free. Paper, 2s. 6d., post free.

War Letters to a Wife. By Colonel Rowland Feilding. Popular Edition, 3s. 6d.; post free 4s.

The Pill Boxes of Flanders. 1s.; post free 1s. 3d.

From Mons to the First Battle of Ypres. By J. G. W. Hyndson, M.C. Price 3/6, post free

YPRES LEAGUE TIES. 3s. 6d. each, post free.

YPRES LEAGUE BADGES. 2s. each, 2s. 1½d. post free.

EMBROIDERED BADGES. 4s. each, post free.

Map and List of Cemeteries in the Ypres Salient. Price 9d.; post free 11d.

Map of the Somme. Price 1s. 8d., post free.

PICTURES.

Burning of the Cloth Hall, 1915. A Coloured Print, 14 in. by 12 in. 1s. post free.

Old Well-known Spots in New Guise.
Prints, size 4¼ x 2¼, recently taken of famous spots in the Ypres Salient, and which may be of great interest to our readers, are on sale at headquarters, price 4d. each, post free 5d. For particulars apply Secretary.

POST CARDS, PHOTOGRAPHS AND ETCHINGS.

Post Cards. Ypres: British Front during the War.
Ruins of Ypres. Price 1s. post free.

Hill 60. Complete Panorama Photographs.
12 in. by 3¾ in. Price 3s., post free; 15 in. by 5 in. Price 3s. 6d., post free.

MODELS OF DEMARCATION STONE.

The model, which is 6 inches in height, may be used for a paperweight or as an ornament. Price 5/-, post free.
Applications to the Secretary, Ypres League.

PHOTOGRAPHS OF WAR-TIME SKETCHES.

Bedford House (Front View), 1916.
Bedford House (Back View), 1916.
Voormezeele Main Street, 1916.
Voormezeele Crucifixion Gate, 1916.
Langhof Chateau, 1916.

Size 8½ in. by 6½ in. Price 2s. 6d. each, post free.

Photographs of the Thiepval and Arras Memorials.
Post card size, price 1s. each, post free.

YPRES TIMES.

The Journal may be obtained at the League Offices.
Back Numbers 1s.; 1934, 8d.; 1935. 6d.

Printed in Great Britain for the Publishers by Ford & Gill, 21a/23, Iliffe Yard, Crampton Street, London, S.E.17.

Memory Tablet.

JANUARY - FEBRUARY - MARCH

January.

Jan. 8th, 1916	...	Gallipoli evacuation completed.
,, 12th, 1915	...	The use of poison gas by Germans reported.
,, 21st, 1915	...	Zeebrugge bombarded by British airmen.
,, 24th, 1916	...	Naval Battle off Dogger Bank.

February.

Feb. 3rd, 1917	...	America broke with Germany.
,, 18th, 1915	...	U-boat "blockade" of England.
,, 18th, 1918	...	German Invasion of Russia.
,, 21st, 1916	...	Battle of Verdun begun.
,, 21st, 1918	...	British capture Jericho.
,, 25th, 1915	...	Allied Fleet attacked Dardanelles.

March.

Mar. 10th, 1915	...	British capture of Neuve Chapelle.
,, 11th, 1217	...	British take Baghdad.
,, 12th, 1917	...	Revolution in Russia.
,, 15th, 1917	...	Abdication of the Tsar.
,, 21st, 1917	...	First British War Cabinet.
,, 21st, 1918	...	German offensive on the Western Front.

The Ypres Times

Communications to
The Editor, "Ypres Times,"
20, Orchard Street, London, W.I.

PRICE 6d.
POST FREE 7d.

VOL. 8, No. 5.   PUBLISHED QUARTERLY   JANUARY, 1937

Ypres Day, 1936

THE WREATH BEARERS.

CPL. A. WILCOX, V.C.,   SGT. O. BROOKS, V.C.,   LT. M. O'LEARY, V.C.

YPRES DAY commemorates the fateful hours of the 31st October, 1914, when 357 Officers and men of the 2nd Worcestershire Regiment conducted themselves with such bravery at Gheluvelt that they saved the Line and enabled that great soldier Brigadier-General Charles Fitzclarence, V.C., Commanding the 1st Brigade, who had assembled all the cooks, orderlies and transport men he could muster and led them against the enemy, to gallop back and deliver the proud message "it's all right, my line holds."

It did hold, and the British Army was never again in such danger till March 21st, 1918, when the Germans launched their overwhelming attack against the Fifth Army.

The Worcestershire Regiment (The 29th) bear the word " Firm " on their badge, and this honour is greatly deserved. I have started this article with these words about the Worcesters for one reason, and that is, that on one occasion I was asked on the Horse Guards' Parade what Ypres Day commemorated.

The 16th Anniversary Commemoration of the Ypres League was held on November the 1st, on the Horse Guards' Parade, St. James's Park, at 11 a.m.

A very large assembly was honoured by the presence of Her Royal Highness, The Princess Beatrice who was received on the Horse Guards' Parade by His Excellency The Belgian Ambassador and Lieut.-General Sir William Pulteney, G.C.V.O., K.C.B., K.C.M.G., D.S.O., etc., Chairman of the Ypres League.

Amongst those present were Lieut.-Colonel Cuny, representing His Excellency The French Ambassador ; Lieut-Colonel Hayes A. Kroner representing His Excellency The American Ambassador ; The Military Attache, Belgian Embassy ; Lieut.-Colonel E. K. Smart, D.S.O., M.C., representing The High Commissioner for Australia ; Lieut.-Colonel F. M. Stanton, representing the High Commissioner for Canada ; Mr. T. H. B. Drew representing The High Commissioner for New Zealand, and The High Commissioner for Newfoundland was also represented ; The Dowager Viscountess Plumer ; Contingents of the O.T.C. ; ' Old Contemptibles' ; St. Dunstans ; 5th Army O.C.A. ; 85th Club and the Ypres League.

The Service commenced with the singing of that beautiful hymn "O Valiant hearts," accompanied by the Band of the 1st Surrey Rifles. At the conclusion of the hymn the Revd. Dr. Joseph Lynn, Hon. Chaplain to His Majesty The King and Deputy Chaplain-General to the Forces, delivered the following prayer :—

" Almighty God who dost order all things well, we thank Thee that in Thy purpose thou hast permitted us to meet here, that we may call to mind the days of old, in which Thou did'st lead the World to victory.

We thank Thee for the example of courage and endurance, of self control and of sacrifice of Thy servants, and we pray for all those who gave their lives in this great cause, as they followed in the steps of our Master. We commit again unto Thee their loved ones, remembering that Life Eternal is Thy gift to those who lived and fought well. We pray that we may never forget them, and that there will always remain a deep and abiding sorrow. We pray for King Edward, Queen Mary and all the members of the Royal Family, beseeching Thee to grant them long life and prosperity. And now, O Lord, we commit ourselves again unto Thy good keeping. Amen."

Then followed The Lord's Prayer and when this was concluded Dr. Lynn addressed the assembly as follows :—

" Comrades of the Ypres League, it is very fortunate that we should meet here together on this day for two reasons. This is the day on which the Church calls to mind *all* those faithful Saints who have fought the good fight, have entered into their rest, and are now sat down on the right hand of God. It was also the day which marked the culmination of that first battle at Ypres when so many of our comrades, whom we meet to-day to remember, paid the supreme sacrifice, as they displayed that gallant spirit of endeavour and resolution which

Dr. J. Lynn, M.A., delivering his Address.

characterized all the hundreds of thousands of men who fought at Ypres throughout the War.

This is a day of commemoration, which I pray we will never allow to lapse. We are not yet so far removed from those days that we cannot call to mind all the fine spirit of comradeship, which was then revealed. Yet it is easy for us in these distracting days of peace to lose sight of each other, and even of the memory of those, who in war were our brethren. Should this spirit ever fail us, then black shame be upon our name.

In the first Article of Association of our League it is written that the League is founded to maintain the spirit of loyalty and of comradeship, while in the last we are told to endeavour to promote the interest and assistance of the rising generation in the great deeds of heroism of the past. To commemoration and comradeship then, we must add consecration. The best way in which we can do justice to the memory of the British Army is to devote ourselves to the service, and, if needs be, to the defence of our country. Thus we will keep alive the spirit for which they fought and died, and preserve our heritage. If we are as willing as they were to make this sacrifice, we can rest assured that our cause will still be maintained.

To-day we bow our heads in humble reverence before Almighty God, as we thank Him again for His great goodness to us, and to those who are now happily united with Him. We pray that He will impart to us the same spirit, the same courage, and the same resolution, and that when we are called upon to do our duty, like them we shall not fail."

Then came that soul stirring Lament " Flowers of the Forest" so well played by the Pipers of 'The London Scottish,' and after a short silence the notes of the 'Last Post' rang out, sounded by the Buglers of the 1st Surrey Rifles.

That wonderful Hymn ' O God our help in ages past " was then sung, followed by the National Anthem and in conclusion the Reveille.

H.E. The Belgian Ambassador and
The Dowager Viscountess Plumer.

The Parade formed up for the march to the Cenotaph, headed by the Band of the 1st Surrey Rifles. At the Horse Guard's Arch Her Royal Highness, Princess Beatrice took the Salute, and later laid the beautiful Ypres League wreath, composed of its cornflower emblems, lilies and white chrysanthemums, at the Cenotaph.

Amongst those who had the honour of being presented to Her Royal Highness were the wreath bearers : Lieutenant M. O'Leary, V.C. (late Irish Guards). Sergeant

O. Brooks, V.C. (late Coldstream Guards), Corporal A. Wilcox, V.C. (late 2/4th Oxf. & Bucks. Light Infantry), and Major L. J. L. Pullar, M.C. (late The Seaforth Highlanders) the new Secretary of the Ypres League.

On the departure of Her Royal Highness at 12.15 p.m. the contingents marched from the Cenotaph back to the Horse Guards' Parade and there dismissed. Prior to the dismissal of the ' Old Contemptibles ' Contingent these old warriors were addressed and inspected by Lieut.-General Sir William Pulteney, who congratulated them on their fine appearance on the Parade. He then took the Salute on the order to dismiss.

Many members of the Ypres League regretted that General Sir Hubert Gough, G.C.M.G., K.C.B., K.C.V.O., etc., Vice-President of the Ypres League found it impossible to be present.

At 12.40 p.m. a Deputation of the Ypres League, headed by Major E. Montague-Jones, O.B.E., T.D., M.A., was received at Westminster Abbey by the Canon in Residence, The Revd. F. Lewis Donaldson, M.A., and a wreath was laid on the grave of the Unknown Warrior. Canon Donaldson addressed the assembly as follows :—

"Members of the Ypres League, it is a great pleasure to meet you here to-day, and I also think how happy it is that we should meet on All Saints Day, which is one of the greater feasts of the Church, followed by that most suitable day for our remembrance here, All Souls Day, which falls due to-morrow.

There is no doubt that among our men who perished on that great occasion, which you represent, there were Saints. One of the most beautiful characters I ever knew in my life was an officer in the British Army. Saints go far beyond the Red Letter days of our Supreme Book, and beyond the black letter days of British History. Let us then offer our prayer to-day for all those who perished in the War, especially to those who are linked to memories in this League, that God will grant to them pardon for their sins, true repentance, light and happiness, and welfare in the world which is unseen. Through Him alone we know what a perfect man should be, Jesus Christ, our Lord both God and Man."

On taking the wreath from Major Montague-Jones, Canon Donaldson uttered the following words :—

"I receive this wreath on behalf of the Dean and Chapter of Westminster, who has asked me to say that we will take the greatest care of it, and that as the people pass from day to day, the Vergers and others will tell them who placed it, on whose behalf, and what for. We, at any rate, of the Chapter will take great care of it. As long as it lasts it will remain there as a lovely symbol, I hope, of what we have been thinking about the last fifteen minutes. It is in their memory and this should bind us together for the noblest ends."

R. HENDERSON-BLAND, Capt.,
late The Gloucestershire Regt.

Lieut.-General Sir William Pulteney, G.C.V.O., K.C.B., K.C.M.G., subsequently received the following letter from Colonel F. E. Packe, M.V.O., Equerry-in-waiting to Her Royal Highness Princess Beatrice :—

KENSINGTON PALACE.

November 15th, 1936.
MY DEAR SIR WILLIAM,

Princess Beatrice wishes me to write and thank you and the Committee of the Ypres League, for your kind letter, and for their appreciation of H.R.H.'s attendance at the Service on November 1st. Her Royal Highness also wishes me to thank you for the report of the Ypres British School.

Yours very sincerely,
(*Signed*) F. E. PACKE.

Twenty Years After—the Somme is Still Stark

Indeed, it can never be "Good-bye to the Battlefields" while these many grim Echoes of the "Blood Bath" remain.

By VICTOR HYDE, M.C.

(*The well-known Writer on the Battlefields, and Author of "Flanders Sleeps," "East of Ypres," and other War Stories.*)

ALMOST arrested as a spy; drinking rum with the Mayor of Martinpuich at a pre-breakfast hour when Britons were still tucked in their beds; route-marching (without pack or rifle) my twenty miles between sun-up and sun-down, and being transformed by a sweltering Somme sun into the semblance of an over-ripe tomato; hanging desparately on to the unaccustomed, in-a-hurry pillion of a friendly British exile's motor-cycle over see-saw French roads — these are some of my adventures in a lightning tour, undertaken last September, in search of an ex-serviceman's Somme, to see the shape of its rehabilitation after the devastation which, beginning twenty years ago last July, ended, four-and-a-half months later, in November, 1916.

I could fill you a book with the drama of the Somme as, footslogging over it in my storming way, I re-discovered it through an old soldier's eye.

For though the Somme is at peace with itself and the world, relics and echoes of the days that you and I both knew still abound. You can neither avoid them nor mistake them.

One moment the Somme will display its war wounds and fangs naked and unashamed; another, and it is at pains to hide them, and you need a keen and trained eye to detect the old ravages. It will be another twenty years before we can say "goodbye" to this blood-soaked Somme that is still so heavily scarred.

Even Albert has not entirely covered up the old sores and fissures. You come upon them in this street and that, but no estate agent publicises them as "commanding sites."

The largest of them is on a big corner near the station; another is the pre-war grotto, ghost of the days when Albert was a second Lourdes, from which they found the money to build the Cathedral that the guns of both sides were so soon to raze. Each is unsightly in its neglect and decrepitude.

In another respect Albert has changed for the worse since I was last in those parts. The post-war English colony has broken up and gone. Except for the cemetery gardeners only one remains, finding a living among the natives and the tourists with a taxi.

But what's this legend calling to me outside my hotel? — "Tea as Mother makes it"? Is it merely an enterprising effort by the owners to draw the itinerant Briton?

Normally the French simply cannot brew tea, so I was dubious as I put the sign to the test of Truth in Advertising. Surprisingly enough, the tea won, for the pot they gave me in those small hours as I set out to gather my raw material for this narrative was certainly up to "Mother's" best standards.

But "Tea Better than Mother makes it!" is how Ex-Chief Despatch Rider C. Smith, mine host of the Prince of Wales Café, in the shade of the vast Thiepval memorial, improves on the old saw. And then, as a timely afterthought to catch the eye of the thirsty pilgrim, "Beer, Cool and Fresh, like Father takes it."

"Father," however, in the person of your humble and perspiring scribe, was in no physical trim for aught but lemonade.

I'm afraid we're wandering. I want you back in Albert for a minute; we'll return all in good time to Thiepval, that's so pregnant with British memories.

Whilst Albert has done many things exceedingly well, she can also do others just as exceedingly badly. The sanitary arrangements are primitive, and would shock your local municipal engineer. In the hamlets to which I am now taking you they are appalling.

The two most difficult accomplishments in Albert are first to buy a railway ticket, and then to get on the platform with it — or even on to the platform at all.

Imagine their shutting all the booking-offices at your local station and locking off all the platforms till a minute before the next train is due ! Well, that's the way of things in Albert. Even a hardened and be-whiskered Frenchman caught my own re-action and fumed.

We'll try to buy a ticket to Hamel for Thiepval. Ah, that's caught them ! They've got one for every other station in France, but not for Hamel, bless my soul, the very next station !

While they're busy on a special bit of paper for us that's going to be too big for our pocket anyway — when they've finished shaking hands with a voluble would-be native passenger who has just pushed past you — and are inscribing it, let's take the motor-bus out to Ovillers and La Boisselle, adjoining hamlets which thousands of "old sweats" have good cause to remember.

Even the Albert-Bapaume bus frightens us. " We are all brothers," runs a Japanese proverb translated into French over the driver's head, " but our banks are not sisters." Sounds uncommonly like an excuse for high bus fares, and the very next one confirms our worst suspicions.

" Roads are like women," it reminds us ; " you need a lot of money to enjoy them ! "

You begin to wish you had walked ; yet even after that dual warning they ask you only three francs (ninepence) (in pre-valuation days).

It's still a wicked approach to Ovillers from the Pozières side. After you have breasted a steep semi-sunken road a fine fruity farm smell greets you in the hamlet where the 143rd Brigade led the ultimate attack that placed the village within our lines. Half-way down on the left is the usual cesspool, or midden.

In the course of my stay the church clock, by way of proving that the Somme can still be perverse, struck the half-hour when its hands showed only 4.20. Yet even this is better than the " old French custom " followed in those off-the-map communes that boast neither post office nor railway ; here they keep the church clocks an hour slow, and will have naught of Summer Time. So, in two villages no more than a mile apart, you may find two entirely different times.

Swinging up again out of Ovillers back to the straight-as-a-die Albert — Bapaume road, now doubly lined throughout its span with rows of pitiably new and fragile poplars in place of the giants that once we knew, a ghostly bank of filled-in dug-outs confronts us, and British barbed-wire flanking the winding roadside.

Here, as we turn into La Boisselle and for the hundredth time are stared at by the field workers as an object of curiosity, is a huge shell-hole filled with the paraphernalia of our fun and games of twenty years ago. It is patently no one's child. Quite stark, this bit.

La Boisselle presents itself to you as a shabbily-rebuilt village, with a church spire like one of those Welsh women's national hats — all " high hat," in fact, stuck unceremoniously on the squat brick-work. It is the same at Auchonvillers.

Only the crater lends La Boisselle any mark of distinction to-day. Containing 60,000 lbs. of gun cotton, it was exploded below the German front line on July 1st, 1916, to form a cavity 100 yards across and 90 feet deep. You will find it by the side of the Albert — Bapaume road, close to its junction with the by-road to Contalmaison. It is colossal.

A quarter of a mile away is another good line in craters. It is well that these things should be preserved.

It was in Ovillers Cemetery that I found the grave of Harry Lauder's son, and in Guillemont Road Cemetery that of Lieutenant Raymond Asquith.

On the La Boisselle-Contalmaison road, they have dumped yet more of the old wire that we put out in no man's land to keep the neighbours off, while so much of it is in permanent employment, looped to our own iron pickets as a fencing to the fields, as long before my pilgrimage was ended to have ceased all together to be " news."

At Auchonvillers, as I made my best way to Thiepval, I all but tripped headlong over an unexploded " five-nine." Frankly, we don't like the look of it, and, as we are not yet tired of life, we will leave it where it is.

Alike at Flers and " Monty Bong," some die-hard has raised the shells we didn't have time to loose off to the " dignity " of a seat on the wayside mile-stones. One of these days someone will get hurt . . . .

An enterprising French firm has acquired the sole " explosive rights " to the " ammo " still being found, and as soon as they have collected a nice fat dump — no hard task, as you will have gathered — they put a match to it to rend the air with another miniature Somme battle.

In the semi-sunken road between Contalmaison and Pozières I heard the unmistakeable sounds of an explosion, repeated at minute intervals. " That," I said, as I swung into the greater safety of an estaminet, " is the dump merchants up to their games." And so was it.

All that my itinerant note-book tells me of Contalmaison that was familiar to all who served on the Somme is of the village geese that, unchecked, peck and strut over the church steps, of the ruins that remain in parts, and of the house that looks suspiciously like a converted orderly room.

You recall the scores of old army Nissen huts in which the peasants of many of these villages live, and say that in a land of economy there is nothing bizarre in living in an orderly room.

Our pilgrimage draws to its curtain. But we must go to Fricourt, where, at the onset of the Somme " push " the " boys " used the bayonet to good purpose . . . .

I find there a field ablaze with the blood-red of the Flanders poppy — hundreds and hundreds of them — and industrious French land women milking the cows in a cowshed perched at an alarming angle in a steep bank over a line of our old dug-outs.

Hallo, what's this ? Just another of those immense yellow, blue and white French sign-boards that give you your direction and shout the village you are entering. Nothing niggardly about these. This is the very one we have been looking for. We are in Geuedecourt.

In the cess-pool quarter of an otherwise aesthetic enough hamlet, they have made half-hearted attempts at rebuilding, but having dumped the new bricks, have washed their hands of the whole thing, and will have none of it. By this refuse heap is an ornate green and blue marquee put up for local whoopee.

Time enough in this " Gerdcour " to look in on the mayor — for he and I are old friends — and toast each other in his excellent white wine and eat his home-made cake.

(*In the* YPRES TIMES *for April Mr. Hyde will continue his story of " The Somme Revisited."*)

PRESENTATION to Capt. G. E. de TRAFFORD, M.C.

After consulting Captain de Trafford's wishes on the matter a beautiful All-Wave Auto Radio Gramophone bearing a plate suitably inscribed has been presented to him.

The balance of the fund (quite a considerable sum) will be handed over to Captain de Trafford to dispose of as he may think fit.

The fund is now closed.

31.12.36.

W. P. PULTENEY,
Chairman.

Ypres in Winter

The " Goldfish " Chateau.

A wintry view of the " Goldfish " Chateau on the Vlamertinghe Road, Ypres, known to every British soldier who fought in the immortal Salient.

Within its walls Marshal Foch (when Commanding the French Northern Army) and Sir John French, afterwards Earl of Ypres, came to the momemtous decision to hold Ypres at all cost, thereby saving the Channels Ports.

Von Kluck occupied the Chateau for one night, and it was freely stated that it escaped destruction from shell fire, because he coveted it as a personal prize, when Germany triumphed at the conclusion of hostilities.

* * * * *

Not Forgotten

Poor Mothers Visit War Graves

Extract from contribution forwarded to the " Southern Datly Echo" by Henry Benson, Esq., M.A., on September 22nd last, and reproduced with their kind permission.

I AM over here with a party of pilgrims to the British War Graves and Memorials in the Ypres Salient, organised by the Ypres League, of which H.M. the King is Patron-in-Chief. This is their last conducted pilgrimage of the year, and includes a number of widows and mothers of men who fell in and around Ypres and who are now through the kindness of the Organisers enabled to visit the last resting places of their loved ones for the first time, free of all cost to themselves.

The fund which allowed this beneficent work to be carried on annually was inaugurated by the late Field Marshal Viscount Plumer, during the time that he was the League's President, and it is supplemented periodically by various small donations. The sole conditions governing this annual Free Pilgrimage are that the pilgrims selected have not previously visited the graves of their fallen relatives, and that their means do not allow them personally to bear the cost of such a visit.

The homes of most of the present party — thirty-four in number — are in the provinces, and they have come from places as far apart as Ripon, Durham, Nottingham, Lancashire, Staffordshire, Bristol, Eastleigh and London. Over here they are one family, united in a common bond.

The present tour extends from 18 - 22 September. The Free Pilgrims travelled from their homes to London on the afternoon of Friday last, and on arrival were met and conducted to a hotel near Victoria Station for the night. Saturday they crossed to Ypres, *via* Ostend, where they are staying in reserved rooms at one of the principal hotels until Tuesday morning. Each pilgrim is taken to the grave of their loved one by private car, and a tour of the battlefields follows. A night will be spent in London on the return journey. The trip throughout is entirely free, the Ypres League bearing all expenses from the moment the pilgrims leave home. Mr. O. Mears, Assistant Secretary to the League, and Conductor of the party, has made every arrangement for the comfort of the visitors, his sole reward being their unbounded appreciation.

Comrades in Arms.

Moreover, they were quick to notice that General and Private rest side by side under the same simple headstones, equally honoured in their deaths for the common sacrifice they were called to make for the freedom of mankind.

Still, I find that what has touched their heartstrings more than all else is the happy tribute that the residents of Ypres pay each evening to the memory of the British dead who fell in the defence of their gallant little city by sounding at nightfall the "Last Post" beneath the central arch of Menin Gate.

Not Forgotten.

The number of visitors to the British War Cemeteries and Memorials in France and Belgium this summer exceeds those of recent years, and in July and August the total was the largest since the corresponding months of 1929.

The following are the figures for visitors signing the books at the various cemeteries and memorials, probably representing about one-third of the total attendance:

1936	Cemeteries	Memorials
July	17,061	11,778
August	23,018	22,815

Another interesting feature regarding visits is the increasing number of organised tours made by Old Comrades' Associations and similar bodies. In the course of the present summer, the Menin Gate Memorial was visited by the following parties: Members of the staff, Players, Ltd. (Nottingham), members of the Royal Welch Fusiliers, the Welch Regiment and the Queen's Westminster Rifles Old Comrades' Associations, by the 9th Congres des Opticiens-Lunetiéres de France, by the Derby branch of the British Legion, by the Anciens Combattants of the French 56th Chausseurs and the 13th Belgian Field Artillery.

Pilgrimages to other cemeteries and memorials have also been made by the Old Comrades of the Cheshire Regiment, the Hampshire Regiment, the Welsh Guards, King Edward's Horse, and by representatives of the 34th Division.

I may add that the Ypres League is open to receive applications for inclusion in their four pilgrimages during the summer of 1937. These should be addressed to: The Secretary, Ypres League, 20, Orchard Street, London, W.1.

Festival of Empire and Remembrance

Royal Albert Hall, November 11th, 1936.

As a result of the consideration and kindness on the part of the British Legion officials the Ypres League were enabled to be represented on Armistice Day last, at their Annual Festival of Rememberance, held at the Royal Albert Hall. This Festival is undoubtedly the greatest thing of its kind held anywhere in the world. The number of applications for seats received each year by the British Legion Headquarters is enormous, and we are therefore most grateful to them for making it possible for our Association to be represented. One of the few tickets allotted to us was allocated to Captain R. Henderson-Bland who has done so much to further the interests of the Ypres League both home and abroad. Captain Bland's impressions of this imposing Ceremony are chronicled in the following article which he has been persuaded to write for the interest of our readers.

THE Correspondent of *The Daily Telegraph*, writing of the scene in the Albert Hall on Armistice Night, referred to it as one of grandeur. Yes, there was grandeur there, but with what touching simplicity His Majesty The King came amongst us. Never have I heard such spontaneous and sincere cheering, as I heard that night when the King entered the box reserved for him.

Standing there in the arena with men of the Ypres League, I caught myself thinking that such a scene was a theme for poets, and it is as a poet I will write of it. When a youth in 1907 I published my second book of poems under the title " Moods and Memories " and that book contained a poem entitled " Patriotism and Reason."

In my very early youth I had been greatly under the influence of Tolstoy, but somehow or other the conviction was borne in upon me that he had set himself an impossible task, and that he was a dangerous guide, and I ventured to reply to his remarks on patriotism in the following poem which was headed by the following paragraphs :—

PATRIOTISM AND REASON.

" I have already several times expressed the thought that the feeling of patriotism is in our day an unnatural, irrational and harmful feeling, and is the cause of a great part of the ills from which mankind is suffering."
—*Tolstoy.*

"Hobbes, like all other speculative Politicians, does not allow for the perplexing irrationality of human kind. As long as the heart of men are thrilled by the sound of their National Hymn and the sight of their National Flag, there is little use in asking them to listen to reason."
The Times Literary Supplement.
August 19th, 1904.

I

O, surely God can think it no bad thing
  For men to love the land that first bestowed
A title proud as any time can bring.
What antique ancestry heaps prouder load ?
    Come out from the sad face
    Of him who holds it dark
  To love the dear birthplace
    Of linnet and of lark.
  O come away ; make no delay
      Lest you betray
  Fair Freedom's Hierarch.

2

Exult, O England ! Isle of rare renown,
  Of freedom loved and lordly punitive ;
All high endeavour finds in thee its crown,
  And of thy sons, though lone and fugitive
    Must you the first love be,
    For gods men are not yet,
  But liker children free
    Who love with no regret.
If love did live with reason, it soon would pass to treason,
    As season succeeds season,
    And soon would all forget.

3

Is it to you as nothing that you bear
  An English name, and with that name a debt
That should be paid if manhood you hold fair?
  Come, give some duty for the good you get.
    Will you let England halt
    While other nations press
      Because you won't exalt
    Your eyes of weariness?
    She has not done, she will not shun
      The task begun,
    And she needs you to help her to success.

4

O, why do we look back on earlier days,
  As we look back upon an old man's prime?
Think not that England walked in fairer ways
  In years agone than these where now we climb.
    Come, let us be strong,
    And go forth on our quest,
    With gladness and with song,
      With joy made manifest:
    For England is yet young, and nations proud among
      She lives the light and tongue
    Of Freedom in her splendour and unrest.

[Photo]   [By courtesy the "Daily Mail."
The Grand Parade at the Royal Albert Hall.

Since the writing of that poem I have been in most of the Capitals of Europe, seen a good deal of the East, spent three years in America, and have done some fighting on the Western Front, but I have nothing to withdraw as far as the poem is concerned. My mind went back to that poem one afternoon in March 1918, during the difficult fighting of the Fifth Army, when I was standing with three weary officers waiting for orders to counter-attack, when, what I thought a very hysterical staff officer, rode up on a sorry horse and exhorted us to " remember England." He promised to send us everything — ammunition — rations — and I think he would have gone so far as to promise a plume from the wing of the Archangel Gabriel. We were silent, and then he turned to me and asked what he could send me. I turned my weary eyes upon him and languidly suggested a " Small Bass."

He rode away into the gathering gloom without another word, We saw and heard of him no more.

I am sure that many will think this a tiresome prelude to an article on the " Festival of Empire and Remembrance," and I am inclined to agree, but I have started in this manner because I wanted to show that though an intransient lover of this Country I was not bound by the deeps of insularity in literature or life. I had weighed and considered the writings of Karl Marx, Henry George, Lassalle, Tolstoy, at a very early age.

The Royal Albert Hall presented a superb and noble appearance on Armistice night. The delicate, tasteful Wedgwood decoration so familiar to Londoners had been enlivened by draperies of blue and yellow, the colours of the British Legion. Over the huge organ hung the handsome curtains of the Legion covering a screen whereon later was shown a film of British War Graves.

During the assembly a March, " The Royal Standard " was played by the massed bands of the Guards conducted by Major Andrew Harris, M.V.O., L.R.A.M., Welsh Guards. This was followed by selections from Leslie Stuart's songs, and Sullivan's Operas. The Conductors being Lieut. J. L. Hurd, L.R.A.M., Irish Guards, and Lieutenant J. C. Windram, L.R.A.M., Coldstream Guards.

Then came a great thrill for the audience. Four trumpeters of the Life Guards with a fanfare of trumpets announced the arrival of His Majesty the King. The massed bands played The National Anthem, but this was hardly heard above the shattering cheers that broke out from that great assembly. The King moved by the warmth of the spontaneous cheering, acknowledged the greeting in a characteristic way. Standing there in mufti he looked so young, and I thought a little lonely, for had not high destiny led him to places where the finger of history traces the things to come. The hearts of people assembled there that night went out to him. After the National Anthem came the entry of Legion Standards, an imposing sight. We all sang with great lustihood "Pack up your troubles," and then Regimental Marches were played.

Then came the march of the Chelsea Pensioners, who received a rousing reception, and "The boys of the Old Brigade" was heartily sung. The march of "Women's War Services" (W.R.A.F., W.A.A.C., W.R.N.S., F.A.N.Y.). The March of the Nursing Services called forth tremendous applause. Most of the men in the arena had reason to be grateful to some nurse. With the entry of the Union Jack with Banners of St. George, St. Andrew. and St. Patrick, the Drums and Fifes of the 1st Battn. Grenadier Guards, 1st Battn. Coldstream Guards, and 1st Battn. Welsh Guards, stirred the audience to enthusiasm,

"Tipperary" was played and sung by the audience and the "March of the Services" was stirring. The Royal Air Force presented a fine appearance and marched to their Regimental March. The Overseas Forces led by Australia roused the audience to enthusiasm. They were followed by The British Army and marched to the tune " Soldiers of the King." The Merchant Navy and Fishing Fleets, marched to " A Life on the Ocean Wave." The Royal Naval Volunteer Reserve ; The Royal Naval Reserve ; the Royal Marines ; and the Royal Navy, marched to " Hearts of Oaks " ; Then came " The Rising Generation, Boys of the Training Ship " Stork " marching to " A Life on the Ocean Wave."

Songs, Choruses accompanied by massed bands and organ, were sung as only soldiers can sing them.

The entry and march of Pipers of the 1st Battn. The Irish Guards, with Drums and Fifes, followed, and were greatly appreciated.

This brought Part I to an end.

Now they are all in position. As a sight it is superb. Right and left of the organ high up are the Legion Standards. The Queen Alexandra Nurses in their scarlet and grey with white head-dresses set off the uniforms of other Nursing Services. The scarlet and gold of the Massed Bands of Guards; the scarlet of the Chelsea Pensioners and the Drummers of the Guards ranged up on the stairways each side of the stage. There are Rough Riders, the yellow khaki of the Overseas Troops, blue-white surplices of the Clergy and Choir boys to make up an unforgettable scene. It should be caught and painted by an imaginative artist for the benefit of history.

Part II begins with Intermezzo — " The Sacred Hour " a magnificent piece of work by Ketelby. I shall be greatly surprised if this fine piece of music does not come to great fame. Then came the entry of Clergy and Choir with Cross and Banners of St. George, St. Andrew and St. Patrick, accompanied by the organ and massed bands. " Onward Christian Soldiers " was sung by all present.

Prayers and then the Anthem " I vow to thee my Country " an Act of Remembrance the audience standing singing " Eternal Father, strong to save " (in grateful and affectionate memory of Admiral of the Fleet, Earl Jellicoe).

There is a Roll of Drums and among the Gardeners and Caretakers from the War Cemeteries of Belgium and France, stands His Majesty The King.

The Last Post is sounded, and very clearly and slowly His Majesty spoke a sorrowing stanza from Mr. Lawrence Binyon's poem, " To the Fallen."

> " They shall not grow old, as we that are left grow old
> Age shall not weary them, nor the years condemn.
> At the going down of the sun and in the morning
> We will remember them."
>
> *And the audience repeated—*
> " We will remember them."

Then very clearly a beautiful voice coming from a high place by the organ began singing " The Supreme Sacrifice " beginning :—

" O Valiant Hearts, who to your Glory came "

That first stanza of this beautiful Hymn was superbly rendered by whom I know not because the programme was strangely reticent on the matter.

The curtains over the screen parted, shewing a picture of war-time graves in the Ypres Salient.

During the singing of " The Supreme Sacrifice " in the dim light, 1,104,890 poppy petals fell in memory of the Empire's dead. Standing at attention in the arena it struck me that they took a long time to fall, then one brushed my cheek and soon they were falling in great numbers as flakes of snow. A Roll of Drums and the 'Reveille' is sounded.

Then followed the Hymn of "Victory" from P. da Palestrina. "Abide with me, fast falls the eventide " accompanied by Massed Bands, organ and choir, was next sung. It was during the singing of this Hymn that the light caught a large Cross made of Flanders poppies, set high over the organ.

Then followed the Blessing, pronounced by the Revd. E. H. Thorold, C.B., C.B.E., D.D., M.A., etc., Chaplain to H.M. The King, Chaplain-General to the Forces.

The Grand March, out of the Hall, followed, to the music of " Homage " by Hayden Wood, and so ended a memorable evening, the sum total of this being Remembrance. Many men made vows in Heaven during the Great War, but never was one so often made as that where men vowed never to forget their dead comrades.

I go so far as to say that this Festival of Remembrance is the most soul stirring Ceremony ever seen in this World. Congratulations to Colonel E. C. Heath, C.V.O. D.S.O., etc., and his staff, for the manner in which they presented and carried out this great and moving Festival of Remembrance.

R. HENDERSON-BLAND,
(Vice-President of The Poetry Society.)

Light and Shade at the Front

VIGNETTES.

SHOT AND SHELL.

(*By an* Ex. R. B.)

WHIZZ-BANG! Boom! CRASH! "Just to introduce ourselves! Good afternoon!"
Shot and shell having played their noisy part, à discrétion and ad extremum, on the mundane stage of the Great War, it may not be untoward to pen a page

(Its szz-szz-szz-ing before it "plopped.")

or two descriptive of this resounding subject. Then, at least, yet another figurative line will have been drawn towards the making of a complete picture of the War.

The standard of a house, that is the state of its interior and its general well-being, may be gauged very fairly by a sight of the front door, and any reader can prove the correctness of that view by strolling round town. So also the identity of a musical instrument is known by its sound; a stringed harp which is heard in Eaton Square, for example, could not be mistaken by any manner of means for the homely and the pleasing notes of mouth-organ which is common to a light-hearted holiday Bank Holiday crowd. And in the same clearly defined way each sort of projectile at the front had its own distinctive note.

The little bullets "pinged"; when, however, they were fired in streams from machine guns their note changed to a long drawn-out shrill cutting whistle. Then there were the minnewerfers, or to use the vernacular term, "toffee-apples." The short range and high trajectory of these could be traced by a small spark and they burst with a deep shattering crash, in marked contrast to the sharp metallic report of shrapnel. The larger shells came over with a whizzing scream or a deeper note, according to size (when and where you didn't like or fancy!).

As readers know, the term " drum-fire " very correctly described a method of firing light shells. Where these were fired at a high speed, as in a creeping barrage or a defensive one, when the gunners' object was to drop a " curtain " of fire between the opposing forces, the rapid explosions of the shells sounded just like the tumultous " thud-thud-thud " of a Brobdingnagian drum, punctuated now and then by the deeper explosion of a heavier shell. The familiar " whizz-bangs " had one distinction (in common with bullets) in that they gave no notice of approach, so that when anyone heard the " phit " he knew he hadn't " stopped " *that* one ! The writer remembers one route where a small notice was fixed : " Whizz-bangs pass six inches above the ground at this point." When a man reached this notice he stopped to read it and then doubled.

In quite another class was the pesky little trench grenade. Take, let us say, a working party who were lightening a parapet ; a shovel would ring against a wiring stake in the darkness and so start the enemy off. Then it was the practice to listen for the " click," drop to cover while the grenade exploded, and on again with the good work. The writer recalls an occasion (common in the line) where a party dodged these grenades the while it did its task, then packed up and moved off like shadows down the dark trench, and these grenades were still being fired when the party was almost out of earshot. Egg bombs, about the size of a small lemon and glossy black in colour, burst with a staccato ring ; so more or less did vein bombs and the metal of these was said to be poisonous. Gas shells differed from the others in this way, their report was very similar to the sound which is made by " cupped " hands.

So much for the small to medium and large. But let us turn to the great projectiles; the largest shells of all. These were by no means unpleasant to listen to when in flight — and nowhere near. They approached at a seemingly steady pace, passed high overhead with a deep thrumming sound like unto a majestic tram-car of the skies, and died away in the distance. And their objective must have been miles behind the line because one seldom or never heard them explode even on the quietest night. When a mine exploded one afternoon on the Vimy front it went up with a roar and a rumble, but even so it fell short, as regards report, of Nature's thunder with its sky-splitting succession of crashes.

Another sort : aircraft bombs. One evening, when the troops were encamped behind the line some enemy bombers paid an evening call, and then followed quite a spirited contest wherein anti-aircraft batteries sent skywards a rapid and accurate fire, upsetting the enemy's aim and causing him to drop " wides," and casualties were few, or none. These aerial bombs burst with an unmistakeably deep resonant boom; anti-aircraft shells were equally distinctive in that they always sounded muffled, a result which was due no doubt to the explosions taking place high up in the sky.

Frontier Camp-cum Pork-and-Beans.

..... " Any more ? " Yes. In taking leave of this iron-rending subject, one must not omit to mention a little projectile which was a near relative of most of the others — the nose-cap — and when one of these was heard " szz-zzz-zzzing " before it " plopped " its exact whereabouts was always a matter of grave uncertainty.

* * * * *

GENERAL PLUMER.

Variety is said to be the spice of life (or is it the salt ?), but let it be spice or salt, the troops often had it in the most unexpected ways.

On an occasion when the Division was moving up to the line the Company pitched its tents in a certain field. At the time of the troops' arrival the colour of this field was a deep restful green, but after a few hours of rain and trampling about its surface changed into the deep brown liquid mud which was a common feature of the Salient. So much for the field. A farmhouse on the further side with smoke curling from its chimnies, some farm buildings on the left facing the road, a watery grey sky, rain slanting down, atmosphere muggy — and the troops marking time in tents. Such was the scenario when word was brought that General Plumer would make an inspection on the morrow afternoon.

The Company paraded on the narrow road, the farm buildings being at its right rear, and presently General Plumer appeared walking towards the right of the line. Of course, as readers are well aware, one's view was restricted when standing to attention (" Stand them at ease ") and it was not much better even when standing " at ease," because the only parts of the body which move on that order are the arms, hands, legs and left foot, but not the head. However, one could always attain a certain obliquity of vision even when keeping the head still, in the same way that a well-trained soldier can see roughly what is on the ground while he is looking " eyes front."

An outstanding feature about General Plumer was his easy bearing — no " fireworks." He was well set-up, of medium height and build, and had thick shoulders for his size, and on this inspection he was in khaki uniform and S.D. hat (the parade was in S.D. caps). As he walked slowly along the line (then drawn up to attention) and scrutinised each man one noticed his heavy white moustache, a thick nose like a wedge broadening out towards the end, a round fresh complexioned face, and light grey twinkling eyes, very quick and searching and wide-awake, and he had that " knowledgable " look which is often associated with the desirable attribute of second-sight.

As to dress, his riding boots of tan leather were polished to perfection, and this was typical of an immaculate appearance from S.D. hat downwards. One must be frank. The Company were only " second " although they had worked hard — at short notice — to put up a smart " turn-out." (Here ! we're not polishin' brasses ? " " 'Ere's a feller askin' for it ! Where's my four-by-two ? " " Hoy ! Don't all shout at once ! Anybody want a wet rag for 'is boots ? " " Where's Bob ? Bob, pass the oil over when you've done y'r butt ! " " All right, soldier ! " " That's right, clumsy ! Tread the mud over 'ere ! " " Hi! throw me over a fag," and like exchanges the while the troops laboured on).

General Plumer stood talking awhile with the captain after the inspection, also to the platoon officers who were called over to where he stood, and then the parade " dismissed." The cooks dished up some fine hot " char " for tea, although they were on this parade, and soon afterwards word got round that the General's remarks as to the inspection were of a satisfactory nature. In other words, " the outlook for spice — or is it salt ? — was promising, and the prospects for the near future were — ' whizzbang ! ' — in the ascendant ! "

J. EDWARDS.

To be continued.

Our Former Secretary's Message of Thanks to Members and Friends

MY dear Members and Friends,
It takes a better pen than mine to find suitable words of gratitude to comrades who have so very generously subscribed towards the testimonial fund kindly organised by headquarters to signal the relinquishment of my much coveted appointment as Secretary of the Ypres League, a post that has been an honour and privilege to fill from May 18th, 1925, to July 6th, 1936.

The general appreciation that has been extended to me completely outweighs my humble services rendered to our Association during the past decade, also I am not only deeply touched, but amazed to peruse the formidable list of members and friends who have associated themselves with this testimonial.

You will be interested to hear that the memento takes the form of an all-wave Auto Radio gramophone, and I desire to convey my congratulations on this excellent choice. The R.G.D. model 645 selected is the "last word" in radio and subscribers will have the satisfaction in knowing that their gift is a real and lasting entertainment to me in my country home, and a luxury that I am proud to share with my relatives and friends.

Headquarters kindly provided a brass plate bearing the following inscription, which I have been proud to affix to the radio set :—

<u>1936</u>
Presented to Captain G. E. de Trafford, M.C.
by Members of the Ypres League
as a token of affection and to mark their appreciation
of his services to the League during the eleven years
that he was Secretary.

Further, the fund has attained such a handsome dimension as to enable me to purchase a quantity of gramophone records to stimulate my passion for music (*not jazz*) and the balance, at my express wish, is being devoted to the Ypres League for the purpose of defraying expenses of one poor relative to Ypres each year so long as the money lasts. I am most grateful to the Committee for allowing me this privilege, because I can happily maintain my interest in the League's charity which is still as close as ever to my heart, as indeed all its activities.

My eleven years Secretaryship will always remain to me a most pleasurable recollection, but I must disclaim any personal credit for the solvent position of the League to-day, and amplify my remarks at the last Annual General Meeting that, the honours are due to the loyal support so readily and ably extended to me from the Committees, Branches and individual members not forgetting the invaluable work of the faithful Assistant Secretary. I thank them all very heartily for this indefatigable co-operation and trust that my depth of gratitude is fully realised.

Needless to say, I sadly miss being detached from the friendship gained during my happy tenure of office, and I hope that my worthy successor, Major Pullar, may enjoy a continuity of the good family spirit, further, that the Ypres League will yet have years of prosperity and prestige for we have great names to support — the immortal name of Ypres alone, our Royal Patrons, our late Presidents, Lord Ypres and Lord Plumer, our President, General Sir Charles Harington, our illustrious Vice-Presidents, and last, but not least, Lieut.-General Sir William Pulteney, to whom we members of the League owe a gratitude that can never be adequately measured or repaid for his services as Chairman.

The thoughtful expression of sympathy in the death of my father so very kindly conveyed in the October edition of the "YPRES TIMES" was greatly appreciated by my family, and I add my own personal thanks. My life has now entered a new chapter, and as the only surviving son it is my duty and pleasure to focus my energy on the management of the Croston Estates, also to play my part in other tasks of exacting nature which I shall endeavour to fulfil to the best of my ability.

The purport of this letter is to say that nothing would give me greater pleasure, had it been possible, than to thank all subscribers personally for their magnificent presentation, but as they are scattered at home and abroad, I must content myself in asking the Editor, "YPRES TIMES" to grant me space in the columns of this issue, hoping sincerely that my expression of thanks will be accepted in a most realistic way, coupled with my everlasting indebtedness for the courtesy and kindness it has always been my good fortune to receive from the Committees and members of the League.

I take this opportunity to wish you all, my dear comrades, a very happy New Year, and conclude with my renewed and overwhelming thanks.

Yours sincerely,

G. E. DE TRAFFORD.

RECRUITING COMPETITION.

The £5 prize awarded to the Branch recruiting the greatest number of new members throughout the year has again been won by our Purley Branch with a total of forty-six new members. The Committee of this progressive Branch have reason to feel proud of their recruiting activities and results, and to them we extend our congratulations and grateful appreciation.

In recognition of the sterling recruiting work of the Purley Branch by winning this prize for the fifth consecutive year, Headquarters presented the Branch on October 2nd last, the occasion of their Re-union Dinner, with a President's Jewel. This token is a very fine piece of work executed to order by one of London's leading Jewellers and is to be worn by the Chairman of the Branch during his term of office.

The Jewel is in the form of a collar, a specially shaded blue ribbon from which is suspended a small oval in gold with the words "Purley Branch" in blue enamel and the badge of the Ypres League, also in blue and gold, dropped from this and held in position by the letter "Y," the initial letter of the word Ypres.

At the Purley Branch Annual Re-union Dinner on October 2nd, out new Vice-President, General Sir Hubert Gough, G.C.M.G., K.C.B., K.C.V.O., etc., who was the Guest of the evening, very kindly consented to present the Jewel on behalf of Headquarters and Mr. A. K. Irens, the Branch Chairman for the year, modestly accepted it on behalf of the Purley Branch amidst much enthusiasm.

YPRES SALIENT NOTICE-BOARDS.

It will be recalled by our members of long standing that several years ago the Ypres League erected in the Salient some forty signposts. The purpose of this was for permanently identifying historic spots, such as Hell Fire Corner, Inverness Copse, etc., for the interest of posterity in general, and the military student in particular. The renovation of these signposts has been necessary from time to time and although the cost for repairing and repainting them is a considerable item the erection and maintenance more than justify the expense. Recently it was observed that several of them required overhauling and orders were given to our Representative for the work to be placed in hand. A fresh colouring has been decided upon and the boards will now have a blue background with lettering in yellow. Captain H. D. Peabody, D.C.M., possessor of an excellent collection of lantern slides has very generously offered to assist the League in the matter of cost for renovating these signposts by way of appeal at his lantern lectures. On Armistice Night at St. Luke's Church Institute, Enfield, a Remembrance Day Festival was organised by the Scouts' Group to which Captain Peabody was invited to give an Illustrated Talk on "The Immortal Salient." An Appeal made during the evening resulted in the sum of £1 6s. 8d. being realised for the sale of Ypres League blue cornflower emblems and this amount together with the cost of the cornflowers was duly forwarded to the Secretary. The accompanying letter stated that Captain Peabody hoped, as a result of future Appeals, to be able to obtain the necessary money to renovate these Ypres Salient Noticeboards without the Ypres League having to encroach on its General Fund. To Captain Peabody we tender our most grateful thanks and wish him success in his loyal efforts.

OUR AMERICAN COLLEAGUES.

Our hearty congratulations are extended to that very loyal and staunch supporter of the Ypres League, Colonel Edward Olmsted, on his recent promotion in the United States Army. On the afternoon of August 22nd last, during First Army manoeuvres at Pine Camp, a simple but impressive ceremony was held in the field adjacent the 44th Divisional Headquarters, at which Governor Harold G. Hoffman of the State of New Jersey, presented Colonel Olmsted, Chief of Staff of the 44th Division, with his Commission as Brigadier-General, United States Army.

General Olmsted was one of the first of our American colleagues who served with the British Forces in the Immortal Ypres Salient, under our late President, the beloved F. M. Viscount Plumer, to become a Life Member of the Ypres League, and we wish him every happiness and further success.

General Leslie Kincaid, another of our American Life Members and keen supporters, recently visited Europe, travelling from America in the German Airship 'Hindenburg.' On his arrival in London one of his first enquries was concerning the Ypres League and its activities. We feel greatly honoured that so distinguished a soldier, believed to be the youngest General in the United States Army, should so kindly remember us, and we are indebted to our old friend, Captain R. Henderson-Bland, for conveying the General's good wishes prior to his departure.

BOUND VOLUMES.

We have received a communication from one of our members to the effect that in view of a move in the near future it may be necessary to dispose of many of his books.

Among these are seven separately bound volumes in green cloth of copies of the YPRES TIMES, some sixty copies in all, and including the four numbers of 1936.

Any member interested and desirous of purchasing these volumes at a cost of three guineas should communicate as early as possible to the Secretary.

Ypres British School

SEVENTH ANNUAL REPORT, OCTOBER, 1936.

The School has now existed for seven years and a few months, not long in the life of schools but long enough to see launched into the world many of the children who were enrolled in April, 1929; children, who but for the inspiration which made the School possible would have been ill prepared to take up any position in England, and as that is the hope of most of our pupils, the School is achieving the aim of its founders.

Our Roll is now 108; it has been 128, but with an increasing number of leavers and fewer new admissions, the lower number is to be expected. With our present accommodation, we are comfortably housed and conform to the Board of Education capacity regulations. The new classroom, adjoining the playground is proving a blessing as the work of the School is easier; we are relieved of the anxiety for children who previously had to cross a busy road several times a day, and there is now peace instead of the noise which at times, had made oral teaching an impossibility. In addition to pupils who come from such outlying places as Vlamertinghe, Poperinghe, Pleogstraat, Poelcapelle and Messines, four children now make the journey from Courtrai daily, a distance of twenty miles. Many more would like to come, but an inadequate and erratic transport service makes it a difficult matter to arrange especially for small children unaccustomed to rail travel. It is obvious from letters I receive that the School has attained a fair measure of publicity and that many people resident in Belgium and France would appreciate having their children enrolled at the School, but as that would entail residence in Ypres, the difficulties are many.

Of the girl leavers, one is employed by a travel agency at Bruges, where she has, to use her own words "easily satisfied" her employers; another has been placed in domestic service in London; a third is nursemaid with an English family in Ypres while a boy leaver is giving satisfaction as an employee in a London Club. Recipients of these Annual Reports will probably recollect that several boys have been accepted at the Chepstow Army Technical School where they have, without exception, done credit to their School at Ypres. I am glad to mention that Jack Blake, the last to leave us for Chepstow, has this year gained a First Certificate in Education, a First Good Conduct Badge and has been promoted Corporal. Two more lads will sit the Entrance Examination in September and as both are keen and intelligent, it is hoped that our list of successes at Chepstow will continue.

After sitting an examination for the Royal Air Force last May, Arthur Batchelor has been offered a place as Boy Entrant. This examination which was competitive and asked for a knowledge of Secondary School subjects, illustrates the standard of work now reached in the top class of the School. Batchelor should do well as he possesses the necessary physical and mental qualifications. Additional classes are held on Saturday mornings for those who intend to sit examinations. In this connection, I am glad to acknowledge the courtesy of Messrs. Isaac Pitman, who have agreed to award Proficiency of the "Queen Mary" for Southampton. We regard our set as a link with Home.

The correspondence with children in other countries continues, and it is hoped that we shall soon be "adopted" by a Tramp Steamer, under a scheme of the L.C.C. by means of which schools will get into contact with vessels sailing to ports in many parts of the world. Cargoes, ports of call, points of interest, etc., will be

Children at the Ypres British School.

Certificates to those of our scholars who qualify in Shorthand under examination conditions, a very helpful gesture which will prove of value to those seeking employment where a knowledge of shorthand and typewriting is essential. Three girls and a boy, who have given evidence of ability in these subjects are having the necessary practice. As many of the boys wish to enter some branch of His Majesty's Forces, a signalling class has been formed, giving them an opportunity to acquire Semaphore and Morse, and having mastered the alphabets, rapid progress has been made in the sending of messages and a new interest infused into the ordinary dictation lesson. Since the issue of the last Annual Report, an excellent wireless set has been installed in the School, the money being raised locally and from friends in England interested in the work of the children. The B.B.C. has given every help by allowing us the use of their booklets so that we are able the better to follow the talks on Travel, History, Geography, etc., while both staff and scholars much appreciated hearing among other events, the various ceremonies attendant on the Proclamation of His Majesty King Edward's Accession and the departure

described by members of the crew and it should prove a useful elaboration of the existing scheme of an exchange of letters, the value of which must of necessity be limited by the age of the correspondents.

Our visits to the local open air baths have been fewer this year due to the inclement weather, but a total of fifteen hours' instruction has resulted in the award of another nine London Schools Swimming Association Certificates, so that 75 per cent. of the children other than infants can now swim. The whole School visited the baths on July 7th to give encouragement to those taking part in events to decide the award of the new Swimming Cup. The sun shone, the end of term was in sight, and the Cup stood, a glistening urge to all competitors to pull their weight. Pulteney House won by 386 points to the Plumer House total of 364. Our visits to these baths have now extended over three years, and it is satisfactory to record that, though they lack many of the amenities of up-to-date English bathing pools, they have not been the cause, so far as I am aware, of one sore throat, nor has any incident occurred which has given us the slightest anxiety.

Again we must blame the weather for a late garden. We have had to return to School several times at a period when seeds should have been planted, and this postponement has meant that crops have matured during the holidays when the gardening class is scattered over Belgium and the British Isles. The advantage of having a garden near the School has been more apparent than ever before, but as has been remarked in a previous report, it is impossible to lease ground for that purpose, unless the house to which it is attached is also taken.

During the autumn, several Nature Rambles were undertaken, and the fruits of various trees and the spoils of many pools brought back to School to provide material for lessons. Calculating the heights of trees from their shadows, gave the older children an out of door arithmetical exercise, which they expressed a willingness to repeat *ad infinitum*. In School, our assortment of silkworms, tadpoles, and fish yield a pleasure out of all proportion to the small trouble in establishing them in their new homes. Special prizes were offered for bean growing last term, and remarkable results were forthcoming, the anaemic growths of the over zealous contrasting with the robust plants of those content to allow Nature her way.

All the games that a small playground permits, the children have enjoyed. Tennis is easily favourite at present, due possibly to the added inducement of a Cup and rackets for the more skilled. The lads have access once a week to the field of the local Cricket Club for which permission I am grateful. Dr. N. Roberts, of the I.W.G.C., having spent a day at the School examining the children, again commented on the improved physique and carriage of the majority, helped undoubtedly by the regular lessons in physical training.

School Staff.
MISS SUMMERS, MR. W. P. ALLEN. MRS. ALLEN.

Previous to the Christmas holiday, the children gave two concerts which were very well attended. Permission had been obtained from the holders of the copyright to allow the performance of a couple of amusing sketches in addition to the School items, and this resulted in a quite unexpected display of histrionic talent by some of the older children. These concerts give immense pleasure to children and adults of the colony and well repay the hours of rehearsal and extra sewing before the actual performances. Again the staff and children much appreciated the Christmas and New Year messages sent by the Bishop of London and Dr. Fleming. As Empire Day fell on a Sunday this year, there was no School celebration as in former years, but an hour was devoted to the singing of patriotic songs and talks on the significance of Empire Day. The children were invited to elect their May Queen, and chose Georgette Piper, a girl of 12½, who having done remarkably well in coming top of the School in examinations and winning two essay competitions, also proved to be the most popular girl of the year, a delightful combination. She was crowned with due ceremony and a two hour programme of singing, dancing and drill followed, witnessed by parents, townspeople and visitors from overseas.

Prize Day was on July 13th. Rain threatened, but fortunately held off to allow us to proceed with the arranged programme in the playground where a large audience had assembled. We were honoured by the presence of the Chaplain General of the Forces, the Rev. E. H. Thorold; Lieut.-General Sir W. Pulteney; Col. F. G. Poole; Mr. P. J. Parr; Mrs. L. K. Briggs and Miss Briggs; Major A. Macfarlane representing the I.W.G.C. and Mrs. Macfarlane; the Rev. G. R. and Mrs. Milner and Father Vanisacker for whose co-operation in taking the Roman Catholics at the Cathedral twice weekly we are very grateful. After presenting the class prizes, again the generous gift of Mrs. Briggs, and the Special Prizes, the Chaplain General spoke to the children in a way they would understand, stressing the pleasure it gave him to be with us on this the most important day of their School year. After a display of dancing, drill and signalling, all joined in the singing of the National Anthem.

Sports Day, held on July 21st, under the auspices of the local branch of the British Legion, on the field of the Ypres F.C., gave the children a day in the open. Fifty-three events were decided in two hours and the children, after a substantial tea, received their prizes. Plumer House gained their first important success with a majority of 284 points over Pulteney House, thus qualifying for the Crouch Sports Cup.

In addition to many parties of tourists, very surprised for the most part to discover an English School in Ypres, our visitors during the year have included : Lady Ware; Sir John and Lady Murray; Sir R. Blomfield; Mr. Stucley and Mr. P. Stucley; Mrs. and Miss Briggs and Mr. Siller of the I.W.G.C. who filmed the children at work and at play. I take this opportunity of thanking the following who have helped in the work of the School by presenting books, special prizes, pictures and cups; while Messrs. Slazenger again presented racquets of their usual excellent quality for competition. The Hon. Mrs. Adeane as always, has been ready with advice and service as to the placing of our girls in England. Whenever help was needed Col. Higginson and the I.W.G.C. has accorded it immediately; I am grateful to Mr. Gill for transport facilities granted us in connection with our May Day ceremony; to Major Macfarlane and Mr. R. J. Parr for kindly reading and adjudicating the essays on Chaucer and *Oliver Twist*; to the Rev. G. Milner for supervising the R.A.F. examination; and finally I acknowledge with gratitude the help and encouragement given by Sir W. Pulteney and Mr. Rich, the Education Officer of the L.C.C., who has allowed us to share and enjoy the privileges usually reserved for the London Shools. WILLIAM P. ALLEN.

Mr. Allen with the Elders.

Sir William and Lady Pulteney; General Harington and Messrs. John Murray; Mrs. L. K. Briggs; Mr. C. H. Babington; Mr. M. Baring; Mr. T. J. Crouch; Mr. Patterson of Belfast; Capt. Peabody and Mr. E. Fletcher,

Since the receipt of the above School Report we have been informed that one of the scholars, named Donald Eaton, has succeeded in passing into the Royal Navy, being placed second out of seven hundred candidates in the examination. This is a very worthy achievement and our heartiest congratulations are extended to both the School and Scholar. To Donald we wish every success in the career he has chosen.

HOTEL
Splendid & Britannique
YPRES

GRANDE PLACE. Opposite Cloth Hall.

LEADING HOTEL FOR COMFORT AND QUALITY, AND PATRONIZED BY THE YPRES LEAGUE.

COMPLETEY RENOVATED

RUNNING WATER. BATHROOMS.

MODERATE TERMS.   GARAGE.

Proprietor—Life Member, Ypres League.

YPRES
Skindles Hotel

(Opposite the Station)

Proprietor—Life Member, Ypres League

Branch at Poperinghe

(close to Talbot House)

Branch Notes

COLCHESTER AND DISTRICT BRANCH.
Armistice Day Memorial Service.

The Chairman, Lieut.Colonel H. W. Herring, M.C., accompanied by a representative party of the Colchester and District Branch, attended the Service of Remembrance at the local Cenotaph on November 11th and at the conclusion of the service placed a wreath on behalf of the Branch. Prayer was said by the Rev. J. Asquith Baker, and the address was given by the Right Worshipful the Mayor (Councillor Gerald C. Benham, M.C.) and Vice-Chairman of the Colchester Branch of the Ypres League. "Last Post" and "Reveille" were sounded by the buglers of the 2nd Battalion, The Lancashire Fusiliers, and the Benediction given by the Right Rev. The Lord Bishop of Colchester. Chopin's Funeral March was played during the placing of the many beautiful wreaths.

Fourth Annual Ball.

The Colchester and District Branch Ball was held on November 12th, at the Red Lion Hotel, Colchester, from 8 p.m. to 2 a.m., and was attended by a record gathering of about 140 people, the function proving both a great social and financial success. This is very encouraging to the Committee and augurs well for the further progress of the League's youngest Branch. The dance music for this occasion was provided by the band of the 2nd Battalion, The Lancashire Fusiliers, and the duties of M.C. were most efficiently carried out by Mr. M. McKinley. The Right Worshipful the Mayor, Councillor G. C. Benham, M.C., and the Branch's Deputy Chairman attended, and parties were brought by the Chairman, Lieut.-Colonel H. W. Herring, M.C., Mr. G. C. Stanford, Mr. D. Shadrach, Captain E. F. Matthews, M.B.E., Major J. A. Thom, Mr. M. McKinley and Mrs. Smythe. Mrs. W. Allen and Mrs. Proctor very kindly assisted in the sale of raffle tickets. To all who

Fourth Annual Ball of the Colchester Branch.

so kindly and generously contributed to the success of the evening the Committee extend their grateful thanks.

Re-union Dinner.

The postponed Fourth Annual Re-union Dinner of the Colchester and District Branch took place on Thursday, December 10th last, at the Red Lion Hotel, and was extremely well attended considering a counter attraction in the town that happened to fall due the same evening.

Lieut.-General Sir William Pulteney, G.C.V.O., K.C.B., K.C.M.G., D.S.O. (Chairman of the Ypres League) had been invited as the Guest of the evening but unfortunately circumstances prevented him at the last moment from being present. Following his earlier notification to the Branch Chairman, Lieut.-Colonel H. W. Herring, M.C., the General very kindly forwarded a telegram which was received during the Dinner, again expressing his deep regret at being unable to attend on this significant occasion and sincerely wished those present a very happy re-union. After reading the message to the gathering the Chairman announced the receipt of another telegram, this from an old friend, the League's former Secretary, Captain G. E. de Trafford, M.C., who sent his cordial greetings, wished all present a jolly re-union and expressed regret that he was unable to accept the Committee's kind invitation to be present.

During the dinner music was provided by the band of the 1st Battalion, The Oxfordshire and Buckingham Light Infantry (*by kind permission of Lieut.-Colonel L. L. Purgiter, D.S.O.*) and the assembly very much appreciated their rendering of old war-time melodies in addition to their other selections.

In view of the programme of entertainment to follow it was requested that the speeches be as brief as possible. Mr. F. S. Collinge opened with proposing the toast of " The Ypres League," to which Major L. J. L. Pullar, M.C., responded. In the course of his remarks Major Pullar thanked very heartily all who had done so much to place the Colchester Branch " on the map," instancing in particular the praiseworthy efforts of the Branch Chairman, Lieut.-Colonel H. W. Herring, M.C., the Deputy-Chairman and present Mayor of the Town, Major G. C. Benham, M.C., whom, it was revealed, had come specially from a Masonic Dinner in order to join old comrades at this Re-union, a gesture that was immensely appreciated, Mr. W. H. Taylor, the Pilgrimage Hon. Secretary and last but not by any means least, Mr. H. Snow, the enthusiastic Branch Hon. Secretary.

The toast to " The Visitors " was proposed by the Chairman, Colonel Herring, who was accorded an enthusiastic reception and the Rev. S. L. Dolph, ex-Australian soldier, and popular favourite with the members duly responded.

As on former occasions of these functions the duties of Toastmaster were carried out by Mr. S. C. Nixon who, needless to add, is now well qualified in this particular art.

The Regina Concert Party took charge for the remainder of the evening and entertained with a high-class programme of mirth and melody which was very cordially acclaimed by all present.

LONDON BRANCH COMMITTEE.

Informal Gatherings.

The first of another series of these Gatherings was held in September last, and the Committee were greatly encouraged by the number of members and friends attending. It is felt, however, that there would be even better attendances if these Meetings were brought to the notice of more of our ex-service comrades. In this connection the Committee appeal to their Branch members to accord them their fullest support for which they would be grateful. Needless to state friends invited would be assured of a hearty welcome.

The Meetings are held on the third Thursday on each month at the Bedford Head Hotel, Maiden Lane, Strand, W.C.2, at 7.30 p.m. Cordial invitation is extended to ladies.

Our October Gathering took the form of a " Steak Supper " over which a member of the Committee, Captain O. G. Johnson, M.A., presided. In view of the apparent popularity of this new venture, it certainly appears that the season's programme will have to include one more such evening if wishing to comply with the many requests from those present on this occasion.

At the November Meeting the gathering were entertained by Miss Glenny who kindly came along and gave a most interesting talk on " Montenegro during the War," explaining how those more obscure sectors fared during the Great War. We were all very pleased to have with us again our old friend, Captain C. Alliston, and more delighted still to observe his general improvement in health which is hoped will be maintained.

The programme for our December Informal Gathering held on Thursday, December 17th, took the form of a variety entertainment, very kindly organised by Mr. O. Mears, of Headquarters. For a number of years now our members have been favoured with a similar programme of entertainment at the December meetings, each one of which has provided us with an extremely jolly evening. The artists procured for this occasion were of the same high standard as formerly and richly deserved the enthusiastic reception accorded them. For another really pleasant evening our grateful thanks are due to Mr. Mears and to those who so kindly extended him their assistance.

The respective programmes for the following three months have been arranged as follows:

January 21st, 1937:
    A Talk on " The naval situation to-day," by Major Gerald Bell, O.B.E.

February 18th, 1937:
    Programme by the " St. Dunstan's " Concert Party.

March 18th, 1937:
    Illustrated Talk by Captain H. D. Peabody, D.C.M.

The Committee have arranged for the Annual Re-union Dinner and Dance to take place on Saturday, April 24th, 1937, at the Palace Hotel, Bloomsbury Street, London, W.C.1, and members are respectfully requested to book this date and help us in making this particular function another great success.

The London Branch Committee takes this opportunity of wishing all its members and friends a happy New Year and earnestly trusts that they may be continued to be favoured with that loyal support in 1937 so generously extended to them in the past.

ANNUAL SMOKING CONCERT.

The Fourteenth Annual Re-union Smoking Concert, arranged by the Committee of the London Branch of the Ypres League, was held on 'Ypres Day' the 31st October last, at Caxton Hall, Victoria, London, S.W.1, and was attended by over five-hundred members and friends.

In the Chair was Major E. Montague Jones, O.B.E., M.A., and gracing the high table with him were ; His Excellency the Belgian Ambassador, Baron E. de Cartier de Marchienne, supported by the Belgian Military Attache, Lieut.-General Baron Vincotte ; Lieut.-Colonel J. Cuny, Military Attache, French Embassy ; Captain J. E. Parks, American Embassy ; The High Commissioner for Newfoundland ; Lieut.-General Sir William Pulteney, G.C.V.O., K.C.B., K.C.M.G., etc. (Chairman of the Ypres League), and Colonel G. T. Brierley, C.M.G., D.S.O.

After the Chairman, in a few well chosen words, had welcomed those present, the "Roosters Concert Party" (late of the 60th Division) and popular Wireless Entertainers, commenced their programme. The reception and applause accorded these artists spoke volumes for the entertainment provided. Whether the items were of a sentimental, humourous, or "service" nature, they were keenly followed and enjoyed and there were many encores. The "Roosters" themselves appeared to be enjoying themselves as much as the audience, entering thoroughly in to the spirit of the occasion and joining in the 'community singing' of the old war-time songs with enthusiasm.

During the evening a telegram, expressing loyalty and devotion to His Majesty The King, Patron-in-Chief of the Ypres League, was despatched to Buckingham Palace, and later the following reply from his Majesty was received and read, amid great enthusiasm, to the assembly : "The King sincerely thanks the Members of the Ypres League assembled at their Annual Re-union for the loyal terms of their message which his Majesty, as Patron-in-Chief much appreciates."

The following message from His Excellency The American Ambassador, who was unable to be present, was then read, "I shall be grateful if you will extend to the members of the Ypres League and their guests, on the occasion of their Annual Re-union, my warmest greetings and best wishes. I am sorry to be prevented from attending the Re-union, and wish all concerned a very enjoyable and successful evening."

Captain G. E. de Trafford, our late Secretary, also remembered us, and sent the following telegram which was likewise read with keen pleasure : " Kindest remembrances and good wishes that your Ypres Day Re-union Concert will be a great success, also that the Ypres League will be well represented at the Commemoration Parade. Regretting very much not being able to be present."

At the end of the first part of the Concert the Chairman referred to the League's activities during the past year, and Lieut.-General Sir William Pulteney followed with a few words of appreciation and encouragement.

In conclusion it may be stated that the evening was most enjoyable and a very gratifying one to the London Branch Committee who wish to thank very heartily all those who contributed to its success.

X. Y. Z.

PURLEY BRANCH.
Re-union Dinner.

The 8th Annual Re-union Dinner of the Purley Branch was held on October 2nd last at the Red Lion Hotel, Coulsdon, when 128 members and guests gathered and enjoyed an extremely pleasant evening. Usually this happy function takes place earlier in the year, but owing to the death of our beloved Patron-in-Chief, King George V, it was naturally postponed to a later date and when the period of mourning was over.

The Guest of the evening was that distinguished soldier, General Sir Hubert Gough, G.C.M.G., K.C.B., K.C.V.O. (War-time Commander of the glorious Fifth Army) and the rousing reception accorded him was eloquent of the esteem and affection these old warriors have for the former Commander.

Those responsible for the selection and *wording* of the menu are to be complimented. With dinner over the inevitable speech making followed, but so unlike the staid after-dinner speeches, those privileged to address the gathering on this occasion certainly did their utmost to be informal and in consequence members and guests were kept in a state of continuous merriment. General Gough accordingly responded in this tone and at least two of his little stories were sufficient to cause everyone to simply rock with laughter. Seated on the General's immediate left at the high table was Private A. K. Irens, the Branch Chairman, who opened his remarks when giving the initial speech of the evening by stating that it was not every day that a "Private" had the honour of being on such terms with a full General. Possibly there was no other country in the world where a similar state of affairs could exist. He could say just what he liked to the General and naively added it was a situation he had sometimes wished for when in the trenches.

In welcoming the guests the Chairman stated how honoured and proud that all were at having with them once again on the occasion of a Branch Re-union Dinner so distinguished and charming a guest as General Sir Hubert Gough. It was earnestly hoped that the General would find it possible to attend a further Branch function in the not too distant future. A cordial welcome was also extended to the new League Secretary, Major L. J. L. Pullar, M.C., and it was noted with pleasure that Mr. O. Mears, his Assistant from Headquarters, was once again with them.

Following the Adjutant's Report which was enthusiastically acclaimed, Commander H. M. Daniel, D.S.O., R.N. (The Crocodile), proposed the toast to "Our Gallant Allies" and after saying his usual few kind words concluded his remarks by hoping to see the guests of that evening with them again next year but not as *guests*. A subsequent report revealed that 24 new members had been recruited during the evening.

General Gough was loudly cheered when rising to respond to the toast and for the next ten minutes the assembly were treated to some very interesting reminiscences and racy stories to the great delight of all present. Before resuming his seat the General presented on behalf of Headquarters a President's Jewel to the Branch in recognition of their sterling recruiting activities and for having won the Recruiting Prize for the fifth consecutive year. Mr. A. K. Irens in accepting the Jewel on behalf of the Branch modestly added that he felt proud in the knowledge that the honour of being the first Chairman to wear this beautiful Jewel should so fortunately fall to himself, a circumstance for which he was most grateful.

Operation Orders indicated "Woodie" as down for the final speech of the evening, subject —the "C.O." but unfortunately, this able speaker, Major S. F. Wood, was prevented from complying through reason of temporary loss of voice as a result of a bad cold. The breach, however, was admirably filled by Captain B. A. Forster who was very heartily applauded.

During the evening the gathering were entertained by an old favourite, Captain Vernon Lee, M.C., who humorous songs and witty bon mots evoked roars of applause and merriment.

At a Branch Committee Meeting prior to the commencement of the Dinner, Major Graham Carr, D.S.O., M.C., was presented with a Jewel, emblematic of the Ypres League, by the members of the Committee. The Jewel was designed specially for him and was awarded as a token of their appreciation of his invaluable services as the Branch Hon. Secretary for many years. It is no reflection on any other member of the Committee, past or present, to say that but for its Hon. Secretary, Major Graham Carr, the Branch would not have attained the esteemed and unique position it enjoys to-day, and the wealth of congratulations which were showered on him as he later appeared wearing the emblem must surely have warmed his heart.

A GUEST.

Armistice Sunday Parade.

Thirty-eight members of the Purley Branch of the Ypres League under the command of the Branch Chairman, Mr. A. K. Irens, attended the United Memorial Service held on Sunday, November 8th, at the Purley Congregational Church, at 3 o'clock p.m.

Annual Dance.

The Third Annual Branch Ball was held on Friday, November 20th, at the Greyhound Hotel Ballroom, Croydon, and once again proved a highly successful function. A company of 317 were present composed of members and their friends.

The Ballroom was tastefully decorated and Tom Newman and his Band were in great form, so all the guests were treated to a most enjoyable evening. The Chairman was resplendent in the new President's Jewel presented to the Branch by Headquarters at the recent Re-union Dinner.

The Committee responsible for the arrangements were greatly helped by the ladies who so kindly volunteered their services in the matter of decorations, presents, and other detail. During the evening the company were entertained at intervals by that stage celebrity, Arthur Prince and "Jim."

It was a great pleasure to welcome Major L. J. L. Pullar, M.C., the Secretary of the League, and we hope he enjoyed the evening. In view of the fact that nearly 100 members had to be disappointed through all available tickets having been sold, it appears very much that the Albert Hall may be required on another occasion.

The financial report on this function has revealed a substantial surplus and the Committee propose to forward a cheque to Headquarters to assist in the League's charitable side of its work. This we hope to do in the course of a few days.

THE ADJUTANT.

SHEFFIELD BRANCH.

Members of the Sheffield Branch paraded with ex-service men of the York & Lancaster Regiment at the Regimental Memorial in Weston Park on Armistice Day for the service there at 11 o'clock a.m.

A wreath on behalf of the Regiment mentioned was placed on the Memorial by Major-General M. H. G. Barker, D.S.O., and the wreath from the Sheffield Branch bearing the following inscription: "Placed in memory of our Comrades who fell in the Ypres Salient, 1914-1918, by the Sheffield Branch, Ypres League," was placed by the Branch Hon. Secretary, Captain J. Wilkinson.

At the Annual Festival of Remembrance held in the evening at 7 o'clock in the City Hall, and arranged by the Sheffield and District Joint Council, the Branch provided a quota of six representative members who attended in conjunction with representatives of the Sheffield and District Council of ex-servicemen's Associations. The first half of the programme was chiefly ceremonial and extremely impressive, while the second half was taken charge of by Murray Ashford and his "Bouquets" Concert Party from the Spa Theatre, Scarborough.

The Branch Secretary Captain J. Wilkinson, wishes to thank those members who so kindly supported him both at the Wreath laying Ceremony and at the Festival in the evening, also those who so generously subscribed to the Wreath Fund. A further cause for congratulation is the manner in which the Branch quota fulfilled their part in the Ceremonial March from the rear of the Hall to the platform at the Evening Festival.

Patron-in-Chief

We have had the honour to receive with great pleasure and gratitude an intimation from the Keeper of the Privy Purse, Buckingham Palace, to effect that His Majesty The King is pleased to permit the Ypres League to continue to show the Sovereign as their Patron during the present reign.

League Secretary's Notes

As we enter upon another phase in the life of our Association, actually the seventeenth anniversary of its existence, we feel that there is justification, in view of the sure and steady progress of the past four years, for permitting ourselves to view the advent of the New Year in an optimistic light.

The past year, 1936, although tinged with a little sadness was, on the whole, one on which we may look back with satisfaction. The steady increase of new members was maintained ; our Travel Bureau report extremely favourable and the Branches recorded their best ever at their respective re-union functions.

Through our Branches lie to a large extent the strength of the League and it is therefore with satisfaction and gratitude that we watch their progress and development. For their loyal support and noble efforts on the League's behalf we extend the respective Committees our grateful thanks and wish them further success in the New Year.

Apart from our efforts in fostering that wonderful spirit of comradeship and close understanding that existed between all ranks during the Great War, the Ypres League have a great duty to fulfil, and that to perpetuate the memory of those 250,000 gallant souls who sacrificed all for the King and Country in the Immortal Defence of Ypres.

In his stirring address at the Horse Guards Parade on the occasion of our last Annual Ypres Day Commemoration the Rev. Dr. Joseph Lynn uttered the following significant words :—

" This is a day of commemoration, which I pray we will never allow to lapse. We are not yet so far removed from those days that we cannot call to mind all the fine spirit of comradeship, which was then revealed. Yet it is easy for us in these distracting days of peace to lose sight of each other, and even of the memory of those, who in war were our brethren. Should this spirit ever fail us, then black shame be upon our name."

Let us all then, in remembering this, try our very best to help strengthen the Ypres League by recruiting to our ranks as many new members as possible, for so long as the life of our Association is assured then we shall not fail in our duty' because our work of commemoration will go on.

Our grateful thanks are extended to the Rev. Dr. Joseph Lynn, M.A., Hon. Chaplain to H.M. The King, and Deputy Chaplain-General to the Forces ; the Band of the 1st Surrey Rifles (now Anti-Aircraft Battalion, Royal Engineers) by kind permission of the Officer Commanding ; and the Pipers of the " London Scottish " by kind permission of Colonel L. D. Henderson, M.C., T.D., Commanding, for their valued support in connection with our Ypres Day Commemoration on Sunday, November 1st, 1936.

As indicated elsewhere in this number, the Purley Branch have again won the Recruiting Prize for the sixth year in succession and receive our heartiest congratulations. We are greatly encouraged by their astonishing recruiting achievements and thank them for such loyal support.

The respective Committees of the Colchester and London Branches are also to be commended for their very creditable efforts for which we are most grateful.

To the Ypres British School we offer our sincere congratulations on their wonderful progress and the high standard attained by their scholars. Some of the essays in particular that we have been privileged to read are remarkable for their knowledge and diction. This can only come about through the painstaking instruction of the teaching staff and happy and contented pupils. Although we have been very much pressed for space in this issue we are glad to include extracts from the Seventh Annual School Report as many members, we fear, are not cognisant of the excellent work that has been done in the past and is being continued at the Ypres British School.

With regard to our Travel Department, enquiries received during the last three months point to a very busy year in 1937 and tours to the Battlefields have already been arranged for units of the Regular and Territorial Armies (Officers' instruction) Old Comrades' Associations, Public Schools and private parties.

It will be of interest to our members to learn that we have had the pleasure to welcome at Headquarters during the past few months representatives and members from the United States of America, France, Belgium, Spain (Madrid), Austria, Australia, New Zealand, South Africa and Uganda.

Before concluding these notes it is desired to take this opportunity of thanking the Committee of the Purley Branch for the cheque so generously donated by them towards our charitable objects.

Wishing all our members a very happy New Year and trusting your endeavours for the welfare of the League will be two-fold.

The Immortal Salient

A British Officer in the third week of October, 1914, ascended the summit of the Cloth Hall at Ypres and surveyed the Plains where the Hosts were marshalling.

He looked over the peaceful landscape for the last time — the picturesque old Chateaux — the dense woods — the shining lakes — the ornamental waters.

Nothing, not a single rood of this was to be spared and from that moment desolation unspeakable was to overspread the land.

One thing only was destined to survive, and that as long as Britain and Britons live can never die. It is the memory of the deaths of a quarter of a million brave men who perished in this bloody ground.

MOTHER'S HOUR.
(November 10th)

You are the world's to-morrow, but to-night
You are my very own. No soldier now,
But just a happy schoolboy, with the light
Of fun and laughter on your freckled brow.
I hear the step that never seemed to tire
As you came running in from school or play,
And sprawling on the rug before the fire,
You'd tell of all the happenings of your day.
This is my hour and these my memories,
And none shall share my joy or know my pain,
Though time may heal the ache and give me ease,
Still, for this evening let me grieve again.
To-morrow's hush may stir my heart to pride—
To-night—I know I loved you and you died.
          HENRY BENSON.

Please book these dates in your diary.

THE MONTHLY
Informal Gatherings
will be held at
THE BEDFORD HEAD HOTEL
MAIDEN LANE, STRAND, W.C.2
on
THURSDAY, JANUARY 21st, 1937.
TALK by MAJOR GERALD BELL, O.B.E., on "The Naval Situation Today."

THURSDAY, FEBRUARY 18th, 1937.
PROGRAMME BY The St. Dunstan's Singers.

THURSDAY, MARCH 18th, 1937.
ILLUSTRATED TALK by CAPTAIN H. D. PEABODY, D.C.M.

From 7.30 to 10 p.m.

If we have had the pleasure of your company we hope to see you again. Also a hearty welcome awaits any friends you may wish to bring along.

An invitation will be sent to any friend by the Hon. Secretary, London Branch Committee, on being supplied with the name and address.

Ladies cordially invited.

CHILDREN'S ANNUAL XMAS PARTY.

The Committee of the London Branch desire to thank all those who so kindly and generously contributed toys and donations to the Children's Annual Xmas Party arranged for January 2nd, 1937, at the Westminster City School, Victoria, S.W.1.

A report of this happy event will be included in our next edition.

BY APPOINTMENT

Carry it with you

It is the lightest of luggage, so take a Bar-Let with you - it only weighs just over eight pounds. Yet it will deal, most efficiently, with all your correspondence and literary work. The Par-Let is so simple to use that you can learn in seven hours to type more quickly than you can write; and the Price is only seven guineas, or 10/- and 10/- a month for 15 months.

BAR-LET
PORTABLE TYPEWRITER
Manufactured by
BAR-LOCK (1925) Co., Nottingham, England.

YPRES LEAGUE TRAVEL BUREAU

CONDUCTED MIXED PILGRIMAGES for 1937

The following Pilgrimages have been arranged for 1937 and the Secretary will be pleased to forward prospectuses to all interested on receipt of application at 20, Orchard Street, London, W.1.

EASTER (March 27th—30th) ... YPRES (Day route *via* Ostend).
WHITSUNTIDE (May 15th—18th) YPRES (Day route *via* Ostend).
WHITSUNTIDE (May 15th—18th) ARRAS (Day route *via* Boulogne).
AUGUST BANK HOLIDAY (July 31st—August 3rd)
                                YPRES (Day route *via* Ostend).
AUGUST BANK HOLIDAY (July 31st—August 3rd)
                                ARRAS (Day route *via* Boulogne).
SEPTEMBER (September 18th—21st)
                                YPRES (Day route *via* Ostend).

Both at Whitsuntide and August Bank Holiday two separate conducted pilgrimages will be organized, one to Ypres (Belgium) and one to Arras (France).

We are pleased to announce that arrangements have now been completed with our Belgian Representatives for the *Rail* journey, Ostend to Ypres and return, to be eliminated in favour of *Charabanc* transport. All persons travelling to YPRES with conducted pilgrimages will therefore, in future be conveyed from Ostend (Maritime Station) by charabanc and the same will apply for the return journey, Ypres to Ostend.

INDEPENDENT TRAVEL.

To those contemplating individual travel, our Travel Department would be pleased to furnish information on all matters connected with trips to any part of the Old Western Front Battlefields.

Apply to Secretary, Ypres League, 20, Orchard Street, London, W.1, for the Ypres League Travel Guide for 1937.

THE BRITISH TOURING SERVICE

Manager—Mr. P. VYNER

Representative and Life Member, Ypres League

10, Station Square
ARRAS
(P.-de-C.) France

Cars for Hire, with British Driver Guides   Tours Arranged

Branches and Corresponding Members

BRANCHES.

LONDON	Hon. Secretary to the London County Committee : J. Boughey; 20, Orchard Street, London, W.1.
	E. LONDON DISTRICT—L. A Weller, 26, Lambourne Gardens, Hornchurch, Essex.
	TOTTENHAM AND EDMONTON DISTRICT—191, Landowne Road, Tottenham, N.17.
	H. Carey, 373, Sydenham Road, S.E.26.
COLCHESTER	H. Snow (Hon. Sec.), 9, Church Street.
	W. H. Taylor (Pilgrimage Hon. Sec.), 64, High Street.
LIVERPOOL	Captain A. M. Webster, Blundellsands.
PURLEY	Major Graham Carr, D.S.O., M.C., 112-114, High Street.
SHEFFIELD	Captain J Wilkinson, "Holmfield," Bents Drive.
BELGIUM	Mr. C. Leupe, 81, Chaussée de Dickebusch.
CANADA	Ed. Kingsland, P.O. Box 83, Magog, Quebec.
SOUTH AFRICA	L. G. Shuter, 381, Longmarket Street, Pietermaritzburg.
KENYA	C. H. Slater, P.O. Box 403, Nairobi.
AMERICA	Representative : Captain R. Henderson-Bland, 110 West 57th Stree New York City.

CORRESPONDING MEMBERS

GREAT BRITAIN.

ABERYSTWYTH	T. O. Thomas, 5, Smithfield Road.
ASHTON-UNDER-LYNE	G. D. Stuart, "Woodlands,", Thronfield Grove, Arundel Street.
BANBURY	Captain C. W. Fowke, Yew Tree House, King's Sutton.
BIRMINGHAM	Mrs. Hill, 191, Cattell Road, Small Heath.
	John Burman, "Westbrook," Solihull Road, Shirley.
BOURNEMOUTH	H. L. Pasmore, 40, Morley Road, Boscombe Park.
BRISTOL	W. S. Hook, "Wytschaete" Redland Court Road
BROADSTAIRS	C. E. King, 6, Norman Road, St. Peters, Broadstairs.
	Mrs. Briggs, North Foreland House.
CHATHAM	W. N. Channon, 22, Keyes Avenue.
CHESTERFIELD	Major A. W. Shea, 14, Cross Street.
CONGLETON	Mr. H. Dart, 61, The Crescent.
DARLINGTON	D. S. Vigo, 125, Dorset Road, Bexhill-on-Sea.
DERBY	T. Jakeman, 10, Graham Street.
DORRINGTON (Salop)	Captain G. D. S. Parker, Frodesley Rectory.
EXETER	Captain E. Jenkin, 25, Queen Street.
HERNE BAY	Captain E. Clarke Williams, F.S.A.A., "Conway," Station Road.
HOVE	Captain G. W. J. Cole, 2, Westbourne Terrace, Kingsway.
LEICESTER	W. C. Dunford, 343, Aylestone Road.
LINCOLN	E. Swaine, 79, West Parade.
LLANWRST	A. C. Tomlinson, M.A., Bod Estyn.
LOUGHTON	Capt. O. G. Johnson, M.A., Loughton School.
MATLOCK (Derby)	Miss Dickinson, Beechwood.
MELROSE	Mrs. Lindesay Kelsall, Darnlee.
NEW BRIGHTON (Cheshire)	E. F. Williams, 5, Waterloo Road.
NEW MILTON	W. H. Lunn, Greywell.

NOTTINGHAM	E. V. Brown, 3, Eldon Chambers, Wheeler Gate.
ST. HELENS (Lancs.) ...	John Orford, 124, Knowsley Road.
ST. JOHN'S (Newfoundland)	Captain L. Murphy, G.W.V.A. Office.
SHREWSBURY	Major-General Sir John Headlam, K.B.E., C.B., D.S.O., Cruck Meole House, Hanwood.
TIVERTON (Devon) ...	Mr. W H. Duncan Arthur, Surveyor's Office, Town Hall.
WELSHPOOL	Mr. E. Wilson, Coedway, Ford, Salop.

DOMINIONS AND FOREIGN COUNTRIES.

AUSTRALIA	Messrs. C. H. Green, and George Lawson, Essex House, (Opposite Anzac Square) Brisbane, Queensland.
	R. A. Baldwin, c/o Government Savings Bank of N.S.W., Martin Place, Sydney.
	Mr. W. Cloves, Box 1296, G.P.O., Adelaide.
BELGIUM	Sister Marguerite, Sacré Coeur, Ypres.
CANADA	Brig.-General V. W. Odlum, C.B., C.M.G., D.S.O., 2530, Point Grey Road, Vancouver.
	V. A. Bowes, 326, 40th Avenue West, Calgary, Alberta.
	W. Constable F. Grece, St. Hilaire Station, Ronville County, Quebec.
CEYLON	Captain F. R. G. Webb, M.C., Irrigation Bungalow, Kalmunai, E.P.
EGYPT	Captain B. W. Leak, M.I.E.E., Turf Club, Cairo.
INDIA	Lieut.-Quartermaster G. Smith, Queen's Bays, Sialkot, India.
IRELAND	Miss A. K. Jackson, Cloneyhurke House, Portarlington.
NEW ZEALAND	Captain W. U. Gibb, Ava Lodge, Puhinui Road, Papatoetoe, Auckland
	S. E. Beattie, P.O. Box 11, Otaki Railway, Wellington.
NEWFOUNDLAND ...	Captain Leo. Murphy, G.W.V.A. Office, St. John's.
NOVA SCOTIA	Will R. Bird, 35, Clarence Street, Amherst.
SOUTH AFRICA	H. L. Versfield, c/o Cape Explosives Works Ltd., 150, St. Georges Street, Cape Town.
SPAIN	Captain P. W. Burgess, Calle de Zurbano 29, Madrid.
U.S.A.	Captain Henry Maslin, 942, President Street, Brooklyn, New York.
	L. E. P, Foot, 20, Gillett Street, Hartford, Conn, U.S.A.
	A. P. Forward, 449, East 80th Street, New York.
	J. W. Freebody, 945, McBride Avenue, Los Angeles.

Membership of the League

This is open to all who served in the Salient, and to all those whose relatives or friends died there, in order that they may have a record of that service for themselves and their descendants, and belong to the comradeship of men and women who understand and remember all that Ypres meant in suffering and endurance.

Life membership, £2 10s.

Annual members, 5s.

Do not let the fact of your not having served in the Salient deter you from joining the Ypres League. Those who have neither fought in the Salient nor lost relatives there, but who are in sympathy with the objects of the Ypres League, are admitted to its fellowship, but are not given scroll certificates.

There is a Junior Division for children whose relatives served in the Salient. It is open also to others to whom our objects appeal.

Annual subscription 1s. up to the age of 18, after which they can become ordinary members of the League.

THE YPRES LEAGUE (INCORPORATED)
20, Orchard Street, Portman Square, W.1.

Telephone: WELBECK 1446.   *Telegrams*: YPRESLEAG, "WESDO," LONDON.

Patron-in-Chief: H.M. THE KING.

Patron:
H.R.H. PRINCESS BEATRICE.

President: GENERAL SIR CHARLES H. HARINGTON.

Vice-Presidents:

THE VISCOUNT WAKEFIELD OF HYTHE.   F.-M. SIR CLAUD W. JACOB.
F.-M. LORD MILNE.   F.-M. SIR PHILIP CHETWODE.
GENERAL SIR CECIL ROMER.   GENERAL SIR HUBERT GOUGH.

General Committee:

THE COUNTESS OF ALBEMARLE.
*CAPTAIN C. ALLISTON.
LIEUT-COLONEL BECKLES WILLSON.
MR. HENRY BENSON.
*MR. J. BOUGHEY.
*MISS B. BRICE-MILLER.
COLONEL G. T. BRIERLEY.
CAPTAIN P. W. BURGESS.
BRIG.-GENL. A. BURT.
*MAJOR H. CARDINAL-HARFORD.
REV. P. B. CLAYTON.
*CAPTAIN G. E. DE TRAFFORD.
*THE EARL OF YPRES.
MRS. C. J. EDWARDS.
MAJOR C. J. EDWARDS.
MR. H. A. T. FAIRBANK.
MR. T. ROSS FURNER.
SIR PHILIP GIBBS.
MR. E. GLOVER.

MR. F. D. BANKES-HILL.
MAJOR-GENERAL C. J. B. HAY.
MR. J. HETHERINGTON.
GENERAL SIR W. C. G. HENEKER.
*CAPTAIN O. G. JOHNSON.
*MAJOR E. MONTAGUE JONES.
MAJOR GENL. C. G. LIDDELL.
CAPTAIN H. D. PEABODY.
*THE HON. ALICE DOUGLAS PENNANT.
*LIEUT.-GENERAL SIR W. P. PULTENEY.
LIEUT.-COLONEL SIR J. MURRAY.
*COLONEL G. E. C. RASCH.
THE HON. SIR ARTHUR STANLEY.
MR. ERNEST THOMPSON.
CAPTAIN J. LOCKLEY TURNER.
*MR. E. B. WAGGETT.
CAPTAIN J. WILKINSON.
CAPTAIN H. TREVOR WILLIAMS.

* Executive Committee.

Bankers:
BARCLAYS BANK LTD., Knightsbridge Branch.

Honorary Solicitors:
MESSRS. FLADGATE & CO., 70, Pall Mall, S.W.

Secretary:
MAJOR L. J. L. PULLAR.

Auditors:
MESSRS. LEPINE & JACKSON,
6, Bond Court, E.C.4.

League Representative at Ypres:
Mr. C. LEUPE,
81, Chaussée de Dickebusch.

League Representative at Cambrai:
MR. A. WILDE,
9, Rue des Anglaises.

League Representative at Amiens:
CAPTAIN STUART OSWALD.
7, Rue des Otages.

League Representative at Arras:
MR. P. VYNER,
10, Place de la Gare.

Hon. Secretary, Ypres British Settlement:
LT. COLONEL F. G. POOLE.

PRIMARY OBJECTS OF THE LEAGUE

I.—Commemoration and Comradeship.
II.—To provide special travel facilities for Members and all interested to Ypres and battlefields, and transport of Members.
III.—The furnishing of information about the Salient; marking of historic sites and the compilation of charts of the battlefields.
IV.—The erection of a Ypres British Church and School which has been completed.
V.—The establishment of groups of members throughout the world, through Branch Secretaries and Corresponding Members.
VI.—The maintenance of cordial relations with dwellers on the battlefields of Ypres.
VII.—The formation of a Junior Division.

Use the Ypres League Travel Bureau for Ypres and Whole of the Western Front.

FOR THE FOLLOWING PUBLICATIONS, Etc., apply:

Secretary, YPRES LEAGUE, 20, ORCHARD STREET, LONDON, W.1.

THE BATTLE BOOK OF YPRES. A history of notable deeds contributed by all regiments. 5s.; post free, 5s. 6d. Compiled by Beatrix Brice with the assistance of Lieut.-General Sir William Pulteney, G.C.V.O., etc.

BOOKS.

YPRES: Outpost of the Channel Ports. By Beatrix Brice. With Foreword by Field-Marshal Lord Plumer, G.C.B. Price 1s. 0d.; post free 1s. 3d.

In the Ypres Salient. By Lt.-Col. Beckles Willson. 1s. net; post free 1s. 2d.

Story of the 63rd Field Ambulance. By A. W. Westmore, etc. Cloth, 3s. 6d., post free. Paper, 2s. 6d., post free.

War Letters to a Wife. By Colonel Rowland Feilding. Popular Edition, 3s. 6d.; post free 4s.

The Pill Boxes of Flanders. 1s.; post free 1s. 3d.

From Mons to the First Battle of Ypres. By the late J. G. W. Hyndson, M.C. Price 3/6, post free.

YPRES LEAGUE TIES. 3s. 6d. each, post free.

YPRES LEAGUE BADGES. 2s. each, 2s. 1½d. post free.

EMBROIDERED BADGES. 4s. each, post free.

Map and List of Cemeteries in the Ypres Salient. Price 9d.; post free 11d.

Map of the Somme. Price 1s. 8d., post free.

PICTURES.

Burning of the Cloth Hall, 1915. A Coloured Print, 14 in. by 12 in. 1s. post free.

Old Well-known Spots in New Guise. Prints, size 4¼ x 2½, recently taken of famous spots in the Ypres Salient, and which may be of great interest to our readers, are on sale at headquarters, price 4d. each, post free 5d. For particulars apply Secretary.

POST CARDS, PHOTOGRAPHS AND ETCHINGS.

Post Cards. Ypres: British Front during the War. Ruins of Ypres. Price 1s. post free.

Hill 60. Complete Panorama Photographs. 12 in. by 3¾ in. Price 3s., post free; 15 in. by 5 in. Price 3s. 6d., post free.

MODELS OF DEMARCATION STONE.

The model, which is 6 inches in height, may be used for a paperweight or as an ornament. Price 5/-, post free.
Applications to the Secretary, Ypres League.

PHOTOGRAPHS OF WAR-TIME SKETCHES.

Bedford House (Front View), 1916.

Bedford House (Back View), 1916.

Voormezeele Main Street, 1916.

Voormezeele Crucifixion Gate, 1916.

Langhof Chateau, 1916.

Size 8½ in. by 6½ in. Price 2s. 6d. each, post free.

Photographs of the Thiepval and Arras Memorials. Post card size, price 1s. each, post free.

YPRES TIMES.

The Journal may be obtained at the League Offices.

BACK NUMBERS 1s.; 1934, 8d.; 1935 6d.

Printed in Great Britain for the Publishers by FORD & GILL, 21a/23, Iliffe Yard, Crampton Street, London, S.E.17.

Vol. 8. No. 6.   APRIL, 1937.

YPRES TIMES

CONTENTS.

H.M. The King.
The Somme—Twenty Years After.
Place Names in Flanders.
Tanks in Action.
Empire's War Graves.
Light and Shade at the Front.
The Late Curé of Ypres.
Ypres British School.
Branch Notes.
League Secretary's Notes.

PRICE SIXPENCE

Memory Tablet.

APRIL - MAY - JUNE

April.

April	5th, 1917	...	United States declares war on Germany.
,,	9th, 1917	...	Battle of Vimy Ridge begins.
,,	9th, 1918	...	Battle of Lys begins.
,,	14th, 1918	...	General Foch appointed Generalissimo of the Allied Armies in France.
,,	22nd, 1915	...	Second Battle of Ypres begins. Germans use asphyxiating gases.
,,	22nd, 1918	...	British Naval attack on Zeebruge and Ostend.
,,	24th, 1916	...	Rebellion in Ireland.
,,	25th, 1915	...	Allied forces land in Gallipoli.
,,	27th, 1915	...	General Sir Herbert Plumer given command of all troops in the Ypres Salient.
,,	29th, 1916	...	Fall of Kut.

May.

May	7th, 1915	...	The *Lusitania* torpedoed and sunk by the Germans.
,,	12th, 1915	...	Windhoek, capital of German South-West Africa, captured by General Botha.
,,	19th, 1918	...	Germans bomb British hospitals at Etaples.
,,	23rd, 1915	...	Italy declares war on Austria.
,,	31st, 1916	...	Sea battle off the coast of Jutland.

June.

June	5th, 1916	...	Loss of Earl Kitchener on H.M.S. *Hampshire*.
,,	7th, 1915	...	Flight-Lieut. Warneford attacks and destroys Zeppelin between Ghent and Brussels.
,,	7th, 1917	...	British victory at Messines Ridge.
,,	29th, 1917	...	General Allenby in command in Egypt.

The Ypres Times

Communications to
The Editor, "Ypres Times,"
20, Orchard Street, London, W.1.

PRICE 6d.
POST FREE 7d.

Vol. 8, No. 6.   Published Quarterly   April, 1937

H.M. King George VI.

Life Story of our Gracious Patron-in-Chief.

National Services in War and Peace.

By Henry Benson, M.A.

AMURATH to Amurath succeeds as Patron-in-Chief of the Ypres League. An intimation has been sent by the Keeper of the Privy Purse from Buckingham Palace that King George VI has been graciously pleased to become Patron-in-Chief of the Ypres League in succession to his elder brother, ex-King Edward VIII. The members of the League and all our other readers will be deeply sensitive of this signal honour and will unite in offering their loyal gratitude to His Majesty.

The King is, as yet, a much less familiar figure to the public than his elder brother or his father; but although naturally he has not enjoyed the unique opportunities provided for the former as Prince of Wales, it is true that he knows the Empire far better than most of his subjects can ever hope to do. At home he has already shown his worth in valuable, if unobtrusive, service. He possesses his brother's gift for understanding the life of the humbler people and he has displayed practical interest in all the social problems of the nation.

The unusual and trying circumstances of his accession have afforded him an exceptionally sympathetic welcome and a special need of loyalty on the part of his subjects throughout the Empire. King George will assuredly add lustre to his ancestral Crown.

Below will be found a brief sketch of his unassuming, but none the less valuable, career.

Early Years.

King George VI—Albert Frederick Arthur George—second son of the late King George V and Queen Mary, was born at York Cottage, Sandringham, on December 14th, 1895, when his parents were still Duke and Duchess of York. Incidentally, his birthday coincides with the death of his great-grandfather, the Prince Consort.

His early years were uneventful. Until Queen Victoria's death, shortly after the child's sixth birthday, his father and mother were still too remote from the succession to be much in the public eye. His boyhood days were spent chiefly at White Lodge, Richmond, and at Sandringham, and his education was entrusted to Mme. Bricka, Mr. Hansell, Mr. Hua and Mr. Walter Jones. In addition, he received instruction in those matters deemed necessary for one of his exalted rank; but he was allowed, nevertheless, to follow the life of a normal English boy. He played football with the village lads at Sandringham and early was taught to ride. He learnt the waltz at Marlborough House and the breast stroke at the Bath Club in Dover Street. Cricket was played at Frogmore and golf wherever the opportunity presented itself. Even before he attained his twelfth birthday he began to play racquets and squash racquets, which gave him a zest for those games that has never left him. As soon as he was old enough, in company with his elder brother, the Duke of Windsor, he was given military drill by a sergeant-major of the Coldstream Guards. All this teaching and training was superintended by his father and mother, and by King Edward VII, who held strong views on the education of his grandsons. From this it will be seen that his youthful upbringing was thoroughly, though unostentatiously, managed.

"Mr. Johnson."

Like his father, King George (King Edward VII's second son) and his great-uncle, the Duke of Edinburgh (Queen Victoria's second son), Prince Albert, the second son, was destined for the Navy, and when he was barely fourteen he entered the Royal Naval College at Osborne as an ordinary cadet, where he remained for two years, afterwards completing a further two years' training at Dartmouth. At both academies there was the customary examinations and the young Prince had to take them with the other boys. Despite the fact that he was rather reserved in private, extremely diffident in public and accustomed to keep himself religiously in the background, he was popular, and was accorded the nickname of "Mr. Johnson"—a title which stuck to him throughout his career in the Senior Service. His father, it may be mentioned, was known in his cadet days as "Sprat." It was at Osborne that King George VI first met Sir Louis Greig, then a doctor on the establishment, who in after years was to become his closest friend.

Just after his seventeenth birthday, at the beginning of 1907, the Prince joined H.M.S. "Cumberland" along with some sixty other naval cadets and, as a cadet, crossed the Atlantic. He visited the West Indies and Canada, receiving a great welcome in the Dominion, on the soil of which he was the first of King George V's sons to set foot. He took the opportunity of going to Montreal, Ottawa and the Niagara Falls. For the rest, he had the life of an ordinary naval officer, learned to swing his own hammock and to make cocoa at all hours. In due course he was gazetted as midshipman to H.M.S. Collingwood in 1913.

Naval Career Interrupted.

A year later Great Britain was at war, and H.M.S. "Collingwood" joined the Grand Fleet with the Prince, still a midshipman, on board. However, much to his dismay, in September, 1914, he was seized with serious illness, transferred to hospital ship and landed at Aberdeen. For some time previously he had been suffering from gastric trouble and he was operated upon for appendicitis. The operation was apparently successful, but unfortunately he did not recover his health as quickly as was hoped. He was allowed to rejoin his ship in February, 1915, but he was found still to be a victim of an obstinate gastric disorder, and during the next two years he was compelled to take several periods of sick leave.

At the Battle of Jutland.

To his great satisfaction, however, he was on duty with the Fleet in 1916 at the time of the Battle of Jutland, and his services as sub-lieutenant, which rank he then held, were mentioned in Admiral Jellicoe's dispatch. As a fact, the Prince saw little of the battle, since his post was with the crew of one of the 12 in. guns in the fore turret. The gun hurled shell after shell at the German Fleet at a range of between 8,000 and

9,000 yards, but neither he nor his fellow gunners had the satisfaction of knowing whether their shells were reaching their target. It was not until afterwards that they learned that the German battleship, "Derfflinger," had been so heavily raked by their fire that she had only just been able to struggle into Kiel.

Soon afterwards an attack of gastric trouble sent him into hospital, and as winter came on he grew worse. Yet, with the spring he was back at sea again in the "Malaya." Not for long. In November that year (1917) a second operation was found to be imperative. Despite the opposition of the late Sir Frederick Treves, Sir Louis Greig had contended in 1914 that the trouble was not appendicitis, but duodenal ulcer, and this proved to be correct. An operation—this time for duodenal ulcer—was performed by Sir Hugh Rigby, since when there has been no further recurrence. This skilful diagnosis of the Prince's illness was mainly responsible for Sir Louis' reputation with the Royal Family. Incidentally, he has now abandoned medicine, and is at present a partner in a well-known stockbroking firm. It may be mentioned that on the occasion of his twenty-first birthday King George V conferred the Garter upon his son.

It had now become evident that the Prince was not robust enough for a life at sea and he was attached to the Victory for duty on the staff of the Commander-in-Chief at Portsmouth. After one more spell of active service with the Fleet, he was on November 12th, 1917, appointed to the Royal Naval Air Force Station, Cranwell. Six months later he obtained his pilot's certificate, and it was as a pilot that he was absorbed, with the rest of his branch, into the Royal Air Force. This provided the opportunity for him to go to France, and he served on the staff of Sir Hugh Trenchard at Nancy until the Armistice. He passed the flying tests in July, 1919, and was appointed a squadron-leader of the Royal Air Force. But a short time after he retired from the active lists, both of the Navy and the R.A.F.

The Prince's first important duty after the Armistice was when he represented his father at the dramatic entry into Brussels of the King of the Belgians in November, 1918.

Undergraduate Days at Cambridge.

In October, 1919, he took the course adopted by so many young men whose education had been cut short by the war and began twelve months' residence at Trinity College, Cambridge. His brother, Prince Henry, now Duke of Gloucester, accompanied him. They did not, however, live in college, but took a house which was run for them by Prince Albert's old comrade, Sir Louis Greig, and his wife.

The two Royal brothers were regular visitors to the Union Society weekly debates, where they occupied chairs in the centre gangway facing the President. On one occasion the Prince vainly tried to elude a Proctor's "bulldog" sent out to apprehend an undergraduate leaving the Union Society smoking a pipe whilst in academical dress, who turned out to be Prince Albert. The Proctor who interviewed the Prince was Mr. T. R. Glover, of St. John's, the present Public Orator. The "Bull-dog," Mr. Lavis, once told me that when he went to collect the fine of 6s. 8d. for the offence, the "victim" invited him to have a drink and was much amused on hearing that he had previously had a narrow escape from being "progged" when leaving the Corn Exchange after an Inter-Varsity boxing match without wearing cap and gown. He had been taken for one of the boxers and consequently was not challenged.

The Prince was well liked at Cambridge, although he was not a very conspicuous member of the University. He took a special course in history, economics and civics, which touched upon such matters of immediate importance as the relation of Capital and Labour, the function of Government and the meaning and quality of citizenship. When he left Cambridge he was well equipped to take his place as the third gentleman in the land.

The Duke of York's Camp.

In the Birthday Honours List of 1920 the Prince was elevated to the Dukedom of York, with the incidental titles of Baron Killarney and Earl of Inverness, and he took his seat in the House of Lords on June 23rd of that year. Of his twelve predecessors in the title five had worn the Crown, under the names of Edward IV, Henry VIII, Charles I, James II, and George V. The public quickly became aware that the young Duke was very much his father's son and that he was inspired by a zeal for effective, if unobtrusive service to the Empire. The period was one of considerable social strain and an endeavour was made to brighten it through the formation of the Industrial Welfare Society, under the direction of Mr. Robert Hyde. The Duke became its President, and he made the office an opportunity for showing an active personal interest in the working life of the people and for encouraging the improvement of conditions in factories and workshops beyond statutory requirements, thereby adding to the security, happiness and health of the working-class community. His countless visits to the industrial areas and mines gave him an encyclopaedic knowledge of the problems both of industrial management and those of the workers themselves. Child welfare was another subject which touched his heart. " Upon the youth of the nation," he once declared, " depends the future of the Empire."

In another way also the Duke helped to promote happiness and fitness among young workers and to bring about mutual understanding and respect between youths of different social classes. " The Duke of York's Camp " is an annual holiday institution which was held first on a disused aerodrome at New Romney and afterwards at Southwold. Two hundred young workers share a week's camp by the sea with two hundred public schoolboys, and the Duke of York—dressed in shorts, pullover and rubber shoes—made a practice of spending two days under canvas with them, living the normal life of the camp. In fifteen years some 6,000 boys have carried back to their homes a sense of comradeship bridging class distinction. Except in 1934, when a poisoned hand temporarily cut him off from active life, the Duke paid his annual visit.

Wedding Romance Delighted whole Empire.

During 1922 there were reported rumours of a romance in the Royal Household. For several seasons the Duke had been the guest of the Earl and Countess of Strathmore at Glamis Castle for the Highland Games, and it was whispered that the daughter of the house, Lady Elizabeth Bowes-Lyon, and the young Duke had become friends. Friendship ripened into love as the young couple walked in the yew-hedged gardens and wooded grounds of Glamis Castle, under the shadow of the Grampian Hills. Then came a Sunday morning stroll near the Earl of Strathmore's other home at Welwyn, in Hertfordshire, when the Duke proposed and was accepted. A story went round that the Duke had to propose three times before acceptance. " Did he ? " said the bride-elect to an inquisitive interviewer. " Do you think it was necessary ? " she added.

In February, 1923, the engagement was announced officially in the Court Circular, and in the following April the marriage was solemnised in Westminster Abbey in the presence of King George V, Queen Mary and a vast congregation. It was the occasion for a day of great national rejoicing, and the heart of the Empire was touched when the bride, on leaving the Abbey, paused to lay her bouquet of white roses on the tomb of the Unknown Warrior. Again, the nation was delighted when the young couple donated a sum of £25,000, which had been subscribed as a wedding gift, to providing treats to poor children in the industrial areas. The honeymoon was spent at Polesden Lacey, near Dorking, and at Glamis. Afterwards the young couple set up home at White Lodge, Richmond.

Empire Tours and State Missions.

After a visit to Northern Ireland in the summer of 1924, the Duke and Duchess made their first Empire tour to South Africa. The birth of Princess Elizabeth on April 21st, 1926, and of Princess Margaret Rose in 1930 further strengthened the bond of sympathy between the British people and the Duke and " the smiling Duchess."

In 1927 they visited Australia and New Zealand, and the Duke opened the new Parliament buildings at Canberra on May 9th amid manifestations of loyalty and jubilation. At a luncheon at the Guildhall, at the conclusion of the tour, the Duke said: " I return to London a thorough optimist. If we hold together we shall win through." Save for those Africa and Australia journeys the King has not spent much time out of England. He has, however, paid a number of brief visits to various European countries, most of them on official missions. An important journey was then made in 1931, when he went to Paris to see the Colonial Exhibition. In proposing the toast of " The Franco-British Entente and the prosperity of France and her Colonial Empire," he said: " Our two Colonial Empires adjoin all over the globe. . . . Our common frontiers, far from creating causes of dissension, encourage us towards an ever friendlier co-operation."

The King's time in the British Isles has been characterized by the assiduous performance of an immense variety of public functions. Among them one occasion stands out. In 1929 the Church of Scotland was able to celebrate its re-union after the long disruption that began in 1843. In this year, so memorable in Scottish history, King George V appointed his son as High Commissioner of the General Assembly.

These years of quiet, painstaking work have given His Majesty his own special place in the regard of his countrymen. The public sees in him a man rich in all his father's virtues, modest, earnest, sincere and admirably conscientious. His sense of duty was never more clearly displayed than last summer, when he travelled down all the way from Scotland to Aldershot to bid farewell to the Service battalion of the Scots Guards, of which he was Colonel, on its departure for the Mediterranean.

His Majesty has always taken an active interest in Masonic affairs, and it was a source of personal pride to him when he was nominated and installed as Grand Master Mason of Scotland during the bi-centenary celebrations of the Grand Lodge of Scottish Freemasons in Edinburgh as recently as last November 30th.

Personal Characteristics.

King George VI, like his father before him, is of a retiring and modest disposition. He has never attempted to put himself in the lime-light, he never envied his elder brother, never sought to undermine his popularity, and never failed to give him loyal, faithful, quiet and dignified advice. He already knows the weight and responsibilities of the Crown, for his father always felt that, with his eldest son unmarried, his second son should be trained, too, for the possible eventuality which might, as it has done, place him on the Throne. Although he has accepted the succession in a spirit of pure and humble service as the rightful heir, he would, nevertheless, have preferred a relative obscurity to the burden and cares of kingship. Like his father before him, he had taken over the Crown as a sacred trust and with his young wife, he has promised to uphold the important tradition of the Royal House.

He would be the first to admit that he lacks some of the personal charm of the Duke of Windsor, but he possesses many outstanding qualities which will stand him in good stead as King and Emperor. He is scrupulously punctual in the fulfilment of his public obligations. He is a good family man, a good son, a good husband, and a good father. And he has one quality which affords supreme confidence to those who know him intimately. He has immense grit. Everything that he takes up he sees through to the end.

Above all else, he is human. He is by no means a "Society" man. Dogs he loves. You could find them all over the place at his late home, 145, Piccadilly. A romp with his dogs and his young daughters in the garden is one of those tonics with which the King, like any ordinary family man, dispels his cares and worries. Again, he likes nothing more than to spend a quiet half-hour reading by the fireside. The classics of English literature and the great writers of ancient Rome and Greece are his well-loved companions.

When His Majesty ascended the Throne on the abdication of his brother, it was not an occasion of transferred allegiance nor shifting loyalty. A steadfast and united Empire was unchanged in its devotion to the Royal House, its fidelity to the Constitution and its sure faith in the principles of free democracy. It augurs well for the future that the King stands for all that is best in the life of the Empire—for service, for devotion to duty and for sympathetic understanding. That he will prove to be a wise and inspiring Sovereign there need be no fear on the part of his people.

On behalf of the members of the Ypres League and of the British community resident in Ypres, I wish His Majesty a long, happy and peaceful reign.

GOD SAVE KING GEORGE VI.

H. B.

Twenty Years After—
The "Blood Bath" Ground is still Red!

WE VISIT HIGH, " LOUSY," BERNAFAY AND " DEVIL'S " WOODS,
AND FIND THE SKYSCRAPER OF PICARDY.

By VICTOR HYDE, M.C.

(The well-known Writer on the Battlefields, and Author of " Flanders Sleeps," " East of Ypres," and other War Stories.)

ALL over the Somme bodies are still being found. They are taking them all home to a last Rest in London cemetery facing High Wood, and the chief re-burial ground for these parts.

There, as I paused awhile last summer with the newly-found Slain, hundreds of wooden crosses were awaiting replacement by the familiar grey-white headstone. For quilts, we have given the boys red roses, beautiful blue nepeta, and many another colourful border.

Each week they are burying opposite the Bois Foureaux, as the French call the stretch of timber that changed hands several times in one day's fighting in the " Blood Bath."

Only the few are identified. I tread softly down the rows and above the beds in the boys' final home, I read, " An Unknown Soldier of the Northumberland Fusiliers," or " A Soldier of the Hampshire Regiment." Over there it is the Manchesters or the Durhams. More often than not it is just " A Soldier of the Great War." For that is all we know. . . .

And thus will it go on. The battlefields have not yet given up all their dead ; bodies still lie in the mines, in the deeper trenches, and in the woods. Still more will be found and reburied in the few cemeteries kept open for the purpose. (Canadian No. 2 at Neuville St. Vaast, and Bedford House cemetery, Zillebeeke, are two others).

Of the 887 bodies found in France in 1934-35, 603 were recovered on the Somme. (As I write, the comparable figures for 1935-36 reach me from the Imperial War Graves Commission, and the proportion of bodies found in that year on the Somme—721 in 821 !—is even higher). That tragic fact alone tells you, if you did not already know, where the fight was fiercest. Do you wonder the late foe called the First Battle of the Somme the "Blood Bath " ? Do you wonder the Somme still lives tragically on ? It will be years yet before the last of the recoverable bones are found, and then there will remain thousands of the Missing who will never find their final grave. Tens of thousands of them, my friends. . . .

Longueval at the junction of the Flers—Bapaume (centre background) and Bazentin-le-Petit and Pozieres Roads, with Delville Wood a quarter of a mile to the right.

The French, who receive a ten francs reward for each body found and reported to the Commission, dig with this pecuniary object in view. They have even perfected a special tool with which, I learned at Delville Wood, they can tell whether their labours have struck wood, steel or — bones. Well, you say, someone must find the boys and bring them home. . . .

Shall I tell you the story of the strangest and loneliest grave of all ? It lies in the corn between Flers and Geuedecourt. "This way to Lord Feversham's grave," a tiny hand-lettered signpost by the roadside informs you. A quarter of a mile through thigh-high crops brings you to a little lych-gate built over a stone flag inscribed " Charles William Reginald, 2nd Earl of Feversham, Lt.-Col. Commanding 21st King's Royal Rifle Corps, killed in action *on this spot*, September 15, 1916." " Flers Day," they call the anniversary of that desperate action in the Blood Bath. The italics are mine.

It is different to every other grave in 770,000 graves, for the Second Earl sleeps alone. The tomb is privately maintained, and as regularly visited. The nearest British cemetery is A.I.F. Burial Ground, by the roadside as you breast the rise into Geuedecourt.

As recently as a few months ago we were given a tragic reminder of Flers' crimson " Day," when forty bodies were discovered, all in a cluster where they fell.

To-day, Flers has licked its sores, and in its renaissance has built itself a brewery and, as in Martinpuich, wired off its thriving crops with a plenitude of our wire and pickets that, even in their decrepitude, still serve. For ten years of " Adoption," Flers " belonged " to Portsmouth — an appropriate godfathering, as you would agree if I had time to tell you the epic of the Portsmouth boys on that historic " Day."

We will have a look at one or two others of the nigh-on a hundred hamlets which we cared for in the early aftermath. In Beaumont Hamel, that Winchester looked after, beside a brave new road of poplars in place of the giants that once we knew, tell-tale chalk mounds mark a line of filled-in trenches. A decayed pill-box lingers on.

For colourful contrast, there's the blood red of the Flanders poppy, massed in the wayside banks.

In this Hamel, too, I counted yet more of our old nissen huts, in which the economical peasant is well content to live.

Nor is Martinpuich, one of Southampton's two " god-children," entirely devoid yet of the old familiar sights. Rows of filled-in dug-outs, clearly visible in the banks of the sunken road as you drop down from Courcelette and the dawn auto 'bus from Albert, provide your first impression of this village.

But it's " Martanpwee " if you would put yourself right with the natives. On that torrid Sunday dawn of late June, my own first contact with them was disastrous. I was nearly arrested.. Shying at my camera and my maps and notebooks, and other paraphenalia of the itinerant journalist, the deputy-mayor advanced menacingly and demanded my " papers." A passing motorist had warned him of my imminent arrival, and without more ado I had been written off as a spy.

The situation threatened to become serious. As peremptorily, however, as my papers were demanded so were they refused. " I'll do as I damn well like ! " I said to myself. But that didn't get me out of an impasse and restore my set schedule.

Time to acquaint this over-zealous official with the real object of my errand (which was to visit the Mayor, but which scarcely concerns or interests you) and to remind him, how, in 1930, he sold back to me some of *our own shell cases* that we had left behind in the village. (Two, they tell me, still grace the Mayor's Parlour in Southampton.)

I was no longer the unwelcome guest.

" Now take me to the Mayor, " I demanded.

We found M. Fournet in his shirt sleeves in the cowshed, with other members of the family. Over a 7.45 a.m. rum in his living room, he proudly produced the mounted enlargement of my own photo taken six years ago at the " disadoption " ceremonies, and presented to his successor in office by the Mayor of Southampton.

Toasts were drunk, and I left His Worship to his cows, for a big itinerary lay in front of me.

Where I had entered Martinpuich suspect, I left it an honoured guest, although I confess to personal prejudices against starting the day from the bottle. . . .

All in the village seemed genuinely glad to see a Briton. A youth dismounted from his cycle and asked, " You are Eengleeshman ? " His eyes lit up at my reply. Perhaps he was thinking of the school treat we provided in 1930.

If my stay in Geuedecourt was shorter, my reception was no less hearty than, ultimately, it had been in Martinpuich.

[Photo. *Victor Hyde.*]
This new angle view of the huge Somme Battle Memorial at Thiepval—as high from base to summit as the Queen Mary from keel to masthead—shows some of the massive piers on which the 73,000 Missing in the " Blood Bath " are named.

Choosing to enter the hamlet as a pillion rider on a Graves Commission official's motor cycle, I found aged Desiré Devillers rounding up his sheep in a lane near his home, a vast blue umbrella tucked underneath his arm, and in his shirt sleeves in the sweltering Somme heat.

There, too, they still have nothing but the happiest memories of those ten " Adoption " years, and the Mayor and his daughter clapped their hands in joy at the thought that Great Britain had remembered the old ties and returned. For that is what took me back to " Gerdcour."

Come, though, let's get back to our woods, which I left to take you rambling about Flers and other parts. High Wood is thick with undergrowth again, and wild roses grow on its fringes. A barbed wire picket aslant and askew in the ditch is the sole evidence of Realism hereabouts.

It is the same at Leuze Wood, which has licked its sores, and where to-day they shoot rabbits and partridges in place of human " cannon fodder."

" Lousy " is green and dense again, except for that shooting drive.

In Delville ("Devil's") Wood, however, the canvas is all together different. There, they have purposely preserved many of the old torn trunks as veterans of the aftermath, and sporadic dumps of war material.

The old drives that intersected " Devil's " are back, too, and little cairns perpetuating the war-time nomenclature bestowed upon them. Thus you come upon your Campbell Street and your Rotten Row, your Princes Street and Regent Street.

At the foot of these bournes are rusted machine gun tripods, and, on the edge of the majestic drive, a warning legend, " Danger — It is forbidden to touch any war material." And, remembering my brute of Auchonviller (see YPRES TIMES, January, page 136), I desisted in time.

Scores of South African oaks, dressed in regular " parade ground " lines, have been planted in that magnificent expanse of turf linking the Longueval-Ginchy road with the Union's memorial, each grown from seeds taken out of the wood by emigrants to the Cape. Not for many a year, however, will they be the giants that once we knew.

Clusters, too, of wild roses flank the approach where it sweeps majestically through the wood. The monument is one of the most striking of all the scores dotted over this resurrected Picardy, with few quite its like.

From the summit of the twin turrets, approached by short, winding stairways, a wonderful panorama of the new Somme is gained, with the lone New Zealanders' Memorial chiselled out in the centre of the canvas. They tell me that, in good visibility, as many as 42 villages can be seen from this monument.

Each turret, liberally signposted in the form of arrow-heads fixed to the circular balustrades, names many of the famous " warm corners " of the Somme. High Wood, Flers, Geuedecourt, Bapaume, Le Transloy, Les Boeufs, Morval, Ginchy and near-by Guillemont and Waterlot Farm, Trones and Bernafay Woods, Arrow Head Copse, " Monty Bong," Pozieres, the Bazentins and Thiepval — the direction of all of them is given to the pilgrim.

But to see " Devil's " as it was you have to cross to its western boundary and read the two remarkable inscriptions there erected.

They plunge you right back into the inferno of 1916, when " Devil's " was more hotly contested than any other part of this vast auditorium of bellicosity, and when many an individual deed of heroism was enacted.

" *Here in a shallow trench,*" says the first, " *stood the battle headquarters of the South African Infantry during the fighting in Delville Wood.*"

The other, in its simple phraseology, and the picture it gives you, is even more historic.

" *Advancing in a north-easterly direction at 7 a.m., on July 15th, 1916, the attacking force of the South African Infantry Brigade entered Delville Wood at this point.*"

Each inscription is cut in the face of a bourne some three feet high. It is well there should be such reminders.

" Delville Cottage " is another high-light of South Africa-sur-Somme. This is the home of Mr. and Mrs. Beckwith, who are in charge of the grounds and the memorial, and which, built in the English style, stands on the Longueval side of the wood bordering the wide drive.

A rest room is set aside in the cottage for any tourist who cares to enter, those from the Union receiving an especially warm welcome.

Across the road from Delville Cottage is Delville Wood Cemetery. South again from the cemetery, the wicket Waterlot confronts you. But it no longer menaces.

Waterlot Farm has been rebuilt on the same site that was once so stubborn, with beet-root fields, a new "sucrerie," and a brickworks clustered round its peaceful quarters. For All's Quiet Now on the " Devil's " Front.

Leave " Devil's," and at the Hebuterne and Longueval cross-roads you express mild surprise at an abandoned and rusted dump of shells and gas-containers and derelict barbed-wire that, like the dumps we remarked in January, is again no one's concern. As the rest, it is a cosmopolitan bag.

The new Longueval is one of the largest of the Somme villages, in which respect it ranks with tee-shaped Pozieres and rambling Combles, which is shaped like a star-fish — all angles.

My visit there coincided with one of those interminable French religious processions, with the choirboys in their picturesque red and white cassocks and bearing banners aloft, girls in the snow-white of their communion dresses, and priests and others chanting as, slowly, they tour the town.

Geuedecourt and " Monty Bong " were similarly occupied, to leave their streets, as Combles had done, strewn with the flowers they drop as a form of sacrificial offering.

Combles is die-hard as these other hamlets we have visited, and is happy enough to retain the squat, tawdry-looking " nissen."

But Daours beats the lot. " This way to the Divisional Baths," I read on a street corner there last summer ! The paint is as fresh as the day those unnamed divisional pioneers daubed it on twenty years ago ! I badly needed a bath, but, like the man who " couldn't find any b ———— Gate to shut," when the old cry went down the ranks, " Last man shut the Menin Gate ! " no sign either could I find of any " Divisional Baths " !

Every house in Daours still carries on its gates its British billeting notices — so many *hommes*, so many *chevaux*.

A strange place, this Daours. "*C'est la guerre !*" is all I could get out of the *patron* of my estaminet when I taxed him with these surprising echoes. We decide we could have told the old chap that ourselves, and, draining our glass, tramp on in further search of our Somme.

Here, hang it, we are supposed to be in Longueval ! May be it was the speed limit that sent us route-marching off to Combles. For, where the fight was to the fastest, they've imposed a twenty-mile limit through the somnolent hamlet. It's the same in Ginchy, where, as in Longueval, the village fathers do not care to be bustled out of their newly-won passivity. Outside Longueval's new church, anti-aircraft guns look grotesquely out of place.

We will run on due east out of Longueval, three miles to another of them, Morval, and try to recapture the scene of another signal British triumph.

A picturesque, elongated village, this new Morval, that has gone one better with the " nissen " and grafted on its own windows and other demilitarised home comforts.

A couple of small factories and the French grid system running down the main street are your chief impressions of a hamlet once razed completely to the ground — these and the inevitable estaminets where you become as inevitably involved over the intracacies of small French change.

We will leave Morval and return to the Somme woodlands. Whereas " Devil's " purposely retains its stricken timbers, the same echoes in Trones and Bernafay Woods linger on because none has bothered to chop them down.

Bernafay, indeed, definitely lives in the past. Five giants that were in the throes of their *rigor mortis* these twenty years ago still rear up out of the new Bernafay, like so many grotesque aerial masts, and you know for a surety that a war once passed that way.

The fact, however, that you can see right through the wood in this instance has no connection with the soldier's Somme: they have merely filched from it for pit props for the northern mines.

On the edge of Bernafay, streamline, in-a-hurry rail cars thunder past Montauban ("Monty Bong") halt on their way from Albert to Peronne. "Monty Bong" itself, an undistinguished hamlet as so many others hereabouts, has been rebuilt an inconvenient half-mile away from its "iron road."

From almost all these resurrected Somme villages, and at practically every compass point, the massive Thiepval Memorial is etched out on the sky-line as a great beacon. You do not ask your direction on the Somme; you take it by Thiepval. It's the skyscraper of Picardy.

I'll say it is as high from base to platformed summit as the "Queen Mary" from keel to masthead, and I won't even bother to check up on my figures. Workmen regilding the flagstaffs on that lofty eminence are as dwarfs in the sky. And yet they tell me it is not as high as originally planned!

In its shade, ex-Chief Dispatch Rider C. Smith keeps the Prince of Wales Cafe afore-mentioned (see your *Ypres Times* for January) and will proudly show you the dais which the Duke of Windsor (as Prince of Wales) and President Lebrun used when His Majesty unveiled the memorial in 1932. After that ceremony, ex-Don. R. Smith chose the only possible title for his premises.

A character, this Smith, whose greatest achievement and pride is to have been foreman of works on the largest of all the British Westfront memorials. Then he rebuilt their local church for them, and is still waiting for his money.

Sooner or later, most pilgrims find their way to his well-stocked bar. His only competitor for the pilgrim's trade is lined and hardy Mme. Doutart Marie Louise, picturesque hostess of the "Cafe of the Heroine of the Ruins," and the first Thiepvalite of all to venture back. She and "Smeeth" are great friends.

It is impossible, in this still heavily-scarred commune, not to run up against them — against ex-Chief Don.R. C. Smith, late 55th West Lancs. Division, and not only mine host of the "Cafe Prince de Galles," but owner, also, of the chateau grounds (the chateau they will never rebuild) and Marie Louise who ekes out a living round the corner from her battlefields comrade, "Smeeth."

Now it is time to turn our backs on the Somme, pondering as we go on John Oxenham's lines that I came upon in the War Park at Hamel. It is only a tiny plaque let into the wall, and you might well miss it.

Tread softly here, go reverently and slow!
God help us if we fail to pay our debt!

Doesn't it make *you* feel humble, too? I'll say you feel the same way about it as I did.

Place Names in Flanders as known to the Troops.

By C. L. BERRY,
Captain, late 13th Welsh Regiment.

THOUGH the pronunciation of English place-names is (or was, until Railways and Radio intervened) essentially traditional, the Englishman strives valiantly to pronounce phonetically the names he meets with abroad. He may be no linguist, but he is essentially conscientious. The results of his efforts are often truly amazing as the Great War illustrated on the Western Front to a degree never before attained.

The names of the two base towns — Rouen and Etaples — were both liable to mispronunciation, though ' Ruin ' was, one suspects, a variant of spurious origin. Etaples, however, was known to the British rank and file as either ' Eat Apples ' or ' Eetaps.' There was no thought of humour in such pronunciations which were the nearest the troops could get to the French sounds. All names were, of course, pronounced in the ' obvious ' way. Thus even the late Earl of Ypres referred always to Saint Omer as if the Saint were a Persian poet.

Those who served in Belgium and in the really Flemish portions of northern France were faced with the greatest difficulties, yet to some extent circumstances favoured them. Lack of intercourse between our troops and the Flemish peasantry, and later the complete devastation of what was left of Belgium, rendered superfluous all niceties of pronunciation and even many of the names themselves. Thus woods, roads, rivers, farms and chateaux were re-named *de novo* by the British Army. No one knew or ever enquired the real names of Admiral's Road, Sanctuary Wood, Irish Farm or Goldfish Château. The Rail-head for the Ypres Salient was Hazebrouck which, when given its normal pronunciation of ' Hazy-brook,' had a delightfully English sound. Ypres itself was, from the first, a source of trouble to the troops. The Commander-in-Chief, Sir John French, as he was then, called it ' Wipers,' and so did most of the ' other ranks ' in the original Expeditionary Force. Soon, however, our troops became aware that this pronunciation was not only incorrect — though really not far from the Flemish — but that it was a subject of ridicule. Immediately it became unpopular and was rapidly dropped, so that after 1916 it was never heard again. Thereafter this ancient town, then but a heap of ruins, was known as ' Eepray ' or ' Eepriz.' Unfortunately we do not know how the name was pronounced by Cromwell's Expeditionary Force, who were among the first to serve in the Salient. Near to, and south of, Ypres were ' Dicky Bush ' (Dickebusch), ' Plug Street ' (Ploegsteert) and 'White Street' (Wytschaete). All these were spontaneous and genuine attempts to pronounce the names as written, and indeed they were very fair approximations. The last syllable of Wytschaete was sometimes pronounced ' shirt ' instead of the more usual ' sheet,' but this was probably a humourous improvement on the natural effort towards accuracy.

Near Poperinghe was the hamlet of Hopoutre, a name almost too good to be true. Naturally it was always called ' Hop Out.' Certain names, in fact, really *were* too good to be true. Noticing the possibilities of the ending common to such names as Erquinghem, Terdeghem, etc., someone (ingenious but unknown) gave the names of Bandagehem, Dosinghem and Mendinghem to certain casualty clearing stations in the Ypres Salient. At least one of these had its own station on our military light railway, where its spurious name was boldly displayed. Years hence some Belgian Place Name Society will ascribe it to a Flemish etymology of respectable antiquity. Goederwearsveldt was, however, no invention of the War, but a genuine name which, if it could not be avoided, was referred to always as ' Gerty wears velvet.'

Farther south was the historic town of Bailleul, generally spoken of as ' Balloo ' by those who knew not Scotland or Oxford. There were other purely French names which assumed strange form in those days. The Village of Choques, near Bethune, was known as ' Shocks.' Sailly-la-Bourse lost in dignity but gained in homeliness when called, as it usually was, ' Sally Booze.' Rue du Bois, near Neuve Chapelle, was ' Roody Boys.' Leuze Wood (Bois de Leuze) was familiarly known as ' Lousy Wood ' — such a description might have been truthfully applied to many places at that time. Mouquet Ferme was either ' Mucky Farm ' or ' Moo-cow Farm,' the latter being the most usual as well as the most attractive name. Chamblain Chatelain was known, half humourously and half in despair, as ' Charlie Chaplain.' Both Fonquevillers and Auchonvillers (near Arras) were easily and inevitably anglicised as ' Funky Villas ' and ' Ocean Villas.' The former was both topical and, in the true Johnsonian sense, temporary while both unexpectedly suggested thoughts of home and peace — the joys of the suburbs or of ' Sea View ' at Margate.

Tanks in Action

By MAJOR W. T. SARGEAUNT,
Editor: *Royal Tank Corps Journal*.

YOUR Editor has asked me to write my experiences of Tanks in action for *The Ypres Times*. I am much flattered, but I am not really the person to do it. I joined the Tank Corps in 1917 and fought with them in France, but I was fortunate enough not to have too many thrilling experiences. One can have too much of that sort of thing!

But I do remember one or two tight corners. I had better tell you about the worst. We were moving up into action on the night of August 7th near Villers Bretonneux.

Photo.] [*Imp. War Museum.*
Battle of the St. Quentin Canal. Mark V Tanks going forward with the "cribs" designed to enable them to cross the Hindenburg Line. Bellicourt, 29th September, 1918.

To achieve surprise, we had moved by night for several days. We were all dog tired. In those days on approaching the Line long white tapes were laid down to guide the Tanks. The Commanders then walked in front guiding the driver either with a shaded light or a cigarette. The Tanks moved slowly in bottom gear to avoid excessive noise.

We were getting near the Line. There was a bit of light shelling. The sky was faintly illuminated with distant Verey lights. It was raining a little. I was leading the first tank of my section, guiding it with a shaded electric torch. A shell burst rather near. Instinctively I ducked and in an instant was caught fast in a loose tangle of barbed wire. In falling I dropped my torch. The tank came slowly on. I shouted. The driver did not hear. The tank came slowly on. I twisted my body round so that I was between the horns. The tank came slowly on. I wondered what it would feel like to be dead, but chiefly how long I should take dying. The tank came slowly on. The belly slopes up in front and for a short time it did not start to squash me. But the tank came slowly on. Now I was right under it. My face was crushed into the wire. I have the marks still. A bolt in the bottom of the tank slowly ripped a groove in my back. The breath was crushed out of my body. But the worst was over. I realised there was just enough clearance. I was saved. The corporal came running out of the side door. I told him exactly what I thought of him and his crew. His only reply was, " Thank God you're alive to swear at me " !

And now extracts from a most vivid account of the first engagements of British and German tanks, written for the Royal Tank Corps Journal by the Section Commander concerned.

" An infantryman jumped out of a trench in front of my tank and waved his rifle agitatedly . . . I slowed down and opened the flap. " Look out, there's Jerry-tanks about," he shouted. This was the first intimation we had that the Germans were using tanks. I gazed ahead and saw three weirdly-shaped objects moving towards the eastern edge of Cachy. Behind the tanks I could see lines of advancing infantry. My attention was now fully fixed on the German tank nearest to me, which was moving slowly. The right-hand gunner, Sergeant J. R. McKenzie, was firing steadily at it, but as I kept continually zig-zagging, and there were many shell-holes, accurate shooting was difficult. Suddenly there was a noise like a storm of hail beating against our right wall, and the tank became alive with splinters. It was a broadside of armour-piercing bullets from the German tank. The crew lay flat on the floor. I ordered the driver to go straight ahead, and we gradually drew clear, but not before our faces were splintered. Steel helmets protected our heads. The left hand gunner was now shooting well. His shells were bursting very near to the German tank. I opened a loophole at the top side of the cab for better observation, and when opposite our opponent, we stopped. The gunner ranged steadily nearer and then I saw a shell burst high up on the forward part of the German tank. It was a direct hit. He obtained a second hit almost immediately lower down on the side facing us, and then a third in the same region.

It was splendid shooting for a man whose eyes were swollen by gas, and who was working his gun single-handed, owing to shortage of crew. The German tank stopped abruptly and tilted slightly. Men ran out of a door at the side.

And here is another story, also from the Journal, of the experiences of an Officer whose tank got right amongst the enemy in the early dawn. He lost his way.

" Owing to the ground mist and darkness, it was impossible to see where they were. They knew they were right in amongst the Germans because of the intense machine gun fire at close range, yet they could not see them. Glanville decided to tackle the situation by driving his tank directly against the bullets in the hope of crushing the machine-guns responsible. But all to no purpose . . . The compass, upset by the firing, was not reading true, and the blackness outside prevented him picking up any landmarks. Bullets had pierced the tank, and he and most of the crew had been wounded ! Trying to think out the best course of action he repeated subconsciously aloud, " What shall I do ? What shall I do ? ' One of the crew, in a state of panic, said : ' Surrender, sir ! Surrender ! Glanville told him brusquely to shut up . . . . He got out in an attempt to find his bearings, but it was no use. Getting in again he told the crew that they must wait until the moon came out, and by it's position he would know which way to steer. About fifteen minutes' suspense followed. Then the moon did come out. He took a bearing by it and the tank started to move back."

When I tell people I am in the Tank Corps they always ask me " Isn't it frightfully hot inside, and *isn't* it awful not being able to see anything when you are all closed down ? " These are standard questions just as people always ask fishermen " How can you have the patience?" It very often is frightfully hot inside. But we who have been infantrymen know that it is very often still hotter outside. And you can see far more peeping out of a slit in a tank that you can lying on your stomach flat, in a shell hole, hoping for the best ! As old Bruce Bairnsfather used to say " If you know's of a better 'ole, got to it." And after three years experience of fighting on my feet I found the Tank Corps decidedly a " better 'ole."

Empire's War Graves

Hallowed Task which Has No Finality.

Pathos and Beauty.

THE Seventeenth Annual Report of the Imperial War Graves Commission has just been issued. As in the past, it contains much interesting matter and some beautiful photographs of the Empire's War Cemeteries and memorials in all parts of the world, bearing testimony to the painstaking and efficient manner in which the graves of the fallen have been constructed and are being maintained.

Impressive Figures.

The total number of the Empire's war dead is 1,104,890. Of that number 587,117 have been identified and buried in war graves, while 513,773 are recorded as "missing." The bodies, however, of 180,861 of the latter have been found but not identified, and have perforce been buried as " Unknown." The names of all the " missing." (including the 180,861), have been engraved on collective memorials erected in the vicinity of the spot where they fell.

It should be explained that these figures are not final — perhaps they never can be — for every week the dead are still being found on the old battlefields. In the course of the twelve months under review 820 bodies of fallen British soldiers were found in France and 63 in Belgium by metal-searchers, French government search parties and farmers. Of the former number, no fewer than 721 were discovered in the area of the Somme. The discovery in every case was reported to the Commission, which arranged for re-burial in a British War Cemetery by its own staff. Notification was sent to the next-of-kin whenever a body was identified. It was found possible during the year to send information of this nature in 96 cases.

During the same period the French officials found and re-buried in one Department (the Pas-de-Calais) alone, the total of 795 French and 810 German soldiers. These figures compare with totals of 732 and 1,679 in 1934-35.

Eton Memorial School.

The Eton Memorial School at Ypres continues to benefit the children of the staff of the Commission who live in that area. Of the 102 pupils attending the school at the time of writing no fewer than 86 are children of men employed by the Commission. The Annual Maintenance Grants, designed to enable parents living out of Ypres to send their children to England to be educated, are much appreciated. Last year forty such children received grants.

Freehold Sites Transferred to Belgian State.

The sites of the British and Dominion memorials in Belgium, owned by British Dominions, by representatives of British units, or by private persons, have recently been transferred to the Belgian State. This transfer has for effect that the freehold of all authorised British memorials of the Great War, not already owned by the Belgian Government, now vest in that Government, but the Dominions, British units, or private owners will continue to enjoy undisturbed possession of the sites as long as they are used for their present purpose. The Imperial War Graves Commission will safeguard their respective interests.

"Last Post" at Menin Gate.

The Commission has placed on record the deep debt that it owes to M. Pierre Vandenbraamsbussche, O.B.E., the Police Commissaire at Ypres, who died twelve months ago. It was he who, in conjunction with M. Kock, proprietor of the Hotel Britannique, Ypres, inaugurated the sounding of the "Last Post" nightly at the Menin Gate. The Surrey Council of the British Legion has presented the Burgomaster of Ypres with a cheque for £400. The annual interest accruing from this capital sum will ensure the continuation of this moving little ceremony of remembrance for all time.

Beautiful Gardens of Sleep.

The number of visitors to our war cemeteries in France and Belgium last summer was quite up to the figure of the previous year, and the Visitors' Books showed that they had journeyed from all parts of the Empire. Many of them were gratified to find that these hallowed God's acres have been laid out, and are being maintained, after the manner of an old-world garden in the British Isles. One of the chief features of the cemeteries, and one which has evoked universal approval and admiration, is the mown grass. These swards, smooth as a Thames-side lawn and yielding softly to the tread, are common to nearly all the cemeteries. In combination with the stately poplars standing sentinel overhead, the spring, summer and autumn flowers following in seasonal succession, and the larks singing their joyous paeons of praise in the sky, they give to these "Silent Cities" an essentially British atmosphere, which is appreciated by visitors from the homeland.

On the occasion of the unveiling by His ex-Majesty King Edward VIII of the National Memorial erected by the Canadian Government on Vimy Ridge, opportunity was taken of conducting many of the 6,000 pilgrims from Canada to the cemeteries and former battlefields of France and Belgium ; and in October, Sir Isaac Isaacs, formerly Governor-General of Australia, made a tour of the cemeteries on the Western Front. At the conclusion of the journey he remarked : " How anyone with any pretence to humanity can glorify aggressive war after seeing or even contemplating the silent testimony of its sin and futility as the cemeteries present, I cannot imagine."

There are few things in the imperfect time through which we are now passing to which the adjective " perfect " can be more truthfully applied than to the work of the Imperial War Graves Commission.

Henry Benson.

* * *

NEXT-OF-KIN.

The Editor, *Ypres Times*.

Sir,

From time to time I receive letters from next-of-kin asking if the remains of a soldier posted as "Missing" are among recent re-burials. May I, through the pages of our leading ex-Service publication, refer all such enquirers to that most humane and solicitous of Government Departments, the Imperial War Graves Commission, at 32, Grosvenor Gardens, London, S.W.1 ? Provided their present addresses are on the files of the Commission, next-of-kin are automatically notified in the case of all identifications twenty years after.

Yours very truly,

Victor Hyde.

THE CLOTH HALL AT YPRES.

Mr. L. N. Murphy, Curator and Founder of the Ypres Salient War Museum, raises an interesting point in a letter to the *Daily Telegraph*.

Mr. Murphy states that the oak used in the Cloth Hall at Ypres was brought as rafts by sea from what is now known as Yugo-Slavia. The beams, being then green trees, became full of salt on the journey to Ypres, and the salt for ever kept the spiders away and even to the last never a cobweb was observed on the beams of this famous building, the first stone of which was laid on March 1st, 1200. Is this not the reason why the death-watch beetle left them alone also ?

Light and Shade at the Front .

(*By an* ex-R.B.)

VILLAGES like Riviéra, Beaumetz, Simoncourt, Grandrullecourt, Neville Vitasse, Aubigny, Dainville and Wancourt, to name a few, are familiar to those readers whom duty called to the Arras Sector, and memories of them naturally will be pleasant or otherwise according to individual experience.

A feature of Wancourt was its little cemetery, on the outskirts, where artificial wreaths and suchlike were scattered pell-mell, but the shell-fire appeared not to have disturbed the coffins underneath. Bearing on this, Neuve Eglise, to the east of Bailleul and just over the frontier (and if it was the *new* church then that building, which lay in ruins, had suffered an early demise) was one of those places where the stone effigy of a saint was fixed so securely to the wall that all the shelling combined had not shifted it ; nor was it broken but looked down calmly on the tumbled rubble and stones.

From what one remembers of Simoncourt that village was a bleak little place. It stood on a plain and was unsheltered from the winds, and was reached by wading through wastes of snow, but although it offered few or no amenities out of the line it was a main route for the transit of mules and horses, presumably for use in the then coming Arras offensive ; incessant strings of these animals led up to the line during the winter, at all times of the day and night. Beaumetz was compact and well built and seemed to have suffered little damage. A long trench (Flank Street) led up from Beaumetz and linked it to the lower end of the village of Riviéra. The depth of the brick work below ground level spoke well for the construction of some of these houses.

Riviéra stood on a slope and its long winding street led up from Flank Street on the left to a trench which opened out on the right and led to Fleet Street, Chancery Lane, and other trenches which all formed part of the system facing the enemy line. A colonial battery was emplaced to the left, down in a hollow behind the houses, and the effect of this position was to throw back an echo so that one always heard a double reverberation after each shot.

A small shop stood a little above the entrance to Flank Street, on the opposite side, and stocked various odds and ends. A young woman served there and was often under shell fire ; at least the shop was and she was in it. Regular features, an olive complexion, hair dressed neatly in the Titian style, and a sedate refinement which masked an underlying strength not apparent to a casual observer. Late one afternoon a shell burst near the back garden, but there were no hysterics about her ; she just went on serving. That little shop must have seen many divisions come and go ; a main route out of the line led off a few yards past there and then Riviéra soon was left behind.

Further up on the same side of the street stood the Convent of St. Sepulcré, with its name emblazoned over the door. This was an austere looking building strongly built of dark grey stone, and its cold flagged interior afforded excellent shelter to the troops. A large shell had damaged the roof, causing the rear half to dip at its forward left corner very similar to a ship which is showing a list on the port bow.

Early one morning after " stand-to," when things were quiet, duty took the writer out of the line into Riviéra, and he arrived about the same time as a desultory shelling. Two women passed presently on their way down to the bomb proof shelters at the lower end, near the First Aid station, and they presented an interesting contrast in bearing. The elder, who was very clean and trim—as they both were—had white hair and the clean-cut resolute features of the " emigré " type ; her companion was taller, sturdier, and much younger, but plainly undecided, and it needed only a glance to see that the old dame was " number one on the gun." Soon after they had gone a stretcher party came down, with their stretcher held at the hip, and a shell screamed over just as they

knew they had reached Sombrin. In the Autumn months the earthy smell of fallen leaves and wet bracken heralded the approach of winter (as does the familiar cry of " Fine wa-al-nut !" at home) and some cold spells in the line, but when this route was made in advanced Spring, after Nature had awakened fully from her lethargy and when everything had sprung to life, then foliage and wild grass abounded and the air was redolent with a woodland perfume.

As one entered Sombrin small farms and cottages extended along on the right in loose order ; on the left one came first to a rough earthern embankment which rose gradually from ground level to a height of six or seven feet and then fell off to a duck pond. A large field sloped back from the pond and in this field, screened from view by some trees, the Company cooker performed its mysteries, and beyond the pond—on a small slope fronting a lime-washed wall—was situate a well. Q.M.S. lay ahead on the right, the Maire's house was beyond that, and further ahead the street merged into open country. Sombrin was off the beaten track, one seldom saw a horse and cart pass, but the staccato thud of the guns was heard day and night, and the skyline beyond the embankment was lit up by the flashes.

It is probable that nothing more stirring than cock-crow was heard in this sleepy little hollow until the war came and then, year in, year out, troops marched in,

" Oh, look at the miles we've done,
Oh, look at the miles we've done,
Oh, look at the miles we've done,
And the miles we have to do !"

and brought with them the cheery yet imperious calls of their regimental bugles.

" Charley, Charley, listen to me-e-e !"

(or a variant : " It's never too late, it's never too late, to me-n-n-d !" or yet another, " You'll never come back, you'll never come back, ali-i-i-ve !")

" Wake up, Charley,
Get your hat and jacket on,
Wake up, Charley,
Get out of be-d-d-d !"

(sometimes Réveillé was played on two bugles, one high and the other low),

" Charley, Charley, get your — "

(CRASH ! The barn door flies open and an N.C.O. tramps in.)

" HI ! SHOW A LEG HERE, WHAT ABOUT IT ? " (inarticulate sounds of anguish). " HI ! COCK YOUR BUSBY ! GET THE STRAW OUT OF YOUR EYES, EVERYBODY ! RIFLEMAN SMITH !"

Rifleman S. : " Corporal ! "

N.C.O. : " You're Orderly Man instead of Brown, reported sick ! "

" Charley, Charley, listen to me-e-e !
Nine-ty two, ni-nety four,
He's never been sick before,
The poor fellow is dead !"

Rifleman S. : " But I did Orderly Man on Wednesday ! "
N.C.O. : " No argument ! WHO'S DOWN THERE IN THE CORNER ? "
Voice : " Me, Corporal."
N.C.O. : " Who's ' me ' ? "
Voice : " Robinson."

N.C.O. : " IF YOU'RE THERE WHEN I COME BACK YOU'LL BE FOR IT ! "

(*Exeunt*, SMASH ! The door bangs to and flies open on the rebound and the day's duties (Sunday) have begun.)

Soon after breakfast, after the Quarter Guard had fallen in,

"Charley, Charley, listen to me-e-e!
Come and do a picket, boys,
Come and do a guard!
It's never very easy
But it isn't very hard!"

and other parties had paraded for fatigues; the day being Sunday and subject to Orders permitting, anyone at a loose end could, if he chose, attend an informal sort of Church Service.

N.C.O. (looking into barn): "Any C. of E.'s or R.C.'s here?" "Where's Dan O'Sh — —? Here, Dan, you lead off with these," and away went Dan O'Sh — — (afterwards Corporal O'Sh — —) with *his* party.

When the fatigues were finished the men dropped in by one's and two's, and attention would turn towards the post,

"Joey, Joey, Joey, Joe-e-e-e-e!"

A shell screamed over

or things would dally along towards dinner, unless —

N.C.O. (looking into barn): "Who's in here? Fall in everybody for baths!"
1st Voice: "Are we supposed to be 'avin' a rest, mate?"
2nd Voice: "Strike me pink, we are an' all!"
1st Voice: "It's enough t' turn a bald man grey!"

As readers know, and so it scarcely needs mention, there were baths at the front —and baths. The man who was on a carrying party for hours in the rain (as the night sped on the harder it rained); the one who slipped on a bit of sandbag by the communication trench and flopped on his back in a puddle; *he* had a bath. ("What did he say? Oh, 'Evins! Pray do not ask!'") This bath at Sombrin was taken in a bucket, and a blanket was hung to screen the men from the wintry winds. Four or five buckets were ranged against the wall, and the sergeant stood outside the blanket and doused each bather with an icy cold sluice from a bucket as he came out from the hot one, this being done to save anyone from catching cold. Long months before that there was an issue of rissoles, and when these rissoles were dished out and the sentry on duty at the Guard Room —

But there, a soldier lives in the present, and dinner made up for it all :
"Charley, Charley, listen to me-e-e !
Come to the cook-house door, boys,
Come to the cook-house door !"
and after dinner the Sunday was one's own excepting for those on duty,
"Rations, rations, ra-tions !"
or defaulters,
"Charley, Charley, listen to me-e-e !
You can be a defaulter as long as you like
So long as you answer your name !"

The writer had a wash and then called at a farm by arrangement to buy some biscuits.

"Bonjour, Madame ; pouvez vous me vendre les biscuits cette aprés-midi ?"
"Certainement ; veuillez vous entrer ?"
and he found company present in the person of Victor and the latter's civilian friend.

Old Vic. was a veteran in uniform, of the type one often saw on duty at railway stations, or quays ; dressed in a dark blue uniform and hooded cloak, kepi, a long rifle with the butt resting on the ground, and a long rakish looking bayonet. Dinner was over and madame sat watching some coffee which was on the hob of the stove ; little Jeannette (aged four) sprawled near her mother's chair.

"Hullo, comment ce va, Petite ?" Silence. "Bon ?" "O-ui."
"Veuillez-vous accepter un peu de chocolat anglais ?" Silence, and a laugh from the company ; a small hand reached out, the chocolate changed ownership, and that was that.

This parlour was very cosy ; the soft light of an oil lamp imparted an agreeable depth and blend of shading to the room ; to the stained oaken table, sideboard and settees, and to the ornaments and china ; the "toute ensemble" was very pleasant, as also was the fragrant aroma of simmering coffee.

The biscuits were bought, a tiny cup or two of coffee paid for and consumed, and then Vic. produced a bottle of "cordial," labelled "Cognac." It was light golden in colour and he and his friend drank thereof with commendable frugality—just one wineglass. But these old stagers were judges. The light which age and a life of hard but honourable toil had dimmed was rekindled ; presently Vic. and his friend started to sing, and after a while, when the short winter afternoon was closing in and the writer rose to take his leave, the old veteran opened out with the "Marseillaise." He rose to his feet on the closing lines, left hand on table and right hand raised, and sung them with a stern vigour :

". . . . . Ils viennent jusque vos bras
Egorger vos fils, vos campagnes !
Aux armes, citoyens ! formez vos bataillons !
Marchons ! Marchons !
Qu-un sang impur abreuve nos sillons !"

Looking beyond the embankment and watching the flashes the thought occurred to one, how this song of Vic.'s had bridged, in an instant, more than a century of time —and France was destined to emerge from this second ordeal again unbroken.

Back to billets to find candles alight, rations laid out on some clean straw, and the troops all up and doing.

"Here he is ! Hoy, you been marking time on the Orderly Men ?" "Been chasing round for those biscuits." "Get any ?" "Two packets." "Good, I've drawn the char," and without more ado tea was in full swing.

Soon after Retreat,
"The pickets are fast retre-ating, boys,
 The distant drum is a-beating, boys,
  Pack up, boys; don't lo-iter now,
 But let us get back to our bivouac, boys!
  Lis-ten to me-e-e!......

and when Officers' Mess had sounded,
"Charley, Charley, listen to me-e-e!
 The Officers' wives have puddings and pies,
 And the sergeants' wives have skille-e-e!
  Oh-h-h, listen to me-e-e!
  Oh-h-h,, listen to me!
 The Officers' wives have puddings and pies,
 And the ser-a-geants' wives have skilly!"

one or two went to a little informal Wesleyan Service. This was held in a small one-roomed school of the "David Wilkie" type and was quite good. The clergyman was killed by a shell during the Arras offensive, and one of his congregation, a Hertfordshire lad, was later on awarded an M.M. at Ypres.

The troops turned in well before First Post, the candles were put out, and soon Sombrin was enwrapped in a stillness which is common to the countryside at night, save only for the reports of the distant gunfire and the clear notes of the bugle,
"Charley, Charley, listen to me-e-e!
 I'm calling, I'm calling,
 Calling, calling, calling,
 I'm calling to you, I'm calling to you,
 I am call-i-ing now to you-u-u."

J. EDWARDS.

(To be continued)

THE TWELFTH ANNUAL

DINNER AND DANCE

ORGANIZED BY THE

LONDON BRANCH COMMITTEE of the YPRES LEAGUE

will be held at the

PALACE HOTEL, Bloomsbury Street

(Nearest Tube Station, Tottenham Court Road)

at 6.30 p.m. for 7 p.m.

On SATURDAY, APRIL 24th, 1937

Evening Dress Optional   Decorations and Medals
TICKETS 6s. 6d. each   **Ladies Cordially Invited**

Early application for tickets, accompanied by remittance, should be sent to the Hon. Secretary, London Branch Committee, Ypres League, 20, Orchard Street, Portman Square, London, W.1., not later than April 22nd.

The Late Curé of Ypres

A Hero of the War.

We are deeply indebted to the Editor of the " Daily Telegraph " for his courtesy in permitting us to reproduce the following article from the pen of Mr. Geoffrey Winthrop Young, who writes :

The Reverend Chanoine Charles Camiel Delaere has died suddenly at the Institute Ste. Camille, near Bruges. He was one of the individual heroes of the War ; a man of unsurpassable courage and resource in action, and of great beauty and independence of character. The pupil and friend of Cardinal Mercier, he had been Professor of Flemish literature and head of the college at Dixmude, had retired to become Curé of St. Pierre, one of the four great churches of Ypres, and had just completed the restoration of his church when the siege began.

After the first battle of Ypres the city itself was left deserted by the surrounding armies and supposedly empty. Into its subterranean cellars and the " caves " in its earthen walls drifted a derelict population, numbering during the autumn and winter of 1914 little fewer than 10,000. Of these, the bombardment took toll day and night. Starvation and epidemics began. Armed deserters, the more dangerous for the uncovering of the 'famous wine cellars, looted freely. The civic government had disappeared. The armies had no means of coping with a population whose presence they had forbidden.

Into this desperate situation the Curé of St. Pierre flung himself with characteristic impetuosity and ability. A Committee of Public Safety was formed in the cellars, under the chairmanship of the gallant M. Stoffel, the leading Freemason, for the Curé smilingly insisted that " the Church ought to take no leading part officially in local government." A hospital was opened in the Asylum of the Sacré Coeur, with the aid of the Friends' Ambulance Unit, for the wounded children found in the cellars. Emergency police, health and salvage services were organized. From a printing press in a half-ruined shed health and other warnings were distributed. Every cellar was visited and order maintained.

The Curé himself, after his house was destroyed, continued to inhabit the Convent Ste. Marie with a few devoted nuns whom he had inspired with his courage. During long months, wherever the 17-inchers fell, crushing some crowded cellar, his tall figure in its black soutane, with grey curls flying back from the high forehead and the aquiline, powerful, humorous face, was always first upon the scene, digging, rescuing, or giving the last consolations to soldier or civilian, in the dark or by the light of conflagration. Usually he was accompanied by the heroic Soeur Marguérite, whose journal of the siege remains as a remarkable record of their work. His curate was killed beside him and, later, his lorry-driver : his soutane was torn on several occasions by flying fragments. But he bore a charmed life. His spirit survived, unshaken, conditions which wore down in the end the strongest nerves, and he possessed a unique power even of banishing panic from among a crowd of children under heavy shell-fire.

In the intervals of bombardment his irresistible energy and ready wit initiated continually new remedial measures. The typhoid epidemic was combated, in collaboration with the Friends' Ambulance, by the distribution of purified water from barrels ; the town swimming bath was similarly purified for the troops ; a dangerous search for typhoid cases and carriers was conducted over the whole devastated area ; more than 30,000 inoculations were given at emergency stations ; typhoid wards were opened, shelled, and again re-opened, and orphanages for girls and boys were established, staffed, and moved again as the firing advanced. In co-operation with the Aide Civile Belge, constituted under Countess Vanden Steen and Countess Louise d'Ursel, milk for babies was distributed over the whole region, hospitals were opened, food and clothes supplied, and even local industries restarted. And all this from a base in a ruined town, continuously shelled and often in flames, and completely cut off from the world by the war zone of the Allied Armies behind, no less than by the trenches in front.

After the battle of April, 1915, what was left of Ypres was destroyed by fire, and the cellars were finally evacuated. The Curé was the last civilian to leave the ruins. But he remained on the edge ; and, day after day, armed with charts and clues supplied to him and commandeering what lorry he might he dashed into the rubble remains of the town and dug up or rescued the buried church vessels, the museum treasures, the historic pictures, and the civic documents. An incident which delighted King Albert was his rescue from a burning house, of the Freemasons' processional flag and its return to the opponents of his Church, with a characteristically witty and courteous message. If Ypres still possesses part of its traditional treasures, and if its citizens have been able to rebuild their houses on the former sites, and, when they wished, in the original style, it is due to the patriotism, forethought, and dauntless courage of this one man.

Ypres destroyed, the Curé withdrew to the headship of one of the orphanages he had created, and devoted himself to collecting funds, organizing relief, and seeing that his orphans were trained as builders, carpenters, etc., ready for the work of reconstruction. On the first day of the Armistice he was back in

Ypres, constructing the wooden shed which he named the first cathedral, school, and town hall of the new city. Instituted as Dean of St. Martin's Cathedral, he threw all his remaining energies into the task of rebuilding the town, its churches, convents, and houses, of which he himself had preserved sample mouldings and specimen fragments as they fell. His great work came to a fitting end when he was able to conduct the re-dedication service of his own reconstructed cathedral. Decorated by the armies, honoured by the friendship of his King and Queen, and looked upon as an almost legendary figure, he then retired, to become director of an orphanage near Bruges which he himself had founded.

Our final memory of him was last year, venerable, upright, and masterful, but infinitely tolerant, and still alert with racy, sympathetic humour, as he walked in his rose garden at sunset, with the children swarming round him, and catching at his hand for the peculiar sanctity of his smiling " Good night " blessing.

* *

We likewise deeply appreciate the following letter received from the War Office :—

The War Office,
London, S.W.1.
3rd February, 1937.

Sir,

I am commanded by the Army Council to say that the Council have noticed with regret the death of the Reverend Charles Camiel Delaere, who in 1914 was Curé of St. Pierre in Ypres, and remained in the city until its destruction. The Council are well aware of the keen interest taken by your League in all those who were concerned in the defence of Ypres, and they desire to express their appreciation of the curé's devoted labours for the succour of all those soldiers and civilians who remained in the city. His heroism and resource must be well remembered by many members of your League, and the Council are confident that his unsparing efforts in the relief of distress will not soon be forgotten.

I am, Sir,
Your obedient servant,
(Signed) A. E. WIDDOWS.

The Secretary,
The Ypres League,
20, Orchard Street,
London, W.1.

Ypres British School

It is pleasing to record the great interest shown by our members in the Ypres British School following the publication in the last issue of the Seventh Annual School Report. Many letters have been received at Headquarters, each expressing appreciation of the splendid work being carried out at Ypres, work of really a national character, and for further information we have pleasure to convey to members an idea of the actual instruction given to pupils and how this instruction has helped to befit them for the battle of life.

The children are taught Arithmetic and English by the individual method, and the apparatus in both these subjects is supplied to meet all grades from three years onwards. A record of each child's progress is kept in the Teacher's record-book and this is studied with the object of arranging the fortnightly programme of work. Practical work is undertaken in " weighing," " measuring " and " shopping." To supplement the childrens' own library a teacher's library is provided to which the children have free access. This library includes " anthologies of poetry " suitable for young children and a collection of stories and myths of all nations and childrens' classics such as " Peter Pan," " Water Babies," etc.

Topical events are followed such as the Johannesburg Flight and the voyage of the sailing ship, " Cap Pilar." History, Geography and Literature play an important role in the studies.

Nature records are kept in the form of "Nature calendars " and the development of bulbs, silkworms and tadpoles are watched. Handwork is a part of the course and includes needlework, knitting, canvas-work, drawing, painting and toy-making with waste-material such as matchboxes, cotton-reels, etc.

Lunch for the little ones is instituted as a set meal ; the tables are prepared and cleared and utensils are washed up by the children themselves. Particular care is taken to train them in being tidy with their cupboards.

Singing, rythmic training and physical exercises are part of the everyday curriculum. That the care and training is beneficial and permanent is borne out by the fact that within the past few years the following positions have been competed for and gained by the " Leavers " of the School : Aircraft Apprentices — Boy Entrants, R.A.F. — Royal Navy Signals — Writer in the Royal Navy — The Army School, Chepstow — Clerks — Poster Designers — Civil Service Examinations — Scholarship to Newcastle — Student in the Nursing Service — Dressmakers — Maids.

For recreation and sports in the School the following are taught and thoroughly enjoyed by the children — Country and Folk Dancing, Swimming (thirty certificates of the L.S.S.A. have already been awarded), Cross-country Running and there are the annual sports arranged to which adults are specially invited, Concerts, Day's Outing to the grounds of the

Marquise du Parc, and annual trips to the seaside for both children and parents.

One cannot speak too highly of this innovation of a British School for the children of Britons who, either from choice or circumstance have taken up residence in a foreign land, and who are thus given the opportunity of preserving the national character in their offspring to a far greater extent than they could possibly do otherwise. Who can deny that, but for the Ypres British School, the character of these children might not become too merged in the Continental and more and more lose touch and sympathy with the land of their fathers, which is their heritage.

All communications on matters concerning the School should be addressed to the Hon. Secretary, Ypres British School, c/o Ypres League, 20, Orchard Street, London, W.1.

Branch Notes

PURLEY BRANCH.
Re-union Dinner.

The Ninth Annual Re-union Dinner of the Purley Branch was held at the Red Lion Hotel, Coulsdon, on Friday, March 5th, and a record attendance gathered to enjoy another of these happy re-unions. The number of guests attending the 1936 Re-union Dinner, held last year in

principal Guests of the evening were General Sir Hubert Gough, G.C.M.G., K.C.B., K.C.V.O., and Lieut.-General Sir William Pulteney, G.C.V.O., K.C.B., K.C.M.G.

A telegram had been despatched to H.M. The King as follows :—

" One hundred and sixty members and guests of the Purley Branch of the Ypres

Photo by courtesy of] ["*The Croydon Advertiser.*"

Ninth Annual Re-union Dinner of the Purley Branch.

October, was 128, then considered an astonishing muster for a Branch function. This year, however, the attendance rose to 154 and but for the fact that no more could be accommodated, the number would have been higher still. Many applicants for tickets had to be disappointed.

The newly elected Chairman for the year, Major S. F. Wood, was in the Chair, and the

League, all members of the fighting forces in the Great War, assembled for their Annual Re-union Dinner at the Red Lion Hotel, Coulsdon, send loyal and devoted greetings to your Majesty " ;

and in the course of the evening the following reply was received :—

"To Chairman of Ypres League Dinner, Red Lion Hotel, Coulsdon. The King sincerely thanks members and guests of Purley Branch, Ypres League, dining together this evening for their loyal greetings which His Majesty much appreciates." (Signed) Private Secretary.

Assembly was timed for 19.00 hours, and at Zero hour the assembly sat down to enjoy the excellent rations provided. Following the toast of "The King" and the "Silent Toast" respectively — enthusiastically and reverently honoured—the Chairman rose to address the gathering and to welcome in particular the two very distinguished guests, General Sir Hubert Gough and Sir William Pulteney. The Chairman thanked them for so kindly accepting the Branch's invitation to their Re-union Dinner and expressed the hope that they would enjoy the evening. Then followed a generous appreciation of the work of his predecessors in general and Private Jim Irens in particular, the Adjutant for his part — incidentally a very great part too — and the Treasurer.

The evening's entertainment was in the capable hands of that old favourite, Captain Vernon Lee, M.C., assisted by a card expert, Corporal Paul Freeman.

The Adjutant then reported on the year's activities which included the winning of the Recruiting Prize for the sixth consecutive year. Membership of the Branch was mentioned as now numbering 309, and during the evening a further twenty-four members were recruited. Major Carr stressed his disappointment at having to refuse so many members who had applied to be present at this Re-union.

The Bombardier (E. A. R. Burden) proposed the toast of the guests in a most delightful and witty speech. It contained much good natured chaffing and did not omit the two distinguished Generals. In similar vein the Generals replied, General Gough concluding with a story of South Africa and General Pulteney one on Waterloo, both of which evoked roars of merriment.

Private MacMilne (A. Milne) paid the C.O. a warm tribute in that light and cheerful tone which marked the evening and the C.O.'s health was drunk with musical honours.

The evening concluded with old war-time songs and the company retired in good order.

* * *

LONDON BRANCH.
Children's Christmas Party.

The rendezvous for this happy function was again the Westminster City School, and on Saturday, January 2nd, one hundred and fifty youngsters gathered to enjoy a most pleasant afternoon and evening. Tea was served in the School dining room, and with the generous assistance of many adult members all were able to satisfy their appetites to the full with the many items on the menu.

After tea the whole party adjourned to the School Hall, which had been tastefully decorated for the occasion, the dominating feature being a very large Christmas tree laden with gifts and lighted with strings of coloured electric bulbs.

For one hour the close attention of the kiddies was confined to a very worthy conjuring and ventriloquial entertainment by Mr. W. G. Atholl. The invitation to several of the youngsters to mount the platform and assist in some of the tricks added greatly to the interest and hilarity of the proceedings.

Mr. Bert Lyons, a clever artist of the "lightning" variety, then proceeded to entertain them with rapid sketches of well-known persons by the aid of a black crayon and large sheets of white paper fixed on an easel. The children were invited to make their own requests for pictures, and it was a noticeable sign of the times that many famous film stars were called for.

With Mrs. Furner at the piano, Community singing then followed, the children singing with great gusto such familiar but old refrains as "Daisy, Daisy, give me your answer do" and "The Man who broke the Bank at Monte Carlo." Under the supervision of Mr. T. Ross Furner games were then indulged in, "Musical Chairs" and "Musical Bumps" being strong favourites. A prize was given to the winner of each event and rivalry for the prize was extremely keen.

Mr. Bert Lyons admirably filled the role of "Father Christmas," and each child at the conclusion of the evening's entertainment received from him a gift taken from the Christmas tree. Following the singing of "Auld Lang Syne" and "God Save The King," each child was given an apple, orange and bag of sweets as they filed out of the hall. A most enjoyable evening for all and great credit to the Organisers. Our grateful thanks to the Governors of the Westminster City School for so kindly granting permission for use of the School premises and also to those friends who contributed in any way, either by gifts or personal service. The obvious enjoyment of the children, however, remains the best thanks for us all.

J.W.F.

* * *

The Informal Gatherings continue to maintain their popularity at the Bedford Head Hotel, Maiden Lane, Strand, W.C.1, and the London Branch Committee hope to record their best ever attendances this year.

These Gatherings which have afforded so much pleasure to the many members and friends attending them in the past, are promoted with the double object of enabling ex-Service men to meet together in convivial atmosphere, to renew old acquaintances, and to further the wonderful spirit of comradeship of the Great War, which is so prominent a feature in the League's great work of Commemoration.

At the January Gathering we were favoured with an extremely interesting Talk by Major Gerald Bell, O.B.E., on "The Naval Situation To-day." The St. Dunstan Singers under the direction of Mrs. Hodson entertained us at the February Informal Gathering, and as on former occasions, their programme was admirably rendered and greatly appreciated. For the March Meeting, Captain H. D. Peabody, D.C.M., gave an Illustrated Talk on "The Ypres

Salient," which was followed with keen interest, members present being much impressed with the excellent slides shown them.

The April Informal Gathering is being held on Thursday, April 15th, at 7.30 p.m., and a programme of entertainment is being arranged for us by the ladies under the direction of Mrs. Stratton.

The London Branch Committee are arranging a seven-day Continental Tour, commencing August 7th next, and the Hon. Secretary will be pleased to forward full particulars to all interested on receipt of application.

* * *

League Secretary's Notes

In welcoming the year 1937 we ventured to predict in the January number another successful year for the Ypres League and, judging by results from the first quarter just concluded the optimistic note was not unjustified. It may be that, with our members co-operation, the Coronation Year of our gracious Patron-in-Chief will be also a red-letter year in the history of our Association.

During the past three months a most noticeable feature has been the increased receipts in regard to renewal subscriptions, receipts under this heading comparing with corresponding quarters for 1934 and 1935 and in advance of those for 1936. This is extremely satisfactory and the best indication of the League's solidity. If renewal subscriptions can be so maintained for the remainder of the year it will greatly encourage Headquarters.

We sincerely thank those members who have so promptly responded to our renewal reminders and also those who have so generously augmented their subscription with a donation to the funds. While on this subject we should like to express our best thanks to that loyal supporter of the Ypres League, Mrs. L. K. Briggs, who has repeated her kindness of former years by forwarding a donation of £5.

Each of our Branches report successful social functions for the past quarter: Colchester—a Whist Drive with 96 players; London—three very enjoyable Informal Gatherings; and Purley their Annual Re-union Dinner with record attendance of 154 (see Branch Notes) at which 24 new members were recruited.

There are distinct sighs that we shall have in the near future quite a strong Branch in the South-Essex area, and so impressed are Headquarters from reports received that it has already been decided to include the name of this Branch with the list of established Branches published on the back page of this journal. Mr. S. H. K. Geller is making every effort to get this Branch going and is confident of the result. We await with pleasurable anticipation a further report of his endeavours. Our hearty thanks and best wishes are extended to him likewise to Captain H. D. Peabody, D.C.M., who so kindly attended the initial gathering of the Branch and gave those present an interesting Illustrated Talk on "The Ypres Salient." From a collection made on the sale of cornflowers a sum of £1 was forwarded to Headquarters towards the Fund for the maintenance of the Ypres Salient Notice-boards.

From our old friends in Queensland, Australia, Messrs. C. H. Green and G. Lawson, we have received a request that in lieu of present Ypres League status as Representatives, they be permitted, together with other Officers, including Lieut.-Colonel Sir Donald Cameron, K.C.M.G., D.S.O., etc., to form a Queensland Branch with the latter distinguished soldier and diplomat as its first President. To this we have readily agreed and are writing them accordingly, at the same time thanking them for their loyal co-operation and earnest endeavours to further the interest of the Ypres League in Australia. We wish them every success.

From America likewise comes the gratifying news that several new members wish to be enrolled and others enquiring about membership. The Branch Recruiting Prize of £5 is again offered to the Branch that obtains the greatest number of new members throughout the year. We anticipate close competition this year, it being hinted to us that a determined effort is being made to wrest the honour from our Purley Branch who have captured the prize for the past six years. We do know, however, that in the event of the honour going to another Branch this year, the first to congratulate them would be the Purley Branch Committee.

Our Travel Bureau is just now working at top speed. A large number of Tours to the battlefields are being arranged for units of the Regular and Territorial Armies (Officers' Instruction); Old Comrades Associations; Public Schools and private parties. This year several Old Comrades Associations are holding their Annual Re-union Dinners in France or Belgium, and the League are being requested to effect all the necessary arrangements on their behalf. Last month a most successful Battlefields Tour was arranged for the 1st (London) Infantry Brigade to Cambrai and Ypres, extending over six days. This Tour of Instruction for Officers was undertaken by nearly 50 members and was accompanied by the G.O.C. the Division and Brigade Commander.

The Chairman of the League, Lieut.-General Sir William Pulteney, G.C.V.O., etc., received subsequently from both these distinguished officers a most satisfactory report, the tour being considered by them an outstanding success.

LONDON BRANCH COMMITTEE.

Informal Gatherings

will be held at the

BEDFORD HEAD HOTEL,

Maiden Lane, Strand, W.C. 2.

on

THURSDAY, APRIL 15th, 1937.

THURSDAY, MAY 20th, 1937.

THURSDAY, JUNE 17th, 1937.

From 7.30 to 10 p.m.

Will you kindly make these gatherings known amongst your own circle and interest some ex-Service man in the Ypres League in order to increase our membership?

Particulars will be sent to any friend on the name and address being supplied, and members are urged to help all they can in this direction.

Ladies cordially invited.

THE ANNUAL MEETING

of the

LONDON BRANCH COMMITTEE

will take place on

FRIDAY, MAY 14th, 1937

at the

YPRES LEAGUE OFFICES

20, Orchard Street,

Portman Square, W.1.

at 7.30 p.m.

The business will be to receive the Report of the London County Committee for the past year and to elect the Committee for the ensuing year. Members are earnestly requested to attend, and the Committee will be glad to receive any suggestions to further the interests of the League in the London area. Should any members have proposals to make, will they please forward them to the Hon. Secretary, London County Committee, Ypres League, at 20, Orchard Street, W.1., by May 15th.

HOTEL

Splendid & Britannique

YPRES

GRANDE PLACE. Opposite Cloth Hall.

LEADING HOTEL FOR COMFORT AND QUALITY, AND PATRONIZED BY THE YPRES LEAGUE.

COMPLETEY RENOVATED.

RUNNING WATER. BATHROOMS.

MODERATE TERMS. GARAGE.

Proprietor—Life Member, Ypres League.

YPRES

Skindles Hotel

(Opposite the Station)

Proprietor—Life Member, Ypres League

Branch at Poperinghe

(close to Talbot House)

Branches and Corresponding Members

BRANCHES.

LONDON	Hon. Secretary to the London Branch Committee : J. Boughey c/o 20, Orchard Street, London, W.1.
	TOTTENHAM AND EDMONTON DISTRICT—E. Glover, 191, Landowne Road, Tottenham, N.17.
	H. Carey, 373, Sydenham Road, S.E.26.
COLCHESTER	H. Snow (Hon. Sec.), 9, Church Street.
	W. H. Taylor (Pilgrimage Hon. Sec,), 64, High Street.
ESSEX (SOUTH)	S. H. Geller, Brielen, 197, Corbets Tey Road, Upminster.
LIVERPOOL	Captain A. M. Webster, Blundellsands.
PURLEY	Major Graham Carr, D.S.O., M.C., 112-114, High Street.
SHEFFIELD	Captain J Wilkinson, "Holmfield," Bents Drive.
QUEENSLAND, Australia	Messrs. C. H. Green, and George Lawson, Essex House, (Opposite Anzac Square) Brisbane, Queensland.
CANADA	Ed. Kingsland, P.O. Box 83, Magog, Quebec.
SOUTH AFRICA	L. G. Shuter, 381, Longmarket Street, Pietermaritzburg.
KENYA	C. H. Slater, P.O. Box 403, Nairobi.
BELGIUM	Mr. C. Leupe, Garage Shannon, Menin Gate.
AMERICA	Representative : Captain R. Henderson-Bland, 110 West 57th Street, New York City.

CORRESPONDING MEMBERS.

GREAT BRITAIN.

ABERYSTWYTH	T. O. Thomas, 5, Smithfield Road.
ASHTON-UNDER-LYNE	G. D. Stuart, "Woodlands,", Thronfield Grove, Arundel Street.
BANBURY	Captain C. W. Fowke, Yew Tree House, King's Sutton.
BIRMINGHAM	Mrs. Hill, 191, Cattell Road, Small Heath.
	John Burman, "Westbrook," Solihull Road, Shirley.
BRISTOL	W. S. Hook, "Wytschaete" Redland Court Road.
BROADSTAIRS	C. E. King, 6, Norman Road, St. Peters, Broadstairs.
	Mrs. Briggs, North Foreland House.
CHATHAM	W. N. Channon, 22, Keyes Avenue.
CHESTERFIELD	Major A. W. Shea, 14, Cross Street.
CONGLETON	Mr. H. Dart, 61, The Crescent.
DARLINGTON	D. S. Vigo, 125, Dorset Road, Bexhill-on-Sea.
DERBY	T. Jakeman, 10, Graham Street.
DORRINGTON (Salop)	Captain G. D. S. Parker, Frodesley Rectory.
EXETER	Captain E. Jenkin, 25, Queen Street.
HERNE BAY	Captain E. Clarke Williams, F.S.A.A., "Conway," Station Road.
HOVE	Captain G. W. J. Cole, 2, Westbourne Terrace, Kingsway.
LEICESTER	W. C. Dunford, 343, Aylestone Road.
LINCOLN	E. Swaine, 79, West Parade.
LLANWRST	A. C. Tomlinson, M.A., Bod Estyn.
LOUGHTON	Capt. O. G. Johnson, M.A., Loughton School.
MATLOCK (Derby)	Miss Dickinson, Beechwood.
MELROSE	Mrs. Lindesay Kelsall, Darnlee.
NEW BRIGHTON (Cheshire)	E. F. Williams, 5, Waterloo Road.
NEW MILTON	W. H. Lunn, Greywell.

NOTTINGHAM ... ... E. V. Brown, 3, Eldon Chambers, Wheeler Gate.
ST. HELENS (Lancs.) ... John Orford, 124, Knowsley Road.
ST. JOHN'S (Newfoundland) Captain L. Murphy, G.W.V.A. Office.
SHREWSBURY ... ... Major-General Sir John Headlam, K.B.E., C.B., D.S.O., Cruck Meole House, Hanwood.
TIVERTON (Devon) ... Mr. W H. Duncan Arthur, Surveyor's Office, Town Hall.
WELSHPOOL ... ... Mr. E. Wilson, Coedway, Ford, Salop.

DOMINIONS AND FOREIGN COUNTRIES.

AUSTRALIA ... ... R. A. Baldwin, c/o Government Savings Bank of N.S.W., Martin Place, Sydney.
Mr. W. Cloves, Box 1296, G.P.O., Adelaide.
BELGIUM ... ... Sister Marguerite, Sacré Coeur, Ypres.
CANADA ... . Brig.-General V. W. Odlum, C.B., C.M.G., D.S.O., 2530, Point Grey Road, Vancouver.
V. A. Bowes, 326, 40th Avenue West, Calgary, Alberta.
W. Constable F. Grece, St. Hilaire Station, Ronville County, Quebec.
CEYLON ... ... Captain F. R. G. Webb, M.C., Irrigation Bungalow, Kalmunai, E.P.
EGYPT ... ... Captain B. W. Leak, M.I.E.E., Turf Club, Cairo.
INDIA ... ... Lieut.-Quartermaster G. Smith, Queen's Bays, Sialkot, India.
IRELAND ... ... Miss A. K. Jackson, Cloneyhurke House, Portarlington.
NEW ZEALAND ... ... Captain W. U. Gibb, Ava Lodge, Puhinui Road, Papatoetoe, Auckland
S. E. Beattie, P.O. Box 11, Otaki Railway, Wellington.
NEWFOUNDLAND .. Captain Leo. Murphy, G.W.V.A. Office, St. John's.
NOVA SCOTIA ... ... Will R. Bird, 35, Clarence Street, Amherst.
SOUTH AFRICA ... ... H. L. Versfield, c/o Cape Explosives Works Ltd., 150, St. Georges Street, Cape Town.
SPAIN ... ... Captain P. W. Burgess, Calle de Zurbano 29, Madrid.
U.S.A. ... ... Captain Henry Maslin, 942, President Street, Brooklyn, New York.
L. E. P, Foot. 20, Gillett Street, Hartford, Conn, U.S.A.
A. P. Forward, 449, East 80th Street, New York.
J. W. Freebody, 945, McBride Avenue, Los Angeles.

Membership of the League

This is open to all who served in the Salient, and to all those whose relatives or friends died there, in order that they may have a record of that service for themselves and their descendants, and belong to the comradeship of men and women who understand and remember all that Ypres meant in suffering and endurance.

Life membership, £2 10s.

Annual members, 5s.

Do not let the fact of your not having served in the Salient deter you from joining the Ypres League. Those who have neither fought in the Salient nor lost relatives there, but who are in sympathy with the objects of the Ypres League, are admitted to its fellowship, but are not given scroll certificates.

There is a Junior Division for children whose relatives served in the Salient. It is open also to others to whom our objects appeal.

Annual subscription 1s. up to the age o 18, after which they can become ordinary members of the League.

THE YPRES LEAGUE (INCORPORATED)
20, Orchard Street, Portman Square, W.1.

Telephone: WELBECK 1446. *Telegrams*: YPRESLEAG, " WESDO," LONDON.

Patron-in-Chief: H.M. THE KING.

Patron:
H.R.H. PRINCESS BEATRICE.

President: GENERAL SIR CHARLES H. HARINGTON.

Vice-Presidents:

THE VISCOUNT WAKEFIELD OF HYTHE.   F.-M. SIR CLAUD W. JACOB.
F.-M. LORD MILNE.   F.-M. SIR PHILIP CHETWODE.
GENERAL SIR CECIL ROMER.   GENERAL SIR HUBERT GOUGH.

General Committee:

THE COUNTESS OF ALBEMARLE.
*CAPTAIN C. ALLISTON.
LIEUT-COLONEL BECKLES WILLSON.
MR. HENRY BENSON.
*MR. J. BOUGHEY.
*MISS B. BRICE-MILLER.
COLONEL G. T. BRIERLEY.
CAPTAIN P. W. BURGESS.
BRIG.-GENL. A. BURT.
*MAJOR H. CARDINAL-HARFORD.
REV. P. B. CLAYTON.
*CAPTAIN G. E. DE TRAFFORD.
*THE EARL OF YPRES.
MRS. C. J. EDWARDS.
MAJOR C. J. EDWARDS.
MR. H. A. T. FAIRBANK.
MR. T. ROSS FURNER.
SIR PHILIP GIBBS.
MR. E. GLOVER.

MR. F. D. BANKES-HILL.
MAJOR-GENERAL C. J. B. HAY.
MR. J. HETHERINGTON.
GENERAL SIR W. C. G. HENEKER.
*CAPTAIN O. G. JOHNSON.
*MAJOR E. MONTAGUE JONES.
MAJOR GENL. C. G. LIDDELL.
CAPTAIN H. D. PEABODY.
*THE HON. ALICE DOUGLAS PENNANT.
*LIEUT.-GENERAL SIR W. P. PULTENEY.
LIEUT.-COLONEL SIR J. MURRAY.
*COLONEL G. E. C. RASCH.
THE HON. SIR ARTHUR STANLEY.
MR. ERNEST THOMPSON.
CAPTAIN J. LOCKLEY TURNER.
*MR. E. B. WAGGETT.
CAPTAIN J. WILKINSON.
CAPTAIN H. TREVOR WILLIAMS.

* Executive Committee.

Bankers:
BARCLAYS BANK LTD., Knightsbridge Branch.

Honorary Solicitors:
MESSRS. FLADGATE & CO., 70, Pall Mall, S.W.

Secretary:
MAJOR L. J. L. PULLAR.

Auditors:
MESSRS. LEPINE & JACKSON,
6, Bond Court, E.C.4.

League Representative at Ypres:
Mr. C. LEUPE,
81, Chaussée de Dickebusch.

League Representative at Ostend:
CAPTAIN P. D. PARMINTER,
16, Galerie James Ensor.

League Representative at Amiens:
CAPTAIN STUART OSWALD.
7, Rue des Otages.

League Representative at Arras:
MR. P. VYNER,
10, Place de la Gare.

Hon. Secretary, Ypres British Settlement:
LT. COLONEL F. G. POOLE.

PRIMARY OBJECTS OF THE LEAGUE

I.—Commemoration and Comradeship.
II.—To provide special travel facilities for Members and all interested to Ypres and battlefields, and transport of Members.
III.—The furnishing of information about the Salient; marking of historic sites and the compilation of charts of the battlefields.
IV.—The erection of a Ypres British Church and School which has been completed.
V.—The establishment of groups of members throughout the world, through Branch Secretaries and Corresponding Members.
VI.—The maintenance of cordial relations with dwellers on the battlefields of Ypres.
VII.—The formation of a Junior Division.

Use the Ypres League Travel Bureau for Ypres and Whole of the Western Front.

FOR THE FOLLOWING PUBLICATIONS, Etc., apply:

Secretary, YPRES LEAGUE, 20, ORCHARD STREET, LONDON, W.1

BOOKS.

YPRES: Outpost of the Channel Ports. By Beatrix Brice. With Foreword by Field-Marshal Lord Plumer, G.C.B. Price 1s. 0d.; post free 1s. 3d.

In the Ypres Salient. By Lt.-Col. Beckles Willson. 1s. net; post free 1s. 2d.

Story of the 63rd Field Ambulance. By A. W. Westmore, etc. Cloth, 3s. 6d., post free. Paper, 2s. 6d., post free.

War Letters to a Wife. By Colonel Rowland Feilding. Popular Edition, 3s. 6d.; post free 4s.

The Pill Boxes of Flanders. 1s.; post free 1s. 3d.

From Mons to the First Battle of Ypres. By the late J. G. W. Hyndson, M.C. Price 3/6, post free.

YPRES LEAGUE TIES. 3s. 6d. each, post free.

YPRES LEAGUE BADGES. 2s. each, 2s. 1½d. post free.

YPRES LEAGUE CUFF LINKS.
3/6, post free.

YPRES LEAGUE SCARVES. 12/6, post free.

EMBROIDERED BADGES. 4s. each, post free.

Map and List of Cemeteries in the Ypres Salient. Price 9d.; post free 11d.

Map of the Somme. Price 1s. 8d., post free.

PICTURES.

Burning of the Cloth Hall, 1915. A Coloured Print, 14 in. by 12 in. 1s. post free.

Old Well-known Spots in New Guise.

Prints, size 4¼ x 2¼, recently taken of famous spots in the Ypres Salient, and which may be of great interest to our readers, are on sale at headquarters, price 4d. each, post free 5d. For particulars apply Secretary.

POST CARDS, PHOTOGRAPHS AND ETCHINGS.

Post Cards. Ypres: British Front during the War. Ruins of Ypres. Price 1s. post free.

Hill 60. Complete Panorama Photographs.
12 in. by 3¼ in. Price 3s., post free; 15 in. by 5 in. Price 3s. 6d., post free.

MODELS OF DEMARCATION STONE.

The model, which is 6 inches in height, may be used for a paperweight or as an ornament. Price 5/-, post free.

Applications to the Secretary, Ypres League.

PHOTOGRAPHS OF WAR-TIME SKETCHES.

Bedford House (Front View), 1916.

Bedford House (Back View), 1916.

Voormezeele Main Street, 1916.

Voormezeele Crucifixion Gate, 1916.

Langhof Chateau, 1916.

Size 8½ in. by 6½ in. Price 2s. 6d. each, post free.

Photographs of the Thiepval and Arras Memorials.
Post card size, price 1s. each, post free.

YPRES TIMES.

The Journal may be obtained at the League Offices.

BACK NUMBERS 1s.; 1935, 8d.; 1936 6d.

Printed in Great Britain for the Publishers by FORD & GILL, 21a/23, Iliffe Yard, Crampton Street, London, S.E.17.

Memory Tablet.

JULY — AUGUST — SEPTEMBER

July.

July 1st, 1916	...	First Battle of the Somme begins.
,, 2nd, 1918	...	1,000,000 Americans transported to France.
,, 9th, 1915	...	Conquest of German South Africa.
,, 18th, 1918	...	General Foch's counter-attack.
,, 28th, 1914	...	Austria-Hungary declared war on Serbia.
,, 30th, 1915	...	First German liquid fire attack.
,, 31st, 1917	...	Third Battle of Ypres.

August.

Aug. 1st, 1914	...	Germany declared war on Russia.
,, 2nd, 1914	...	German ultimatum to Belgium.
,, 3rd, 1914	...	Germany declared war on France.
,, 4th, 1914	...	Great Britain declared war on Germany.
,, 8th, 1918	...	Great British Offensive launched in front of Amiens.
,, 10th, 1914	...	France declared war on Austria-Hungary.
,, 12th, 1914	...	Great Britain declared war on Austria-Hungary.
,, 16th, 1914	...	British Expeditionary Force landed in France.
,, 23rd, 1914	...	Japan declared war on Germany.
,, 27th, 1916	...	Rumania entered the war.

September.

Sept. 3rd, 1916	...	Zeppelin destroyed at Cuffly.
,, 5th, 1914	...	End of retreat from Mons to Marne.
,, 6th, 1914	...	First Battle of Marne begins.
,, 15th, 1914	...	First Battle of Aisne begins.
,, 23rd, 1914	...	First British air raid in Germany.
,, 25th, 1915	...	Battle of Loos.
,, 27th, 1917	...	Hindenburg Line broken.
,, 29th, 1918	...	Bulgaria surrendered.

The Ypres Times

Communications to
The Editor, "Ypres Times,"
20, Orchard Street, London, W.1.

PRICE 6d.
POST FREE 7d.

VOL. 8, No. 7.   PUBLISHED QUARTERLY   JULY, 1937

H.M. The Queen
An Intimate Story of Her Majesty's Life

A VERY GRACIOUS LADY.

(Specially Contributed to the *Ypres Times*).

By HENRY BENSON, M.A.

[*In the April issue of " The Ypres Times " there appeared from my pen a brief sketch of the life of his Majesty King George VI. The Editor has asked me to contribute to the July issue a companion life of the King's Gracious Consort, Queen Elizabeth.—H. B.*]

QUEEN ELIZABETH! What visions this name conjures up to most of us—a gaunt, red-headed, militant and domineering monarch, living in rough and almost uncivilised grandeur. When Edmund Spenser wrote his beautiful " Faerie Queen " in 1589 it was known that he alluded thus to Queen Elizabeth in allegorical manner, which meant to flatter her, but the poem was never taken by her subjects to be a correct or suitable way of describing " Good Queen Bess." Anything less like a fairy could not well be imagined.

To-day we have another Queen Elizabeth to gladden our hearts. No one could be a greater contrast, for where her undoubtedly brilliant predecessor was gaunt, she she is plump; instead of a redhead she is a brunette; and she is certainly not militant or domineering in any way.

AN EARLIER SCOTTISH QUEEN-CONSORT.

Queen Elizabeth—Elizabeth Bowes-Lyon by birth—is the youngest daughter of the Earl and Countess of Strathmore, and who was born on August, 4, 1900. There is a general tendency to stress that she is Scottish. True, that her family are Scots, but the birth took place at the parents' Hertfordshire home, St. Paul's, Waldenbury, on the outskirts of London, near Welwyn. Although with her family she paid regular visits to Glamis Castle, that ancient grey pile with its " pepper-box " turrets in Forfarshire (or as they like to call that part of Scotland, Angus), most of her young life was spent in England. In fact, the Queen has not the slightest trace of Scottish accent which might have been hers had she been more in the beautiful and rugged land north of the Tweed. Another point about her family is that her mother is a Cavendish-Bentinck, who, had she been a boy would have been Duke of Portland.

Of course, hereditarily, she is a Scotswoman, and she is the first woman of Scottish nationality to sit on the English throne since Matilda of Scotland, daughter of King Malcolm III, married Henry I. Their wedding, like her own, took place in Westminster Abbey, on November 11th, 1100, and though Norman nobles tauntingly referred to the Sovereign and his bride as " farmer Godru and his cummer Godgifu," the union was both popular and significant. It was the beginning of a very long historical process which united two nations.

THE QUEEN'S NOBLE ANCESTRY.

The ancestral home of Queen Elizabeth's family, Glamis Castle, is as old as Scottish history itself, and it occupies the most picturesque situation of any inhabited British castle to-day. From its battlements there is a superb view over Strathmore and the Grampians. Malcolm II is said to have been murdered here and, as Macbeth was Thane of Glamis, popular imagination has associated Shakespeare's Macbeth with the castle. Locally, the great story of Glamis is the secret chamber, the entrance to which is known to only three members of the family—the Earl, the heir-apparent, and any third person in whom they may wish to confide. According to popular rumour, the chamber once housed a monstrosity.

An ancestor of her Majesty, Sir John Lyon of Forteviot, married in 1376, a daughter of the Scottish King, Robert II, and was granted the dormant Thanage of Glamis. Still more interesting is the fact that it was a raid against Robert II which led to the title of the Duke of York being bestowed upon one of the foremost fighters in that raid.

The present castle owes its aspect to the first Patrick Lyon, a Lord of the Treasury, who was made Earl of Strathmore in 1677. Before that date the Lyon chieftain bore the title of Baron Glamis. In 1557, Lady Glamis, the widow of the sixth Baron, was burnt as a witch on the Castle Hill at Edinburgh. The estates were forfeited to the Crown, and her son, the seventh Baron, was imprisoned. Later, the accuser confessed that the whole story was a fabrication, and the Baron was released. The Lyons were staunch Jacobites, and the fifth Earl was killed in battle during the rising of the "Fifteen." For a time, James III, the Old Pretender, held his court at Glamis. Towards the end of the eighteenth century, the ninth Earl assumed the additional name of Bowes, and until the recent Coronation, Queen Elizabeth's father, sat in the House of Lords as Baron Bowes.

From this it will be gathered that if you see Queen Elizabeth wearing the Royal Stuart tartan, it must not be thought that it is by virtue of her marriage into the British Royal House. On the contrary, it is of her own right, and all her family are entitled to it.

"MERRY MISCHIEF."

As a child, Lady Elizabeth Bowes-Lyon—she became " Lady " Elizabeth on the death of her grandfather in 1904—was known as " Merry Mischief." She was then not above rigging up spoof spooks for the benefit of unwary visitors to Glamis Castle, and once she laid up a store of provisions with the object of running away from home, but was detected. She had her own pony, kept Persian cats, fowls and tortoises and, with the other children of the famliy, had great affection for the animals in the farmyard. Her mother taught her to read and write, as well as the first steps in music, dancing and drawing.

In the early years of this century cricket was a very popular game at Glamis, and the Earl of Strathmore ran a family cricket eleven which played matches against the various Forfarshire sides. The Earl's eleven was composed of himself, his brother, his sons,—all useful players, and the domestic staff. A friend of mine recalls one match at Glamis in 1906. The visiting eleven was batting and, while his side was waiting for their knock, they were entertained by a little girl of six summers. " Do you know the man who is bowling?" she asked. They confessed their ignorance. " That is the man I am going to marry," she explained gravely. The little girl of six is now Queen of England. The " fiancé " was James, a Glamis footman, and the fast bowler of Lord Strathmore's team.

Happy and Care-free Girlhood.

Lady Elizabeth, as I will call her for the present, was taught at home by governesses, and led the life of the average well-to-do child, without any " frills " or airs and graces. She was quite unspoilt, though permitted to enjoy a good deal of latitude in her young days. Lessons never seemed hard to her, because she was endowed by nature with a quick brain. When in London there was special music tuition from a well-known pianist and a French governess introduced her to that language, which she now speaks with fluency. Sewing and embroidery as well as painting, have always been considered part of a well-brought-up girl's education, and in these accomplishments she had the help of her mother. In addition, she was taught to cook, and baked traditional scones with great success.

Lady Elizabeth was highly popular with her girlhood companions. A good tennis player, a motorist, and an exceptionally graceful dancer, she was also a keen sportswoman, fishing making the strongest appeal of all. She had learned to ride over the moors on hardy little Scots ponies almost as soon as she could walk, and knew much of the wild life of Forfarshire. Extremely vivacious, she showed also a strength of mind which, with her persuasive tongue, enabled her to make other people fall in enthusiastically with her wishes.

The young girl, like many children of her generation, learned of the War in her early years, for she was in her 'teens when Glamis Castle was turned into a hospital for soldiers. Too young to nurse, her high spirits helped in many ways to entertain the wounded and assist the nurses. Life at Glamis was normally that of an ideally happy family circle, though, during the War, losses and anxieties took their toll.

The Gipsy's Prophecy.

In due course, childhood days and ways were left behind, and in 1919 Lady Elizabeth " came out " into Society. There were no Courts then at which she could be presented, and the first ones after the War were not until 1920, when they were stripped of much of their glory, for neither trains nor veils and feathers were worn. Still, she went to the usual functions common to her circle, and a curious and outstanding incident is associated with her attendance at Ascot in 1921.

After lunching at the Bachelors' Club with a party of friends, Lady Elizabeth and Mrs. Donald Forbes were making their way across the course to the Royal Enclosure—a passage always difficult owing to the crowd surging around, and the club tents being on the far side of the course. In this melée she and Mrs. Forbes were stopped by a gipsy who rushed forward, caught their hands and insisted on telling their fortunes. It is an absolute fact that this gipsy prophesied that Lady Elizabeth would be a Queen, and the mother of a great Queen! Her prediction for Mrs. Forbes was that she would be famous in five continents. This Mrs. Forbes is the Rosita Forbes of to-day, whose explorations are world known, but who had done no travelling at the time.

A Romantic Betrothal.

Lady Elizabeth was five when she first met Prince Albert of Wales at a children's party. With this pretty girl he was greatly taken; they pulled crackers together and crowned each other with paper caps. Thirteen years later, when he met her again at the house of Lady Leicester, they recalled the frolic of the previous occasion. In 1920 he was one of a house party at Glamis, and in the next year King George V and Queen Mary paid a visit to the Castle. Friendship developed between the young couple and the future Duchess was a bridesmaid at the wedding of the Princess Royal, this being the first occasion on which she was introduced to the larger public. Incidentally, she was the first of Princess Mary's bridesmaids to become herself a bride.

Rumours of a ripening romance was on every tongue and these were confirmed in the Court Circular of January 15th, 1923:—

" It is with the greatest pleasure that the King and Queen announce the betrothal of Their beloved son, the Duke of York, to the Lady Elizabeth Bowes-Lyon, to which The King has gladly given his consent."

So, for the first time for 250 years, a Prince in the direct line of succession was betrothed to a commoner. Country and Empire rejoiced that such a striking example of the new spirit of democracy, of the breaking down of the antiquated barrier between class and class, which had swept over the world after the war, should be manifest in the Royal Family itself. On the other hand, Lady Elizabeth was by no means the first member of an aristocratic family to marry into the Royal circle, for only fourteen months earlier the Princess Royal had taken as her husband Viscount Lascelles, now Earl of Harewood. And very much earlier Queen Victoria's daughter, Princess Louise, had been permitted to marry the Marquis of Lorne, son and heir of the Duke of Argyll. It will be recalled that, when an old crofter woman on the Duke's Scottish estates was told of the betrothal, she remarked, " Aye, and it's a proud day for the Queen of England."

The Abbey Wedding.

Three months of intensive preparation, three months during which the engaged pair lived in a blaze of publicity, and then the wedding took place in Westminster Abbey on April 26th, 1923, amid great national rejoicing. The Duke was attended by the Prince of Wales (now Duke of Windsor), and Prince Henry (now Duke of Gloucester). Actually the April day when this auspicious event took place was not at all spring-like. It was quite chilly, and Lady Elizabeth was provided with a cloak of ermine to wear to and from the Abbey. Her wedding dress reached to the ground, and was mediaeval in design. If I remember rightly, it was of white moiré, with long sleeves of lace and adorned with embroidery in beads and silver. The bridegroom was in the azure dress of the Royal Air Force, and King George in that of an Admiral of the Fleet. Of special interest to women, perhaps, is the fact that the bride wore no gloves and carried a litte white Dorothy bag decorated with orange blossom. A touch which moved everyone was the beautiful thought of the young Duchess to drop her bouquet on the tomb of the Unknown Warrior as she passed down the aisle after the ceremony.

Enormous crowds greeted her on the drive from the Abbey to Buckingham Palace and there were expressions of delight everywhere. Her smile became famous, and from that day onwards the people took the daughter of the House of Lyon to their hearts.

It may be mentioned that, although her father is not what one would call particularly wealthy, the young bride did not come empty-handed to her Royal bridegroom, and that she did have a dowry.

Overseas Tours with the Duke.

The honeymoon began at Polesden Lacey, after which the Duke and Duchess went to Glamis and then to Frogmore. They afterwards settled at their new home, White Lodge, Richmond. It was there, too, that Queen Mary went to live after her marriage and within its walls the Prince of Wales (now Duke of Windsor) was born.

The first autumn of the Duchess's wedded life took her away from England on a visit of ceremony—the pioneer of many to come. She and the Duke travelled to Serbia, in order that the latter might personally act as godfather to the baby son of the ill-fated King Alexander. On the return from this journey a large number of public engagements in London pressed upon the young couple and they found White Lodge too far away. Consequently, Chesterfield House, Mayfair, was lent to them by the Princess Royal. An official visit to Ireland, a little holiday in Scotland, and then the Royal pair had to make their plans for a trip to East Africa in the autumn of 1924, during which, the Duchess had splendid opportunities of enjoying the excitement of hunting.

On April 21st, 1926, Princess Elizabeth was born, but only a few months had passed when her mother, thoroughly happy in the company of her baby, had to interrupt that domestic pleasure for the purpose of making a long overseas' tour. With the Duke, she left Portsmouth in H.M.S. Renown on January 6th, 1927. The main purpose of the journey was to visit Canberra for the opening of the Federal Parliament House, but this permitted also of a stay in New Zealand. There the Royal couple were received with tremendous enthusiasm, but the continual round of engagements entailed very great strain, the unfortunate consequence being that the Duchess had to abandon part of the programme. However, she made a quick recovery, and in due course the journey to Australia was continued, where again there was a wild welcome. More than once she recognised and spoke to soldiers whom years before she had met at Glamis during the period that the Castle was a military hospital. The most democratic of all the Dominions loved her, as much as anything, for the obvious delight she took in shaking hands with as many people as she could. Those handshakes strengthened the bonds of Empire. One amusing incident came when a well-wisher handed the Duchess a threepenny piece with the request that it should be put in little Princess Elizabeth's money-box.

A Devoted Wife and Mother.

Eventually the long tour came to an end, and nowhere was the return of the travellers more welcome than at their London home, where their little daughter was getting old enough to recognise her parents. On August 21st, 1930, a second child was born—Princess Margaret Rose. Then started the new home life at 145, Piccadilly—the Royal house which looked just like any other of its neighbours. There never was a sentry outside it, nor anything remotely resembling the appearance of a Royal Palace. The only difference after the accession was the presence of two policemen at each gateway.

Throughout these years the Duchess ministered to her little daughters with unaffected pleasure, but she did not allow her motherly care to interfere with an enormous amount of public work. Her interests expressed themselves in highly-varied activities, and more firmly than ever she endeared herself to the whole country. She and her Royal spouse have now stepped into History. And it may well be that when that History is written, it will be said: " She had a gift of making others happy. Her husband first, and then his people."

Personal Characteristics.

Possibly some of those who are reading this have never seen Queen Elizabeth in person. For them I will try to give a brief detailed description. First of all, she is not tall, being about five feet five inches. Her hair is dark, not black, but of a quite dark brown. There is just a suspicion of a coil at the nape of the neck, and the rest is waved and parted at the centre. True to her early taste her Majesty keeps to her " fringe," though it seems to me that there is now less of this. There are only a few hairs cut short across the forehead, which certainly is becoming to her shape of face. Her eyes are blue, but not a very deep colour, though the fact that they have naturally dark lashes enhances their tone and, unlike so many women who have their eyebrows plucked, the Queen has always left hers as nature intended them, and their clearly marked outline lends character to her entire face. The " Royal smile," is a notable feature,—a real smile, not only shown in the mouth, but which creeps over the face and has its accompanying response in the expression of the eyes. It is a gentle smile, a kind smile, and an understanding smile. People feel when in her presence that they are talking to someone who is not being merely polite. There is no wandering of the eyes elsewhere, for she looks at one straight and frankly.

In common with her sister-in-law, the Princess Royal, blue is her favourite colour, and her favourite jewels are sapphires and pearls. With jewels, as with clothes, the trend is for simplicity. On her wedding day she wore a double row of pearls and ever since she has remained faithful to those gems. There is one piece of jewellery which is certain always to attract all who have the pleasure of meeting her. That is her engagement ring, which is a large oval sapphire with diamonds each side.

THE QUEEN'S KISS FOR HER MAID.

In the past, Queen Elizabeth has to a great extent supervised the domestic side of her life, and although, of course, there was a housekeeper in charge of the general work at 145, Piccadilly, she always kept her fingers on the strings. The daily menus were invariably submitted for her approval. She is a wonderfully kind and considerate mistress, and there are seldom changes in the household.

Her personal attendant, Miss Catherine Maclean, has accompanied her Majesty to Buckingham Palace. Miss Maclean, the daughter of a Dingwall (Ross-shire) builder, has served her mistress—as Lady Elizabeth Bowes-Lyon and as the Duchess of York—for twenty-five years, but she doubted if she could serve her as Queen of England. Queen Elizabeth, however, dispelled her doubts. " If you cannot do it for me, Catharine," she said, " who can? I cannot do without you now." With that, her Majesty threw her arms around Miss Maclean's neck and kissed her, remarking, " I shall try to make Buckingham Palace as bright, cheerful, and homely as 145, Piccadilly."

That God will bless Queen Elizabeth with a long and happy life is the earnest prayer of the whole Empire.

H. B.

* * *

The Coronation, May 12, 1937

THE last time I had the honour to write for *The Ypres Times* was on the occasion of the Festival of Empire and Remembrance at The Royal Albert Hall when I referred to King Edward VIII in these words: "Standing there in mufti he looked so young, and I thought a little lonely, for had not high destiny led him to places where the finger of history traces the things to come? " What prompted me to write that I know not, but this I know, that the finger having written moves on and waits for no man. I feel that the great affection ex-service men had for their King is not something that can be lightly set aside, and I venture to state that all will join me in the hope that he and his Duchess may look forward to a happy private life.

Another life has now been dedicated to the service of the People. For the first time in the history of the world the peoples of the world shared in that dedication. Watching the faces of those around me on Constitutional Hill I was sensible of the seriousness of their demeanour as the words of the Abbey Ceremony were broadcast.

Some mighty and centripetal force seemed to be merging on that Abbey scene, and I am one who dares to think that the man who set out to ride among his people that day knew that he had been set apart, and given up to service.

So much has been written, spoken, and photographed of the ceremony of Coronation that I feel it would be useless for me to embark on a tide of praise in the space allotted me, but a few words concerning the significance to the nation of this great event might not come amiss.

That great leader of men, Cromwell, once spoke these words with a deep sincerity: " We are a people with the clear stamp of God upon us." That is the utterance of a great and fearless man, and it would not be out of keeping with this hour in our history to dare to believe as he believed without any hypocrisy. Of course there have been things, events in our history that any right thinking man or woman must deplore, but even at the time of their happening voices were raised in strong condemnation. Somehow a lesson was learned and so was built up the greatest Empire the world has ever known.

The Throne is the Great Symbol Of Imperial Unity.

It is the centrifugal rays from the Throne that hold the Empire together. Without the Throne the Empire would crumble and the Dependencies would become parochial in aim. The Very Revd. W. R. Inge, in an article on the Coronation, asked wonderingly if any people witnessing the Ceremony or Procession had in mind Carlyle's " Sartor Resartus," I can say that I had, and the line from that great book that occurred to me was " Friend, thou seeest here a living link in that Tissue of History which inweaves all Being: watch well, or it will be past thee, and seen no more."

Then a sentence from the essay on History by Emerson obtruded itself: " To the poet, the philosopher, to the saint, all things are friendly and sacred, all events profitable, all days holy, all men divine. For the eye is fastened on the life, and slights the circumstance!

Yes, the eye is fastened on the life!

There are many who look upon all ceremonial as trumpery trappings surviving from Mediæval times, and looked at with the eye of reason they may be right. However, there is more in it than that, and it is when the spiritual supersedes the reason and passes into the regions of the unseen that the office of the symbol becomes apparent.

Misraim, who built cities in Egypt, was the first man to assume the title of King, and it is interesting to note that there was prescribed a very definite code for his direction.

The hour of rising, the portion of time for religious exercises, the administration of justice, the quality of his food, the rank of persons by whom he was served.

It is all very different now, but there still remains the dedication to the life of service. We stand to-day at the greatest turning point in the history of the world, and unless we are to decline upon a futile attitude of despair we must all serve.

It was Hobbes, the philosopher, who likened the body politic to a Leviathan, and it would be idle for us to deny that there are not many sores on our body politic to-day, but surely it is apparent that in no country in the world is there such a spirit of good will.

It is not so many years ago when a visitor abroad heard, and saw written words that confidently asserted that Britain was a crumbling power—was finished.

All that is changed now. All eyes are upon her, and she stands in the very van of the eternal march towards a better world. In Westminster Abbey on the day of Coronation were gathered distinguished men and women of every race to render homage to the Throne. That homage was rendered with no sense of fear, coercion, or compulsion of any kind. It was the free and loyal homage of hearts drawn by an eternal principle that is weaving at the roaring loom of Time a garment that will eventually envelope the world.

The Procession as a spectacle was superb. There was a fairy-like something mingled with the pomp and power of a great nation. The splendid dignity of it clothed on with a high seriousness that should accompany all high ceremonial because it is interpretative, and speaks of the things of the spirit.

When the late King George V came to the throne I wrote the accompanying poem which appeared in a book entitled " Poetical tributes to the Memory of King Edward the Seventh." The poem might stand for the present occasion.

1

What though we be all saddened now
  By memories of solemn rites,
Yet must we turn to one whose vow
  Leads where Hope with Love unites.
The Nation looks to him whose heart
Oft on the wide sea stood apart
While thinking on this England and her ways.

2

Not that she struck with heavier hand
  Than other nations pledged to power—
Nor that her statesmen surely fanned
  The flame of hate in a chosen hour—
Not for the stubborn wills she breeds;
  Nor because of her people's needs:
No, not for these things are her paths so many,

3
But because in a wilful fashion
 Her noblest sons have groped for God,
Of whom the tasks, and eager passion
 That led them where their lone feet trod.
And she to be strong and and endure
 Must ever be blind to the lure
Of fools who see no purpose in her might.

4
Our sailor-king so oft has seen
 Our flag flung wide 'neath other skies,
And known where English feet have been,
 And marked such noble enterprise,
That we may look with fervent hearts—
 With highest hope that faith imparts
And know that he will strive and fail us not.

R. HENDERSON-BLAND.

* * *

Light and Shade at the Front

(By an ex-R.B.)

FLOWERS OF THE FOREST.

JOHN PEEL was a regular. It followed that, being a Regular, he could not be mistaken for anything else, and so far as could be seen at the time there were several reasons for this. There can be no doubt that Army routine was second nature to a Regular soldier and ample evidence of his training could be seen with half an eye, not only in the long service chevrons worn at the cuff, but also in the set of the face, the erect carriage, and in his general bearing. Perhaps the most salient trait of any was the habit which he appeared to have of methodically doing the right thing at the crucial moment. And while on this subject, and although it may seem something of a paradox when speaking of soldiers of the War, so far as the writer could judge the practice of " grousing " was somewhat foreign to the Regulars' ken; they were on the contrary quiet and self-contained. It may be, indeed, that War's discomforts had become a habit, and that their matter-of-fact coolness was proof against anything which was not outside the then everyday run of events.

The writer was on a working party one night cleaning out a trench, and the job was a tough one. The mud underfoot was thick and sticky and shifting it was anything but easy. This trench was of the narrow but high variety and by looking up out of the darkness one had an excellent view, if that sort of thing interested him, of a dazzlingly brilliant moon and stars. There was not much traffic but a carrying party filed by while the work was being done, and there was grumbling at the sticky going. One of the party, a tall strapping fellow, had some trouble with his rifle and bags of rations, the trench being narrow, and while he was trying to squeeze past a member of the working party his equipment became entangled with the other fellow's, and to make matters worse his feet stuck in the mud. " Halt in front ! " passed from man to man along the trench, and as the equipment wallah laboured to break away he expressed his feelings to the full in the manner which was then typical of the line. (How does Will Shakespeare put it, " Full of strange oaths "?) But that man was not a Regular.

John Peel's Service Dress Khaki was worn and weather stained but it fitted him all right; it set off a strong wiry physique and the buttons being black did not show the stain. It is probable that khaki stands the mud and the weather better than any other shade, and khaki putties possess the additional merit of affording excellent protection to the legs, at least that is how the writer found it. The mud caked on the outside and the inner folds kept dry. And more than that the putties were a good buffer against the many obstacles one collided against in the dark; in fact, it is safe to say that putties saved many a shinbone from a nasty crack.

Peel was not a talkative sort, he was reserved, and this trait may have commended itself to the village folk; at any rate he had a seat at the cottage stove, and when one chanced to see him make a slice of toast it was quite an education. First he would cut off a round of bread, and he performed this operation with the precision that one expected to see in an experienced S.B.; then he toasted it carefully both sides in front of the glowing little fire. Spreading the butter evenly and with economy came next, and after that was done he laid the buttered toast on the grid while he replaced the lid on the butter tin. The next act in the art of "ye compleat toast-maker" was to cut the round of toast into butter fingers with his jack knife as the toast lay on a clean plate, and when that was done *then* he ate his toast piece by piece at his leisure.

One night a bullet "pinged" out of the darkness from the front line, having missed its objective there, and killed a man who was filing on with a working party quite a good distance behind the line. Said John Peel the next day: "It hit him plumb in the forehead." One felt a little diffident about asking John to dress any common

Is it far?

or garden cut, such for example as a mishap with a tin-opener. Of course he would dress the cut, and as was usual with him would make no comment, but at times looks are more eloquent than words; and John's look seemed to say, "It's quite right to look after small cuts, but you should have seen some of the wounds that I've dressed!"

A morning came when the Company paraded en route for the line. Troops forming and on the march have a fascination for the young, and children stood by the cottage where Peel made his toast and watched the platoons numbering and forming fours. On the order, "Quick March!" their quick glance singled out John Peel, and as the S.B. passed they called out in their clipped English: "*Gooddbye, Johng Pill!*" A few weeks after that the Company found itself in a hot quarter during the Arras offensive, and when later on it came out of the line John Peel was not on the strength, the reason being, to quote the familiar words, he was "far, far away."

* * * * *

The writer happened to be in a Recreation Hut near Boulogne (on an occasion already referred to in these articles) when he was asked by a—But let us begin at the beginning.

Sector: The Salient. Position in the line: A low front line trench. Hour: It was near zero hour for the attack, a little after dawn. Weather: Well, a paragraph is needed adequately to describe the weather. The sky was of that familiar colour which is called " grey "; it was " grey " with rain clouds; the morning was bleak, the rain pelted down, and everywhere was yellow mud. Slimy mud oozed under the feet, mud dropped from the trench, No Man's Land was a quagmire of mud, the shell-holes were sloughs of yellow mud, service dress, putties and equipment were plastered with mud, hands and faces were begrimed with mud, the rifles got fouled with mud in spite of the utmost efforts which were made to keep them clean, the pull-throughs were dirty with mud, the rations were not free from mud—in a word the weather's name was MUD, and one cannot put it plainer than that.

The front line was the assembly trench, and the writer was one of the troops in support who occupied the front line as soon as the attack was launched. He was not an eye witness of the incident which he is about to relate, but it was narrated afterwards by one of the attacking party.

The weather conditions were unfavourable to attack and the German section of front line was not captured, but the troops consolidated in shell holes on No Man's Land, and this was an appreciable gain considering the heavy fire which the attack faced and the number of men who fell. One of the officers in command of the attack was held up by the enemy wire and a guttural voice called out in English: " Will you surrender? " " No! " shouted the officer, and the next moment he fell dead under the enemy's fire.

When the writer was in the Recreation Hut already referred to, he was approached by one of those officials whose task it was to enquire into cases of " reported missing." Curiously enough, his first question was about this officer who was killed in the attack at Ypres, and although the writer did not tell him definitely that the officer *was* killed, as he was not an eye-witness of the incident, he stated the other facts and let the official draw his own conclusions.

* * * * *

The St. Quentin Sector has been a good deal in the public eye, within recent times, as being the jumping off ground of the German attack in March, 1918, but when the troops first took over this sector of line from the Allies its quietude had to be experienced to be believed. Things livened up after a while but even then a wide distance always separated the opposing lines. And not only was that the case between the opposing lines, but the distance behind our own line from front line to support, from support to reserve, and from post to post, was considerable.

Visualise a dark night, quiet, the fresh odour of damp country earth, and a chilly rawness in the air which was the forerunner of rain. The relief had filed into a new stretch of line behind the guides, and an outpost squad was about to look round and take bearings in its new position, when a message was received, and leaving the rest of the squad the N.C.O. departed to take over a carrying party of six duty men and two officers' batmen. This party was filing over the top to draw supplies from the Reserve Line when it sighted another party which was moving along in the trench below, and was in charge of Corporal Imber.

Corporal Imber was of slim build, height about 5 feet 7½ inches, oval face, clear complexion, he was aged about 22 or 23, and his general bearing was pleasant. The parties halted and question and answer were spoken in low tones. " Is that E——? " " Yes, what are you on? " " Wiring, but we have to find some wire first. Where is the Lewis gun post? " " Take the first trench on the left, walk straight along it, and you'll see the Lewis gun post near the further end." " Is it far? " " Yes, a goodish way." " D'ye know if there is any wire there? " " I expect there are two or three coils dumped outside." One or two further remarks followed and then the parties led on.

Some time afterwards, as the carrying party was loading up in Reserve, the Germans opened up a heavy fire, and the Captain, who was near the Stores dump talking to the Q.M.S., asked for someone to go to the front line and get a report as to what was happening there. The N.C.O. was senior rank of the party present so away he went to get it, doubling over the top to save time, and because the communication trench was bad going, working parties being newly in.

Cutting a corner he slipped on a greasy plank which had been put there to reinforce the parapet, and somersaulted into the trench. But equipment and putties absorbed the shock and he was up and away again in double quick time on his errand. Out with the password ("Seven nine five") to a row of men facing rear in the support trench with levelled rifles—best not to wait! (the supports were facing rear in view of a possible attempt by the enemy at a turning movement) a jump between their shoulders and on to the front line. Back to Reserve with the report " . . . . . . the enemy are firing minnewerfers into the front line, and there is a shortage of Véry Lights and S.O.S.'s" A hop, skip and a jump with these, and then back once more to Reserve as the firing slackened. This firing brought on rain.

And so - Vale!

The carrying party was soon ready and after the N.C.O. had received a welcome " tot " from the Q.M.S., he joined the party and it headed into a stiff downpour and a wind that blew in gusts. This night came over to be the blackest that the writer ever met with at any time before or since. It must have been as black as the Styx across which Charon ferries his boatloads of immortals. This was the night when two orderly men fell into the trench with the dicksey of tea. Luckily, the dicksey reached the ground first and so they weren't scalded.

Progress was slow but the party dropped into the trench (Maze trench) on the last lap without any mishap, the N.C.O. falling to the rear, and then each man kicked against a heavy object that was laying in the bottom of the trench. This proved to be a " dud " and later on it was reported and shifted. (One evening in the Arras Sector the writer saw an officer smash the nose cap off a " dud " with an axe, and there was no resultant explosion). Near home a stretcher party was sighted keeping direction on top by the trench, and after a brief exchange: " Who's on there, Taff? " " Corporal Imber." " Is he hurt much? " " Think so; he was hit on a wiring party," and the parties led on their respective ways and so—Vale!"

(To be continued)

One Night in Flanders

OR, THE STORY OF TWO VERY BRAVE MEN.

On the Eve of the 20th Anniversary of the Onset of the Third Battle of Ypres, our Contributor Dips into the Past with the following True Story.

By VICTOR HYDE, M.C.

(The well-known Writer on the Battlefields, and Author of " Flanders Sleeps," " East of Ypres," and other War Stories.)

ONCE more I am back in Flanders, thinking of my Hauptmann, and that grand fellow, Cyrus Q. Wollheim, late of Cincinnati, Ohio. You see, as near as makes no difference, it's all of Twenty Years After . . . I'll tell you the story.

The story of a night and a day, east of Ypres, two decades ago, and a year before the Armistice which seemed, then, as if it would never come. St. Julien had fallen, and my platoon had been ordered forward from brigade reserve for the escort of prisoners. But we never saw the enemy—not the ones we were to bring back to the cages—and a peregrinating platoon, fresh and forty strong, proved too tempting a morsel for a commander in action, with a thin outpost line likely to be counter-attacked at any moment, to miss.

This was not at all my idea of a Sunday in brigade reserve. I protested it was not what I came for, and that he had no authority over me whatever. All I got in return was to be told to stay where I was. I was thinking of the men, not of myself. If a squad of C3 bakers from the Base who didn't know the butt from the barrel had descended on St. Julien in that moment of crisis, Major Thompson would still have sent them into the breach. All the things I could call myself for missing the enemy would not alter the position. We were in the soup.

Our orders were to find and fill a 600 yards gap left in our front line after the attack that morning. Entering the line was a nightmare. The Ypres Salient—that vast featureless bog—was at its very worst. The ground had been bored and pocked by shell fire into countless pits and craters, anything from twenty to thirty feet in circumference, and three to twenty feet deep, with only a small and treacherous margin between the lip of one and the rim of the next. Every shell-hole spelled potential death. When you slithered off the lips of these filthy excavations you pitched into a stinking, clinging morass from which there was often no succour. At the bottom of each, splayed round its sides, jagged bits of metal gone to earth, pieces of human flesh, bits of horses and mule, and worse abominations than those. Over all, the pungent smell of cordite and the stench of death. . . . If this were not a respectable publication I could mention them; as it is, I leave it to you to imagine them.

Into these diabolical cavities rain had fallen pitilessly and continuously, and it was easy to sink waist-deep and beyond in that glutinous, embracing bog. Many were drowned in the Salient without even being hit.

Twice I sank to my armpits in that vile slime. I lost my watch, my helmet and my temper. I took a tin hat off a corpse. It had a hole punched neatly through the front . . . . .

The danger, on a night like this, when none knew quite where our line lay, of overstepping your own outposts and walking into the enemy lines, was very real.

When we ultimately reached the line of our deepest advance that day, the Germans were only forty yards away, still on the higher ground. I filled that ominous gap by the usual expedient of scattered outposts.

All evening we were shelled to blazes. At any moment we expected the barrage to lift and a counter attack to develop. But none came. The guns spewed up their destruction. The orchestra played on. It was one of the worst bombardments even the Salient ever saw.

How any human being lived through that inferno passes comprehension. Not one of us had a vestige of cover. Our khaki, caked and sodden, clung to frozen, half-starved bodies. I gave orders for iron rations to be eaten.

God was surely with us that night. Thousands of shells fell all around us, yet not a man was hit. And the boys of whom I was so proud had once again emerged triumphantly from the greatest test of all. To sit, helpless, without even the chance of doing battle, under a merciless bombardment, strained the nerve as nothing else.

Then things began to happen. The principal actors, on and off stage, were " A Captain in the Royal Sussex Regiment," sundry Brass Hats and Staff Big Wigs, an American Army doctor, and a platoon divorced from its parent body of the " Elegant Extracts."[1]

Towards midnight our first guest arrived. " Can you direct me to Langemarck? I've lost my way."

He's a hell of a long way from Langemarck, but there's plenty of time before dawn. You can see from his badges—the eight-pointed star and Cross of St. George —he is a captain in the Royal Sussex regiment, and those funny little crossed pick-axes tell you, the expert on badges you involuntarily became after three years of war, that he has strayed from a Pioneer battalion. He is making roads, as Pioneer battalions do, or did. In other words, he is " Labour." Being P.B.I., you feel a trifle superior about it.

He is asking you for whisky, and you hand him water from a petrol can because you haven't any Haig, and even if you had there isn't a corkscrew. What a war !

" The chloride's better to-night," you say, by way of being bright and chatty, and simulating the perfect host, as chalk and petrol vie for predominance in a liquid you optimistically like to think of as " water." There is precious little H_2O about it to-night, however. Yet even chloride can be as nectar. It depends on the circumstances.

It is just too bad about that working party; two hundred men, making roads, three kilometres away. That is why he is so anxious to get back to Langemarck. You think of Michael Fairless's classic story, " The Roadmender," and wish you had that book and the old roadmender's philosophy to-night.

He is too full of questions, however, this Captain in the Royal Sussex Regiment, to take any serious interest in Langemarck. The whole place is in ruins, and probably there isn't any beer, and road repairing is only a step above duckboard mending, so, after all, he will stay where he is. And as we said, there is plenty of time before dawn.

He has the talking mood on him tonight. You know what it is. Chatter, chatter.

" What regiment are you?
" How long have you been in the line?
" How many men have you?
" Who's your brigadier?
" What's that pill-box over there?
" Did you hear of their moving G.H.Q.?
" Where are your reserves?
" What are your casualties?
" Do you think they'll attack on the Somme? "

A Man seeking Information.

You may as well have the last Act. It was Curtain and Finality—Epilogue—in one. It was the Brass Hats and Staff Big Wigs who ordained it. That is our only excuse for dragging them into the story. The script read something like this—

" *A member of the enemy secret service was executed at dawn on the 27th for espionage behind the Allies Lines.*"

---

[1] Royal Fusiliers.

Hauptmann, I salute you! You assumed a role I would not have had the courage to assume. You were a pretty good actor, *Hauptmann,* but not quite good enough to see it through. You recall, of course, how, when I challenged you and said, " You are a Captain in the Sussex? " you squinted down your nose at your badges before replying? It was only momentary, *Hauptmann,* and you recovered yourself, yet after that I was merely playing with you. And you did ask rather a lot of questions, didn't you? And leading questions in the front line, as you know, were not encouraged.

Even when I sent you down to battalion headquarters under the promise—or was it a threat?—of a bed, you didn't know then I had spotted your little game, did you, *Hauptmann?* Both those men had their orders in case you tried any funny little tricks, so you had it coming to you either way, *Hauptmann.*

And why, when you had so many to choose from, did you pick on the badges of the old 35th and 107th Foot? I am a man of Kent myself, *Hauptmann,* and so not jealous, but then, I suppose they were the first that came to hand?

Anyway, *Hauptmann,* you've had a mighty fine sleep, and Langemarck wasn't high up on the list of front line spas, was it? So perhaps you are better off where you are . . . .

Nine o'clock the following morning, and another guest—and Another Very Brave Man. And for no better reason than to distribute largesse to the nearest troops he could find. Those troops, unfortunately, were ourselves, for daylight visitors who gave away your position to the enemy were not encouraged. I am afraid I was very rude to him.

He was as plain as a pikestaff to the foe who was either lazing, or waiting to see where he went to earth and then register us to the fraction of an inch. In any case, Cyrus's mind was not on bullets.

This product of an American medical school, in his first week of active service, and finding time hanging on his active young hands, proceeded to unload enough cigarettes and tobacco to open a kiosk. Cyrus had done his good deed for the day. For such a trivial reason, indeed, and no more, he had forsaken the relative safety of a dressing station for the uncertainty and lurking death of a front line shell-hole never for a moment beyond enemy observation. Who was it who said, " What fools men are?" . . . .

It was the kind of thing you did only in the first flush of active service. But only a damn fool did it. Later, if you lived, you acquired wisdom. Strange to say, Cyrus did live, but not for very long.

One would not have taken a penny-piece on his life as he picked his way back to his bandages. Nevertheless, when he disappeared over the skyline, he was intact. Like the draft-dodgers at the Base, and the man who pulled the pin from a Mills " to see what happened," that was just another of the war's wonders. Cyrus did not know quite how lucky he had been.

At midnight, after a repetition of the previous nights's shelling, we were relieved. Never did I move out of the line so speedily on top of my relieving troops as then. Cheddar Villa[1] was going to seem very sweet indeed. But first I had a duty call to make on Cyrus. Having had time to cool off, I now wished to offer him the apology I failed to give at the time.

In such chastened spirit I entered the dressing station. Cyrus Q. Wollheim was there, but under a ground sheet. Cyrus Q. Wollheim, in fact, was dead.

---

[1] *A one-room winter residence standing in its own grounds, facing east. Commanding, but never at any time even remotely desirable. Uninterrupted views in all directions, and good shooting over the district. Likewise bed and " bored." The mortality figure was high, however, and long leases were not guaranteed. The garden was a bit out of condition, and the neighbours had acquired a nasty habit of throwing things over the fence when you weren't looking. The last tenants left complaining of the smell. For keys to view, apply Mr. S. Alient, St, Julien, or direct to the P.B.I.*

He had been out in the open, succouring the wounded, when a five-nine took his own stomach away. Thus passed A Very Gallant Gentleman.

I forgot all about that inferno; I forgot all about our own hungers and thirsts and miseries. I felt I had lost a friend. I could not even say I was sorry. So if you don't mind, I'll apologise now, Cyrus. Atta boy, doc.!

In other words, dear friends, A PILL BOX . . . .

They put him in a steel casket and sent him home with 40,000 other dough-boys.[1] Then when the final American reckoning was made, as the battlefields became cemeteries, the cost of 80,000 steel coffins presented a barrier even to an America that wanted to do right by its dead. So they left the half of them and took the rest. They took Cyrus Q. Wollheim, who risked his life for a fag for others.

(The rest of Mr. Hyde's article is held over owing to pressure on space).

[1] *Seventy-six thousand seven hundred and forty-nine American soldiers were killed in the Great War; 46,214 were returned to the United States for reburial, and the rest, 30,535, were interred in Europe, where they remain.*

* * *

The Advance from Mons

(VON BLOEM).

AN APPRECIATION.

By MAJOR L. J. L. PULLAR, M.C.

(Late 1st Battalion, The Seaforth Highlanders)

IT is not possible within the space at my disposal to adequately appreciate such an excellent work as has been given to us from the pen of the soldier-author Von Bloem, entitled "The Advance from Mons" (published by Messrs. Peter Davies of 30, Henrietta Street, London).

The book itself is not a text-book or intended as such, but a vivid narrative of events during that rapid movement through Belgium and Northern France, as they actually occurred and were experienced by the author himself—a well-known German novelist—who was, prior to hostilities, a Captain on the Reserve in that famous Regiment the 12th Brandenburg Grenadiers, a Regiment which formed part of the III Corps of General Von Kluck's First Army.

Writing immediately, as he did, after the actual events the book records his impressions before time or other influences blurred or distorted them. It should of course be remembered that Von Bloem was a novelist and some may argue that there appears a tendency to gloss over, and in some cases ignore, certain happenings which might not be too acceptable to his own countrymen. Be that as it may, the record of his experiences as a junior regimental officer, carrying out a subordinate, albeit a most important role, that of Company Commander on the field of battle must be of interest to those officers who have been, and invaluable to those who may be, similarly employed.

The work should be particularly instructive to the junior officer and the senior non-commissioned officer, since it is the junior in rank on the battlefield who can see and feel first hand the good or bad effects of a training system on his fighting personnel when confronted with the unforeseen and frightful.

The Great German General Staff violated the neutrality of Belgium and entered the war conscious of the fact that they were wrong to do so, but convinced that their organisation and efficiency in the art of war permitted it and relied on a swift and sweeping victory to put matters right afterwards.

It is of course possible that they hypnotised themselves, and that part of Europe that threw in their lot with them that their course of action was proper and it is probable that they could not see the reverse side of the picture.

For years they had regarded the British Army as insignificant and the shock they received on their first contact with it had very far reaching results.

In this connection quoting Von Bloem " Reports coming in seemed to confirm the fact that the English were in front of us. We knew what they looked like by the Comic Papers. There was much joking about this, and also Bismarck's remark of sending the police to arrest the English Army."

So incredible did it seem to them that the terrible casualties they were suffering could come from the British soldiers that they thought at once—we are being fired on by our own troops in error. Again quoting Von Bloem, " It must be our troops but luckily we had a way of stopping that, who has the red flag? Grenadier Just produced it and waved it wildly. No result, in fact the fire became even heavier. Lie down Just, good fellow, it's no use, they must see, but they won't believe." It never occurred to them that any other troops but their own understood even the elementary principles of fire tactics.

After the first clash with the British the following conversation between Von Bloem and his Battalion Commander is significant. " I don't know yet how the other Battalions have fared, but it seems to have been terrible for them all. What a day Bloem, perfectly ghastly, the battalion is all to pieces, my splendid battalion."

Again quoting Von Bloem, " Then they did know something about war, those cursed English, a fact soon to be confirmed on all sides, wonderful how they had converted every house and every wall into a little fortress; the experience no doubt of old soldiers gained in a dozen colonial wars. A bad defeat, there could be no gainsaying it, in our first battle we had been badly beaten and by the English we had so laughed at a few hours before."

And so ended the first clash, which after all was but a rearguard action, covering a brilliantly executed withdrawal of the British Expeditionary Force, step by step, to other positions in rear, inflicting again and again such terrific losses on the " invulnerable " German Army in its advance as to cause the gravest anxiety to the Great German General Staff, and to destroy for ever that quality they then possessed to a considerable degree, a quality that cannot be learned since it is a " gift "— " conceit."

The Retreat to the Seine and the Battle of the Marne was a magnificent exhibition, the like of which the world had never seen before, of marching, endurance, fighting, discipline and shooting. The rifle shooting of the British troops was of an amazing standard, particularly its rapid fire, called the " Mad Minute." On many occasions it was this latter type of fire that gave rise to the German belief that the British were armed with thousands of machine guns, instead of only two per Battalion of Infantry and two per Cavalry Regiment. It was this type of fire that harassed the Germans so much in their advance from Mons.

Von Bloem's experience as a Company Commander in the German Advance from Mons, covers useful ground to a military student, embracing as it does a variety of factors. Von Bloem deals with propaganda and condemns much of it as totally untrue. That propaganda of a certain type was used by nearly all the belligerents is undoubtedly true. It is based on the tenets of Von Clausewitz, i.e., to stir up the national emotion of peoples to give a suitable motive for war. Clausewitz states " War is a conflict between States, carried on by violence in which each side employs force, such a conflict involves not merely the intention but the feeling also and is always accompanied by an explosion of hostile passions and is a trinity composed of (i) Brute force, hate and hostility; (ii) Play of chance and probability; (iii) Its nature as a political instrument.

Hence propaganda must always play an important part. The stronger the motives of a war, the more they will embrace the whole nation.

As regards the tactical side of Von Bloem's experience he lays stress on the value of enfilade fire and the importance of making use of dead ground in his forward rushes. He suffered very much from the accuracy of the British fire. He was astonished at the ingenious manner in which the British troops made use of buildings and walls to deliver that fire with the most deadly effect and the minimum of danger to themselves. The incessant and unexpected harassing fire tactics of the rear parties of the rearguard itself caused many casualties to the advancing German troops and robbed them of much needed morale, and what was equally important, forced them to abandon their fast moving formations in order to deploy to overcome the resistance. Sometimes a few rifle shots were sufficient to make a whole column deploy.

Von Bloem goes on to say " It was occasional surprises that one noticed the men, and oneself as well, were not steady under fire. A fear almost amounting to panic seemed to overtake the columns, such as rarely occurred in the middle of a battle."

Discipline in Von Bloem's Command was undoubtedly of a high order and not the iron-handed variety one has been given to believe existed throughout the whole German System. He is a little reticent about some things, but candidly admits that his men did go about in search of food in an improper manner, which, after all, was not terribly serious. He never failed to administer reprimand or punishment sufficient to meet the case. Certain also was it that he had the confidence and affection of his troops and there is only one way an officer can get that and keep it.

The discipline and morale of the British Army in 1914 was the wonder of the civilised world and the reason is not difficult to find. It was a discipline induced by the confidence and affection the rank and file had for their superiors in rank, the inculcating into the minds of men that there can never be a loss of dignity or self respect in obedience to reasonable commands, and that such surrender of one's independence as may be necessary to gaining a desired end, when that end is for the good of the whole, of which the individual forms a part and must therefore share in the benefit that follows.

Subservience to discipline does not mean that one surrenders one's individuality to a superior in rank, but that one trains oneself to think on the same lines as the superior and carry out the orders in the spirit they are issued.

It appears certain that Von Bloem did not share the belief that a rigid form of discipline was essential to military success, and maybe there were many others like him of whom we know nothing.

In any event it may be truthfully said that the Germans were brave and worthy foes.

Public Schools O.T.C. Battlefields Tour

Arrangements for the fourth annual Public Schools O.T.C. Battlefields Tour, which took place from April 10th to 13th, were, as on the three previous occasions, placed in the capable hands of the Ypres League. Major E. Montague Jones, O.B.E., M.A., was in charge of the party, which numbered some eighty officers and cadets, and Mr. O. Mears, from League Headquarters, accompanied the party as the League Representative.

In buoyant mood and eagerly looking forward to their forthcoming adventure, the party assembled at Victoria Station on Saturday morning, April 10th, and were greeted by Lieut.-General Sir William Pulteney, G.C.V.O., K.C.B., K.C.M.G., D.S.O., Chairman of the Ypres League, and Lieut.-General the Baron Vincotte, the Belgian Military Attache. The appearance of these two very distinguished soldiers at so early an hour to see the party off was deeply appreciated by all. Sir William Pulteney generously presented to each cadet a map depicting the battlefields to be visited.

The reservations for the party had been altered at the last moment to a little later train and at 9.38 a.m. the first part of the journey, London to Dover, was commenced. The crossing from Dover to Ostend, fortunately, did not prove a formidable one on this occasion and very few casualties were reported as a result of mal-de-mer.

On arrival at Ostend production of the "laissez-passer" so courteously granted by His Excellency, the Belgian Ambassador, made the passage through the Customs a mere formality, and within a very short time the whole party were aboard the motor coaches, which were found waiting to receive them at the Maritime station. On former occasions the journey to Ypres had been made by rail. The extra comfort afforded the party, apart from time saved and better facility for viewing the country, as a result of the League's new arrangements, was much appreciated.

Accommodation at Ypres had been reserved at Hotel Skindles and Hotel Splendide & Britannique and within a few minutes of arrival all had been safely deposited in their respective rooms. At 7.0 p.m. all were ready for the initial meal at Ypres and at 8.30 p.m. the party assembled at Hotel Skindles for an Illustrated Talk by the Official Lecturers to the Tour. With the kind permission of the War Office, Lieut.-Colonel The Viscount Bridgeman, M.C., and Major C. P. Warren, M.C., had journeyed from London specially for the occasion, and their talk on the Battlefields was listened to with intense interest. The cadets were taken over the ground they were to cover during the following two days' tour and information conveyed to them at these lectures would be amplified by further explanations and personal reminiscences on the actual ground. In this connection the above mentioned officers was assisted by Major S. Jones, M.C., Rifle Brigade, who had also kindly made the trip in order to make the Tour both interesting and instructive for the cadets.

The Ypres League's Chairman, Sir William Pulteney, who had, as stated, seen the party off at Victoria, travelled over to Ypres by a later train and still further showed his practical interest in these particular Tours by being present at the Lecture, a gesture which was unanimously appreciated and applauded.

On Sunday morning a trip was made to Poperinghe to visit the famous old house of "TOC H." Here the party was privileged to listen to an interesting talk on "Toc H" and its work by Major Paul Slessor, who had made special arrangements to be on hand this particular morning in order to receive the party. The Cadets appeared very impressed as they were conducted through the various rooms by Major Slessor, especially on reaching the Chapel used by the gallant fellows who fought in the defence of the Salient.

The party returned to Ypres in time to attend a service in the Ypres British Church, afterwards assembling in the School playground for

Photo]   [Evening News.
Lieut.-General The Baron Vincotte, Belgian Embassy and Lieut.-General Sir William Pulteney with the Cadets at Victoria.

the usual group photograph. This was followed by a wreath of red poppies being placed by Major E. Montague Jones, O.B.E., M.A., on behalf of the Public Schools O.T.C. at the Ypres Town War Memorial.

The card attached to the wreath bore the folloing inscription :—

" In memory of the fallen soldiers of our gallant Belgian Ally who fought side by side with our British Armies in the Immortal Defence of Ypres, 1914—1918."

From the Officers and Cadets of the English Public Schools, O.T.C.

The Cadets formed up three sides of a square opposite the Memorial and after the wreath was placed in position by Major Jones a one-minute's silence was observed.

The Departure

Photo] [*Evening News*

Dispersing quietly many took advantage of the short interval before lunch to visit the Cathedral and view the ruins of the old Cloth Hall.

After lunch a tour of the Ypres Salient Battlefields was undertaken, halts being made at the many outstanding places of interest and also at several spots where the lecturers were able to relate their personal reminiscences, which were found highly interesting. The previous evening's Illustrated Talk considerably helped the party to comprehend the significance of the ground over which they were now travelling.

Returning to Ypres in time for dinner the cadets were assembled again at 8.45 p.m. for a further Illustrated Talk, this time at the Hotel Splendide & Britannique. At the conclusion of an extremely interesting and instructive Talk by Lord Bridgeman and Major Warren, the party showed their appreciation of the efforts of these two Officers on their behalf by giving them three resounding cheers, which indeed they had well earned.

The following day was the occasion for a whole-day battlefields tour into France as far south as Vimy Ridge. As on the previous day, the Officers spared no effort in interesting the cadets en route, halts being made at several places and battles and outstanding engagements described to them. Vimy Ridge in particular proved quite an attraction, the cadets being very thrilled with all to be seen there; the gigantic Canadian Memorial; the trenches and tunnels, and general war debris lying about. The last stand on the return to Ypres was on Kemmel Hill, where usually a wonderful panoramic view of the Salient can be obtained. Visability on this occasion, however, was not of the best, but compensation was afforded by the vivid descriptions of the fighting in that area by the Staff Officers.

On the last evening at Ypres the whole party assembled at 8.45 p.m. for a short Service prior to the sounding of the " Last Post " at the Menin Gate. The Revd. G. R. Milner, M.A., conducted the Service, and among the notable people present were the Burgomaster of Ypres and the Chief of Police. A wreath was then placed at the Memorial on behalf of the Officers and Cadets by the senior Officer present. The inscription on the card attached was as follows :

" In proud memory of the glorious British Dead who fell in the immortal Defence of Ypres, 1914—1918, and who have no known graves but whose names are inscribed on this Memorial."

From the Officers and Cadets of the English Public Schools, O.T.C.

Tuesday morning saw the party off on the return journey to London, which was reached at 4.30 p.m. after another pleasant channel crossing, this time on the s.s. Prince Baudouin, undoubtedly the best boat on this service.

Observing the animation of the cadets as they greeted their folk at Victoria it was apparent that the Tour had been a huge success and for this happy state of circumstances the thanks of all are due to Viscount Bridgeman, Major C. P. Warren, and Major S. Jones; to Major E. Montague Jones, The Ypres League under whose auspices the Tour was organised, and their League representative at Ypres, Mr. C. Leupe.

Representative Party of the Fourth Annual Public Schools O.T.C. Tour Assembled in The Ypres British School Playground.

Photo] *[Daniel, Ypres.*

The "Shinies" Back Again

Whitsuntide Battlefields Tour to Ypres and The Somme.
Dedication of a Banner at St. George's Church, Ypres.

By C. D. Planck.

The second Battlefields Tour of the "Shiny Seventh" took place at Whitsuntide last, and was undoubtedly a great success. Forty members of the 7th (City of London) Battalion, The London Regiment, O.C.A., left Victoria on Saturday, the 15th May, this being a far greater number than on our previous Tour, and included five members who were with us on that occasion.

We were fortunate in having with us a member with a cine-camera and pictures were taken throughout the tour with a view to showing them at our next Annual Dinner.

One of the chief objects of this year's visit was to dedicate a Banner at St. George's Church, Ypres, in memory of all Ranks who fell in the Great War.

On arrival at Ostend, following a very pleasant crossing, we were conducted to the motor coach which was to convey us to Ypres, instead of making the journey as formerly by rail. This new arrangement by the Ypres League for parties travelling under their auspices was much appreciated and, apart from the extra comfort, permitted us to do some sight-seeing en route.

Our party, which was graced by the presence of six ladies, also included two ex-tommies with artificial legs and one minus an arm lost at Loos; the latter assured us that he intended to find the spot where the damage was done.

We were soon on our way along the front to Nieuport where, in passing, we were able to obtain a good view of the pleasantly situated British Memorial to the Missing.

One or two members could be observed examining the sketch diagram of the route, which had been issued to the party in the form of blue prints to enable them to follow the itinerary. We had to ease up to pass a horse and cart and as a matter of interest to the company the writer asked them to note the single rope used as a rein, a great laugh went up when it was seen on passing that the horse was being driven with leather reins—however, the driver of our motor-coach came to my assistance by saying "It is the only pair in Belgium, you will not see any more "; and neither did we.

Proceeding on our way to Dixmude we passed a Belgian Cemetery, all thought how nice it looked and how attractive were the headstones, each bearing, in a small circle, the Belgian National colours. A halt was made at Poelcappelle and after viewing the monument to the French Air Ace, Guynemer, I walked over to the ruined tank just too late to hear Hill's lecture on tanks generally.

Our next stop was at Tyne Cot Cemetery, where we paid our respects at the grave of Major H. S. Green, who was killed in September, 1917; he was the brother of Colonel C. J. Salkeld Green, D.S.O., M.C., whom we were very delighted to have travelling with us. The panel containing the names of missing "7th" men was also inspected and everyone was full of praise for the splendid condition of the Cemetery. Continuing we reached the Menin Road at Gheluvelt and eased up to get a view of the Memorial to the Worcesters who filled the gap on a certain historic occasion early in the War and I believe finished up at about the same spot at the Armistice. Ahead of us could be seen the Memorial to the Gloucesters and close by the site of Clapham Junction with a view to one side of the road of Glencorse, Nonne Bosschen and Polygon Woods. It was just off Clapham Junction on 15th September, 1917, that the "Shinies" made a successful raid on a German stronghold. Lieut. B. N. Cryer was unfortunately killed in this raid, and the stronghold became known as Cryer Farm in his memory. Although previous attacks on this strong point had failed, the "7th" succeeded, ten of the occupants were killed and thirty six taken prisoners, our casualties were comparatively small; a determined counter attack the following morning was held off. Within a few days of this the 1st Battalion of the 7th London Regiment, left the Salient after eleven months' continuous service in the Ypres area.

Our next point of interest was Hooge Cemetery which has been constructed on the site of the old craters, our cookers used to be at the far end near Zouave Wood, many possibly will recall the difficult journeys of the ration parties over the brushwood track from the cookers to Clapham Junction, under observation the whole way. Who can remember our daylight relief and again the day when we ourselves were relieved by the Australians and left Clapham Junction, six at a time, to make our own way to Cafe Belge?

On past Hell Fire Corner and through the Menin Gate to the Hotel Splendide, where after a wash and brush up, we all enjoyed the excellent dinner provided.

At 9 p.m. we assembled at the Menin Gate for that impressive ceremony of the "Last Post," after which Colonel C. J. Salkeld Green placed a wreath on behalf of the Old Comrades' Association in memory of those who made the great sacrifice. The evening was fine and the opportunity was taken for a stroll around the town. At a neighbouring estaminet a large

The Dedicated Banner.

number of German ex-service men were encountered and several interesting conversations were held, songs were sung by both parties, but chief honours went to Danny Steele for his song rendered from the balcony. Two of our number played billiards, but found the absence of pockets rather a handicap.

Everyone was up in good time on Sunday morning and all made for the British Church of St. George's, where the short Dedication Service was to be held preparatory to the unveiling of the 7th London Banner, which had been brought over with us and placed in position overnight. The Service was conducted by the resident Chaplain, the Revd. G. R. Milner, M.A., who, with well chosen words, spoke of the significance of our gathering together that day, and also of that very fine spirit of comradeship shown by all who served. A few simple prayers and the Banner was unveiled with appropriate words by Colonel C. J. Salkeld Green. Following a one minute's silence, the hymn "O God Our Help In Ages Past" was sung, and the Service concluded with the National Anthem. The Banner seen now for the first time hung in position looked well, the design appears splendidly proportioned and has been carried out in the regimental colours of scarlet and buff.

Our coach awaited us and very shortly afterwards we were on our way to Arras and the Somme. Out of Ypres, on past the London Scottish Memorial at Messines then the Ploegsteert Memorial and shortly after, the frontier at Le Bizet. Here formalities were soon over and 10.30 a.m. found us passing through Armentieres. Further on we halted to get a view of "The Christ of the Trenches" and eased up upon passing the Indian and Portuguese Memorials, continuing on, we reached Le Touret Memorial and here viewed the panel to the missing "7th" men.

The next stop was at the Festubert cross roads by the Church and the position of the old front line of 1915. Outside, the village was searched for and found, also Dead Cow Farm and the spot where Major Barnes was wounded.

Twenty-two years ago to the very date the " Shinies " moved into this part of the line for the first time.

Our journey continued over the La Bassèe Canal, where Michael O'Leary won the V.C., and on through Cambrin where Mr. S. H. Geller (Ypres League Representative accompanying the party) pointed out No. 1 Harley Street, a large corner building used as a dressing station during the War and which still stands in its original state.

The ladies of our party were immensely interested by the large number of little girls whom we saw all dressed in long white silk dresses and veils on their way to their first Communion Service. Re-entering our coach, we then travelled on via Vermelles to Dud Corner Cemetery, Loos, where again as last year, the battle positions were discussed, and our friend Johansen was satisfied that it was on this part of the road that he lost his arm.

This cemetery, like all others, is beautifully kept, the panel to the Missing "7th" men was viewed, and the names revived many memories to some of the party present who had gone over the top with them.

This cemetery contains 1,800 graves and records 20,693 Missing. Time was getting on, but we could not leave Loos without visiting the Loos British Cemetery. The number of grave stones with the "7th" badges on in this cemetery with the inscription "Known unto God" underneath is appalling; here let me explain—and I have it on good authority that these men who fell at the Battle of Loos all received a proper burial, and each man had a wooden cross erected over his grave, nearly all were buried near the Crassier. Subsequently, however, this ground was fought over again and eventually the bodies were discovered and buried as unknown.

Full speed ahead for Vimy, after a view of the immense Canadian Memorial the trenches and tunnels were visited, and the half hour spent here was most interesting, particularly to the ladies who saw for the first time something of the conditions under which many of us existed during the War.

The party were now feeling a little hungry— we being about an hour behind schedule. However, ten minutes later saw us at Arras and very soon we were getting on the right side of a good dinner which was thoroughly enjoyed by all.

In view of the pressure of business thrown on his own establishment during this particular week-end by the sudden influx of visitors to Arras, the proprietor of the Hotel Moderne had very kindly arranged for our party to take lunch at Le Pré Fleurie, thinking that in the circumstances we should be more comfortable and obtain quicker service. This arrangement suited us very well indeed and was much appreciated. Le Pré Fleurie is noted for its open air dance hall and fine band, the hotel itself stands in extensive grounds which contained swings, see-saws, a zoo, and last, but not least, a donkey. It was upon the latter that Gardner mounted and with the attendant's peak cap on back to front, caused great amusement by passing Captain Head at the Salute. Our cine-camera was again hard at work, and one of the ladies decided to try her luck on the donkey, but had only gone a few yards when the saddle slipped and so did she. I fancy that the cine-camera just failed to record this event. Meanwhile Addison and Marett were busy on the swings and one way and another the cine-camera was in great demand. Following this little recreation, " All Aboard " was called, and very shortly we were heading for the Somme. Skirting Bapaume we took the road to Albert and pulled up at Warlencourt Cemetery; here everyone was struck with the magnificent show of violas which occupied the fronts of the two centre rows of headstones throughout the entire depth of the cemetery.

A large number of " 7th " men lay buried here, including Captain Flower whose grave, with others, comes under the heading of " Special Memorial," as he is " believed to be buried here."

On again, past the Butte de Warlencourt, which now looks vastly different from the old days, through Martinpuich to High Wood, here at the Memorial of the 47th Division a wreath was placed by Colonel C. J. Salkeld Green.

After this ceremony we walked to the edge of the wood and Colonel Green explained the position of the 7th London and the direction of the attack made on 15th September, 1916, when tanks were first used. Four days fighting at High Wood cost the Division just over 4,500 officers and men in casualties. We drove up to the entrance of the South African Memorial and then proceeded past Flat Iron Copse, the gun positions for High Wood and on via Contalmaison to La Boisselle. Here we halted to have a look at the gigantic crater; George Hill paced round the lip and it was estimated to have a diameter of 100 yards. In this area one still has to be careful of strands of barbed wire sticking out of the ground. One lady did tear her coat on some barbed wire, but the remarks were very different to those used by troops in similar circumstances. Several old shells were found and the ladies got a good idea of how muddy a trench could be, from the mud we all collected in walking up the road. Travelling on to Pozieres, we obtained a view of the Australian Divisional Memorial, and then took the road to Thiepval to view the Memorial to the Missing on the Somme. Apart from the very long panel of " 7th " men who were " missing," many of the party had relations whose names were on panels connected with other regiments; many photographs were taken. Everyone appeared overawed with the size and beautiful setting of this Memorial.

A welcome cup of tea was obtained at a near-by café, but, owing to our large number, I am afraid we put a great strain on the teapot, and for a few the tea, although wet and warm, was of a doubtful quality. Latecomers were served in small basins, reminiscent of the way we used to have " café au lait " in the old days.

Twelve members of the party who were with the "Shinies" at Festubert twenty-two years ago.

At 7.15 "All aboard" again and after a good run a halt was made at Arras, and from here onwards we had a very enjoyable sing song chief honours for leading going to the ladies, Mrs. Holmes in particular, well supported by George Hill and the entire company. All the old war-time songs came to life, including our Regimental March "Lady Greensleeves," "Away to the Old Canteen" and " Spit and Shine," the psalm of the " Shiny Seventh."

En route we were afforded a final view of the Canadian Memorial at Vimy, as this can be seen for miles around when floodlit, and looks very imposing. Passing Hulloch, the Regimental March " Lady Greensleeves " was whistled. The frontier was reached and, after a ten minute stop we were again on our way and our Hotel was reached at 11 p.m., after a wonderful trip of approximately 145 miles. We all did justice to the splendid dinner prepared for us by the Proprietor of the Splendide and so to bed.

The following morning some of the party were early astir, visiting the Menin Gate and Ramparts, and at 9.30 we took our seats for a short trip of the Salient. Passing through Lille Gate, I noticed an invitation to visit the tunnels in the ramparts which seemed fresh to me. From beyond Lille Gate and looking back we had a good view of the Ramparts Cemetery, further up the road we passed Shrapnel Corner and Woodcote House, Mount Kemmel could be seen clearly in the distance. Bedford House Cemetery was reached and a halt was made at the Canal Bank by the Demarcation Stone. Here it was arranged for some of the party to walk up the Canal Bank while the remainder went with the charabanc via St. Eloi to the Bluff to meet the walkers.

Spoilbank and Chester Farm Cemeteries were visited, in the latter are buried several of 300 men of the 25th London who were drafted to the 7th London and joined the Regiment at Halifax Camp.

The bolder spirits of the party decided to climb and explore Spoilbank; this they did, crossed the Canal higher up and made for the White Chateau which was captured by the " Shinies " on 7th June, 1917. The remains of the Chateau are now being used as the last resting place of two French officers. A grass track surrounds the moss-covered ruins and in a small recess under the ruins behind a glass panel can be seen the skull and bones, presumably of the two officers referred to, and to whom a stone pillar has been erected on the boundary of the land. The party at St. Eloi visited Bus House Cemetery, and upon the walking party returning we headed for Ypres and an early lunch was taken.

Before taking our seats on the coach for the return journey to Ostend, we assembled outside our Hotel for a photograph. This completed, we were soon travelling out of Ypres past Salvation Corner on to Essex Farm, with the Memorial to the West Riding Division in the background. Our driver, M. Cyrille Leupe, deserves our hearty thanks for his steady driving, and on the route we were now travelling he proved most interesting, as he had fought in this area during the War with the 1st Carinbineers. We eased up to view the Gas Memorial and M. Leupe pointed out the positions of the front where the gas attack was made. We were now running parallel to the old Belgian front line and many signs are still visible, especially about Ramscappelle. At Nieuport we had a view of the trenches retained by the Belgians for exhibition, the proceeds obtained being for the Belgian ex-service men.

Along the front between Nieuport and Ostend several remains of concrete pill boxes can still be seen.

At Ostend we went straight on board the Princess Astrid and had a most enjoyable return trip. The weather was good, everyone had thoroughly enjoyed themselves, and Danny Steele caused great amusement on the boat by his imitations of a hawker selling tooth powder, he brought forth roars of laughter with his efforts to advertise a famous hair restorer, and again as a ladies' barber. It will be some time before we forget his efforts as a showman with the "Sleeping Beauty." Danny's conjuring with a banana, roll and a camp stool were highly amusing, and his spontaneous wit brought tears to our eyes, through so much laughter.

Nearing Dover a message in a bottle was flung overboard, and the whole party sang " That old bass bottle."

At Dover we were soon through the Customs and on the train for London which was reached at 10.30 p.m., to find ourselves all mixed up with the crowds who had been viewing the Coronation decorations.

For so pleasant and interesting a Tour we are grateful to the Ypres League for arrangements made on our behalf and to their representative, Mr. S. H. K. Geller, who proved extremely helpful to us throughout the trip.

THE
ANNUAL GENERAL MEETING
OF THE
YPRES LEAGUE
WILL BE HELD ON
MONDAY, JULY 19th, at 6 p.m.
At Headquarters Offices:
20, ORCHARD STREET,
LONDON, W.1.

7th Lincolnshire Regiment O.C.A.

BATTLEFIELDS TOUR TO ARRAS.

On Saturday, May 15th, a party of fourteen ex-members of the above Battalion, together with a few friends gathered at Victoria Station for a tour to the battlefields which was arranged for them by the Ypres League.

Actually, the party consisted of members who survive from some forty or more who joined up from the same London business house in September, 1914, and was therefore in the nature of a re-union.

As soon as the train departed from Victoria the " flood gates " as it were, were opened, and yarns were spun, reminiscences exchanged, making the journey to Folkestone appear an extremely short one. Most of the party weathered the choppy crossing to Boulogne well, but the writer has a suspicion that at least one or two were relieved when Boulogne was reached! There was some delay in getting away from the Douane and again at the Ville station, reminding one of the irritating delays experienced during the War, so " Grousing, grousing, grousing " simply had to be sung. However, once on the move, Amiens was soon reached and the necessary change here and short wait for the Arras train permitted time for a little refreshment. At Arras accommodation had been reserved for the party at the Hotel Moderne, and after depositing suit-cases and experiencing the welcome reviver of a wash and brush-up we were quite ready for the excellent dinner provided. Later the party explored, in twos and threes, the sights of Arras.

After breakfast next day, the party left for a whole-day tour of the Somme battlefields by motor coach, returning to Arras on conclusion of a most interesting and enlightening trip. Monday morning saw the party off again, this time for a Tour as far northwards as Ypres. At the Immortal City the short stay of one hour passed all too quickly. In the afternoon a tour of the Salient Battlefields and Memorials were undertaken, the party being most impressed with the beauty of the Cemeteries and the dignity of the Memorials.

During the two days' tour the graves of many of the original 7th Lincolnshire were seen. It was a comfort to the party, as it must be to the relatives of the Fallen, to know how carefully and tenderly these graves are maintained by that wonderful organisation, The Imperial War Graves Commission.

The last evening at Arras was made cheerier through being joined by several ex-tommies from other parties, all battlefield visiting.

All were agreed that the Tour had been a great success and the party expressed its appreciation of the services rendered by Mr. W. Hole in initiating the Tour and looking after things generally, and to Captain R. P. Pridham, M.C., who accompanied the party as Ypres League Representative.   F. B.

7th Lincs. O.C.A. Party at the Canadian Memorial, St. Julien.

Fifth Army (1916-1918) Old Comrades Association

Whitsuntide Battlefields Tour of the Somme.

Several friends were at Victoria Station on Saturday morning, May 15th, to see our party off on the first stage of our journey to Amiens. Thirty two members were taking part in this Tour including six ladies.

The bustle incidental to the departure of a boat train reminded some of us of the " going over " under other conditions, when the railway officials were not in evidence to " punch our tickets." The crossing from Folkestone to Boulogne was extremely pleasant, although one of our number thought it " rather rough." The weather was warm, if a little dull, and on landing at Boulogne all appeared to be in good spirits. " Is it to be Martin's Camp, or are we going up this afternoon? " was asked, recalling experiences of twenty years ago. The usual peace-time push and scramble off the boat and through the Customs, then very shortly we were aboard the train for Amiens. En route, many were watching for remembered wayside stations, and ere long that well-known place, Etaples, was reached. Some may have recalled it on account of its snow or mud—or its heat and dust—others, perhaps of a glorious bathe at the Paris Plage—or a meal in comfort with a cloth on the table at Le Touquet, or was it the hospitals?

Reaching Amiens eventually, we were welcomed at the station by the Amiens Ypres League Representative, Captain Stuart Oswald, M.C., late K.R.R.C., who, after arranging for the transport of our hand luggage, conducted us to the Hotel de la Paix, where accommodation had been reserved for the party. After the welcome dinner, Captain Oswald took us along to one of the more popular cafés, where we had not been seated long before a rather motley torchlight procession, complete with bands in uniform, passed along the street. The remainder of this evening was mainly spent in exploring the city and its cathedral.

We were early astir on the Sunday morning, and by 8.0 a.m. our motor coach, with Mr. Bristow (late British Army) as driver appeared on the scene, ready to transport the members on the first stage of the battlefields tour. The route taken was via the Albert Road to Pont Noyelles, Corbie, Bray, Mametz, Albert, Thiepval to Bapaume. Here lunch was taken, and afterwards the journey continued to St. Quentin via Gouzeacourt and Vermand, several stops being made on the way to visit cemeteries. Vermand, incidentally, is the suggested site for the Fifth Army Memorial. Arriving at St. Quentin, we found the town en fete, the many attractions and bands helping to pass the evening very enjoyably.

Monday morning we left St. Quentin for Peronne, passing Cerisy, La Fère, Pithon, Ham, Athies, Le Mesnil en route. Lunch had been arranged for us at Peronne, and at 3.0 p.m. we were off again, heading this time for Noyon, where the night was spent. Our itinerary took us through Misery, Licourt, Nesle and Roye. Nesle was the one-time headquarters of our Commander, General Sir Hubert Gough. A number of photographs were taken of the H.Q. in the main street, and we tried to visualise, on this peaceful afternoon, the coming and going that must have marked the activities of those carrying out the wishes and orders of our General.

Eventually we arrived at Noyon and at the Hotel St. Eloi, where we were to be " billetted " that night, the party were pleasantly surprised to find the hotel so beautifully situated, standing in its own grounds amongst masses of trees. The cathedral is still in the course of reconstruction, and many houses remain in ruins.

As this was our last night of the Tour we followed the dinner by honouring the Loyal Toast, also remembering our fallen comrades and absent friends.

By 8.30 a.m. on the Tuesday morning we set off for the return journey to Amiens, prior to catching the evening boat from Boulogne for home. As a good many had not seen the "Big Bertha" near Proyat it was decided to slightly alter the itinerary and include a visit there. On the way, however, the road became little more than a farm track and the path to the big gun gave a fair idea of the Somme mud. Afterwards the journey continued via Warfusée, Abancourt and Villers Bretonneux, arriving at Amiens 1.30 p.m.

Captain Oswald greeted us, full of sympathy for the bad weather he apparently imagined we had been having; we, however, was able to assure him that rain, at least, had not worried us at all.

An excellent lunch was served at the Hotel de la Paix, and afterwards the party split up to make purchases of souvenirs and presents for those at home.

At 4.45 p.m. Captain Oswald and Mr. Gordon (late Australian Army) came and saw our party off at Amiens Station for the journey to Boulogne wishing us bon voyage. Another smooth channel crossing and an uneventful journey from Folkestone found us at Victoria about 11.50 p.m.

Several letters have been received from those taking part in the Tour, expressing their great satisfaction with all arrangements made on their behalf. One member writes to pay tribute to the Imperial War Graves Commission for the beautiful way in which the cemeteries are tended and maintained. In this regard no matter how many cemeteries we visited there was always the same dignity and beauty, the grey stones and the green grass, the flowers, rosemary, lavender, and in several the rose bushes —just ready to burst into bloom, one rose over each grave—a veritable Garden unto God.

For a wonderful Tour and pilgrimage we acknowledge our indebtedness to the Committee of the Fifth Army O.C.A., The Ypres League; Captain Stuart Oswald and his staff; Mr. Gordon and Mr. Bristow; and finally to Mr. J. Boughey, who accompanied our party throughout as Ypres League Representative, and proved most helpful. We are looking forward to the next Tour, which we hope will be as successful.

H. D. BRADFORD, Captain.

The Party at Proyat (Big Bertha).

Matey

By Patrick Macgill.

Not comin' back to-night, matey,
And reliefs are comin' through,
We're all goin' out all right, matey,
Only we're leavin' you.

Gawd! it's a bloody sin, matey,
Now that we've finished the fight,
We go when reliefs come in, matey,
But you're stayin' 'ere to-night.

Over the top is cold, matey—
You lie on the field alone,
Didn't I love you of old, matey,
Dearer than the blood of my own.

You were my dearest chum, matey—
(Gawd! but your face is white)
But now, though reliefs 'ave come, matey,
I'm goin' alone to-night.

I'd sooner the bullet was mine, matey—
Goin' out on my own,
Leavin' you 'ere in the line, matey,
All by yourself, alone.

Chum o' mine, and you're dead, matey,
And this is the way we part,
The bullet went through your head, matey,
But Gawd! it went through my 'eart.

Correspondence

Newborough,
Nr. Rotherham.
22nd May, 1937.

Dear Sir,

I must apologise for the unavoidable delay, owing to pressure of business, for not writing you earlier to thank you very very much indeed and to express my gratitude for the wonderful trip I had last week-end to Ypres. I am sure no one could wish for more. Everything was carried out with such smoothness, and I can safely vouch for the fact that every one of the party was highly satisfied.

I would like to add a further word of praise for the Ypres League Representative, conducting. I am sure that without his help and advice and cheerfulness the trip would have lost much of its interest. He is a highly delightful man to come in contact with, and carried out his duties admirably.

It was with regret that I left Ypres last Tuesday, but at the very first opportunity I intend to avail myself again of this wonderful trip.

Again thanking you for your valued help and co-operation,
Yours truly,
H. J.

29th May, 1937.

May I pass on to you the appreciation of members who went on the recent Fifth Army O.C.A. Tour, re the splendid arrangements throughout the Tour.

Yours sincerely,
G. S. B.,
Hon. Sec., Fifth Army
O.C.A. Committee.

Dear Sir,

My son told me he had a delightful time at Ypres and enjoyed every moment of it. He only wished it had been longer.

Yours very truly,
M. C. F.

26/11/36.

Dear Sir,

I am in receipt of your letter of 25th inst., with railway tickets, which appear to be in order. I would like to thank you for the care taken in making arrangements for our tour, and have pleasure in enclosing my cheque.

Yours faithfully,
W. S. P.

Ypres British School

Coronation Day celebrations were an outstanding success and were attended by practically the whole British Community around Ypres, some coming from as far afield as Mons.

The celebrations were held in the Theatre which was kindly lent to the school for the occasion through the generous efforts of the Burgomaster, M. Vanderghote.

To the rhythm of Chopin's Marche Militaire, played as a duet by girls of the School, the children took up their positions. The Schoolmaster, Mr. C. Yorath, welcomed the parents and visitors and then announced a Parade of Shields depicting the Royal Coats of Arms since the reign of Edward the Confessor. The fourteen shields had been splendidly designed and painted by the boy pupils. The history of two of the shields which were carried by the smaller children was explained by girl pupils. Following the Parade the shields were then hung and formed a background replete with colour after which the younger children gave a remarkably good performance of the "Queen of Hearts" directed by Miss Summers.

A pageant of some of the Kings and Queens of Britain was then introduced and was received with enthusiastic appreciation, King Charles II and Henry VIII receiving prolonged applause. Having but recently assumed their duties in control of the school, Mr. and Mrs. Yorath are to be congratulated for the excellent display prepared in the brief period at their disposal. They were fortunate in securing the kind co-operation of a number of local residents.

The singing by the school children, under the direction of Mrs. Yorath, was noticeably good, and the folk songs, included in this feature, added a typical British atmosphere. The elder children recited clearly and with feeling the Poet Laureate's Prayer for the King. Souvenir mugs and medals were then distributed to the one hundred and sixty-four children present and, after the Revd. G. R. Milner, M.A., had read to the assembly the text of a telegram received from His Majesty's Private Secretary, the programme concluded with the National Anthem.

School Sports

In spite of the inclemency of the weather the sports programme was run to schedule and in this connection mention must be made of the kind assistance given by Mr. Gill and Mr. Piper of the Imperial War Graves Commission in laying out the field. The sports were thoroughly enjoyed by spectators and those taking part. The prizes were presented by Miss Summers to the successful competitors and this lady was herself presented with a bouquet of flowers in token of the high appreciation felt by all for her strenuous and unsparing efforts on behalf of her young charges in the Ypres British School.

A very enjoyable tea followed and at 6.30 p.m. the children, tired but very happy, were shepherded home. Later, the adult visitors were entertained at a dance which was graced by the presence of a number of distinguished Belgian and French guests.

Arrangements were made for the elder children to 'listen in' to His Majesty's Broadcast Speech at 8 o'clock that evening.

Thus ended a most enjoyable and instructive day, one which will be remembered by the British Community at Ypres for a long time to come.

Miss Summers' Farewell

On Friday, June 4th, a large proportion of the Ypres British Community assembled to bid farewell to Miss Summers upon the termination of her four years' service as teacher to the younger children at the Ypres British School. On behalf of those present the Revd. G. R. Milner, M.A., presented Miss Summers with a memento in the form of a silver hand-mirror and hair-brush and Mr. C. Yorath addressed the gathering as follows:—

"Ladies and Gentlemen, the British Community at Ypres has, I think, one very marked and pleasing characteristic. It is ever ready to show its warm appreciation of the efforts made on the children's behalf. I am pleased, therefore, to see so many present this evening to say goodbye to Miss Summers, who, for four years had worked unceasingly for the children's welfare; to say good-bye to a charming, talented and very industrious lady. The sterling qualities of her personality will live in the children and as they grow up and progress in life, will doubtlessly recall the tireless and effective work of Miss Summers on their behalf. Miss Summers leaves behind a record of splendid educational achievement. Having exploited no eccentric methods it will be a pleasure to carry on her work and we all sincerely hope that back in England Miss Summers will find happiness and further success. Miss Summers—the passing of the years will not obliterate your splendid work. We will remember you with gladness in our hearts."

* * *

The Annual Prize-giving will take place at Ypres on Saturday, 24th July, at 9.30 a.m.

Branch Notes

PURLEY.

Further records of the Branch were broken when 48 members took part in the Coronation Golf Meeting on May 13th at Woodcote Park Golf Club, Coulsdon.

The Competition was 18 Holes versus Bogey on the Stapleford points system, and the first prize was a special Silver Coronation Wipers Cup with a further Cup for the second. The weather was fine and the course was in good shape when shortly after 2 a.m., the Chairman, Major S. F. Wood, led off the competitors and started off with a nice birdie. The majority of members played later and between 4.30 and 5.30 there were many Wipers ties on the first Tee. Early starters did not do too well, and for a quite a long time 33, produced by Major S. F. Wood and Pte. A. K. Irens, were the best returns: then Lieut. H. L. W. Hancock brought in 35½, Dvr. C. C. Wood 37½, Major G. Carr 35½, but the last man in was the winner, Cmdr. R. H. Shelton, with a magnificent score of 40 (and this on a handicap of 10 reduced to 8 owing to a previous win).

The supper which followed was almost too well attended, 45 remaining to the feast, and a very cheery evening was spent. The Chairman was in great form and imposed the usual penalty on all those who failed to make a return. Subsequent explanations for lack of success were both interesting and highly amusing. The evening concluded with a hearty vote of thanks to the Host Clerk.

THE ADJUTANT.

LONDON BRANCH COMMITTEE.

Informal Gatherings.

The programme for our April Gathering was in the charge of the ladies and as in the case last year when they kindly took over for the evening, the occasion was a most enjoyable one. To Mrs. Stratton and the artistes who rallied to her support we say " jolly good " and look forward to the next " Ladies' Night."

No set programmes were announced for either the May or June Informals, both being impromptu affairs, but nevertheless those present were afforded the opportunity of passing extremely pleasant evenings in very congenial company.

We have now completed another season as far as there Gatherings are concerned, and to all who have so kindly given their patronage and assistance we extend our grateful thanks. A pleasing feature has been the number of fresh patrons attending these Informals. To all we extend a hearty welcome and hope very much they will continue to accord us their support.

Very shortly we shall be preparing the programme for the next season's Gatherings and the Hon. Secretary would be very pleased to hear from anyone kindly disposed to arrange an evening's entertainment for our members and friends.

Annual Re-union Dinner and Dance.

Many enjoyable evenings have been spent on the occasions of the eleven preceding Annual

Re-union Dinners organised by the London Branch Committee, but the Dinner and Dance held this year on Saturday, April 24th, at the Palace Hotel, Bloomsbury, W.C. may be stated to have surpassed previous efforts. This function, the Twelfth Annual Re-union and Dance, coincided with the Coronation festivities of the historical event which was to take place at Westminster Abbey on May 12th, and it was in a spirit of respectful homage and gladness that the company assembled and lent itself to several hours' enjoyment.

Major E. Montague Jones, O.B.E., M.A., Chairman of the Branch Committee, presided at the Dinner which was honoured by the presence of General Sir Hubert Gough, G.C.B., G.C.M.G., K.C.V.O., etc., accompanied by his charming daughter. The vociferous welcome were to their Hon. Secretary, Mr. John Boughey, upon whose shoulders fell the bulk of the work entailed in connection with these events.

Selections from popular airs were rendered during the Dinner by the Al. Berry Band, and later on these same musicians provided the dance music in the adjacent dance hall to where the assembly had adjourned. The M.C., Mr. W. Parker, soon had the dancers tripping the light fantastic toe in the intricacies of a variety of old and modern steps to the obvious enjoyment of all.

It is very gratifying to record that twelve years after the inauguration of these particular functions we should witness the best attendance ever, a pleasing feature being the large number of new members present as well as the

Photo] **Twelfth Annual Re-union Dinner and Dance of the London Branch.** *[R. A. Wood.*

accorded the General was eloquent of the respect and popularity with which he is held to this day by the men who were " out there " with him. We were all very delighted to have also with us the League's distinguished Chairman, Lieut.-General Sir William Pulteney, G.C.V.O., K.C.B., K.C.M.G., D.S,O,, in fact no Ypres League function would seem complete without him. There were renewed rounds of applause when General Gough in the course of his speech, in proposing the Toast of the London Branch referred to Sir William's enthusiastic and selfless efforts on the League's behalf. He commended the sterling work of the Ypres League in its numerous activities at home and abroad. Major Montague Jones also spoke of the League's work in general and likewise referred to the many functions arranged by the London Branch during the year, adding how very grateful the Committee usual muster of those staunch old friends. Obviously the spirit of comradeship born of the War is far from dead and is being successfully fostered by the good people of the Ypres League. A. R. F.

Branch Continental Tour.

Arrangements are in hand with headquarters for an eight-day Tour in August to the delightful and interesting Ardennes country. The party will leave Victoria Station on Saturday, August 7th, and proceed to Brussels via Dover-Ostend route, where they will remain until the following day. After this they will visit and stay in turn the following places—Rochefort, Virton, Luxemberg, St. Vith, Malmedy, Liege, Diest, Antwerp, Malines, Louvain, Waterloo, returning eventually to Brussels and then to Ostend. No rail journeys will be undertaken on the Continent, a motor-coach de luxe being at the party's disposal from the time of arrival at Ostend until our return there on 14th.

We enjoyed a most successful Tour last year, and a hearty welcome is extended to any member or friend who would like to join us on this occasion. There are a few vacancies at the time of writing, so if this trip should appeal to you please communicate with Mr. J. Boughey, Hon. Secretary, London Branch, who will be delighted to forward all particulars.

League Secretary's Notes

We welcome very heartily all who have become members during the past quarter and thank them for their esteemed support. Among those joining our ranks during this period are a number of Colonial Ex-Servicemen who have been visiting this country for the Coronation Ceremony and celebrations, and have taken the opportunity of making a pilgrimage, under our auspices, to the battlefields. It was most refreshing to receive these old comrades from overseas and the facilities we were able to extend to them in connection with their pilgrimages was a pleasure to us and appreciated by them. They all promised to make known our League to their friends on returning home and to broadcast the warm welcome and assistance they will receive from the Ypres League on visiting the " Old Country."

It is interesting to observe the keenness that survives among ex-servicemen generally by way of re-visiting the battlefields with their comrades. There are also many relatives who live in hope that one day they will visit the grave or memorial of a loved one.

Apart from the many pilgrimages arranged for small parties and individuals the Ypres League have so far this year organised the following battlefield tours.

March 10th—15th. 1st (London) Infantry Brigade Tour of Instruction for Officers.

March 27—30th. Eastertide Mixed Pilgrimage to Ypres.

March 27th—30th. Colchester Branch Tour to Arras.

April 10th—13th. Public Schools O.T.C. Battlefields Tour to Ypres.

May 15th—18th. Whitsuntide Mixed Pilgrimage to Ypres.

May 15th—18th. Fifth Army Old Comrades' Association Battlefields Tour to the Somme.

May 15th—17th. 7th City of London Regimental Old Comrades' Association Battlefields Tour to Ypres and Somme.

May 15th—18th. 7th Lincolnshire Regimental Old Comrades' Association Battlefields Tour to Arras.

June 5th—8th. Mixed Pilgrimage to Ypres.

July 9th—11th. Manningtree, Mistley and District Branch, British Legion. Battlefields Tour of forty members to Zeebrugge, Ypres and Arras.

In this issue space does not permit of a detailed account of each of the above-named tours, but as far as possible two or three interesting accounts have been included elsewhere in this number. Perusal of them may serve to illustrate what has already been stated, i.e., the spirit of the ex-serviceman is to-day as strong as ever, and forms a real factor in our national life. This comradeship and commemoration must, if pride of race and endeavour is to continue, never be permitted to wane.

At the recent Review in Hyde Park of ex-servicemen by Their Majesties the King and Queen a contingent representative of the Ypres League took part in the Parade. One enthusiastic member came from as far afield as Sunderland and another from Dublin.

With regard to the Ypres British School, it is gratifying to observe the excellent start made by the two new Principals, Mr. and Mrs. Clifford Yorath, in their new sphere. We desire to extend to them our hearty congratulations. Miss Ryder who succeeds Miss Summers, following the latter's four years devoted service, also seems to have made a happy beginning.

Although fuller particulars will be announced in the next edition of the " Ypres Times," we wish to draw our members' attention to our Ypres Day Commemoration Parade in the hope that as many as possible will earmark the date and support us on this memorable occasion in record numbers. The event takes place on the Horse Guards' Parade this year on Sunday, October 31st, the actual date, as it happens, of the anniversary of Ypres Day.

PLEASE MAKE A NOTE OF THIS DATE.

FIFTEENTH ANNUAL RE-UNION

SMOKING CONCERT

(Organised by the London Branch Committee)

will be held on

Saturday, October 30th, 1937

at 7.30 p.m.

Caxton Hall, Caxton St., Victoria Street, S.W.1.

Programme to be announced later.

♦·······♦

Come and join us at this jolly Re-union. Tickets already on sale. We fear a number of our supporters were occasioned disappointment last year through failure to obtain tickets at the last moment. We therefore advise early application for tickets to Mr. J. Boughey, Hon. Sec., London Branch, c/o 20, Orchard Street, London, W.1.

EMBROIDERED BADGES.

These badges which can be suitably worn on pockets of sports jackets may be supplied on application to the Secretary, Ypres League, 20, Orchard Street, London, W.1. Price 4/- post free.

YPRES LEAGUE BADGE.

The design of the badge—a lion guarding a portcullis gate—represents the British Army defending the Salient, which was the gate to the Channel Ports.

The badge is brilliantly enamelled with silver finish. Price 2s., post free 2s. 1¼d. (pin or stud, whichever is desired).

Obtainable from Secretary, Ypres League, 20, Orchard Street, London, W.1.

PHOTOGRAPHS OF WAR GRAVES.

The Ypres League is able to supply photographs (negative, and one print, postcard size, unmounted) of graves or memorials situated in the Ypres Salient, and in the Hazebrouck and Armentieres areas, at the price of 10s. each.

All applications for photographs should be sent to the Secretary, together with remittance, giving full regimental particulars of the soldier.

WREATHS.

Arrangements are made by the Ypres League to place wreaths for relatives on the graves of British soldiers situated in France and Belgium on any day throughout the year.

The wreaths may be composed of natural flowers, laurel, holly or poppies, and can be bought at the following prices—10s. 6d., 12s. 6d., 15s. 6d., and 20s., according to the size and quality of the wreath.

MODELS OF DEMARCATION STONE.

Plaster models of the Demarcation Stone can be supplied from Head Office.

All members are aware that 240 granite demarcation stones stretch from the Swiss border to the sea, marking the extreme line of advance of the German invasion.

The model, which is 6 inches in height, may be used for a paperweight or as an ornament. Price 5s., post free in United Kingdom. Applications to the Secretary, Ypres League.

YPRES LEAGUE TIE.

Dark shade of cornflower blue relieved by a narrow gold stripe. In good quality silk.

Price 3/6d., post free.

Obtainable from Secretary, Ypres League, 20, Orchard Street, London, W.1.

BURNING OF THE CLOTH HALL, 1915

A few remaining coloured prints now in stock are being offered to our members at the reduced rate of 1s. each, post free.

Since further copies are unobtainable we would advise those interested to make their purchase without delay.

THE BRITISH TOURING SERVICE

Manager—Mr. P. VYNER

Representative and Life Member, Ypres League

10, Station Square

ARRAS

(P.-de-C.) France

Cars for Hire, with British Driver Guides   Tours Arranged

Ypres League Travel Bureau

CONDUCTED PILGRIMAGES

Attention of members and friends is drawn to the remaining Conducted Pilgrimages for Season of 1937.

August Bank Holiday, July 31st — August 3rd.
   PILGRIMAGES TO YPRES AND ARRAS.

September 18th — 21st.
   PILGRIMAGE TO YPRES.

Prospectuses will be gladly forwarded on application to the Secretary, Ypres League, 20 Orchard Street, London, W.1.

HOTEL
Splendid & Britannique
YPRES

GRANDE PLACE. Opposite Cloth Hall.

LEADING HOTEL FOR COMFORT AND QUALITY, AND PATRONIZED BY THE YPRES LEAGUE.

COMPLETEY RENOVATED

RUNNING WATER. BATHROOMS.

MODERATE TERMS.   GARAGE.

Proprietor—Life Member, Ypres League.

YPRES

Skindles Hotel

(Opposite the Station)

Proprietor—Life Member, Ypres League

Branch at Poperinghe

(close to Talbot House)

Branches and Corresponding Members

BRANCHES.

LONDON	Hon. Secretary to the London Branch Committee: J. Boughey c/o 20, Orchard Street, London, W.1.
	TOTTENHAM AND EDMONTON DISTRICT—E. Glover, 191, Landowne Road, Tottenham, N.17.
	H. Carey, 373, Sydenham Road, S.E.26.
COLCHESTER	H. Snow (Hon. Sec.), 9, Church Street.
	W. H. Taylor (Pilgrimage Hon. Sec.), 64, High Street.
ESSEX (SOUTH)	S. H. Geller, Brielen, 197, Corbets Tey Road, Upminster.
LIVERPOOL	Captain A. M. Webster, Blundellsands.
PURLEY	Major Graham Carr, D.S.O., M.C., 112-114, High Street.
SHEFFIELD	Captain J Wilkinson, "Holmfield," Bents Drive.
QUEENSLAND, Australia	Messrs. C. H. Green, and George Lawson, Essex House, (Opposite Anzac Square) Brisbane, Queensland.
CANADA	Ed. Kingsland, P.O. Box 83, Magog, Quebec.
SOUTH AFRICA	L. G. Shuter, 381, Longmarket Street, Pietermaritzburg.
KENYA	C. H. Slater, P.O. Box 403, Nairobi.
BELGIUM	Mr. C. Leupe, Garage Shannon, Menin Gate.
AMERICA	Representative: Captain R. Henderson-Bland, 110 West 57th Street, New York City.

CORRESPONDING MEMBERS.

GREAT BRITAIN.

ABERYSTWYTH	T. O. Thomas, 5, Smithfield Road.
ASHTON-UNDER-LYNE ...	G. D. Stuart, "Woodlands,", Thronfield Grove, Arundel Street
BANBURY	Captain C. W. Fowke, Yew Tree House, King's Sutton.
BIRMINGHAM	Mrs. Hill, 191, Cattell Road, Small Heath.
	John Bunman, "Westbrook," Solihull Road, Shirley.
BRISTOL	W. S. Hook, "Wytschaete" Redland Court Road.
BROADSTAIRS	C. E. King, 6, Norman Road, St. Peters, Broadstairs.
	Mrs. Briggs, North Foreland House.
CHATHAM	W. N. Channon, 22, Keyes Avenue.
CHESTERFIELD	Major A. W. Shea, 14, Cross Street.
CONGLETON	Mr. H. Dart, 61, The Crescent.
DARLINGTON	D. S. Vigo, 125, Dorset Road, Bexhill-on-Sea.
DERBY	T. Jakeman, 10, Graham Street.
DORRINGTON (Salop) ...	Captain G. D. S. Parker, Frodesley Rectory.
EXETER	Captain E. Jenkin, 25, Queen Street.
HERNE BAY	Captain E. Clarke Williams, F.S.A.A., "Conway," Station Road.
HOVE	Captain G. W. J. Cole, 2, Westbourne Terrace, Kingsway.
LEICESTER	W. C. Dunford, 343, Aylestone Road.
LINCOLN	E. Swaine, 79, West Parade.
LLANWRST	A. C. Tomlinson, M.A., Bod Estyn.
LOUGHTON	Capt. O. G. Johnson, M.A., Loughton School.
MATLOCK (Derby) ...	Miss Dickinson, Beechwood.
MELROSE	Mrs. Lindesay Kelsall, Darnlee.
NEW BRIGHTON (Cheshire)	E. F. Williams, 5, Waterloo Road.
NEW MILTON	W. H. Lunn, Greywell.

NOTTINGHAM	E. V. Brown, 3, Eldon Chambers, Wheeler Gate.
ST. HELENS (Lancs.)	John Orford, 124, Knowsley Road.
ST. JOHN'S (Newfoundland)	Captain L. Murphy, G.W.V.A. Office.
SHREWSBURY	Major-General Sir John Headlam, K.B.E., C.B., D.S.O., Cruck Meole, House, Hanwood.
TIVERTON (Devon)	Mr. W H. Duncan Arthur, Surveyor's Office, Town Hall.
WELSHPOOL	Mr. E. Wilson, Coedway, Ford, Salop.

DOMINIONS AND FOREIGN COUNTRIES.

AUSTRALIA	R. A. Baldwin, c/o Government Savings Bank of N.S.W., Martin Place, Sydney. Mr. W. Cloves, Box 1296, G.P.O., Adelaide. J. C. Correll, Port Vincent, South Australia.
BELGIUM	Sister Marguerite, Sacré Coeur, Ypres.
CANADA	Brig.-General V. W. Odlum, C.B., C.M.G., D.S.O., 2530, Point Grey Road, Vancouver. V. A. Bowes, 326, 40th Avenue West, Calgary, Alberta. W. Constable F. Grece, St. Hilaire Station, Ronville County, Quebec.
CEYLON	Captain F. R. G. Webb, M.C., Irrigation Bungalow, Kalmunai, E.P.
EGYPT	Captain B. W. Leak, M.I.E.E., Turf Club, Cairo.
INDIA	Lieut.-Quartermaster G. Smith, Queen's Bays. Sialkot, India.
IRELAND	Miss A. K. Jackson, Cloneyhurke House, Portarlington.
NEW ZEALAND	Captain W. U. Gibb, Ava Lodge, Puhinui Road, Papatoetoe, Auckland S. E. Beattie, P.O. Box 11, Otaki Railway, Wellington.
NEWFOUNDLAND	Captain Leo. Murphy, G.W.V.A. Office, St. John's.
NOVA SCOTIA	Will R. Bird, 35, Clarence Street, Amherst.
SOUTH AFRICA	H. L. Versfield, c/o Cape Explosives Works Ltd., 150, St. George Street, Cape Town.
SPAIN	Captain P. W. Burgess, Calle de Zurbano 29, Madrid.
U.S.A.	Captain Henry Maslin, 942, President Street, Brooklyn, New York. L. E. P. Foot. 20, Gillett Street, Hartford, Conn, U.S.A. A. P. Forward, 449, East 80th Street, New York. J. W. Freebody, 945, McBride Avenue, Los Angeles.

Membership of the League

This is open to all who served in the Salient, and to all those whose relatives or friends died there, in order that they may have a record of that service for themselves and their descendants, and belong to the comradeship of men and women who understand and remember all that Ypres meant in suffering and endurance.

Life membership, £2 10s.

Annual members, 5s.

Do not let the fact of your not having served in the Salient deter you from joining the Ypres League. Those who have neither fought in the Salient nor lost relatives there, but who are in sympathy with the objects of the Ypres League, are admitted to its fellowship, but are not given scroll certificates.

There is a Junior Division for children whose relatives served in the Salient. It is open also to others to whom our objects appeal.

Annual subscription 1s. up to the age of 18, after which they can become ordinary members of the League.

THE YPRES LEAGUE (INCORPORATED)
20, Orchard Street, Portman Square, W.1.

Telephone: WELBECK 1446.   *Telegrams*: YPRESLEAG, "WESDO," LONDON.

Patron-in-Chief: H.M. THE KING.

Patron:
H.R.H. PRINCESS BEATRICE.

President: GENERAL SIR CHARLES H. HARINGTON.

Vice-Presidents:

THE VISCOUNT WAKEFIELD OF HYTHE.	F.-M. SIR CLAUD W. JACOB.
F.-M. LORD MILNE.	F.-M. SIR PHILIP CHETWODE.
GENERAL SIR CECIL ROMER.	GENERAL SIR HUBERT GOUGH.

General Committee:

THE COUNTESS OF ALBEMARLE.	MR. F. D. BANKES-HILL.
*CAPTAIN C. ALLISTON.	MAJOR-GENERAL C. J. B. HAY.
LIEUT-COLONEL BECKLES WILLSON.	MR. J. HETHERINGTON.
MR. HENRY BENSON.	GENERAL SIR W. C. G. HENEKER.
*MR. J. BOUGHEY.	*CAPTAIN O. G. JOHNSON.
*MISS B. BRICE-MILLER.	*MAJOR E. MONTAGUE JONES.
COLONEL G. T. BRIERLEY.	MAJOR GENL. C. G. LIDDELL.
CAPTAIN P. W. BURGESS.	CAPTAIN H. D. PEABODY.
BRIG.-GENL. A. BURT.	*THE HON. ALICE DOUGLAS PENNANT.
*MAJOR H. CARDINAL-HARFORD.	*LIEUT.-GENERAL SIR W. P. PULTENEY.
REV. P. B. CLAYTON.	LIEUT.-COLONEL SIR J. MURRAY.
*CAPTAIN G. E. DE TRAFFORD.	*COLONEL G. E. C. RASCH.
*THE EARL OF YPRES.	THE HON. SIR ARTHUR STANLEY.
MRS. C. J. EDWARDS.	MR. ERNEST THOMPSON.
MAJOR C. J. EDWARDS.	CAPTAIN J. LOCKLEY TURNER.
MR. H. A. T. FAIRBANK.	*MR. E. B. WAGGETT.
MR. T. ROSS FURNER.	CAPTAIN J. WILKINSON.
SIR PHILIP GIBBS.	CAPTAIN H. TREVOR WILLIAMS.
MR. E. GLOVER.	

* Executive Committee.

Bankers:
BARCLAYS BANK LTD., Knightsbridge Branch.

Honorary Solicitors:
MESSRS. FLADGATE & Co., 70, Pall Mall, S.W.

Secretary:
MAJOR L. J. L. PULLAR.

Auditors:
MESSRS. LEPINE & JACKSON,
6, Bond Court, E.C.4.

League Representative at Ypres:
Mr. C. LEUPE,
Garage Shannon, Porte de Menin.

League Representative at Ostend:
CAPTAIN P. D. PARMINTER,
16, Galerie James Ensor.

League Representative at Amiens:
CAPTAIN STUART OSWALD.
7, Rue des Otages.

League Representative at Arras:
MR. P. VYNER,
14, Rue Chanzy.

Hon. Secretary, Ypres British Settlement:
LT. COLONEL F. G. POOLE.

PRIMARY OBJECTS OF THE LEAGUE

I.—Commemoration and Comradeship.
II.—To provide special travel facilities for Members and all interested to Ypres and battlefields, and transport of Members.
III.—The furnishing of information about the Salient; marking of historic sites and the compilation of charts of the battlefields.
IV.—The erection of a Ypres British Church and School which has been completed.
V.—The establishment of groups ot members throughout the world, through Branch Secretaries and Corresponding Members.
VI.—The maintenance of cordial relations with dwellers on the battlefields of Ypres.
VII.—The formation of a Junior Division.

Use the Ypres League Travel Bureau for Ypres and Whole of the Western Front.

FOR THE FOLLOWING PUBLICATIONS, Etc., apply :

Secretary, YPRES LEAGUE, 20, ORCHARD STREET, LONDON, W.1

BOOKS.

YPRES: Outpost of the Channel Ports. By Beatrix Brice. With Foreword by Field-Marshal Lord Plumer, G.C.B. Price 1s. 0d.; post free 1s. 3d.

In the Ypres Salient. By Lt.-Col. Beckles Willson. 1s. net; post free 1s. 2d.

Story of the 63rd Field Ambulance. By A. W. Westmore, etc. Cloth, 3s. 6d., post free. Paper, 2s. 6d., post free.

War Letters to a Wife. By Colonel Rowland Feilding. Popular Edition, 3s. 6d.; post free 4s.

The Pill Boxes of Flanders. 1s.; post free 1s. 3d.

From Mons to the First Battle of Ypres. By the late J. G. W. Hyndson, M.C. Price 3/6, post free.

YPRES LEAGUE TIES. 3s. 6d. each, post free.

YPRES LEAGUE BADGES. 2s. each, 2s. 1½d. post free.

YPRES LEAGUE CUFF LINKS. 2/6, post free.

YPRES LEAGUE SCARVES. 12/6, post free.

EMBROIDERED BADGES. 4s. each, post free.

Map and List of Cemeteries in the Ypres Salient. Price 9d.; post free 11d.

Map of the Somme. Price 1s. 8d., post free.

PICTURES.

Burning of the Cloth Hall, 1915. A Coloured Print, 14 in. by 12 in. 1s. post free.

Old Well-known Spots in New Guise.

Prints, size 4¼ x 2¼, recently taken of famous spots in the Ypres Salient, and which may be of great interest to our readers, are on sale at headquarters, price 4d. each, post free 5d. For particulars apply Secretary.

POST CARDS, PHOTOGRAPHS AND ETCHINGS.

Post Cards. Ypres: British Front during the War. Ruins of Ypres. Price 1s. post free.

Hill 60. Complete Panorama Photographs. 12 in. by 3¼ in. Price 3s., post free; 15 in. by 5 in. Price 3s. 6d., post free.

MODELS OF DEMARCATION STONE.

The model, which is 6 inches in height, may be used for a paperweight or as an ornament. Price 5/-, post free.

Applications to the Secretary, Ypres League.

PHOTOGRAPHS OF WAR-TIME SKETCHES.

Bedford House (Front View), 1916.

Bedford House (Back View), 1916.

Voormezeele Main Street, 1916.

Voormezeele Crucifixion Gate, 1916.

Langhof Chateau, 1916.

Size 8½ in. by 6½ in. Price 2s. 6d. each, post free.

Photographs of the Thiepval and Arras Memorials. Post card size, price 1s. each, post free.

YPRES TIMES.

The Journal may be obtained at the League Offices.

BACK NUMBERS 1s.; 1935, 8d.; 1936, 6d.

Printed in Great Britain for the Publishers by FORD & GILL, 21a/23, Iliffe Yard, Crampton Street, London, S.E.17.

Vol. 8. No. 8.　　　　　　　　　　　　　　　　　　　OCTOBER, 1937.

YPRES TIMES

CONTENTS.

The Princesses Elizabeth and Margaret Rose.
Memories of the Tower.
What does Ypres mean to me?
Light and Shade at the Front.
An Old Soldier writes to his Pal.
Ypres British School.
The King Albert Army and R.A.F. Memorial.
Ypres Day, 1937.
Pilgrimages and Battlefield Tours.
League Secretary's Notes.
Branch Notes.

PRICE SIXPENCE

Memory Tablet.

OCTOBER - NOVEMBER - DECEMBER

OCTOBER.

Oct.	4th, 1914	...	Russian ultimatum to Bulgaria.
„	5th, 1915	...	Allied Forces land at Salonika.
„	9th, 1914	...	Antwerp occupied by Germans.
„	10th, 1916	...	Allied ultimatum to Greece.
„	14th, 1915	...	Bulgaria at war with Serbia.
„	18th, 1918	...	Belgian coast clear.
„	20th, 1914	...	First Battle of Ypres begun.
„	25th, 1918	...	Ludendorf resigned.

NOVEMBER.

Nov.	1st, 1918	...	Versailles Conference opened.
„	3rd, 1918	...	Austrian surrender. Kiel Mutiny.
„	4th, 1917	...	British troops in Italy.
„	5th, 1914	...	Great Britain declares war on Turkey.
„	6th, 1917	...	British storm the Passchendaele Ridge.
„	9th, 1918	...	Marshal Foch receives German Envoys. Abdication of the Kaiser.
„	10th, 1918	...	Kaiser's flight to Holland.
„	10th, 1914	...	"Emden sunk."
„	11th, 1918	...	Armistice Terms accepted.
„	18th, 1917	...	General Maude's death in Mesopotamia.

DECEMBER.

Dec.	8th, 1914	...	Naval Battle off Falklands.
„	9th, 1917	...	British capture Jerusalem.
„	15th, 1915	...	Sir Douglas Haig C.-in-C. in France.
„	16th, 1914	...	Germans bombarded West Hartlepool.
„	19th, 1915	...	Withdrawal from Gallipoli.
„	24th, 1914	...	First air raid on England.

The Ypres Times

Communications to
The Editor, "Ypres Times,"
20, Orchard Street, London, W.1.

PRICE 6d.
POST FREE 7d.

VOL. 8, No. 8.   PUBLISHED QUARTERLY   OCTOBER, 1937

Their Royal Highnesses
The Princess Elizabeth and Princess Margaret Rose

(*In recent issues of the "YPRES TIMES" I have written brief sketches of the lives of the more prominent members of the Royal Family, commencing in April, 1936, with one of our late ever-lamented and much-loved Sovereign, King George V., and followed later on by those of ex-King Edward VIII. and his present Majesty, King George VI., all three of whom were in succession Patrons-in-Chief of the Ypres League. The July issue contained a short pen-picture of the life of Queen Elizabeth.*

In response, I believe, to requests from readers of the "YPRES TIMES," the Editor has asked me to continue the series to the third generation with an outline of the juvenile lives of the heiress to the Throne, Princess Elizabeth, and her younger sister, Princess Margaret Rose. No Royal group, however limited, would be complete without a tribute to the life-long and devoted services of Queen Mary, and with that I shall conclude the present series in the next issue.

A new series on the military careers of the League's three successive Presidents—the late Field Marshal the Earl of Ypres, the late Field Marshal the Viscount Plumer and General Sir Charles Harington—will possibly follow in the course of 1938.—H.B.)

(Specially Contributed to the "Ypres Times")

By HENRY BENSON, M.A.

THE most important little lady in the land to-day is Princess Elizabeth. On the accession of her father, King George, she became Heiress-Presumptive to the Throne. Next in order of succession comes her younger sister, Princess Margaret Rose. Consequently, they might be considered to be in the same relation to the Crown as were the Princess Mary and her half-sister, the Princess Elizabeth, to their half brother, King Edward VI from 1547 to 1553, were it not for the fact that various Acts of Parliament then in existence had imposed disabilities on both the daughters of King Henry VIII.

DAUGHTERS AND THE THRONE.

The position with regard to the immediate succession is now different both from that which existed in the sixteenth century during the reign of King Edward VI and in the seventeenth and nineteenth centuries during the reigns of King William III and King William IV, because then a single Princess in each case, the Princess Anne and the Princess Victoria, was Heiress-Presumptive. A theory is sometimes held that as no rule of succession as between two daughters has yet been laid down in England, all daughters have an equal claim. The theory is accidentally supported by the fact that on the only two occasions when two sisters have stood next in succession, special Acts of Parliament have been passed.

The first occasion was when Parliament decided that Mary I should come before Elizabeth, the second was when Mary II (William and Mary) came before Anne. On both these occasions, however, there were other reasons for the Acts. In the first case to straighten out the matrimonial tangle of Henry VIII. In the second to keep the Catholic descendants of James II from the Throne.

When Princess Margaret Rose was born, very careful enquiry established that daughters, like sons, succeed in order of birth, and statutory provision was made this year to remove any possible doubt in the matter.

The Line of Succession.

Apart from the two little Princesses in the direct line of succession, never has the British Throne been more plentifully supplied with heirs than at the present time. There are 130 direct descendants of Queen Victoria living, without going back to those of her uncles, the Dukes of Cumberland and Cambridge. Actually, the line of succession goes into most of the Royal Families of Europe. The Queen of Norway (King George VI's aunt) is 14th in order of succession.

The rule of descent is simple in itself, but difficult to trace out. It is King's children first, brothers taking precedence of sisters, then King's brothers and sisters, children of elder brother coming before younger brother. Then King George V's sisters' children. Then Queen Victoria's second son's descendants, then third son's descendants, then fourth son's decendants, then eldest daughter's descendants (this is where the ex-Kaiser comes in), and so forth.

"Most Popular Baby in Great Britain."

Princess Elizabeth was born on April 21st, 1926, when (to quote his own words), King George VI became the father of "the most popular baby in Great Britain." Many people even then realised the significance of the event, which took place at the home of Queen Elizabeth's parents, 17, Bruton Street, Mayfair. There was much anxious waiting until it was know that all was well and a baby daughter had been born. Bruton Street being so close to the heart of things, leading into Bond Street at one end and into Berkeley Square at the other, it was part of the routine of many of the women workers in the neighbouring shops to make a pilgrimage past No. 17 daily.

They all hoped either to see the Royal mother taking an airing or to have a glimpse of the baby and her nurse. This "nanny" was an old servant of the Strathmore family, for she was first of all nurse to Queen Elizabeth and afterwards went to nurse the children of Lady Elphinstone, her Majesty's sister, although it was understood that she would leave Lady Elphinstone when her sister's first baby arrived. And this duly took place.

Princess Elizabeth was a great favourite with her grandfather, King George V— his little "Lilibet"—and "Uncle David," ex-King Edward, was always very close to the child's heart; while she spent a good deal of time with her grandmother, Queen Mary, particularly when her parents were away on their Empire tour. On her fourth birthday she was presented with her first pony, the gift of her grandfather. From Queen Mary she received a miniature Zoo.

Attending public functions with her father and mother has always delighted her, and she takes the liveliest interest in the proceedings. At Olympia, during the Royal Tournament and at the Circus, she is an excited spectator, clapping the various items

Photo] [Marcus Adams.

and frequently turning to her mother to point out things she has noticed with all the spontaneity of childhood.

Early Education.

Princess Elizabeth is being fitted for the responsible role she will play in later years. She is in no danger of being spoilt. The Queen has set a sound curriculum for her, and the fact that she is next to the Throne itself is not allowed in any way to interfere with her education.

At the age of five, a governess, Miss Marian Crawford, from Dunfermline High School, was appointed to teach her the elements of reading, writing and arithmetic. Tutors and extra governesses have recently been appointed for special subjects to fit her for the high position which in due course she will probably inherit.

In view of that great future which may be hers, she has to learn some things more seriously than other girls of her age—such as languages, the duties of a hostess, and constitutional history.

Her self-possessed, yet perfectly childish deportment when she appears with her mother in public, demonstrates clearly that the training of this important little girl, who may one day be Queen Elizabeth II of England, is proceeding on the right lines for the happiness of both herself and of the country over which she eventually may have to rule.

When there came to her—she had not then reached double figures—the shadow of her grandfather's death, and she was sent home from Sandringham lest the sight of sorrow should wound her too deeply, her demeanour at Wolverton Station and in the great dingy, glazed cavern of Liverpool Street was that of a mourning Princess—serious, attentive, and aloof. There, too, her control of the younger sister was perceptible though unostentatious. The latter was not old enough to sense the trouble that had come; not old enough, too, to sustain the gravity that occasion demanded, lapsing from easy tears to easy laughter. But always the elder sister was at her side, dominating her by personality and instructing her by example.

Princess Margaret Rose.

The happily-named Princess Margaret Rose was born at Glamis Castle on August 21, 1930, being the first Princess of the Blood Royal to be born in Scotland since the Union of the Crowns. She has inherited her mother's good looks and keen intelligence. Already she had had a great deal of tuition in many subjects, can write excellently, and has a talent for knitting.

Some time ago it was noticed that she delighted to seat herself at the piano, where she strummed out tunes. Though she could play them with only one finger, it was obvious that she had an unusually keen memory for musical airs. So music lessons were included in her curriculum—at a much earlier age than originally intended.

She has also inherited a pretty, tuneful voice, which is being carefully trained. Both she and Princess Elizabeth are encouraged to take an interest in gardens.

Out-door hobbies appeal strongly to Princess Margaret Rose and she loves collecting leaves and flowers and preserving them in books. She is taking swimming lessons with her sister and has become a " Brownie " in the Girl Guides Company—consisting of friends and daughters of regular Palace visitors—in which Princess Elizabeth is a guide.

Influencing Children's Fashions.

The two little Princesses have their own jewels. Like many other children of well-to-do parents, they are given a pearl every birthday, and they now have quite a few mounted in a chain, which will gradually increase in length as the years go by.

Princess Elizabeth became a depositor in the Post Office Savings Bank last January. This was revealed by Queen Elizabeth when she visited the Post Office

Stand at the British Industries Fair. The Princess, however, is not the first youthful member of the Royal Family to become interested in the savings movement. Prince Edward, infant son of the Duke and Duchess of Kent, owns a Post Office " home safe." The Duke accepted it when he attended the seventy-fifth anniversary celebrations of the Post Office Savings Bank.

Naturally, the two Princesses are the leaders of children's fashions throughout the country. Simplicity has always dominated their clothes—little silk or fine woollen frocks hanging straight, sometimes with a small yoke, with tiny puffed sleeves, and, for special occasions, with a frill round the hem, have been their general wear. For cold days, plain woollen jumpers and tweed skirts—the latter often in raspberry mixture shades.

The children's hats have always been simple, and in their earliest years both wore bonnets, thereby reviving a child fashion, which had fallen into disuse. Often they wear no hats—most striking influence of all, perhaps, that the Royal children have had upon the children of the country.

When it was first stated that the Duchess of York's little girl had been out in public with coat and gloves on, but no hat, lots of folks did not believe it. Since then, one of the most pleasing sights in London has been to see her and Princess Margaret Rose with the light shining on their uncovered fair hair, waving their hands in greeting to the people.

The Children's Hour.

Queen Elizabeth is a very devoted mother. This point hardly needs mentioning, for the public are quite accustomed to seeing her going about with her children on every possible occasion. In this she is following Queen Mary's custom, for she used to be seen everywhere with her sailor-clad boys looking spruce in their white-duck outfits in the summer.

At home the little Princesses are not left merely to their governesses and nurses. Their happiest time is when " Daddy and Mummy " join them in the nursery. King George is, above all else, a family man and he has always made it a rule with his wife that when their official duties allowed them to be in London, or in more recent years at their Windsor home, they should spend one hour together with their children, like any ordinary father and mother, with the cares of State forgotten, and dolls' houses, pet dogs and childish games all important. This is a very wholesome atmosphere for Royal children, and I think there can be no doubt that it will pervade the Palace and the Court and so, indirectly, freshen society in general.

There will be fewer of these spare hours in future, more's the pity; but I am sure that both the King and Queen will make time for as many as possible. The tea-hour is the one usually chosen for the two children to meet their parents, when they romp just like any lesser ones. Incidentally, I may mention that the Queen is one of the growing number who think tea-time an infinitely more cheerful hour than the cock-tail one.

As a treat, the two Princesses, with their mother, visited the Lyceum pantomime, " Puss in Boots," last February. The Queen has none of those old-fashioned ideas that children should be kept to a rigid rule of life, which chills and cramps their warmest feelings. Recently two footmen have been specially detailed to look after them in their " nursery flat " on the second floor of Buckingham Palace, in addition to Mrs. Knight, the chief nurse, and her assistant.

The decision not to have individual mention of the name of Princess Elizabeth, as heiress to the Throne, in the loyal toasts was due to the express wish of the King and Queen. This will be included when she attains her eighteenth birthday. She was, however, a bridesmaid at the wedding of the Duke and Duchess of Kent, and her face was engraved on the Canadian Silver Jubilee postage stamps.

The two little Princesses are fortunate in their father and mother!

H. B.

Memories of the Tower

By Michael Irwin.

THE Tower of London has a perennial fascination for me, for it was here that I spent the early days of the Great War as one of the garrison. Fifteen years ago I marched, with "pack upon my back" and rifle upon my shoulder, into the venerable precincts of the Tower. This happened to be my very first visit and I remember feeling distinctly proud of the fact that my regiment had been chosen to garrison one of the Guards' Barracks.

For a period of six months I was stationed within the Tower and thus had ample opportunity to absorb some of the charm and wonderment of the place. Yes, wonder-

The Tower of London

ment, for the Tower casts a magic spell on those who live within its precincts. One lives in the past with those who walked and talked within those walls. And what a company they were! Kings, Queens, Dukes and Ladies! Traitors and Martyrs! Rich and Poor! Old and Young!

During normal times the Tower is always garrisoned by one of the Battalions of Guards. It was this fact that made the Commanding Officer of my regiment (a Territorial one) particularly anxious that our own military efficiency should not fall below the standard of the Guards. Our sergeant-major, himself a Scot's Guardsman, shared a similar anxiety, as well we knew to our sorrow at times.

The famous moat which surrounds the Tower was the drill ground and it is interesting to note here that this moat was when the Thames overflowed its banks some time ago. It was in this moat that we were "licked into shape" for the army.

A few days ago I sat in the Tower Gardens which overlook the moat and let my mind wander back to the early days of the war. Yes, although it all seems a dream now, I had formed fours, formed two-deep, right-turned, doubled, marched, sloped arms and a hundred other military evolutions in that very moat now lying before my eyes. It used to be one of the sergeant-major's stock jokes to get one of us recruits to drill the squad. He would then tell the squad to march forward and just as it was fast disappearing in the distance he would turn to the poor unfortunate who was drilling the squad and tell him to recall it. Thus requested, the recruit would almost burst his lungs in trying to get the squad to hear. All the time the sergeant-major would encourage him to shout louder telling him that he was only whispering. It usually happened that the sergeant-major was forced to recall the squad, which he did in a voice that seemed to shake the very walls of the Tower.

Apart from the drill the mounting of guards was the principal military function in the Tower. Several guards had to be furnished each day. Thus the Wharf Guard, as its name denotes guarded the Wharf and was in charge of the " drunks " which the military police had arrested within the City. These " drunks " were more often than not men home from the Front, who had been celebrating well but not wisely. They were put into cells and usually allowed to go free in the morning providing they had not overstayed their leave.

The Wharf Guard was the most interesting of the guards, for one could watch the shipping coming and going all night. It was rather an eerie sight to see the Tower Bridge slowly open at the dead of night to allow some ship to pass.

Then there was the Main Guard which guards the Crown Jewels and is the Guard which performs the ceremony of the Keys. This guard also is responsible for the posting of a sentry outside the Governor's residence. The Spur Guard is the guard that provides sentries at the main entrance to the Tower.

There was one particular guard, however, which every man envied. This guard was not actually a Tower Guard but is always found by the garrison of the Tower. I refer to the Bank Guard. This is a guard which sets off every night from the Tower and marched to the Bank of England which it guards until daybreak the next day. This guard was especially favoured by the men for the simple reason that it was followed by a day's leave. Moreover each man received a new shilling from the Bank Authorities. The officer in charge received a guinea and a bottle of wine and could invite two friends to dinner with him.

Many a night have I stood in the courtyard of the Bank and heard coins sliding down a shoot into the vaults below.

During my stay at the Tower about seven spies were shot. I have had many a talk with them when mounting guard over them and with one exception they seemed decent enough fellows. The exception proved rather a handful to us for he tried to burn his cell down and once threw a scalding hot cup of coffee into the sergeant's face. I'll pass over what the sergeant-major said.

Few people realise that the Tower has a large civilian population within its walls and boasts of a day school. It was one of our fatigue duties to clean out the school every morning before school opened . . . . a duty no-one objected to. This was probably not unconnected with the fact that the schoolmistress was young and particularly good-looking.

The Tower has its own Church, or Chapel Royal called St. Peter and Vinculum. When one of the Yeoman Warders was showing me round the Tower a few days ago he pointed out this Church to me. Little did he know that many a time had I been deputed to blow the organ on a Sunday many years ago.

Yes, the Tower will always hold wonderful memories for me . . . nights when I tramped the Wharf . . . the first time I challenged the King's Keys . . . seeing the moon rise over the White Tower in the early morning . . . the croak of the ravens breaking an eerie stillness . . . the distant roar of London's traffic . . . the pale face but the erect head of a spy as he was led away to be shot . . . and that last look round at the White Walls as we left one morning for France.

> "And when the stream
> Which overflowed the soul was passed away,
> A consciousness remained that it had left
> Deposited upon the silent shore
> Of memory images and precious thoughts
> That shall not die, and cannot be destroyed."

* * * * *

What does Ypres mean to me

By R. H. Mottram.

IT seems worth while to answer such a question because I do not think any place on the whole lengthy battle front from Britain to the furthest corners of the Seas can be so utterly and completely a British memory as the half-dozen miles around Ypres we call the Salient.

We took it over before the line had been stabilised on the spot on which it was to remain for so long, and although there were at first French to left and right of us, and they came to our assistance again for a short time in 1918, the actual Salient remained with us.

I was not a professional soldier and know nothing of those first months and the two crucial battles of that time, except what I hear from soldiers and a few members of Territorial and Colonial units who were there. That is the first thing that cannot be said too often about the Salient, we held it for just four years and in that time there grew up different generations of us. There was that of the First Battle, the army of the Marne and the Aisne, who held up that terrific onslaught with their rifles. There was the generation of the second battle, who contrived (it remains something of a miracle to this day) to make good against the entirely novel use of gas.

I belonged to the next, the New and Territorial Army formation that gradually replaced the survivors of the race of heroes who had gone before. Ours was not a glorious period at Ypres, and the subsequent offensive towards Passchendaele was infinitely more spectacular, the retreat to the line I always think of as "our" line more thrilling, the final advance more decisive.

Yet we played our part and it was not a particularly easy one. It lacked completely the urgency of greater moments. It did not take the person of average intelligence, such as myself, very long to see that we were besieged there, and that we must make the very best of increasing autumn darkness and mud and the preoccupation of the enemy.

We were not soldiers. Few of us had any pre-war military training, nay, any idea that we should ever be thrust into the fore-front of a European War. In the battalion to which I belonged, the Colonel, the Adjutant, the Regimental Sergeant Major, and perhaps a dozen N.C.O.'s had a period of regular service behind them, generally some years behind, and two officers and a few other ranks, bore the South African ribbon as a result of voluntary service. I doubt if that experience was of much value, the conditions were so utterly different.

I had the luck to be sent up two days before to look at the line we were to take over from a celebrated battalion. I remember it as if it were yesterday the utter emptiness of the landscape through which two or three of us plodded with a guide, the constant noise, the excitement of picking up a piece of a driving-band that fell at my feet from one of the frequent shrapnel bursts. There, by an utterly wrecked cottage, a grotesquely murdered cottage, its inside flung out all over its little garden, we entered a shallow roughly-made communication trench and began to wade, while overhead I heard that sound that no one will ever forget, the whisper and ear-splitting crack of a long-distance bullet. I think I can say without boasting that we were not scared. We had volunteered to take on this job, and we took it on, accepting as part of it the walking wounded, the stretchers we met and the sight of plunging shells of a heavy howitzer sending up great columns of earth and debris. The thing which did daunt us, was that there seemed nothing to be done. Here and there individuals were hunting for snipers, or a machine-gun would come spasmodically into action, on some communication trench of the Germans, and our artillery could be heard firing overhead and the bursts observed amid the mud-coloured hummocks a hundred yards away. But it was clear enough that we were besieged and that, on the whole, the enemy was more numerous, plentifully provided with ammunition, and in possession of the high ground.

However, our spirits were high and our sense of duty if possible higher, and we smiled grimly at the remarks passed by the battalion we were relieving:

" What's this lot, Bill? "

" Noo Army ! "

" We'll be coming back to-morrow night, to retake these b——y trenches ! "

We said to ourselves: " Oh, will you ! "

They didn't.

Such was the situation when two nights later we undertook the march in the dark into those flooded and often blown-in or collapsed trenches. We broke up into artillery formation on leaving the canal bank, and plodded along, shepherded back into the communication trench, if we tried going over the open, by stern voices:

" What the —— are you comin' near these guns for? " At last ! there we were. The men crouched on the fire steps. We had a first attempt at sending out patrols, But the Germans knew all about us and our relief. The parapets were carefully traversed every few minutes, the communication trenches enfiladed, the dumps and company headquarters (such as they were: " a quarter of an inch of corrugated iron and six inches of water " someone said) and anything else, shelled. I forget what our casualties were, that first tour, doing nothing. However, we got used to it and many other things, but I still marvel. I remember when I had disposed of my platoon to the best advantage I could think of, screwing myself up behind a battered tree trunk and gazing round. From Boesinghe in the north, by Hooge, near by, and dying away southward beyond St. Eloi, we seemed to be surrounded by a ring of fireworks. Flares soared up incessantly with greenish light, hung poised and sank. Rifles and machine-guns spluttered and shells roared (fortunately) over us. We had no steel helmets, mills grenades, rockets, or other resources. We were even green enough not to have taken dry kindling (that was remedied the second tour).

" They call it a baptism of fire, don't they? I prefer the old wet one myself ! "

We joked, we had to, there was nothing else to be done. We could not imagine a line that would run, one day through Passchendaele and Messines, much less Roulers. We hung on to what we had, it was not much, and cost a lot. That was the contribution of my generation.

Light and Shade at the Front

By an Ex-R.B.

The Christmas Spirit.

AT times a detail looms so largely in the scheme of things that it may be a moot point whether the term is not a misnomer. Even admitting that too much attention to detail is likely to conduce to a narrow view, but as meticulous care focussed on pawns in the chess game is apt to cramp the planning and execution of a player's strategical movements.

"Tink-tink-tinkety-tink" (or "tink-tink-tink-tink") was the sound which was made by a loose mess-tin on the back of a pack or haversack. Usually the "tinkety-tink" (of which more anon) kept time with the movement of the file like the tap of

Passchendaele. Author's eyewitness impressions.

a drum at the head of a column, but as soon as anyone who was irked by this unsoldierly way of carrying the tin produced a piece of string, and tied the small attachment on the tin to a strap, the troops were able to file on in silence.

Night's shadow is visibility's cloak, and as readers well know, where a party on No Man's Land stood stock still in the light of an enemy Vérey, it more often than not escaped notice. But even a small light suffices to remove that figurative cloak; the luminous dial of a wrist watch was surprisingly visible in the darkness and when, as in the St. Quentin Sector, one of a party roaming round wore this detail of personal adornment and doubtful utility (wrist watches always stopped at unexpected moments) his attention was drawn to the fact "for necessary action, please."

"Put that cigarette out, there!" That order, of course, was not often called for in the line at night, and where the need for it arose it usually was enforced in strong language. But the writer knew of a case (behind the line) where the lack of a match to strike a light put a man into the most perplexing of dilemmas. The incident occurred on the Division's way out when the platoon billetted for the night in a barn.

This was a fine barn, built in the best French style, large, dry, and swept quite clean. A low partition divided it into two unequal sections, all equipment being dumped in the larger section around which the troops were sleeping, but as the small opening for the pitching of straw was set high up the interior was dark.

In the silent watches, while the troops were "peacefully sleeping," a duty man rose to leave the barn, but not having a match he missed the small gate in the partition, and after groping round came to a halt in the far corner; as luck would have it on a sleeper's face. When the commotion consequent on this act had quietened down he had another try. The writer, as did others, heard him feeling his way and, after what seemed a long while, the riot broke out afresh. Luck again—and the same face; the lay of the equipment led that way. In the outburst of verbal pyrotechnics which followed the disturber of the peace was equally vehement, and it was left to the lighting of but a single match to remove his difficulty.

Probably if one views this term "detail" in the light of function rather than size it is a misnomer. The pin which held the striker of a rifle grenade before the grenade and stick were fired was one of the smallest of the parts. In fact so small as to be only a detail. And yet when on a certain occasion a man put down his bag of grenades at a halt, and then noticed that a pin had worked loose to the point of falling out, see how tenderly he re-adjusted it! Yes, little things do matter. On an occasion when enemy gas was "in the offing" it was not easy for a sentry to distinguish between ground mist and the other sort, but the coming of a slight wind which drove the mist up from our own rear lines promptly settled the doubt. Details. A button missing from a shoulder tab, the length of the rifle stock, a mistake in the spelling of a village name, a broken bootlace, the lack of a "four-by-two," a shortage of oil, the counting of the turnings past a shattered cottage, care to extract the "one up the spout," each detail being fraught with more or less important results.

Everywhere events appear to hinge on detail. There is, or was, a type of engine which registered the water in the boiler by a small, thick glass tube. Let this tube get fouled and then what happened! Why, away went the engine. Along the rails? No, up in the air. The swarthy natives of those climes where the deep blue of the spacious Pacific is set off by the light yellow of the pampa have no reverence or respect for explosives; incorrigibly so. And when two or three of them scrambled lightheartedly aboard a couple of cars—loaded with explosive—which were side-tracked in the interior, why, what is more pleasant than a quiet nap out of the noon-tide heat and a "lift"? And a leisurely smoke before going to sleep. After all, what is a cigarette but a detail. This explosion did some damage and when, in a moment of idle curiosity, the writer later on asked a ganger what happened to the "boys," all *he* said, with a lift of the eyebrow and a shrug of the shoulders was, "No hay!" Which being interpreted means, "Reported missing."

Colour and its arrangement exercise a decided effect on temperament; red is startling, light brown is cosy, and Venetian red darkened with Rembrandt brown is an aid to reflection. A black helmet, red jacket and white slacks seems to be a curious sort of uniform for a fireman to wear, but it was worn by the volunteer firemen of those parts only on ceremonial occasions. Calls to a fire were attended in "civvies," plus the helmet, and a lot of good work was done. As to the alarm, this was sounded by the energetic ringing of church bells.

"The bells, bells, bells . . . . . .
"How they clang and clash and roar!"

taken up all over the town, and as the resultant din was unmistakeable and exhilarating, everyone sprang to his duty with a zest. And then a detail made its modest début, a detail of change. The ringing of the church bells was dropped and the blowing of rams' horns was substituted therefor. And as everyone knows, the blowing of a ram's horn is the nearest parallel to "medicine man's music" that it is possible to imagine. It starts on a husky, tremulous note, rises slowly into a strangulated wail of anguish which merges into a howl, and then dies away in a moan. But in spite of all these merits it was not compelling enough. The night came when a fire broke out and the bells no longer clanged their brazen, tumultous summons. Instead these rams' horns wailed and moaned in the deserted streets, but in vain; the fire blazed up fiercely and the firemen—slept on. They were not " attuned " to the new signal; Morpheus had closed their eyelids and Novelty could not re-open them. Late one night a big fire broke out in Valparai—But " Halt !" This is going off the route with a vengeance, and space is limited. Suffice it to say that where the word " detail " associates unimportance with something just because it is small, it could be profitably bracketed with the word " impossible " in a certain well-known dictum.

These questions relating to " detail " arose from casual thoughts on Passchendaele. Each sector of the Western Front had its own characteristics; compare, for example, the deeply-wooded slopes which the Division passed as it moved by easy marches up to St. Quentin, with the tortured mud and unrest of the Salient and its environs.

It has been said that the opening shell fire of the Passchendaele offensive broke down the dykes, and if that statement be correct it would explain the abundance of water, looking like miniature lakes, which was present in addition to the water in the craters and shell holes. Although soldiers are not easily impressed by the conditions which are incidental to their trade, the general atmosphere of Passchendaele undoubtedly was funereal. A dreary skyline helped to this view, as also did the winding paths and duckboard tracks which led up through the mud, these latter often passing close to water, or between accumulations of water, and over ground which bore striking evidence of the mortality. This prevalence of water would explain, or at least be one of the reasons, why at times the top layer of earth or mud was too sparse to cover in the dead bodies. If one may suggest a parallel it is probable that the desolate, cheerless appearance of Passchendaele closely resembled that of this best of all worlds at a remotely early period of the world's history; that is, before it was graced by any living thing, and when lifeless land and water struggled with each other for the mastery.

And yet, writing as one found it, although Passchendaele (and the Salient) were, to put it mildly, so insalubrious, one never met with a case of typhoid; no doubt the strict discipline which was enforced in the matter of burning or burying all refuse and filth was one of the several reasons for that immunity.

Winter brought frosts which hardened the ground and snow which whitened it. And a glorious moon shone out, glorious in the sense that it was surpassingly brilliant. But one can have too much of a good thing (the platoon tragedian: " A-ha, my proud beauty, what of Sir Jasper now?" " Sir Jasper? A-ha ! I killed him because I loved him so !") objects on the snow being sharply outlined; a short stretch from the post back to cover was " taped," and visibility is an aid to sniping.

Boxing Day was very quiet, following a desultory shelling on the Christmas, and in the late afternoon, while yet daylight, the squad suddenly caught the faint but unmistakable " tink-tink-tinkety-tink " (or " tink-tink-tink-tink ") of a mess-tin " on the move." As the sound came nearer a voice was raised to check it—sound carries on the snow—and the squad deduced the coming of the relief. So did the enemy. In a few moments shells whizzed and screamed and bullets hissed. The relief threw caution to the winds; shouts of command were heard, presumably ordering men to cover, the opening up of heavy returns by the home artillery added to the racket, and in this duty of " getting out " Chance did what Design might have failed to accomplish. The enemy snipers and machine gunners packed up; by looking through an opening in the post one could see them doubling back for cover, and when the fire slackened and the relief came in the squad were able to walk out, smartly, across the enemy front without a shot being fired.

The Division went into rest billets on the outskirts of St. Omer, and at the Company's Christmas dinner the best efforts of the cooks were supplemented by a small cask of real beer. A ration of this beer was duly allowanced to the Quarter Guard, which was installed in a little shack outside the hamlet, the N.C.O.'s remaining in billets, a brazier on a tripod was placed outside the shack, and in the charge of the Guard was a genial colonial who was attached to the R.B.'s. He was just back from " Blighty " leave, was in funds with a remittance which he had not had the time to spend, and he was " clinked " for a nominal offence.

A rumour reached the " Guard Room " in the forenoon that a tiny estaminet some distance out held a stock of champagne, in bottles, and in the afternoon this rumour was confirmed. Rumour has been called a lying jade, but often in the matter of good news she flies on the wings of truth.

Towards evening there was a general air of cheerfulness about the Guard, which spoke well for the quality of that real beer, and later on, when darkness had fallen and

EXTRACT: "and guard all property within sight of your post."

the hamlet slept, anyone passing the Guard Room might have chanced to witness a festive scene which was joyous to behold. The Guard and the " prisoner " were doing a wild dance round the brazier in the snow while the sentry looked stolidly on. Presently one of their number, a sturdy lad who was awarded an M.M. in the Ypres Sector, stumbled and lost his balance and sat in the brazier, and this incident illustrates the truth of the saying that " it is better to be born lucky than rich." The brazier had just been recharged with more fuel; there was a quick rush and he was pulled off before his slacks were scorched.

An early rouse, careful attention to detail, and the Guard put up a smart " turn-out." They passed the inspection, and then the rest of the day was their own.

J. EDWARDS.

An Old Soldier writes to his Pal

(*By* D. H. ROWLANDS, author of " For the Duration ").

DEAR JIM,
I was dreaming the other evening—of you and the old Battalion. My wife and son had wanted me to go with them to the Pictures, but I was not feeling in the mood; so I stayed at home and had a nap instead. I had just been turning out some of the *souvenirs de la guerre* and teaching the boy a few Army phrases, so it was no wonder that I dreamed of the old days.

The house was very quiet, and it was warm by the fire. There was a spot of Johnny quite handy; altogether, the atmosphere was just the sort to send a fellow off to sleep. I must have started to doze very soon after the family had gone out, because it was quite a long dream that I had; anyway it was long enough to include most of the things that happened to us " out there." Nearly all our experiences together seemed to belong to the present once again, though I would not dare suggest that they came back to me in proper sequence.

There was that twenty hours' journey from Havre, in crude waggons labelled " *Chevaux (en long)*, 8; *hommes*, 35-40 "; the ceaseless song of the wheels, " on-a-bit, stop-a-bit; on-a-bit, stop-a-bit; P——— B——— I———." And the sweltering march over miles and miles of *pavé*. I seemed to hear the sergeant shouting, " Left-right, left-right "; I saw the eternal parallel of poplars; I smelt the familiar sweat of men and horses.

Somewhere in the dream came our short period of training near Armentières and the journey south to take over from the French. You will remember, of course, that night when we sat on our packs in the deserted village just behind the line, waiting for the *poilus* to come out and looking at a roadside crucifix silhouetted against the moonlit sky; the dreary winter of 1915, the lonely sentry duty, the rain and slime, the outsize rats, the meagre bread-ration, the creepy night-patrol, the constant shovelling of muck.

The Somme, too—the Battalion making that ghastly attack towards Pozières; the moving wall of steel and earth and flame; the hissing of machine gun bullets, the gaps in each advancing line of khaki, the fierce struggle in the enemy trenches, the trailing processions of wounded, some on foot, some on stretchers; the tragic roll-call at the end.

The Battle of the Ancre in the following November; the snow falling as the Battalion moved into position; the fiercer storm next day that claimed still more of the old originals.

Arras again—the skyline ablaze with the flashes of guns; the inferno that greeted our assault, the Colonel falling mortally wounded, the crowd of big Bavarians surrendering to a handful of Londoners about half their size.

Then there was the move to the Ypres Salient and all that followed. The camps we used to occupy near Locre, Kemmel, Ypres, St. Jean and other places; the long trail to the forward area and back; the lousy trenches providing little in the way of comfort or protection; the concrete pill-boxes which Jerry's artillery tried out with various kinds of bowler, fast and slow; the shell-hole line where life hung by a very thin thread; the working parties which, like a pestilence, pervaded every interval between tours of the line. I recalled in my dream our last journey back from the trenches, the night we left the Salient for good. I saw the ghostly gleam on the tin hats of the fellows in front and on the wreckage that piled out of the great pools on either side of the Menin Road; but I heard no sound save the distant rumble of guns, mingling with the trudge of leaden feet and the rustle of equipment.

I re-lived, too, some of those dark days in the Spring of 1918; the hurried move southwards; the rushing here and there in motor lorries; the atmosphere of rumours and lies and wind-up.

Also the advance which began in the month of August; our new experience of going after Jerry and not coming back; the feeling that the statement on a field post-card, " I hope to be discharged soon " would read, some day, like the truth.

Then the Armistice—finding it hard to believe that the war was over at last; realising the loss of many old comrades so near the end; trying feebly to celebrate in the little town where joy had not been known for over four years; losing our hearts to the pretty girl in our billet.

I was just enjoying the fun at one of our Battalion concerts when I received a vigorous shaking and heard my son saying, " Come on, Dad, show-a-leg; what's the joke? "

So much for the dream of this old soldier. How are things with you these days? A safe job, good pay and plenty of rations, I hope.

I notice that the date of the next Re-union Dinner has already been fixed, and I am counting on your being there. Meanwhile, cheerio and all the best.

Your old pal,
BILL.

* * * * *

Ypres British School

The Earl of Cavan Presents the Prizes.

A New Wave of Progress.

THE Eton Memorial School at Ypres, like the time-honoured foundation from which it originated, continues to " flourish " and an observant visitor cannot fail to be impressed with many recent improvements.

The eighth annual Prize-Day took place on Wednesday, July 21, when the awards were distributed by Field Marshal the Earl of Cavan. Lady Pulteney, Mrs. L. K. Briggs, M. de Beyser, the Third Army and Cheltenham College, as usual, donated prizes of a varied and suitable character.

This year's programme was more comprehensive and ambitious than on recent anniversaries, containing, as it did, items from Shakespeare, which included two scenes from " A Midsummer Night's Dream " and the " Witches " scene from " Macbeth."

It was also pleasing to note that songs occupied a prominent place, the dances being somewhat curtailed.

Lord Cavan, in a happily-worded address, congratulated the school on its general efficiency and commented on the smart bearing of the scholars. The vote of thanks was proposed by Sir William Pulteney.

In his report, Mr. C. Yorath, the new headmaster, who, together with his wife, entered last March upon a four-years' period of office, mentioned that at the opening of the September term the school roll would have increased from 88 to 97. Two boys and one girl were leaving—Paul Cassin (awarded the " Plumer " scholarship for 1937) to the Gordon Home at Woking, William Crouch to take an advanced commercial course, and Georgette Piper (whose name has figured prominently in successive annual prize-lists) to Kent College, Folkestone.

It is hoped next summer to take 30 or 40 of the older children on a school excursion to England for about a fortnight, it being felt that such a trip to the Mother Country would not only be of exceptional interest, but also of real educational value to the pupils.

Meantime, special preparatory courses in English literature and the geography and history of the British Isles are to be arranged, in order that the youngsters may take full advantage of the tour.

It is pleasing to note that the Union Jack has been embodied in the school badge, which will make the scholars more readily distinguishable from those of similar local establishments.

The Ypres British Cricket Club has kindly granted the use of its ground and gear to the boys on two evenings a week, and the local Belgian Football Club has offered similar facilities for the winter sport. For the girls net-ball apparatus has been installed in the school playground, this being an ideal team game were limitations of space have to be taken into consideration.

As already mentioned in a previous issue, the British community in Ypres has showed its appreciation of the services of Miss M. L. Summers, the late assistant mistress, by presenting her with a silver-backed hand mirror and hair brush. Miss Summers returned to England last Spring after four years' devoted and successful work in the infants' classes.

Mr. and Mrs. Yorath and their capable assistant, Miss Ryder, have entered upon their respective tasks with the full energy and enthusiasm of youth. Already they have made many friends among both the Belgian and British communities.

Mr. Yorath has joined the British Cricket Club as a playing member and has also accepted membership of the Belgian Football Club. The latter is an excellent move, which cannot do otherwise than create good feeling and *camaraderie*. Again, it must be remembered that many of the mothers of the pupils are either French or Flemish by birth. Very wisely, the three new teachers have been quick to realise that the social side of their duties is all-important and must not be neglected if their period of office is to prove the success that is generally anticipated. Of one thing I am assured. Visitors to the school from any part of the Empire will be accorded a hearty welcome.

In conclusion, I would mention that the school library is by no means as well supplied with books as it should be. Gifts of standard English works and other literature, suitable for children, are urgently needed. The long winter evenings are now upon us, when reading occupies more time than it does in the summer months. *"Bis Dat Qui Cito Dat."*

H. B.

* * *

Ypres Day

THIS year, the Ypres League Annual Commemoration will be held on **Sunday Morning, 31st October,** and the following programme has been arranged :—

10.30 a.m. Assemble on the Horse Guards' Parade.

11.00 a.m. Address by the Rev. J. Lynn, C.B.E., D.D., B.A., Deputy Chaplain-General to the Forces, Hon. Chaplain to H.M. The King, who will conduct a short service, followed by the "Lament" by Pipers of the 2nd Battalion Scots Guards.

March to Cenotaph.

Laying of the Ypres League wreath on the Cenotaph.

March back to the Horse Guards' Parade.

Dismiss on the Horse Guards' Parade, and at 12.20 p.m. a deputation of the Ypres League will proceed to the tomb of the Unknown Warrior in Westminster Abbey and place a wreath.

H.R.H. Princess Beatrice has graciously consented to attend the Ceremony.

King Albert Army and R.A.F. Memorial

READERS will recall the form of Memorial selected was to fill the Rose Window in the restored St. Martin's Cathedral, Ypres, with fine coloured glass, a window of 250 square feet, containing 62 figures, and Crests of the British Army and Royal Air Force; of Belgium, and the 5th Royal Inniskilling Dragoon Guards.

The sum required was subscribed by all units and ranks of both the men and women's services. The Window is nearly completed and it will be erected during the winter months and, it is hoped, unveiled about Eastertide next.

There will be an Inscription Memorial Tablet in English fixed in the wall under the great organ to be used for the Unveiling Ceremony, and in consequence future British visitors and pilgrims to Ypres can read and comprehend the purpose of this Memorial gift. Lt.-General Sir William Pulteney has had a photograph taken of this Tablet before its transportation next month and a reproduction is enclosed in this number of the Journal.

The Tablet is eight feet by three, a panel and frame of pale grey sycamore wood, letters painted in oil and sealed behind plated glass, on which is engraved the crests in colour. Special consideration had to be given this in view of the damp nature of the Ypres climate. The *Crest of the British Army* is here used for the first time and was given to that Service by the late King George V.

The *Crest of Belgium* is of carved wood and is here shown surrounded by the British Order of the Garter.

The *Crest of the 5th Royal Inniskilling Dragoon Guards* is shown in its new design (since the War two Regiments have been amalgamated). King Albert was Colonel-in-Chief of the Regiment and H.M. King Leopold is the present Colonel.

The general design of this Tablet was assisted by a young architect, Mr. Stanley Marsh, a member of the Inn's of Court Regiment.

G. C.

FOOTNOTE.—*In the January, 1938 edition of the "* YPRES TIMES *" it is hoped to give full details of the Unveiling Ceremony and plans made by the Ypres League in regard to travel to Ypres and hotel accommodation.*

* * *

Manningtree, Mistley and District Branch British Legion Battlefields Tour

A LONG anticipated visit to the battlefields was made by a party of thirty-eight members of the Manningtree, Mistley and District Branch of the British Legion, under the auspices of the Ypres League, on July 9th last.

The party assembled at the Legion Headquarters and were conveyed by motor-coach to Parkeston Quay, where we embarked on the L.N.E.R. steamer "Archangel." The steamer was rather crowded, and in consequence very few sleeping berths were available. This, however, did not damp the spirits of 'the troops,' and ere long all had settled themselves as comfortable as possible for the crossing.

On arrival at Zeebrugge we were met by Mr. O. Mears, from Ypres League headquarters, who had arrived with the necessary transport from Ypres ready to conduct the Tour throughout.

Travelling along the coast via Blankenberghe, our first stop was at Ostend, where a Continental breakfast had been arranged for us and the short stay permitted a hasty wash and brush-up. From Ostend we proceeded to Moere to view the Big Gun which shelled Dunkerque, some 28 miles distant, during the War. Keen interest was shown in this gun and its emplacement, so cunningly concealed that it remained undiscovered until the Germans themselves were finally driven out.

Leaving Moere, we then followed the route to Ypres via Nieuport, Dixmude and Boesinghe, travelling, as it were, along the old Yser Battle Front. Ypres was reached about 11 o'clock and, after depositing our light baggage, the time until lunch was spent in exploring this historical and tragic city. A small party visited the Rifle House Cemetery, Ploegsteert, and, after placing a wreath on the grave of Harry Marchant, joined in a short service, conducted by our Chaplain, the Rev. E. F. Hemming, at the graveside.

The Party photographed from the Eastern Side of the Menin Gate Memorial.

Following an excellent lunch at Hotel Skindles, the party then undertook a tour of the Ypres Salient Battlefields and Memorials. Passing through the Menin Gate Arch the first place of interest reached was Hell Fire Corner, although now a very quiet spot on the countryside, the significance of the name was vividly recalled by Mr. Mears in his interesting talk at this stand. Potijze, St. Jean, Wieltje, St. Julian, Vancouver Cross Roads, Gravenstafel and Passchendaele were then visited and passed in turn. At the Tyne Cot Memorial, Passchendaele, a visit was made to view the panel on which the name of H. Vincent, Essex Regiment, is commemorated.

The tour continued, after leaving Tyne Cot, to Broodseinde, Becelaere, Kruiseecke, Gheluvelt, Inverness Copse, Clapham Junction, Hooge, Maple Avenue, Sanctuary Wood, Menin Road, Zillebeke, Hill 60 (tunnels, trenches, museum visited), Transport Farm, Shrapnel Corner, Lille Gate, Ypres.

By this time all were apparently ready for dinner, and the Proprietor is to be congratulated on the excellent fare provided. Shortly prior to 9 o'clock the party marched to the Menin Gate Memorial where a wreath of Flanders Poppies was placed. A short but impressive service was held, conducted by our Chaplain, and following the sounding of the ' Last Post ' all joined in very heartily in the singing of the National Anthem. We were both interested and greatly pleased to observe the presence of a party of Germans, who reverently joined in the service.

The following morning everyone was up early and, after an English breakfast, departed by motor-coach for a whole day tour as far as Arras via Bedford House, Wytschaete, Messines, Hill 63, Hyde Park Corner, Strand, Ploegsteert and Le Bizet (frontier). On French soil the journey continued through Armentieres, Fleurbaix, Fauquissart, Neuve Chapelle, La Bassee, Hulloch, Lens to Vimy Ridge. Vimy Ridge was one of the most important stragetic positions on the Western Front and witnessed some of the fiercest fighting of the War. All were impressed by the strength of the position, which dominates the country for miles. At Vimy the first thing was to view the magnificent Canadian Memorial erected on the Ridge, which stands at 475 feet above sea-level. This Memorial commemorates the names of 11,000 brave Canadians who lost their lives on French soil during the Great War and who have no known graves and are recorded among the " Missing."

Afterwards the trenches and subterranean tunnels were visited; these are maintained in a permanent state of preservation and a reminder of the nature of fighting that took place at this spot. Here can be seen the Canadian Front Line trench separated from that of the enemy by a " no man's land " in the way of a mine crater twenty yards wide and approximately thirty feet deep. Needless to add, all were deeply impressed with Vimy Ridge and what can be seen there.

On arrival at Arras a small party visited the Brown Copse Cemetery at Roeux, where a wreath was placed on the grave of F. W. Ley-Flurrie and prayers offered by our Chaplain.

The return journey proceeded by Maison Blanche, La Targette, Souchez, Notre Dame de Lorette, where a visit was paid to the impressive French Memorial, Aix Noulette, Grenay, Bethune, Locon, La Gorgue, Estaires, Bailleul, Locre, La Clytte, Dickebusch, Ypres, Thourout, Bruges.

At Bruges, dinner was taken at the Hotel Cosmopolite, where every courtesy and kindness was extended to our party. Afterwards an hour or so was spent sight-seeing. The town was en fete in commemoration of the anniversary of the Belgians gaining their freedom from the French in 1300. Our members mingled with the thousands who thronged the square opposite the renowned " Belfry," listening to the fanfare of trumpets. Time was all too short, as very soon we had to be on our way to Zeebrugge for the return journey to England. For the crossing Zeebrugge to Parkeston Quay we were more fortunate than on the out-going journey, as on the steamer " St. Denis " all were allotted sleeping berths, which permitted a welcome good night's sleep.

Parkeston Quay was reached next morning at 6 o'clock a.m. and from here the party embarked on the final stage of the journey home by motor-coach.

Everyone appeared tremendously impressed with all that had been seen during the tour, particularly so in the cemeteries, all so beautifully laid out and so carefully maintained.

The organisation of the tour by the Ypres League was perfect; all went like clockwork, nothing having been left to chance. The memory of this week-end will live in the minds of all who took part in the Tour. F. V. C.

Editor's Note.—*The Ypres League desire to express to Mr. F. V. Crisp their appreciation and grateful thanks for his active co-operation in the organisation of above Tour.*

London Branch Tour

It is difficult to write on this week's tour in the Ardennes without writing at some length but I am informed by the Editor that space in this issue will not permit this, so herewith a record of the salient features of the London Branch's peregrinations during their tour from the 7th to the 14th of August, 1937.

Some twenty members of the Branch assembled at Victoria Station on the 7th of August, at 8.15 a.m. All were acquainted with each other through the Monthly Informal Gatherings and most had mutual happy memories of last year's tour. On arrival at Dover we found the boat, the "Prince Charles" already crowded with passengers but being a beautiful day no one appeared to be disturbed very much by this.

At Ostend we were met by the Ypres League Representative at Ypres, Mr. C. Leupe, with his comfortable looking motor-coach, the "Shannon" and in short time we were on our way to Brussels via Bruges and Ghent. The journey to Brussels was a lengthy one, although interesting, and we were quite ready for the excellent dinner at the Hotel Bedford on arrival. For some obscure reason the ex-Artillery men of the party were not quartered in the main hotel with the others but were hidden away round the corner at the annexe. The time after dinner was spent exploring the City in little groups and it was very peculiar how frequently these groups ran into each other in so large a place as Brussels.

We were all early astir the next morning and after breakfast entered our coach for the long trip to Rochefort, in the south, passing en route Wavre (near where is Waterloo, which was to be visited later), Gembloux, Namur, Dinant and Han. The country through which we passed appeared more beautiful, perhaps an idea by reason of our being on holiday. It certainly seemed, however, to be a tremendous improvement on the country around the coast. After passing through Namur, with its old fortress high above the Meuse, we arrived at Dinant where we remained for lunch. Outside the town of Dinant is a Plaque commemorating the names of civilians who were executed on that spot during the War.

The afternoon tour brought us to the Grottos of Han. These underground caves, now lighted by electricity consist of a series of vast caverns in Devonian limestone below carboniferous rock, with a total length of two miles. Though their existence had been known for centuries, the caves were first explored in 1814. The chief caverns are the Salles des Mamelons (60 ft. high) with curious stalactites resembling dried tobacco leaves. Visitors leave the caves by boat along the river Lesse, a cannon being fired to produce an echo through the caves. After being underground for more than one and a half hours we welcomed the fresh air and sunshine on reaching the exit.

From here our journey carried us to Rochefort, a quiet place but typically Continental. Nothing very much to do after dinner but sit outside our hotel and give the waiter an opportunity to improve his fair knowledge of the English language. I am afraid the Proprietor would have been disappointed had we retired before midnight. The next day we left Rochefort for Luxembourg via Bouillon. At Bouillon there is a fort perched on top of a Gibraltar-like rock and passing under the archway one beholds a scene of complete tranquility and beauty too amazing to describe, the valley of Semois, with anglers of both sexes each completely detached in their own thoughts and pastime. For anyone desirous of leaving the hustle and anxiety of modern life, I commend them to Bouillon. The history of the Castle here dates back to the remotest period and at the Hotel de la Poste nearby, Napoleon III spent the night of the 3rd September, 1870, as prisoner of war.

On the way to the next stopping place, Virton, one of the artillery members was dressed up with the willing assistance of the ladies, and padded out with bits of paper until he made a fair imitation of the weaker sex. When joined by another old comrade, also an ex-artilleryman, disguised with a false moustache shaped like a set of rabbit's teeth, the pair looked a perfect burlesque of a honeymoon couple on holiday from a rag and bone emporium. With the remainder of the party simply convulsed with laughter we just had to stop the coach and make them face a battery of cameras by the road-side.

We eventually arrived at the town of Luxembourg at 5.30 p.m. well pleased that we could look forward to a long evening there. Outside the Hotel Staar where the party were accommodated we were greeted by a stray dog; a cross between a dachshund and retriever. This animal appeared to take a keen interest in us and apparently awaited our arrival. The next morning he greeted us as our luggage was being placed aboard the coach, afterwards lying down under the front axle. Metaphorically speaking, he had neither beginning nor end as far as we were concerned.

Leaving Luxembourg it seemed impossible that it could be so early in the week, for we appeared to have been travelling for months. All too soon we were to feel that it was strange our week could be nearly ended. Between Luxembourg and St. Vith, where we were to stop for lunch, is Vianden, with steeply descending streets and set amongst the finest scenery we encountered on the whole of our trip. The ever-changing hillsides, prolifically endowed with trees rising in masses from the little valleys, were all around and many a chateau and ruined castle gave an added beauty. Lunch was taken at the Hotel Genten where we were waited upon by the whole of the Proprietor's large family; the artillerymen by two small girls. Continuing our journey after lunch the next halt was made at Spa where tea was taken. Some of the party visited the pump room in the square and had a glass of the famous water which cost twenty-five centimes and tasted just like Stephen's blue-black ink. Here in Spa one member searched indus-

once more for Brussels, the route selected being via Malines and Louvain. The towering and beautiful spire of Malines Cathedral impressed us very much. During the tea interval at Louvain, M. C. Leupe told us many stories of the hardship and sufferings of the people of Louvain during the war.

Thursday evening was quite an eventful one, since a member of the party was suddenly taken ill and was quickly conveyed to hospital in Brussels. Appendicitis was diagnosed which necessitated an urgent operation and I think everyone of our members remained up until 2 a.m. the next morning. Before we left Brussels on the Friday morning however, information was passed round that the patient had successfully undergone the

The London Branch Party at Bouillon.

triously through the town for a mouth organ and after much bargaining managed to obtain an instrument for forty francs. Our next place of call was Liège where headquarters was made for the night. After dinner we spent an adventurous evening, and needless to add, a good many francs.

On Wednesday we left Liège to the strains of "Tipperary" and at 10.30 a.m. passed through the Dutch Frontier to Maastrich. In turn Hassell, Diest and Lier were visited before reaching our next headquarters, Antwerp. Following dinner here our party, or most of them, adjourned to a nearby café where there was an excellent band rendering the type of music appreciated by all.

Thursday morning was spent in visiting the Antwerp Zoo, many photographs being taken, and before lunch several paid a visit to the Cathedral. The afternoon found us bound

operation and was well on the road to recovery. In the afternoon two or three visited the hospital and the remainder undertook a trip to the battlefield of Waterloo.

On Saturday the whole party, minus the invalid, departed Brussels for Ostend to catch the afternoon boat to Dover. Several remained behind, however, to continue their holidays at such places as Blankenberghe, Ostend or Ypres.

The cordial thanks of the party are due to the organisers and to the gentleman who compiled the descriptive brochure, the tour being in every way a great success and enjoyed by all. The ladies proved themselves great sports and Cyrille as good a driver as we could possibly have had.

And now we have commenced saving for next year's tour.

F. H. B.

The September Pilgrimage to Ypres

With the kind permission of the Editor, "Edinburgh Evening News," we reproduce herewith for the interest of our readers, an article contributed by their Special Correspondent that appeared in a recent issue

THIS summer there have been more pilgrims, visitors, and organised parties to our war cemeteries and memorials in France and Belgium than in any similar period during the past decade.

The Ypres League, of which the King is Patron-in-Chief, has conducted a dozen separate pilgrimages since Easter, one of them being confined to members of the Public Schools Officers' Training Corps. This was made up of boys from Eton, Winchester, Marlborough, Rugby, Rossall and Cheltenham.

Widows, Mothers and Sisters

I am now over here with the League's last party of the year. This is mainly composed of widows, mothers, and sisters of men who fell in and around Ypres, who are visiting the last resting-places of their loved ones, free of any cost to themselves.

The fund, which permits the League to carry out this beneficent work annually, was inaugurated by the late Field-Marshal Viscount Plumer ten years ago, during the time he was the League's president, and it is supplemented periodically by donations, the sole conditions being that the pilgrims have not previously visited the graves of their fallen relatives and that their means do not allow them personally to bear the cost of such a journey.

The tour extends from 18th to 21st September. The provincial pilgrims travelled from their homes to London on the afternoon of last Friday, and on arrival were met and conducted to an hotel near Victoria Station for the night.

Last Saturday they crossed to Ypres, via Ostend, where they are staying in reserved rooms at one of the principal hotels.

Pilgrims at the Grave

Each pilgrim is taken to the grave of her loved one by private car, followed by a tour of the Ypres Salient Battlefields, halts being made at many outstanding places of interest.

Yesterday there was a whole-day tour into France as far south as Vimy Ridge, where the gigantic Canadian Memorial, the trenches and the tunnels are always an outstanding attraction.

On the return journey a stop was made at Mount Kemmel, from which a wonderful panoramic view of the Salient was obtained.

Several of the women have confided to me that they were overawed by the majesty and dignity of the Menin Gate Memorial, which will for ever remain an inspiration to them, and all are unanimous in their gratitude to the Imperial War Graves Commission for the emerald lawns that cover and the flowers that adorn each grave in our beautiful war cemeteries. They were quick to notice that general and private rest side by side, under the same simple headstones, equally honoured in their deaths for the common sacrifice they were called to make.

Still, I find that what has touched their heart-strings more than all else is the tribute that the residents of Ypres pay each evening to the memory of the British dead who fell in the defence of their gallant little city by sounding, at nightfall, the "Last Post," beneath the central arch of Menin Gate.

A Remarkable Record

One of the members of the present party lost six brothers in the war, and she is now visiting the graves of three of them for the first time.

"I shall never forget the experience as long as I live," she told me, "and I cannot thank the Ypres League enough for giving me the opportunity. My twin brother, who was in the Northumberland Fusiliers, was killed in the Salient in October, 1917. I had a photograph of his grave, but little did I imagine from it that it was so neatly and beautifully tended.

"The rose tree planted on it and the flowers around are just what I should have wished, and I shall return home much comforted by what I have seen.

"It was a proud, though sad, moment to stand beside his grave after all these years have passed. I never expected to see his grave, but now I have once been there I want, if it is at all possible, to come again. My eldest brother is buried at Pozieres, and a third, who also fell in Flanders, lies at Ploegsteert. I am to visit their graves before I return, thanks to the kindness of the Ypres League.

"Another of my brothers was killed in Palestine, and two others died of wounds in hospitals in England. I lost my husband three years ago, and two of my sons are at present in the Navy."

LONDON BRANCH
Monthly Informal Gatherings
WILL BE HELD AT
The Bedford Head Hotel, Maiden Lane,
STRAND W.C.2.
On **THURSDAY, 21st OCTOBER, 1937**
THURSDAY, 18th NOVEMBER, 1937
THURSDAY, 16th NOVEMBER, 1937
At 7.30 p.m.

You are kindly asked to support these gatherings as much as possible. All are welcomed. Particulars will be gladly sent to any friend on receipt of name and address.

Please help to make them a success.

OBITUARY

We regret to announce the death of Mr. Charles John Parminter, who passed away peacefully after a long and painful illness, on Tuesday, 31st August last. Affectionately referred to as "Jack" among his many friends, he was the junior partner of the transport business the "Wipers Auto Service" of which his elder brother, Captain P. D. Parminter, at Ostend, is the head. Always of a cheery disposition and a regular encyclopedia on the battlefields of Belgium and France, he will be remembered by our members as the Ypres League Representative at Ypres for so many years and pilgrims who have travelled under our auspices will recall with gratitude his ready advice and assistance during their visit to the Immortal City of Ypres. It was his failing health that prevented him from continuing as active Representative of the League at Ypres. We beg to tender our deepest sympathy to his widow and family in their bereavement. A service was held in the Ypres British Church on Friday, 3rd September, at 2.30 p.m., attended by one of the largest congregations ever assembled there. In accordance with our instructions Mr. C. Leupe, the Ypres League Representative at Ypres duly conveyed a wreath on behalf of the Ypres League to the Church with card attached bearing suitable inscription.

COLONIAL SUPPORT

Recently we were favoured with a charming letter and pamphlet of poems from a member resident in Johannesburg, South Africa. The member states that he is the author of the poems and it is his intention to donate the royalties on the first thousand copies sold to the Ypres League General Fund if the Committee will accept. The royalties amount to threepence per copy and we have been pleased to write and accept this enthusiastic member's generous offer and to thank him very heartily for such sterling support. May the sales exceed expectations.

* * *

THE OLD CONTEMPTIBLES

Our readers may be interested to hear that on the eve of Ypres Day this year, 30th October, the B.B.C. are going to broadcast a Dramatic Sequence, describing the great feat of arms—MONS to YPRES, 1914. The script has been prepared by Beatrix Brice and has been passed by the 30th Historical Section as accurate.

We understand that it will be performed with sound effects and should prove a very moving drama.

Beatrix Brice will be remembered as the Author of those two Ypres League publications the Battle Book of Ypres and the Guide Book Ypres: Outpost of the Channel Ports.

WREATHS.

Arrangements are made by the Ypres League to place wreaths for relatives on the graves of British soldiers situated in France and Belgium on any day throughout the year.

The wreaths may be composed of natural flowers, laurel, holly or poppies, and can be bought at the following prices—10s. 6d., 12s. 6d., 15s. 6d., and 20s., according to the size and quality of the wreath.

* * *

The above photograph depicts one of the many wreaths the Ypres League have placed on the graves of soldiers killed in the Great War, at the request of relatives and friends.

* * *

MODELS OF DEMARCATION STONE.

Plaster models of the Demarcation Stone can be supplied from Head Office.

All members are aware that 240 granite demarcation stones stretch from the Swiss border to the sea, marking the extreme line of advance of the German invasion.

The model, which is 6 inches in height, may be used for a paperweight or as an ornament. Price 5s., post free in United Kingdom. Applications to the Secretary, Ypres League.

League Secretary's Notes

We have now reached that period of the year when travel activities give place to social functions, i.e. Re-union Dinners, Dances, Annual Concerts, Informal Gatherings and such like. It is at this time we look forward to enrolling the major portion of the year's recruits.

Reverting to the travel season just concluded, we look back with some satisfaction on what has been accomplished. Apart from small parties and individual travellers, more than a dozen pilgrimages and battlefields tours have been organised and conducted since March last. The many testimonials received at Headquarters, and which are open to any member's scrutiny, speak much for the care and general efficiency of our Travel Bureau Service. A goodly percentage of those who have visited the Battlefields, Cemeteries and Memorials of France and Belgium, under the auspices of the Ypres League this past year have notified their intention to go again with us either as a party or individually.

On the occasion of our last conducted Pilgrimage to Ypres, 18th-21st September, a number of Free Pilgrims were included. The funds at our disposal are now practically exhausted but a special effort was made to maintain continuity in this branch of our activities. It is earnestly hoped that funds will be forthcoming in the near future to enable us to reduce the ever-growing list of applications from poor mothers and widows who can never hope to see the graves of their loved ones without the aid of the Ypres League. A report on this particular Pilgrimage by a News Correspondent who accompanied the Pilgrimage is included elsewhere in this issue of the Ypres Times.

In our April edition we ventured to comment on the gratifying manner in which membership subscriptions had been paid for the first quarter of the year, but since then we regret to observe a retrograde state of affairs. Maybe many members have overlooked the matter of their subscription, holidays or an unusually busy season, being the prime cause of the renewal form placed aside for the moment and then forgotten. In this hope we are sending to each member whose subscription became due during the past three or four months, and in respect of which no remittance has been received a "reminder form" and we earnestly trust they will see their way clear to continue their subscription. We value the support of our members and it is only by subscriptions that we can continue to produce this unique and purely ex-serviceman's little journal, besides continuing with the other and varied branches of our work.

As previously stated it is about this period of the year we hope for new recruits to fill gaps which have for one cause and another occurred in our ranks. The Great Reaper is responsible in part this last year and a certain number have reluctantly resigned. We especially appeal to all existing members to rally round and help to make good the loss in number, nothing can make good the actual loss.

During the past Travel Season ex-Servicemen and others with whom we have come in contact for the first time, have expressed a wish to join the League and have shown some surprise that such an Association was in existence. It is on account of our own experience in this that we ask members to advertise the League and its aims as much as possible. It must always be borne in mind that the British Empire owes in very large measure its present existence as a free people to those gallant heroes of Mons—Le Cateau—The Aisne and Ypres, and it is one of our aims to ensure that the memory of these men shall not fade. To successfully pursue the objects for which the Ypres League was founded and has survived for a period longer than any similar organisation, members and more members are essential.

With regard to the popular little journal itself, we take this opportunity of thanking with all our heart those authors who have so kindly and unsparingly contributed the interesting articles, sketches and photographs for the benefit of the whole. We are anxious to maintain the undoubtedly high standard the journal enjoys—obviously through the authors referred to—but as time goes on articles, etc., from the pens of reputable writers must become fewer so we should be glad to hear from any member who is in possession of suitable articles or subject matter or would be willing to write his reminiscences for inclusion in the Ypres Times.

Ypres Day, 31st October, 1914, when the great crisis around Ypres occurred and was so magnificently overcome, is commemorated annually by the Ypres League on the nearest Sunday to the 31st October at a Memorial Parade, falls this year on the actual Ypres Day itself. Details of this ceremony will be found elsewhere in this issue. The Committee of the Ypres League hope that as many members as possible will rally to support the occasion. Her Royal Highness The Princess Beatrice, our beloved Patron, has graciously promised to attend the Ceremony should the weather conditions be favourable.

We cannot conclude without asking our Branches, Corresponding Members, Representatives, and all individual supporters to accept our expression of gratitude for valuable co-operation with Headquarters and to all members of the Ypres League, at home and abroad, we wish a happy Christmas and a peaceful and prosperous New Year.

Branch Notes

Colchester Branch

A General Committee Meeting of the Colchester Branch was held at the Red Lion Hotel, Colchester, on Friday, 10th September, when Major G. C. Benham, M.C. (Vice-Chairman) presided in the absence of the Chairman, Lieut.-Colonel H. W. Herring, M.C.

The Meeting was attended by Captain A. C. Palmer, Hon. Treasurer; Mr. W. H. Taylor, Hon. Pilgrimage Secretary; Mr. H. Snow, Hon. Secretary; Captain E. F. Matthews, M.B.E.; Captain C. E. Rooney, M.C.; Mr. M. McKinley, Mr. D. Shadrach and Mr. S. Farran.

The Meeting was held with the object of arranging the social programme for the winter season, 1937-8, and as a result the following events and dates were decided.

Fifth Annual Re-union Dinner, Red Lion Hotel, Colchester, 9th November, 1937.

Fifth Annual Ball, Red Lion Hotel, Colchester, 26th November, 1937.

Annual Whist Drive, Spring of 1938, date to be fixed later.

In connection with the latter event Mr. H. Snow will be assisted, as formerly, by Captain C. E. Rooney, who will between them decide the actual date.

A separate Sub-Committee was appointed for both the Re-union Dinner and the Ball with Lieut.-Colonel H. W. Herring and Major G. C. Benham as Chairman respectively.

* * *

LONDON BRANCH

Fifteenth Annual Re-union Smoking Concert

The London Branch Committee announce that they are holding their Fifteenth Annual Re-union Smoking Concert on Saturday, 30th October, 1937, at 7.30 p.m. at the Caxton Hall, Caxton Street, Victoria, S.W.1, when Major E. Montague Jones, O.B.E. Chairman of the Branch will preside.

The following distinguished guests have already accepted invitations to be present:— H.E. The Belgian Ambassador; Lieut.-General The Baron Vincotte, Military Attaché, Belgian Embassy; General A. Lelong, Military Attaché, French Embassy; Captain R. R. Studler, Assistant Military Attaché, American Embassy; Lieut.-General Sir William P. Pulteney, G.C.V.O., K.C.B., K.C.M.G., D.S.O., and Colonel G. T. Brierley, C.M.G., D.S.O.

The programme this year is being arranged by the "First Army Follies Concert Party" under the personal direction of Mr. Will. Burnes, originally of "Splinters" (Les Rouges et Noirs). This Concert Party, originated during the War on the Western Front, returned from France in May, 1919, and have carried on as the "First Army Follies Concert Party" ever since. They have performed before the late King Albert of the Belgians and a number of the War Lords including the late Lord Milner, the late Admiral Jellicoe and the late Admiral Beatty. Their entertainment provided a wonderful tonic and diversion to thousands of Tommies at the Front at such places as Poperinghe (POP), Armentieres, Bethune, Arras, etc. In their programme for 30th October they will present tit-bits from their varied war-time numbers and sketches including all the popular songs and features of that period. Community singing will be conducted by an Old Time Music Hall Chairman.

A strong appeal is made to all members to do their best to make this year's function one of the most successful ever held. Last year we did extremely well and we are optimistic enough to believe that this year can be even better. We therefore appeal to members to extend us their support for this occasion, bring along a friend if possible, and help us to achieve our objective.

Cornflowers will be on sale at the Hall, price 2d. each, and all present are kindly asked to wear one.

Application for tickets, price 5/-, 2/6, and 1/10, should be made as early as possible to the Hon. Secretary, London Branch Committee, Ypres League, c/o 20, Orchard Street, London, W.1. Ladies are cordially invited.

Owing to the limited accommodation reserved seating arrangements must of necessity be restricted. The 5/- tickets will be automatically reserved, and 2/6 seats can be reserved on payment of 6d. extra per ticket. Applications for reserved seats cannot be considered after 16th October.

It is hoped that as many members as possible will apply for tickets for sale amongst their friends, and in the event of those prevented from being present, the Committee respectfully appeal to them to purchase a ticket on behalf of some ex-service man who might not otherwise be able to attend, or to assist their funds.

Arrangements are being made for the fixing of a stall at the entrance to the Concert Hall at which Ypres League badges, ties, cuff-links, maps, literature and particulars of the League can be obtained. The stall will be in the charge of Mr. C. Page.

Informal Gatherings

The first of the season's Informal Gatherings was held on Thursday, 16th September, when Mr. Geo. A. Goodall, Hon. Social Secretary, Hampton Wick Branch, British Legion, very kindly provided the evening's entertainment with his "Bing Boys" Band and "Whoopee" Girls in mirth, music and dance.

For an exceptionally entertaining and jolly evening we extend our grateful thanks to Mr. Goodall and his young artists, all of whom thoroughly deserved the appreciative applause accorded them at the conclusion of the programme.

The London Branch Committee earnestly trust that greater effort will be made by members to bring these Gatherings to the notice of friends. Hundreds of thousands of ex-service men passed through the Salient during the Great War and there must be at least one whom you come in contact with. Why not bring him along? He is assured of a hearty welcome.

Notice of these Gatherings will be gladly sent to any of your friends upon name and address being supplied to the Hon. Secretary.

Monthly Informal Gatherings

will be held at The Bedford Head Hotel, Maiden Lane, Strand, W.C.2, on

Thursday, 21st October, 1937
Thursday, 18th November, 1937
Thursday, 16th December, 1937

from 7.30 p.m. to 10 p.m.

Particulars of programmes arranged for these evenings will be forwarded on application being made to the Hon. Secretary, London Branch Committee.

* * *

PURLEY BRANCH.

Bombardier's Foursomes 1937.
First and Second Battles.

Disappointment was caused this year by the smaller entry than usual: many well-known pairs were absent, and there were not enough newcomers to compensate.

The troops engaged received Operation Orders on the eve of summer time, and soon afterwards the First Battles were on.

Results of 1st Battles:—

Capt. G. B. Mutton (18) and Lieut. A. D. Duncan (11) beat Major W. F. Topley (18) and Lieut. F. B. Jones (9), 4 and 2.

Lieut. C. J. Frost (10) and Rfmn. G. D. Green (6) beat Capt. D. H. Morgan (24) and Lieut. S. V. Smith (11), 1 up.

Pte. A. K. Irens (4) and Corpl. J. E. A. Davies (6) w.o.; Lieut. J. H. Heines (12) and Capt. E. L. Vaus (12), scratched.

Corpl. C. T. Taylor (9) and Capt. F. W. Douse (7), w.o., Major J. S. Hall (18) and Capt. G. E. E. B. Nichols (24), scratched.

Major L. Meakin (16) and Major J. Wayte (18) beat Major H. G. Harris (16) and Capt. N. W. Streat (12), 4 and 3.

Gnr. J. K. McFarlane (13) and Gunner W. Kerr (11) beat Bomdr. E. A. R. Burden (2) and Lieut. H. L. W. Hancock (10), at 19th. (The Bombardier says it was robbery!)

Capt. S. T. Grant (13) and Sergt. D. L. Greig (8) beat Lieut. C. P. Humphery (18) and Capt. E. A. O. Wever (20), 1 up.

Pte. A. Milne (14) and Trooper F. Skade (18) beat Pay. Commdr. F. L. Monk (16) and Capt. S. Murray (14), 5 and 4.

Major S. F. Wood (8) and Capt. E. A. S. Lund (16) beat Pte. H. Boon (16) and Lt.-Col. A. M. Wilkinson (18), 4 and 3.

Capt. E. Featherstone (1) and Major G. Carr (9) beat Lieut. E. W. Bennett (11) and Lieut. A. H. Pollard (18), 1 up.

Capt. J. Saul (4) and Capt. W. R. Williamson (11) beat Capt. G. D. Gooch (10) and Capt. W. E. Philpots (8), 6 and 5.

Capt. A. S. Green (11) and Major D. H. Leck (6) beat Capt. B. A. Forster (8) and Commdr. R. H. Shelton (10), 1 up.

C.S.M. N. L. Way (12) and Corpl. E. A. Satchell (16) beat Major J. F. Legg (22) and Major R. H. Forster (20), 2 up.

The Second Battles followed at once and brought in all those who had escaped the First through byes: results were:—

Major E. H. Coe (11) and Lieut. S. Newman (10) beat Mutton and Duncan.

Irens and Davies beat Frost and Green, at 19th.

Meakin and Wayte, w.o., Taylor and Douse, scratched.

McFarlane and Kerr beat Grant and Greig.

Milne and Skade beat Wood and Lund, 2 and 1.

Featherstone and Carr beat Saul and Williamson, 4 and 3.

Green and Leck, w.o., Way and Satchell, scratched.

Major L. W. Alderson (5) and Corpl. A. A. Meredith (10) beat Corpl. C. Stroud (14) and Major A. G. Grutchfield (18), 7 and 6.

Third Battle Results:—

Coe and Newman beat Irens and Davies, 2 up.

Meakin and Wayte beat McFarlane and Kerr, at 19th.

Milne and Skade beat Featherstone and Carr, 3 and 2.

Green and Leck beat Alderson and Meredith, 1 up.

Fourth Battle Results:—

Meakin and Wayte beat Coe and Newman, 3 and 1.

Green and Leck beat Milne and Skade, 2 up.

And so the 5th and Final Battle lay between the two Croydon M.O.'s and a Woodcote Park pair: the Bombardier's report on the match is as follows:—

The Final of the Bombardier's Foursomes.
Coulsdon Court, 18th July, 1937.

The Bombardier was honoured by an invitation to Referee the final of the Foursomes with which his name is associated and it need not be said that he appreciated at once that his duties would be purely nominal. Amongst such old campaigners and such gallant sportsmen, infraction of the Rules, even involuntary ones, were not likely to be brought to the notice of the Referee. He was able, therefore, to confine his attention to producing a report of as gallant a fight as ever took place in his not inconsiderable experience.

Of the contestants, Green alone was a past winner. His partner, Leck, cut his first tooth on a cleek which still adorns his bag and probably knows more about the game than all the others put together. The two Doctors, one felt, had reached the final by sheer persistence, and by the fortunate production of the " wizard " shot at the critical moment. They produced several such shots in the final, but not with sufficient regularity to ensure their occupation of the premier position at the Annual Dinner of the Branch. Sad to relate, the gift of six shots was not sufficient to enable them to capture the Cups.

The game started spectacularly. Leck placed his drive in an ideal position at the tricky first hole, Green hit a moderate approach and Leck holed an 'ell of a putt for a birdie 3, which gave them the hole despite the concession of a stroke. The same pair also won the second hole where both sides seemed reluctant to hole out.

Neither side reached the green at the short third, but Wayte missed a short putt to win the hole and Leck and Green halved a hole they looked like losing. They were unsteady at the fourth however, and their lead was reduced to one.

At the fifth, the Doctors received their second stroke but a pulled approach by Wayte (a favourite stroke of his in the early stages of the game) and a lovely approach putt by Green, robbed them of the win they seemed to have in their pockets. They were generous at the sixth also where they played the better tee shot and proceeded to concede a half by a wild first putt. The seventh provided the first thrill for the indulgent spectators (amongst whom were recognised several reprobates from a neighbouring Club). Wayte's drive, with the magnificent pull we have already remarked on, finished in the trees on the left, from which position Meakin was able to hit the ball only a few feet. Leck hit a fine drive down the middle into the exact spot for his partner to place the next on the green. The shot however, seemed to be struck with the grip rather than the head of the club and the ball disappeared into the bushes on the right and all began to wonder whether it would ever be found. By a miracle, it was found to have hit a branch and it lay clear, from which fortunate position, Leck hit another off the socket which finished below the green on the right. Meanwhile the Doctors had reached the back of the green in 4, from whence Meakin laid a skilful putt dead. To the relief and I am confident, the surprise of their supporters, Green and Leck produced a fair approach and a long putt and won the hole to make themselves two up again.

At the eighth, the Referee had exhausted all his fingers and had started counting on his toes when Leck and Green resigned the hole. No more need be said than that Meakin and Wayte reached the bunker at the hole side in two and subsequently holed out in seven and won the hole by the length of a street.

After the Doctors had had an argument with the trees at the ninth, their opponents won the hole to become two up at the turn.

The tenth was won by the Doctors in three after a visit to the Spinney, a tortuitous and unexpected recovery, and so was the eleventh, where they received a stroke and also got a three. They lost the twelfth however, after a wild pull by Wayte and struggled a half at the 13th with their stroke. Still one down.

At the fourteenth, Meakin's drive, strategically hit all along the ground, escaped several thousand obstacles and reached the fairway, from whence, with the others in a series of bunkers, they won the hole to become square.

For the Doctors, the 15th was a tragedy for after the better drive and a wicked approach by Green they twice missed easy approaches and lost the hole to be one down again.

The 16th saw them produce a win which looked to those watching very like a loss. Neither pair was on at this short hole but Green was short to the right whilst Meakin was away to the left in the neighbourhood of some tree trunks which his ball hardly missed. Wayte's approach overran the green and lay a full 15 yards from the hole. Leck's run-up was six feet too strong and then the gallant Meakin, after long and prayerful deliberation, hit the back of the hole, jumped into the air and fell in. Naturally the others missed. ALL SQUARE; TWO TO GO AND A STROKE AT THE 17th. Things looked good for these medicos.

Wayte produced a fizzer from the tee and so did Leck. Green, from a grand position, underclubbed and was short. The Doctors were in a shallow bunker by the green in two. Leck played the odd which made them two more with the stroke and then these Doctor people played a couple of terrible shots and scrambled a six and a half. All square and one to go. Visions arose of the 19th with, Heaven only knows why, a stroke to come, and the Bombardier recalled his own fate when he and Hancock, having taken two good Scottish locals to the 18th with the match still alive, had to concede a stroke at this 19th. What a hope!

However, the impeccable Meakin pulled under a tree and in three they were nearly in the Moat. Even then, with the green yawning in front of him, Leck shanked and just missed sand on the right of the green; but they still achieved a four and won a great battle.

It would not be fair for an onlooker, however impartial, to say much about the play. Nobody played well. Many shots were produced which were unworthy of the strikers. Let us say that Leck drove well and Meakin putted grandly at times and leave it at that.

THE BOMBARDIER.

The Ypres League (Incorporated).

Head Office Balance Sheet, 31st December, 1936.

FUNDS AND LIABILITIES.

	£ s. d.	£ s. d.
General Fund—		
Balance at credit, 1st January, 1936	168 19 10	
Add Balance at credit for year to 31st December, 1936	30 5 6	
		199 5 4
Free Pilgrimage Fund		47 9 8
Reserve Fund—In respect of Life Membership Subscriptions		300 0 0
Ypres Times Maintenance Fund		64 18 5
Hostel Fund		322 19 10
Maintenance Fund—Ypres Salient Notice Boards		6 16 9
Sundry Creditors		62 0 1
		£1,003 10 1

ASSETS.

	£ s. d.	£ s. d.
Cash at Bank and in hand—		
Free Pilgrimage Fund	49 9 6	
Head Office Account	37 16 6	
		87 6 0
Halifax Building Society—		
Deposit Account "A"	324 4 8	
Deposit Account "B"	216 3 1	
		540 7 9
Add Interest accrued		13 12 4
		554 0 1
Hostel Fund Investment—		
£323 2s. 11d. War Stock 3½%		322 19 10
Sundry Debtors and Pre-payments, etc.		29 19 4
Stocks at Head Office—		
As per Head Office Records		9 4 10
		£1,003 10 1

E. MONTAGUE-JONES } *Members of the*
G. T. BRIERLEY } *General Committee.*
BEATRICE BRICE-MILLER }

REPORT OF THE AUDITORS TO THE MEMBERS OF THE YPRES LEAGUE, INCORPORATED.

We beg to report that we have examined the above Balance Sheet with the Head Office Books and relative Documents of the Association and have obtained all the information and explanations we have required. In our opinion such Balance Sheet is properly drawn up so as to exhibit a true and correct view of the state of the Association's affairs, according to the best of our information and the explanations given to us and as shown by the Head Office Books of the Association.

Dated this 29th day of April, 1937.

LEPINE & JACKSON, Chartered Accountants,
6, BOND COURT, WALBROOK, LONDON, E.C.4. *Auditors.*

Head Office

Income and Expenditure Account for the year ended 31st December, 1936.

EXPENDITURE.

	£	s.	d.
To Salaries	318	10	0
,, Rent and Rates	249	3	2
,, Printing and Stationery	22	6	1
,, Postages and Telegrams	40	9	6
,, Prospectuses, Publicity Leaflets, etc.	18	6	6
,, Telephone and Insurances	27	12	9
,, Lighting and Heating	7	19	9
,, Accountancy Charges	21	0	0
,, "Ypres Day" Expenses	17	13	4
,, General Expenses	82	14	0
	805	15	1
,, Balance—Surplus carried to General Fund	66	18	6
	£872	13	7

INCOME.

	£	s.	d.
By Subscriptions	437	4	1
,, Donations	140	3	8
,, Travel Bureau	275	0	10
,, Publications, etc. Account	2	12	7
,, Interest	17	12	5
	£872	13	7

Head Office

General Fund for the year ended 31st December, 1936.

EXPENDITURE.

	£	s. d.	£	s.	d.
To The Ypres Times—					
Cost of Printing, etc.	308	7 7			
Less Sales and Advertising Revenue	23	16 2	284	11	5
,, Travel Bureau—					
Adjustment in respect of year to 31st December, 1935			19	14	6
,, Balance—Carried to Balance Sheet			30	5	6
			£334	11	5

INCOME.

	£	s.	d.
By Income and Expenditure Account. Surplus for the year transferred.	66	18	6
,, Legacy	50	0	0
,, Ypres Times Maintenance Fund Amount appropriated towards cost of The Ypres Times.	217	12	11
	£334	11	5

THE FIFTEENTH

RE-UNION OF MEMBERS AND FRIENDS

Organized by the London Branch Committee of the Ypres League,

WILL BE HELD AT THE

CAXTON HALL, CAXTON STREET, VICTORIA STREET, S.W.1.

ON

SATURDAY, OCTOBER 30th, 1937

All Members of the Ypres League and their friends are cordially invited by the London Branch Committee to meet together at the Caxton Hall, when a

GRAND SMOKING CONCERT

will be given. The Chair will be taken by

MAJOR E. MONTAGUE JONES, O.B.E., M.A.

(Chairman of the London Branch Committee)

The following will also be present:

H.E. The BELGIAN AMBASSADOR; LIEUT.-GENERAL BARON VINCOTTE, Miltary Attaché, Belgian Embassy: GENERAL A. LELONG, Military Attaché, French Embassy; CAPTAIN R. R. STUDLER, Assistant Military Attaché, American Embassy: LIEUT.-GENERAL SIR W. P. PULTENEY, G.C.V.O., K.C.B., K.C.M.G., D.S.O.; and COLONEL G. T. BRIERLEY, C.M.G., D.S.O.

An excellent programme has been arranged by

The First Army Follies

And **WILL BURNES**, Originally of SPLINTERS (Les Rouges et Noirs)

From the Savoy, Queens & Coliseum Theatres, London.

Doors Open at 7 p.m.   Concert Commences at 7.30 p.m.

ADMISSION ... 5/-, 2/6, and 1/-.

Owing to limited accommodation at the Hall reserved seating arrangements will be very restricted. The 5/- tickets will be automatically reserved and a certain number of 2/6 seats can be reserved on payment of 6d. extra per ticket. Application for reserved seats cannot be considered after October 16th.

Last year we had a record attendance and again this year we anticipate a full Hall. Early application, therefore, accompanied by a remittance, should be sent to the Hon. Secretary, London Branch Committee, c/o Ypres League, 20, Orchard Street, Portman Square, W.1.

YOUR SUPPORT ON OCTOBER 30th WILL BE APPRECIATED.

Branches and Corresponding Members

BRANCHES.

LONDON	Hon. Secretary to the London Branch Committee: J. Boughey, c/o 20, Orchard Street, London, W.1.
	TOTTENHAM AND EDMONTON DISTRICT—E. Glover, 191, Lansdowne Road, Tottenham, N.17.
	H. Carey, 373, Sydenham Road, S.E.26.
COLCHESTER	H. Snow (Hon. Sec.), 2, Church Street.
	W. H. Taylor (Pilgrimage Hon. Sec.), 64, High Street.
ESSEX (SOUTH)	S. H. Geller, "Brielen," 197, Corbets Tey Road, Upminster.
LIVERPOOL	Captain A. M. Webster, Blundellsands.
PURLEY	Major Graham Carr, D.S.O., M.C., 112-114, High Street.
SHEFFIELD	Captain J Wilkinson, "Holmfield," Bents Drive.
QUEENSLAND, Australia	Messrs. C. H. Green, and George Lawson, Essex House, (Opposite Anzac Square) Brisbane, Queensland.
CANADA	Ed. Kingsland, P.O. Box 83, Magog, Quebec.
SOUTH AFRICA	L. G. Shuter, 381, Longmarket Street, Pietermaritzburg.
KENYA	C. H. Slater, P.O. Box 403, Nairobi.
BELGIUM	C. Leupe, Garage Shannon, Menin Gate.
AMERICA	Representative: Captain R. Henderson-Bland, 110 West 57th Street, New York City.

CORRESPONDING MEMBERS.

GREAT BRITAIN.

ABERYSTWYTH	T. O. Thomas, 5, Smithfield Road.
ASHTON-UNDER LYNE	G. D. Stuart, "Woodlands,", Throntield Grove, Arundel Street.
BANBURY	Captain C. W. Fowke, Yew Tree House, King's Sutton.
BIRMINGHAM	Mrs. Hill, 191, Cattell Road, Small Heath.
	John Burman, "Westbrook," Solihull Road, Shirley.
BRISTOL	W. S. Hook, "Wytschaete" Redland Court Road.
BROADSTAIRS	C. E. King, 6, Norman Road, St. Peters, Broadstairs.
	Mrs. Briggs, North Foreland House.
CHATHAM	W. N. Channon, 22, Keyes Avenue.
CHESTERFIELD	Major A. W. Shea, 14, Cross Street.
CONGLETON	Mr. H. Dart, 61, The Crescent.
DARLINGTON	D. S. Vigo, 125, Dorset Road, Bexhill-on-Sea.
DERBY	T. Jakeman, 10, Graham Street.
DORRINGTON (Salop)	Captain G. D. S. Parker, Frodesley Rectory.
EXETER	Captain E. Jenkin, 25, Queen Street.
HERNE BAY	Captain E. Clarke Williams, F.S.A.A., "Conway," Station Road.
HOVE	Captain G. W. J. Cole, 2, Westbourne Terrace, Kingsway.
LEICESTER	W. C. Dunford, 343, Aylestone Road.
LINCOLN	E. Swaine, 79, West Parade.
LLANWRST	A. C. Tomlinson, M.A., Bod Estyn.
LOUGHTON	Capt. O. G. Johnson, M.A., Loughton School.
MATLOCK (Derby)	Miss Dickinson, Beechwood.
MELROSE	Mrs. Lindesay Kelsall, Darnlee.
NEW BRIGHTON (Cheshire)	E. F. Williams, 5, Waterloo Road.
NEW MILTON	W. H. Lunn, Greywell.

NOTTINGHAM	E. V. Brown, 3, Eldon Chambers, Wheeler Gate.
ST. HELENS (Lancs.) ...	John Orford, 124, Knowsley Road.
ST. JOHN'S (Newfoundland)	Captain L. Murphy, G.W.V.A. Office.
SHREWSBURY	Major-General Sir John Headlam, K.B.E., C.B., D.S.O., Cruck Meole, House, Hanwood.
TIVERTON (Devon) ...	Mr. W H. Duncan Arthur, Surveyor's Office, Town Hall.
WELSHPOOL	Mr. E. Wilson, Coedway, Ford, Salop.

DOMINIONS AND FOREIGN COUNTRIES.

AUSTRALIA	R. A. Baldwin, c/o Government Savings Bank of N.S.W., Martin Place, Sydney.
	Mr. W. Cloves, Box 1296, G.P.O., Adelaide.
	J. C. Correll, Port Vincent, South Australia.
BELGIUM	Sister Marguerite, Sacré Coeur, Ypres.
CANADA	Brig.-General V. W. Odlum, C.B., C.M.G., D.S.O., 2530, Point Grey Road, Vancouver.
	V. A. Bowes, 326, 40th Avenue West, Calgary, Alberta.
	W. Constable F. Grece, St. Hilaire Station, Ronville County, Quebec.
CEYLON	Captain F. R. G. Webb, M.C., Irrigation Bungalow, Kalmunai, E.P.
EGYPT	Captain B. W. Leak, M.I.E.E., Turf Club, Cairo.
INDIA	Lieut.-Quartermaster G. Smith, Queen's Bays, Sialkot, India.
IRELAND	Miss A. K. Jackson, Cloneyhurke House, Portarlington.
NEW ZEALAND	Captain W. U. Gibb, Ava Lodge, Puhinui Road, Papatoetoe, Auckland
	S. E. Beattie, P.O. Box 11, Otaki Railway, Wellington.
NEWFOUNDLAND ...	Captain Leo. Murphy, G.W.V.A. Office, St. John's.
NOVA SCOTIA	Will R. Bird, 35, Clarence Street, Amherst.
SOUTH AFRICA	H. L. Versfield, c/o Cape Explosives Works Ltd., 150, St. George Street, Cape Town.
SPAIN	Captain P. W. Burgess, Calle de Zurbano 29, Madrid.
U.S.A.	Captain Henry Maslin, 942, President Street, Brooklyn, New York.
	L. E. P, Foot, 20, Gillett Street, Hartford, Conn, U.S.A.
	A. P. Forward, 449, East 80th Street, New York.
	J. W. Freebody, 945, McBride Avenue, Los Angeles.

Membership of the League

This is open to all who served in the Salient, and to all those whose relatives or friends died there, in order that they may have a record of that service for themselves and their descendants, and belong to the comradeship of men and women who understand and remember all that Ypres meant in suffering and endurance.

Life membership, £2 10s.

Annual members, 5s.

Do not let the fact of your not having served in the Salient deter you from joining the Ypres League. Those who have neither fought in the Salient nor lost relatives there, but who are in sympathy with the objects of the Ypres League, are admitted to its fellowship, but are not given scroll certificates.

There is a Junior Division for children whose relatives served in the Salient. It is open also to others to whom our objects appeal.

Annual subscription 1s. up to the age of 18, after which they can become ordinary members of the League.

THE YPRES LEAGUE (INCORPORATED)
20, Orchard Street, Portman Square, W.1.

Telephone: WELBECK 1446. *Telegrams*: YPRESLEAG, "WESDO," LONDON.

Patron-in-Chief: H.M. THE KING.

Patron:
H.R.H. PRINCESS BEATRICE.

President: GENERAL SIR CHARLES H. HARINGTON.

Vice-Presidents:

THE VISCOUNT WAKEFIELD OF HYTHE.   F.-M. SIR CLAUD W. JACOB.
F.-M. LORD MILNE.   F.-M. SIR PHILIP CHETWODE,
GENERAL SIR CECIL ROMER.   GENERAL SIR HUBERT GOUGH.

General Committee:

THE COUNTESS OF ALBEMARLE.
CAPTAIN C. ALLISTON.
LIEUT-COLONEL BECKLES WILLSON.
MR. HENRY BENSON.
*MR. J. BOUGHEY.
*MISS B. BRICE-MILLER.
COLONEL G. T. BRIERLEY.
CAPTAIN P. W. BURGESS.
BRIG.-GENL. A. BURT.
*MAJOR H. CARDINAL-HARFORD.
*MAJOR GRAHAM CARR.
REV. P. B. CLAYTON.
CAPTAIN G. E. DE TRAFFORD.
MRS. C. J. EDWARDS.
MAJOR C. J. EDWARDS.
MR. H. A. T. FAIRBANK.
MR. T. ROSS FURNER.
SIR PHILIP GIBBS.
MR. E. GLOVER.

*MAJOR H. G. HARRIS.
MR. F. D. BANKES-HILL.
MAJOR-GENERAL C. J. B. HAY.
MR. J. HETHERINGTON.
GENERAL SIR W. C. G. HENEKER.
*CAPTAIN O. G. JOHNSON.
*MAJOR E. MONTAGUE JONES.
MAJOR GENL. C. G. LIDDELL.
*CAPTAIN H. D. PEABODY.
*THE HON. ALICE DOUGLAS PENNANT.
*LIEUT.-GENERAL SIR W. P. PULTENEY.
LIEUT.-COLONEL SIR J. MURRAY.
*COLONEL G. E. C. RASCH.
THE HON. SIR ARTHUR STANLEY.
MR. ERNEST THOMPSON.
CAPTAIN J. LOCKLEY TURNER.
*MR. E. B. WAGGETT.
CAPTAIN J. WILKINSON.
CAPTAIN H. TREVOR WILLIAMS.

* Executive Committee.

Bankers:
BARCLAYS BANK LTD., Knightsbridge Branch.

Honorary Solicitors:
MESSRS. FLADGATE & CO., 70, Pall Mall, S.W.

Secretary:
MAJOR L. J. L. PULLAR.

Auditors:
MESSRS. LEPINE & JACKSON,
6, Bond Court, E.C.4.

League Representative at Ypres:
Mr. C. LEUPE,
Garage Shannon, Porte de Menin.

League Representative at Ostend:
CAPTAIN P. D. PARMINTER,
16, Galerie James Ensor.

League Representative at Amiens:
CAPTAIN STUART OSWALD.
7, Rue des Otages.

League Representative at Arras:
MR. P. VYNER,
14, Rue Chanzy.

Hon. Secretary, Ypres British Settlement:
LT. COLONEL F. G. POOLE.

PRIMARY OBJECTS OF THE LEAGUE

I.—Commemoration and Comradeship.
II.—To provide special travel facilities for Members and all interested to Ypres and battlefields, and transport of Members.
III.—The furnishing of information about the Salient; marking of historic sites and the compilation of charts of the battlefields.
IV.—The erection of a Ypres British Church and School which has been completed.
V.—The establishment of groups of members throughout the world, through Branch Secretaries and Corresponding Members.
VI.—The maintenance of cordial relations with dwellers on the battlefields of Ypres.
VII.—The formation of a Junior Division.

Supplement to *The Ypres Times*, October, 1937.

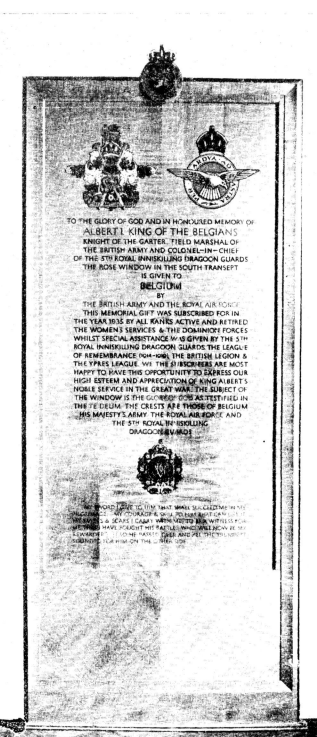

Copy of Inscription Tablet Words :—

To the Glory of God and in honoured Memory of ALBERT I, KING OF THE BELGIANS, Knight of the Garter, Field Marshal of the British Army and Colonel-in-Chief of the 5th Royal Inniskilling Dragoon Guards, the Rose Window in the South Transept is given to Belgium by

THE BRITISH ARMY and ROYAL AIR FORCE.

This Memorial Gift was subscribed for in the year 1935 by all Ranks active and retired, the Womens' Services and the Dominion Forces, whilst special assistance was given by the 5th Royal Inniskilling Dragoon Guards, The League of Remembrance (1914-19), the British Legion and the Ypres League. We, the subscribers, are most happy to have this opportunity to express our high esteem and appreciation of King Albert's noble service in the Great War.

The subject of the window is The Glory of God as testified in the *Te Deum*.

The crests are those of Belgium, His Majesty's Army, the Royal Air Force, and the 5th Inniskilling Dragoon Guards.

" 'My sword I give to him that shall succeed me in my pilgrimage, and my courage and skill to him that can get it. My marks and scars I carry with me, to be a witness for me that I have fought His battles who will now be my rewarder.' So he passed over, and all the trumpets sounded for him on the other side."

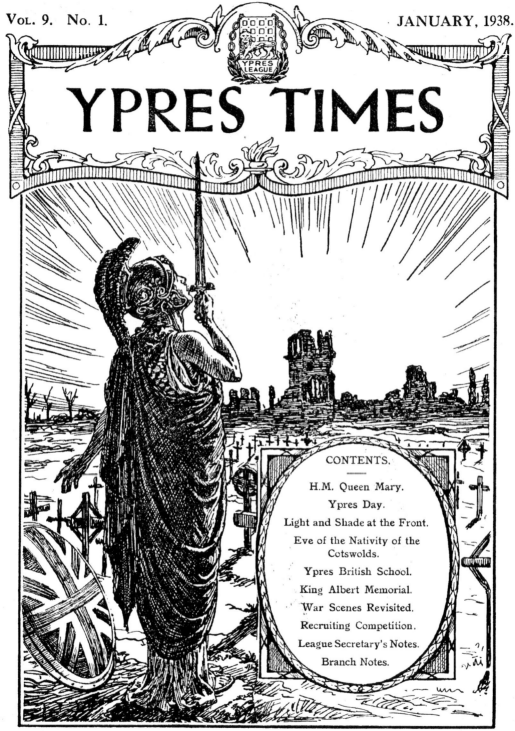

Memory Tablet.

JANUARY - FEBRUARY - MARCH

January.

Jan.	8th, 1916	...	Gallipoli evacuation completed.
″	12th, 1915	...	The use of poison gas by Germans reported.
″	21st, 1915	...	Zeebrugge bombarded by British airmen.
″	24th, 1916	...	Naval Battle off Dogger Bank.

February.

Feb.	3rd, 1917	...	America broke with Germany.
″	18th, 1915	...	U-boat "blockade" of England.
″	18th, 1918	...	German Invasion of Russia.
″	21st, 1916	...	Battle of Verdun begun.
″	21st, 1918	...	British capture Jericho.
″	25th, 1915	...	Allied Fleet attacked Dardanelles.

March

Mar.	10th, 1915	...	British capture of Neuve Chapelle.
″	11th, 1917	...	British take Baghdad.
″	12th, 1917	...	Revolution in Russia.
″	15th, 1917	...	Abdication of the Tsar.
″	21st, 1917	...	First British War Cabinet.
″	21st, 1918	...	German offensive on the Western Front.

Communications to
The Editor, "Ypres Times,"
20, Orchard Street, London, W.1.

PRICE 6d.
POST FREE 7d.

Vol. 9, No. 1.   Published Quarterly   January, 1938

H.M. Queen Mary

A Small Tribute to a Life of Sacrifice and Service.

(*Specially contributed to the* "Ypres Times")

By Henry Benson, M.A.

IN writing this for the "Ypres Times"—the last of a series of brief pen-pictures of the careers of the more prominent members of our Royal Family—I would preface it by stating that in any sketch, however inadequate, of the life of Queen Mary, the honest difficulty lies in tracing on her shield, prior to the past decade, any of those shadows without which the lights are apt to seem monotonous and unreal.

The same qualities—courage, energy, gentleness, loyalty, patience, right judgment—marked her early years no less than those which have been exposed to public view; and one cannot paint the shadows which one does not see. For the most part, her career has been the sunniest of landscapes. The Queen's story is the story of a woman born and bred in the England she loves so deeply. From her birth to the present day she has been part of the life of the country, and to millions she typifies English womanhood at its best.

Early Years at Richmond.

Her Majesty was born at Kensington Palace on 26th May, 1867, and the event was received with public delight in a degree usually only associated with the birth of a direct descendant of the ruling Sovereign. Congratulations poured in, the bells of Kensington Church rang out merry peals, and more than 1,000 enquirers signed the visitors' book. Perhaps some of them already saw significance in the birth of a daughter to the Duke and Duchess of Teck. In any case, Disraeli, who became Premier in the following year, with almost uncanny presentiment, remarked at the time, "A cousin—but not too near a cousin—to the two little boys at Marlborough House."

An entry in Queen Victoria's journal for June, 1867, records a visit to Kensington Palace in an "open carriage and four through the densely crowded Park to see dear Mary Teck." In an upstairs room, "the former bedroom in which Mamma and I slept," she found the Duchess of Teck, "Aunt Cambridge," and the future Queen Consort of England—"a very fine baby, with pretty little features, a quantity of hair and a tiny rosebud of a mouth. In a word, a model of a baby." Queen Mary's infant days were spent at White Lodge, Richmond, generally, under the care of the head-nurse, "Girdie" (Mrs. Girdlestone) and Ellen, a favourite housemaid. In the summer of 1868 her Majesty had the first and only serious illness of her life—gastritis—and for forty-eight hours the doctors held out little hope.

The Duchess of Teck, whilst loving her only daughter with doting affection, held what would nowadays be regarded as extremely strict views concerning her upbringing and training for whatever the future might hold for her. To Queen Alexandra she once confided: " A child has quite enough to do in learning obedience, in attending to her lessons, and to grow, without parties and late hours. They take the freshness away from childhood, and the brightness and beauty from girlhood. There are too many grown-up children in the present day."

On the other hand, she showed her broad-mindedness and her unselfishness conspicuously when any question arose of her young daughter doing good to others. From her earliest years she was taught to be courteous to everyone, helpful to the poor, kind to animals, and not to injure the plants or flowers in the garden. Shortly after her tenth birthday, Dr. Carr Glyn, then Vicar of Kensington, came twice a week to Richmond to give her lessons.

" Mary."

Queen Mary's earliest public appearance was at the opening of the Colonial and Indian Exhibition by Queen Victoria in 1886, and she was also present at the Drawing-rooms and State Ball in the same year. In May, 1893, the late King George (then Duke of York) proposed to his cousin and was accepted. They had been playmates since childhood, and had little to learn or unlearn about each other. The wedding took place in the following July. The Duke of Windsor was born at White Lodge on 23rd June, 1894, and thereby for the first time in the nation's annals the succession was secured for the fourth generation.

When King Edward, universally beloved and mourned, passed away in 1910, her Majesty, on becoming Queen Consort, was faced with a decision regarding her name. She possessed eight—Victoria, Mary, Augusta, Louise, Olga, Pauline, Claudine, Agnes—but she chose the second one, Mary.

The great qualities of her Majesty found full scope during her husband's reign, and she shared in full his responsibilities and cares. Once reads much of Queen Mary's thoroughness, culture, knowledge of art and of old furniture, and of her additions to the treasures in the royal palaces; but when these things are half-forgotten people will talk of and hand down to their children the story of her deep interest in the poorer subjects of the Crown, her practical suggestions for their comfort, her eagerness to help them, her courage, and perhaps more than all else her magnificent work during the War years, when she shared with millions of women their anxieties and fears. She knew the feelings of the mothers with sons at the front, and she bore in her heart the griefs of the forlorn and bereaved.

War Work.

The War set a seal upon the link between the royal family and the nation. Her Majesty worked early and late for the sick and wounded, she visited hospitals and brought brightness to the patients. Well do I recall, in 1915, her sympathetic homely words, " My poor boy," addressed to a battery commander, who already wore his Military Cross and his Legion of Honour, when she observed that half the hand with which he saluted her was missing. She organised, she inspired others, and like ordinary folk, she economised and endured discomforts. I remember a visit paid in 1917 to the royal farm at Windsor where in the dairy I saw butter being made up for the Castle. Each pat had a crown stamped on it; but each pat contained no more than the meagre allowance to which every housewife's ration-card entitled her. " Queen's orders," I was told.

The Shadows Fall.

King George V's illness in 1928! His subjects went to Buckingham Palace, quietly; read the bulletins, questioned each other. The King was something more to all of us than a head on a penny. Good news, recovery! The Jubilee of 1935! That procession must be fresh in everybody's mind. The King sitting up straight, with very bright blue eyes—his mother's eyes—smiling at the crowd; Queen Mary

deeply affected. We all remember that, and the magnificent summer weather that came for a day or two, just to give the finishing touch to a splendid pageant. I would rather think of that procession, its warmth of welcome, its colour, the family quality of its rejoicing, than the mournful procession which followed in the January of 1936.

Throughout the short reign of her eldest son, Queen Mary was very closely present in the thoughts and prayers of the people. They all hoped that the continuity of public service, which she had promised to them, might be easy for her and that no heavy burden of duty might be added to the load of sorrow she had been called upon to bear. *Dis aliter visum.* The racking anxiety that afflicted the whole Empire in December 1936 fell with direct and merciless force upon the mother of the Sovereign. Yet all of us were aware that throughout the tormented negotiations Queen Mary was always at hand, ready to give help and counsel, for the good of her people as well as of her children. Not only was comfort sought from her by all her sons in turn, and by their wives whom she had made her daughters, but Ministers also withdrew themselves from the deep disquiet of Cabinet debates to refer to Queen Mary a problem beyond the power of statesmanship to solve.

The people came through the great ordeal without bitterness, with their affection for their lost leader unimpaired, yet ready to give their ancient loyalty with full devotion to his brother who was crowned amid the Empire's rejoicings last May, but no one can estimate how much was owed to the wise and gracious influence that worked in the background. Moreover, let it be remembered that while thus bravely working for the public good, Queen Mary had throughout to contemplate, and is now suffering, a very great personal sorrow. The tragedy necessarily involved for her, late in life and close upon her greatest bereavement, separation from her eldest son. That is a blow which can scarcely be softened. It is only possible to assure her Majesty of the boundless gratitude, sympathy, and love of many peoples, who, having received such inestimable benefits at her hands, devoutly trust that her life of service to them may never again lead her into further paths of tragedy.

PERSONAL CHARACTERISTICS.

Queen Mary has never had the desire to lead the " smart set " and it is sometimes the sneer of the latter that she is prone to indulge in " middle-class virtues." But it is precisely those traits in her character—her domestic accomplishments, her devotion to her late husband and her children and her unaffected kindliness—which have securely enthroned her in the hearts of the British people.

Foremost I would place, not her knowledge and grasp of affairs, but her patience and consideration.

I remember a party one day at which her Majesty was present. There was an old lady very blind. The Queen went up to her at once and took her arm to help her to a chair. She said: " How are you, dear Lady ——? " The old lady replied: " Who are you, my dear? I recognise your voice, but I am so blind these days." The Queen said: " I am Mary." " Yes," said Lady ——, " but there are so many Marys. Which Mary are you? " " Well—you see, I am the Queen."

Again, when visiting one of the Children's hospitals in London recently, she paused at the cot of a three-year-old patient. " Well, little dear," enquired her Majesty, " how are you and where do you live? " " Near St. Pancras station," replied the toddler, " and where do you live? " " Near Victoria station," said Queen Mary laughingly.

There is hidden in these two little anecdotes the Queen's sense of humour,—her own well-exercised quality, which once made the late Keir Hardie exclaim, " When that woman laughs, she does laugh."

The King's mother has a place of her own in the hearts of his subjects who have watched for years her unselfish devotion to duty, her understanding of the problems of everyday life as few queens have done in the past. Never before has the Royal House been in closer sympathy with the Empire than at the present time. To that we owe much to Queen Mary.

H. B.

Ypres Day, 1937

THE Seventeenth Annual Commemoration of the Ypres League was held on October 31st, officially known as "Ypres Day." This particular day marked the crisis of the First Battle of Ypres, 1914, when our line was re-established at Gheluvelt, thus deciding the fate of the Ypres Salient.

The Dowager Viscountess Plumer very kindly extended us the honour of deputising for Her Royal Highness, The Princess Beatrice who, through indisposition, was unable to be present.

Lady Plumer, representing H.R.H. Princess Beatrice, and His Excellency the Belgian Ambassador with the four V.C.s at the Cenotaph.

Among those present were: His Excellency The Belgian Ambassador; Lieut-General The Baron Vincotte, Military Attaché, Belgian Embassy; Colonel Martin Scanlon, Military Attaché for Air, representing the American Ambassador; Colonel Ruggeri-Laderchi, representing the Italian Ambassador; A Military Attaché, representing the Portuguese Ambassador; Lieut-Colonel E. K. Smart, D.S.O., M.C., representing the High Commissioner for Australia; Major C. G. Arthur, D.S.O., representing the High Commissioner for Canada; H. T. B. Drew, Esq., representing the High Commissioner for New Zealand; D. J. Davies, Esq., C.B.E., The High Commissioner for Newfoundland; H. R. Rainsford-Gordon, Esq., representing the High Commissioner for South Africa; Lieut-General Sir William Pulteney, G.C.V.O., K.C.B., K.C.M.G., etc., Chairman of the Ypres League; Major E. Montague Jones, O.B.E., T.D., M.A., The Hon. Alice Douglas Pennant; Captain and Mrs. R. Henderson Bland and Representatives of the U.S.A. Legion. The parade comprised contingents of The Old Contemptibles commanded by the Marquis of Carisbrooke, G.C.B, G.C.V.O., etc.; The Fifth Army, O.C.A., St. Dunstans; 85th Club (3rd London Territorial Field Ambulance), Officers Training Corps Cadets and the Ypres League.

At 11 a.m. the Service opened with the singing as a solo, verses of "Land of Hope and Glory," beautifully rendered by Miss Iris Wade. It is no easy matter to sing in the open with good effect, but Miss Wade, the South African-Danish soprano, who had the honour of appearing at the December Command Performance before Their Majesties, succeeded wonderfully and that her effort was greatly appreciated was evidenced by the gracious words addressed to her afterwards by the distinguished personages present.

Then followed the singing by all present of the hymn "O Valiant Hearts," accompanied by the band of the 1st Surrey Rifles (35th Anti-Aircraft Battalion, R.E.).

At the conclusion of the hymn the Reverend Dr. Joseph Lynn, C.B.E., etc., Hon. Chaplain to His Majesty the King, and Deputy Chaplain-General to the Forces offered the following prayer:—

"Almighty God, in whose hands are all our lives, we thank Thee that in Thy Providence we are privileged again to meet here, in order that we may acknowledge our gratitude to Thee.

We thank Thee for the comradeship of all who served in The Great War, and for their courage and cheerfulness throughout the years. We remember before Thee all those who gave their lives in defence of their King and Country, and commend again unto Thy fatherly care and keeping their loved ones. We pray for Thy blessing on our Sovereign Lord King George, Queen Elizabeth, Mary the Queen Mother, and all the members of the Royal Family, beseeching Thee to grant them long life and prosperity. Once again we commit ourselves to Thy goodness through Jesus Christ." Amen.

Then followed The Lord's Prayer, and when this was concluded Dr. Lynn addressed the assembly as follows:—

Comrades of the Ypres League, last year in my address to you I spoke of the triple spirit of commemoration, comradeship and consecration. To-day I wish to dwell on this last thought for a brief time.

Recently we have had many anniversaries of great events in the history of our race, from Hastings in 1066 A.D. to Balaclava in 1854 A.D. Agincourt and Trafalgar appear prominent among great victories gained by our arms. We look back with pride on these feats, and feel that our fathers have handed down to us a great heritage. It is our privilege, and our duty, to transmit it unsullied to our children, and for this purpose we do well to meet here, and, remembering the great victory we gained under God's providence this day, to reconsecrate ourselves to the service of our Country, and this League.

Loyalty, then, is our first watchword, loyalty to our leaders and our cause. If this spirit is present, there can be no doubt as to the continued success of our efforts. Without it, dissension and difficulty may combine to destroy our work.

Leadership is essential to any enterprise and we look with good reason to our leaders in Church and State to show us the way, and here I would fail in my duty to my sacred calling, if I did not point you to Him who is our great spiritual leader, "The Captain of our Salvation."

From these two ideas should flow what I may call a 'Liveliness' in our outlook. There is a tendency as the years pass and we grow older for us to slacken in our interest and effort, and to leave it to the younger generation to carry on. But we are heirs to a heritage, which no one, who is not of our generation, can understand and appreciate. We stood shoulder to shoulder in those dark days, "our backs against the wall," and we alone can speak of the result. So we must, while God spares us, with voice and heart and action tell with enthusiasm of the great days and great deeds, through which we passed, and hand them down to our children's children to cherish and to follow."

Then came the soul-stirring Lament, "Flowers of the Forest," by Pipers of the 2nd Battalion, Scots Guards. At the termination of the "Lament," which was superbly rendered, the "Last Post" was sounded and when ended all present sang the old hymn "O God Our Help In Ages Past."

Dr. Lynn then bestowed the Blessing which was followed by "God Save the King."

After Reveille had been sounded the Parade moved off behind the band to the Cenotaph where, the Dowager Viscountess Plumer, assisted by His Excellency the Belgian Ambassador, laid the beautiful Ypres League wreath composed of corn-flower emblems, liles and white chrysanthemums, on the National Shrine.

The wreath bearers were the following four V.C.s:—Captain W. E. Boulter, V.C.; Sergeant O. Brooks, V.C.; Lieut. Michael O'Leary, V.C.; Corporal H. Wilcox, V.C.

At 12.20 p.m. a Deputation of the Ypres League, headed by Major E. Montague-Jones, O.B.E., T.D., M.A., was received by the Rev. Canon V. F. Storr, Sub-Dean of Westminster.

After a wreath had been placed on the Tomb of the Unknown Warrior by Major E. B. Waggett, C.B.E., D.S.O., etc., Vice-Chairman of the Ypres League, Canon Storr addressed those present, as follows:—

The four V.C.'s, reading from left to right:—Captain W. Boulter, Sergeant O. Brooks, Corporal H. Wilcox and Lieut. M. O'Leary. (Sgt. Brooks greeting an American Legionaire).

The Rev. Dr. Joseph Lynn, C.B.E. (Deputy Chaplain-General to the Forces), officiating at the Ypres Day Ceremony.

"Your Annual Visit here we very much appreciate and we record it in our Chronicles.

We have to tend a welcome to all present here of the Ypres League and in the name of the Chapter we bid you, welcome.

YPRES, what a name of memories and associations, sad and glorious, are recalled. I think it is a name never to be forgotten.

Now it seems to me that the work which the Ypres League is doing is something, of which, results cannot be judged on the surface. The amount of work which you are doing, by the comfort you bring in Pilgrimages, by the Spirit and ties of fellowship that you create and your ideals which are inspiring and, if I mistake not, that kind of thing is the start from which the individual qualities of character are made and redeem life from its drabness and sadness. I believe what you are doing is wanted at this time lest the great spiritual values of life shall become obscure. The things that you stand for are valueable. We see a world of strife, jealousy, and we in England see ideals being lost, but you know the peoples are for peace and quite slowly under the surface, the hope of peace is growing, and I believe that these clouds will pass and that there will come a period of peace.

This day we that are living think of those that have passed beyond out of our sight. After all there is only one family in Heaven and on earth there is only one God, and before I end with a short prayer, I suggest that we, by silent thought, will think of those who fell at YPRES, and those months of strife and suffering for the cause which we all think and believe to be sacred."

At the conclusion of the Service I had the pleasure of shewing to two representatives of the American Legion the framed Congressional Medal of their own country brought to England and presented by General John Pershing. They told me that they were very deeply impressed by the Ypres Day Commemoration. I told them that the Ypres League was proud and happy to welcome them.

THE SPIRIT OF THE LEAGUE.

I should like to be permitted to tell the following little story as it emphasises so well that spirit of the Ypres League of which we, as members, are proud.

Following the Unveiling Ceremony in 1936 of the Canadian Memorial at Vimy Ridge one of our members, upon learning of the financial struggle in which a number of Canadian mothers had been able to make the long pilgrimage, sent a donation to the League headquarters for distribution to one of the most deserving cases. This was in due course forwarded to the proper quarter and the gift was eventually handed over to a poor widow who had eleven sons in the War, six of whom were killed in action.

So impressed was the donor with the fortitude and sacrifice of this dear old Canadian mother that a further gift has been sent this year to the Ypres League with the request that it be forwarded to the same widow.

I cannot conclude without a reference to the sterling work performed by the League headquarters and our thanks are due to Major L. J. L. Pullar, M.C., and his assistant, Mr. O. Mears, for the admirable manner everything connected with this moving Commemoration was carried out.

R. HENDERSON BLAND, Captain,
(Late The Gloucestershire Regiment).

* * *

Light and Shade at the Front

(By An Ex-R.B.)

" Milk! Milk! Fresh Dairy Milk-O!"

IT was the month of June and the beginning of a Divisional rest and La Belle France was in a sunny mood. The troops saw sweetly scented new grass instead of trenches and trench mud; the billet huts, which lay almost hidden in wide untrodden fields adjacent to some trees, looked quite small by comparison, and the War being out of sight it was also, for the most part, out of mind.

Sang Shu——y,
 " Oh, oh who'll buy my lavender,
  My newly cut sweet lavender?
 The more you buy, the more you want,
  Oh, oh who'll buy my lavender?"

and on the afternoon on which this story opens the immediate outlook of the troops was further brightened when orderly men set the dicksey down, took the lid off, and by so doing released a cloud of steam and the refreshing odour of tea.

Bre—st—r reached the hut as the dicksey was being taken away. A ready, " meet-you-more-than-halfway " manner identified him as one of that elk who enliven our days (alas, not so much in these times as formerly) with their musical yodels, and if further proof of his " civvy " activities had been needed it was to be seen in a fresh " out-of-door " complexion, and a slight stoop which persisted in spite of army drills. A glance at the dicksey moving off, and then he asked the natural question:

" Anybody drawn my char? "

" Anyone drawn Bre—st—r's char? "

" Yes, and the " buckshee " as well. You didn't say you were going out."

" Only been to change a tin 'at," and then, turning to a " mucker-in," " Did you get some cake? "

" 'Ere, 'ere's a bloke wants jam on it! He's askin' for some cake!"

A small four feet by three canteen had opened up and sold slabs of cake and tins of salmon.

" I said ' cake ' and I won't say ' No ' to a slice of it."

" 'Ere you are then, Milky! Did you get a hat? "

" Yes, but they only had this one; it flops about a bit."

" Why not swop it with that new chap, What's-his-name? "

" No good; his tin 'at's about the same size as mine."

" Then why not tighten the strap? "

" Never mind, I'll make it do. This char's all right! It's only about six sizes too big."

" Well, if it's only six sizes too big why not use it as a dug-out? "

An eminent man of letters (Tents? Camp. Breakfast? Bacon!), once wrote down two lists of trite little proverbs, his object being to show that each proverb was flatly contradicted by another. Our Bacon is not to hand at the moment; at least, the food for the body is but not the food for the mind, and so the following examples are not culled from his collection, but they will serve. (a) " To save time is to lengthen life," but (b) " 'Ware speed-hogs or die an early death." (a) " Absence makes the heart grow fonder," not forgetting, however, that (b) " Too long an absence makes one forget." (a) " A rolling stone gathers no moss." Well, one wouldn't expect a rolling stone to gather moss; there are some pretty mossy old stones to be seen in churchyards. The correct riposte, however, to (a) is (b) that " a standing stone stands to be sat on." (a) " Least said soonest mended." An old wife's tale. (b) " Half confidences are worse than none," and yet a number five (space will not go to a number nine) " A stitch in time saves nine." So saith the busy housewife, but for anyone who lacks a huzzif (b) " Use bachelor's buttons and no stitches are needed." A proverb that would appear to have no counter is " It's an ill wind that blows *no good*," and Bre—st—r's tin hat was destined to afford an excellent example of that truth.

The Division went from rest billets into the Salient, an initial view of the then conditions presenting itself when a small party of scroungers touched off a booby trap. One night, about the time when the Company was moving up on " relief," the enemy opened up with a shelling, and a halt was called pending a slackening of the fire, the platoon being in a communication trench which had been dug from shell-holes. This trench sloped and crumbled on both sides, and in contour it was more like a V-shaped hollow.

The shelling was kept up all night, one shell bursting on the inner side of the slope, near the top, and in the vivid light of its momentary flash the troops could be seen stooping on one knee, rifle butt on ground, and patiently waiting. The " new chap " was getting his baptism of fire in a warm quarter, and several minutes elapsed before it was noticed that he was dead. Just at this juncture a four-handed stretcher case came up from the left, and on the stretcher being eased down among the troops that also halted.

The " lead-on " was given at about day-break, and at the next " halt!" a section of the platoon found itself under the lea of a sunken road. Just about here the water in the shell-holes was deep red and two blackened corpses within a few feet of each other lay in an advanced state of putrefaction.

No further order reaching the section they strolled about within the confines of the " halt," and presently lighted on an eighteen-pounder that had been spread-eagled by a direct hit, and on certain articles of equipment that were scattered about. A water allowance doesn't go far, and just at that time water-cum-chloride—cum-petrol was scarce in the section. So a water-bottle of good make and shape near the gun was picked up and its contents sampled. Ye gods! It was not water, it was—S.R.D. *undiluted*. So happeneth the unexpected.

At dusk the troops were a biscuit throw from the front line, and as Sergeant H—— came up he said, in casual tones, " Move up a

" Oh, oh who'll buy my lavender?"

bit, you blokes, we're going over in the morning." The whispered orders were, "The platoon is to get out into shell-holes. The K.R.R.'s will attack in the morning with this platoon in support on their right flank." The way out was by a tiny sap, footed by two sand bags, which was "taped" by machine-gun fire, but the troops aided by the darkness nipped out between bursts, crawled into shell holes, and waited. With the coming of dawn they expected to hear the signal shell, see an officer pop up, and the racket begin. But nothing happened. The attack was made the next morning by other troops from another point.

It was eased down.

A popular song in the Great War (and also in the Crimea) was, of course, "Annie Laurie," and it is interesting to remark that although "Marching to Georgia" was often played in the War, and was sung countless times to the vernacular one never heard "Wait till the clouds roll by" (adapted to the music of Handel's March in Scipio). A relative of a Crimea soldier told the writer that "Wait till the clouds roll by, Jenny" was a marching song in that war, and if that be so it would be senior by several years to "Marching to Georgia." The reason why "Jenny" was not sung in the Great War would appear to be that "Tipperary" eclipsed it.

"Annie Laurie," ending as each verse does with the line "I'd lay me down and dee," is singularly suggestive of the way of all flesh. And that being so, it is only reasonable to assume that where troops are laying out at night on a long wait, in readiness to attack at a stated hour, even the most matter-of-fact type of man so employed will devote at least a few moments to thinking privately, in a detached sort of way, as to the sort of " packet " he is likely to get, and in the event of that " packet " being a " daisy-rooter " (quoting the vernacular of the period) whether he will be any the wiser for it?

This is an interesting point because, taking the average soldier on active service in the field, there is no doubt he is as alert and physically fit as anyone could be. Especially so is that the case in these days where machinery and mechanical aids displace so much physical exercise, and as a result thereof healthy muscular developement suffers severely in proportion. The question which suggests itself, therefore, is that where a soldier with all his senses alert is within, quite probably, a few seconds of making a speedy exit from this world's stage, can he then see behind the scenes? As to the writer's own experience, such as it was, frankness compels him to say that at no time in the line was his vision wider than at any other time. The veil was impenetrable.

Turner's painting in the National Gallery, entitled " Night on Waterloo," which depicts an angel hovering down over the battlefield, and inspecting in the light thrown from a celestial lamp the faces and figures of the fallen, is one of the purest expressions extant of solicitude for the fallen in battle. But even allowing for the Divine and all-important attributes of instinct and a moral sense, who can say that once the voyager has set foot in Charon's boat his entity thenceforward is not merged inseparably with the shades?

Sergeant H. and the writer were in the same shell hole, and pending new orders, it was decided to wait until dusk and then crawl back. Snipers were posted on each side of the line, the enemy snipers using telescopic sights, the backsight being an upright open ring, fixed, and about the size of a sixpence. If the trigger were pulled as soon as an object seen through the backsight was approximate dead centre with the foresight, a hit at short range was practically assured. Presumably the design was to allow of speedy sighting at short range.

The enemy shelled the front line in the forenoon for an hour or two without drawing our fire, and after that a couple of planes flew low raking likely spots and then packed up. Feeling peckish about noon a light lunch was made off iron rations, some broken biscuit and a drink from the water bottle, and then things settled down to that postprandial state of repose which is common the world over. Suddenly the sharp report of rifle shots brought rifles to the ready, and next moment a figure loomed up, fell forward, and crashed full length on to the two occupants of the shell hole. This was Bre—st—r, and his first words were, " I'm hit in the nut!"

Here was an example of a lucky escape of which doubtless there were many in the Great War. Feeling thirsty, and things being quiet, Bre—st—r had risen from cover and doubled for the line, and was hit twice before coming to earth. One bullet entered the left side of his tin hat but did not mushroom as the range was so short. It then passed out of the helmet about an inch and a quarter from the point of entry without grazing him. Another bullet struck him as he twisted for cover and it furrowed a shallow wound at the base of the shoulder blades. First aid was given, also a quencher of water, and at dusk when the troops crawled back he was " sent down."

It is generally agreed that Science and Invention have made great strides, and it has been claimed that as a result thereof life's ageing stream is rejuvenated by as much as twenty years or so. True, there are certain people who claim, and probably they are right, that for every " good " that Science and Invention achieve they also do a corresponding " ill "; that they have that boomerang effect. Anyway, however

— The voyager. —

that may be it is hoped that Bre—st—r is as active as ever, and is still busy on his round. " Milk ! Milk ! Fresh Dairy Milk-O ! And I'm coming along !"

(To be continued)

J. EDWARDS.

* * *

The Eve of the
Nativity of the Cotswolds

SHEPHERDS WHO STILL WATCH.

THREE years ago, on Christmas afternoon, immediately preceding the late King George's broadcast message as father of a world-wide family, there came over the ether an expression of loyalty and devotion from one of the humblest of his subjects—an old shepherd living in a lonely hamlet away on the Cotswolds. The greeting was simply phrased and delivered in the homely accent of the western uplands. It followed similar greetings from all parts of the Empire, and I cannot recall a broadcast with such a magnificent climax.

A MEMORABLE NIGHT.

A few years ago it was my great privilege to pass the Eve of the Nativity in the company of a shepherd on the Cotswolds. It was a clear, still night, and a solemn haunting silence wrapt the earth in mystery. The vast sweeping wolds, the scattered copses and weather-worn hamlets lay out in the starlight—a forgotten land, breathlessly waiting for the mid-night of the Great Birth. From this upland track the lights of villages and farmsteads far below glowed cheerfully; whilst the vault above was purple-blue with the fires of Heaven itself.

I have wandered far among sheep and shepherds. I know their watchings and waitings at all seasons of the year. With the cold, grey light of early dawn there is the survey of the vast table-land of grass, so that straggling sheep may be returned to their proper pastures. At dusk, when the west is ablaze, the flock is mustered beneath the copses and round the folds. In storm, there is a flurry of white, and many an anxious hour is spent until the sheep are found and tracks beaten so that they may come to the stores of hay and turnips.

Controlling the Staples of Ypres and Calais.

Cotswold was full of delights and mystery this Christmas Eve. What must it have been before the wolds were enclosed in those rambling low stone walls, when the huge flocks, each worth a King's ransom, mingled ownership at their edges?

Six centuries ago the Cotswold country was reckoned the richest zone in all England. Its wool controlled the staples at Ypres and Calais, together with the markets of all Flanders and Europe, and brought much profit to King and country. In those days no one thought the Woolsack an uncommon seat for the King's Chancellor in the House of Lords. It represented England's richest trade.

Watching the Flocks at Night.

The shepherd and I walked in silence towards the sheep, the old collie at his master's heels, apparently taking not the slightest notice of the flock clustered about the hollow. The sheep were quite visible as grey patches in the clear starlight. The lamps of Heaven were lit in honour of the Saviour's birth. We abandoned the car-haunted road, and the feeble glimmering of distant farms, and villages seemed far away over the edge of another world.

As we approached the flock in the moist mist a decided tang of wool-scent arose from the fleeces; then a husky cough, a rustle, a voice-rumble as the nearest sheep sensed the coming of a stranger.

My Companion Meditates.

This Christmas Eve the air was so clear and still that the stars peered down with amazing penetration. As we walked alone, I heard more of this. My companion agreed that even a frosty night was less vivid in lights and shadows among the mighty hills. He spoke slowly, as though to himself, about the Eve we were celebrating.

"My grandfather used to say that Cotswold was once all wool-country; that the present sheep came later; but old times or new, there is always beauty in the tending of a flock. On Christmas Eve, we shepherds are forced back to think of the World's Greatest Day, when it was men of our craft who were sent to greet the new-born Saviour. And, though we may not go to church on Sundays, we have pride in this fact. The old shepherds used to have a lock of wool buried in their hands, so that on the Resurrection Morn there would be no doubt about their honourable calling in life."

A Soul-Inspiring Experience.

While he spoke the mid-night bells rang out in the distant villages, a tinkle of the various notes stealing over the edge of the hills from the churches in the glades below.

I shall come to see the flock, and to visit once again the vast silent land which has a vision to the Severn and to Wales beyond. Yes, my delight is in the quiet corners of the world, mostly because of their lovable people:—

"In the highlands, in the country places,
Where the plain old men have rosy faces
And the young fair maidens quiet eyes."

It was soul-inspiring to be with the flocks, to hear the sonorous pealing of distant bells, and to know that low down in the vale, the waits and choirs were singing "Adeste Fideles" and the old familiar Christmas carols.

H. BENSON.

Children at the Ypres British School, 1937.

Ypres British School

Extract from the 1937 Report.

Upon completion of their term of office Mr. and Mrs. W. P. Allen returned to England in March last after four years' hard work and devoted service. They had admirably continued the splendid traditions set by their predecessors, Mr. and Mrs. Morris—the first Principals of the School.

With the assistance of Miss Ryder, both Mr. and Mrs. Yorath are looking forward to their four years in office. They are determined to maintain that undoubtedly high standard of learning and deportment for which the Ypres British School has become so well known, as well as cementing the cordial relationship which exists between the School and the inhabitants of Ypres.

No sooner had the new Principals established themselves at the School than preparations were made for the Coronation Celebrations. It was desirable that the British Colony in and around Ypres should spend a patriotic and eventful day and the preliminaries necessitated an enormous amount of labour. The results, however, amply justified such effort.

The inclement weather prevented the display taking place in the School Playground, but through the kind offices of the Burgomaster, M. Vanderghote, the Theatre was placed at the Organisers' disposal, a gesture which was tremendously appreciated. The Celebrations were attended by practically the whole British community around Ypres, some coming from afar afield as Mons. The children did wonderfully well, and after the various patriotic displays a commemorative mug and medal was distributed to each child.

In the afternoon a grand sports meeting was held and among the interested spectators were Colonel Higginson and Commander Mackenzie of the Imperial War Graves Commission, Arras. The kind assistance rendered by the Revd. G. R. Milner, M.A., Mr. O. L. Gill and Mr. A. E. Piper with the many items of the sports programme was the contributing factor to its success. A tea tastefully arranged by Mrs. Milner and the Ladies' Committee was followed with the presentation of prizes by Miss Summers. The parents completed a memorable day by attending a dance in the evening which was graced by the presence of a number of distinguished French and Belgian guests.

With the balance of the Coronation Celebrations Fund, kindly donated by the Committee, a netball apparatus has been purchased and with deft instruction by Miss Ryder the children have shown much enthusiasm and considerable skill. This game has the advantage of tennis in that it is less individual, less expensive, and half the School can be pleasantly exercised in the time occupied by four playing tennis.

The visit of Field-Marshal the Earl of Cavan to distribute the prizes on July 21st was immensely appreciated by both parents and children, and Sir William Pulteney expressed the feelings of all when thanking Lord Cavan for his kind interest and efforts on the School's behalf. At this Prize-giving the pupils entertained their elders with two of Shakespeare's plays, "A Midsummer Night's Dream" and "Macbeth," the first time in the history of the School that Shakespearean plays have been attempted. For the splendid prizes given the School are particularly grateful to the Viscountess Albemarle, Lady Pulteney, Third Army Corps, Cheltenham College, Mrs. Briggs, Captain Peabody and M. de Beijser.

Special mention is made of the encouraging support accorded the new staff by the School's great benefactor, Lieut.-General Sir William Pulteney during their first months of office.

Apart from the three under-mentioned pupils who are leaving for the reasons stated, the number of children attending the School is ninety-six.

Georgette Piper, winner of many prizes, including the Cheltenham College prizes, in two successive years, goes to Kent College, Folkestone.

William Crouch leaves to take an Advanced Commercial Course.

Paul Cassin, awarded the Plumer Scholarship (Ten Pounds) for 1937, goes to the Gordon Boys' Home, Woking, for an Advanced Vocational Training.

It may be of interest to give the particulars of how the following three boys, who were educated in the School at Ypres and who joined the Army Technical School at Chepstow, have progressed; the particulars have been kindly supplied by the Commandant.

J. Blake.

Joined the School during the Summer of 1934 and left to join the Royal Army Service Corps in June, 1937.

His conduct was excellent and he rose to be a boy N.C.O., i.e., Apprentice Tradesman Corporal. His work in the workshops was above standard. He obtained a First Class Certificate of Education, he had a natural aptitude for games and was a good all-round performer.

W. A. Elridge.

Joined the School in January, 1937, and is due to join the Corps in January, 1940. His conduct is very good, he has obtained a Second Class Certificate of Education with high marks and is sitting for two subjects for his First Class Certificate this month; he is above the average, his work in the Shops is very satisfactory and in his group at present stands eighth out of fifty.

C. S. Harper.

Joined the School January, 1937, and is due to join the Corps in January, 1940. His conduct has been very good and he is up to standard as regards his trade training; he is in possession of a Second Class Certificate of Education and is sitting this month for two subjects towards his First Class.

Seventeen newcomers joined the School at the beginning of September this year, no less than seven of them speaking no English though all of them have English fathers; fortunately the children learn English very quickly, but it can be realised what extra difficulties are imposed upon the teachers.

It is not generally recognised how much the School is appreciated by parents of children who do not reside in Ypres. Appended is a list of children coming from outside with distances in kilometres:—

Children				
2	from	Harlebeke	...	39 kms.
1	,,	Courtrai	...	34 ,,
7	,,	Passchendaele	...	14 ,,
4	,,	Wulverghem	...	14 ,,
3	,,	Poelcapelle	...	13 ,,
7	,,	Poperinghe	...	11 ,,
5	,,	Vlamertinghe	...	5 ,,
6	,,	Kemmel	...	10 ,,
1	,,	Messines	...	10 ,,
1	,,	Langemarck	...	10 ,,
3	,,	St. Jean	...	3 ,,

There is also one girl boarded in Ypres from the Arras District for the purpose of attending the School.

The heavy expense of bringing these children from the outlying districts is borne by the Imperial War Graves Commission.

In the matter of finance a loss was sustained on the year. This is mainly attributed to loss of subscriptions through death, a matter which is causing the Committee the gravest anxiety. A few more Public Schools have promised their support and Lieut.-General Sir William Pulteney would be most grateful to hear from anyone interested in this work of such national importance willing to be numbered among the subscribers.

* * *

King Albert Army and R.A.F. Memorial

(Reproduced by courtesy of the Editor of "The Times.")

The stained-glass rose window which is to be placed in Ypres Cathedral, and which is the gift to Belgium of the British Army and Royal Air Force as a memorial to King Albert, has now been completed. The work has been carried out at Fulham to designs by Miss Geddes, whose work in Canada and Ireland is well known. The window is being transported to Ypres in sections. The ceremony of unveiling, which it is hoped will be undertaken by the King of the Belgians, will probably take place on April 30, 1938.

The sum of £2,000 for the work was subscribed by all ranks and units in modest amounts which were received from all parts of the Empire. The subject of the window is "The Glory of God" as expressed in the Te Deum. The size is 250 sq. ft., with a diameter of 25ft.

The central light shows Christ seated on the Rainbow of Peace and at His feet the earth while two symbolic soldier saints kneel on each side. In the circles are lights with figures of Apostles, Prophets, and Martyrs. In small surrounding windows are the crests of Belgium, the British Army, the Royal Air Force, and the 5th Royal Inniskilling Dragoon Guards, of which regiment King Albert was Colonel in Chief.

Inscription on Tablet.

A tablet which has been added as part of the memorial will be affixed to the main pillar in the chancel of the Cathedral. It is of grey sycamore wood in natural grain and will bear the crests of the British Army, of Belgium, and of the 5th Royal Inniskilling Dragoon Guards, and inscriptions as follows:—

To the glory of God and in honoured memory of
Albert I, King of the Belgians,
Knight of the Garter, Field Marshal of The British Army, and Colonel in Chief of the 5th Royal Inniskilling Dragoon Guards,
The Rose Window in the South Transept is given to
BELGIUM
By
The British Army and the Royal Air Force.

This Memorial gift was subscribed for in the Year 1935 by all ranks, active and retired, the Women's Services, and the Dominion Forces, whilst special assistance was given by the 5th Royal Inniskilling Dragoon Guards, the League of Remembrance (1914-1919), the British Legion, and the Ypres League. We, the subscribers are most happy to have this opportunity to express our high esteem and appreciation of King Albert's noble service in the Great War.

"My sword I give to him that shall succeed me in my pilgrimage. My courage and skill to him that can get it. My marks and scars I carry with me, to be a witness for me that I have fought His battles who will now be my rewarder."

So he passed over, and all the trumpets sounded for him on the other side.

FURTHER GIFTS.

Further gifts of stained glass for the Cathedral are the three chief windows in the east end, which have been presented by families living in the War area of Ypres. The subjects of these windows are St. Martin, St. George, and St. Michael. It is hoped that the unveiling of these windows will take place at the same time as the ceremony of unveiling the British memorial. The Ypres League will arrange for a pilgrimage to Ypres to coincide with the ceremony, and it is hoped that other ex-Service men's organisations will take the opportunity of arranging for the presence of members at the service.

The Earl of Athlone is chairman of the Presentation Committee, and the other members are His Excellency the Belgian Ambassador, Lieut.-General Sir W. P. Pulteney, Lieutenant-General Sir Tom Bridges, L'Abbe Vermaut, the Doyen of Ypres, Major-General Sir Neill Malcolm, Air Vice-Marshal Baldwin, and Captain Guy Cassie (Secretary).

As stated in our previous issue a special pilgrimage will be organised in connection with this Unveiling Ceremony which is provisionally fixed for Saturday, April 30th, 1938, and the pilgrimage will depart from London on the Friday, April 29th. Applications from those wishing to take part are requested to be forwarded to the SECRETARY, YPRES LEAGUE, 20, ORCHARD STREET, LONDON, W.1, as early as possible as only a limited number of seats in the Cathedral will be available to those travelling under the League's auspices.

* * *

Tomb of the "Soldat Inconnu," Paris, upon which a wreath, five feet in height and comprising over one hundred roses, was placed on behalf of the Ypres League on Ypres Day, October 31st, 1937, by Colonel Beckles Willson (Founder of the Ypres League) accompanied by the American Military Attache. We are indebted to Colonel Beckles Willson for sending a duplicate of the Memorial Card which reads as follows "In memory of our gallant French Comrades who served and perished in the Immortal Defence of Ypres, 1914-1918."—*The Ypres League*.

War Scenes Re-Visited

ROSES FOR MEMORY.

[The following interesting review was left over from our last edition through lack of space.]

To re-visit the battlefields of Belgium and France is the wish of every ex-service man and this year I made my second pilgrimage to many a spot where I held a rifle. My first visit was when the scars of war were still fresh and unhealed in the countryside, now they are healed and man and nature have covered up that which was broken or destroyed. It is possible to mark the area in which one soldiered; the writer could make out the line of country along which he trudged from St. Jean to Passchaendaele over duck-board tracks above shell-holes whose lips touched in seemingly endless succession. But the country is now like that of England, sheaves of corn are stacked where twenty years ago was a sea of mud. Round Le Cateau where we advanced in the days of victory it is the same as then— it was open fighting in our days and shell-fire had not done a great deal of damage. Aulnoye where my battalion had almost its last fight is quiet and sleepy as if war had never troubled it, or its railway bridges had never gone up into the air the result of delayed action mines. In what was the British lines can still be seen the corkscrew piles for wiring and elephant iron is still being used as roofs for poultry and cattle houses. Cartridge cases, bullets and shrapnel can be picked up and some areas are closed to the public owing to the danger of unexploded shells and bombs. Many of the war memorials —this applies only to the Belgian—are weather-worn owing to the soft stone upon which they were carved and details of figures are disappearing. All the cemeteries are as we should wish them to be. The German cemeteries are also now cared for. The British cemeteries are like God's acre at home, the headstones are becoming mellowed by age, English roses bloom on each grave and they are quiet well-kept sanctuaries, fitting resting places for comrades who gave all. Visitors to the cemeteries, who did not suffer the loss of a near one, look in the book recording the names of those who rest there and find one who is dear to a friend in some English town or village and from his grave they take a leaf from a shrub to hand over as a trust to those who bear his memory as fresh as the day when he passed over.

Starting on a tour which embraced most of what is known as the Ypres Salient, the writer saw his first British Cemetery at Ramscapelle. The headstones are becoming dulled by time, roses and tree lupins adorned each little plot and in every sense it was an English garden Further along the road was a Belgian Military Cemetery, with the headstones in a semi-circle. All the graves in the Belgian cemeteries are of unknown soldiers—as where they were known they were taken back to their village or town churchyards. A Belgian observation tower at Pervyse is hidden by trees from view, but the place is preserved as a notable landmark of the war. At Dixmude the remains of the famous Flour Mills, a German strong point and the Trench of Death are preserved, to tell of the heroic fights of the Belgian Army. An imposing memorial stands close to a bridge at Steenstraete, where the Belgians were called upon to withstand the first gas attack. They were pushed back a short way, but recaptured the lost positions, the Ostend Regiment faring badly and have only just been re-formed as such. Near here it was where the Belgians flooded the land to strengthen their defences. Next came Boesinghe, which was for three long years the northern boundary of the British Army and from which the gates to the Channel Ports were held remorselessly and stubbornly. Officers and men of the 49th (West Riding) Division lie in pretty Essex Farm Cemetery and here reposes a very gallant young warrior, aged 15, the youngest British soldier killed in the war. Salvation Corner, where troops heaved a sigh of relief if they were going down the line and otherwise if they were going up, is now only dangerous if motorists take the bend too swiftly. Then came Ypres, with that magnificent memorial, the Menin Gate. The city is full of associations for those whom the call of duty took to the Salient—no other place has the same proud appeal as this Flemish city, which has arisen from piles of rubble.

Canada's Tribute.

Through the Menin Gate we went, then turned along a new road, lined with Maple Trees to Mount Sorrel (Hill 62), where the Canadians have built a dignified memorial. Only a slight rise in the flat country, the hill was of great importance and gave command over a large area. Tenaciously held by the Canadians from 1915 until the withdrawal in the spring of 1918, they have erected a low-lying terraced monument, formed into a miniature park, with trees and shrubs brought from Canada, the whole aspect being quiet and beautiful. Adjacent are the trenches of Sanctuary Wood, still in a fair state of preservation, rifles, exploded gas bombs, flying pigs, helmets and shell-cases litter the ground, giving a vivid impression of what the front line was like in those really far-off days. Sanctuary Wood was so called because a General placed troops there in "Sanctuary" and commanded that they were not to be used without his orders.

Retracing our way we had lunch in Ypres in an up-to-date restaurant against the road where once we slogged along for the line. Then up towards the apex of the Salient through Potijze, where there are several cemeteries; then left along Junction Road and close to Vinery, where once the light railway ran. Past Mill Cottages, where fatigue parties assembled and along Oxford Road (close by is Oxford Road Cemetery), then on to Wieltje and by L.R.B. Cottage. How vivid and real came back the scenes of twenty years ago. Broken pill-boxes in close proximity, stood out from fresh-cut cornfields. Away stretched the low-lying undulating country, golden with the stubble of corn and squared with green hedges. Once shell craters linked lip to lip, mud would swallow a man in its grip and duck-board tracks carried the ceaseless flow of soldiers to and fro, but now with the summer sun shining, it was as peaceful and serene as Earlswood Common. Away in the distance stood the white headstones of Tyne Cot Cemetery. The Canadian memorial of a soldier with bowed head, where Imperial troops were called upon to undergo the first gas attack, stands at the St. Julien crossroads in a pleasant park-like enclosure, as neatly trimmed as some cool retreat in a garden. Here in 1917 the 39th Division was engaged in terrific fighting and held the ground they won, withstanding powerful German counter attacks. Nature has recovered with her green mantle all that was torn and blasted. At Poelcappelle came the German line and nesting in the angle of a fork road, with young trees around were rows of small black squat crosses. They were the well-kept graves of German soldiers. A little further on was another German cemetery, but here the headpieces were in the shape of Iron Crosses. Plain and neat were these two cemeteries—no flowers adorned the graves of those who sleep away from their Fatherland.

The Belgian Line.

Then, finally, we came back to the Belgian line—Houthulst Forest—standing back from the narrow road. To the Belgians Houthulst is what Ypres is to the British and Verdun to the French. The wood is green, the young branches are thickly crowned with leaves, but standing above, gaunt and brown in colour, are dead trees, reminders of the days that are gone. The wood is closed to the public because of the danger of unexploded bombs, which lie just under the surface of the ground. Only last summer some children were killed there. The tour concluded with a visit to the big gun of Leugeboom at Moere, which the Germans used on Dunkirk, twenty-eight miles away. The monster with its massive breech casing is rusty, grass and bushes are growing over the concrete basin embrasure, but bared to sight is the broken lip into which the Germans fired in the hope that the shell would rebound and smash the gun, but instead it crashed its way through.

And so ended a tour, brimful of memories of days when the Great Adventure thrilled us young men. Our comrades sleep in hallowed spots where English roses bloom and all is well with them. They are not forgotten.

C.W.P.

* * * *

Lantern Slide Lectures

A feature of the League's many activities is the holding of Lantern-slide lectures and reviews, a department that is being given special attention in view of the interest and requests from groups of ex-service men and friends. These Illustrated Talks will be gladly arranged by League headquarters for any organisation or party on receipt of their request.

We reproduce below, with kind permission of the Editor of the local Gazette, a commentary that appeared in their publication of a Lantern-slide Review arranged by headquarters on Armistice Night for the Grange Park Comradeship of Remembrance at Woodford Green.

Mr. W. J. Morrison, referred to in the report, is one of our staunchest members and the possessor of a wonderful collection of slides dealing with the work of the Y.M.C.A. during the War. His talks are really most interesting and his services are cheerfully given. Headquarters of the Ypres League value his co-operation very much.

A happy group of "Old Contemptibles" in sheepskin coats toasting the camera-man in cups of steaming cocoa, Christmas, 1914, introduced Mr. W. J. Morrison's lantern talk to Grange Park Comradeship of Remembrance and friends from the Ypres League, assembled to commemorate the coincidence of the Comradeship's tenth anniversary and of Armistice Day.

Mr. Morrison's anecdotes and photographs rolled back the veil of the passing years and revealed the battlefields as ex-servicemen knew them—waterlogged trenches and shell-holes, tangles of rusty barbed wire, mine craters, dug-outs, tree stumps that had been woods, broken and discarded equipment, devastated towns and villages. Lumps came into one's throat at the sight of wounded men forcing sad smiles for the camera—and the little isolated crosses. . . .

Mr. Morrison showed pictures of once familiar Y.M.C.A. huts and astounded his hearers with figures that proved the immensity of the Y.M.C.A.'s war-time activities.

Mr. O. Mears of the Ypres League spoke of the work of the War Graves Commission, and showed slides of the Cemeteries and Battlefield Memorials. He also explained the objects of the Ypres League and described the pilgrimages to the battlefields organised by the League—Ypres, Loos, Cambrai, Vimy, Arras, Somme, Messines, St. Quentin, Zeebrugge—tragic but glorious names to our generation.

A hearty vote of thanks was accorded the speakers and the meeting was closed with the appropriate Ritual.

The Ypres Day Broadcast

"FROM MONS TO YPRES."

We owe this admirable and stirring piece of work to the poetess Beatrix Brice-Miller, one of our earliest members of Committee, to whom the League owes a heavy debt of gratitude for her several literary productions, specially written for us.

This, her latest achievement, recalls in the most vivid fashion the early incidents of the War, from the first contact with the Enemy through the Retreat and the Advance, finishing with a most striking presentation of the First Battle of Ypres.

As a literary effort this was, as one would expect from such a powerful pen, a record of the most inspiring quality. Those who missed it, missed a page of War literature of the very first importance. We are happy to learn that a repetition will be given on a future occasion. Meanwhile, we send hearty thanks to the poetess for one more invaluable contribution to the literature of the War.

E. B. W.

* * *

Our Ypres Representative

The Ypres League representatives at Ostend, Arras and Amiens are doubtless so well known to the travelling members of the League that it would be somewhat superfluous to make any reference to them here except to say that all of them have given of their best by way of loyal service and advice whenever called upon so to do. In this connection, therefore, it may not come amiss if we pen a few words about our present Representative at Ypres, M. Cyrille Leupe.

He was appointed to take the place of our late and deeply lamented Representative, Mr. "Jack" Parminter, who found, to our great regret, that persistent ill-health prevented him from continuing as our active Representative. That he did not survive very long after giving up his active association in our interests we deeply deplore.

M. Leupe is a very fine type of ex-serviceman. He enlisted in Belgium's "gallant little Army" in September, 1914, at a place called Lierre, near Antwerp, and found himself, very early in his service, in the fighting retreat of the Belgian Army to the Yser battle line, the position from which the Germans were never able to drive them.

On reaching Nieuport, he was sent to an Instructional Camp, somewhere in France, and on completion of his training was posted to the 1st Regiment of Carabineers. Early in 1915 saw him in action with this Regiment during the first gas attack at St. Julien, the 1st Carabineers being on the immediate left of the Canadians in that momentous battle. For their heroic part in this fighting the 1st Carabineers have their name commemorated on the French Memorial at Steenstraate.

M. Leupe next found himself on the Yser in front of Dixmude and he was one of those gallant defenders of that much assaulted bridgehead of the Yser Battle Line. As is well known the fighting at Dixmude during the desperate efforts of the Germans to break through was of the most fierce and savage imaginable and in this fighting M. Leupe was in the forefront. For a particularly gallant exploit he was awarded the Croix de Guerre with palm, granted ten days' special leave and an account of the exploit which gained him this coveted decoration was ordered to be published in Regimental Orders of the 1st Carabineers. M. Leupe was twice wounded and in 1916 he was sent to

M. Cyrille Leupe.

England where his skill as a metal turner was put to account by the British and he instructed war convalescents in the art of shell-making. He subsequently rejoined his Regiment and on the Armistice he was at Obbercassel. His demobilisation took place on August 29th, 1919, at Neuss on the Rhine.

During the Battle of Kemmel in 1918 his home at Poperinghe was damaged by shell-fire and his mother and two sisters sought refuge in France. Both his brothers were at this time still fighting in the Line.

At the special invitation of the Ypres League M. Leupe came to England recently and attended the Ypres Day Commemoration Ceremony on 31st October and had the honour of being presented to His Excellency the Belgian Ambassador.

Recruiting Competition

As is well known to members of the Ypres League, the Purley Branch of our Association has won for six consecutive years the Annual Recruiting Prize, so it may perhaps be forgiven us at H.Q. for assuming that they would win again, having a substantial lead up to a fairly recent date. The London Branch, up to the time of holding their Annual Concert, were behind Purley in the numbers of new members recruited to the League, but realising that the race is never over until the tape is broken and that there was still a chance of gaining this distinction—the prize in itself is but secondary —put forth a truly noble effort and spurted up the straight to such purpose that they succeeded in passing the post a winner for the first time.

It was a close finish, the figures being as follows:—London Branch thirty-nine and Purley thirty-three. It goes without saying that our Purley sportsmen will be among the first to congratulate their London comrades and to do their utmost to win next year.

It will be appreciated from the above figures that the contest was a close one and we congratulate both Branch Committees and in particular the respective Hon. Secretaries, who work so very hard and loyally for the welfare of the Ypres League and their own Branches in every possible way.

We hope with all our heart that this friendly rivalry will continue as it not only gives a stimulus to the League in general but gives us at H.Q. the opportunity of welcoming many new members to the roll, and we feel sure our members would like to know how much this Annual Competition has helped to this end. Since the first year of the competition, in 1931, the Purley Branch of the Ypres League have recruited the remarkable number of three hundred and twenty members, and for the London Branch to have snatched the palm in the seventh year, even if it has been on the post, is something for which they deserve congratulation. We are confident that they will be delighted at having gained what has so persistently evaded them after much striving, for we know at H.Q. that they have tried hard in past years, and taken in a very sportsmanlike way their defeats.

This time next year we may be reporting the success of another Branch in this recruiting competition, and not necessarily a "Home One." In any event we look forward to an equally close finale.

In conclusion may we further wish our Branches good fortune in their splendid efforts to keep the Ypres League alive and interesting by way of their re-union functions and sporting events, and to end by congratulating the London Branch Committee for winning in 1937 the seventh Annual Recruiting Ribbon and to Purley for their efforts to keep it in Surrey.

* * *

Cartoon by Wyndham Robinson (signed) presented to the Ypres League by the "Morning Post" last year and reproduced with their kind permission.

THE FOURTEENTH ANNUAL

Children's Christmas Party

organised by the
LONDON COUNTY COMMITTEE
will take place at the
**WESTMINSTER CITY SCHOOL,
55, PALACE ST., VICTORIA ST., S.W.1.**
(By permission of the Governors of the School)
On SATURDAY, JANUARY 15th, 1938,
at 4 p.m.

Admission:
**Junior Division Members, Free.   Friends 6d.
each.**

Applications for tickets should be made to the Hon. Secretary, London County Committee, Ypres League, at 20, Orchard Street, W.1, not later than January 12th, 1938.

Please book these dates in your diary.

THE MONTHLY
Informal Gatherings

FOR JANUARY, FEBRUARY, AND MARCH
will be held at
**THE BEDFORD HEAD HOTEL,
MAIDEN LANE, STRAND, W.C.2**
on
THURSDAY, 20th JANUARY, 1938.
  Review (Lantern Slides) "Principal Events and Battles up to Second Ypres."
THURSDAY, 17th FEBRUARY, 1938.
  Programme by the St. Dunstan's Concert Party.
THURSDAY, 17th March, 1938.
  Programme arranged by the Ladies.

Start the year by paying us a visit at our Gathering on Thursday, 20th January, 1938. A very hearty welcome awaits you and any ex-service friend whom you may wish to bring along.

Full particulars of the Gatherings will be sent by the Hon. Secretary, London County Committee, to a friend on receipt of name and address. Ladies are cordially invited.

HOTEL
Splendid & Britannique
YPRES

GRANDE PLACE. Opposite Cloth Hall.

LEADING HOTEL FOR COMFORT AND QUALITY, AND PATRONIZED BY THE YPRES LEAGUE.

COMPLETEY RENOVATED

RUNNING WATER. BATHROOMS.

MODERATE TERMS.   GARAGE.

Proprietor—Life Member, Ypres League.

YPRES
Skindles Hotel

(Opposite the Station)

Proprietor—Life Member, Ypres League

Branch at Poperinghe

(close to Talbot House)

Correspondence

Matlock, Derbyshire.
8.11.37.

Dear Major Pullar,

I have the sorrow to inform you that my dear mother passed away in January last. I had intended writing the League before, but of course you, unlike Captain de Trafford, had not met her. I think all members who had will agree that she was a very wonderful as well as a dear woman. Although 82 years of age she travelled alone from Nottingham last year to join the Whitsuntide Pilgrimage to Ypres which was conducted by the Assistant Secretary, Mr. Mears. On her behalf I enclose a small subscription towards the maintenance of the "Ypres Times." You will of course in future only forward one copy. The journal, by the way, I pass on to our local ex-service men's Club.

In connection with my mother's last trip to Ypres there was a very beautiful incident which I want to express gratitude for, and if you choose to publish this letter, or part of it, you are at liberty to do so. On the Whit Sunday in Ypres my mother did not feel equal to getting up for the 8 o'clock service but went to St. George's Church for Matins. Thinking there would be Holy Communion after service she remained in her seat. The church, however, emptied and finally the Padre came down the aisle dressed for leaving. He stayed to speak to my mother and she explained that she had thought there would be a Communion. "And so there will be," was the Padre's instant response, and approaching two tourists on a sight-seeing expedition, invited them to partake in the service which was then held for my mother's benefit. This touched and comforted her more than words can tell, and to me it is a very lovely and significant thing that the last Communion my mother partook was there on that sacred soil and near to her beloved son's grave. I am extremely grateful to the Vicar of St. George's for his act and I hope to thank him in person on my next visit to Ypres. Please let me have travel itineraries as soon as published.

Just one thing more, I would also like to thank all members who were so kind to my mother on her trip with the Whitsuntide Pilgrimage mentioned. I have not written to them personally for I did not know them, but on her return she was full of the kindness and attention she had received during the trip. Through you, Mr. Secretary, I say "thank you, one and all who helped to make my mother's last pilgrimage such a happy one."

Yours very sincerely,
J. M. D.

* * *

Brisbane, Australia.
5.10.37.

Dear Sir,

Please find enclosed Money Order for one Ypres League badge as advertised in the "Ypres Times."

London is a long way from here, but my memories of the Pilgrimage last year and the kindness I received from your Representatives during my stay in the Old Country will always remain a pleasant memory.

Christmas greetings to yourself and my fellow members of the Ypres League.

H. G.

* * *

East Withering,
Sussex.
4.11.37.

Dear Sir,

I have pleasure in sending my subscription to the Ypres League. I am always grateful to the League for arranging my journey to Ypres to see my brother's grave. The "Ypres Times" is much appreciated; there are seven or eight ex-service men here and they all read it.

Yours faithfully,
H. P.

* * *

Roath,
Cardiff.

Dear Sir,

I enclose a donation towards the "Ypres Times Fund." It gives me great pleasure to contribute my mite. I should miss my quarterly number dreadfully if I did not receive it.

Yours faithfully,
A. T. D.

* * *

Cross Lane,
Congleton.
13.12.37.

Dear Sir,

I do not know what amount my husband usually sends to the League, but if you will kindly let me know I will post the amount on to you. My husband, unfortunately, is in the Memorial Hospital; he underwent a serious operation last August. I should like to continue with the "Ypres Times" as I enjoy reading it myself.

Yours faithfully,
M. H.

* * *

Bronx,
New York, U.S.A.
2.12.37.

Dear Major Pullar and Mr. Mears,

I wish to thank you for the very fine reception that you accorded me during my recent visit to your country and I hope that some day I will be able to do the honours for you when you come to America. With my best wishes for a jolly Christmas and a very Happy New Year. My motion pictures of the Ypres Day Commemoration came out splendidly and I will show them at the Veterans' Meeting when I attempt to talk Ypres League to them; anyway, I'll do my very best.

Very cordially and sincerely yours,
B. R.

Saskatoon,
Canada.

Dear Sir,

I am enclosing a mite with the hope that it will help towards the "Ypres Times Maintenance Fund" and make sure to us such a periodical as the "Ypres Times."

Yours very truly,
E. H.

Victoria, British Columbia.
10.12.37.

Dear Sir,

I am to-day forwarding a Money Order towards the carrying on of the "Ypres Times." Personally I look forward to the time when I am to receive another number and always find something interesting in it, and would miss it very much.

Yours sincerely,
C. H.

* * *

League Secretary's Notes

A year ago we ventured to foretell another successful year of effort for our Association and studying the reports from the various Branches and Departments we feel justified in stating that the year of 1937 has been a satisfactory one in many respects. The principal event of the Ypres League is of course the Annual Ypres Day Commemoration Parade and Ceremony, held on the Horse Guards Parade, St. James's Park, on the nearest Sunday to Ypres Day itself, namely the 31st October. This last year's Parade fell on the actual day and was attended by a gathering which eclipsed in numbers any previous one by over a thousand.

Our Branches reported most successful social sporting events and functions throughout the year; travel and pilgrimages were well maintained and many new friends and members resulted from these. In addition several Organisations favoured us with their Battlefield Tours and numbered among these were one or two who came to us for the first time. We have ample evidence that satisfaction was given them in every way and we have hopes that their future tours will be conducted under our auspices.

During the year we had the honour of being visited by a number of Colonial and American ex-comrades-in-arms, all of whom were impressed with what they saw and heard at Head quarters. Several have promised not to forget that the Ypres League exists and two have returned home with the intention of forming Branches.

In regard to the "Ypres Day" Commemoration Parade and Ceremony of 31st October last, the weather was again fine and the sun shone throughout. This was remarkable in view of the very bad weather preceding and following the Ceremony. The one great disappointment of the day was the unavoidable absence of our beloved Patron, Her Royal Highness Princess Beatrice, who, had she followed her own wish instead of accepting the wise advice of her doctors, would have been present. That this very gracious Lady and friend of the Ypres League be spared for years to attend our Ypres Day Commemoration is the heartfelt wish of every member of the League.

The membership roll has been most satisfactorily added to, and our grateful thanks are given to the Branches of the League and certain individuals for their interest and help in this way. Reference has been made elsewhere in this issue of the "Journal" to the recruiting duel between the Purley and London Branches. Reverting to the Ypres Day Parade, we were very gratified to welcome thereon a number of Colonial members and their friends—visiting the "Old Country" as well as representatives of the American Legion. There is much scope for better liason between us and our Colonial, American and Continental ex-service comrades, and it is our wish in this new year before us—the eighteenth year of the League's life—to see this developed.

We are happy to announce the unanimous election to the Executive Committee of the Ypres League of Major H. G. Harris, founder of the Purley Branch, and Major Graham-Carr, D.S.O., M.C., its indefatigable Honorary Secretary.

The Ypres British School continues to advance in prestige and popularity and we have included elsewhere in this issue extracts from the School Report for 1937.

The unveiling Ceremony of the "King Albert Memorial Window" by His Majesty King Leopold III, at the Ypres Cathedral has been fixed provisionally for 30th April next and members and friends who wish to be present are requested to notify us as early as possible in view of the limited accommodation available. A special Pilgrimage is being organised under our auspices for this Ceremony. Reference has been made elsewhere to our normal conducted pilgrimages for 1938 and we look forward to meeting once again those members who so regularly take part in these tours. We also welcome any new travellers and feel sure that once they come with us they will favour us again. A number of Battlefield Tours have been arranged to date for Units of the Regular Army, the Territorial Army (officers' instruction), Old Comrades Associations, Public Schools Officers Training Corps, and private parties. The travel season for the League has every indication of being a busy one.

Before concluding these Notes we desire to express our deepest thanks to those members who have so generously contributed to the "Ypres League Maintenance Fund," for without help in this direction we should experience the greatest difficulty in producing the unique little "Journal" four times a year.

Finally, may we wish all our members a very happy and successful New Year.

Branch Notes

COLCHESTER & DISTRICT BRANCH.

Re-union Dinner.

The 5th Annual Re-union Dinner took place on Tuesday, November 9th last, at the Red Lion Hotel when the number of members and friends attending was smaller than on previous occasions. This is attributed to the unfortunate fact that the date selected for this function again fell on the same evening as the equally important—to many members of the Colchester Branch, Ypres League—Masonic Banquet. In the circumstances we are deeply grateful to Major G. C. Benham, M.C., the Branch Vice-Chairman and Deputy Mayor of Colchester, for dividing his time between the two functions.

Lieut.-Colonel H. W. Herring, M.C., Chairman of the Branch, presided and the guest of honour was Lt.-General Sir William Pulteney, G.C.V.O., K.C.B., C.M.G., D,S,O., Chairman of the Ypres League.

During the dinner music was provided by the band of the 5th Royal Inniskilling Dragoon Guards and afterwards there was a delightful entertainment by the Regina Concert Party.

Submitting the toast "The Ypres League," Major Benham said that those who served in the Ypres Salient had a very great deal in common, and could appreciate that the underlying object of the Ypres League was the great ideal of comradeship. The League, he said, was doing a great deal to cement friendship between all the Allies and Colonial forces. Speaking of foreign affairs and the present world unrest, Major Benham commented that they could liken the situation to being at cross-roads—there were many dangers, but there were also safeguards. They wanted to see that all our safeguards were well maintained, a situation which was more likely to prevent a clash than anything else. He would say that military tradition with a love of peace was particularly English, and one of the strongest factors for the peace of the world to-day. Military tradition without a love of peace could be most dangerous, while love of peace without military tradition was absolutely futile. The Ypres League stood for peace, improved conditions, comradeship and all those things that make life worth while.

Sir William Pulteney on rising to respond to this toast was given an enthusiastic reception and in the course of his remarks said that those who had served in the Ypres Salient would always remember it.

The duties of toastmaster were once again carried out by Mr. S. C. Nixon and in the general arrangements Mr. H. Snow (Hon. Secretary) was ably assisted by Captain H. C. Palmer.

Armistice Day Memorial Service.

The Chairman, Lieut.-Colonel H. W. Herring, M.C., accompanied by a representative party of the Colchester and District Branch, attended the Service of Remembrance at the Colchester War Memorial and at the conclusion of the service Colonel Herring placed a wreath on behalf of the Branch. The wreath of natural flowers in the League colours, blue and gold, bore a card with the following inscription:— "In memory of all who gave their lives in the Great War, 1914-1918 for the British Empire and for civilisation—From the Colchester and District Branch, Ypres League." "Last Post" and "Reveille" were sounded by the 1st Battalion, The Oxfordshire and Buckingham Light Infantry, and the blessing was bestowed by the Right Revd. the Lord Bishop of Colchester. Chopin's Funeral March was played during the placing of the many beautiful wreaths.

Annual Ball.

November 26th, 1937, was the occasion of the Fifth Annual Ball of the Colchester and District Branch. Although well supported, the attendance was not so good as last year, the reason possibly being due to the foggy weather prevailing on this particular evening. The function was organised by a Committee comprising Mr. W. H. Taylor, Mr. S. Farran, Captain A. C. Palmer, Mr. M. McKinley, Mr. D. Shadrach and headed by Major G. C. Benham (Vice-Chairman of the Branch), with the duties of Hon. Secretary jointly shared by Mr. McKinley and Mr. Shadrach.

The dance music throughout the evening was rendered by the 2nd Battalion Lancashire Fusiliers (by kind permission of the Officer Commanding, Lieut.-Colonel J. S. Fulton, O.B.E., M.C.), and the duties of M.C. were in turn taken over by Major Benham, Captain Palmer and Mr. Shadrach.

Parties were brought by the Branch Chairman, Lieut-Colonel H. W. Herring, M.C., Major G. C. Benham, M.C., Captain M. Leach, M.C., Captain E. F. Matthews, M.B.E., G. C. Stanford, Esq., and C. Rabatt, Esq. A member of the Dance Committee, Mr. M. McKinley, who brings a party each year to this function, was unfortunately prevented at the last moment from attending.

A large box of chocolates, kindly presented by Lieut.-Colonel H. W. Herring, was put up for competition and the holder of the lucky number was Mrs. Liddell, wife of Major-General C. G. Liddell, C.B., C.M.G., C.B.E., D.S.O., Commanding 4th Division, Colchester.

The dancing extended from 8 o'clock p.m. until 1 o'clock a.m., and the occasion was greatly enjoyed by all present, for which circumstance we are very grateful to the Organisers.

LONDON BRANCH COMMITTEE.
Annual Smoking Concert.

The Fifteenth Annual Re-union Smoking Concert, arranged by the London Branch Committee of the Ypres League, was held on October 30th last at the Caxton Hall, Victoria Street, S.W.1, and was attended by over five hundred members and friends.

In the Chair was Major E. Montague Jones, O.B.E., M.A. (Chairman of the London Branch Committee), and gracing the high table with him were: His Excellency the Belgian Ambassador, Baron E. de Cartier de Marchienne, supported by the Belgian Military Attaché, Lieut.-General Baron Vincotte; General Sir Hubert Gough, G.C.B., G.C.M.G., K.C.V.O., D.S.O., and Lieut.-General Sir William Pulteney, G.C.V.O., K.C.B., K.C.M.G., D.S.O. (Chairman of the Ypres League).

The programme for this occasion was provided by the First Army Follies Concert Party under the personal direction of Mr. Will Burnes, originally of Splinters (Les Rouges et Noirs), and after the Chairman had welcomed those present the entertainment commenced. The artistes, attired in khaki uniforms, with aid of an old-time Chairman, true to type, and "Mademoiselle from Armentieres," put over a magnificent show and every turn was keenly followed and enjoyed. The atmosphere introduced by the artistes was typical of those days old soldiers recall so well, and a sketch showing the interior of an estaminet with soldiers enjoying a smoking concert prior to leaving for the Front Line fairly brought down the house. Led by the old-time Chairman the audience joined lustily in the singing of popular war-time melodies and at the conclusion of the programme the artists were accorded a thoroughly deserved applause.

During the evening Major E. Montague Jones read the following message which had been addressed to H.M. the King:—

"To His Majesty the King, their Patron-in-Chief.
Members of the Ypres League assembled at their Annual Re-union beg to send expressions of their unfailing loyalty, devotion and homage."

and later the following reply was received and read, amid much enthusiasm, to the assembly:

"Chairman, Ypres League, Caxton Hall.
The King sincerely thanks the members of the Ypres League assembled at their Annual Re-union for their loyal assurances, which His Majesty as Patron in Chief much appreciates."

The Chairman also read a telegram received from His Excellency the American Ambassador.

"To the Chairman.
I appreciate this opportunity of conveying to the members of the Ypres League an expression of friendship from comrades in arms across the sea on this occasion of their Re-union. I sincerely regret that it is impossible for me to be with you."
(signed) ROBERT W. BINGHAM.

After the various distinguished guests had been thanked by the Chairman for being present, Sir William Pulteney rose to express the special thanks of all to His Excellency the Belgian Ambassador, who has the interest of the League so much at heart and attends their functions regularly year after year. Tremendous applause greeted these remarks and the audience rose and heartily sang "For he's a jolly good fellow."

The evening proved very enjoyable and again showed how popular are these Re-unions among old war comrades. As long as there are veterans of the Great War surviving these Reunions will find favour. The Committee wish to thank very heartily all those who contributed to its success.

J. M.

* * *

As stated in the previous issue the first of the present series of Informal Gatherings was held on September 16th, when Mr. Geo. A. Goodall, Hon. Social Secretary, Hampton Wick Branch, British Legion, very kindly provided the evening's entertainment with his "Bing Boys" Band and "Whoopee" Girls. The programme of mirth, music and dance was thoroughly enjoyed and we hope that at some future date Mr. Goodall will be kind enough to oblige again. We extend him and his capable young artistes our very grateful thanks.

Our October Gathering took the form of a "Steak Supper" over which a member of the Committee, Mr. F. W. Stevenson, presided. A very pleasant evening was spent and the League Secretary, Major L. J. L. Pullar, who had accepted the invitation to be present, was asked to address the gathering with a few words about the League generally. To this request Major Pullar was happy to respond, commenting how delighted he was to be among such jolly company and expressing the hope that all present would strive their utmost to enthuse their friends in the League's work and so help to increase still further the membership of the League.

The November Gathering were entertained by Mr. R. S. Beck who gave a most interesting Cinematograph Talk on the Isle of Man and North-west England.

The programme for the December Informal held on Thursday, December 16th, was kindly provided by Mr. O. Mears, of Headquarters. In view of the entertainment provided on previous occasions at the December Informals it is no surprise to find these particular Gatherings well patronised, and shortly before 8 o'clock on the evening of December 16th one could observe that our accommodation would be highly taxed. Members and friends had come along in anticipation of the usual jolly evening in keeping with the festive season and by the reception accorded the various artists during the following three hours' entertainment they had not been disappointed. Mr. Mears has generously provided these "end of the year" Informal programmes for the past six years and with all due regard to those artists who have so ably supported him in the past it was freely expressed, afterwards, that the high standard of entertainment had not only been maintained but on this occasion excelled. For another really pleasant evening our grateful thanks are due to Mr. Mears and to those who extended him their kind support.

The respective programmes for the following three months have been arranged as follows:—

Thursday, January 20th, 1938.—Illustrated Review of "The principle events and battles up to the Second Battle of Ypres," by Major L. J. L. Pullar, M.C.

Thursday, February 17th, 1938.—Programme by the "St. Dunstan's" Concert Party.

Thursday, March 17th, 1938.—Programme provided by our Lady Members.

Annual Children's Party.

Our Fourteenth Annual Children's Christmas Party takes place on Saturday, January 15th, 1938. By kind permission of the School Governors the spacious hall at the Westminster City School has again been placed at our disposal and with the co-operation of members we are hoping to stage another successful event. To many of the children who attend, this is perhaps the only treat enjoyed by them during the Christmas season and we therefore appeal very earnestly to members to help us swell the bag of Father Christmas and so ensure each child receiving a present. Gifts of toys or donations will be thankfully received by the Hon Secretary, London Branch Committee, at 20, Orchard Street, London, W.1.

Re-union Dinner and Dance.

May 7th is the date arranged for the Annual Re-union Dinner and Dance to take place, as last year, at the Palace Hotel, Bloomsbury Street, London, W.C.1. Members are respectfully requested to book this date and help us in making this particular function another great success.

Continental Tour.

A ten-days' Continental Tour has been arranged for August, 1938, from the 6th to the 15th, and the itinerary will be via Ypres, Strasbourg, Verdun and Paris. Our two previous tours proved highly successful and many applications are anticipated for this year's tour. Numbers, however, are limited, and those interested are therefore advised to communicate with the Hon. Secretary, London Branch, as early as possible when full particulars will be gladly forwarded.

The London Branch Committee takes this opportunity of wishing all its members and friends a very Happy New Year and thanks them for the support accorded them during the past year. It is sincerely hoped that members will help us to increase our numbers during 1938 and that the Committee will continue to be favoured with that loyal support throughout the New Year.

PURLEY BRANCH.

Armistice Sunday Parade.

Over fifty members of the Ypres League Purley Branch, a record muster, assembled for this Parade under the command of the Branch Chairman, Major S. F. Wood, on Sunday, November 7th last, and attended the United Memorial Service held at St. Mark's Church, Purley.

Fourth Annual Ball.

The Fourth Annual Ball was held on Friday, November 19th last, at the Greyhound Hotel, Croydon, and, as on former occasions, proved an immense success. It was again necessary to restrict the number of members and guests in view of the limited space available, but over three hundred gathered to enjoy the dancing to Tom Newman's Band. There is always that wonderful friendliness and jollity at the "Purley" functions, especially so at the Annual Dance, and this year was as gay as ever. At supper time the atmosphere was made still gayer by the distribution of unique and snappy paper hats which put the finishing touch to the artistic and well-decorated Ballroom. Later in the evening the assembly were given a breezy entertainment by those well-known and popular artists—the Western Brothers.

Major L. J. L. Pullar, M.C., the Secretary of the Ypres League, honoured us with his presence and we hope he enjoyed the evening. The Branch Chairman, Major S. F. Wood, was in attendance supported in good number by members of his Committee. The duties of M.C. were ably carried out by Mr. N. A. Zinn to whom our thanks are extended as also to the Dance Committee again led by Captain R. L. Haine, V.C., M.C., who had made every possible provision for the comfort and enjoyment of the guests.

The Adjutant.

* * *

SHEFFIELD BRANCH.

Members of the Sheffield Branch paraded at the Lancashire and Yorkshire Regimental Memorial on Armistice Day for the 11 o'clock Service held there annually, and a wreath on behalf of the Branch was laid by Cadet Keith Wilkinson, junior member of the Ypres League.

In the evening a representative party of Sheffield and Chesterfield Members of the League took part in the Annual Festival of Remembrance at the Sheffield City Hall. This Festival is arranged by the Sheffield and District Joint Council of Ex-service Associations.

The Hon. Secretary of the Branch, Captain Jack Wilkinson, wishes to thank those members who so kindly supported him at the Wreath-laying Ceremony and also at the Festival.

EMBROIDERED BADGES.

These badges which can be suitably worn on pockets of sports jackets will be supplied on application to the Secretary, Ypres League, 20, Orchard Street, London, W.1. Price 4/- post free.

* * *

YPRES LEAGUE BADGE.

The design of the badge—a lion guarding a portcullis gate—represents the British Army defending the Salient, which was the gate to the Channel Ports.

The badge is brilliantly enamelled with silver finish. Price 2s., post free 2s. 1½d. (pin or stud, whichever is desired).

Obtainable from Secretary, Ypres League, 20, Orchard Street, W.1.

* * *

YPRES LEAGUE TIE.

Dark shade of cornflower blue relieved by a narrow gold stripe. In good quality silk,

Price 3/6d., post free.

Obtainable from Secretary, Ypres League 20, Orchard Street, London. W.1.

* * *

PHOTOGRAPHS OF WAR GRAVES.

The Ypres League is able to supply photographs (negative, and one print, postcard size, unmounted) of graves or memorials situated in the Ypres Salient, and in the Hazebrouck and Armentieres areas, at the price of 10s., each.

All applications for photographs should be sent to the Secretary, together with remittance, giving full regimental particulars of the soldier.

WREATHS

Arrangements are made by the Ypres League to place wreaths for relatives on the graves of British soldiers situated in France and Belgium on any day throughout the year.

The wreaths may be composed of natural flowers, laurel, holly or poppies, and can be bought at the following prices—10s. 6d., 12s. 6d., 15s. 6d., and 20s., according to the size and quality of the wreath.

The above photograph depicts one of the many wreaths the Ypres League have placed on the graves of soldiers killed in the Great War, at the request of relatives and friends.

* * *

MODELS OF DEMARCATION STONE

Plaster models of the Demarcation Stone can be supplied from Head Office.

All members are aware that 240 granite demarcation stones stretch from the Swiss border to the sea, marking the extreme line of advance of the German invasion.

The model, which is 6 inches in height, may be used for a paperweight or as an ornament. Price 5s., post free in United Kingdom. Applications to the Secretary, Ypres League.

YPRES LEAGUE TRAVEL BUREAU

CONDUCTED MIXED PILGRIMAGES for 1938

The following Pilgrimages have been arranged for 1938 and the Secretary will be pleased to forward prospectuses to all interested on receipt of application at 20, Orchard Street, London, W.1.

EASTER (April 16th—19th) ... YPRES (Day route *via* Ostend).

(April 29th)
Special Pilgrimage to Ypres in connection with the Unveiling of the "King Albert" Memorial Window at St. Martin's Cathedral, on Saturday, April 30th, 1938. (April 30th is the date provisionally fixed and Pilgrimage will depart Victoria Station on Friday, April 29th.

WHITSUNTIDE (June 4th—7th) YPRES (Day route *via* Ostend).
WHITSUNTIDE (June 4th—7th) ARRAS (Day route *via* Boulogne).
AUGUST BANK HOLIDAY (July 30th—August 2nd)
    YPRES (Day route *via* Ostend).
AUGUST BANK HOLIDAY (July 30th—August 2nd)
    ARRAS (Day route *via* Boulogne).
SEPTEMBER (September 17th—20th)
    YPRES (Day route *via* Ostend).

Both at Whitsuntide and August Bank Holiday two separate conducted pilgrimages will be organised, one to Ypres (Belgium) and one to Arras (France).

The Pilgrimages organised to Ypres via the Dover-Ostend Day Service are arranged to avoid the irksome rail journeys, Ostend to Ypres and return, these journeys now being made by motor-coach transport.

INDEPENDENT TRAVEL.

To those contemplating individual travel, our Travel Department would be pleased to furnish information on all matters connected with Pilgrimages to Cemeteries, Memorials and trips to any part of the Old Western Front Battlefields.

Apply to Secretary, Ypres League, 20, Orchard Street, London, W.1, for the Ypres League Travel Guide for 1938.

THE BRITISH TOURING SERVICE

Manager—Mr. P. VYNER   10, Station Square

Representative and Life Member,   ARRAS
Ypres League   (P.-de-C.) France

Cars for Hire, with British Driver Guides   Tours Arranged

Branches and Corresponding Members

BRANCHES.

LONDON	Hon. Secretary to the London Branch Committee : J. Boughey, c/o 20, Orchard Street, London, W.1.
	TOTTENHAM AND EDMONTON DISTRICT—E. Glover, 191, Lansdowne Road, Tottenham, N.17.
COLCHESTER	H. Snow (Hon. Sec.), 2, Church Street.
	W. H. Taylor (Pilgrimage Hon. Sec.), 64, High Street.
ESSEX (SOUTH)	S. H. Geller, "Brielen," 197, Corbets Tey Road, Upminster.
LIVERPOOL	Captain A. M. Webster, Blundellsands.
PURLEY	Major Graham Carr, D.S.O., M.C., 112-114, High Street.
SHEFFIELD	Captain J Wilkinson, "Holmfield," Bents Drive.
QUEENSLAND, Australia	Messrs. C. H. Green, and George Lawson, Essex House, (Opposite Anzac Square) Brisbane, Queensland.
CANADA	Ed. Kingsland, P.O. Box 83, Magog, Quebec.
SOUTH AFRICA	L. G. Shuter, 381, Longmarket Street, Pietermaritzburg.
KENYA	C. H. Slater, P.O. Box 403, Nairobi.
BELGIUM	C. Leupe, Garage Shannon, Menin Gate.
AMERICA	Representative : Captain R. Henderson-Bland, 110 West 57th Street, New York City.

CORRESPONDING MEMBERS.

GREAT BRITAIN.

ABERYSTWYTH	T. O. Thomas, 5, Smithfield Road.
ASHTON-UNDER-LYNE	G. D. Stuart, " Woodlands,", Thronfield Grove, Arundel Street.
BANBURY	Captain C. W. Fowke, Yew Tree House, King's Sutton.
BIRMINGHAM	Mrs. Hill, 191, Cattell Road, Small Heath.
	John Burman, "Greenfields," Hampton Lane, Solihull.
BRISTOL	W. S. Hook, "Wytschaete" Redland Court Road
BROADSTAIRS	C. E. King, 6, Norman Road, St. Peters, Broadstairs.
	Mrs. Briggs, North Foreland House.
CHATHAM	W. N. Channon, 22, Keyes Avenue.
CHESTERFIELD	Major A. W. Shea, 14, Cross Street.
CONGLETON	Mr. H. Dart, 61, The Crescent.
DARLINGTON	D. S. Vigo, 125, Dorset Road, Bexhill-on-Sea.
DERBY	T. Jakeman, 10, Graham Street.
DORRINGTON (Salop)	Captain G. D. S. Parker, Frodesley Rectory.
EXETER	Captain E. Jenkin, 25, Queen Street.
HERNE BAY	Captain E. Clarke Williams, F.S.A.A., "Conway," Station Road.
HOVE	Captain G. W. J. Cole, 2, Westbourne Terrace, Kingsway.
LEICESTER	W. C. Dunford, 343, Aylestone Road.
LINCOLN	E. Swaine, 79, West Parade.
LLANWRST	A. C. Tomlinson, M.A., Bod Estyn.
LOUGHTON	Capt. O. G. Johnson, M.A., Loughton School.
MATLOCK (Derby)	Miss Dickinson, Beechwood.
MELROSE	Mrs. Lindesay Kelsall, Darnlee.
NEW BRIGHTON (Cheshire)	E. F. Williams, 5, Waterloo Road.
NEW MILTON	W. H, Lunn, Greywell.

NOTTINGHAM	E. V. Brown, 3, Eldon Chambers, Wheeler Gate.
ST. HELENS (Lancs.) ...	John Orford, 124, Knowsley Road.
ST. JOHN'S (Newfoundland)	Captain L. Murphy, G.W.V.A. Office.
SHREWSBURY	Major-General Sir John Headlam, K.B.E., C.B., D.S.O., Cruck Meole, House, Hanwood.
TIVERTON (Devon) ...	Mr. W. H. Duncan Arthur, Surveyor's Office, Town Hall.
WELSHPOOL	Mr. E. Wilson, Coedway, Ford, Salop.

DOMINIONS AND FOREIGN COUNTRIES.

AUSTRALIA	R. A. Baldwin, c/o Government Savings Bank of N.S.W., Martin Place Sydney.
	Mr. W. Cloves, Box 1296, G.P.O., Adelaide.
	J. C. Correll, Port Vincent, South Australia.
BELGIUM	Sister Marguerite, Sacré Coeur, Ypres.
CANADA	Brig.-General V. W. Odlum, C.B., C.M.G., D.S.O., 2530, Point Grey Road, Vancouver.
	V. A. Bowes, 326, 40th Avenue West. Calgary, Alberta.
	W. Constable F. Grece, St. Hilaire Station, Rouville County, Quebec.
CEYLON	Captain F. R. G. Webb, M.C., Irrigation Bungalow, Kalmunai, E.P.
EGYPT	Captain B. W. Leak, M.I.E.E., Turf Club, Cairo.
INDIA	Lieut.-Quartermaster G. Smith, Queen's Bays, Sialkot, India.
IRELAND	Miss A. K. Jackson, Cloneyhurke House, Portarlington.
NEW ZEALAND	Captain W. U. Gibb, Ava Lodge, Puhinui Road, Papatoetoe, Auckland
	S. E. Beattie, P.O. Box 11, Otaki Railway, Wellington.
NEWFOUNDLAND ...	Captain Leo. Murphy, G.W.V.A. Office, St. John's.
NOVA SCOTIA	Will R. Bird, 35, Clarence Street, Amherst.
SOUTH AFRICA ...	H. L. Versfield, c/o Cape Explosives Works Ltd., 150, St. George Street, Cape Town.
SPAIN	Captain P. W. Burgess, Calle de Zurbano 29, Madrid.
U.S.A.	Captain Henry Maslin, 942, President Street, Brooklyn, New York
	L. E. P. Foot. 20, Gillett Street, Hartford, Conn, U.S.A.
	A. P. Forward, 449, East 80th Street, New York.
	J. W. Freebody, 945, McBride Avenue, Los Angeles.

Membership of the League

This is open to all who served in the Salient, and to all those whose relatives or friends died there, in order that they may have a record of that service for themselves and their descendants, and belong to the comradeship of men and women who understand and remember all that Ypres meant in suffering and endurance.

Life membership, £2 10s.

Annual members, 5s.

Do not let the fact of your not having **served in the Salient** deter you from joining the Ypres League. Those who have neither fought in the Salient nor lost relatives there, but who are in sympathy with the objects of the Ypres League, are admitted to its fellowship, but are not given scroll certificates.

There is a Junior Division for children whose relatives served in the Salient. It is open also to others to whom our objects appeal.

Annual subscription 1s. up to the age of 18, after which they can become ordinary members of the League.

THE YPRES LEAGUE (INCORPORATED)
20, Orchard Street, Portman Square, W.1.

Telephone : WELBECK 1446.   *Telegrams* : YPRESLEAG, " WESDO," LONDON.

Patron-in-Chief : H.M. THE KING.

Patron
H.R.H. PRINCESS BEATRICE.

President : GENERAL SIR CHARLES H. HARINGTON.

Vice-Presidents :

THE VISCOUNT WAKEFIELD OF HYTHE.   F.-M. SIR CLAUD W. JACOB.
F.-M. LORD MILNE.   F.-M. SIR PHILIP CHETWODE.
GENERAL SIR CECIL ROMER.   GENERAL SIR HUBERT GOUGH.

General Committee :

THE COUNTESS OF ALBEMARLE.
CAPTAIN C. ALLISTON.
LIEUT-COLONEL BECKLES WILLSON.
MR. HENRY BENSON.
*MR. J. BOUGHEY.
*MISS B. BRICE-MILLER.
COLONEL G. T. BRIERLEY.
CAPTAIN P. W. BURGESS.
BRIG.-GENL. A. BURT.
*MAJOR H. CARDINAL-HARFORD.
*MAJOR GRAHAM CARR.
REV. P. B. CLAYTON.
CAPTAIN G. E. DE TRAFFORD.
MRS. C. J. EDWARDS.
MAJOR C. J. EDWARDS.
MR. H. A. T. FAIRBANK.
MR. T. ROSS FURNER.
SIR PHILIP GIBBS.
MR. E. GLOVER.

*MAJOR H. G. HARRIS.
MR. F. D. BANKES-HILL.
MAJOR-GENERAL C. J. B. HAY.
MR. J. HETHERINGTON.
GENERAL SIR W. C. G. HENEKER.
*CAPTAIN O. G. JOHNSON.
*MAJOR E. MONTAGUE JONES.
MAJOR GENL. C. G. LIDDELL.
*CAPTAIN H. D. PEABODY.
*THE HON. ALICE DOUGLAS PENNANT.
*LIEUT.-GENERAL SIR W. P. PULTENEY.
LIEUT.-COLONEL SIR J. MURRAY.
*COLONEL G. E. C. RASCH.
THE HON. SIR ARTHUR STANLEY.
MR. ERNEST THOMPSON.
*MR. E. B. WAGGETT.
CAPTAIN J. WILKINSON.
CAPTAIN H. TREVOR WILLIAMS.

* Executive Committee.

Bankers :   *Honorary Solicitors* :
BARCLAYS BANK LTD., Knightsbridge Branch.   MESSRS. FLADGATE & CO., 70, Pall Mall, S.W.

Secretary :   *Auditors* :
MAJOR L. J. L. PULLAR.   MESSRS. LEPINE & JACKSON, 6, Bond Court, E.C.4.

League Representative at Ypres: **League Representative at Ostend:**
Mr. C. LEUPE,   CAPTAIN P. D. PARMINTER,
Garage Shannon, Porte de Menin.   16, Galerie James Ensor.

League Representative at Amiens: **League Representative at Arras:**
CAPTAIN STUART OSWALD.   MR. P. VYNER,
7, Rue des Otages.   14, Rue Chanzy.

Hon. Secretary, Ypres British Settlement:
LT. COLONEL F. G. POOLE.

PRIMARY OBJECTS OF THE LEAGUE

I.—Commemoration and Comradeship.
II.—To provide special travel facilities for Members and all interested to Ypres and battlefields, and transport of Members.
III.—The furnishing of information about the Salient ; marking of historic sites and the compilation of charts of the battlefields.
IV.—The erection of a Ypres British Church and School which has been completed.
V.—The establishment of groups of members throughout the world, through Branch Secretaries and Corresponding Members.
VI.—The maintenance of cordial relations with dwellers on the battlefields of Ypres.
VII.—The formation of a Junior Division.

The Ypres Times

Communications to
The Editor, "Ypres Times,"
20, Orchard Street, London, W.1.

POST FREE
To all Members.

Vol. 9, No. 2.   Published Half-Yearly.   July, 1938.

Our Presidents

We have great pleasure in presenting to our readers the first of a series of articles written on the lives of our Presidents, past and present, and other distinguished members of the Ypres League. For this we are indebted to that brilliant scholar and writer, Henry Benson, Esq., M.A., so well known to members for his many interesting contributions and who has so kindly consented to write this series at our special request. (Editor—" Ypres Times").

Field-Marshal The Earl of Ypres

LIKE Nelson, Wellington and Kitchener, Field-Marshal the Earl of Ypres was born in one of those little out-of-the-way places solely associated with the peaceful pursuits of country life. Ripple is a pleasant hamlet in Kent, which requires a very keen eye to discover it on the map. Here, on September 28th, 1852, the only son of Captain French, R.N., and Margaret, daughter of William Eccles, made his first tiny commotion in the world.

The Orphan Boy.

The boy, who was christened John Denton Pinkston, had the misfortune to lose both parents at an early age, and after the first easy lessons had been learned as he sat beside his sister, who in after-life became Mrs. Despard, and is happily still with us, he was sent to a preparatory school at Harrow—not the great public school that crowns the hill, but a much humbler institution in the vicinity.

Like his colleague, the late Earl Kitchener, French (as we will call him for the present) neither went to a public school nor entered the lecture room of a university college. Of his scholastic successes or failures, we know nothing, but of his kindness of heart—a predominant characteristic throughout life—a delightful little glimpse is afforded us by one of his mother's maids.

"One morning," she relates, "in the depth of winter, when I went downstairs, I found Master Johnny kneeling on the dining-room hearth trying his best to light a fire. Disappointedly, he said, " I meant to have a good fire for you, but it would not burn.' "

Midshipman Who Became Soldier.

When the time came for him " to put away childish things," the question of a career for " Master Johnny " had to be considered. It was solved by putting him into the same profession as his father, and the lad was sent to Eastman's Naval Academy at Portsmouth to study for the entrance examinations that would admit him to the "Britannia." He passed successfully, and served for four years as a cadet and midshipman on board H.M.S. "Warrior." This vessel was one of the squadron of ironclads to which the ill-fated "Captain" was attached when she went down with 600 of her crew in a furious gale in the Bay of Biscay in 1870.

Midshipman French eventually decided he was far more suited to the army than to the navy. He left the sea, and entering the militia, obtained a commission as lieutenant in the 8th Hussars, which regiment he joined in 1874.

About this change an excellent story is told. A number of naval officers were dining with some military men, when one of the former remarked, "You have not got a leader worth a cent with the exception of one man, French, and he's a sailor!" "Yes," retorted a soldier, "he was in the Navy just long enough to see what a wretched service it was. Then he chucked it, and went into the militia, where he learnt to become what he is now!"

The young soldier's service with his first regiment was not of long duration. He was gazetted lieutenant on February 28th, 1874, and tranferred to the 19th Hussars on the 11th of the following month, where he remained until he commanded it. He became Adjutant in 1880, and in April of the following year accepted a similar position in the Northumberland Yeomanry, in which he served for four years, re-joining the 19th Hussars as Major in September, 1884.

The Battle of Abu Klea.

French's first experience of active service was in the Soudan Campaign of 1884-5, when as second in command of the 19th Hussars, he accompanied Sir Herbert Stewart in the abortive attempt to relieve General Gordon who was surrounded by Arabs at Khartoum. The force reached the Gakdul wells and occupied them, and after further troops had been fetched up the march across the desert commenced on January 8th, 1885. Eight days later it became very obvious that they were not to be permitted to reach their objective unmolested, but a force of 11,000 of the enemy was scarcely anticipated. The opposing forces met at the wells of Abu Klea, where, to quote a famous war correspondent "the most savage and bloody action ever fought in the Soudan by British troops took place." Notwithstanding the numbers and valour of the Arabs, that they penetrated the square, and that they inflicted on the troops a loss of nine officers and sixty-five men killed, and nine officers and eighty-five wounded—ten per cent. of the entire force—they were driven from the field with great slaughter and our Desert Column camped at the wells. It was in this battle that Colonel Burnaby, a cavalry officer of note in his day, but now, of course, quite forgotten, was struck down by an Arab spear. Sir Herbert Stewart was himself wounded.

So Charles Wilson then assumed command. You know the remainder of the sad story. Gordon had been murdered forty-eight hours before Wilson reached Khartoum.

French and others had remained at Metammeh. On February 15th, Sir Redvers Buller, the new commander of the Desert Column, reached Abu Klea, and was successful in getting into touch with Wilson's troops and leading them back to Korti. Buller was deeply impressed by the soldier-like qualities displayed by French, and mentioned him in despatches, to this effect: " I wish expressly to remark on the excellent work that has been done by a small detachment of the 19th Hussars, both during our occupation at Abu Klea and throughout our retirement. And it is not too much to say that the force owes a great debt to Major French and his thirteen troopers."

Rapid Promotion.

In February, 1885, French was made a Lieutenant-Colonel and given the command of his Regiment. Six years later he saw service in India, and in 1893 was employed as Assistant-Adjutant General of Cavalry on the staff, in which position he remained until August, 1895, when he was appointed Assistant-Adjutant-General at the War Office, where he had the opportunity of superintending the full introduction of what is known as the squadron system, which he had first established in his own regiment.

Photo] FIELD-MARSHAL THE EARL OF YPRES. [Alex Corbett

His next promotion came in May, 1897, when he was given command of the South-Eastern District, with headquarters at Canterbury. In January, 1899, French, now temporary Major-General, took over the command of the 1st Cavalry Brigade at Aldershot, where he remained until the following September, when he was nominated to lead the Cavalry Brigade in the Natal Field Force as full Major-General.

A record such as this conveys nothing to the lay mind of the amount of down-right hard work that French put into the service, but it is noteworthy that Sir Redvers Buller would hear of nobody but French as leader of the cavalry in the Boer War. He knew his man, he appreciated what he had done in the Soudan, and he understood exactly what he had accomplished after that time. The official leader of the cavalry was therefore passed over in favour of French, whose wonderful performances in the manoeuvres of 1898 had been the admiration of most military men.

French and Napoleon.

French was a fervent admirer of Napoleon, and had he tried on one of the Emperor's uniforms, it would not have been a misfit. He would have been Napoleon without the Napoleonism. Quite apart from metaphor, he was of similar build to the Emperor, although he bore no facial resemblance to him.

One of the maxims of Napoleon may well be used to sum up the military characteristics of French: " The first qualification in a General-in-Chief," said the Emperor, "is a cool head which receives just impressions, and estimates things and objects at their real value. He must not allow himself to be elated by good news, or depressed at bad. The impressions he receives either successively or simultaneously, in the course of the day should be so classed as to take up only the exact place in his mind that they deserve to occupy; since it is upon a just comparison and consideration of the weight due to different impressions that the power of reasoning and of just judgment depends. Some men are so physically and morally constituted as to see everything through a highly-coloured medium. They raise up a picture in the mind on every slight occasion, and give to every trivial occurence a dramatic interest. But whatever knowledge, or talent, or courage, or other good qualities such men may possess, nature has not formed them for the command of armies, or the direction of great military operations."

French neither used rose-coloured spectacles nor smoked glasses, and was invariably level-headed. It was Christian de Wet, a military genius of no mean order, who remarked of French that " he was the one Boer General in the British Army," thereby paying him the highest compliment he could call to mind.

Personal Characteristics.

A rigid disciplinarian, the General was called in the Army " Silent French." At Aldershot he once had occasion to reprimand a private. " Old French don't bark a bit," said the soldier in question to a comrade, " but don't 'e bloomin' well bite !"

French had no characteristics that suggested a machine other than an amazing capacity for sustained effort. A study of what he said and wrote on the function of the Cavalry branch of an Army illustrates his belief in initiative and elasticity. " My conception of the duties of the mounted arm " he wrote, " is not to cut and hack and to thrust at your enemy whenever and however he may be found. The real business of cavalry is so to manoeuvre your enemy as to bring him within effective range of the corps artillery of your own side, for which a position suitable for battle, and commanding a field for an infantry engagment, if necessary, would previously have been selected."

French possessed a keen sense of humour, and although his wit was sharp it was not barbed. It never left a nasty wound. When he was labouring at the old War Office in Pall Mall, he was rather fond of visiting the House of Commons, especially when a military debate was on. After one of these sittings he casually remarked to a friend, " I think I shall turn politician." " What do you mean: what do you know about politics?" asked the other, in considerable amazement. " Quite as much as most of those who have been speaking to-night about the Army," replied French.

(To be continued)

British Army and R.A.F. Memorial
to
Albert I, King of the Belgians

CEREMONY OF UNVEILING AND DEDICATION OF ROSE WINDOW AND TABLET.

I AM privileged to write a few notes for the YPRES TIMES on the unforgettable Ceremony performed on Saturday, May 21st, 1938, at 11.00 a.m. by His Majesty King Leopold III, and graced by the presence of the Queen Mother. Conceiving the scheme, carrying it through with its many interests and anxieties naturally made the final stage one greatly looked forward to and one that should do all honour possible to the importance of its purpose and those attending for Belgium and our own country. I am pleased to say that, considering all, the Committee, the Subscribers, and those who had worked for that moment have nothing with which to reproach themselves. His Majesty, together with Queen Elizabeth have graciously expressed their pleasure of the Memorial Gift and Ceremony of Honour carried out on this Saturday at Ypres.

There are many, both Belgian and British, whom one would like to thank; some indeed whose names are not even known, but whose kindly help and instant response will be gratefully remembered. There is the Priest who taught the Flemish Choir to sing our English hymns, and wonderfully well did they sing them; the translating of the numerous letters and messages which passed between the two countries. The small brown-faced gardener who, to make the wreaths of the correct British colours rose and caught the 5 a.m. train to Brussels, in order to obtain the flowers, and also the friends who gave instant help in connection with finding and bringing to the Cathedral in time, the programmes which had been mislaid somewhere in Belgium.

The day of the Ceremony, despite the rain and the cold, found Ypres early on the move. Belgian flags were to be seen everywhere and the principal streets were lined with citizens anxious to see and welcome their King and the Queen Mother. Her Majesty was making a very rare public appearance at an official ceremony. The carillon of the belfry started at 10.30 a.m. at which time the detachments of picked troops of the 5th Royal Inniskilling Dragoon Guards and Royal Air Force, with the Band of the Royal Fusiliers, paraded opposite the West Door of the Cathedral. These troops had arrived from Ostend in motor char-a-banes under arrangements made by the Ypres League, and were under the command of their own officers and a stirring spectacle they made. Long before 11 a.m. the Cathedral was packed with about 2,500 people, including many very distinguished officers and members of the Government. Khaki, which was generally worn, was enlivened by glittering orders and medals and made a most impressive sight.

There were also present a large number of guests, which included members of Old Comrades' Associations, some still disabled by war wounds, and about a hundred British children from the Ypres British Settlement School, who were, to their delight, delight, seated next to the British soldiers.

The Rose Window glowed with its rich colours of Ruby—Blues and Gold. The Tablet was draped with a five-yard Union Jack kindly provided by the Ypres League. The red, white and blue wreaths of natural flowers represented " Those absent who know not of this Memorial."

Monseigneur Lamiroy, the Bishop of Bruges, together with Monseigneur Colle, Chaplain of the Court, with the Cathedral Clergy moved down to the West Door. The British Ambassador, Sir Robert Clive, together with the Earl of Athlone, arrived, and were received by the official delegates, whose senior member laid a wreath of poppies on the City's Memorial.

The British Army was represented by Field-Marshal Sir Claud Jacob, G.C.B., etc.; Field-Marshal Sir Cyril Deverell, G.C.B., etc.; General Sir Edmund Ironside, K.C.B., etc.; Lieut-General Sir Reginald May, K.C.B., etc.; Lieut.-General Sir Hugh Elles, K.C.B., etc.; and Major-General Sir John Capper, K.C.B., etc.

The Royal Air Force was represented by Marshal of the Royal Air Force Sir Edward Ellington, G.C.B., etc; Air-Marshal Sir Arthur Longmore, K.C.B., etc.; Air-Marshal Joubert de la Ferte, C.B., etc.; Air-Vice-Marshal J. E. Baldwin, C.B., etc.; and Miss Blair, Matron-in-Chief, R.A.F.N.S.

The Committee of the Memorial consisted of: Major-General The Earl of Athlone, K.G. (Chairman); Lieut.-General Sir William Pulteney, G.C.V.O., etc.; Major-General

[Photo]   [Central Press

H.M. King Leopold III with the Queen Mother, at moment of Unveiling the Tablet in Ypres Cathedral. The Royal Air Force contingent in foreground.

Sir Neil Malcolm, K.C.B., etc.; Air Vice-Marshal J. E. Baldwin, C.B., etc., and Captain Guy Cassie, M.C. (Hon. Organising Secretary).

His Majesty, having inspected the Belgian Guard of Honour on his arrival at Ypres station, proceeded to the Town Memorial, with the Burgomaster of Ypres, the Minister of National Defence, the Governor of Western Flanders (Lieut.-General de Haene), Lieut.-General the Baron Vincotte, Lieut.-General Le Manton and others.

The Procession formed and entered the Cathedral, led by King Leopold in khaki uniform and wearing the Blue Riband of the Garter. The Queen Mother walked by his side, a quiet, small but very distinguished figure in black, and wearing her senior British decoration.

The Service commenced in accordance with the programme and when the Flemish choir sang so beautifully the hymn "Praise My Soul" in perfect English, all present had brought home to them the special significance of the joint Belgian and British Ceremony of Honour—Protestant and Catholic, united to do solemn tribute to his late Majesty, King Albert's memory.

The height of the Ceremony was reached immediately after the unveiling of the Tablet by the King. The National Anthems were played, trumpets sounded, and the Bishop dedicated the Window. King Leopold then laid a magnificent wreath, over six feet high, of pink flowers on the Tablet steps, with the red, white and blue British wreaths at the side. Both the King and Queen Elizabeth took a long look at the Memorial and slowly returned to their Thrones.

Monseigneur Colle then delivered an impressive Address from the Altar, first in English and afterwards in Flemish as follows:

Ave Maria,
Sire, Madam, My Lord,

It is not, without a deep emotion, but with far greater feelings of respect and gratitude, that I have the honour of addressing so distinguished an audience, and in such moving circumstances as this Commemoration of our late beloved King, H.M. Albert I of Belgium.

But, as we are here, my dear Brethren, united in the first place to give thanks to God, by way of the interpretation of that splendid "Te Deum" Window, which has been Unveiled, just now, by H.M. the King, and consecrated by H.E. Mgr. Lamiroy, Bishop of Bruges, it seems, that the best text of our Holy Books, which could ever be chosen as a concrete interpretation of that glorious hymn of colours yonder and of the whole signification of this ceremony, is Luke, Ch. II, v. 14: Glory to God in the Highest and on earth, peace to men of good will: Gloria in Excelsis Deo et Pax hominibus bonae voluntatis," and this, for the following reason:

This, my dear brethren, is not a civil solemnity, not even a military one, notwithstanding all this military display and splendour. I daresay that it is in the first place an essentially religious Commemoration, the real and profound signification of which is peace: that peace, everlasting, complete, interior and exterior, individual as well as public, but international also, that peace, which is one of teh most sensible attributes of God, all-peace Himself in his unmutable nature . . . . and altogether one of godliest favours to mankind.

Therefore, I thank God Almighty for having the honour of delivering this short address in the presence of both Your Majesties: in the presence so august of His Majesty the King, son and successor to our great King Albert and inspired continuator of his policy of peace, not only within the boundaries of this beautiful realm, but towards anyone of his neighbours . . . in the gracious presence, which shall be a great joy for all, here assembled, the presence, Madam, of Your Majesty, the faithful companion of King Albert's great struggle for peace, and the confidant of his innermost thoughts.

With the august presence I have the honour of associating that of His Highness, the Earl of Athlone, as a chief and a head to all those noble representatives: Field-Marshals, Generals, and other Officers of the great Monarch and the glorious Army, Navy, and Air Force of the largest Empire of the World. Honour, too, to the whole great British nation, that stands behind its Statesmen, in their patient and splendid struggle for lasting peace.

Yes, we ought to say again: Glory to God in the Highest and on earth, peace to men of good-will.

That idea of seeing in this day of Remembrance a day for glorification of peace, has been suggested by the foresight in the imagination of all the surroundings of place, atmosphere and feeling, in which we are moving, just now. Indeed, everything, in this marvellous Cathedral is sounding like a trumpet of peace and most of all that beautiful Rose Window, which shall remain there to the honour of God, with the blessed denomination of "Te Deum" Window, as an eternal

The Memorial Window.

reminder of friendship between our two nations. And here are they assembled, the sons of both, in the house of the Lord of Peace, God Almighty, whose nature is peace, and whose Son, denominated already by the Prophet Isaiah as: "The Wonderful . . . the Prince of Peace," Is. x, 7, whose Son, our Lord Jesus Christ, as says St. Peter in the Acts x, 36, and as sung by the Angels at his Nativity, came into this world, sent by His Heavenly Father, in order to bring His peace to mankind.

Here, we are in His House, Here we know Him to be present, in His Eucharist, here we look at Him, crowned with thorns on His Cross, Him, the eternal Preacher of charity and peace, buying with the price of His divine Blood, that peace, which was His salute again and again after His Resurrection, His blessing for His Apostles. Here we admire Him, in the centre of that glorious Window, sitting, nay, enthroned on the rainbow, that sign of the first covenant between God and man: For, said the Lord: This is the sign of the covenant, which I give between Me and you: Dixitque Deus ad Noë: Hoc erit signum foederis, quod constitui inter Me et Te" (Gen. ix, 12). We look at Him, there, in this bright centre, Lord of the world, surrounded in the same way, as He is followed in the Te Deum itself, by all His illustrious messengers of peace: those sixteen Prophets of the Old Testament, who announced His Kingdom of Peace, Te Prophetarum Laudabilis numerus, by His Apostles, whom He sent all over the world to preach the good news, the new law of love and peace, His Gospel, to all nations, unto the farthest limits of the earth: Te gloriosus Apostolorum Chorus. And again, there we behold those sweet figures of our Belgian Martyrs and Saints: Te martyrum candidatus laudat exercitus, who here, in this country were the heroic heralds of his peace, who shed their blood and casted away their lives to redeem their brethren, giving, what the Lord Himself said to be the greatest token of love. How could they be lacking there, those dear Brethren of Heaven, the Angels: Tibi omnes Angeli, who announced the immediate coming of peace into the world and most, into the hearts of all men of good-will.

Really, it has been with the kind promoters of this ceremony, with the generous donors, with the artist, who designed that wonderful work, it has been a magnificent conception to glorify by means of that radiant hymn to God, such a warrior for peace, as was H.M. our late King Albert. For, again, we should not forget, that here we are in the temple of that God of peace, Whom the King worshipped so simply, but so nobly, Whom he possessed in his christian and manly heart. Yes, here we are gathered to celebrate that great war hero, who was none the less a noble champion of peace. Although H.M. King Albert was, from the beginning, resolved to fight to the bitter end, war was never his aim. Neither did he wish for the title of War-Lord, and when he was forced by sheer necessity to draw the sword, the world was filled with admiration; beholding his manly and gallant mien he never desired war for fighting sake, nor for personal glorification. He fought for justice alone and through justice for peace, as say the Holy Word of God: the work of justice shall be peace. Et erit opus Justitiae: Pax. (Is. xxxii, 17).

His was a character of meekness with strength, which means peace with all, even with one-self . . . that peace, which is God in one's heart, but altogether calm and lasting. Therefore, no text could be better applied to that great King, and partly to your Majesty, his successor, than those splendid words, taken from Bunyan's Pilgrims' Progress, "The passing of a valiant," there for ever on that fine tablet: "My sword I give to him, that shall succeed me in my pilgrimage, and my courage and skill to him, that can get it." My marks and scars I carry with me to be a witness for me, that I fought HIS battle, WHO will be my rewarder. So he passed over, and all the trumpets sounded for him on the other side."

Inspiring, as are these words of human language, our Lord said: "Blessed are the meek, for they shall inherit the earth . . . Beati Mites, quoniam ipsi possidebunt terram" (Matt. v, 4).

Therefore, the Lord blessed the King, blessed his weapons, blessed his cause, for from the first days during that unprovoked and ill-conceived attack on Belgium, the King and his Army were championed by that great nation across the sea. They crossed the Channel, those peaceful and heroic sons of Britain, not so "contemptible" it transpired, they came by thousands, soon by millions to fight our battle, that battle for justice and freedom. They came to restore to our dear country that peace we pray may never again be violated. As words of fire before my mind, are those words of the Psalmist: "Mercy and Truth have met each other: Justice and Peace have kissed: Misericordia et Veritas obviaverunt: Justitia et Pax osculatae sunt." Ps. lxxxiv, ii.

Thousands of them fell: splendid heroes in those awful battles around Ypres and when we now cross those peaceful fields and look down, with gratitude on those thousands of simple white tombstones at Ypres, Poelcapelle, Passchendaele, Langemarck, St. Julien and so many other sacred spots, we sing in our hearts, Te Deum laudamus; we glorify God in those heroes—the flower of manhood, who fought His battles of justice. They shall have their reward for, sayeth the Lord: "Blessed are the Peacemakers: for they shall be called 'the children of God': Pacifici, quoniam filii Dei vocabuntur." Matt. v, 9.

Sire, Madam,

Your Majesties came here in order to join the glorious sons of England, of whose Army, King Albert was a Field-Marshal and part of which have Your Majesty as their Colonel-in-Chief, but, as in our Royal Family and most in Our Sovereigns beats the heart of the whole Belgium nation. It is for your humble and devoted subjects a cause of great joy and blessing to show in our most sincere manner, to the representatives of the King and people of the British Empire the gratitude of the Royal Family, and of the whole of our nation.

[Photo] [Central Press

H.M. King Leopold; The British Ambassador, Sir Robert Clive; The Earl of Athlone and Lieut.-General Sir William Pulteney at the Menin Gate.

After the Addresses a further English Hymn was sung, followed by the Te Deum in Latin. Then special prayers for His Majesty, preceded the Bishop's Blessing and the great service came to a finish.

Their Majesties, followed by all the delegates, then joined the British Ambassador at the Menin Gate where further wreaths were laid. The 5th Royal Inniskilling Dragon Guards and the Royal Air Force afterwards formed up behind the Band of the Royal Fusiliers and marched past the King, who took the Salute. A return was then made to the Hotel de Ville, where some presentations were made and the Golden Book of Ypres City was signed by His Majesty, the Ambassador and the distinguished guests. After the departure of the King and Queen Mother from Ypres, the Burgomaster and Counsellors of Ypres gave a luncheon at Skindle's Hotel to the Delegates and Memorial Committee. Truly a great day for Ypres, and for those fortunate enough to be present. It should be borne in mind that the Memorial Gift is a lasting one and it is hoped that in future years many will be able to visit it and ponder on all that it means, the present and the past.

GUY CASSIE.
(Hon. Secretary to Memorial).

* * *

A Touching Ceremony at Meteren

FOLLOWING the Unveiling Ceremony of the " King Albert " Memorial Window at Ypres Cathedral on Saturday, May 21st, Lieut.-General Sir William Pulteney, G.C.V.O., K.C.B., K.C.M.G., etc., accompanied by the following officers: Major L. J. L. Pullar, M.C., Captain J. F. Miller, Captain G. M. Wingate and Captain R. H. Bland motored across the Franco-Belgian Frontier to Meteren where a touching little ceremony of friendship and remembrance took place.

The object of the visit was to restore to the Commune of Meteren a beautifully fashioned Crucifix in bronze, erected in 1740, which had been rescued by a Canadian soldier during a severe bombardment in the Great War and taken away by him as a memento. The Crucifix had been sent to the Ypres League some little time ago with a request that it should be returned to its original place near Meteren, and General Pulteney—Chairman of the Ypres League, undertook to command in person the delegation.

A Civic Reception was arranged at the Town Hall of Meteren, and the Mayor, M. Cesar Herreman, who has the honour of being a Conseiller d'Arrondissment, a Commander de Merité Agricole and a Chevalier de la Legion d'Honneur, was supported by his Deputy-Mayor; the Counsellors of the Municipality of Meteren and the assembly was further graced by the presence of the Member of the French Parliament for Bailleul-Merville, M. Plichon. The Church was represented by the Abbé Thorez Dean of Meteren.

General Sir William Pulteney and party were welcomed outside the Town Hall and introductions took place. Afterwards the assembly entered the building and the Municipal Band struck up the British National Anthem. In the centre of the group of people who had ranged themselves at the " High Table," Sir William Pulteney, speaking in French, explained the purpose of the visit, and on conclusion of his speech handed over the Crucifix to the Abbé Thorez. The General's words were received with very great applause and the Mayor, facing Sir William, read the following Address in French:—

It is in the name of the whole population of Meteren that the Municipal Council and the Religious Authority, in the person of M. le Doyen Thorez, in the presence of M. le Député Plichon, our representative in the French Parliament, of M. Perrier, Conseiller Général du Nord, and M. Notteau, Conseiller d'Arrondissement, have been pleased to greet in you one of the high dignitaries of the British Army and to bid you welcome in our modest Community, raised from its ashes after its annihilation in 1918.

Your visit honours us exceedingly, we greatly appreciate the admirable gesture which led to it, and I am happy to be able to express to you, as Mayor of the Commune, our very deepest gratitude. Inspired by a sentiment, full of dignity, dear General, you have wished to bring back yourself this Christ, emblem divine, worshipped by all true believers, so that it may once more take its place on the road through our fertile country in the same spot where on two occasions the German invasion was stopped. While awaiting the decisions taken in the matter, Monsieur le Doyen undertakes the duty of guarding the precious trust.

Your presence, dear General, takes us back naturally to the time, which still seems near, when the English troops were among us; it recalls their bravery on the battlefields of our Flanders where, side by side with our French soldiers, so many of your tommies fell in fighting for the noble aim of safeguarding right and liberty.

The mission which you have come to fulfil to-day brings us fresh evidence of the friendship of your great Nation towards France. We shall record the event in the Archives of the Commune, and in order to keep a tangible memory, we should be deeply grateful if you would grant us an autograph in the Book of Gold, which we shall take the liberty of presenting to you and to the distinguished colleagues who accompany you.

Some years before the war in the unforgettable period when the "entente cordiale" was at full expansion, I had the good fortune to visit, with a group of friends, the magnificent hop-fields of Kent. Throughout the streets and in the happy countryside surrounding Canterbury and Maidstone, we were received, because we were French, with the heartiest cheers. Even though it is now somewhat distant, I recall this memory still more gladly because this friendship between our two nations still subsists. At the present time, indeed, in full agreement with France, the intense diplomatic activity shown by the British Government and its resolute attitude during the course of difficult discussions and proceedings, have led to a notable relaxation in the international situation which was brought about by grave events that might have threatened world peace.

Therefore, in my turn, and as the mouthpiece for my co-citizens, it is with pleasure that I repeat with the same heartfelt enthusiasm :

Long live England; and at the same time, Long live France.

After the Mayor's address and general fraternising, the whole party, led by the Abbé Thorez, proceeded to the Church and were shown over the Sacred Building, erected on the ruins of the one destroyed in the Great War.

This most interesting visit over, the delegation, watched by practically the whole town of Meteren, walked over to the local War Memorial, upon which Sir William Pulteney laid a wreath, and taking the time from the General everyone present stood at attention and observed one minute's silence.

M. Plichon, Member of the French Parliament for Bailleul-Merville, kindly invited Sir William Pulteney and officers to dinner, which the General most reluctantly had to decline owing to an engagement at Ypres. Captain J. F. Miller, The Seaforth Highlanders, deputised for the General and, accompanied by Captain R. H. Bland, was regally entertained.

During the leave-taking the band played both British and French airs and the cars containing the delegation left Meteren to the strains of the British National Anthem. The object of the pilgrimage had been religiously carried out, and the feeling of affection that strongly exists between the two great Nations was never more obvious than on this occasion. The return visit to which the delegation was cordially invited will be looked forward to with the greatest pleasure.

* * *

Memories of the Ypres Salient

By Claud V. White, late Lieutenant, Machine-Gun Corps.

RUPERT BROOKE said "there is a place which is forever England." If the Great War ever created such a place, surely it is the Ypres Salient, which, as R. H. Mottram points out in the October issue of the YPRES TIMES, was held practically by British troops alone for four years? Although soldiering is not my profession, I think masters of military strategy will agree that the Salient was the pivot around which the world-war raged.

My memories of the Salient began when I joined my unit at Albert after that great gun-wheel-to-gun-wheel Battle of the Somme. I was merely one of the "loots" on the inventory which was carefully prepared before every big engagement with a really uncanny accuracy as to estimated losses. It was on the trek across country from Albert to Reninghelst that my troubles began. Being at Grantham a Staff Instructor on poisonous gasses and bombs to the Machine-Gun Corps, I had been excused that awful ordeal called a riding school, but when actually on the Western Front, I found that, as a M.G.C. Section Commander, I was to be allocated a "charger." Seeing that I am no taller than was Napoleon, one can imagine my dismay when the C.O., out of a sense of humour I believe, assigned to me one of the largest horses I have ever seen. My first hour or so in the saddle in front of marching troops may be better imagined than described.

What with the increasing ache in the hips, the continual passing of lorries and my steed so often on the edge of a deep escarpment, I wisely vacated the saddle, leaving " the charger " to be led by a trustworthy corporal. This horse, however, had its virtues, for he made me the most popular officer among " the foot-sloggers," who, when out of the line, were only too glad to exercise him for me. My unit occupied the line about Vierstraat opposite the Wytschaete Ridge. Rest billet was at La Clytte, and one day, when on leave from the line, I felt I would like to see Ypres, for although only some ten or twelve kilometres away I had never been nearer than this distance to the City. So I mounted, and off to Ypres I went. As I entered the ruined City, an anti-aircraft gun on the road must let fly, causing my " charger " to so jump as to almost unsaddle me. I passed the famous Cloth Hall, now but a pile of brick rubble with one torn finger rising out of the ruin, pointing, as it were, a digital emphasis of the City's suffering. Scarcely had I got into the place before I found myself and horse suddenly pulled into what I took to be the large basement of a town hall. I don't think that any human creature was so " straffed " in all his life. " Did I not know that no horse was allowed in the City since——" but, of course, I did not know. Anyway, my bland ignorance was forgiven, and I had a good tea. At six o'clock pip emma, I was advised to get out, for the enemy had a way of opening up on his favourite target a little after dusk. I set out to return, but somehow did not like the way my horse pricked up his ears. I had not gone far before I heard a tremendous crash to my rear, and a regular inferno started. Straight down the road to Reninghelst I went like John Gilpin. I learned afterwards that I was the last man ever to leave Ypres on a horse, and I was promptly told that I was lucky not to be court-martialled, whereby I came to know that there really was a terrible to-do about the safety of " a charger," but not too much concern about the human creature on his back.

But glad indeed I was to be back in my little cottage-billet at La Clytte only to find the old, one-eyed Belgian woman looking out of her window, wringing her hands in excitement as each enemy shell crashed in the city of eternal torment. " Allemand win ! Allemand win !" she repeated again and again in a voice of utter despair.

On the Vierstraat Ridge my dug-out was the cellar of a cottage and screened from the enemy by the broken village of Vierstraat. A stretched wire-mesh, covered with sandbags, was my bed, and with army blankets gave me one of the most comfortable beds I had ever known. In fact, for the first month or so, I got undressed and went to bed in my pyjamas with gum-boots ready to hand and a loaded Colt on the box by the head of the bed. I wonder whether this entitled me to another court-martial? Thus for six months I led the life of a quaint country squire, visiting my machine-gun posts once by day and once by night. This duty was not arduous, since being responsible for 1,000 yards of lateral front as regards machine-guns, I naturally looked in at each infantry dug-out where I was welcomed with " a toddy " and the usual duck-board gossip. Those wonderful days of trench warfare, one can never forget. There was an *espirit de corps* among all ranks, a real unselfishness, a sincerity and a nobility which I have rarely encountered since the War. I am no apologist for war in any of its forms, but I have often longed since 1918 that mankind might show in peace that graciousness of the human spirit which only a dire wholesale slaughter seems to bring out.

I had intended to tell you something about " Smiler." He was the fellow who got so much C.B. because he was always smiling. He had the " undisciplinary look."

[Continued at foot of Page 50

Light and Shade at the Front

(By an ex-R.B.).

Round About.

THERE is little doubt that if a student of first causes were asked to name the one or more reasons for the term "roundabout," as applied to a favourite form of rural amusement, he would promptly include in his answer the words "round about." And if he were asked *why,* he would probably reply, that, reasoning back from effect to cause, the words "round about" describe more accurately than any others the circulatory route that passengers take when on a roundabout, and then, switching back to cause and effect, he would assert that the description of the movement came to be used as descriptive of the thing, and that as a result of frequent usage the two words merged by easy stages into "roundabout," and so added a new word to our language.

The word in question is not of increasing recurrence, because it is not easy in these days of bricks and mortar and kindred constructive materials to find a roundabout that does function within a nodding distance of leafy trees and open to the wind and weather, urban expansion having spelt rural extinction. But even so, a roundabout, merry reminder of the bracing countryside, is to be found even in London, the Mecca of bricks and mortar, although it is more than likely that if anyone starts out to seek it without first taking cue by way of direction, and the cue is given in these lines, he will walk himself to a standstill without finding it.

However, at the moment of writing, we are less concerned with a roundabout than with the subject of "round about." But a recent sight of the former, in the course of our travels, having suggested the latter, from "round about" to the in and out and about and round outlined of a trench is but a step, and so yet again, figuratively and by the natural course of cause and effect that is where we find ourselves.

Limiting one's remarks to a period not later than the Great War, it would seem that modern wars, although each new war put improved lethal weapons into the field, have differed but little from each other in the general method of campaign, the trench warfare of the Great War being an exception. The trench was of course no innovation, but trench warfare on such a vast scale undoubtedly was something new.

It is recorded of Wellington's men,

> "I'm sick of this marching,
> Pipeclaying and starching,
> How neat we must be
> To be shot in a trench!"

but whether the trenches of those days, not excepting the works laid down by the engineers in the lines of Torres Vedras, were furnished with such shelters as dugouts and funk-holes is a moot question.

So far as the writer recalls, round about in a trench usually brought the troops to a dug-out, or if not to a dug-out then to a funk-hole, or to a substitute of one sort or the other for either. A waterproof sheet sometimes served for cover, as also did a camouflage of light bracken, the bracken being arranged across the top of the trench (Ypres) and the feeling of security that was imparted by this slight cover was noteworthy. As regards strength and security of cover the pill-box was at the other extreme, and not only did it answer as a substitute for all the other forms of cover in use at that time in a trench, it also stood in a class by itself.

A funk-hole, as readers know, was a hole dug in the side of a bank with an entrenching tool, or sometimes a shovel, and maybe funk-holes were a close parallel on a small scale, to the caves of our ancient forebears. In devising a means of protection the twentieth century recruited antiquity to its aid. But one may venture to take exception to the term "funk-hole" as being descriptive of that form of cover having regard to the fact that anyone who took shelter therein, as all the troops did at times, took his life in his hands, the average funk-hole being likely to cave in and bury its occupant at any odd moment.

Of dug-outs there was a large variety, but, unlike the periwinkle of the epicure, they were not all "fine, large," or even "all fresh!" and, as readers will recall, they varied between small, medium and large, good, bad and indifferent. The more rough-and-ready dugout was just a man-made cave underground and was reached by descending several deep, irregular steps. The sloping stairway was shored with timber and a stout framework was fitted at the entrance opening in from the trench, not much timber being used in the construction. A feature of this sort of dug-out was that the troops had to bend double on entering or leaving it; where anyone on coming up for a look round left his helmet below, then perchance—crack!—it was a case of wood against wood, and having learnt his lesson in the best school he wore his helmet next time.

Not much cheese.

Far be it from us to seem to belittle in any way the solid advantages that were afforded by the dug-out but it was a fact that at times the ventilation was not, well, quite perfection. When a fire was alight at night the dug-out was filled with a more or less perceptible blue haze of wood smoke, and usually the first thing that one noticed on turning in from the trench was a smell of wood smoke. But all things are relative, to quote a well-worn platitude, and where a sentry on the step in driving wet snow, that found every crevice and froze without freezing, had been trying to pierce the darkness towards the enemy line and stamping his feet to promote circulation, was relieved off the step, then did he find the smell of wood smoke quite welcome. And when he descended into the dug-out, treading the slush in on the top steps, and opened out his rations by candlelight; bread, cheese (not much cheese), butter and a cigarette issue; why, the blue haze of wood smoke meant real enjoyment.

From the viewpoint of ventilation it is probable that the direct opposite to a seat on the top of foothills, with nothing stretching in front of one but the downward slopes of timeworn rock and the boundless expanse of ocean, is a stand in a crowded lift where everyone is packed like sardines. Civilisation trying to "put one over" Dame Nature, who exacts a requital in oxygen. But the writer recalls an occasion when things were even more congested, when the troops were scotching up in the Vimy offensive and marked time in a smallish enemy dug-out. The interior was cramped and the air shaft had been damaged by shell fire. Presently word was passed from the other end, " Pass it up, we're suffocating," followed a few minutes later by another message, " Pass it up, urgent, we're going black in the face !" And it being a case of " Hobson's choice," orders were given to lead out, and the troops had to quit.

Under a strong guard.

It can be seen, quite readily, when travelling in the depths, how water oozes through from above, and that failing is reminiscent of a dug-out in the Arras Sector (of the sort with which readers are familiar), where the water dripped down steadily and formed puddles on the chalky floor and the troops looked just like the hands in a plasterer's shop. The art here was not to choose a dry place on the floor, that being much of a muchness, but to find a spot where the water didn't drip down one's neck. But difficulties always give way before energy and practical knowledge, and perhaps it is a mistake to suppose that a little knowledge is always a dangerous thing, that stricture being limited to one's chief occupation.

A lost art in these days, although it was quite common during the war, is that of keeping a light on at night by the simple expedient of "nursing" candle gutterings and a small piece of wick. Ingenuity, too, was often exercised in the changing of wet conditions into dry ones, the scraping down of earth from the sides of a sap, for example, the tramping in of sandbags, and the raising of the level on a gradient as a drain-off, serving to turn a wet sap into a dry one.

It is not difficult to visualise the feelings of a hungry man who, having a tin of Frey Bentos in his hands, lacks an implement with which to open it. Something of the same problem arose with some of the biscuit issues. Readers may recall that a biscuit in common issue to the troops was dull white in colour, about three inches square, and equal in unyielding hardness to a Delft kitchen tile. The problem therefore was " How to eat them?" and a way was soon found. Break them up with a coke hammer (or usually an entrenching tool handle), allow them to be boiled for two or three hours in the soup, and treated in that way they were quite palatable. A broken biscuit issue, also white in colour, could be eaten off-hand, but the best biscuits issued were not white, but more like standard flour, baked a golden brown, and could also be eaten off-hand. They were the same size as the white biscuits, a trifle thicker, and equal to " Ship's first saloon." One morning, when the troops were on the steps of an enemy dug-out during the attack on Wancourt, they sampled a small bag of German biscuits. These were round in shape, quite small, and light in colour, but being unsweetened they tasted rather " flat."

A characteristic about enemy dug-outs, at least of the larger sort, was a profusion of timber that was used in their construction. This timber was all of good lengths, board or plank width, straight, dry and sound, and its unstinted use extended also to the standing bunks of the built-up box type.

Mention has been made of pill-boxes, and these were an example of something new, in the way of ideas, being fashioned in principle to the design of something old. It may be said, with truth, that a tree trunk is one of Nature's most effective ways of breaking the force of fierce storms, seeing that the circular shape of the bole tends to deflect force instead of flatly resisting it, and the shape of a lighthouse is a close parallel. In design the pill-boxes were mostly round and the compass small, although at times the dimensions were larger and the design adapted to shelter several persons. These shelters, as readers will recall, were built at a suitable level and were camouflaged by the trench or the surrounding ground, the material used in their construction being a sort of reinforced concrete of considerable thickness and hardness, and they withstood the severest tempests, although admittedly these were of shell fire and not of howling winds and raging seas. When a shell struck a pill-box the impression that the troops formed was that it bounced off, and where it did explode at the point of contact apparently no damage was suffered— by the pill-box, which stood firm in a wrack of destruction. One pill-box that the writer was in was fitted with a small gunmetal slide which covered an aperture. A sentry could closely observe the enemy line through this opening and close and re-open the slide at will.

Anyone in the field is apt to learn, more readily than elsewhere, that " man needs but little here below," and that truism was often exemplified in the making of tea. Readers of course do not need reminding that tiny splinters of wood, pared off with a jack-knife, sufficed for the boiling of water in Salient trenches. But given the right conditions elsewhere a good fire could be made, although it may be said en passant that this remark has no reference to the large dumps that one occasionally saw burning at night in the distance. The lurid glare of the flames lasted all night and these fires were a subject of much conjecture.

Soon after daybreak one morning, about the time when the cyclonic fury of the Arras offensive had slackened off, and both sides were settling down into their new positions, there was a nip in the air, not to say a rime of late frost, that made one's fancy lightly turn to thoughts of an early morning canteen of tea. So a spot was chosen at the foot of a bank, where it was hidden by a winding approach, some earth was put ready as a damper and the fire was started, a time honoured way being the cutting of a small V-shaped groove out of the ground. Dry wood was plentiful, and as it was thrown on it blazed and flashed without smoke, and the tea was ready within five minutes. It tasted slightly woody but then, if report be believed, so does ye Wine from ye Woode.

Nothing seems to stale the infinite variety of worldly affairs. Things seem to run mostly in pairs, or else in threes, the eternal old triangle, one of a three being the " fine old crusted " of vintage fame. Another fine old crusted which is said to " ripen " with age is, of course, cheese. Possibly a third, one which looks crusty even if it isn't crusted, is that type of nondescript sausage, tied tightly round with string, which may be seen on one's travels as it hangs suspended from aloft by a hook. The reference to cheese reminds the writer of a small cheese, of civilian days, that was sent out across the ocean packed in a strong container. On arrival at its destination it was issued to table from Stores and one or two guests speared a tiny morsel out of the container. However, in response to the mute but eloquent appeal of the company they carefully replaced the lid and so effectively applied the closure.

Normally one would not expect to see a fire in a cemetery, given over as these silent last resting places are to the " cold, dull ear of death." On an occasion when the battalion was out of the line the body of a French general who had died in the line was brought back to a local cemetery for burial. French troops in field blue and steel helmet formed a guard lining the cemetery and the battalion furnished a firing party. On the firing of the second round, " Reload, Present, Fire !" when all the rifles discharged into the air as one, smoke was seen coming from an adjacent grave, and when the troops filed out after " Last Post " it was seen that an ejected blank had fallen on to an artificial wreath and ignited it.

Certain of our readers may have seen the picture of a horse standing by its dead rider on the battlefield, but a repetition of such an incident promises to be a thing of the past. Faced by mechanisation the horse is now in the " last ditch," and it is pleasant while penning these lines to recall the finest horse of its type that the writer ever saw. This was in Doullens as the Division was moving off. At a moment when the Company was in the act of wheeling at the lower end of the street a French orderly appeared leading Bucephalus by its bridle. What a picture! Jet black in colour, small well shaped head, wavy mane, arched back, well rounded quarters, long wavy tail reaching to the ground, wide open nostrils, eyes like pools of fire, tapered legs, very small hooves, and every movement one of lightness and grace. Alas! Compare that superb specimen with the awful relics of horses seen in certain South American towns on the Pacific Coast; harnessed to frowsy dirty old landaus and in the last stages of disease, harness sores, starvation and general neglect. What a commentary, on human nature.

The Grey of Dawn.
Yorks & Lancs taking over.

Memories of places round about the Front rest naturally on one's individual service, and space permits the mention of only a few. Locre was a bright little place in the fine weather; there were plenty of troops there, many of whom were Anzacs. One afternoon when an Anzac Division was moving up within sight of the battered ruins of Ypres a Maori sounded his war cry. Perhaps "the spirit moved him." This war cry was primeval in character, welling fierce and unrestrained, and it was well calculated to "move" anyone, especially on a dark night. The writer and a friend visited a small camp cinema near Locre; the films had seen a lot of "-action," as was evidenced by the many little white spots showing up on each reel. In Locre, too, was a six feet by four little general shop that stocked a mild brand of cigar, so mild as to be almost anaemic, and it is probable that these cigars were closely related to some tobacco leaf seen drying in a small lean-to open shed near Locre.

St. Omer was very quiet. A restaurant on the further side of an open square provided an excellent service of eggs and chips. The price? Oh, quite moderate; about half a franc at francs 25 to the £. And St. Omer removed a doubt which may beset any observer when looking at certain of the portraits painted by Old Masters. To wit, whether ye Olde Master tried to improve on nature by adding a few touches of his own. When off duty one morning the writer and a friend strolled into the town and bought one or two things at a small stationer's shop and they were served by a young girl in the 'teens who, as regards likeness, might have stepped direct out of one of Greuze's or Romney's paintings, the salient features apart from good looks being a fair, perfect complexion unspoiled by the addition of any cosmetic, and clear grey eyes that spoke of sunny fields and a distant horizon. Needless to say the two customers were careful, on a point of etiquette, to keep their opinion strictly to themselves. Outside St. Omer, and off the beaten track, was a farmhouse that was approached by a country lane and flanked by a very picturesque mellow red brick wall. One assumes that callers were few, but excellent coffee was obtainable.

At Meteren the Company was billetted in a rambling old brasserie, with plenty of landing space, and a "striking" feature just across the street was a small turret clock. In the early hours one could hear its tranquil bell, "ding-dong, ding-dong, ding-dong, ding-dong," the one settled note of serenity in the then unsettled strife of war. Meteren was said to have been the scene of a cavalry skirmish early in the war, and at night on the outskirts one could see the Vereys tracing their slender pencils of light in the line. There was a small narrow street in this village that might well have been termed "Vanishing Street" although that was not its name. Coffee was on sale during the day but after dark the street was blacked right out, not a vestige of light showing.

It may not be untoward to close this brief desultory sketch of the line by relating an incident that occurred in Meteren and where history repeated itself, although as usual with a difference. Late one night, we will call him X.Y.Z., was reported missing from billets, and news of him reached the Guard-room when the innkeeper of a small beerhouse presented himself to make a report. Said he, resting his head on his hand, "Ze Tommy 'e iss—dormant." Presently the rumble of a wheel was heard on the cobble stones, and this heralded the arrival of a wheelbarrow in which the missing file lay "dead to the wide." And the words that greeted him were not ". . . . . and pass, all's well!" as in the case of a certain well-known hero of fiction, but something quite different.

J. EDWARDS.

(*To be continued*)

Continued from Page 44]

I saw him in the ranks in England in two units, and then at Poperinghe, and last of all at Passchendaele. Some one came and told me that in that awful battle of the mud "Smiler" was down. When things quietened a bit, I went out from the recently captured dug-out to explore. Yes, there he lay dead, but was he really dead, for he still had that wonderful smile on his face. Then, again, I wanted to tell you about little Tina of Bailleul, that sweet girl who attended officers in the town's bodega-place, and made us sign her tablecloth which was covered with the signatures of some of the most famous men engaged in the War. Tina knew them all. Tina with her Clicquot cheered the boys up when out for a few days rest from the line, but none of us ever answered Tina's many questions as to how long we had been out, or from what part of the line we had come, etc., excusing ourselves that we were out for a holiday and didn't want to talk shop. One day Tina was no longer at her bonny bodega, and we often wondered what had become of her. After the unhappy fate which was eventually meter out to Bailleul, we again wondered.

CLAUDE V. WHITE.

Public Schools Battlefield Tour

FROM Saturday, April 23rd to Tuesday, April 26th, over eighty public school cadets were privileged to make a tour of the Battlefields under the auspices of the Ypres League, in co-operation with the Officers Training Corps Club. But it was a tour that ended in a pilgrimage, for as one looks back on those four days it appears all the more strongly that the seeing of places which have been hallowed for all time by the sacrifice of the men of a whole generation opens our understanding to their crusade in a way that nothing else can. So we will call ourselves pilgrims; and as befits all good pilgrims, many of us rose very early on that Saturday morning in order to be at Victoria Station at 9.15 a.m. A little too early, perhaps, as we had to wait till 10.30 before we got away for the coast, but once in the train we realised that we were to be well looked after. We were given a map of Ypres Salient and surrounding country—presented, we learnt later, by Lieut.-General Sir William Pulteney (Chairman of the Ypres League) to each pilgrim—as well as some notes on the actual fighting which took place over the ground we were to see next day. This careful attention to the details of the tour was expressive of much that was to come, and when we were ushered through the customs at both ends without the necessity of opening a single bag we knew at once we were travelling under a privileged organization. The sea was kind, the boat comparatively steady and in a few hours we were standing on Belgium soil. H.M.S. Vindictive was no longer lying in the Ostend Harbour; had she been, a grim relic of the war would have welcomed us, but her disappearance was symbolic of much that lay beyond for we were to find a land nursed back to beauty with the scars of war scarcely visible until they were pointed out by the story of the fighting.

The drive in char-a-bancs from Ostend to Ypres gave us an opportunity of realizing the flatness of the country which made possible the flooding of the vast area which we were to see along the Yser on our return trip on the following Tuesday, and it also gave us our first view of two outstanding memorials of the war which were to be indelibly impressed on our minds during the next 48 hours—the divisional memorials standing at the junctions of the roads, all differing in shapes and sizes which we were continually to find along our pilgrimage and the resting places of those who had passed beyond the sight of men. We were to know more of these.

Arrived at Ypres we were soon settled in the hotels allotted for our stay, some at Hotel Splendid and Britanique, in Grande Place, and others at Hotel Skindles in Station Place. That evening after dinner we all met at Hotel Skindles and we were given a very interesting lantern lecture on some general aspects of the Ypres Salient and on the places we were to see during the next two days. It was hard for some of us to realise as we walked through the streets of Ypres that evening the total extent of the havoc that had been wrought in that place and yet some were beginning to seek out already the new life that had been built on the old, and in that seeking were to learn the extent of sacrifice. The evening lecture had introduced us to the two staff officers who had been granted permission by the War Office to accompany the tour—Major M. Lee-Cox, 34th Training Battery, R.A. Depot, Royal Artillery, Woolwich, and Major J. M. West, Master of Shrewsbury School, O.T.C. Their presence helped in no small measure to make the tour such a success. Their collection of stories from first-hand knowledge and from the letters and diaries of those who had seen fighting in some of the places we were to visit, added just that intimacy which turned the ditch, the cross-road, the sloping green field and the ridge from a peaceful countryside into the battlefield where courage and devotion had hallowed the ground for ever for us who only dimly remembered their sacrifices.

Sunday began for some with a service of Holy Communion at 8 a.m. in the Ypres British Church, and at 9 a.m. the entire party attended morning service there, taken by the Rev. G. R. Milner, M.A. This was followed by the laying of a wreath on the Town Memorial by Major Montague Jones, with the party standing in silence, in homage of the Belgium dead—the inscription on the card attached was—

"In respectful memory of the fallen soldiers of our gallant Belgian Ally who fought side by side with our British Armies in the Immortal Defence of Ypres, 1914-1918."

"From the Officers and Cadets of the English Public Schools O.T.C."

The next move was to Poperinghe, where the home of Toc H breathes the atmosphere of pilgrimages new and old. "Dull would he be of soul" who could have entered that "Old House" and not caught something of the spirit which expressed itself more fully in the little Chapel at the top of the House. Some of us would have liked to have stayed longer, for the walls carried pictures and notices and letters which took us back over the twenty years in a moment of time, but we had to get back in readiness for the tour round the Ypres Salient in the afternoon.

Driving out North East from Ypres through St. Julien, our first stop was at the Canadian Memorial and from there we were able to look back and see the full extent of the Salient. A list of names conveys very little to most people, but for us there was to be a great awakening to reality as we passed the New Zealand Memorial, the Tyne Cot Cemetery and Memorial to the missing at Passchendale; nobody could walk here without a feeling of sorrow and pride as he viewed the rows and rows of headstones, surrounded by lovely English flowers and lawns, with names engraved on the memorial stones telling us, who had been too young for the fray, that our heritage had been dearly and nobly defended—surely here at any rate was a reason for our pilgrimage—none of us could ever have imagined the glory of that spot and none of us could have left it without a firm resolve that their sacrifice must not have been made in vain and that a real and lasting peace among nations of the earth must be the answer to that glory. And then we moved on down south, past the 7th Division Memorial to Gheluvelt, whose history was told us by Mr. Mears and on to Hill 62 were a few trenches in the form of a museum gave us an idea of the conditions of trench life. Although they were preserved for sightseers there was enough reality in them to contrast with the beauty and stillness of the Memorial which stood over above them. The contrast was a lesson in itself. And so back to Ypres, entering by the south gate.

After dinner there was a further talk on the tour for the following day and Major J. M West must be congratulated on giving us some extracts from the diary of an officer, which was to cover just part of the route we were to take. It was these single stories taken from odd places that enabled us to build up again the trials which men had to face—and it is good to remember those trials.

Monday saw us moving down South into France as far as Arras, after visiting Hill 60 with its tunnels, the Messines ridge with its craters, on past the London Scottish Memorial, across the frontier, through Armentieres, past the Indian and Portuguese Memorials, over the battleground of Loos, through Souchez until we came to Vimy Ridge. Here a halt was called and from a vantage spot we were able to look down into the flat country below and realise the magnitude of the task which fell to those who captured and held the ridge.

At Arras we enjoyed a hot lunch, and after a short stay which gave us a chance of seeing the restored Cathedral and the Grande and Petite Places we moved out to Monchy where Major Lee-Cox gave us a vivid description of the fighting which ended

The Public Schools O.T.C. Contingent, photographed in the Ypres British School Playground, following the morning Service in St. George's Church, Ypres. Seated in the front centre of the group is Major E. Montague-Jones, O.B.E., etc., Chairman of the London Branch of the Ypres League and inspiring leader of these Annual O.T.C. Battlefields Tours.

in its capture. Then back again to Vimy via Arras, where the amazing Canadian Memorial took our breath away with its grandeur and its challenge—a broken column telling of victory but witnessing to the sorrow and sadness which swamps mankind when the dogs of war are loosed.

And so we began the homeward journey. A stop for tea at Bethune soon found us moving on until, the frontier crossed, we came back to the foot of Kemmel Hill, that dominant feature overlooking the Salient. Most of us found enough energy to climb this on foot, and well were we rewarded, for here below us lay the Salient. It was a fitting end to a memorable day. From north to south and back again and still we knew in our hearts that it was the Salient, pushed out from Ypres, with its roads along which men had gone gloriously to pass beyond the sight of their fellows, that must remain as one of the greatest battlefields which history will ever know. And it was our pilgrim place.

That evening at 9 p.m., as a fitting ending to our pilgrimage we laid a wreath at the Menin Gate Memorial after the moving ceremony—so simply and strangely kept —of the sounding of " The Last Post." The words of the inscription must sum up our thoughts as we thankfully look back to the Battlefield Tour which had been thus made possible—

" In proud memory of our glorious British Dead who fell in the Immortal Defence of the Ypres Salient, 1914-1918, and who have no known graves but whose names are inscribed on this Memorial."

" From the Officers and Cadets of the English Public Schools O.T.C."

And what of the memories we carried home with us—what had it meant to the boys? Perhaps the experience of one who was there may be the experience of the many, for he got up at 6 o'clock on the last morning and with the dawn breaking as he walked under the Menin Gate he made a lone pilgrimage out along the Gheluvelt road to a wayside cemetery because he wanted to learn again the meaning of sacrifice.

O. R. F.

* * *

YPRES DAY, 1938

This year the Ypres League Annual Commemoration will be held on **SUNDAY MORNING, 30th OCTOBER**, and the following programme has been arranged:—

10.30 a.m.   Assemble on the Horse Guards' Parade.

11.00 a.m.   Address by the Rev. Joesph Lynn, C.B.E., D.D,, B,A,, Deputy Chaplain-General to th Forces and Hon. Chaplain to H.M. The King. Dr. Lynn will conduct a Short Service which will be followed by the " Lament," by Pipers of the Scots Guards.
March to the Cenotaph, and laying of the Ypres League Wreath thereon. March back to the Horse Guards' Parade, dismissing there.

12.20 p.m.   A deputation of the Ypres League will proceed to the Tomb of the Unknown Warrior in Westminster Abbey and place a wreath.
It is hoped that H.R.H. Princess Beatrice will graciously attend the Ceremony.

Douai after Twenty Years

Capture by 2nd Middlesex Celebrated.
A Memorable Trip.
Battalion's War-Story Re-lived.

Invited by the Mayor of Douai—the historical old French town situated due east of Vimy—to attend a Civic Reception on Easter Sunday, April 17th, 1938, commemorating the capture of the town by the 2nd Battalion, the Middlesex Regiment, on October 17th, 1918; the Commanding Officer on that date together with those Officers who had served under him at the time, planned a week-end Tour covering all the battle fronts of the Battalion in France and Belgium from November, 1914, to November, 1918.

The Tour was organised under the auspices of the Ypres League and Captain R. P. Pridham, M.C., was deputed to accompany the party throughout as their Representative.

The party, numbering twenty-one, included Major A. M. Toye, V.C., and we were privileged to enjoy the personal services of Mons. C. Leupe, the Ypres League's Representative at Ypres, who endeared himself to all by his courtesy and ready assistance in all circumstances.

From the moment of assembling at Victoria Station on Good Friday until the time of our return, we were indeed a very happy family. Not a hitch of any kind interrupted the good fellowship of the party throughout. The Tour proper commenced at Ostend, when Colonel E. E. F. Baker, C.B.E., D.S.O., M,C., T.D., took his place beside the driver, M. Leupe, and proceeded to lead the party with the same distinction as he had led the Battalion to victory in the closing months of the War. Colonel Baker, who had commanded the 2nd Middlesex Regiment from June, 1918 to April, 1919, had made the most thorough preparation for the Tour, so much so that his study had cleared up several obscure points in the Official History. As the result of his labours every member of the party was enabled to live again the magnificent war-story of the 77th Regiment and to feel a deep sense of gratitude to Colonel Baker for so unique an experience.

Approaching Ypres from the direction of Roulers we were able to appreciate the importance of the Passchendaele Ridge which so dominates the country north, east and south of Ypres. Colonel Baker interested us with a brief explanation of the Ypres Battles, 1915, 1917 and 1918. Entering our own battlefield area one and a half miles north of Passchendaele we soon came to Teal Cot which was identified with difficulty. Here on March 3rd, 1918, the Battalion captured six prisoners in a raid at the expense of one casualty, the latter continuing, however, to remain on duty afterwards. The appalling conditions of the Salient during the winter of 1917—1918 were recalled—the mud and the shell-holes—where men were in danger of drowning once they left the duck-board tracks.

Between Passchendaele and Zonnebeke we crossed the Line held prior to the first gas attack in April, 1915, and both at this place and on the Westhoek Ridge, we fought again, as it were, the Battles of July 31st and August 16th, 1917. Before reaching Ypres we passed one of the 240 demarcation stones placed to mark the furthermost points reached by the Invader. After dinner at Ypres a pilgrimage was made to the Menin Gate Memorial, where a brief but nevertheless impressive service preceded the sounding of the "Last Post." Walking round to the Lille Gate a visit was made to the guard-room (mess) and dug-outs (sleeping quarters) in the ramparts used by the Battalion H.Q., after it had been shelled out of the Cavalry Barracks in 1917. Both Colonel Baker and Major Toye were able to identify the bunks they had used on that occasion.

On Saturday morning, we again boarded our very comfortable motor-coach, and departed Ypres via the Lille Gate, crossing the Ypres-Comines Canal from where we could observe Hill 60 some two miles distant. We were next shown the general Line from 1914 to 1916 and from the 7th kilometre stone, south of Messines, we stopped to see the spot from where the Battalion first advanced into the Line on November 15th, 1914. At this place we had a short discussion on the results of the Battles of Messines and the German Advance in April, 1918. Continuing our journey, we passed Ploegsteert and then on to the frontier post at Le Bizet. The next two places reached were Armentières and Pont de Nieppe, the latter recalling to many how certain two French Madamoiselles, by name "Lanoline" and "Vaseline" joined the British Concert Party there during the first winter of the War.

Fleurbaix was the next place of interest to our party, it being remembered as being at the edge of the peaceful billetting areas used by the Battalion from December, 1914 until March, 1916, and from there we converged on the Line held at various times by the Battalion between Neuve Chapelle and Bois Grenier. Passing Fauquissart we soon arrived on the Aubers Ridge Battlefield, May 9th, 1915, and the next place of call was at a point slightly north of Neuve Chapelle where our first officer casualty occurred: Lieutenant Harvey while stalking a German sniper. We viewed the ground over which the Battalion made its first attack on March 10th, 1915, when casualties were suffered to extent of 16 officers and 449 other ranks. Of this Battle of Neuve Chapelle, Colonel Baker gave us a vivid description of the fighting and related how he was wounded by a bullet which passed through the peak of his cap at the front and emerged from the side of it. He described the flooded trenches which were afterwards transformed into massive breast-works and which remained the British Front Line until the great German Offensive in 1918.

Continuing we passed the scene of the many fruitless attacks at Richebourg and Festubert in May, 1915, and proceeded to Cuinchy where the Battalion, after the terrible hammering it received at Ovillers on July 1st, 1916, was put into the Line with its left resting on the La Bassée Canal. Later Colonel Baker described talion's entry into the Arras sector, and the Canadian Cross, well-known as a rendezvous for guides. Arras was then reached and from here to Bapaume, we passed through country abandoned by the Germans when they withdrew to the Hindenburg Line in March, 1915.

Our next contact with Battalion history was at Le Transloy, where we picnicked for packet lunch, and from where we were afforded a good view of the site of Zenith Trench which was captured on October 23rd, 1916, with a loss of nine officers and 226 other ranks. Re-entering our coach the Tour continued along the main Bapaume-Peronne Road with the well-known places of the central Somme area on our right

Colonel Baker and his party standing at attention before the French Memorial at Douai.

to us the fighting in the Battle of Loos, September, 1915, and he recalled how he was shelled out of his bath while enjoying a much-needed clean-up following a protracted sojourn in the sector.

Returning to the La Bassée-Lens Road we came to Cité St. Elie, Hulloch, Lens and thence to the famous Vimy Ridge. It did not require much imagination to appreciate the importance of this great feature overlooking the Douai Plain and why the enemy made such strenuous efforts to retain it. The size and beauty of the Canadian Memorial on the Ridge, in the form of a "broken column" impressed us all immensely. Descending from the Ridge we continued our journey via Thelus, passing en route the scene of the Bat- and after passing Sailly-Saillisel we were afforded an excellent panoramic view of the St. Pierre Vaast Wood just to our left.

Approaching Rancourt we were reminded that the Battalion took over the Line here in January, 1917. Probably on no other part of the Western Front were there so many British, French and German corpses lying in No Man's Land as were found here when the Battalion took over on the date mentioned.

In the trenches limbs protruded from the sides and it was hopeless to attempt to dig anywhere without disturbing half-buried bodies. At a later period the ground in this sector was frozen so hard that it was impossible to bury our own dead.

As we approached Bouchevesnes, the scene of a raid on February 27th, 1917, Colonel Baker recounted how the Battalion followed up the enemy from here to the Hindenburg Line, escorted by General Seeley and his dashing mounted Colonial Snipers. As we descended the valley into Peronne we were afforded an extensive view of the Somme Valley, and all were eager to hear the exploits of the Battalion in the 1918 fighting there. Major Toye and Captain Birdwood vividly described the actions in which the Battalion were involved here, at the same time in what has been considered one of the most gallant fights ever put up by the 77th. Here it was that Major Toye won his Victoria Cross.

Turning east at Villers-Carbonnel and looking southwards we followed the country over which the Battalion so magnificently resisted the great German onslaught of 1918. In the fighting, the odds against us were overwhelming, and we lost 12 officers and 300 other ranks. We then turned in the direction of Villers-Bretonneux where on April 24th to 26th, 1918, the Battalion drove off the last desperate German assaults with heavy losses to the attackers, and with only 39 survivors the battalion counter-attacked on April 27th. This great effort was not without its price, since the Battalion suffered the loss of 13 officers and 500 other ranks out of a total of 585 all ranks.

At Foucancourt we turned northwards, and reaching Chingnes we stopped to inspect Big Bertha, the famous long-range German gun, also the interesting little war museum. Crossing the Somme at Bray, we saw Suzanne through the trees, where in January, 1917, General Heneker first met the Battalion, which, as he often said, never let him down. Passing through Bray, we soon reached the top of the hill and a splendid view of the whole Somme area unfolded itself to our gaze. We also saw Albert with its famous spire before us. Descending to Meaulte we continued towards Albert, and were ready for tea. Albert, we remembered gratefully, as being the first place in 1916 where good baths and other comforts could be enjoyed in our rest billets. Leaving by the Bapaume Road we stopped at La Boisselle and viewed the mine craters made on the 1st July, 1916. We looked across to Orvillers where on this memorable 1st July, 1916, we had our share of the colossal casualties of the Somme Battle, no less than 22 officers and 590 other ranks out of a total of 23 officers and 660 other ranks who advanced to the assault. Colonel Baker recalled how he had sadly handed over his Company to a senior Captain a month earlier and, having been left out of this Battle, found himself in command of the remnants of the Battalion for two days. We then made for the heart of the Somme area, visiting the South African Memorial at Delville Wood and making north for Bapaume via Geudecourt, we reached the road to Arras, an eventful day charged full with memories.

Easter Sunday, 1938, will be remembered as a day of days by everyone in our party. We had been justly proud of our Commanding Officer, when in 1918 he had led us in one successful action after another up to the capture of Douai in October 17th of that year, and finally to Maisieres on the outskirts of Mons on November 11th, 1918, but never did Colonel Baker rise so high in our esteem and affection as he did at Douai this 17th April, 1938. We reached Plouvain, occupied by the Battalion on October 5th and some recalled how at dawn on October 7th we captured the Fresnes-Rouvroy Line and the village of Biache-St. Vaast, and at dawn on October 9th the village of Vitry-le-Marais and the Queant-Drocourt Line fell to our attack. We likewise recalled, with pride, the exciting events which followed our attacks which culminated at 8.30 p.m. on October 17th, when under the personal supervision of Brigadier-General St. V. Grogan, V.C., etc. and Colonel Baker, the 2nd Middlesex Regiment hoisted the Union Jack together with the French National Flag on the Hotel de Ville at Douai.

Now, twenty years after, we were again at the same Hotel de Ville, but what a different setting and what a different scene met our eyes. Waiting to greet us in the Court of Honour were the Mayor and Town Councillors of Douai, the President and members of the British Club, and the principal officials of the town's Societies. Fanfares of welcome were blown by the trumpeters of the Association Philanthropique who, garbed in full hunting kit, presented a picturesque sight. The Douai Flag was borne by Lieut. Chevens, who fought in the South African War as well as the late War. There were several French flags being carried by officers, in addition to the emblems of the Societies, and Veteran War Associations. The Mayor, after greeting Colonel Baker, led the assembly into the White Hall for the official reception. The Mayor, addressing Colonel Baker, touchingly spoke as follows:—

"Having the great honour of receiving you in our Town Hall, together with the officers who helped in the deliverance of our town twenty years ago, it gives me very great pleasure to tend to you the homage of the Douai Municipal Authorities and to give you a most cordial and affectionate welcome. We shall never forget that on the 17th October, 1918, the town of Douai was freed from its terrible plight by a British Regiment under your command. It was to commemorate this happy event that a Tricolour Flag was, on the 19th May, 1919, embroidered by the women of our town and offered to you as a token of our admiration and gratitude. A few months later you had the gracious thought of presenting to the women of Douai a Regimental Flag with the Badge embroidered upon it as a symbol of the affection which you felt towards our old city, and of the unbreakable friendship which now unites our two Nations. We keep faithfully both the Flag, which is now placed in our museum, and the moving letter which you sent with it. Since then we have been visited by groups of former British soldiers and on the 21st July, 1935, we welcomed Lady Haig in this room. Let us take this opportunity of remembering once more the name of the great Field-Marshal, worthy soldier colleague of Marshal Foch, and to honour the memory of them both. All these Associations keep alive in our French and "Douaisien" hearts feelings of gratitude and brotherhood, of which I am proud to assure you. These feelings are kindled each time we visit the innumerable graves in which your dead are now lying so close to ours in the Cemeteries which spread along the former battle-line and where you know so well how to honour your dead heroes. And so at the same time as we have such pleasure in welcoming you on the twentieth anniversary of your entrance into our re-won city, we greet you not only as the agents of deliverance, but also as messengers of peace and goodwill. For our two peoples, who have worked so hard together, who have fought and suffered so much for the freedom of the world, cannot forget the blood shed side by side and for the most sacred of Causes. All good Frenchmen who have faith in the future of our two countries are agreed that our two nations must remain friends, etc., etc."

On conclusion of the inspiring Address, the Mayor raised his glass and toasted Colonel Baker and his party. This was followed by a most impressive manifestation of the Entente Cordiale, as our hosts and ourselves touched glasses containing the champagne, and the Mayor's toast was drunk.

Speaking in excellent French, Colonel Baker replied as follows:—

"Mr. Mayor, Municipal Councillors and our friends of Douai,

"In October, 1918, the Fates had put my Battalion in the line opposite Douai. Thus it was to us that the honour was given of being the troops who drove the enemy out of your ancient and historic town. Proud as we were of that honour, we are even more proud to-day of the honour you do us by this magnificent reception at the Town Hall.

"We proudly carry the Douai flag, as we call it—the treasured flag which was embroidered by the fairy fingers of the ladies of Douai. It has lost some of its original brightness, but since the war the Battalion has been on foreign service in Egypt, Singapore and India, where silk is harmed by the climate, necessitating the protection of the material by net. But I always think that historic treasures are valued more and more by a regiment with the passing of years. I am very glad that you have been good enough to afford us the opportunity of displaying once more in Douai this bond of friendship, so to speak, between the people of the two great democracies. We were comrades in arms and we remain comrades—comrades in peace. Neither the French nor the English desire war; we firmly believe that trade is the foundation of prosperity and all we want is to carry it on so as to insure that all our people can live in happiness and peace, enjoying such blessings as heaven sends us. So we must go forward side by side, always on friendly terms, making it plain that we ask for no more than peace and justice for all; and if aggressors refuse to allow it, we shall oppose them with the whole combined might of the two nations.

"When we entered Douai in 1918, we found it sacked. Curtains were hanging out of the windows; cross-roads were blocked by craters; débris lay everywhere. In the houses, drawers had been wrenched out; forks, plates, and overturned chairs and tables lay on the floors. Everything was in disorder. To-day we are very glad to see the town in its restored condition.

"We were disappointed not to find any people in Douai, but to-day, after twenty years, we feel very pleased and honoured to meet our friends at last.

"This occasion will remain treasured in our memories till the end of our lives, and we thank you profoundly and sincerely from the bottom of our hearts."

Loud and prolonged applause followed Colonel Baker's speech and fraternising with our French friends continued. Later we were shewn the splendours of the Hotel de Ville, pausing for a moment of silence at the War Memorial in the building. A procession was then formed and, headed by the Mayor and Colonel Baker, we proceeded to the Douai War Memorial where Colonel Baker laid a wreath of poppies, to which was attached a card bearing the following inscription:—

"A NOS CAMARADES DOUAISIENS MORTS POUR LA FRANCE."

A regal luncheon followed, our hosts being the Douaisis British Club, whose President, le Docteur Faucheux, for the occasion took the Chair. The hospitality given at this function will ever be remembered for its generosity, and after the usual complimentary speeches, Colonel Baker was elected an Honorary Vice-President of the Club.

The remainder of the Sunday was spent in the neighbourhood of the Vimy Ridge, and, although the new Canadian Memorial impressed us tremendously, quite naturally it does not hold for us the same associations as the War-time Canadian Cross at Thelus.

One of the great thrills of the whole tour was to find again the actual site of Crucifix Corner, just out of Arleux-en-Gohelle. This was made possible by having with us the actual trench-map used in the capture of Britannia Trench and the village of Arleux-en-Gohelle on September 27th, 1918. On Easter Monday, we went through areas which we had known as

Colonel Baker and the Officers.

camps or billets. At a regenerated La Targette we saw the ruined tower of St. Eloi, and the re-built Neuville St. Vaast. We also crossed the road by which Colonel Baker, as Commanding Officer, led us into the Line in July, 1918. Passing Cabaret Rouge, where Captain Bairnsfather made many of his drawings we came to Souchez and Notre Dame de Lorette. Here we realised the price paid by the French while we were training our National Army. On the way to Noeux-les-Mines we saw Bully-Grenay, Mazingarbe and Vermelles, and later Labourse and Beavry. Next came Bethune, and making an unexpected detour through Steenwerck reached once more the Franco-Belgian Frontier and so to Ypres for luncheon. This was to be our last set meal on this trip, so the opportunity was taken to express the thanks of the party to those who had given us such an unforgettable tour. To Captain Taggart who acted as Secretary; to M. Leupe for his many services; to Captain Pridham, the Ypres League representative, and above all to Colonel Baker, whose health was proposed with musical honours.

Resuming our journey, we saw where the Yser-Ypres Canal held up the great German attack of April-May, 1915, and M. Leupe pointed out places of interest in the Belgian Line and told us, by special request, where and how he had gained the coveted distinction of the Croix de Guerre with Palm, and where the sluice gates were opened at Nieuport, flooding the Maritime Plain of Flanders in the Battle of the Yser, 1914.

The Party near Le Transloy partaking of a wayside lunch. Site of Zenith Trench may be seen near skyline.

Shortly afterwards we reached Ostend, and the never-to-be-forgotten battlefields tour was at an end.

A. MONTGOMERY MANN,
Captain.

* * * * *

Fifth Army O.C.A. Battlefields Tour

In glorious sunshine, a mixed party of some thirty-two members of the Fifth Army O.C.A., left Victoria Station on Saturday, June 4th, for a tour of the Ypres Salient and Somme Battlefields. We were favoured by the elements for the Channel crossing, Dover to Ostend, and this particular part of the journey, generally viewed with apprehension, was on this occasion extremely enjoyable.

On arrival at Ostend, and after passing through the Customs, we boarded our motorcoach and in quick time were on the way to Ypres, the route followed being Nieuport, Dixmude, Poelcappelle, Boesinghe, Elverdinghe, and Vlamertinghe. Dinner was awaiting us at Hotel Skindles, and our party were quite ready to do justice to the excellent repast. At 9 p.m. we attended the impressive ceremony of the sounding of the "Last Post" at the Menin Gate Memorial and the next hour or so was spent in the usual convivial manner. With exception of one member all were in their billets before the hour of midnight.

Sunday morning at 9 a.m. found us ready for a tour of the Ypres Salient, and a most interesting trip was enjoyed prior to our returning to the hotel at 1 p.m. for hot lunch. The afternoon, being free, was mostly spent by individual members purchasing souvenirs, visiting the museum, ramparts or the British Settlement. We were joined in the evening by members of other parties travelling under the Ypres League's auspices with the resultant jolly time and inevitable relating of Great War experiences.

Arranged for our party next day, Whit-Monday, was a whole-day battlefields tour from Ypres to the Somme area. Numerous places of interest were visited en route and many stops made, but space here permits me to mention only a few. The journey out from Ypres to the frontier at Le Bizet was made via Messines and Ploegsteert and after passing through Armentieres the route continued via Fleurbaix, Fauquissart and Neuve Chappelle, thence on to the main La Bassee-Lens road. A stop was made at Neuve Chapelle to enable the party to view the Indian Memorial and the Portuguese Memorial and Cemetery. Reaching the La Bassee-Lens road our journey continued past Hulloch, Loos, Lens and then straight on to the Vimy Ridge. The best part of an hour was spent on the Ridge, visiting the Canadian Memorial, trenches and subterranean tunnels and then on to Arras, where hot lunch was ready for us at the Hotel Moderne.

After lunch the tour continued in the direction of Albert, visiting among other places en route, Newfoundland Park and the Cemetery at Hedauville. Passing through Albert, we made our way to Cerisy-Gailly to enable one of our party to make the pilgrimage to the grave of his "pal". Time was passing quickly, and when the return journey from the Somme was commenced, we were behind schedule. The route followed to Bethune, where billets had been arranged for us for the night, was via Bapaume, Arras, St. Nicholas and Souchez. Excellent accommodation and dinner was awaiting us at the Hotel Vieux Beffroi, Bethune, and as we did not arrive there until 9.30 p.m. it will be appreciated that we were quite prepared for the meal.

On Tuesday morning at 8.30 a.m., we departed Bethune and made our way to Bruges via Estaires, Kemmel, Ypres, Westroosbeke and Thourout. A splendid lunch was enjoyed at the Hotel Cosmopolite and after a brief tour of this famous old city the final stage of the tour was commenced. Ostend was reached at 3.45 p.m., and shortly afterwards all were aboard the steamer to enjoy what proved to be another excellent crossing. Eventually arriving at 9.40 p.m. in London, the party dispersed to their respective homes all thoroughly satisfied with their four days "over there".

The Ypres League must be congratulated on the splendid arrangements made on our behalf, the accommodation and meals being excellent, and the coach placed at our disposal by their representative at Ypres, M. Cyrille Leupe, being all that could be desired.

F. W. S.

The Editor acknowledges with grateful thanks the following comment dated June 24th, 1938, from the Vice-Chairman, Fifth Army, O.C.A., in connection with the above Tour :—

"I feel I must express the thanks of our Association, as well as those who were on the Tour, for your help in organising and carrying out all the arrangements. Next year I hope to be able to go myself."

The Fifth Army O.C.A. Party at the Indian Memorial at Neuve Chapelle.

Attention is drawn to impending change of address of the Ypres League Headquarters.

On and after September 1st all communications should be addressed to

22, ORCHARD STREET, LONDON, W.1.

The Queen's Westminsters at Gavrelle

The Whitsuntide week-end of 1938 was made the occasion for a Pilgrimage and Battlefields Tour by a party of fifty-nine Old Comrades of the Queen's Westminster Rifles. The Tour was organised under the auspices of the Ypres League and one of the items on the itinerary was for a visit to be made to the small village of Gavrelle, approximately six kilometres N.E. of Arras, with a view to the unveiling there a Bronze Plaque, to the memory of the Queen's Westminster Rifles, and especially to those who fell during the gallant stand made by the Regiment in the defence of Gavrelle in March, 1918, the time of the great German Offensive.

Under the command of Lieut.-Colonel G. H. Lambert, O.B.E., T.D., the party arrived in Gavrelle on the morning of Monday, June 6th, and were accorded an enthusiastic welcome by the local officials and inhabitants. In brilliant sunshine and in the presence of M. Lequette, Mayor of Gavrelle; the Municipal Council of Gavrelle, Colonel Higginson (Imperial War Graves Commission), Sapeurs Pompiers, Les Anciens Combattants and a large gathering of local inhabitants an Address of Welcome was read by the Deputy-Mayor. Following the Address, Colonel Lambert laid a wreath on the Gavrelle War Memorial and then the whole assembly marched, in procession, to the Mairie, where the Mayor, M. Lequette, addressed the party as follows:—

Colonel and gentlemen,

In the name of the Municipality and of the people, I express to you all the satisfaction with which we view your visit. You have come to-day to erect a Plaque to the Regiment of Westminster. You are going to leave us here at Gavrelle, where so many of your comrades fell so gloriously, a souvenir in memory of the heroism of those dear comrades. For a very long time, this Plaque will resist all injury from the weather and will recall to the younger generation, how your soldiers have suffered to save France and liberty. Not only, gentlemen, have you been such a great help in securing victory, but, after the Armistice, remembering the ruins accumulated here by rifle and shell-fire, and in memory of soldiers who fell on our soil, the City of Westminster brought monetary aid to help our little village. This generous and kindly act, gentlemen, we have not forgotten, that is why Gavrelle receives you with all the joy and good wishes that she owes not only to an ally, but to a benefactor.

It would please us much, dear Colonel, upon this occasion, if you would renew to the Mayor of Westminster, all our sentiments of true gratitude for the generosity of his City towards our dear Commune. To you, gentlemen, be well convinced that your Commemorative Plaque will be the object of our affection. It will be, for you, a very suitable Memorial, and to strangers it will be a new tangible and inspiring proof of the union and alliance of our two countries to defend peace and liberty

. . . . Vive WESTMINSTER ! . . . . Vive ANGLETERRE !

Colonel Higginson very kindly translated the speech and Colonel Lambert replied as follows:—

Your worship the Mayor, Ladies and Gentlemen,

We are here to-day to hand over to the safe-keeping of the Village of Gavrelle, a Plaque in memory of our comrades of the Queen's Westminster Rifles who fell during the Great War, and especially to the memory of those who fell at Gavrelle on March 28th, 1918. We desire to thank you with all our heart, M. le Maire, and all the members of your Council for having accorded us the privilege of fixing this Commemorative Plaque on the wall of your Mairie. We sincerely hope that France will never again have to submit anew to invasion by an enemy and the horrors of war which result thereby.

A wreath was then placed beneath the Plaque by Captain G. A. N. Lowndes, M.C., followed by the sounding of the "Last Post" and Reveille, between which, one minute's silence was observed. The calls were sounded by Corporal C. J. Timney, a bugler in the present Battalion. Prior to proceeding to the site of the Towy Post the party were entertained, most hospitably, by the Mayor and Council with a "Vin d'Honneur." It was at Towy Post that Captain Lowndes as O.C. of "B" Company was in command on

Colonel Lambert unveiling the Memorial Tablet to the Queen's Westminster Rifles at Gavrelle.

that memorable day when such a spirited and invaluable defence was put up by the "Queens Westminsters" and he gave us a vivid description of the varied phases of fighting during the battle.

On the Saturday previous to the Gavrelle visit, the party had undertaken a tour of the Ypres Salient Battlefields and Memorials, concluding with a special trip to Poperinghe. The purpose of the visit to Poperinghe was to unveil a small bronze Plaque in Talbot House to commemorate the close connection of the Regiment with the foundation of TOC H. Special arrangements had been made for the reception of the party at Talbot House for the particular purpose and

Chairs. The Memorial Banner was unveiled by Colonel Lambert and following a most bright and impressive service, the Banner and Memorial Chairs were dedicated by the local Padre, the Rev. G. R. Milner, M.A. Afterwards the party assembled in the adjoining School Playground where a group photograph was taken, and then an interesting tour was made of the School and the School work inspected.

On the Sunday a battlefield tour was made to Arras and the Somme areas and a most interesting day it proved, stops in particular being made at Vimy Ridge, Cambrai, Newfoundland Park and Hebuterne. At Cambrai, Captain Lowndes gave an account of the Westminster's capture of 1,000 yards of the famous Hindenburg

The Queen's Westminsters' O.C.A. Party with the Rev. G. R. Milner, M.A., at Ypres.

after the unveiling ceremony we were conducted over the "Old House" by Major Paul Slessor.

The Plaque was unveiled by Colonel Lambert and afterwards dedicated by the Rev. P. B. Clayton, more affectionately known to us as "Tubby". A short service was subsequently held in the "Upper Room" so well known to us, and which the Regiment had helped to furnish.

Lunch was taken this day at Skindles Hotel, Poperinghe, and in the early afternoon the return was made to Ypres where another impressive little ceremony was to take place at St. George's Church. The occasion was the placing of a Memorial Banner in the British Church and the installing of Memorial

Line, including Tadpole Copse, on November 22nd, 1917. Newfoundland Park was much appreciated as being so well preserved and at Hebuterne, the scene of the Regiment's most tragic day, one hour was spent in going over the ground and in visiting the cemetery. As is customary when visiting this cemetery, sprays of Rosemary were once again deposited by our members. On the return to Arras, where we were to spend the night, the usual pilgrimage was made to Dainville Cemetery to visit the grave of Colonel Glasier.

After the Gavrelle visit on Monday morning, the Tour continued to Armentieres and Houplines, in which sector the Battalion first went into the line in 1914, and here the party were welcomed by the inhabitants with great joy. The site of the old Front Line was visited, as also was the church and cemetery. In the church is a very beautiful Memorial to the Curé, M. Bailleul, who was killed on May 3rd, 1915. After much difficulty, the members of our party were eventually got together for the next stage of the journey, to Ypres, where we arrived just in time for dinner. After dinner all assembled at the Menin Gate for the sounding of the "Last Post", where we lined up with the South African Pilgrimage Party who were over on a special visit to Ypres. On behalf of the party a wreath was placed at the Memorial by Mrs. Ims. At 10 p.m

The party marching from the French Memorial to the Mairie at Gavrelle.

Captain Lowndes describing the fighting at Gavrelle on the actual site of Towy Post.

the return journey was commenced from Ypres to Ostend and then home.

For so memorable a Tour the thanks of us all are hereby recorded to the Ypres League for the arrangements made on our behalf; to M. Leupe, "Cyrille" to us, their Ypres representative, for some wonderful time-keeping throughout the trip in France and Belgium; to Mr. and Mrs. C. Page (Ypres League representatives accompanying party) for such cheery companionship; to the Mayor of Gavrelle for his great welcome and hospitality, and to Colonel Higginson for his many services at Gavrelle in connection with our visit.

E. P. L.

QUEEN'S WESTMINSTER RIFLES ANNUAL MAIDAN DINNER

The Annual Re-union Maidan Dinner will be held on

SATURDAY, NOVEMBER 5th, 1938,

AT HEADQUARTERS, 51, BUCKINGHAM GATE, S.W.1.

This Re-union is confined to all surviving members of the 1st Battalion, Queen's Westminster Rifles, who sailed to France on November 1st, 1914, on the S.S. MAIDAN.

The "Shinies" again "Over There"

On Friday night, June 3rd, 1938, a party of twenty-six members of the 7th (City of London) Regiment, Old Comrades' Association, left Victoria for their third annual Battlefields Tour. At Dover we were joined by two more members, and on arrival at Ostend, a further four members, who had been holidaying on the Continent, joined the party.

The night journey across the Channel was made in very calm sea, and all appeared very fit on arrival at Ostend. Following a good breakfast at the Hotel St. Sebastien, we boarded the char-a-banc placed at our disposal by the Ypres League and commenced the initial stage of our battlefields tour. The route taken was via Nieuport and Dixmude and on to Poperinghe where arrangements had been made for our party to visit Talbot House, more familiary known as TOC H. The Guide who conducted us over this famous old place so well related to us certain facts and incidents in connection with the place that we were enabled to a certain extent, to recapture the spirit that pervaded Talbot House during the War.

Leaving Poperinghe we made for the frontier post at Bailleul and after crossing the frontier our compass was set for Bethune, where a visit was paid to the Civil Cemetery wherein rest the remains of both English and French soldiers. Here we found the grave of Lieutenant J. H. B. Fletcher, who will always be remembered by the "Shinies" for his noble effort in founding a fund to assist Old Comrades of the Regiment in distress. The graves of 2/Lieut. L. C. H. Squires, Private G. Moore and Private A. J. Harvey were also located, as also was the grave of Brig.-General G. C. Nugent, M.V.O., of the 141st Brigade.

Our next place of pilgrimage was the Cemetery at Noeux-les-Mines, where silent tribute was paid to the memory of Private G. W. Rose, whose father and brother were with us on this Tour. Altogether we succeeded in finding the graves of at least a dozen soldiers of our Regiment, who were killed during the September, 1915, fighting. We next climbed the heights of Lorette on the summit of which stands that very fine French Memorial and beautiful Church, Notre Dame de Lorette. The interior of the Church is decorated with small coloured stones set in mosaic design. The Ossuary, with its coffins and the enormous number of crosses in the adjacent grounds are a grim reminder of the terrible sacrifices the French made in this area. From Lorette we resumed the tour towards Arras, passing en route Cabaret Rouge and the large German Cemetery at La Targette. Thanks to the arrangements made on our behalf by the Ypres League, we were able, on reaching the Hotel Moderne at Arras, to occupy our rooms, indulge in a refreshing wash and brush-up, and be seated in the dining-room all within the space of fifteen minutes. At 4 p.m. we were on the road again, this time to complete a short tour arranged for the Somme area, the first stop out from Arras being made at Mailly-Maillet. Our journey then continued to Beaumont Hamel (Newfoundland Park Memorial) where an interesting visit was made to the original trenches, the ladies of the party experiencing the thrill of walking round the trenches on the old duckboards. Within short distance of this Memorial Park of some eighty acres stands the Ulster Memorial to the 36th Division, and a little further beyond, the huge brick Memorial of Thiepval on which are commemorated the names of 73,367 "Missing".

An interesting feature of this monumental Memorial is to observe the Union Jack and the Tricolour flying side by side at the top of the tower. On one of the panels are commemorated the names of one hundred and forty Officers and Other Ranks of the "Seventh" London Regiment, these having no known graves.

From Thiepval we proceeded to Pozieres, the furthermost southerly point of our Tour, and from there the return journey was commenced to Arras, travelling via Bapaume. Many Cemeteries and Regimental Memorials were passed en route, and we were afforded a very good view of High Wood and the Butte de Warlincourt. Arras was eventually reached at 8 p.m. where another excellent meal awaited us at the Hotel Moderne. After dinner a number of the party took the opportunity to explore the city of Arras, visiting the Grande and Petite Places, etc., but somehow or other we all managed to meet later at a neighbouring hotel, where a jolly hour or so was spent with the inevitable good old sing-song.

Everyone was down in good time next morning for breakfast, and with the aid of the driver, who had, by the way, made himself quite popular with our party by his skilful and careful driving, sounding the motor horn by request of the "knocker-up", we were all soon aboard our chara and making our way to the Faubourg d'Amiens Memorial. On the panels of this beautiful Memorial, are inscribed the names of 35,600 "missing", and in the centre of the Memorial is a special Memorial erected to the memory of the "Missing" of the Royal Air Force who died on all parts of the Western Front, and who have no known graves. Seventy-six names of the Shiny "Seventh" are recorded on the panels of the Arras Memorial.

Returning to Arras, to get back on to the Bapaume Road, we passed through the Grande Place and Petite Place, where there are interesting remains of Spanish architecture. At Bapaume we turned due east for Haplincourt and from there proceeded to Bertincourt, Bus, Ytres and Lechelle. It was at the latter place where our Battalion was disbanded in January, 1919, when a mock funeral was held and a cross erected in memory of the "Shinies".

Our journey continued to Trescault and Ribecourt, but before reaching the former place we were afforded an excellent view from the road of Havrincourt Wood. Situated on the cross-roads at Ribecourt is the site of the old billet used by No. 1 Platoon of "A" Company.

Leaving Ribecourt we travelled on to Flesquieres and saw the old water-splash, still in existence, and proceeding along the sunken road observed with interest the position of our old Front Line. Bourlon Wood came next into view as we made our way towards the villages of Graincourt and Anneux. At Anneux, we found eleven graves of old "Shinies", none of whom, however, were known to any of our party. On the sunken road skirting Bourlon Wood we had another of our old Front Line positions pointed out to us. It was from this spot that the Shiny "Seventh", using only two Companies, made a raid and captured 52 German prisoners and 18 machine-guns. This exploit was rewarded by a congratulatory message from the Army Commander.

Louveral Memorial which stands on the main road near Doignies. It may be interesting to note that this Memorial commemorates those "missing" from November 20th to December 3rd, 1917 only, and records in that brief period over 7,000 names. One of the panels contains the names of fifty-five soldiers originally of the 25th London Regiment, but who were transferred to our Regiment on their arrival in France.

Back in Arras we were not long in settling down to the excellent dinner provided and this over, we joined party with another batch of Old Comrades, the London Irish, who were also over on a similar mission, and a really jolly evening resulted. At one period a competition of sorts was held, the London Irish singing "Tipperary" and we "Pack up your troubles, etc." both at the same time.

A Group of the "Shinies" Party at Cambrai.

Arriving at Cambrai we visited the large Cemetery, so beautifully planned and so well maintained. It has a centre path which opens out to wide circles, in the centre of which, is a large stone cross. Around this cross in successive circles are German graves. The Cemetery contains 8,312 German graves, and to one side of the Cemetery we observed nearly 250 graves of Russians, presumably prisoners of war transported to the Western Front to assist in the construction of the Hindenburg Line. Beyond the graves is a mound over three feet high, beneath which lie the remains of 2,738 German soldiers who could not be identified. A little beyond this mound we found the grave of Private A. H. Walker of the "Shinies" who, judging from the data on other graves nearby, had unfortunately lost his life on the very last day of the War.

From Cambrai we proceeded via the Bapaume road to Fontaine Notre Dame, where a brief halt was made to view the ruins of the old sugar factory. The next stopping place was at the

Next morning saw our party depart Arras for Ypres, travelling via Dud Corner, Loos, Vermelles, La Bassee, Neuve Chapelle and Armentieres. On the journey from the frontier to Ypres a halt was made at the Canal Bank to enable those interested to view the ruins of the old Lock Gates. Ypres was reached in good time and thus permitted our party time to visit the Menin Gate, and the Ypres British Church, wherein hangs the "Seventh" Banner.

At the Hotel Splendid and Britannique, we were cordially welcomed by the proprietor, M. Koch, and given a jolly good lunch. Shortly after we were off once again, this time for Ostend where, it was ascertained on arrival, the mileage covered by our party since the Saturday morning exceeded 350 miles.

Comfortable seats were obtained on the boat for our return journey, the sea was like a millpond, and the crossing was enjoyed by all. Those who read my report of last year's Tour may recall that, off Dover, we placed a message in a bottle and threw it into the sea. It may be of interest, therefore, to record that the message was returned to us two months later, having been picked up off the coast of Holland. This year another message was despatched in similar manner.

In conclusion, I would like, on behalf of the Old Comrades, to tender our thanks to the Ypres League, for all the arrangements they made for our comfort. We accomplished all we set out to do and our accommodation and food wherever we went was first class, the meals being served without any delay, thereby greatly assisting us to complete our itinerary. As on former occasions we were favoured with perfect weather throughout.

C. D. PLANCK.

* * *

Ypres British School

The number of children attending the School at the time of these Notes is ninety-eight. Twenty of the pupils are corresponding with over thirty children in different parts of the world.

A past pupil, Louise Francis, is to be awarded a Parchment by the Royal Humane Society for diving, fully clothed, into the Fossé du Chateau, Ypres, to rescue a three-year old British boy, now a pupil at the School.

Forty of the children were taken on a trip to Antwerp, the original intention being to visit the School "Adopted" Ship, s.s. Hartismere. Unfortunately, the boat had to leave hurriedly, so a visit was paid to the Zoo, where the youngsters had a thrilling and interesting time. Afterwards a short trip was made on the River Scheldt.

For the Unveiling Ceremony in St. Martins Cathedral of the "King Albert" Memorial Window on May 21st, the School were granted a privileged position in the Cathedral, the children being placed next to the British Army and Air Force Contingents, a situation which they greatly enjoyed. From this position a good view was obtained of the general proceedings and the children were privileged with a close-up view of King Leopold and the Queen Mother. It was unfortunate that the inclement weather disturbed original arrangements for the children to march to the Menin Gate after the Ceremony in the Cathedral.

On June 4th, an Exhibition of Children's Work was arranged and prizes were awarded for Writing Exercises, Essays, Letter Writing, Drawings, Paintings, Stencils, Designs, Lino-Block Printing, Leatherwork, Raffia Work, Fretwork, Bamboo Pipe Making, Sewing and Embroidery. A Verse-speaking Competition also was held.

The Exhibition over, the pupils then entertained the gathering with the following three plays which they had for some weeks been preparing: Youngest School, "Snow White"; Middle School, "Roast Pig"; Upper School, "The Queen's Ring" (historical). Scenes from these will probably be given with other work on Prize Day, Saturday, July 16th.

For Sports Day held on July 2nd, Lieut.-Colonel F. G. Poole, D.S.O., O.B.E, Hon, Secretary of the Ypres British Settlement, very kindly donated a silver cup to be presented to Victor Ludorum. A report of the Sports Meeting will be incorporated in the next issue of the "Ypres Times."

Hopes are still maintained of taking some of the children to England on an educational tour.

A year ago an Appeal was made for children's books of every description. Thanks to the efforts of the School Committee we were able to purchase at an extremely low figure one thousand class-books, and for the first time in the School's history we have now complete sets of suitable history books, geography books, arithmetics and anthologies of English verse. Our need and intention is to stock the School as are the Schools in England with materials for all kinds of hand-work; arts and crafts, carpenter's benches, planes, chisels, saws, etc., lino-cutting tools and materials; stencil knives, looms for weaving, cane-work and basketry materials and book-binding tools. The pupils pay a small school fee, but this does not, by any means, meet requirements of handiwork and sport materials. For a sum of £20 to £30 the whole of the School's requirements in this direction could be met.

Regarding sports gear — footballs, cricket bats (size 5 and 6) which cannot be purchased in Belgium, netballs and matting for physical jerks are all badly needed. We therefore appeal to our friends in Britain to be kind enough to spare a thought for the School when they are reviewing their donation list or their own children, having outgrown sports impedimenta, are at a loss to know what to do with them.

We are grateful for the recent gift of sports gear, which has so delighted both boys and girls, privately given by headquarters of the Ypres League which we hope will prove an impetus in the direction we are aiming. Strong and healthy bodies in these young British subjects, resident abroad, contribute largely to obtaining the best results from the teaching we impart.

C. YORATH, Principal.

Since the receipt of above School Notes an Appeal was made at the last Monthly Gathering of the London branch of the League, and resulted in the gift of two footballs and one netball which are being forwarded to Mr. Yorath.—(Ed)

* * * *

ANNUAL PRIZE GIVING

The date of the Annual Prize-Giving at the Ypres British School has been fixed for SATURDAY, JULY 16th, 1938, at 10.30 a.m.

Gift of Oak Cabinet to the Ypres British School

A magnificent oak cabinet, the gift of Mr. George H. Lawrence of Sheffield, together with a library of 750 books, the gift of the people of Sheffield, will be handed over to the Ypres British School on Saturday, July 9th, by the Lord Mayor of Sheffield in the presence of a distinguished gathering including the Vice-Chairman of the Imperial War Graves Commission, Major-General Sir Fabian Ware, K.C.V.O., K.B.E., C.B., C.M.G., and Lady Ware,

are eighteen compartments for books, fitted with glass-fronted sliding panels which lift up and slide into the Cabinet on ball bearings.

Surmounting the top left-hand side is a shield exquisitely carved by Mr. Clarkson, with the Sheffield Coat of Arms, and a correspondingly fine shield on the other side with the Coat of Arms of the Cutlers' Company in Hallamshire. The centre of the cabinet at the bottom has four drawers with a brass plate bearing the inscrip-

The gifts are the result of the efforts of the Sheffield War Graves Pilgrimage Association, who made known to the people of Sheffield the requirements of the Ypres British School.

The cabinet has been made by Messrs. Swift & Goodinson, Ltd., Sheffield, and the carving is by Mr. J. Clarkson, A.R.C.A., one of the masters of the Sheffield College of Arts and Crafts. It is of light English oak to match the Old Etonian Memorial Panel which is already in the school-room of the British School. There

tion: "This library, the gift of the people of Sheffield (the cabinet the gift of George H. Lawrence, Esq.) opened by the Lord Mayor of Sheffield (Ald. E. G. Rowlinson) on July 9th, 1938—W. G. Turner, O.B.E. (Chairman), Ernest A. Beasley, Hon. Secretary."

The Belgian Government very generously waived the transfer (luxury) tax, and the usual permit as well as the certificate of origin, in order to make its conveyance to Ypres as easy as possible.

Obituary

MAJOR E. MONTAGUE-JONES

We deeply regret to announce the death of Major Edgar Montague-Jones, O.B.E., T.D., M.A., who succeeded Major D. Ramsdale as Chairman of the London branch of the Ypres League in 1923. He passed peacefully away in his sleep at a London clinic on June 30th last, at the age of 72 years.

His loss will be felt by more Associations than our own since he was an active, a very active member of many, which included — Life Membership of the National Rifle Association; Hon. Secretary of the O.T.C. Officers' Club; President of the St. Alban's branch of the "Old Contemptibles' Association"; a Life Governor of the Freemasons Hospital; a member of the Council and Executive Committee of the National Playing Fields Association; President of the Hereford Chess Association and Dorset Chess Association and Chairman of the Executive Committee of the British Chess Federation.

Major Montague-Jones was a distinguished scholar. He gained the Wills Scholarship and the Merchant Venturers' Exhibition at Bristol, where he was educated before winning the coveted open Mathematical Scholarship which took him to New College, Oxford. From the University he graduated with first-class honours in mathematics and physics and obtained as a result the senior mastership in mathematics and science at Edinburgh Collegiate School. He was eventually appointed headmaster of St. Albans School, where he remained until retiring from scholastic life, in 1931.

Not the least of his achievements was his successful co-operation with Lord Haldane, then Secretary of State for War, in the formation of the Officers' Training Corps. With Colonel C. H. Jones, his brother, and one or two other enthusiasts, he interviewed the Secretary of State for War and attended certain conferences which resulted in the O.T.C. coming into force.

During the Great War, Major Montague-Jones served in France and Flanders with the 4th (Guards) Brigade, and was the proud wearer of the 1914 Star, in other words he was an "Old Contemptible." His keen interest in all matters concerning soldiers and soldiering continued up to the time of his death. He was to be seen every year at Bisley Camp, organising, commanding and taking part in the rifle shooting competitons.

He was, in his youth, a noted athlete, having captained Oxford against Cambridge in cross-running contests and was also a Rugby football player of repute. On most mornings, up to the last three or four months, he was to be seen entering the sea for a bathe, winter and summer alike, for not even the bitterest cold morning deterred him.

It is no exaggeration to say that he literally gave his life to the service of others, for he never really picked up from the heart attack which followed his strenuous tour of the battlefields of France and Flanders in connection with the Public Schools Instructional Tour, which took place between April 23rd and 26th of this year, and which was under the auspices of the Officers' Training Corps Club and the Ypres League. We of the Ypres League will never be able to fill his place, either in the work he did for us or in our hearts. He was a dearly loved man and we take some comfort in the thought that he was spared suffering, and had, after his strenuous, selfless and useful life, a beautiful end.

The funeral took place at Golders Green Crematorium on Saturday, the 2nd July last, and in addition to the family mourners, representatives were present from: the War Office; St. Albans branch of the "Old Contemptibles"; The O.T.C. Club; Westminster City School (Headmaster); Public Schools Rifle Association, and General Viscount Gort, V.C., President of the O.T.C. Club; London branch of the Ypres League and Headquarters of the Ypres League. There were also present General Sir Hubert and Lady Gough with Miss Gough.

* * *

CAPTAIN J. S. PARKER, O.B.E.

We regret to record the death of Captain J. S. Parker, O.B.E., Chief Horticultural Officer to the Imperial War Graves Commission, who passed away on February 11th last at his residence near Bristol.

Eldest surviving son of the late Canon Charles J. Parker, he was a keen horticulturist and an authority on all kind of trees. In 1917, he became one of the first two horticultural officers appointed in the Graves Registration Unit, in which capacity he went to France. At the end of the War, he was transferred to the Imperial War Graves Commission as Chief Horticultural Officer and remained in charge until his retirement in February, 1935. He was awarded the O.B.E. in 1924.

While engaged in these duties he was one of those deputed to conduct King George V on his tour of inspection of the British War Cemeteries in France and Italy.

It is doubtful whether anyone could have carried out the work of beautifying the cemeteries in France and Belgium with such remarkable success as did Captain Parker, thanks to his untiring energy, skill and devotion. He established four large nurseries for the propagation of the plants needed for the cemeteries in France and Flanders, and carried out the work of turning desolate cemeteries covered with untidy heaps of sterile soil, exposures of bare chalk, and areas of blown sand into fertile spots where now flourish smooth green lawns and beds of flowering shrubs and herbaceous plants.

Looking to-day on these well-kept and beautiful British gardens, it is difficult to realise the extent of the work carried out by Captain Parker and his staff. Nothing was too hard for him, and he laboured with his own hands and suffered every sort of privation and hardship in order to get it done properly and at the right time.

In the War days and afterwards, most of his garden labourers were not gardeners but mostly old soldiers who had been wounded, and had little energy or interest in the work. Parker, however, with his energy and enthusiasm, roused his men to an active response, and in spite of many setbacks achieved his end. Many a man might have given up the task in despair when a beautiful cemetery in a forward area was blown up or fell into enemy hands or when more than one well-stocked nursery was destroyed and the hardly won results of a year or more were hopelessly lost. Despite all this Parker remained undaunted, cheerful and full of hope; always making fresh efforts, travelling from one end of his territory to another, advising and encouraging and advancing the works. Later he did equally good work in the Italian cemeteries and in those of Gallipoli, Greece and the Near East.

No one can visit the cemeteries in France, Flanders or Italy to-day without a feeling of pride in the charm and beauty of the resting places of our dead. We are afraid, however, that it is not realised how much is due to the great labours so cheerfully undertaken by Captain Parker who was never known to complain of the hardships and difficulties he encountered on all sides.

At the graveside, buglers of the Depot Battalion of the Gloucester Regiment sounded the "Last Post" and "Reveille." Among the many floral tributes, which included a wreath from the Chairman of the Imperial War Graves Commission, Major-General Sir Fabian Ware, was a wreath sent by the gardeners over whom Captain Parker had supervision in France. The flowers had been picked from every war cemetery which came under Captain Parker's charge and had been sent to Arras, where they were assembled as a wreath and brought to England by those who attended the funeral.

INFORMATION WANTED.

The Editor will be grateful for any information concerning the following enquiries which have been received at H.Q. of the Ypres League.

1. Private John Nichols, No. 9401, late 2nd Battalion The Devonshire Regt., reported missing in December, 1918, in the Neuve Chapelle Sector. His mother is still hoping for news from someone who could give her any information or knew him on the battlefield.

2. Private J. Borman, late 7th Battalion, King's Royal Rifle Corps, afterwards transferred to the 2nd London Royal Fusiliers about June, 1918. His Comrade-in-Arms enquiring.

3. Gunner E. M. Stone, 153rd Battery, R.F.A. Fell in action July 24th, 1917. His mother is asking for anyone who knew him to get in touch with her through the Ypres League.

* * *

1st WEST LONDON CADET CORPS.

The above Corps has four companies—Westminster, Kensington, Chelsea, Putney. Each company is affiliated to a parent unit of the Territorial Army. There are vacancies in each company for youths between the ages of 12 and 18 years, and sons of members of the Ypres League are cordially invited to join. All information concerning the Unit will be gladly given to anyone interested, by Cadet Captain R. S. Pitt-Kethley.

The Cadet movement seeks to teach young men the ideals of British citizenship, and, in this respect, is akin to the aims of the Ypres League itself. The company at Westminster is equipped as a Scottish Lowland Regiment in diced glengarry—khaki tunic and webb belt—tartan trews and black boots.

* * *

A GIRL'S HEROISM.

We reproduce a translation of a report which appeared in a recent Continental newspaper concerning the heroic act of Miss Louise Francis, who learnt to swim while a pupil at the Ypres British School, referred to under School Notes.

On Monday, at about mid-day, two children were playing at a spot known as "Fossé du Château". Suddenly one of them, little Rolfe Kennett, living in the rue de l'Industrie, and aged three years, fell into the water. His young companion called for help, and his sister, Miss Louise Francis, aged 18, took off her shoes and jumped, fully clothed, into the water. She succeeded in seizing the child by the hair as he was about to sink.

The poor child was carried unconscious to the house of Mr. Francis, where, after artificial respiration had been administered, he recovered. The Kennett and Francis families are of English nationality.

Miss Francis's courageous act deserves recognition.

Editor's Note.—This heroic act has received recognition by the award of a certificate from the Royal Humane Society.

Correspondence

April 28th, 1938.

Dear General,

Having been privileged to meet you when at 20, Orchard Street recently, I would like to tell you how satisfactory were the arrangements for my Tour at Easter. Major Pullar and Mr. Mears could not have taken more trouble to ensure success: M. Leupe was a tower of strength at all times, willing, agreeable, obliging and extremely helpful. Mr. Vyner, aided by Mr. Richards of the Arras Branch of the British Legion gave us much assistance with the intricacies of the reception at Douai, and the unanimous vote of the party was, that it was the best four days they had ever had—an expression which was actually used half a dozen times on the way home by different people.

Our grateful thanks to the Ypres League.

Yours sincerely,

(Signed) E.E.F.B., Colonel.

* * *

April 11th, 1938.

My dear ———,

I think you know that this Battalion has just completed a battlefield tour for which the arrangements were made by the Ypres League. The greatest trouble had been taken to ensure that we were comfortable everywhere, that the transport arrangements should work without a hitch, and we did appreciate very much, etc., etc.

(Signed) W. F., Lt.-Colonel.

May 2nd, 1938.

Dear Sirs,

I am writing to say how successful the arrangements were for the recent battlefields tour in the Ypres sector, and how much it was appreciated by everyone concerned. I would be grateful in particular if you could convey my thanks to the driver of the charabanc who was extremely helpful both in his actions, and suggestions. He was a valuable asset to the tour.

Yours faithfully,

(Signed) L. B. W., Major.

* * *

May 1st, 1938.

Dear Major,

I am writing to thank you for the excellent arrangements made for the Easter Pilgrimage to Belgium and France. The Conductor, Mr. Mears, was most attentive and helpful to everyone. He gave us a very clear explanation and history of each of the many places visited.

I am looking forward to making another trip, and if I hear of anyone wishing to make a pilgrimage I shall most certainly recommend them to go through your League.

Yours truly,

(Signed) H. W.

The above photograph of the 128th Field Company, Royal Engineers, O.C.A., is of special interest to members of the Ypres League. It portrays a re-union at a London Hotel in February last, of the first Old Comrades Association directly affiliated to the Ypres League. Members attending this Re-union function journeyed from all parts of the Kingdom and numbered nearly eighty ex-members of the above mentioned war-time Unit. A special invitation to League headquarters to be present was deeply appreciated and enthusiastically accepted.

League Secretary's Notes

Our Members, particularly those of long standing, must have felt a little disappointed at receiving a notification in March last, to the effect that the "Ypres Times" would, in future, be issued half-yearly instead of quarterly. From the earliest period of the League's life, the "Ypres Times" has been published regularly every quarter and from the many letters received at Headquarters from time to time, one can appreciate how much this little journal is welcomed, especially by members resident abroad, whose only contact, in many cases, with their old comrades of the Great War, and in some instances even with their Mother Country, is through the medium of the "Ypres Times".

At a Committee Meeting of the Ypres League, held in February, 1938, two major items were on the Agenda for discussion and decision, one, the increasing cost of production of the "Ypres Times" and the other, the question of premises. The latter became necessary on account of the existing lease expiring in September, 1938. After lengthy discussion and consideration, it was unanimously agreed that the time had arrived when the purpose of the "Ypres Times" could still be served by producing it twice a year, i.e., in the months of January and July, thereby saving the League a not inconsiderable expense.

It is fully intended to maintain the high standard of the journal, and when practicable to produce these half-yearly numbers with increased subject matter. Shortly after the issue of the notice sent out to all members concerning the above, a considerable number of readers were kind enough to write expressing their full agreement with the Committee's decision, stating that they were quite happy to receive their copy half-yearly.

In regard to the second problem before the Committee, i.e., Headquarters premises, it was decided to vacate the present offices at 20, Orchard Street, W.1, although better terms were offered by the existing landlord if the League would remain. The Committee decided that in September next, a move would be made to some very suitable premises vacant at No. 22, Orchard Street, W.1, only two doors away in the same block, and nearer to Oxford Street itself. Therefore as from September next, there will be a slight amendment to the League's address — from No. 20 to No. 22 Orchard Street, London, W.1.

The past half-year has been very busy, strenuous and eventful as regards the League's Travel Bureau, no fewer than fourteen Pilgrimages and Battlefields Tours have been organised to date, and there are several more to be arranged ere the season closes.

It is very pleasing to record that, on the occasion of the Ceremony of the Unveiling of the "King Albert" Memorial Window in Ypres Cathedral on May 21st last, arrangements affecting the distinguished guests, which included delegates fom the Army and Royal Air Force, were entrusted by the War Office to the Ypres League, and in addition transport and certain feeding arrangements for troops of The 5th Royal Inniskilling Dragoon Guards, The Royal Air Force Contingent and the Band of The Royal Fusiliers. It is, perhaps, hardly necessary to add that the organisation and labour required for this large and important event threw much additional strain on the Headquarters staff of the Ypres League, whose reward came subsequently in the receipt of numerous gratifying letters intimating that all arrangements went without a hitch. In this connection it must be pointed out that the H.Q. staff in London are by no means unmindful of the fact that a large slice of the congratulations for the League's success must go to its Ypres representative, M. Leupe, for his part in undertaking and carrying out so efficiently the many requirements for transport. It has therefore been noted in the records of the League, a grateful appreciation to M. Leupe, and to the respective hotel proprietors at Ypres, Madame Bentin and her staff at Skindle's Hotel—Monsieur and Madame Koch of the Splendid and Britannique Hotel, for their loyal support, unreservedly accorded to the Ypres League during this most eventful week-end.

Last, and by no means least, are those pillars of support of the League in its many activities; we refer to the voluntary worker. In this connection grateful thanks are extended on behalf of H.Q. of the League to the following for so kindly helping the Travel Bureau by ably conducting certain of its Battlefields Tours and Pilgrimages; Mr. John Boughey; Mr. F. W. Stevenson; Mr. J. M. Finn; Mr. C. Page, and Mr. C. D. Planck.

Many interesting accounts have been forwarded to H.Q. by members taking part in the recent battlefields tours and we are pleased to include a number of these in this issue of the League's Journal. These reports are among the best ever submitted to us for publication and it is a matter for regret that space alone has compelled us to considerably reduce them both as regards the number and subject matter.

For the remaining months of the year, our attention must be directed to membership, and in this connection an appeal to all members to do their utmost to help in filling the gaps which have unavoidably occurred. Both our London and Purley Branches are doing trojan work in the matter of recruiting and there is ample evidence that another tussle between them will take place before the end of the year, to win the Branch recruiting prize of £5, offered by H.Q.

As will be observed from the Branch Notes there has been plenty of activity in respective Branches since the last issue of the "Ypres Times". Their social functions and re-unions are an immense help in maintaining the enthusiasm and interest of members and we heartily congratulate the respective committees and wish them every success with their forthcoming autumn and winter programmes.

Branch Notes

COLCHESTER BRANCH.

The Colchester and District Branch of the Ypres League held its fifth Annual Whist Drive on May 9th, 1938, at Jacklin's Cafe, Colchester, and 108 players enjoyed a good game of Military Whist. The Master of the Ceremonies for the occasion was Mr. F. J. Eves, assisted by the following, acting as Stewards: Mr. H. Snow (Hon. Secretary of the Branch), Captain C. E. Rooney, M.C. and Mr. Hull.

The excellent arrangements for the event, which were carried out by Mr. and Mrs. H. Snow, included two competitions, and prizes were generously donated for these and the "Drive" itself by Lieut.-Colonel H. W. Herring, M.C. and Mrs. Herring, Major G. C. Benham, M.C., and other staunch supporters of the Branch.

The attendance was most gratifying and speaks for itself of the energy expended by the promoters and the support of the members and their friends. H.Q. of the Ypres League beg to offer hearty congratulations on the record attendance at this social event.

The Fifth Annual General Meeting of the Branch took place at the Red Lion Hotel, Colchester, on Monday, January 31st, 1938, at 8 p.m. Major G. C. Benham, M.C., in the absence of the Chairman, Lieut.-Colonel H. W. Herring, M.C., unavoidably prevented from attending on account of illness, presided.

The following were re-elected for 1938. Lieut.-Colonel H. W. Herring, M.C., Chairman of the Branch. Major G. C. Benham, M.C. as Vice-Chairman Mr. H. Snow, as Hon. Secretary. Mr. H. Taylor, Pilgrimage Hon. Secretary and Captain E. F. Matthews, M.B.E. was elected Hon. Treasurer in place of Captain A. C. Palmer, who has been compelled to relinquish this office on account of ill-health.

The following were re-elected en bloc to the General Committee of the Branch: G. E. Stanford, Esq.; Captain C. E. Rooney, M.C.; M. McKinley, Esq.; D. Shadrack, Esq.; S. C. Nixon, Esq; S. Farran, Esq.; M. A. O'Halloran, Esq.; with the additional three members, Captain E. Vinson, D.C.M., Captain J. Oxley, and J. W. Demaine, Esq.

* * *

LONDON BRANCH.

Annual Children's Party.

From 3 pm. to 4 p.m. on Saturday, January 15th, 1938, passers-by could not fail to notice small groups of happy and excited children in the neighbourhood of Victoria, making their way towards the Westminster City School. The occasion was the Annual Children's Christmas Party arranged for them by the London Branch of the Ypres League, an event which is eagerly looked forward to, particularly by those fortunate enough to have attended before.

At 4.30 p.m. over 150 children sat down to tea in the large dining hall of this famous old school and did full justice to the fare provided. Parents and friends gladly allied their services to those of the League Members in the matter of waiting on the youngsters at the table, and in other helpful ways, thereby adding considerably to the enjoyment of the children.

After tea a move was made to the main hall of the School, lavishly decorated with flags and bunting, and in which reposed a huge Christmas Tree laden with toys and presents. This was the centre of interest to the children. The next hour was given to a conjuring entertainment, the "wizard" being Mr. H. H. Bekker, who has that happy knack of making these entertainments both mysterious and amusing. When the last rabbit had been taken out of the hat, Mr. Lines followed with a series of clever lightning sketches portraying certain celebrities. The youngsters were invited to call out the names of notable people they would like to see drawn and subsequent requests revealed surprising knowledge and intelligence.

A rollicking game of "musical chairs" followed and was obviously much enjoyed, the next item "musical bumps" being also much appreciated, albeit a little more strenuous. After the games came the prize distribution with a gift from the Christmas Tree to every child present. The gifts were handed to each child by Father Christmas (suspiciously resembling a member of the London Branch Committee), and finally the jolly evening was brought to a close by the singing of "Auld Lang Syne" and the National Anthem. As each child passed out of the Hall he or she was given an orange and a bag of sweets to further cheer them.

We were very pleased to have with us, among others, Major L. J. L. Pullar, M.C., Secretary of the League, and his energetic Assistant, Mr. O. Mears, both of whom took a hearty interest in the proceedings.

The Committee once again thank those who helped so much to make the occasion the great success it was—the Headmaster and Governors of the Westminster City School—the friends who spent many tiring hours decorating the Hall, the generous contributors to the Fund, and to Mrs. Glover and her devoted band of lady helpers who toiled unseen in the kitchen below, attending to the many matters so necessary at such jollifications.

J.W. F.

Annual Re-union Dinner.

The Thirteenth Annual Re-union Dinner and Dance was held on May 7th, 1938, at the Palace Hotel, Bloomsbury, in an atmosphere of enthusiasm and spirit of sociability.

It was with regret that those present learned that our esteemed Chairman, Major E. Montague Jones, O.B.E., M.A., T.D., would be unable to be present owing to illness and the wish was expressed that he would make a speedy recovery. At very short notice Captain O. G. Johnson, M.A., kindly consented to deputise as Chairman for the evening and very ably conducted the proceedings. In a short but pithy speech, he referred to the various activities of the London Branch and stated how pleased he was to learn that the Branch Recruiting Prize had at last been won by the London Branch. He spoke of the great encouragement this would give the untiring Hon. Secretary, Mr. J. Boughey, and concluded his remarks by telling two very amusing stories which moved the assembly to hearty laughter.

Delightful rendering by the Al Berry's Band of popular airs during the Dinner evoked much applause and we were privileged to have the same musicians provide the music for the Dance that followed.

The whole of the arrangements for this most enjoyable evening were carried out by Mr. J. Boughey, who goes to great trouble to entertain and interest members of the Branch and their friends. It is hoped, therefore, that London members will continue to support as many of the Branch functions as possible and thereby show our appreciation of his generous labours on our behalf and for our Association.

F. W. S.

For the January Meeting, the first of the year, we were entertained with a Lantern Lecture kindly given by Major L. J. L. Pullar, M.C., assisted by Mr. O. Mears. The slides shown were most interesting and the Talks much appreciated by all present.

At the February Gathering, our friends from St. Dunstans came along and, as in past years, gave us a most entertaining evening of song and mirth. It is hoped we shall be privileged to enjoy another such evening from these talented artists in the not too distant future.

The March Informal programme was in the capable hands of the ladies, and for the excellent entertainment provided by them we have nothing but praise. Ladies—we thank you, and regard "Ladies' Night" as a fixture in our programme!

April was a truly "Informal" affair, members and friends present enjoying an impromptu programe provided by themselves. For the May Informal Gathering we had the pleasure of an interesting Talk on "Zeebrugge" kindly given by Mr. Moyse.

The season's Informal Gatherings closed with the June Meeting, when eighty-one members and friends sat down to enjoy a steak supper. Mr. Mears, from Headquarters, was prevailed upon to take the Chair, and apart from other humorous references, he, quite naturally, had something to say about the holding of a hot steak supper in flaming June. The evening proved an extremely jolly one from beginning to end, and it would be difficult to imagine a season's gatherings concluding on a happier note than this Informal provided. Our thanks are extended to Mr. H. Foster and his friend, Mr. Smith, for their musical and breezy entertainment following the "Supper."

Smoking Concert.

The Committee have arranged to hold the Sixteenth Annual Branch Smoking Concert on Saturday, October 29th, 1938, at 7.30 p.m. Particulars appear elsewhere in this issue.

Details of programme, etc., will be posted to members in due course. It is hoped that as many members and friends as possible will support this Annual Re-union, and in the case of those prevented from attending, the Committee appeal to them to purchase a ticket on behalf of some ex-service man who would not otherwise be able to be present, or to assist their funds.

Continental Tour.

Arrangements have been concluded for a ten-day Tour to Paris via Ypres, Charleroi, Strasbourg, Chateau Thierry and Verdun. Two or three places only remain vacant, so any person interested is advised to communicate at the earliest opportunity with the Hon. Secretary, London Branch, c/o, 20, Orchard Sreet, London, W.1.

Resignation.

The Committee regret to report the resignation from the Board of Mr. C. H. Hambrook, owing to business reasons. They desire to extend to Mr. Hambrook their grateful thanks for his support and valued co-operation during his term of office on the Committee.

Annual General Meeting.

The Annual Meeting of the London branch will be held at the end of September, the actual date will be duly notified to members in the Notices sent out in connection with the September Informal Gathering.

In conclusion, the Committee wish to draw members' attention to the question of the Branch Recruiting Prize of £5, offered by Headquarters each year for the greatest number of new members recruited. We managed to secure the Prize last year for the first time and we are hopeful of retaining the honour for 1938. To enable us to achieve our object many more new members are required, so to any of our London London members who can help us in this direction we shall be most grateful.

LONDON BRANCH
Monthly Informal Gatherings
WILL BE HELD AT
The Bedford Head Hotel, Maiden Lane,
STRAND, W.C.2.

On **THURSDAY, 15th SEPTEMBER, 1938.**
THURSDAY, 20th OCTOBER, 1938.
THURSDAY, 17th NOVEMBER, 1938.
THURSDAY, 15th DECEMBER, 1938.
At 7.30 p.m.

Your support to the above Informals would be greatly appreciated.

Notice of these Gatherings will be gladly sent to any of your friends upon name and address being supplied to the Hon. Secretary.

PURLEY BRANCH.

The Tenth Annual Re-union Dinner of the Purley Branch was held at the Red Lion Hotel, Coulsdon, on March 4th, 1938, and may, with justice, be said to have established this popular function more firmly than ever in the minds of those members and guests for whom room could be found.

It is remarkable that each succeeding year should bring a greater demand for seats and for the second year in succession the Committee has been compelled to publish "House Full" notices some time prior to the final date allotted for application. This year 160 members and guests assembled, twelve of whom paraded at the last moment to fill vacancies available through certain members preventing from attending, one member being actually fetched from his home after the general assembly had been announced.

No greater tribute could be paid to the popularity of the event and it speaks highly of the efficiency with which the Adjutant and Committee carried out their duties that such arrangements could be made.

This year the Chair was occupied by Captain Bernard Smither, one of the most loyal supporters of the Branch since its inception, and who performed the duties in the high tradition of his distinguished predecessors. He was ably supported by the Adjutant, Major Graham Carr, on whom the bulk of the work of organisation falls and on whom the burden seems to sit with increasing lightness as the years pass.

The guests of the Branch included our beloved and valued friend, General Sir William Pulteney, whose genial presence is essential to the success of the gathering. It is to be regretted that another old friend and regular supporter, General Sir Hubert Gough, was unable to be present owing to the coincidence of what he described in his letter of regret as "an equally important function," and one which he had accepted before receiving his invitation to Purley.

The Branch was also honoured by the presence of Colonel Willans (Brigadier Willans to be), who has been selected for the command of the London Territorials, and Major Pullar of the Headquarters Staff of the League.

The company settled down to examine the Menu, which, as has been the custom for many years, is an example of the ingenuity of the Chairman rather than an accurate and intelligible guide to the repast to come. This year, certain anagrams were devised and the company were mystified and occasionally somewhat shocked (if it is possible to shock ex-soldiers), by some of the corruptions of the names of ordinarily delectable dishes.

The toast of "The King" was loyally and musically honoured, and the Chairman afterwards read a telegram received from His Majesty acknowledging the loyal greetings of those present. Then came the Silent Toast, which brought back vivid memories of old friends and companions left behind, and the impressive rendering of the famous lines of Laurence Binyon, "They shall not grow old as we that are left——"

Having consumed the food and pronounced it good, despite the slightly pornographic descriptions, the company hitched up its slacks and prepared itself for the fusilade of the C.O., which revealed itself in an excellent address.

There followed the presentation to the winners and runners-up of the Bombardiers Foursomes, the former, Major Leck and Captain Green, having got the better of two distinguished medicos, Majors Meakin and Wayte, in a homeric contest which was described in a recent issue of this Journal.

Captain Vernon Lee, M.C., provided the inimitable entertainment which is such a delightful feature of all our Dinners, and the rafters rattled the sound of the old old songs, which are ever new to those who sang them in days gone by.

When the Adjutant rose to deliver his report, he was greeted affectionately and vociferously, and it is to be hoped that his dear old heart was gratified by the obvious appreciation of his great work for the Branch. He told the same old story of the growth of the Branch, of the hard work of the Committee (genial eye-wash), and announced that in future the Branch would collect its own subscriptions, to be fixed at 10/- per annum, of which sum 5/- would be forwarded to the parent League and a like sum retained to meet any charitable or benevolent calls which might be made upon our funds.

The hush which followed was broken by a sudden rush of warm air as Captain Sydney Green rose to propose "Our Gallant Allies," a no longer very effective disguise for the toast of the guests. It might have been observed that Sydney was facing a situation which had its parallel in the old days of "wind up," but he did his stuff bravely and very effectvely, scoring many a bull with his sallies at the expense of the distinguished guests. One particular point made in reference to Colonel Willans was received with much applause and with obvious appreciation by its victim. He recalled the time when Colonel Willans, then a private in the Artists, was being rallied by the S.M. because of the bad shape of his pack, which, on being opened to discover the cause, was found to contain an immature Field-Marshal's baton.

The replies to Sydney's welcome were made by General Pulteney, to whom the Branch is always delighted to listen, and Colonel Willans, who treated us to a vivid and happily phrased speech which revealed the brain behind the man chosen by the new Minister for War.

An able speech by Captain R. McDonald, proposing the health of the Chairman, equally ably replied to, and a few remarks by the President, most beloved of men, who with characteristic modesty, endeavoured to explain away the choice of the Branch for his high office, and a little more of Vernon Lee brought the evening to its climax and the final adieux.

Another Annual Dinner has come and gone, and we parted with the happy reflection that the Branch is stronger than ever and that the old friendships will stand the test of many further years.

THE BOMBARDIER.

The Spring Golf Meeting

This Meeting was held at the Purley Downs Golf Club on the 12th May last, and attracted 54 members of the Branch. The trophy to be won was the 13th Wipers Cup, and there was also a prize for the "runner-up". The competition took the popular form of a points-scoring bogey competition.

There were a few early starters about 2 o'clock and contrary to what has happened in the past, it turned out this year that the first two returns provided the winner and second. Corporal C. Stroud (14) making a return of 40½, and Major L. Meakin (14) 39½.

The weather was beautifully fine, and the course in very good order considering the long drought; this exceptional weather has not always been provided by Purley Downs where we have often had wet and stormy conditions.

The supper which followed in the Club-house was delayed a little by the late arrival of the last Competitors and this delay is something which we shall avoid another time, but the Steward as usual provided a splendid supper.

In the unavoidable absence of the Chairman, Captain B. Smither, the President of the Branch, Major H. G. Harris, took the Chair, and presented the prizes, and for the first time not one single member failed to return his card, and in consequence there were no delinquents to explain why they had failed. The winner was able to satisfy the members by his explanation, and liquid refreshment supplied by him followed. Unfortunately the "runner-up" was not able to stay, so the Secretary spent some of his "sweep-money" for him.

A number of excellent stories were told, and so another enjoyable evening came to a close.

The Bombardier's Foursomes.

It is somehow usual to expect new records in the Branch in all its events, and pleasant to record that this year's entry is the biggest ever in the history of the Competition, numbering forty pairs. This comprises pairs from a wider selection of Courses than ever, and is the first time that Coulsdon Court, unfortunately, has no representatives owing to its compulsory acquisition; but its old members have issued their usual strong challenge from all the other courses that have since taken them in.

The first Battle was timed to commence at the beginning of summer time and actually on the day previous (April 9th) Operation Orders were received by all the competing Foursomes; the numbers are too big to report individual matches at length, but briefly, this is how the day went in the first Battle:—

Mutton and Duncan beat Frost and Green 6/4; the latter just could not go right.

Irens and Chorley beat Legg and Scott 6/5 on their own course, which is a little rude.

Stroud and Grutchfield w.o., Morgan and Liell scratched owing to Liell's engaging in 'flu.

Coe and Newman beat Hall and Nicholls 3/2; no frills, just efficiency.

Featherstone and Carr met the whole might of Scotland in Kerr and McFarlane, and just got away with it, winning 1 up; it was St. George's Day.

Way and Satchell beat Drynan and Carter 4/3 on their own course, showing what an influence the Treasurer must have.

Hancock and Simpson beat Boon and Knight 4/3, but no details as to the manner of it arrived.

Saul and Williamson beat Alderson and Meredith 2/1, and are understood to have had a fine match and a fine evening afterwards.

The second Battle:—

Mutton and Duncan beat Irens and Chorley 2/1 at Kingswood; a good win.

Coe and Newman met Stroud and Grutchfield the day after Stroud had won the 13th Ypres Cup, but his side could not produce the same form so they lost by 5/4.

Grant and Greig beat Salmon and Bell without disclosing the margin.

Green and Leck, last year's winners, beat Bennett and Pollard 2 up, at Woodcote Park.

Hines and Vaus beat Haine and Jackson 5/3; played on one of their own courses obviously rather ruthlessly.

Monk and Murray beat Squires and Cole 3/2 at home at Woodcote Park.

Smither and White beat Douse and Ashby 1 up; good for the Chairman.

Cox and Topley beat Humphery and Wever 7/6 at Woodcote; there was nothing more to be said.

Birrell and North beat Skade and Milne, but Milne says they were lucky—very lucky!

Pool and Bingham beat Wood and Ling; a runner came in with the result immediately.

Forster and Shelton beat last year's finalists Meakin and Wayte 3/2; a little late at that!

Baldwin and Jones w.o., Broadway and Jenkins scratched; the penalty of waiting until the last day when, of course, it rained hard.

Hazell and Parkes beat Crump and Smith 1 up Chipstead does favour the home side.

Davies and Randolph beat Harris and Streat; no margin declared, in fact very little news.

Way and Satchell beat Featherstone and Carr 2 up; finishing rather rudely with one putt on the last two greens.

Hancock and Simpson beat Saul and Williamson 2/1 one Sunday morning at Woodcote.

The third Battle:—

Mutton and Duncan beat Coe and Newman at Kingswood at the 19th; another wet evening.

Grant and Greig destroyed Green and Leck, last year's winners, 5/3, at Addington Palace.

Monk and Murray played scratch golf and beat Hines and Vaus 6/5 in a very cavalier fashion.

Smither and White beat Cox and Topley 1 up at Chipstead.

Pool and Bingham beat Birrell and North 3/2; no details supplied.

Forster and Shelton beat Baldwin and Jones 1 up; again a little late.

Davies and Randolph beat Hazell and Parkes 6/4.

Hancock and Simpson beat Way and Satchell at the 19th after being 3 down with 4 to go, on the enemy's course.

So these are the last eight, and their exploits in the 4th, 5th and 6th Battles will follow in a later bulletin.   THE ADJUTANT.

YPRES LEAGUE TRAVEL BUREAU

CONDUCTED PILGRIMAGES

Attention of members and friends is drawn to the remaining Conducted Pilgrimages for Season of 1938.

August Bank Holiday. July 30th—August 2nd.
  PILGRIMAGE TO YPRES.

September 17th—20th.
  PILGRIMAGE TO YPRES.

Prospectuses will be gladly forwarded on application to the Secretary, Ypres League, 20, Orchard Street, London, W.1.

THE BRITISH TOURING SERVICE

Manager—Mr. P. VYNER

**10, Station Square
ARRAS
(P.-de-C.) France**

Representative and Life Member, Ypres League

Cars for Hire, with British Driver Guides   Tours Arranged

HOTEL
Splendid & Britannique
YPRES

GRANDE PLACE Opposite Cloth Hall.

LEADING HOTEL FOR COMFORT AND QUALITY, AND PATRONIZED BY THE YPRES LEAGUE.

COMPLETELY RENOVATED

RUNNING WATER. BATHROOMS.

MODERATE TERMS. GARAGE.

Proprietor—Life Member, Ypres League.

YPRES
Skindles Hotel
(Opposite the Station)

Proprietor—Life Member, Ypres League

Branch at Poperinghe
(close to Talbot House)

EMBROIDERED BADGES.

These badges which can be suitably worn on pockets of sports jackets will be supplied on application to the Secretary, Ypres League, 20, Orchard Street, London, W.1. Price 4/- post free.

* * *

YPRES LEAGUE BADGE.

The design of the badge—a lion guarding a portcullis gate—represents the British Army defending the Salient, which was the gate to the Channel Ports.

The badge is brilliantly enamelled with silver finish. Price 2s., post free 2s. 1½d. (pin or stud, whichever is desired).

Obtainable from Secretary, Ypres League, 20, Orchard Street, W.1.

* * *

YPRES LEAGUE TIE.

Dark shade of cornflower blue relieved by a narrow gold stripe. In good quality silk,

Price 3/6d., post free.

Obtainable from Secretary, Ypres League 20, Orchard Street, London. W.1.

* * *

PHOTOGRAPHS OF WAR GRAVES.

The Ypres League is able to supply photographs (negative, and one print, postcard size, unmounted) of graves or memorials situated in the Ypres Salient, and in the Hazebrouck and Armentieres areas, at the price of 10s., each.

All applications for photographs should be sent to the Secretary, together with remittance, giving full regimental particulars of the soldier.

WREATHS

Arrangements are made by the Ypres League to place wreaths for relatives on the graves of British soldiers situated in France and Belgium on any day throughout the year.

The wreaths may be composed of natural flowers during the spring, summer and autumn months and obtained at the following prices— 10s. 6d., 12s. 6d., 15s. 6d., and 20s. During winter months only artificial wreaths, laurel, holly or poppies, can be supplied.

Wreaths are placed on graves and memorials by the League's Continental Representatives and photographs forwarded to relatives.

The above photograph depicts one of the many wreaths the Ypres League have placed on the graves of soldiers killed in the Great War, at the request of relatives and friends.

* * *

MODELS OF DEMARCATION STONE

Plaster models of the Demarcation Stone can be supplied from Head Office.

All members are aware that 240 granite demarcation stones stretch from the Swiss border to the sea, marking the extreme line of advance of the German invasion.

The model, which is 6 inches in height, may be used for a paperweight or as an ornament. Price 5s., post free in United Kingdom. Applications to the Secretary, Ypres League.

THE SIXTEENTH ANNUAL
RE-UNION OF MEMBERS AND FRIENDS

Organized by the London Branch Committee of the Ypres League,

WILL BE HELD AT THE

CAXTON HALL, CAXTON STREET, VICTORIA STREET, S.W.1.

ON

SATURDAY, OCTOBER 29th, 1938.

All Members of the Ypres League and their friends are cordially invited by the London Branch Committee to meet together at the Caxton Hall, when a

GRAND SMOKING CONCERT

will be given. The Chair will be taken by

The Chairman of the London Branch Committee.

General SIR CHARLES H. HARINGTON, G.C.B., G.B.E., D.S.O., President of the Ypres League hopes to be present.

An excellent Programme is being arranged

of which Members will be notified in due course.

DOORS OPEN AT 7 P.M.   CONCERT COMMENCES AT 7.30 P.M.

ADMISSION ... 5/-, 2/6 and 1/-.

Owing to the limited accommodation at the Hall reserved seating arrangements will be very restricted. The 5/- tickets will be automatically reserved and a certain number of 2/6 seats can be reserved on payment of 6d. extra per ticket. Application for reserved seats cannot be considered after October 17th.

Last year we had a record attendance and again this year we anticipate a full hall. Early application, therefore, accompanied by a remittance, should be sent to Hon. Secretary, London Branch Committee, c/o Ypres League, 20, Orchard Street, Portman Square, W.1.

YOUR SUPPORT ON OCTOBER 29th WILL BE APPRECIATED.

Branches and Corresponding Members

BRANCHES.

LONDON	Hon. Secretary to the London Branch Committee: J. Boughey, c/o 20, Orchard Street, London, W.1.
	TOTTENHAM AND EDMONTON DISTRICT—E. Glover, 191, Lansdowne Road, Tottenham, N.17.
COLCHESTER	H. Snow (Hon. Sec.), 2, Church Street.
	W. H. Taylor (Pilgrimage Hon. Sec.), 64, High Street.
LIVERPOOL	Captain A. M. Webster, Blundellsands.
PURLEY	Major Graham Carr, D.S.O., M.C., 112-114, High Street.
SHEFFIELD	Captain J. Wilkinson, "Holmfield," Bents Drive.
QUEENSLAND, Australia	Messrs. C. H. Green, and George Lawson, Essex House, (Opposite Anzac Square) Brisbane, Queensland.
CANADA	Ed. Kingsland, P.O. Box 83, Magog, Quebec.
SOUTH AFRICA	L. G. Shuter, 381, Longmarket Street, Pietermaritzburg
KENYA	C. H. Slater, P.O. Box 403, Nairobi.
BELGIUM	C. Leupe, Garage Shannon, Menin Gate.

CORRESPONDING MEMBERS.

GREAT BRITAIN.

ABERYSTWYTH	T. O. Thomas, 5, Smithfield Road
ASHTON-UNDER-LYNE	G. D. Stuart, "Woodlands,", Thronfield Grove, Arundel Street
BANBURY	Captain C. W. Fowke, Yew Tree House, King's Sutton.
BIRMINGHAM	Mrs. Hill, 191, Cattell Road, Small Heath.
	John Burman, "Greenfields," Hampton Lane, Solihull.
BRISTOL	W. S. Hook, "Wytschaete" Redland Court Road
BROADSTAIRS	C. E. King, 6, Norman Road, St. Peters, Broadstairs
CHATHAM	W. N. Channon, 22, Keyes Avenue.
CHESTERFIELD	Major A. W. Shea, 14, Cross Street.
CONGLETON	Mr. H. Dart, 61, The Crescent.
DARLINGTON	D. S. Vigo, 125, Dorset Road, Bexhill-on-Sea.
DERBY	T. Jakeman, 10, Graham Street.
DORRINGTON (Salop)	Captain G. D. S. Parker, Frodesley Rectory.
EXETER	Captain E. Jenkin, 25, Queen Street.
HERNE BAY	Captain E. Clarke Williams, F.S.A.A., "Conway," Station Road.
HOVE	Captain G. W. J. Cole, 2, Westbourne Terrace, Kingsway.
LEICESTER	W. C. Dunford, 343, Aylestone Road.
LINCOLN	E. Swaine, 79, West Parade.
LLANWRST	A. C. Tomlinson, M.A., Bod Estyn.
LOUGHTON	Capt. O. G. Johnson, M.A., Loughton School.
MATLOCK (Derby)	Miss Dickinson, Beechwood.
MELROSE	Mrs. Lindesay Kelsall, Darnlee.
NEW BRIGHTON (Cheshire)	E. F. Williams, 5, Waterloo Road.
NEW MILTON	W. H. Lunn, Greywell.

NOTTINGHAM	E. V. Brown, 3, Eldon Chambers, Wheeler Gate.
ST. HELENS (Lancs.) ...	John Orford, 124, Knowsley Road.
SHREWSBURY	Major-General Sir John Headlam, K.B.E., C.B., D.S.O., Cruck Meole, House, Hanwood.
TIVERTON (Devon) ...	Mr. W. H. Duncan Arthur, Surveyor's Office, Town Hall.
WELSHPOOL	Mr. E. Wilson, Coedway, Ford, Salop.

DOMINIONS AND FOREIGN COUNTRIES.

AUSTRALIA	R. A. Baldwin, c/o Government Savings Bank of N.S.W., Martin Place Sydney. Mr. W. Cloves, Box 1296, G.P.O., Adelaide. J. C. Correll, Port Vincent, South Australia.
BELGIUM	Sister Marguerite, Sacré Coeur, Ypres.
CANADA	Brig.-General V. W. Odlum, C.B., C.M.G., D.S.O., 2530, Point Grey Road, Vancouver. V. A. Bowes, 326, 40th Avenue West. Calgary, Alberta. W. Constable F. Grece, St. Hilaire Station, Ronville County, Quebec.
CEYLON	Captain F. R. G. Webb, M.C., Irrigation Bungalow, Kalmunai, E.P.
EGYPT	Captain B. W. Leak, M.I.E.E., Turf Club, Cairo.
INDIA	Lieut.-Quartermaster G. Smith, Queen's Bays. Sialkot, India.
IRELAND	Miss A. K. Jackson, Cloneyhurke House, Portarlington.
NEW ZEALAND ...	Captain W. U. Gibb, Ava Lodge, Puhinui Road, Papatoetoe, Auckland S. E. Beattie, P.O. Box 11, Otaki Railway, Wellington.
NEWFOUNDLAND ...	Captain Leo. Murphy, G.W.V.A. Office, St. John's.
NOVA SCOTIA ...	Will R. Bird, 35, Clarence Street, Amherst.
SOUTH AFRICA ...	H. L. Versfield, c/o Cape Explosives Works Ltd., 150, St. George Street, Cape Town.
SPAIN	Captain P. W. Burgess, Calle de Zurbano 29, Madrid.
U.S.A.	Captain Henry Maslin, 942, President Street, Brooklyn, New York L. E. P, Foot. 20, Gillett Street, Hartford, Conn., U.S.A. A. P. Forward, 449, East 80th Street, New York. J. W. Freebody, 945, McBride Avenue, Los Angeles.

Membership of the League

This is open to all who served in the Salient, and to all those whose relatives or friends died there, in order that they may have a record of that service for themselves and their descendants, and belong to the comradeship of men and women who understand and remember all that Ypres meant in suffering and endurance.

Life membership, £2 10s.

Annual members, 5s.

Do not let the fact of your not having served in the Salient deter you from joining the Ypres League. Those who have neither fought in the Salient nor lost relatives there, but who are in sympathy with the objects of the Ypres League, are admitted to its fellowship, but are not given scroll certificates.

There is a Junior Division for children whose relatives served in the Salient. It is open also to others to whom our objects appeal.

Annual subscription 1s. up to the age of 18, after which they can become ordinary members of the League.

Printed in Great Britain for the Publishers by FORD & GILL, 21a/23, Iliffe Yard, Crampton Street, London, S.E.17.

THE YPRES LEAGUE (INCORPORATED)
20, Orchard Street, Portman Square, W.1.

Telephone: WELBECK 1446.   *Telegrams*: YPRESLEAG, " WESDO," LONDON.

Patron-in-Chief: H.M. THE KING.

Patron:
H.R.H. PRINCESS BEATRICE.

President: GENERAL SIR CHARLES H. HARINGTON.

Vice-Presidents:

THE VISCOUNT WAKEFIELD OF HYTHE.   F.-M. SIR CLAUD W. JACOB.
F.-M. LORD MILNE.   F.-M. SIR PHILIP CHETWODE.
GENERAL SIR CECIL ROMER.   GENERAL SIR HUBERT GOUGH.

General Committee:

THE COUNTESS OF ALBEMARLE.   MR. E. GLOVER.
CAPTAIN C. ALLISTON.   *MAJOR H. G. HARRIS.
LIEUT-COLONEL BECKLES WILLSON.   MR. F. D. BANKES-HILL.
MR. HENRY BENSON.   MAJOR-GENERAL C. J. B. HAY.
*MR. J. BOUGHEY.   MR. J. HETHERINGTON.
*MISS B. BRICE-MILLER.   GENERAL SIR W. C. G. HENEKER.
COLONEL G. T. BRIERLEY.   *CAPTAIN O. G. JOHNSON.
CAPTAIN P. W. BURGESS.   MAJOR GENL. C. G. LIDDELL.
BRIG.-GENL. A. BURT.   *CAPTAIN H. D. PEABODY.
*MAJOR H. CARDINAL-HARFORD.   *THE HON. ALICE DOUGLAS PENNANT.
*MAJOR GRAHAM CARR.   *LIEUT.-GENERAL SIR W. P. PULTENEY.
REV. P. B. CLAYTON.   LIEUT.-COLONEL SIR J. MURRAY.
CAPTAIN G. E. DE TRAFFORD.   *COLONEL G. E. C. RASCH.
MRS. C. J. EDWARDS.   THE HON. SIR ARTHUR STANLEY.
MAJOR C. J. EDWARDS.   MR. ERNEST THOMPSON.
MR. H. A. T. FAIRBANK.   *MR. E. B. WAGGETT.
MR. T. ROSS FURNER.   CAPTAIN J. WILKINSON.
SIR PHILIP GIBBS.   CAPTAIN H. TREVOR WILLIAMS.

* Executive Committee.

Bankers: *Honorary Solicitors*:
BARCLAYS BANK LTD., Knightsbridge Branch.   MESSRS. FLADGATE & CO., 70, Pall Mall S.W.

Secretary: *Auditors*:
MAJOR L. J. L. PULLAR.   MESSRS. LEPINE & JACKSON, 6, Bond Court, E.C.4.

League Representative at Ypres:
Mr. C. LEUPE,
Garage Shannon, Porte de Menin.

League Representative at Amiens: **League Representative at Arras:**
CAPTAIN STUART OSWALD.   MR. P. VYNER,
7, Rue des Otages.   14, Rue Chanzy.

Hon. Secretary, Ypres British Settlement:
LT. COLONEL F. G. POOLE.

PRIMARY OBJECTS OF THE LEAGUE

I.—Commemoration and Comradeship.
II.—To provide special travel facilities for Members and all interested to Ypres and battlefields, and transport of Members.
III.—The furnishing of information about the Salient; marking of historic sites and the compilation of charts of the battlefields.
IV.—The erection of a Ypres British Church and School which has been completed.
V.—The establishment of groups of members throughout the world, through Branch Secretaries and Corresponding Members.
VI.—The maintenance of cordial relations with dwellers on the battlefields of Ypres.
VII.—The formation of a Junior Division.

The Ypres Times

Communications to
The Editor, "Ypres Times,"
22, Orchard Street, London, W.1

POST FREE
To all Members.

Vol. 9, No. 3.   Published Half-Yearly.   January, 1939.

Our Presidents

By Henry Benson, M.A.

Field-Marshal The Earl of Ypres.

The South African War.

(Continued from issue of July, 1938.)

THE immediate cause of the South African War was the ill-considered invasion of the Transvaal by Dr. Jameson and some 600 mounted men in 1895. Instead (as Jameson expected) of there being an armed rebellion of the voteless Europeans, or Uitlanders, as they were called—who formed a majority of the population—the farcical affair ended in the surrender of the little army and the sending of the famous—or rather infamous—telegram by the ex-Kaiser to President Kruger, congratulating him on his success.

Thus the match was applied to highly combustible material, and in 1899 the South African Republic and the Orange Free State broke into a blaze. On the 9th October, the Boer ultimatum was handed in, the chief demands being the withdrawal of troops which had reached South Africa since the 1st of the previous June, and the calling back of all troops then on their way.

The result was war, the invasion of Natal and Cape Colony by the enemy, and the unpreparedness of Great Britain.

A Self-Sacrificing Commander.

No sooner had General French arrived in South Africa than he proved himself a most valuable lieutenant to his superior officer, Sir George White, and he met with an immediate success in the battle of Elandslaagte. When Sir George decided not to evacuate Ladysmith—a town, incidentally, named after the writer's great-aunt—but to hold it, French managed to slip out by the last train. He made his escape lying under the seat of a carriage—a necessary precaution, because the train was fired at as it proceeded on its journey. He reached Pietermaritzburg, and was sent to protect Nauwport, an important junction which it was essential to hold if the central portion of the colony was not to be open to the enemy. Everywhere else disaster attended the British arms, but French by masterly tactics pushed the Boers back steadily without once giving battle.

With the beginning of February, 1900, the time had arrived for French, in accordance with instructions received from Lord Roberts, to make his preparations for the important share he was to take in the relief of Kimberley. He had shown extraordinary prowess on the field and done all that was expected of him, never sparing himself and setting a wonderful example to his men. On one occasion he did not so much as take off his boots for three days and three nights, but contented himself by snatching a brief interval of sleep when opportunity offered.

THE SURRENDER OF CRONJE.

Later in the same month, orders came from Lord Kitchener directing that French should set out and prevent Cronje, who was in retreat, from seizing the Paardeberg Drifts. That accomplished, and the enemy held in check until sufficient reinforcements were brought up, it was made possible for him to be surrounded.

The General and some 2,000 men, not particularly fresh but thoroughly determined, started at midnight on 17th February; the river was reached, and the enemy sighted. The guns were placed in position. Cronje, suddenly discovering his position, attempted to seize a hill, but was foiled. Then the Boers began to entrench their ground, and as they bent their backs to the task, the battle raged furiously. On the following morning, the British brigades had surrounded them.

French had stemmed the tide, but there were no fewer than 1,100 British dead and wounded. Next day, Roberts came up with additional men, Cronje's camp was bombarded and he was forced to surrender.

There is something truly noble in the words that Roberts spoke to the Boer general as he met him.

" I am glad to see you," he remarked. " I am glad to meet so brave a man."

" Wherever French has gone," wrote the late Sir Arthur Conan Doyle in his *Great Boer War*, " he has done well, but his crowning glory was the movement from Kimberley to head off Cronje's retreat."

THE SURRENDER OF BLOEMFONTEIN.

An advance on Bloemfontein, the capital of the Orange Free State, was the next item on the British military programme, and again French had an important part to play. The first movement was an attempt to envelop the Boers at Poplar Grove. It failed, largely on account of the slowness of the Cavalry Division; but although French was unable to cut the enemy's line of retreat, he was so far successful that he compelled De Wet to abandon an exceedingly strong position. " In war you can't expect everything to come out right," was the only comment made by Lord Roberts, recognising that French's troopers were fighting with tired horses and on all but empty stomachs.

Gradually, however, the British force drew nearer to Bloemfontein, and French not only secured a range of hills which almost commanded the town, but blew up a railway culvert, that prevented supplies from leaving the place before it was taken or capitulated. The latter alternative happened, and on 13th March, Bloemfontein surrendered to French, who had threatened to bombard it if the reply was in the negative.

A GREAT CAVALRY CAMPAIGN.

While Lord Roberts remained at Bloemfontein preparing to march on Pretoria, the capital of the Transvaal, French was busy securing the submission of the Boers outside the city. Everything perfected for the great advance, French's Division, which was attached to the Army of the Centre, left Bloemfontein in the first week of May, 1900, and good progress was made, the march being relieved from tediousness by intermittent skirmishes and the seizure of Diamond Drift, which opened the way to Kroonstad, the second capital of the Orange Free State.

On the 30th, French was at Driefontein, and Johannesburg surrendered. Giving his troops and horses but two days to rest, the General with his cavalry, forming to the left of the enemy, set out on the road to Pretoria, but while pressing forward to secure the Pietersburg railway, disarmed Boers informed him that Pretoria had fallen.

" Thus ended," said Mr. H. W. Wilson, the famous war correspondent, " the cavalry's great march of 280 miles from Kroonstad, a distance covered in a fortnight by horses overladen and in bad condition, with a uniform success and rapidity that cowed the Boers and reflected the utmost credit upon the active and daring General French."

A Fine Cavalry Leader.

To follow the guerilla campaign which was the closing phase of the South African War would require the whole of the pages of this issue of the "YPRES TIMES." It was not until the beginning of 1901 that Kitchener instituted the wonderful series of "drives" which eventually swept the enemy into his numerous nets. That in the Eastern Transvaal, the greatest of them all, was entrusted to French, who had seven columns for the task, starting from different points, but keeping in touch with each other. By the first week in April he had accomplished his work with complete success.

In June, French, worn in health but energetic as ever, was entrusted with similar sweeping operations in Cape Colony, where rebels were numerous and sedition plentiful. Finally, on the 31st May, 1902, peace was signed at Pretoria. Unlike so many of his colleagues holding high rank in the service, the General left South Africa with a greatly enhanced reputation. It was recognised beyond question that he was the first cavalry leader in the British Army.

Well-Merited Honours.

Like his chief, Lord Roberts, French was a commander in whom "Tommy Atkins" placed entire trust. In the trenches in France and Flanders soldiers who went through the Boer War were wont to relate those little personal anecdotes which so intimately reveal the type of man under whom they were serving. One of them has to do with certain happenings at Strydfontein at the close of an unusually exhausting day. After searching about for some considerable time, French and his staff found a house containing only one bed. The General willingly surrendered it to an officer. " I don't care where I sleep," he said, as he flung off his boots and stretched himself on the floor. And there he remained until the next morning.

While he was carrying on his notable work in South Africa, French was promoted to the rank of Major-General, and was mentioned in despatches many times. He was made a K.C.B. in 1900, K.C.M.G. in 1902, G.C.V.O. in 1905, and G.C.B. in 1909.

From 1901 until 1907, he commanded the 1st Army Corps, becoming in the latter year Inspector-General of the Forces and First Military Member of the Army Council, with the rank of General. These offices he retained until the " Curragh Episode," when he resigned. He became a Field-Marshal in 1913.

H.B.

(To be concluded.)

* * * * *

It's "Ieper" Now

MANY of the pilgrims who visited the battlefields of Belgium last summer under the auspices of the Ypres League were doubtless surprised and probably perplexed to find that the French names of the streets and railway stations at the holiday resorts on the littoral and throughout Western Flanders had disappeared.

Formerly, the names were prominently displayed both in French and Flemish, but the language question has once again become an acute and bitter political controversy, with the result that last spring orders were given that the French names were to be removed and only the Flemish to remain.

On the station platform at Ypres, for example, the familiar " Ypres " has given place to the purely Flemish, " Ieper," and the tortuous street, "Rue Au Beurre," which winds its way to the Menin Gate, has become " Boterstraat."

The alteration also applies to the Government discs officially used in the local post-offices for the cancellation of letters and similar purposes.

It may be added that the step has the full support of the majority of the local population, who are anxious to suppress the use of the French language in every way. On the other hand, some of the bourgeoisie, realising what a handicap an ignorance of French would be to their children in after-life, are sending them to schools in Lille and elsewhere, in Northern France.

"English Spoken" Police Badge.

A Union Jack in miniature on the left arm of a gendarme at Ostend denotes "English Spoken." This was an innovation during the season of 1938, which British tourists, whose knowledge of French and Flemish is limited, have found both useful and welcome.

H.B.

* * * * *

The Fourteenth Division

First Annual Re-union and Dinner.

Lord Nuffield's Generous Gift.

NEVER was the familiar adage, "Better late than never," more appropriately exemplified than on Friday evening, 25th November, when the late 14th Division B.E.F. (France), held its *first* annual re-union and dinner.

The function took place at the Allenby (Services) Club, High Holborn, the chair being occupied by Lord Gorell—probably better known to the majority of those present as Major Barnes—and among others supporting him was the genial Rev. P. B. ("Tubby") Clayton of "Toc H."

The company totalled about 90, and a thoroughly enjoyable evening was spent. Reminiscences were exchanged and acquaintanceships renewed, the gathering demonstrating once again that friendships formed in the mud of Flanders stand the test of time.

Naturally, the name of Gilbert Talbot, 7th Rifle Brigade, and "Toc H.," Poperinghe, founded in his memory, figured prominently in the speeches. The Rifle Brigade was well represented, but it is hoped that next year there will be a stronger muster of "Gunners."

A special greeting was extended to Serjt. Arthur Rainbow, M.M., the "baby" of the party, who responded to the country's call in the first year of the War at the early age of sixteen, and saw continuous service until after the conclusion of hostilities.

It was decided to make the re-union an annual function, and the next dinner was provisionally fixed for October, 1939. Full particulars may be obtained from Mr. St. J. C. Shepherd, "St. Hilda's," Lampitts Hill Lane, Corringham, Essex.

£3,000 From Lord Nuffield.

It should be mentioned that shortly before Christmas, Lord Nuffield, with characteristic generosity, sent £3,000 to the Veteran's Association, which owns and administers the Allenby (Services) Club for ex-Servicemen. The gift will enable the Association to pay off the balance of the mortgage in connection with the reconstruction and enlargement of the club as the national memorial to the late Viscount Allenby. Ex-Servicemen are provided by the Association with a residential club, financial help, clothing and an employment bureau.

H.B.

Ypres Day, 1938

THE Eighteenth Annual Commemoration of the Ypres League was held on October 30th last, on the Horse Guards' Parade, St. James's Park, London, and was attended by the largest gathering since its inauguration.

Once again the "Old Contemptibles" formed the backbone of the parade, turning out in strength, and with their twenty banners presented an imposing sight

Another outstanding feature of the parade was the greatly increased attendance of the Public Schools' O.T.C. Contingents; who numbered about 250 strong as against a score in previous years. Their smartness on parade and general turn-out was very favourably commented on by the distinguished General Officers present and their officers were subsequently congratulated, one by one, by his Excellency the Belgian Ambassador.

Congratulations were also offered to Major J. M. West, of Shrewsbury School, whose keenness and energy was so largely responsible for marshalling such a parade of Cadets.

Ex-Servicemen from the Queen's Westminster Rifles—7th City of London Regiment—the Fifth Army—19th Div. Artillery O.C.A.—the 85th Club (R.A.M.C.)—the Ypres League—St. Dunstans—Chelsea Pensioners—ladies of the Ypres League and other Associations supported the "Old Contemptibles" and the uniformed troops, in the hollow square formation.

Among the guests of the Ypres League were:—His Excellency the Belgian Ambassador, Captain de Brantes (representing the French Ambassador), Major Samuel Greenwell (representing H.E. the American Ambassador), Colonel Ruggeri-Laderchi (representing the Italian Ambassador), the Military Attaché (representing H. E. the Portuguese Ambassador, D. James Davies, Esq (the Commissioner for Newfoundland), H. Rainsford Gordon, Esq. (representing the Commissioner for South Africa), Lieut.-General the Baron Vincotte (Military Attaché the Belgian Embassy), Lieut.-General Sir William Pulteney, G.C.V.O., etc. (Chairman of the Ypres League), the Dowager Viscountess Plumer, Mrs. E. H. Gibson (representing the League of Remembrance), Colonel L D. Henderson, C.M.G., Colonel Maurice Browne, M.C., Major A. Dunton, M.C. (representing the Royal Chelsea Hospital), Major J. M. West (representing the Public Schools' O.T.C.), Captain A. G. D. Denoon, M.C. representing the Seaforth Highlanders), and Captain J. H. Miller (the Seaforth Highlanders), who marshalled the distinguished guests.

The Service commenced with "Land of Hope and Glory," sung as a solo by Mrs. Pullar, wife of Major L. J. L. Pullar, M.C., Secretary of the Ypres League, the gathering joining very heartily in the chorus. After leading the Parade in prayer, the Rev. Dr. Joseph Lynn, C.B.E., Hon. Chaplain to H.M. the King and Deputy Chaplain-General to the Forces, addressed the assembly as follows:—

Comrades of the Ypres League and other friends—

We are met again to-day on the 24th Anniversary of that great day when the 'Old Contemptibles' stemmed the mob in Ypres and saved the day for England. Round this day, centre the activities of our League, as this the Symbol of all that WE stand for in our Association, which was practically the first Ex-Servicemen's Association formed after the war.

This then is chiefly a day of Commemoration of the Defence of Ypres, where over a quarter of a million British soldiers gave their lives with their backs to the wall during the four years of the Great War, that they might protect our Country. In the Salient the Old Contemptibles exhibited a wonderful heroism, which has rarely been paralleled in British military history, and which provided a standard for Kitchener's Army and the great National Army which took their place as well as for the Territorial Army. We would fail in our duty if we did not pay our respect to them and to their memory.

For those of us who have been spared to see this day, it is also a day of Comradeship, on which we can once more stand shoulder to shoulder with those who, like us, fought the good fight. But this comradeship is perhaps best shown in the work carried on by the League in helping to find employment for those of its members, who have fallen on evil days, and in securing for them, whenever possible, more generous provision through pensions for their needs.

No Ex-Serviceman or relative, who has appealed to the League for advice, is ever turned away without every attempt being made to assist him. This is a very practical example of the value of comradeship, and one which deserves the interest of all members.

But there is one other aspect of the work of the League, which should not be forgotten—its charity, in helping to provide for the visits each year of poor pilgrims to the Graves and memorials of their lost sons and relatives. Only poor widows and mothers are considered, although arrangements are made for all others to proceed at very reasonable charges, in organised bodies.

These women are brought from their homes, often as far afield as Scotland, and back again at no expense to them. For this work an appeal is made to the members of the League, its supporters, and to the general public in order that no deserving person may be refused. Indeed the Ypres League itself needs and deserves much more financial support than it receives, and as, being a small body, is in danger of being forgotten around the many other claims upon the purses of our people. Strict economy is practised, but if the League is to survive, not only to pay tribute to the glorious deeds of the past, but also to make its contribution to the present, and hand down its traditions to our children, it should—indeed must—receive more support.

The " Lament," played by pipers of the 1st Scots Guards, under their Pipe-Major, followed Dr. Lynn's address and greatly stirred all present. The Pipers were in full dress, as were the two buglers who subsequently blew the " Last Post." They and the Pipers had journeyed up from Windsor, by kind permission of Lieut.-Colonel G. L. Tyringham, the Commanding Officer of the 1st Scots Guards.

On conclusion of the Service on the Horse Guards Parade ground, the assembly marched to the Cenotaph, led by the Pipers, the O.T.C. contingents and the " Old

Photo]   *[Photo News.*
Captain D. W. Belcher, V.C., Captain W. C. Boulter, V.C., and Corporal A. Wilcox, V.C., with the Ypres League Wreaths.

One of the twenty "Old Contemptibles" standards at the Parade.

Contemptibles," and on arrival there units formed up on three sides and, amidst an impressive silence, the three V.C. heroes present, handed the Ypres League wreath to the Dowager Viscountess Plumer (who was deputising for H.R.H. the Princess Beatrice), and Lady Plumer, assisted by his Excellency the Belgian Ambassador, laid the wreath on the Cenotaph.

The units then returned to the Horse Guards Parade, led by the band of the 35th Anti-Aircraft Battalion, who "played" them all the way. They were in attendance again this year by kind permission of their Commanding Officer, Lieut.-Colonel R. C. Foot, M.C. On forming close column, the units and contingents were inspected by his Excellency the Belgian Ambassador and Lieut.-General Sir William Pulteney, the latter not failing to recognise and say a few words to all comrades who fought under him in both the South African and the Great War.

After the "Dismissal," a delegation proceeded to Westminster Abbey for the purpose of laying a second Ypres League wreath upon the Tomb of the 'Unknown Warrior.' The delegation was welcomed by the Rev. Canon Barry, D.D., etc., and then the wreath was deposited on the Tomb by Major F. B. Waggett, C.B.E., etc., from his invalid chair. After the placing of the wreath Canon Barry gave the following address:—

"Lady Plumer, Major Waggett, and all of you members and friends of the Ypres League—

"It is my privilege on behalf of the Dean and Chapter once again this year to accept the wreath which you have brought to this Perpetual Shrine of Memory in immemorial remembrance and honour of those who endured and suffered in defence of the Salient and in the hardships and ardours at Ypres. Year by year you have come, and as the years go by we of that generation are getting older than we were and we are now in the minority of the population of this country, and the younger people wonder, not fully understanding quite what it is that we observe in this annual Commemoration, and why, as it seems to them, that we have, to be looking back and not looking forward. But what we went through in those years must always be for us who shared in them the decisive experience of our lives, and we do not think that our memories are merely sentiment, for we learnt there some secret of brotherhood in service, by which we believe that the world may be saved. The ideal of brotherhood in arms is one which we hope by God's mercy our world is outgrowing. A brotherhood in service and in mutual responsibility that ideal is imperishable, and we dare to offer it sometimes in the House of God and to claim for it the blessing of Christ.

"During the last few weeks torturing thoughts have haunted the minds of all of us whether that sacrifice has been made in vain. I think we can answer confidently that it was not. Within the hearts of the unknown people, the unknown soldiers of every nation, there is rising still an anxious desire for a world of peace in which men and women can live and work together as one family at the real tasks of life, and there is no doubt that among the changes that will make for the peace of the world at last none is so strong as that we have learnt together something not only of the dreadful causes of war, but something of the discipline and brotherhood of loyalty and consecration, which are the last and richest resources of the people.

"So in this year of crisis, which has meant for a number of us such a searching of our souls, we come again to the Abbey to pay our tribute to the representative of those known and unknown warriors of every nation who were brought into the storm of the World War.

"We pray and hope for all those unknown workers of every nation who are seeking to build a world of peace."

Before concluding, reference must be made to the following account which appeared in the *Daily Sketch* on Monday, the 31st October, for which acknowledgment is hereby made:—

Standing in the misty rain before the Cenotaph yesterday morning I found a "little old lady" looking at a bunch of flowers she had just placed on the cold slab, writes a *Daily Sketch* reporter.

There were tears in her eyes. In the distance the wailing of the pipes of the Scots Guards and the tramping of ex-Servicemen died away down Whitehall.

"Beside that beautiful wreath this seems so poor," she whispered to me.

And together we looked at the great blue-and-white Ypres League wreath, fragrant with carnations and chrysanthemums, which had just been laid on the Cenotaph.

Then she stepped forward and laid her bunch of small brown chrysanthemums at the foot of the great wreath.

"My husband was killed at Ypres . . ." she told me later. "I am Mrs. Ethel Graham, from Australia. I've come all the way here, travelling steerage, so that I could be at the Cenotaph on Ypres Day."

She smiled sadly. "That was 21 years ago, the battle of Ypres. Twenty-one years of loneliness. Thank God we have peace to-day!"

Her eyes grew sad again. I knew she was thinking of the young upright youths in the O.T.C. units who had listened to the "Lament" of the pipes.

"Let's pray there won't be another war." she whispered, and walked slowly away.

* * * * *

Obituary
Major E. B. WAGGETT

WE deeply regret to announce the death of Major Ernest Blechynden Waggett, C.B.E., D.S.O., V.D., etc., Vice-Chairman of the Ypres League and one of its greatest supporters. His loss will be most keenly felt not only by the Ypres League and other kindred ex-Servicemen's Associations but by the whole medical fraternity, for Major Waggett had a most distinguished medical career. He was particularly notable for a courageous decision that was to save him much suffering and which was of inestimable value to the medical profession. A few years ago he was suffering intolerable agony in his legs, so he decided to have them amputated, which gave him relief and restored him to almost normal health. He very nobly and calmly recorded his sensations of the pain endured and subsequent operations so that science might benefit. Major Waggett very rarely failed to attend the meetings of the Ypres League Committee, of which he was Vice-Chairman, and his advice and practical help was ever forthcoming when needed.

A Requiem at All Saint's, St. Margaret's Street, London, W., was held on Saturday morning, the 7th January last, when over five hundred people attended, including many distinguished surgeons, physicians, soldiers and others.

A Personal Tribute

The following tribute from the pen of Captain G. de Trafford, M.C., will be of interest to our readers:—

The late Major E. B. Waggett was Vice-Chairman of the Ypres League during the time it was my honour to act in the capacity of Secretary of the Association from May 1925 to July 1936.

My constant co-operation with the Major proved his sound judgment on all matters the Committee or myself desired to consult him for the welfare and prestige of the League and above all his friendship.

Efficiency and straightforwardness were the interpretations of his demeanour and, indeed, testimony of his labours.

To me, his regular attendances at the League Committee Meetings, and personal attention to detail in the various departments of the work was a very great support when taking into account his distinguished medical career, and the innumerable important tasks in other spheres with which his life was so closely associated, and yet, while engaged in League affairs he conveyed the impression that it was "the one job that mattered" and to which he was giving his best.

The fact that he allowed his patronage of the Meetings and interest to continue, despite intense suffering, and after the amputation of both legs was characteristic of his indomitable enthusiasm.

On the occasion of the last Annual General Meeting it was my pleasure to attend in company with Major Pullar, neither of us can ever forget his generous appreciation of my humble endeavours coupled with a sincerely encouraging welcome to my successor.

Major Waggett's passing must be an incredibly severe loss to the Ypres League, but he has taught an example that may be hard, nevertheless precious to follow.

G. E. de TRAFFORD.

* * * * *

Light and Shade at the Front

By an Ex-R.B.

IN FANCY'S GUISE.
(*Circa: The Great War.*)

WELL, I suppose I 'ad better be my own Master of the Ceremonies an' introjuce meself, because if I don't 'ow are you to know who I am or what I am? You all know what a pack is? That's what I am; the pack! Not the butcher; the block!

No, I don't look too bright just at the moment but I don't expect to, not in the line. *Out* of the line is when you ought to see me if you want to see a smart turn-out, or better still, when I was a new issue, canvas and straps brand-new an' buckles as bright as a new coin from the mint. It's a surprisin' fact though, although you mightn't think it, but a new pack isn't always popular an' the reason is that it *is* stiff an' it takes time to get set. It's like a pipe that you're used to; you don't like a new one so well. But mind you there's an art in packin' a pack as you'll find out for yourself at the first start-off. Take a dekko at a greatcoat khaki an' then at the pack it 'as got to go into an' naturally you'll say, "Why, it's like tryin' to put a gallon into a pint can!" But when the coat is folded in a certain way an' *dropped* into the pack, not squeezed in, you'll see that packin' a coat is one of the arts of soldierin'; what is more I say that when a lucky lad can pack 'is coat like that 'e 'as in 'im the makings of a soldier.

What 'as the pack to do with soldierin'? The pack 'as a lot to do with it. For one thing nimble 'ands make a nimble 'ead and a nimble 'ead is something more than an ornament as soon as a lad finds 'imself in the line. One ounce of practice in the line is worth a ton of it on the barrack square. Wait till 'e 'ears a thumpin' great Jack Johnson a-waltzin' near 'is fairy feet; strike-a-light! 'e'll be nimble enough, not 'alf 'e won't!

Of course, barrin' Quarter Guard, if you want to see the pack at its best you must turn out on Battalion Parade—"Marker-r-rs, Steady!" Once when Tommy an' me was on a Battalion Parade we watched the Colonel gallopin' 'is fiery charger up an' down the field while the Companies marched up an' were dressed into alignment. Suddenly 'e calls out : " h'Orderly, hold my horse, please ! " an' then 'e dismounted for the inspection while the band played dreamy tunes. After we 'ad waited a tidy while the Colonel and 'is staff reached the rear of our rank an' walked slowly along it till they came to Tommy an' then they stopped. Presently an officer gave me a push 'ere, a poke there, an' then 'e tugged at a buckle, after which the Colonel and 'is officers stood talkin'. Thinks I, " This doesn't look too good ; it's Tommy for the 'igh jump ! " But it wasn't ! Better to be born lucky than rich. No, the pack isn't always carried. F'rinstance, " Dress, walking-out ; " belt polished extra bright an' a cane. An' assumin' that you 'ave plenty of what our Major spoke of when we was in France, *esprit de corps*, which means 'aving a pride in your regiment, *I'm* tellin' you that you'll buy a cane that 'as a solid silver mount !

Well, as to soldierin' bein' a gentleman's life, why, I dessay that it is—sometimes. P'raps it is in the early days when you are in barracks or in huts, when you can get plenty of buckshee in the canteen an' you 'ave a pleasant time walkin' out in the evenin's. An' the same remark applies to instruction, musketry instruction, when the platoon are out seated on the grass before tea an' you can 'ear the bugles a-practisin' a field or two away. The instructor speaks quietly, no shoutin' : " . . . being careful to take a six o'clock aim take the first pressure of your trigger and then fire, and if you have judged your range correctly you will hit the object at which you have aimed." Easy, just like that. Of course it's diff'rent at bay'net practice ; then it's all energy an' action ; " IN ! OUT ! ON GUARD ! " Doublin' with fixed sword ! " LOOK FIERCE AND GRIT YOUR TEETH ! " " Forward ! Long point ! Short point ! " an' at it you go 'ard at the innards of the old straw dummy. " ON AGAIN ! " an' away you go full pelt at a six-foot trench, jumpin' down one side an' scramblin' up the other. Naturally in givin' orders the instructors' voices are adjusted accordin'.

No, those days will never come back. " Come to the cookhouse door, boys ! Come to the cookhouse door ! " Hurrah ! RISSOLES FOR BREAKFAST ! Give the old squire three 'earty cheers ! Hurrah ! hurrah ! hur—— But listen ! what's the old squire sayin' ? Let 'im speak ! " …and so on second thoughts I think it best to put 'em back in the old oak chest because——" What a shabby trick ! Look, 'ere comes the Orderly Officer ! " ORDERLY OFFICER ! ANY COMPLAINTS ! " An' at that a lance-jack stands up to attention an' 'e ses : " Sir ! about these 'ere rissoles. . . ." While 'e was talkin' the Orderly Officer stood listenin' calm, cool an' collected—the SOLDIER'S GUIDE BOOK, boys ! " In all times of doubt, difficulty and danger keep calm, cool and collected "—an' presently 'e ses, " Hum ! " (Strike-a-light ! they wasn't 'alf hummin' an' all !) " fetch the Q.M.S., an' when 'e 'ad had a talk with the Q.M.S. e ses : " There is nothing the matter with these rissoles ; what you notice about them is the flavouring. However, the rissoles are being taken away and cheese will be issued in their stead." An' so rissoles it wasn't an' cheese it was.

For the Front at last ! " Wake up Charley, get your hat and jacket on ! " and nobody was slow at showin' a leg. Blanket rolled on pack an' two days' rations—" All present and correct, Sir ! " The Colonel inspected the parade ; 'e was tall an' spare in build, an' 'ad a white mustache, an' 'aving seen 'is first Foreign Service many years ago 'e addressed a few words to the troops before they marched off : " You are going away now," 'e ses, " to fight for your King and Country. When you are in action, as no doubt you will be before long, always obey orders quite regardless of difficulties or of odds. Do your duty well and in all that you do prove yourselves to be good soldiers, and in that way not only will you maintain, you will also help to augment, the traditions of your regiment." 'E paused for a moment or two an' then 'e said in a measured sort of way, " Some of you will not come back." Only natural. One of the last of that parade doubled up early one misty mornin' ; thud ! thud ! thud ! pounded the shells an' just before 'e reached the post up went a tree stump in the air. It is not always the 'eat of the sun that makes the sweat stand out on a man's face in big drops, an' a resolute man at that ! " Where's the Company Officer?" 'e called out, an' after giving 'is message an' doublin' away agen 'e never came back.

BANG-BANG-BANG! on the drum an' away through the town. It seemed funny to be passin' all the old places, p'raps for the last time, but the troops soon get used to losin' old faces an' to meetin' with new ones. Nor do they think o' the future because what's the use of it when, as often 'appens in action, a fellow is goin' to be lucky if 'e sees to-day out? True, 'ere an' there a lad *is* careful about the future an' on the eve of a big action 'e will make out what 'e calls 'is Last Will and Testyment, but Sanferian! why, that's worse than paradin' for your next-of-kin! Down on the platform the troops danced to "The girl I left be'ind me;"

"Oh, ne'er shall I forget the night,
 The stars were bright above me,
 And gently shed their silv'ry light
 When first she vowed to love me:"

"The dirty old man 'e washed 'is pan in 'alf a pint of wa-ter, an' then 'e did a mike for a week because 'e thought that 'e ough-ter." These 'ere songs on Foreign Service are all right:

"Jenny, my own true loved one
 Wait till the clouds roll by!"

But what about when the bold soldier boy 'as done "carvin' 'is way to glory?" Will the bright flame that lighted 'is departure 'ave been quenched by the doubts of War's uncerta'nties? Explain meself? What do I mean? Why, when 'e comes back will 'is Jenny then revive the tender blossom of 'er love? All right, I'm only askin'! Because that's the right sort o' Jenny.

No, as I've already said the pack isn't always carried but even so it manages to see a fairish bit of action. It's all much of a muchness, though; either you wind up as a casualty or else you do not, an' seein' that soldierin' is a trade, just like any other trade, the old pack don't look to open up much about "shop." Any more, f'rinstance, than a plumber at 'is Union's Annual Ball is expected to talk about the burst pipes an' the leaky valves that 'e 'as been called in to mend. Granted, some things in action you do notice in partic-lar; f'rinstance, the cavalry who fell in action one mornin' on the Arras front—"Last noon beheld them full of lusty life!"—as the day waned their lifeless forms were slowly hidden by the shades of night, an' as the day reawakened there they lay, 'orses an' men extended on the snow in their last sleep. One afternoon, as an officer was makin' 'is way along a Y'pres trench 'e stooped down to look at the face of a man who 'ad been killed; "Who is this?" 'e asked; it was one of the Batt. we 'ad just relieved. It is the small things that you notice. "How is the attack going?" asked an officer; this to another officer who passed by the troops with a wound in 'is arm; "We are held up by machine-gun fire!" I dessay you 'ave 'eard of the weakling who suffered as a result of 'is two strong neighbours bein' at war? The same thing 'appened to the rations one mornin' followin' a raid: "Look!" ses one of the lads, "this 'ere rooty ain't 'alf been through it!" "rooty" o' course bein' our name for bread.

(*To be continued.*) J. EDWARDS.

* * *

Ypres British School

Extract from Ninth Annual Report.

The Annual Prize-giving took place on July 16th, 1938, when Lieut-General Sir William Pulteney, G.C.V.O., K.C.B., K.C.M.G., etc., kindly attended to distribute the books. Sir William was warmly applauded by the parents and children and subsequently thanked by Mr. O. L. Gill, M.B.E., for his continued generous support and interest in the School.

The year has witnessed large scale developments in the School, the Roll of which has continued in the neighbourhood of 100—never being less than ninety-seven. Twenty-five new children have been enrolled, seven of whom are attending their first school. The attendance has been good and the health of the children has been generally sound. The physique has improved owing to increase of

Cricket, Football and in particular Netball. The School are now proud possessors of twelve footballs, given by individual members of the Ypres League and the 11th Lewisham Battalion of the Royal West Kent Regiment. The children are in consequence better exercised and happier, and improvement in games is most noticeable.

Much has been done during the year past to stock the School as an English school at home and also to provide well-balanced Class libraries. One thousand school books have been taken into use and for the first time complete sets of Geography, History and Arithmetic books are available.

In their first year of office the Principals have striven to fix firmly the fundamentals of Primary Education—not forgetting the important art of speaking sense distinctly. At the same time individual interests have been encouraged and developed and in 1939 they intend to press for a further intensification of the academic work and an increase of interest, enthusiasm and skill in the Crafts.

* * *

League Secretary's Notes

During the latter half of 1938 circumstances with which we are all familiar had an adverse effect on our Association. Activity in the Travel Bureau practically ceased, a number of members lapsed in their subscriptions and there was a considerable falling off in donations. During this period our headquarters had already been committed to a removal to less expensive premises but which necessitated certain expenditure by way of refitting the new offices. In consequence of the new and difficult position it was decided to call a Special Meeting of the Committee to consider the financial situation and the League's future. The meeting took place in November last when it was decided to effect still further economies in the League's administration and under this axe fell the head of our popular little journal, the "Ypres Times." While maintaining its high standard it was resolved, for the time being, to reduce its pages to sixteen. In the meantime a Special Appeal for funds was made through our Chairman to all Life Members, which met with an immediate and encouraging response. Further Committee Meetings were held in December and January and, at the latter, the Auditors' Report and Balance Sheet was discussed.

We earnestly trust that each one of our loyal supporters will appreciate the position when their copies are received and that the curtailed issue means a considerable saving of expense to the League. It is hoped very much that we may shortly be in a position to revert to the old standard "Ypres Times," and for the present we crave our readers' indulgence.

* * *

Branch Notes

COLCHESTER & DISTRICT BRANCH.

Re-union Dinner.

The Sixth Annual Re-union Dinner of the Branch was held at the George Hotel, Colchester, on Thursday, November 17th, 1938, and proved a most successful function. Under the Chairmanship of Lieut.-Colonel H. W. Herring, M.C., a company of over seventy assembled for the occasion and the chief guest of the evening was the Mayor of Colchester, Councillor H. H. Fisher, J.P.

From Headquarters came the League Secretary, Major L. J. L. Pullar, M.C., and whose presence was much appreciated.

The Toasts of the evening were brief, the only speech of any length being that of Major Pullar's in response to the Toast of 'The Ypres League'. The company listened with great interest as he recounted the great work performed by the League and its Branches since its inception. Members present were delighted to learn also of the new Branch formed in Queensland, Australia, under the Chairmanship of Lieut.-Colonel Sir Donald Cameron, K.C.M.G., D.S.O.

As on previous occasions the duties of Toastmaster were ably carried out by Mr. S. C. Nixon and his services were greatly appreciated. To the delight of the Company appropriate music was rendered during the Dinner by Frank Baynton's Trio and later in the evening entertainment was provided by Messrs Cowper and Jones (melody and mirth) Mr. C. D. Dennis (Piano Accordion) and Mr. J. Holt (Piano). In addition the Company were entertained and immensely amused by the Branch's own impromptu Concert Party under the leadership of Captain E. F. Matthews, M.B.E.

The evening was undoubtedly a great success and with a record number attending the

Officials are encouraged in the belief that the occasion augurs well for the future of the Branch.

Armistice Day Memorial Service.

The Chairman, Lieut.-Colonel H. W. Herring, M.C., accompanied by a representative party of the Colchester and District Branch, attended the Service of Remembrance at the Colchester War Memorial on Armistice Day, 1938. Prior to the Sounding of the 'Last Post' by the 2nd Batt. The Somerset Light Infantry, and the observance of the two minutes 'silence' The Right Worshipful the Mayor of Colchester (Councillor H. H. Fisher, J.P.) uttered the following short prayer:—"In remembrance of those who made the great sacrifice, O God, make us better men and women, and give peace in our time". Following 'Reveille' and the singing of a Hymn the Mayor then delivered a Prayer and Address. The Blessing was subsequently bestowed by the Right Revd. The Lord Bishop of Colchester and the many beautiful wreaths were then placed on the Memorial. Accompanied by Mr. H. Snow and Mr. H. Shaw, the Chairman placed a wreath on behalf of the Branch.

Annual Ball.

For this jolly and popular annual event over two hundred members and friends assembled at the George Hotel, Colchester, on December 8th, 1938, and very few left before the finish at 2 a.m. Parties were brought by the Chairman, Lieut.-Colonel H. W. Herring, M.C., the Vice-Chairman, Major G. C. Benham, M.C., Captain C. Vinson; Captain M. Leach, M.C., G. C. Stanford, Esq; H. G. V. Rumball; M. McKinley, Esq., and M. O'Halloran, Esq. There was lively competition for the prizes ultimately presented to the lucky winners by Mrs. H. W. Herring, wife of the Chairman.

The Ball Committee, Messrs. D. Shadrach, M. McKinley, S. Farran and W. H. Taylor with Major G. C. Benham as Chairman, are to be heartily congratulated on the admirable arrangements made for the reception of so goodly a muster. Such good staff work could not have resulted in the occasion being other than what it proved to be, a tremendous success.

* * * *

PURLEY BRANCH.

Armistice Sunday Parade.

There was a very good attendance of the Branch at the Annual Parade held on the occasion of the Armistice Sunday Service in the afternoon of Sunday, November 6th. The Party numbering nearly 50 marched under the C.O., Captain B. Smither, to the Purley Congregational Church where a United Memorial Service was held in which the Churches of all denominations took part.

The arrangements made this year omitted a Sermon altogether but a very impressive Service was arranged and once more we remembered and honoured the Fallen.

Fifth Annual Ball.

On Friday, November 18th, the Greyhound Hotel, Croydon, was again the rendezvous for some 300 members of the Purley Branch and their guests for the Annual Dance. The Ballroom was delightfully decorated and on the back of the stage was to be seen the badge of the League and blue and gold were the colours of the decorations. Tom Newman and his Band provided music, and the Members and their friends made merry with their usual zest.

This is one of those evenings which does not take any time to warm up: the Members bring some kind of cheery spirit with them which warms the air at the moment they arrive and the evening goes with a bang straight away.

In such a wonderful company it is impossible to mention the names of those present, but the Branch was delighted to have Major L. J. L. Pullar, M.C., and Mrs. Pullar as their guests. The Chairman, Captain B. Smither had a large party and was supported by his Committee. As usual the arrangements were made by a Sub-Committee of which Captain R. L. Haine, V.C., M.C., is Chairman and the arrangements for dancing as well as rationing (both wet and dry), left little to be desired.

No Cabaret appeared this year for the first time and most Members appeared to approve this innovation as they preferred to have all the time available for dancing.

2 a.m. arrived all too soon and this wonderful evening was over for another year.

* * * *

LONDON BRANCH COMMITTEE.

Annual Smoking Concert.

The Sixteenth Annual Re-union Smoking Concert, arranged by the London Branch Committee, Ypres League, was held on October 29th, 1938, at Caxton Hall, London, S.W.1, and as usual was supported in strength. In the chair was our newly-elected and popular Branch Chairman, Captain O. G. Johnson, M.A., and gracing the High Table with him were His Excellency the Belgian Ambassador, Baron E. de Cartier de Marchienne, Lieut-General Sir William Pulteney, G.C.V.O., K.C.B., D.S.O., and representatives from the Colonies and Dominions, France and America.

The programme, well presented and enjoyed by all, was provided by the Roosters Concert Party, and the war years of 1914-18 were recalled when the artists entertained us with a series of sketches. During the evening a telegram was received from our Patron-in-Chief, His Majesty The King, thanking all members present for their loyal assurances and wishing the Assembly a jolly evening. The telegram was in reply to the message previously addressed to His Majesty.

"To His Majesty The King, their Patron-in-Chief.

"Members of the Ypres League assembled at their Annual Re-union beg to send expressions of their unfailing loyalty, devotion and homage."

A telegram was also received from His Excellency The American Ambassador, which the Chairman was pleased to read to the Assembly.

Captain Johnson, in making his first speech to members as Chairman of the Branch, spoke of the great loss sustained by the Branch and the Association generally by the death of Major E. Montague Jones, O.B.E., M.A., since the last Re-union. He felt that members could honour his memory in no better way than by striving their very best to obtain new members and so add strength to the Ypres League for whom Major Montague Jones had himself done so much and for whose cause he had so much at heart.

Space forbids a fuller report on this Re-union but suffice it to say that another jolly and convivial evening was enjoyed and the Committee extend their hearty thanks to all present for their kind support.

Annual Children's Party.

Our Fifteenth Annual Children's Christmas Party took place on Saturday, January 7th, 1939, when 182 children made merry for over four and a half hours. As on former occasions the event was held at the Westminster City School and we are very grateful indeed to the Governors and Mr. J. C. Dent, the headmaster, for so kindly placing this spacious building at our disposal for the afternoon and evening. Several members of the Branch had been for hours preparing the tea and during the meal were again busily employed replenishing the tables with appealing fare for the sturdy youngsters. Tea over, the party were entertained to a Marionette Show and after this games were enjoyed and the winners awarded prizes for their efforts. All eyes were then turned on the large Christmas Tree, now lit up, and after "Father Christmas" had made his appearance and spoke a few words of welcome each child was presented with a toy from the tree. Following the singing of Auld Lang Syne and the National Anthem the happy function was drawn to a close, but prior to departing each child was handed a bag of sweets, fruit and a bonbon to cheer them on their way. To many of the kiddies present this was the only real treat they had enjoyed during the festive season and we are grateful to those who so generously contributed donations and gifts of toys and so made it possible for us to entertain such number. We are also indebted to those who so willingly gave their time and services to the occasion.

Re-union Dinner and Dance.

Our Annual Re-union Dinner and Dance is fixed this year for Saturday, April 1st, at Gatti's Restaurant, Strand, W.C., and members are asked to make a note of the date and support the Committee by their presence. Friends of members will be heartily welcomed and we can assure all of the usual jolly time.

Annual Continental Tour.

The ten-day Continental Tour organised by headquarters for the Branch in August last was another great success and it is proposed to hold a similar Tour this year. The ground to be covered will differ of course from previous tours and will not extend, for convenience of several wishing to take part, beyond one week, i.e., from Saturday to Saturday. France, Belgium and Holland as well as the Duchy of Luxemburg will be visited and those interested are invited to apply to Mr. J. Bougney, Hon. Secretary, as early as possible for full particulars in view of the limited number it is proposed to accept.

Informal Gatherings.

These Gatherings were recommenced in September last when Mr. Geo. A. Goodall, Hon. Secretary, Hampton Wick Branch, British Legion, very kindly brought along his team of boy and girl artists and entertained the members with an excellent programme. October was an Open Meeting and the St. Dunstan's Singers under the direction of Mrs. Hodson provided the programme for the November Informal. It was with regret that we learned that this would most probably be the last occasion we should have these talented artists with us as a party, but it is hoped their members will continue to patronise our gatherings whenever they find it convenient. The December programme was once again kindly provided by Mr. Mears from headquarters and before a very full house his artist friends gave their usual breezy entertainment and one befitting the festive season. For the January Informal we were privileged with a Lantern Slide Talk by the League Secretary, Major L. J. L. Pullar, M.C., which was followed by a short talk on the War Memorials and the work of the Imperial War Graves Commission by Mr. Mears.

Apart from the honour of winning the Branch Recruiting Prize of £5 for the year the Committee have every justification for feeling satisfied with the past year's achievements and to all who have so kindly accorded them their support the London Branch Committee extend their most grateful thanks.

To those members and friends who have not found it possible to attend recent gatherings of the Branch we respectfully draw their attention to the dates on which these are held and look forward with pleasure to their attending one or more of these, when they can be assured of a hearty welcome. The gatherings are held on the third THURSDAY in each month at 7.30 p.m. at the

BEDFORD HEAD HOTEL,
MAIDEN LANE, STRAND, W.C.2
(Admission Free).

Branches

LONDON	Hon. Secretary to the London Branch Committee: J. Boughey, c/o 22, Orchard Street, London, W.1.
	TOTTENHAM AND EDMONTON DISTRICT—E. Glover, 191, Lansdowne Road, Tottenham, N.17.
COLCHESTER	H. Snow (Hon. Sec.), 2 Church Street.
	W. H. Taylor (Pilgrimage Hon. Sec.), 64, High Street.
LIVERPOOL	Captain A. M. Webster, Blundellsands.
PURLEY	Major Graham Carr, D.S.O., M.C., 112-114, High Street.
SHEFFIELD	Captain J Wilkinson, "Holmfield," Bents Drive.
AUSTRALIA, (Queensland)	Messrs. C. H. Green, and George Lawson, Essex House, (Opposite Anzac Square) Brisbane, Queensland.
CANADA	Ed. Kingsland, P.O. Box 83, Magog, Quebec.
SOUTH AFRICA	L. G. Shuter, 381, Longmarket Street, Pietermaritzburg.
KENYA	C. H. Slater, P.O. Box 403, Nairobi.
BELGIUM	C. Leupe, Garage Shannon, Menin Gate.
AMERICA	Representative: Dr. William Rich, 156, West 165th St., New York City.

Corresponding Members

DOMINIONS AND FOREIGN COUNTRIES.

AUSTRALIA	R. A. Baldwin, c/o Government Savings Bank of N.S.W., Martin Place, Sydney.
	Mr. W. Cloves, Box 1296, G.P.O., Adelaide.
	J. C. Correll, Port Vincent, South Australia.
BELGIUM	Sister Marguerite, Sacré Coeur, Ypres.
CANADA	Brig.-General V. W. Odlum, C.B., C.M.G., D.S.O., 2500, Point Grey Road, Vancouver.
	V. A. Bowes, 326, 40th Avenue West, Calgary, Alberta.
	W. Constable F. Grece, St. Hilaire Station, Ronville County, Quebec.
CEYLON	Captain F. R. G. Webb, M.C., Irrigation Bungalow, Kalmunai, E.P.
EGYPT	Captain B. W. Leak, M.I.E.E., Turf Club, Cairo.
INDIA	Lieut.-Quartermaster G. Smith, Queen's Bays, Sialkot, India.
IRELAND	Miss A. K. Jackson, Cloneyhurke House, Portarlington.
NEW ZEALAND	Captain W. U. Gibb, Ava Lodge, Puhinui Road, Papatoetoe, Auckland
	S. E. Beattie, P.O. Box 11, Otaki Railway, Wellington.
NEWFOUNDLAND	Captain Leo. Murphy, G.W.V.A. Office, St. John's.
NOVA SCOTIA	Will R. Bird, 35, Clarence Street, Amherst.
SOUTH AFRICA	H. L. Versfield, c/o Cape Explosives Works Ltd., 150, St. Georges Street, Cape Town.
SPAIN	Captain P. W. Burgess, Calle de Zurbano 29, Madrid.
U.S.A.	Captain Henry Maslin, 942, President Street, Brooklyn, New York.
	L. E. P. Foot, 20, Gillett Street, Hartford, Conn, U.S.A.
	A. P. Forward, 449, East 80th Street, New York.
	J. W. Freebody, 945, McBride Avenue, Los Angeles.

Printed in Great Britain for the Publishers by FORD & GILL, 21a/23, Iliffe Yard, Crampton Street, London, S.E.17.

THE YPRES LEAGUE (INCORPORATED)

22, Orchard Street, Portman Square, W.1.

Telephone: WELBECK 1446. *Telegrams*: YPRESLEAG, "WESDO," LONDON.

Patron-in-Chief: H.M. THE KING.

Patron
H.R.H. PRINCESS BEATRICE.

President: GENERAL SIR CHARLES H. HARINGTON.

Vice-Presidents:

THE VISCOUNT WAKEFIELD OF HYTHE.
F.-M. LORD MILNE.
GENERAL SIR CECIL ROMER.
F.-M. SIR CLAUD W. JACOB.
F.-M. SIR PHILIP CHETWODE.
GENERAL SIR HUBERT GOUGH.

General Committee:

THE COUNTESS OF ALBEMARLE.
CAPTAIN C. ALLISTON.
LIEUT-COLONEL BECKLES WILLSON.
MR. HENRY BENSON.
*MR. J. BOUGHEY.
MISS B. BRICE-MILLER.
COLONEL G. T. BRIERLEY.
CAPTAIN P. W. BURGESS.
BRIG.-GENL. A. BURT.
*MAJOR H. CARDINAL-HARFORD.
*MAJOR GRAHAM CARR.
REV. P. B. CLAYTON.
CAPTAIN G. E. DE TRAFFORD.
MRS. C. J. EDWARDS.
MAJOR C. J. EDWARDS.
MR. H. A. T. FAIRBANK.
MR. T. ROSS FURNER.
MR. E. GLOVER.
*MAJOR H. G. HARRIS.
MR. F. D. BANKES-HILL.
MAJOR-GENERAL C. J. B. HAY.
MR. J. HETHERINGTON.
GENERAL SIR W. C. G. HENEKER.
*CAPTAIN O. G. JOHNSON.
MAJOR GENL. C. G. LIDDELL.
*CAPTAIN H. D. PEABODY.
THE HON. ALICE DOUGLAS PENNANT.
*LIEUT.-GENERAL SIR W. P. PULTENEY.
CAPTAIN J. F. MILLER.
LIEUT.-COLONEL SIR J. MURRAY.
*COLONEL G. E. C. RASCH.
*MR. H. SNOW.
THE HON. SIR ARTHUR STANLEY.
MR. ERNEST THOMPSON.
CAPTAIN J. WILKINSON.
CAPTAIN H. TREVOR WILLIAMS.
*CAPTAIN G. M. WINGATE.

* Executive Committee.

Bankers:
BARCLAYS BANK LTD., Knightsbridge Branch.

Honorary Solicitors:
MESSRS. FLADGATE & CO., 70, Pall Mall, S.W.

Secretary:
MAJOR L. J. L. PULLAR.

Auditors:
MESSRS. LEPINE & JACKSON,
6, Bond Court, E.C.4.

League Representative at Ypres:
Mr. C. LEUPE,
Garage Shannon, Porte de Menin.

League Representative at Amiens:
CAPTAIN STUART OSWALD.
7, Rue des Otages.

League Representative at Arras:
MR. P. VYNER,
14, Rue Chanzy.

Hon. Secretary, Ypres British Settlement:
LT. COLONEL F. G. POOLE.

YPRES LEAGUE TRAVEL BUREAU.

For information and advice (gratis) regarding Battlefield Tours or individual visits to War Cemeteries and Memorials in France or Belgium, apply Secretary, Ypres League, 22, Orchard Street, London, W.1.